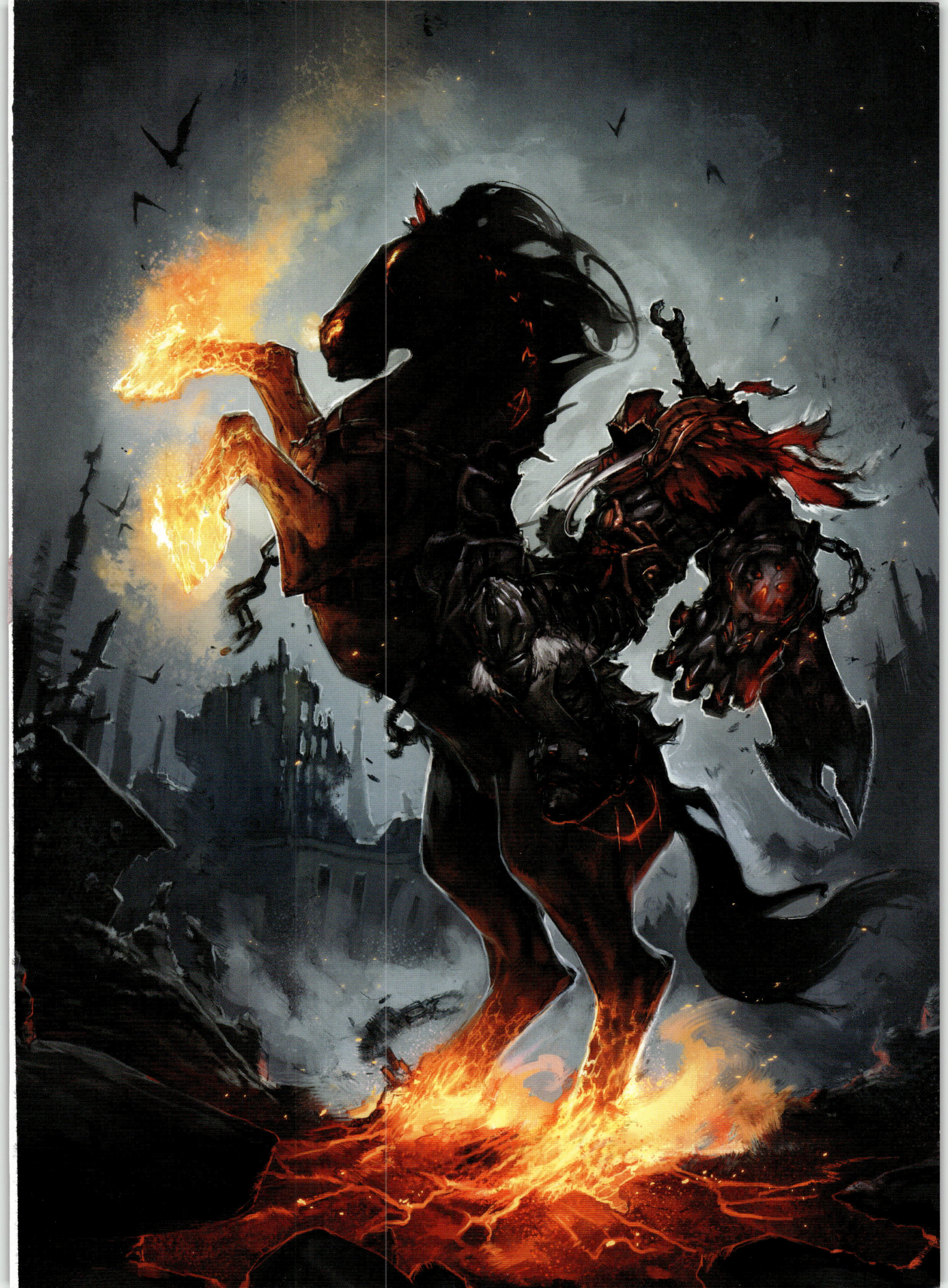

The Art of DARKSIDERS™

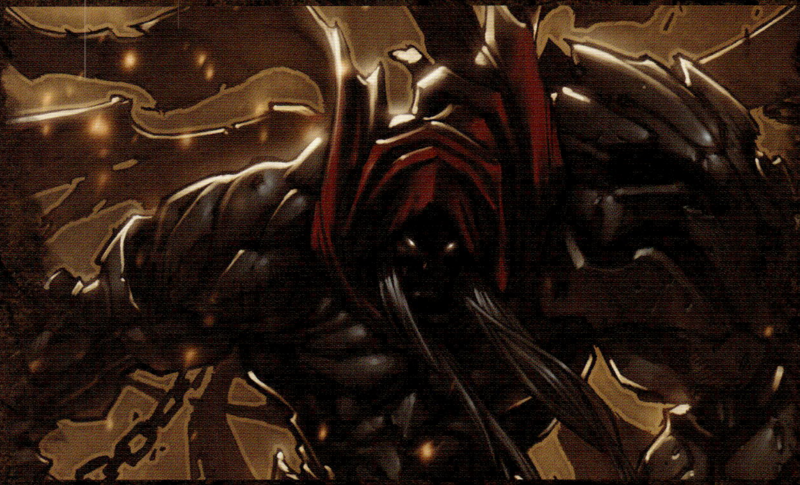

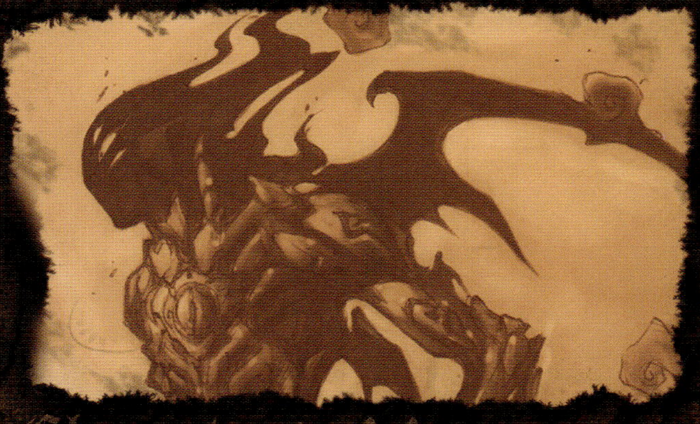

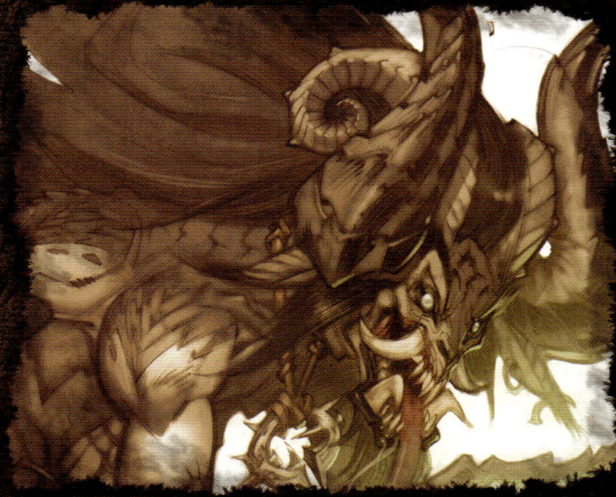

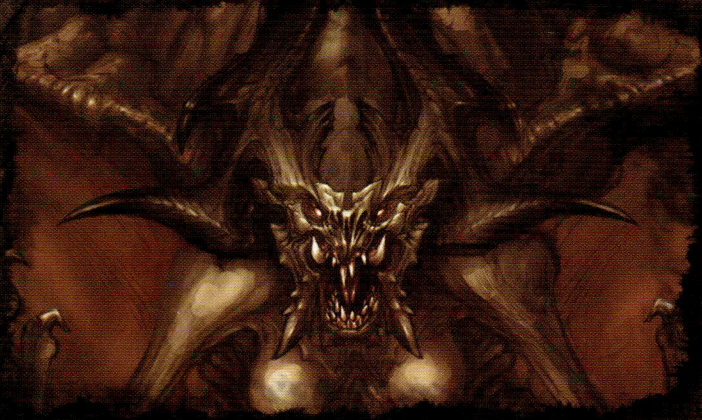

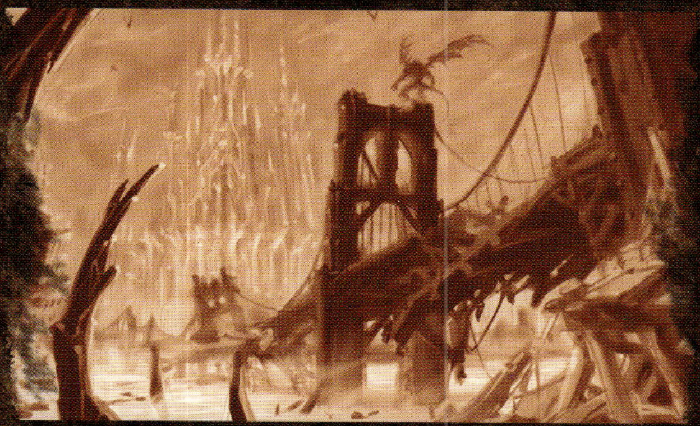

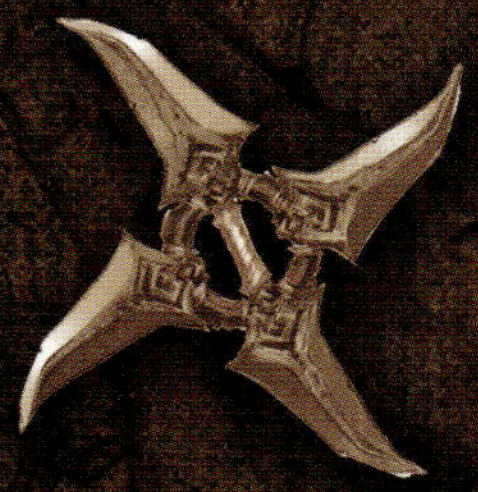

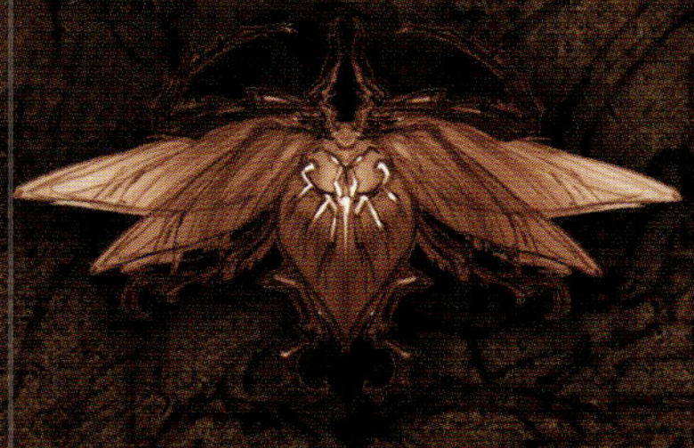

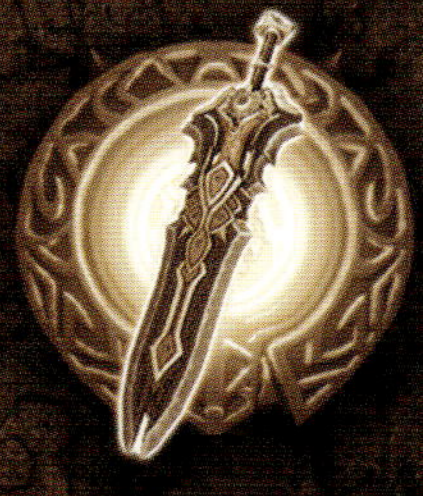

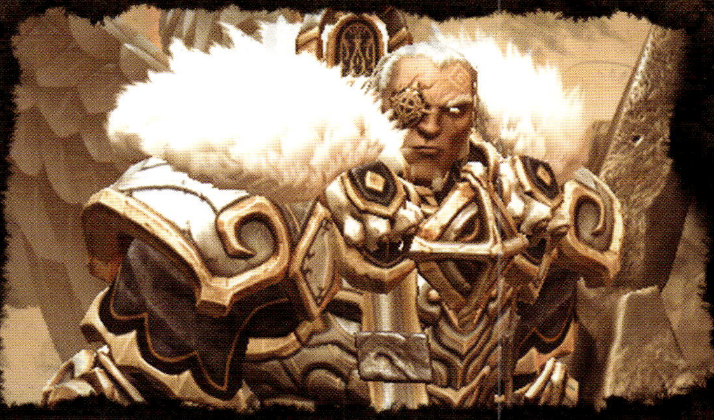

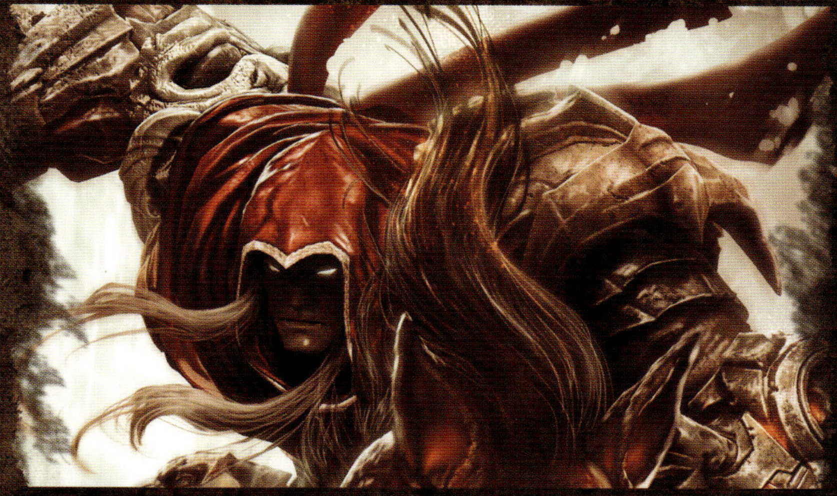

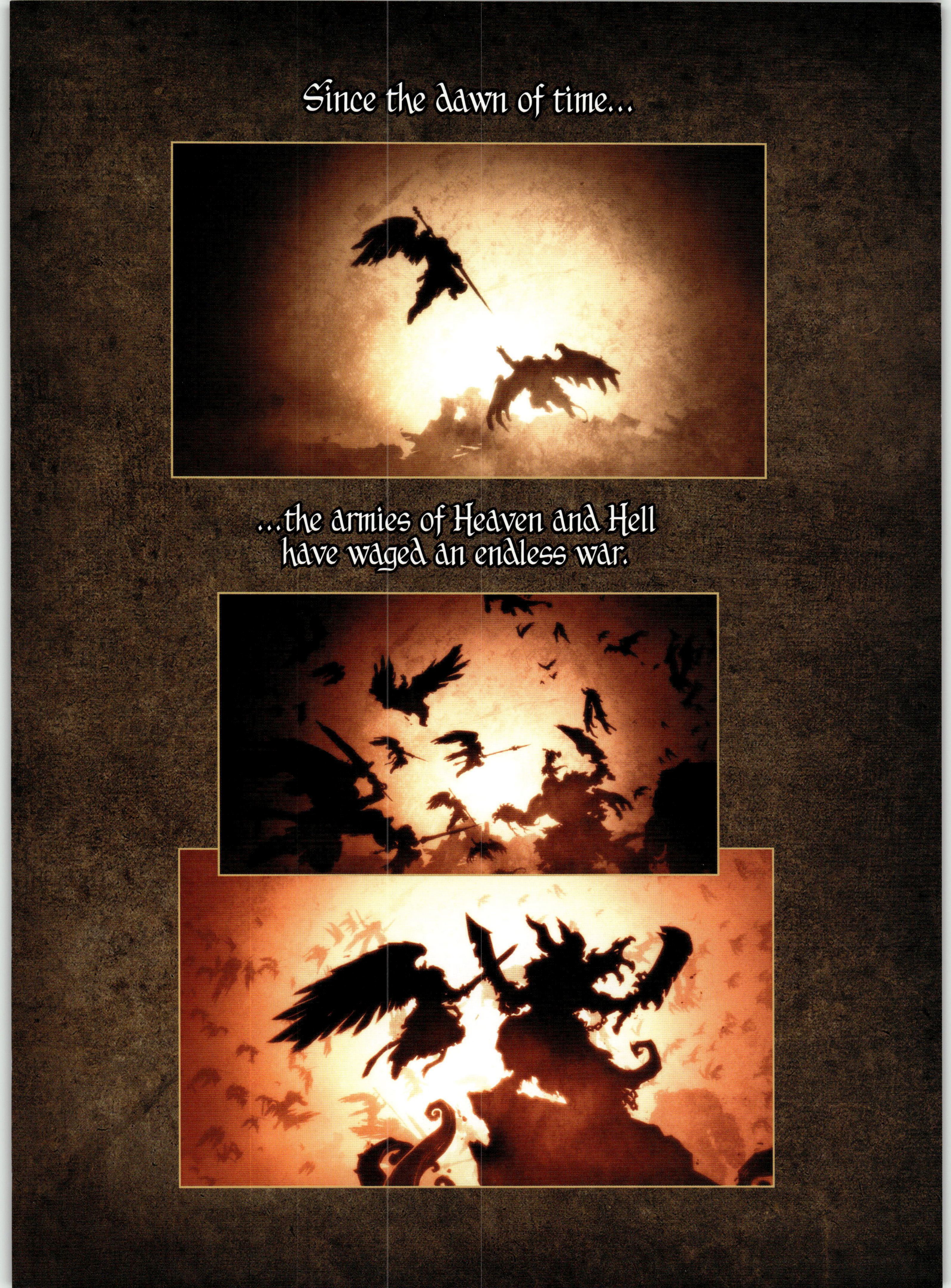
Since the dawn of time...
...the armies of Heaven and Hell have waged an endless war.

Drawn to the conflict was the Charred Council, an entity bound by ancient laws to preserve order and balance.

It held that any great power, unchecked, threatened the very fabric of the universe.

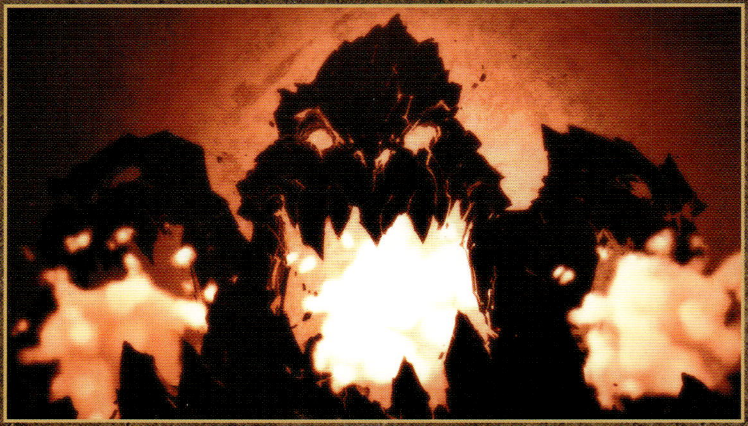

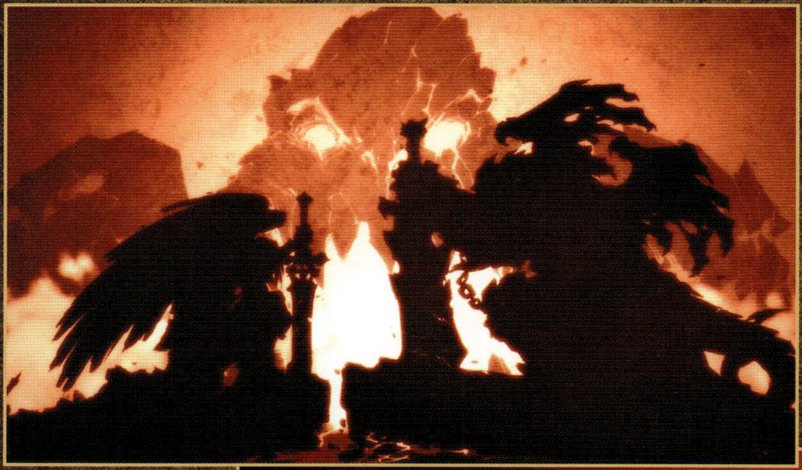

In time, Heaven and Hell came to honor the council and its laws, for none were beyond the swift and terrible justice of the council's enforcers, a fearsome brotherhood known as the Four Horsemen.

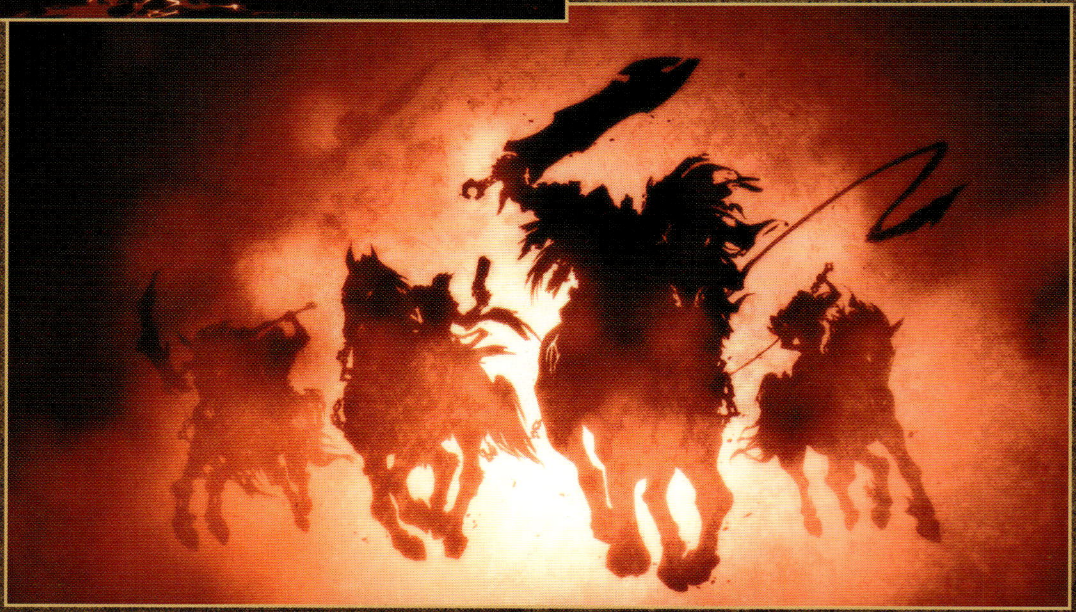

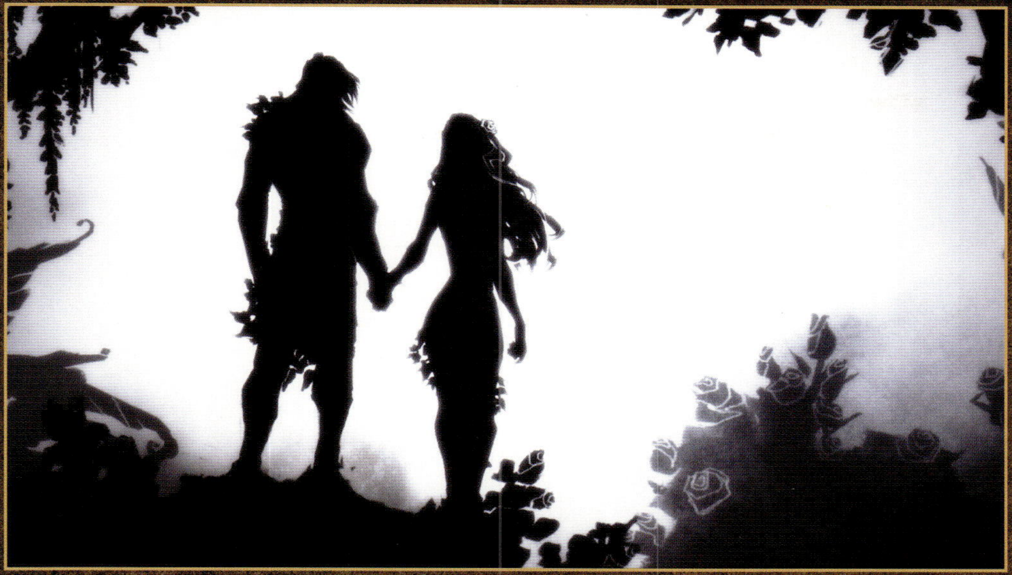

Amid the turmoil, the first humans emerged. The council foretold that these weak, but cunning creatures would someday be integral to the balance.

Thus, a third kingdom was named – the kingdom of man.

By order of the council, a truce was forged between Heaven and Hell.

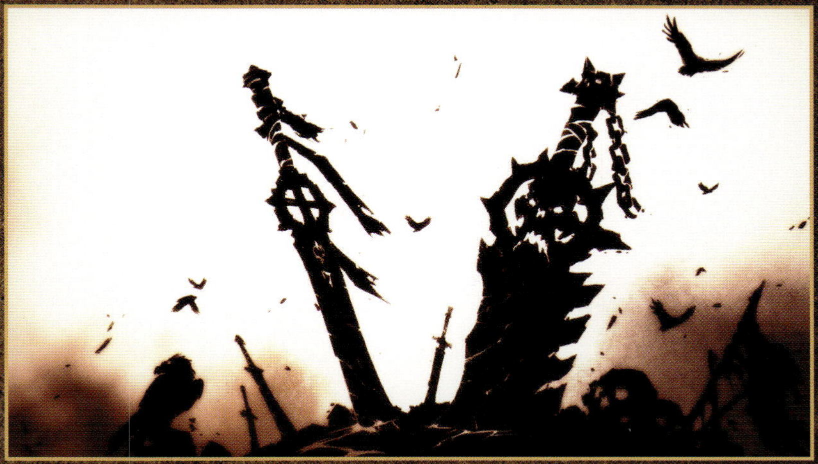

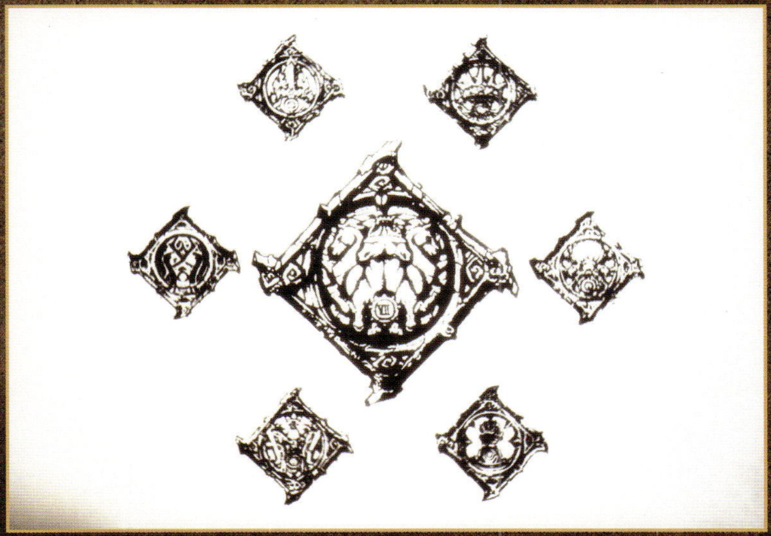

The great pact as bound by seven seals, to be broken at the appointed time when man's kingdom stood ready for the endwar – a battle that would bring balance and determine the ultimate fate of the three kingdoms...

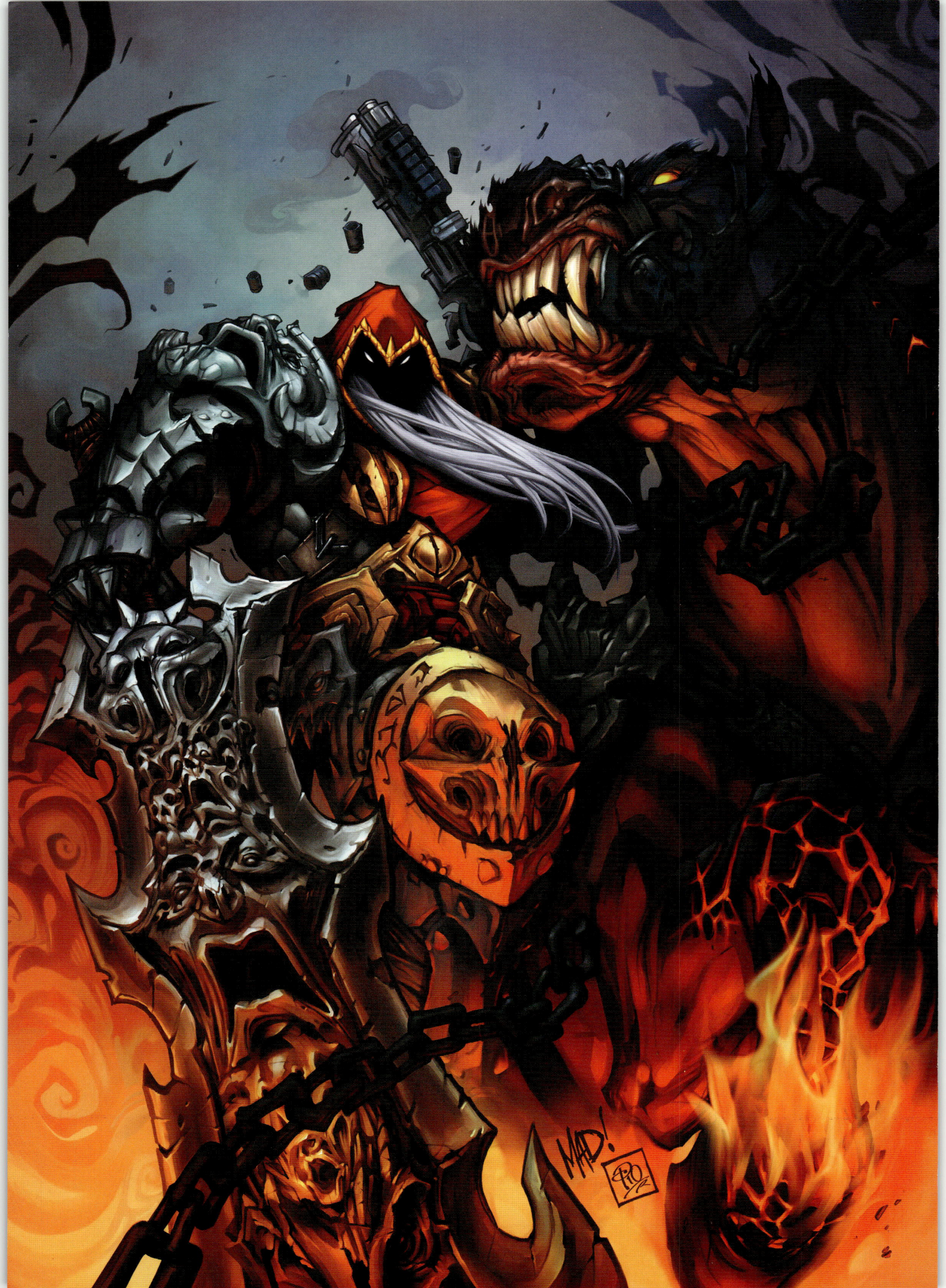

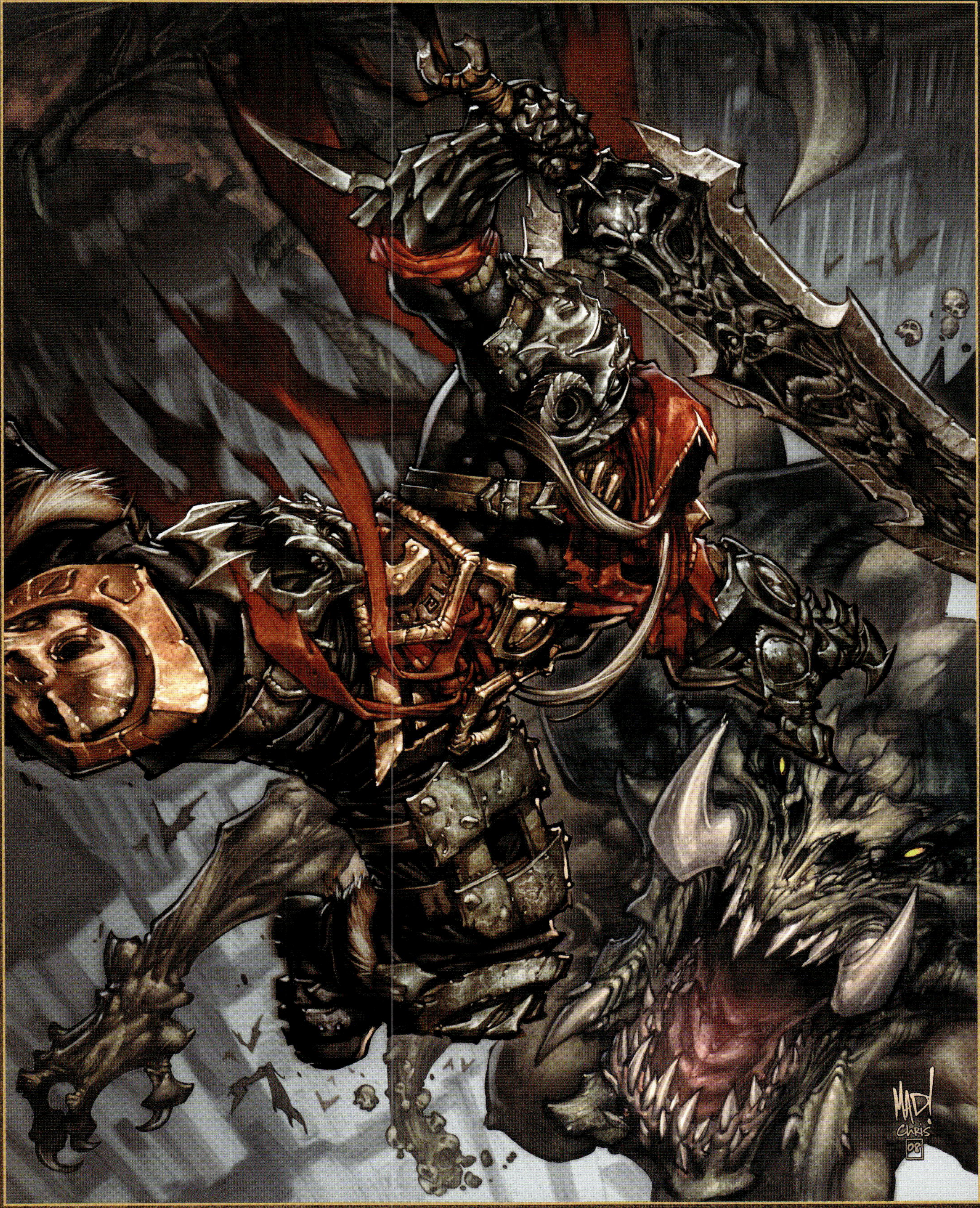

PLAY MAGAZINE COVER

<< PLAY MAGAZINE COVER

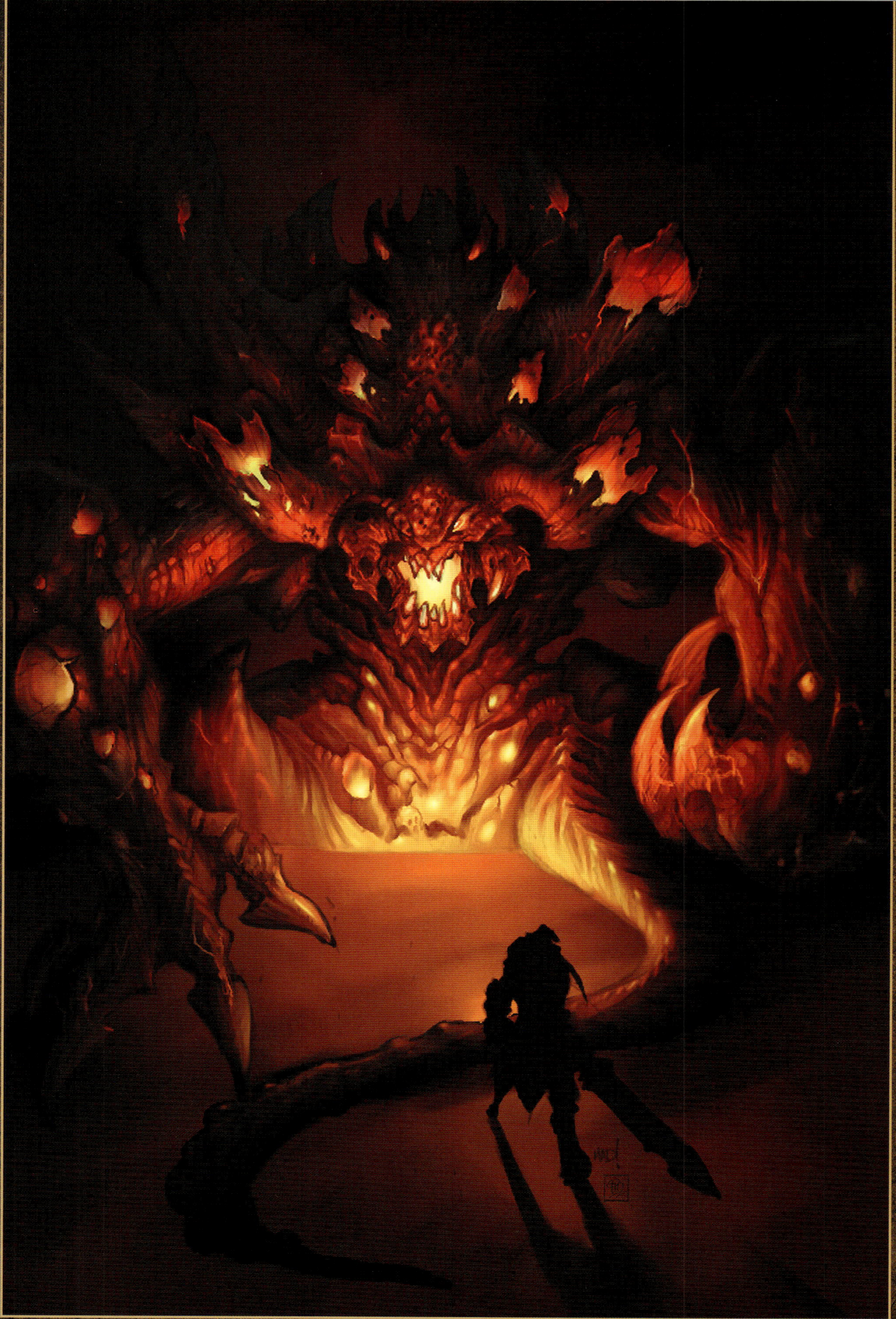

PROMOTIONAL ILLUSTRATION

WIZARD MAGAZINE COVER >>

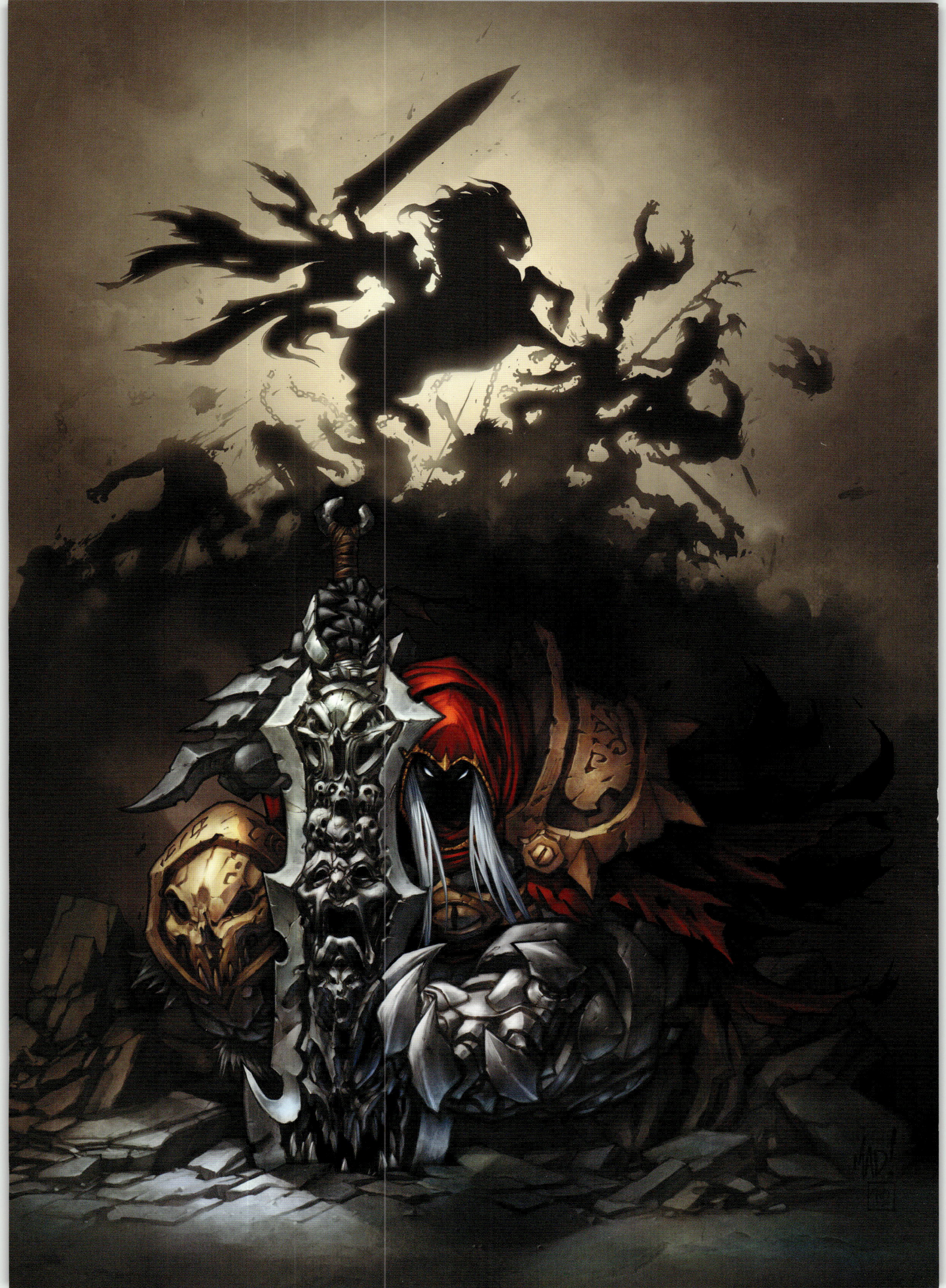

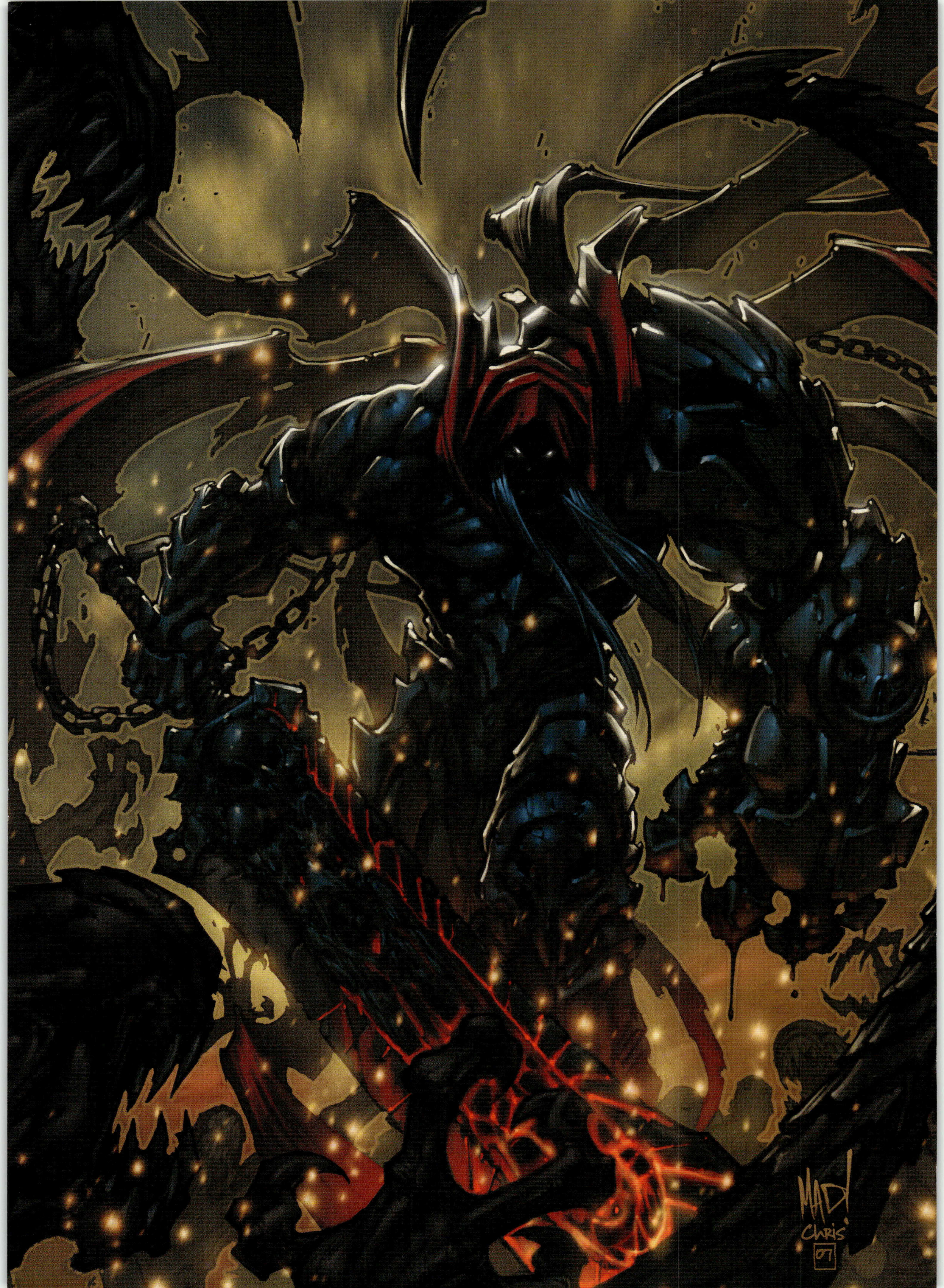
MAD!
Chris
07

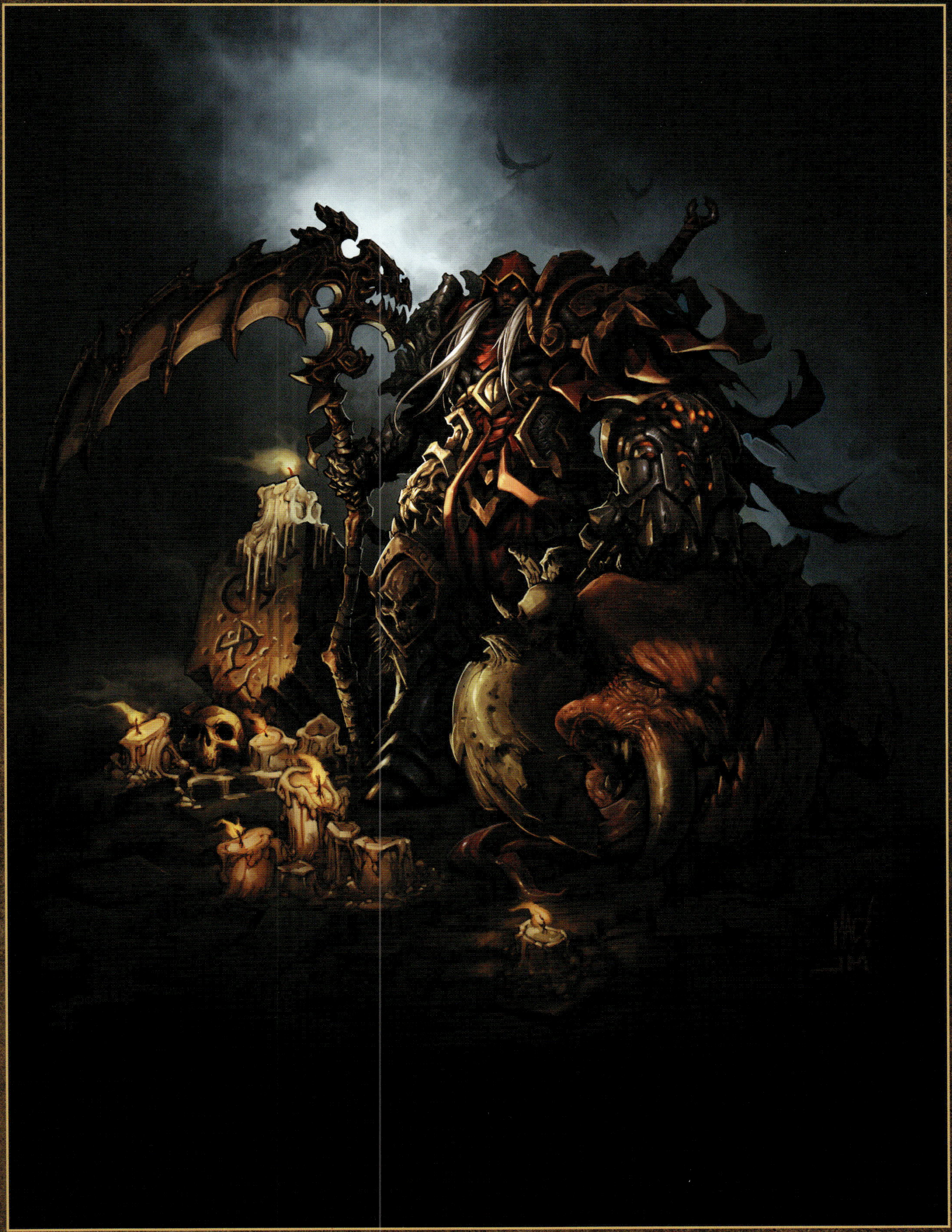

GAMESTOP POSTER

<< PROMOTIONAL ILLUSTRATION

War

The Horseman War has charged into countless battles astride his spectral steed Ruin, leaving a trail of blood and bones in his wake. His eyes and hair are as white as the chill he casts on angels and demons alike, for the fury of his massive sword is unmatched in combat. As unyielding as time itself, War is both honorable and savage.

When summoned to the Final War, the Horseman's task was to purge the Earth and bring the Kingdoms of Heaven and Hell into a new era. But he was betrayed, and his actions wrote the end to the chapter of man. I have heard that War now seeks his revenge. Surely, only the Horseman's wrath can burn away the pure evil of the Destroyer's reign.

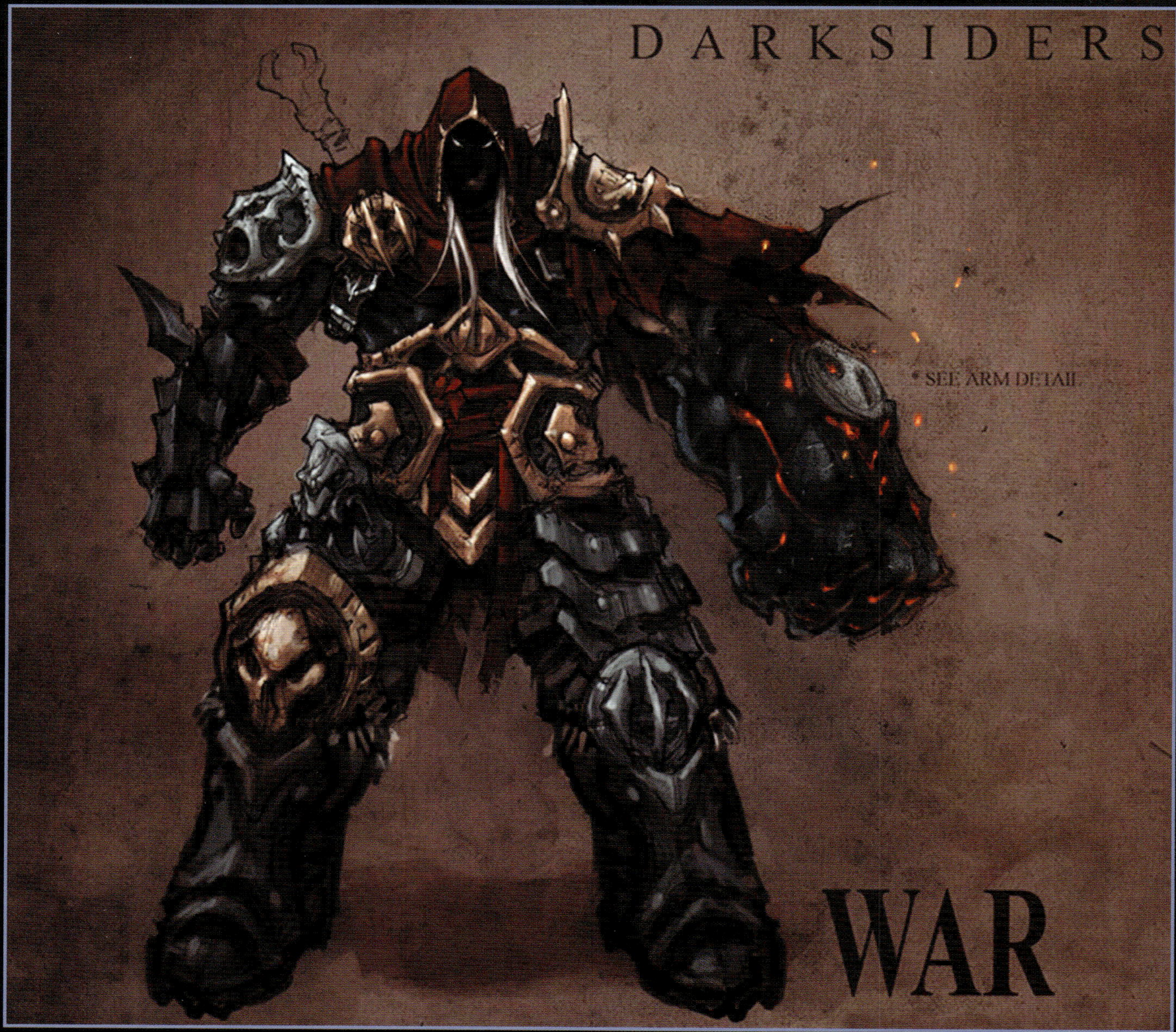

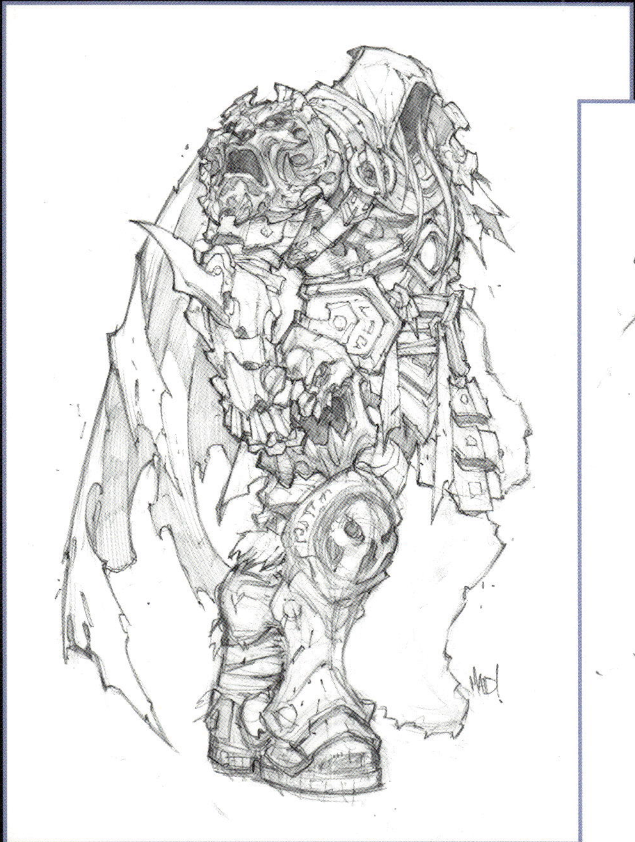

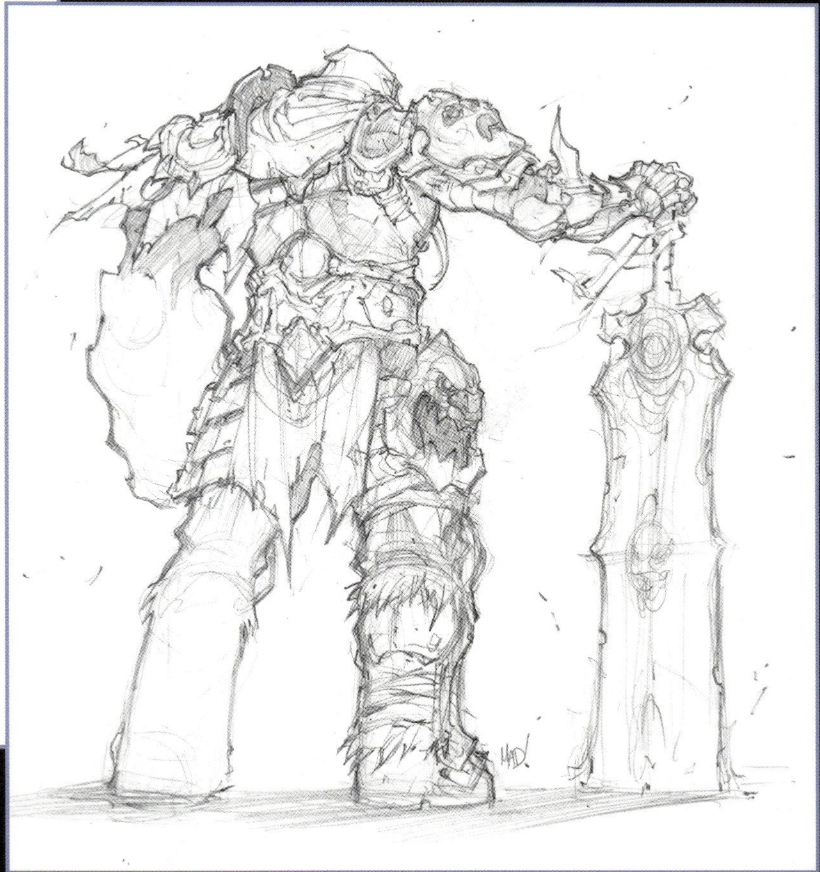

TURNAROUNDS

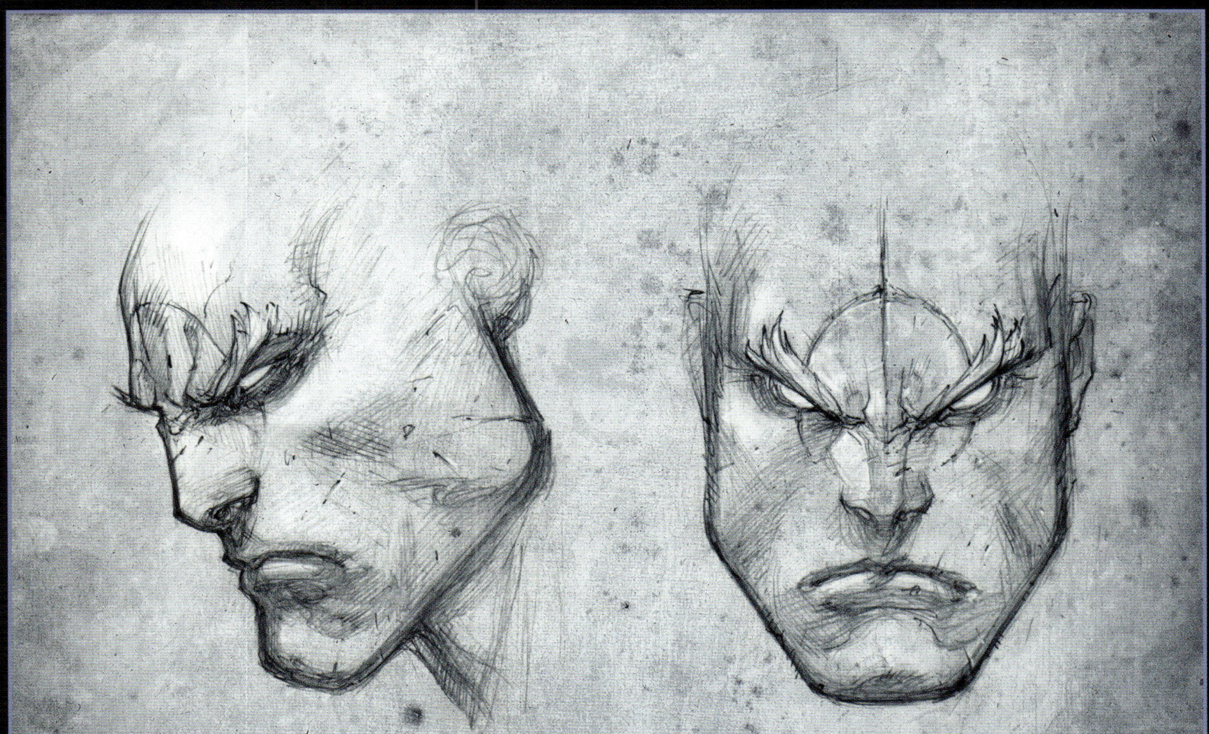

HEAD DETAIL

EARLY CONCEPTS - "BLADE HAND"

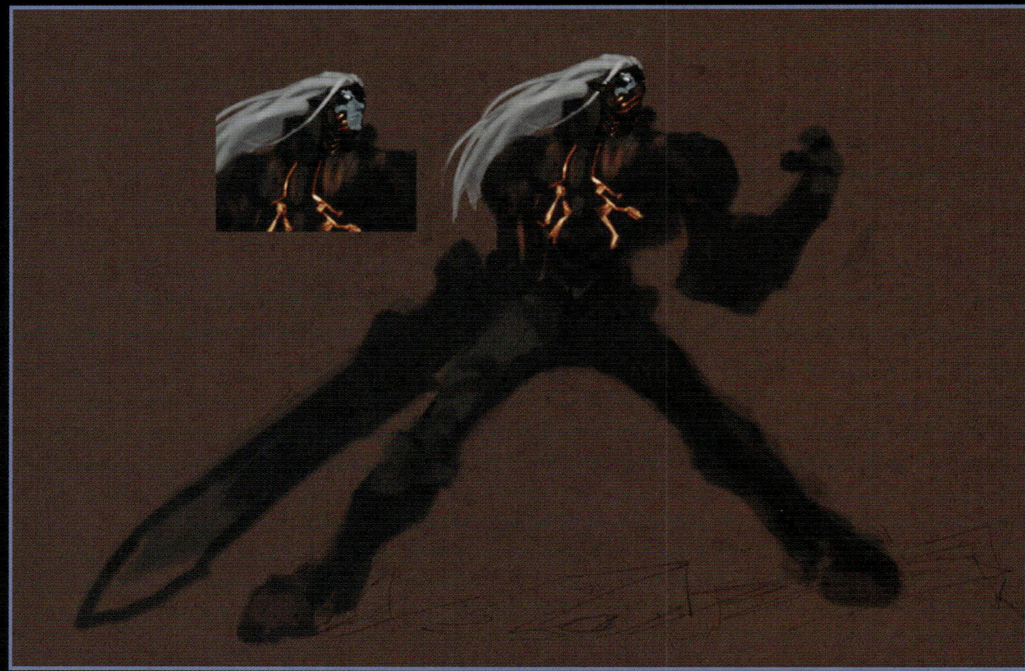

EARLY CONCEPTS - ARMOR DESIGNS

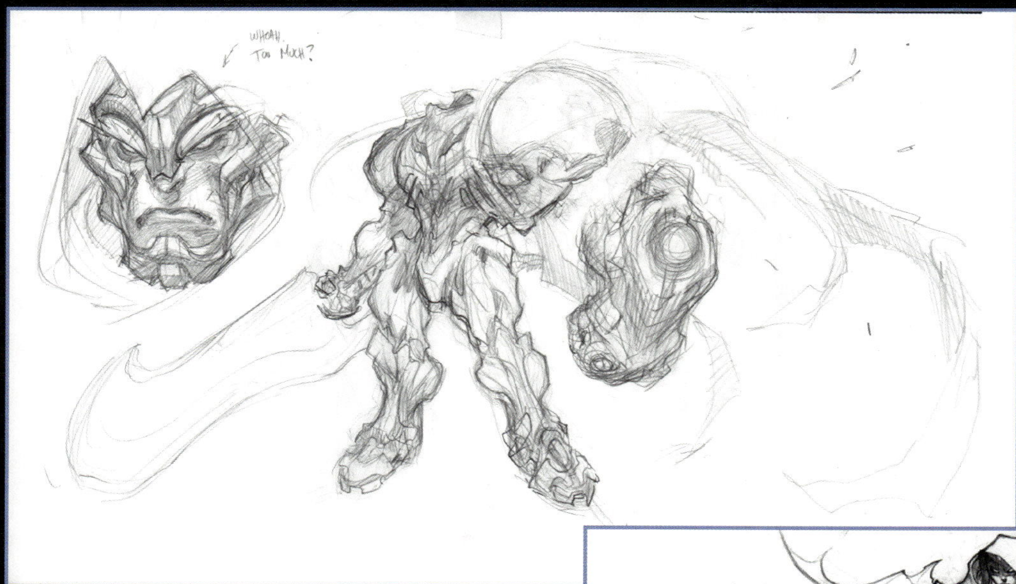

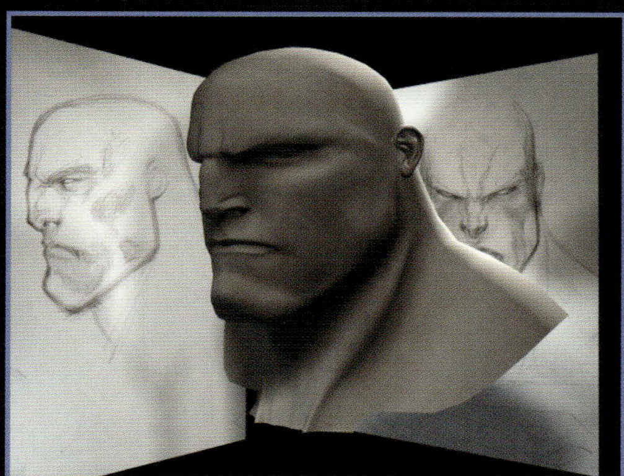

HEAD RENDER

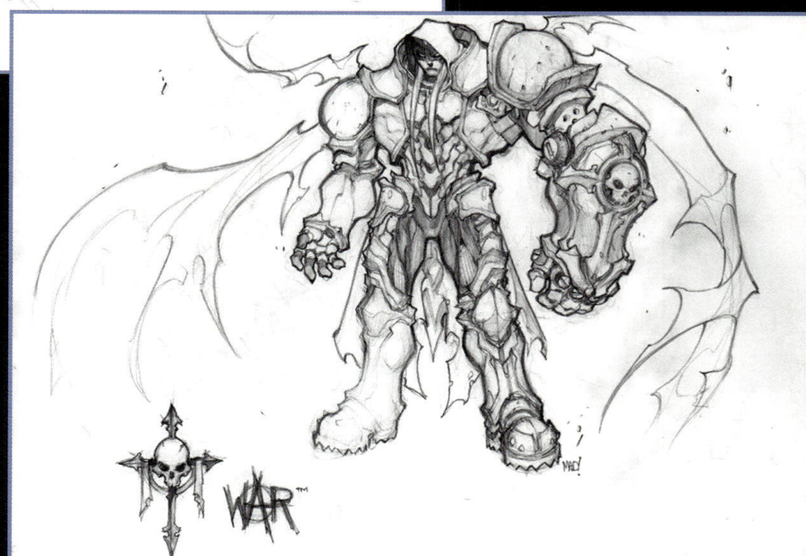

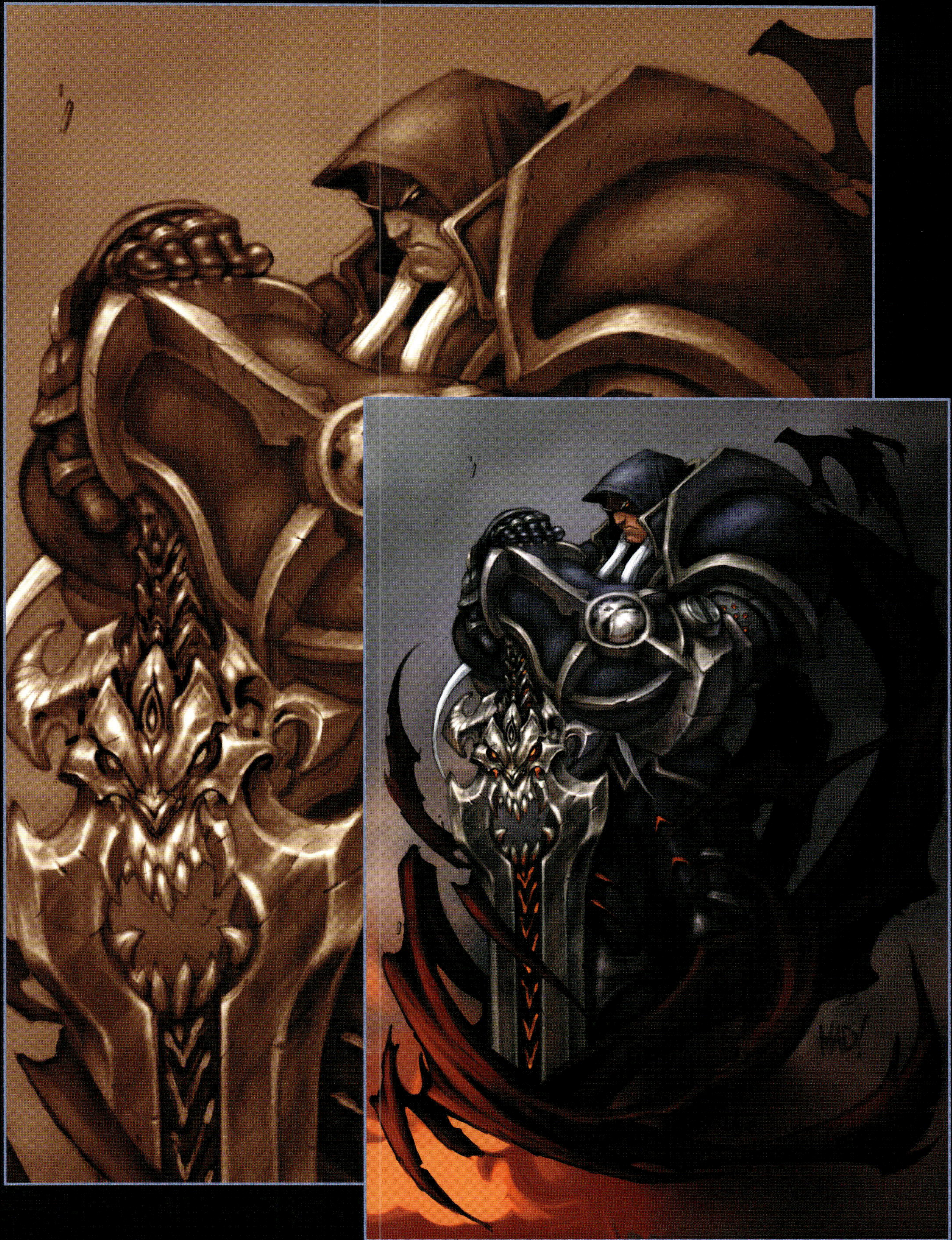

EARLY CONCEPTS - "GUY WITH A SWORD"

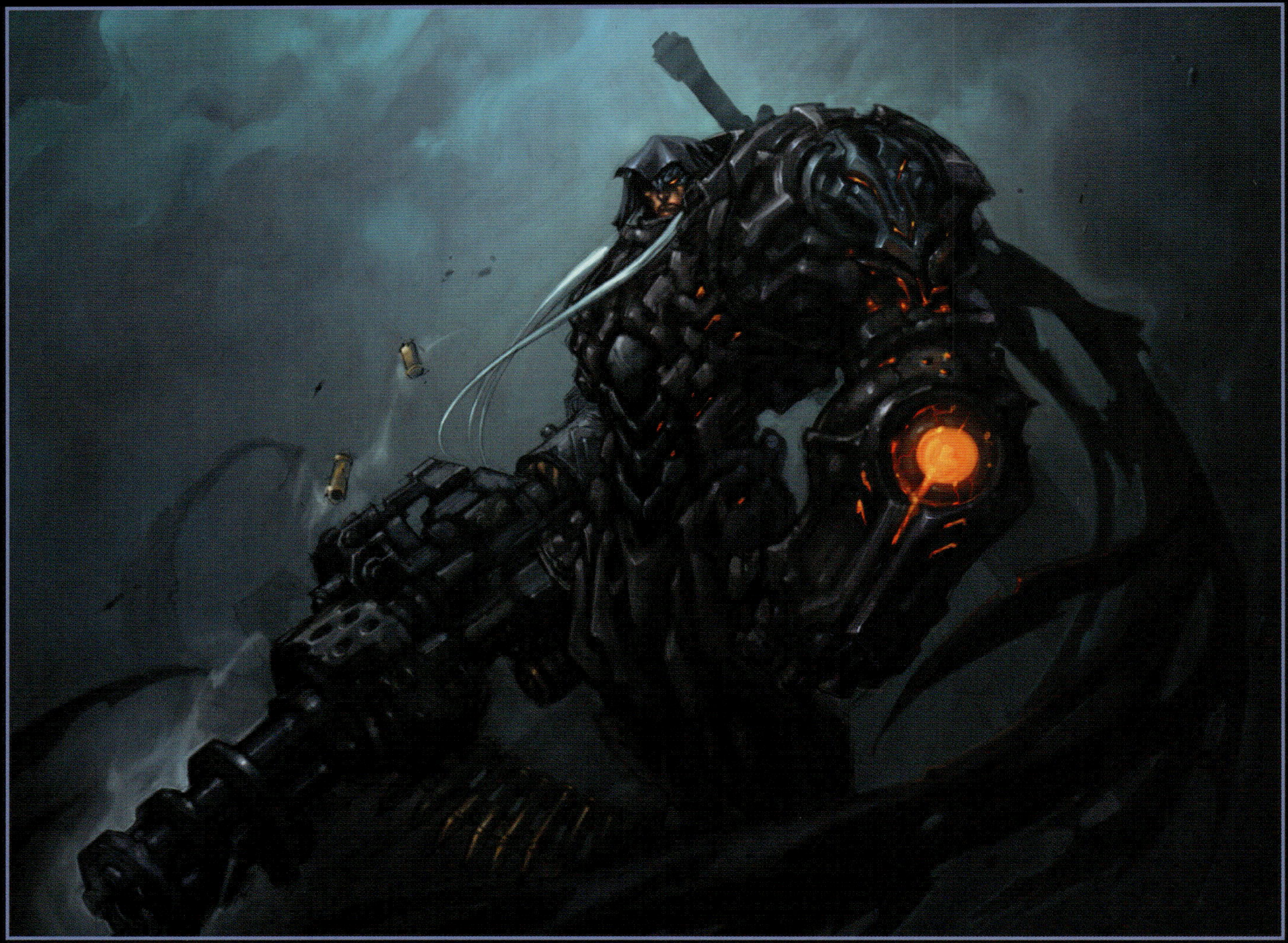

EARLY CONCEPTS - "FUTURE WAR"

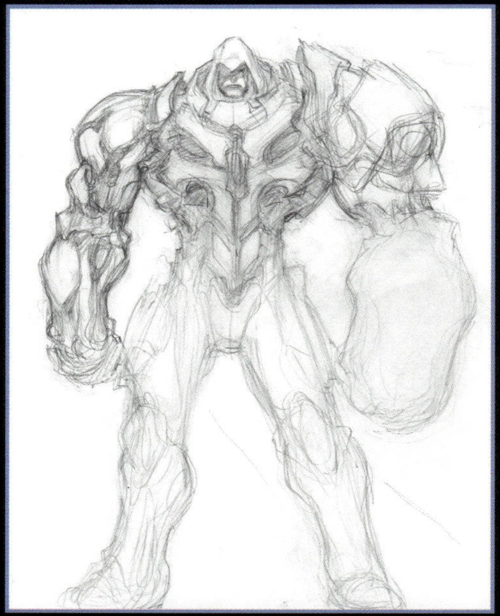

ARMOR SKETCH

TEST RENDERS

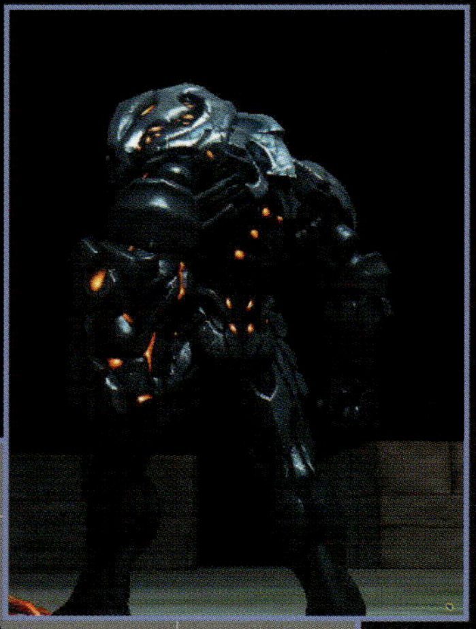

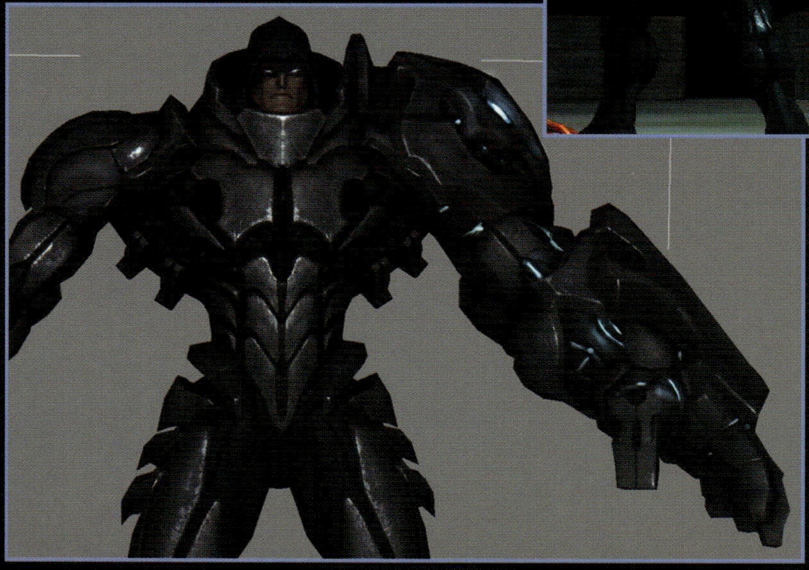

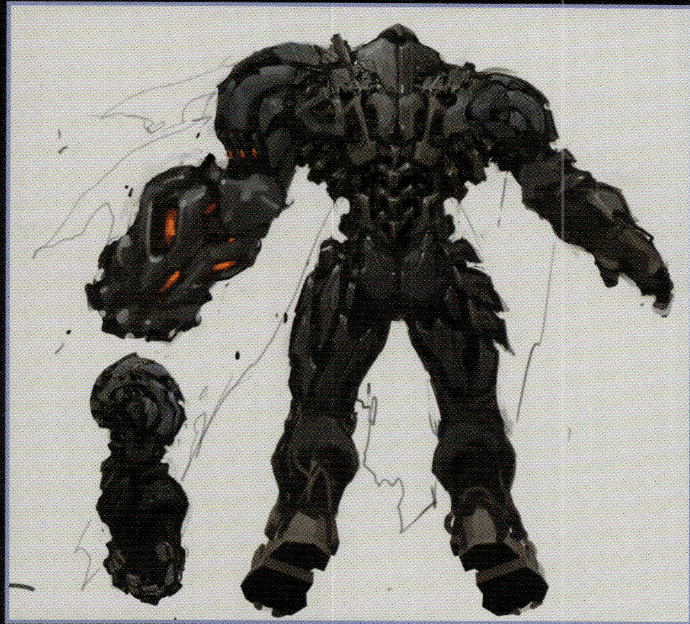

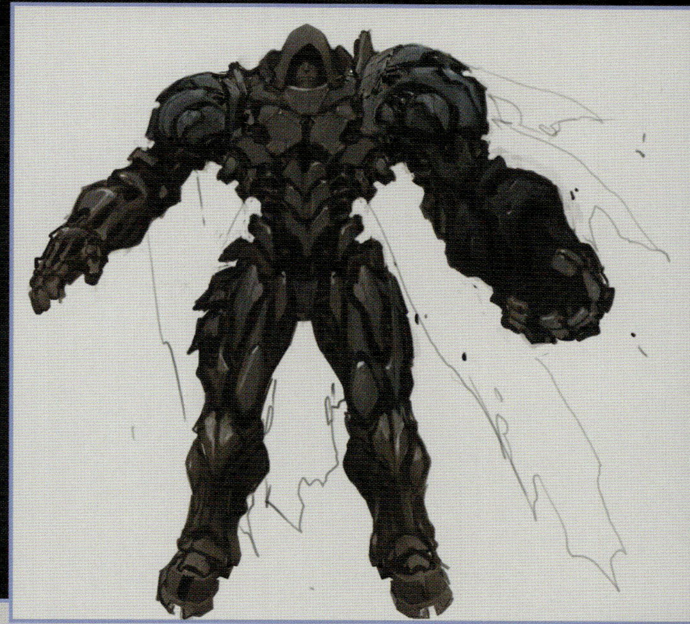

TURNAROUNDS

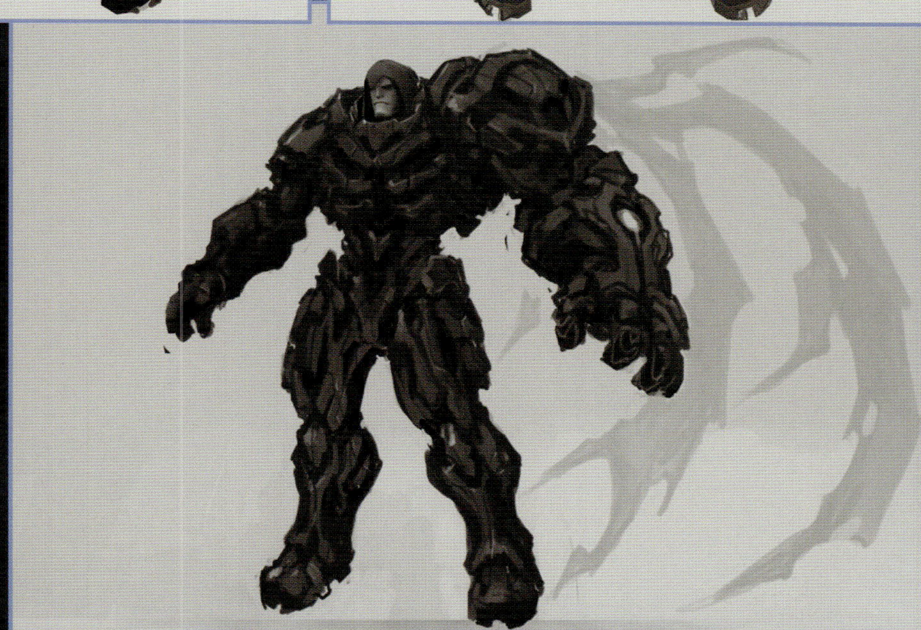

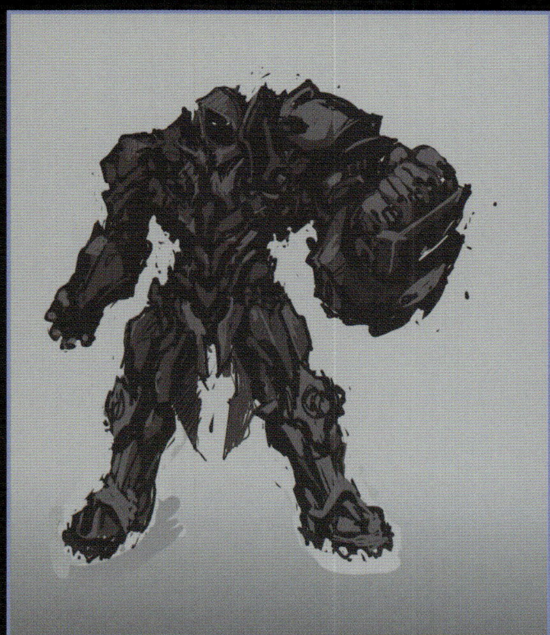

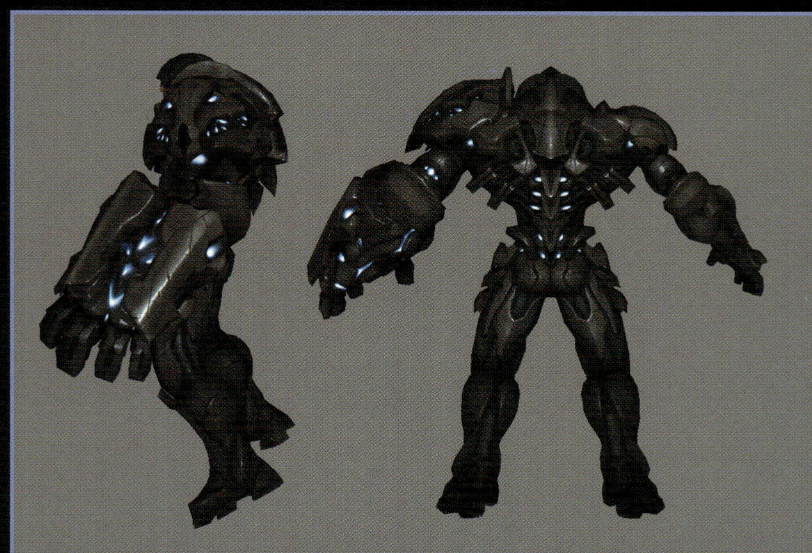

TEST RENDERS

ARMOR SKETCH

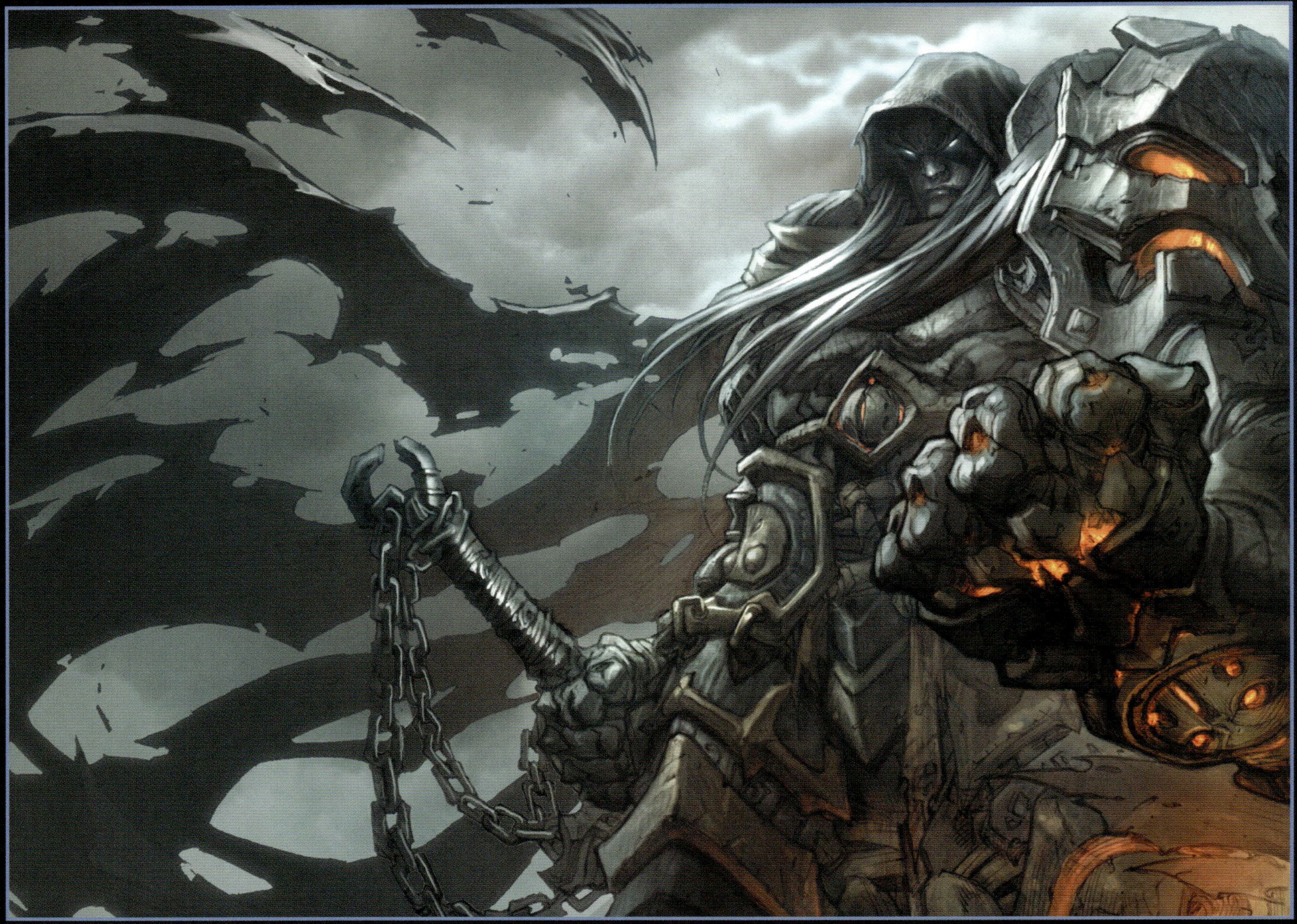

EARLY CONCEPTS - "ANCIENT WARRIOR"

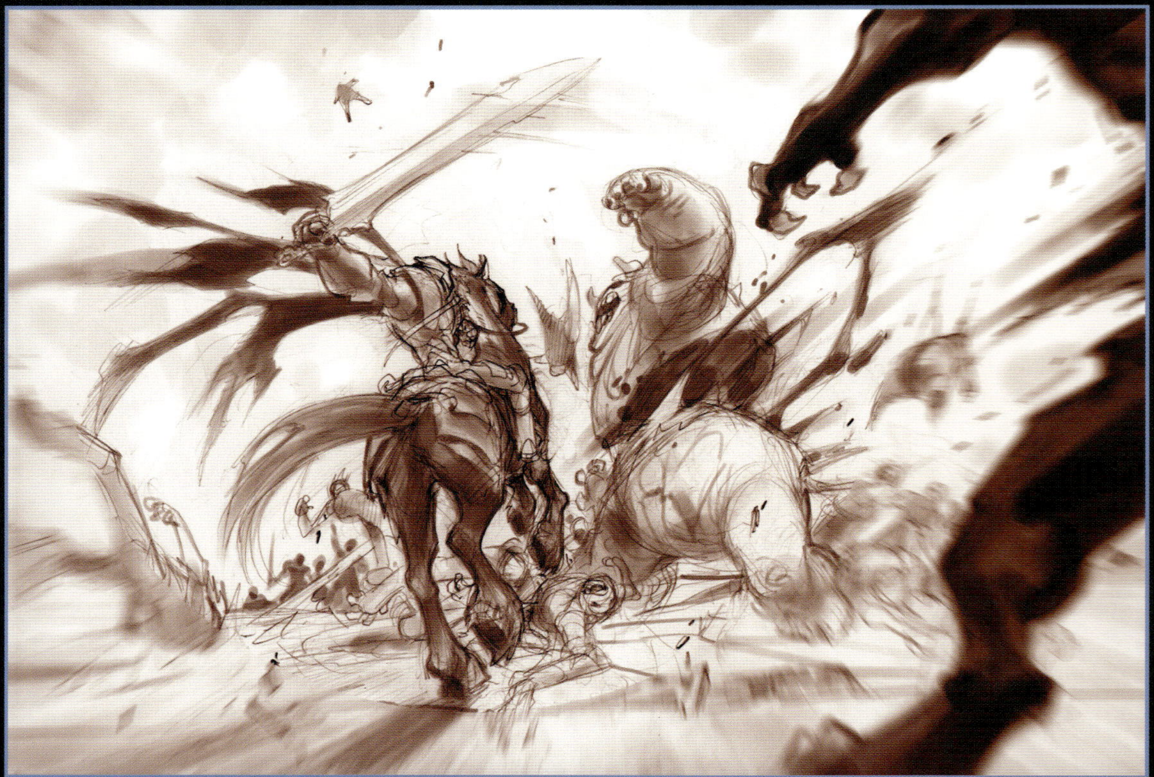

ACTION SKETCH

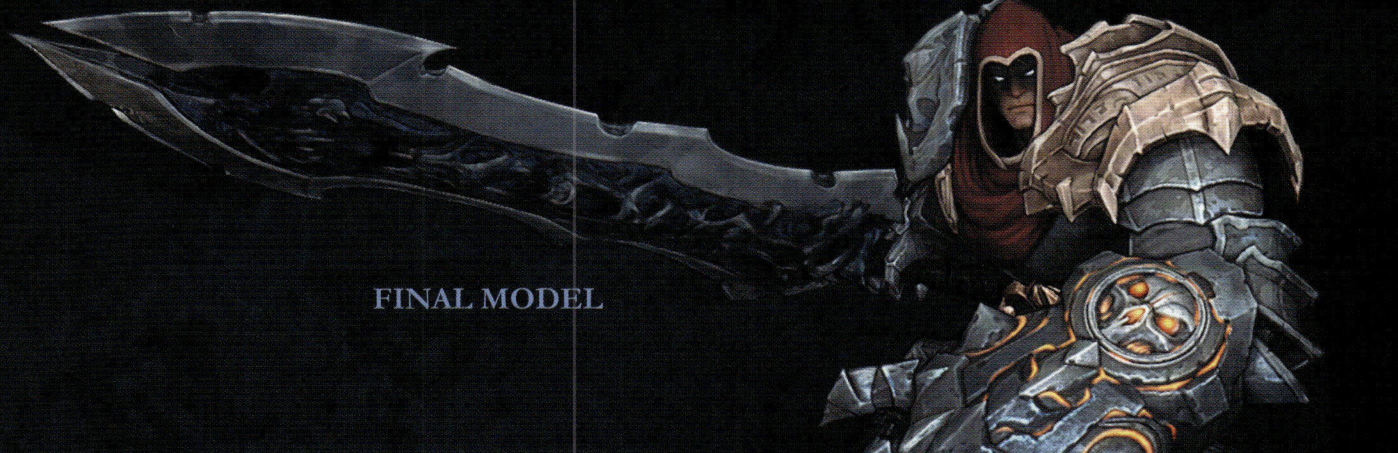
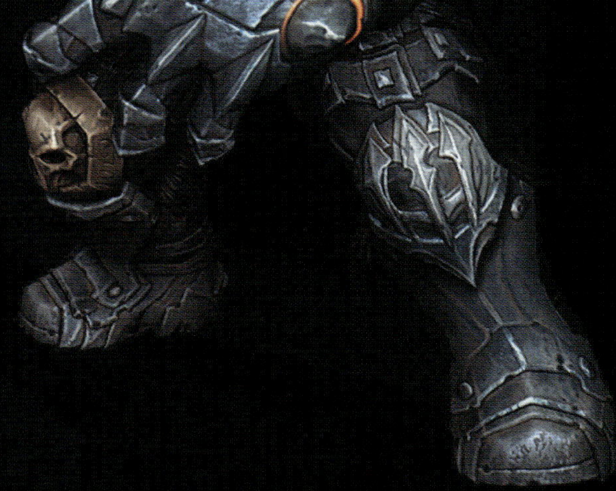

FINAL MODEL

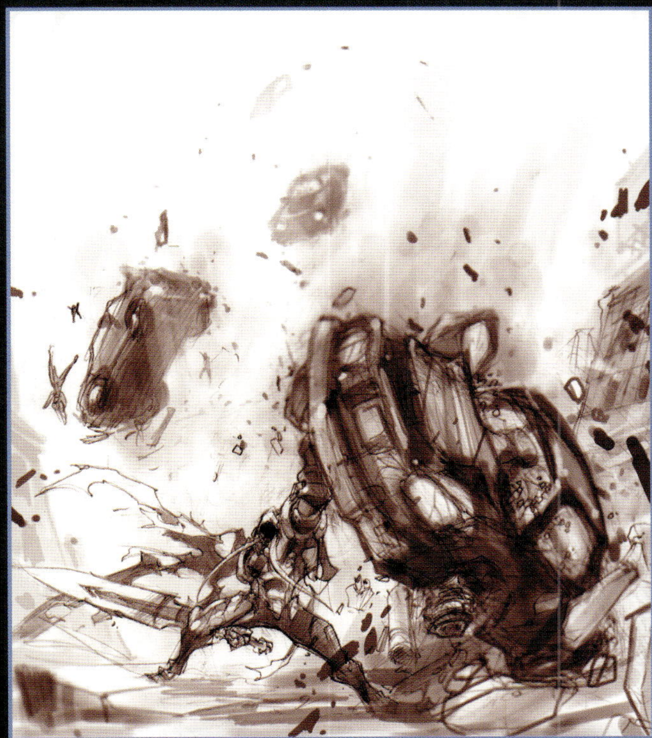

ACTION SKETCH

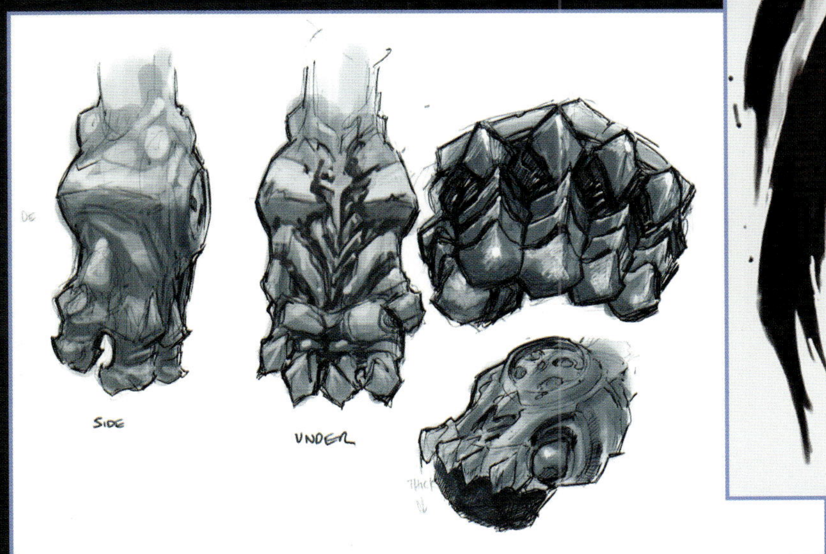

GAUNTLET CONCEPT

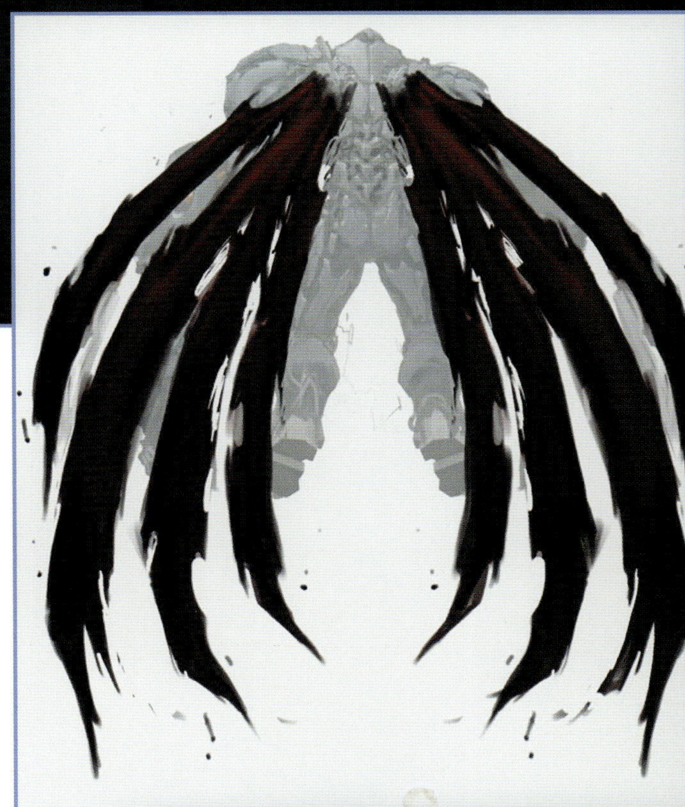

SHADOWFLIGHT CONCEPT

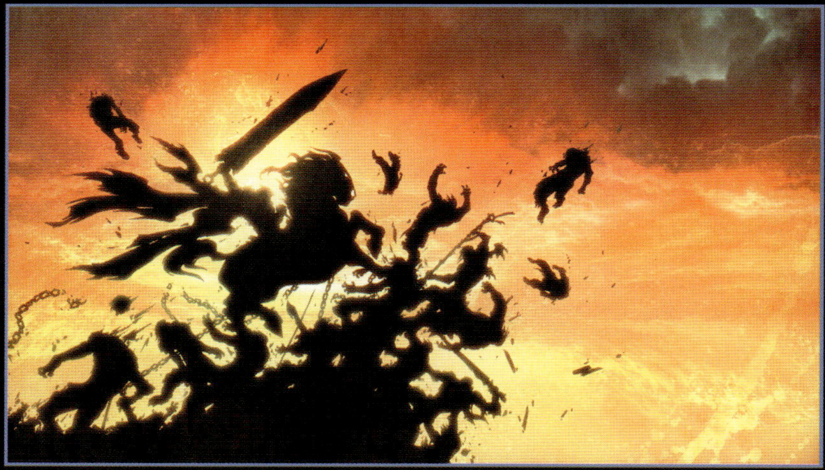

Ruin

Ruin is the legendary red steed of the Horseman War. When astride Ruin, War strikes harder, faster, and wider, his powers somehow magnified by the stallion beneath him. Ruin himself is a deadly opponent. I have seen Ruin burst from the earth in a cloud of smoke and slashing hooves then vanquish demons in cascades of swirling flame.

Like two suns, Ruin and War join to burn all the brighter. If they were to unite on the cursed planes of Earth, nothing could escape their blazing union.

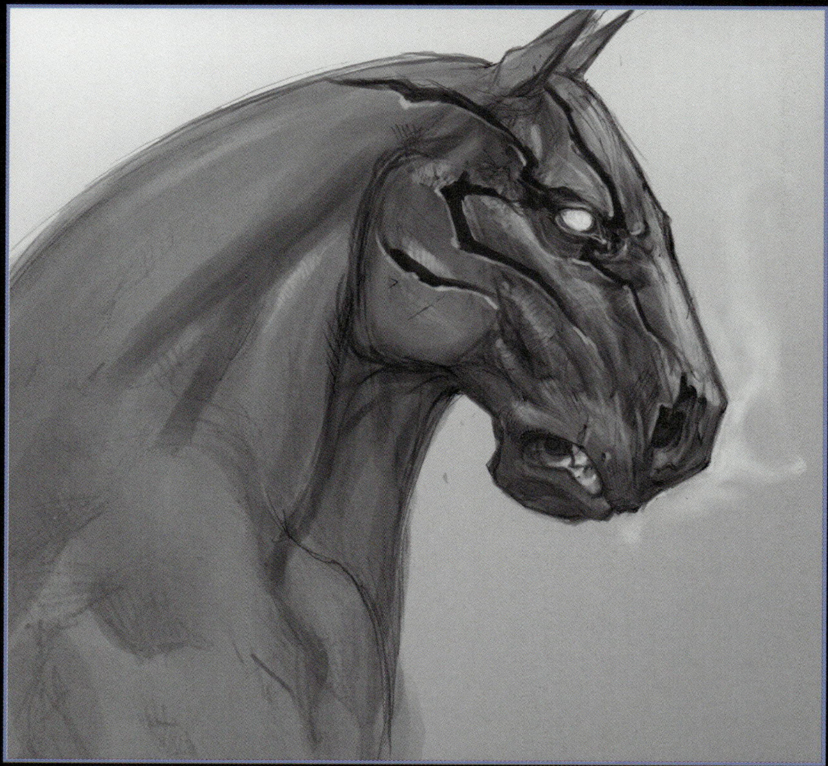

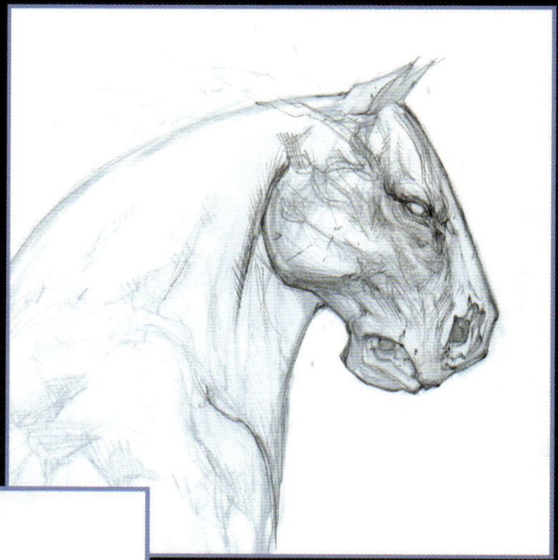

HEAD CONCEPTS

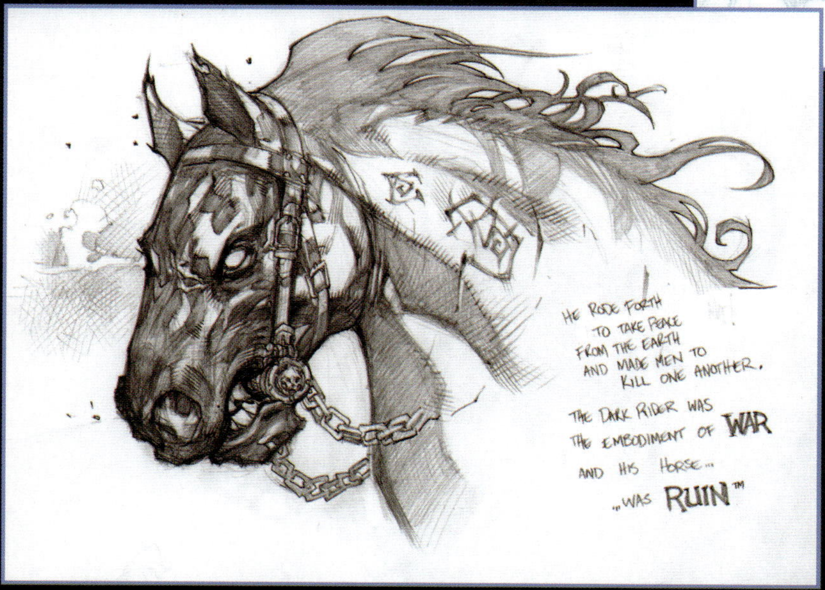

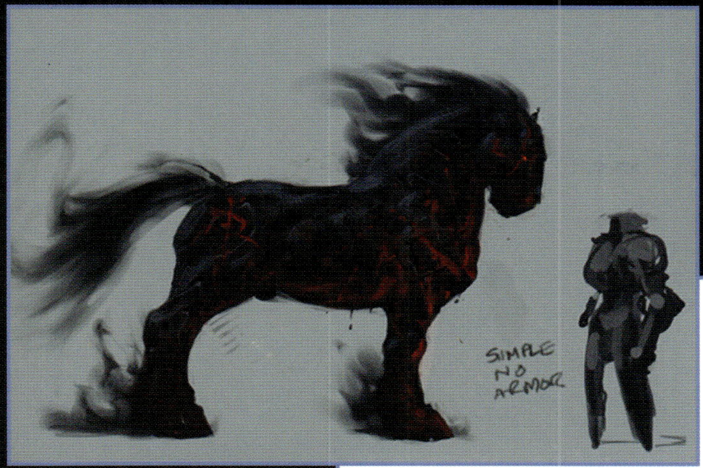

WITHOUT ARMOR

RUIN WITH ARMOR

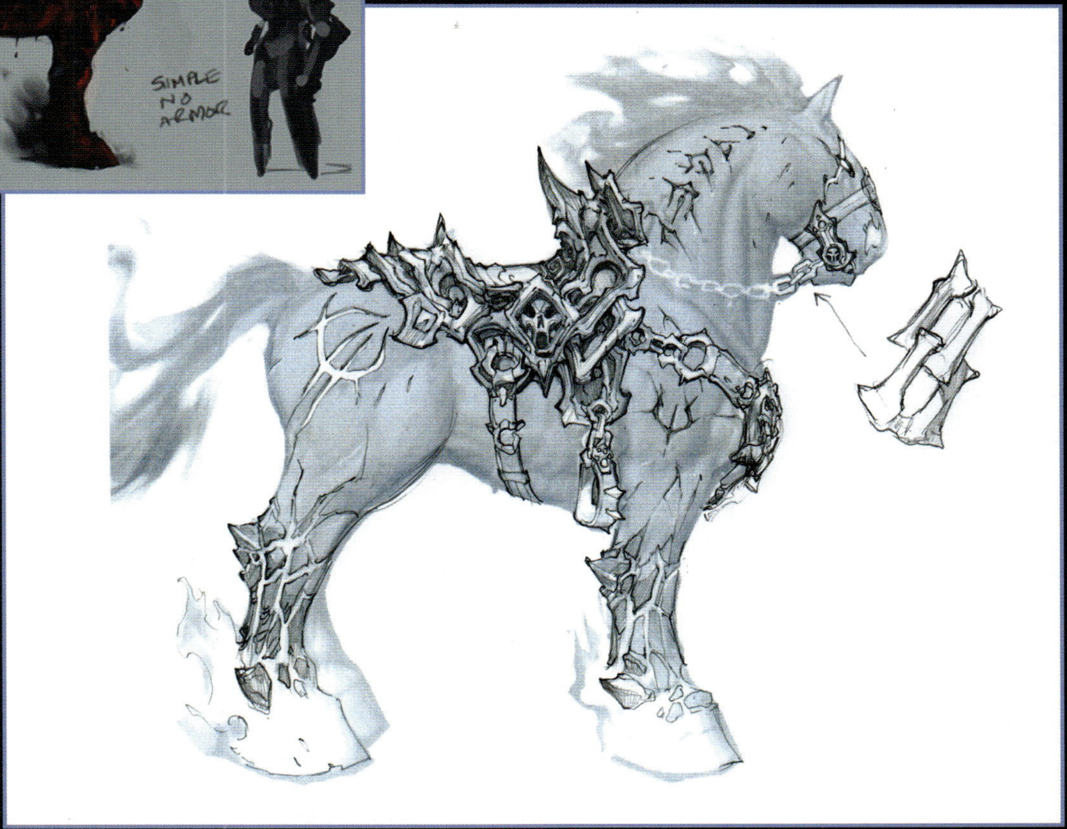

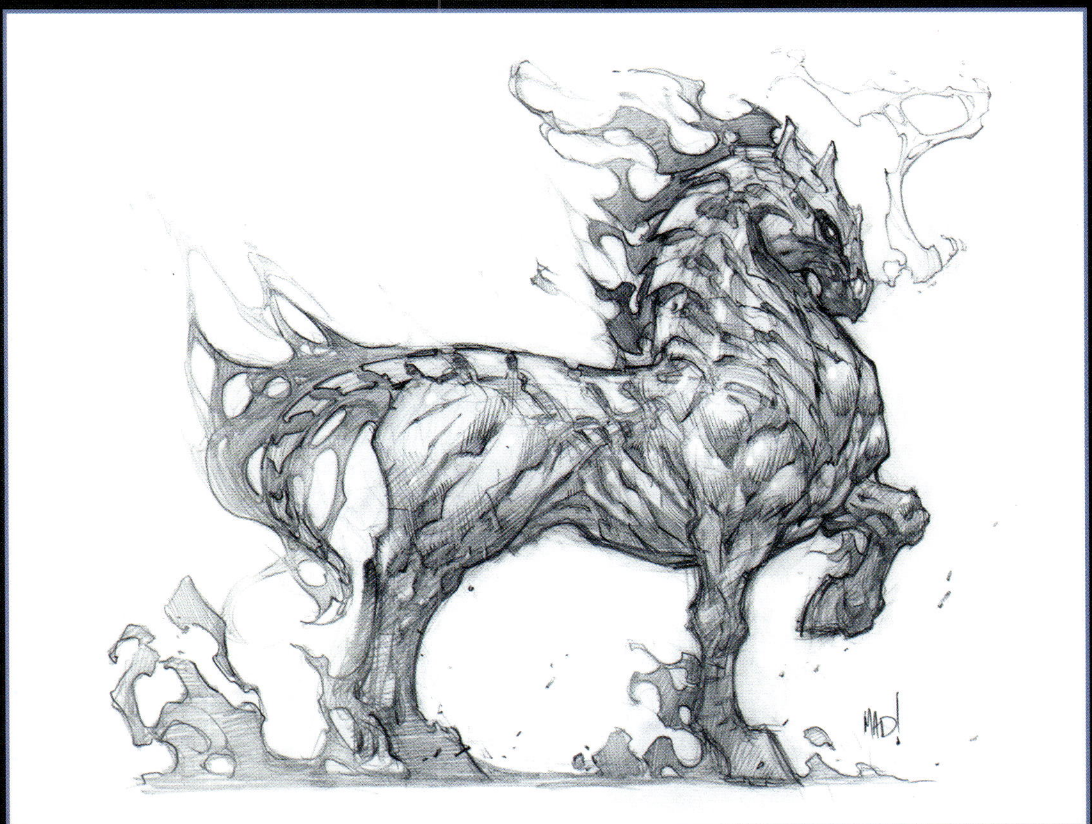

ALTERNATE DESIGN

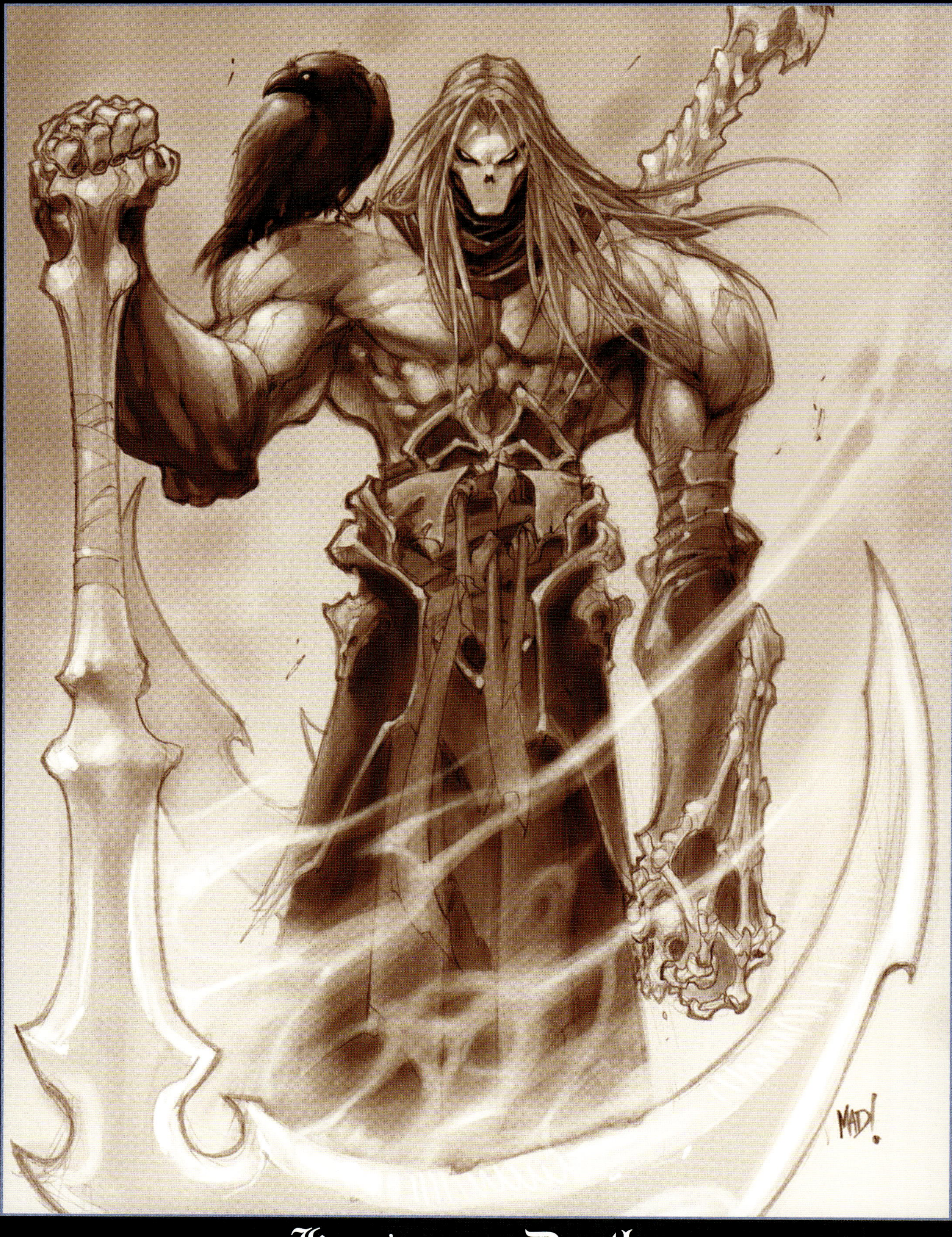

Horsemen: Death

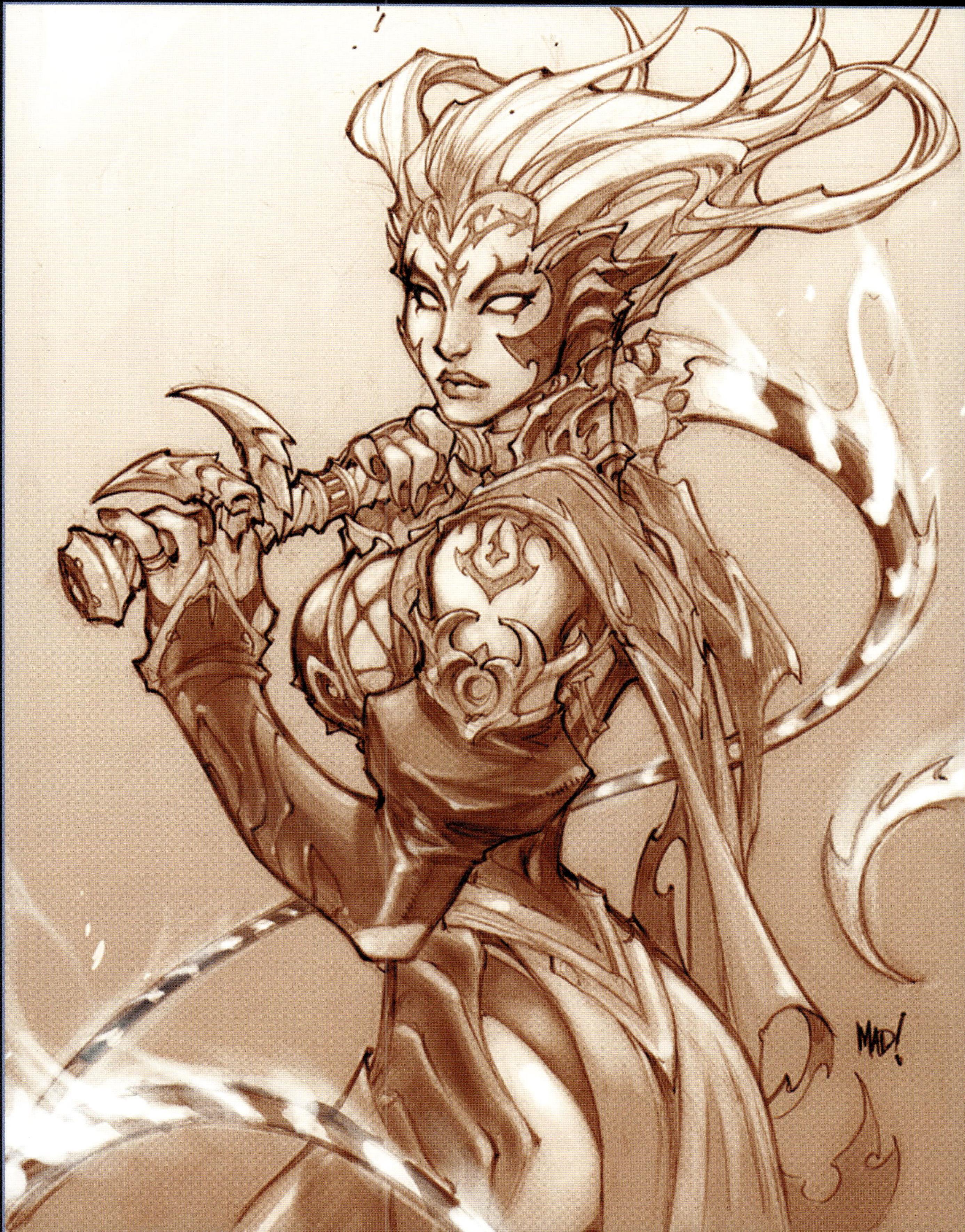

Horsemen: Fury

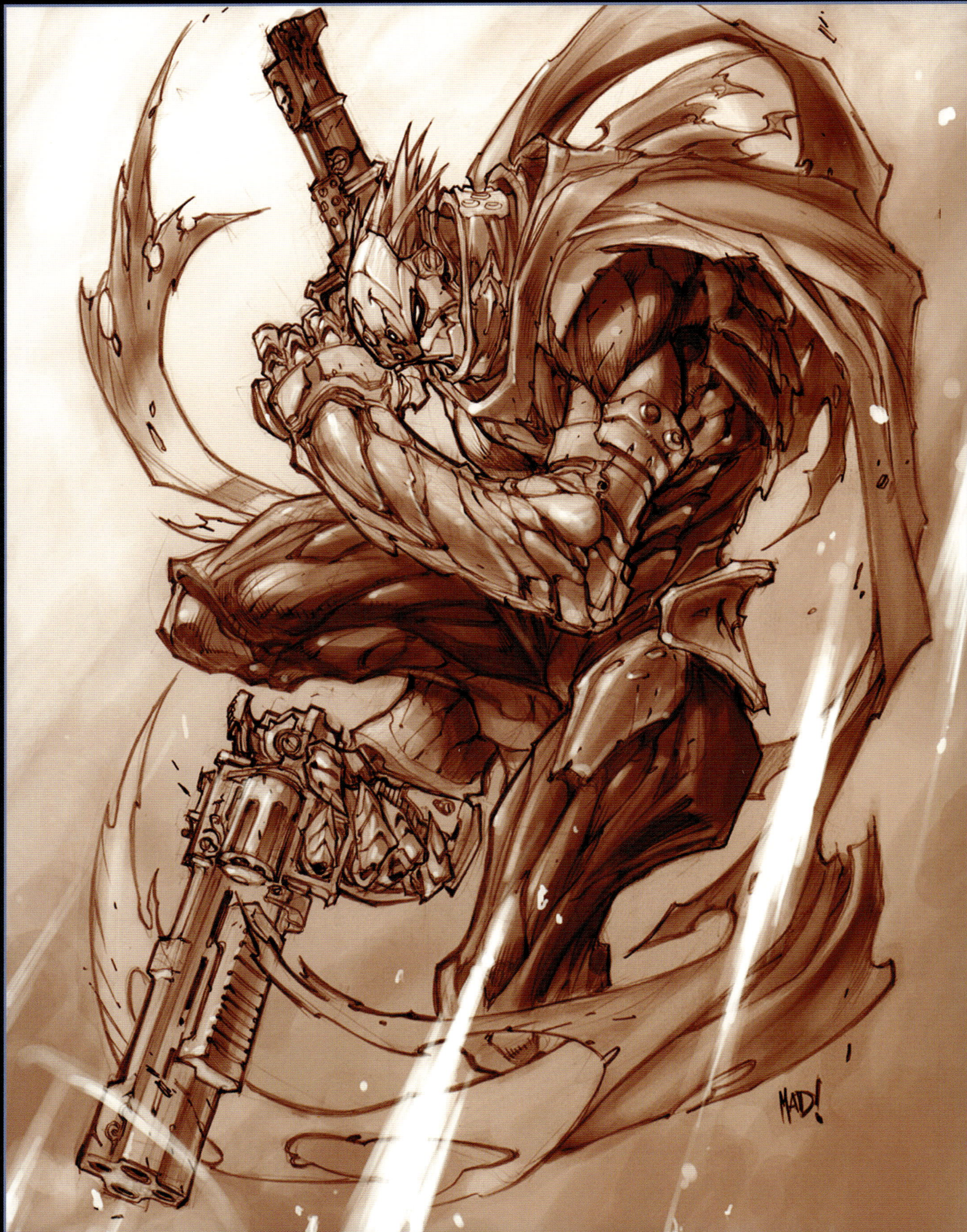

Horsemen - Strife

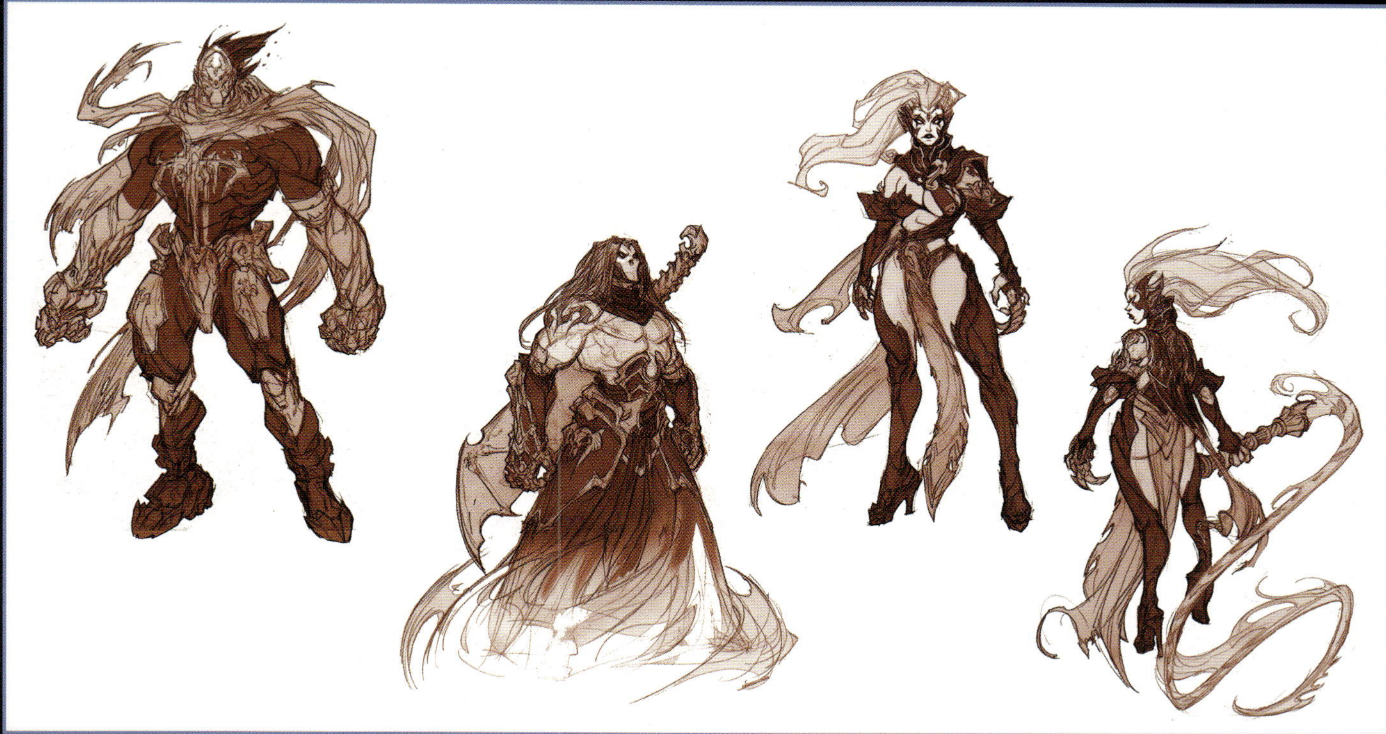

BODY SHOTS

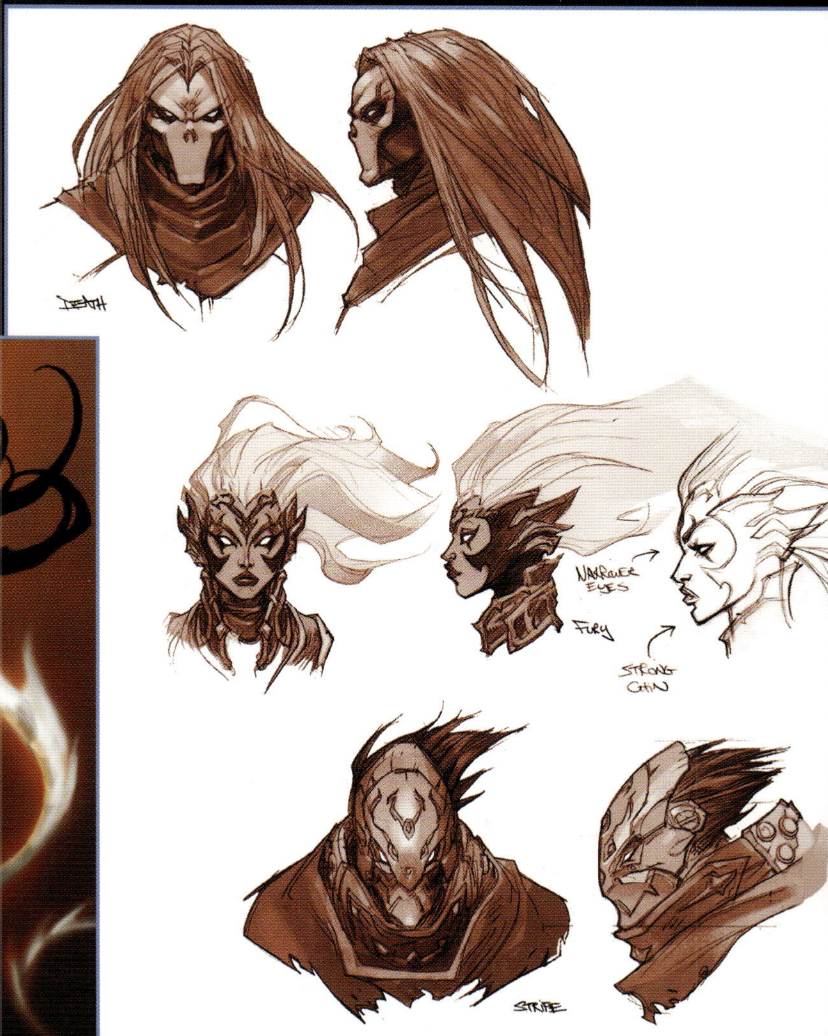

HEADSHOTS

COLOR TEST

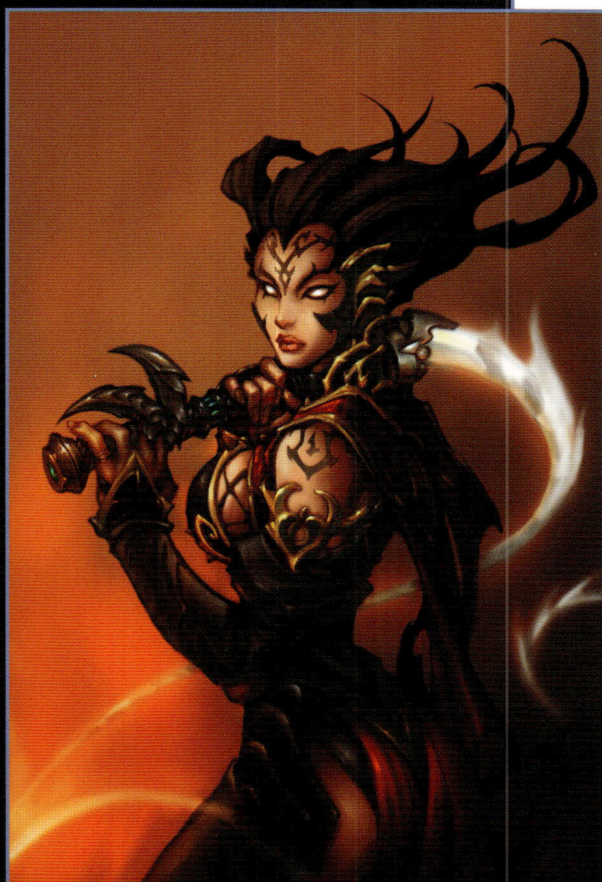

The Charred Council

There is but one authority in the universe that cannot be questioned—the Charred Council. These three omniscient beings, bound by ancient laws, are charged with preserving the balance between Heaven, Hell, and the Kingdom of Man. To oppose the Council's edicts is to invite terrible retribution at the hands of its enforcers, the dreaded Four Horsemen.

The Council is not known for its mercy. I feel the shadow of the Horsemen looming over the world. We will all answer for the Destroyer's crimes, and "balance" will be measured out in blood and fire.

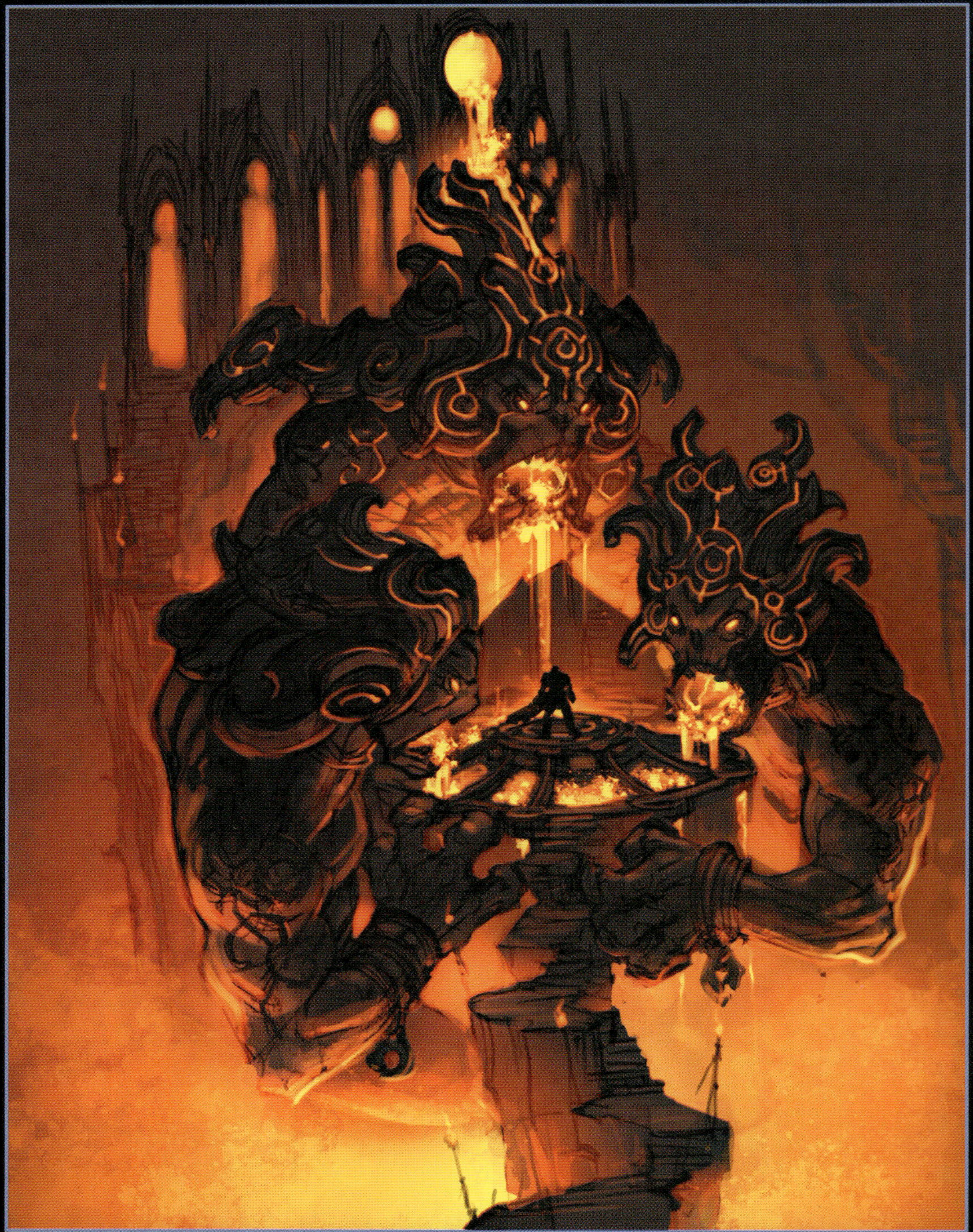

CONCEPT

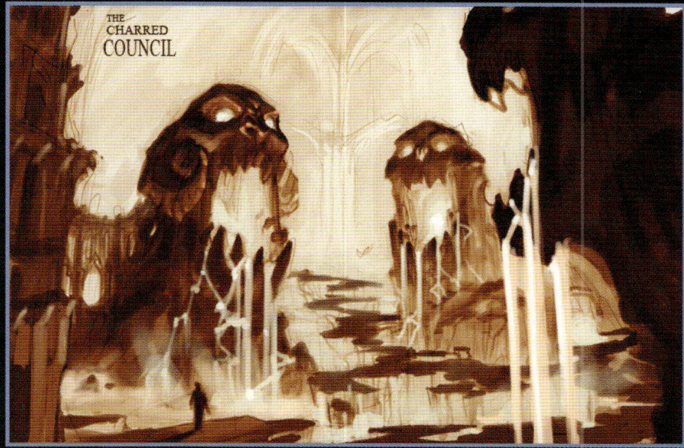

CONCEPTS

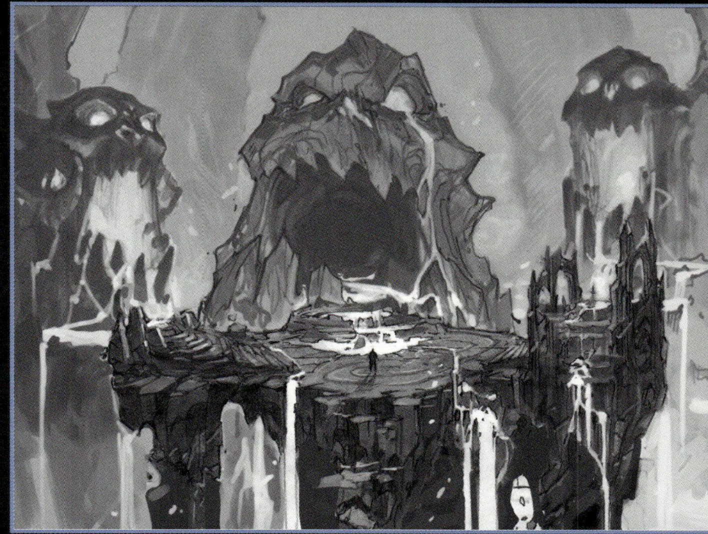

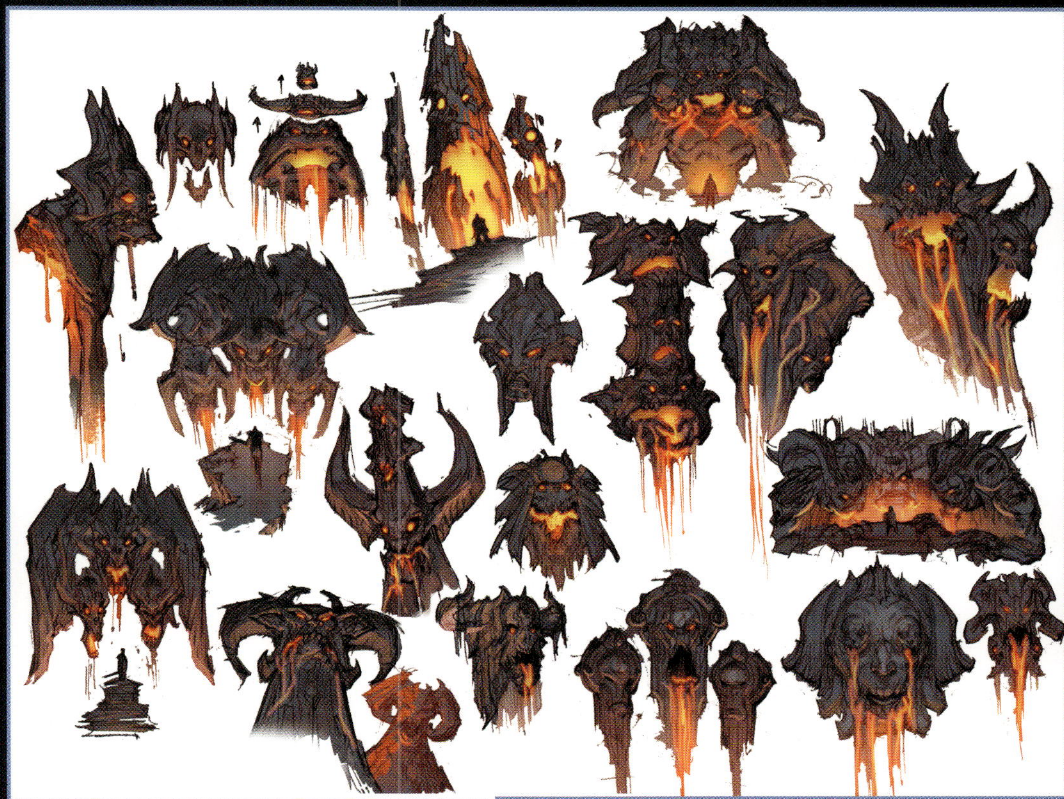

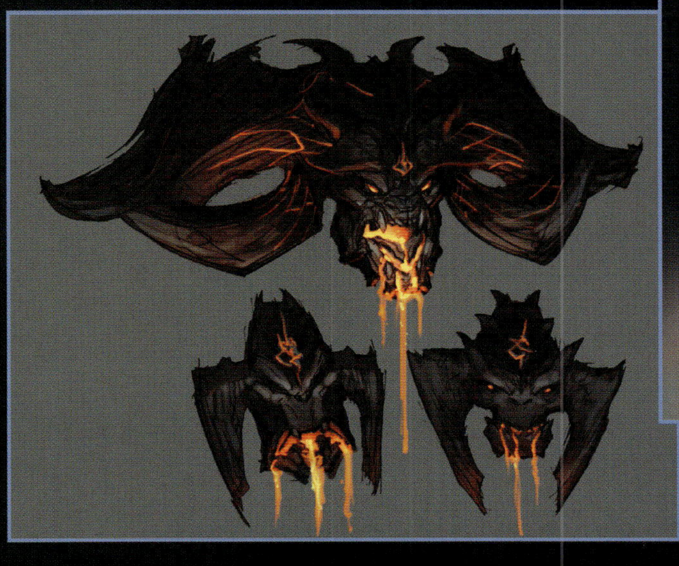

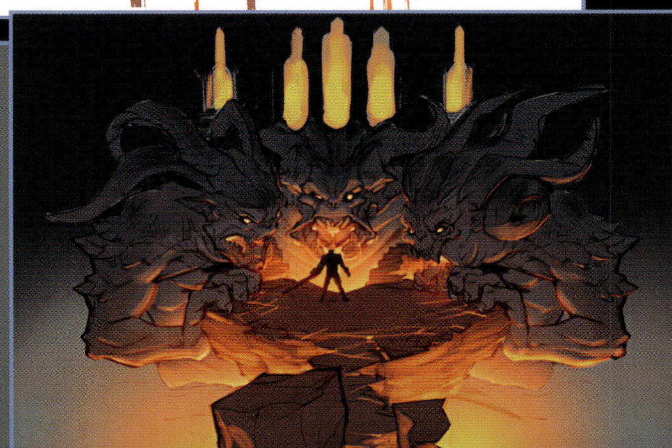

CONCEPTS

Vulgrim

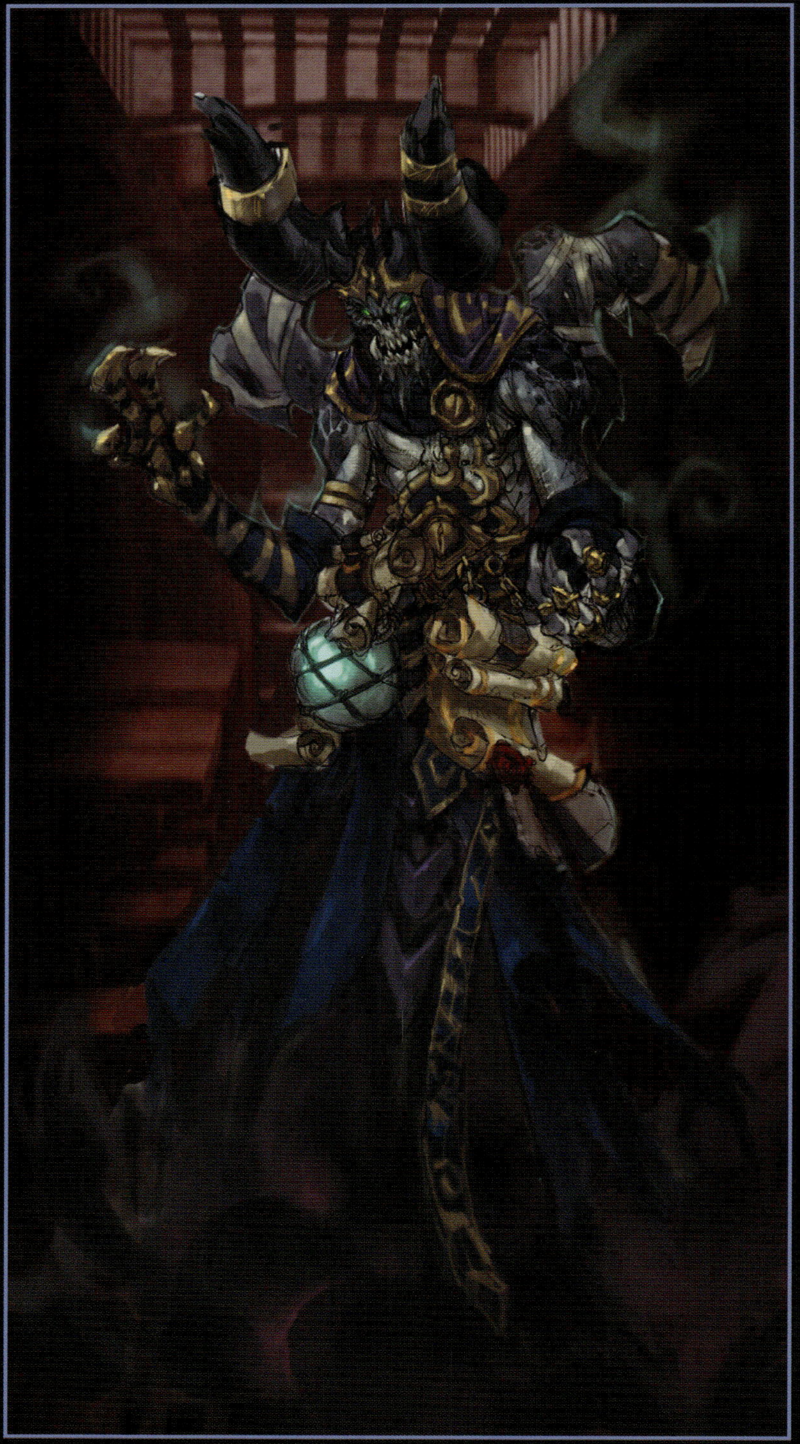

Vulgrim's twisted mind spins with so many detestable schemes that I doubt he even trusts himself. Indeed, he has grown even more devious since mankind exhaled its last breath. If this wretched demon's business is collecting souls, his pleasure is devouring them.

Always ravenous, Vulgrim will beg, steal, or kill for souls. He has also been known to trade for them. A desperate warrior might find such a black bargain palatable. To find him, one need only seek Vulgrim's glyphs, burned into the ground beneath demon haunts and the broken shells of buildings.

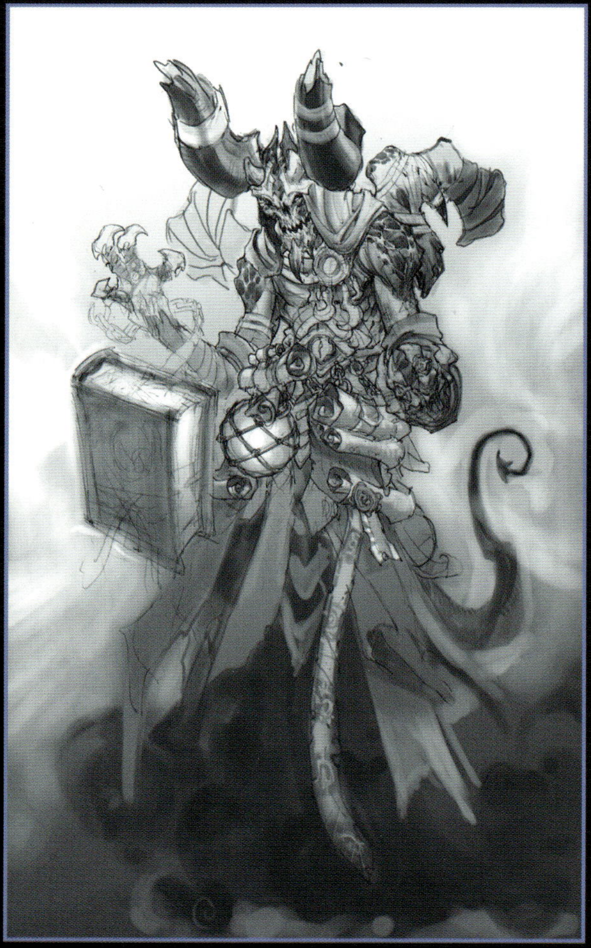

SKETCH

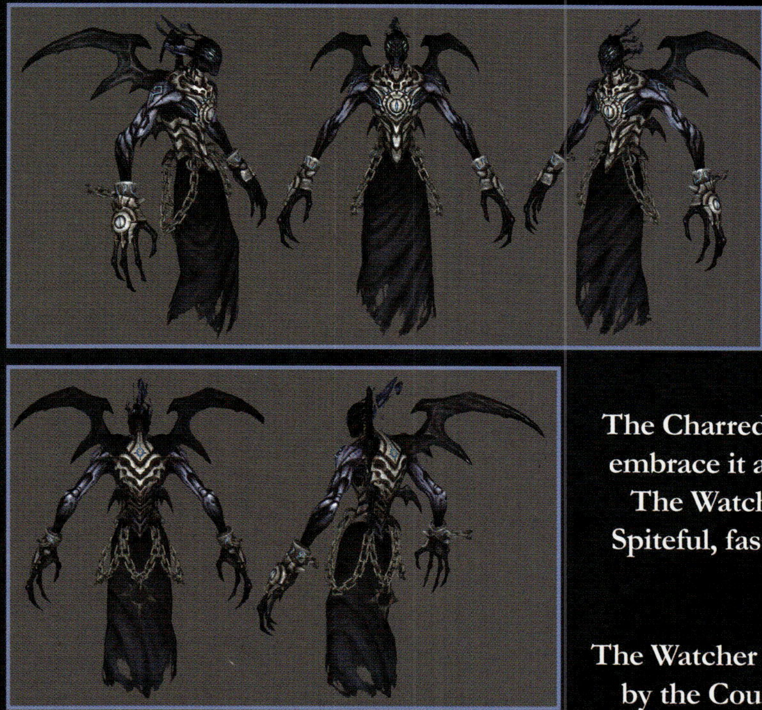

CG TURNAROUNDS

The Watcher

The Charred Council is not averse to evil. If anything, they embrace it as part of the balance they're sworn to protect. The Watcher is a troubling example of such tolerance. Spiteful, fast-talking, and cruel, he is one of the Council's most trusted servants.

The Watcher delights in the suffering of others. Empowered by the Council, he flagrantly tortures and humiliates his charges, dripping poisonous insults and sarcasm onto their prostrate forms. I long for the day when the Watcher's leash is broken and his cruelty is repaid in kind.

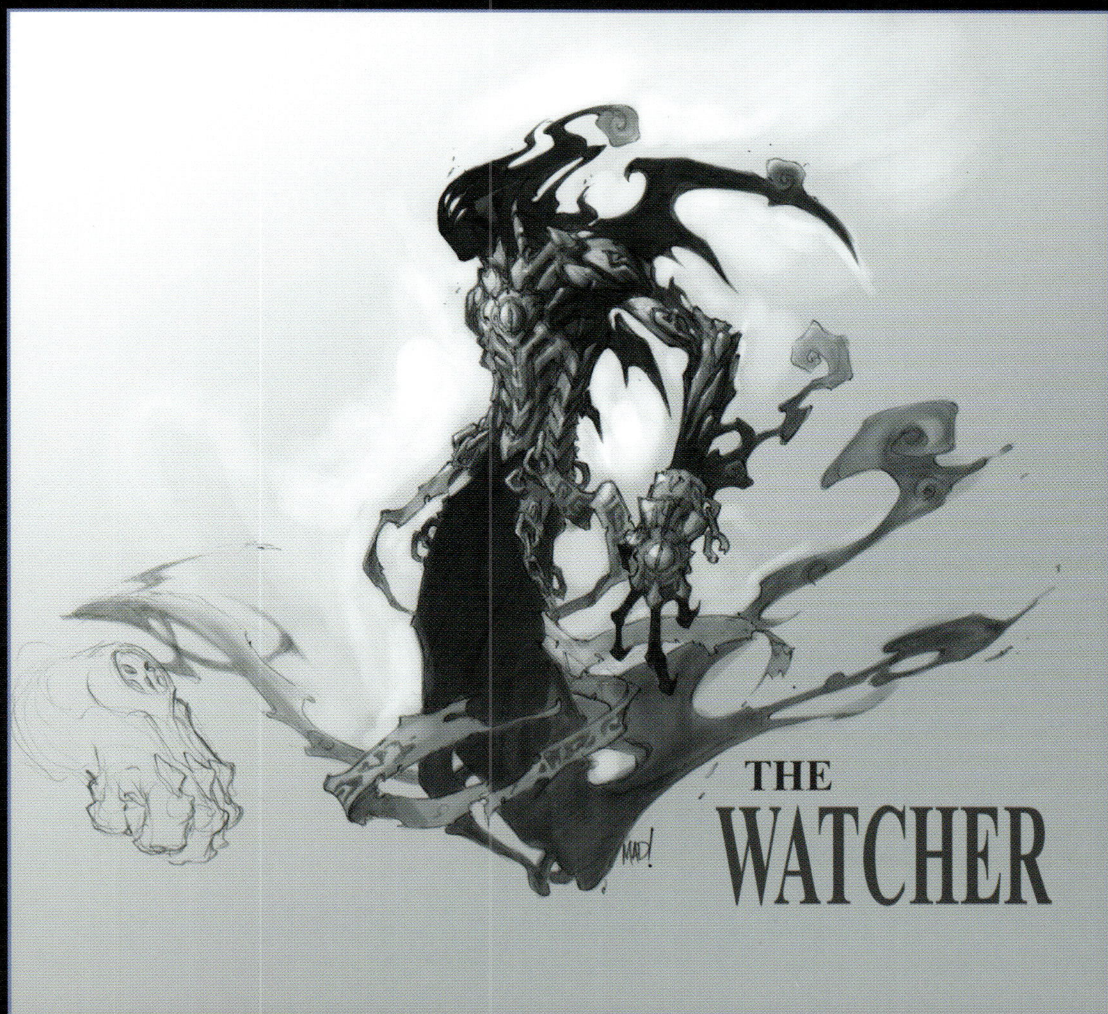

SKETCH

Ulthane

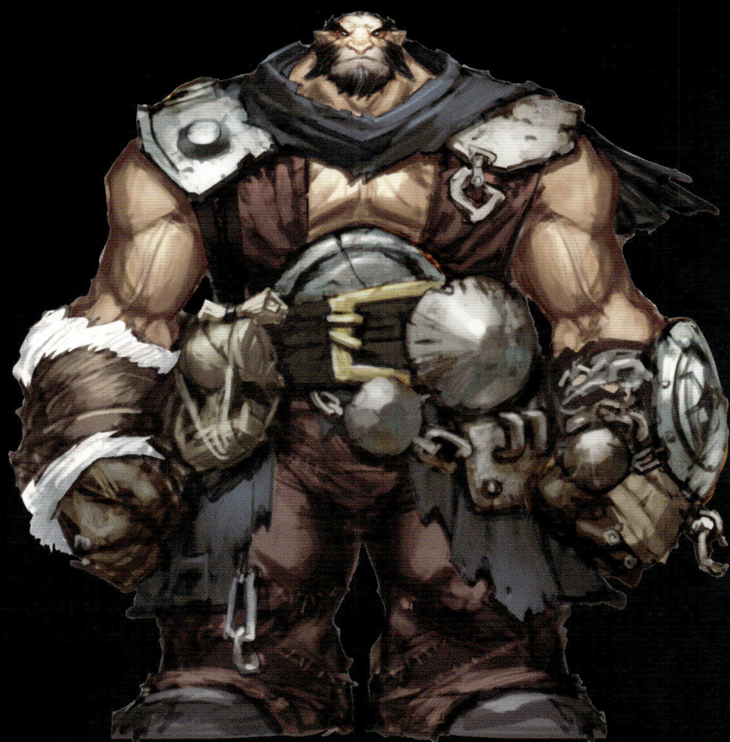

Ulthane is an Old One with a unique perspective on the endless machinations of Heaven and Hell—they don't concern him one bit. He greets demons and angels alike with a wink, a merry whistle, and the business end of his black hammer. Through the dark lens of his twisted humor, all is a lark.

The only thing Ulthane takes seriously is the shaping of steel. Among the ranks of legendary weapon-makers, he is unmatched. I have held the Great Smith's craftsmanship myself, his own strength manifest in every line and curve—a sword that could kill a god. The Destroyer will not allow such a weapon to be forged again.

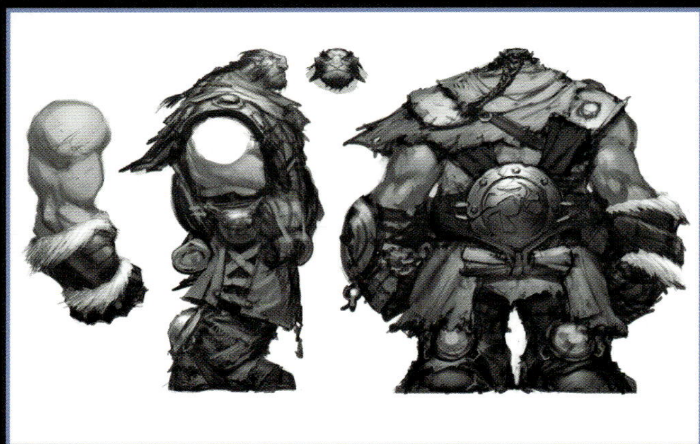

TURNAROUNDS

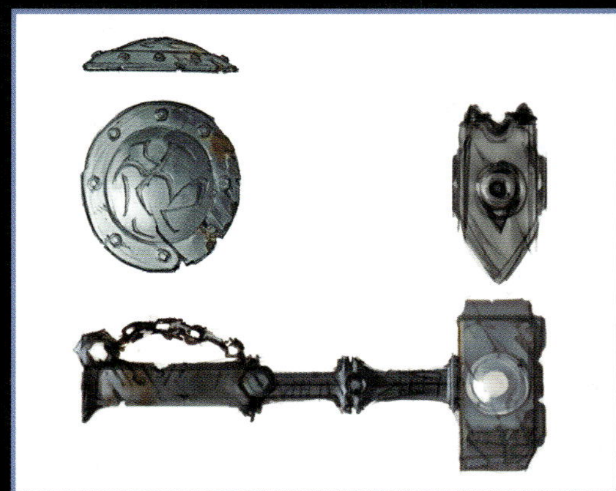

WEAPONS

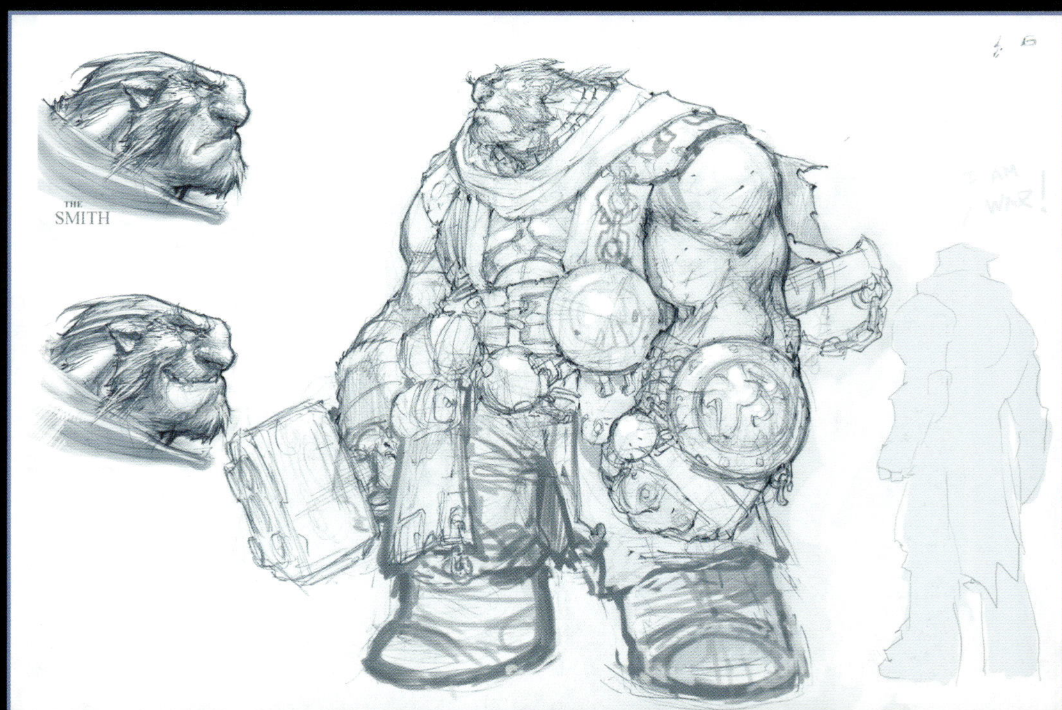

SKETCH

Abaddon

The archangel Abaddon was once a valiant warrior of the Light, feared by Hell's minions and respected by the angels who served under him. His fierce determination to rid the world of infernal corruption was as strong as any weapon. But in the heat of battle, even an iron will can be sundered.

Abaddon led the Heavenly Host into combat during the first desperate hours of the Apocalypse, slaughtering uncounted demons—until the Horseman War distracted him. An instant's hesitation was all that the demon Straga needed to crush Abaddon and drag him into the depths of Hell. The Army of Light has yet to recover from the shattering loss of their champion.

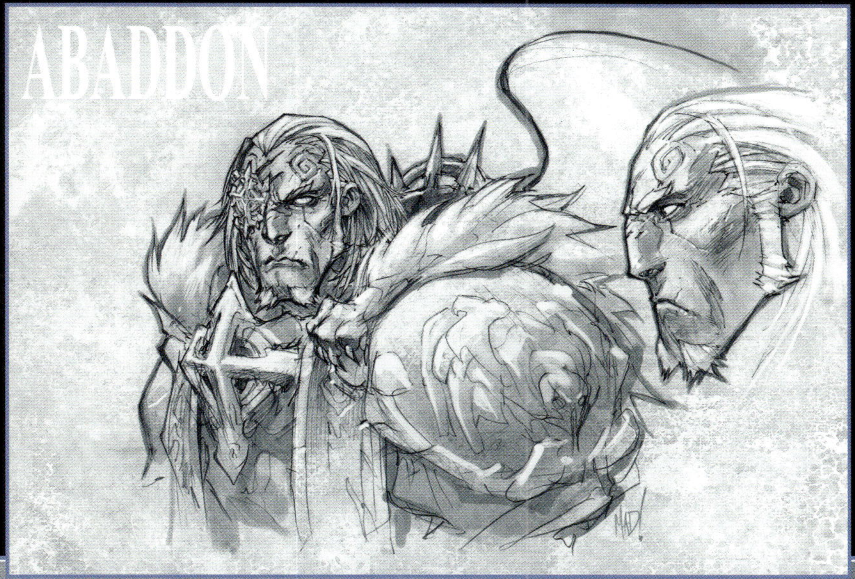

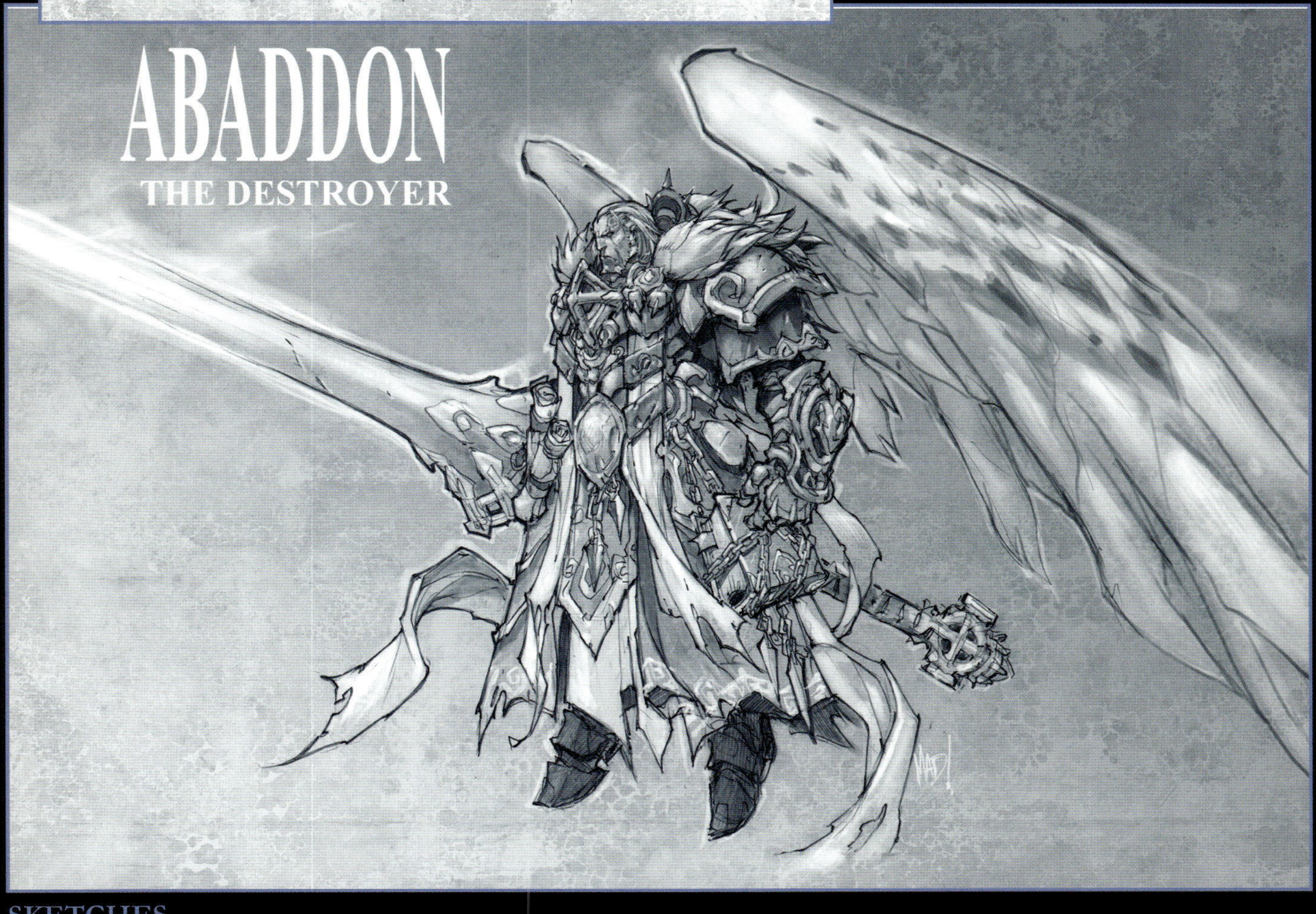

SKETCHES

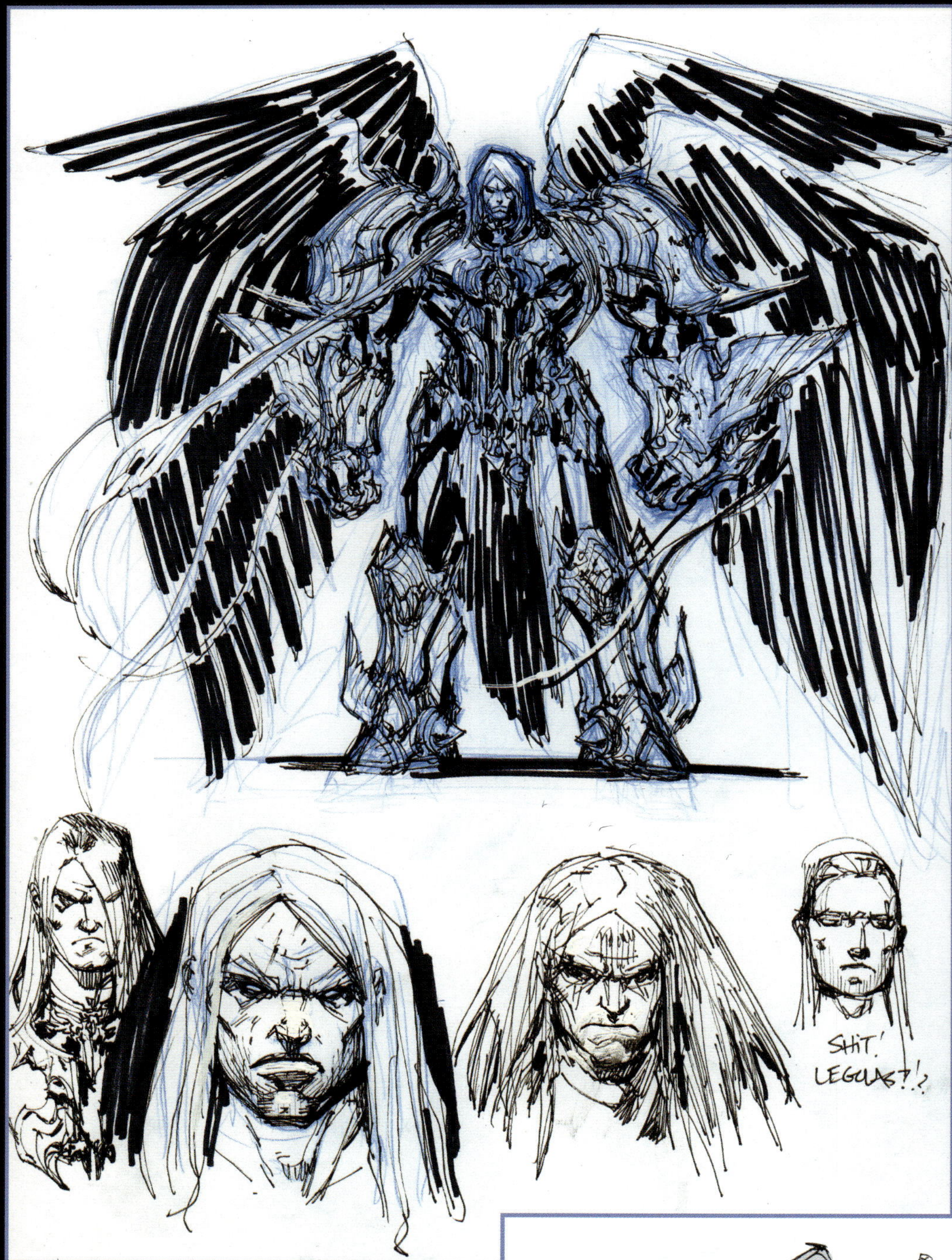

DEVELOPMENT SKETCHES

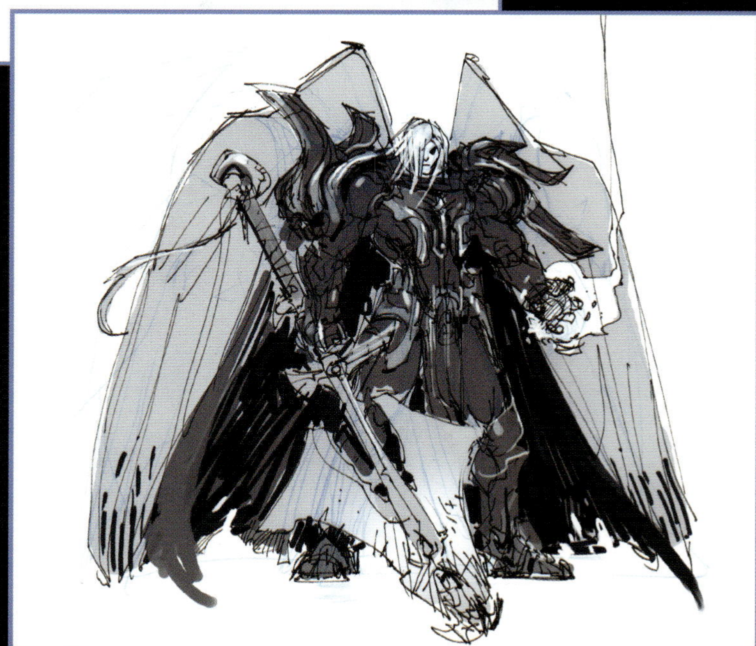

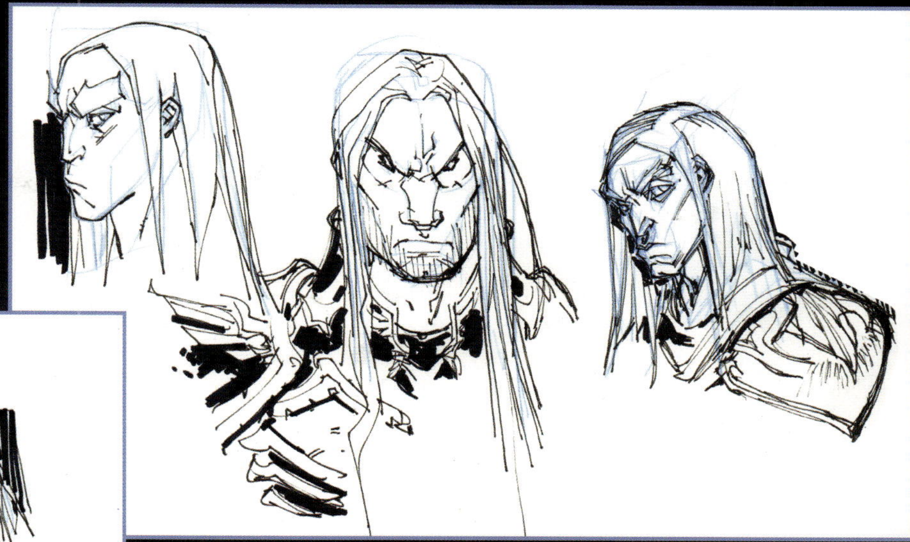

DEVELOPMENT SKETCHES

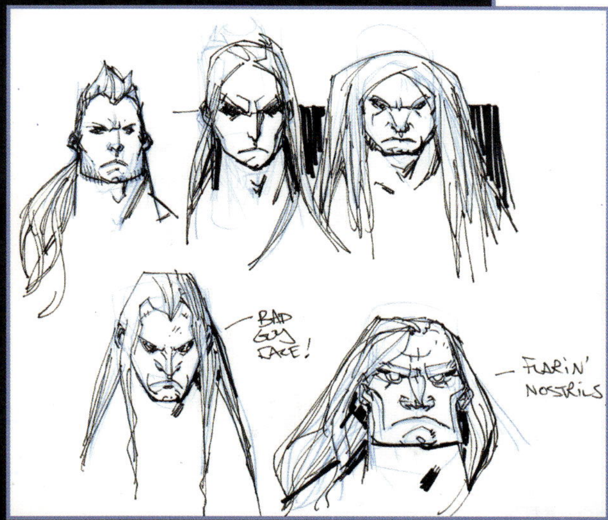

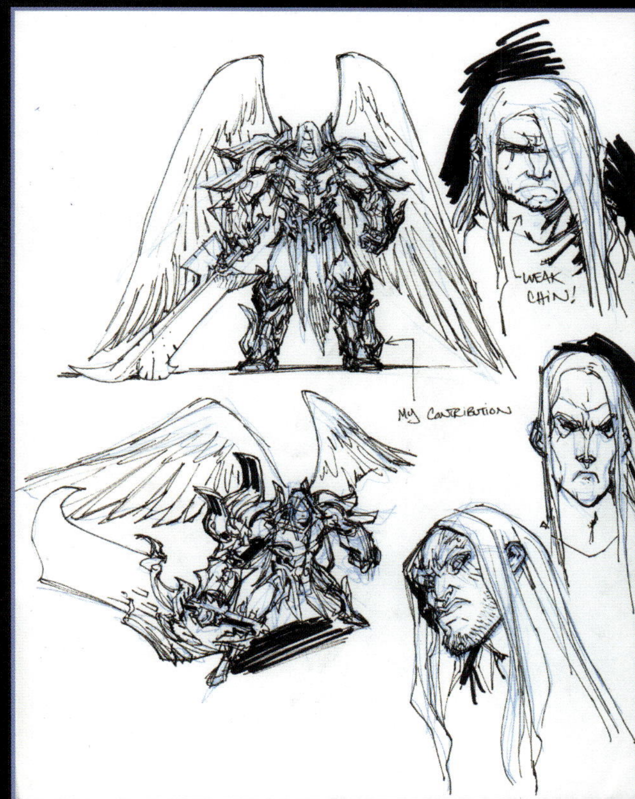

DEVELOPMENT SKETCHES

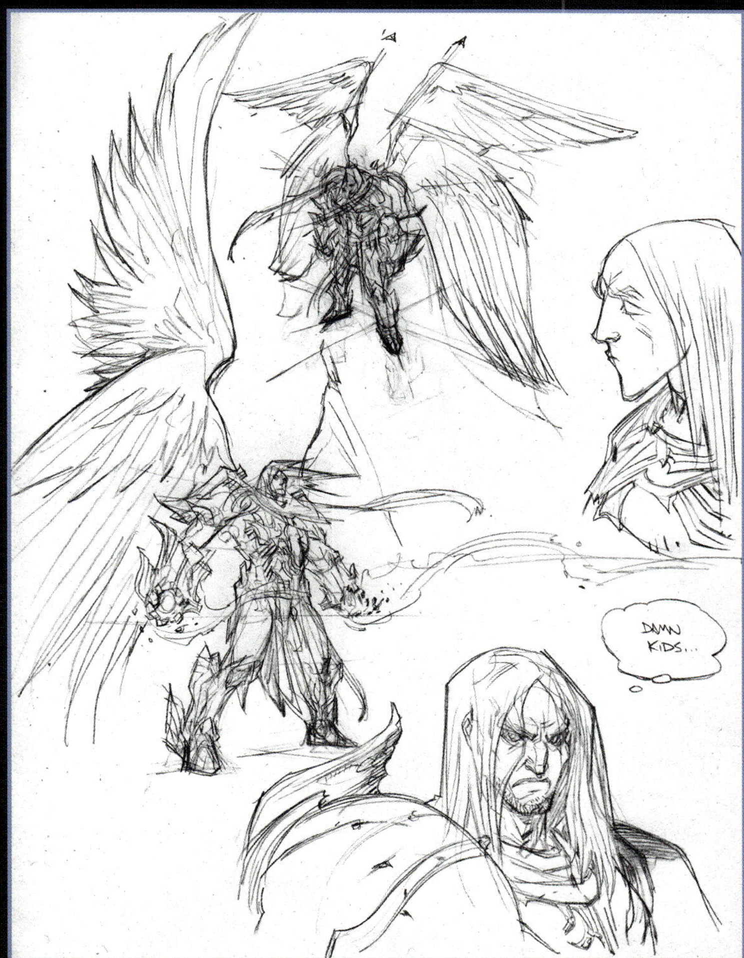

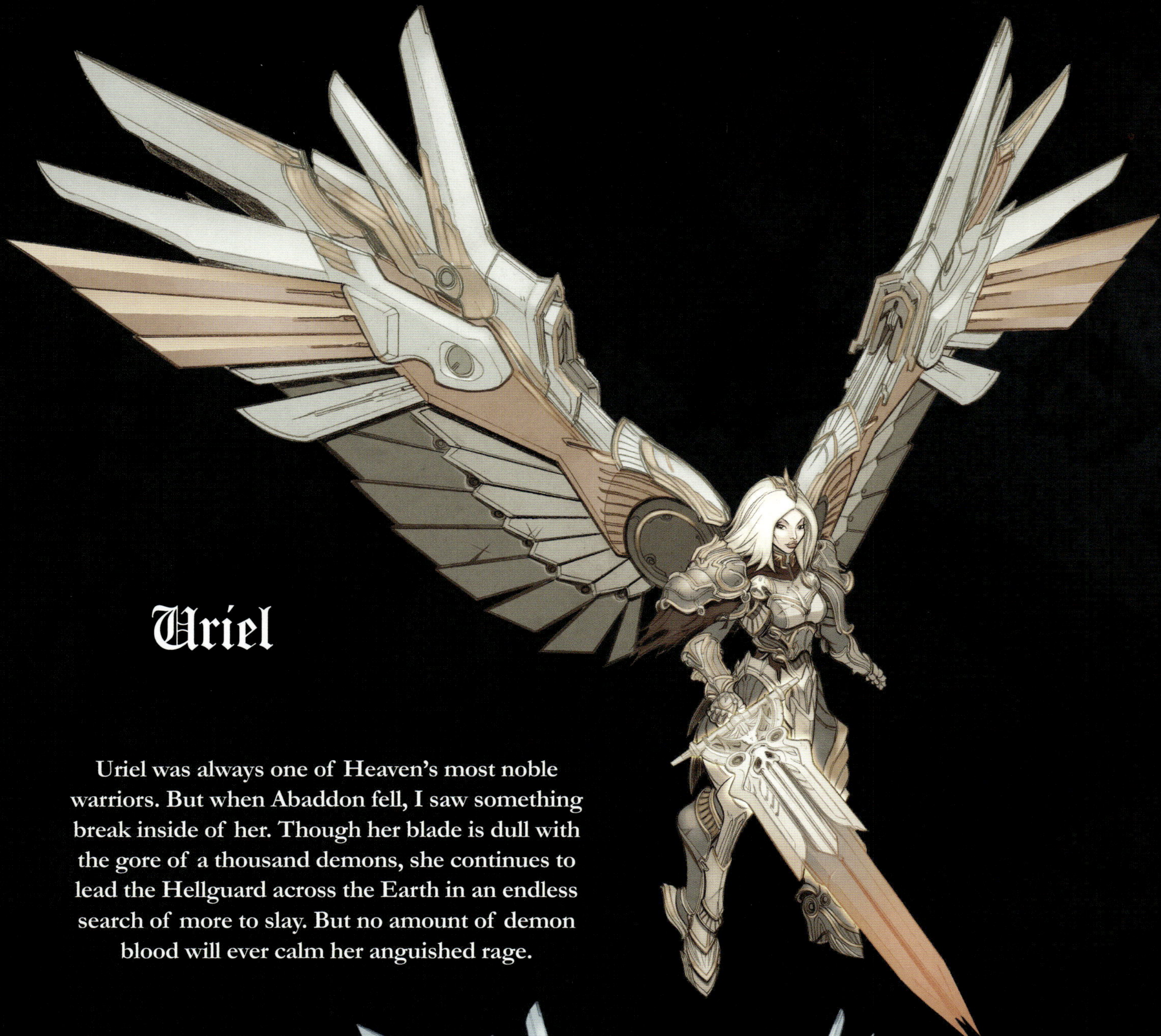

Uriel

Uriel was always one of Heaven's most noble warriors. But when Abaddon fell, I saw something break inside of her. Though her blade is dull with the gore of a thousand demons, she continues to lead the Hellguard across the Earth in an endless search of more to slay. But no amount of demon blood will ever calm her anguished rage.

WING CONCEPTS

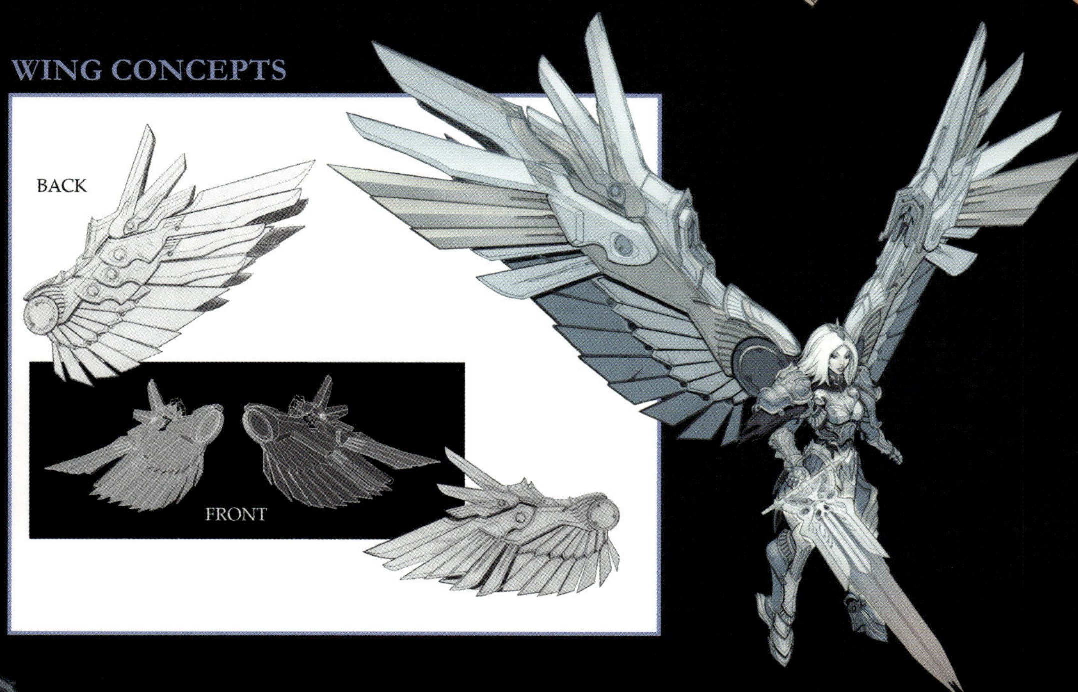

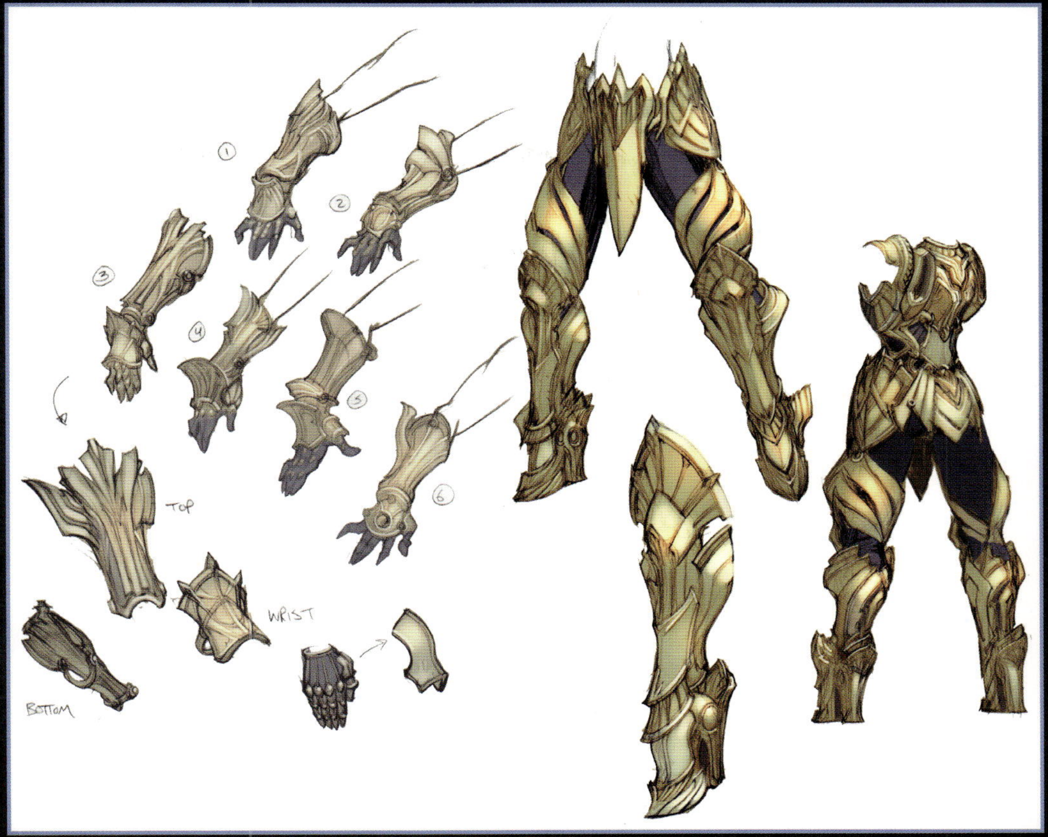

ARMOR DESIGNS

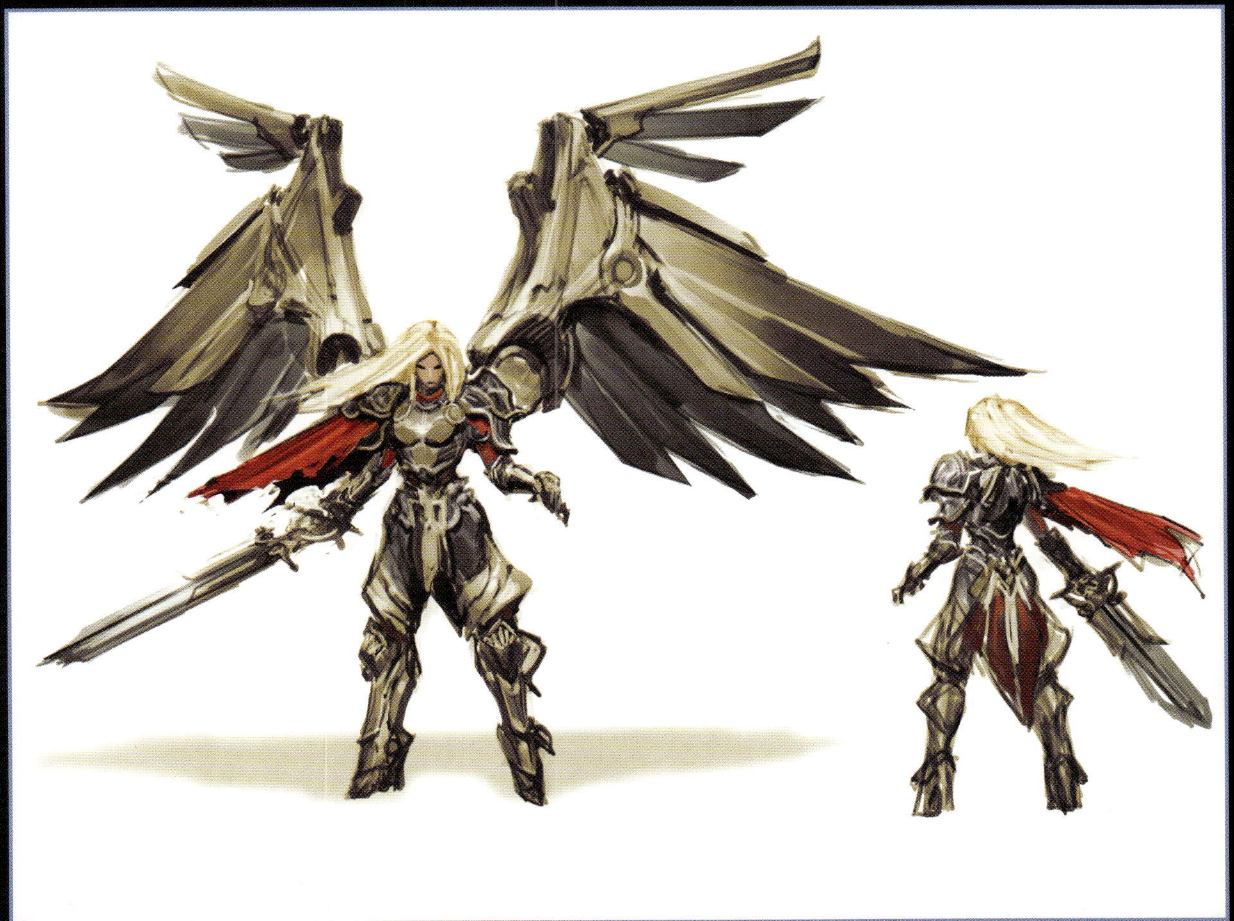

CONCEPTS

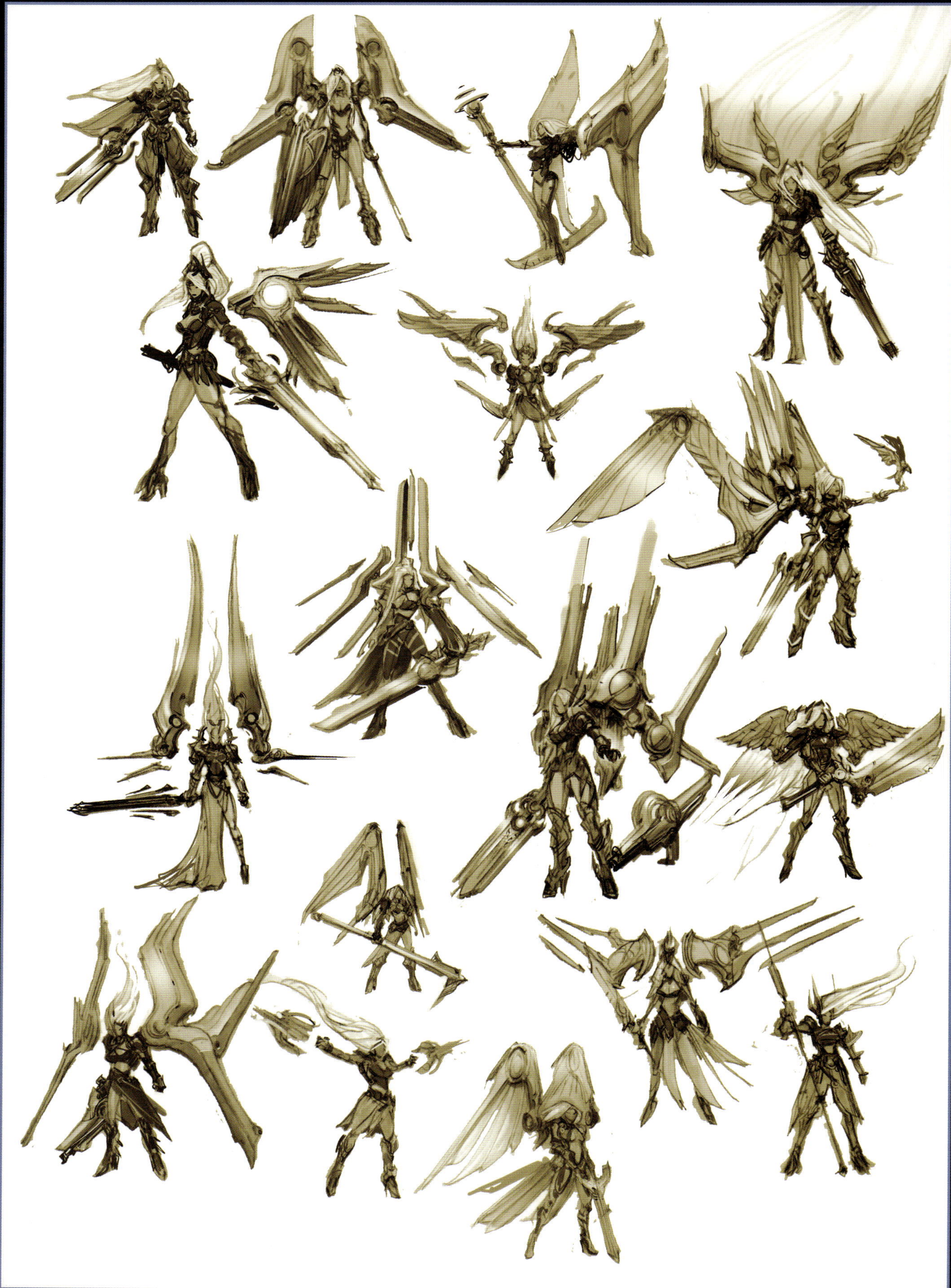

DEVELOPMENT SKETCHES

HEAD DESIGNS

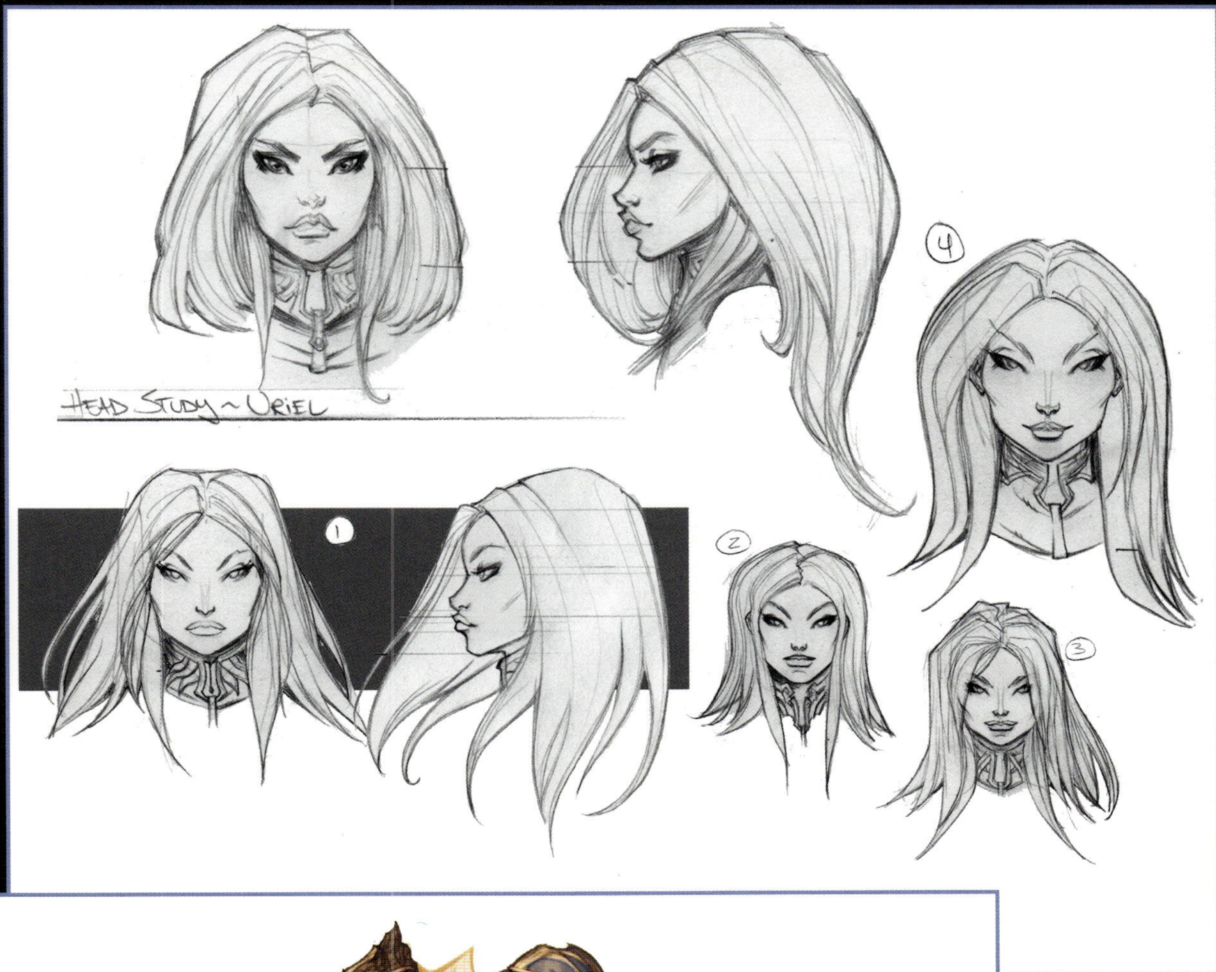

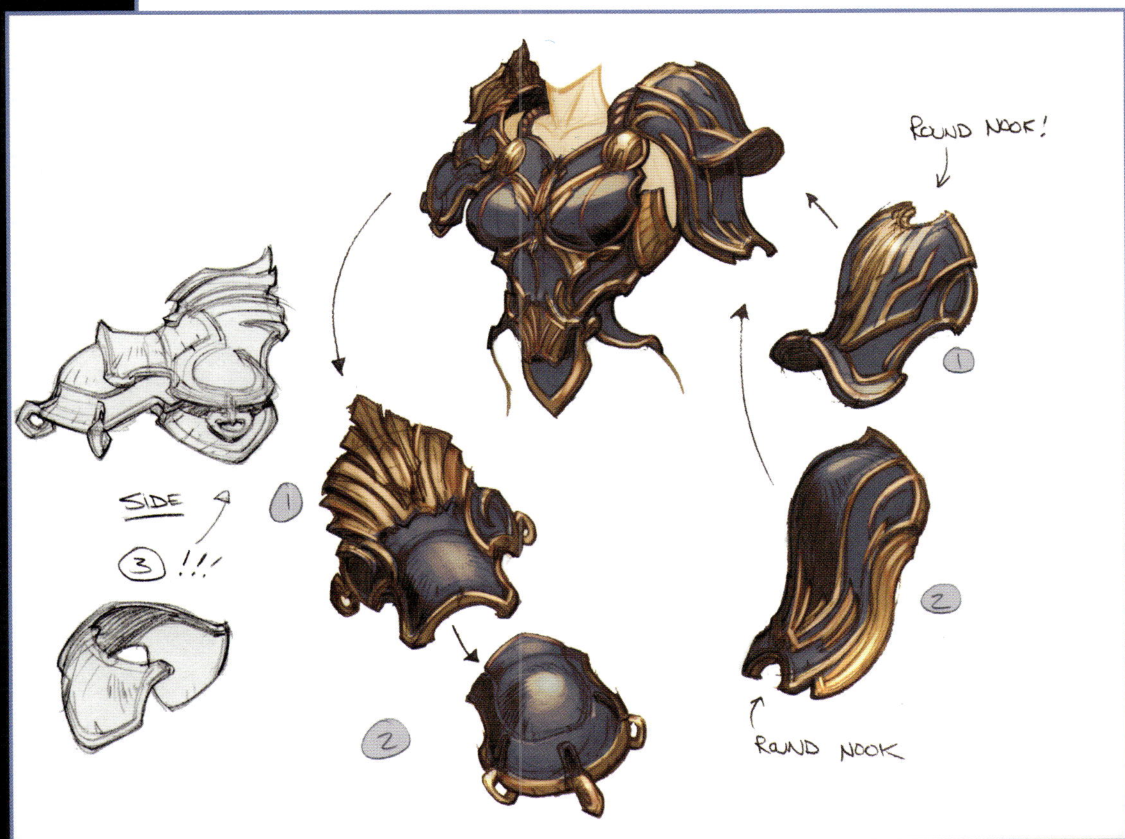

ARMOR DESIGNS

Azreal

HEAD DESIGNS

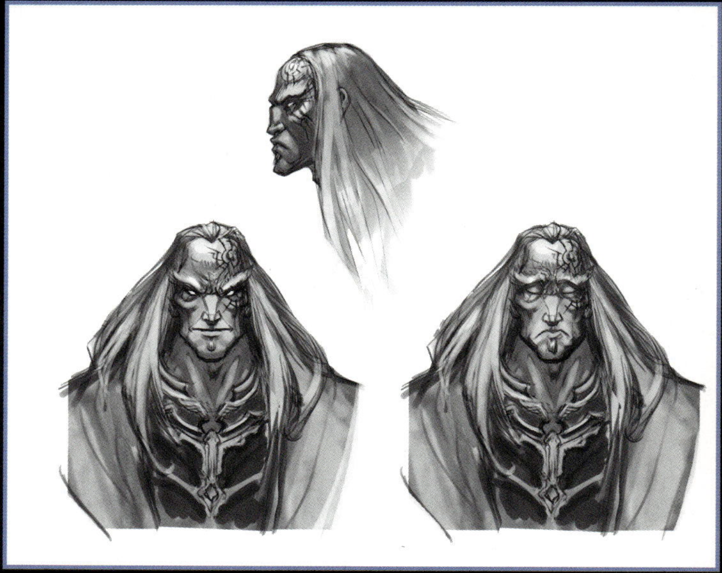

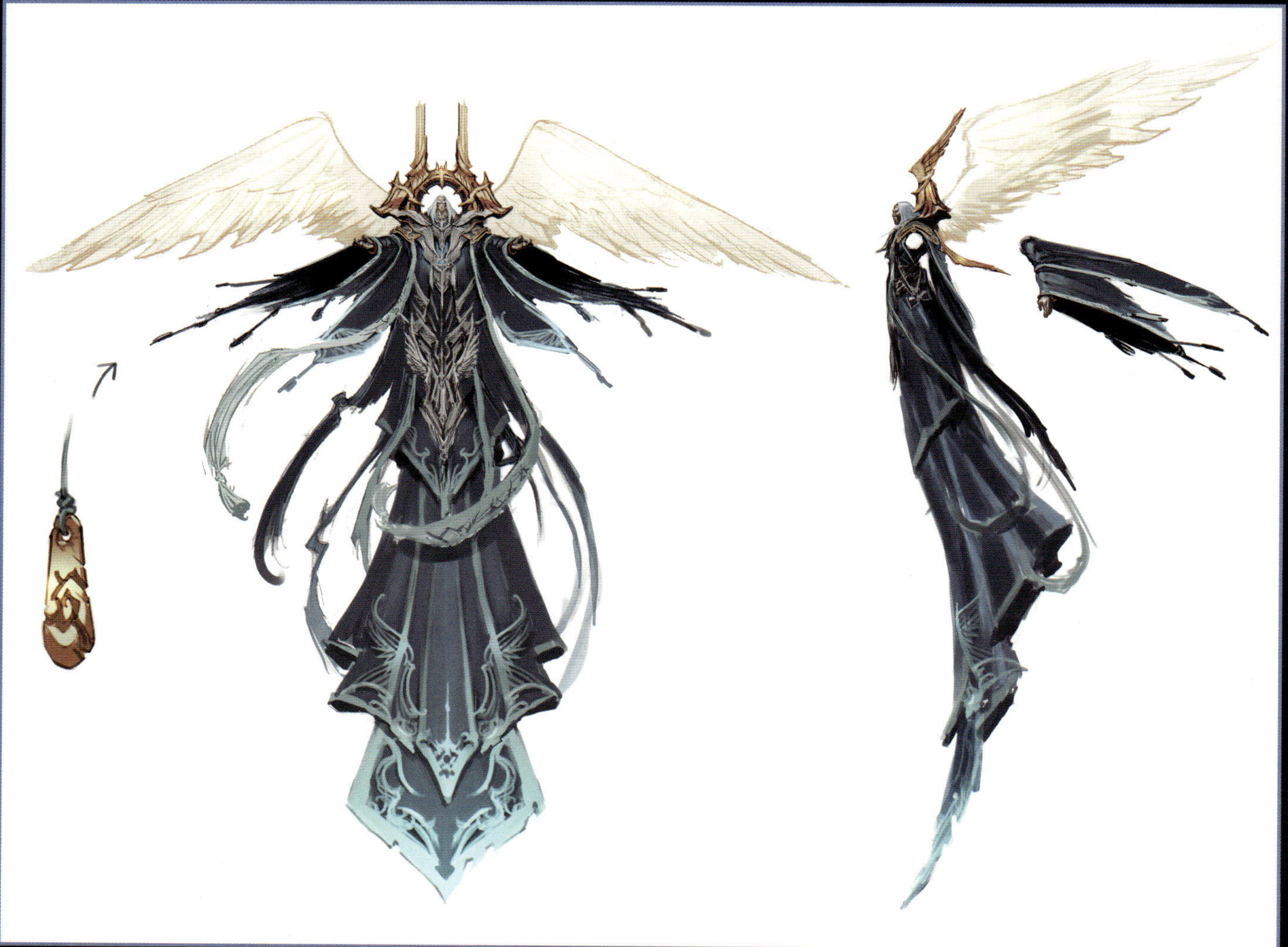

TURNAROUNDS

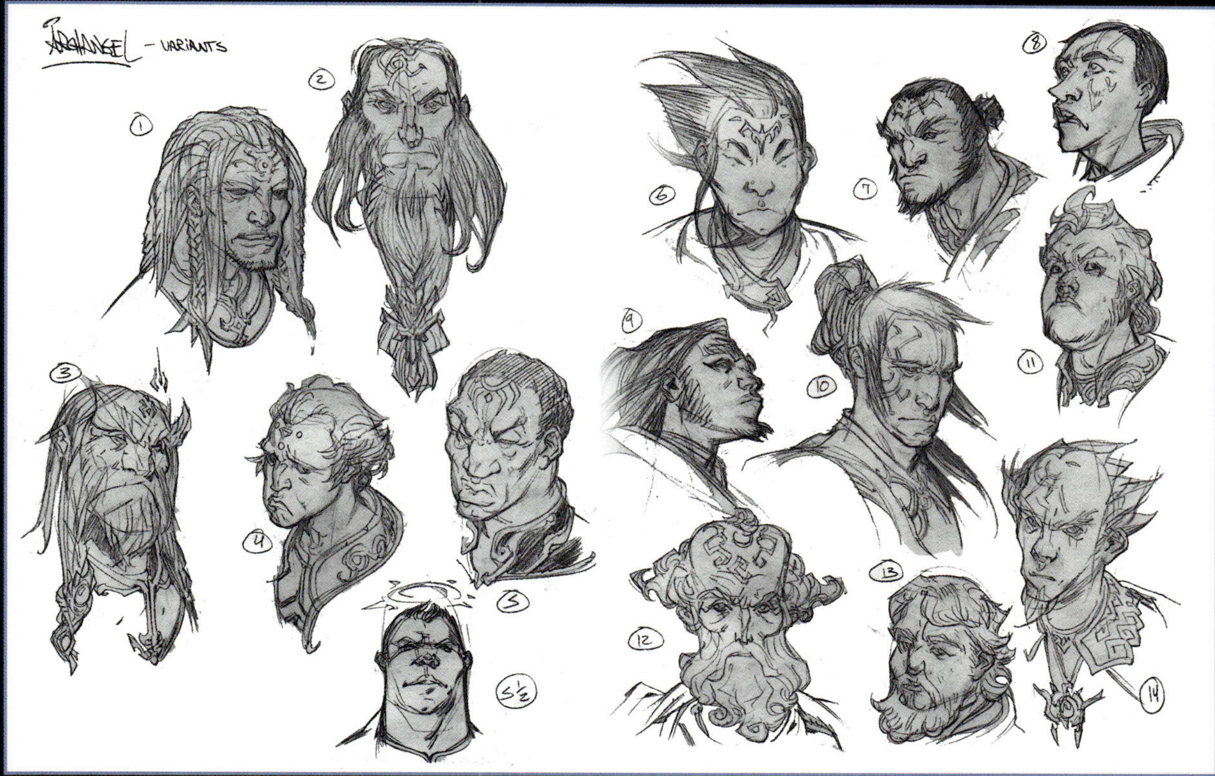

HEAD DESIGNS

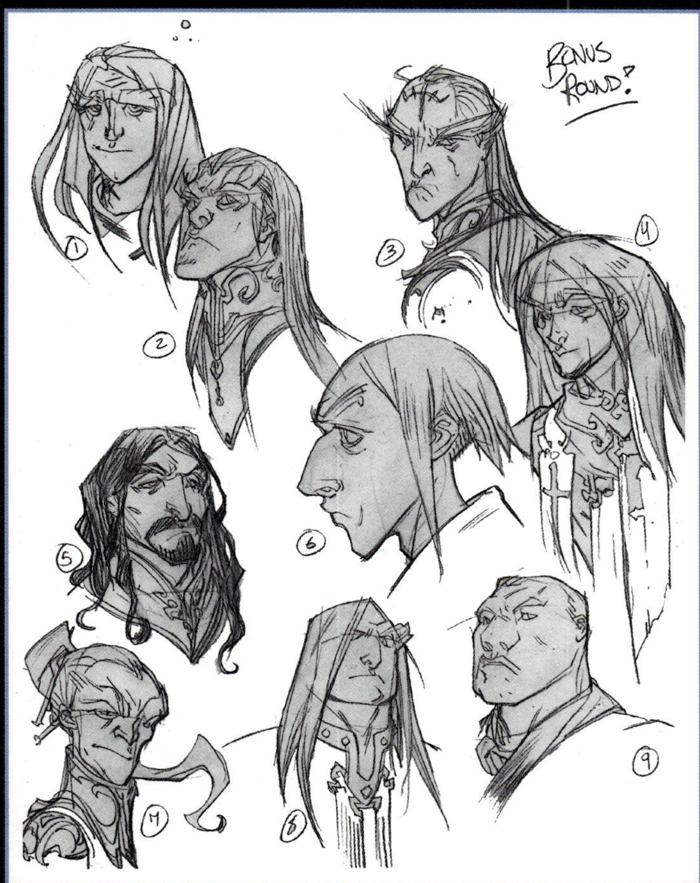

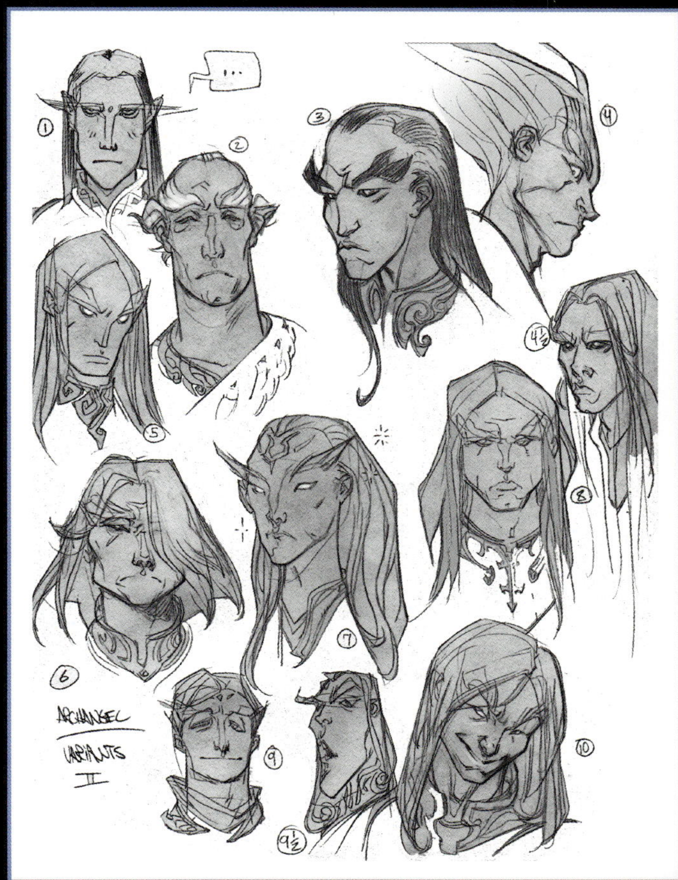

Samael

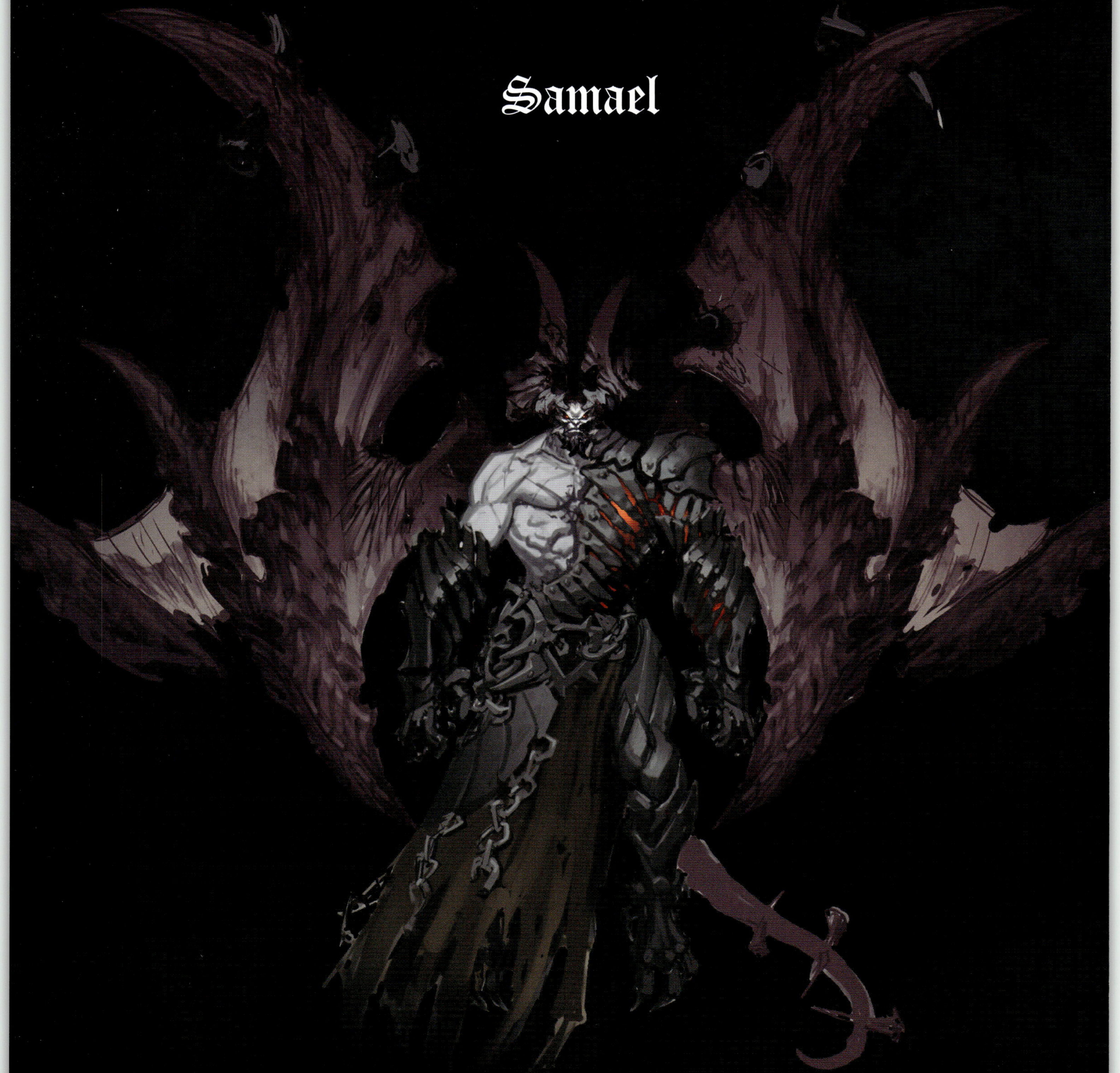

Samael is a demon of terrible power and warped beauty. His black wings are hideously inverted, a cruel mockery of the angels he has battled against for so long. To look upon Samael is to know the true face of evil.

Samael rejected The Destroyer's rule. For this, Samael was imprisoned for eternity. Now, his every thought is of vengeance. I feel his rage throbbing from the heart of the Scalding Gallows, and wonder…could the redemption of this bleak world lie with one so utterly consumed by fury?

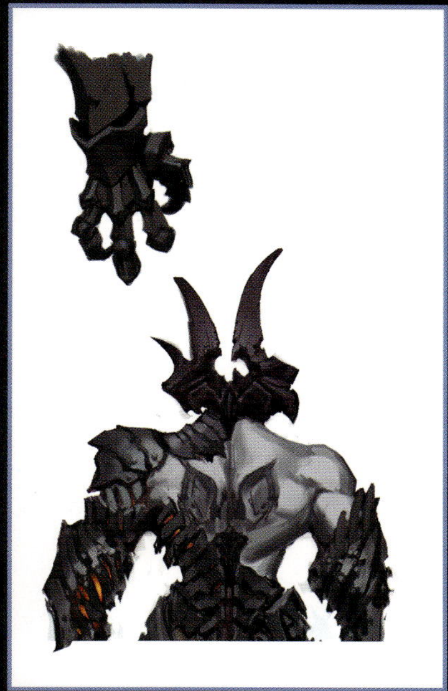

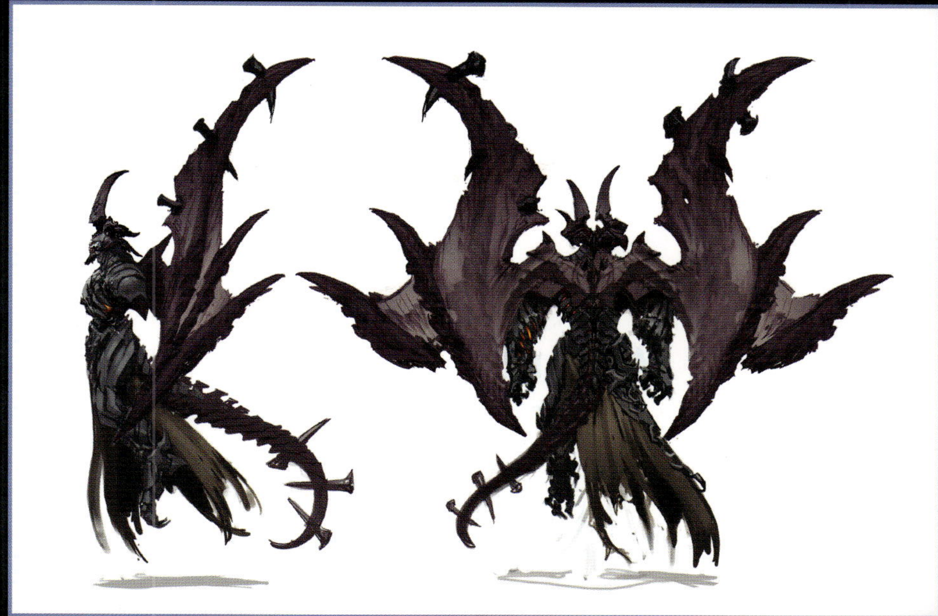

TURNAROUNDS

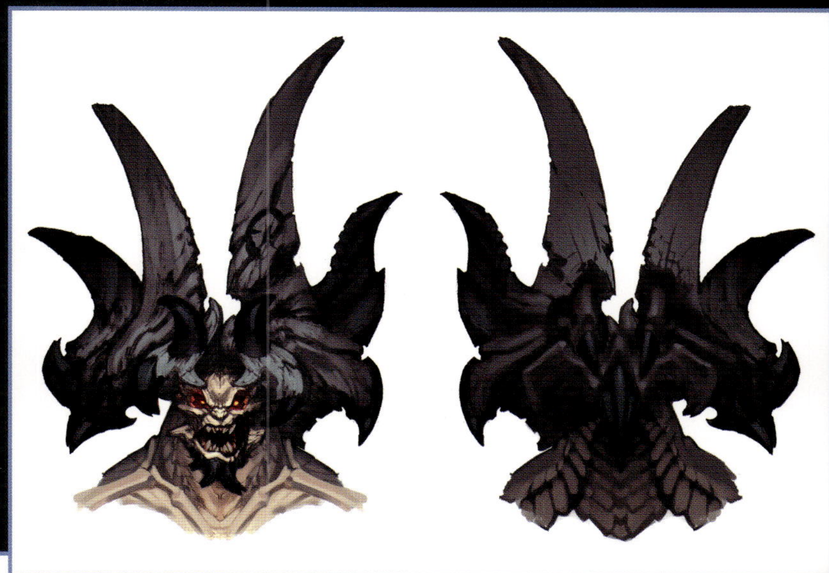

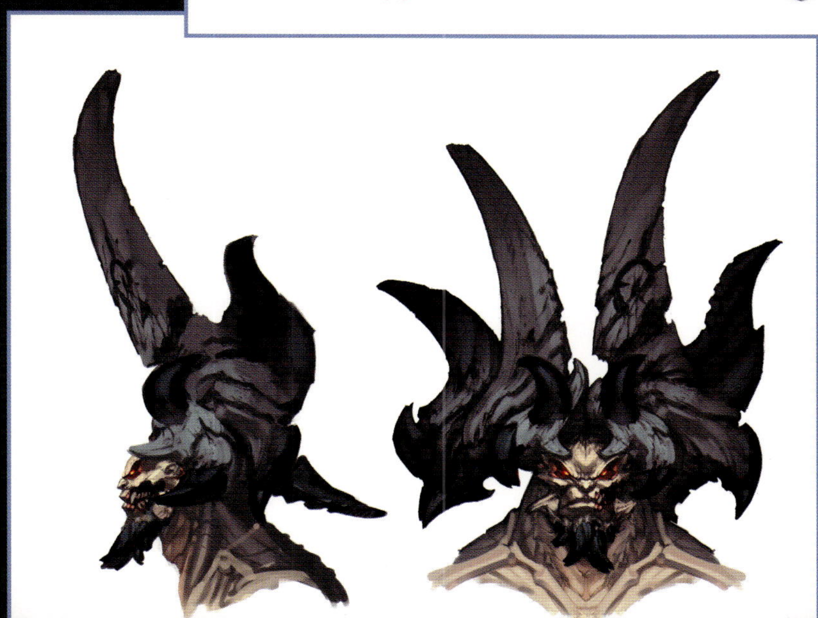

HEAD DESIGNS

HEAD DESIGNS

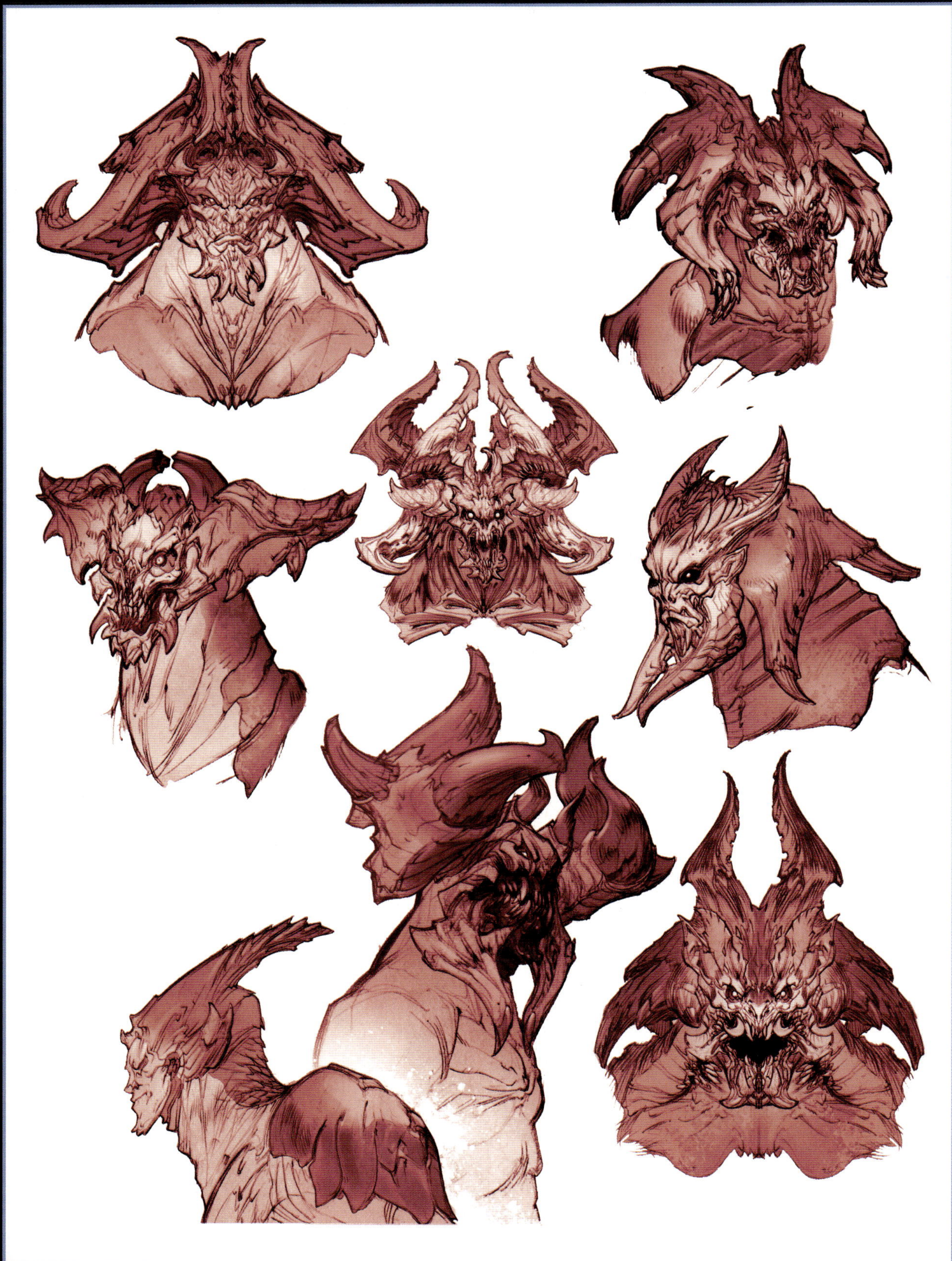

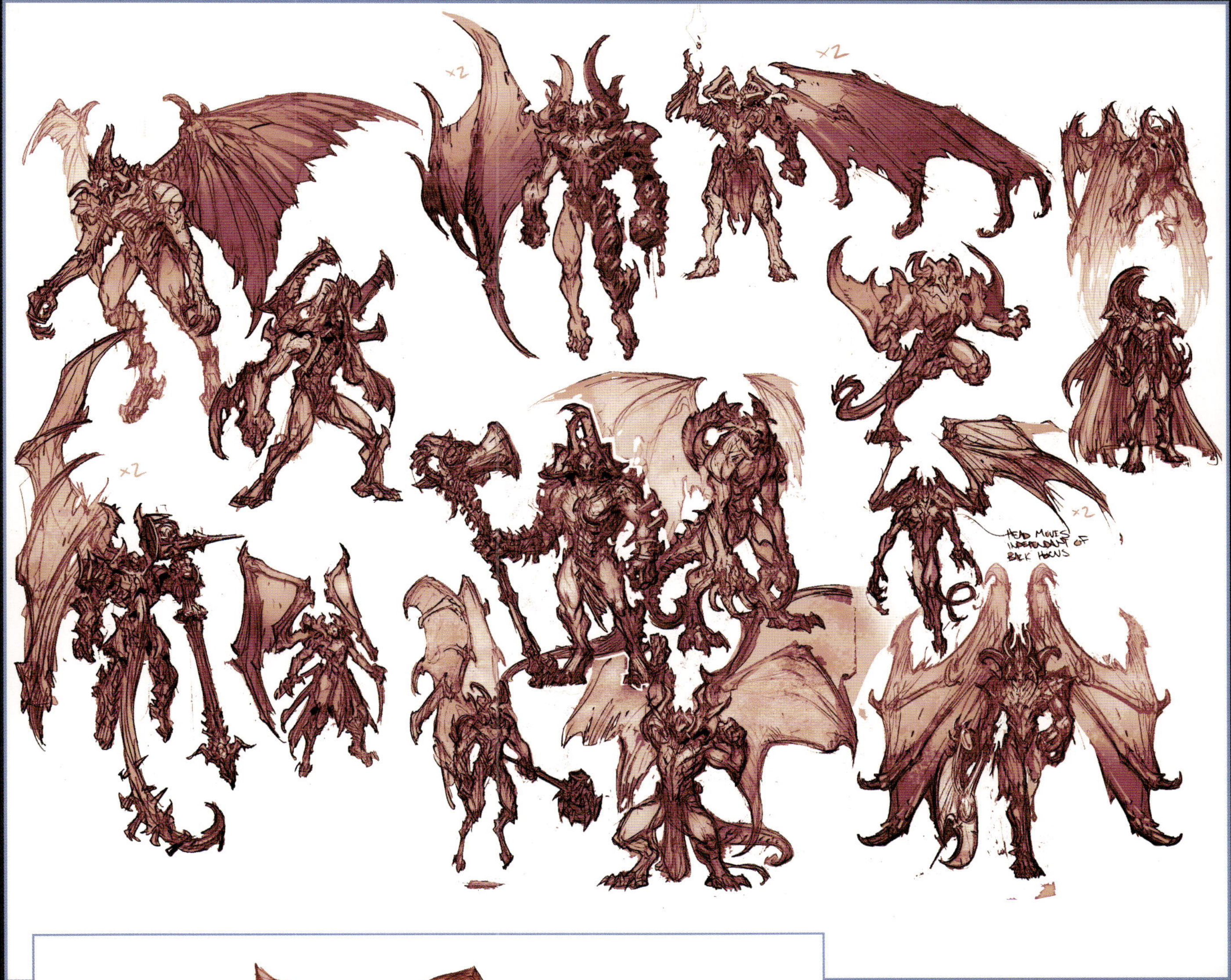

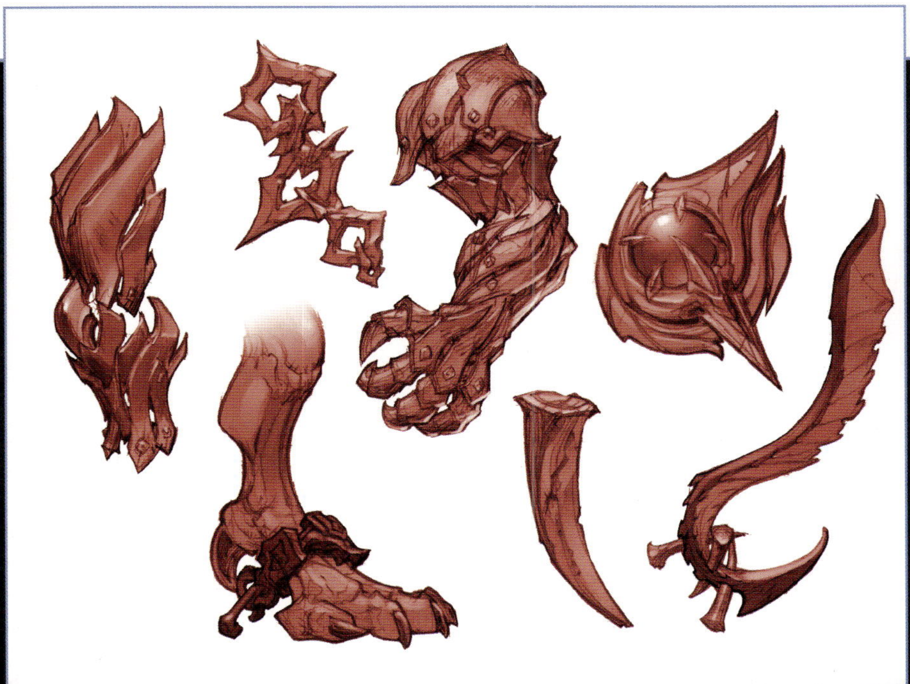

DEVELOPMENT SKETCHES

Lilith

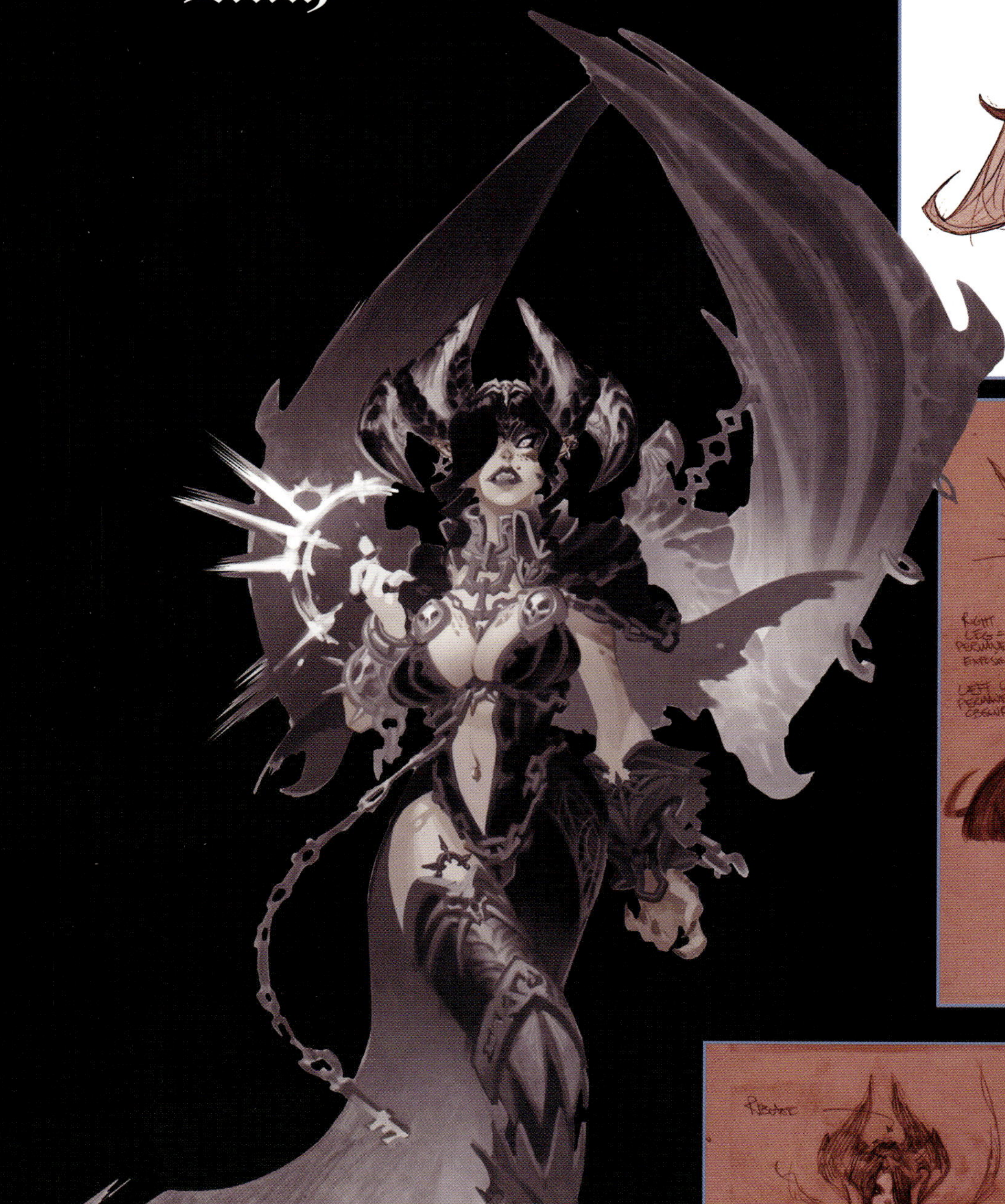

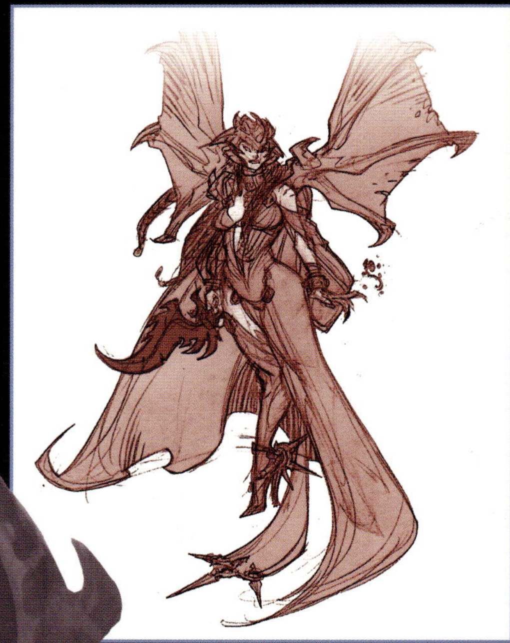

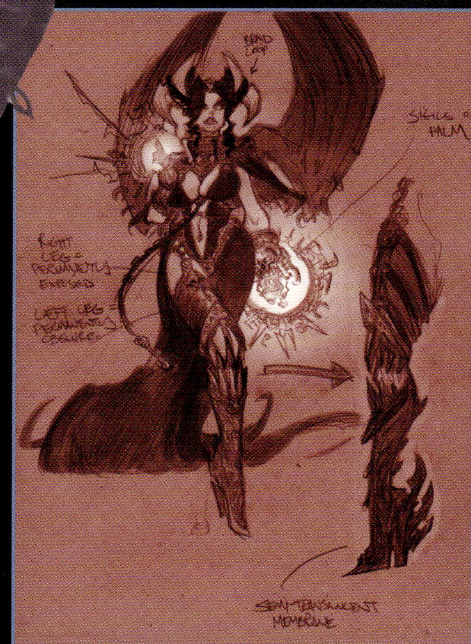

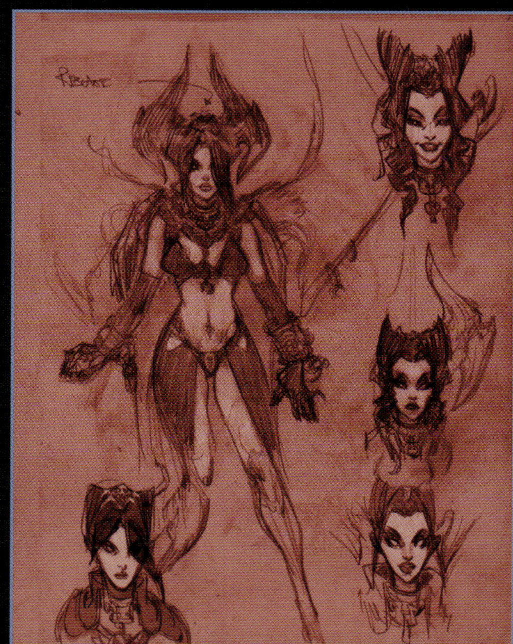

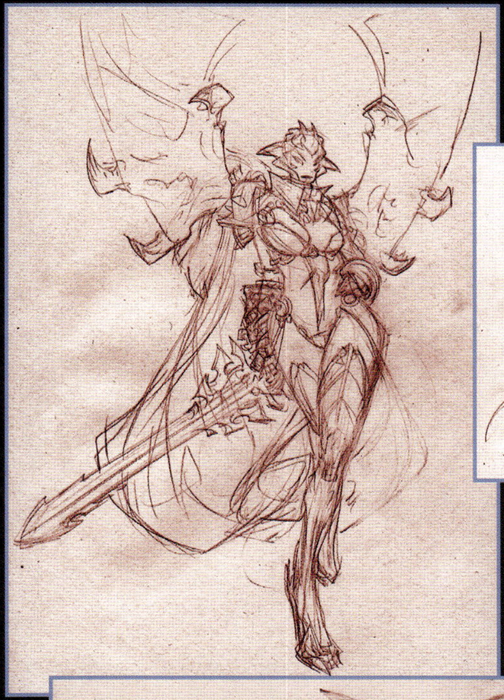
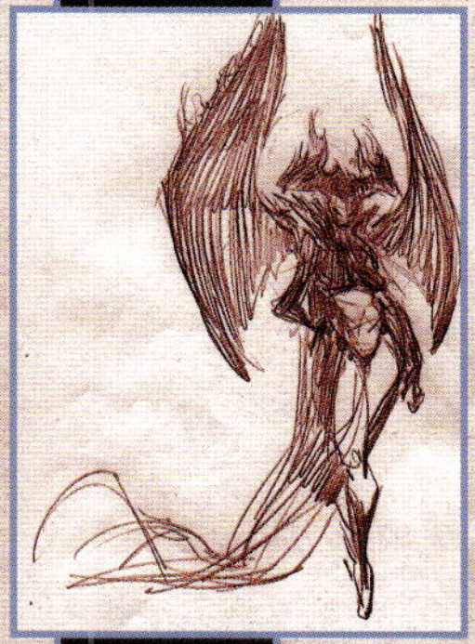
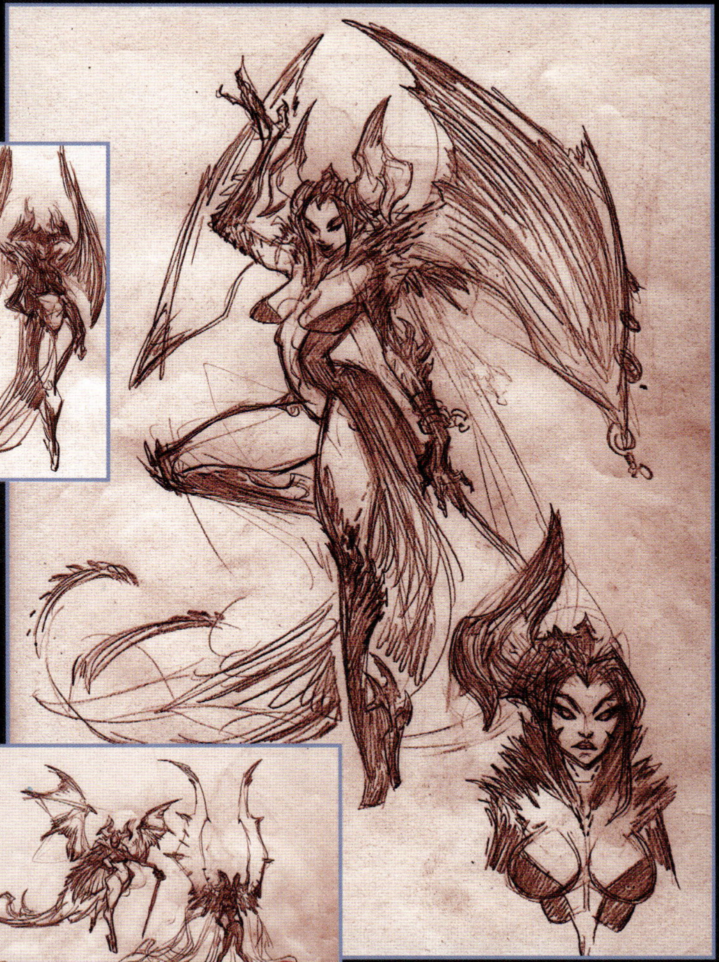

DEVELOPMENT SKETCHES

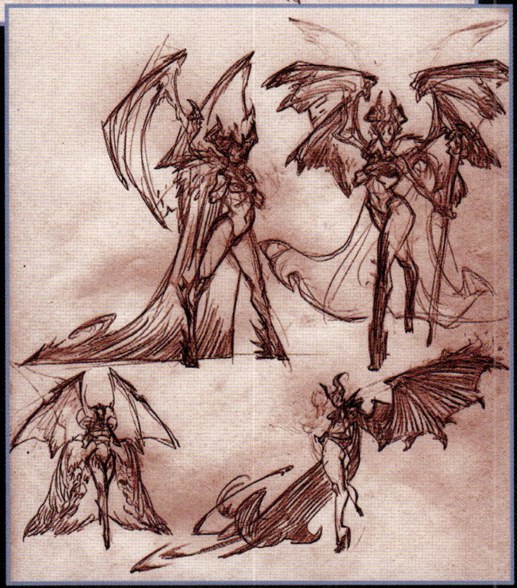
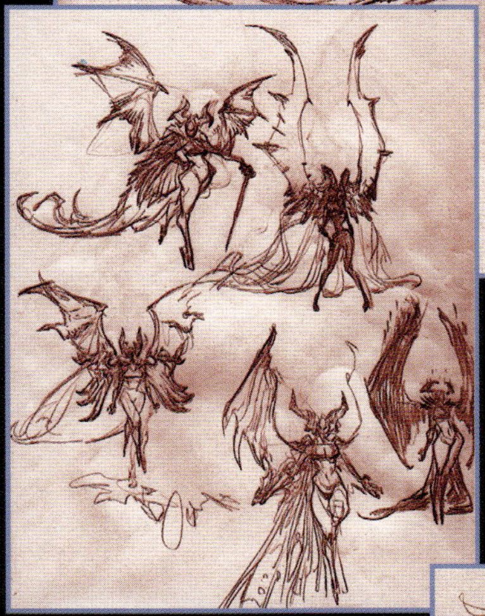
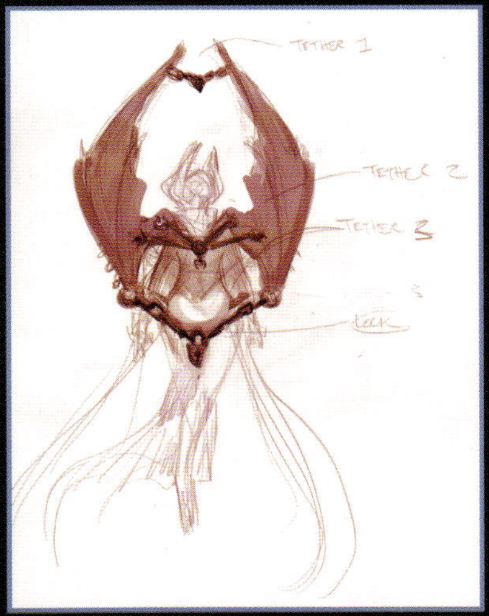
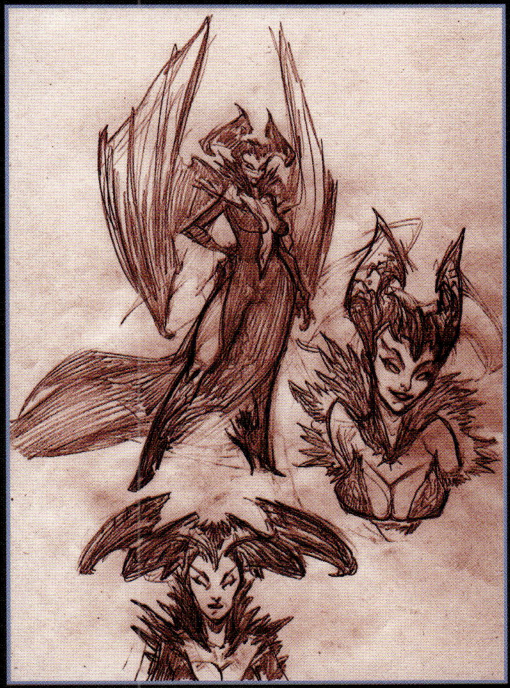
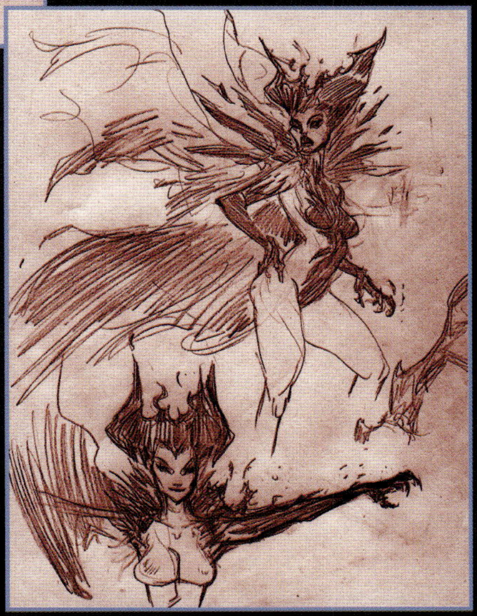

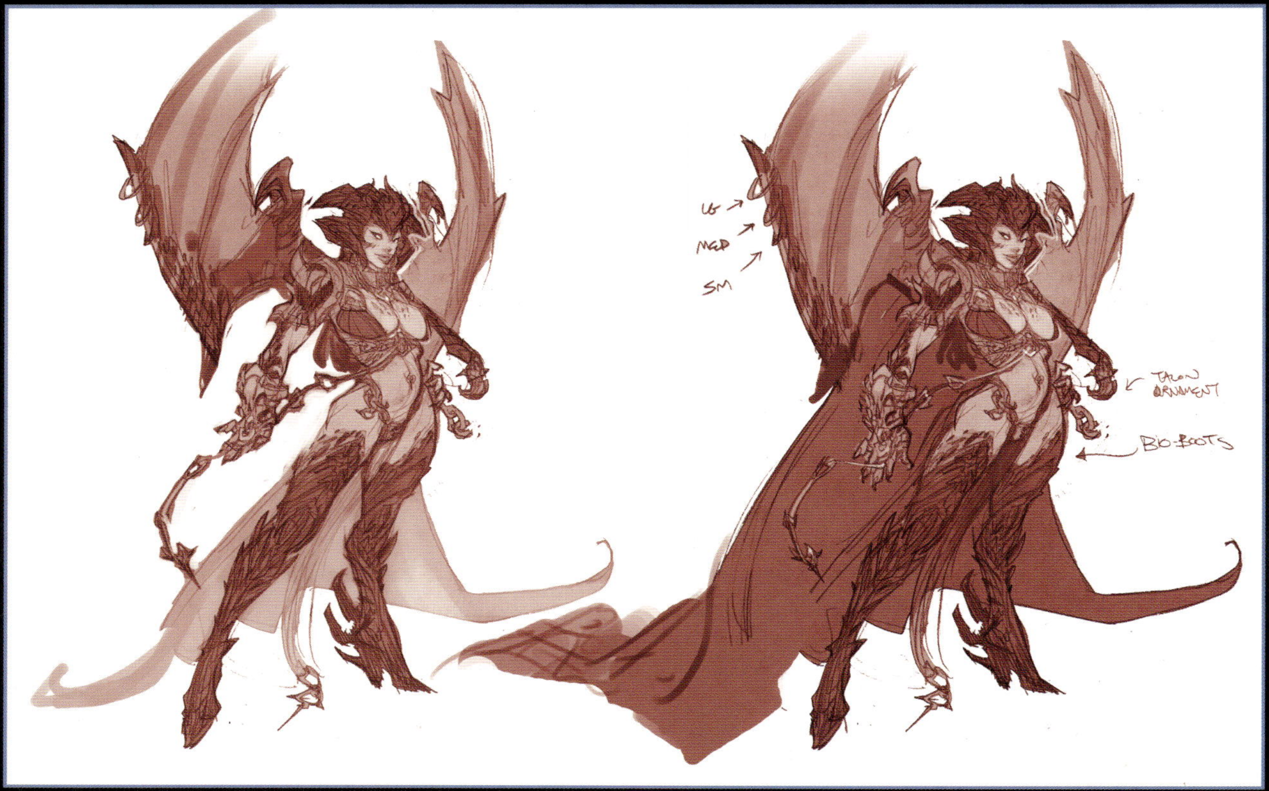

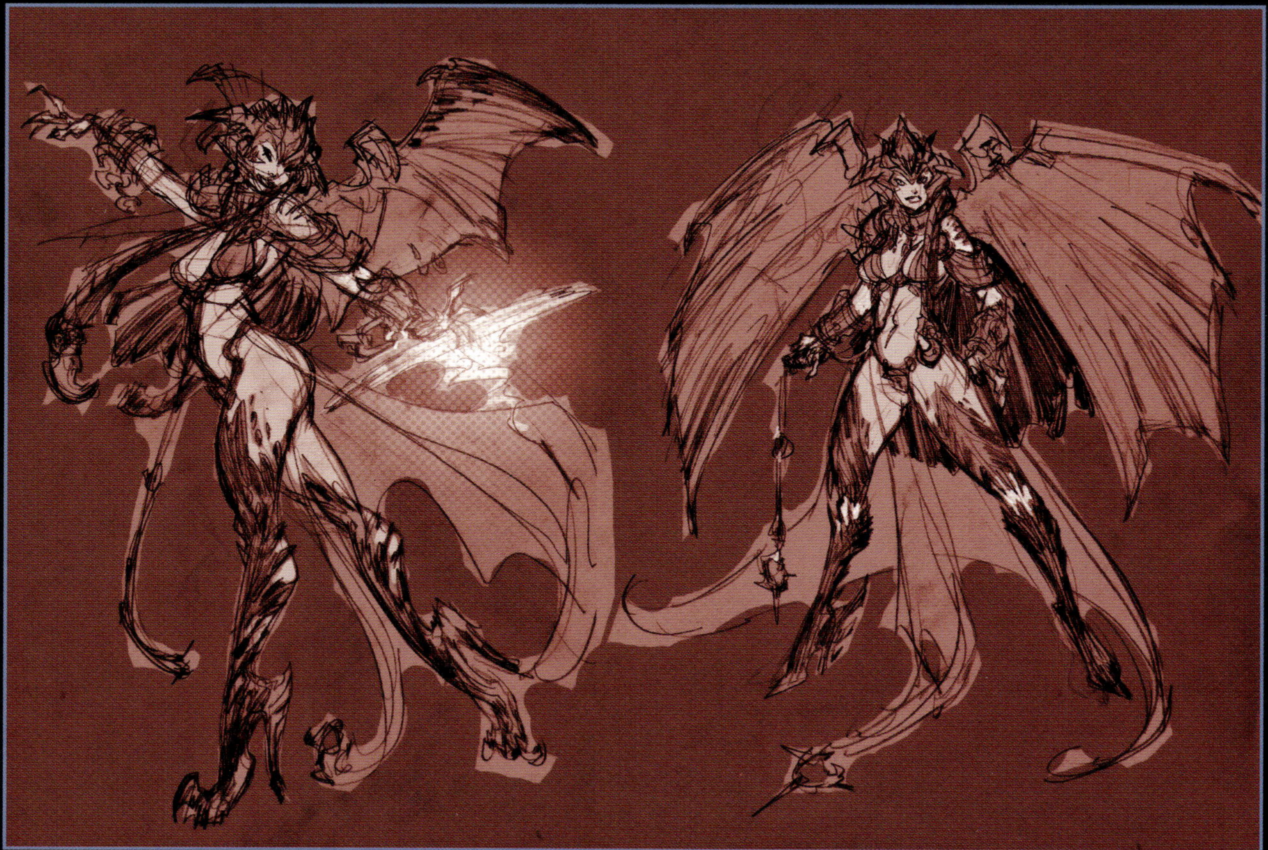

DEVELOPMENT SKETCHES

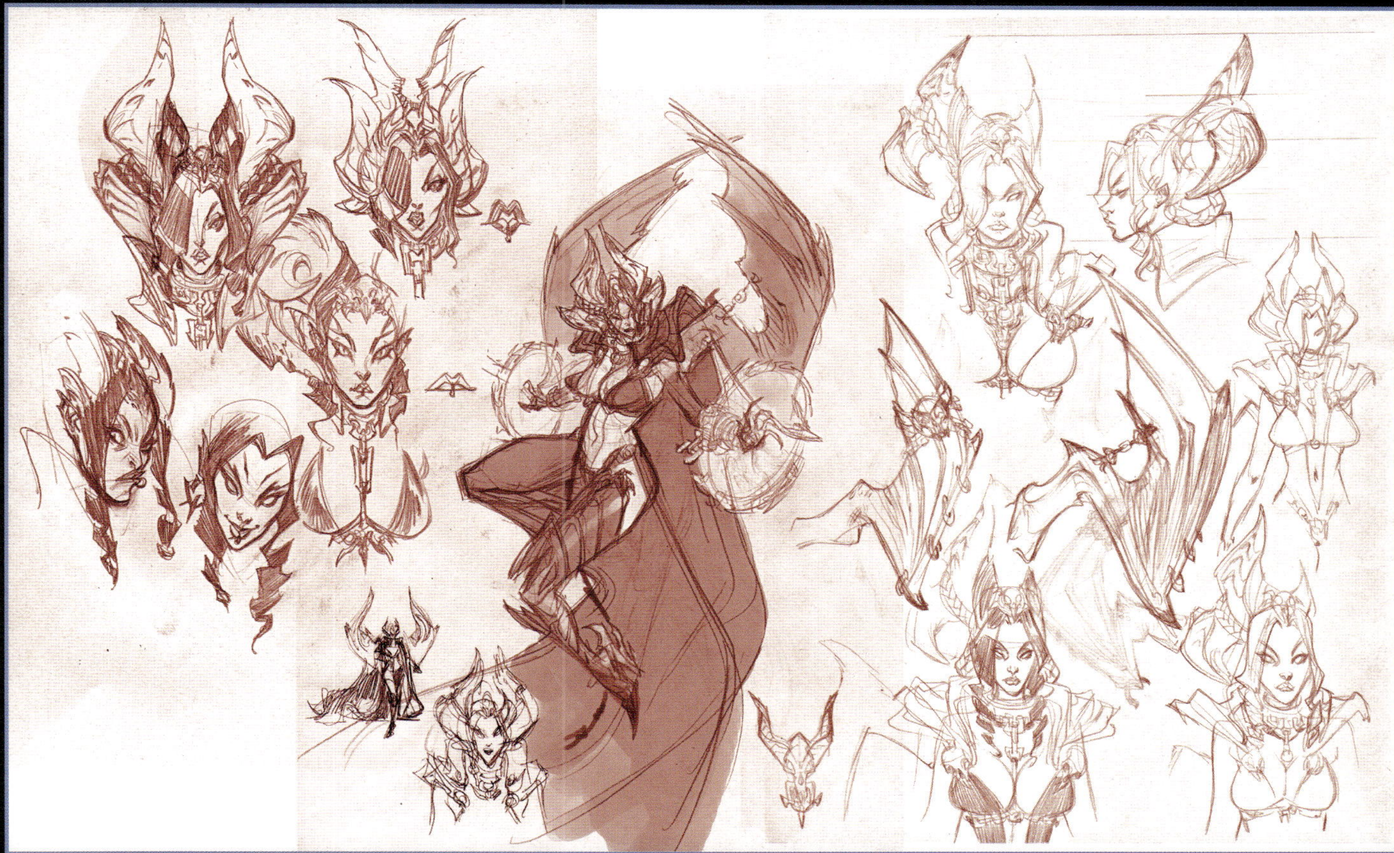

DEVELOPMENT SKETCHES

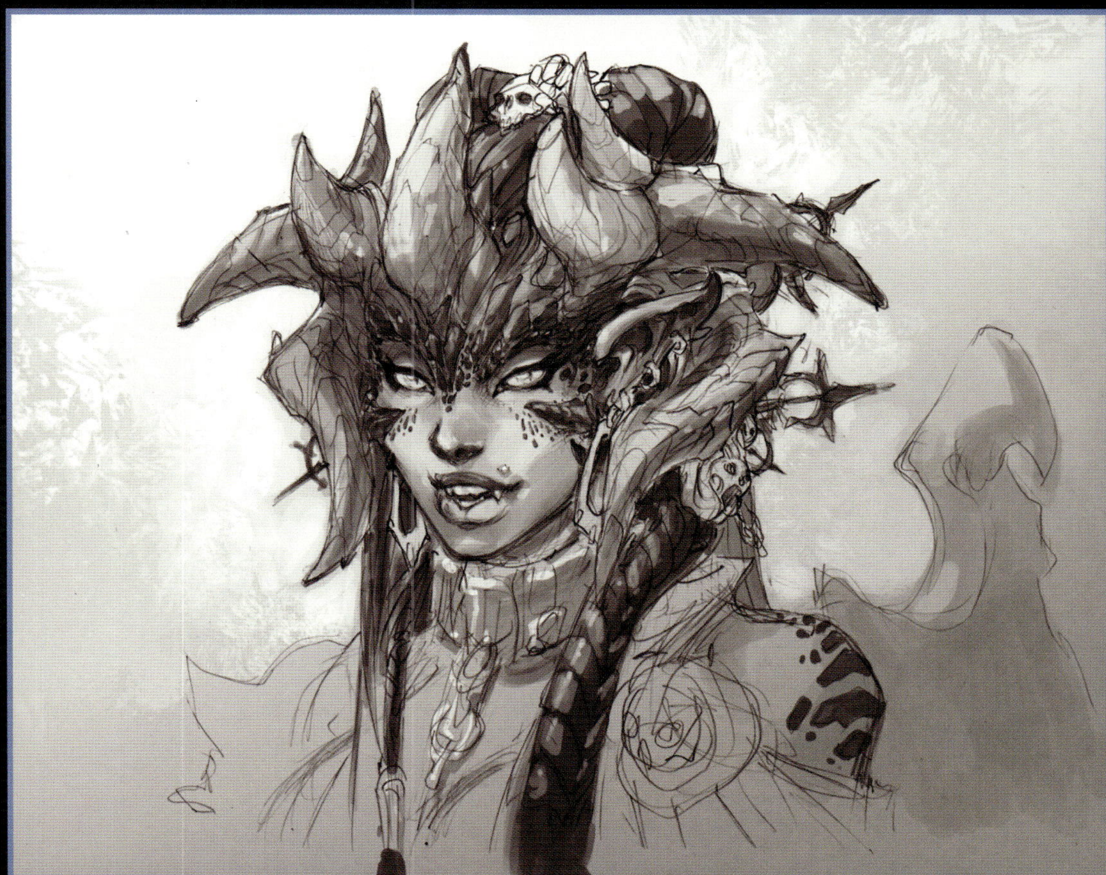

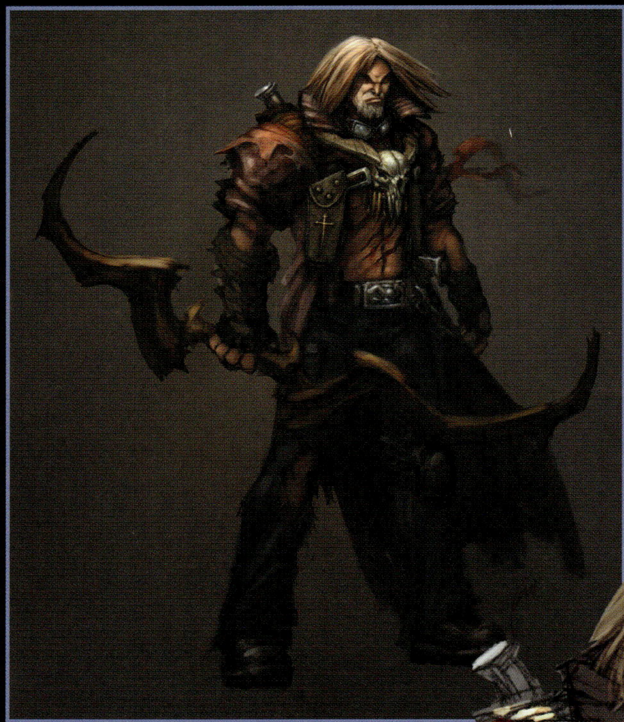

HEAD DESIGNS

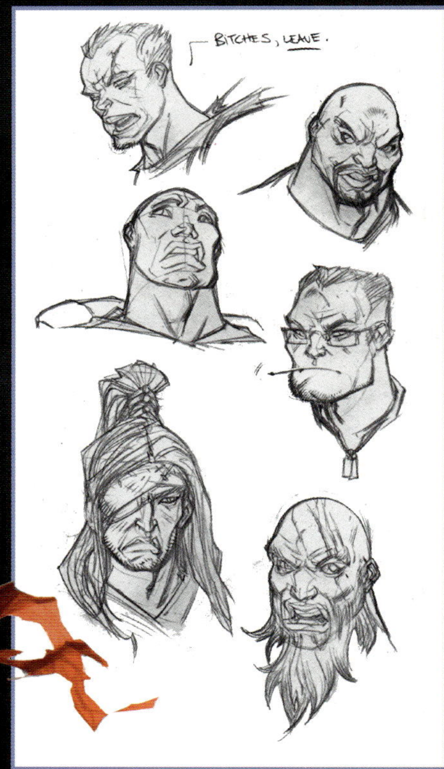

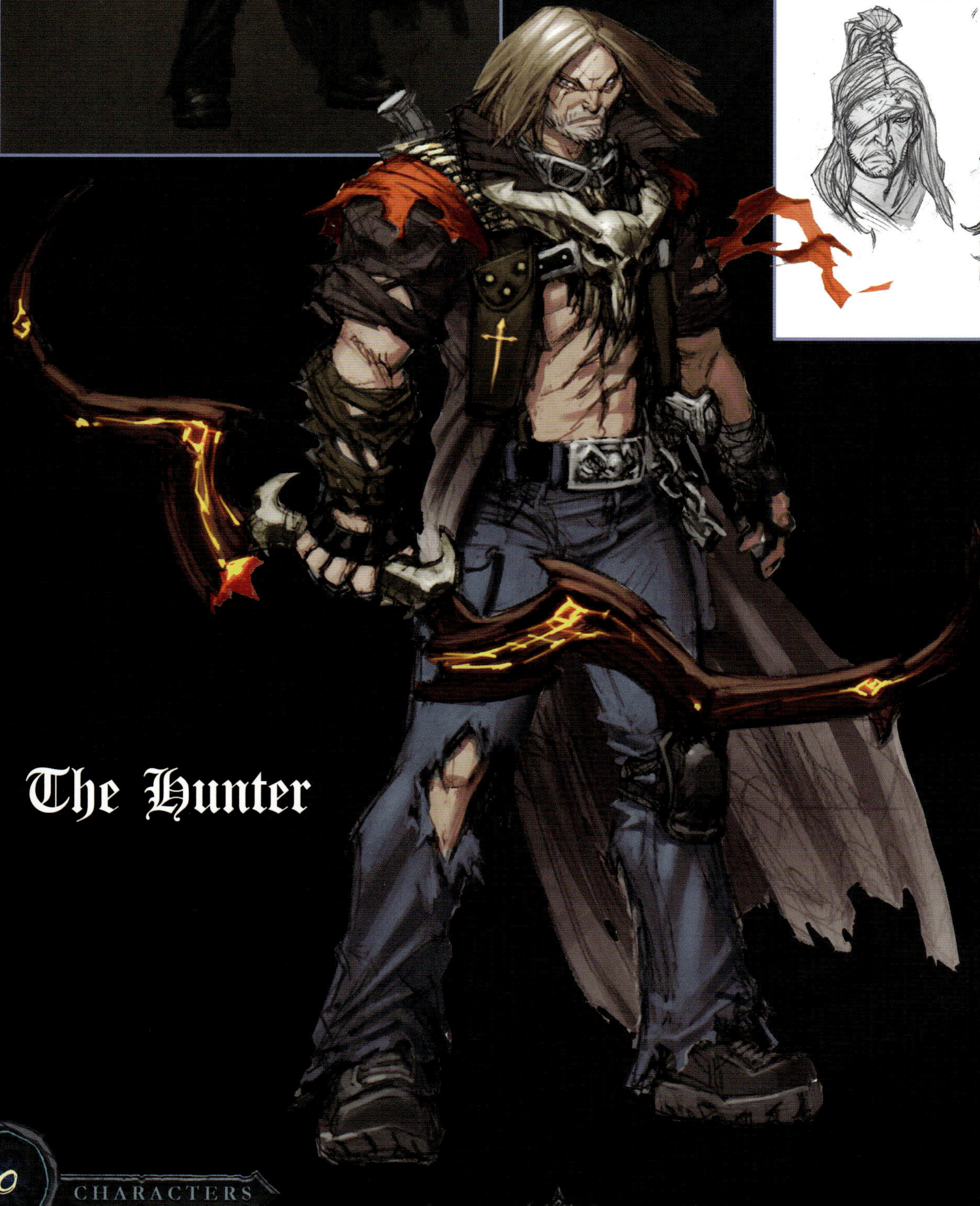

The Hunter

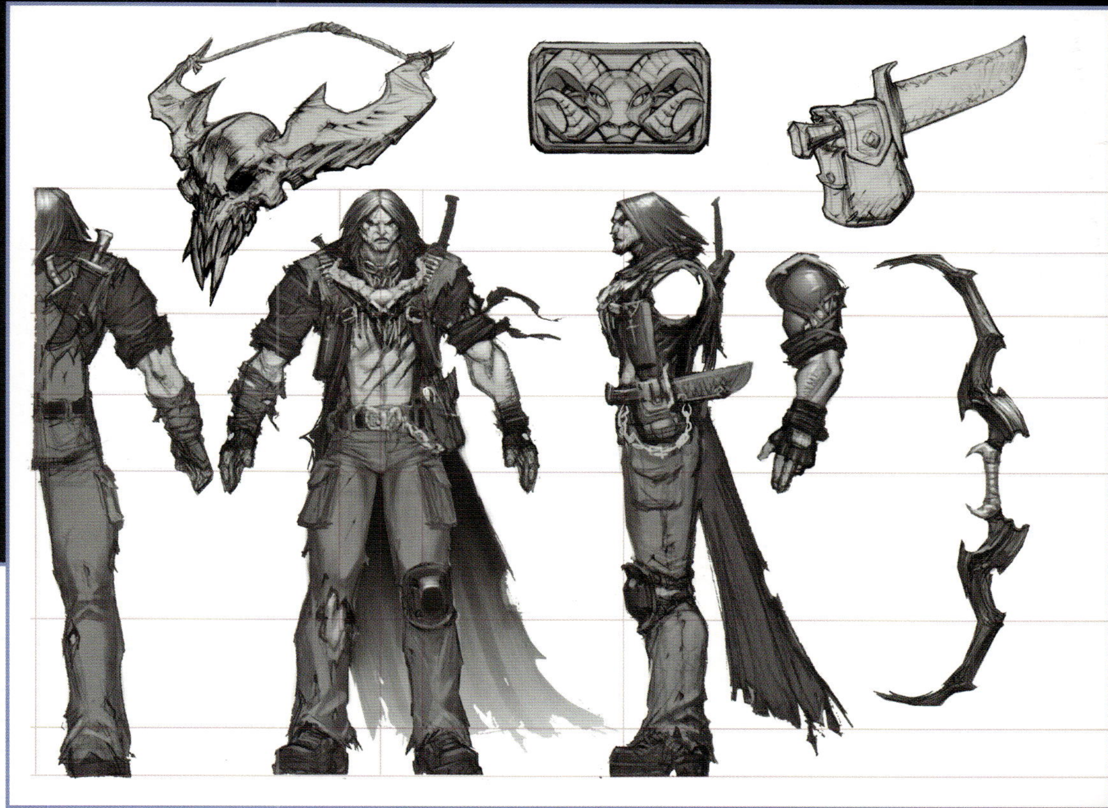

TURNAROUNDS

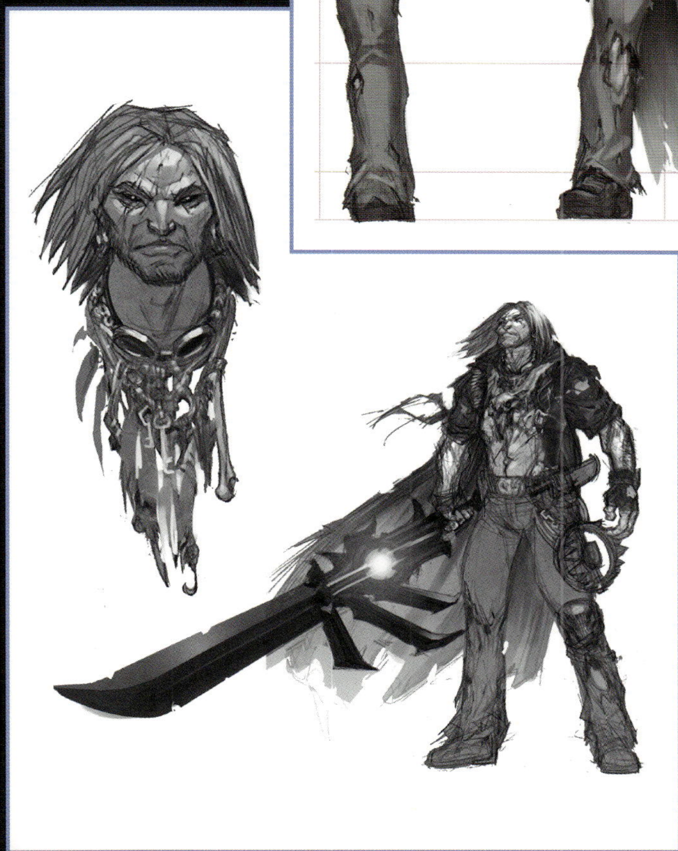

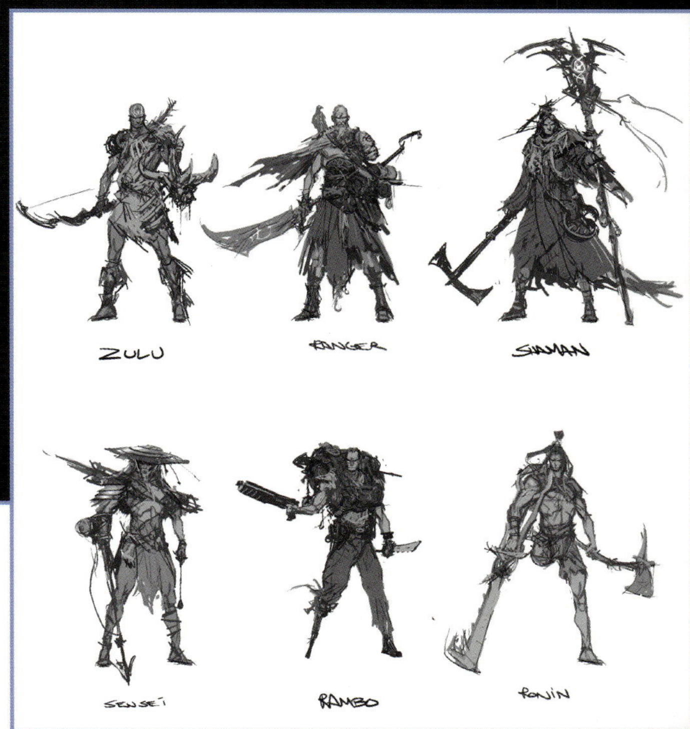

DEVELOPMENT SKETCHES

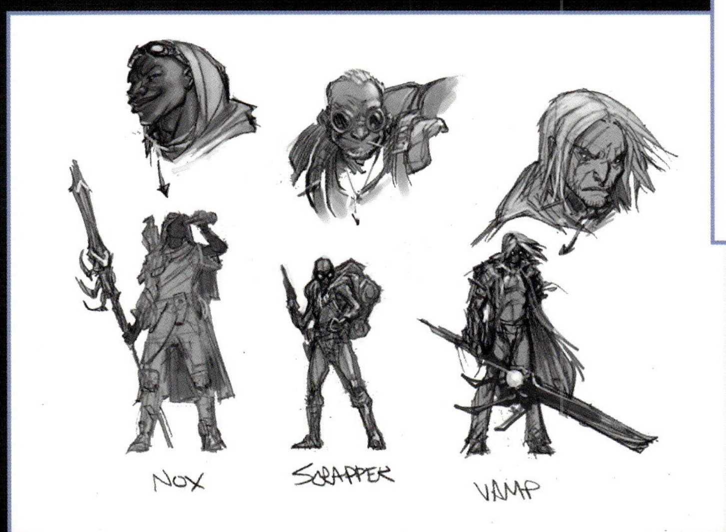

The Wicked

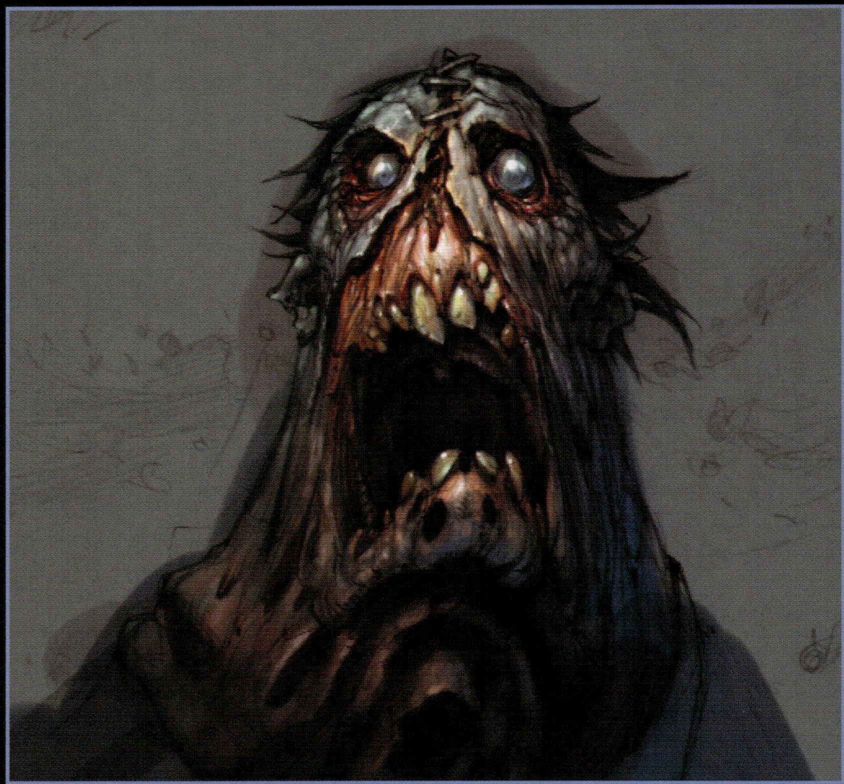

CLOSEUP PAINTINGS

Countless corpses have been raised to bolster the Destroyer's army. But even more have risen on their own, fueled by the agony of their evil souls.

A great number of the Wicked roam this darkened world. Their clothes and skin have long since moldered to dust, exposing tendon, bone and the crusted scars of their death-wounds. Driven to madness by their eternal torment, these fiends will attack anything in their paths with the tenacity of jackals.

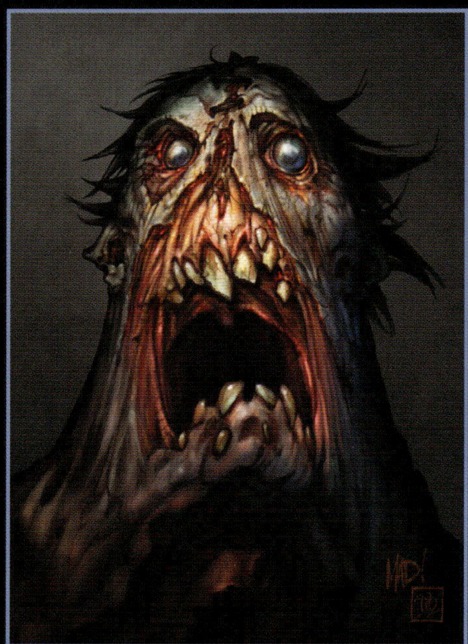

VARIATION

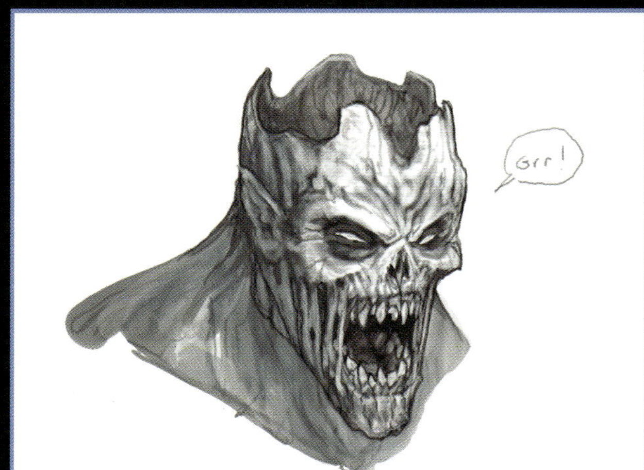

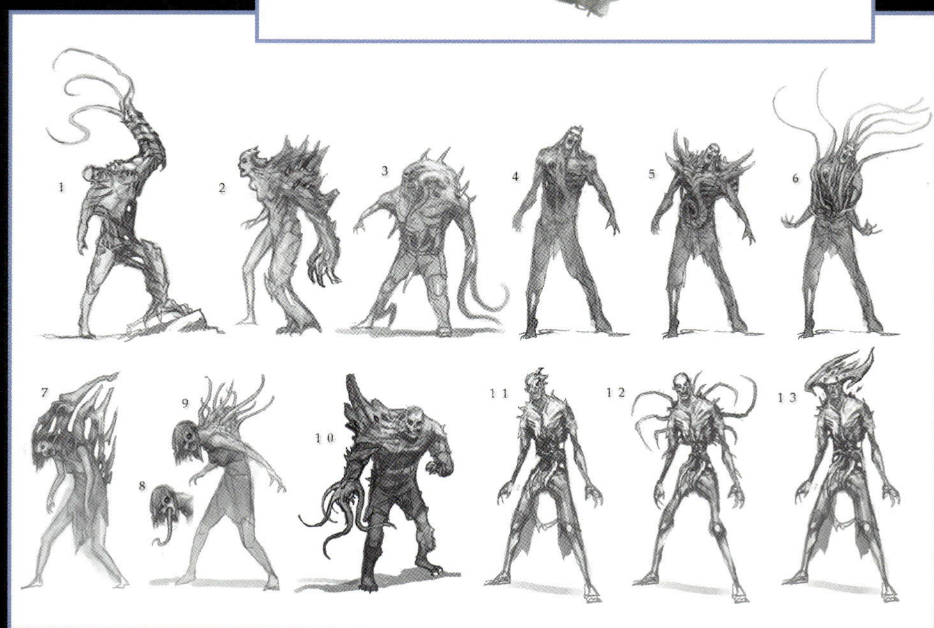

DEVELOPMENT SKETCHES

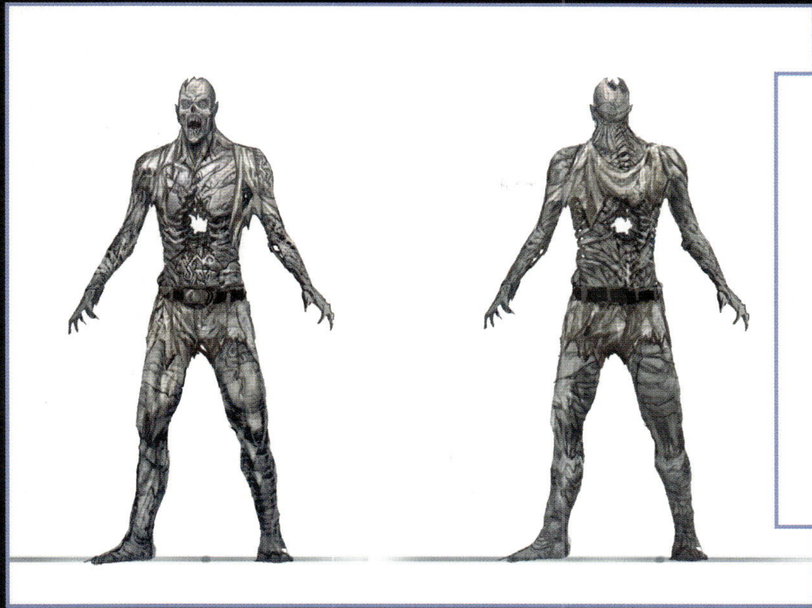

TURNAROUNDS

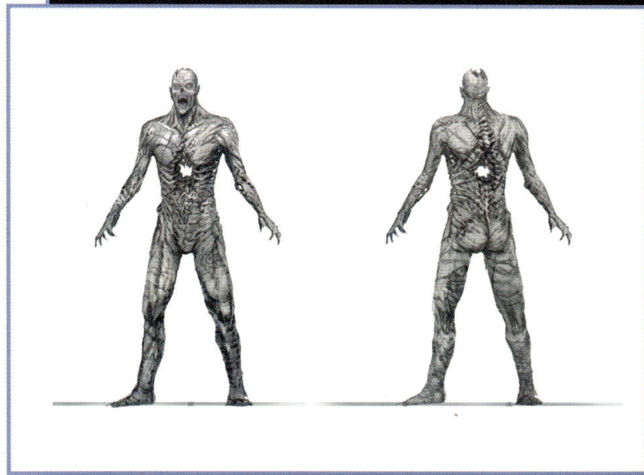

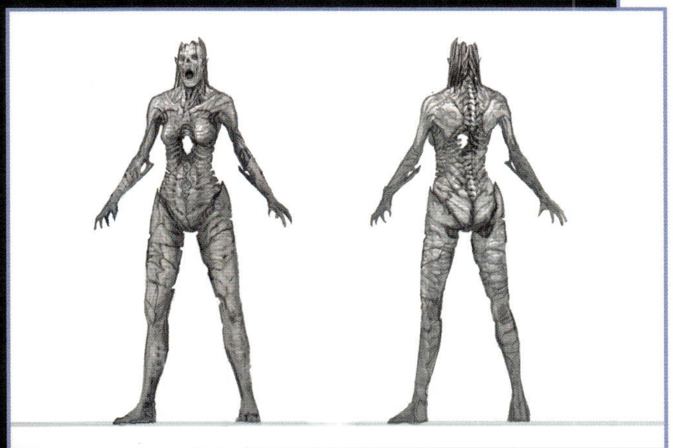

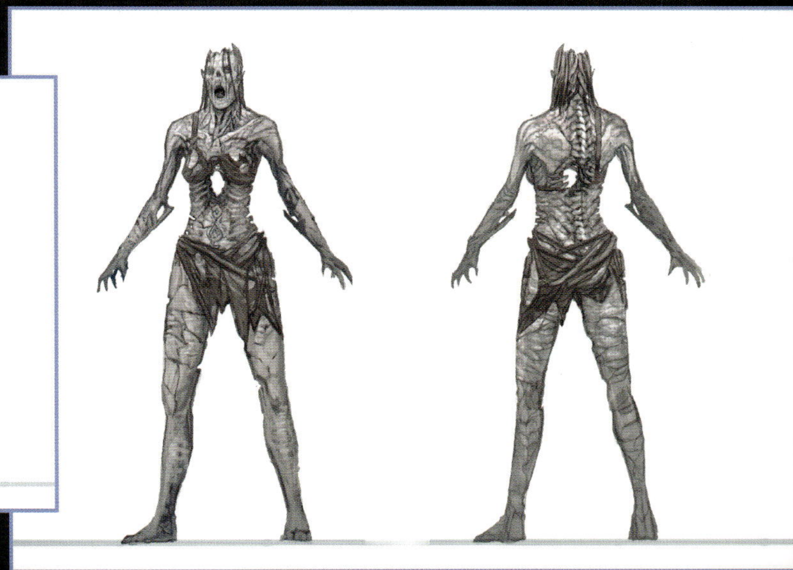

TURNAROUNDS

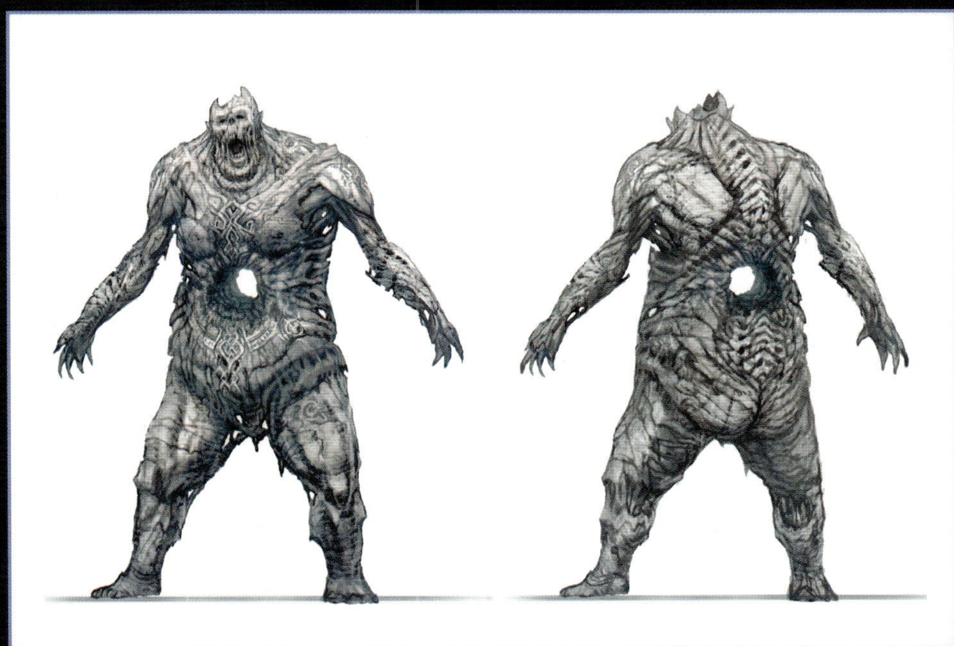

TURNAROUNDS

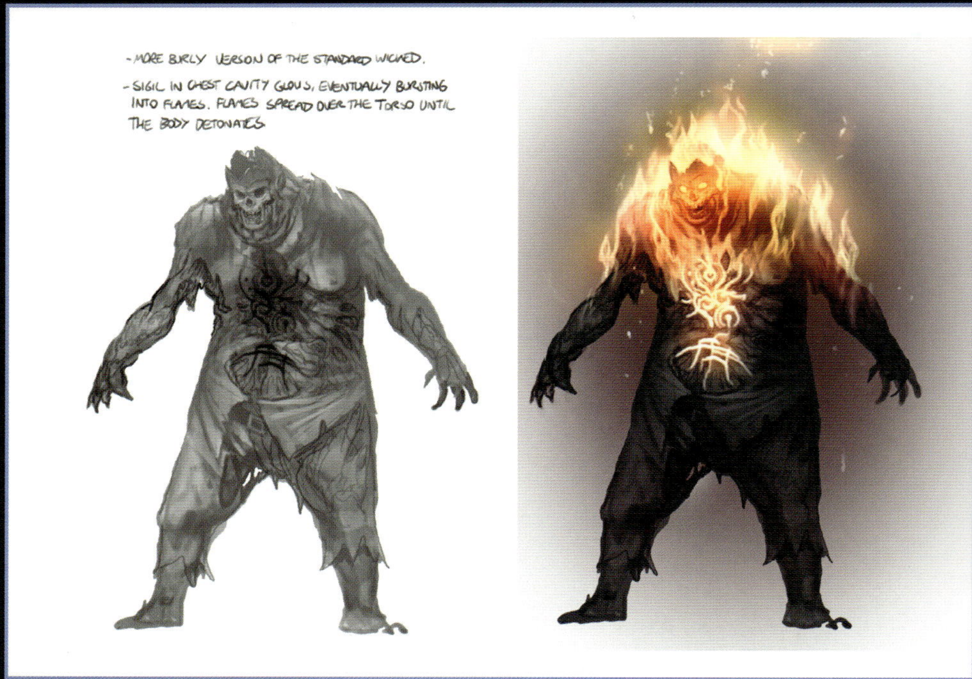

DEVELOPMENT SKETCHES

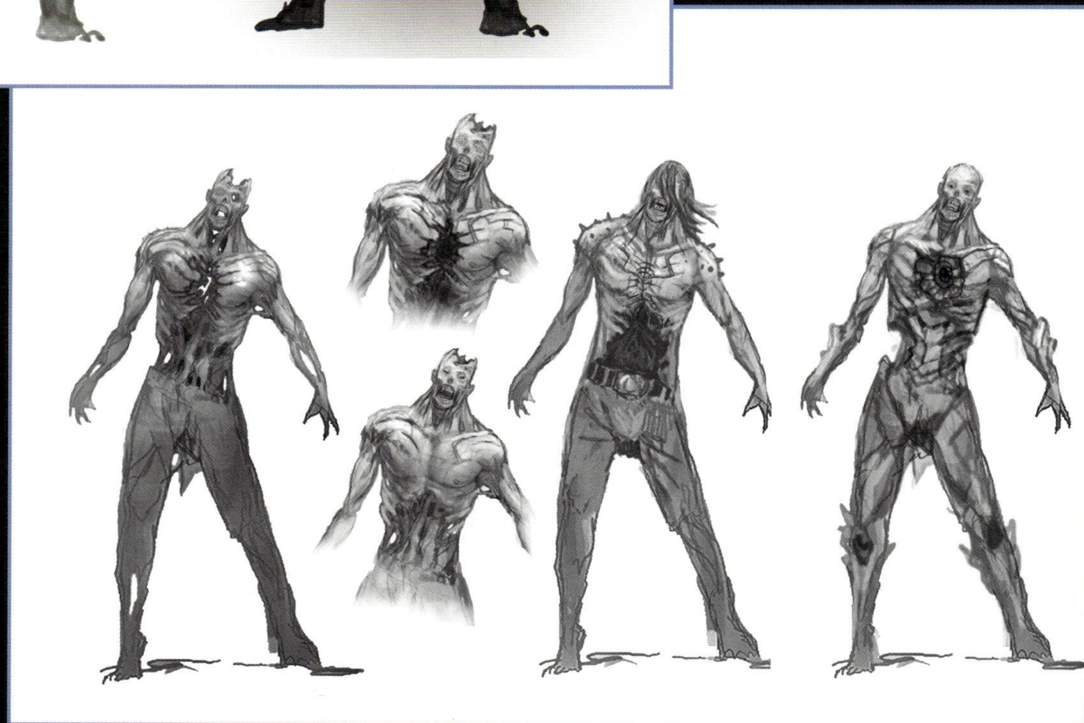

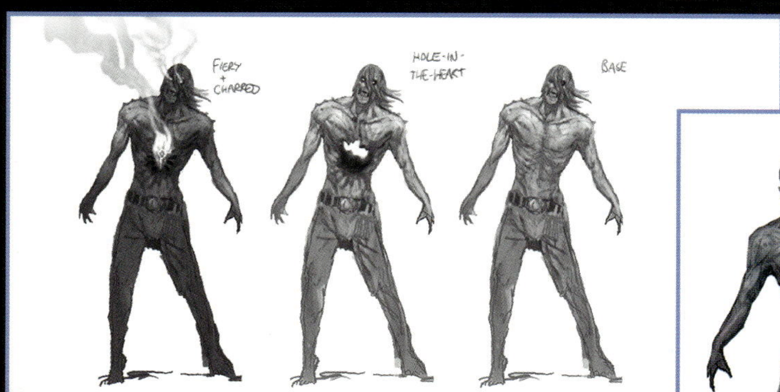

DEVELOPMENT SKETCHES

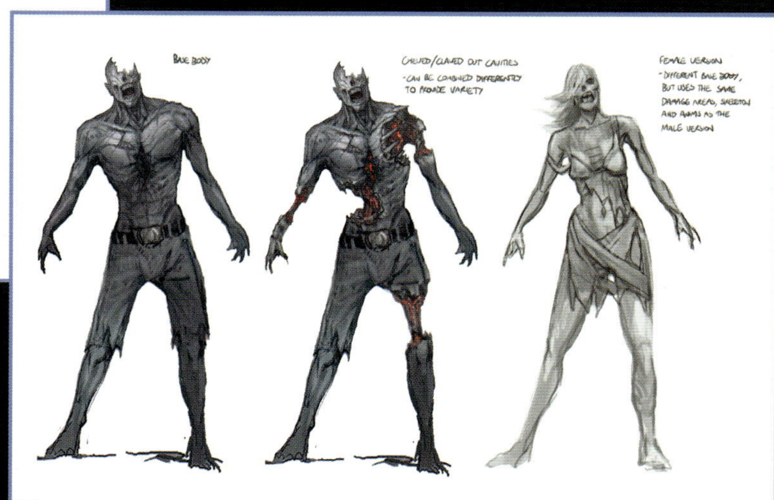

LINE ART

Minions

The Minions are the Destroyers hounds, pack hunters that scour the wastelands for prey. Their misshapen masses of heads, torsos, and limbs are fused into a hideous array. Over the decades, their prey has grown brutally scarce. What will the foul Minions kill when even Angels are no more than heaps of bone?

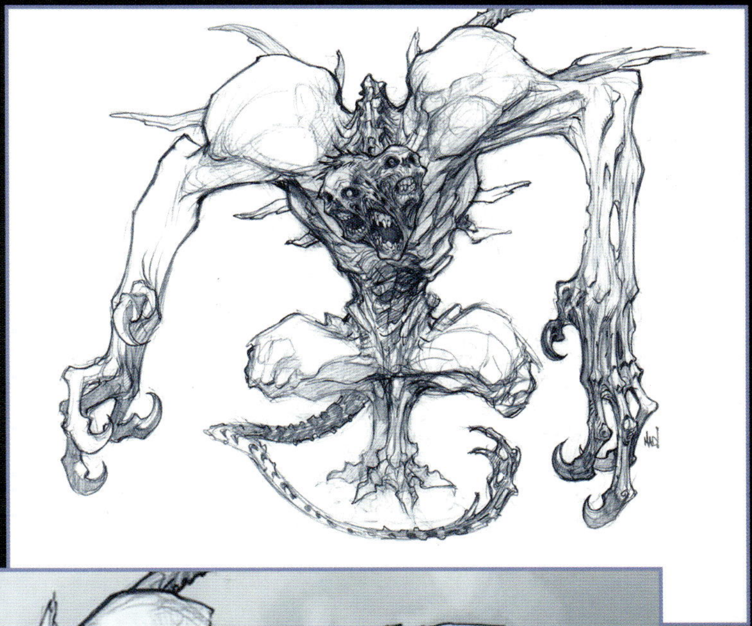

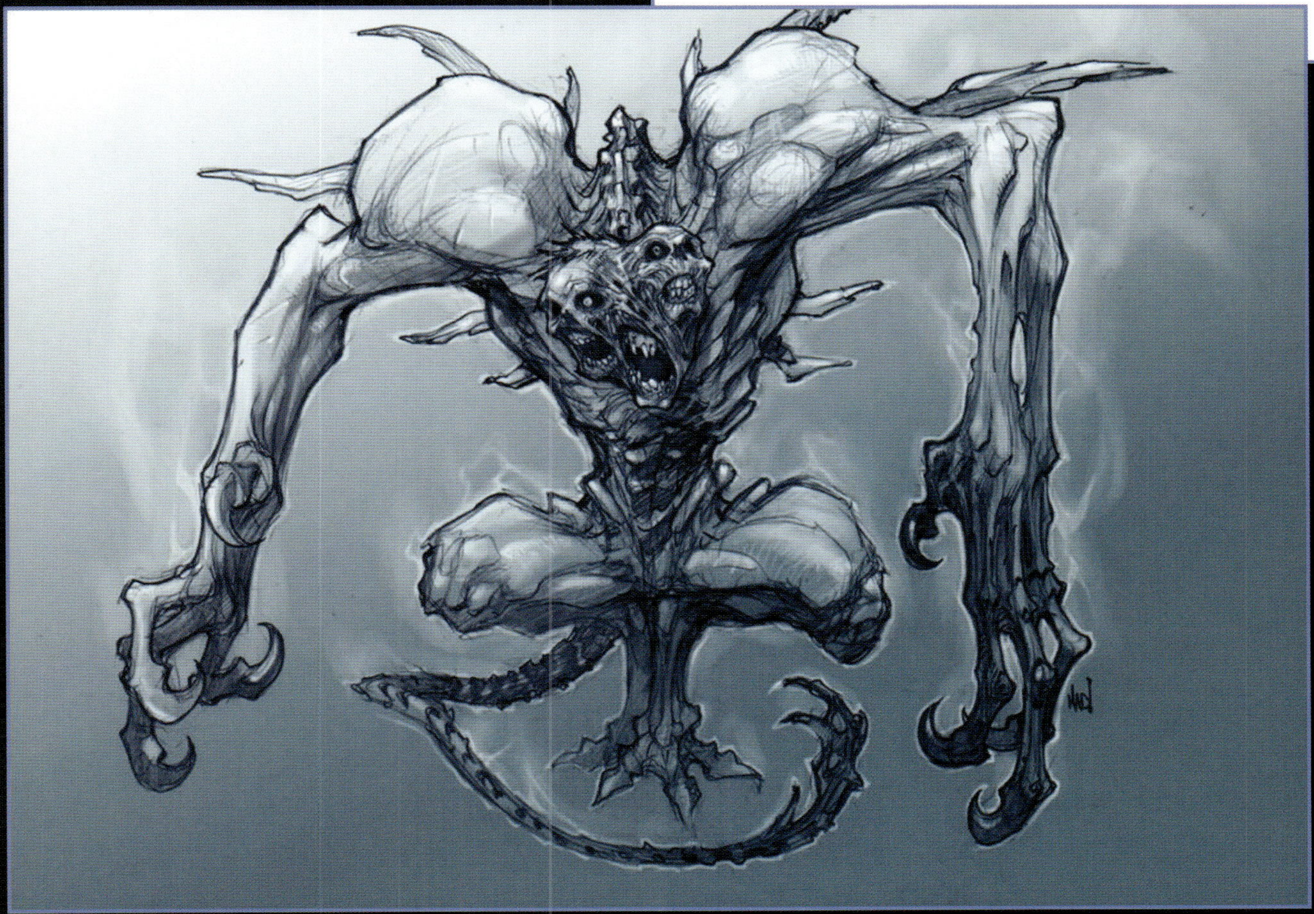

PENCIL ART

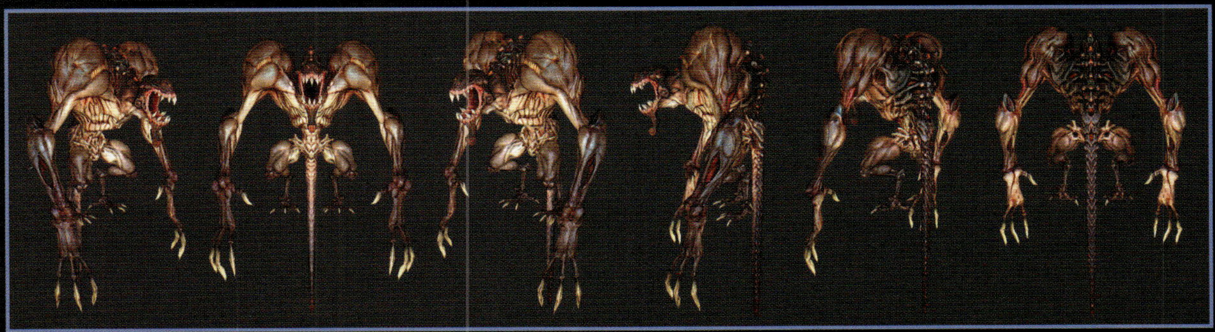

CG TURNAROUNDS

Undead

It is troubling that in the war between Heaven and Hell humanity found no escape—not even in death. Animated by the Destroyer's power, the Undead corpses of man still creep across the Earth, their empty eye sockets burning with their master's will.

The Undead are relentless foes, as they sense neither pain nor fear. Projectile weapons do not seem to slow their drive to destroy. Indeed, these mindless slayers have been known to walk through a hail of gun fire just to get close to their prey. This is a most challenging enemy, for how might a warrior kill that which is already dead?

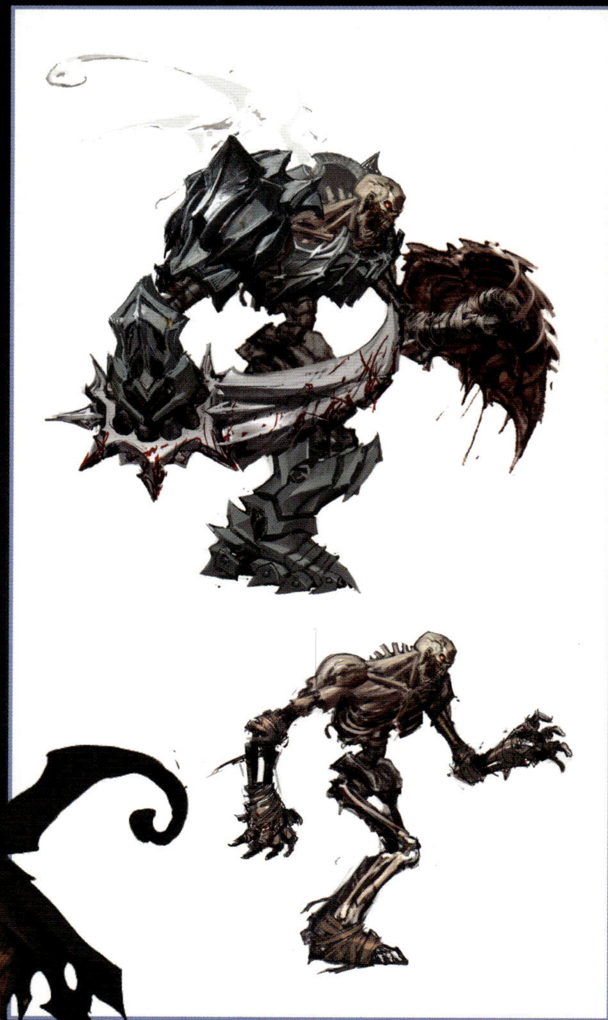

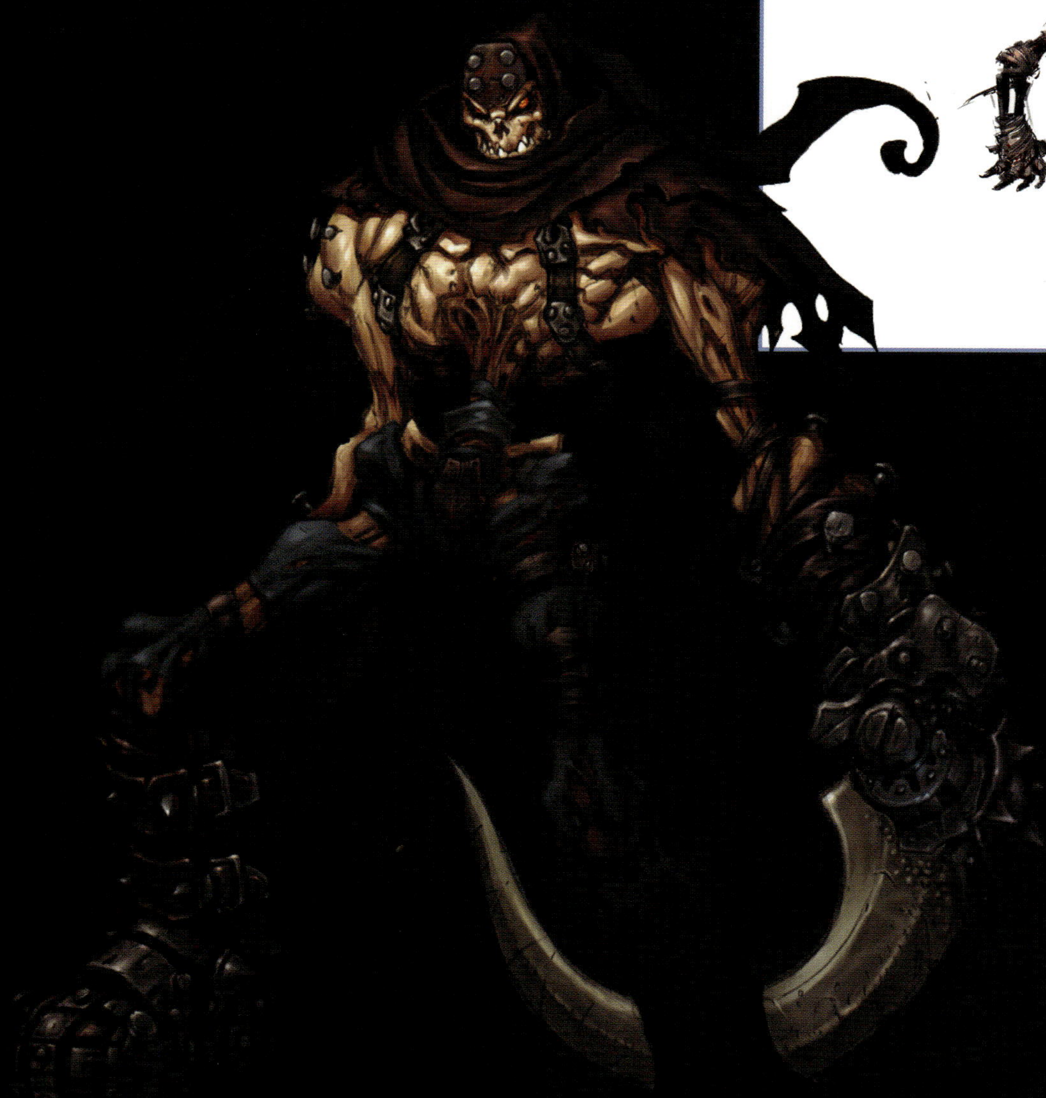

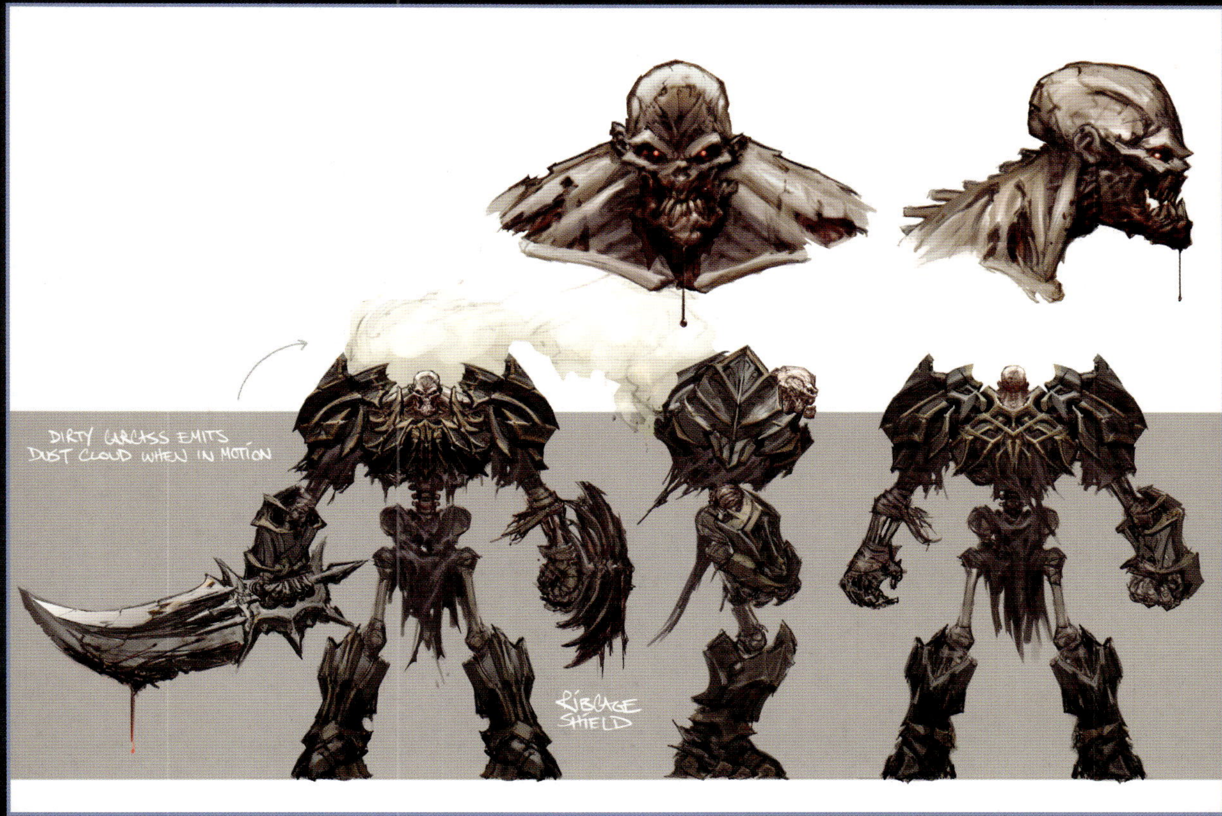

TURNAROUNDS

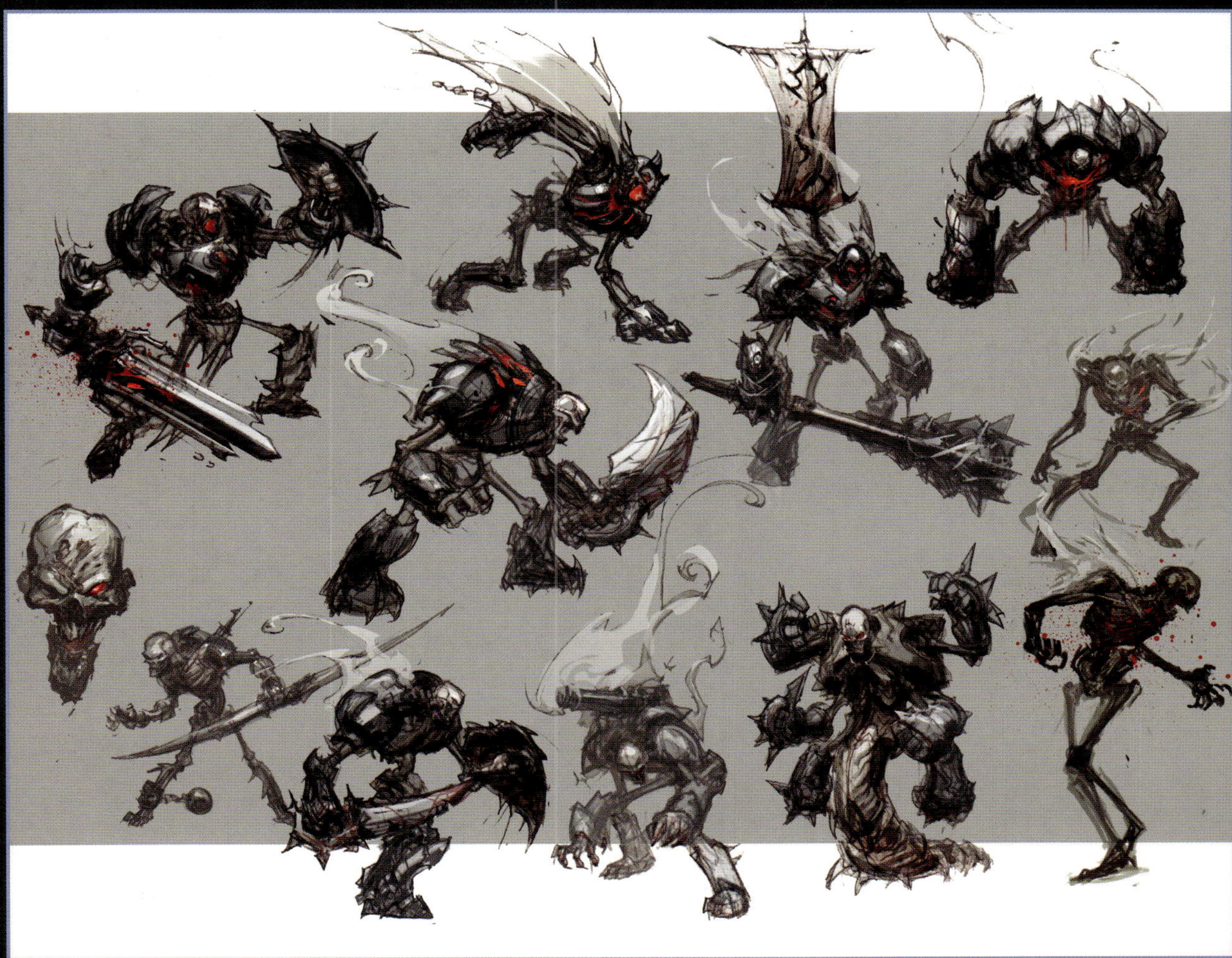

DEVELOPMENT SKETCHES

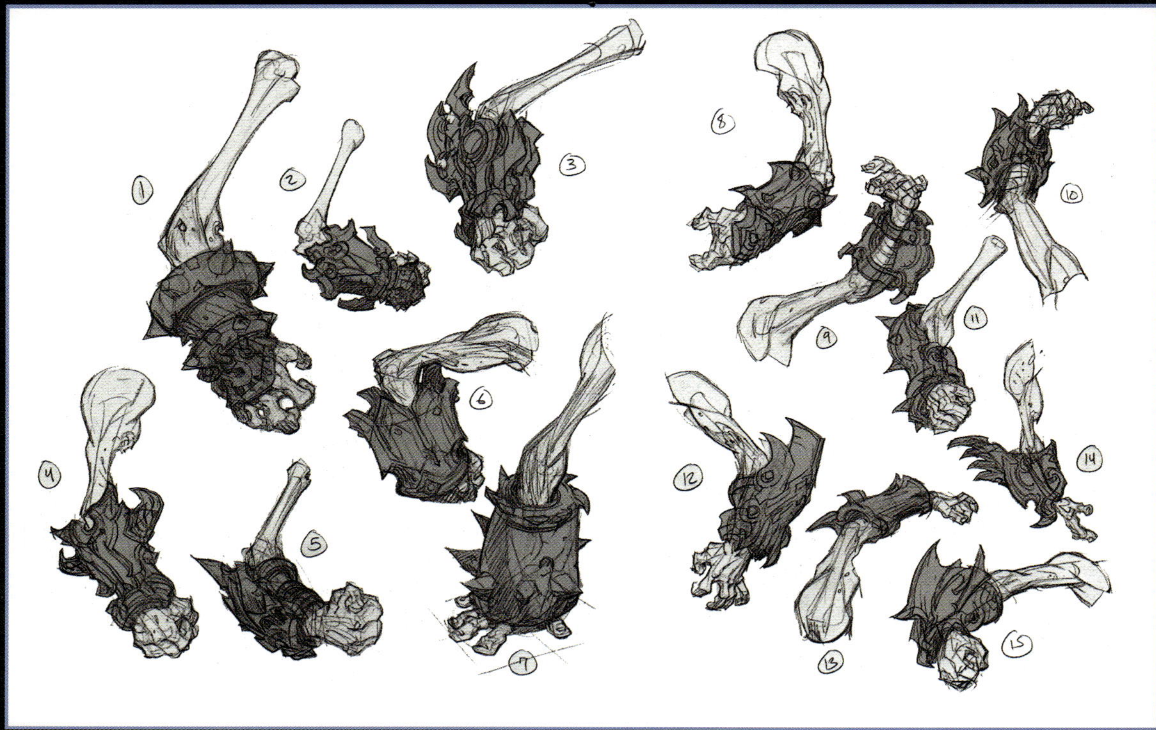

UNDEAD ARM DESIGNS

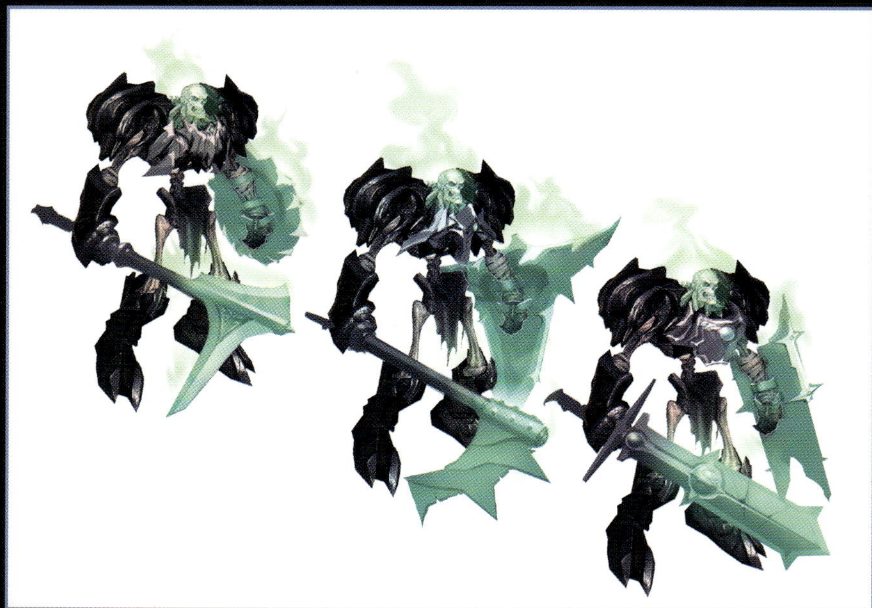

SHIELD LORD TURNAROUNDS

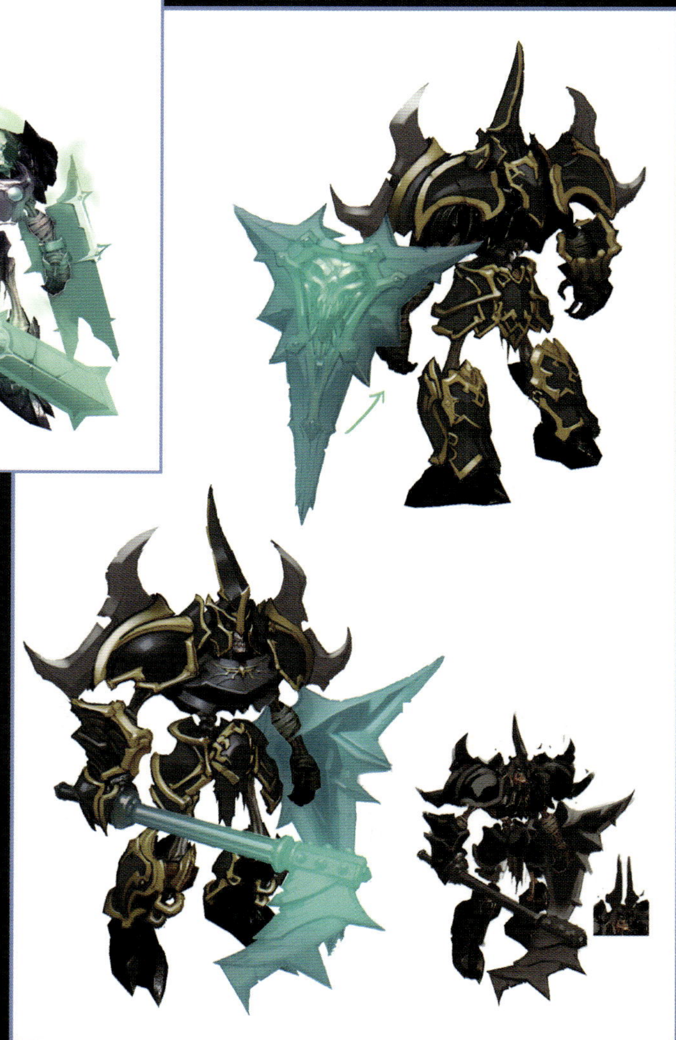

Undead Shield Lord

The Undead Shield Lords are among the most dangerous of the living corpses who serve the Destroyer. Their dark armor bristles with spikes and thorns. Their shields are razor-sharp, tapering down to a vicious point that the creatures seek to drive into their prey.

Hidden beneath such a shell, little about the Shield Lords seems human. Only the stench that follows them, that of soured blood and desecrated graves, hints at their unspeakable origin.

PLAGUEBEARER TURNAROUNDS

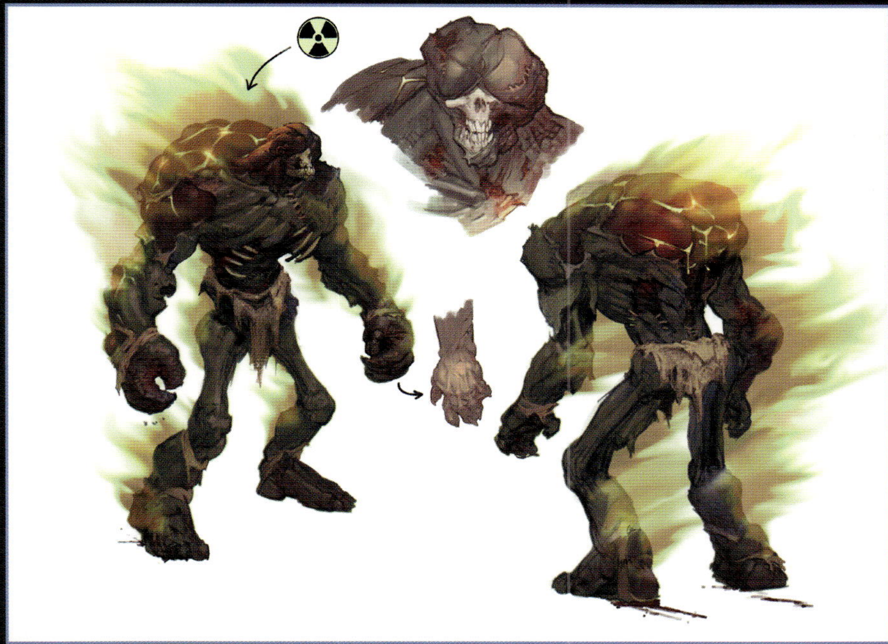

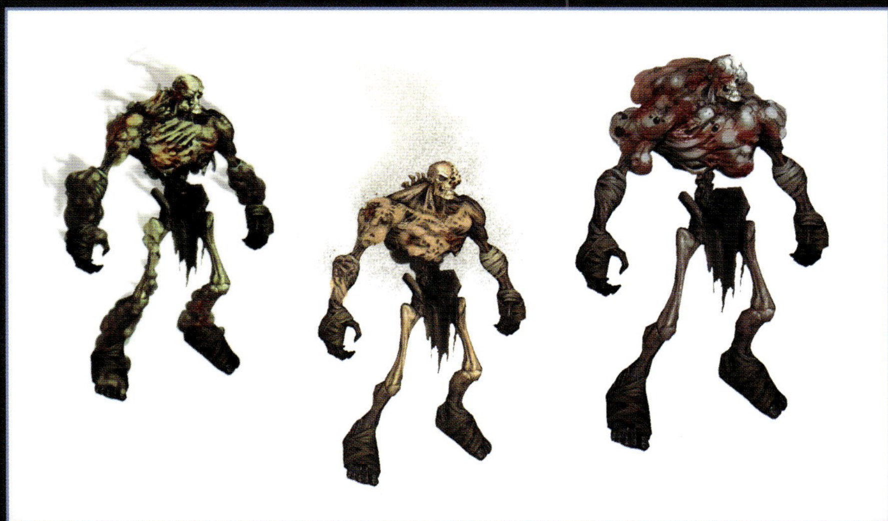

Undead Plaguebearer

The Destroyer has left the Earth a corrupted, diseased shadow of its former self. The Undead Plaguebearer is yet another manifestation of how twisted the world has become.

A toxic green haze oozes from the folds of the Undead Plaguebearer's skin. Anything caught within this noxious cloud of gas instantly begins to decay. Flesh putrefies and weapons lose their edge. Protected by this fetid mist, the Plaguebearers mount furious melee attacks. Only when stunned does this cloud dissipate, leaving the Plaguebearer vulnerable for a brief moment. The only sure defense against this relentless foe is to kill it—again.

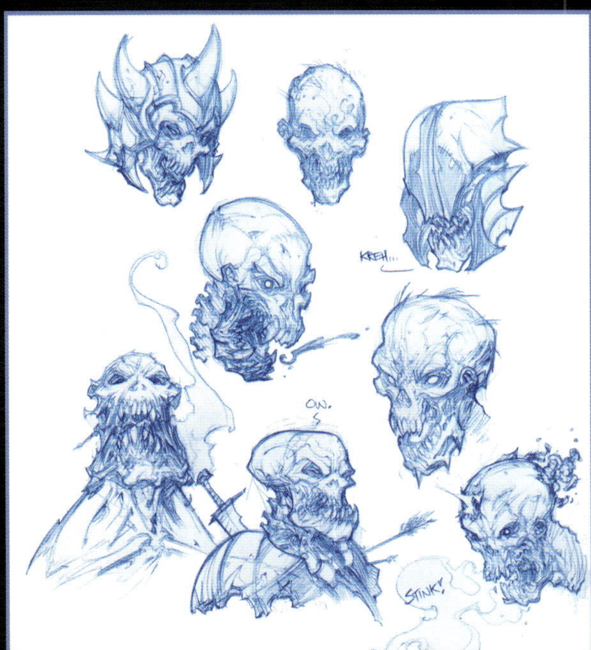

UNDEAD CONCEPTS

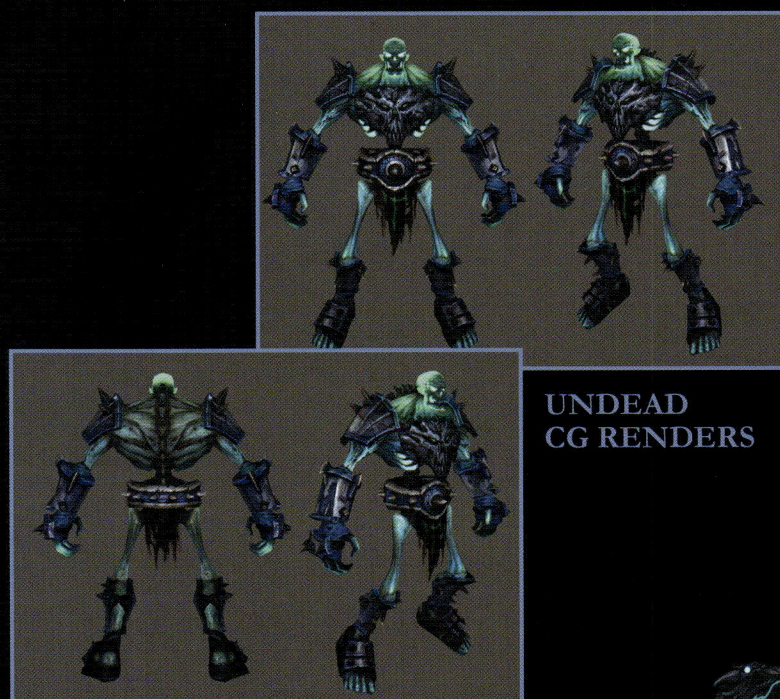

UNDEAD CG RENDERS

Phantom Guard

From the greatest of Infernal Lords to the lowest of Wicked, Hell's legions still spread across the desolate Earth. The Phantom Guard form the backbone of the Destroyer's army.

They are hideous to behold, with craggy faces, stunted wings, and armor as jagged as their flesh. For years the Phantom Guard hunted the remains of mankind without pity. Now, these demons battle the valiant angels who patrol the scorched sky, and sate their bloodlust on those they bring to ground.

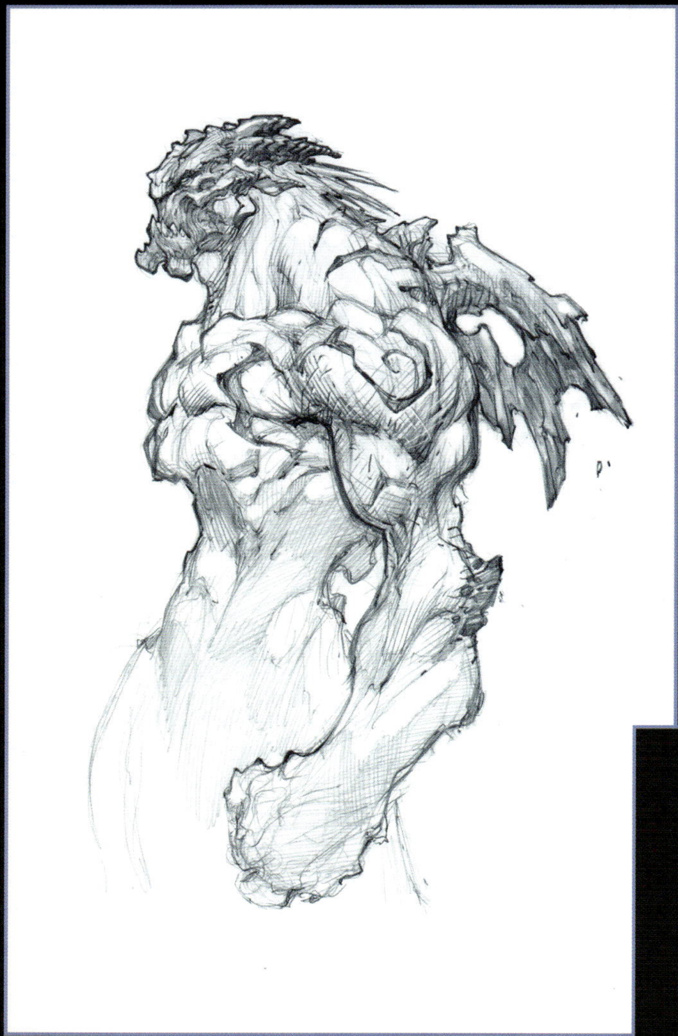

TORSO SKETCH

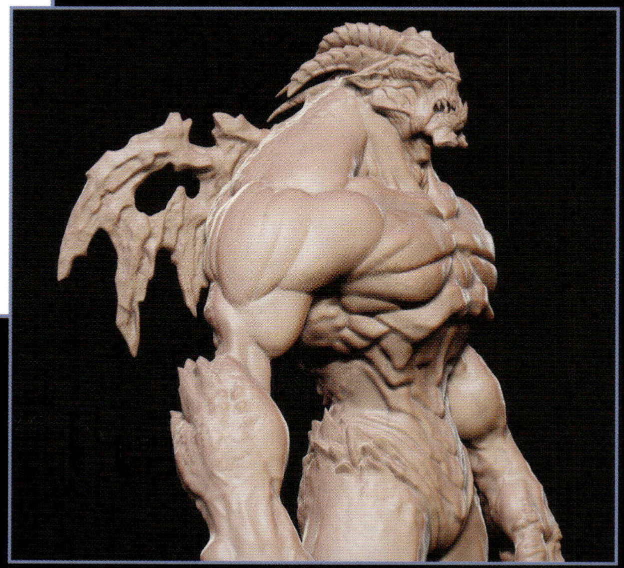

CG MODEL RENDER

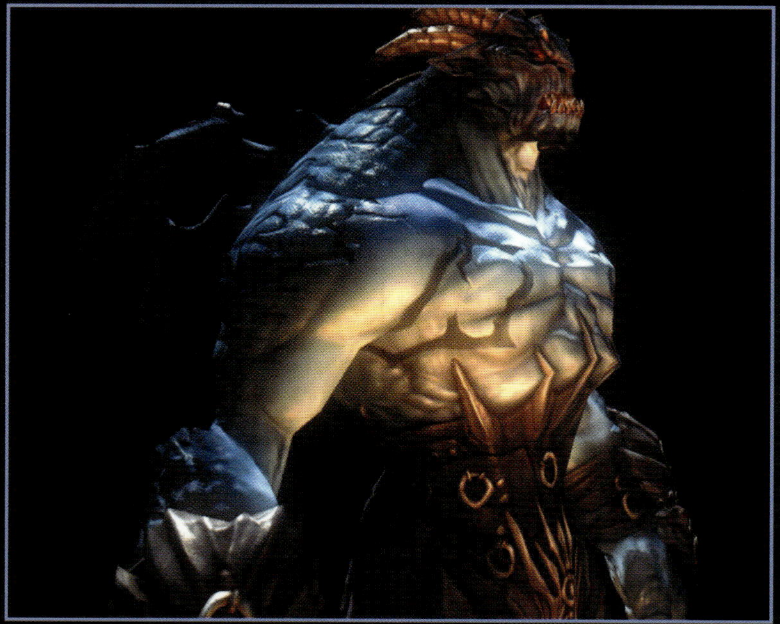

CG TEXTURED MODEL RENDER

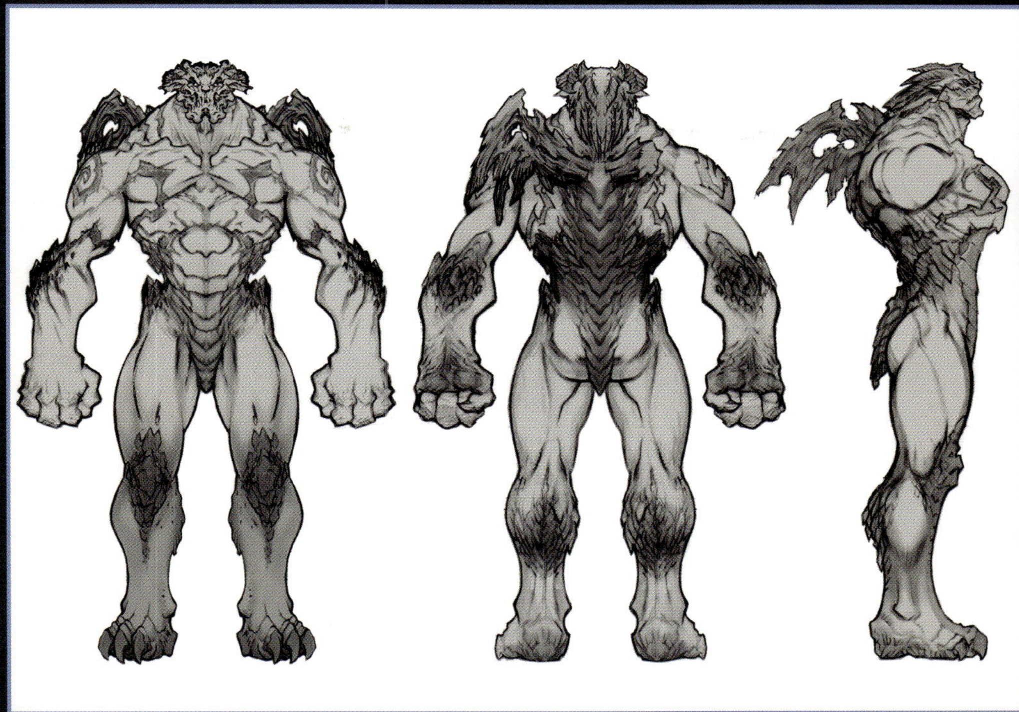

SOLDIER TURNAROUNDS

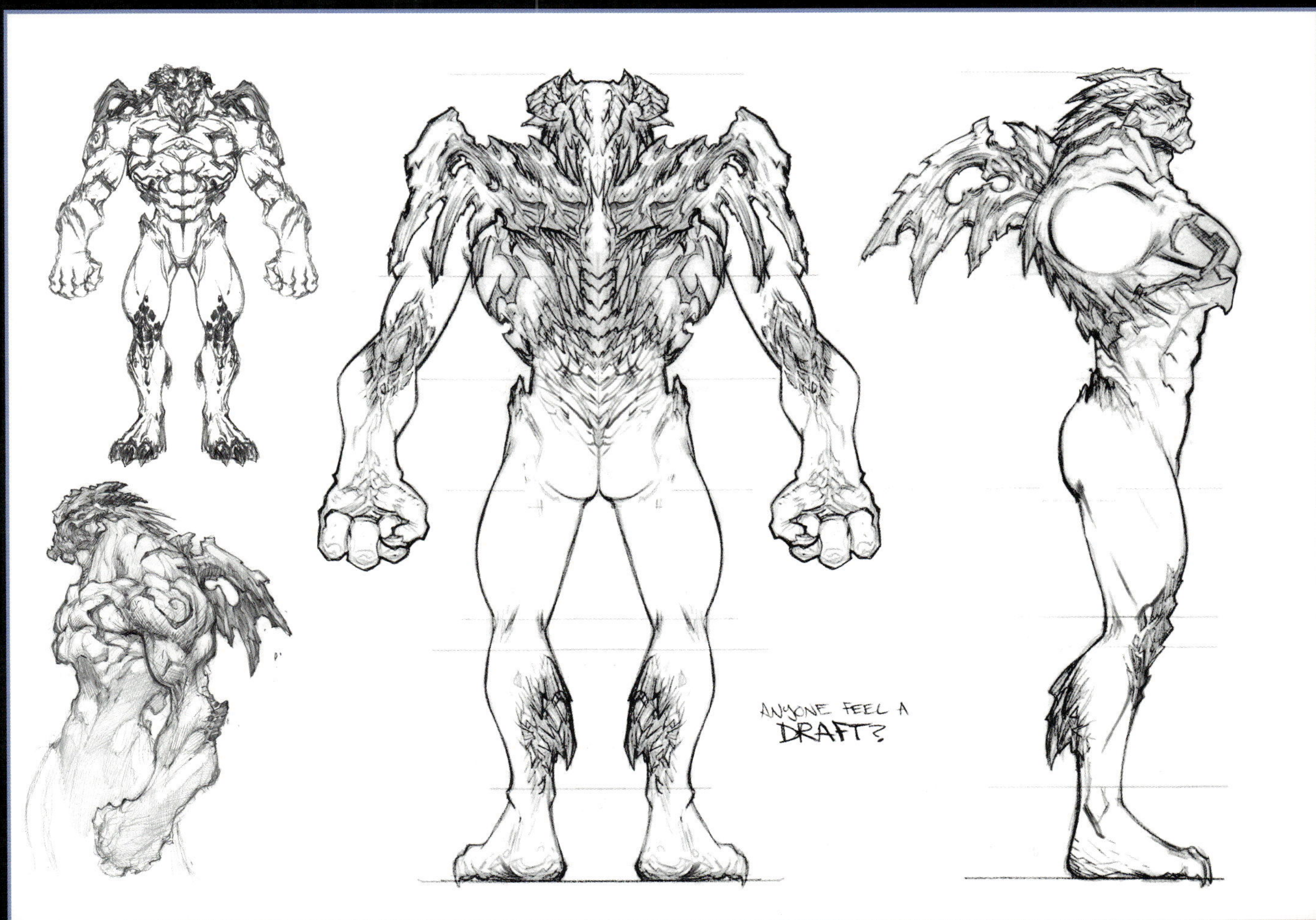

SOLDIER TURNAROUNDS

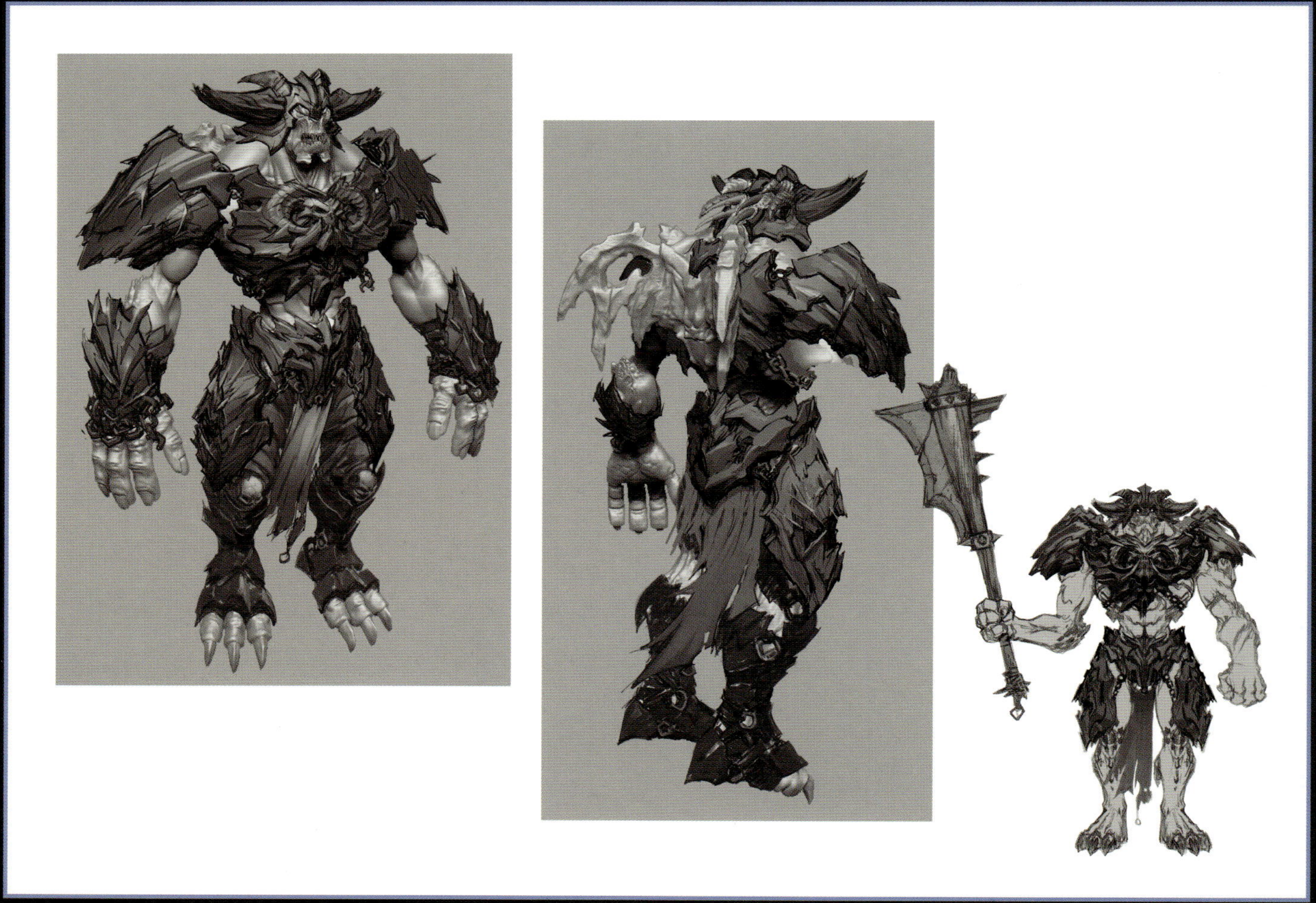

PHANTOM GENERAL TURNAROUNDS

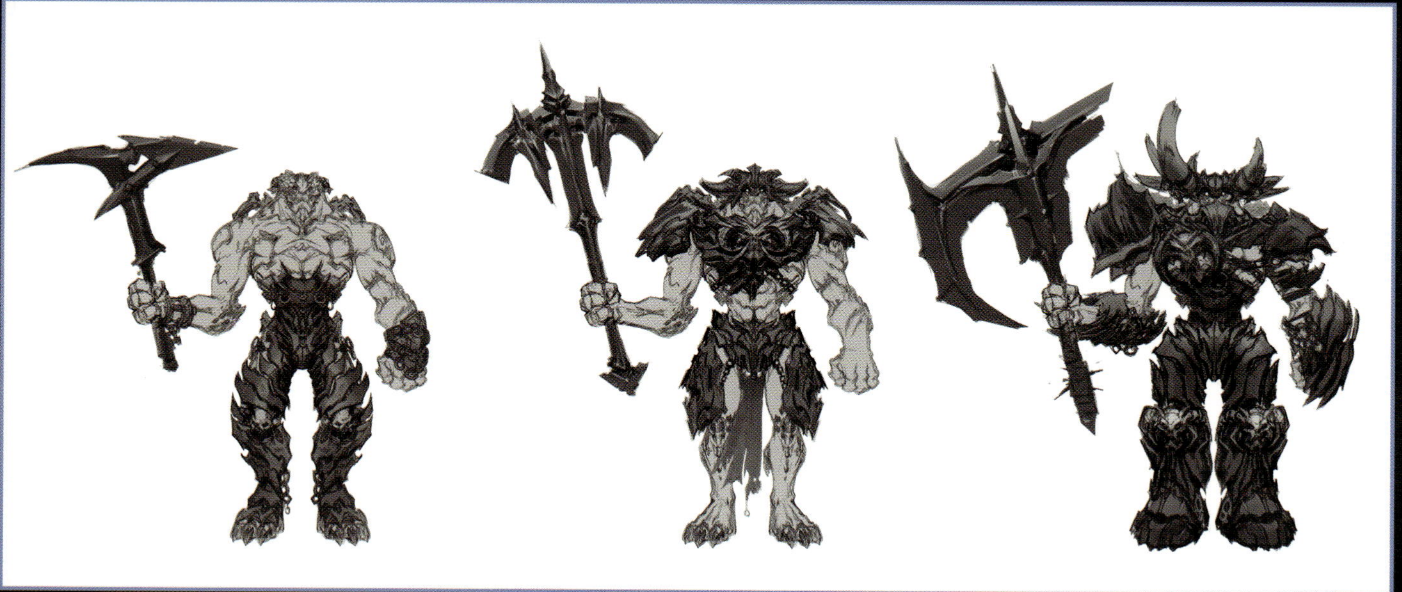

SIZE COMPARISON

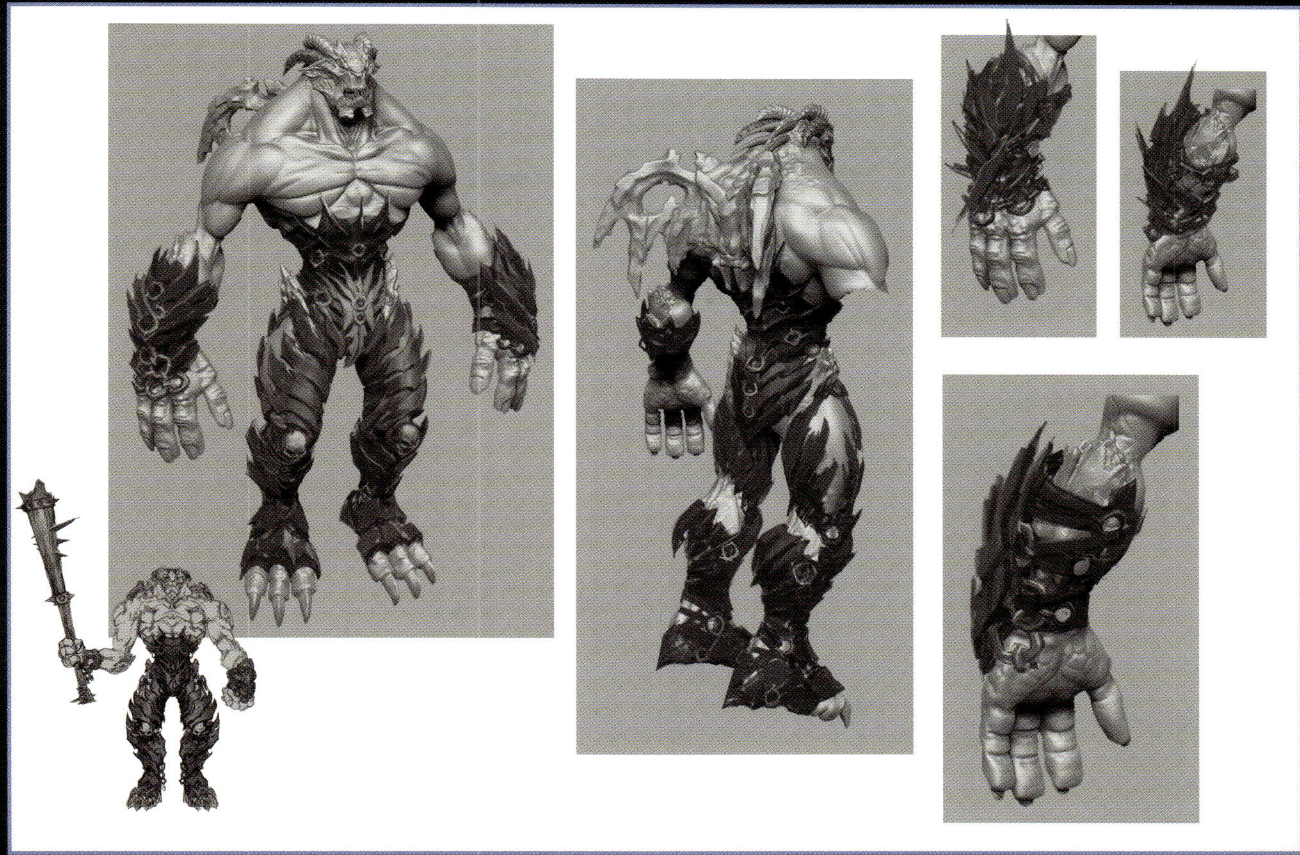

SOLDIER TURNAROUNDS

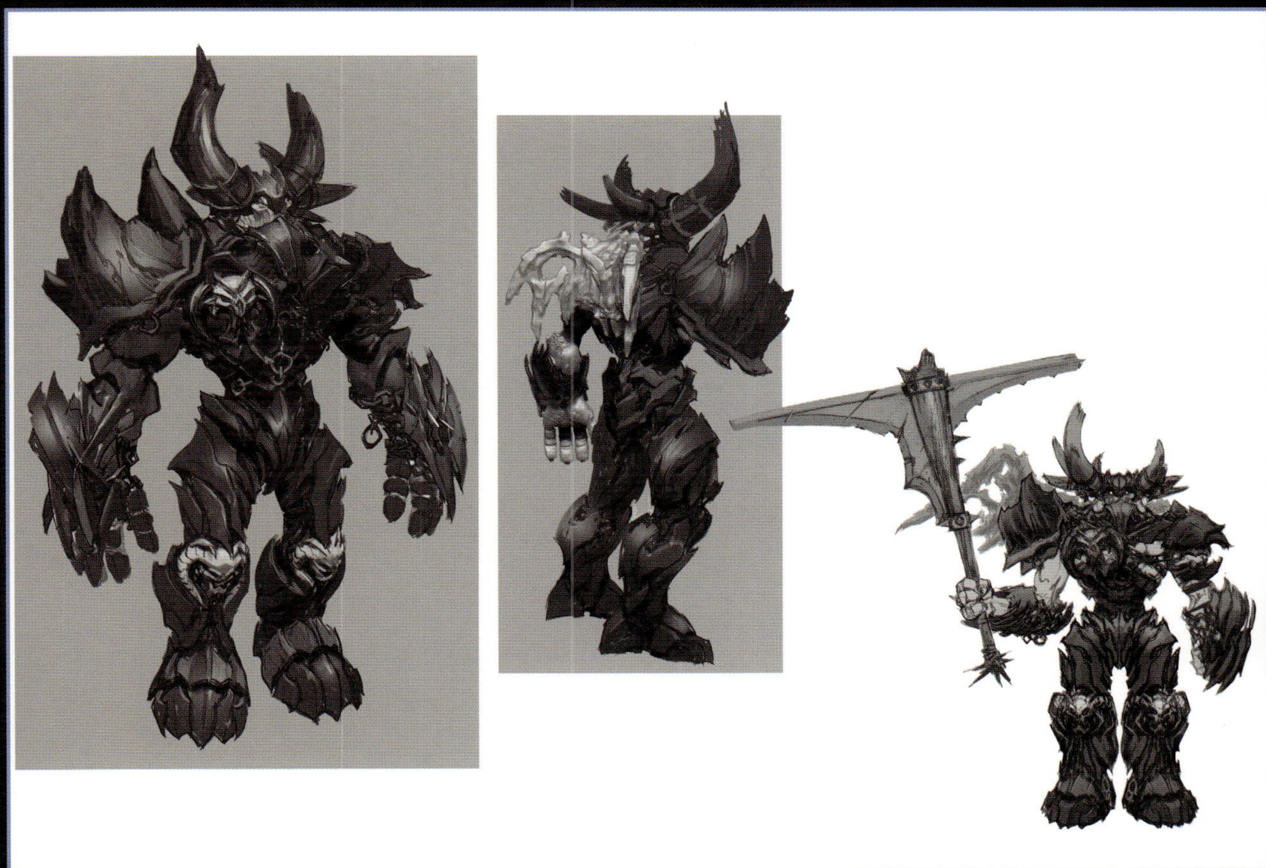

BERSERKER TURNAROUNDS

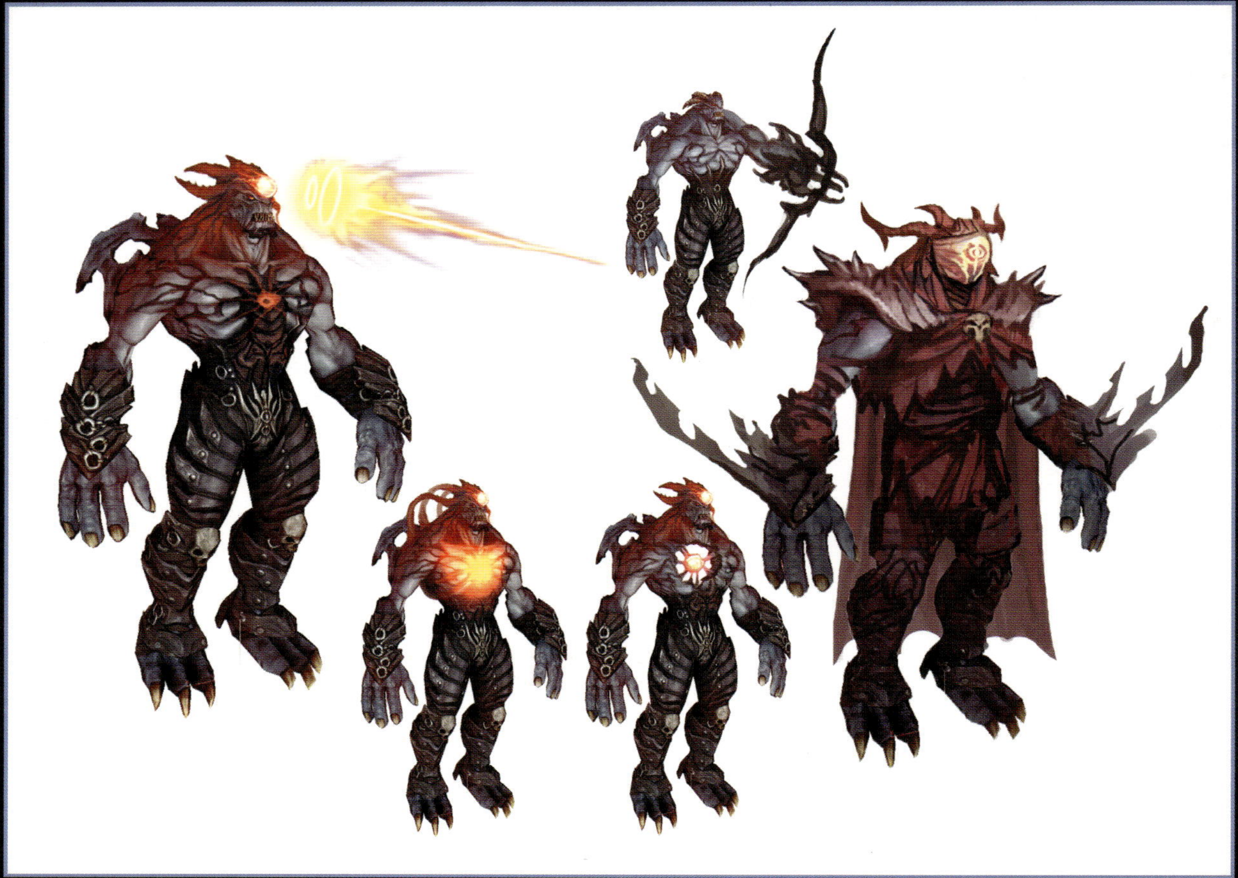

PHANTOM GUARD SHAMAN CONCEPTS

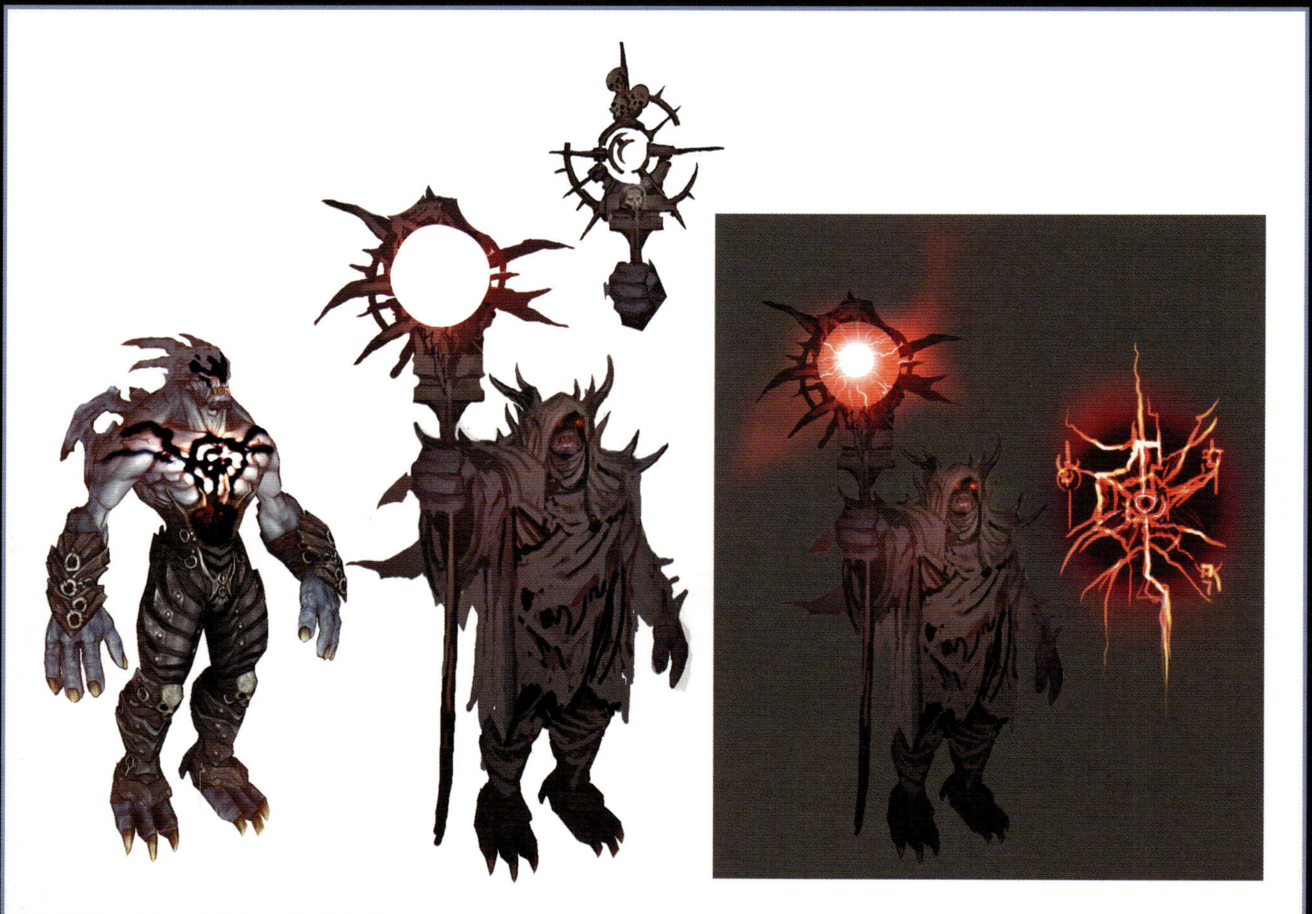

PHANTOM GUARD SHAMAN CONCEPTS

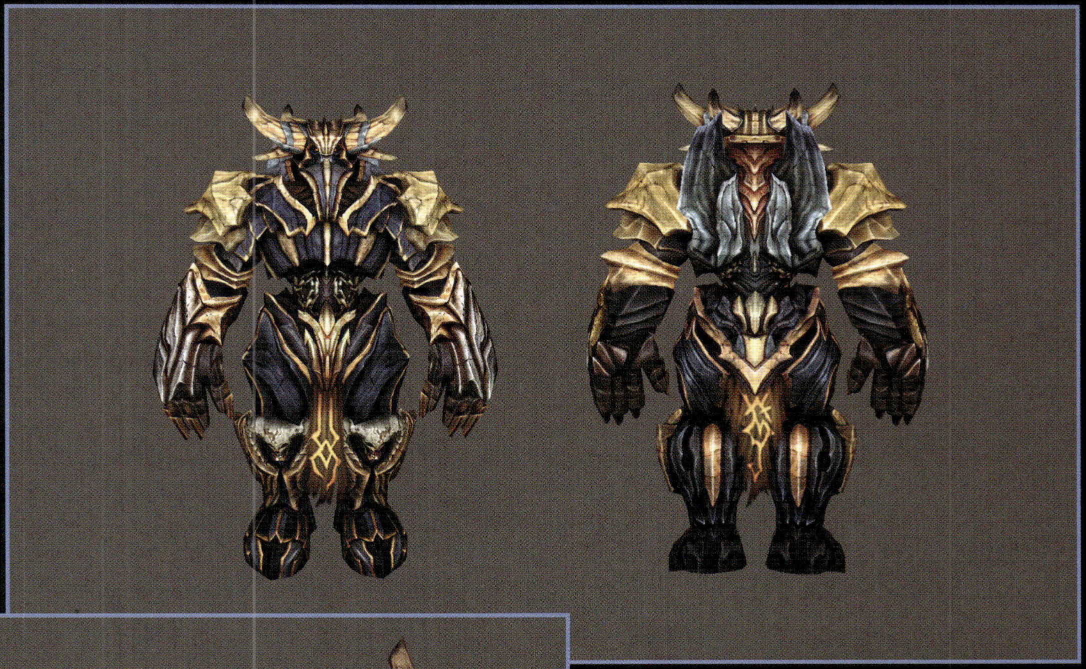

CG TURNAROUNDS

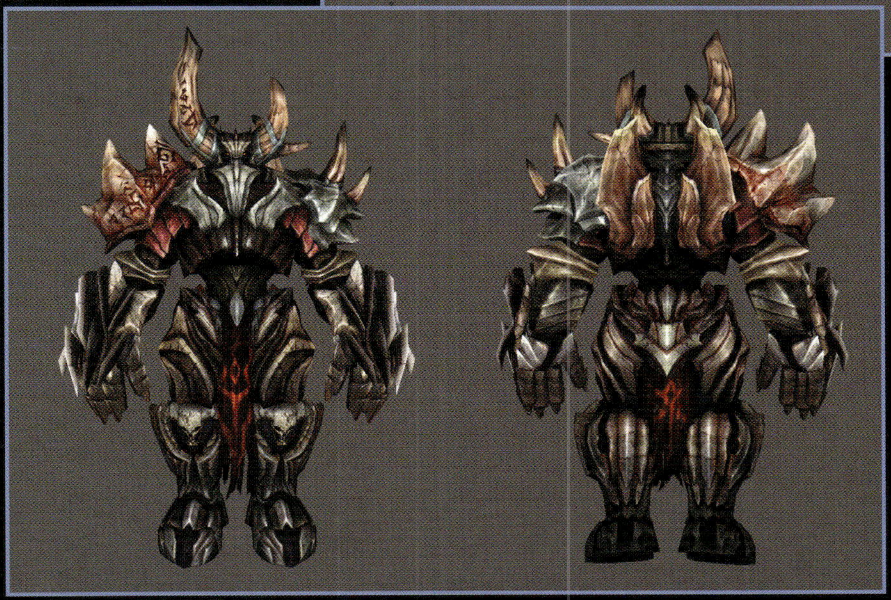

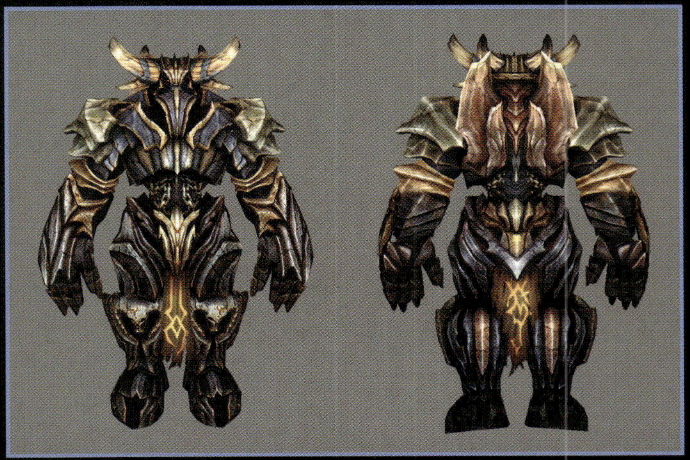

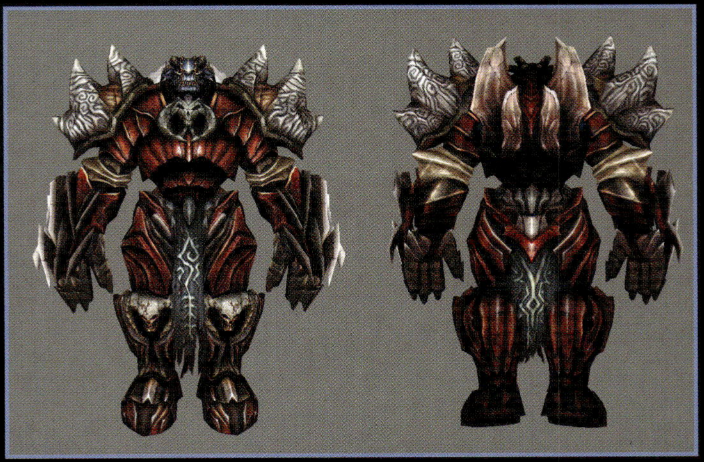

CG TURNAROUNDS

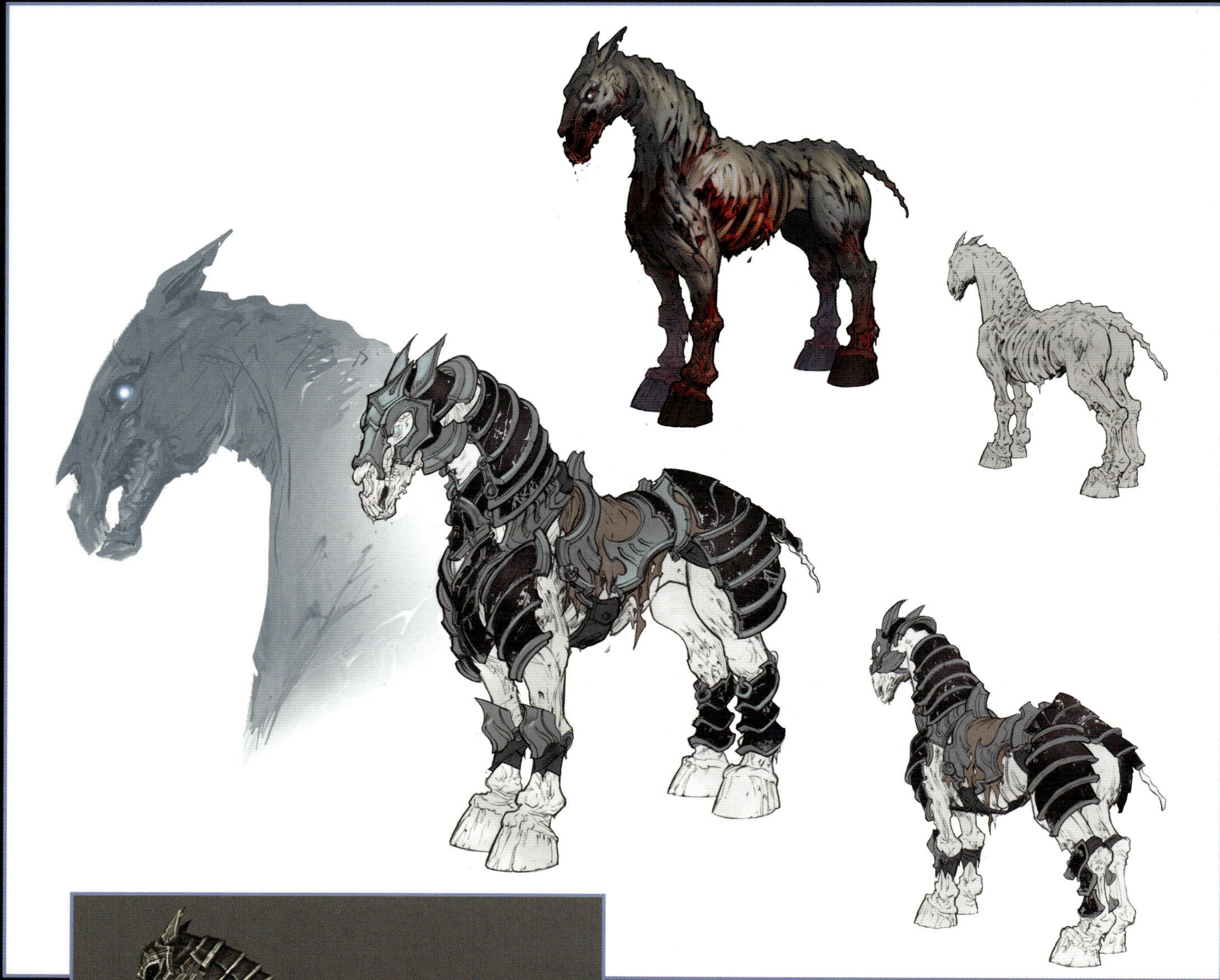

HORSE DESIGNS

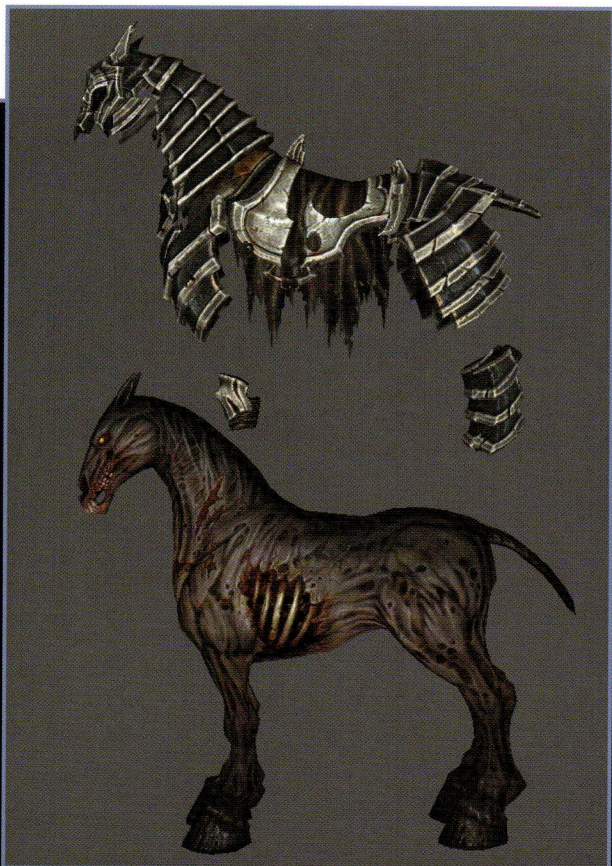

ARMOR DESIGNS

Abyssal Riders

The Abyssal Riders are the Destroyer's cavalry. Beneath their armor, these pitiless horsemen are cracked and pale, their flesh barely able to contain the hellfire that roils within.

They can release this energy in sorcerous attacks, or channel it into their phantom steeds which shriek with the agony of their Riders' tortured souls. From the bleak place of my captivity, the pounding hoofs of the Abyssal Riders sound like the distant beat of Death's Drum.

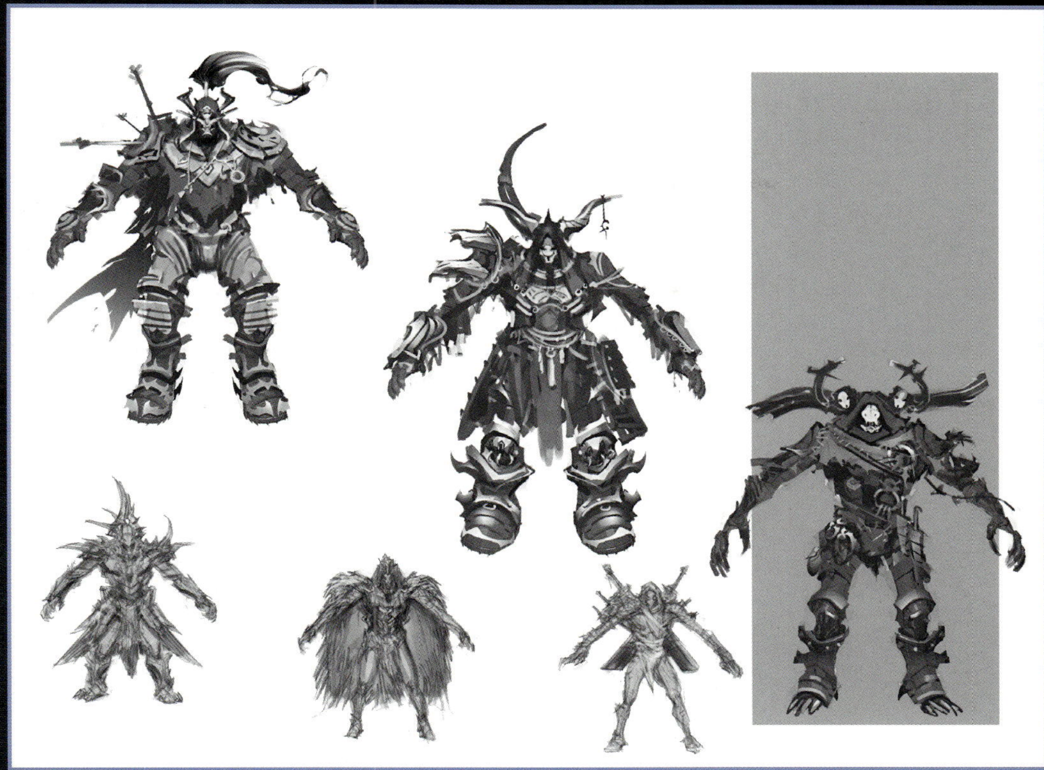

RIDER DESIGNS

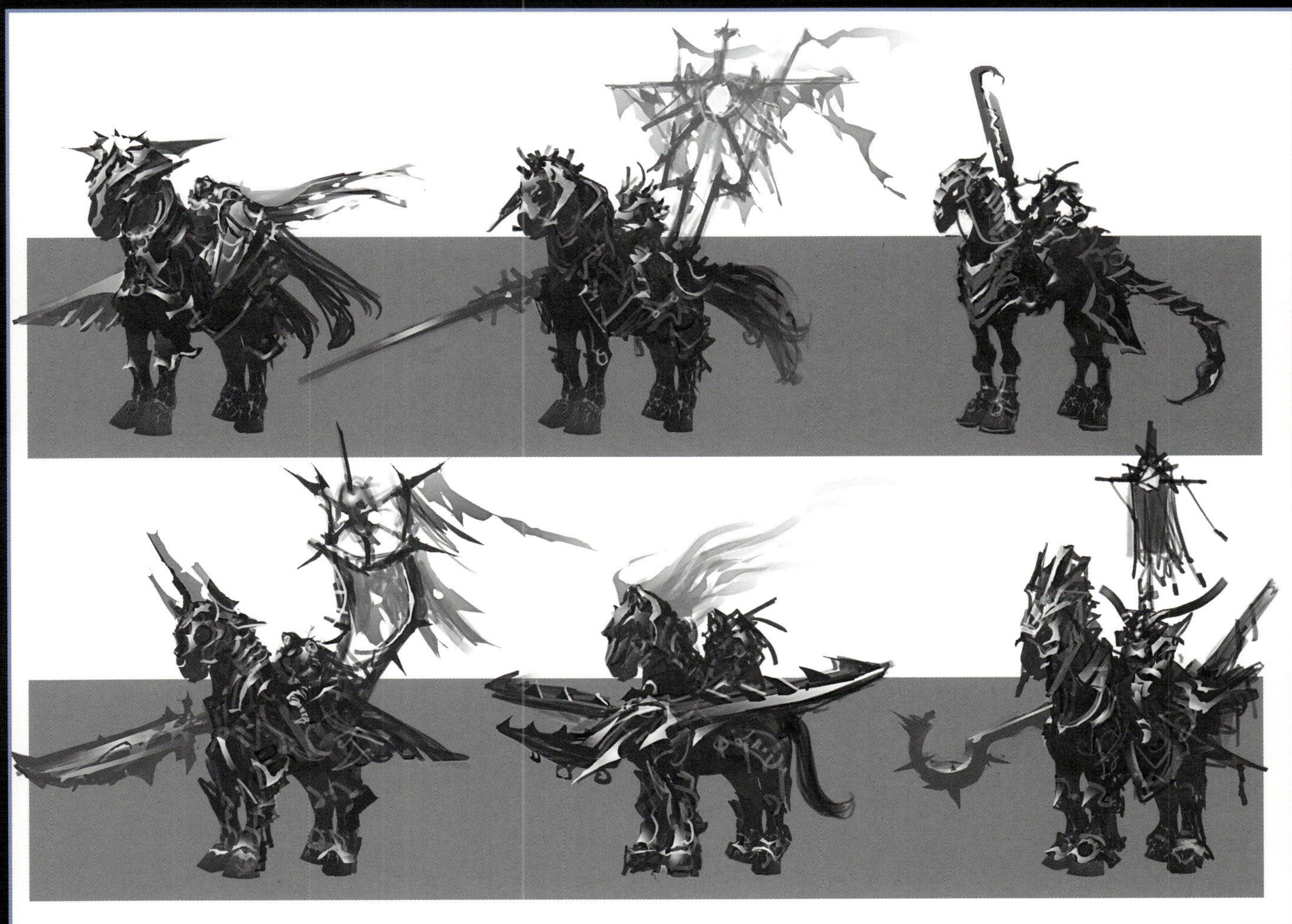

DEVELOPMENT SKETCHES

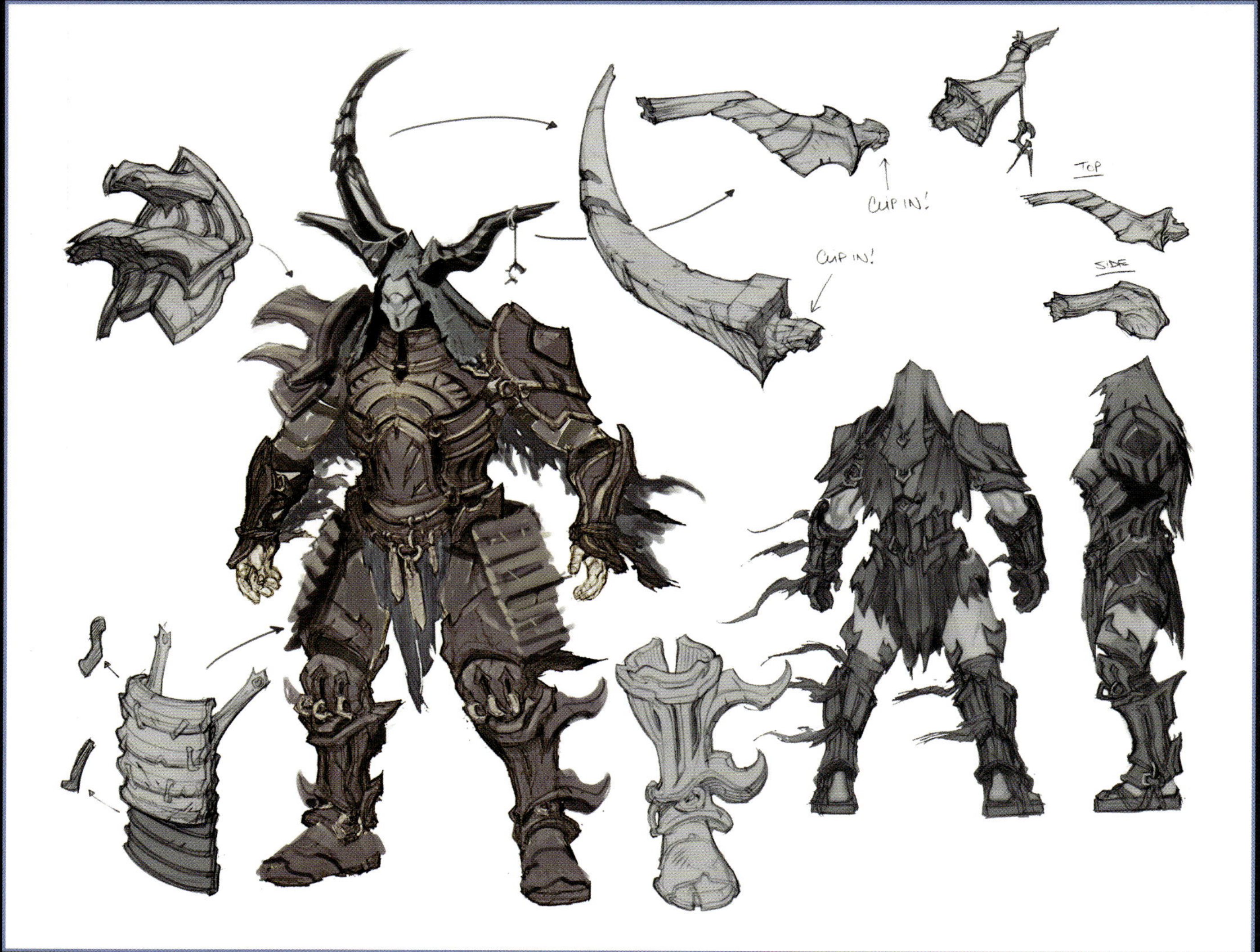

ARMOR DESIGNS

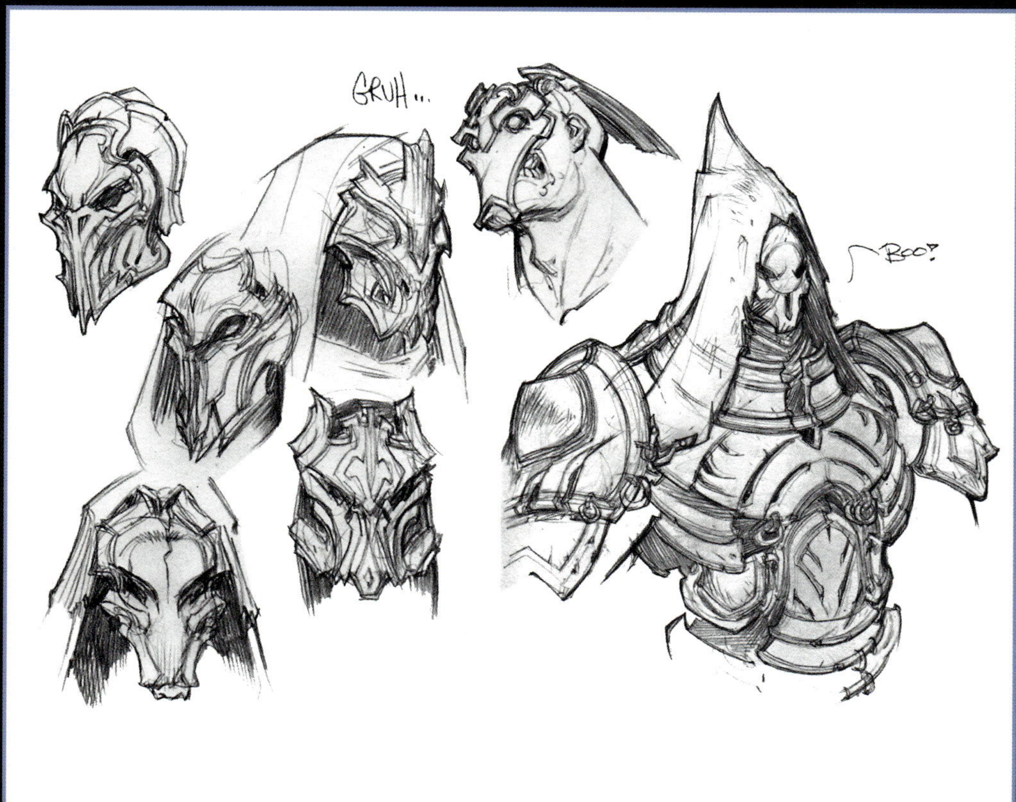

HEAD CONCEPTS

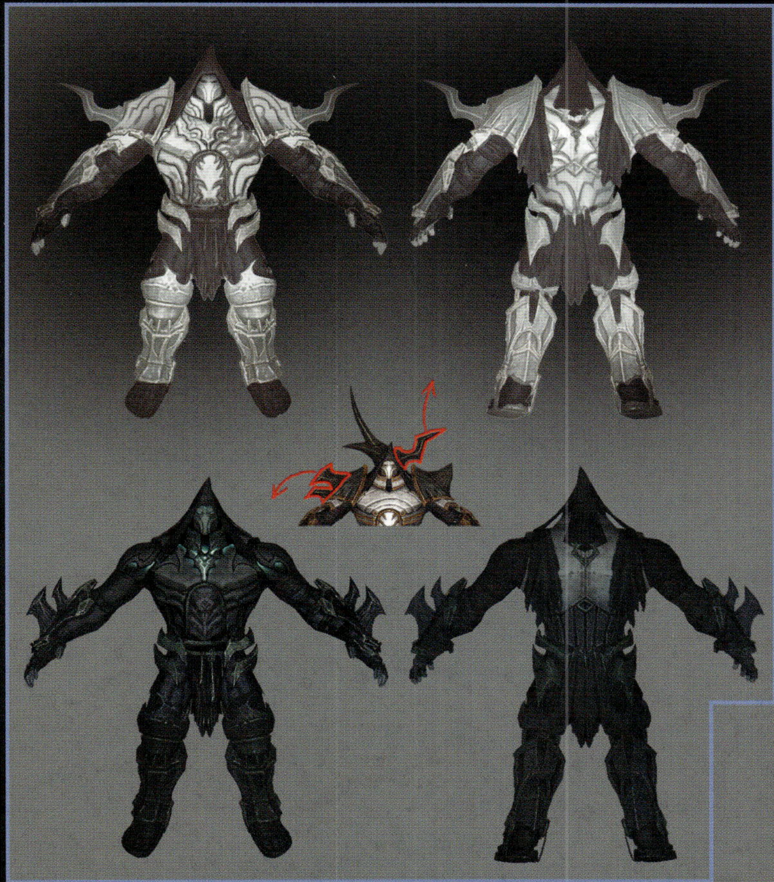

TURNAROUNDS

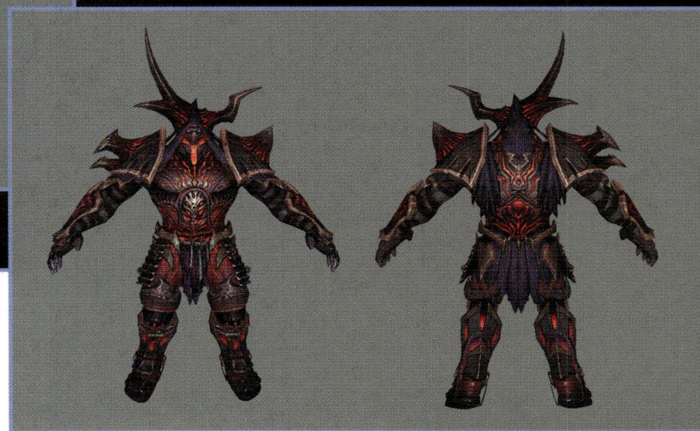

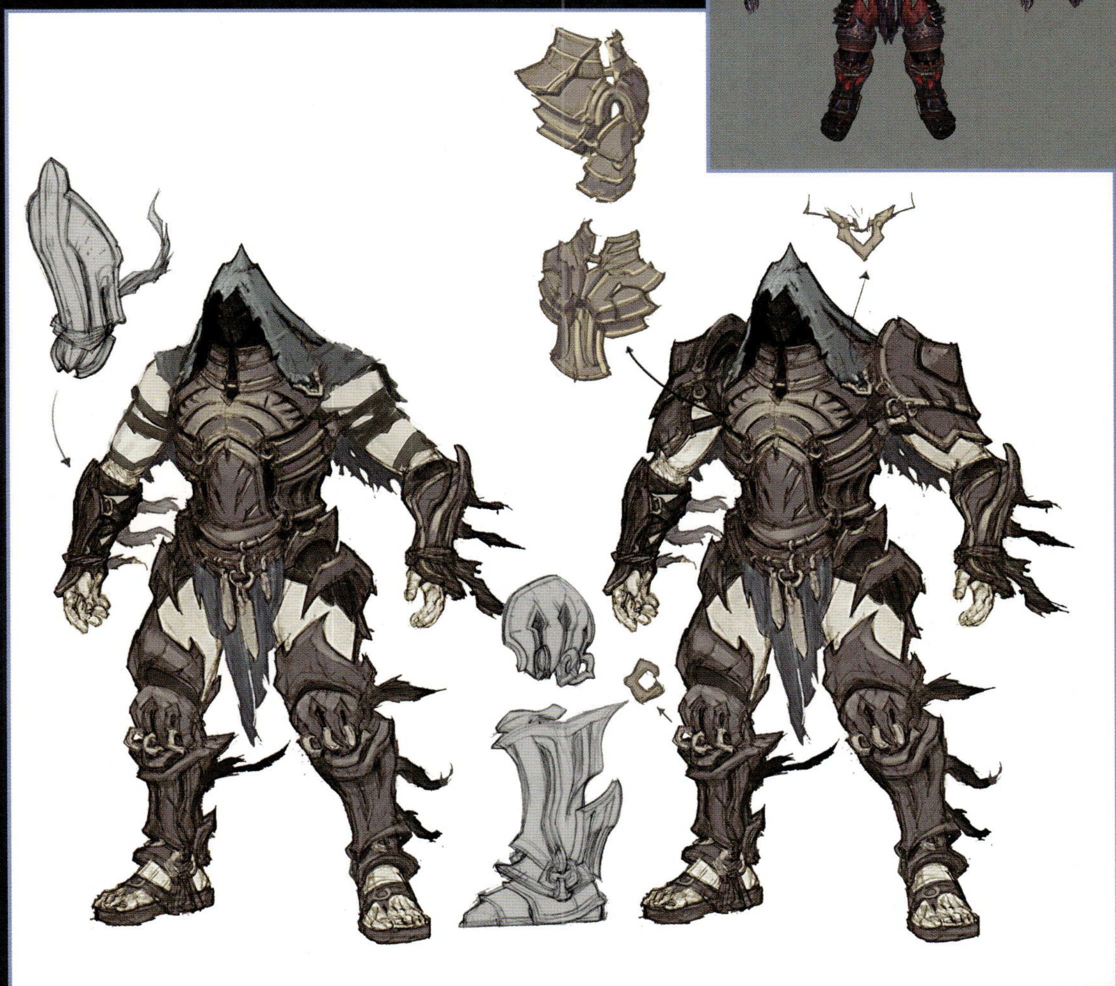

ARMOR DESIGNS

The Jailer

The Jailer's hulking torso is formed from the remains of countless cadavers. Hanging from this shroud of decayed flesh are cages where the souls of those killed by the Jailer remain trapped. These souls can be summoned as rotting corpses to serve the Jailer's command. As the undead mob harries his prey, their master crushes the victim beneath his cage. The demons hint that some darker secret lies hidden within the Jailer's hideous frame.

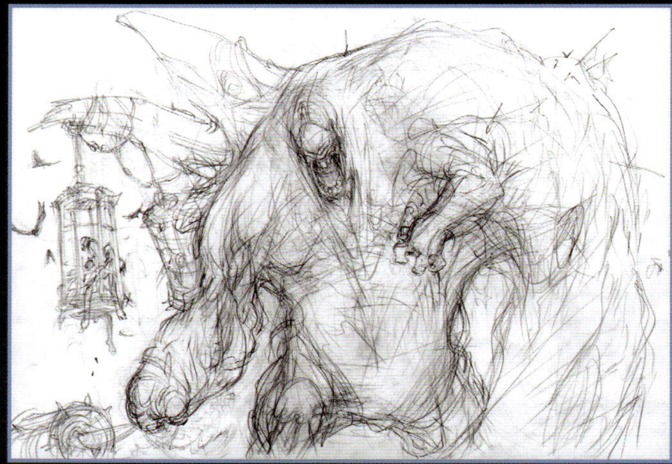

SKETCH

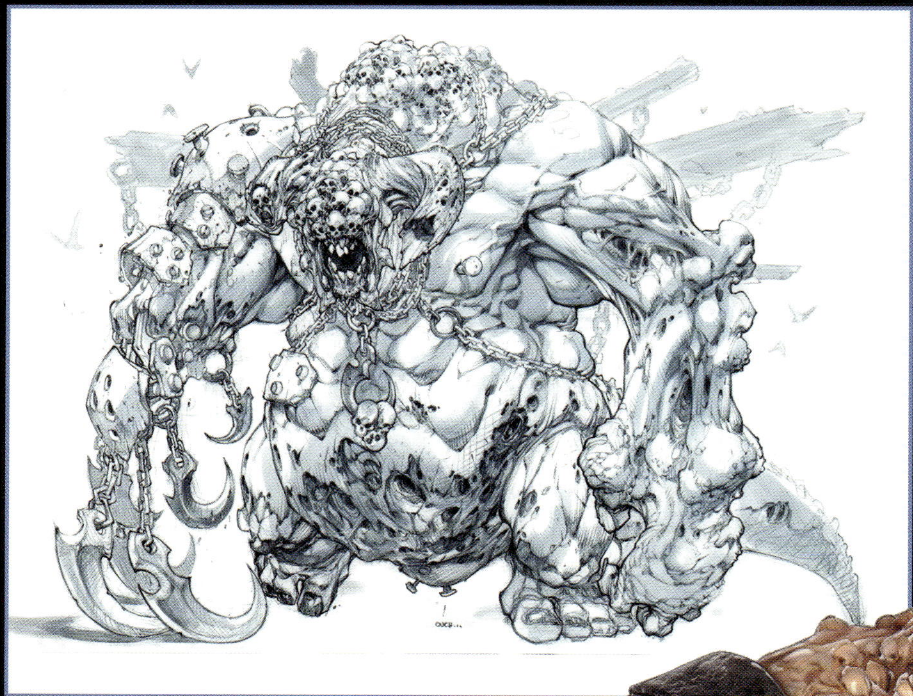

EARLY CONCEPT

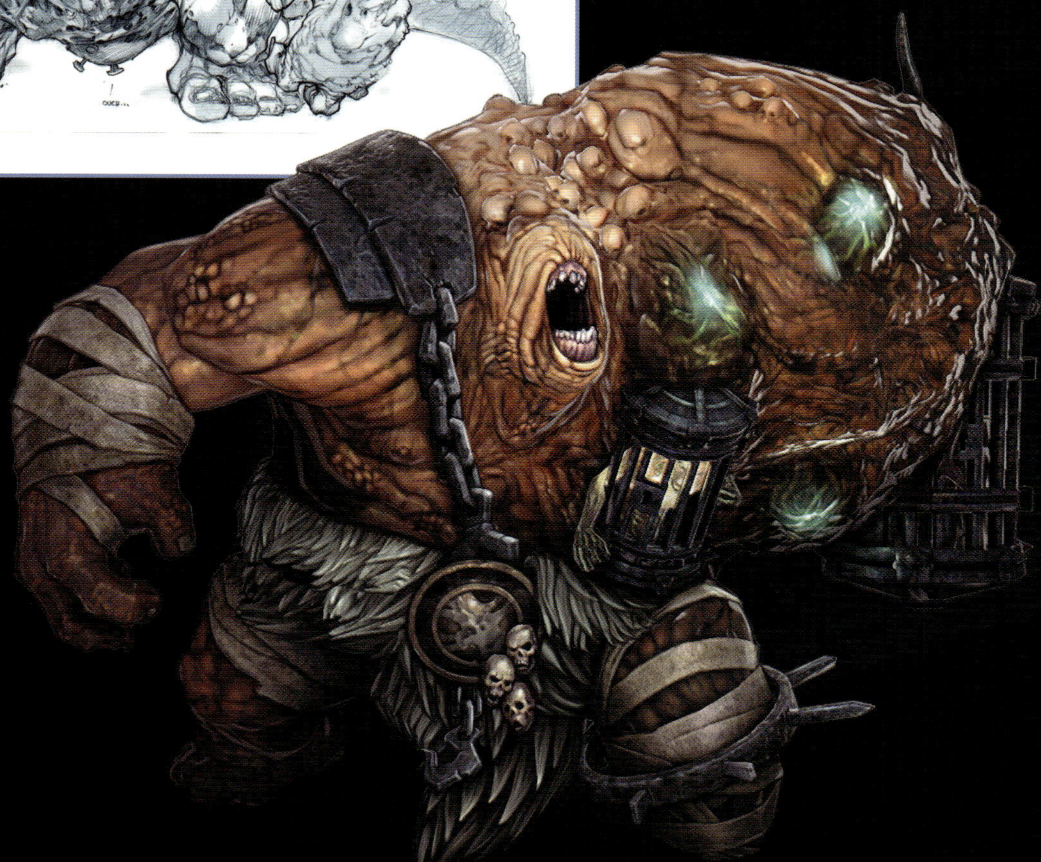

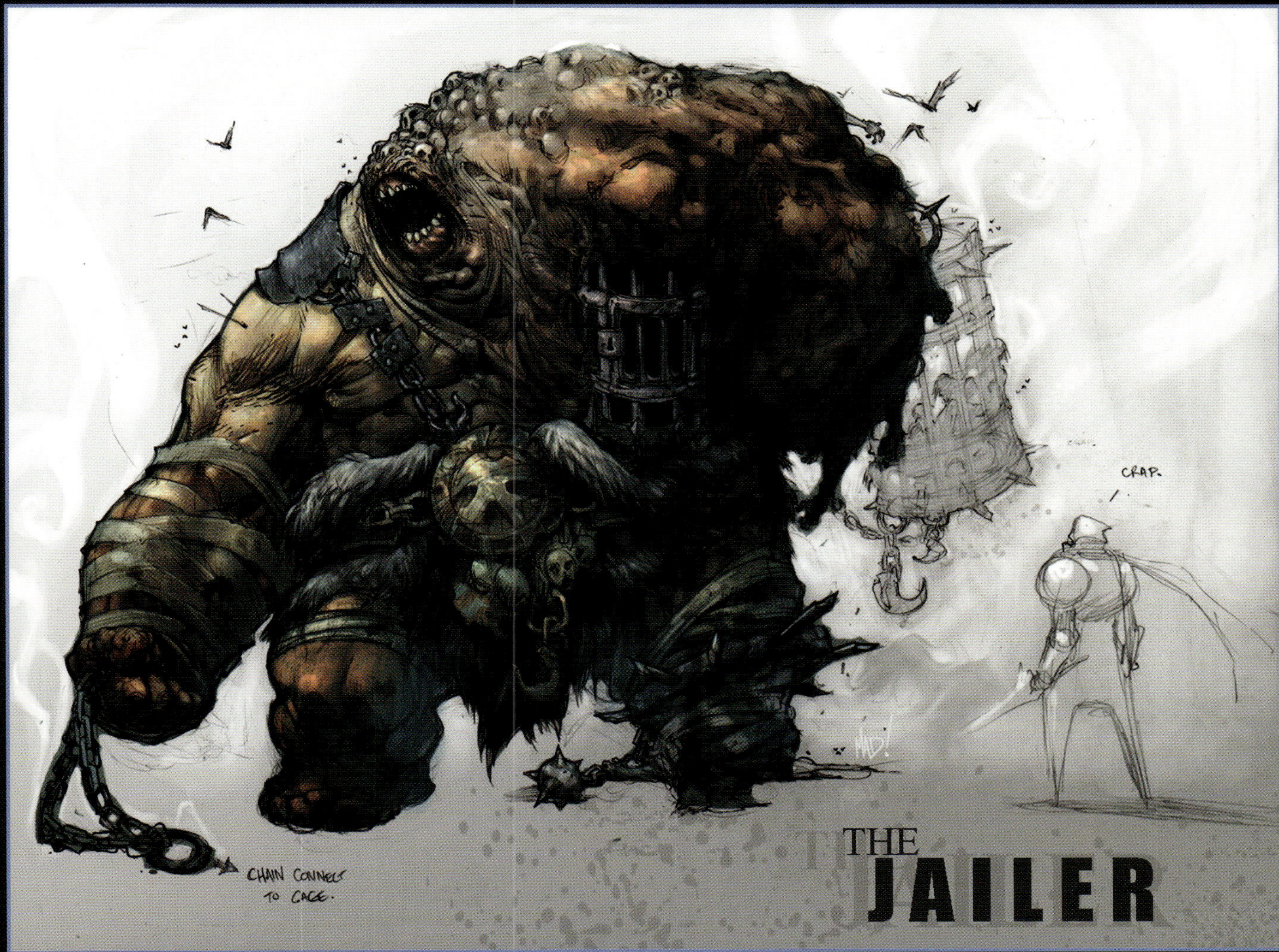

FINAL DESIGN

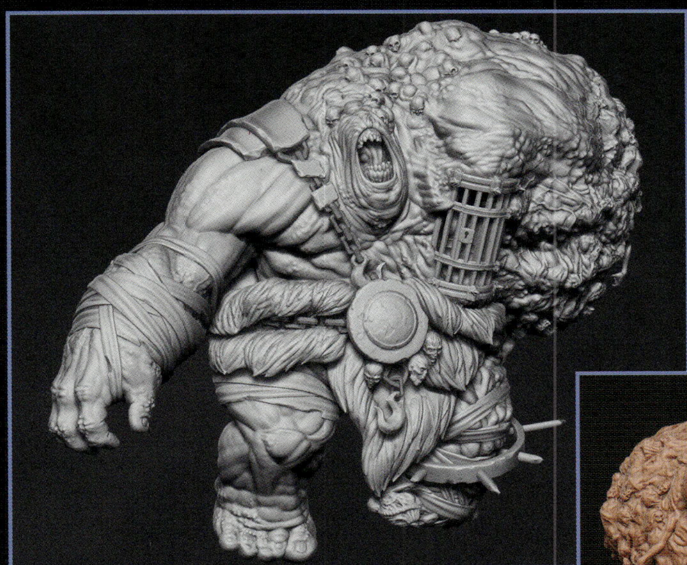

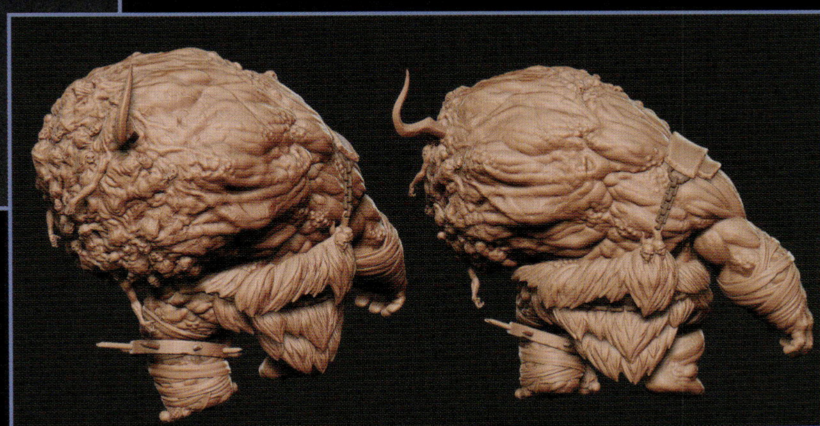

CG RENDERS

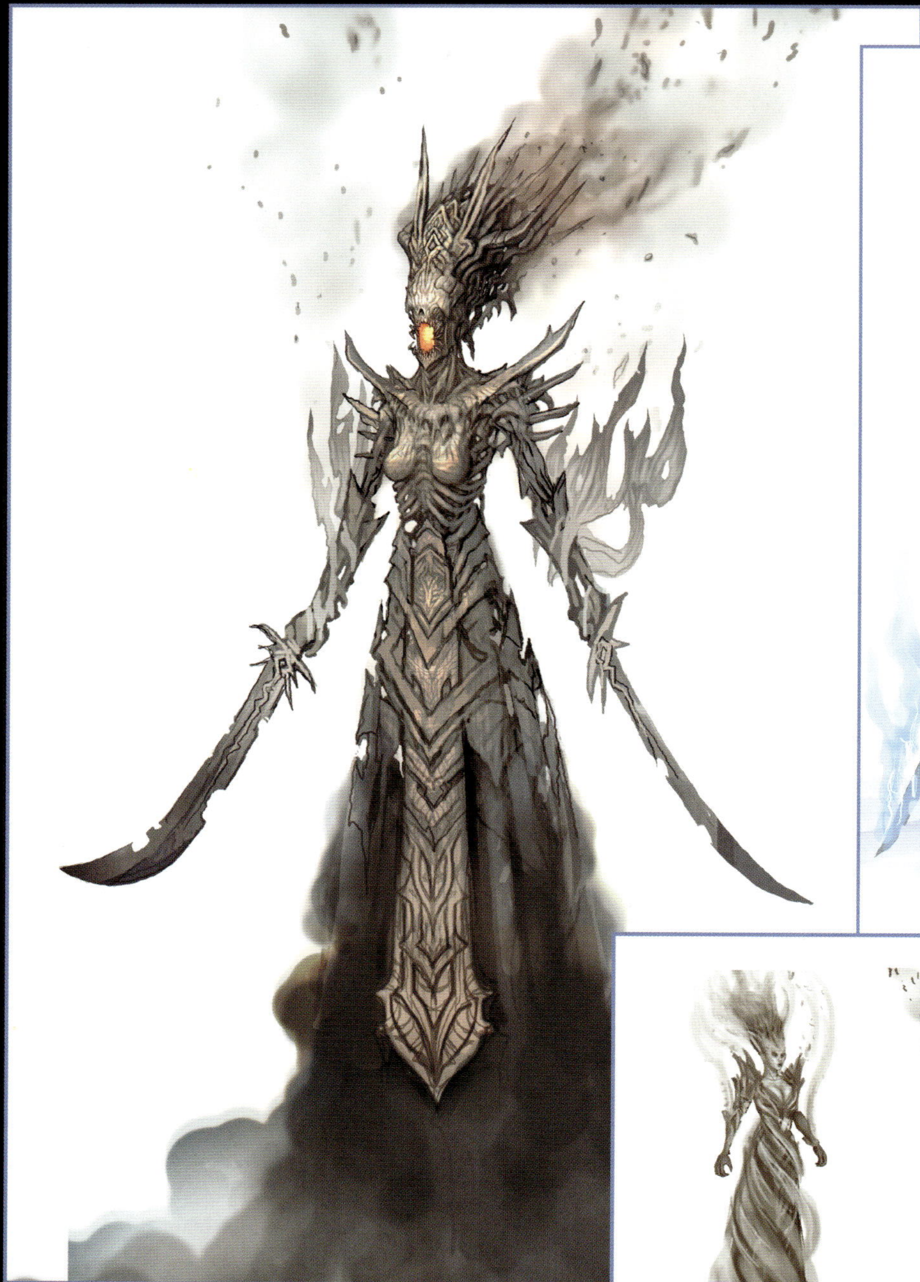

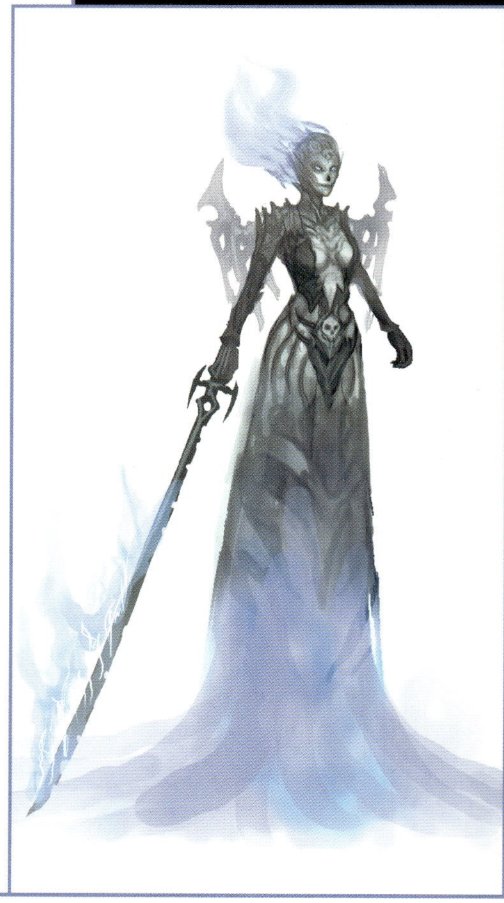

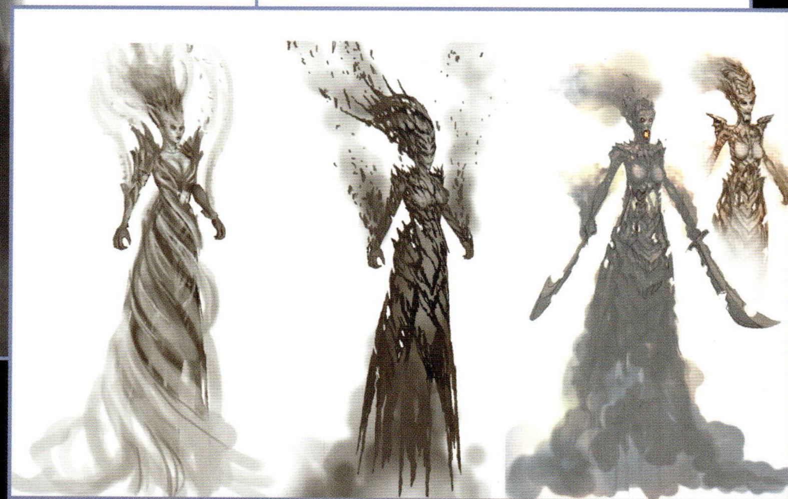

WRAITH CONCEPTS

Wraith

Among the horrors of Hell there is also seductive beauty. The Wraiths float alluringly above the wastes, their tattered garments billowing gently in the breeze. But beneath a Wraith's delicate facade there is only hunger. These she-demons devour life force, mercilessly extracting it from any who stumble near. Their prey are left mere husks, the cast-away shells of an unholy sirens' feast.

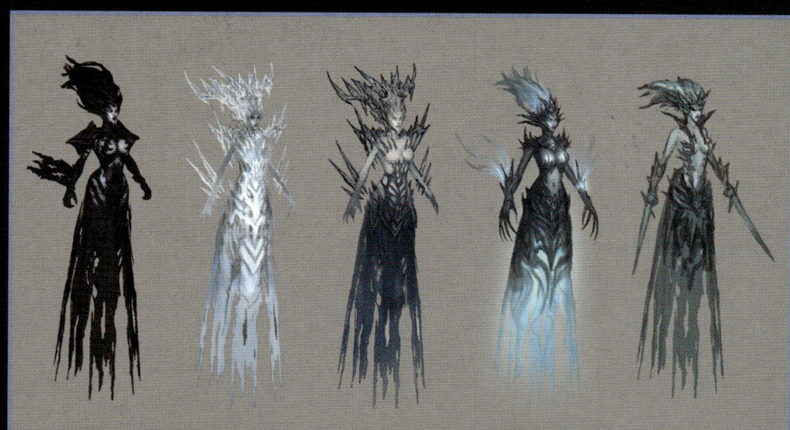

WRAITH CONCEPTS

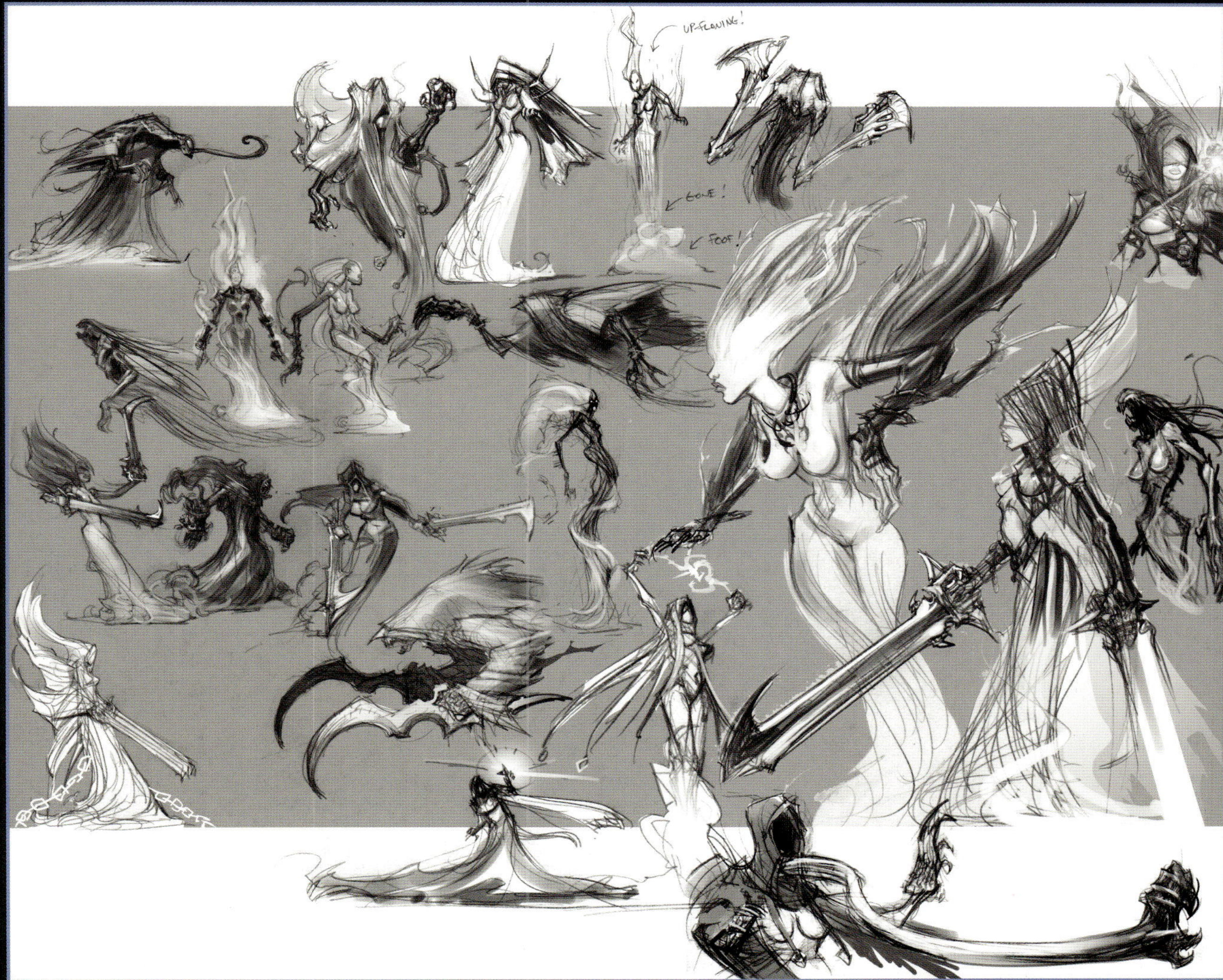

DEVELOPMENT SKETCHES

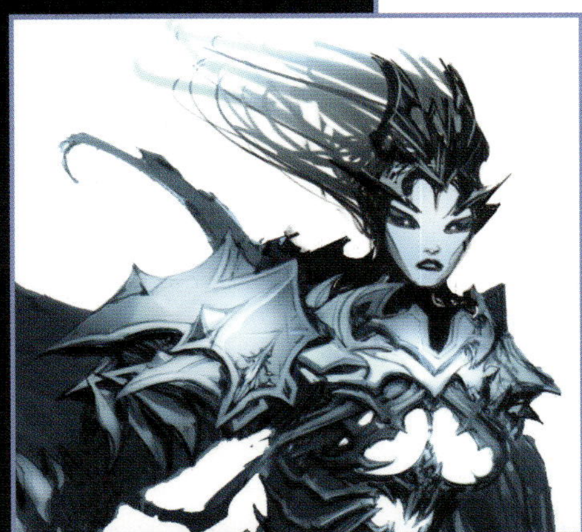

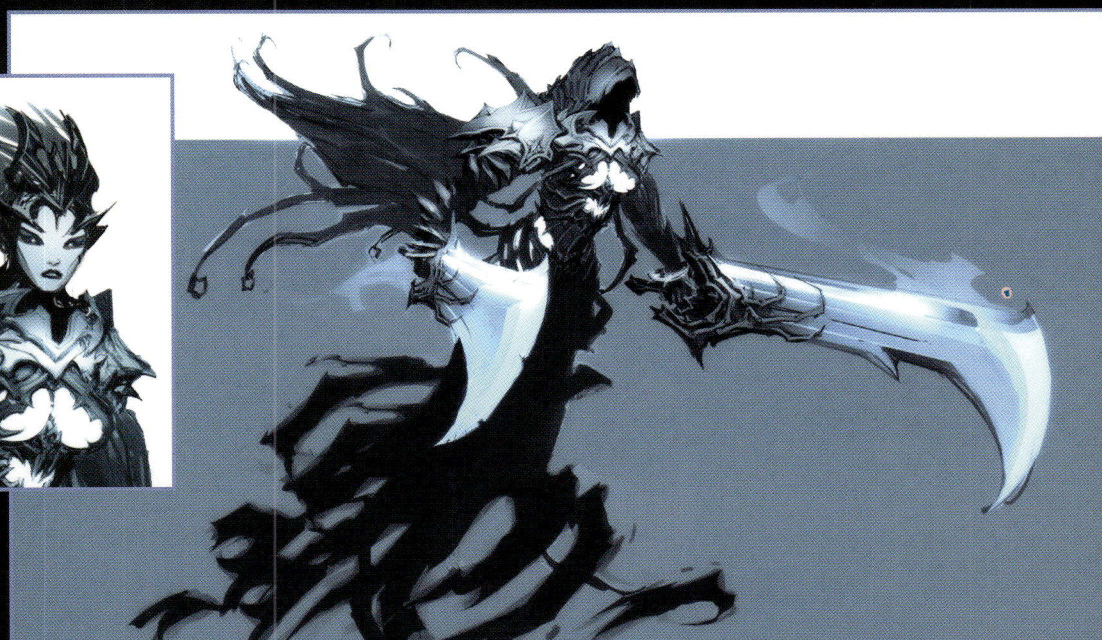

DEVELOPMENT SKETCH

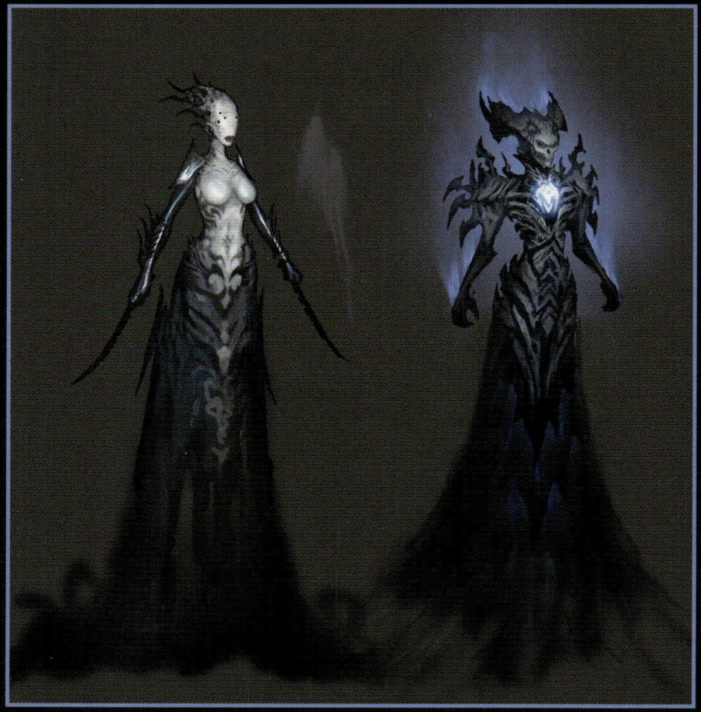

CG RENDER

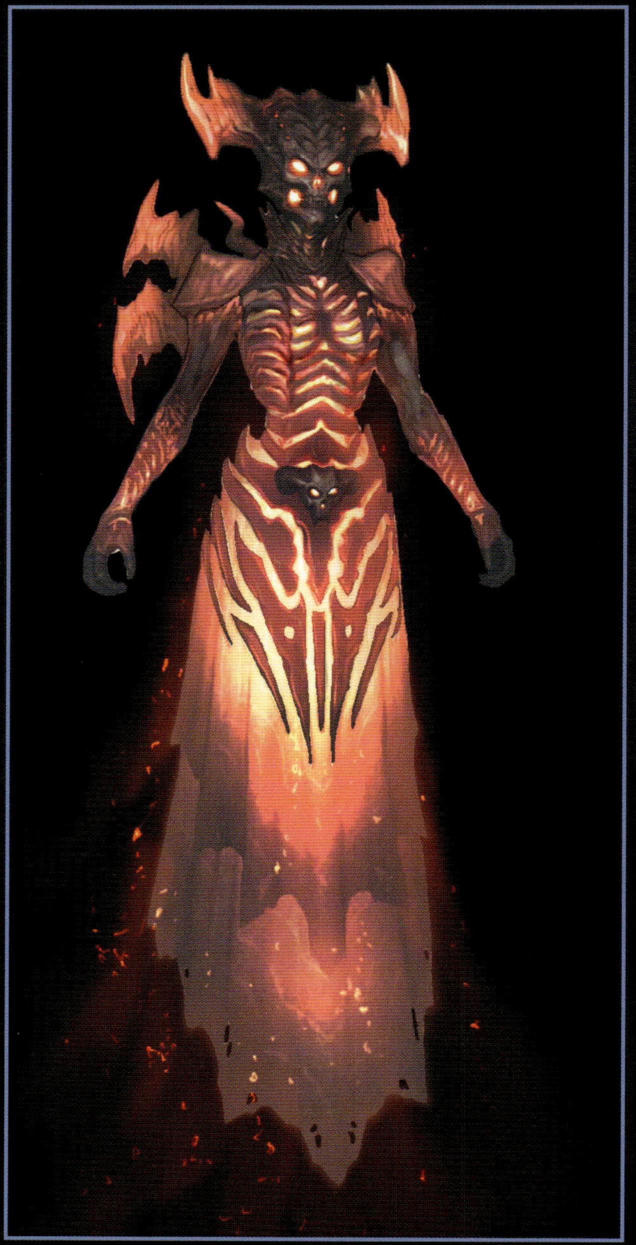

CG RENDER

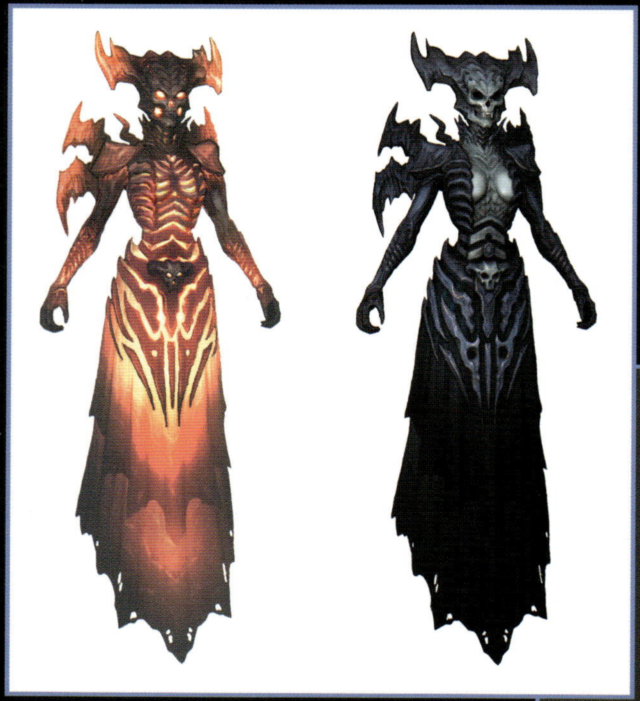

CG RENDER

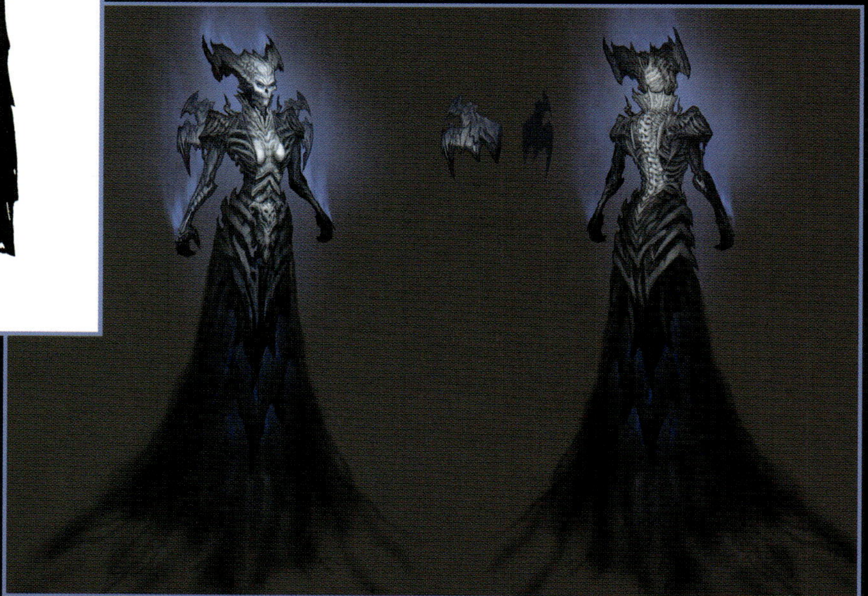

CG TURNAROUNDS

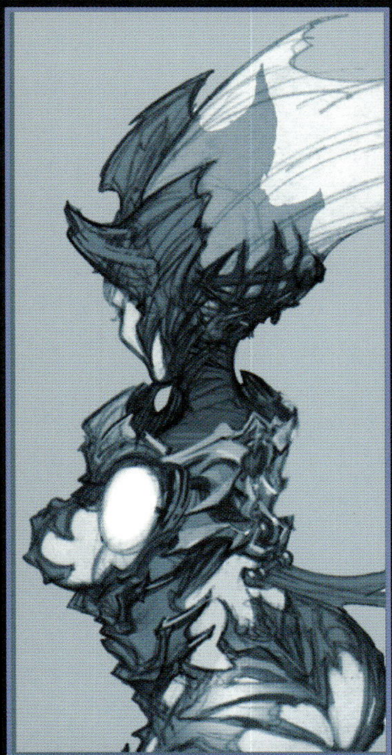

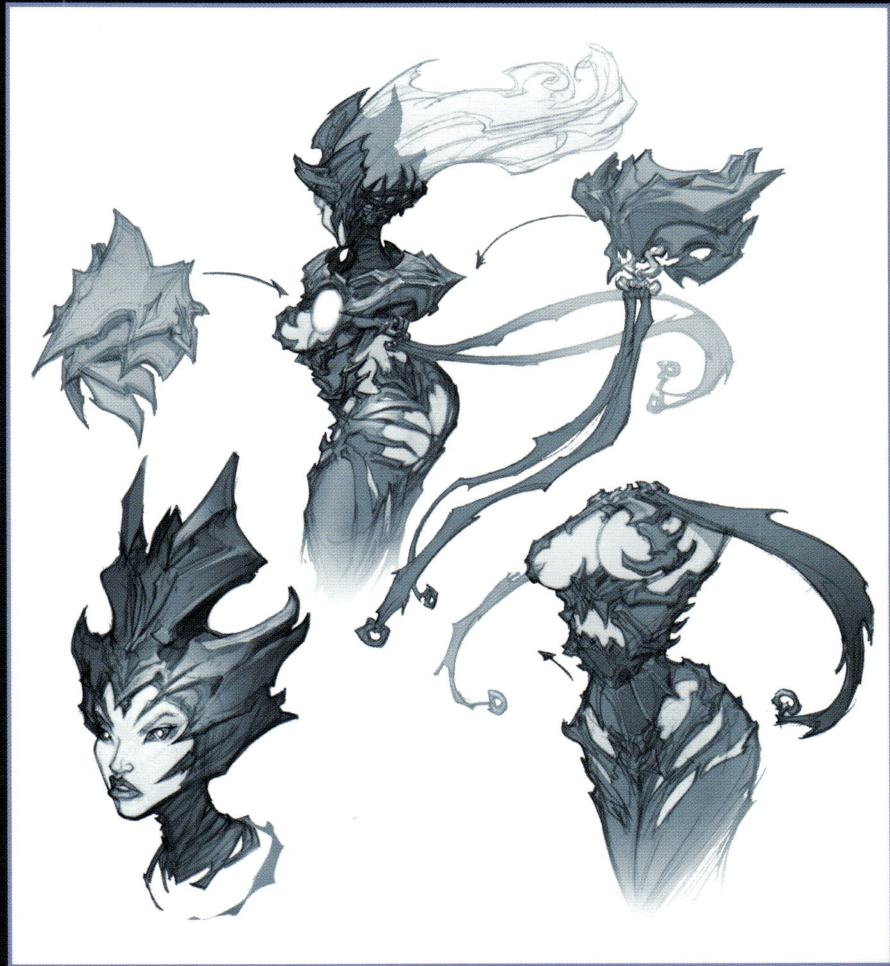

DEVELOPMENT SKETCHES

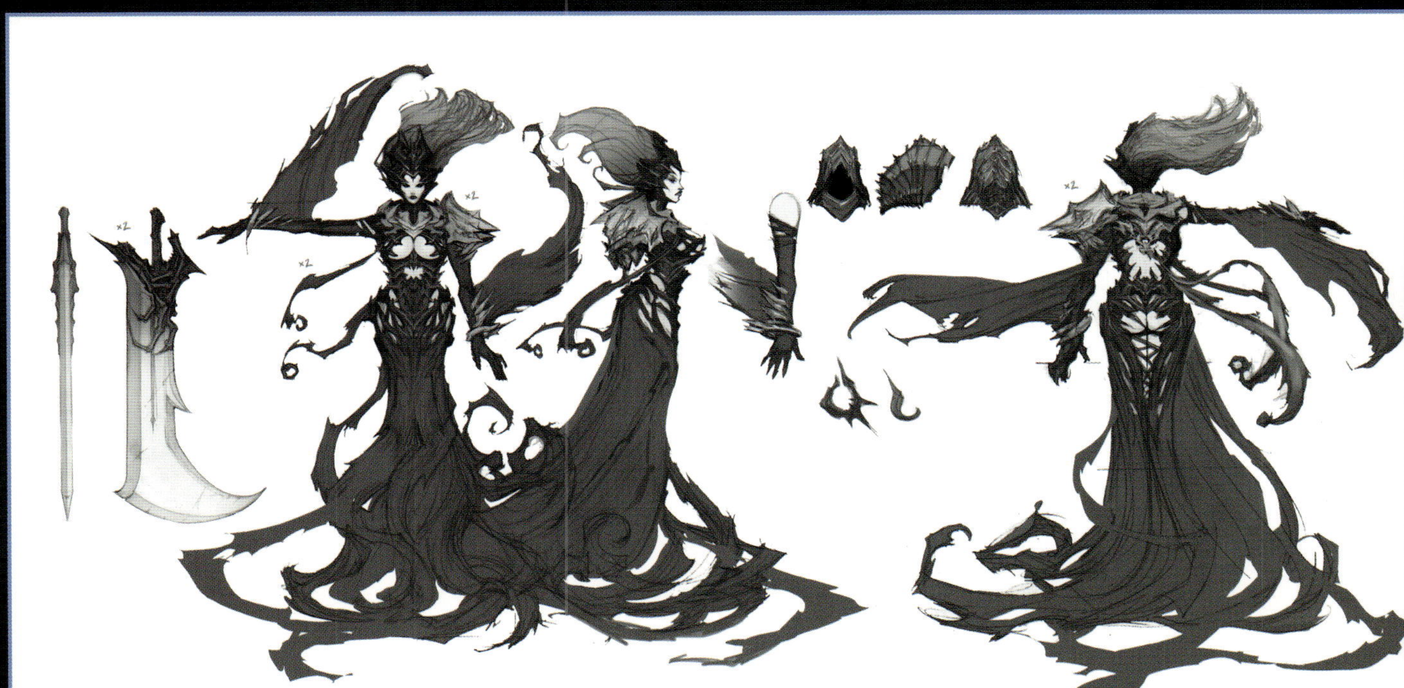

TURNAROUNDS

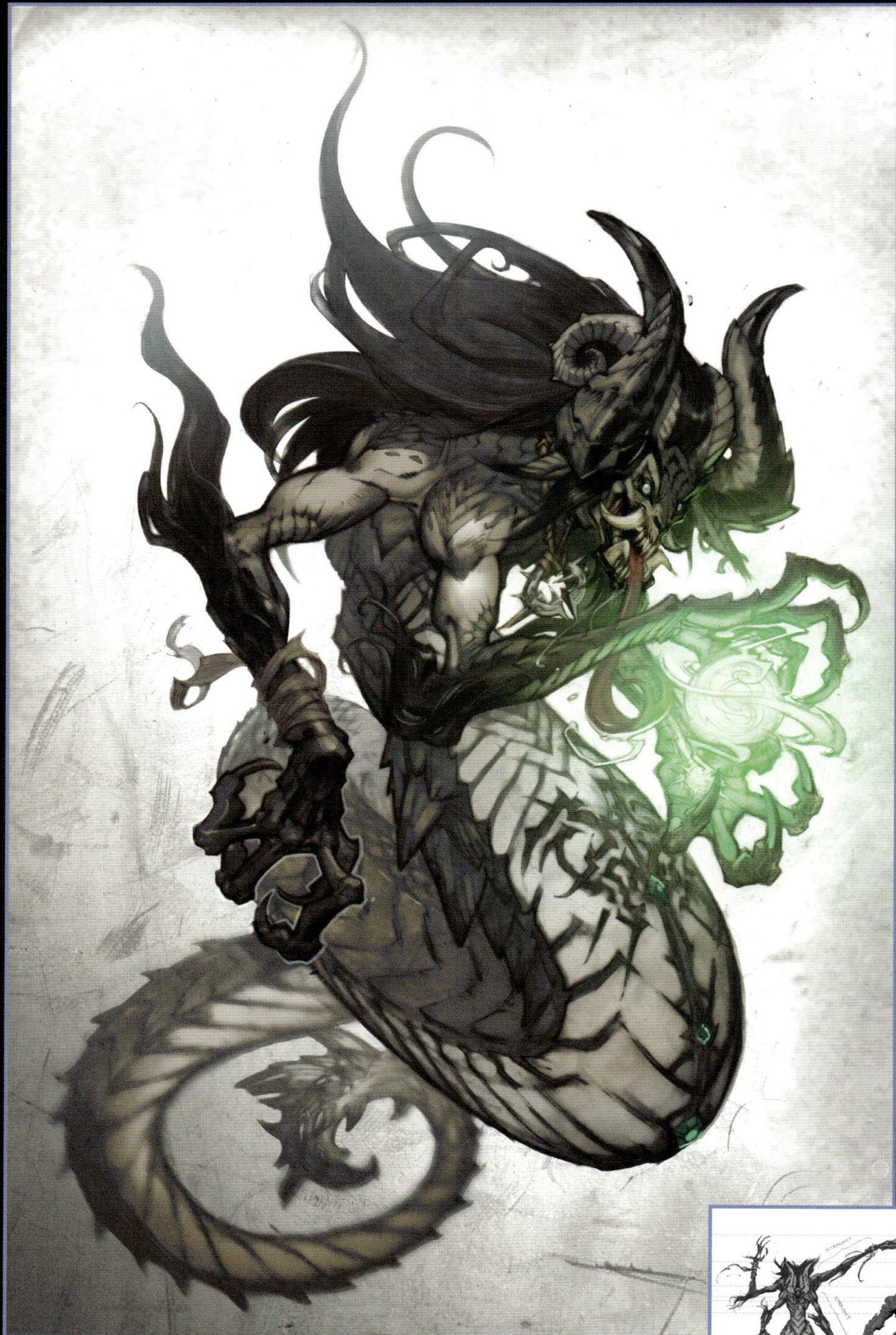

Caster

A journey through the Destroyer's kingdom is one few survive. His servants watch every street, with ears cocked for the slightest sound. And some, like the serpentine Casters, are impossible to evade. These demons do not rely on sight—they can taste vibrations on their snaking tongues. An errant soft footfall on powdered ash will drive them to a murderous frenzy.

Once prey is targeted, the Caster's clawed hands knead energy into crackling balls of fire, which explode in all directions. This hell-bred beast will attack until it tastes the sweetest vibration of all—the last shallow beat of a dying heart.

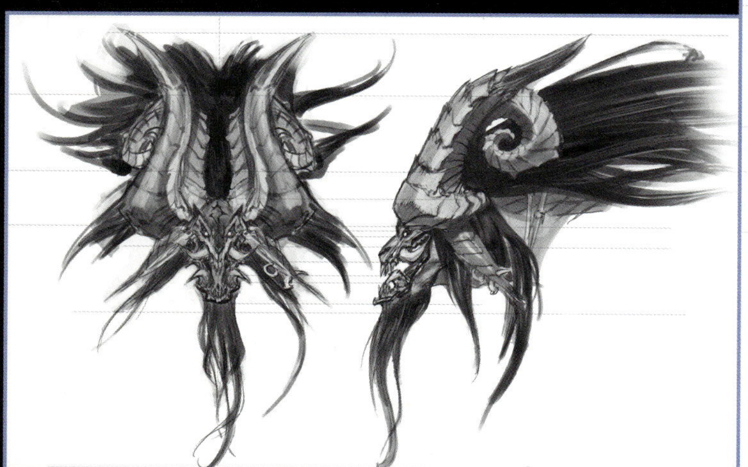

HEAD DESIGNS

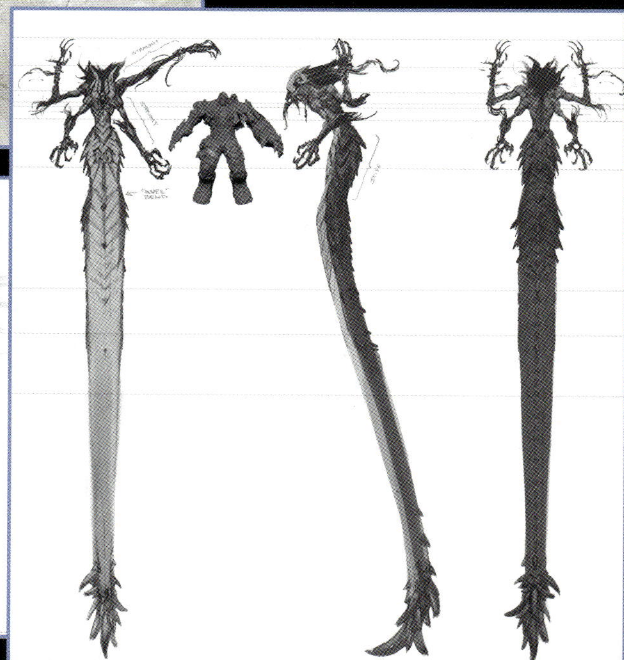

TURNAROUNDS

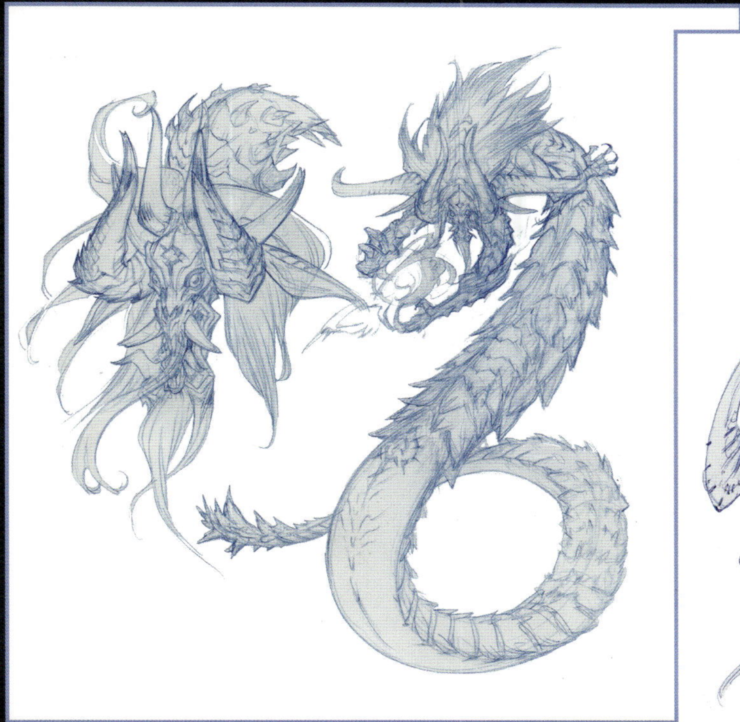

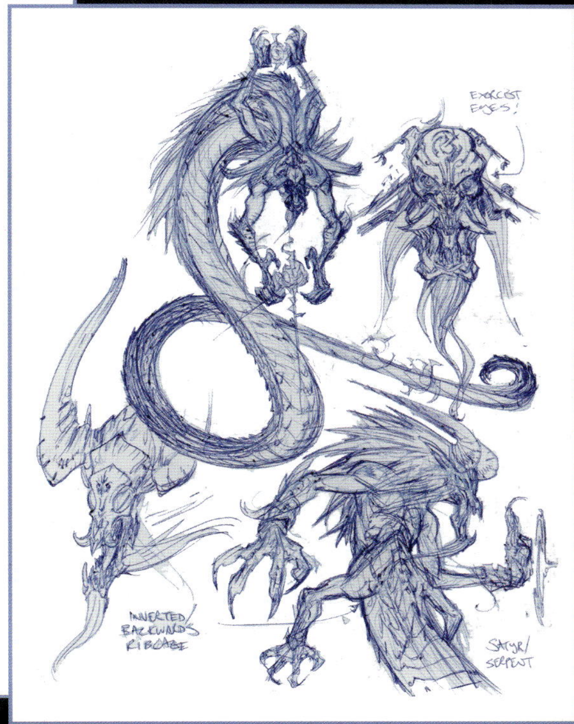

CONCEPT SKETCHES

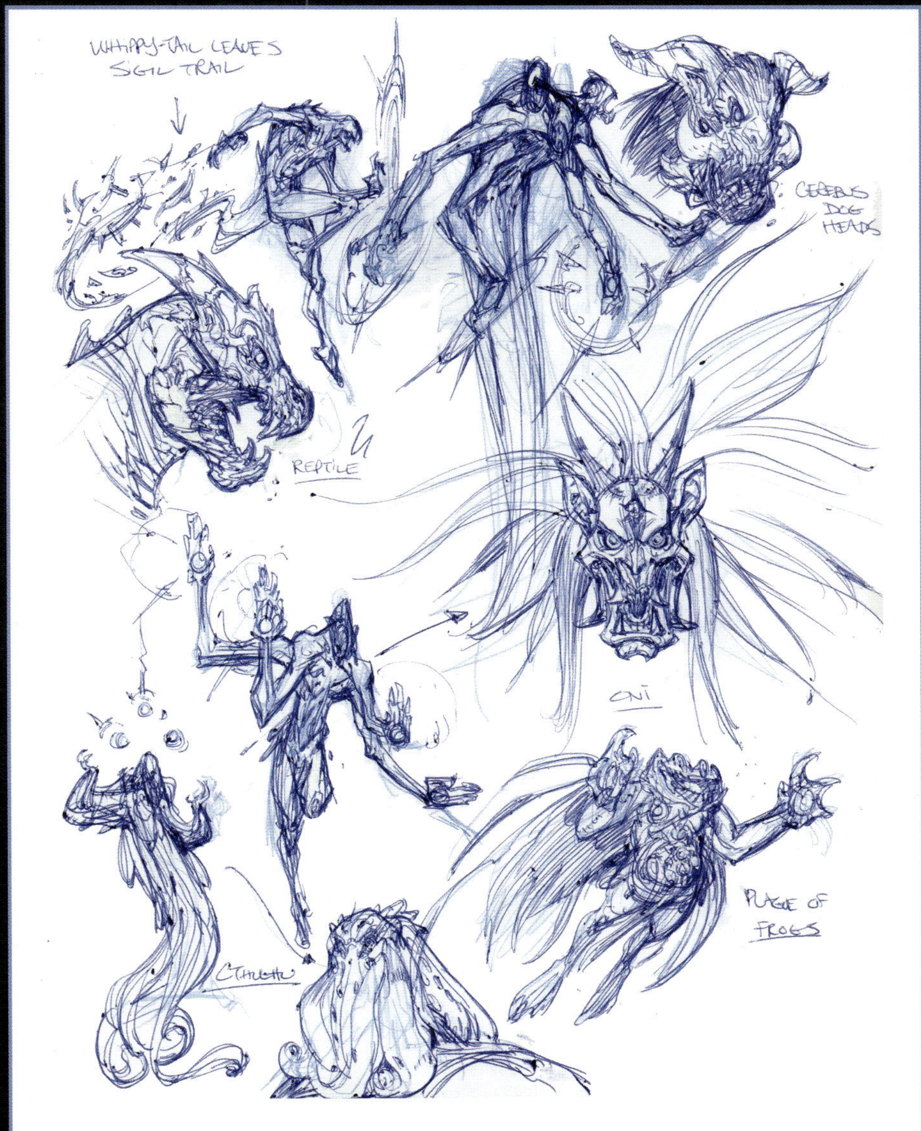

CONCEPT SKETCHES

The Fallen

The Fallen are the twisted shadows of their angelic brethren. They are opportunistic hunters, prowling the skies over destroyed cities. I have seen them dive on their prey without warning, their shrieks echoing through the bone-strewn canyons of mankind's remains. I have also seen their dark silhouettes dancing in battle with angels far overhead.

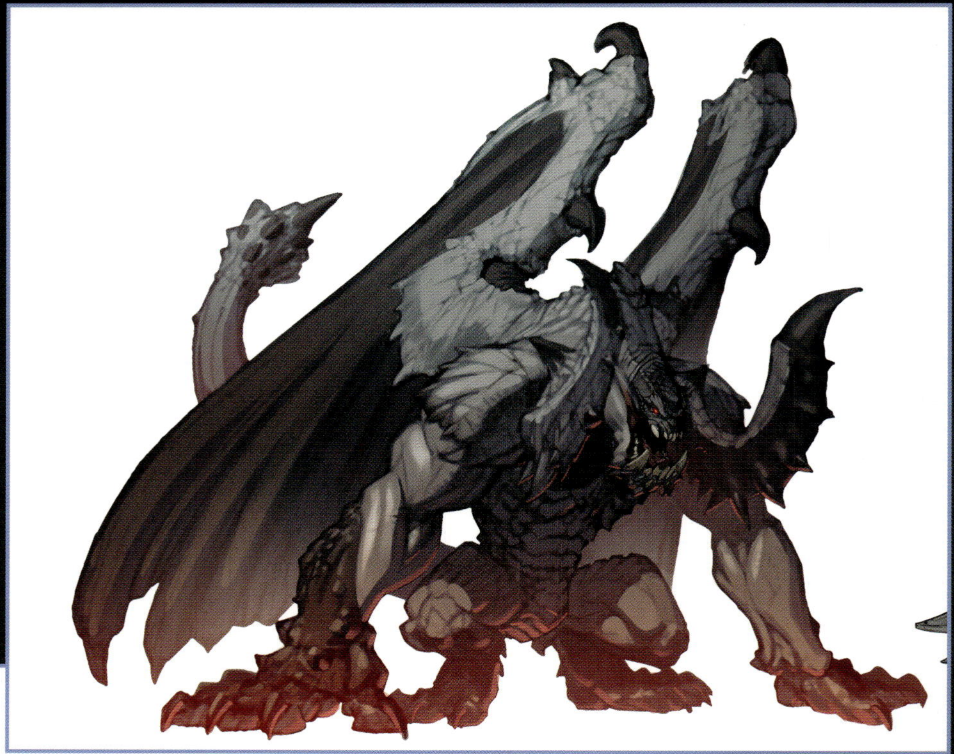

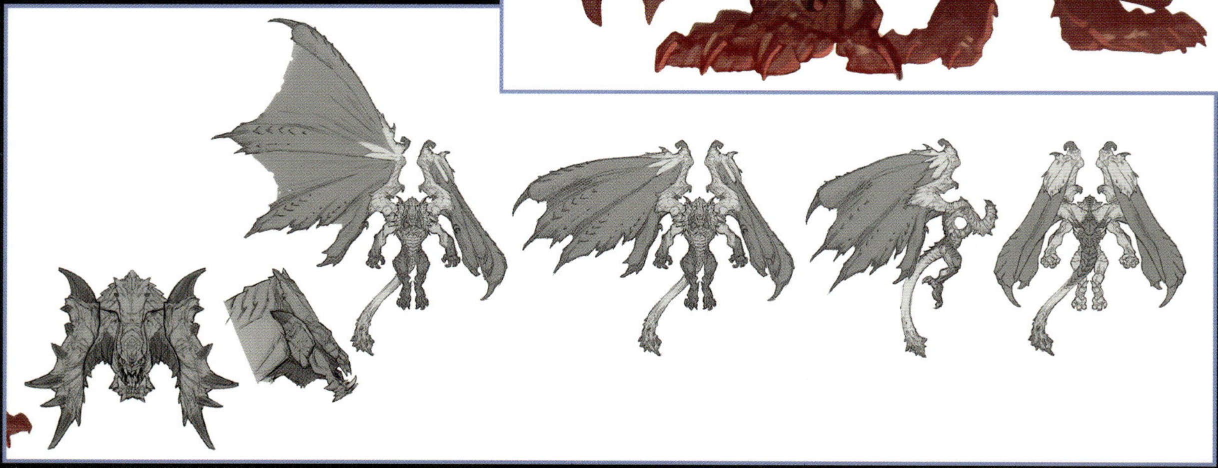

TURNAROUNDS

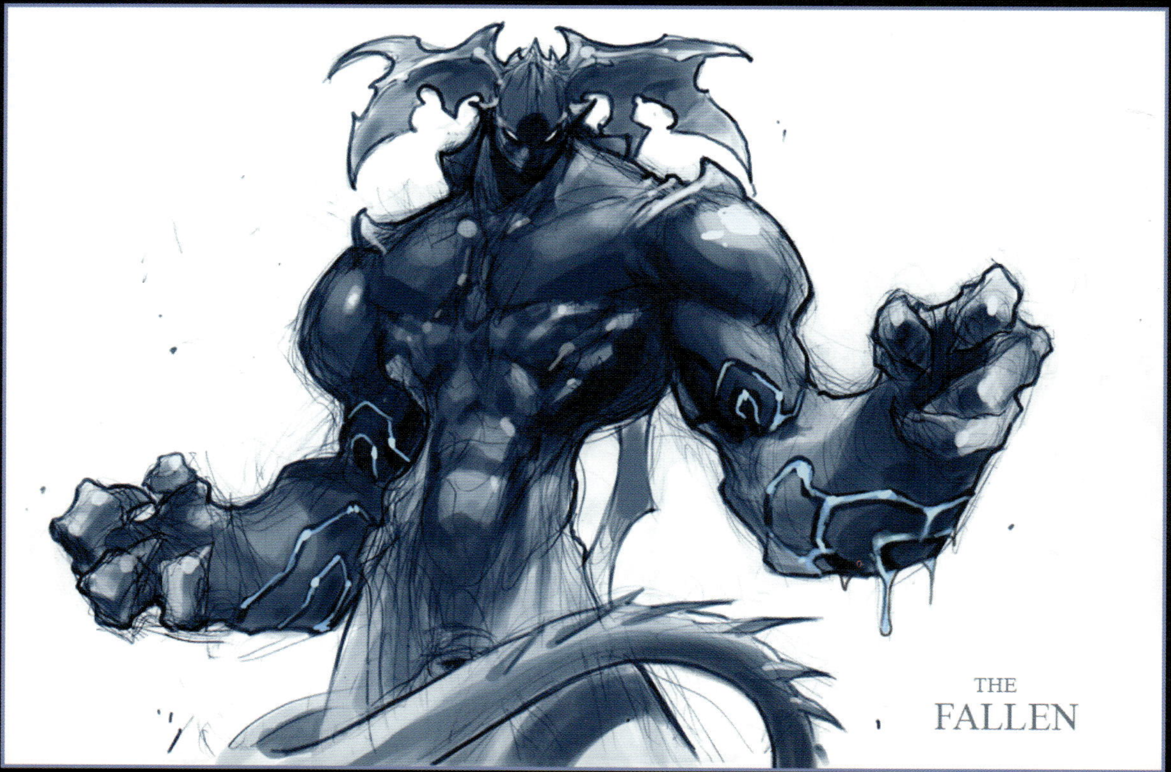

EARLY CONCEPT

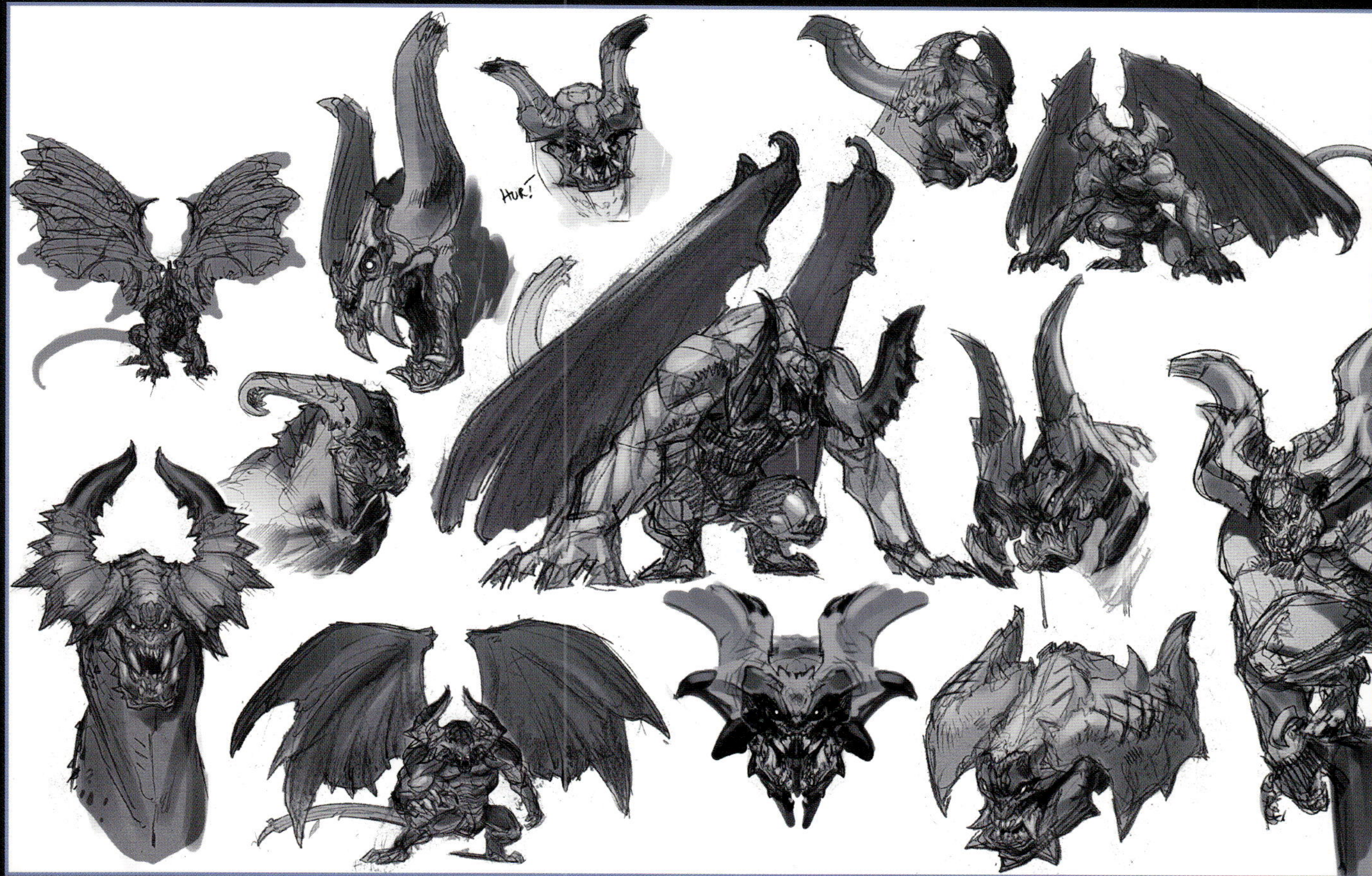

CONCEPT SKETCHES

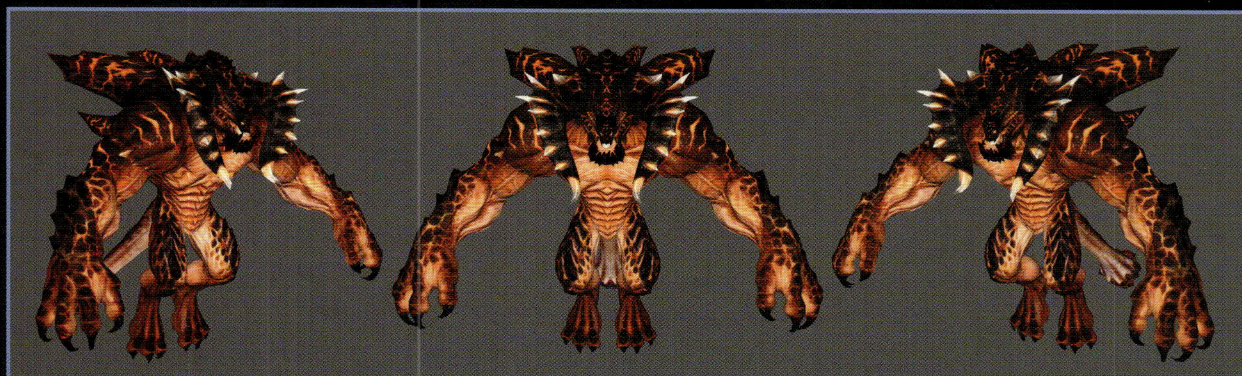

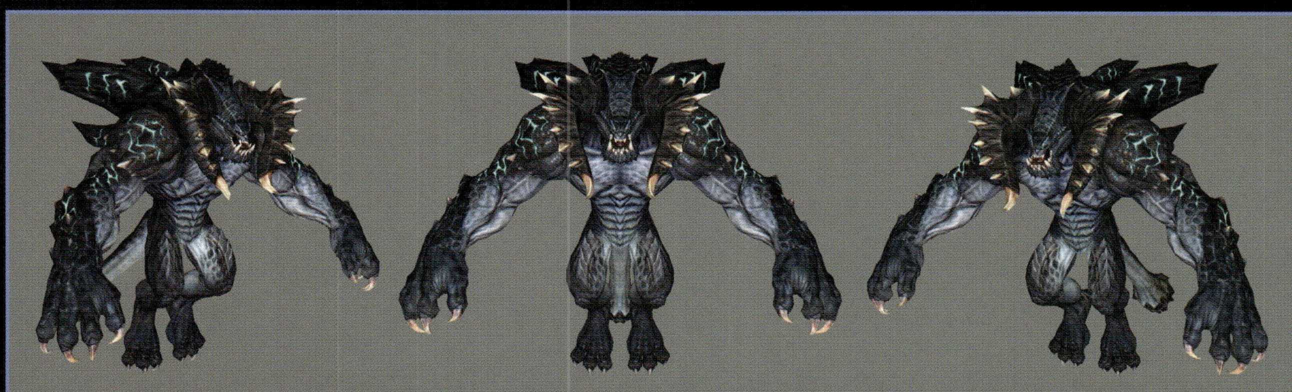
GRAPPLECLAW CG TURNAROUNDS

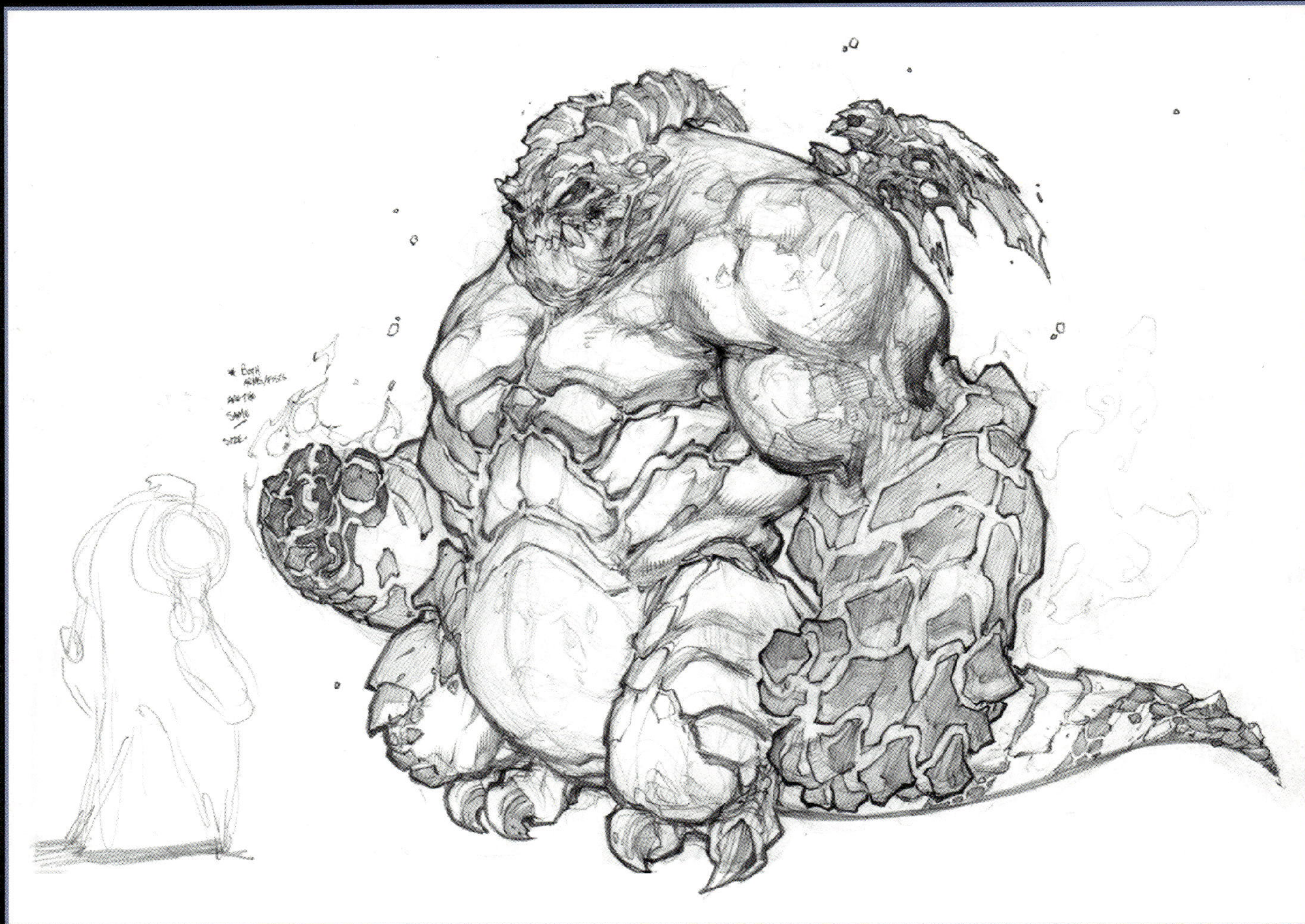

PENCIL ART

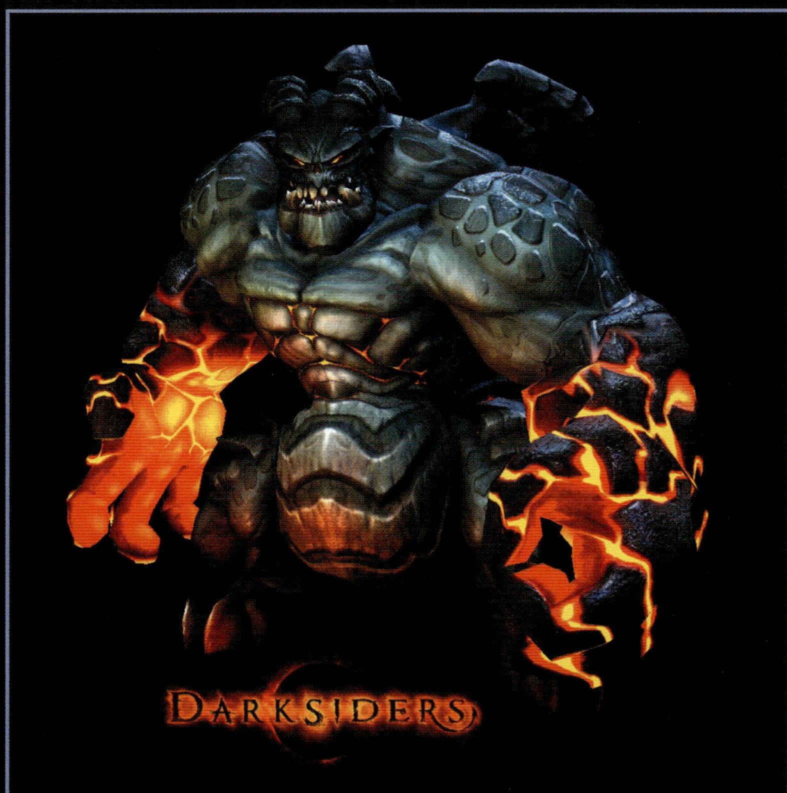

CG RENDER

Gholen

There is nothing subtle about the massive Gholens. The very ground trembles under their monstrous weight. Each hand is impossibly hard and smolders with fire that cannot be quenched. Gholens shake off blows that would fell trees, and crush skulls as if they were clay. When enraged, I have seen them rip up lengths of street and smash the ground to create mammoth concussion waves.

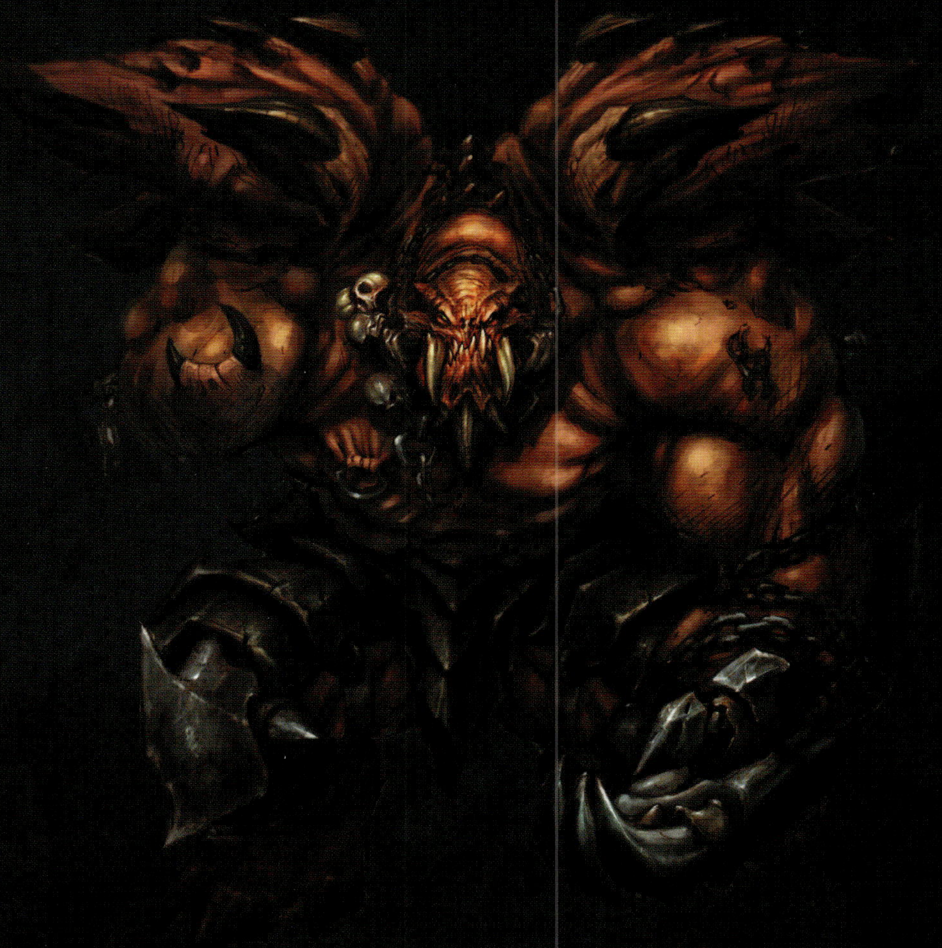

Trauma

There are many hellish creatures in the Destroyer's army, but few can match the savage strength of the Trauma. The chains that once bound them hang loosely from their hands and neck. The colossal beasts have mammoth claws on each hand that can shred steel as easily as flesh. I have seen them skewer cars and other debris from Man's reign to hurtle at passing angels. Their brutality is fearsome to behold.

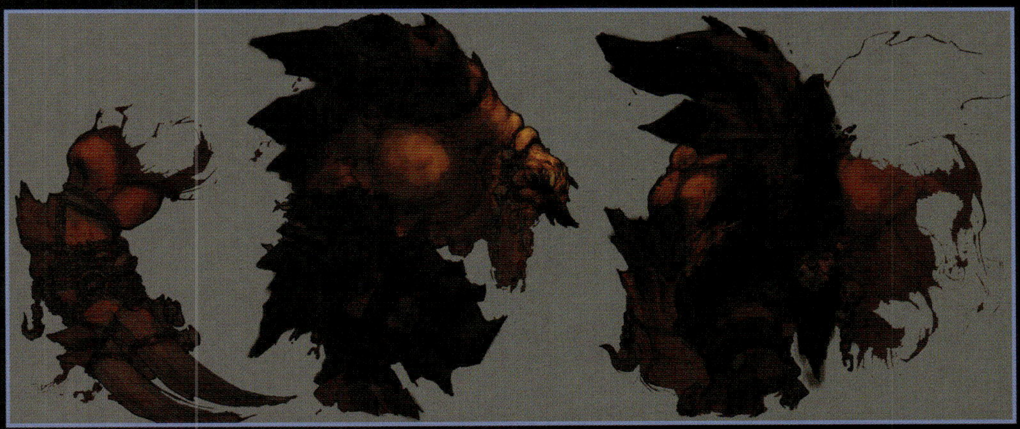

TURNAROUNDS

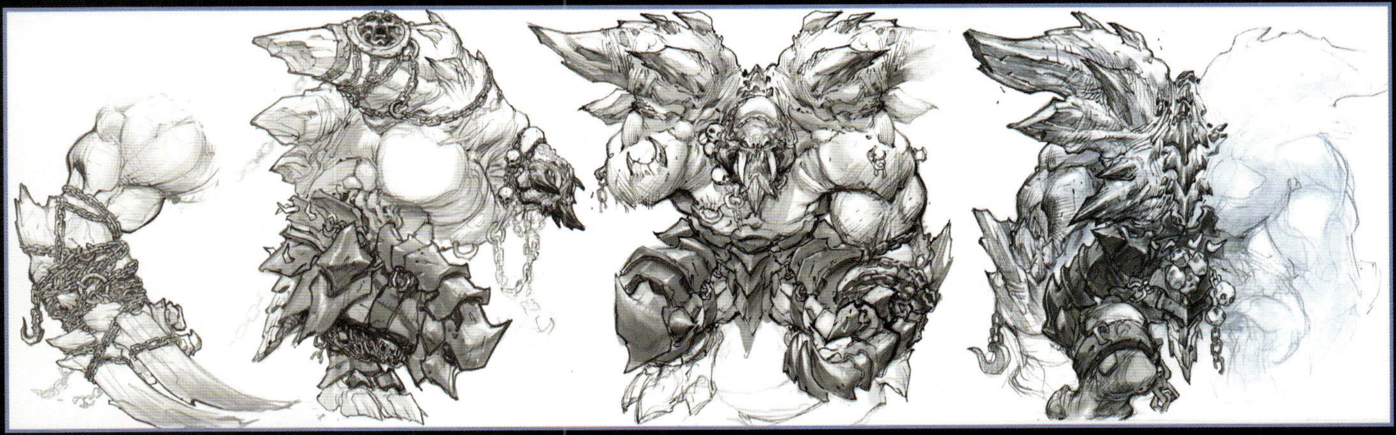

PENCIL ART

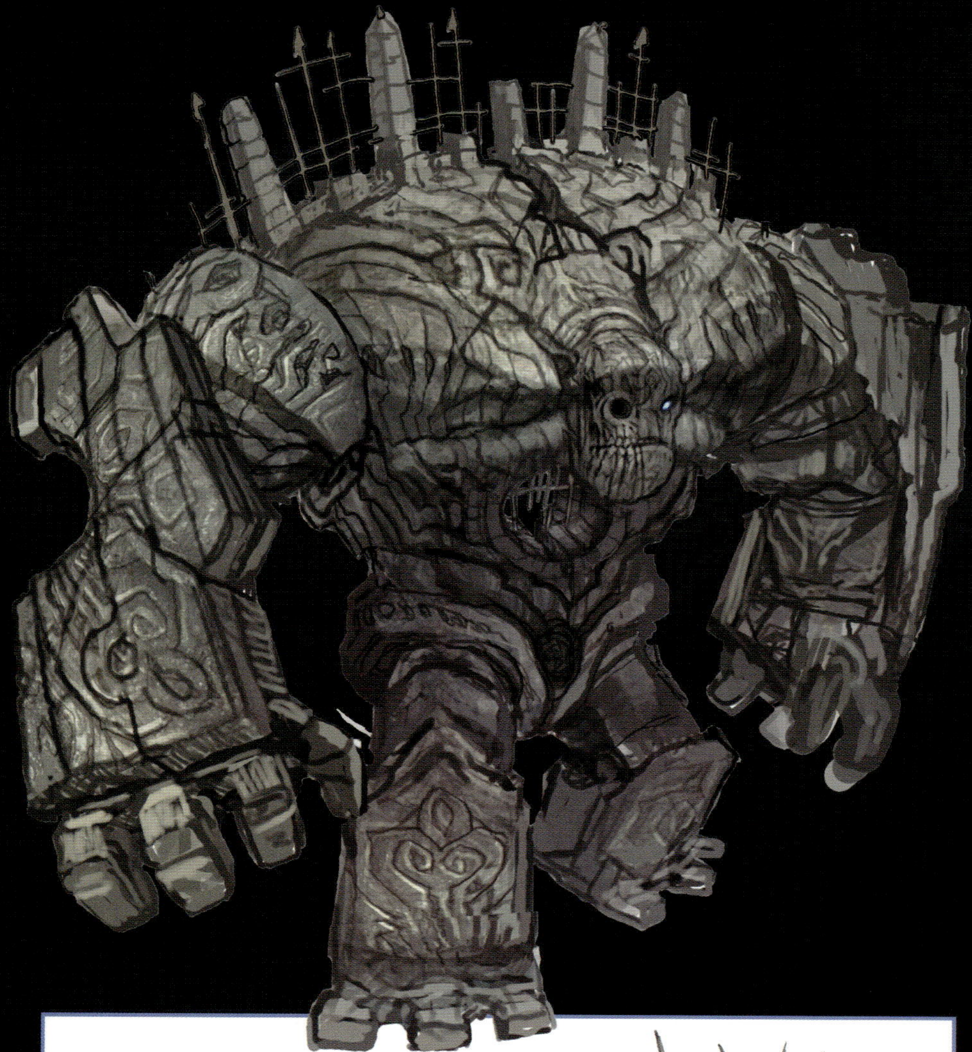

Tormented Gate

The Tormented Gates are massive creatures that have been enslaved by the Destroyer. Their huge stone arms can fold into a massive rock wall, a trait the Destroyer has used to turn these gentle beasts into towering barricades. I have heard of a horn that can awaken these gates, but that relic has fallen into evil hands that will not part with it lightly.

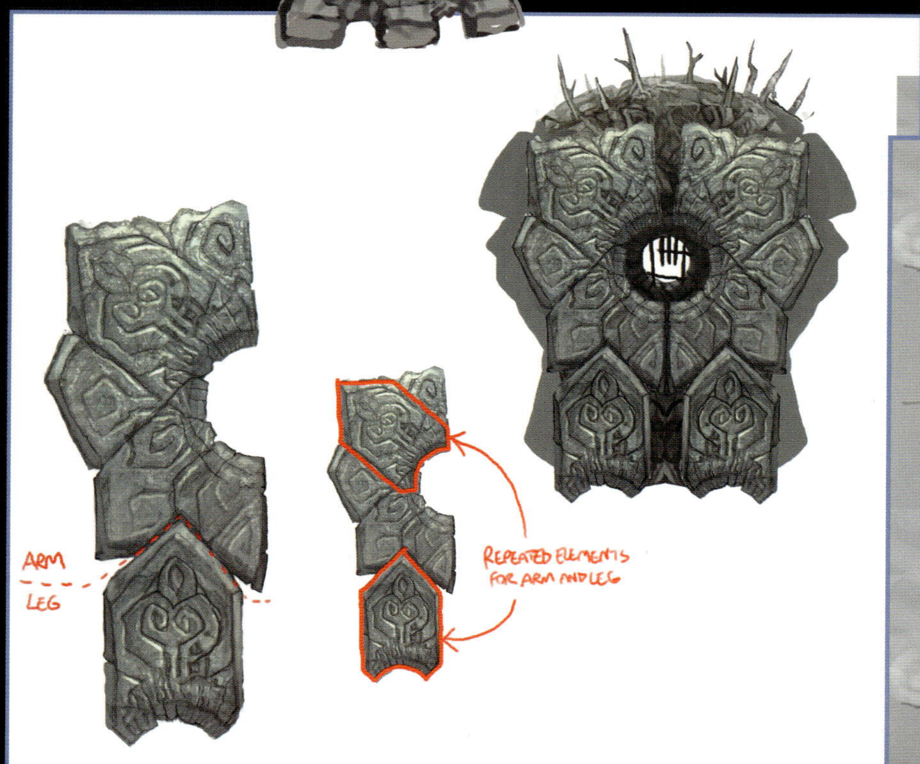

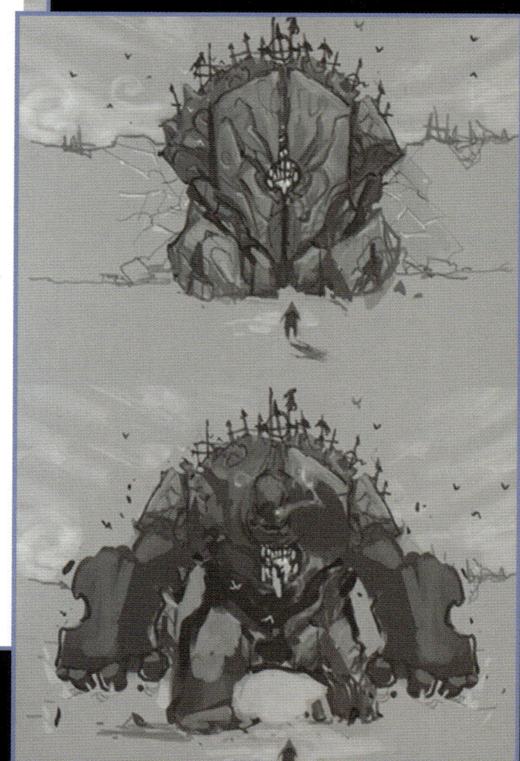

TRANSFORMATION CONCEPTS

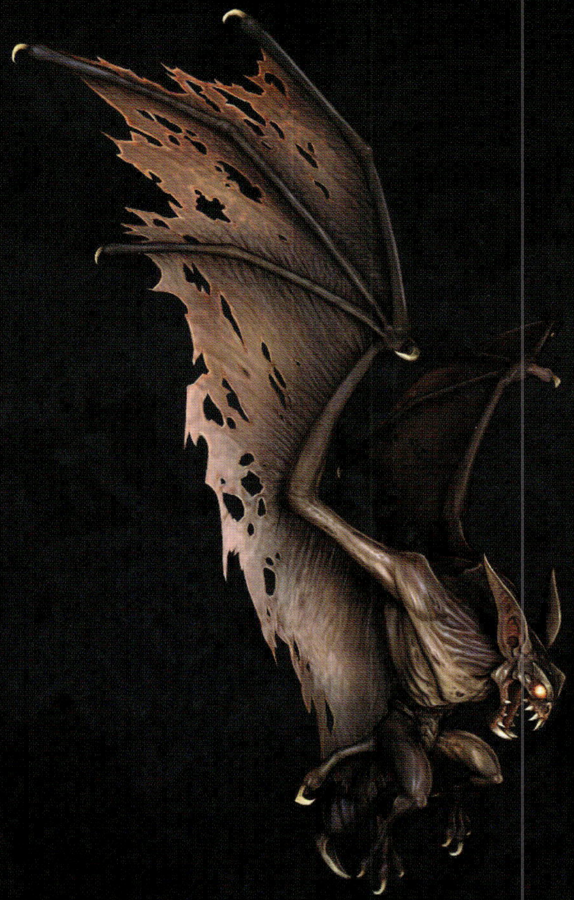

Duskwings

I have not seen the sun in over a hundred years. The sky itself is choked with ash and pestilence. And then there are the living clouds—the black and ravenous Duskwings.

Hovering on tattered wings, Duskwings are forever in search of carnage. With claws, fangs, and fury they render their victims a bloody smear. Even the rusting hulks of Man's wheeled machines are but toys to them. These vile creatures live only to kill, and their numbers seem to have no end—Duskwing eggs are scattered wide across the ruined city. I fear the sun may never shine again.

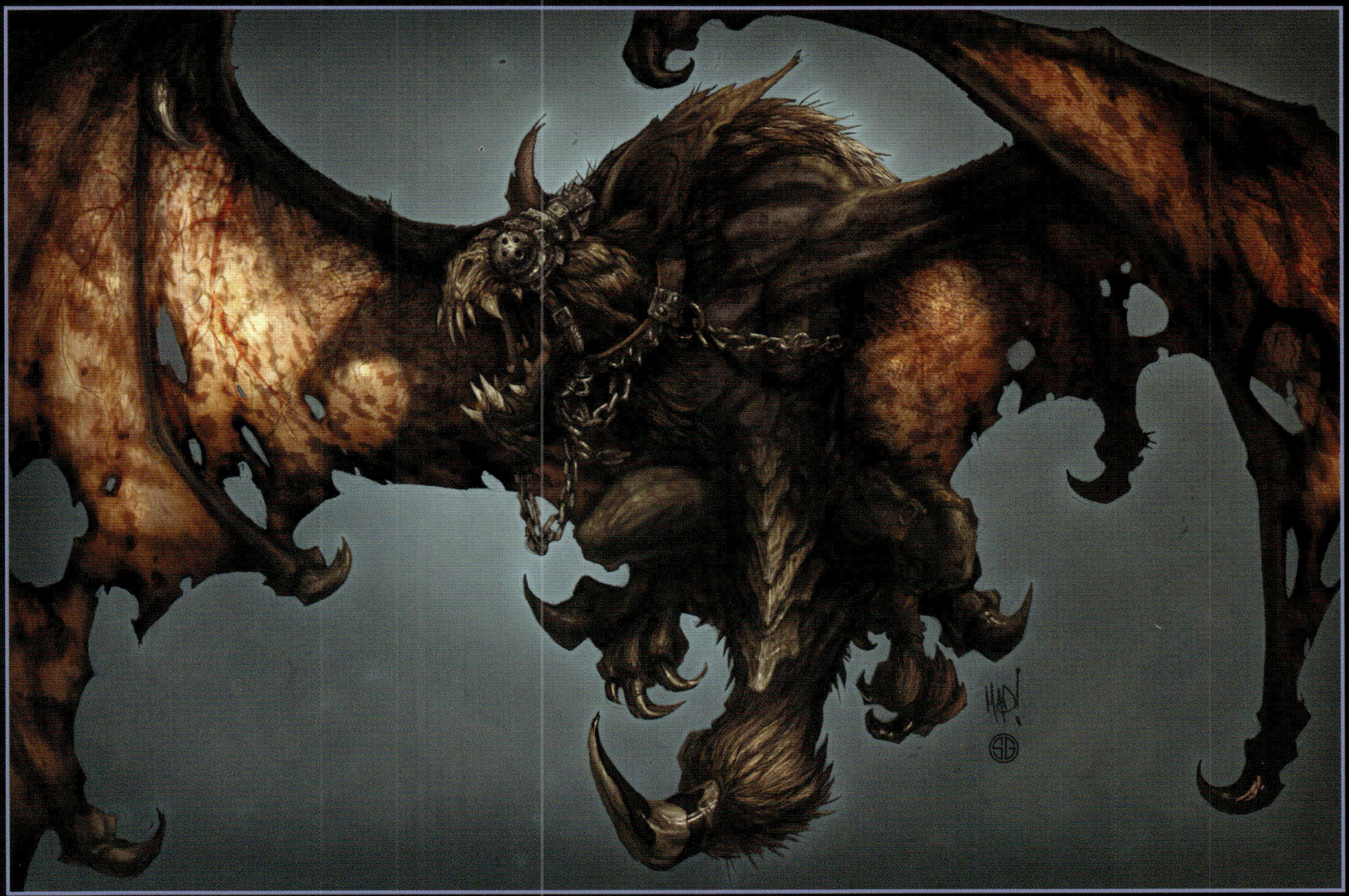

PAINTED ART

Broodlings

Silitha's Loom is a maze of web and fire-husked buildings, so silent that the patter of crumbling concrete echoes for miles. But these ruins are not unoccupied.

Hidden throughout the moldering towers are birthing sacs, globular growths that pulse with life. When the sacs burst, Broodlings are strewn onto the ground. These spiny-backed monsters know only ravenous hunger. They engulf any living thing that intrudes on the Loom. In seconds, their vicious mandibles can pick a victim's bones clean. With each passing day the swarm grows ever larger.

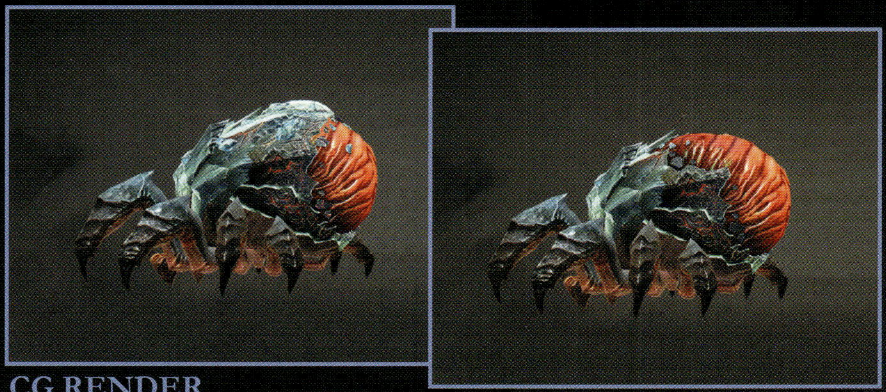

CG RENDER

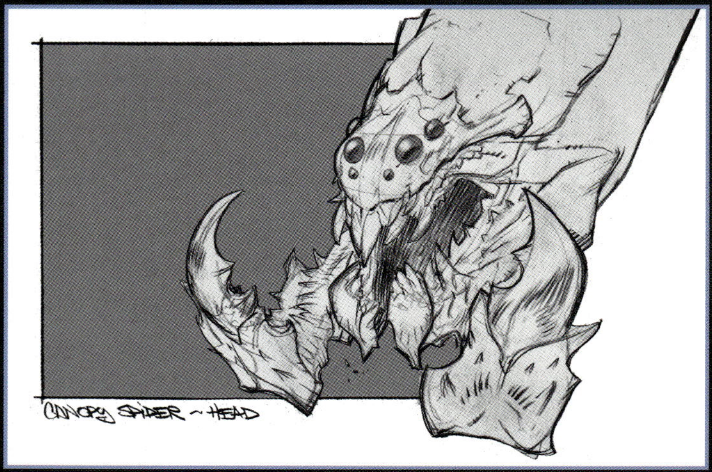

PENCIL ART

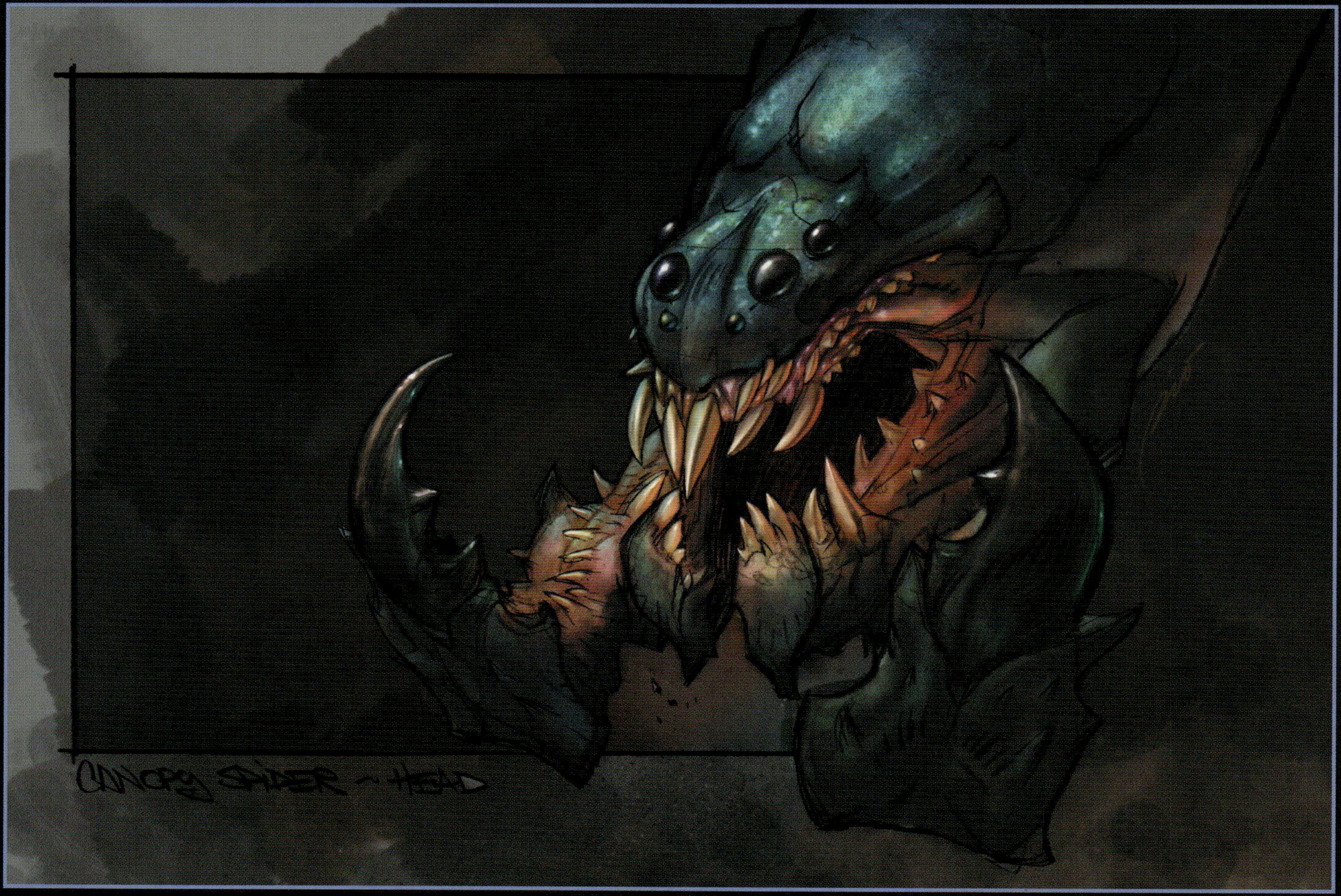

HEAD SHOT

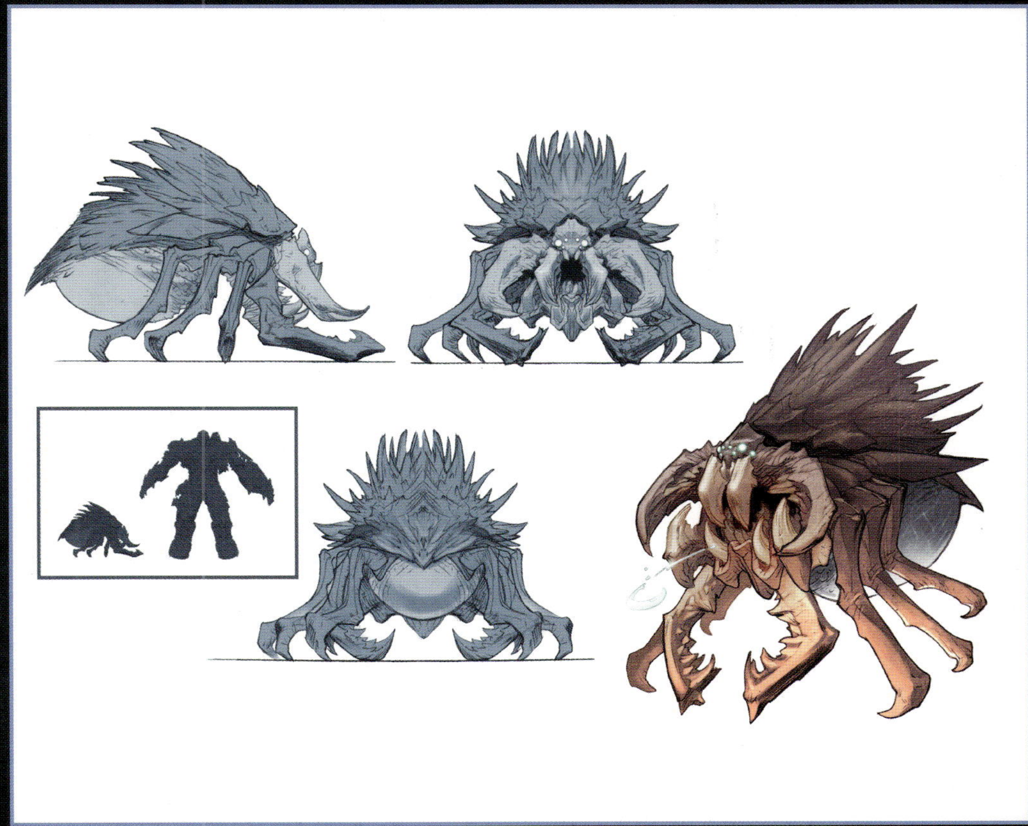

TURNAROUNDS

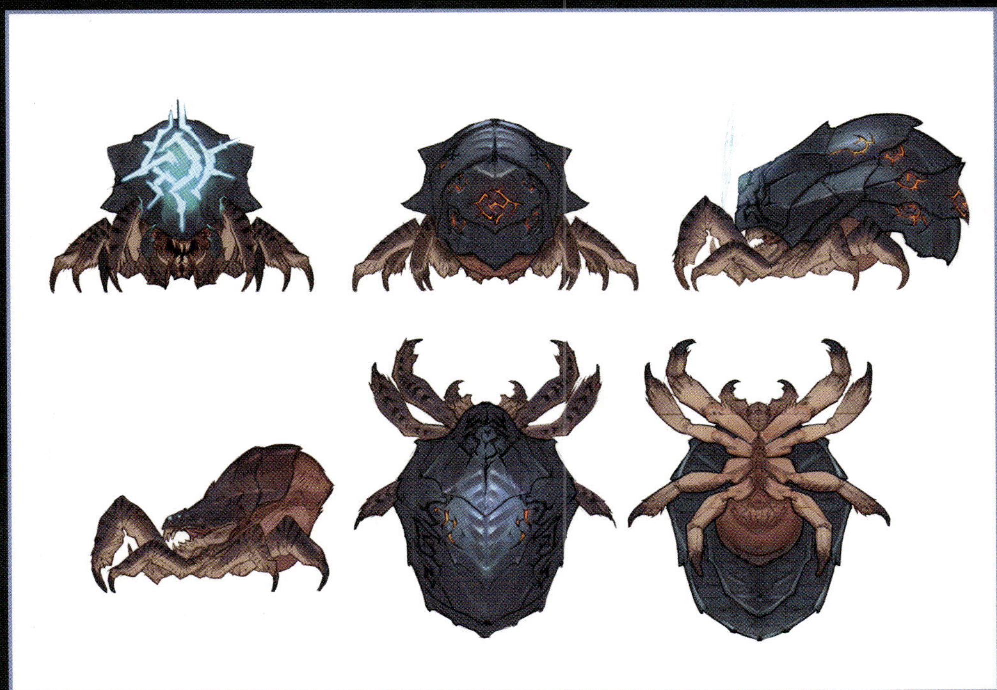

TURNAROUNDS

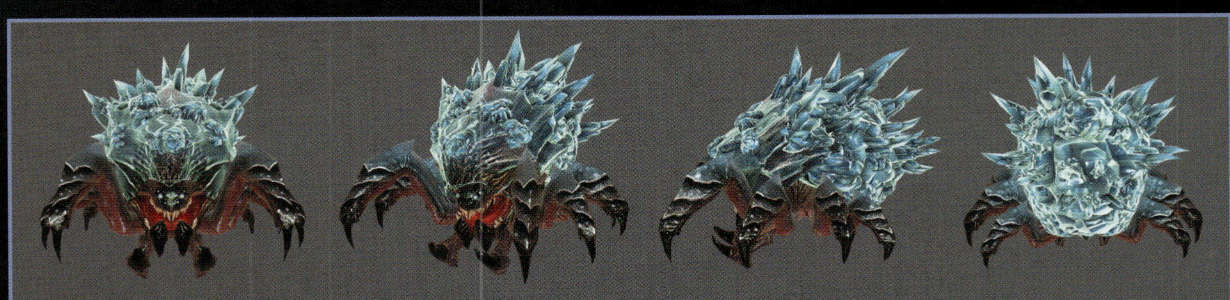

BROOD MOTHER CG TURNAROUNDS

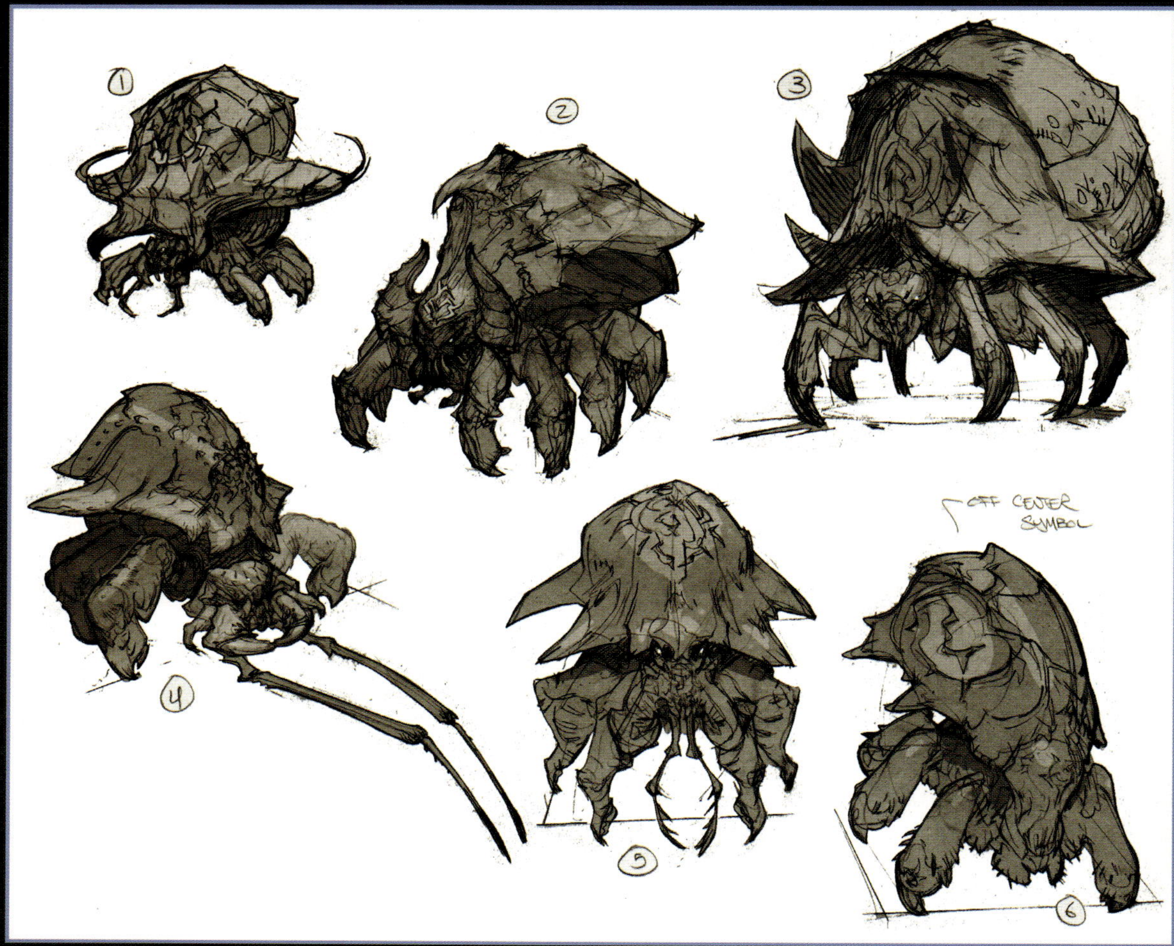

CONCEPT SKETCHES

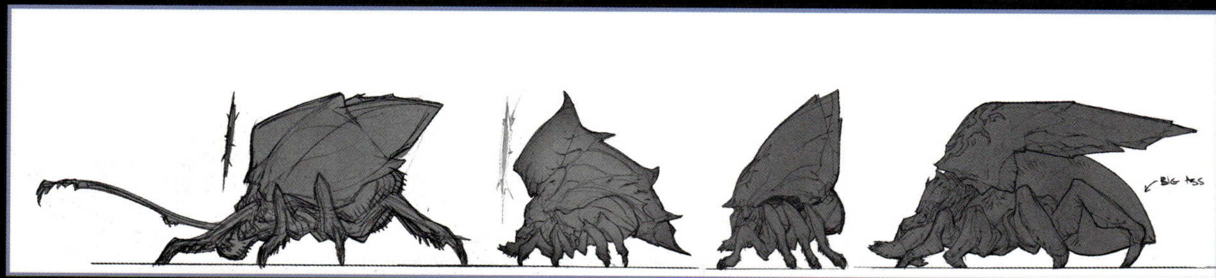

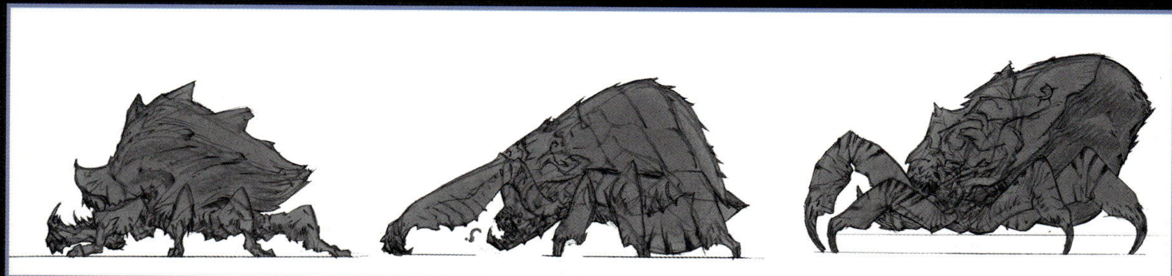

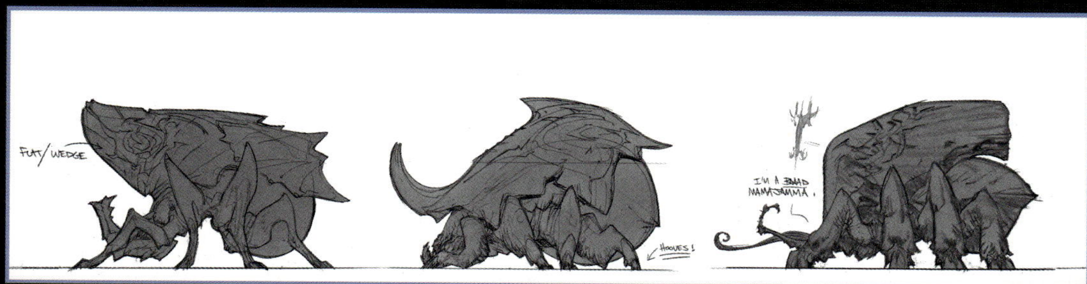

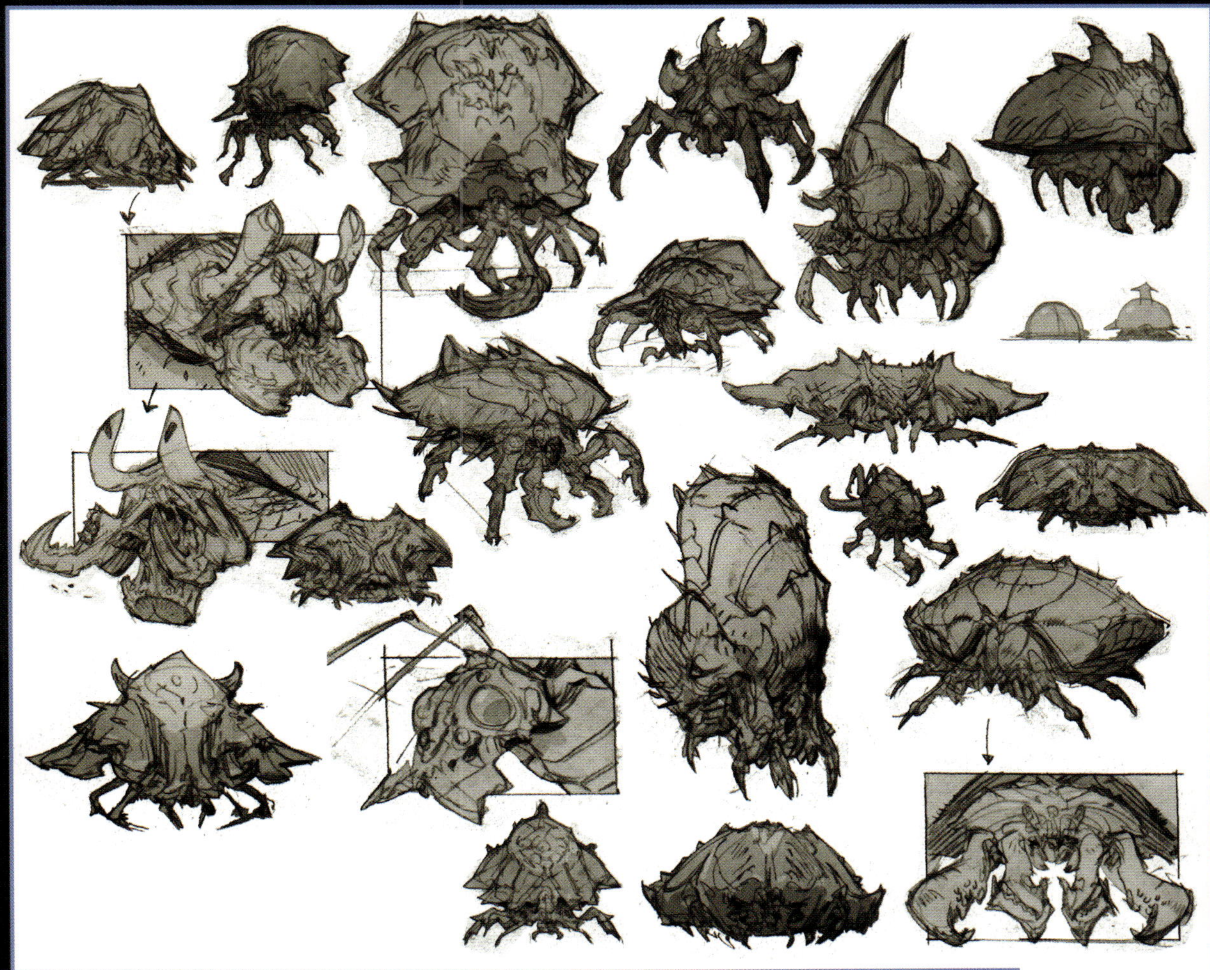

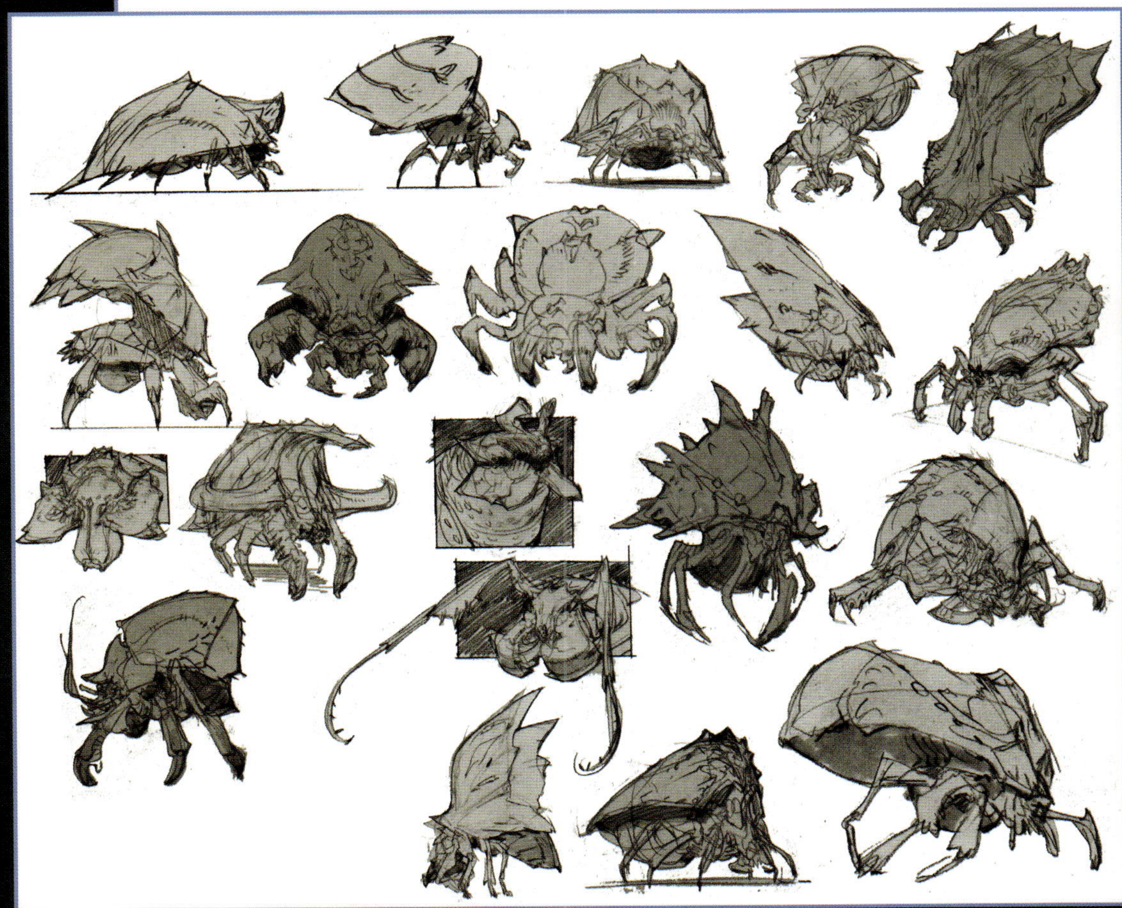

CONCEPT SKETCHES

Torture Coil

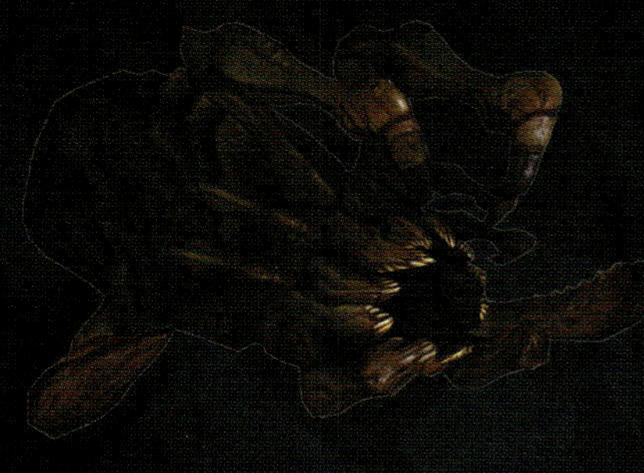

CG HEADSHOT

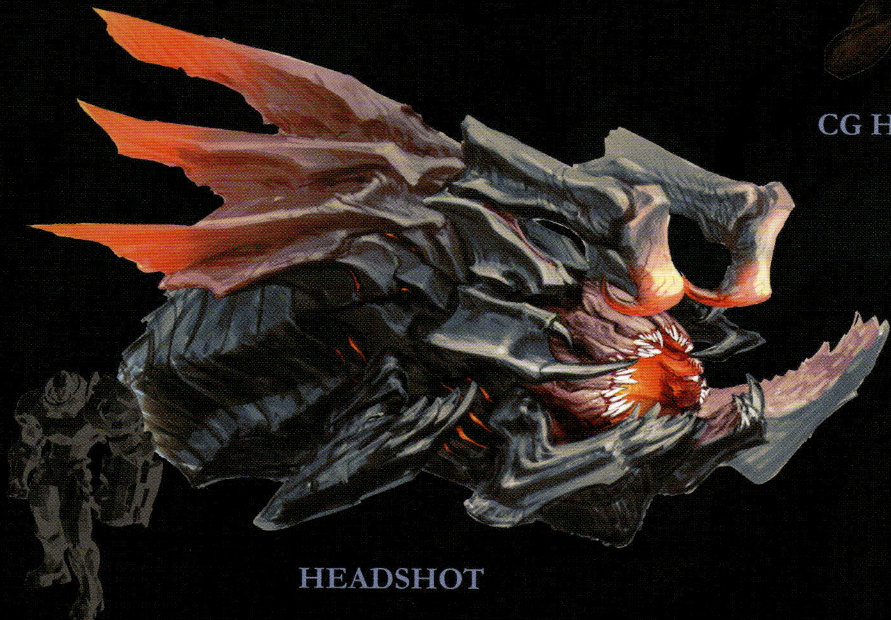

HEADSHOT

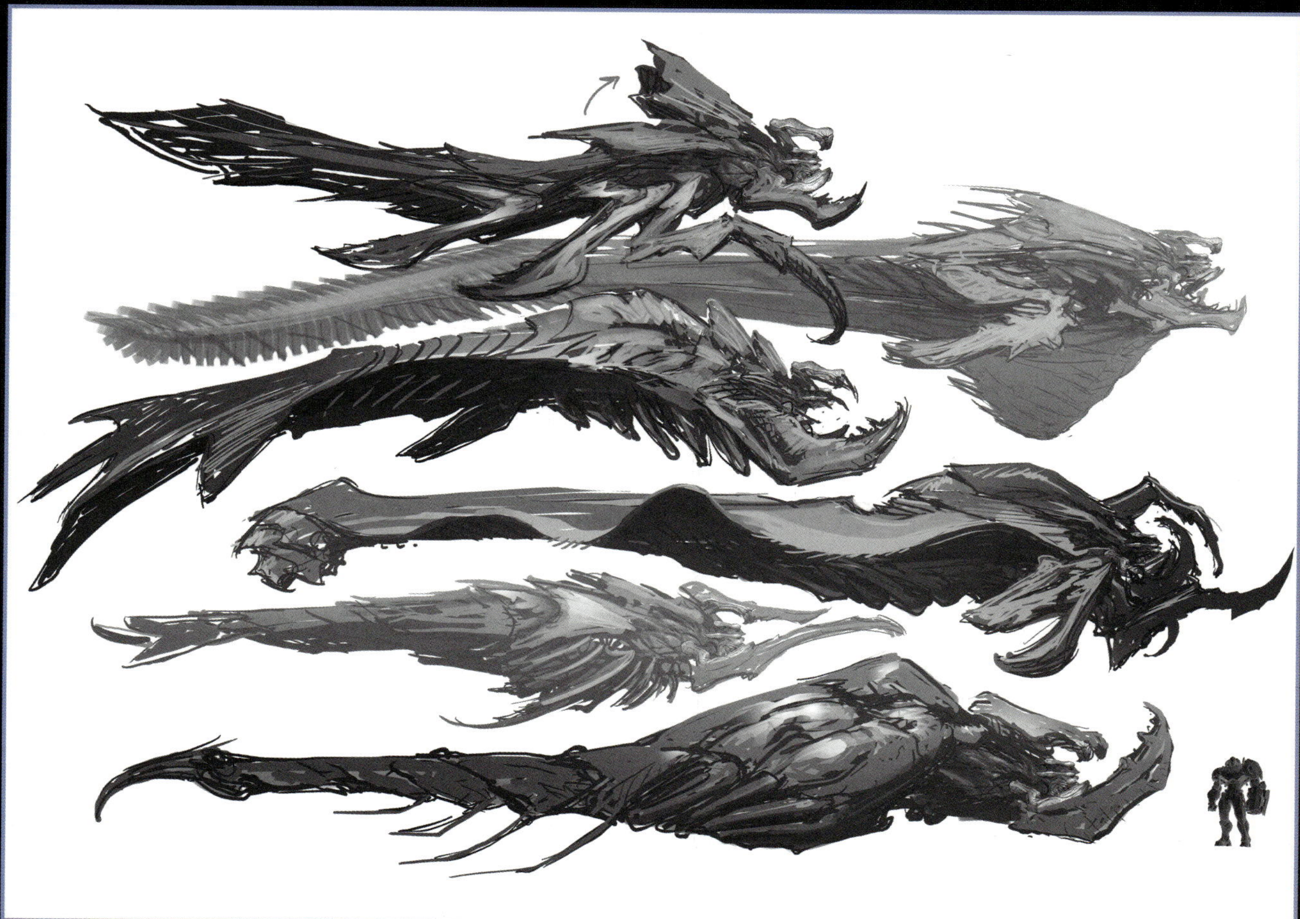

CONCEPTS

Ash Titan

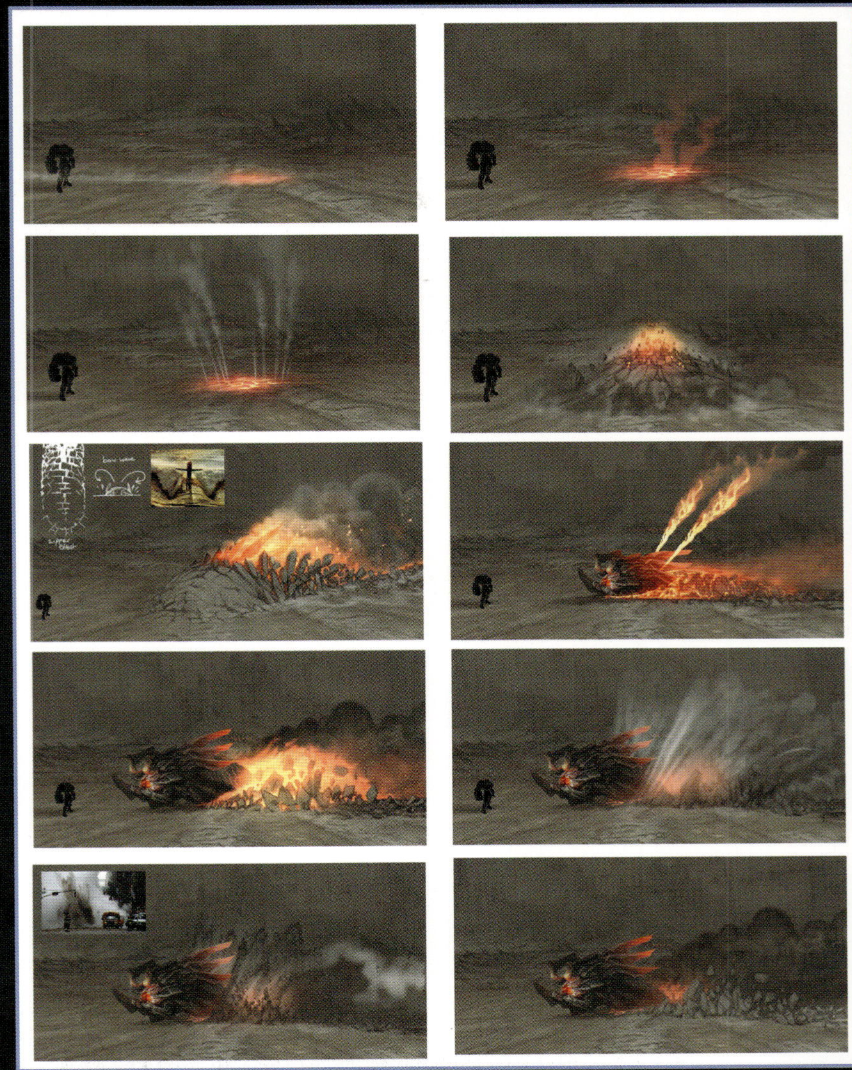

TRAIL CONCEPTS

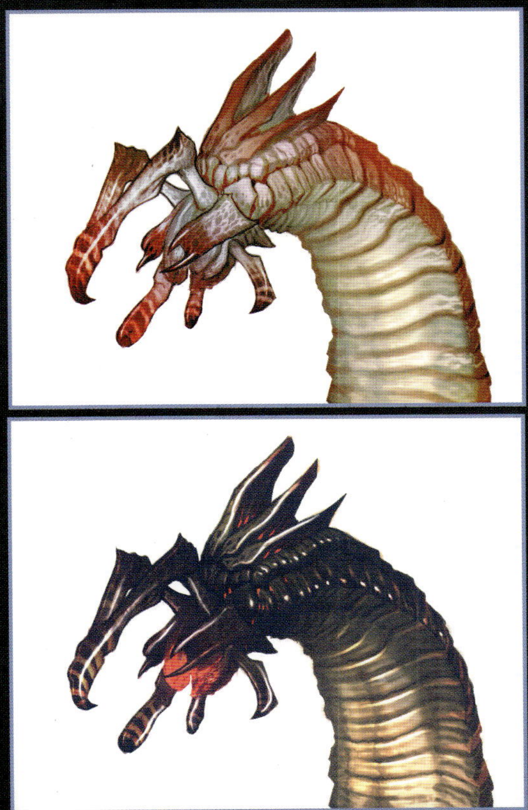

HEAD DESIGNS

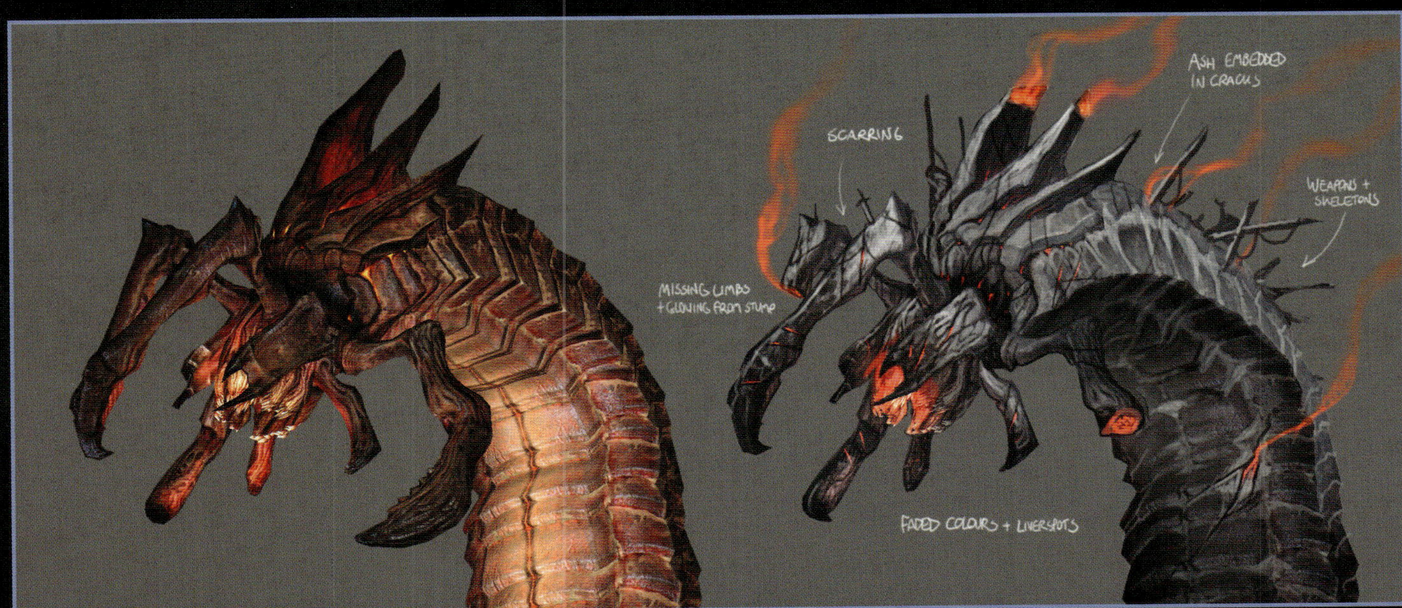

HEAD DESIGNS

Light Angels

When the Archangel Abaddon fell, the Army of Light dimmed irrevocably. Yet the surviving Light Angels continue to battle against the forces of Hell.

I see them from my prison, white dots on a sea of black. Their golden armor is smeared with ash, but their will is untarnished. They glide over the ruined skyscrapers and broken streets, laying waste to demon hordes with blazing guns and flashing swords. I wish I could say that they seek to redeem the world…but it is vengeance that fires their hearts.

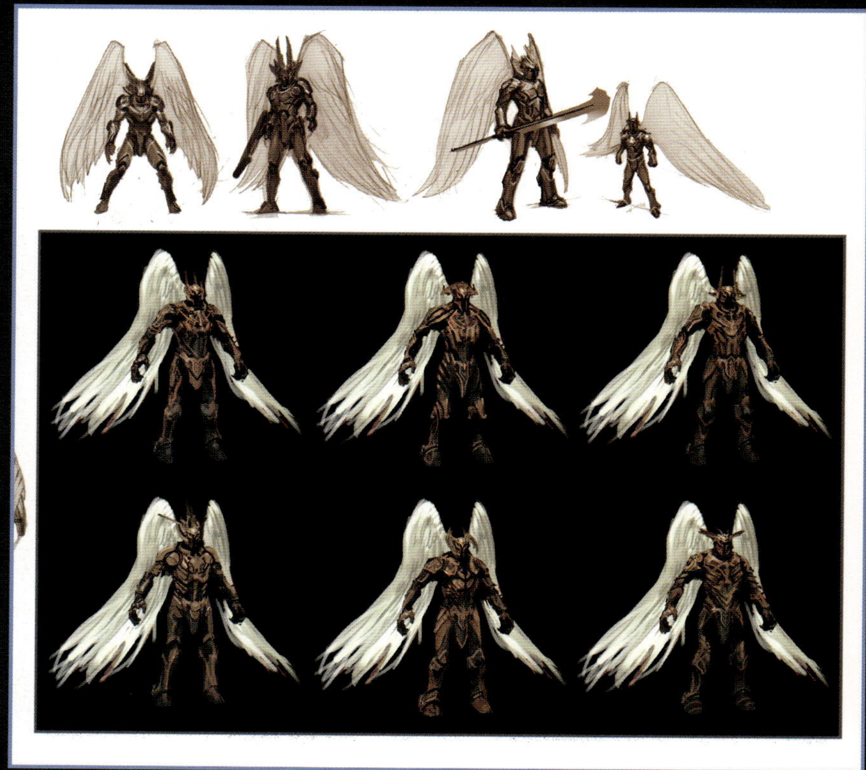

ARMOR CONCEPTS

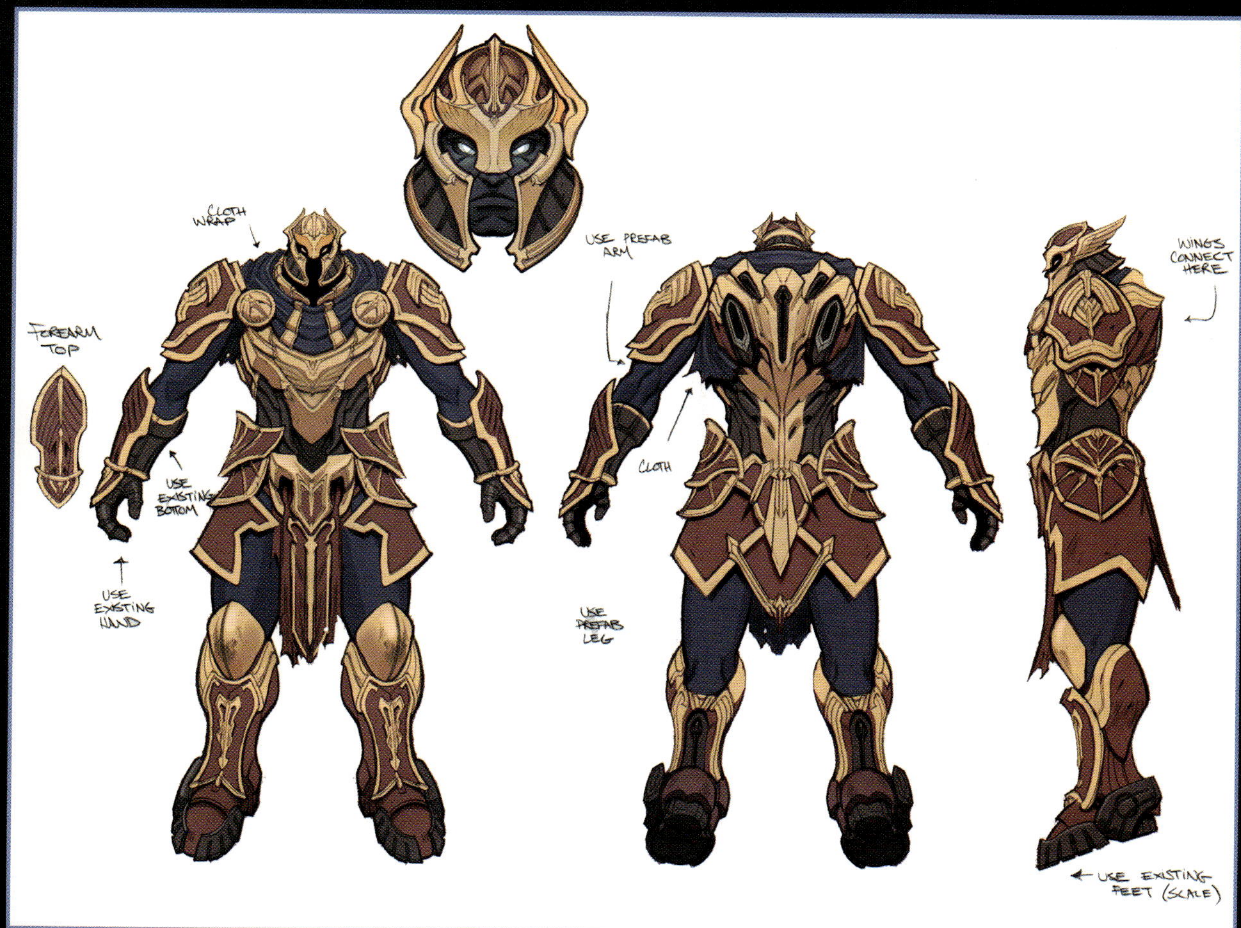

TURNAROUNDS

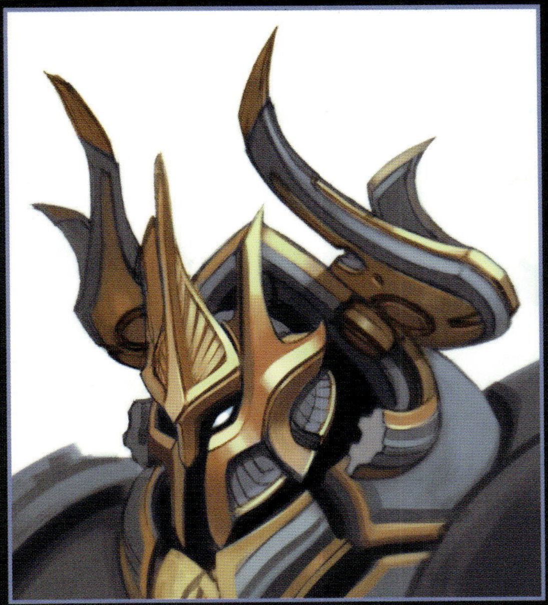

HEAD SHOT

Angel Champion

Though most were murdered, broken, or exiled, there are still some Angel Champions on Earth. These deadly seraphim lead the charge against the Destroyer's armies, floating on armored, flame-spewing wings.

When airborne, they can weave through hell growth, ruins, and killing blows with an agility as impenetrable as any shield. They wield energy swords, with blades hot enough to slice hides that have been battle-cured by hellfire. At the hand of one true Champion of the Light, a legion of lesser demons may be decimated.

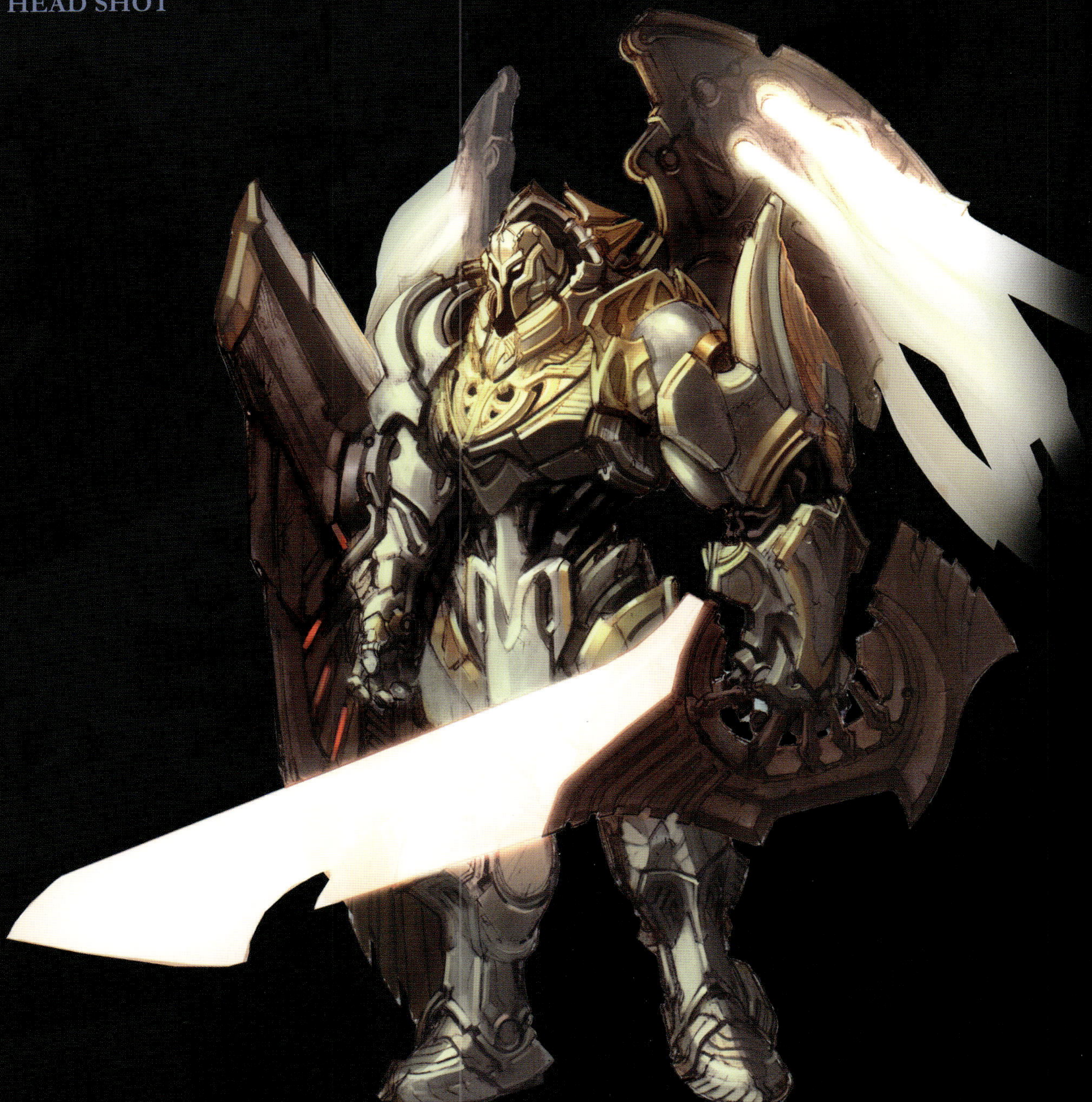

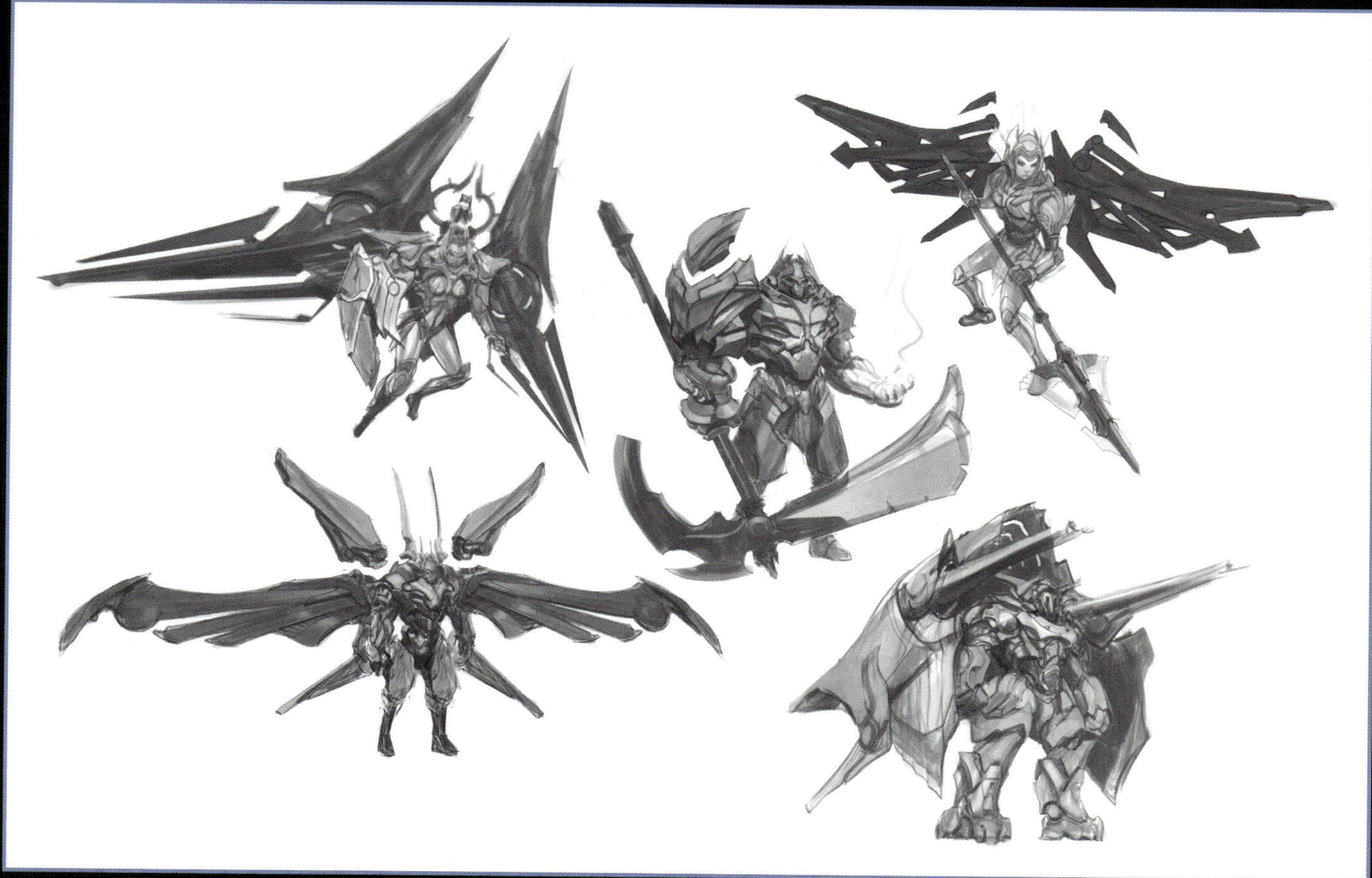

DEVELOPMENT SKETCHES

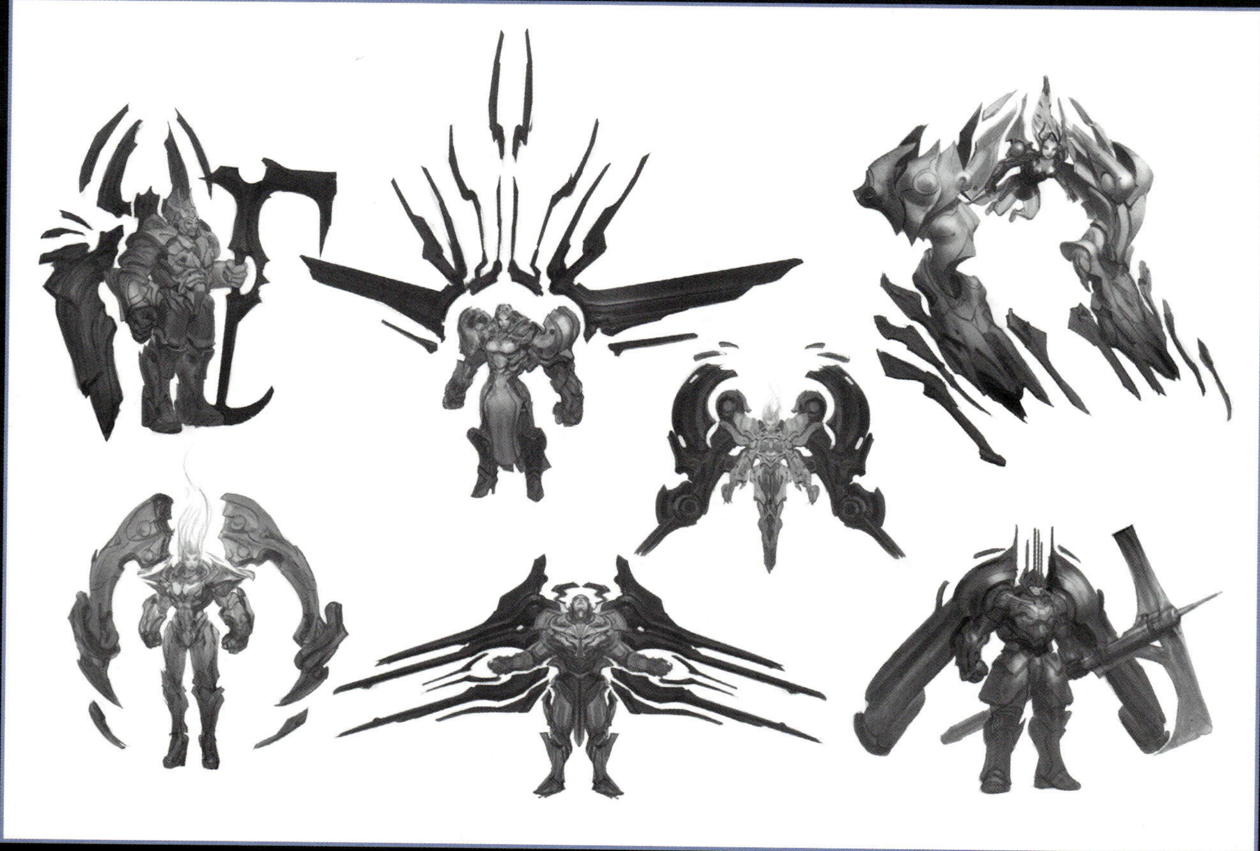

DEVELOPMENT SKETCHES

DEVELOPMENT SKETCHES

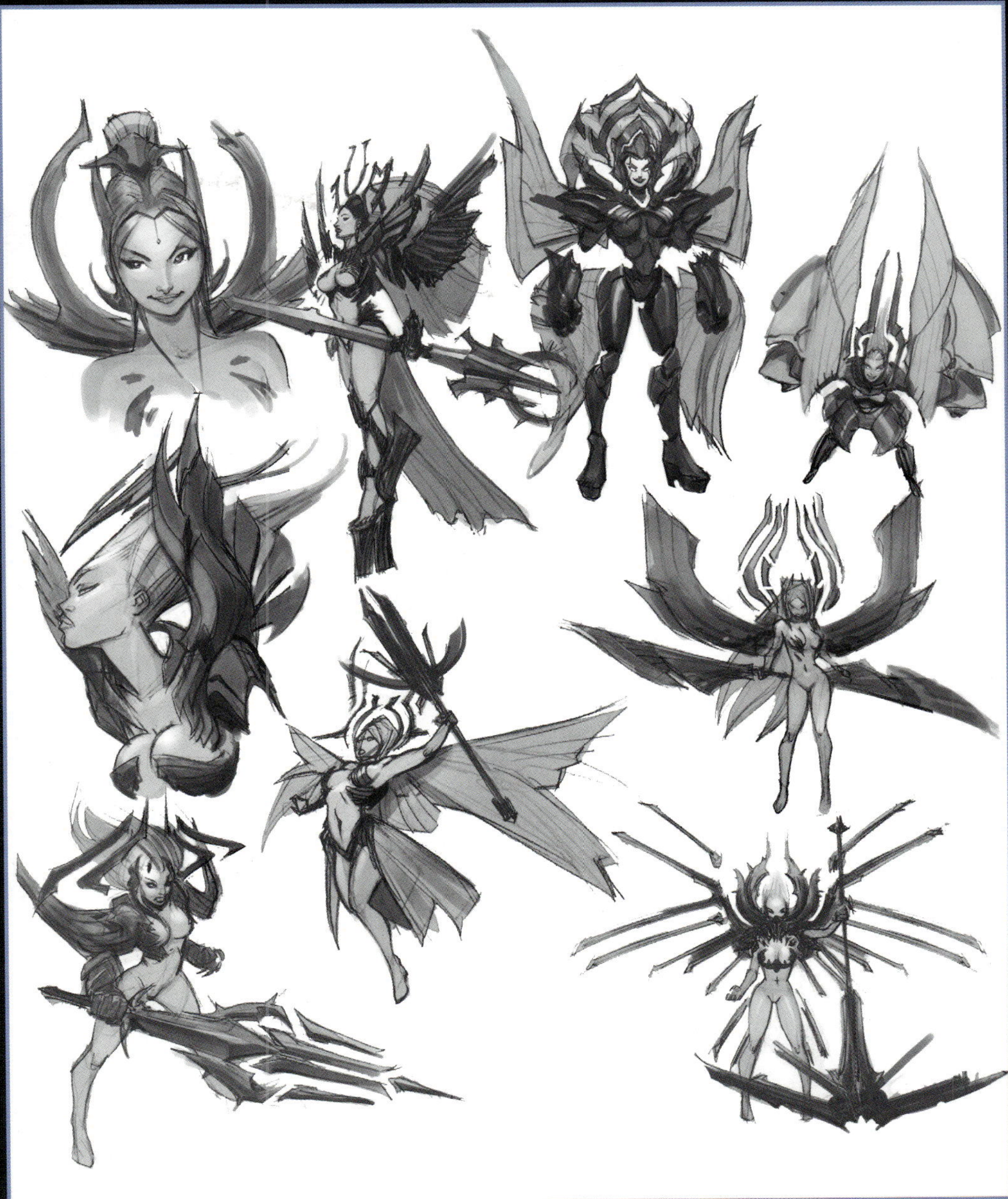

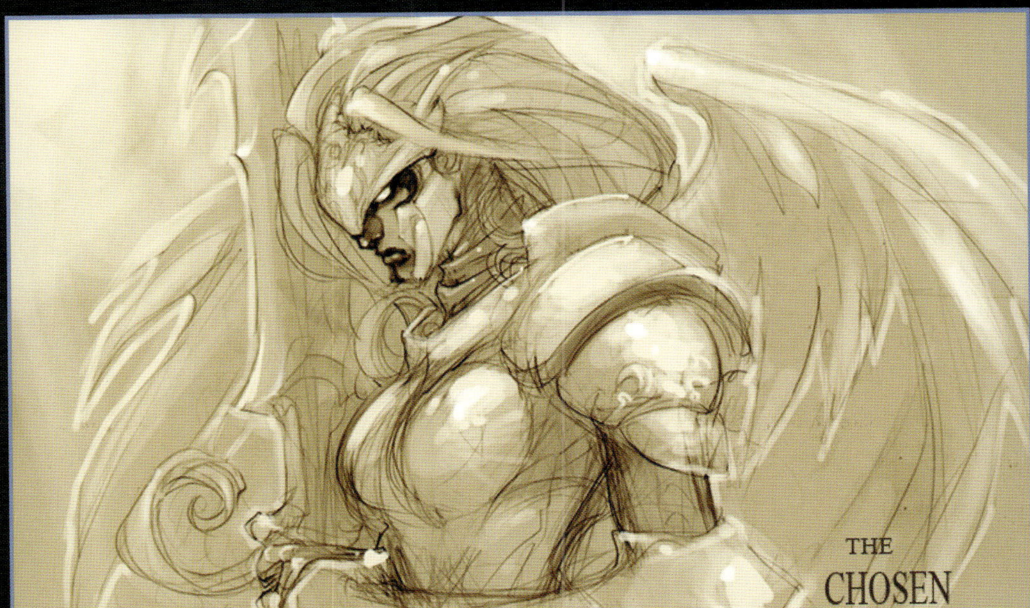

SKETCH ART

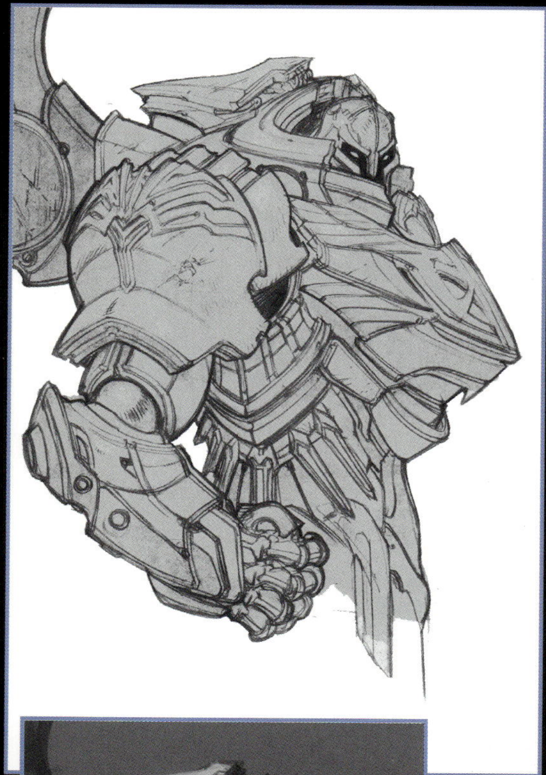

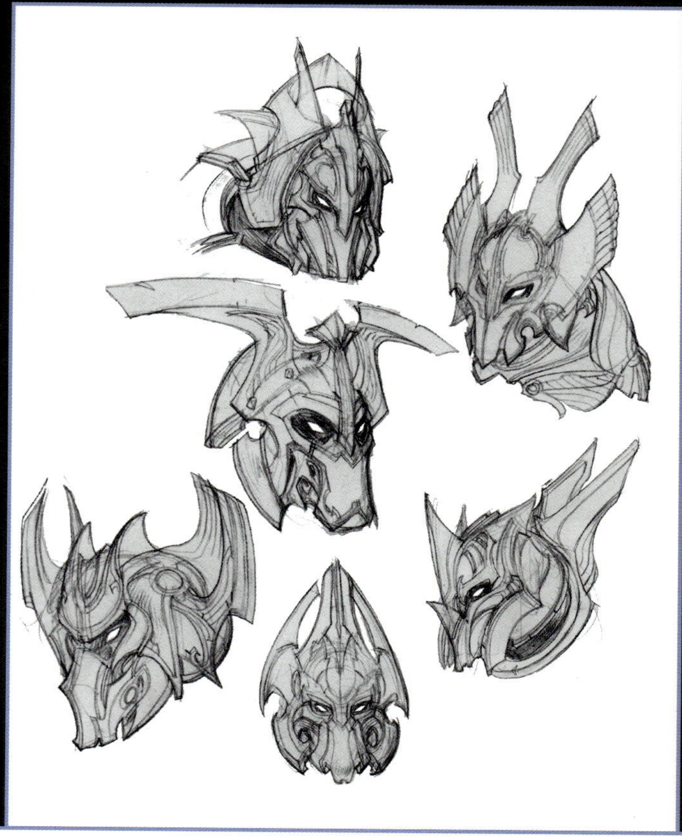

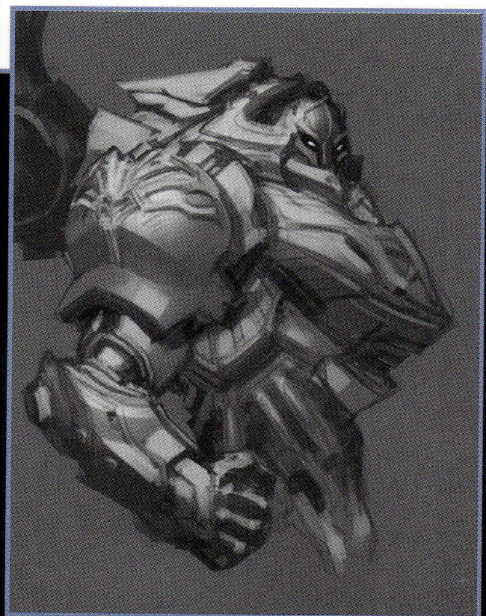

ARMOR CONCEPT

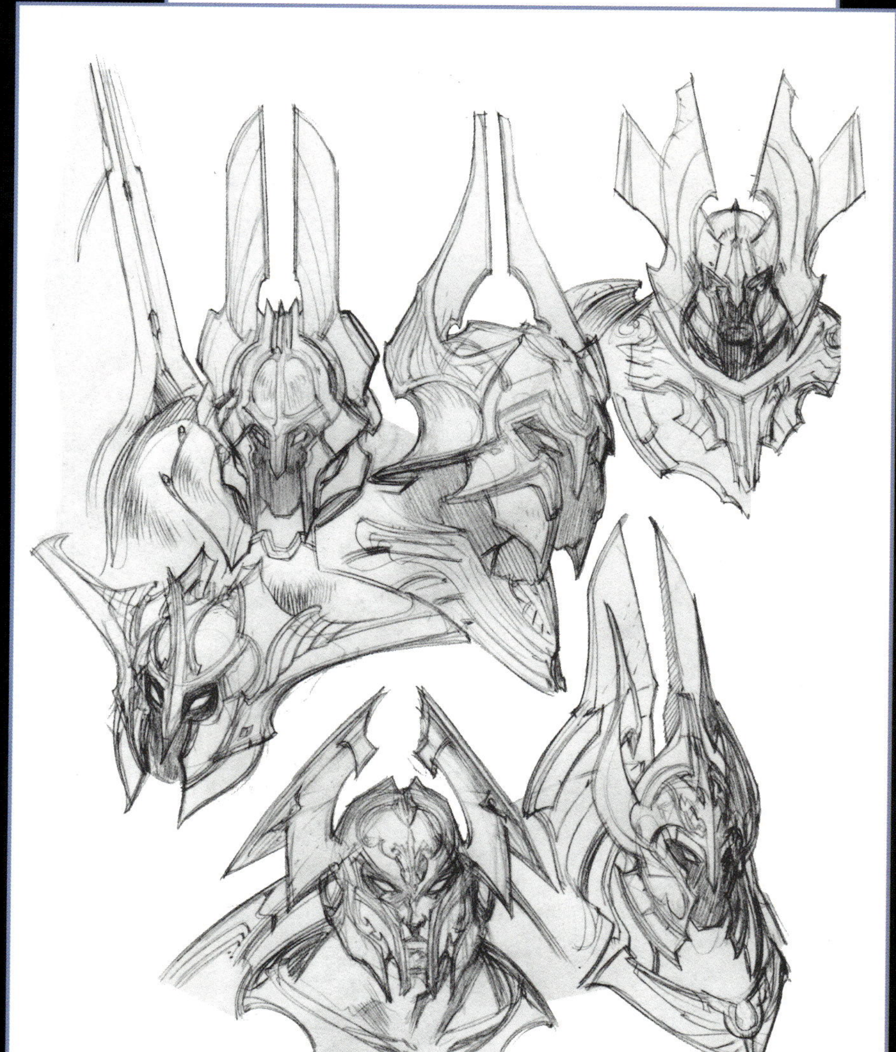

HELMET CONCEPTS

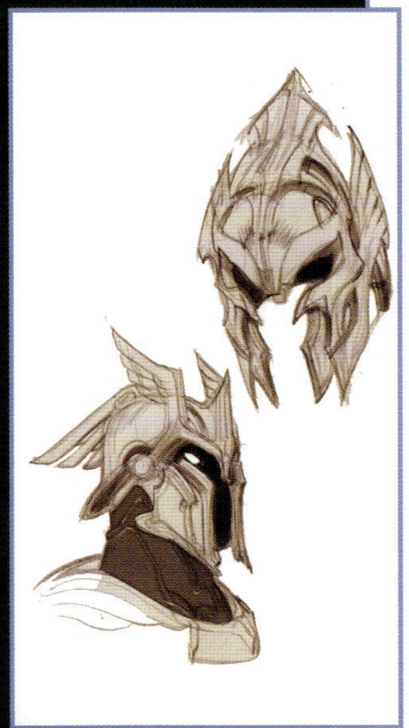

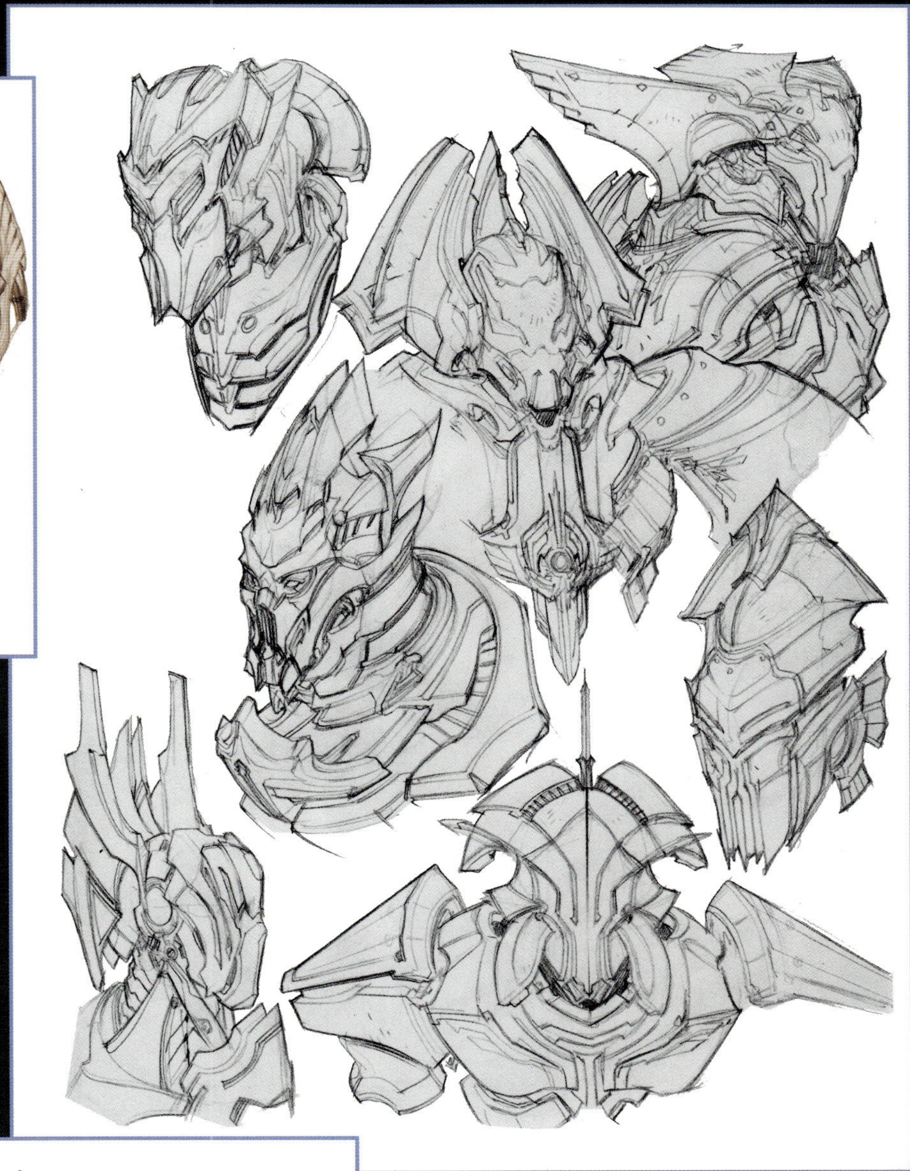

HELMET CONCEPTS

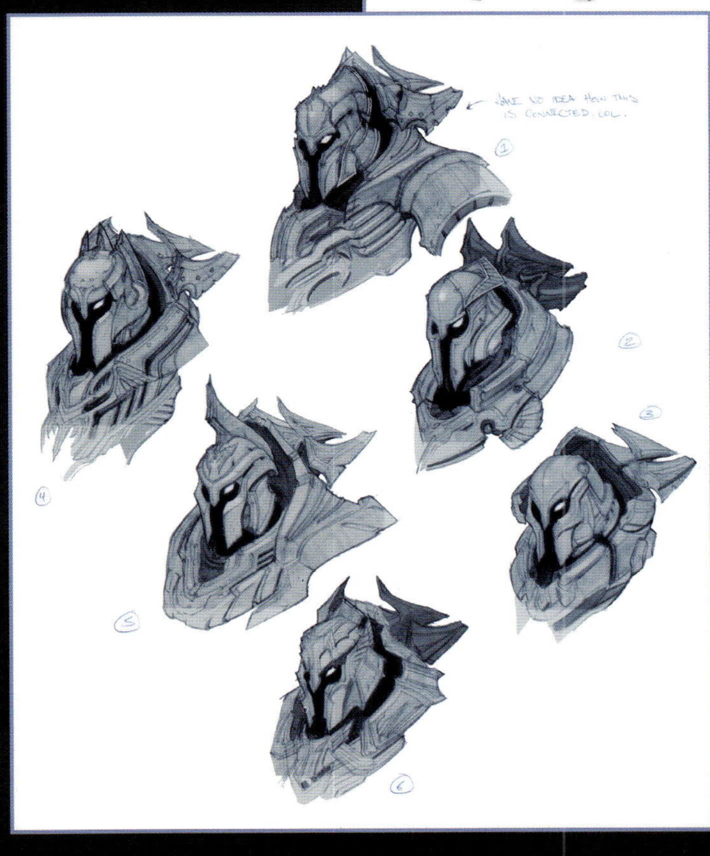

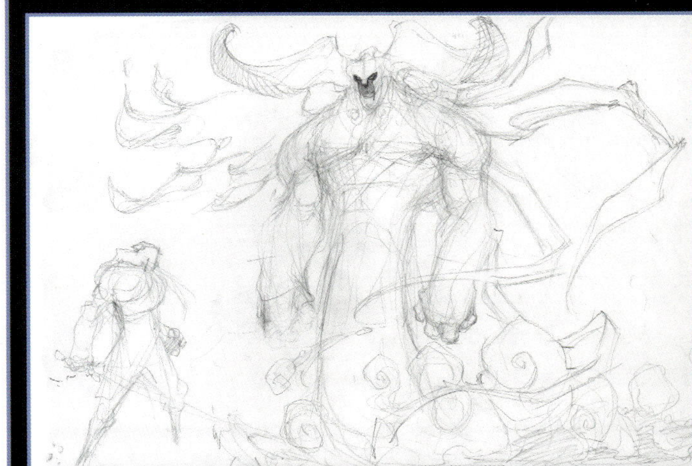

CONCEPT SKETCH

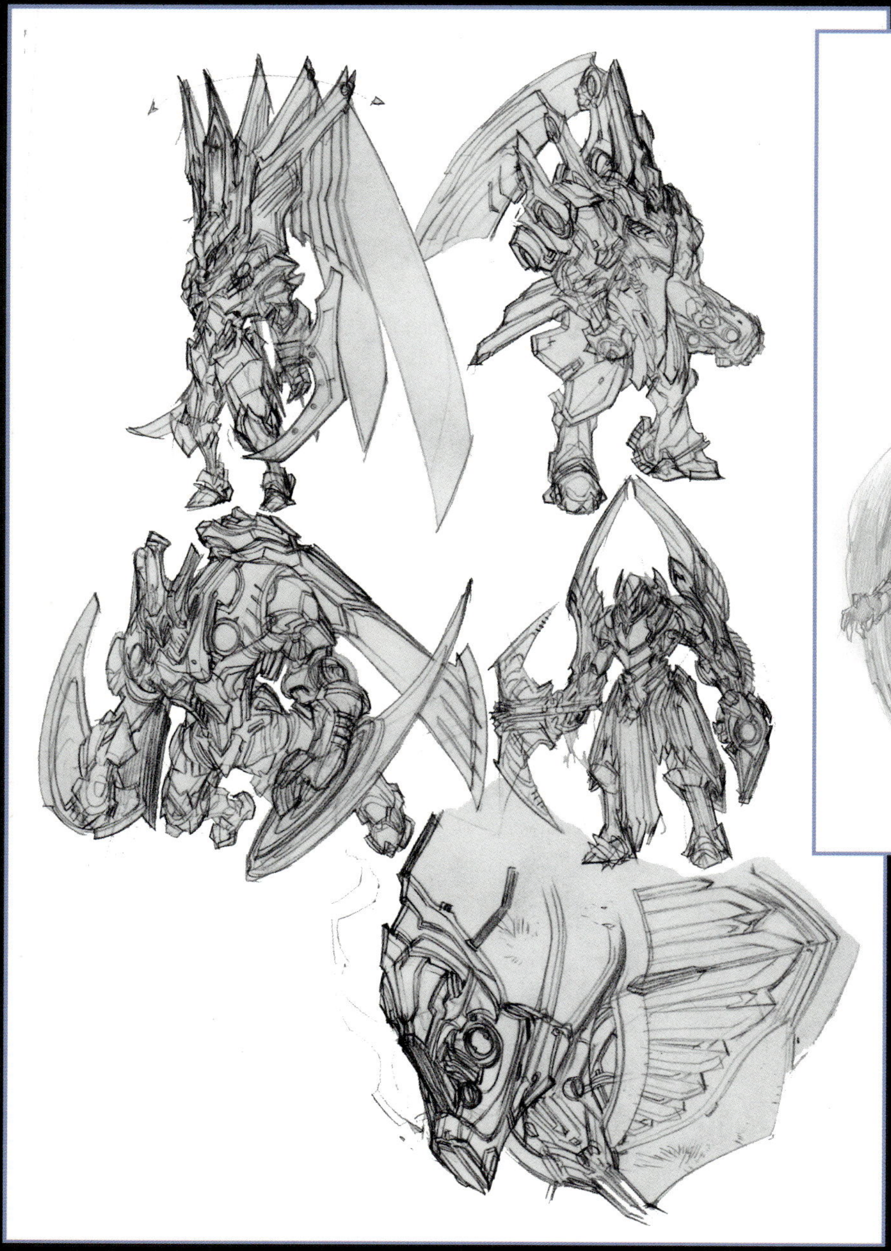

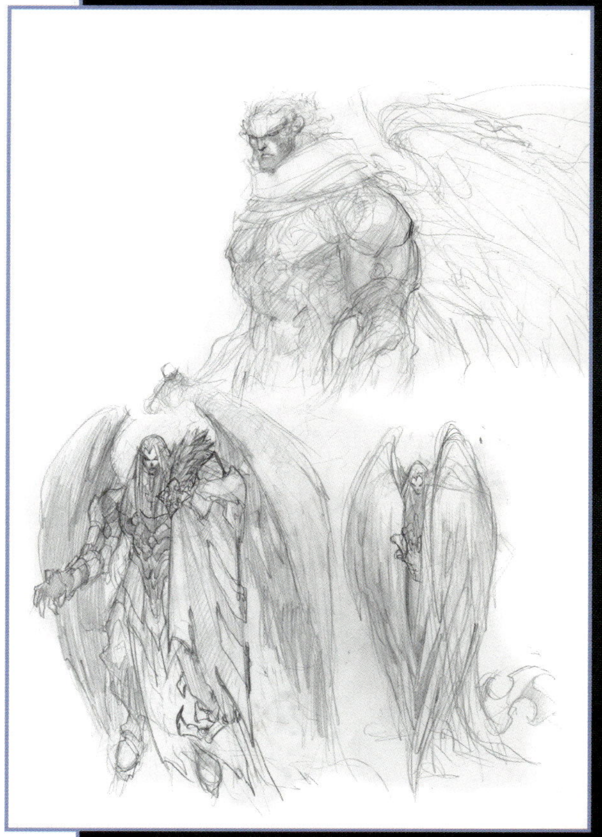

ARMOR DESIGNS

FALLEN ANGEL
CG TURNAROUNDS

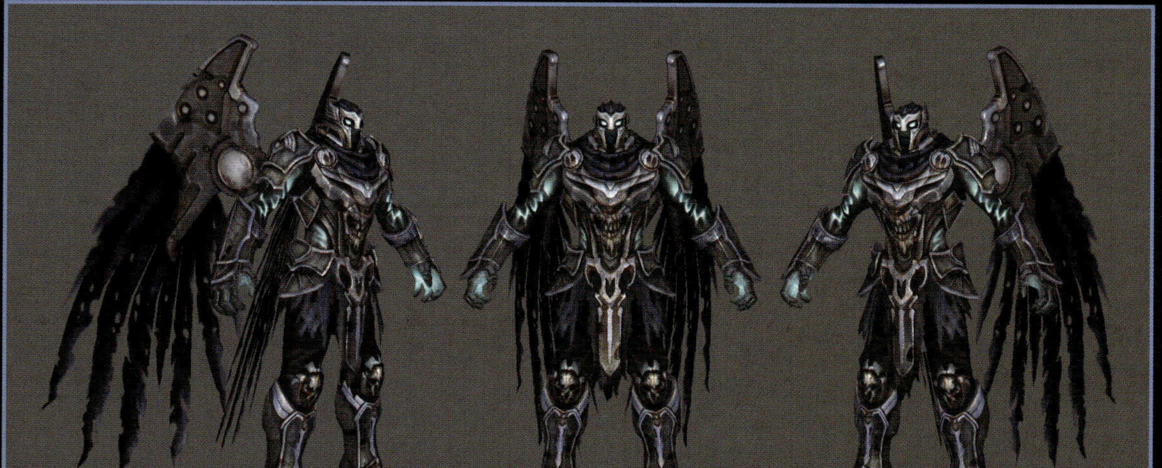

ARMOR DESIGNS

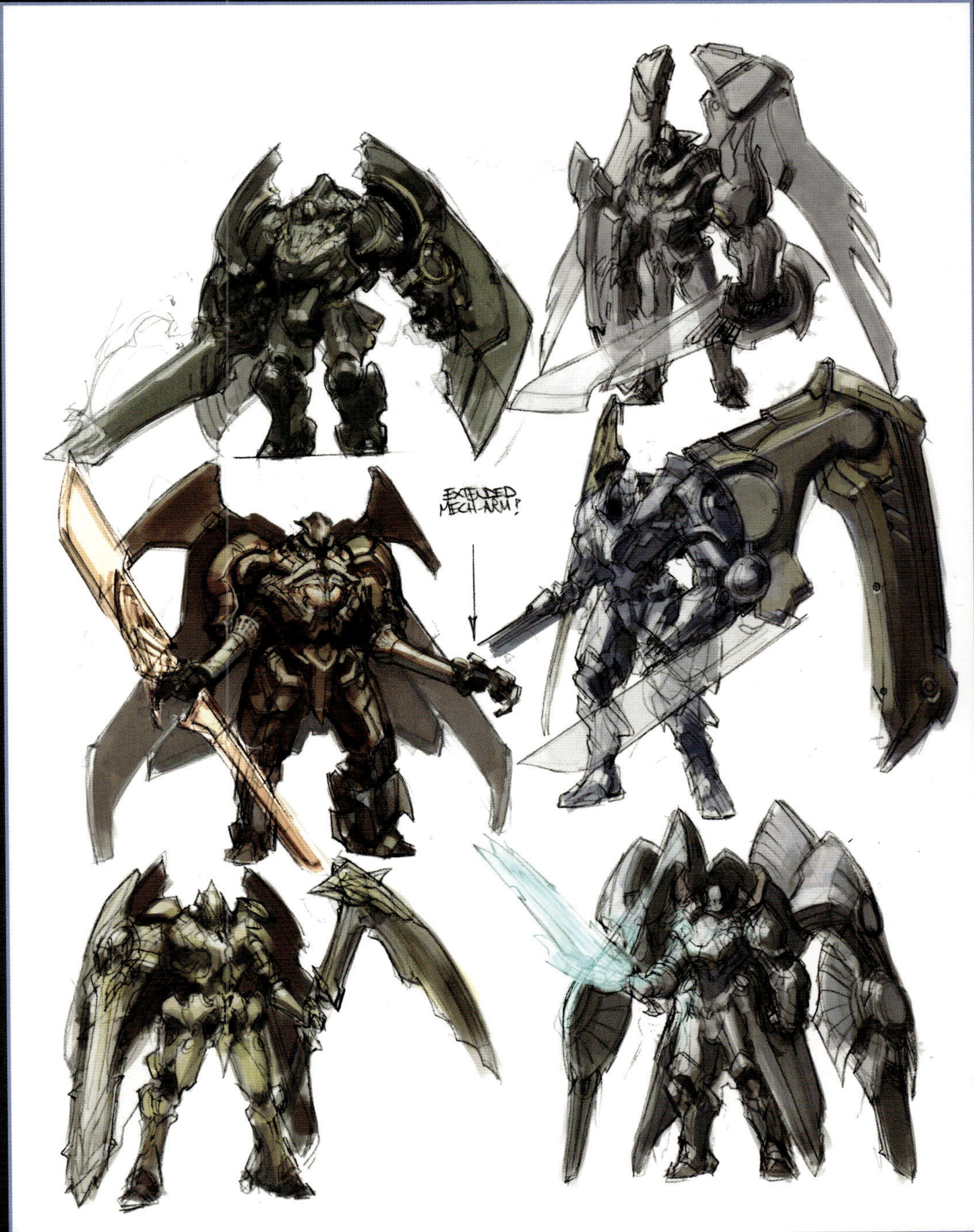

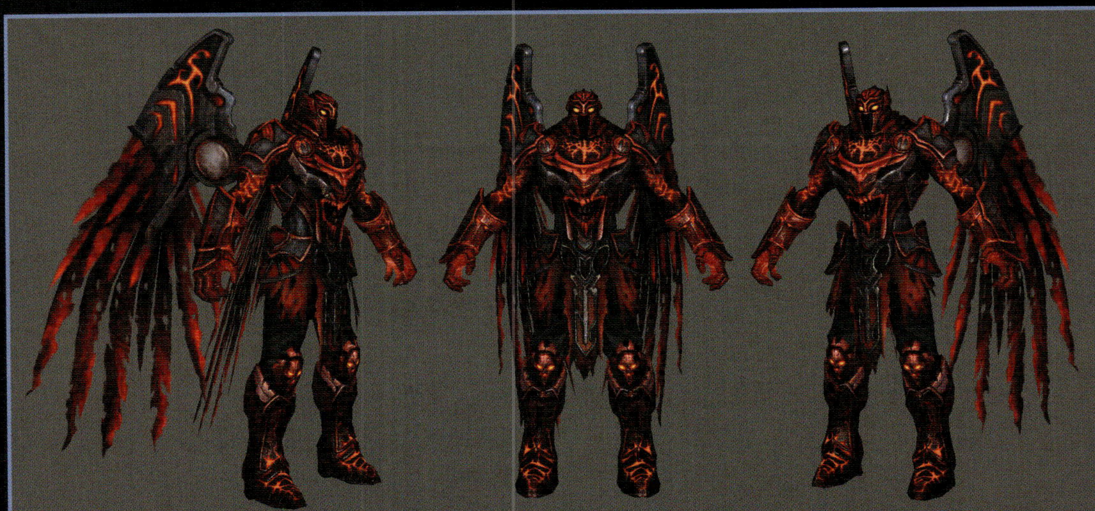

FORSAKEN CG TURNAROUNDS

Angelic Mount

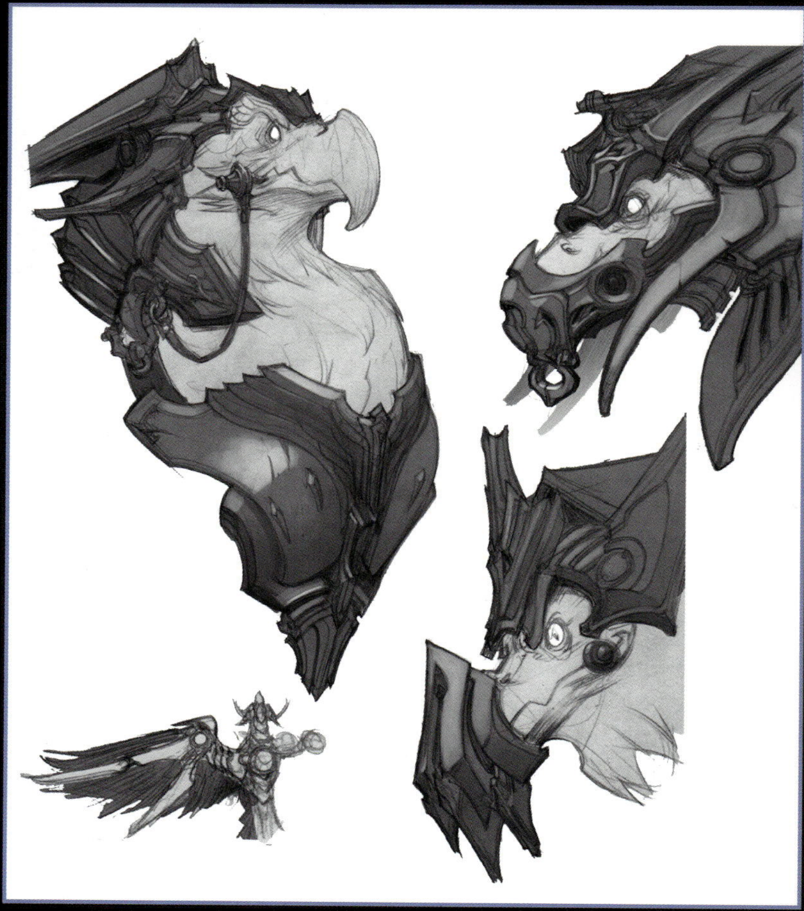

HEAD DESIGNS

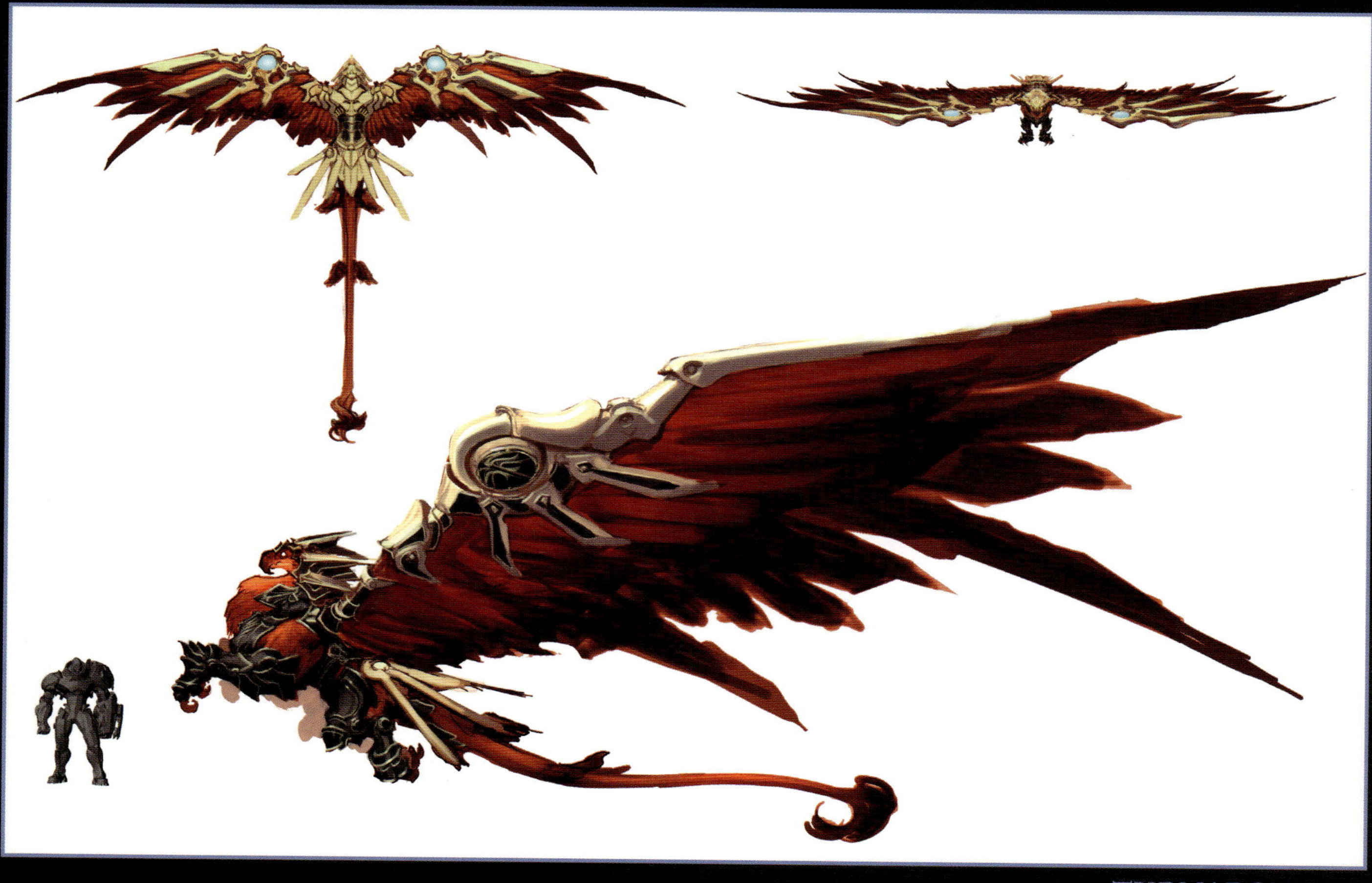

TURNAROUNDS

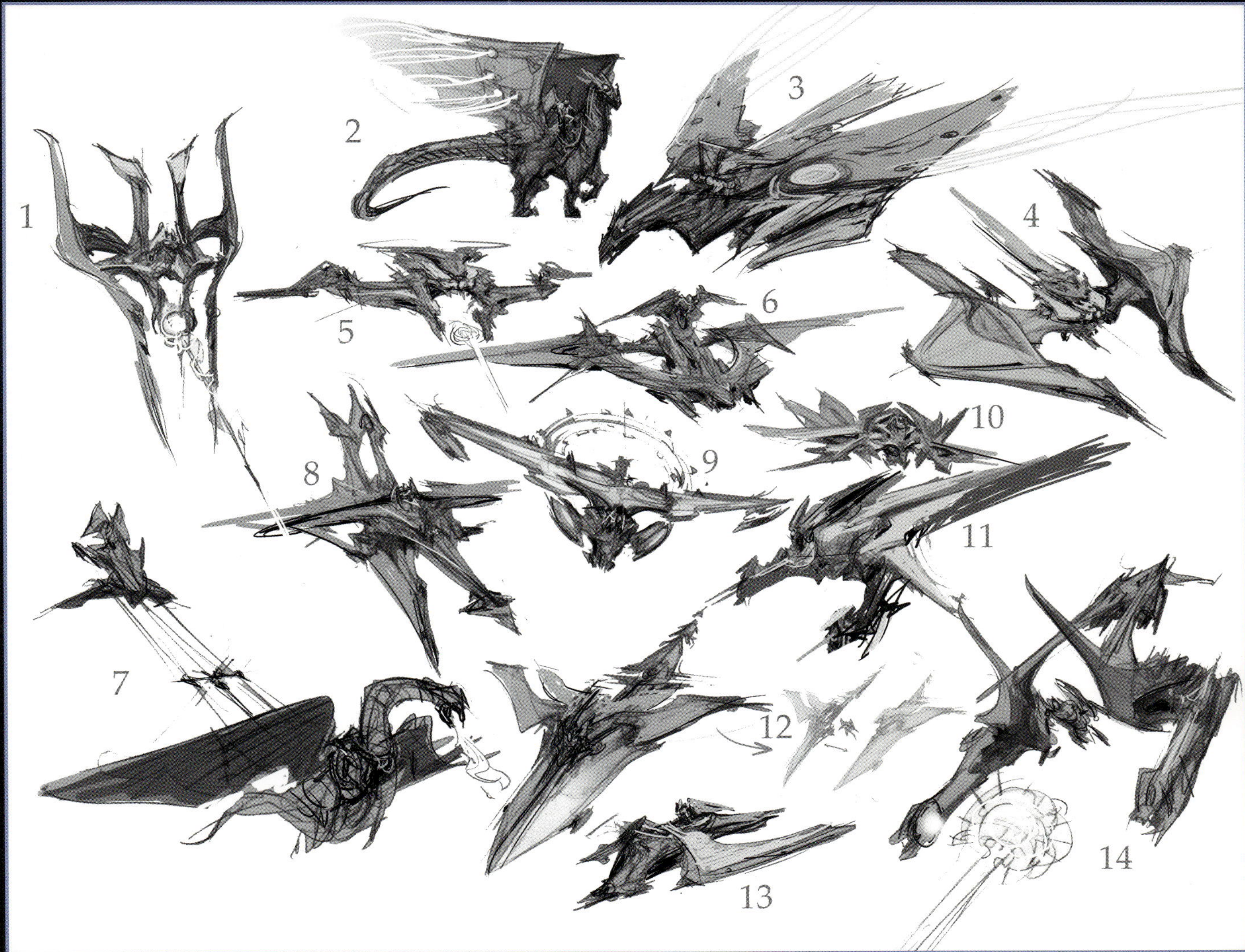

DEVELOPMENT SKETCHES

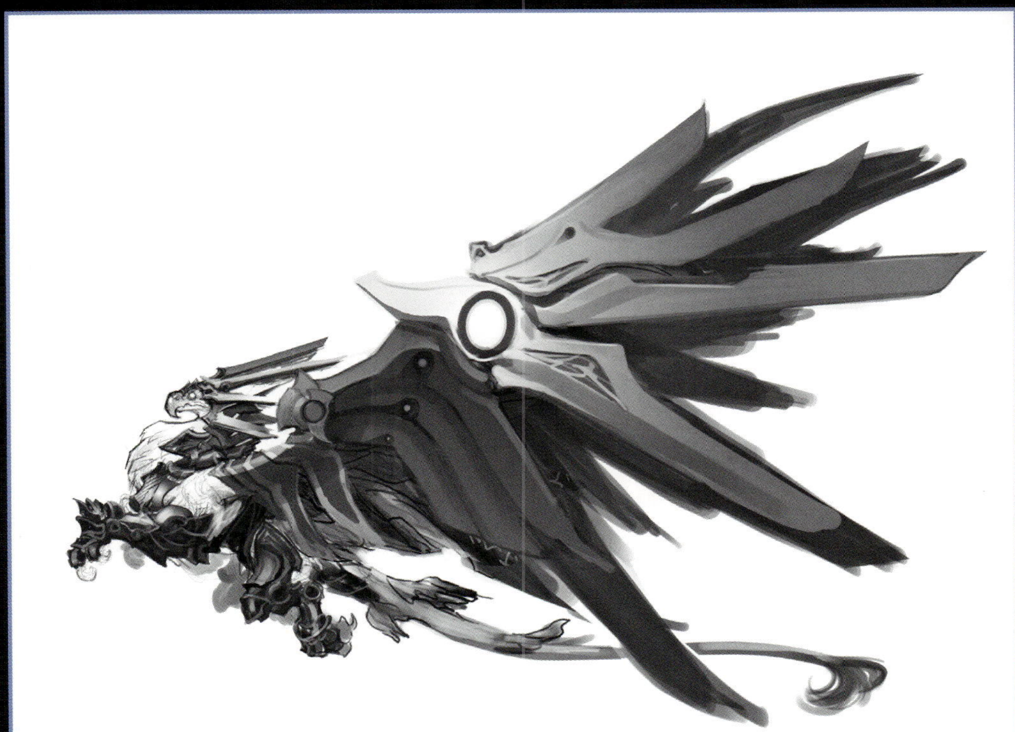

CONCEPT SKETCH

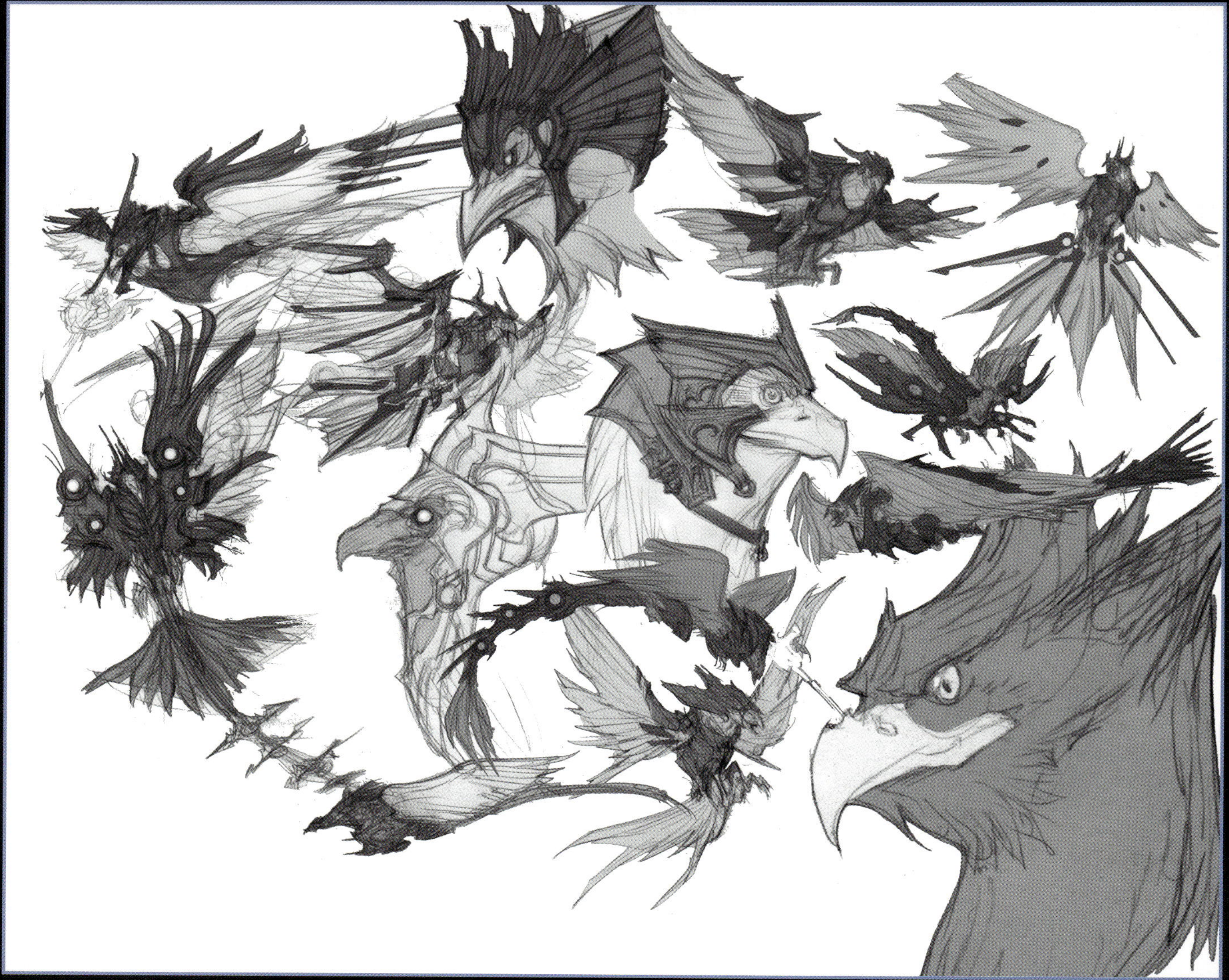

DEVELOPMENT SKETCHES

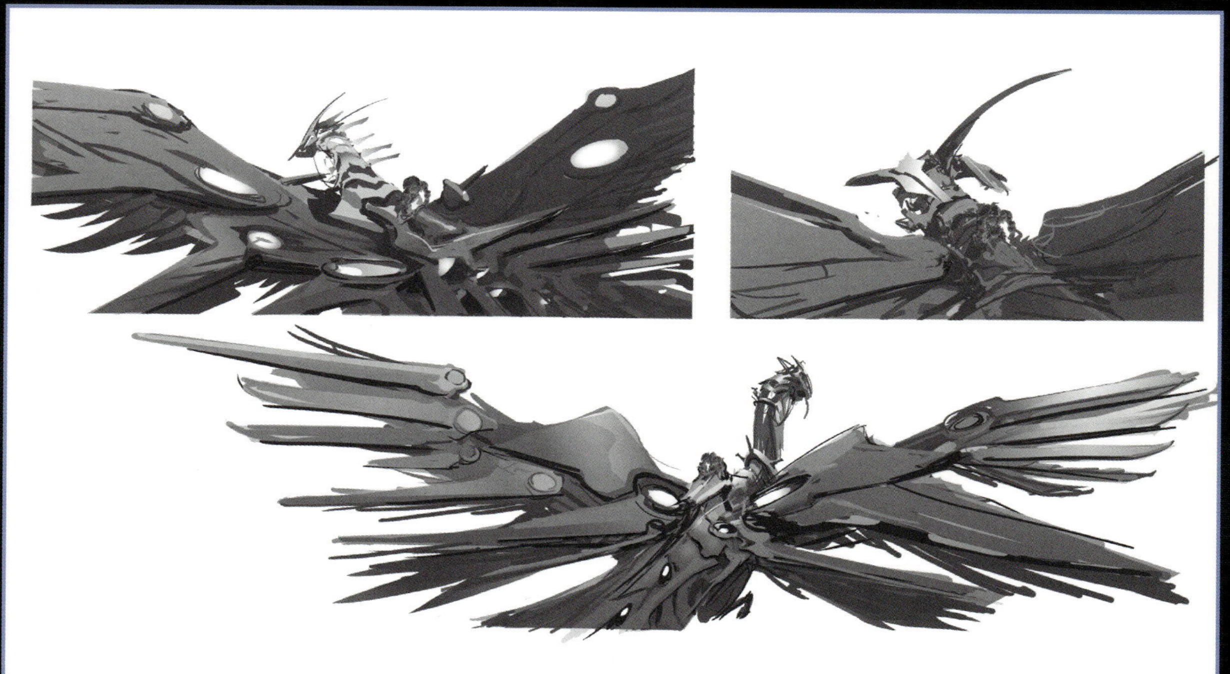

WING CONCEPTS

Animals

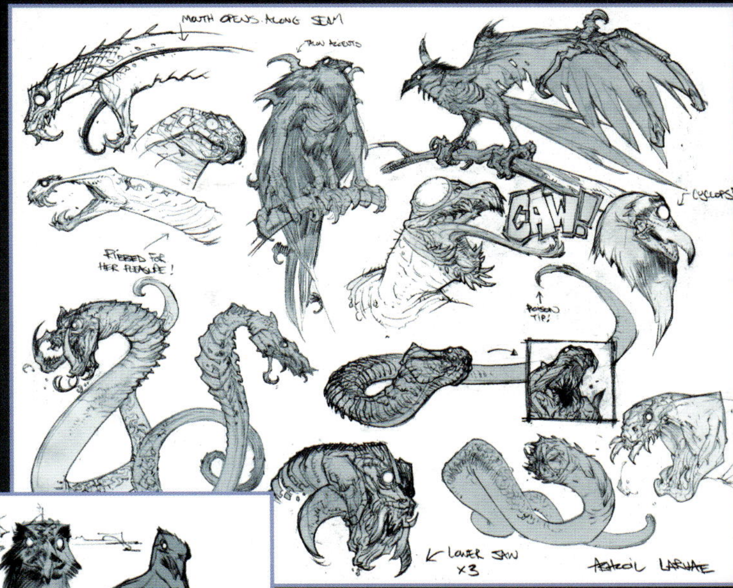

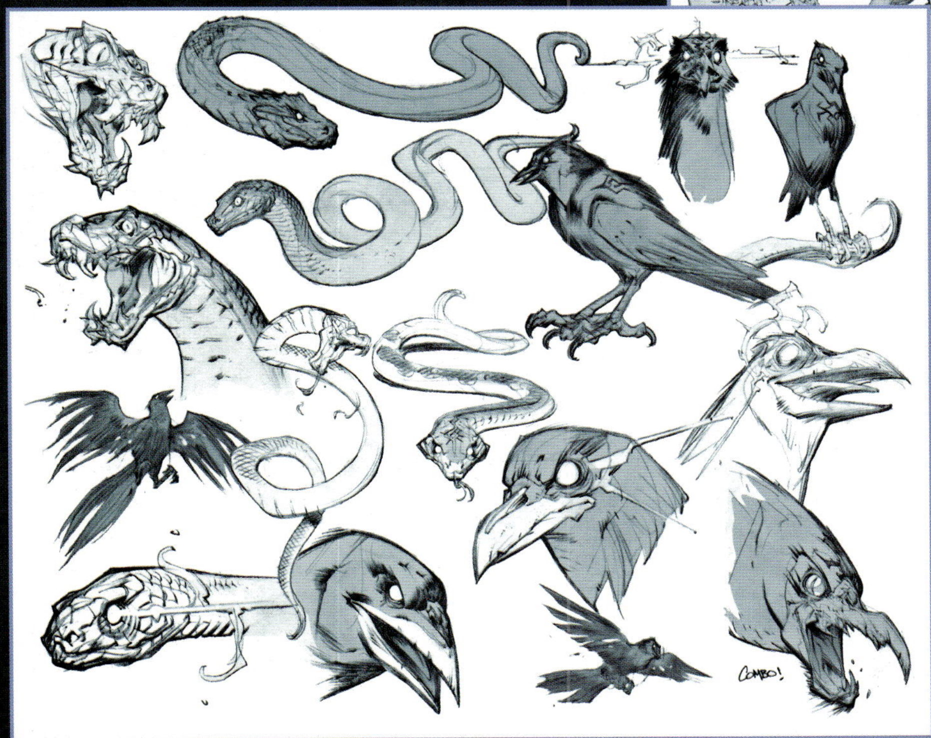

CROW AND SNAKE CONCEPTS

Goremaw

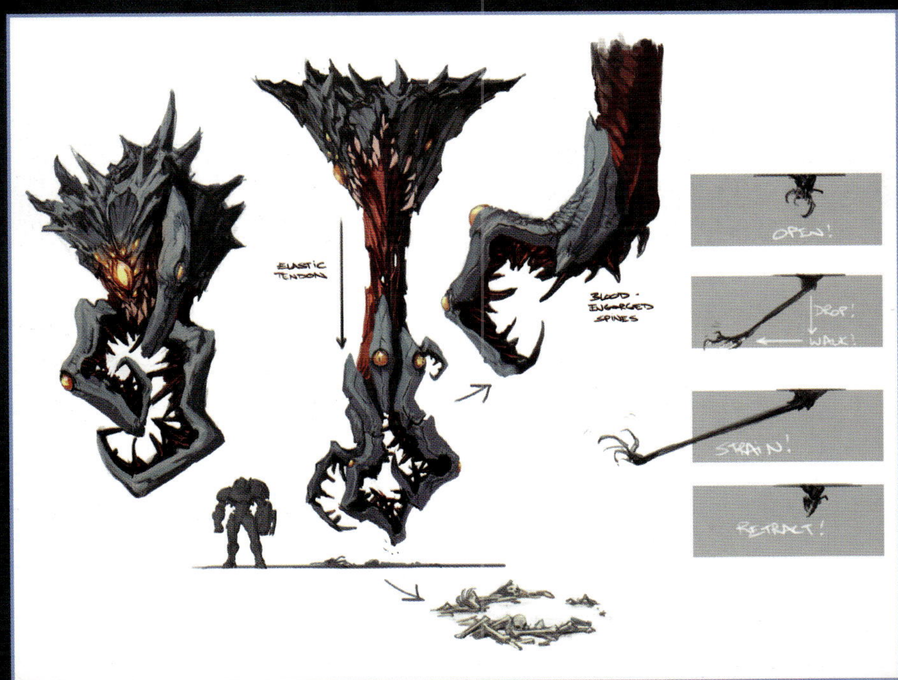

GOREMAW DESIGNS

Guardian

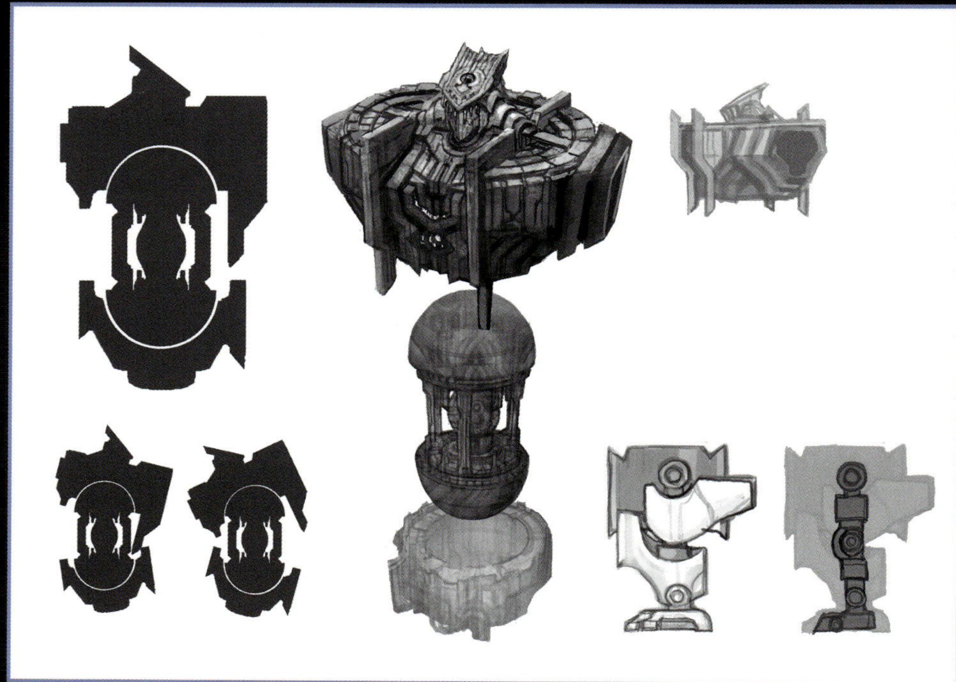

MECHANISM DESIGNS

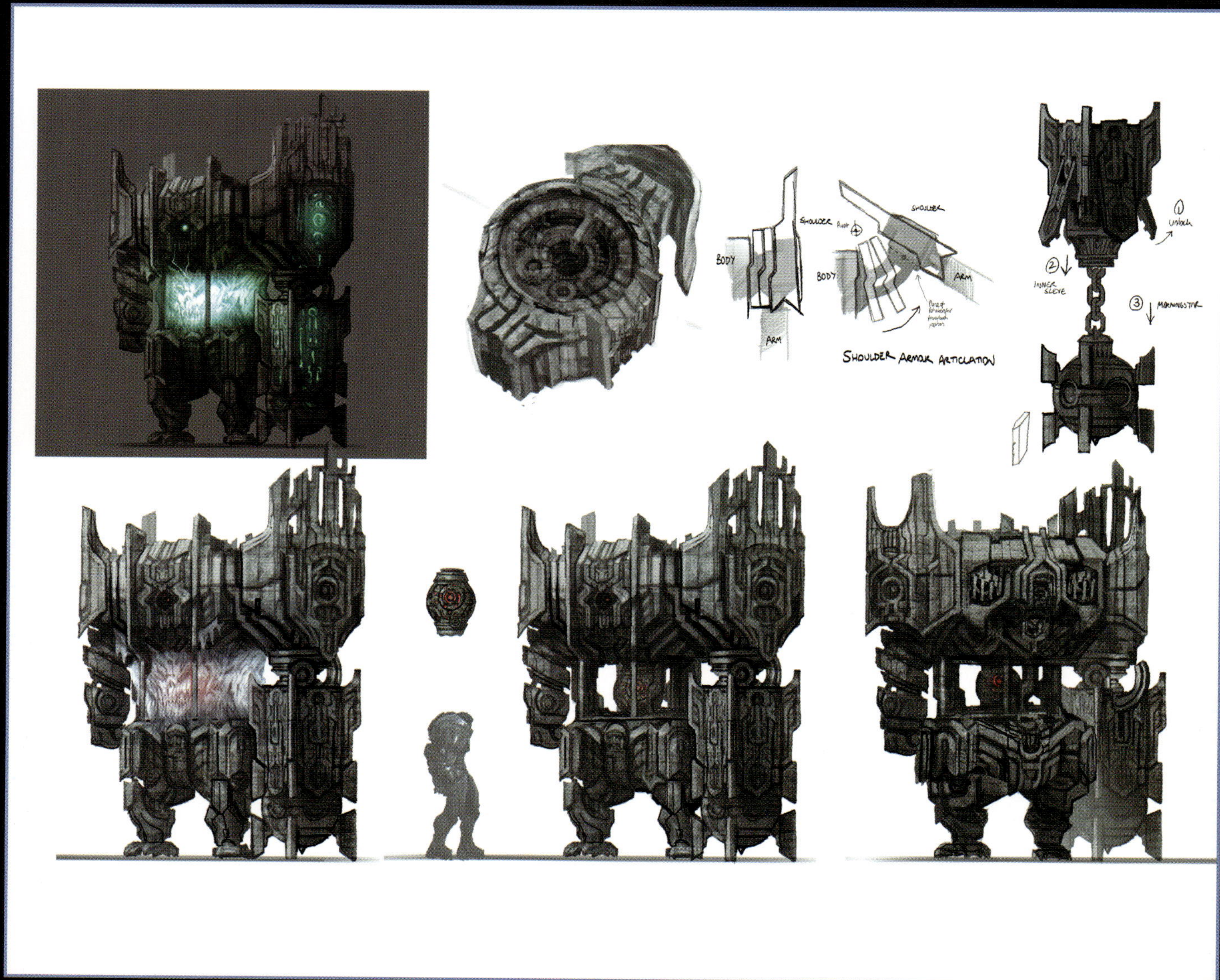

TURNAROUNDS

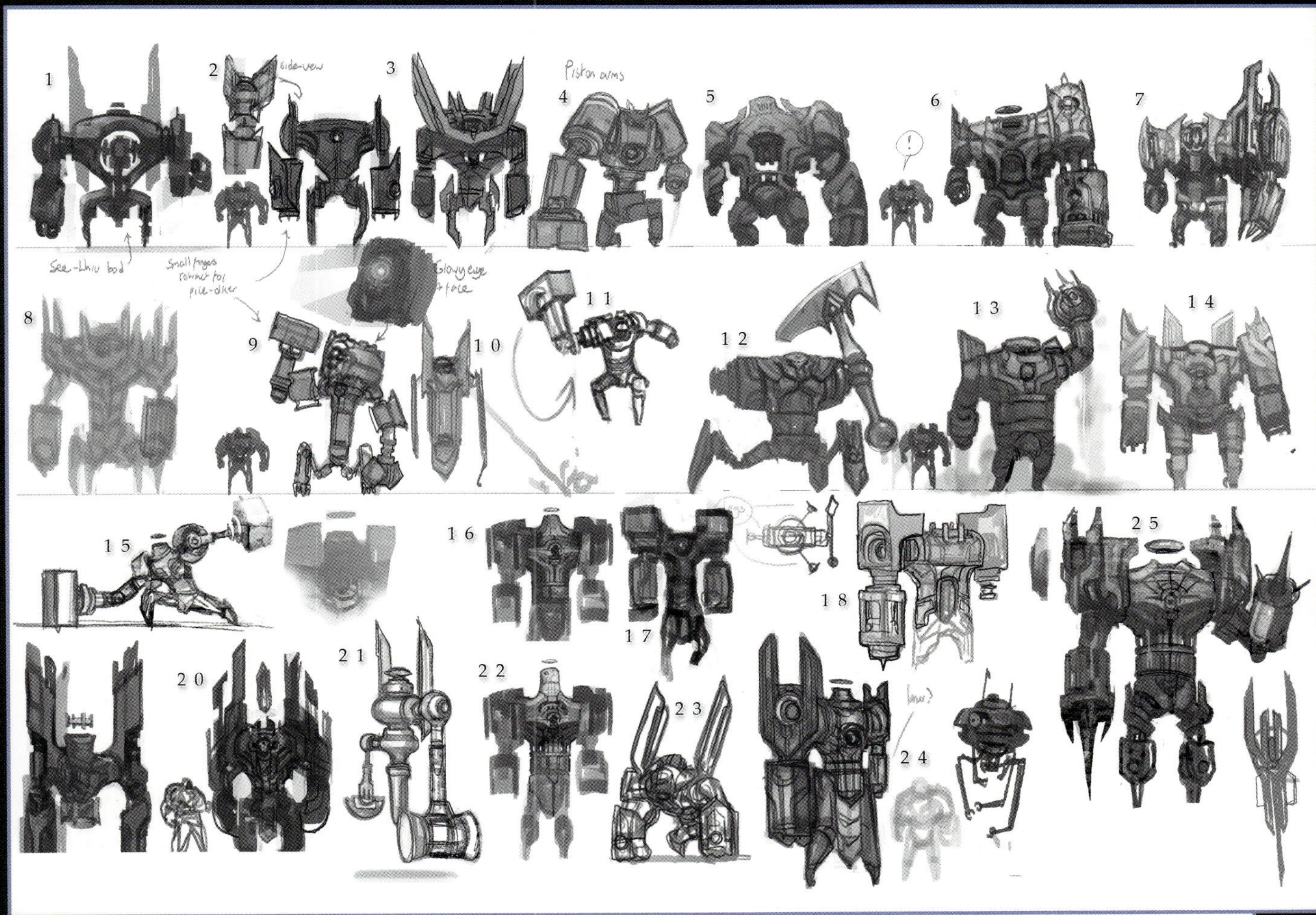

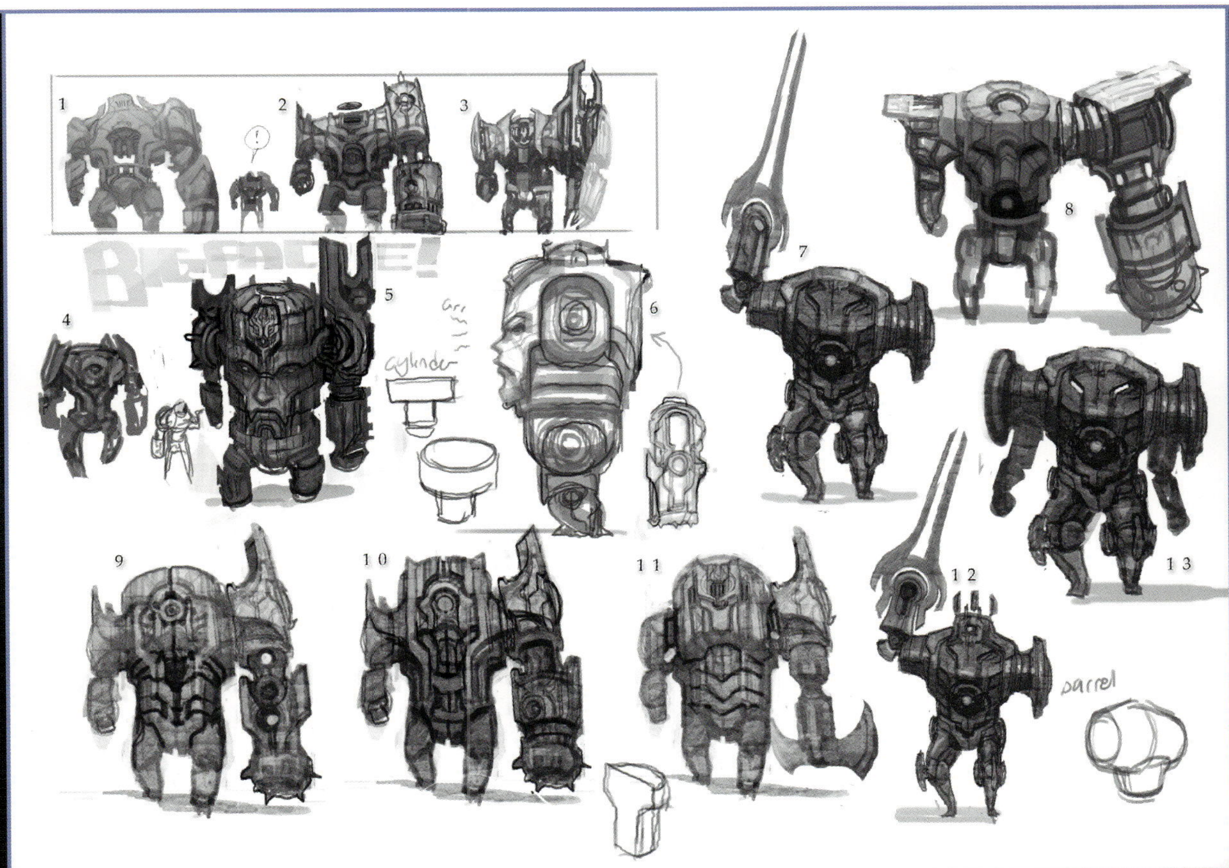

DEVELOPMENT SKETCHES

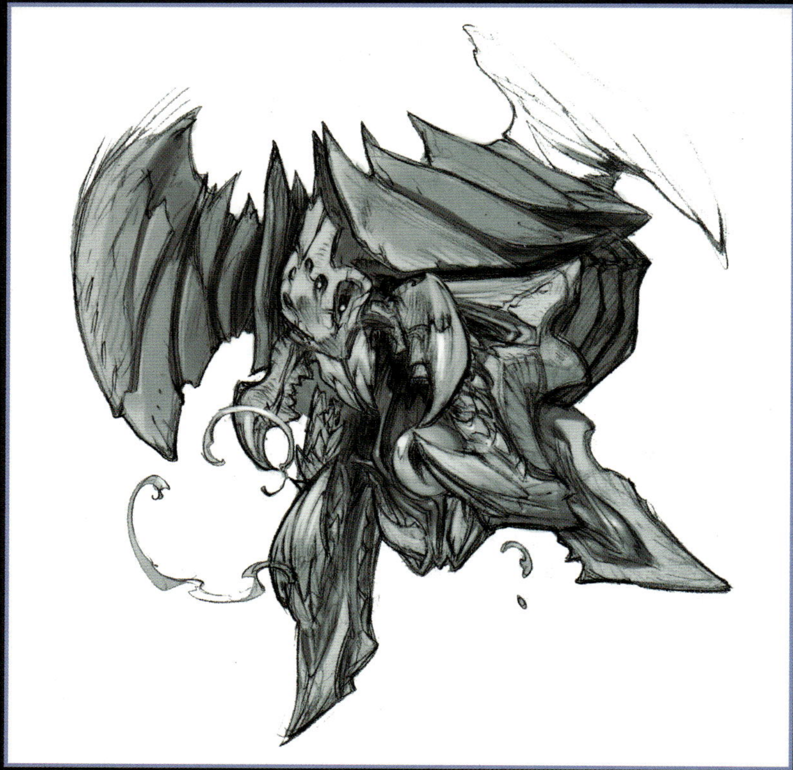

HEAD DESIGN

Silitha

Many unfortunate creatures find themselves trapped in Silitha's intricate webs, a silken snare strung across a corner of the Destroyer's city. She takes great pleasure in cracking bones between her fangs to suck out the marrow, or casting them into the chittering jaws of her children.

But sometimes, Silitha preserves her prisoners, to better enjoy their slow agonies. For the Spider Queen spins more than webs. She spins sadistic tales of woe, and writes their unhappy endings in her own venom.

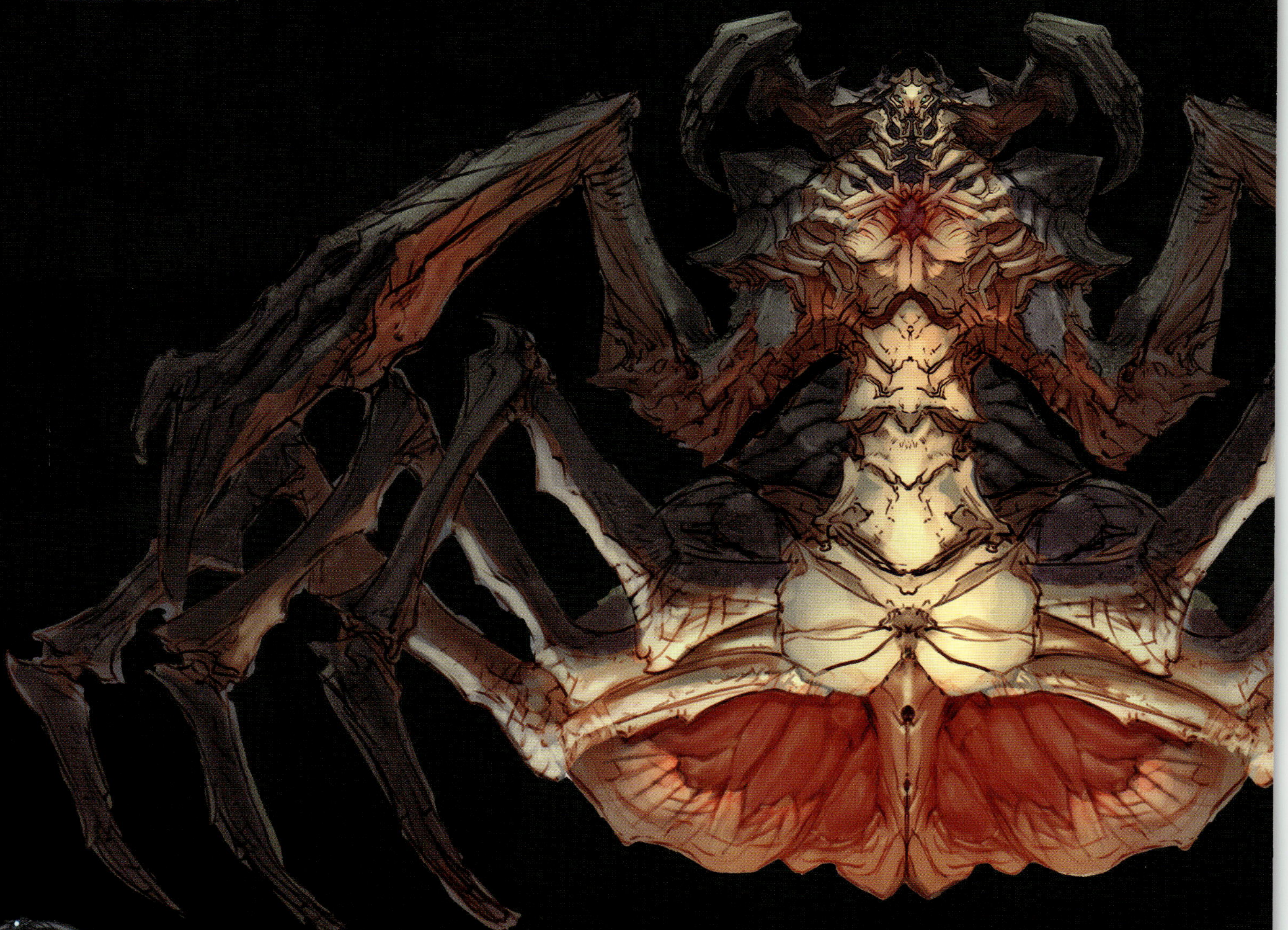

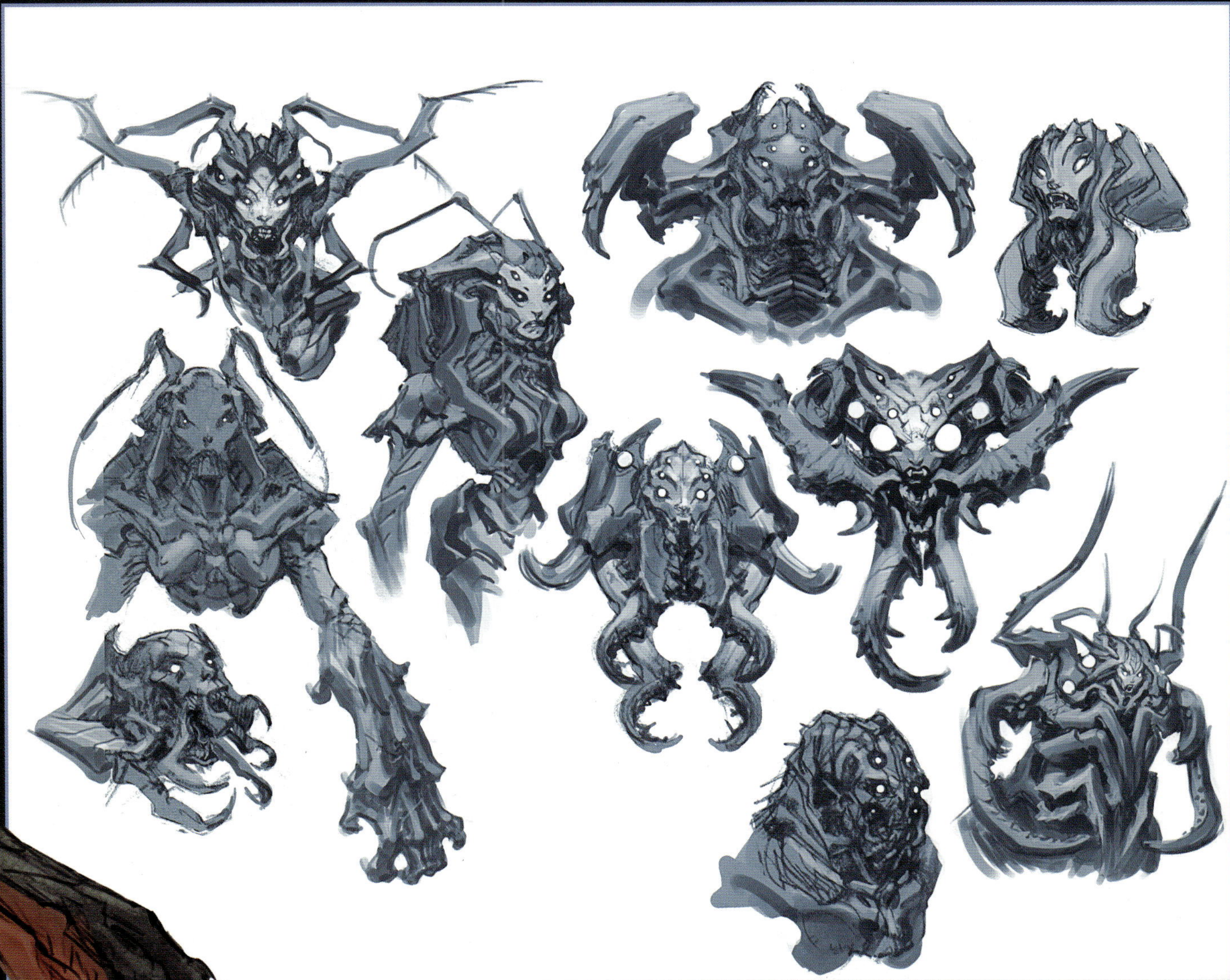

DEVELOPMENT SKETCHES

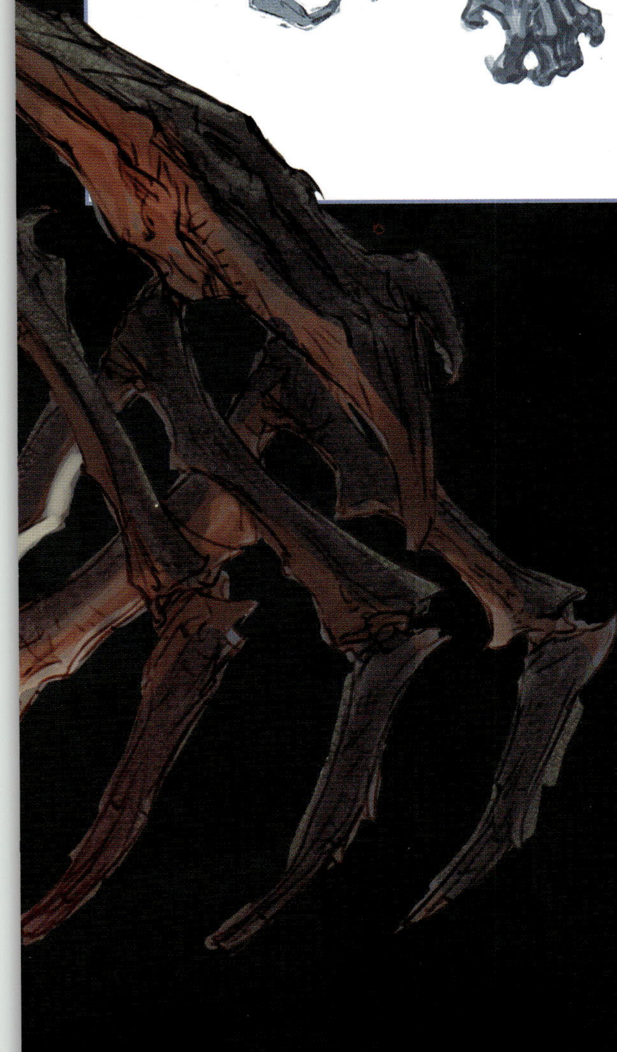

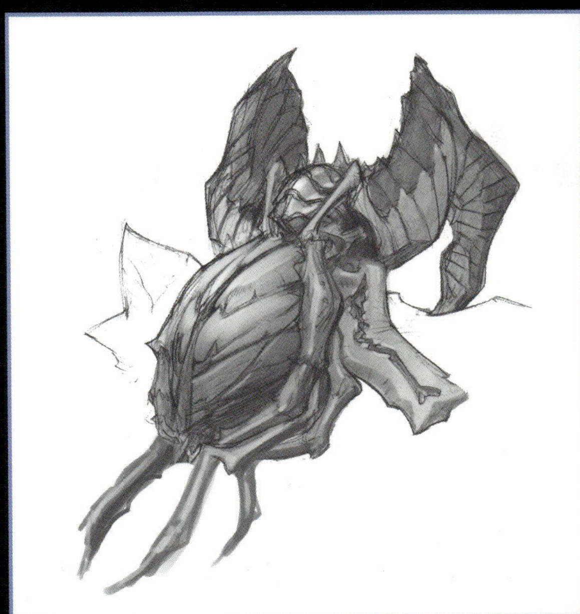

REAR HEAD DESIGN

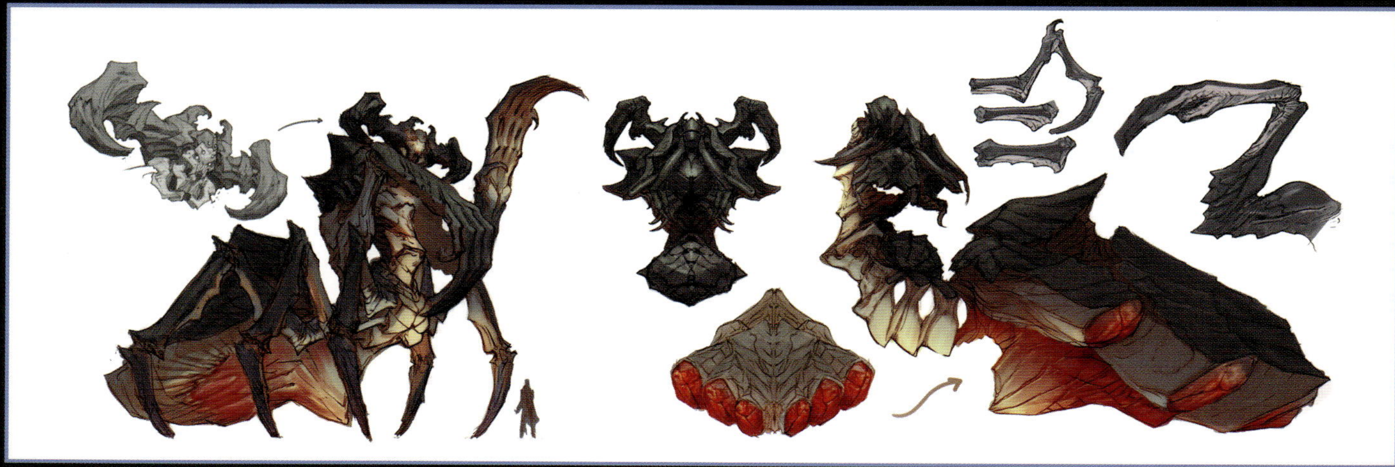

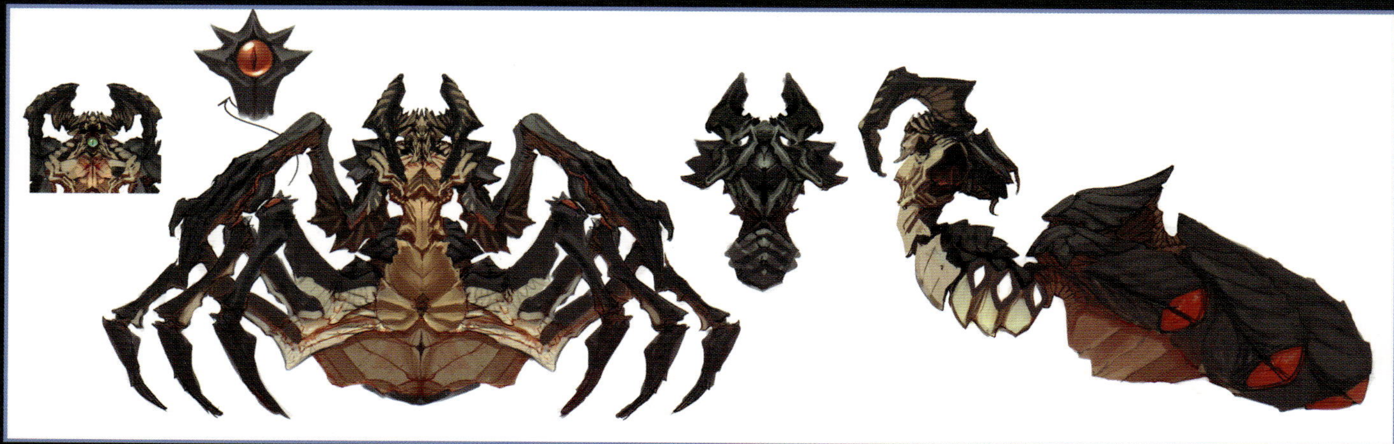

TURNAROUNDS

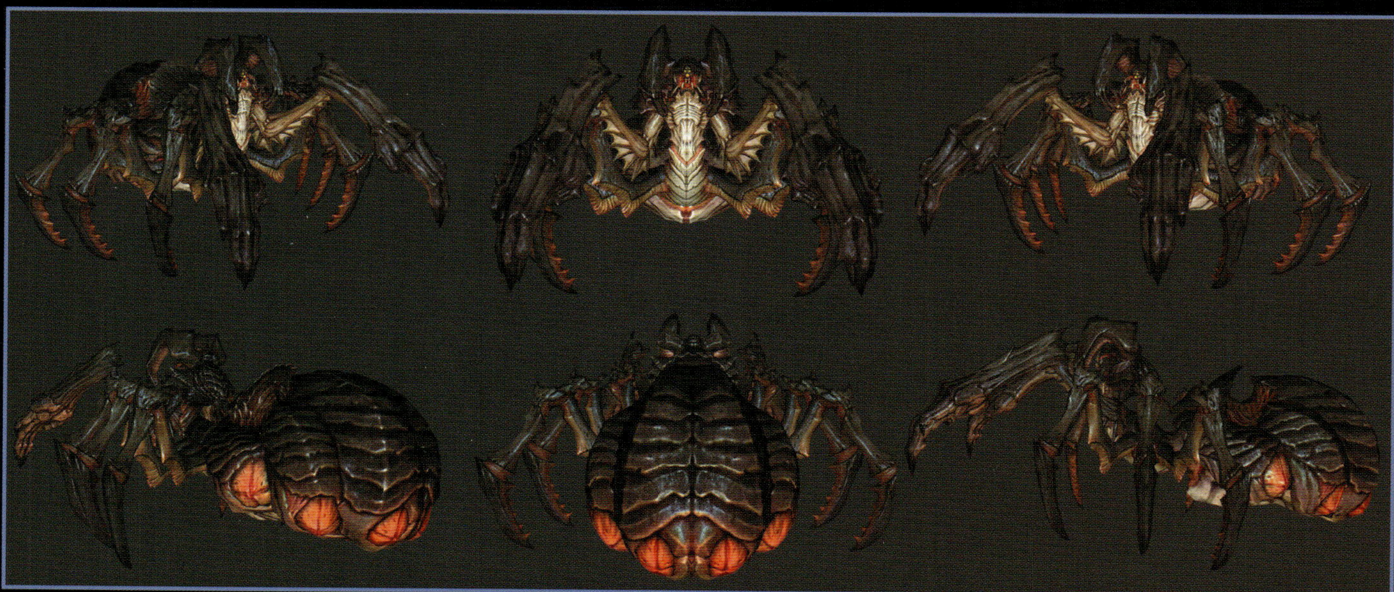

CG TURNAROUNDS

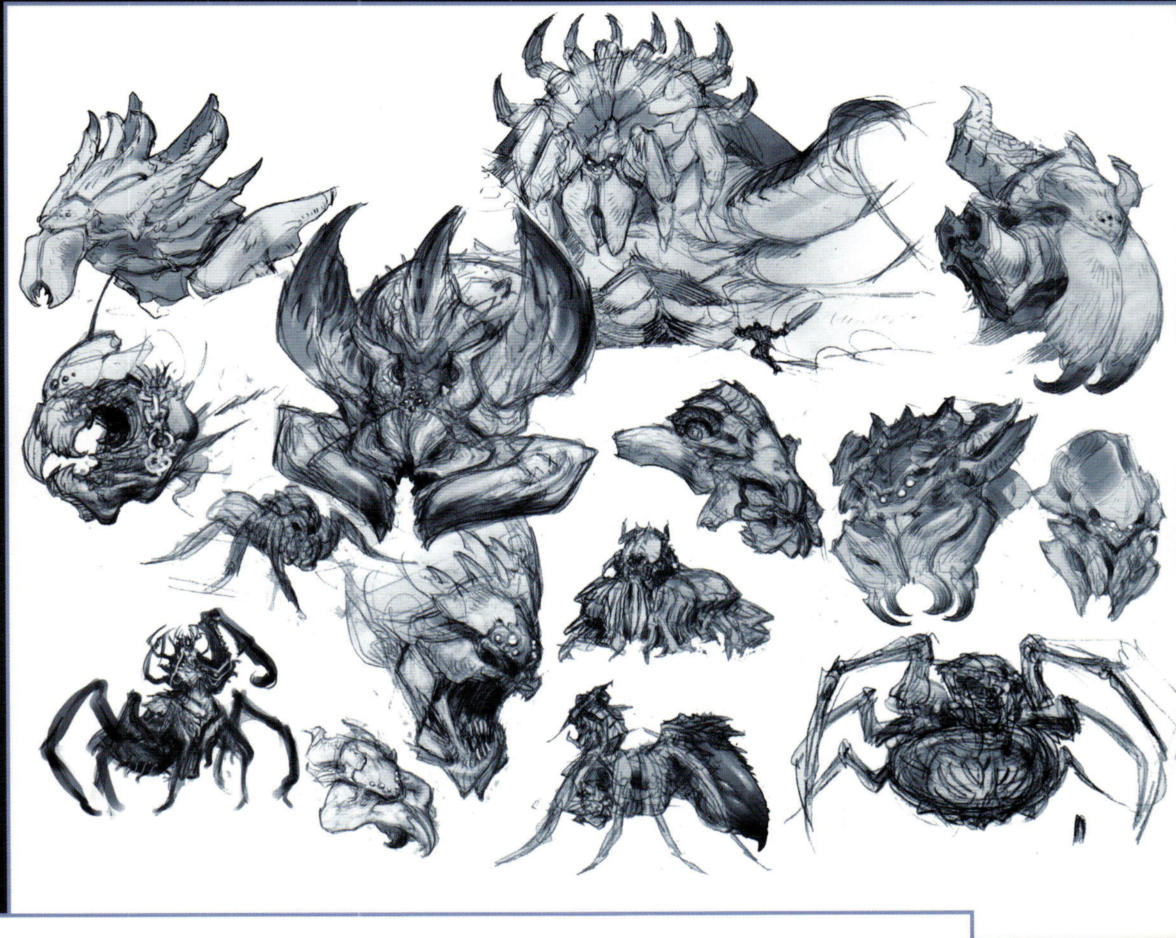

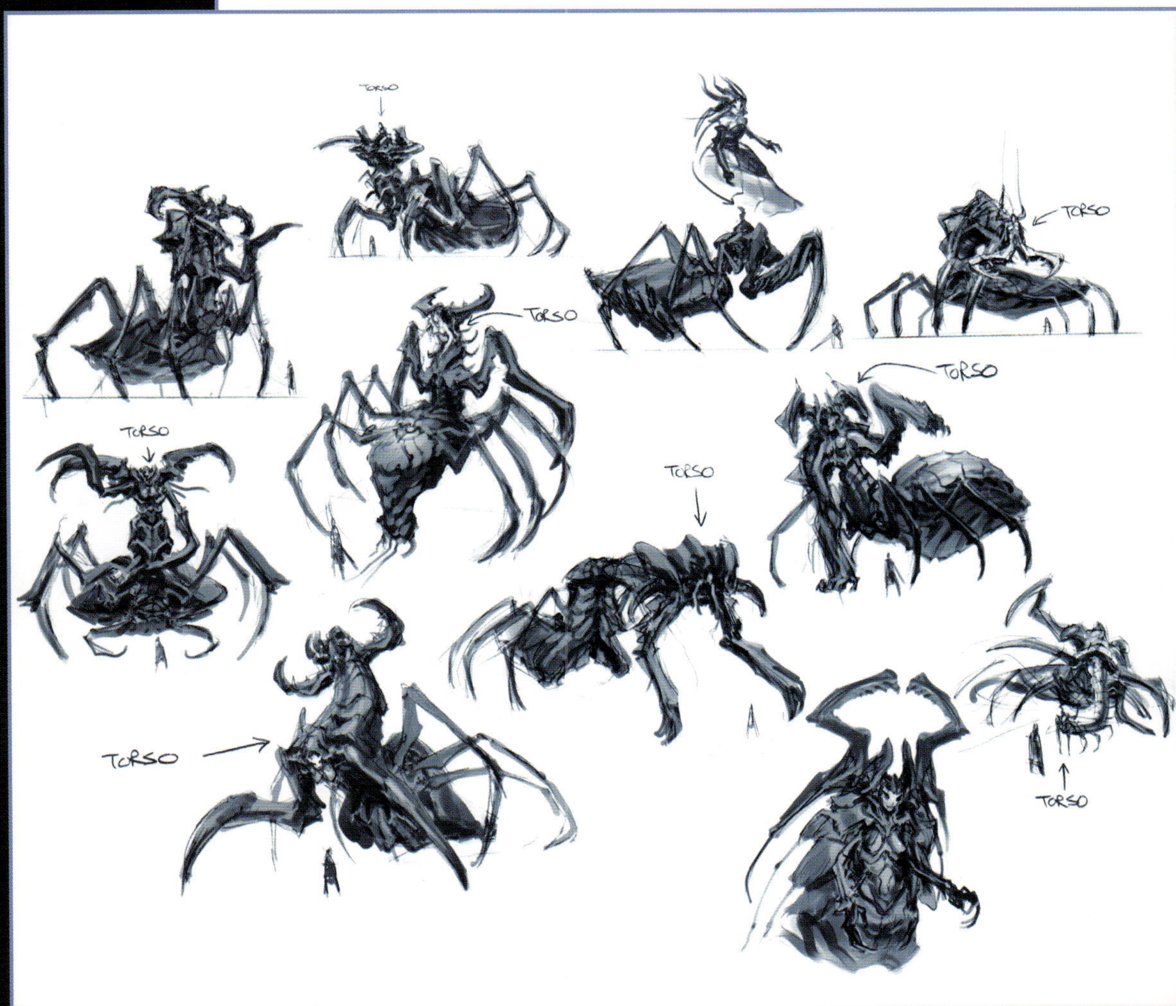

DEVELOPMENT SKETCHES

Tiamat

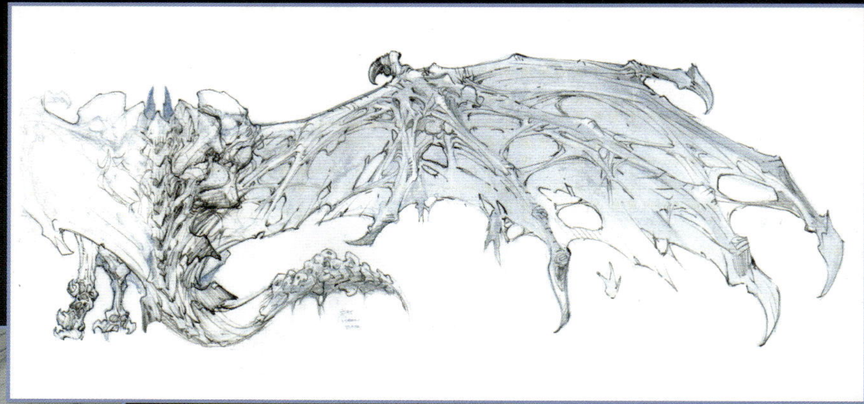

REAR WING DESIGN

HEAD DESIGN

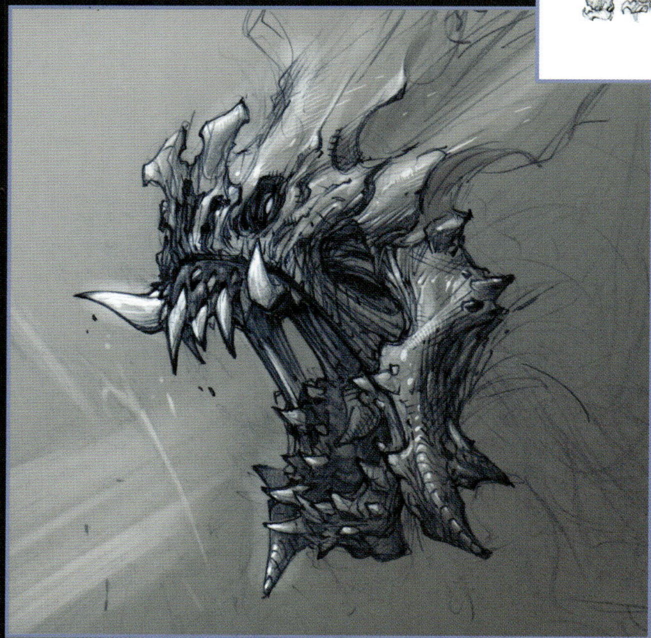

Among the Destroyer's feared Chosen, there are none more savage or sadistic than Tiamat, the Dusk Queen. This monstrous, bat-winged demon lurks in the shadows of the Twilight Cathedral, once-sacred ruins now littered with the rotting carcasses of her prey.

I have seen her foul jaws shred flesh to bloody ribbons, and her club-like tail shatter skulls. But, far worse, I have heard the screams of Tiamat's less fortunate victims, whose agonies are prolonged with cruel and fiendish torture.

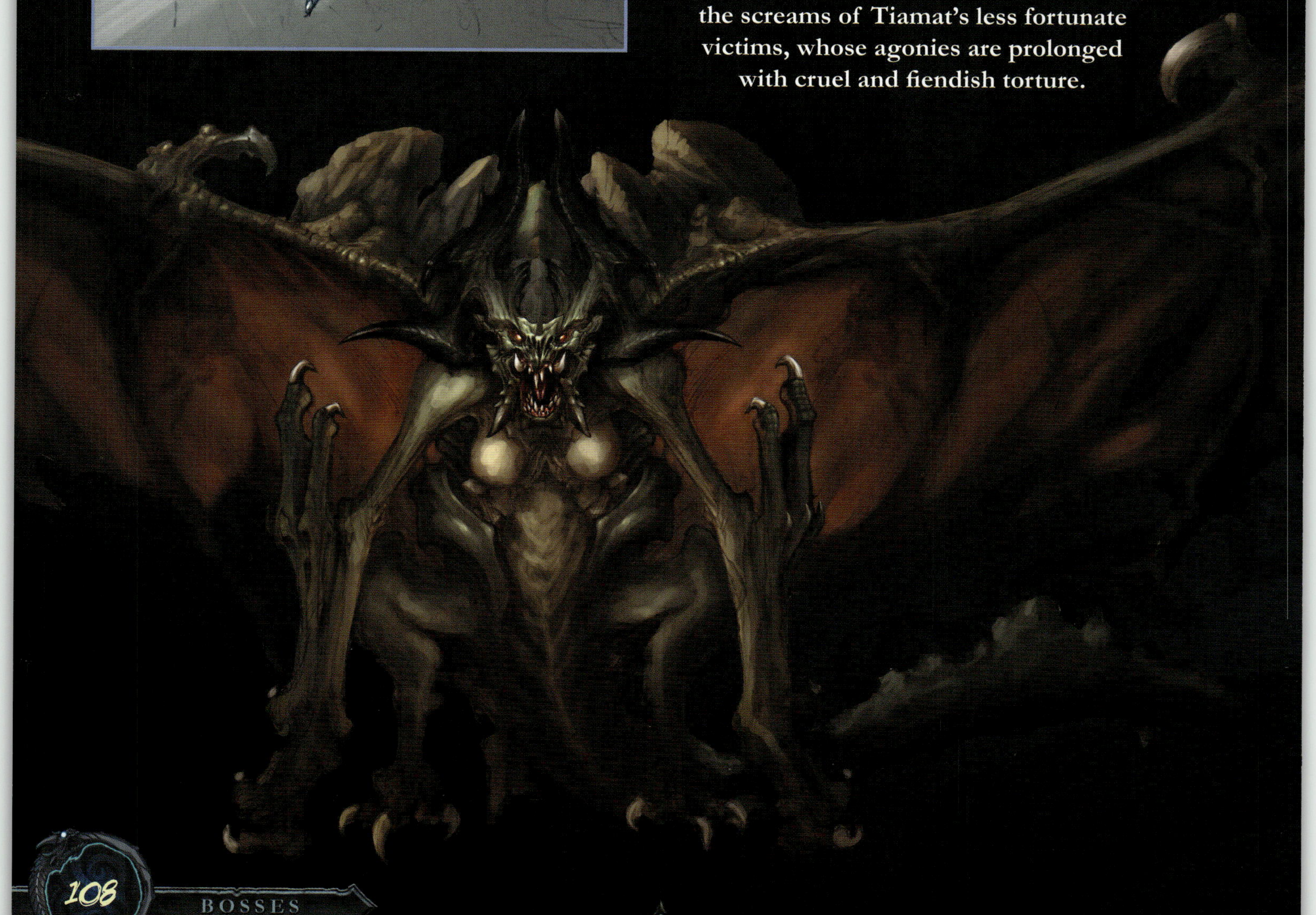

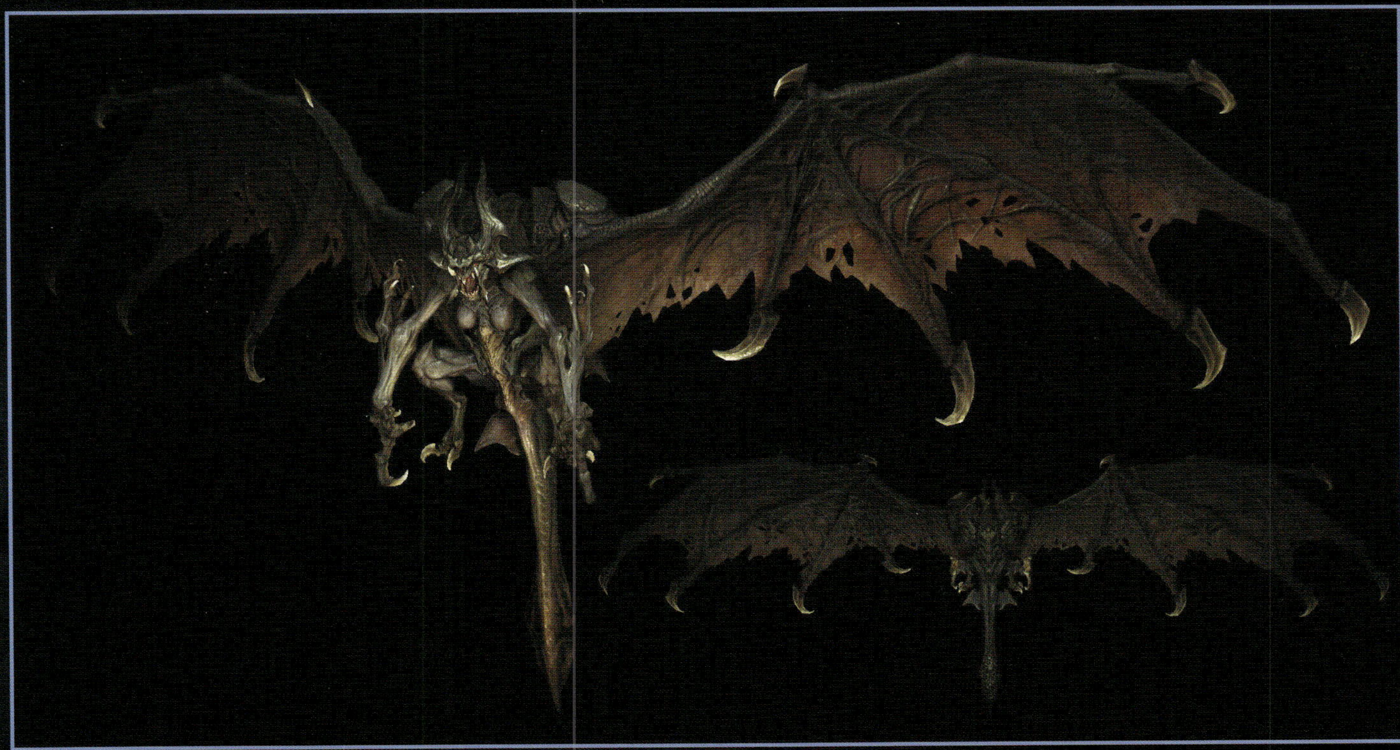

CG TURNAROUNDS

The Stygian

A century of feasting on the remains of man has only whet the appetite of massive demonic worms.

I have watched demon bands enter the wastes, only to disappear amid distant plumes of ash and razor fins. The half-eaten survivors speak of craggy skin that blunts even the sharpest blade, and terrifying mouths that open like black holes. The perverse pleasure in their voices when they describe such horrors…it is no small wonder the demons have raised an arena above the ash, where they can sate their unending bloodlust.

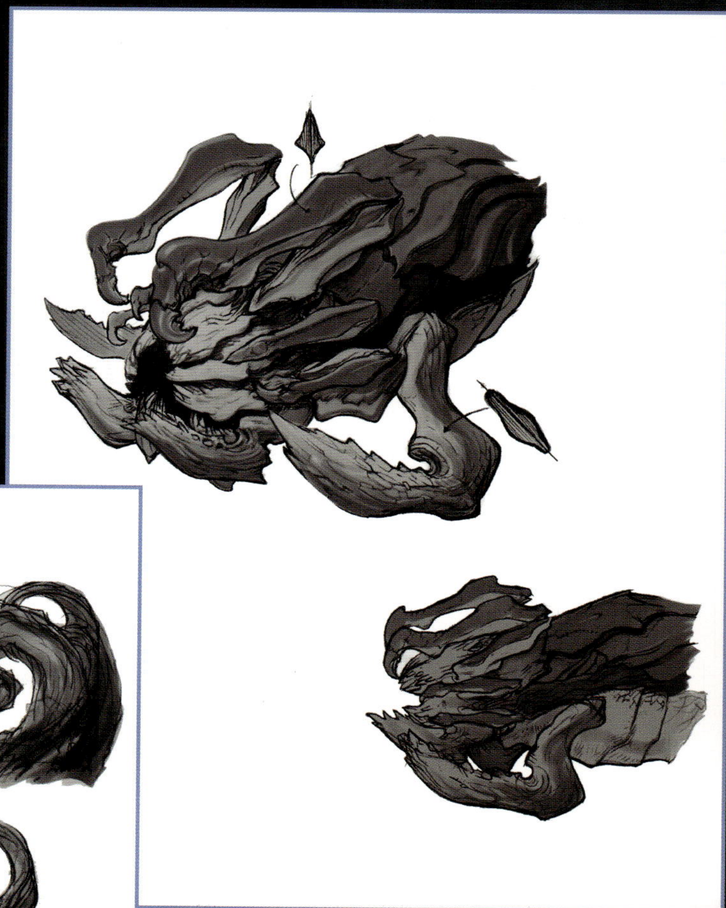

HEAD CONCEPTS

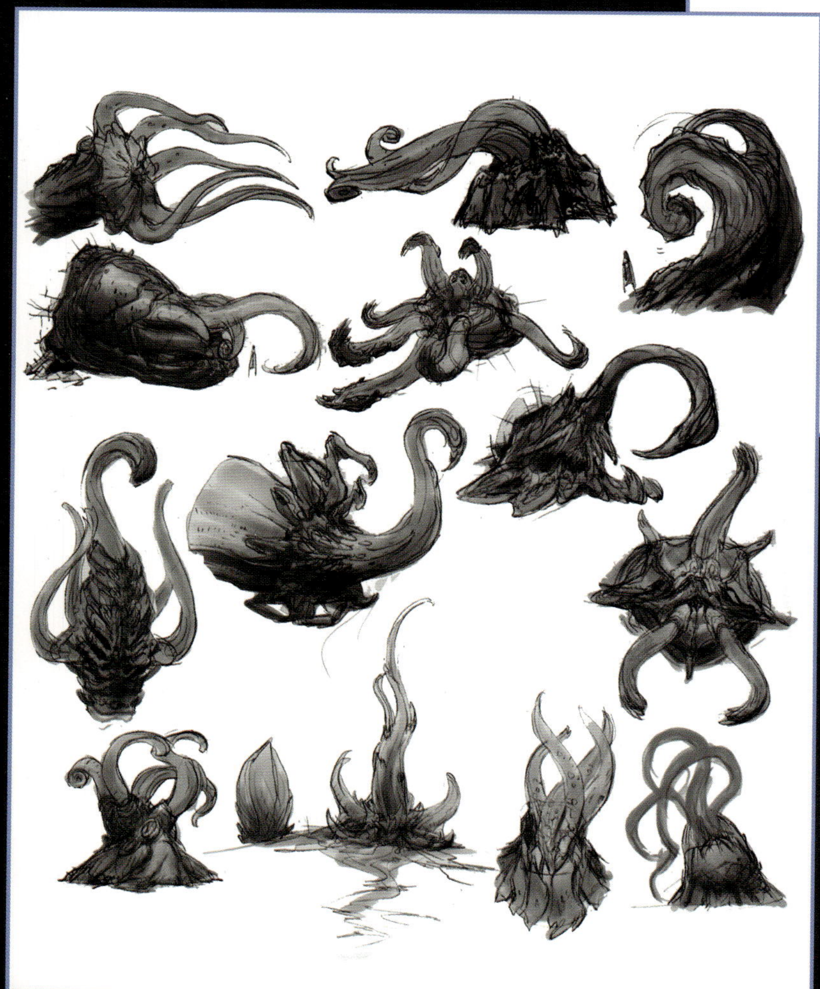

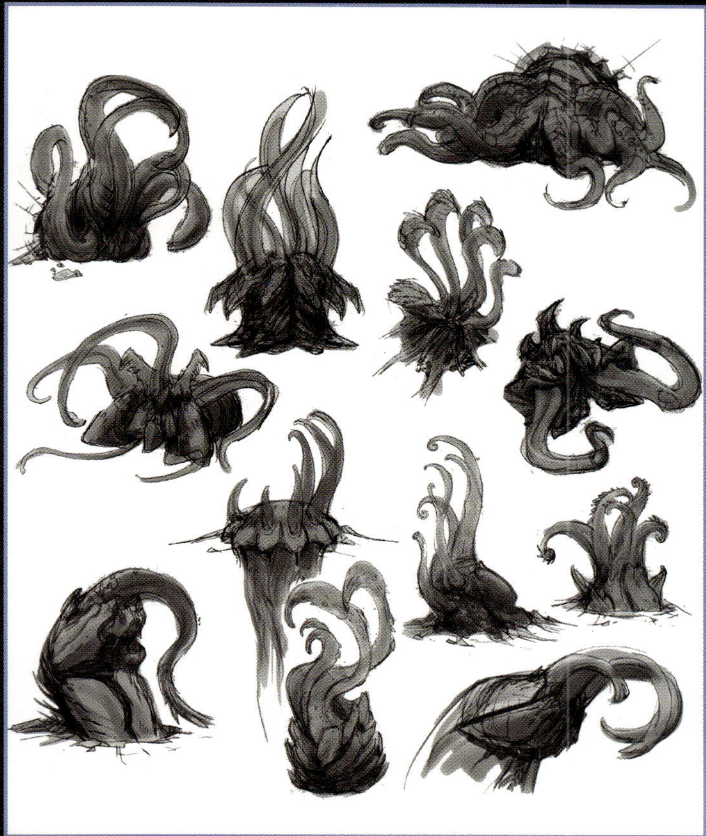

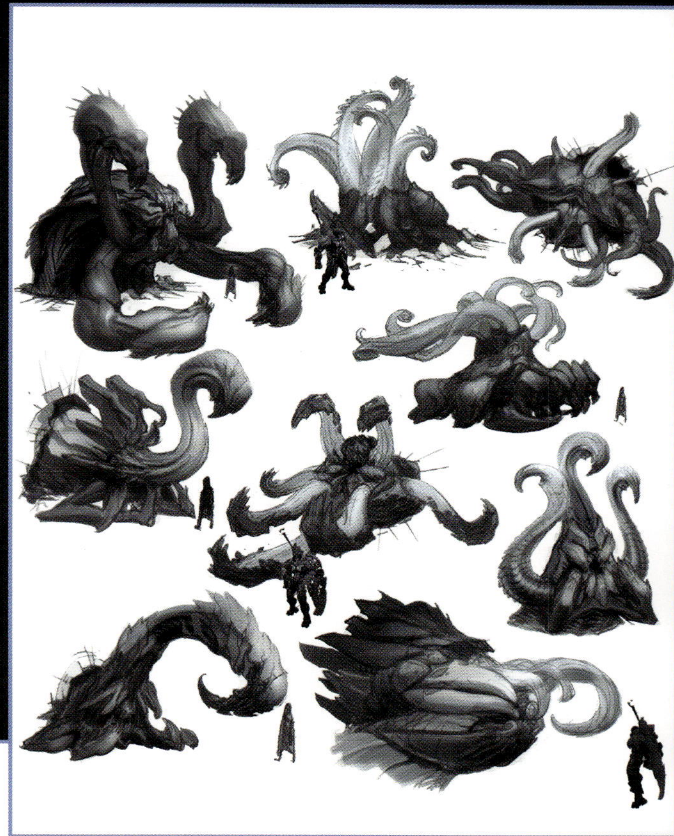

DEVELOPMENT SKETCHES

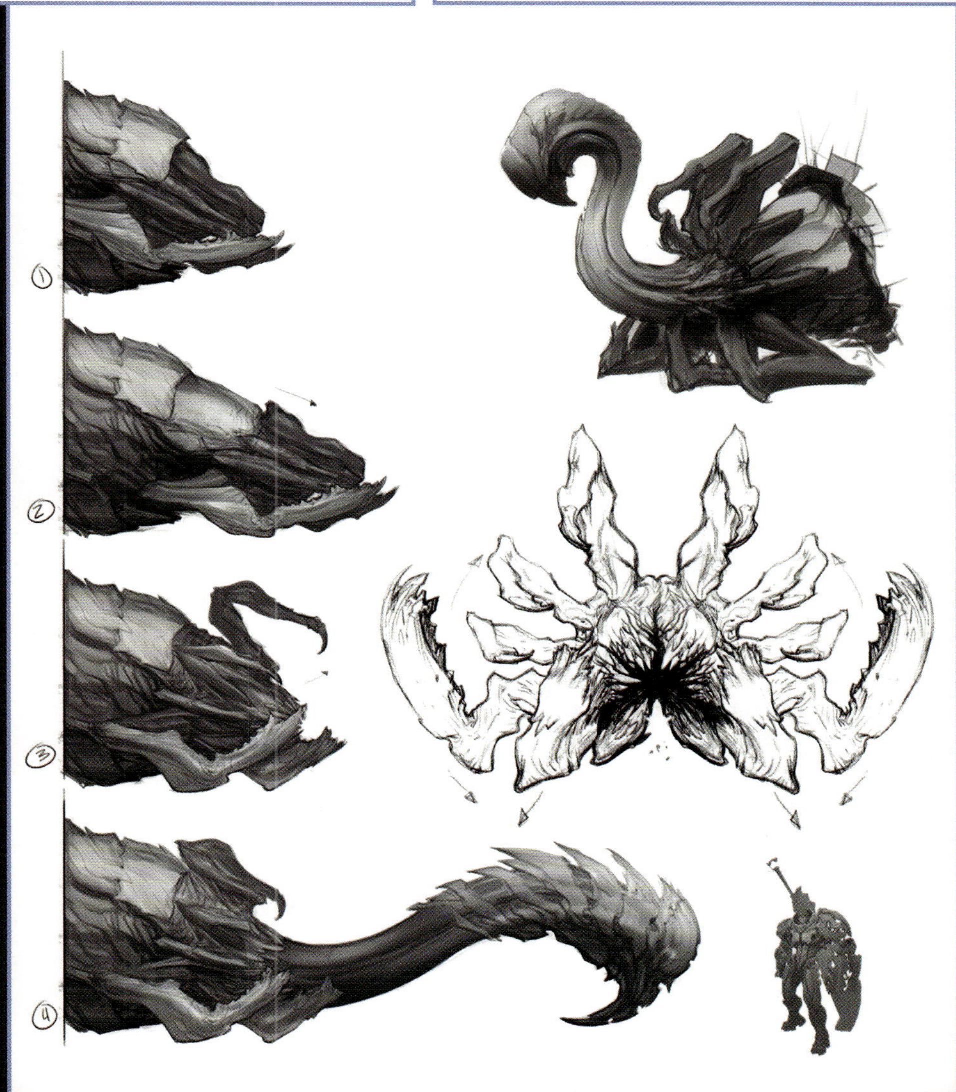

Straga

The demon Straga has long been known as a brawny, dimwitted behemoth. But I never took true measure of his strength until both Abaddon and the Horseman War were crushed beneath his fists. I did not fare much better.

Straga revels in his new role as the Destroyer's champion, a one-demon phalanx between the Dark Prince and all who would oppose him. Chained beneath the shadow of Straga's monstrous bulk, I see no escape. Who could defeat such a fearless, bone-splintering force of nature?

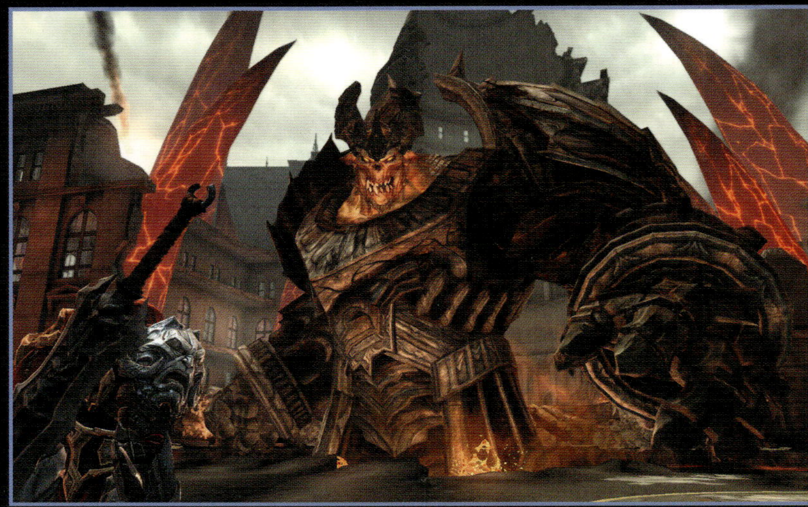

FINAL IN-GAME DESIGN

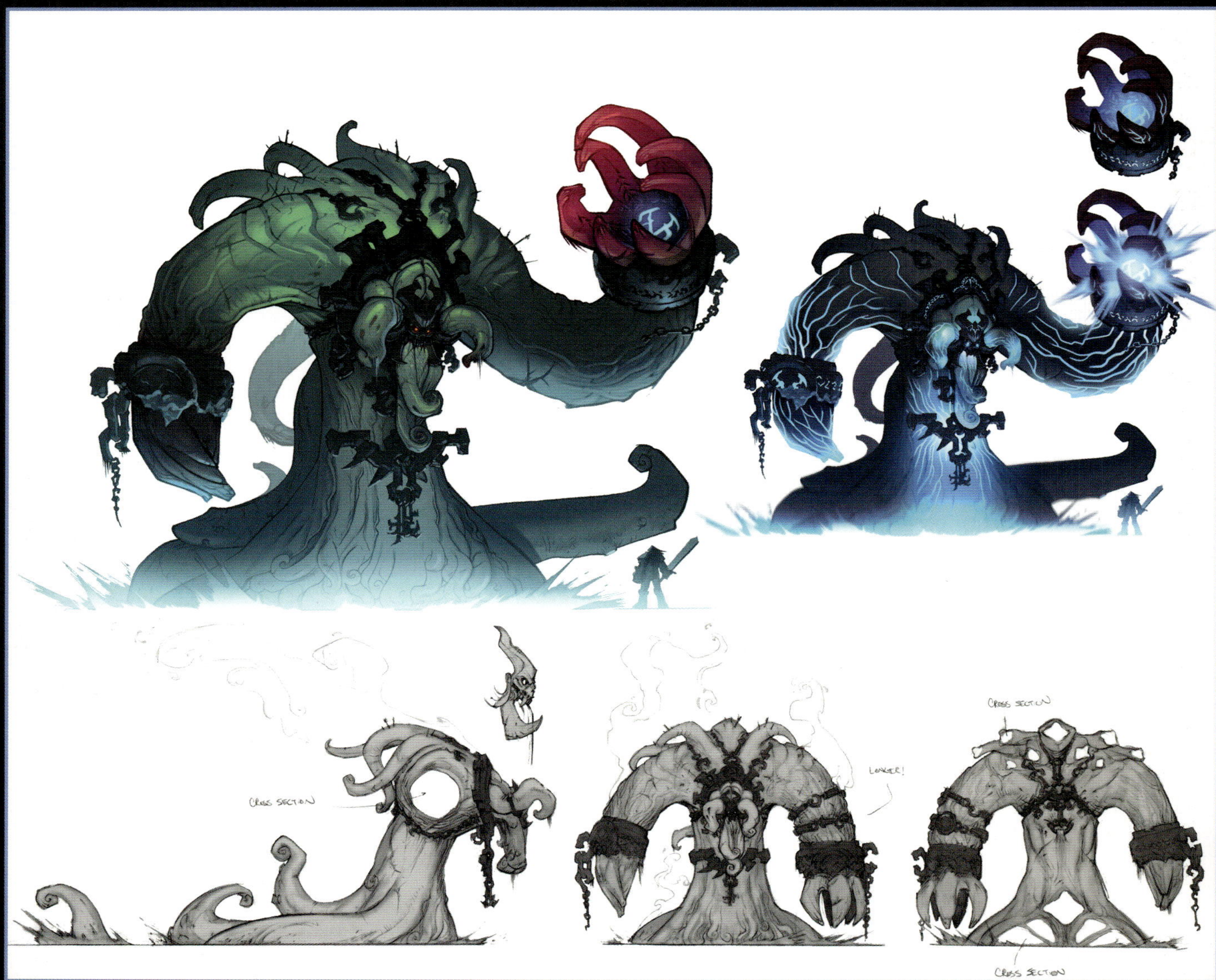

DEVELOPMENT ART

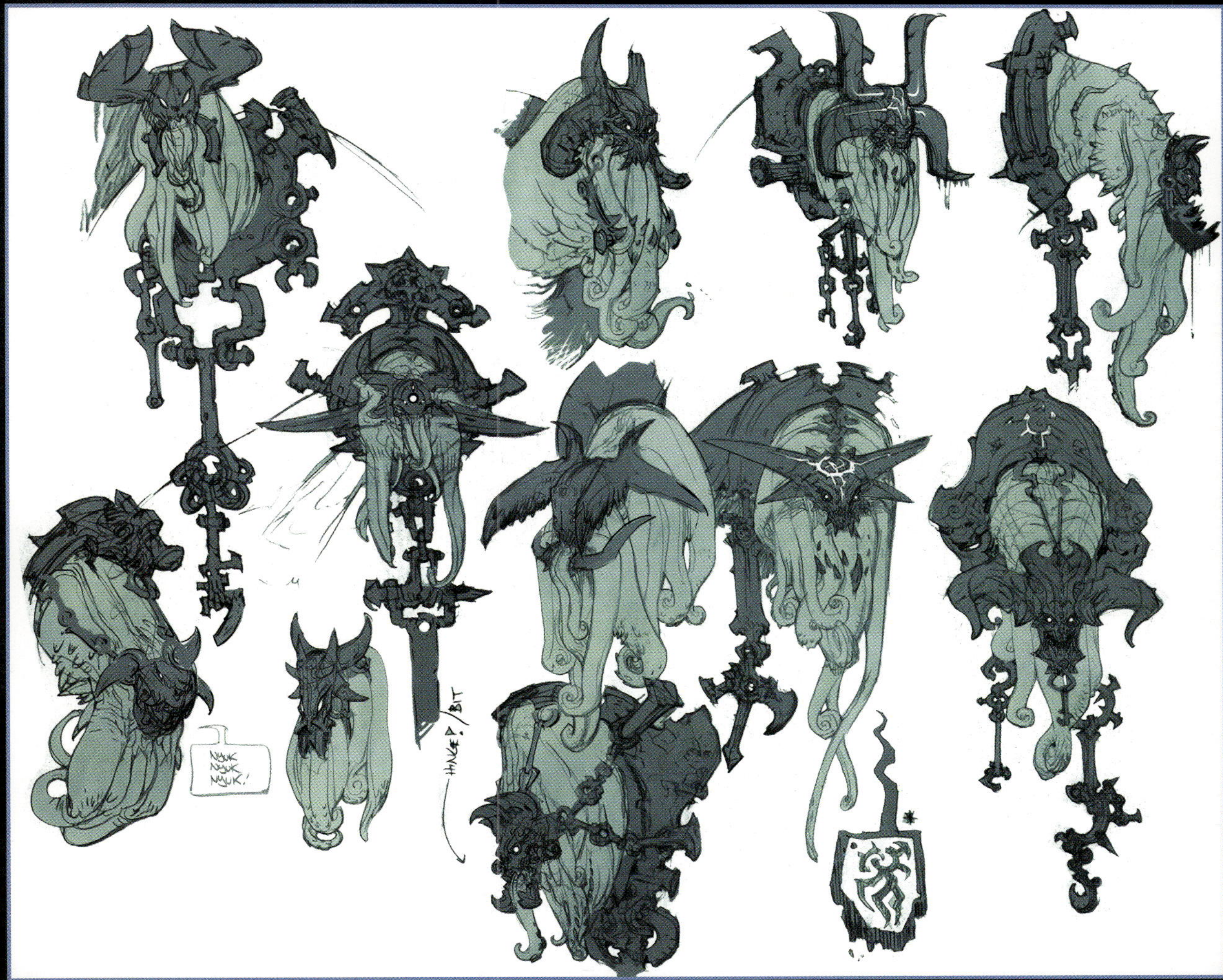

DEVELOPMENT SKETCHES

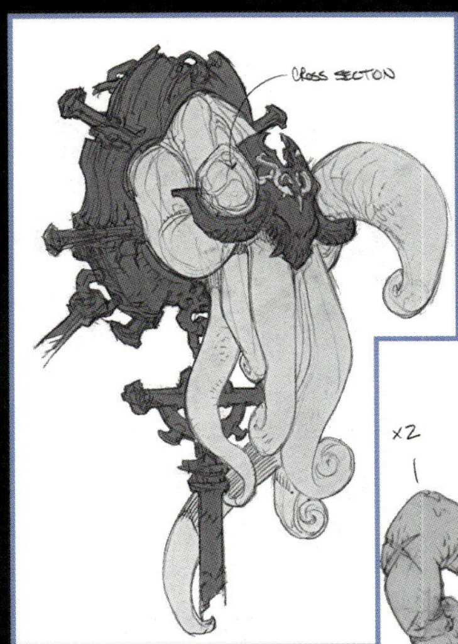

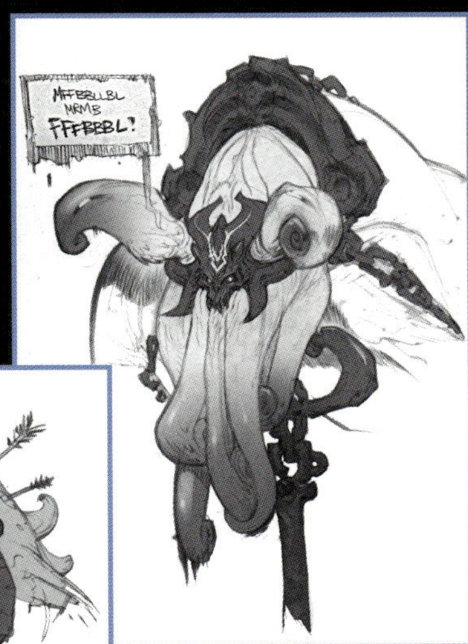

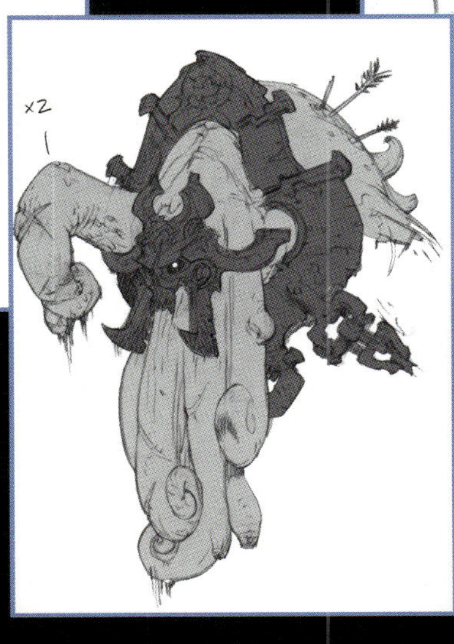

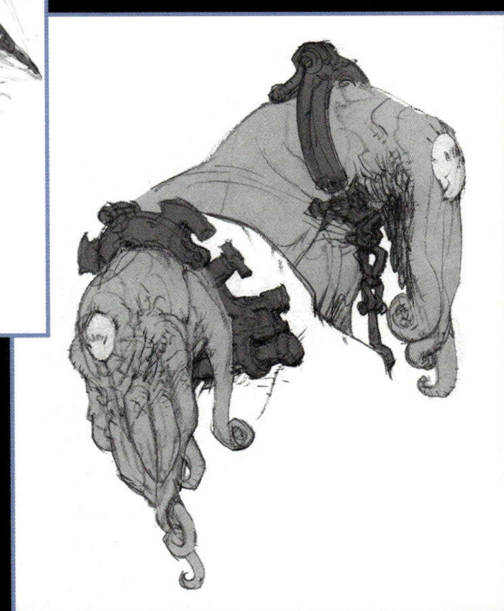

HEAD CONCEPTS

The Destroyer

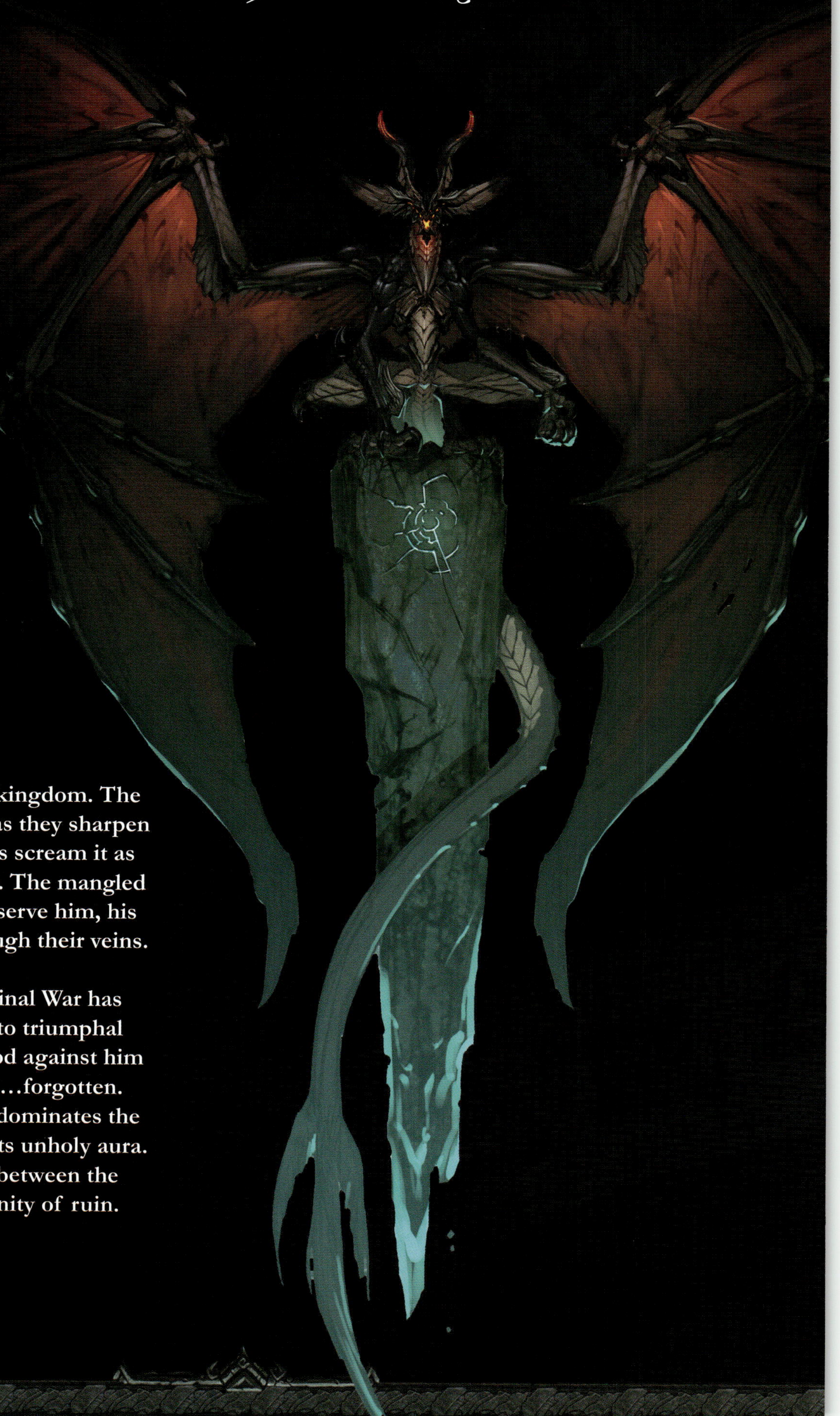

This is the Destroyer's kingdom. The demons howl his name as they sharpen their knives. The angels scream it as their flesh is shorn away. The mangled corpses of man rise to serve him, his black will coursing through their veins.

Hell's victory in the Final War has carried the Destroyer to triumphal heights. Those who stood against him were slain or shackled…forgotten. Now his Black Throne dominates the horizon, crackling with its unholy aura. I fear nothing stands between the Destroyer and an eternity of ruin.

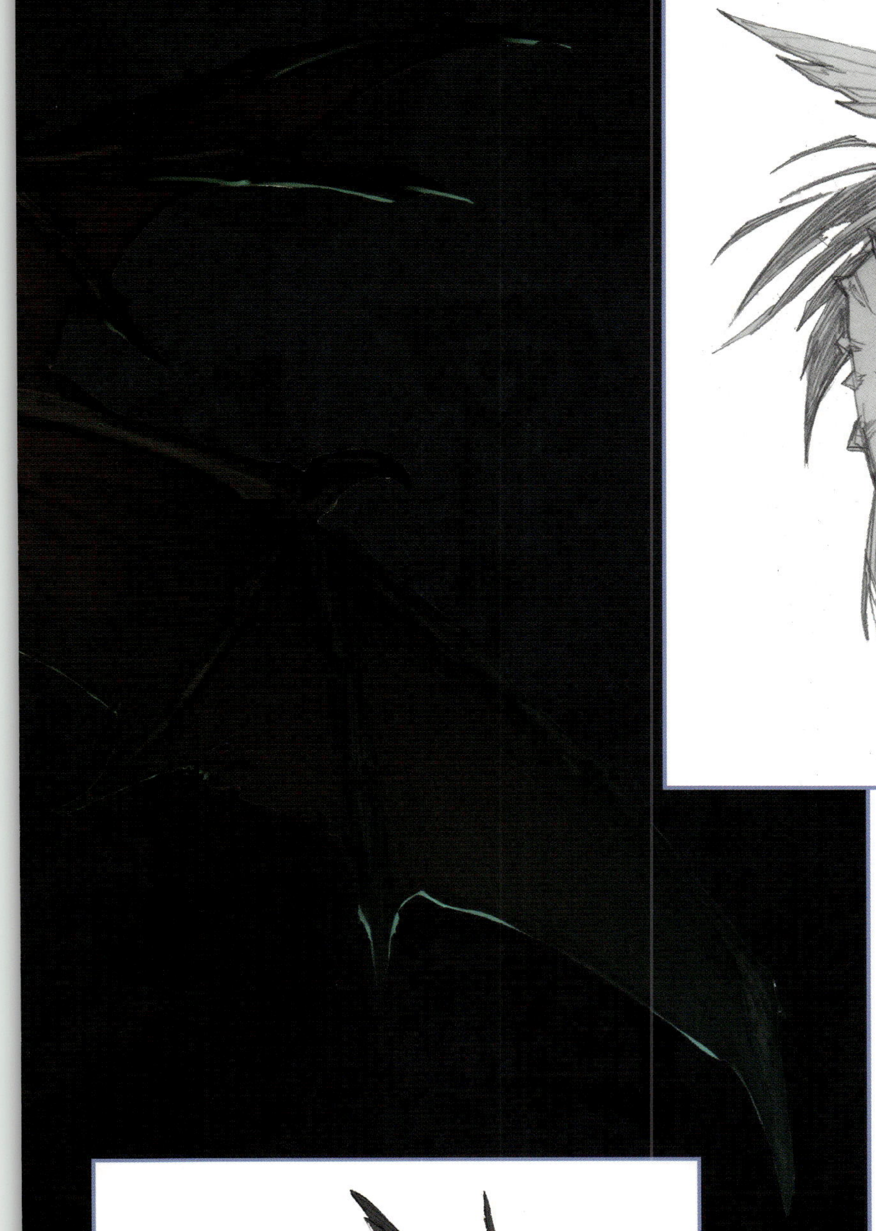

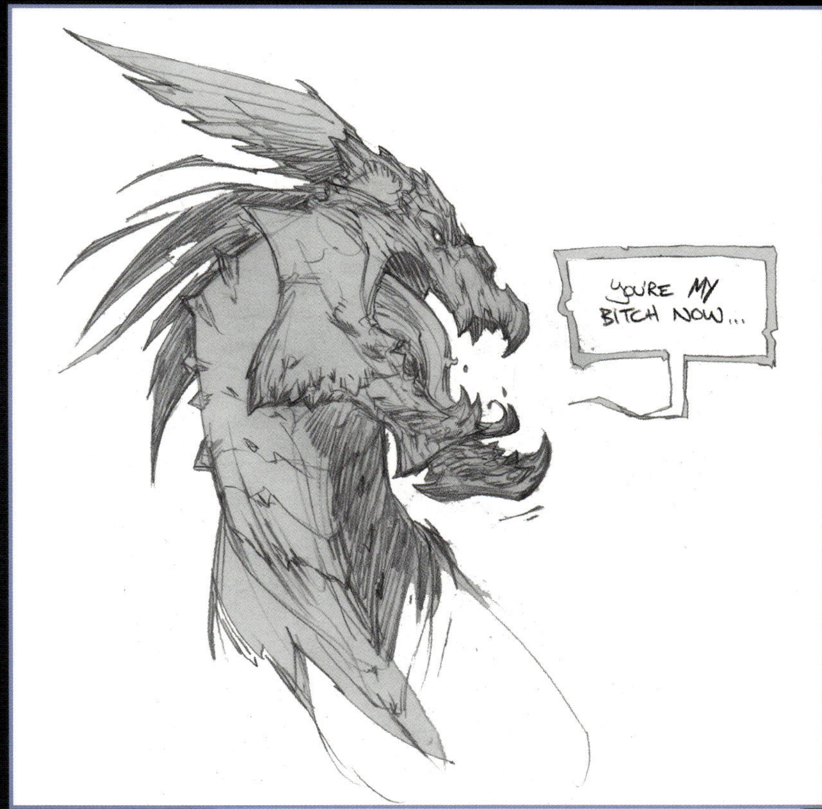

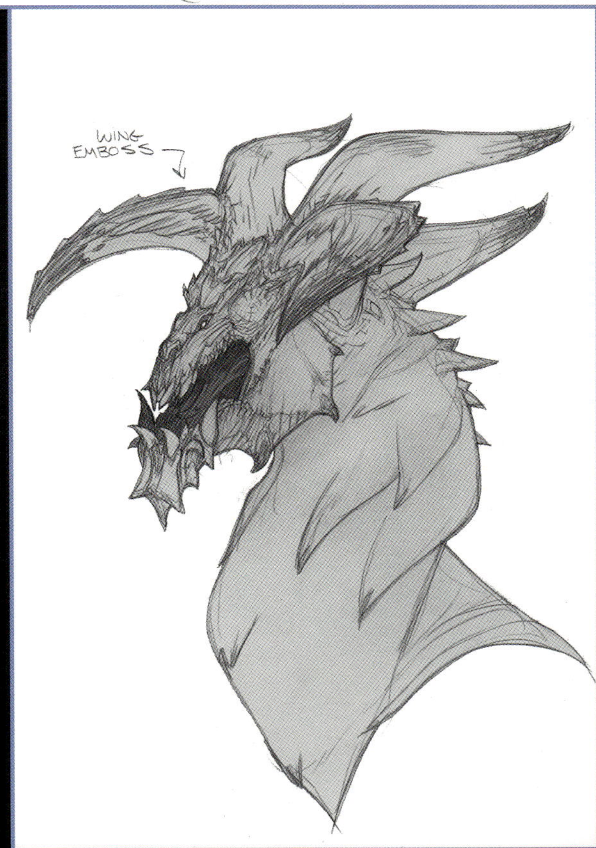

HEAD DESIGNS

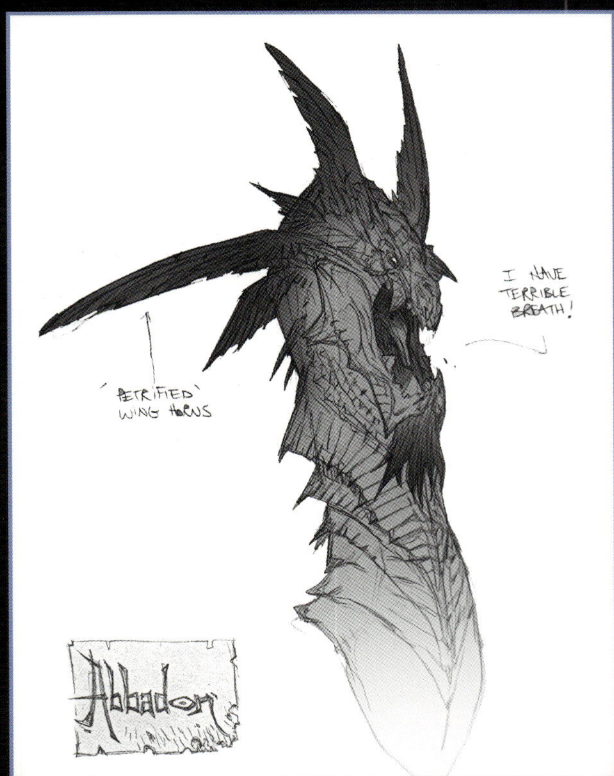

HEAD DESIGN

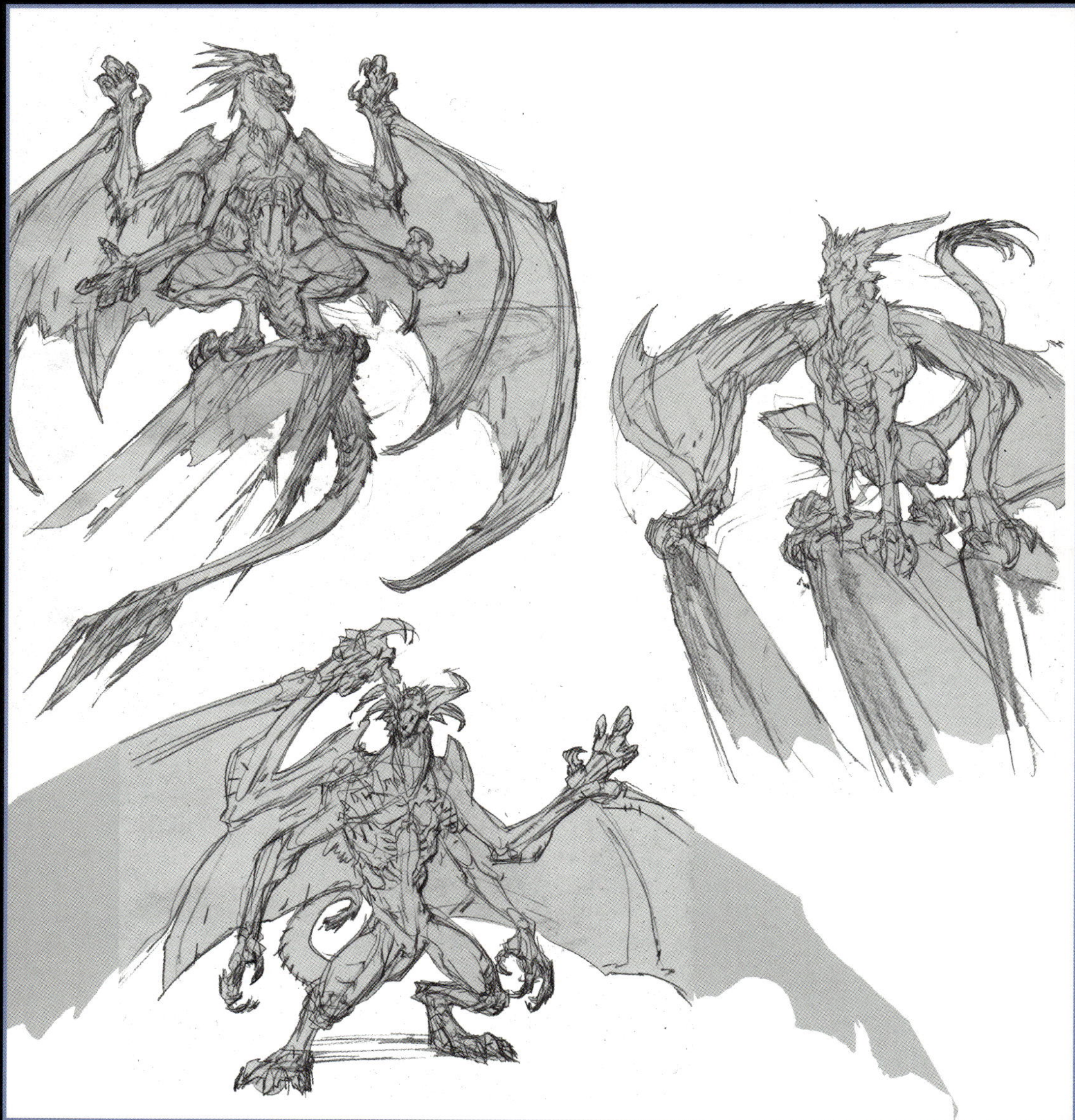

DEVELOPMENT SKETCHES

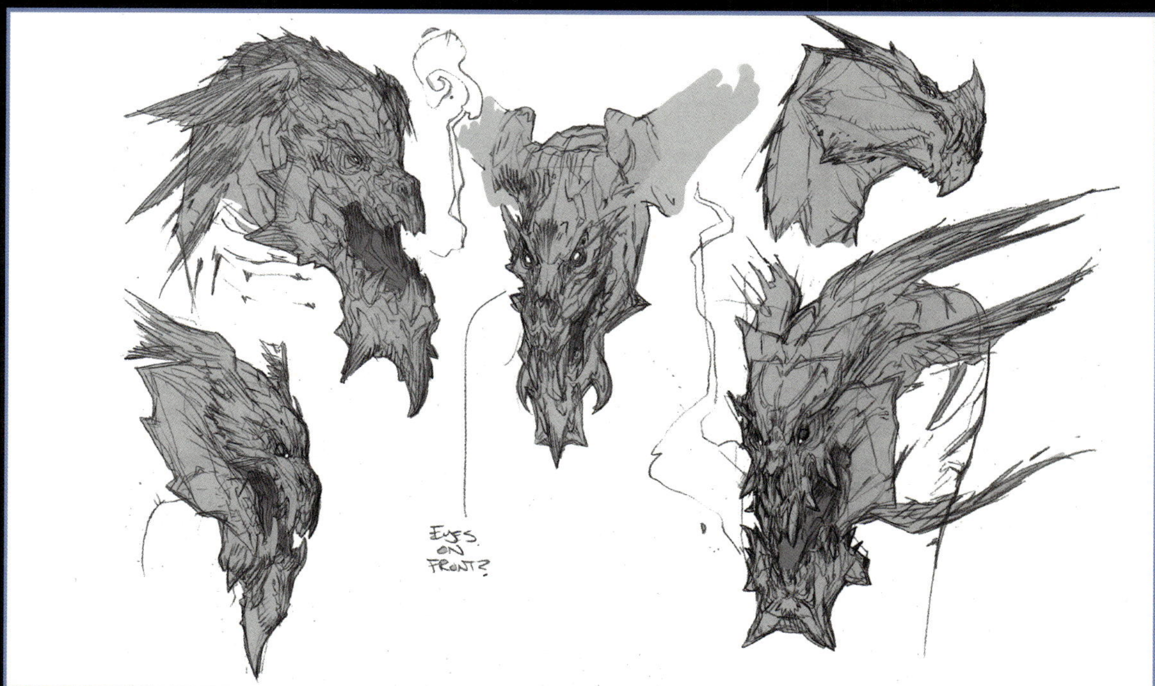

HEAD DESIGNS

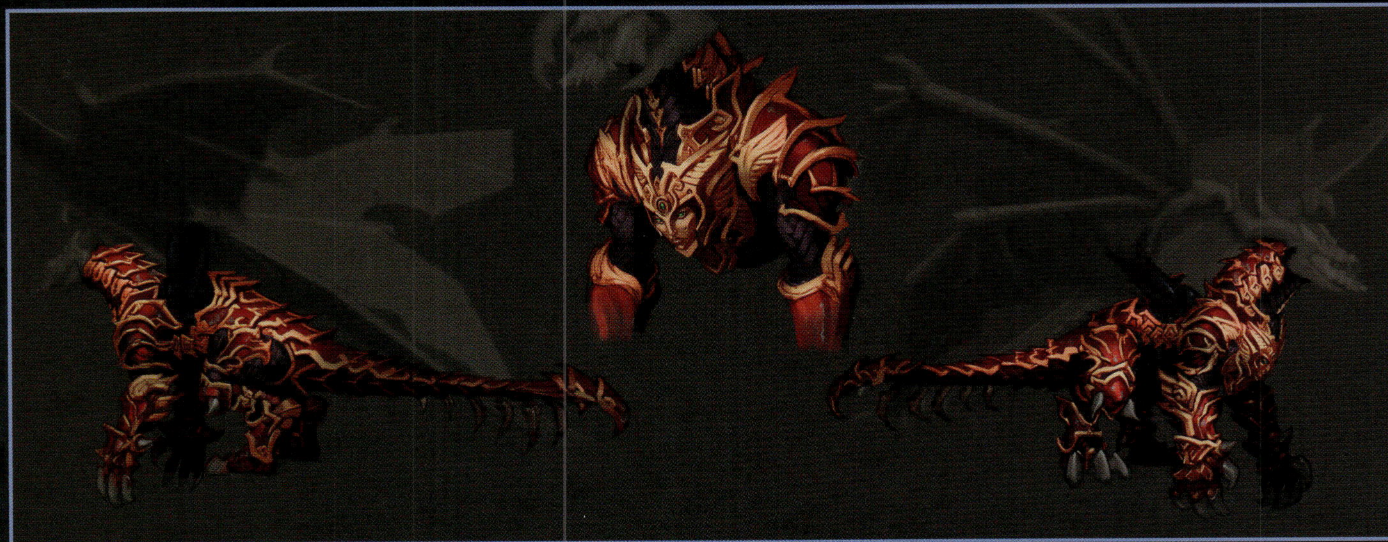

ARMOR CONCEPT

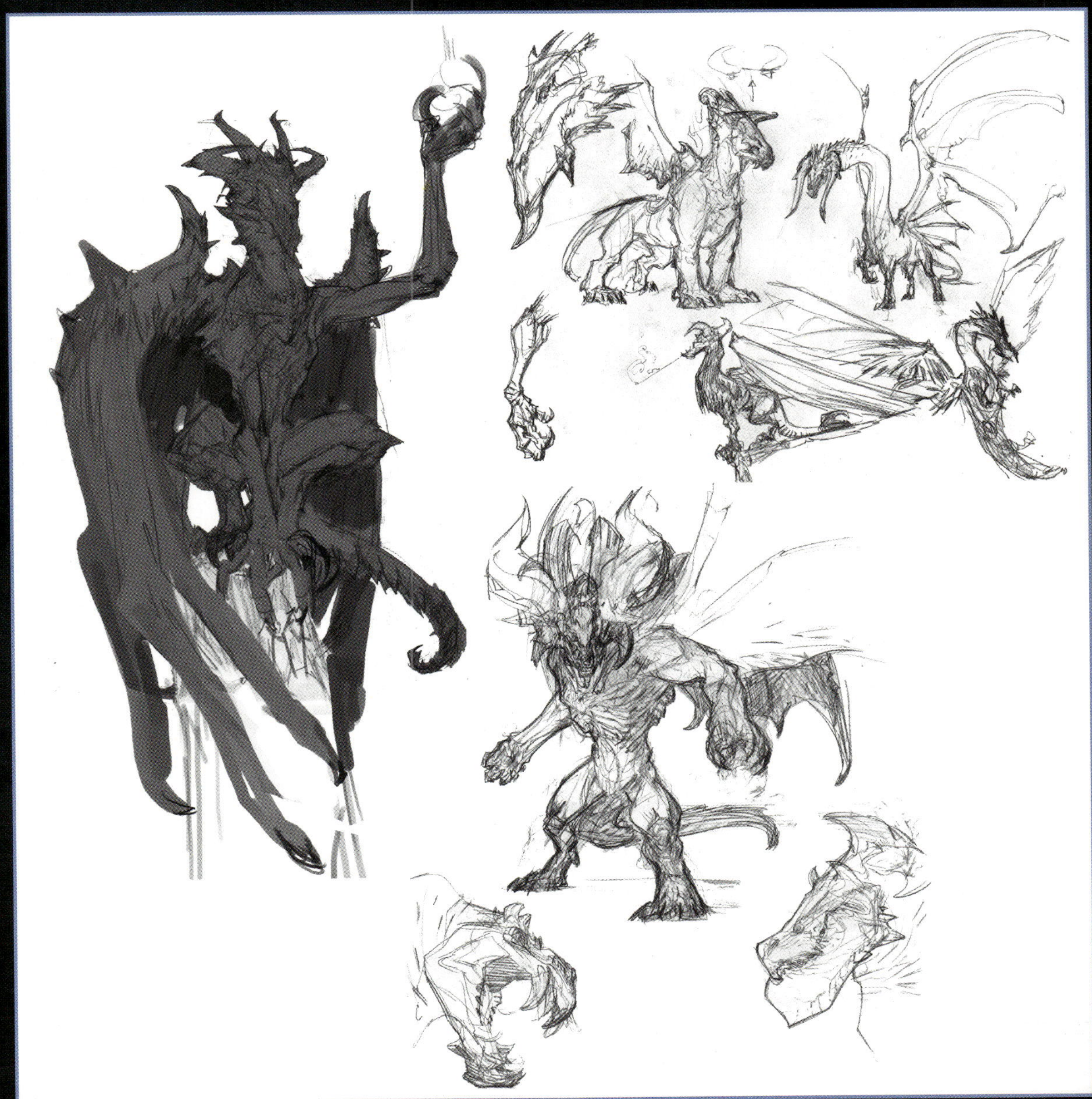

DEVELOPMENT SKETCHES

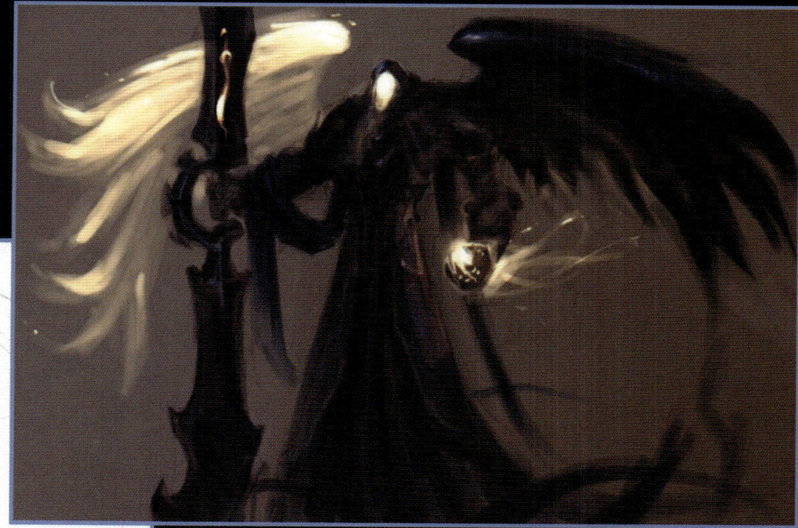

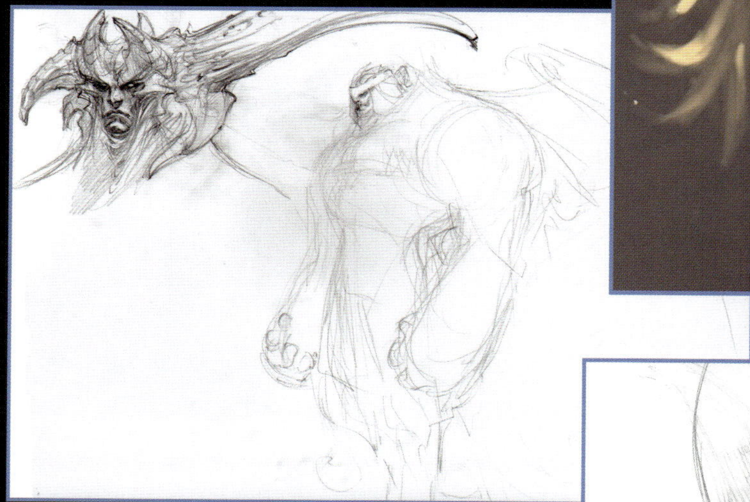

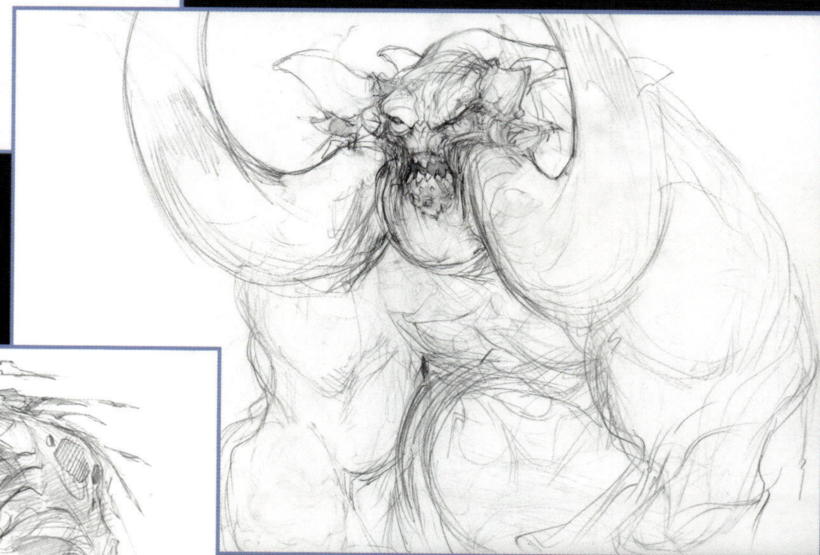

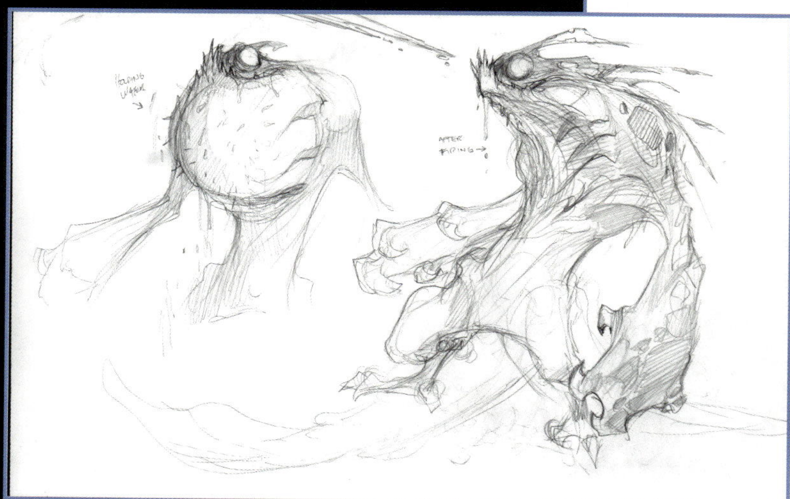

Unused Designs

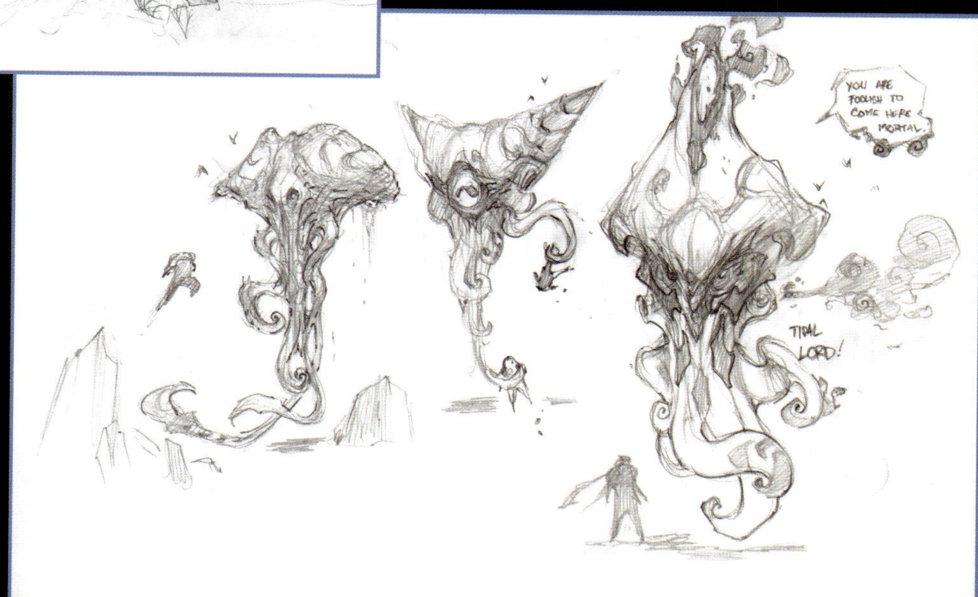

Additional Sketches

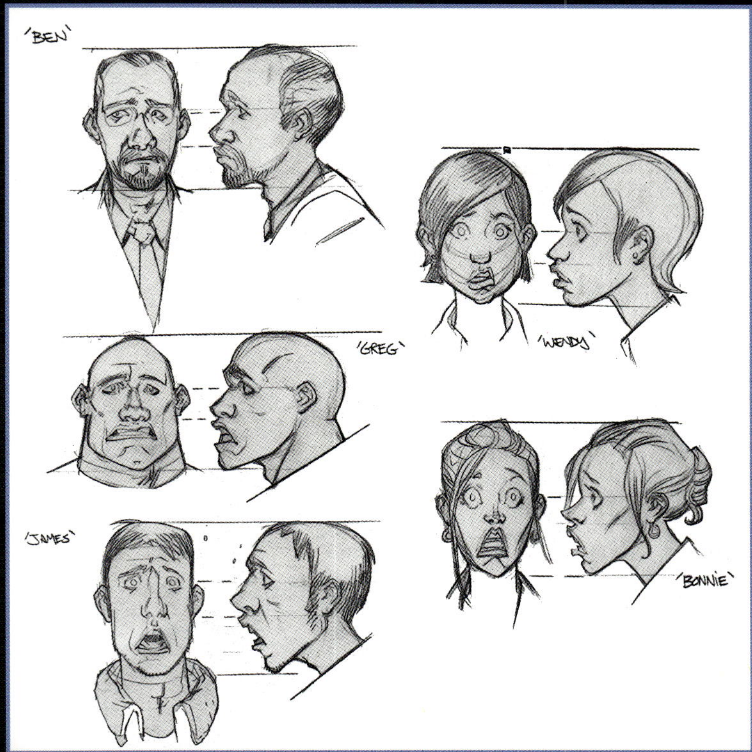

HUMANS

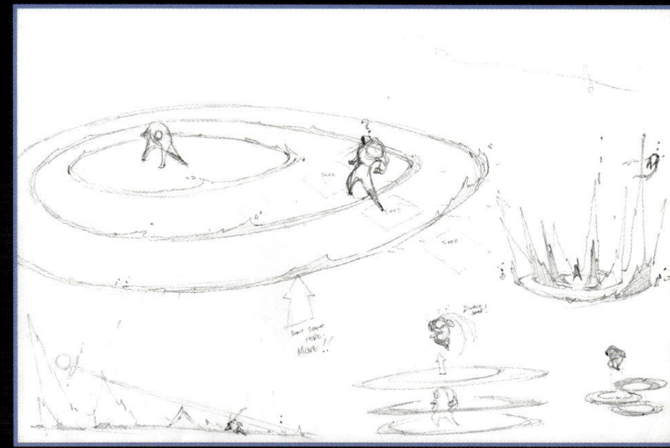

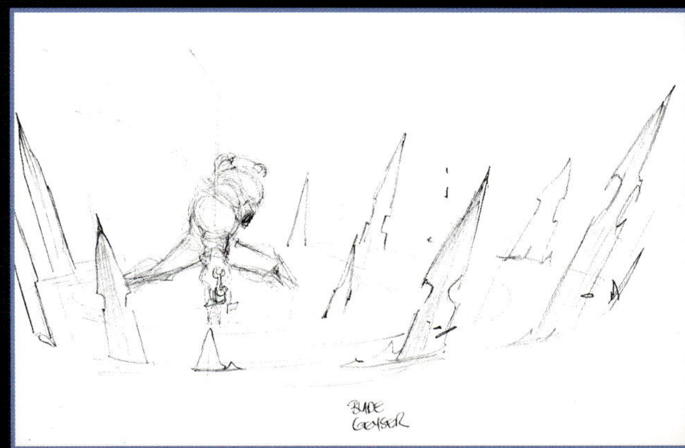

BATTLE CONCEPTS

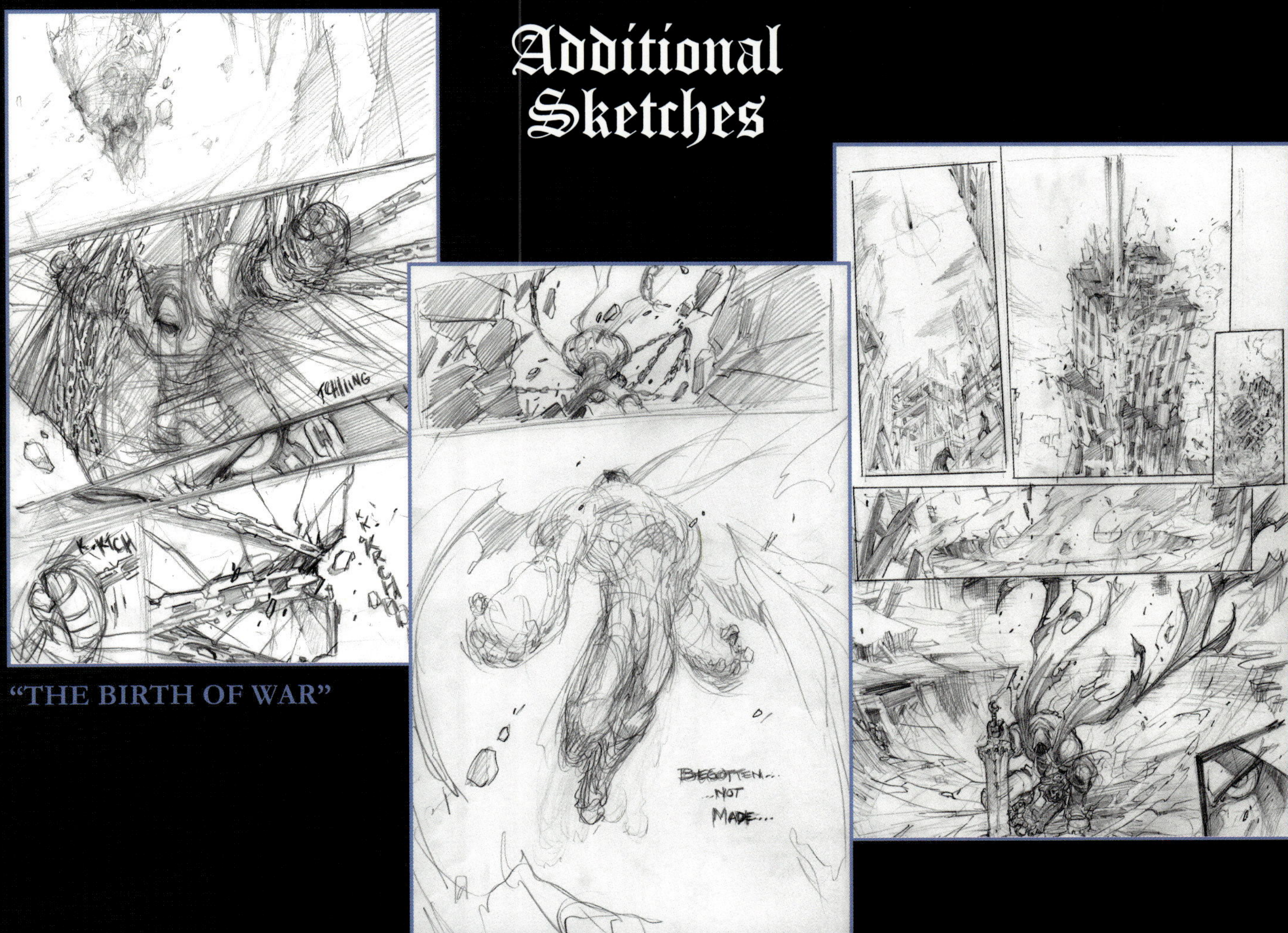

"THE BIRTH OF WAR"

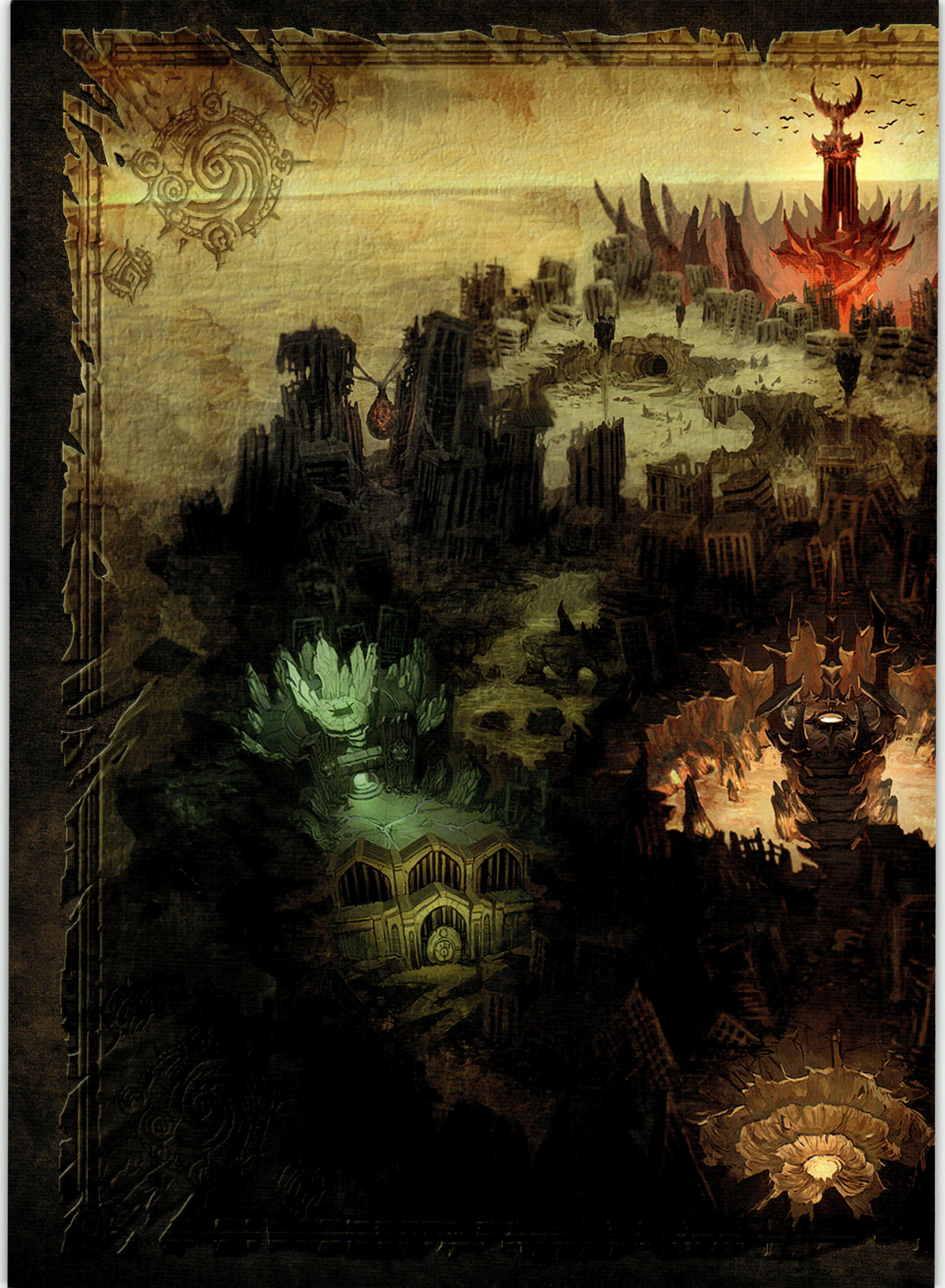

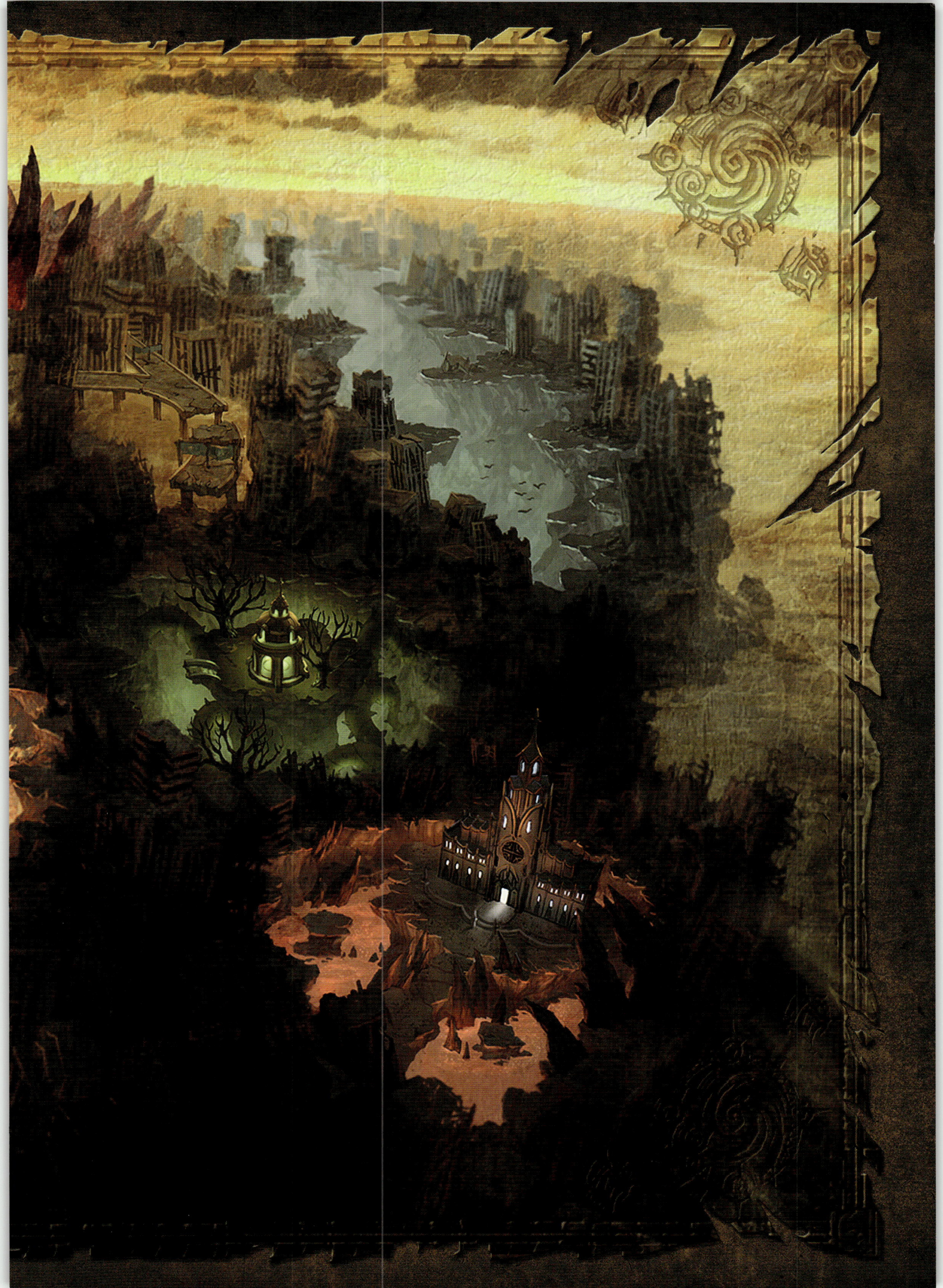

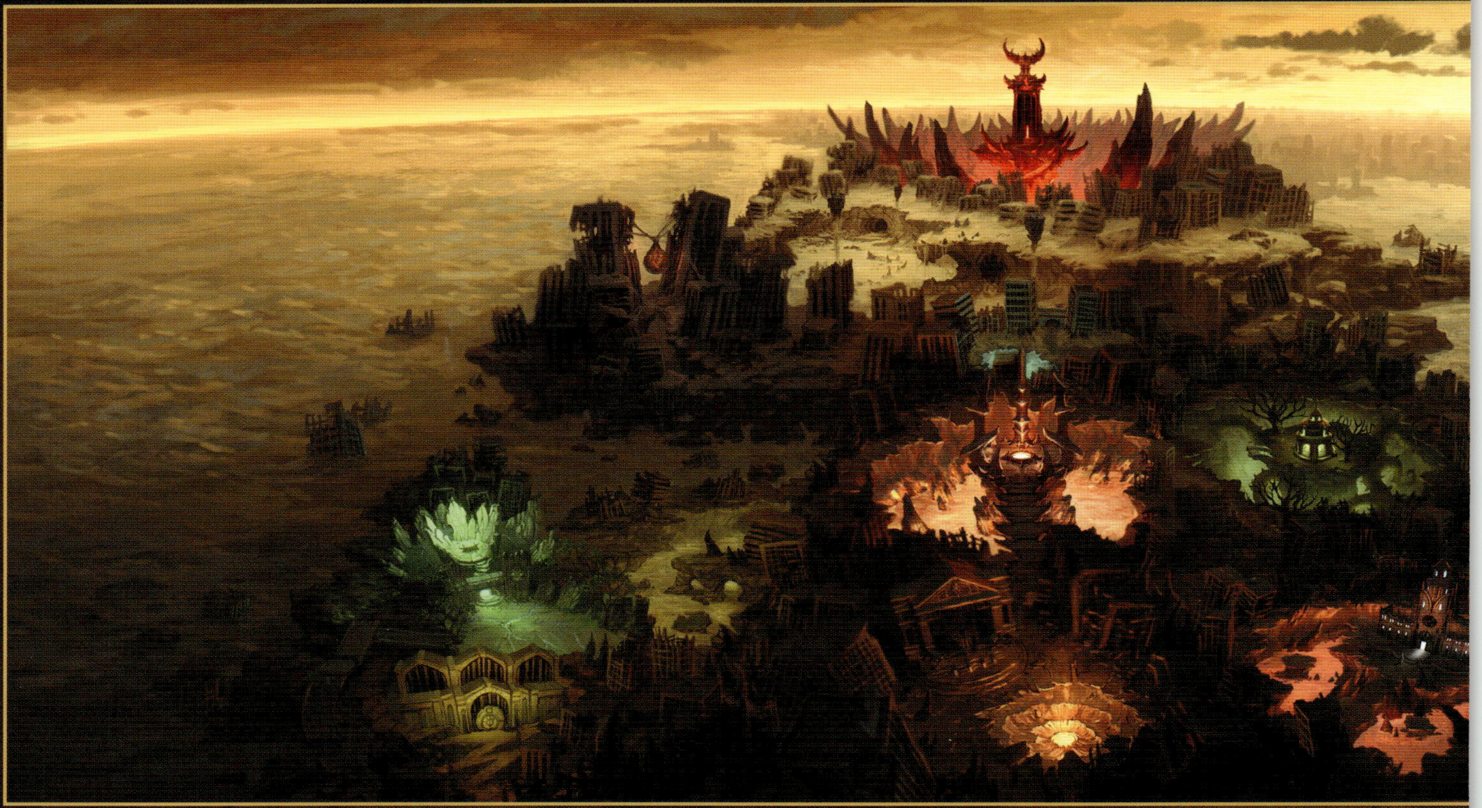

NEAR FINAL MAP ILLUSTRATION

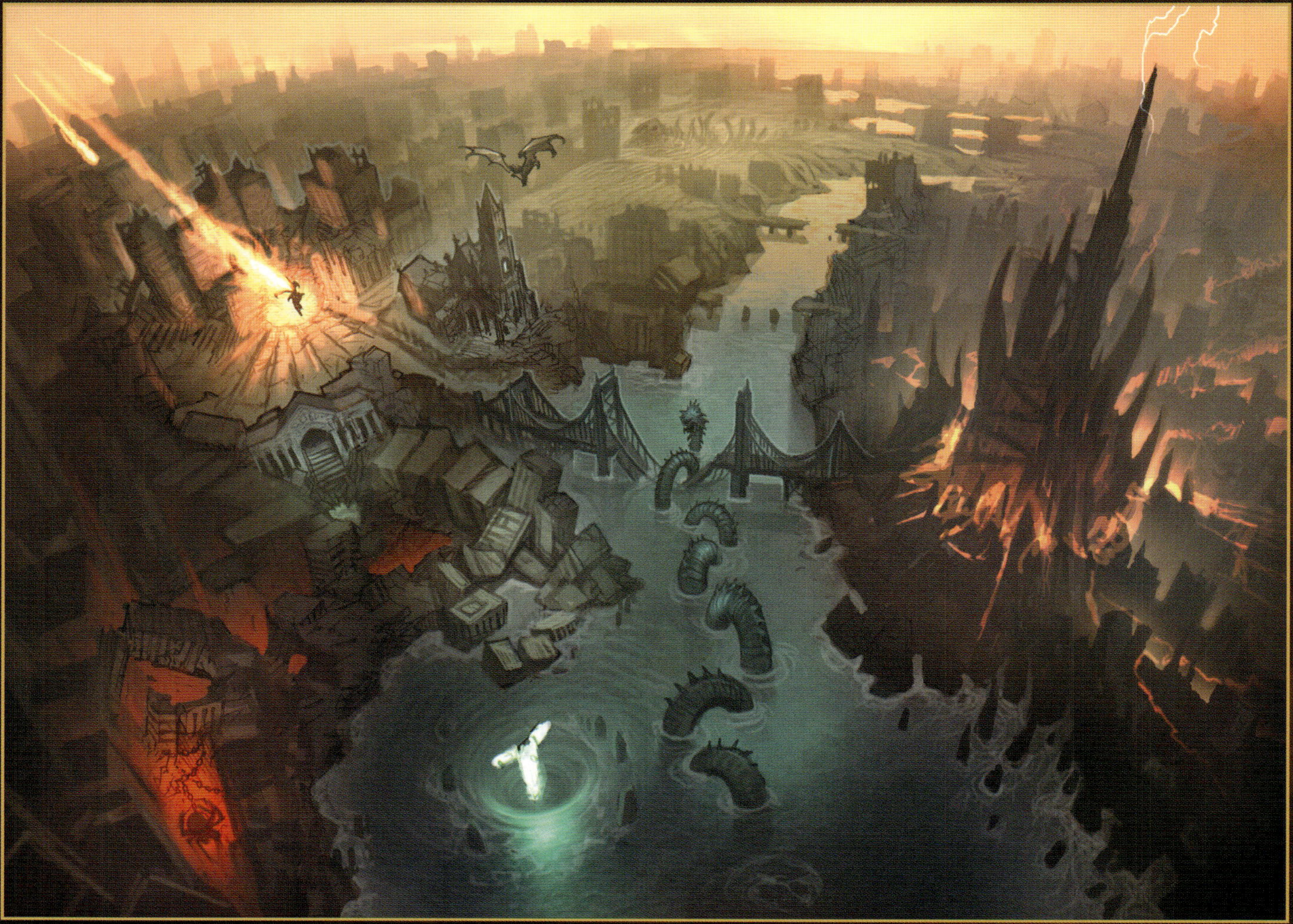

EARLY MAP CONCEPT

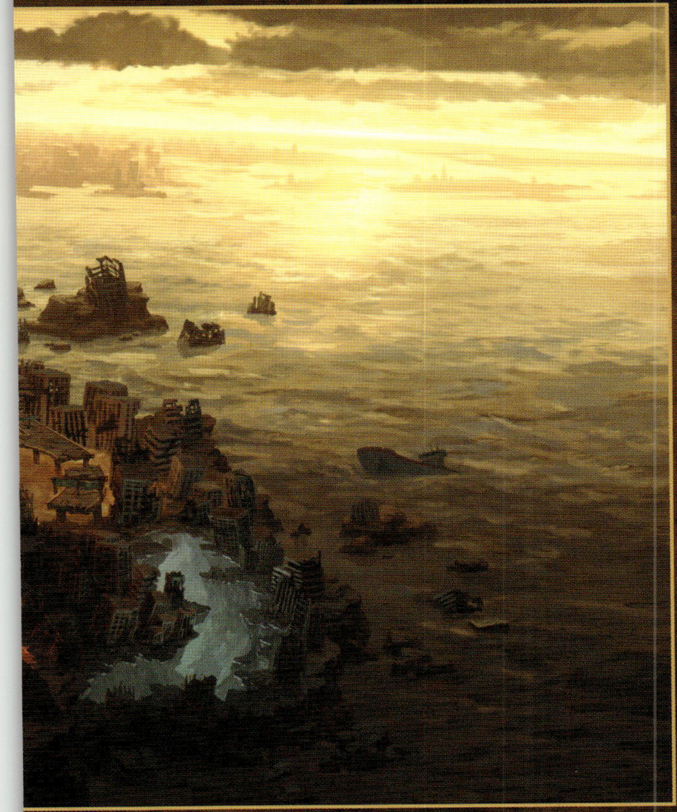

Maps

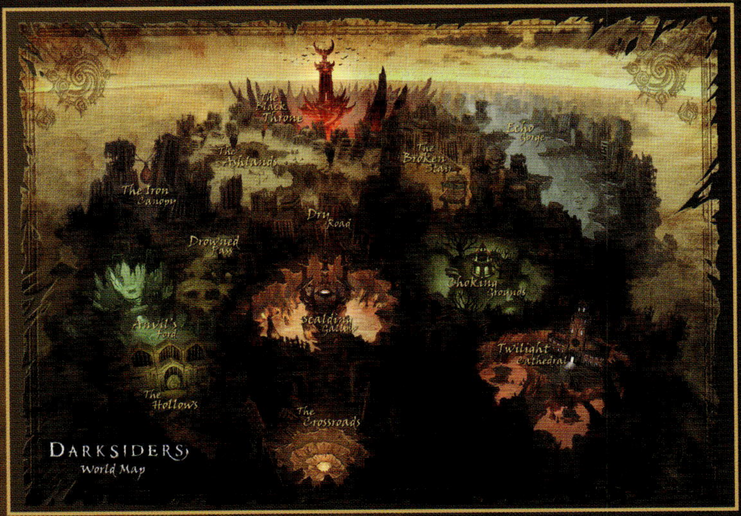

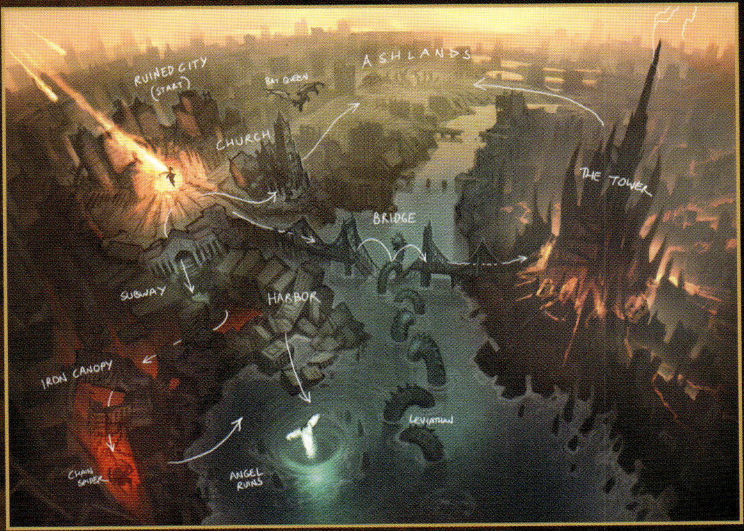

LABELED MAPS

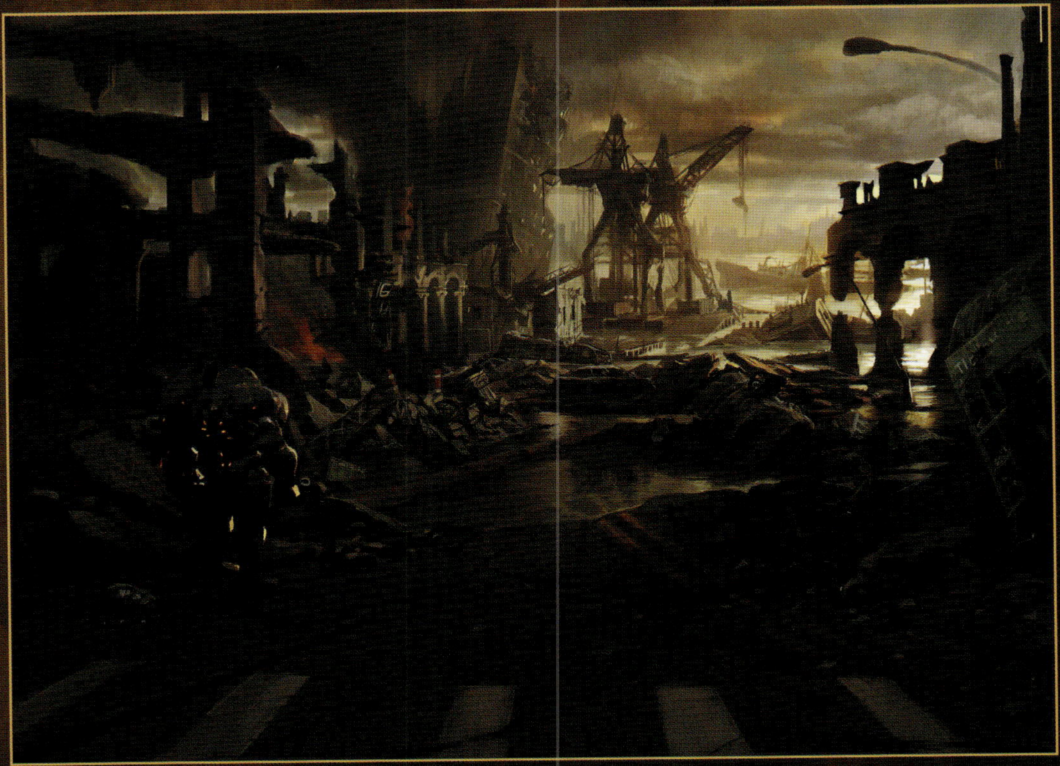

CITY CONCEPT

The Crossroads

It is the sight of the familiar, turned a perverse shadow of itself, which makes the Crossroads truly horrifying. Here, buildings that were once hotels, museums, and apartments are now tombs which spill their dead onto the sundered pavement. The Wicked continually roam the streets, still oozing gore after a hundred years. Scattered around them are impassable thickets of black stalagmites that smell suspiciously like burning blood. Many parts of the city have been corroded by pure evil or claimed by howling demons—but it is at the Crossroads where Hell and Earth truly meet.

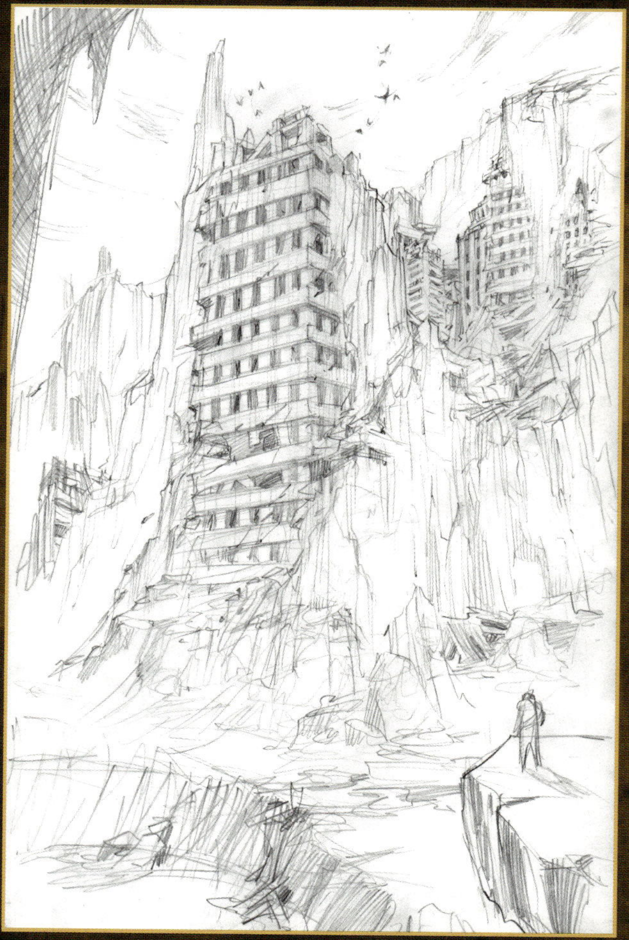

CLIFF BUILDING SKETCH

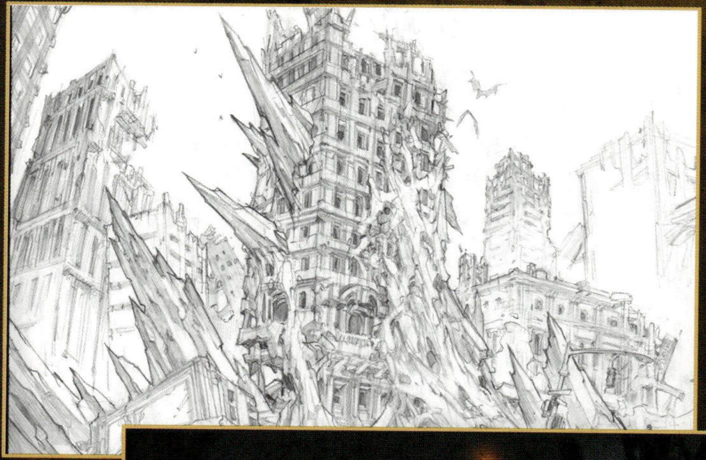

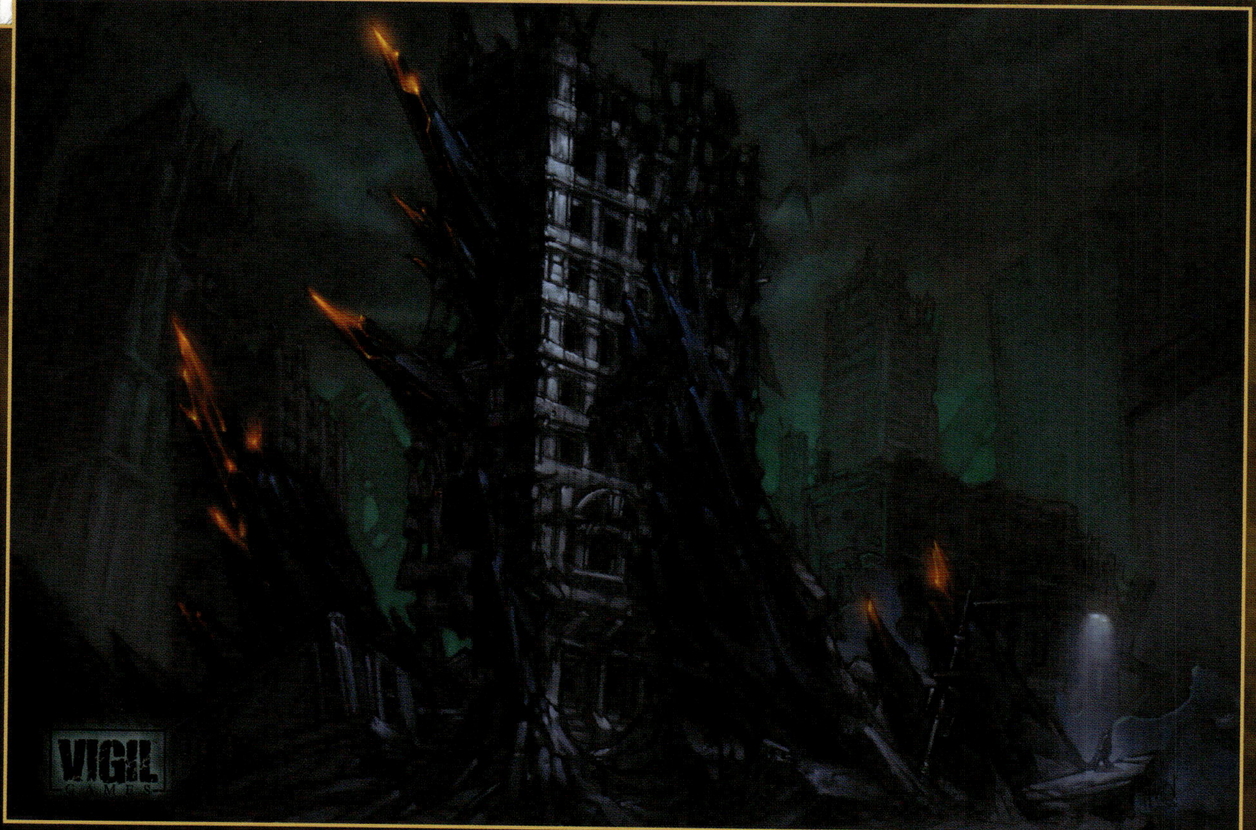

BUILDING CONCEPT

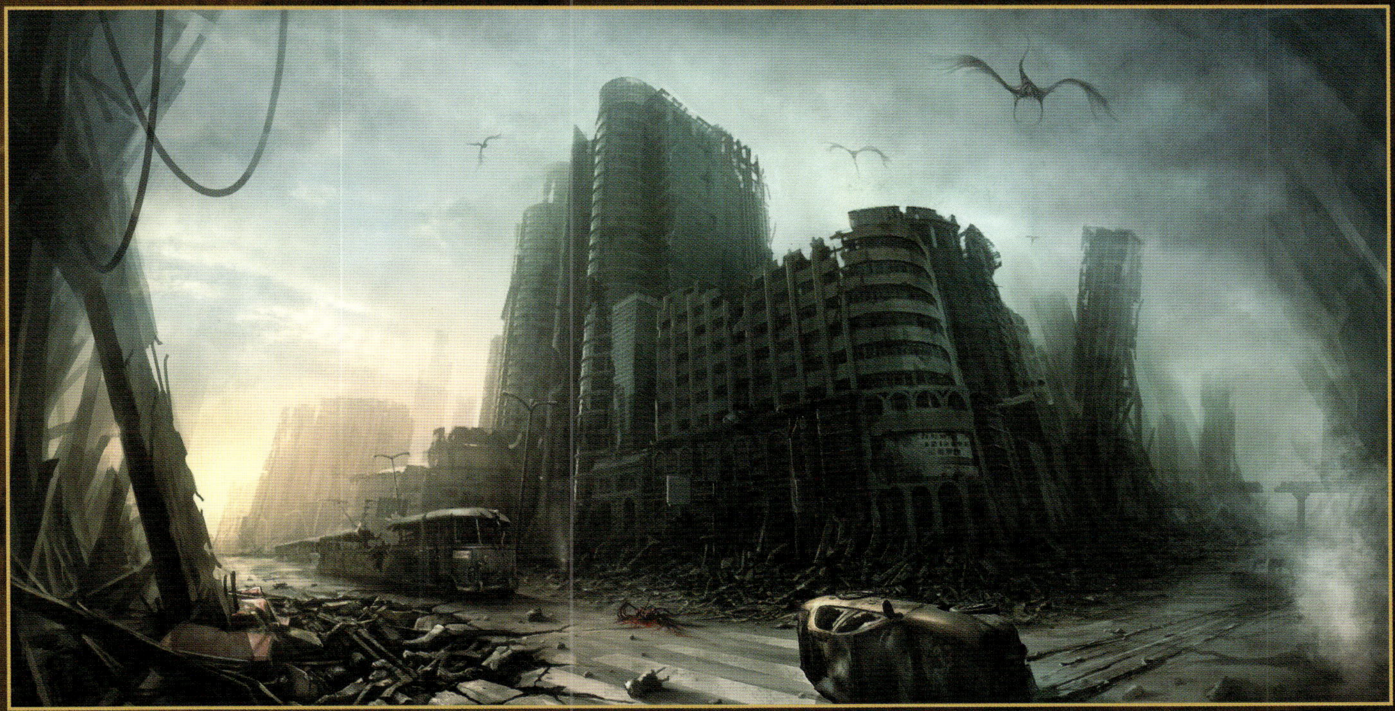

CITY CONCEPT

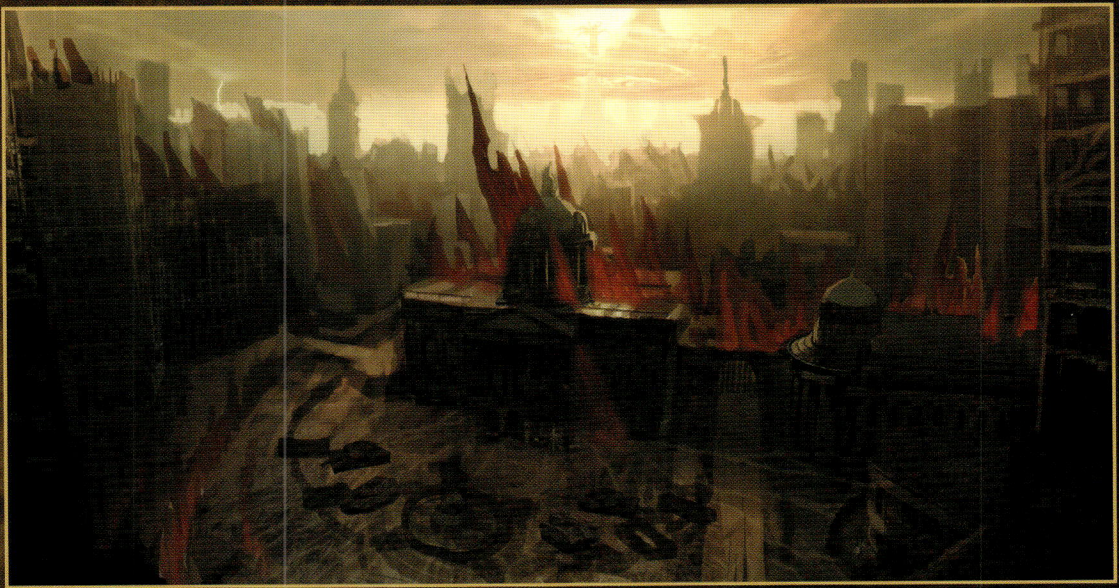

CITY CONCEPT

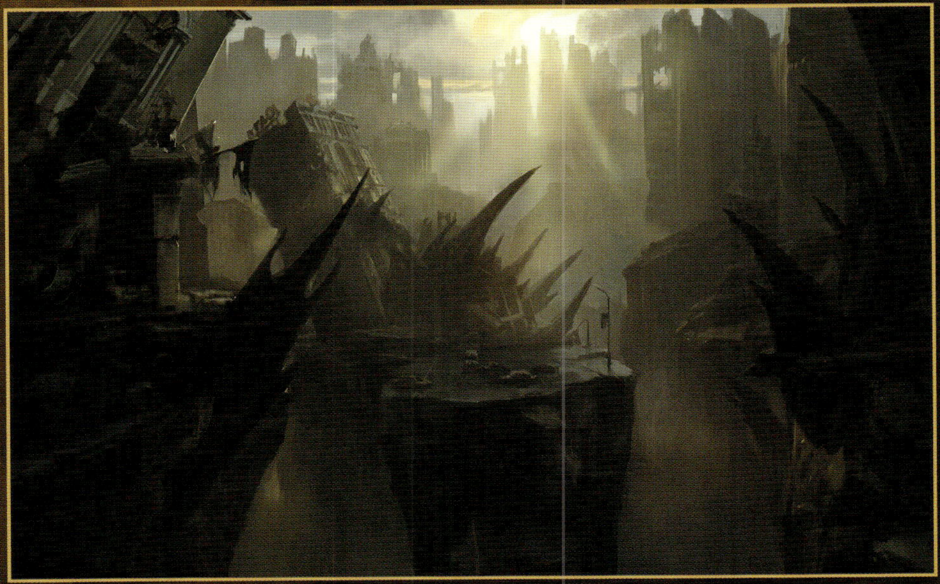

CANYON CONCEPT

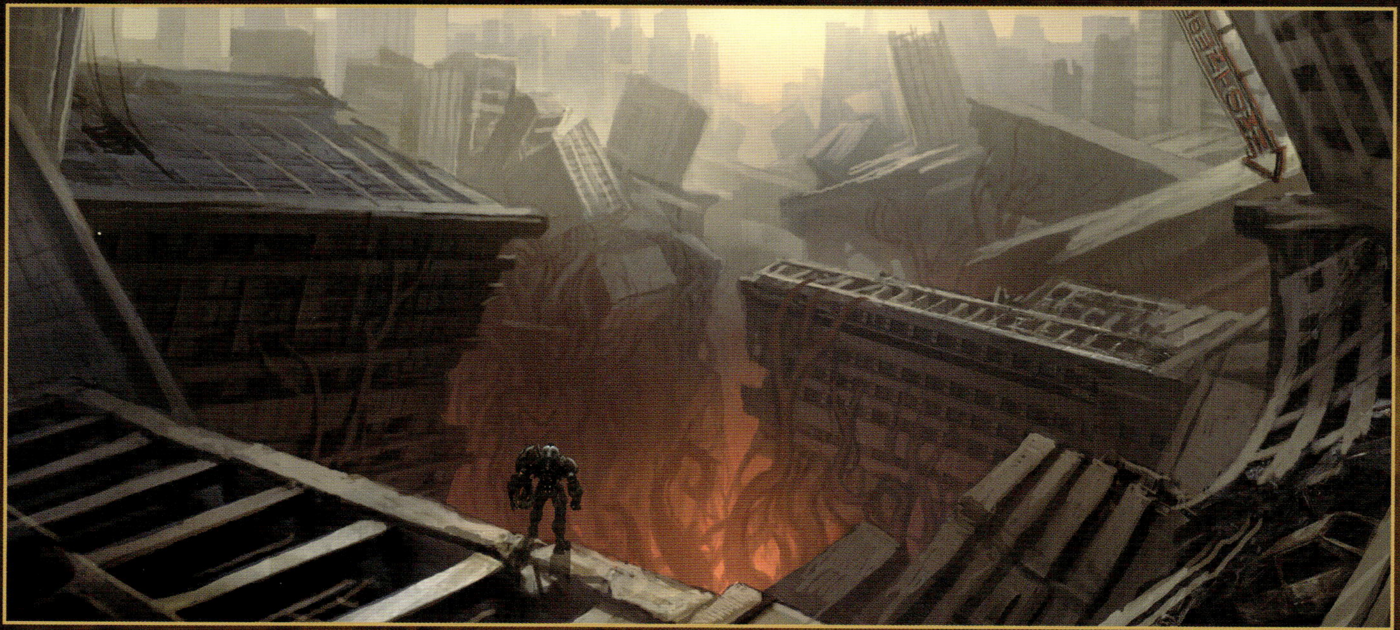

CITY CONCEPT

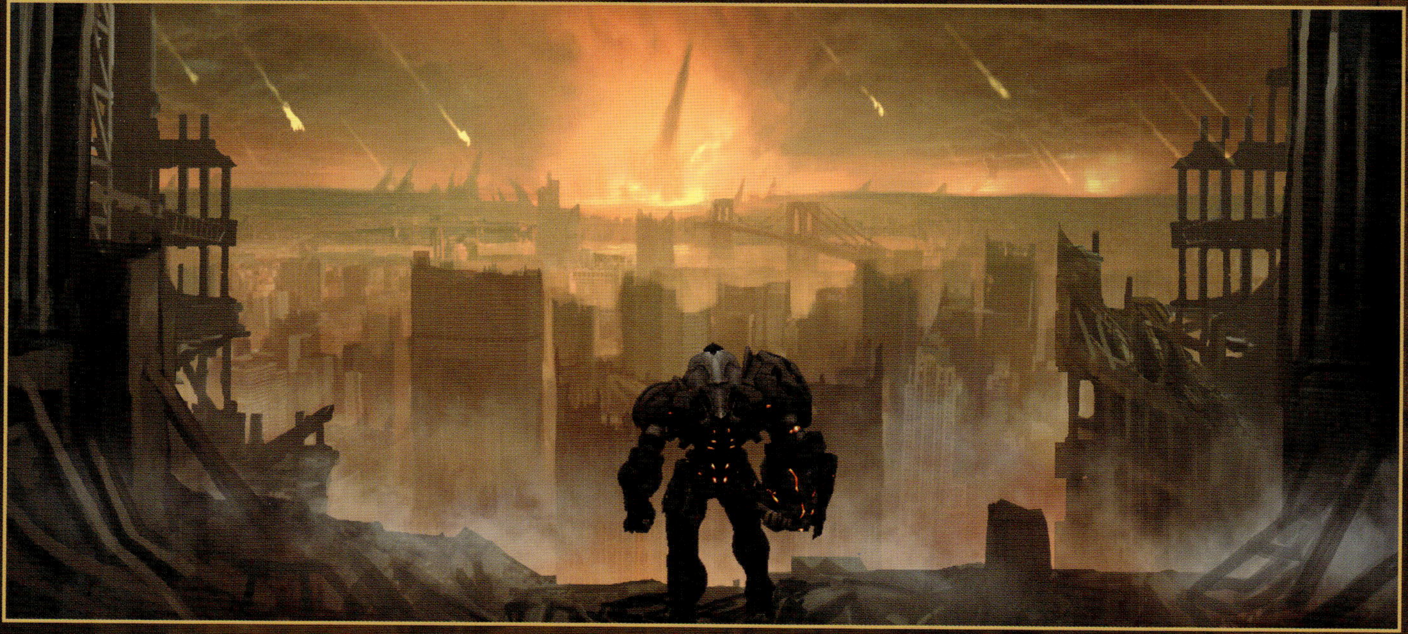

CITY CONCEPT

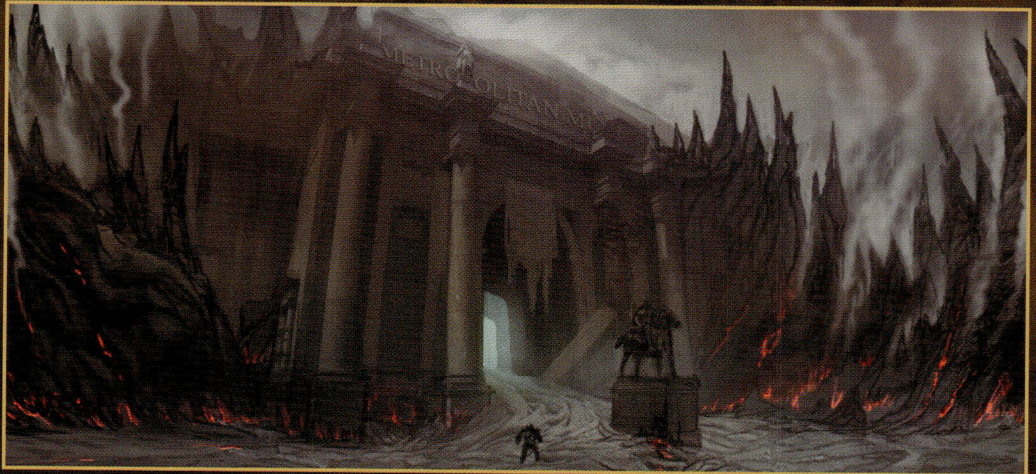

BUILDING CONCEPT

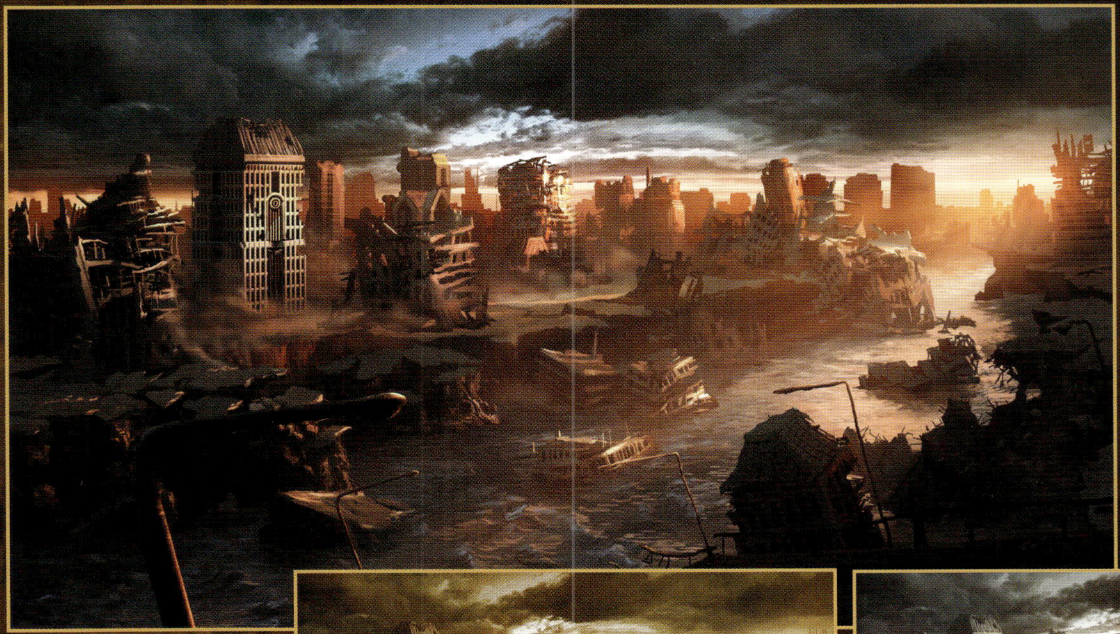

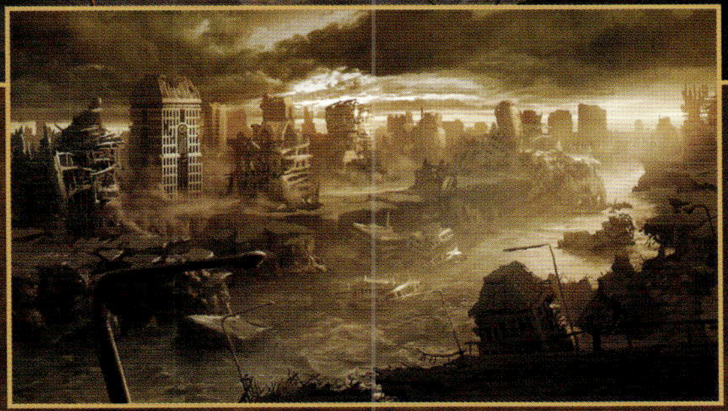

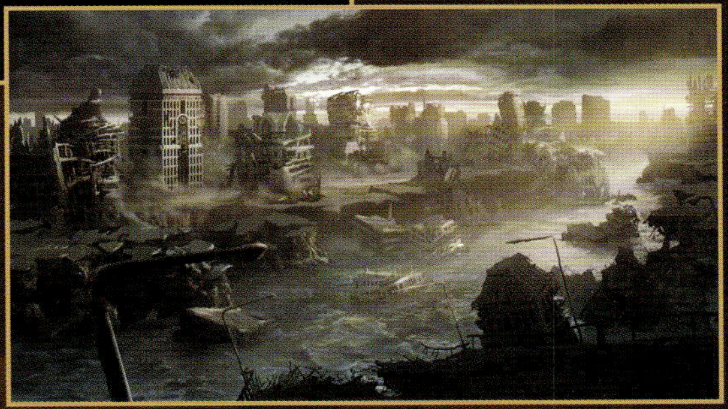

FLOODED SUBWAY CONCEPTS

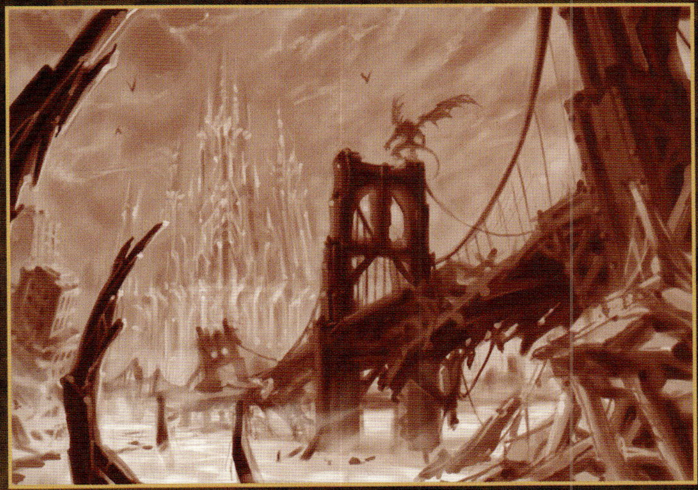

BRIDGE SKETCH

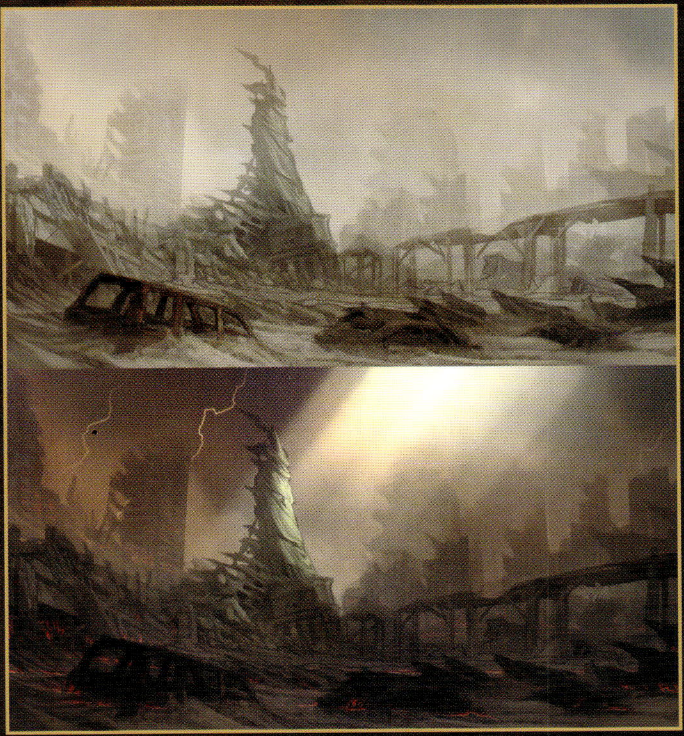

COLLECTOR CONCEPTS

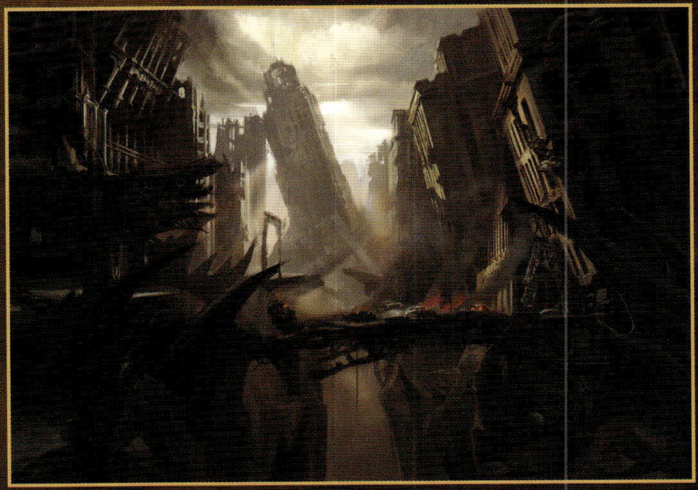

CITY CONCEPT

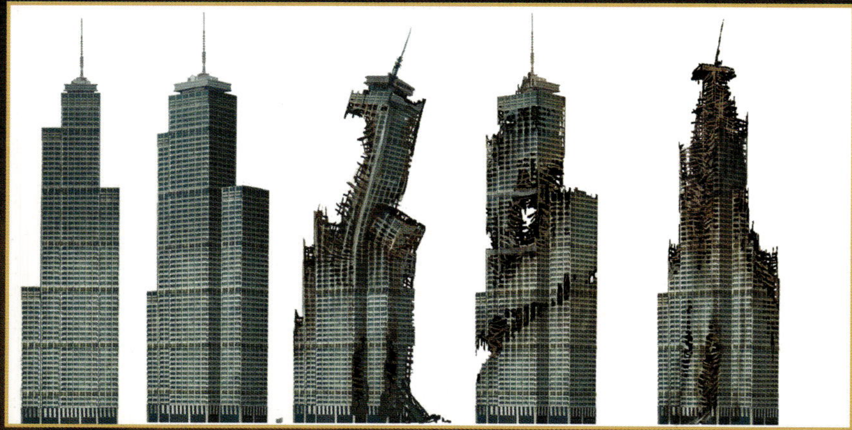

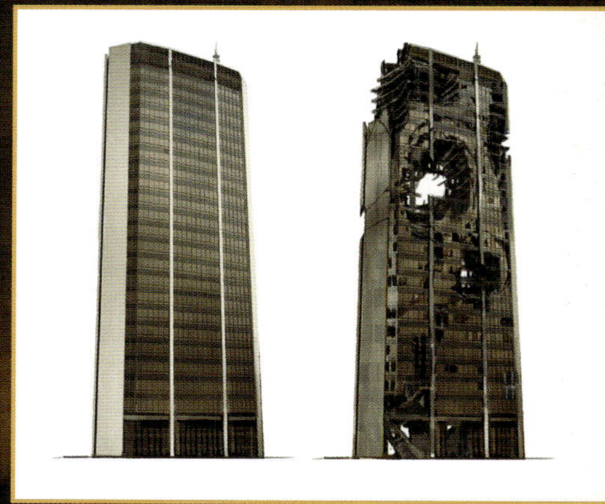

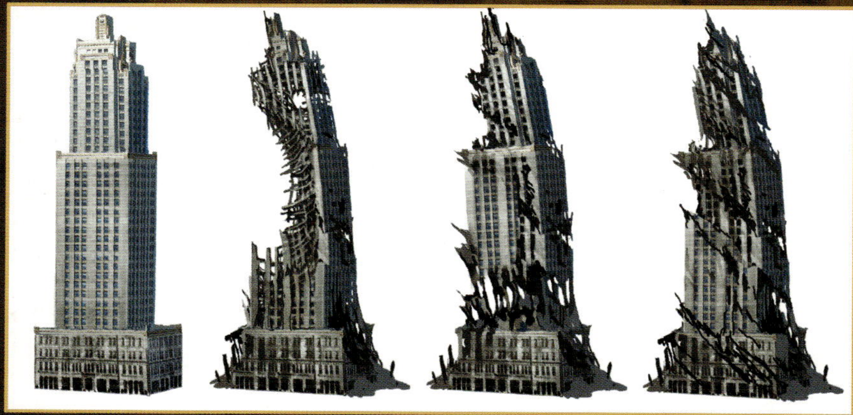

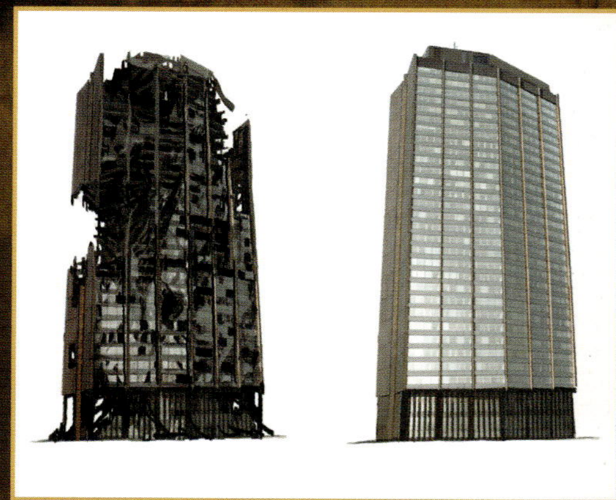

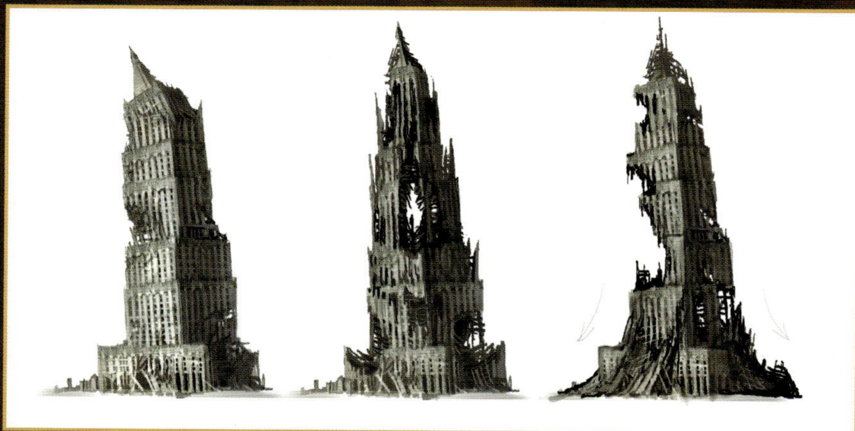

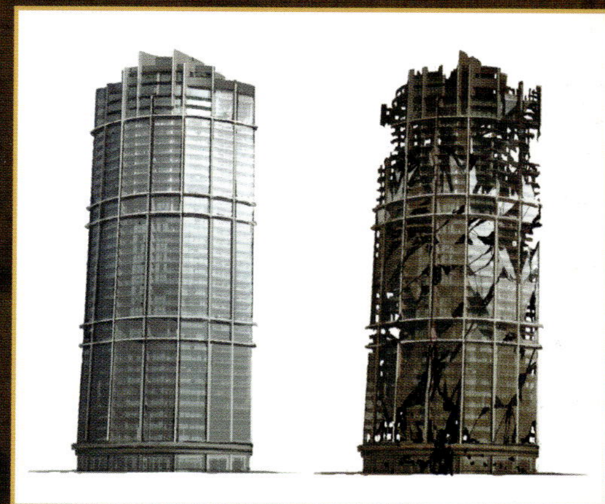

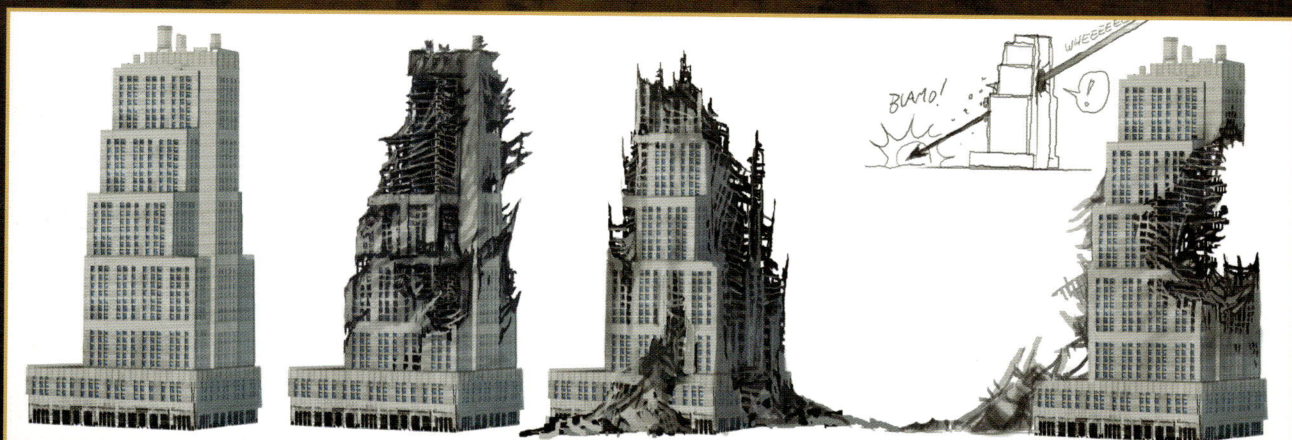

BUILDING DESIGNS

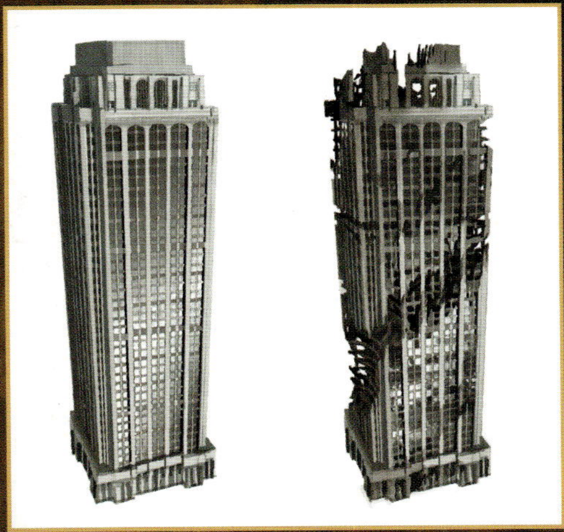

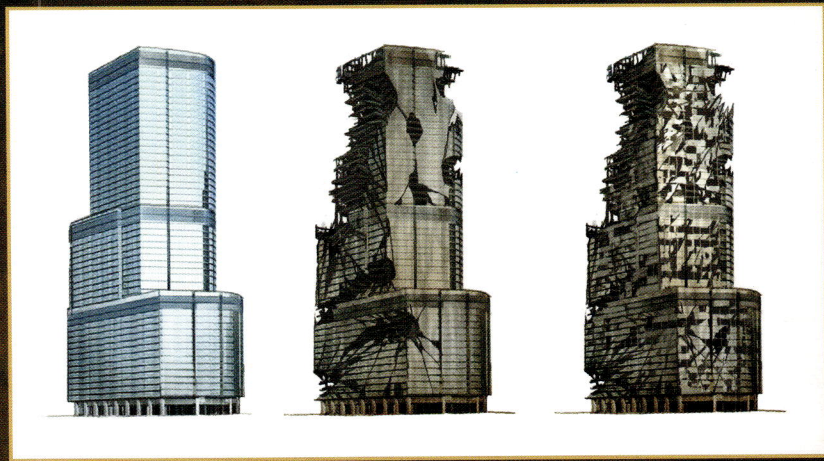

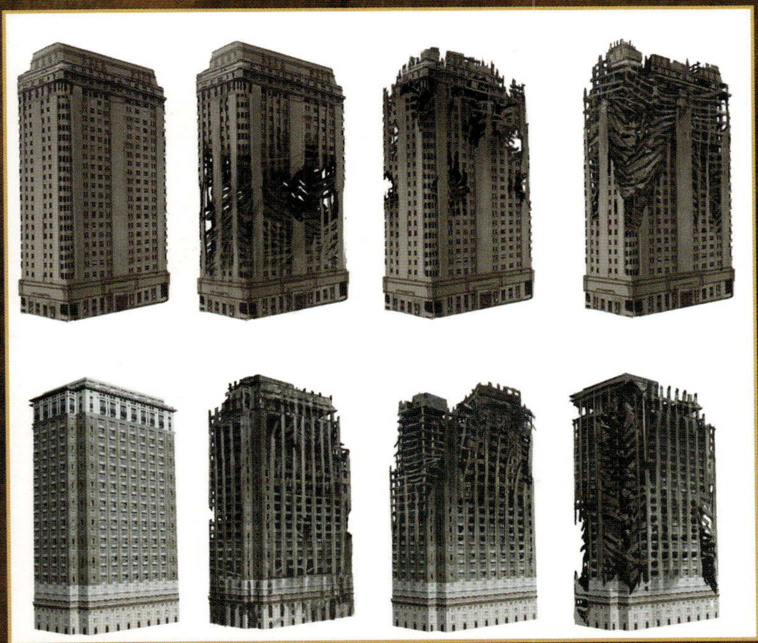

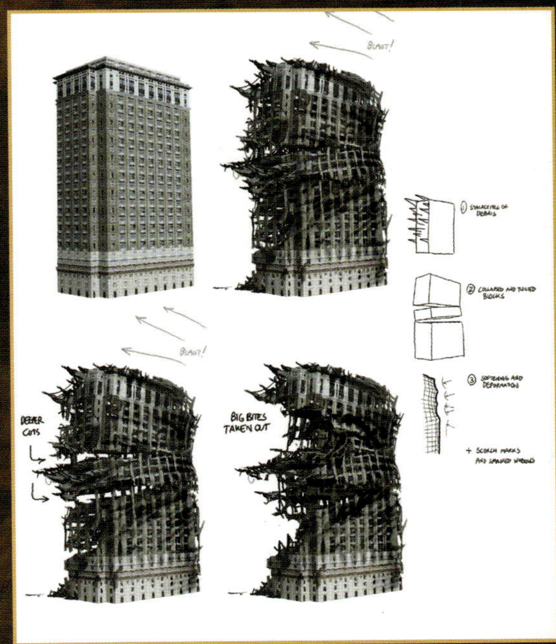

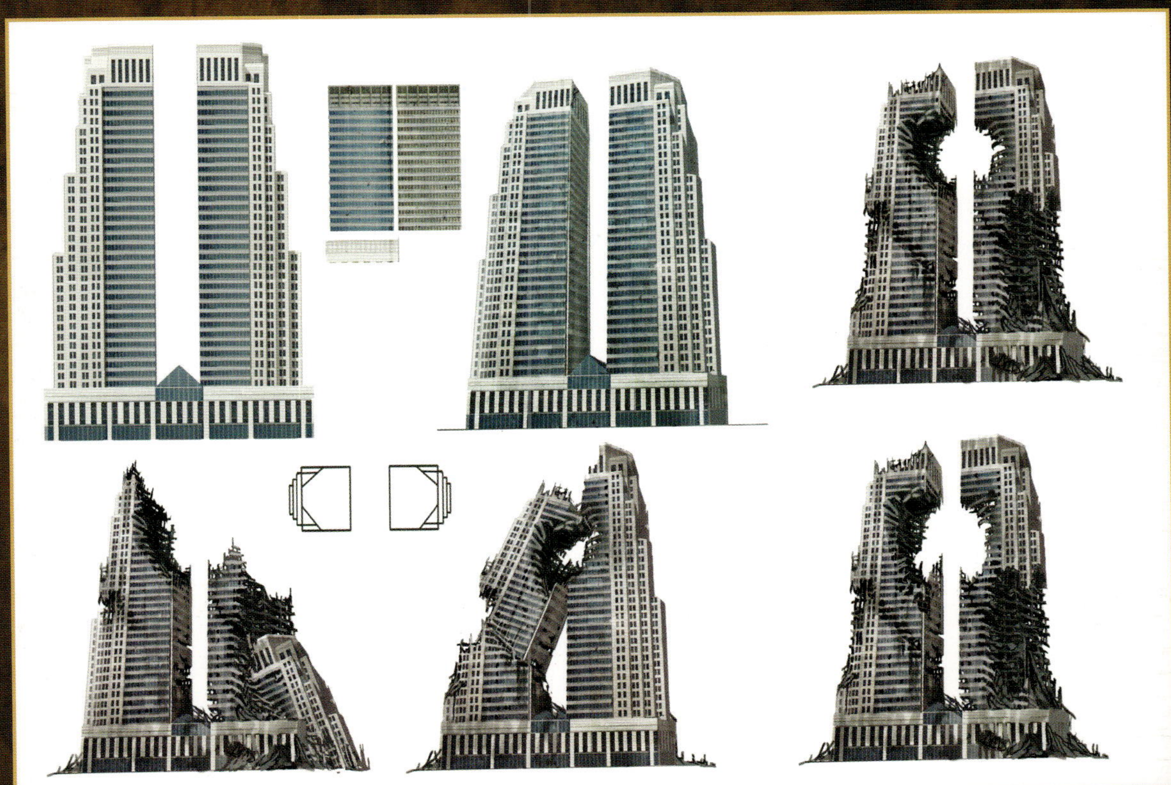

BUILDING DESIGNS

BRIDGE CONCEPT

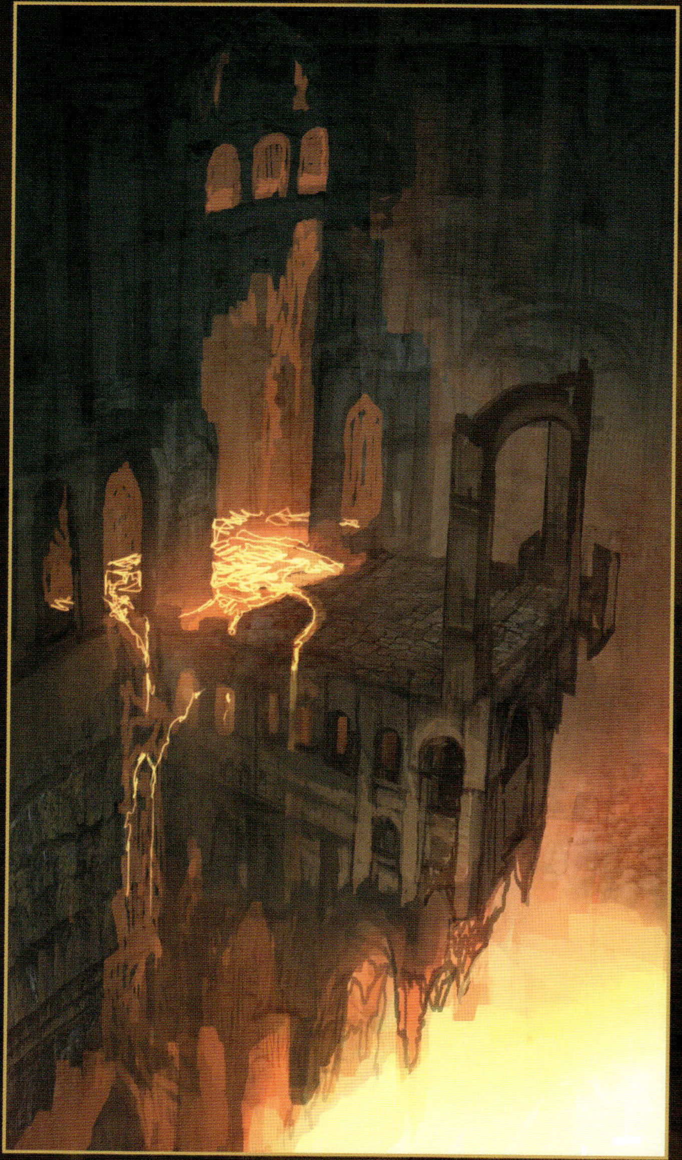

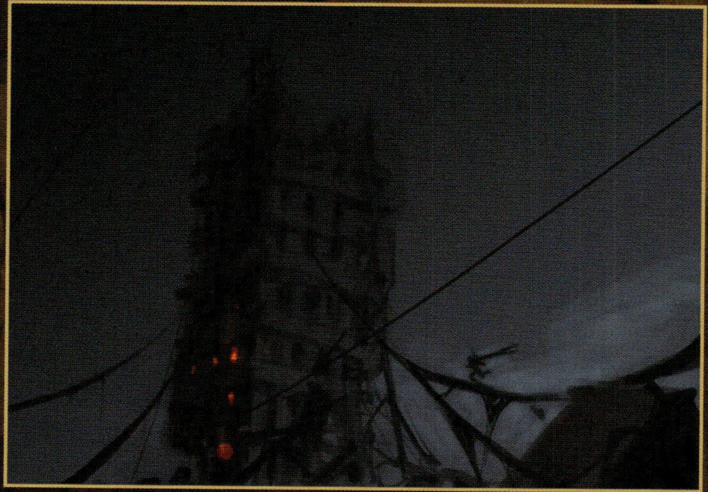

BUILDING CONCEPT

LAVA CONCEPT

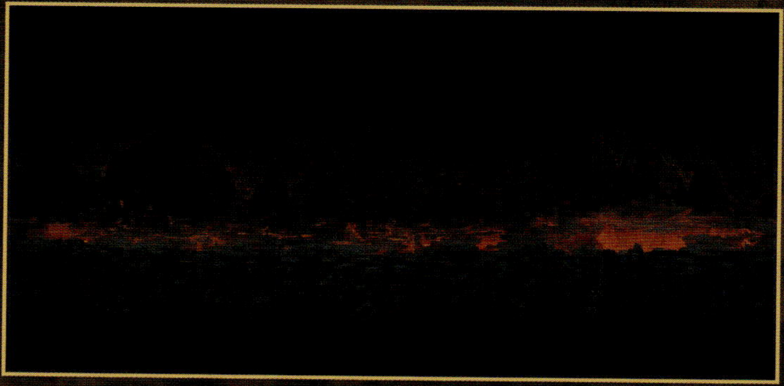

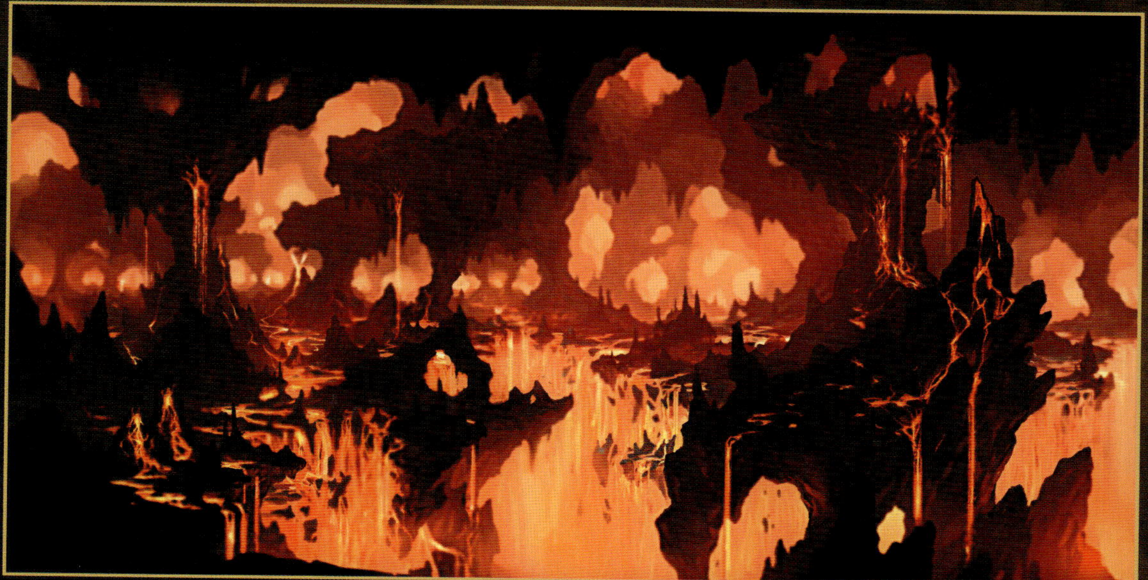

LAVA CONCEPT

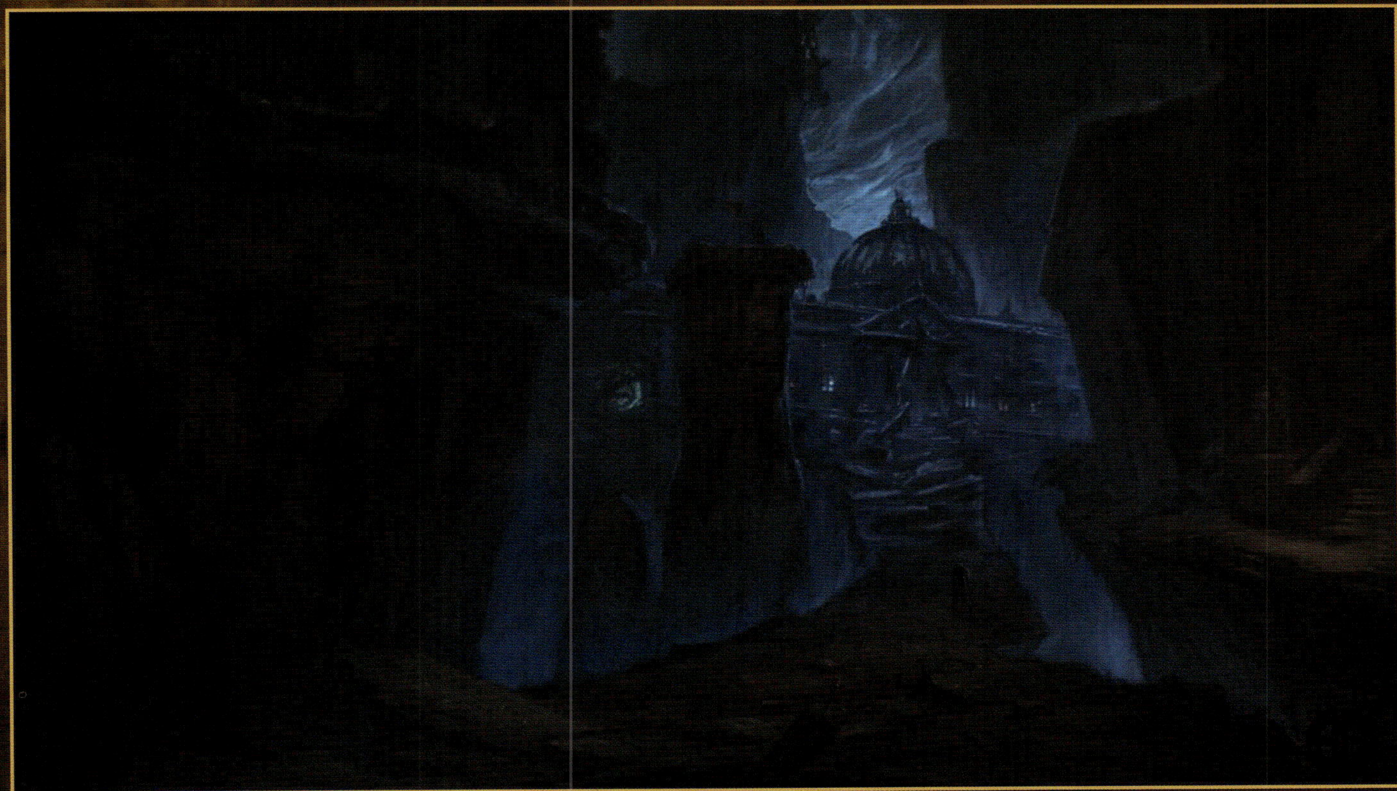

LIBRARY CONCEPT

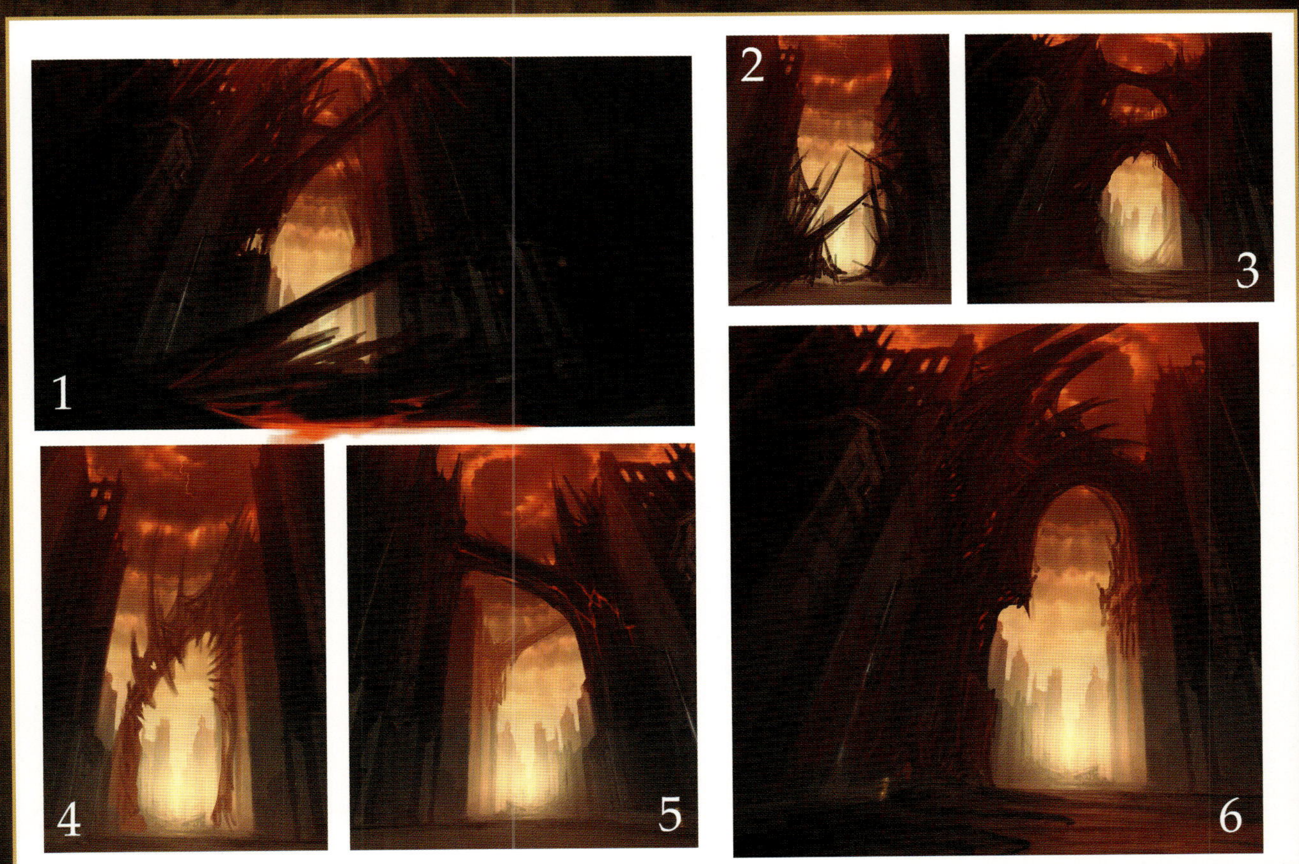

CITY FORMS

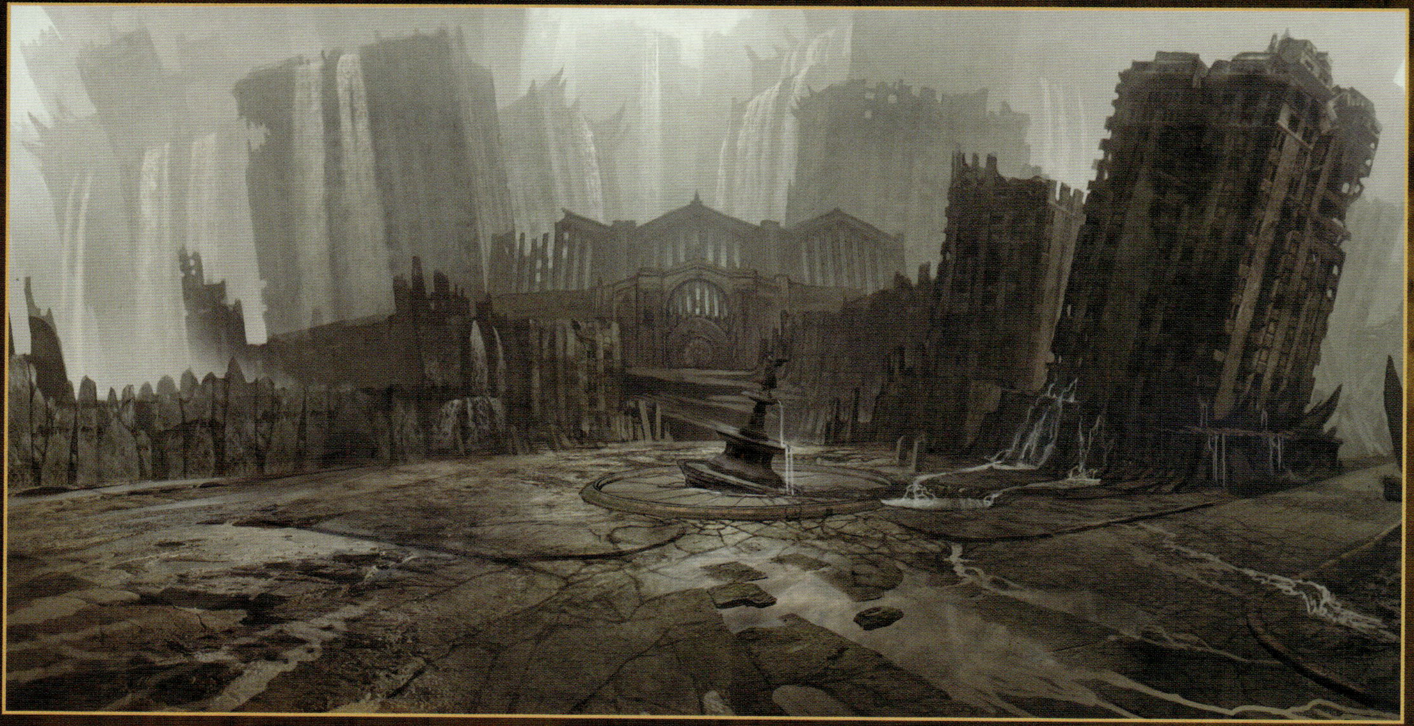

SUBWAY TERMINAL

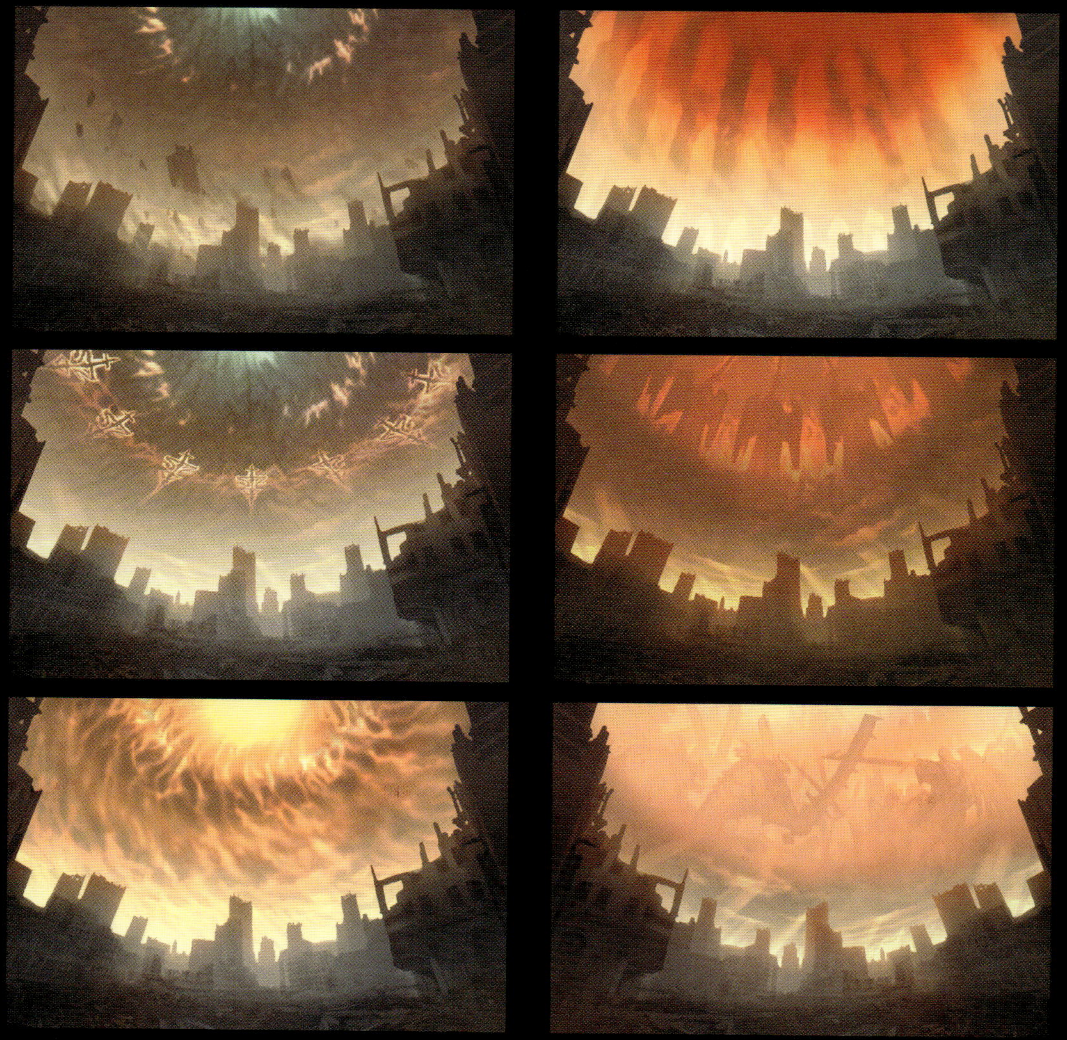

SKY CONCEPTS

ECHO GORGE

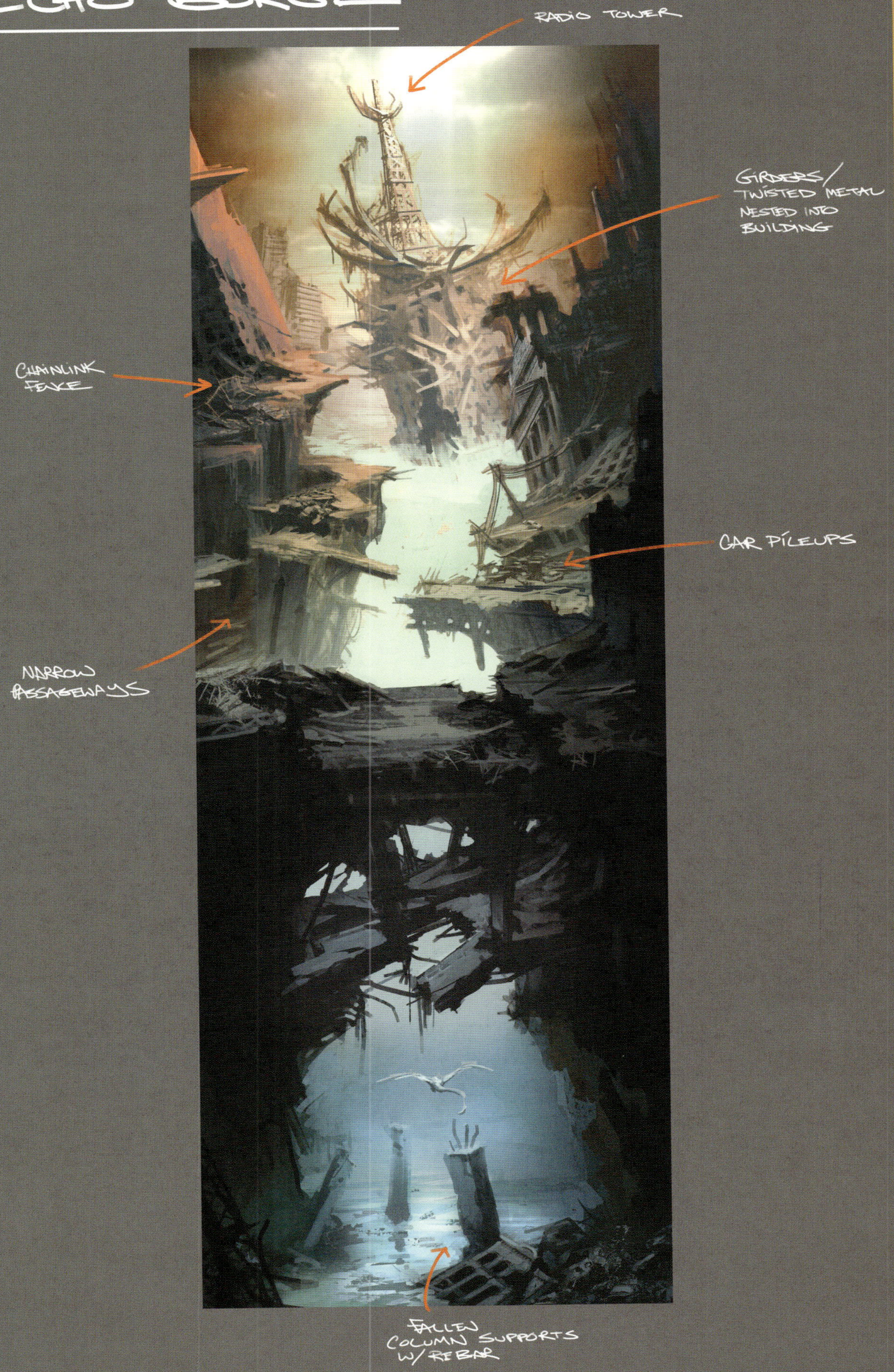

ECHO GORGE CONCEPT

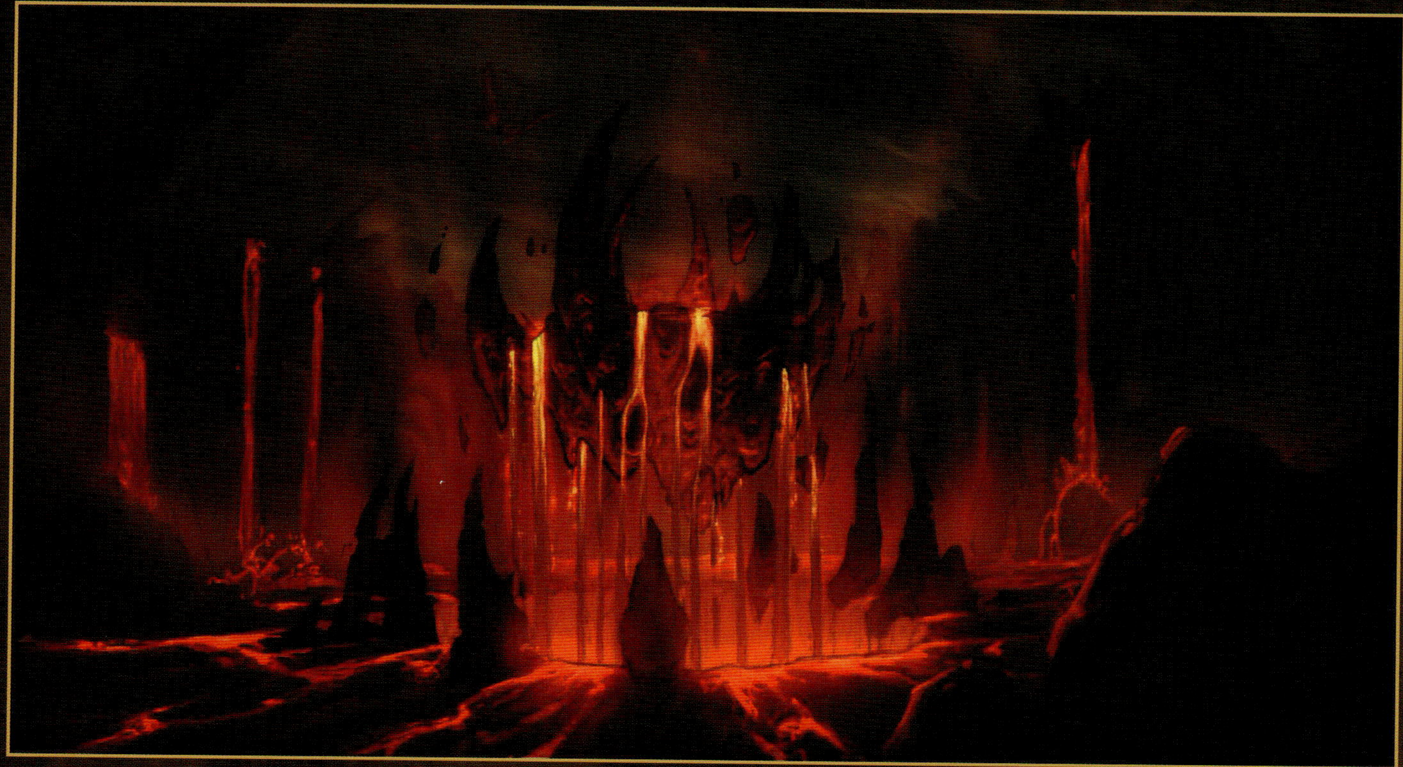

SCALDING GALLOWS CONCEPT

The Scalding Gallows looms ominously over a lake of fire, its curved spires grasping at the foreboding skies. When Samael dared to defy the Destroyer, he was imprisoned within the hellish confines of the Gallows. Samael was a demon lord of legendary dark power, yet even he was broken by the Destroyer's might. Will the Horseman face a similar fate?

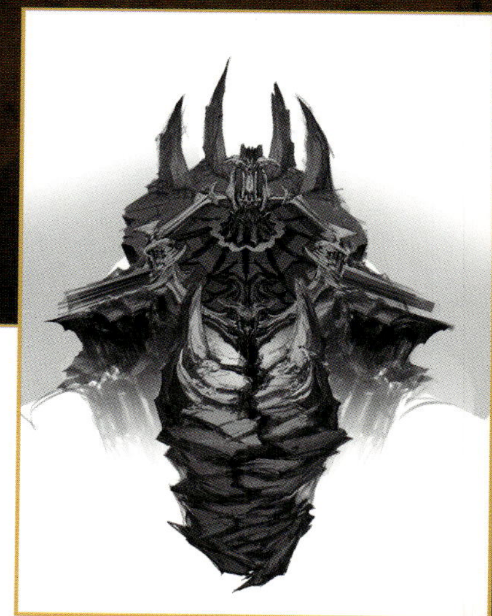

Scalding Gallows

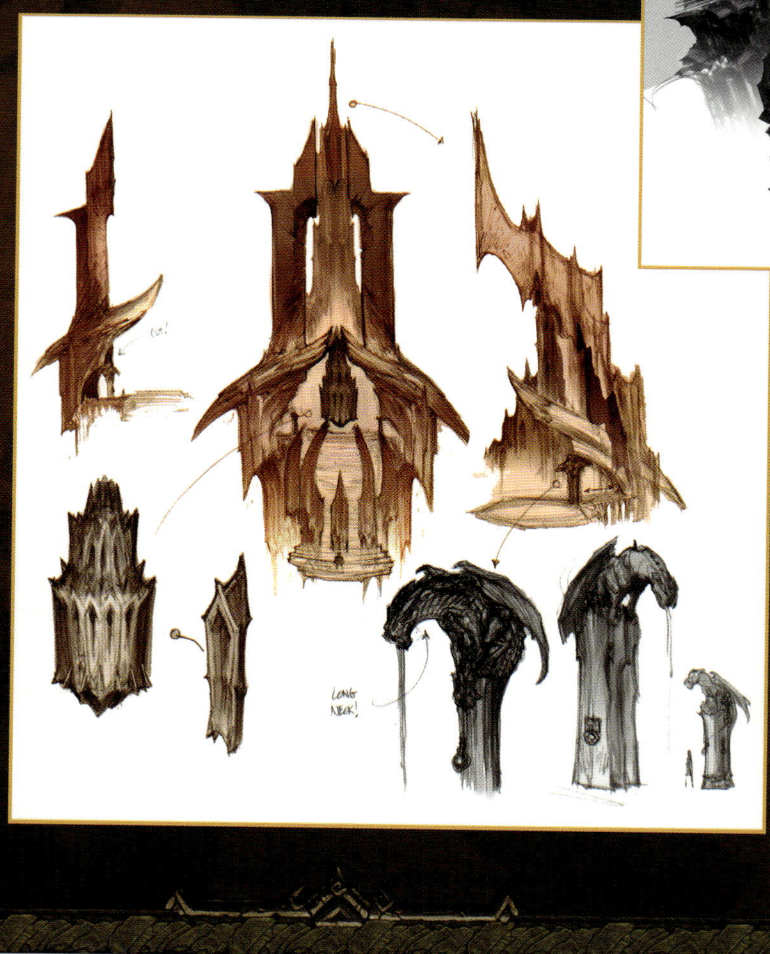

SAMAEL'S PRISON CONCEPTS

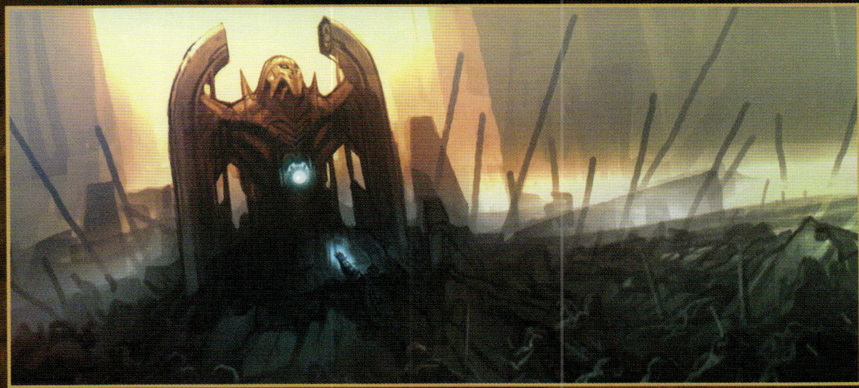

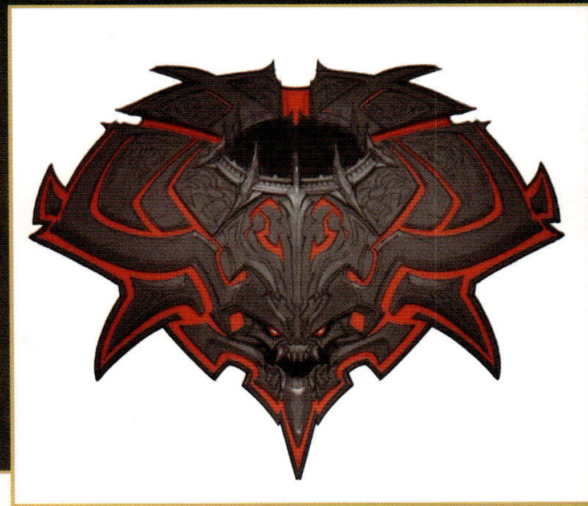

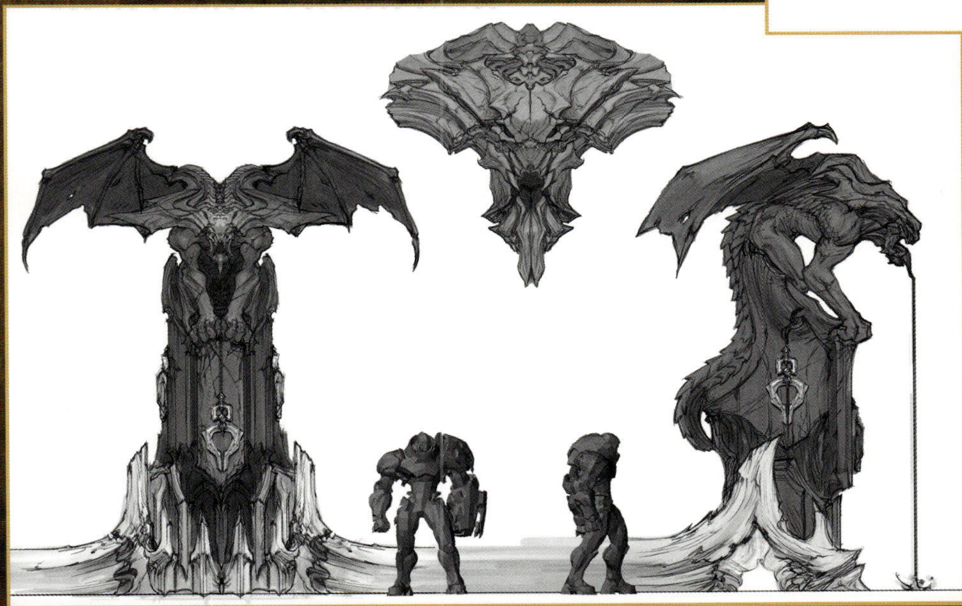

SAMAEL'S PRISON CONCEPTS

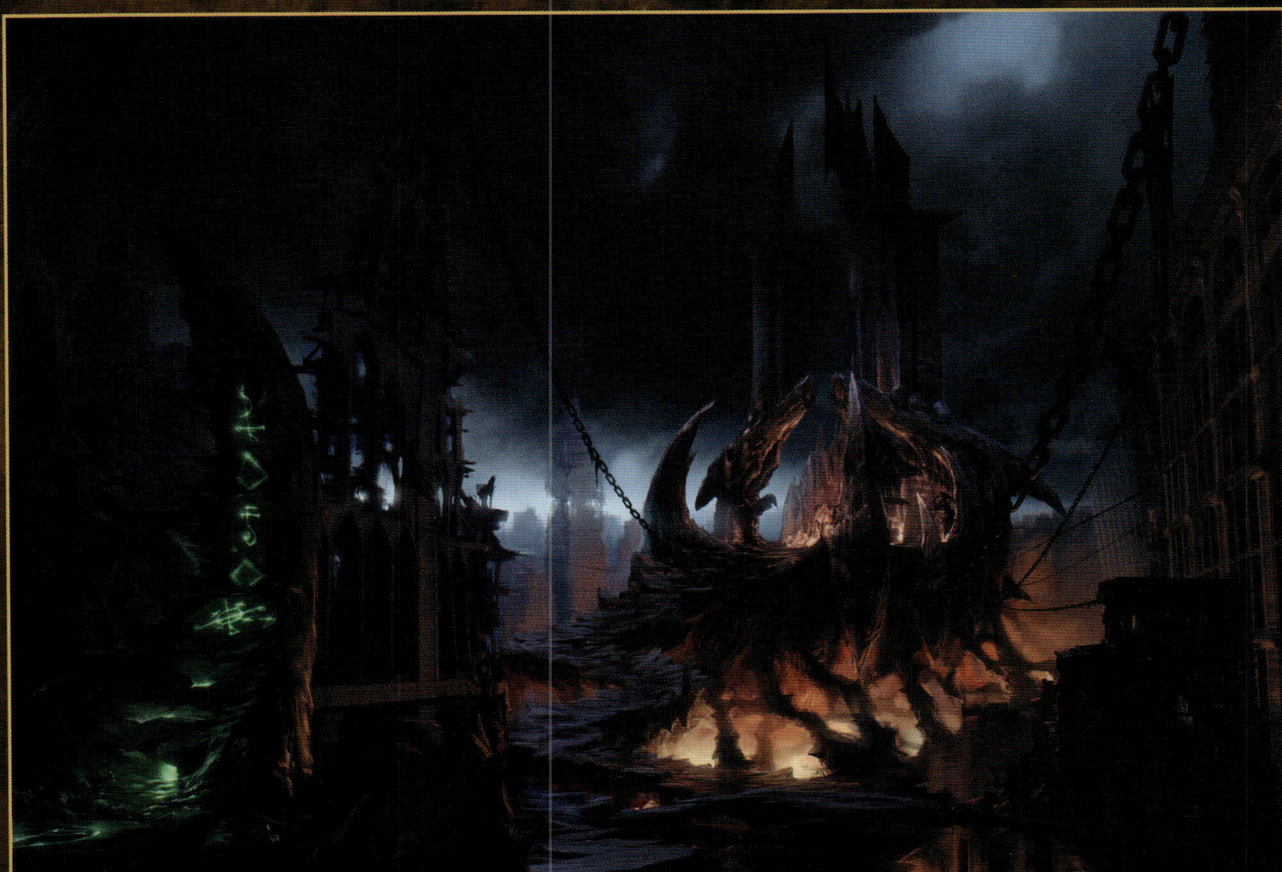

SCALDING GALLOWS CONCEPT

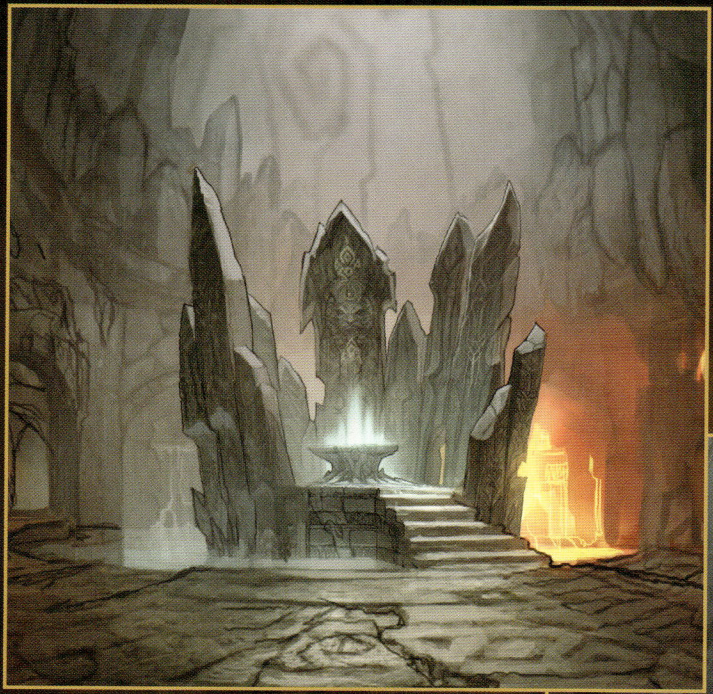

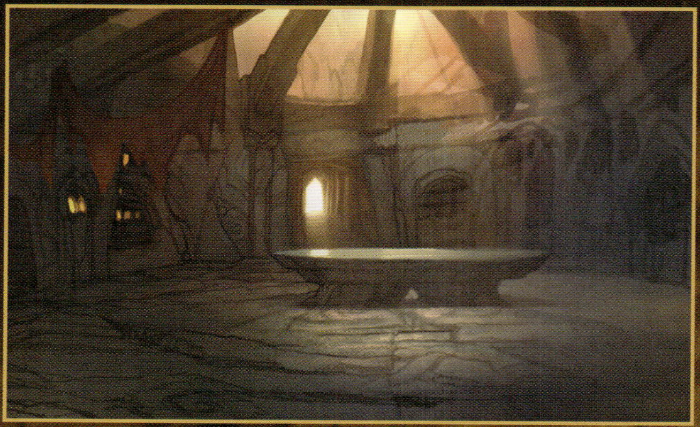

FORGE CONCEPTS

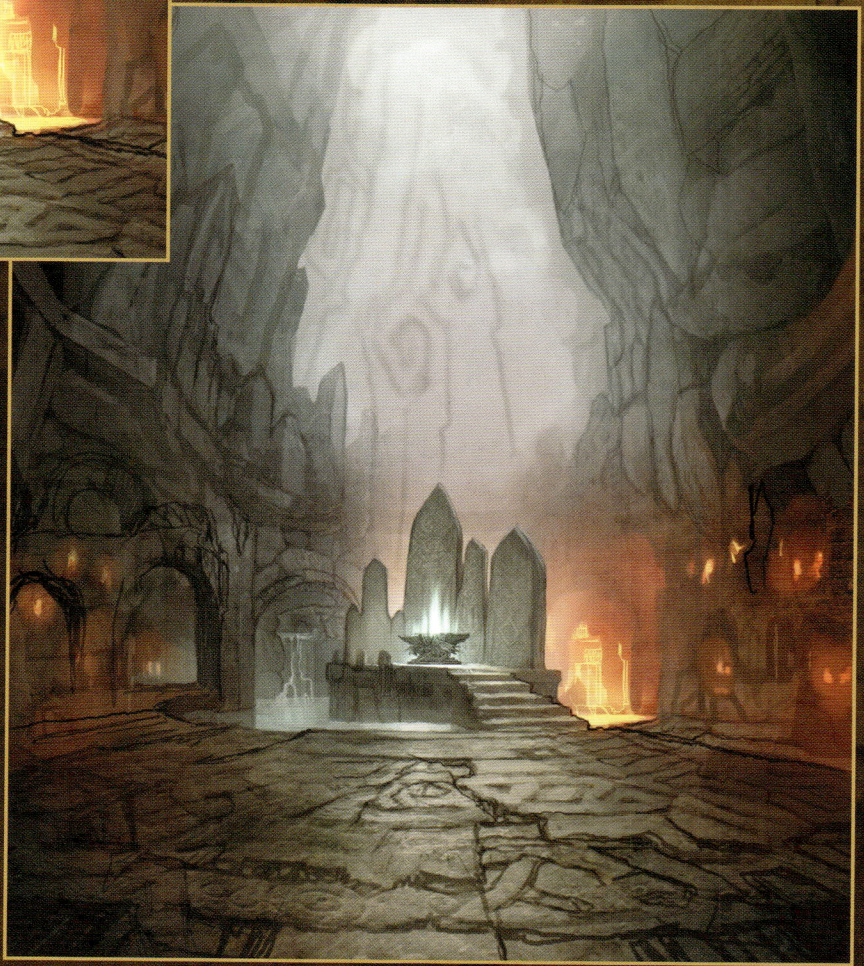

Anvil's Ford

The Anvil's Ford is hidden in the wastes. Here, sparks leap from an anvil as steel is flattened and honed. Above this blazing forge leans Ulthane, a being far older than the war between Heaven and Hell. With each clang of metal on metal, Ulthane perfects legendary arms and armor. On his walls are spears to fell sky-borne demons and swords to pierce the blackest of hearts.

Ulthane will need such an arsenal if he is to survive the demon hordes. I suspect his smithy cannot remain hidden for long.

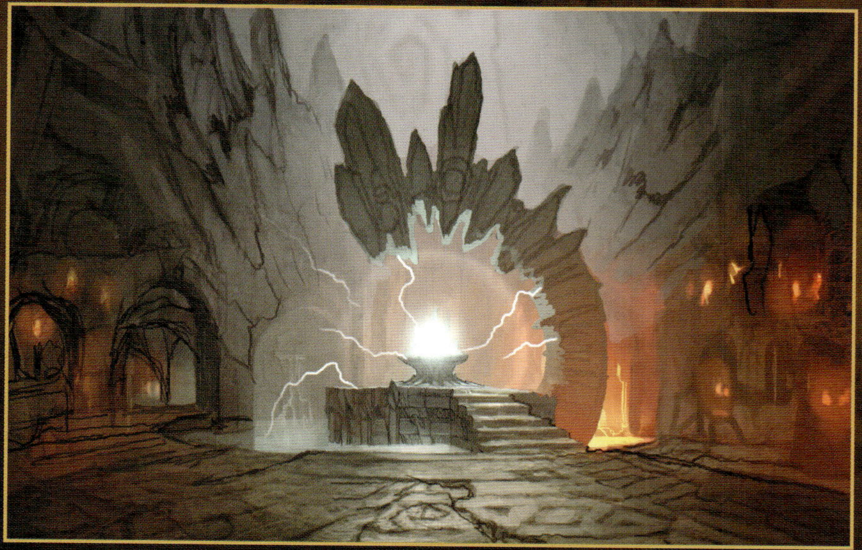

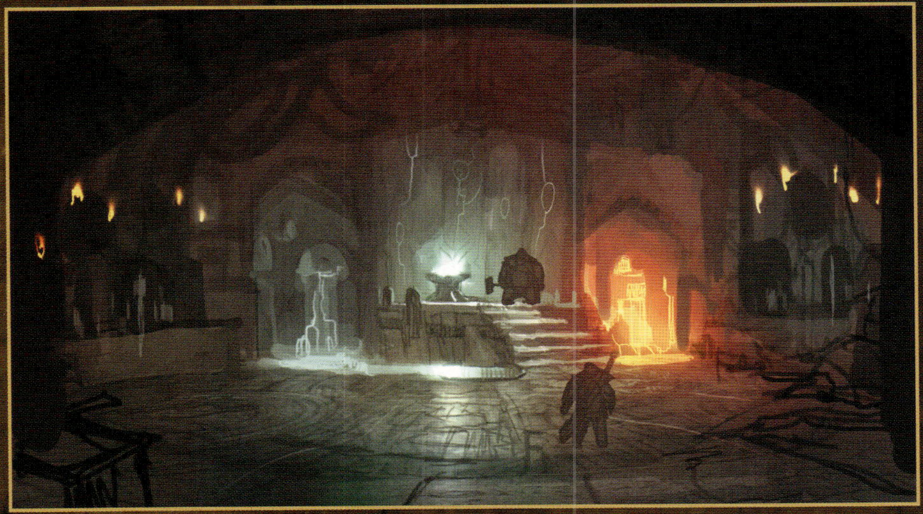

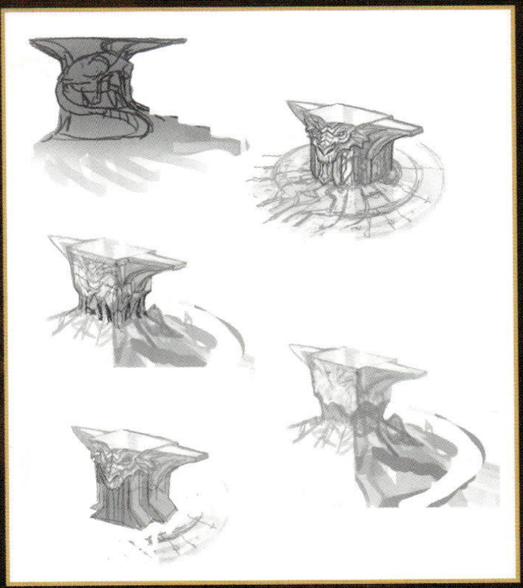

FORGE DESIGN

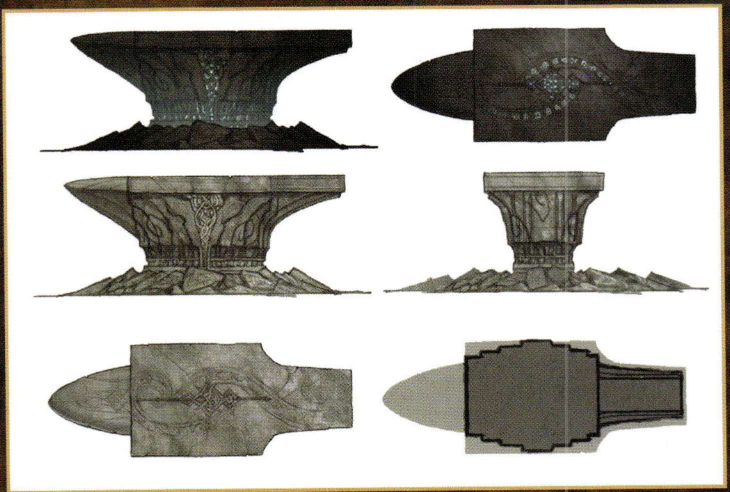

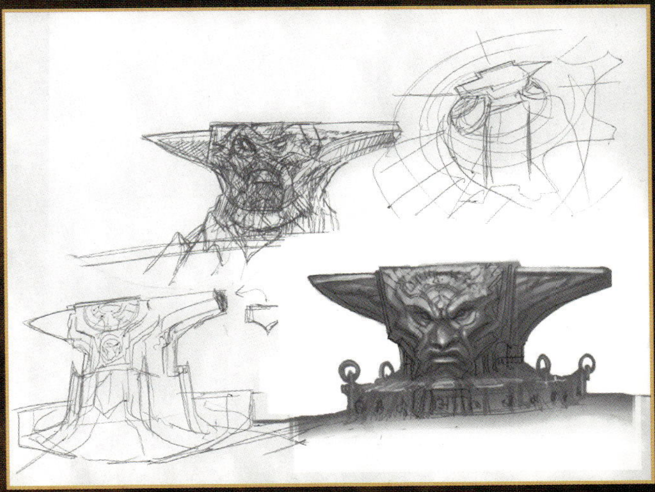

ANVIL DEVELOPMENT SKETCHES

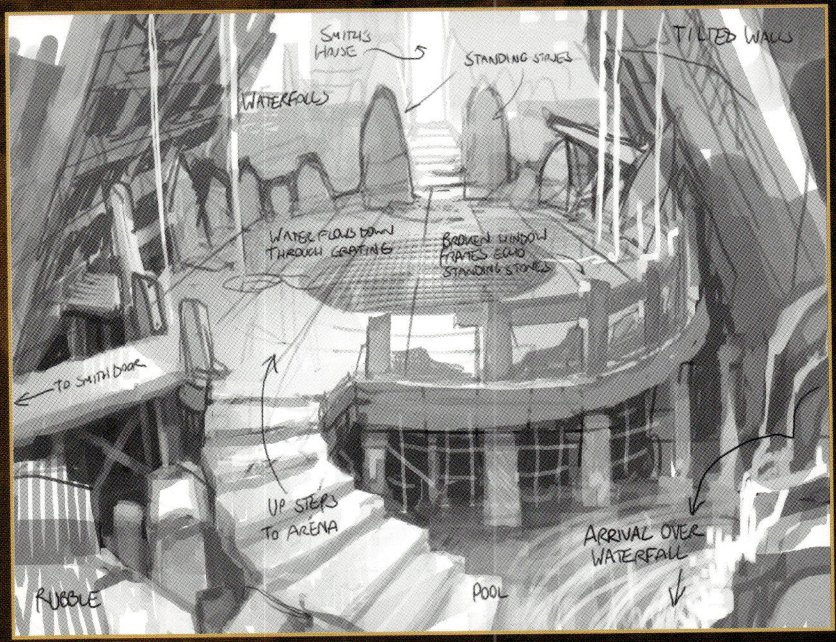

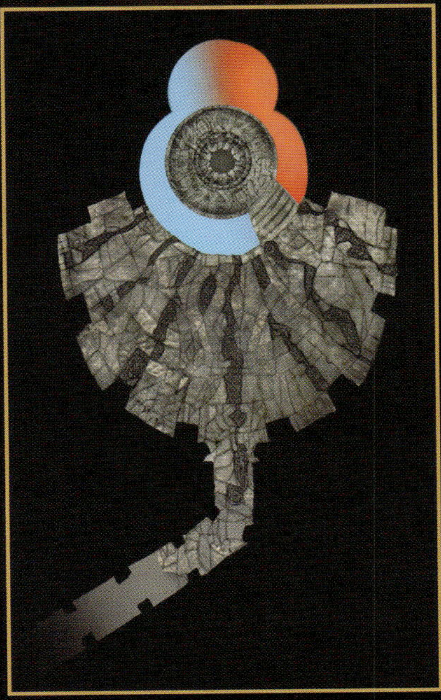

LAYOUT SKETCHES

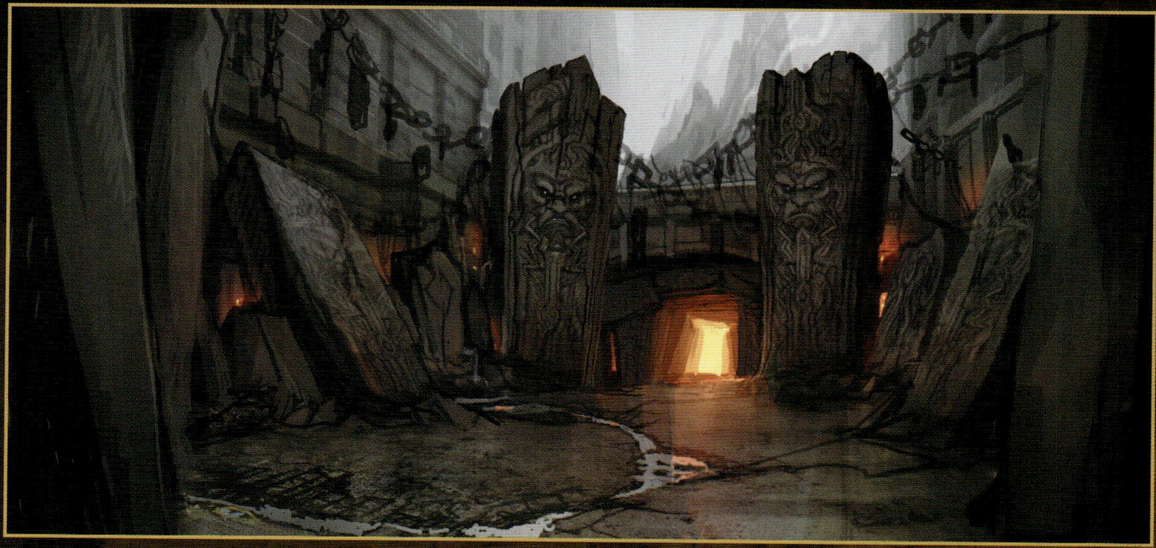

ENTRANCE CONCEPT

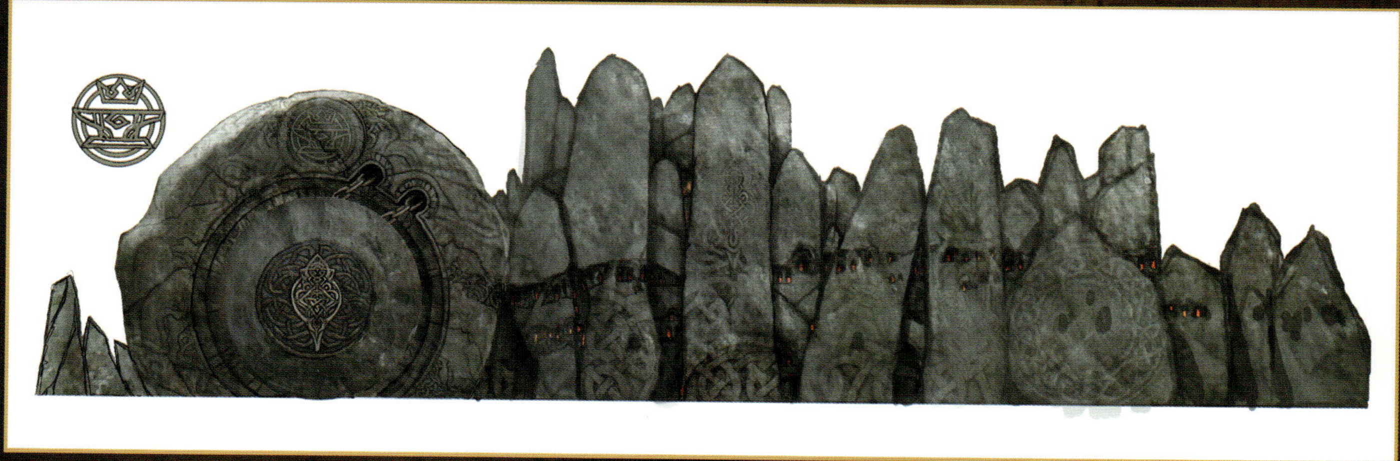

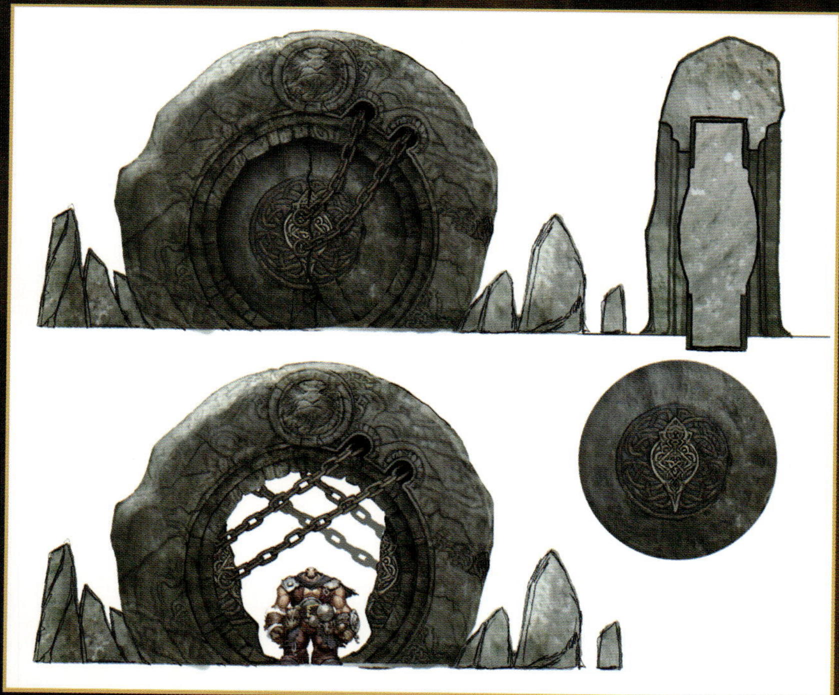

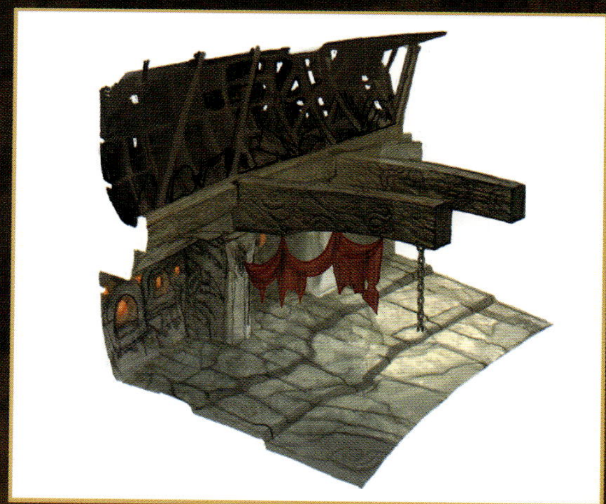

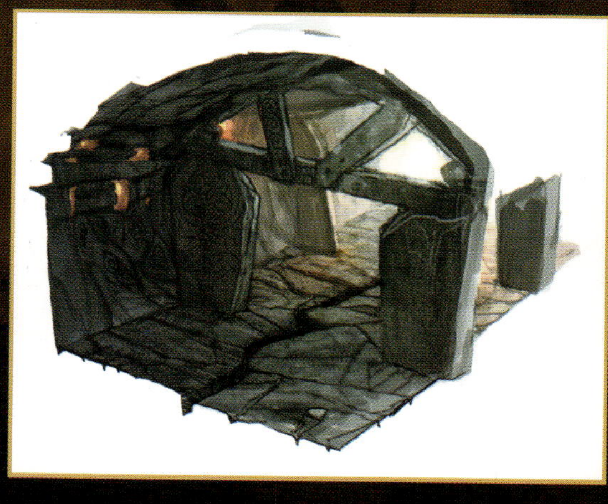

WALL & DOOR DESIGNS

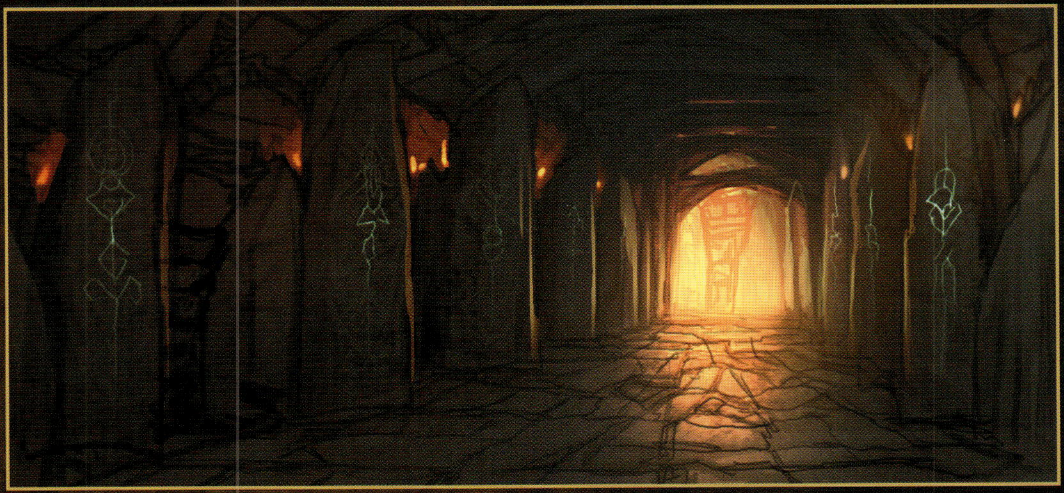

ENTRANCE CONCEPT

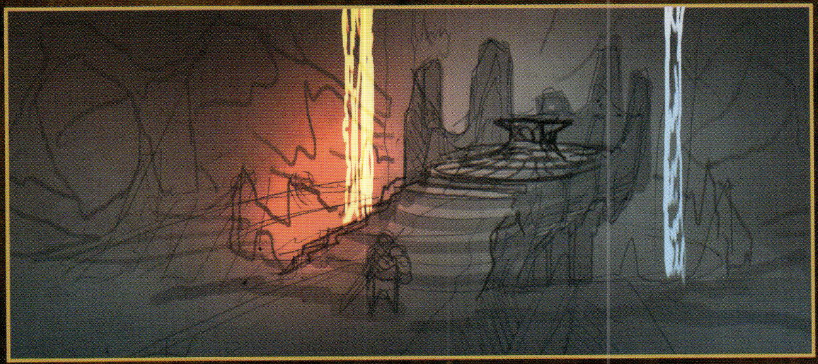

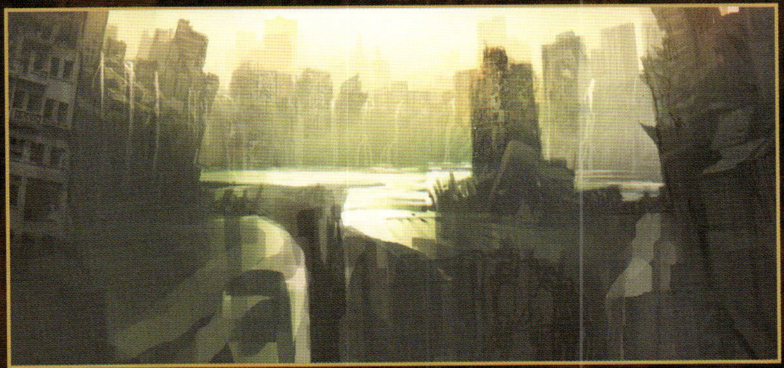

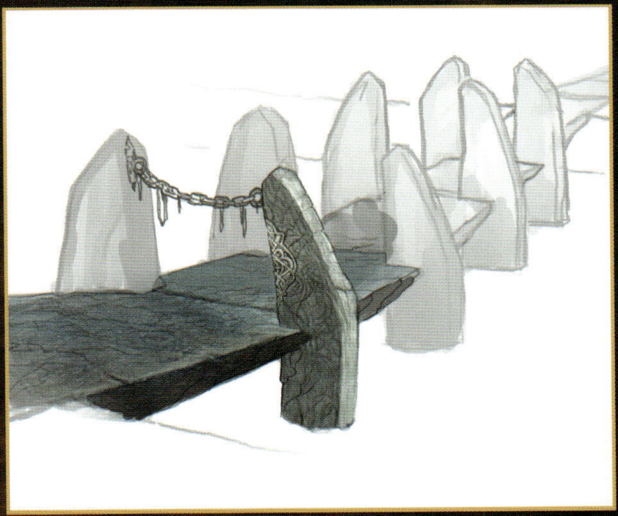

BRIDGE CONCEPT

ANVIL'S FORD CONCEPTS

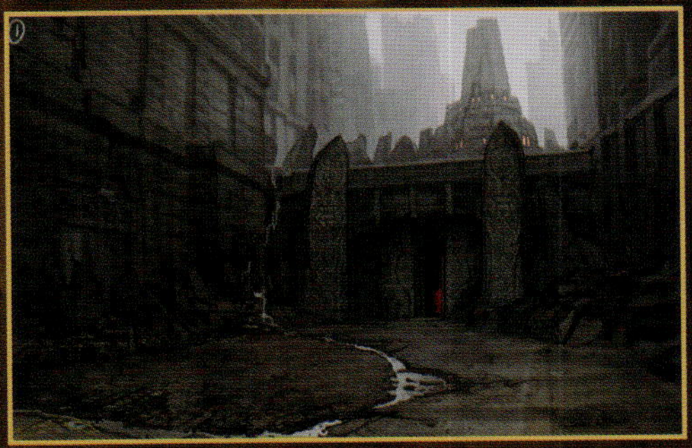

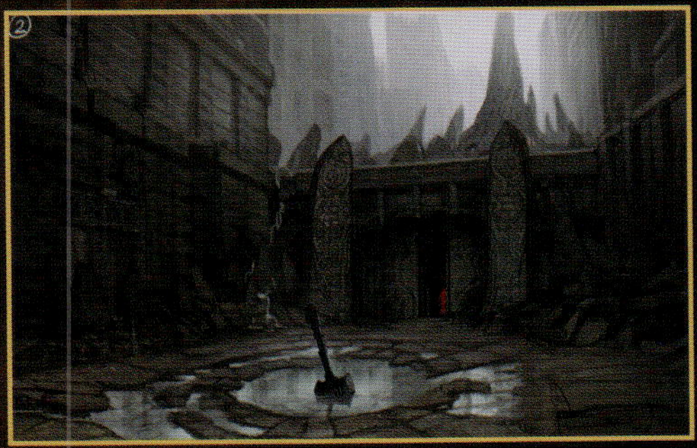

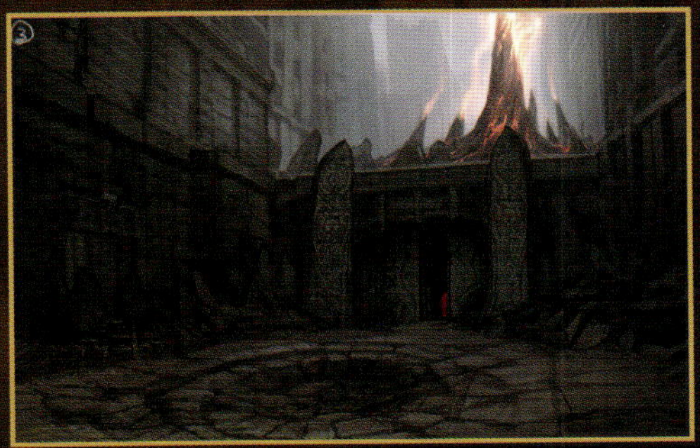

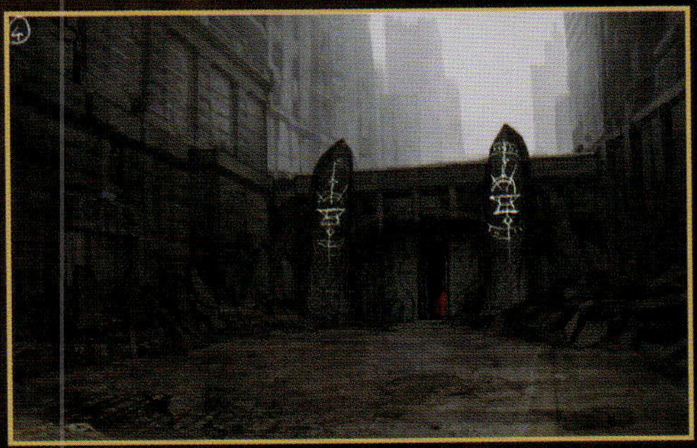

ENTRANCE CONCEPTS

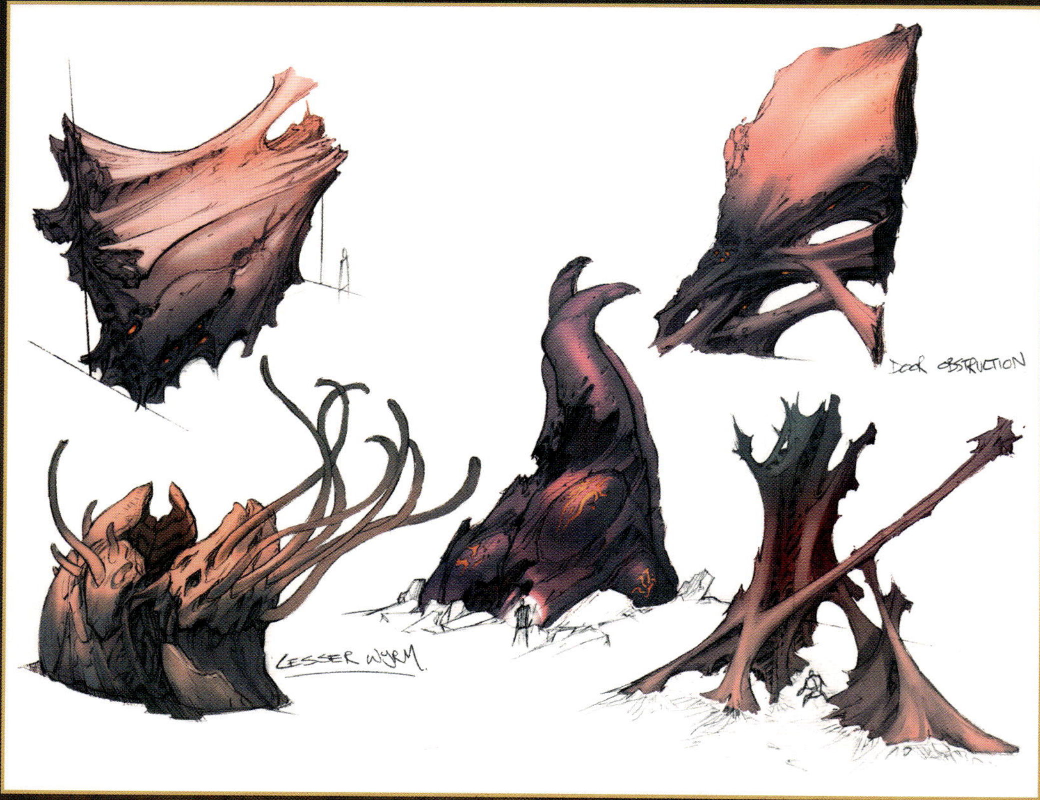

FORM CONCEPTS

Hellgrowth

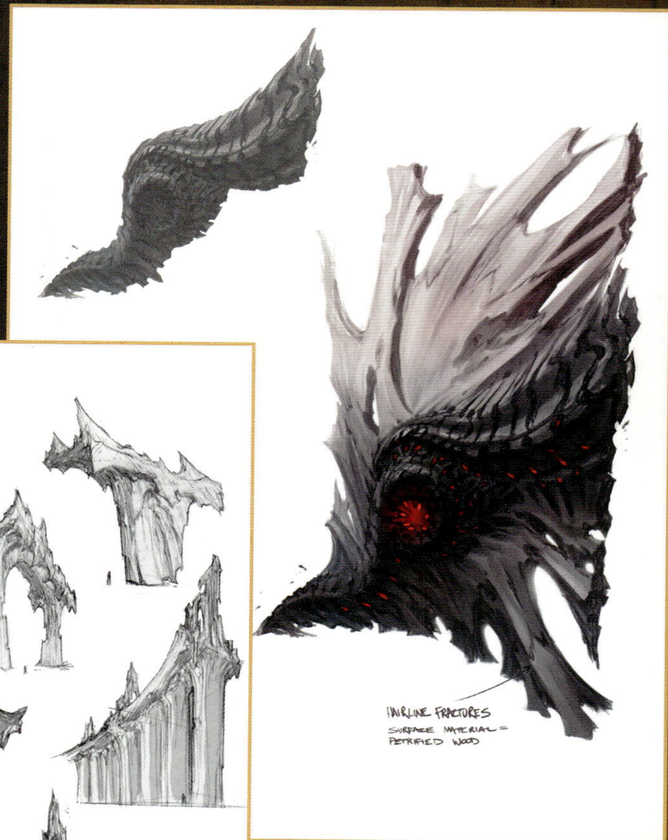

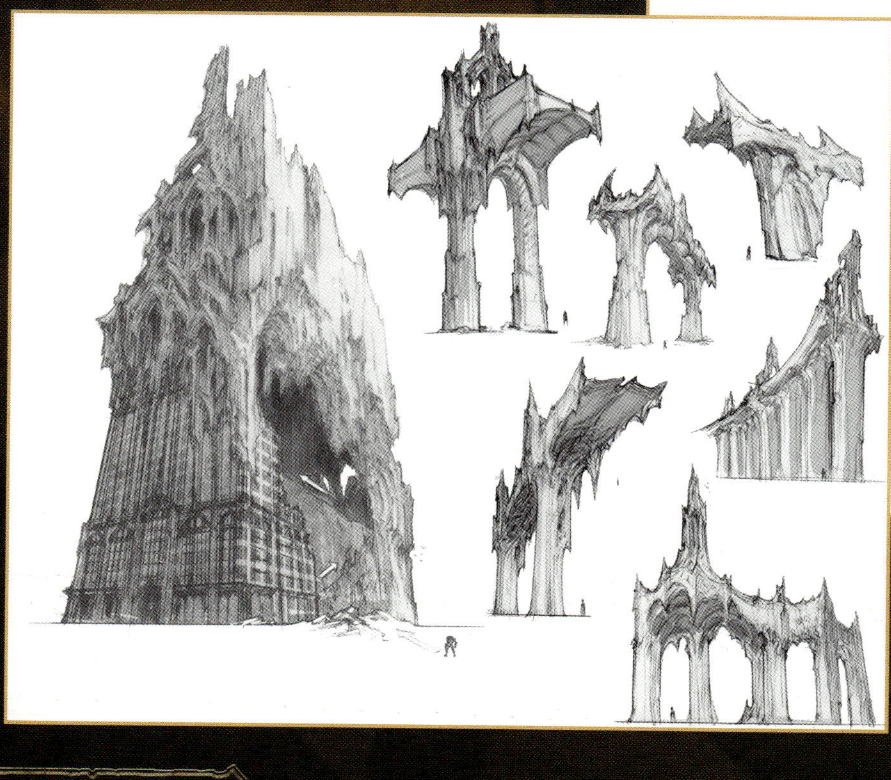

FORM CONCEPTS

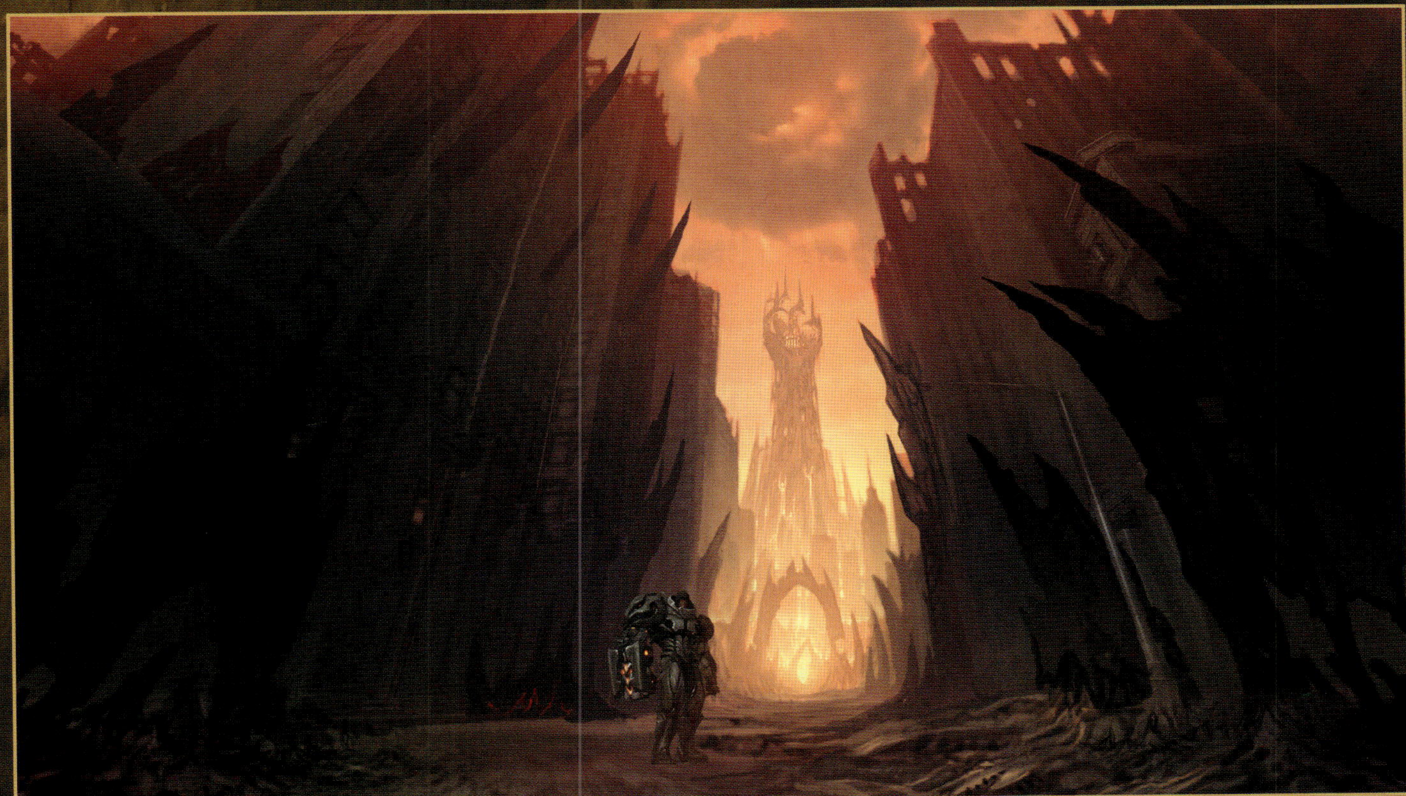

STREET CONCEPT

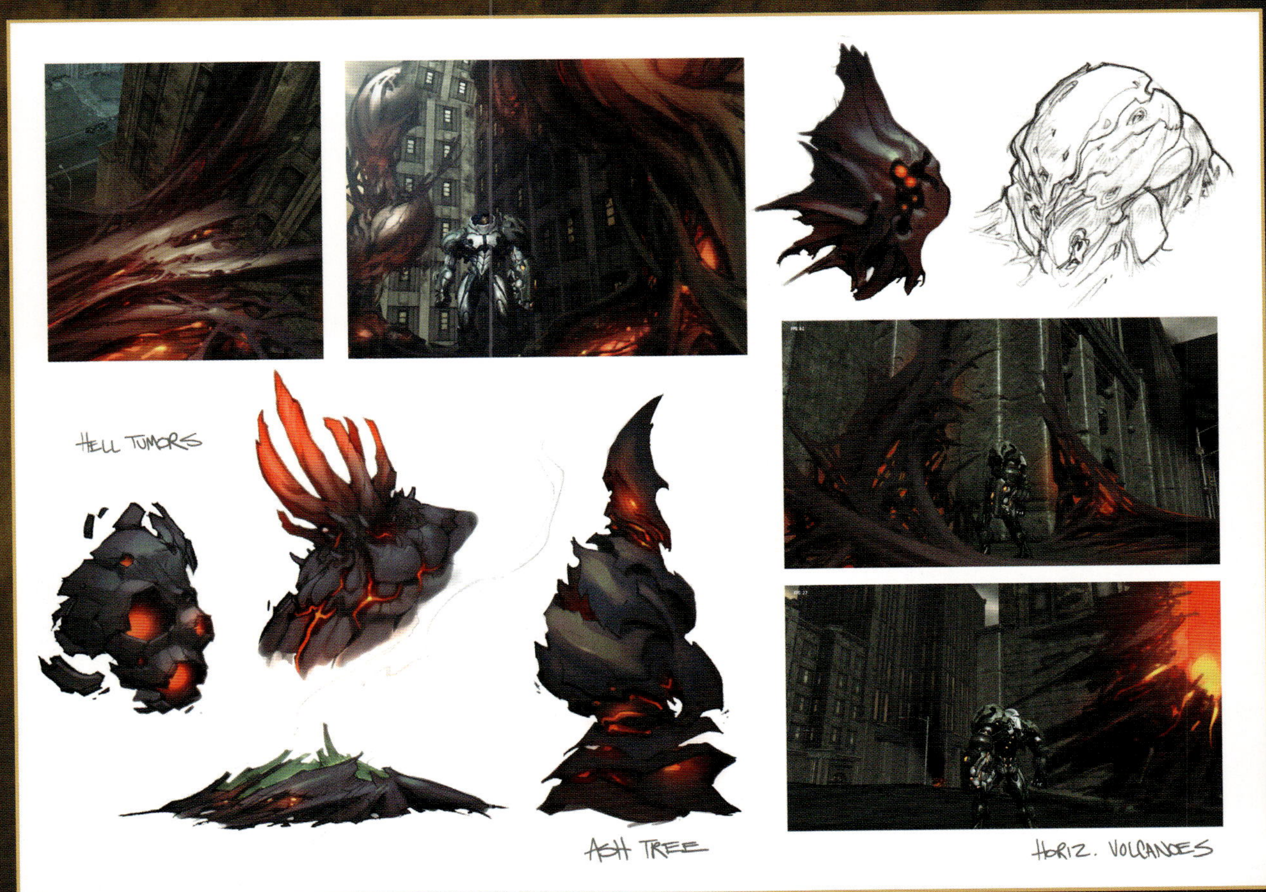

FORM CONCEPTS

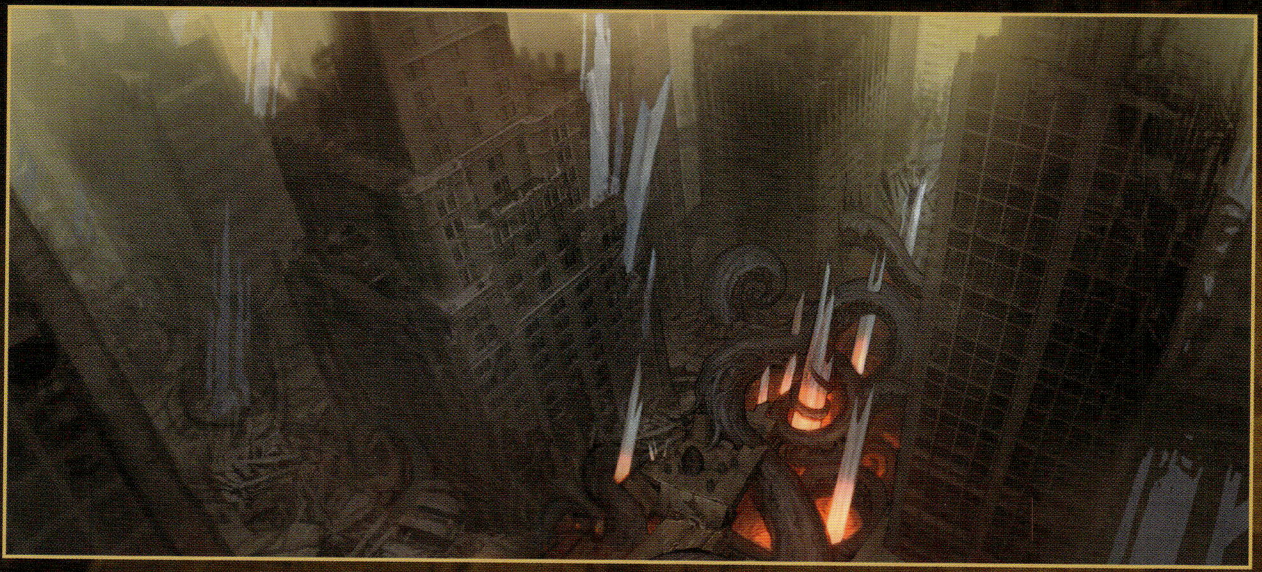

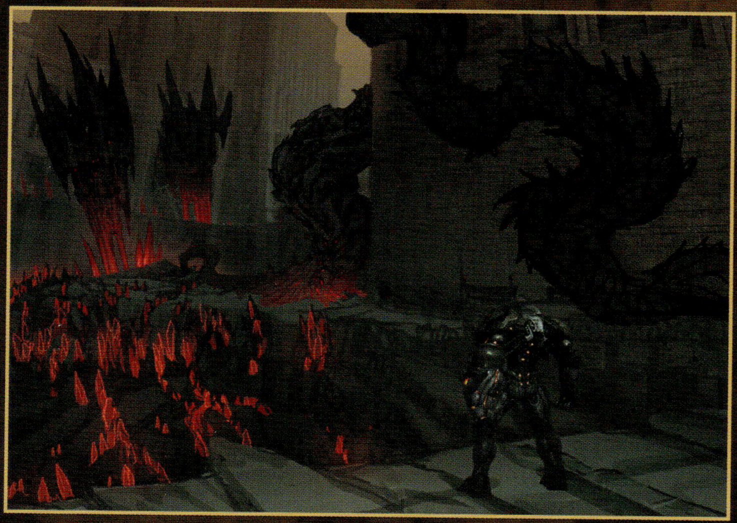

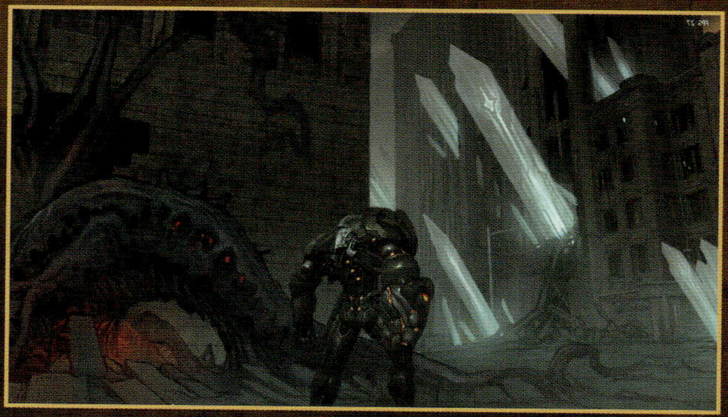

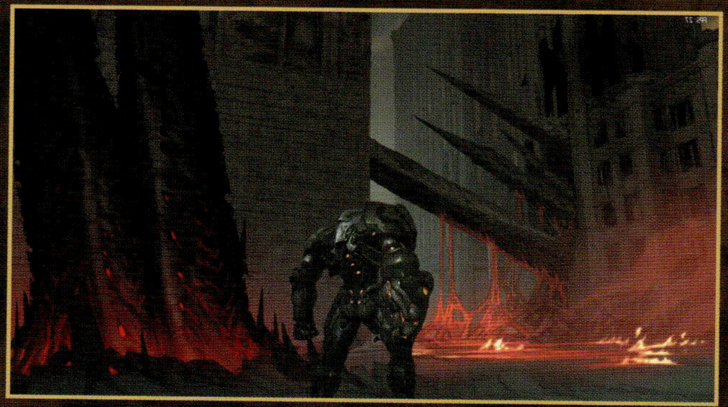

HELLGROWTH CONCEPTS

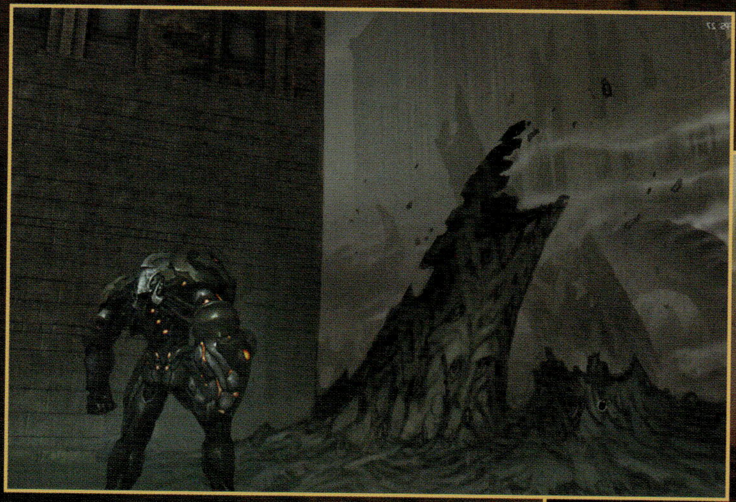

HELLGROWTH CONCEPTS

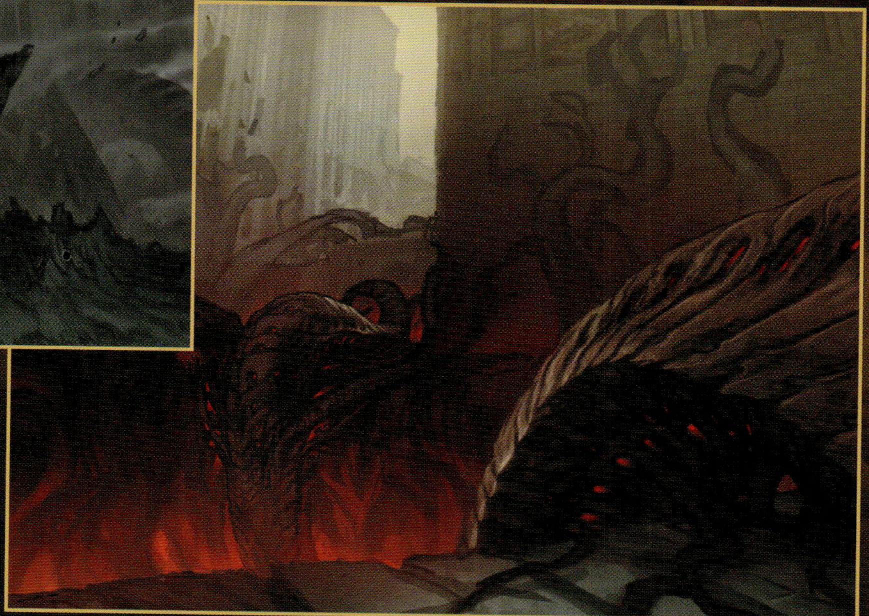

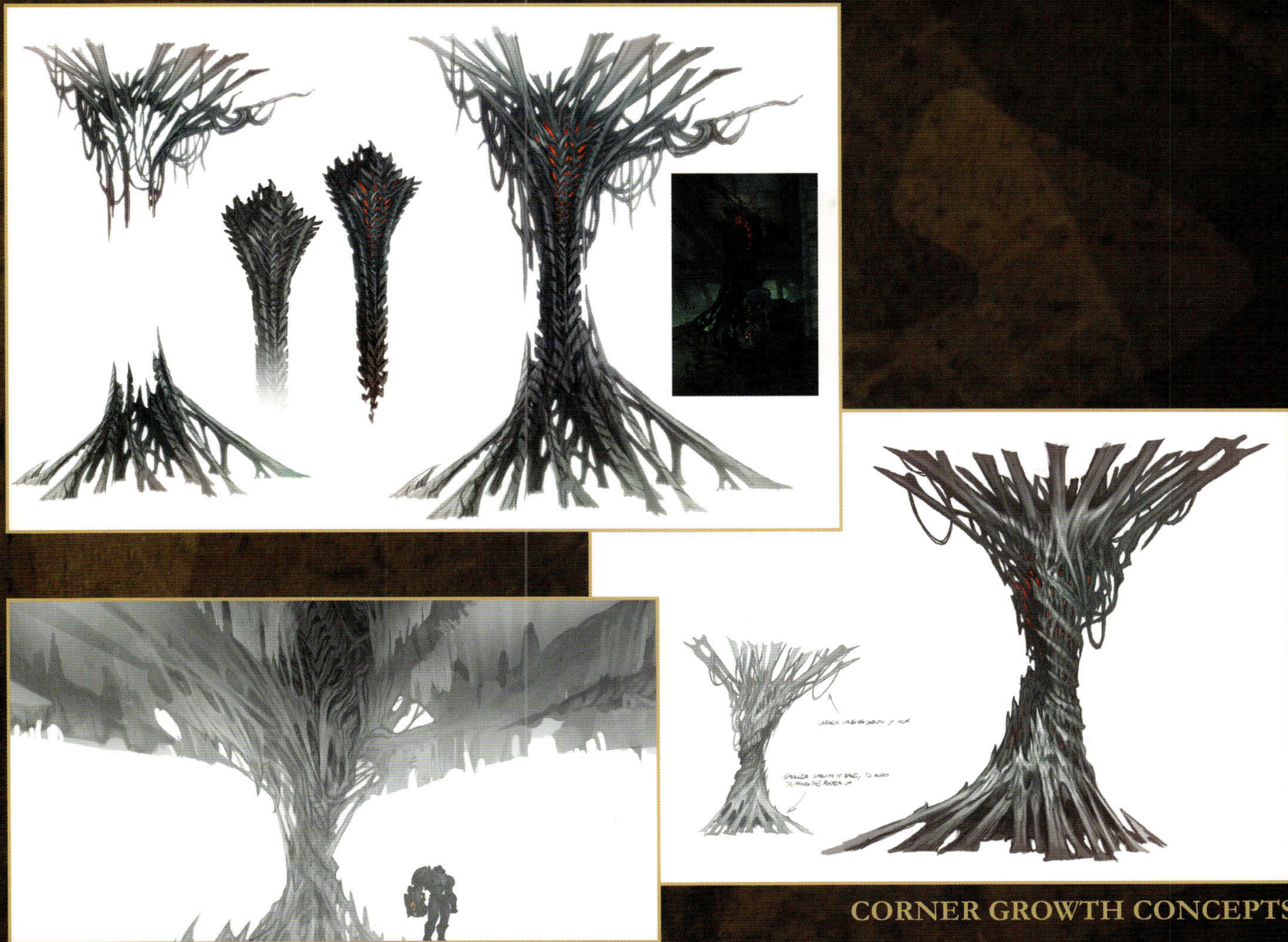

CORNER GROWTH CONCEPTS

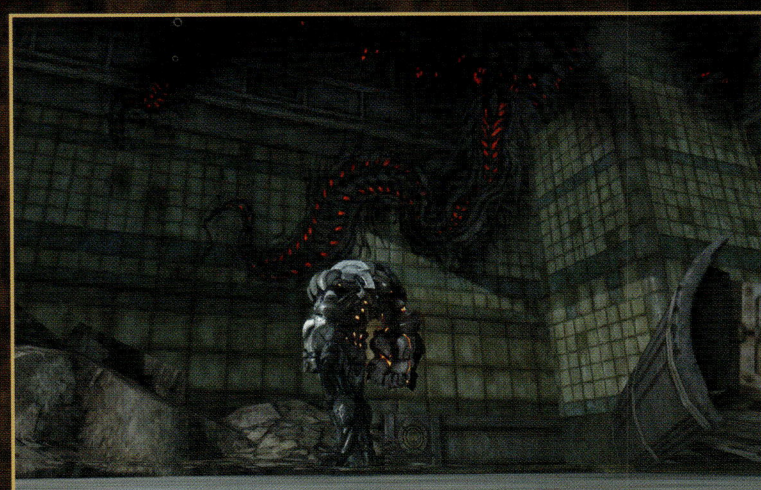

HELLGROWTH CONCEPT

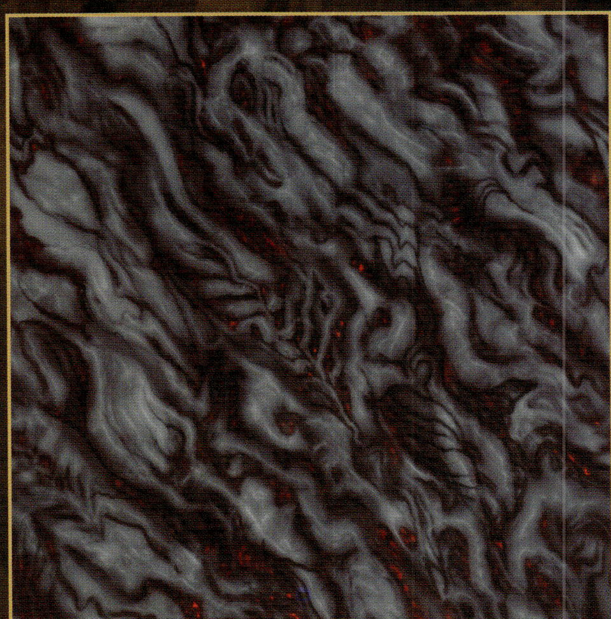

HELLGROWTH TEXTURE DETAIL

HELLGROWTH FORM CONCEPS

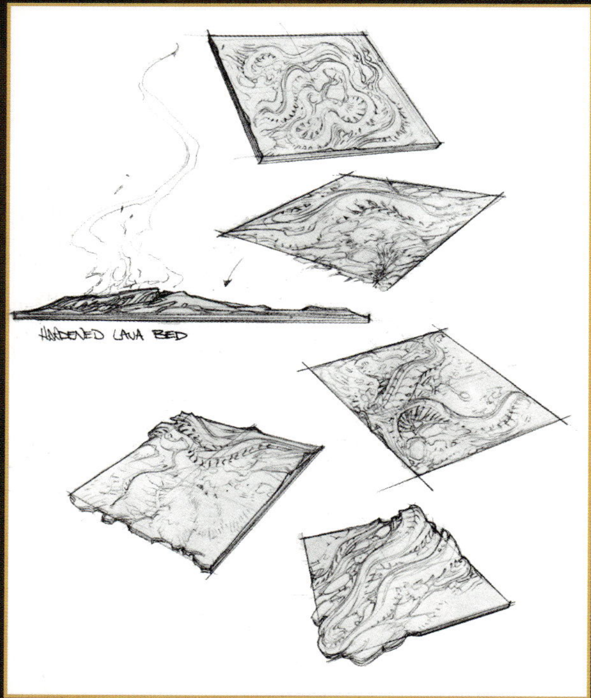

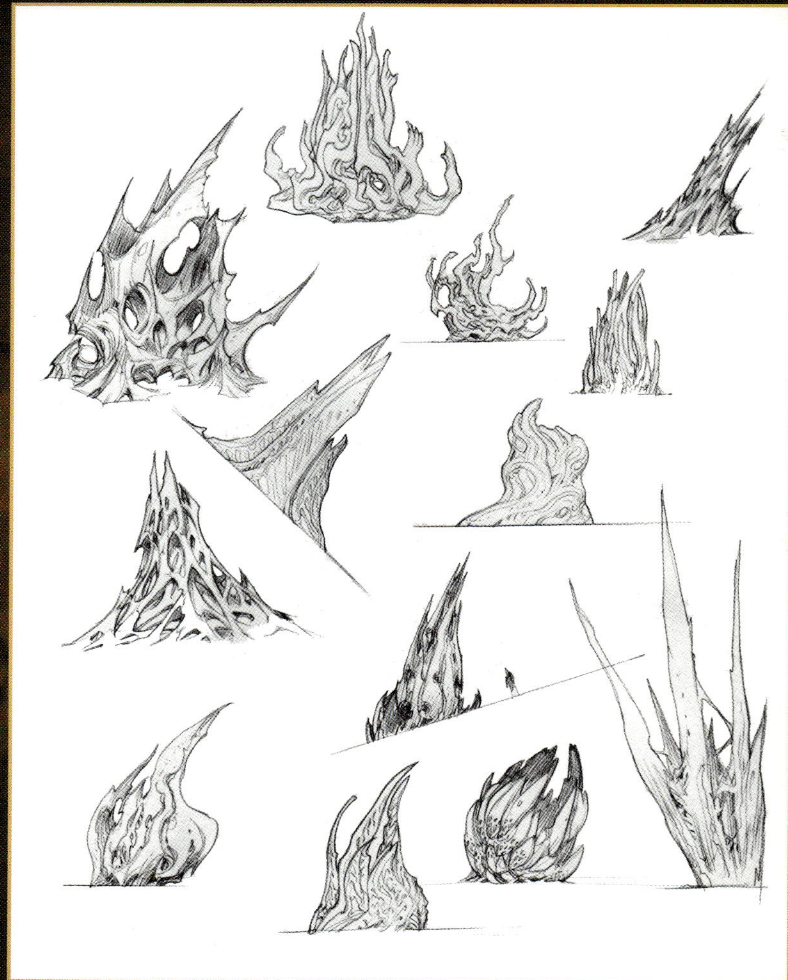

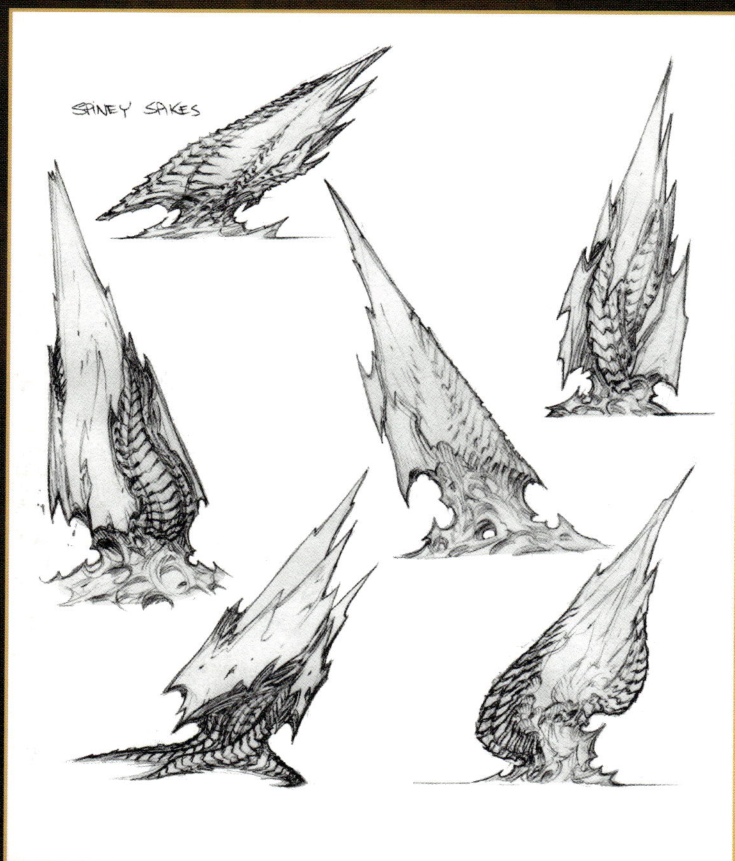

FORM CONCEPS

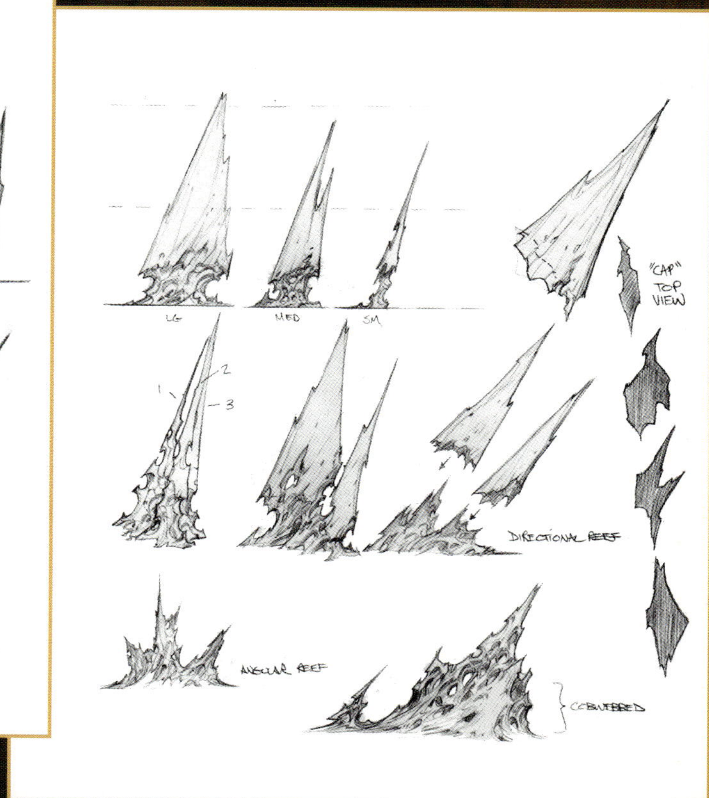

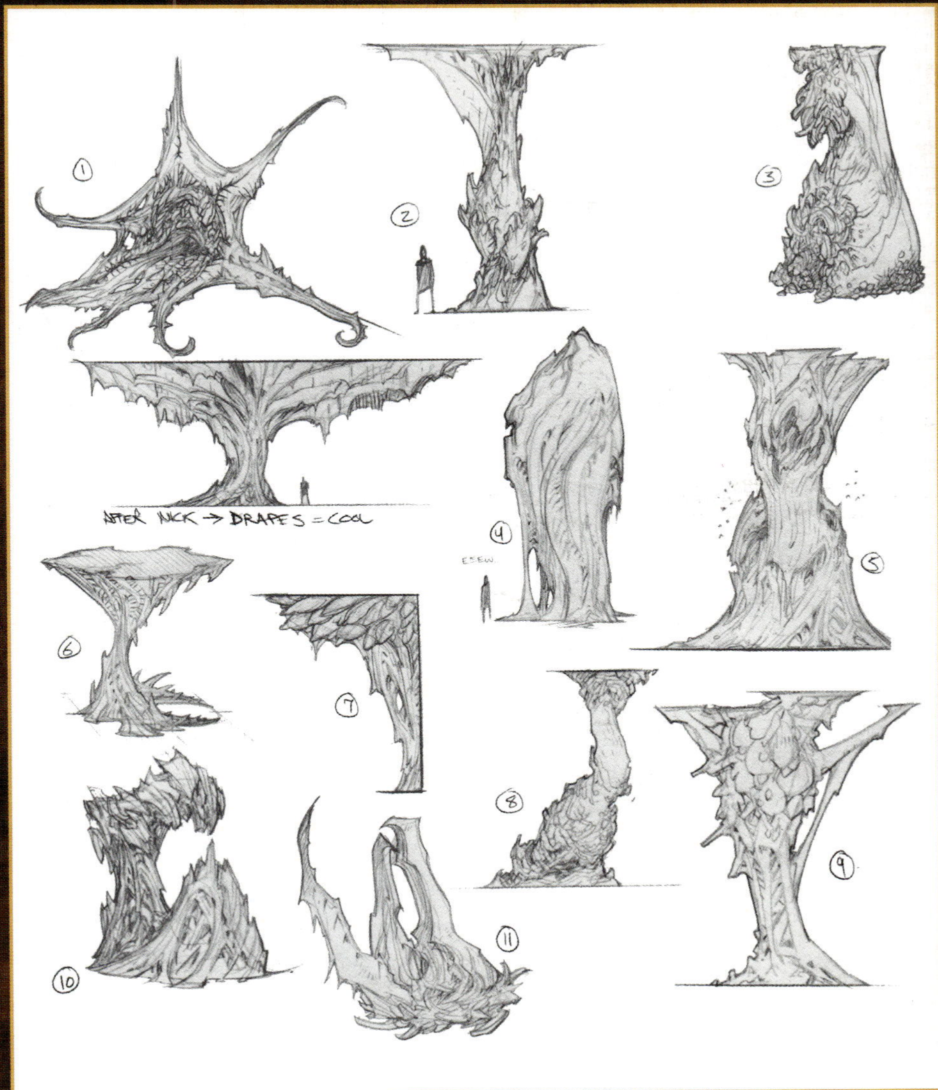

FORM CONCEPS

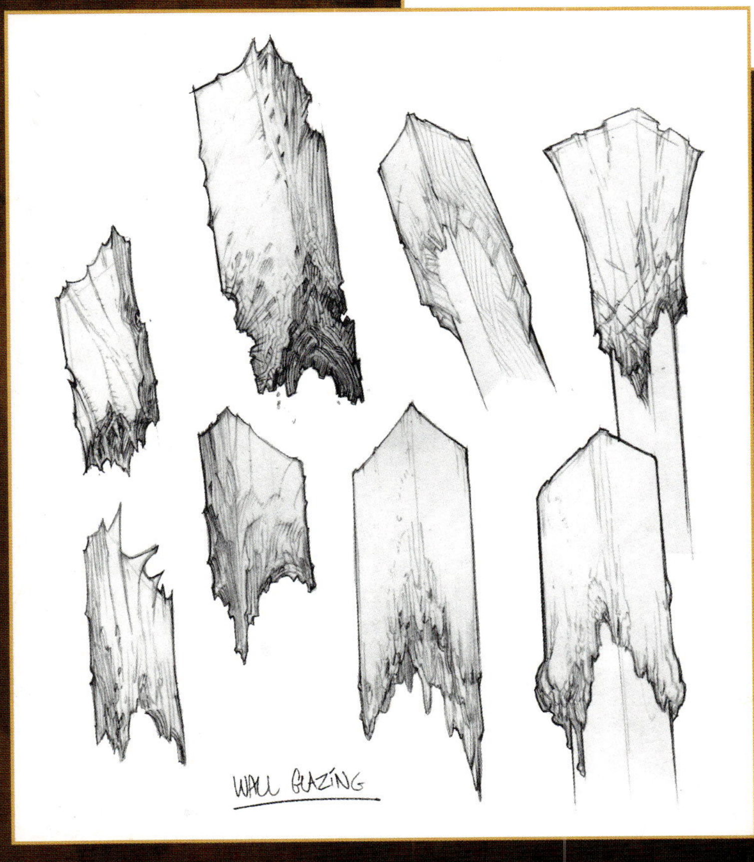

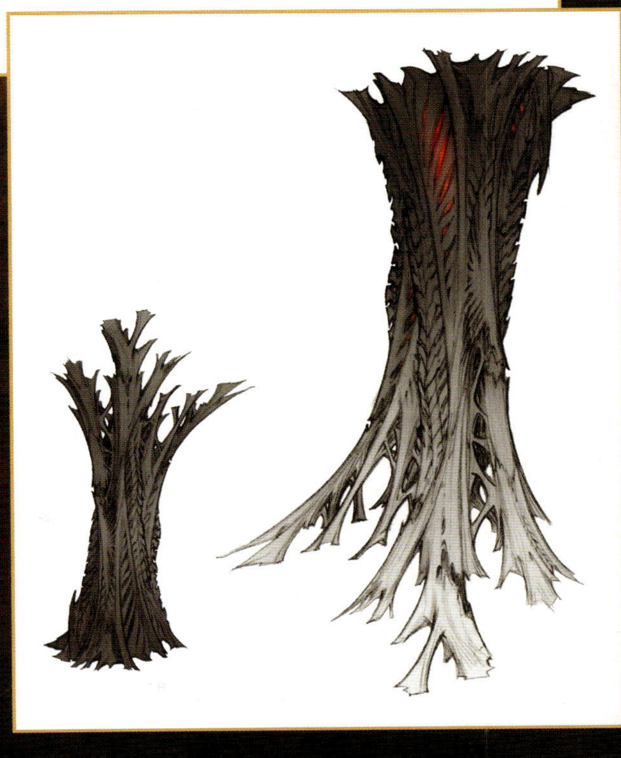

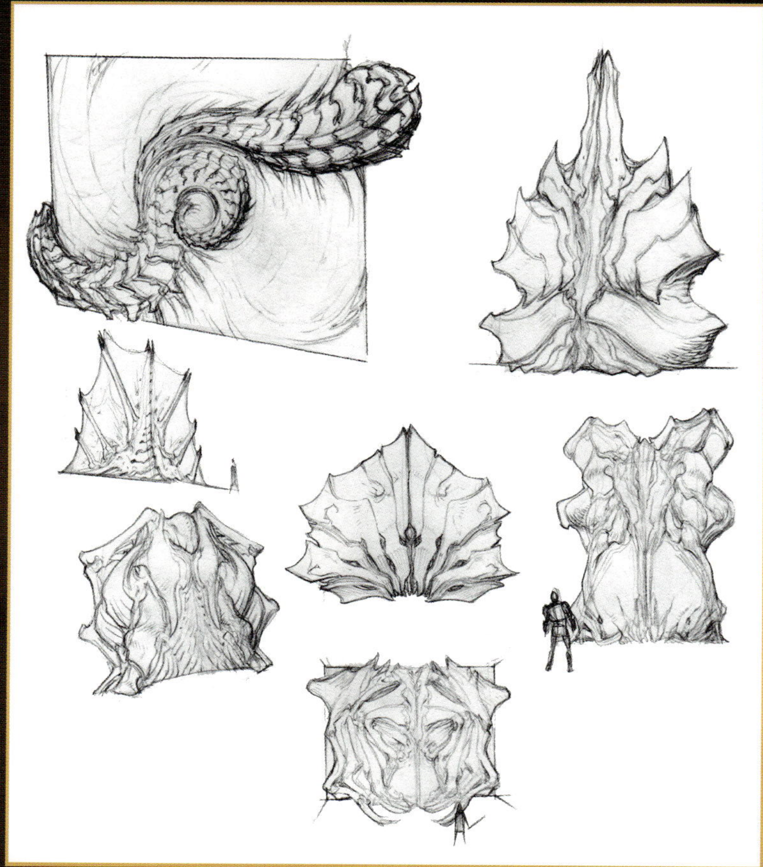

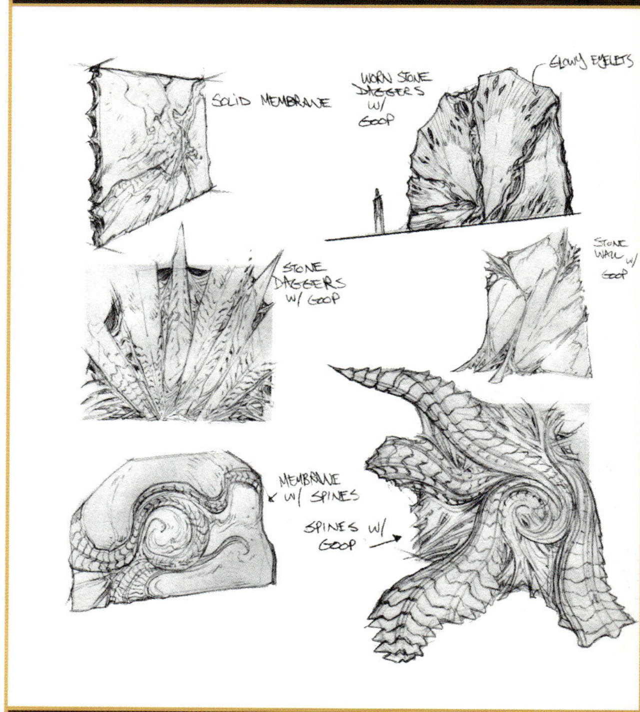

HELLGROWTH
FORM CONCEPTS

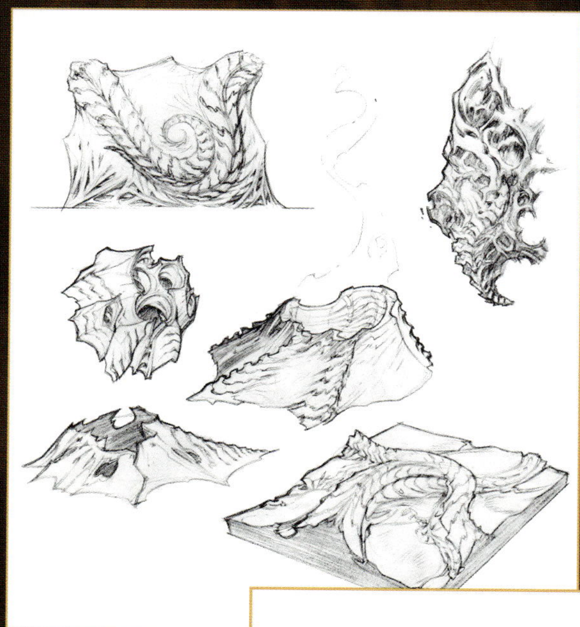

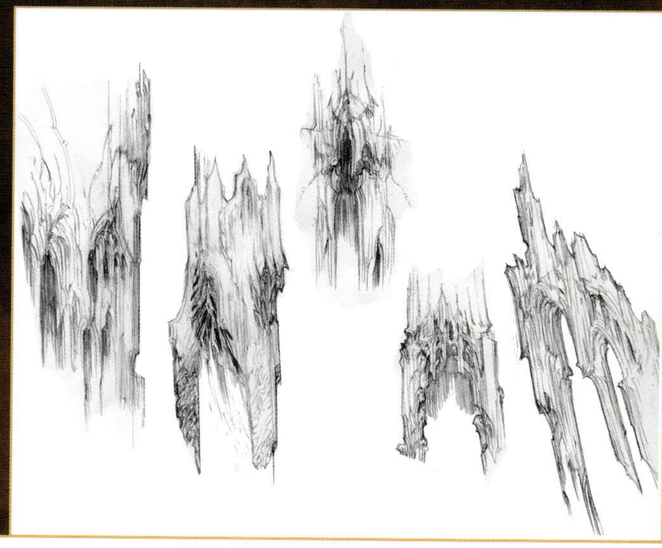

FORM
CONCEPTS

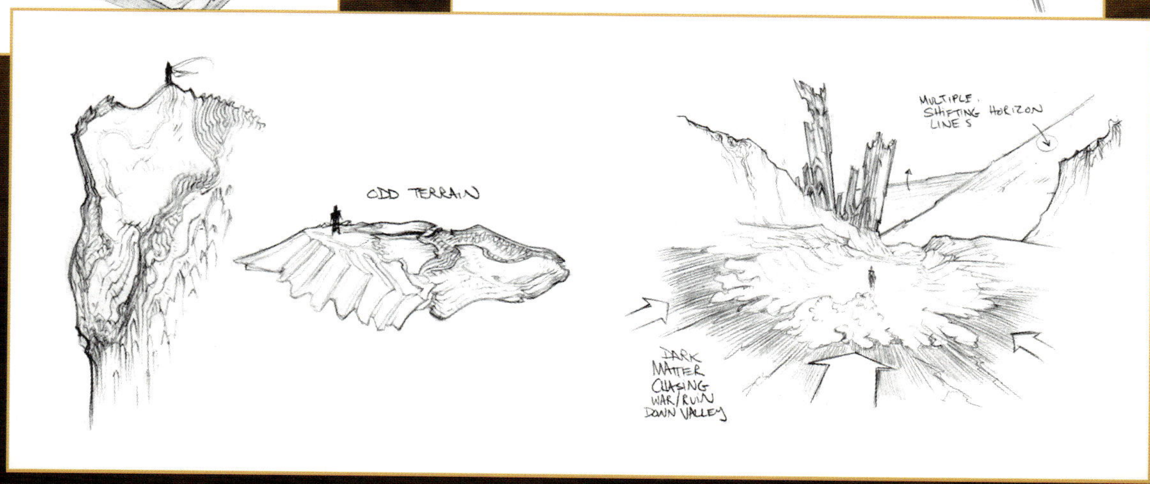

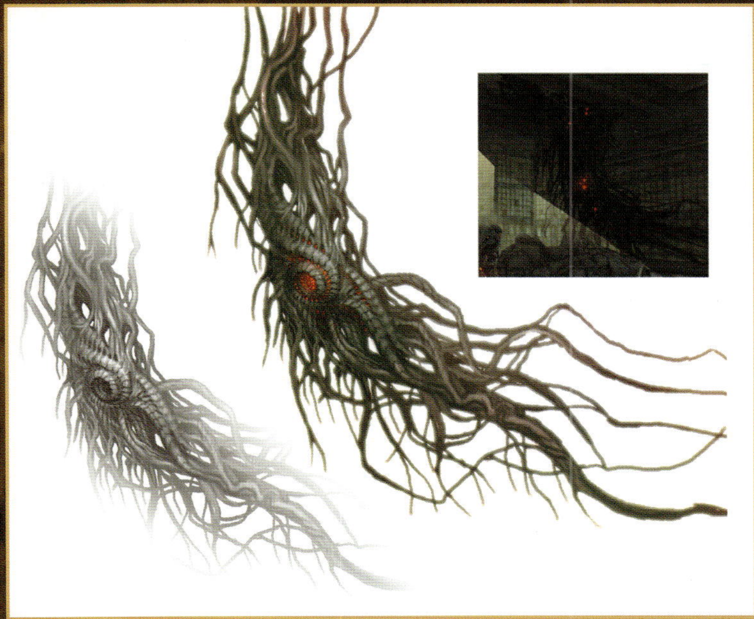

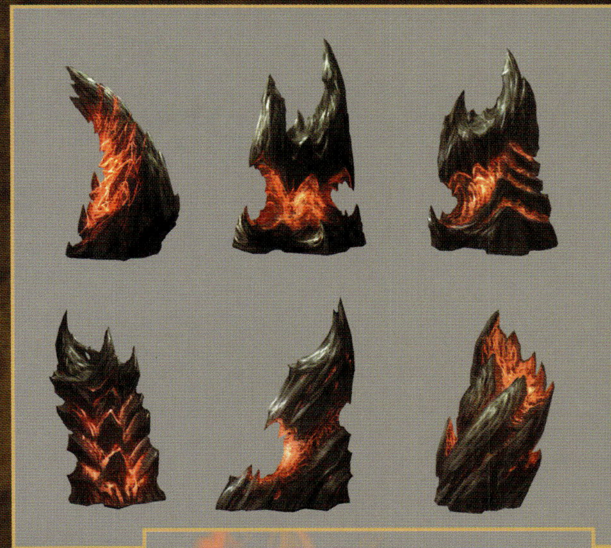

FORM CONCEPTS

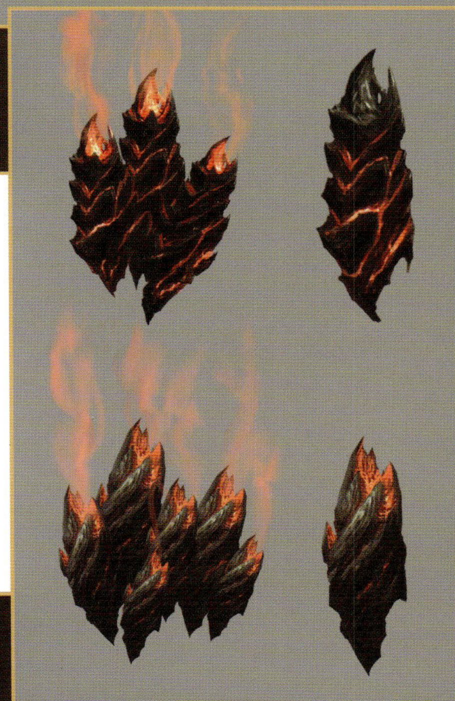

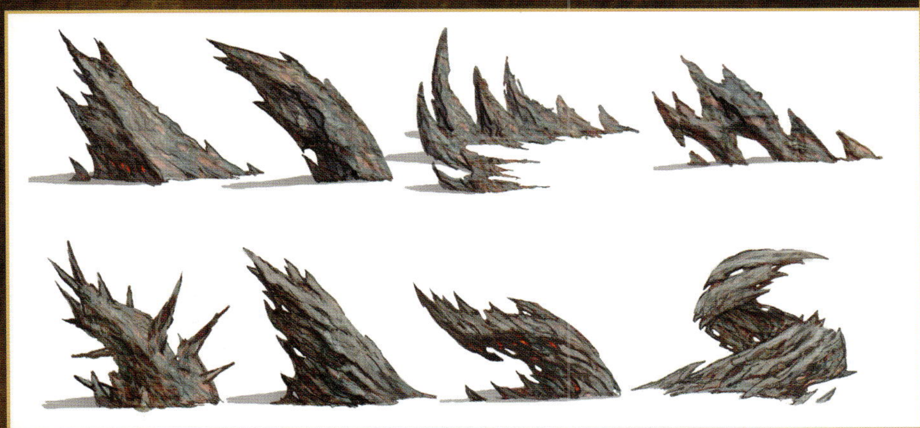

FORM CONCEPTS

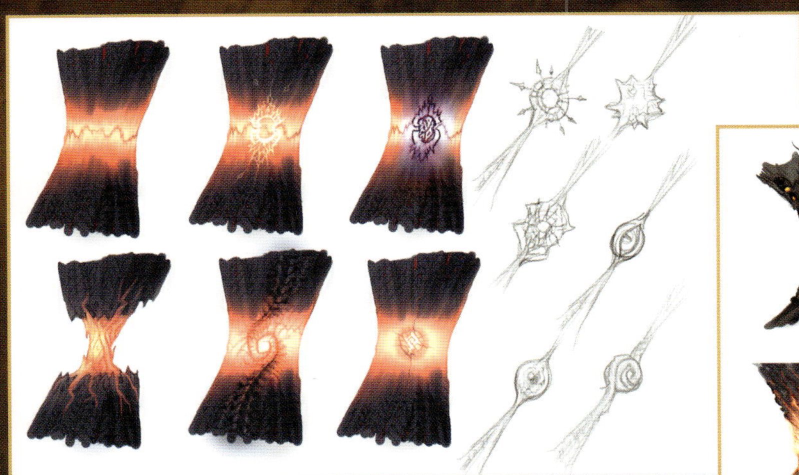

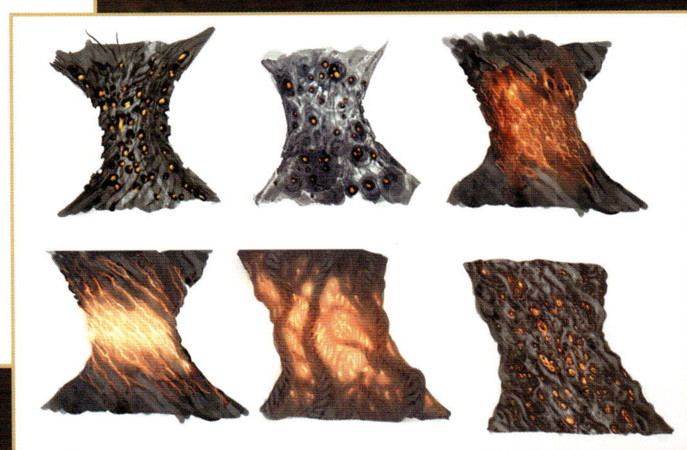

COLUMN CONCEPTS

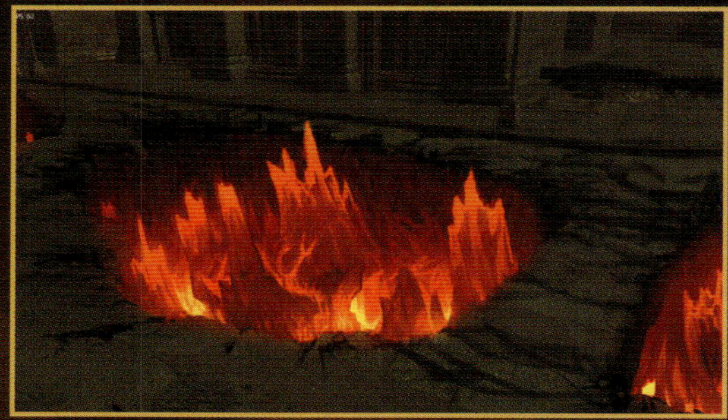
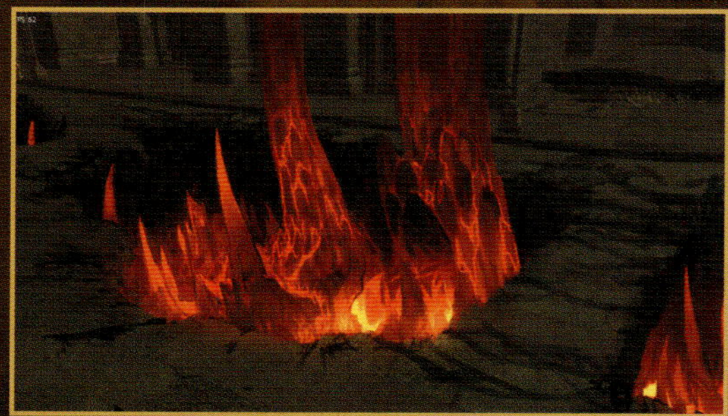
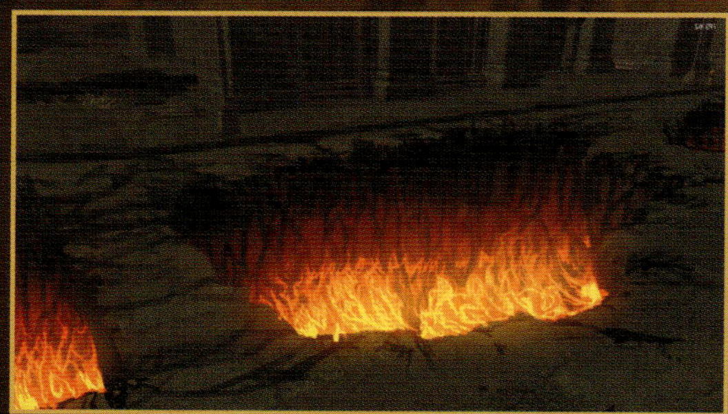
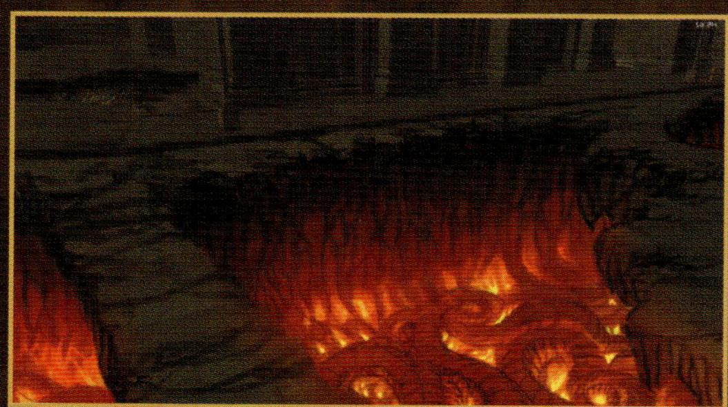
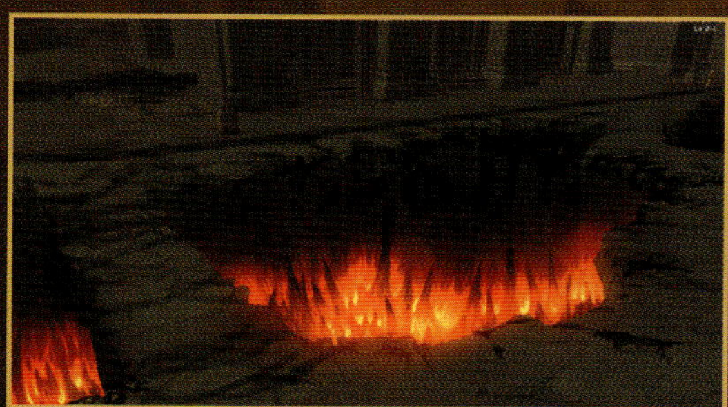

PIT CONCEPTS

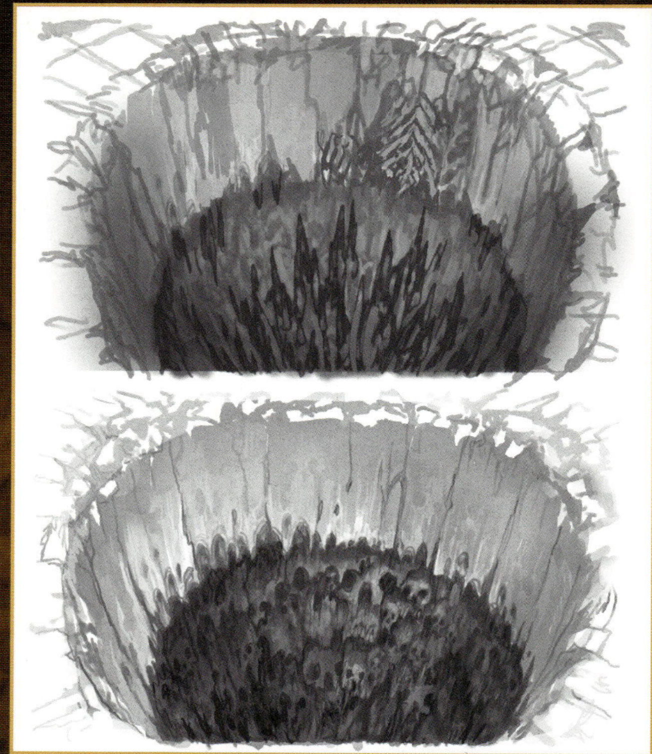

HELLGROWTH BOMB DESIGNS

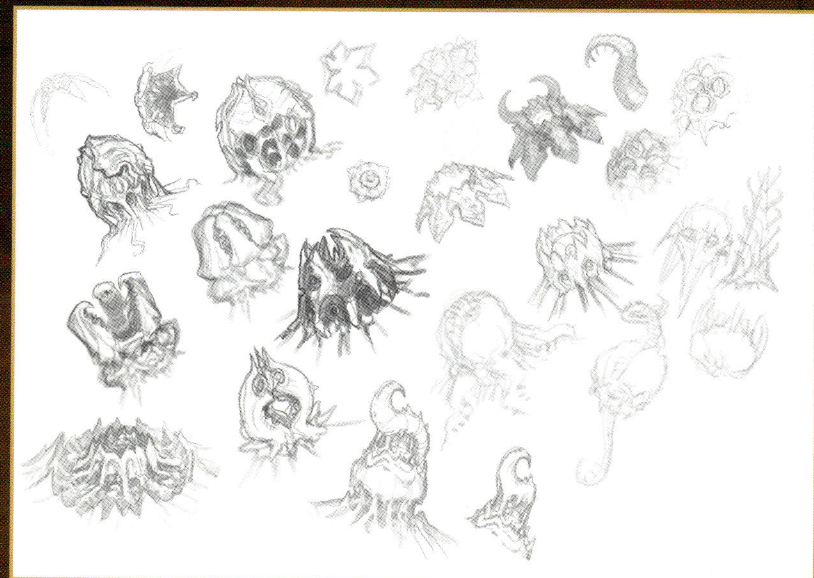
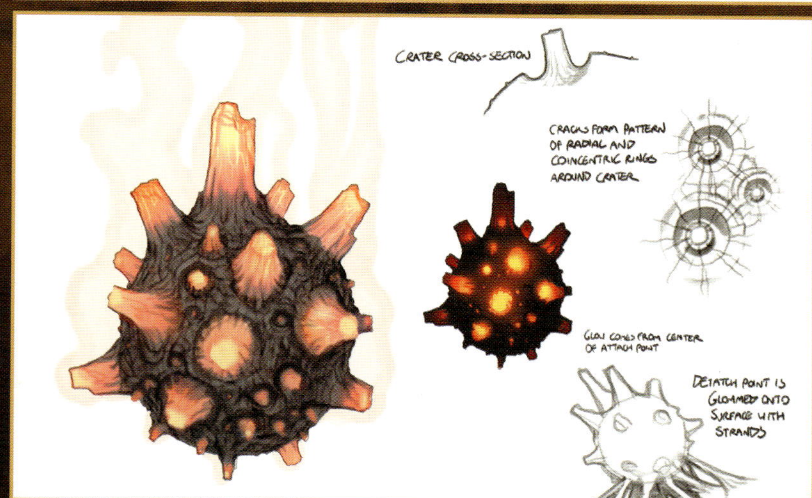

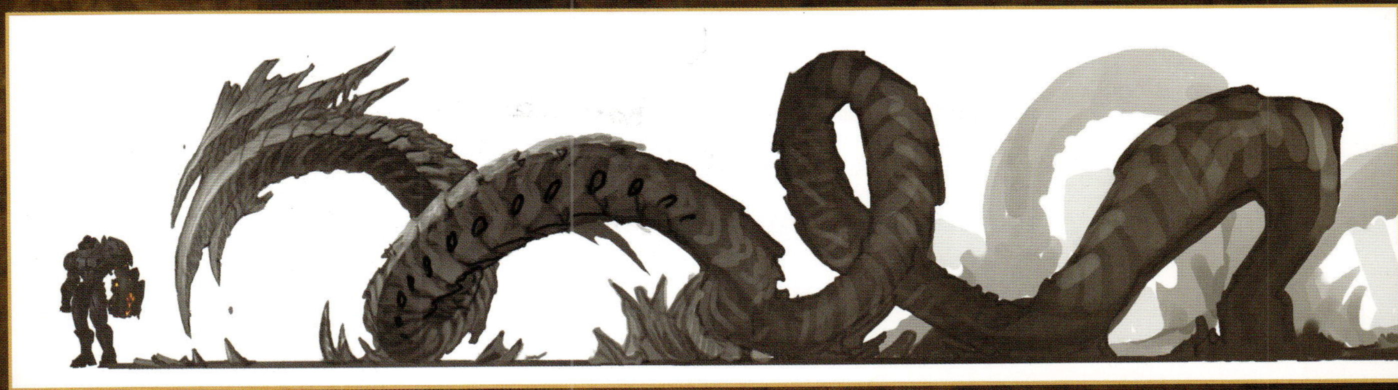

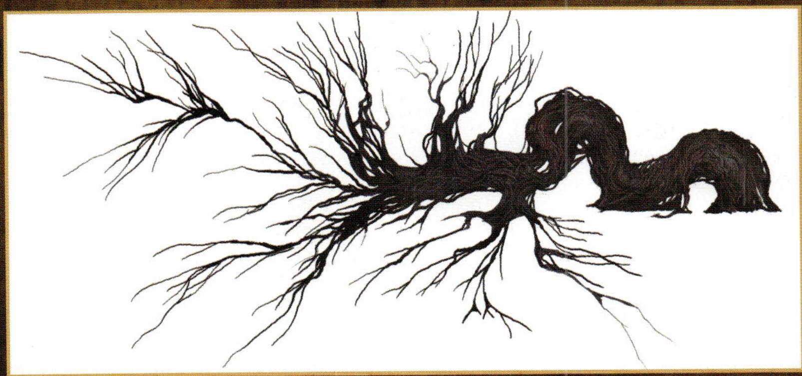

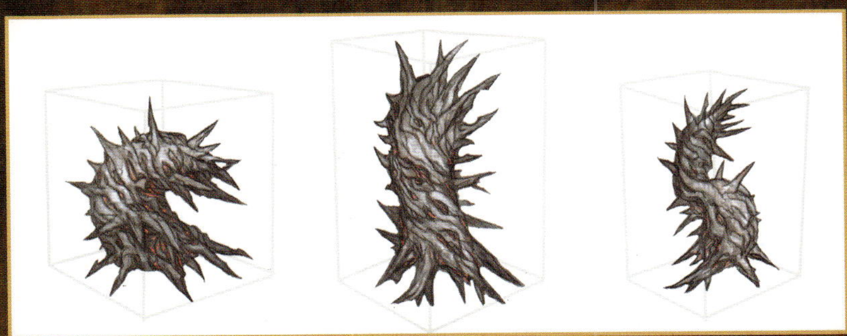

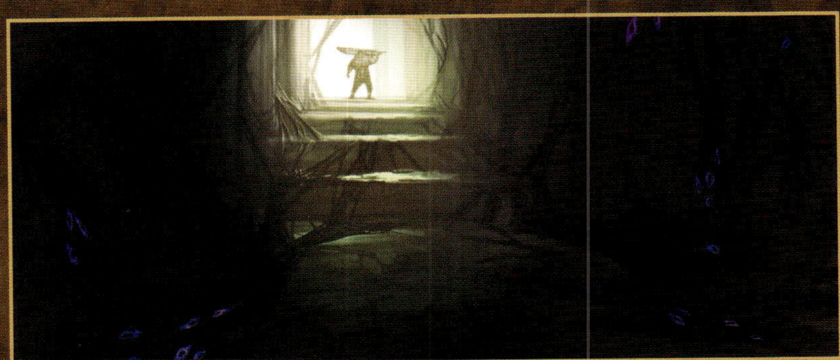

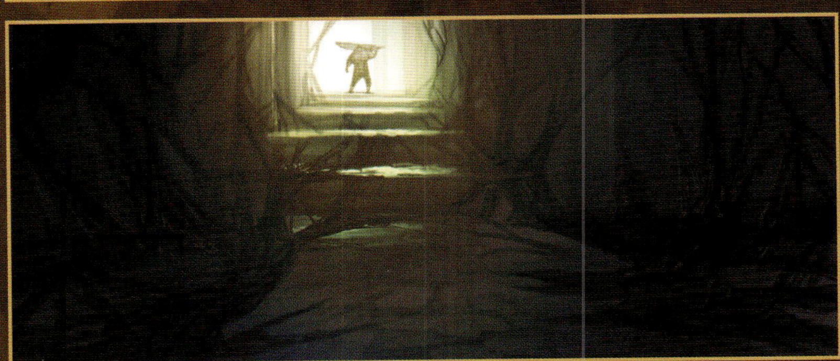

HELLGROWTH CONCEPTS

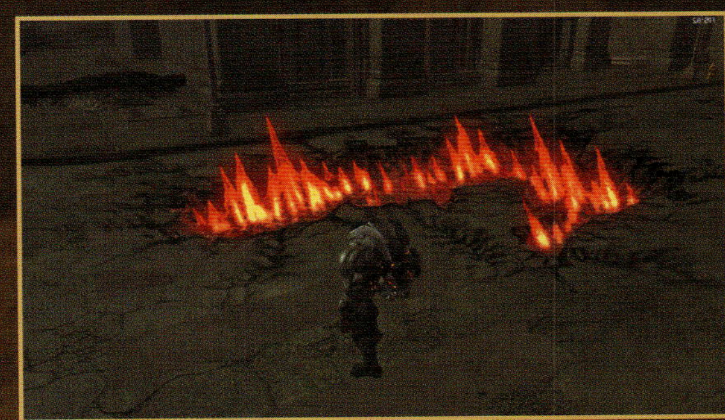

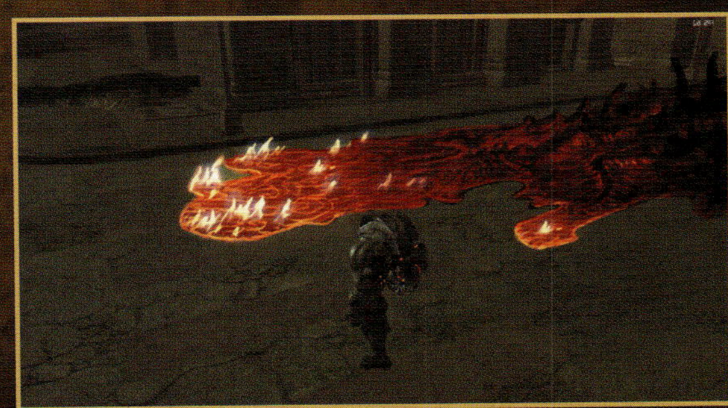

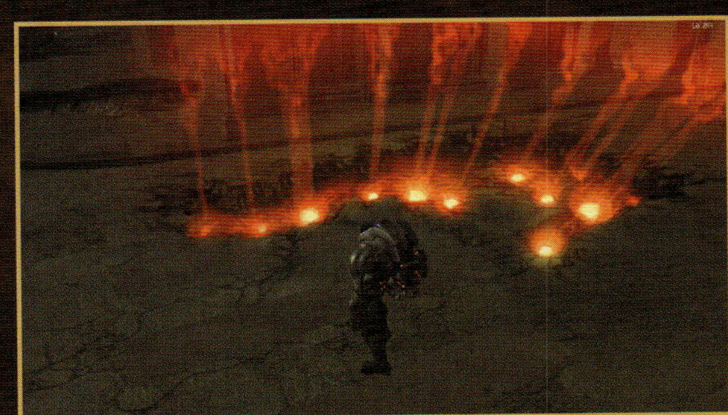

HELLGROWTH HAZARD CONCEPTS

Silitha's Loom

Silitha's Loom stretches for miles, a tangled labyrinth of cobwebs that cling to the toppled city towers, suspended above the earth. Cocooned within are angels, mummified humans, and other horrors. Some are still alive, hung like preserved meat for the Canopy's mistress. Others are corpses missing limbs and heads and torsos, mere snacks for her many-eyed children.

Travelers would be wise to avoid Silitha's Loom, lest they become one more entrée on a nightmare's menu.

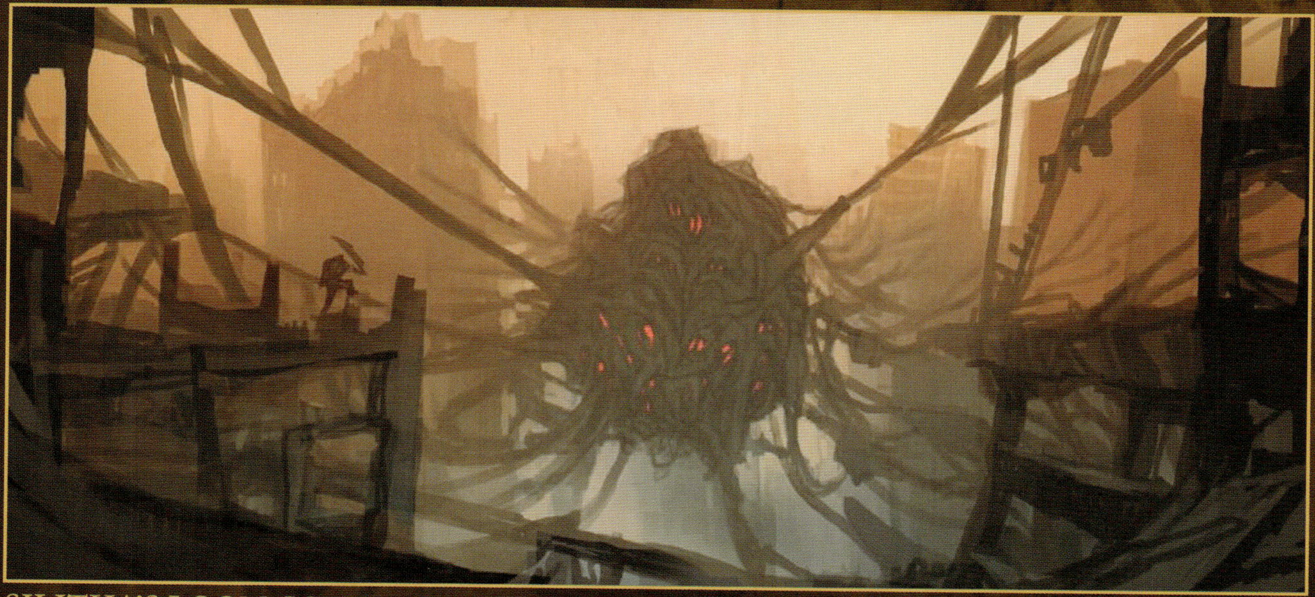

SILITHA'S LOOM CONCEPT

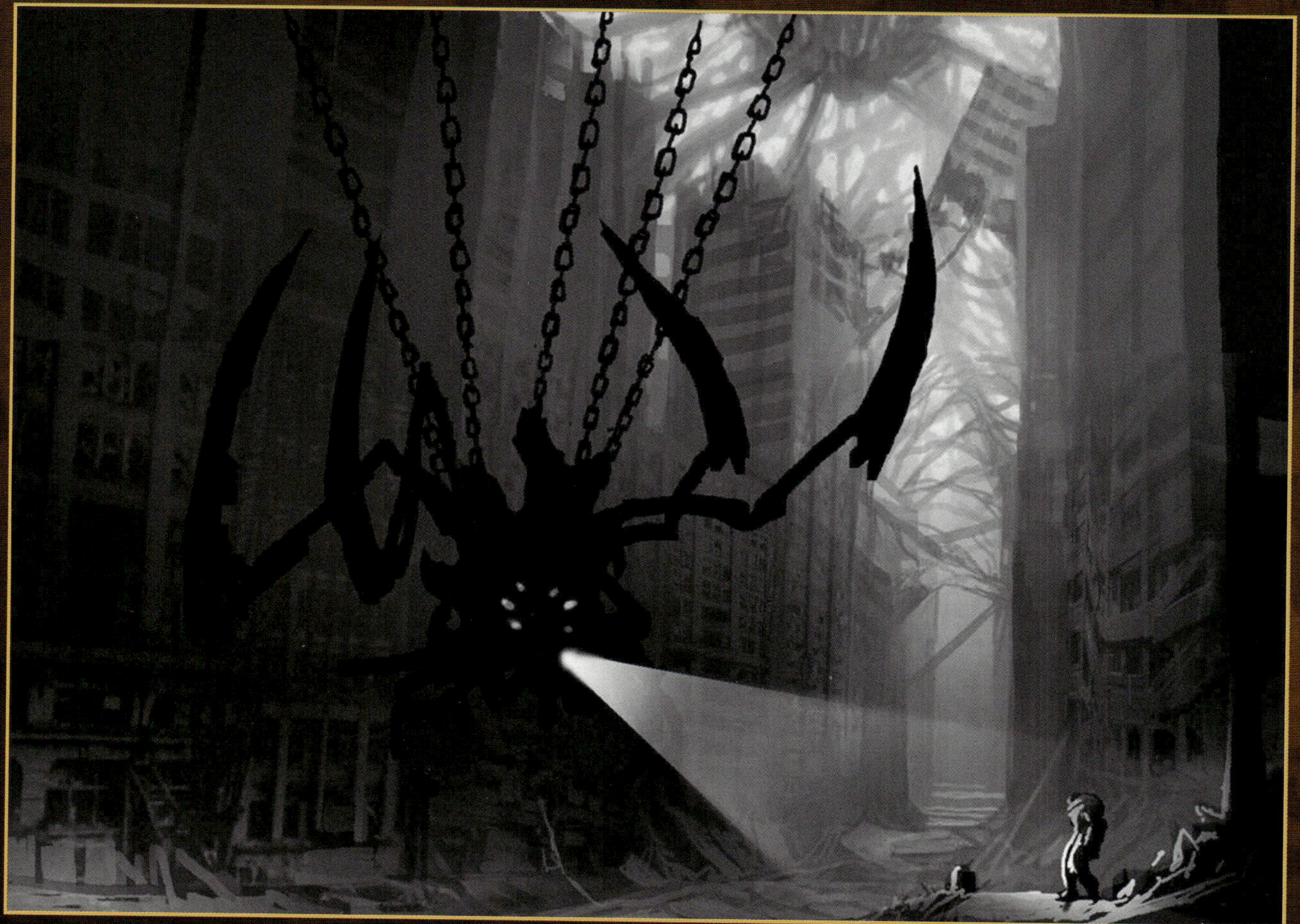

SILITHA'S LOOM CONCEPT

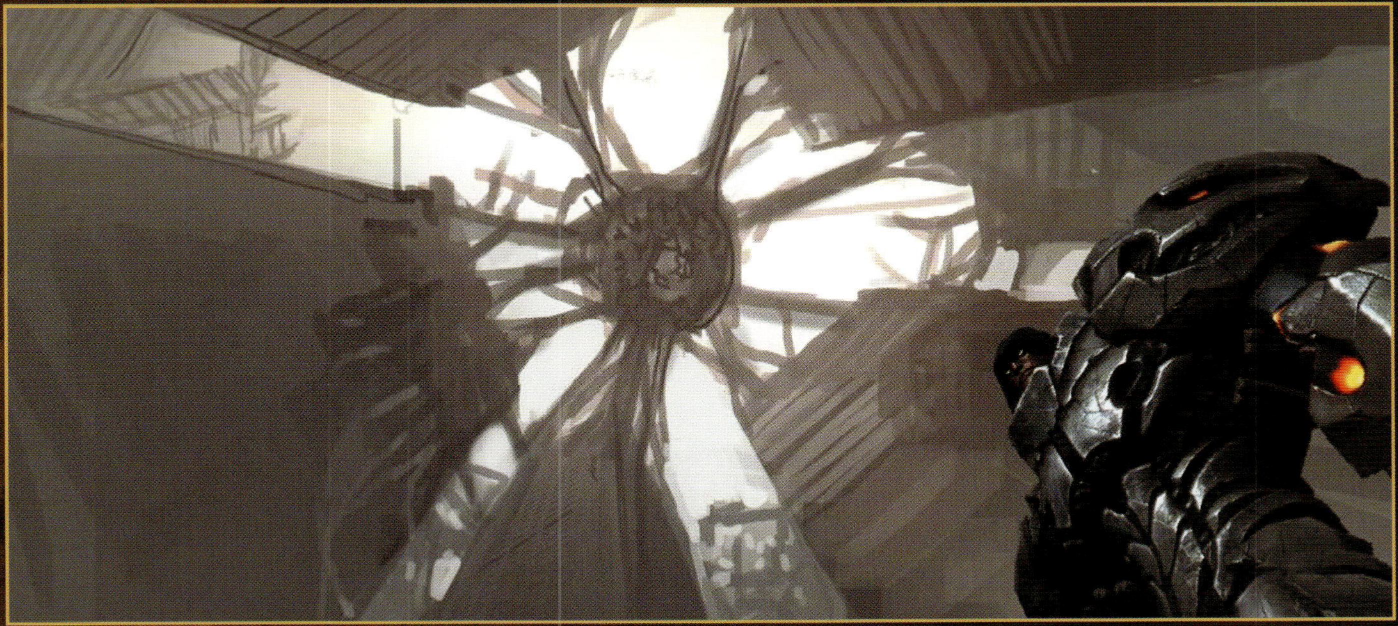

CEILING CONCEPT

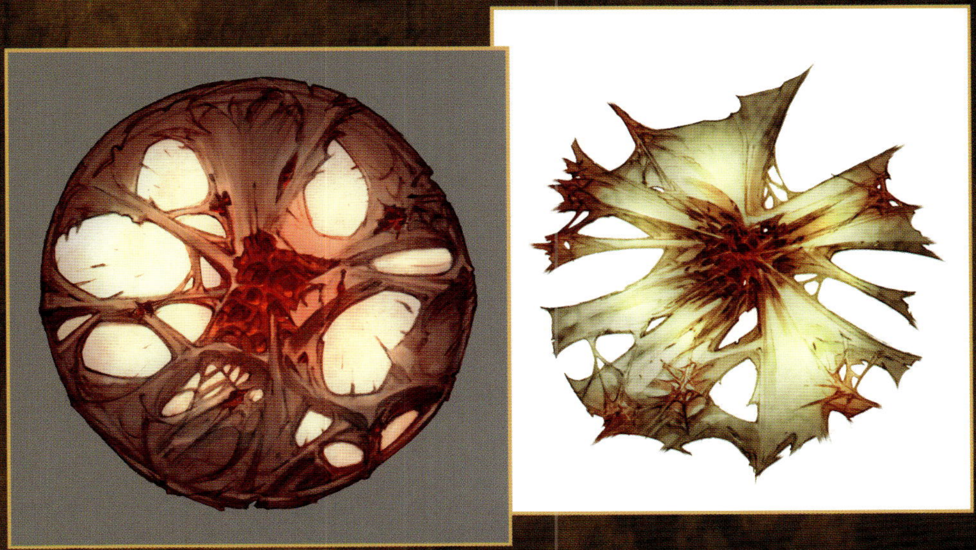

CEILING CONCEPTS

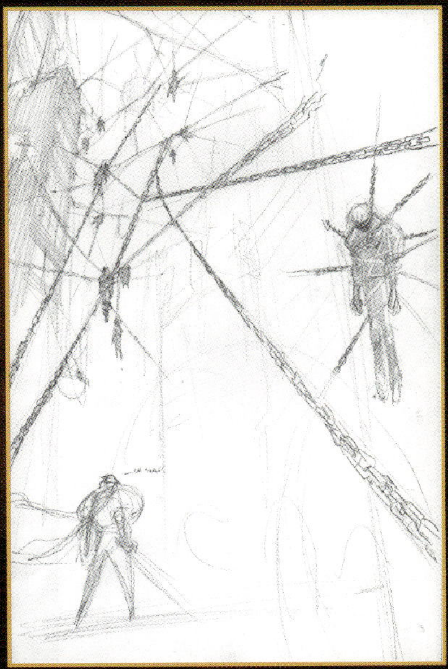

CHAINWEBS CONCEPT

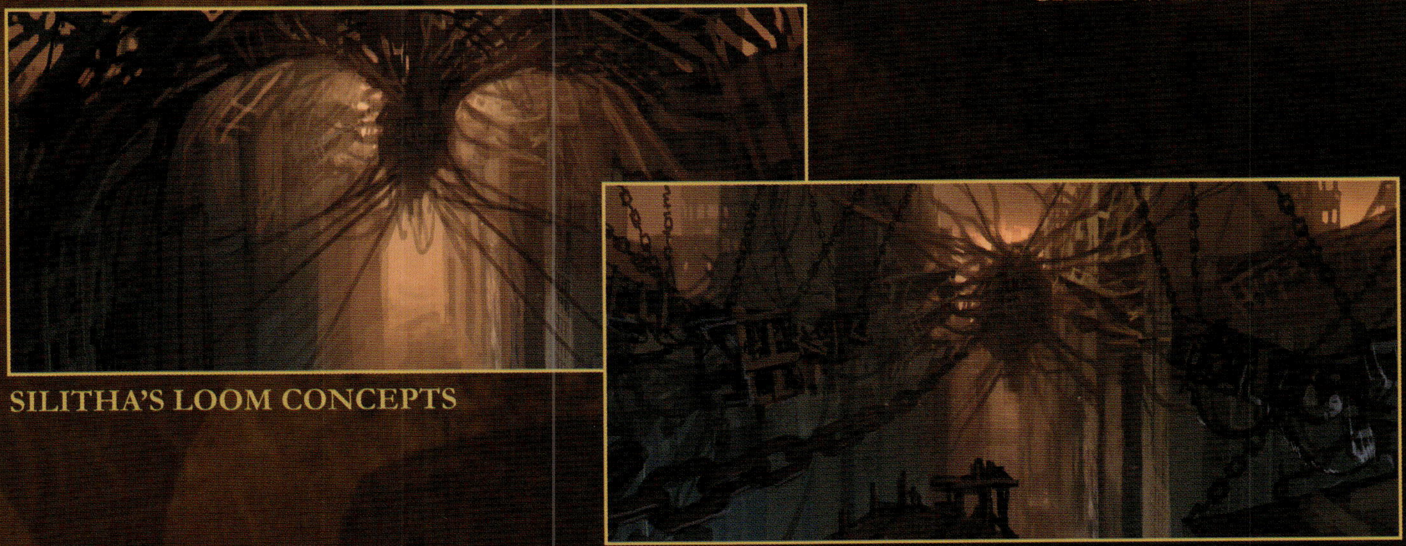

SILITHA'S LOOM CONCEPTS

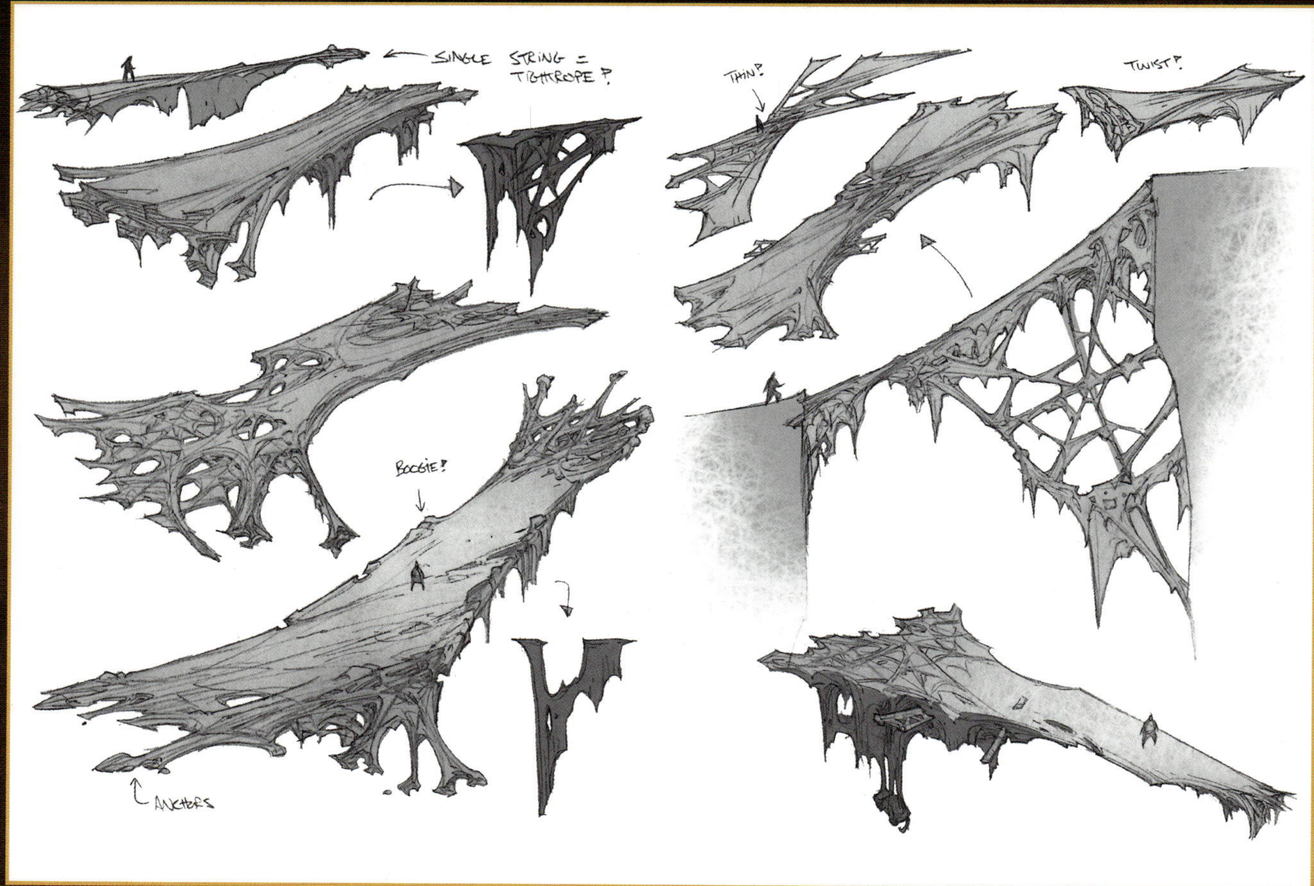

WEB CONCEPTS

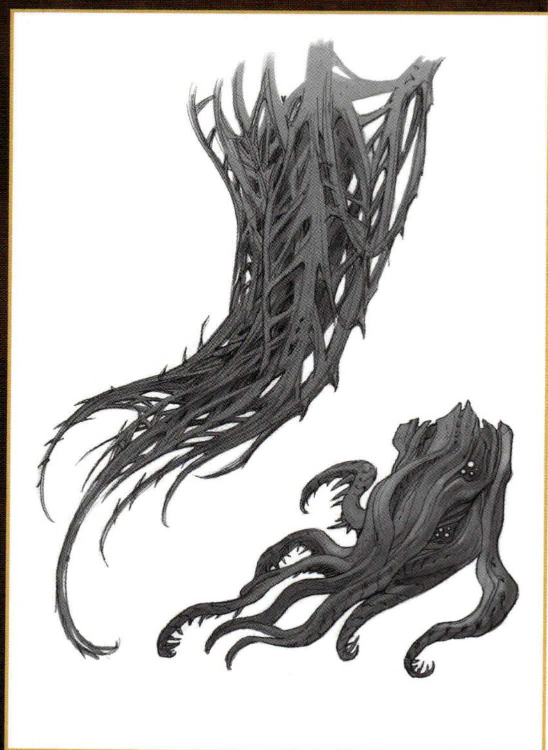

WEB CONCEPTS

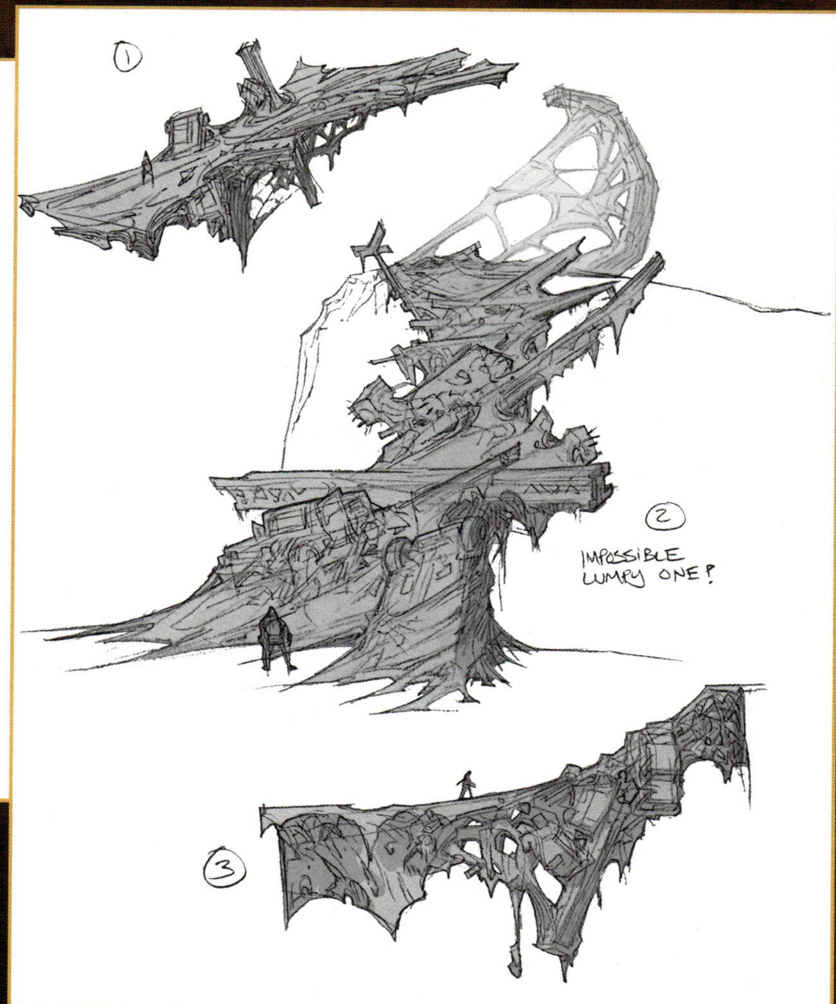

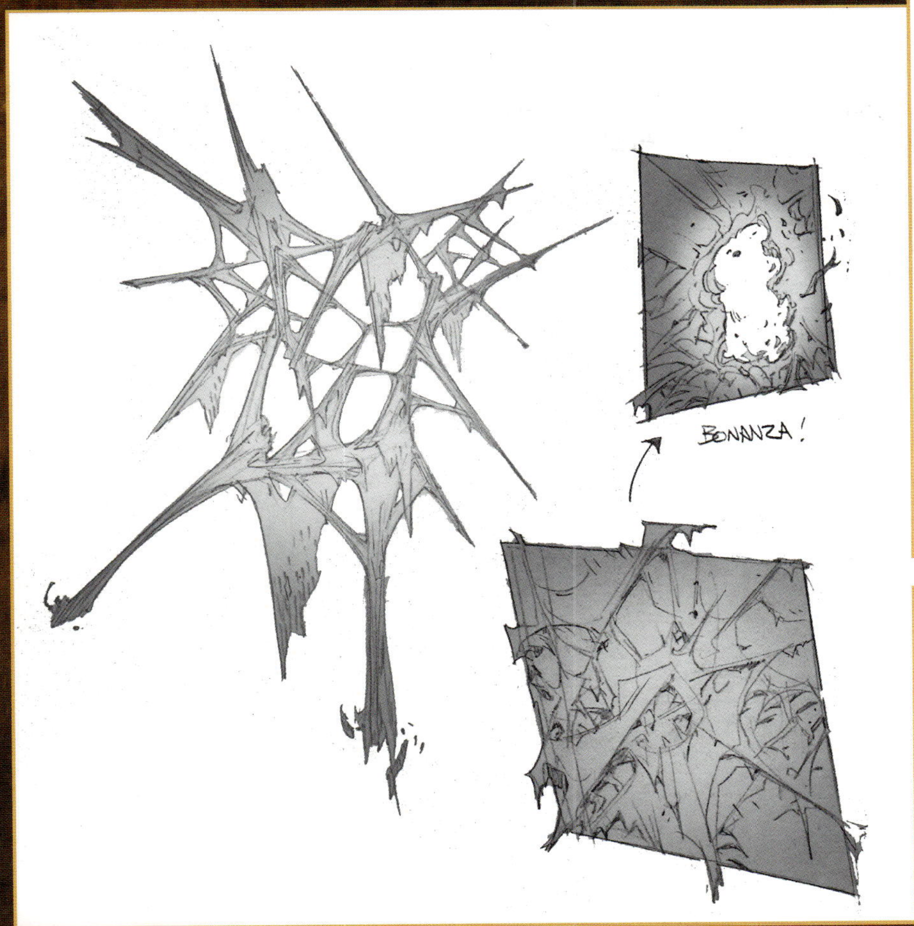

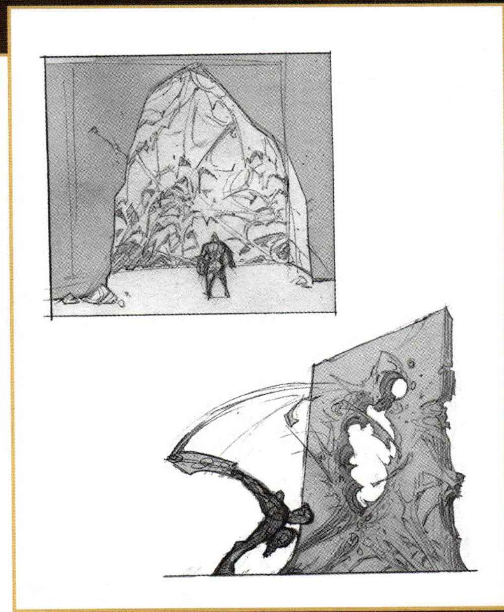

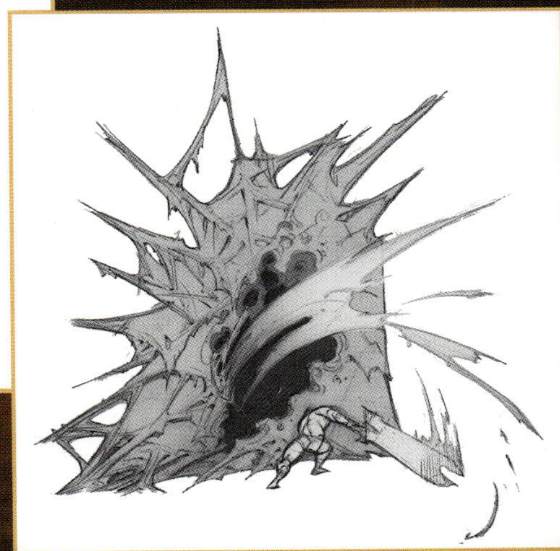

WEB DOOR CONCEPTS

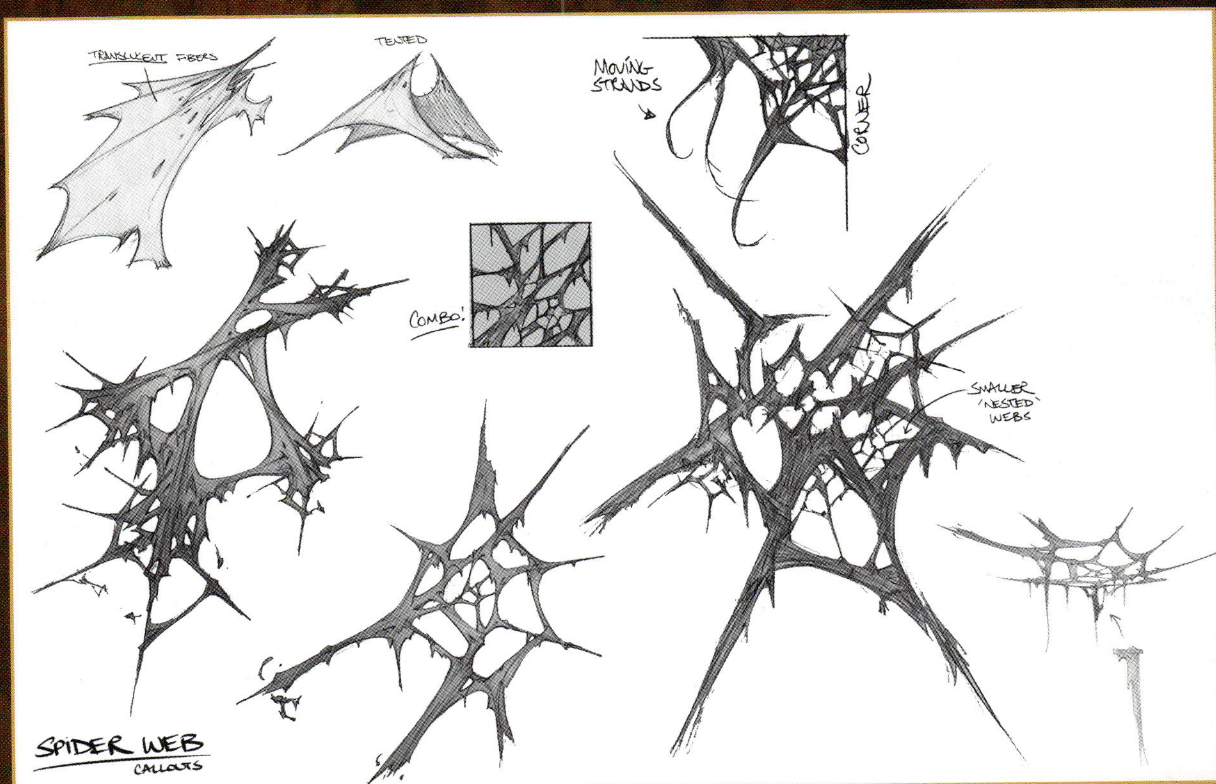

WEB CONCEPTS

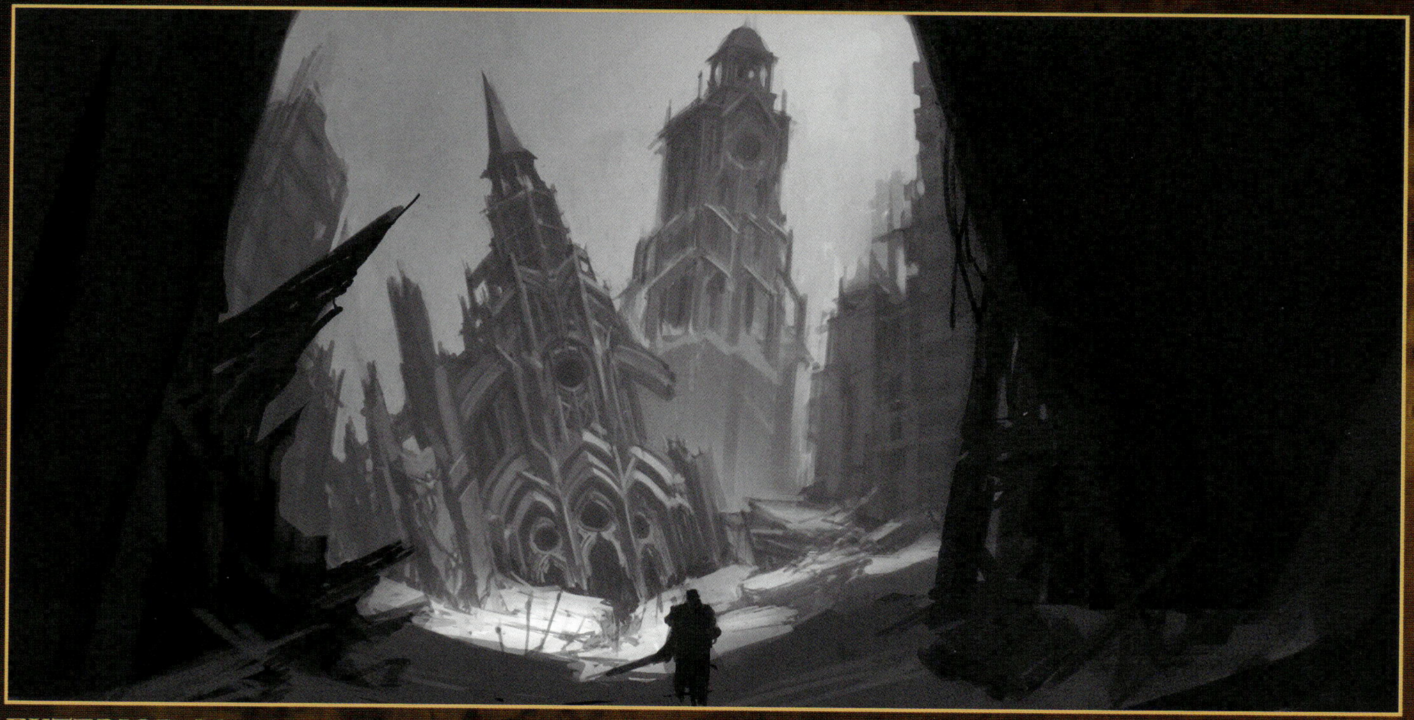

EXTERIOR CONCEPT

INTERIOR CONCEPT

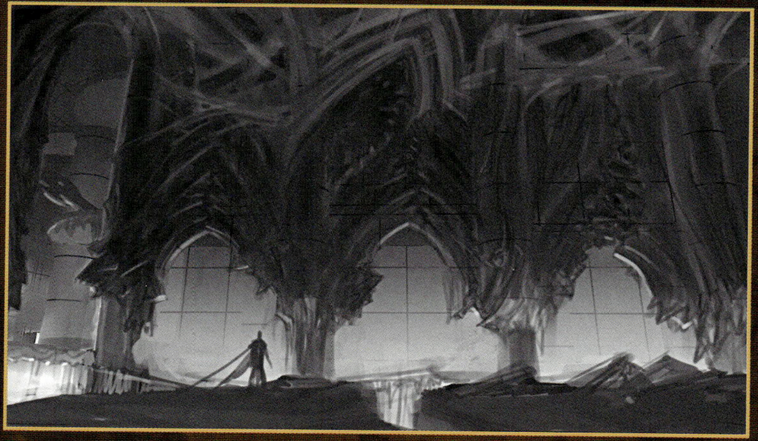

Twilight Cathedral

Within the sacred halls of churches, mankind once found refuge from the evils of the world. But, in the End of Days, even the houses of God were ground to dust. Only the Twilight Cathedral was left standing, and it has festered into something truly unholy.

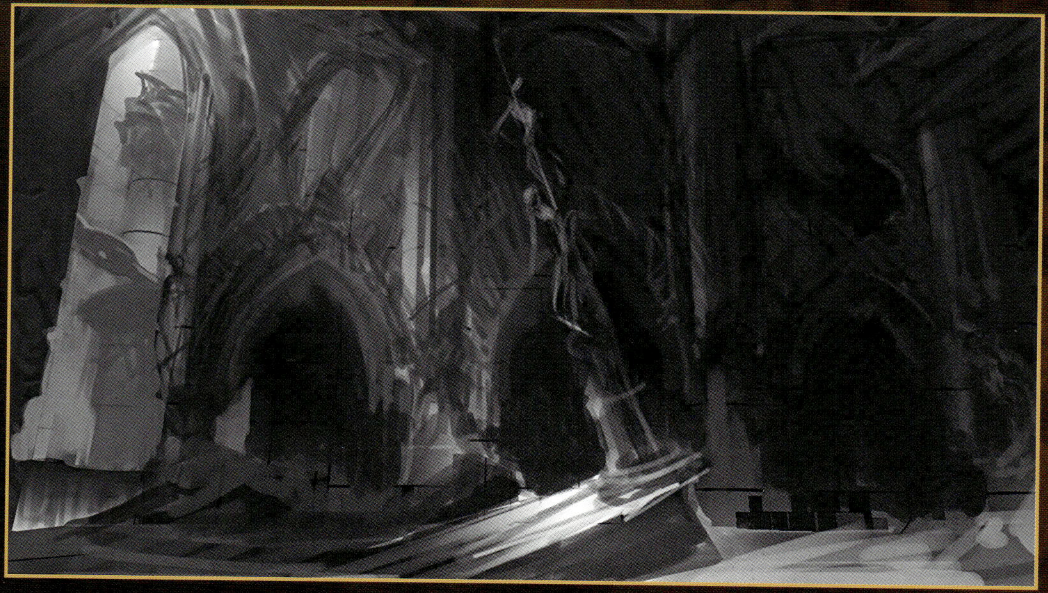

The cathedral has been claimed by the Bat Queen Tiamat. Its walls are stained with the blood of her prey, and hellfire boils through the stone floor. The tower teems with winged demons who worship their sadistic queen. The only hymns now heard in the Twilight Cathedral are the screams of the tormented.

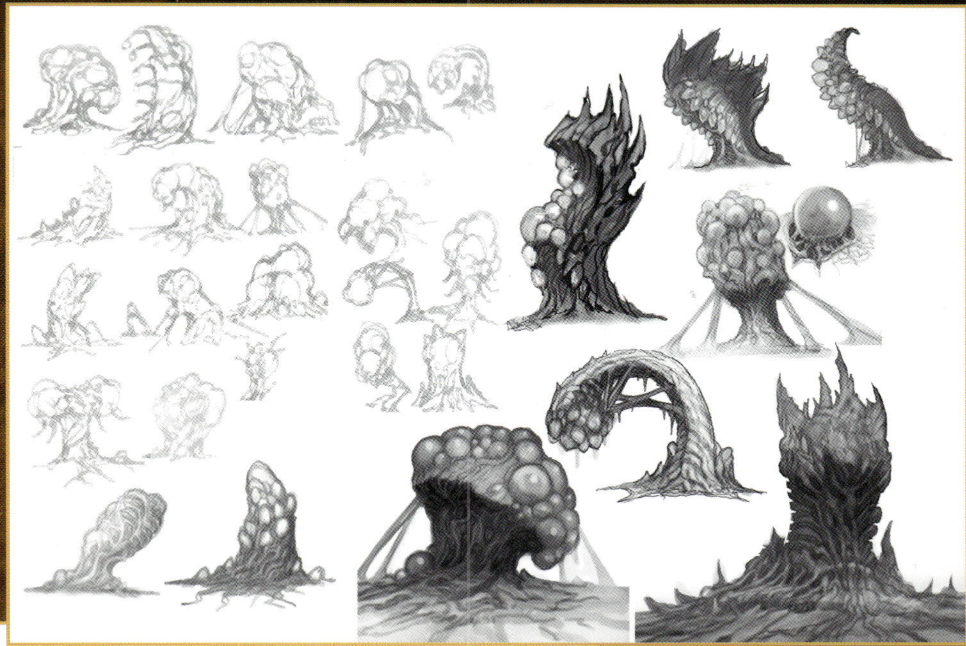

BATGROWTH DEVELOPMENT SKETCHES

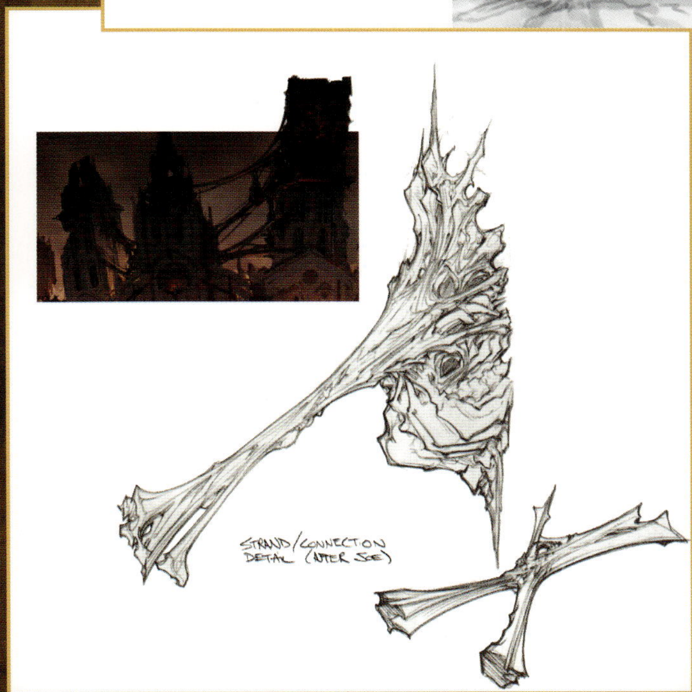

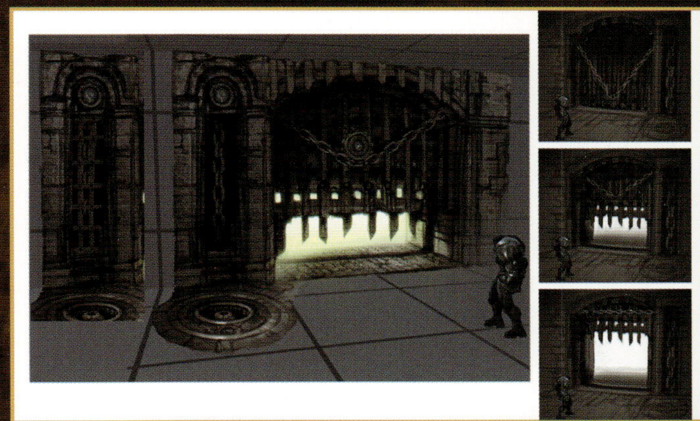

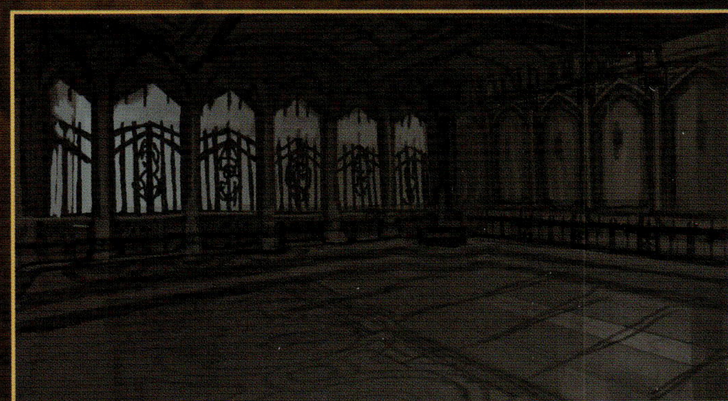

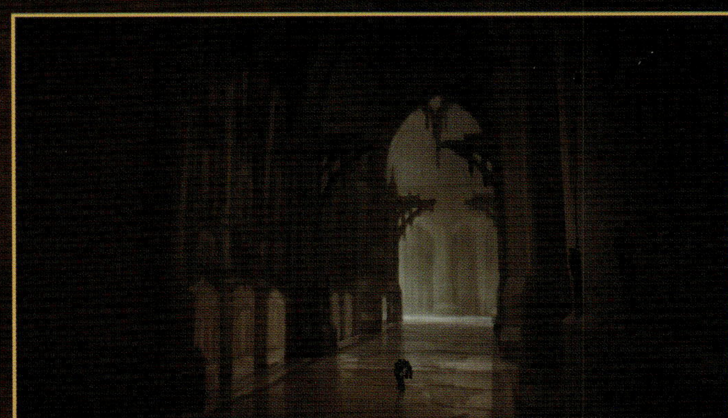

INTERIOR CONCEPTS

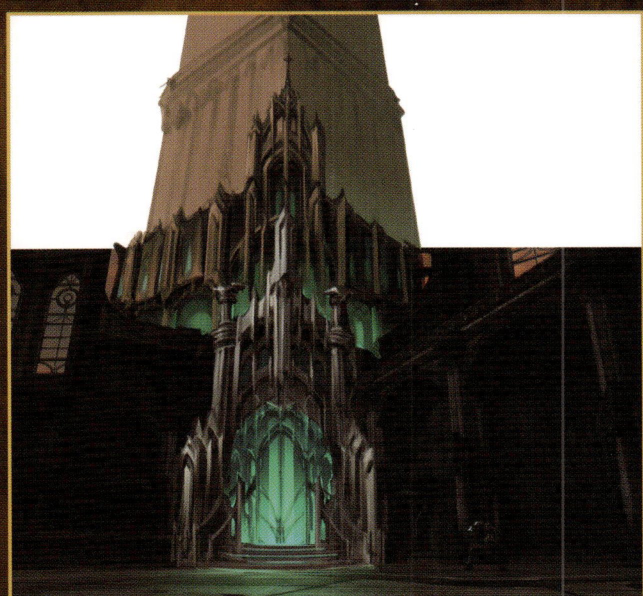

EXTERIOR CONCEPT

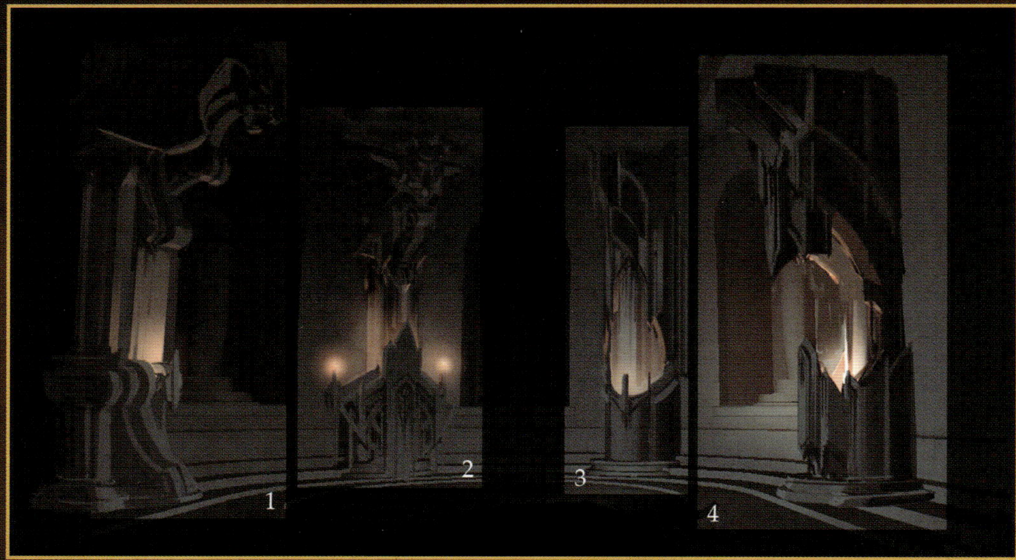

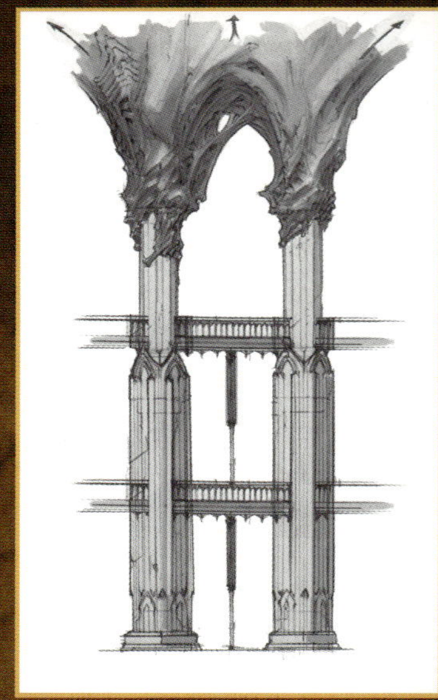

COLUMN CONCEPTS

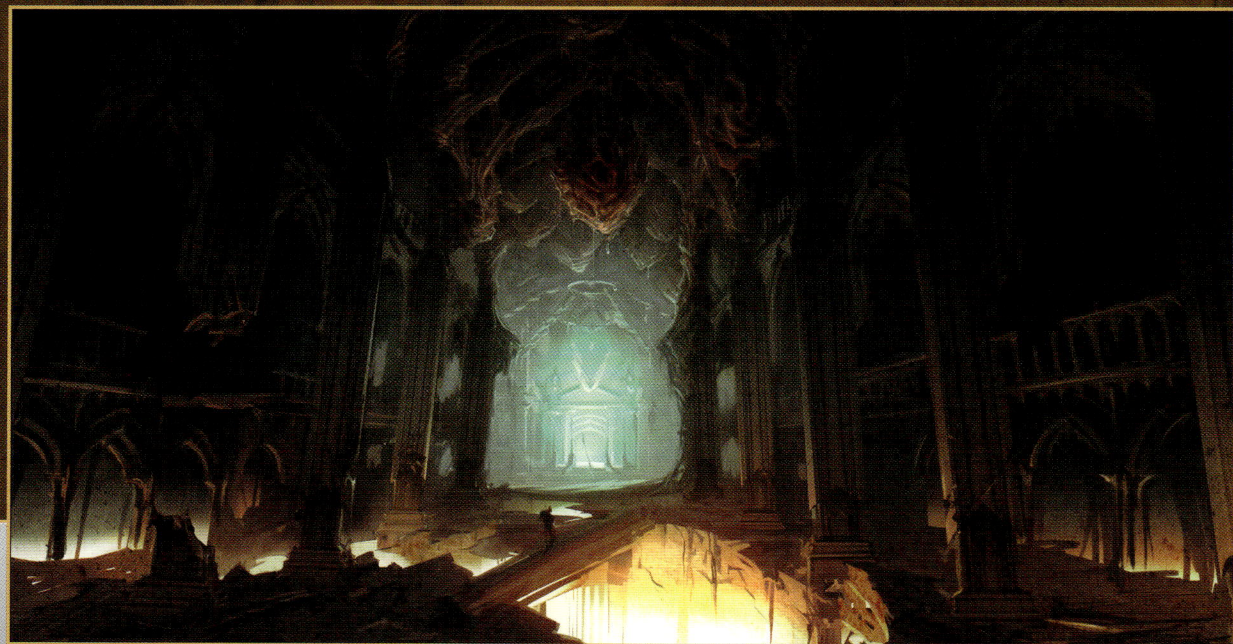

MAIN ROOM CONCEPT

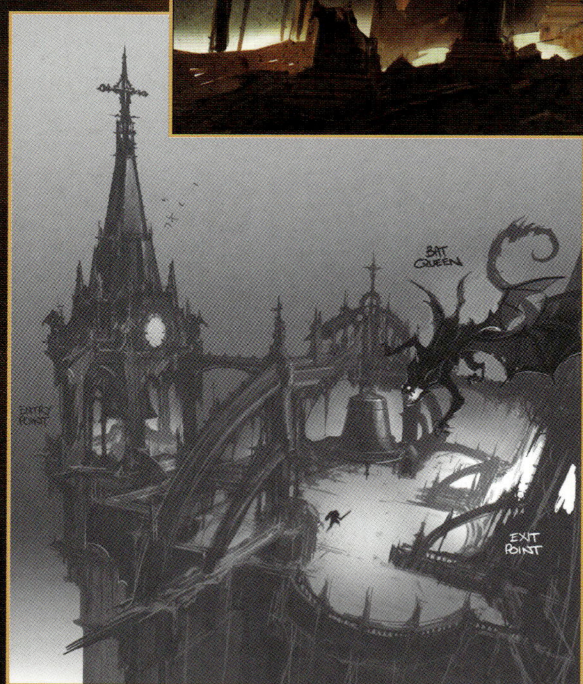

LOCATION CONCEPT

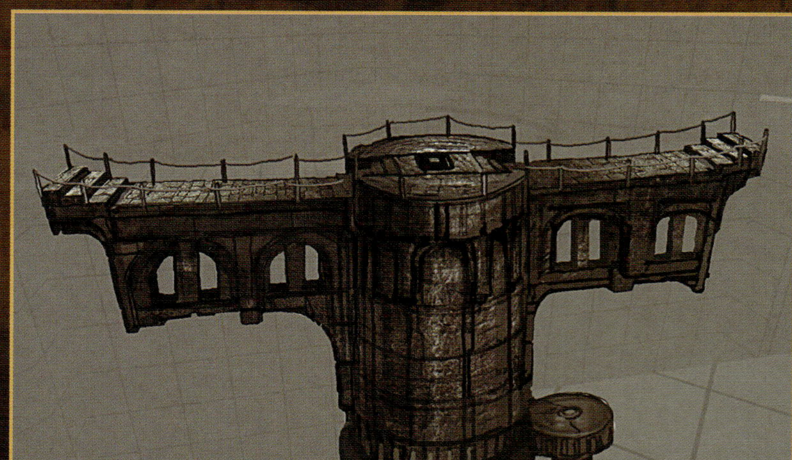

BRIDGE CONCEPT

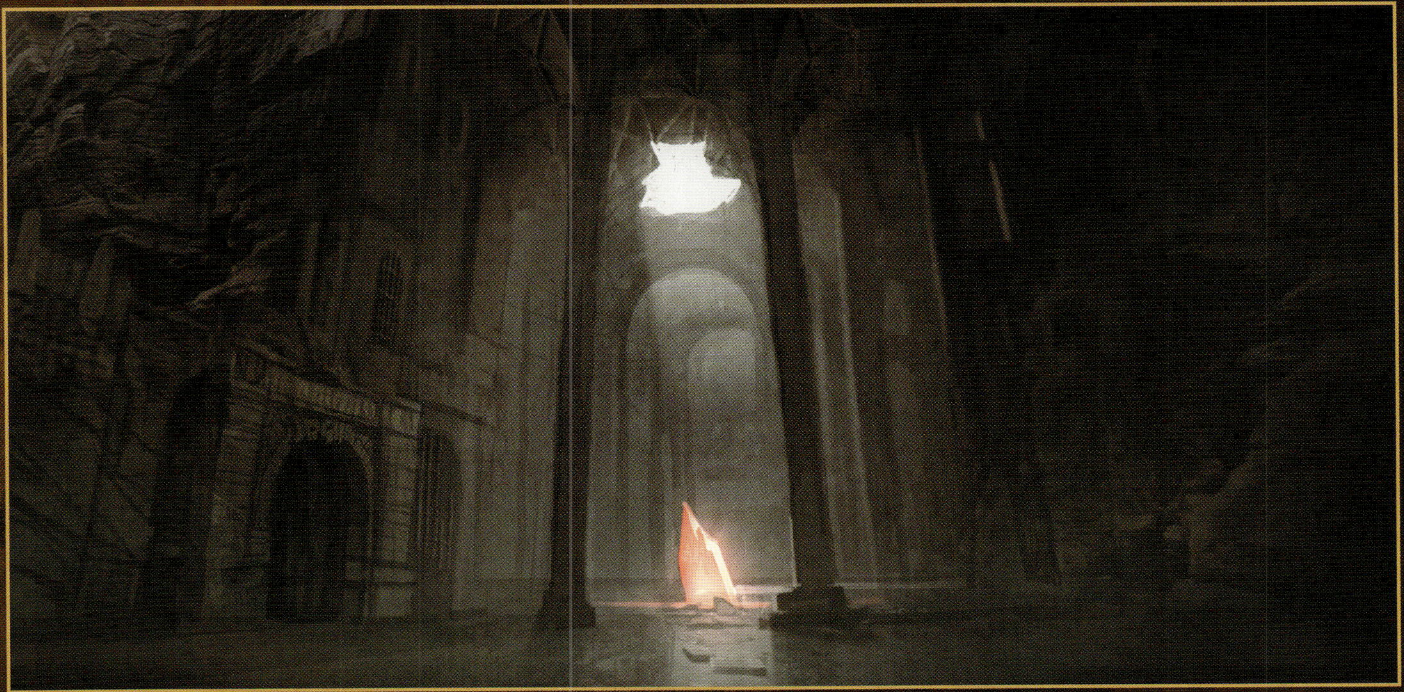

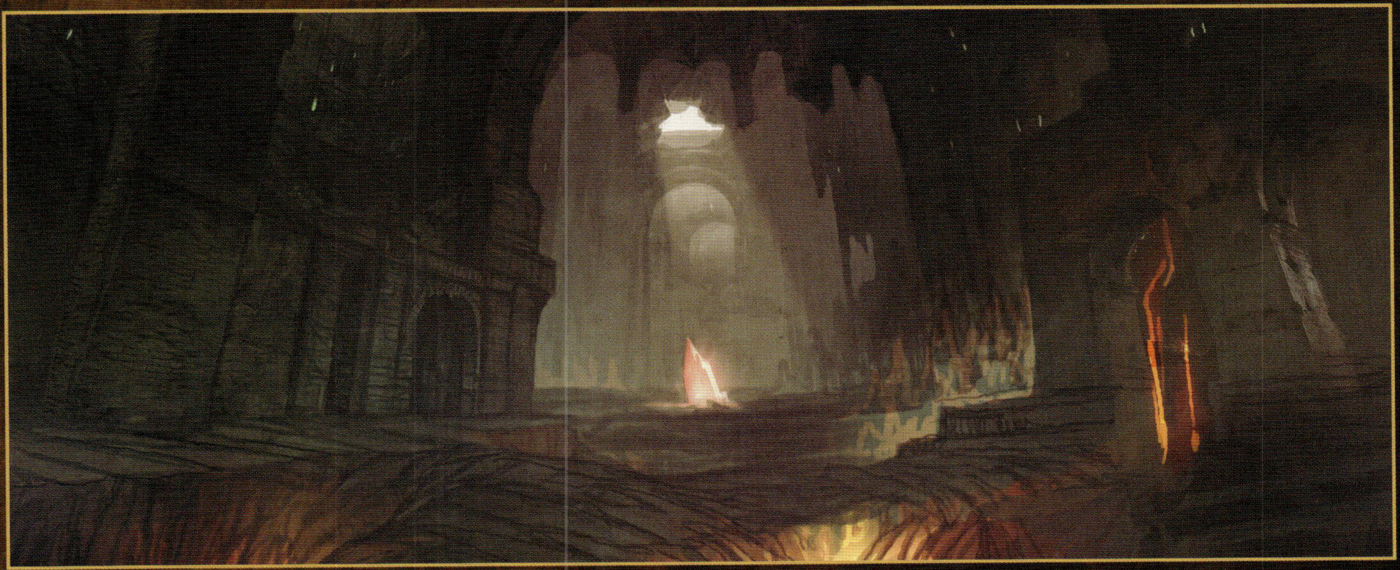

CATACOMBS ENTRY CONCEPTS

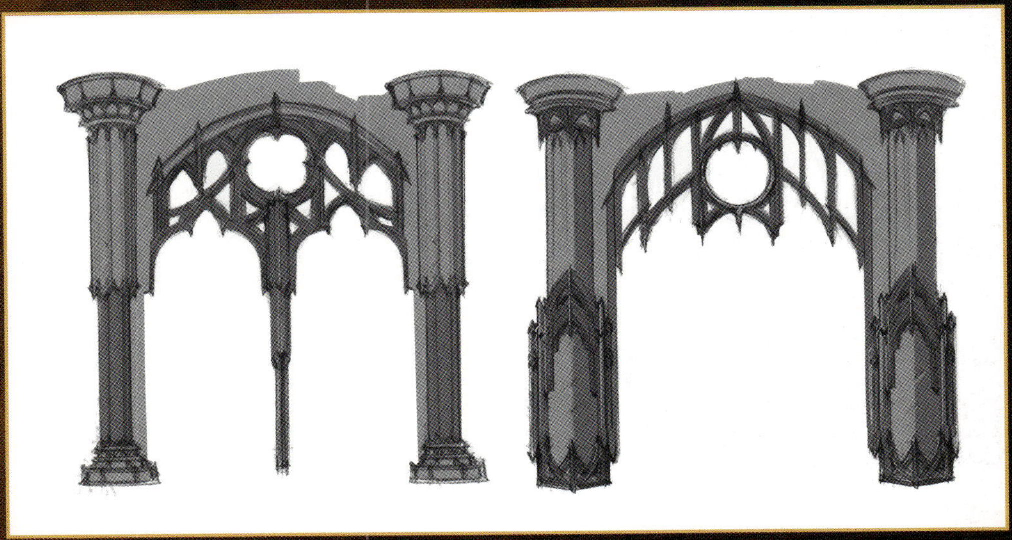

ARCH DESIGNS

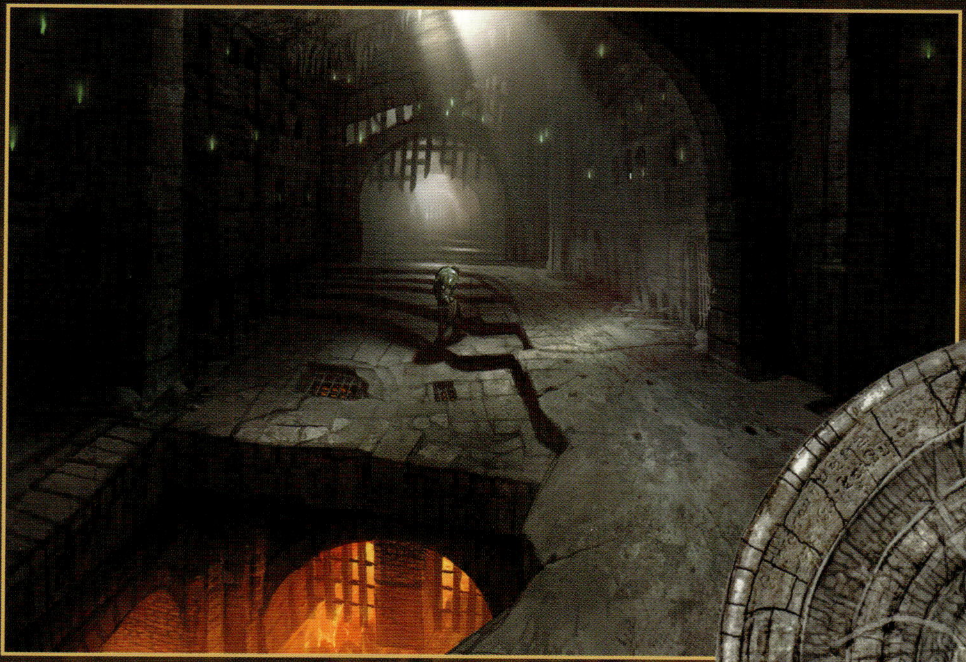

CORRIDOR CONCEPT

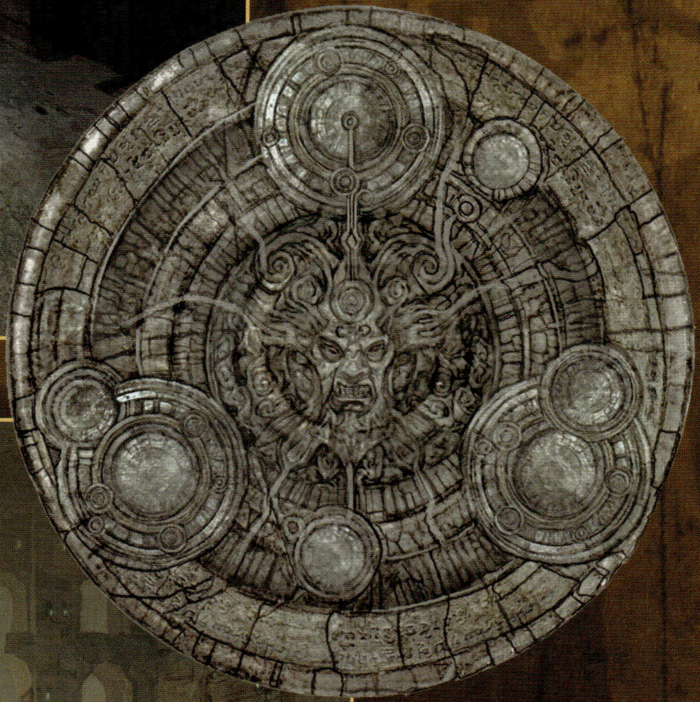

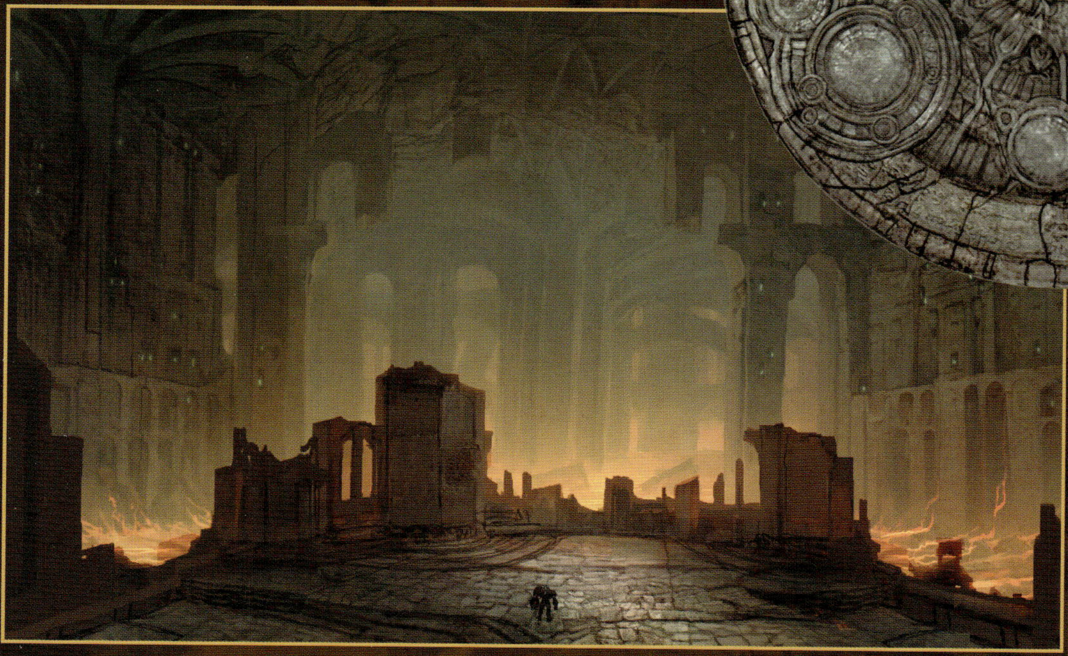

VISTA ROOM
CONCEPT

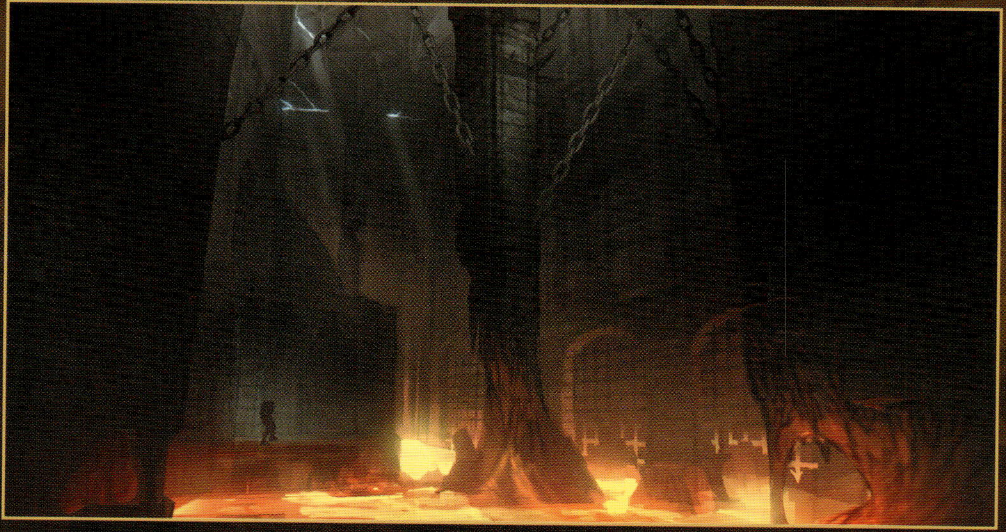

FLOOR BREAKER CONCEPT

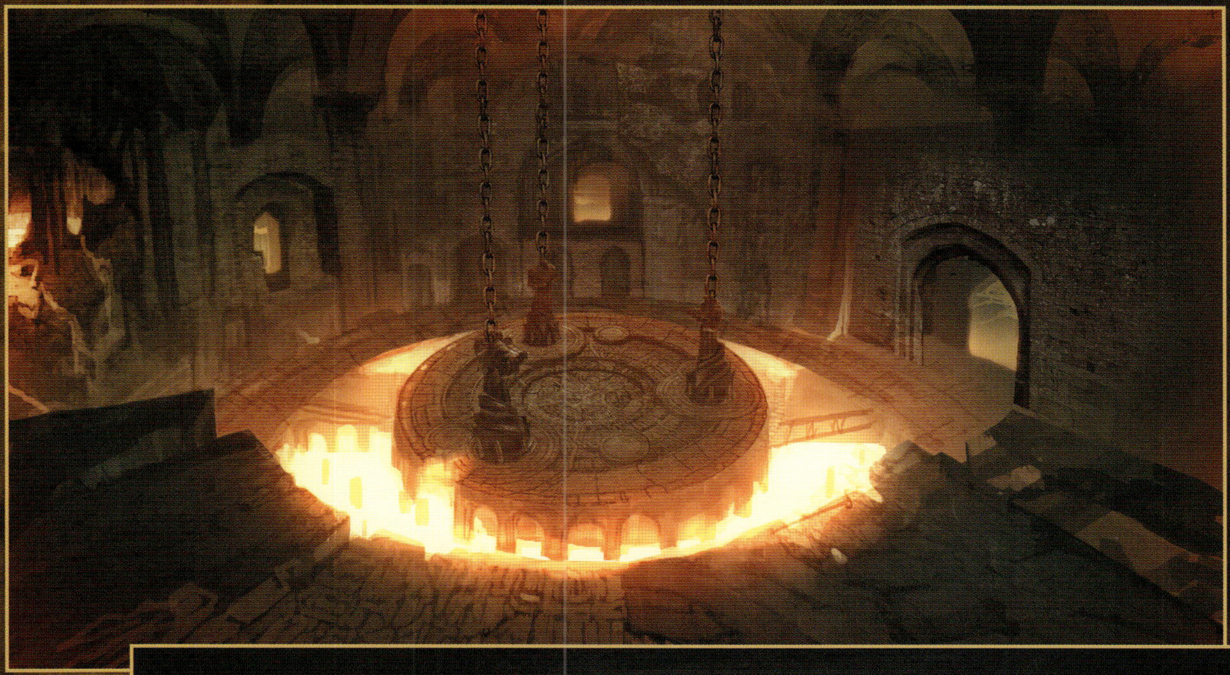

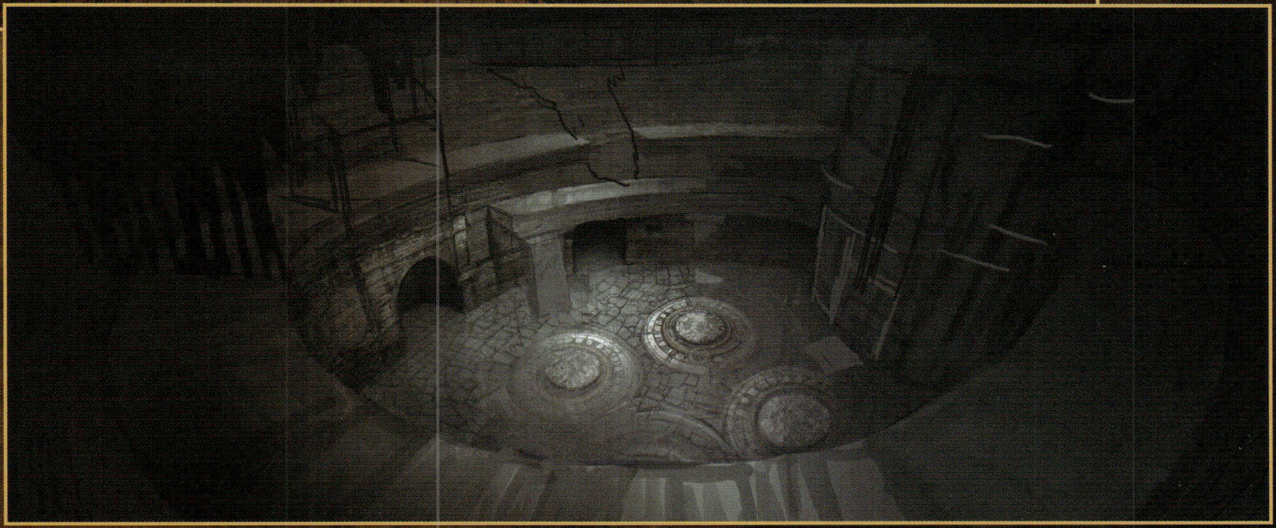

LIFT ROOM CONCEPTS

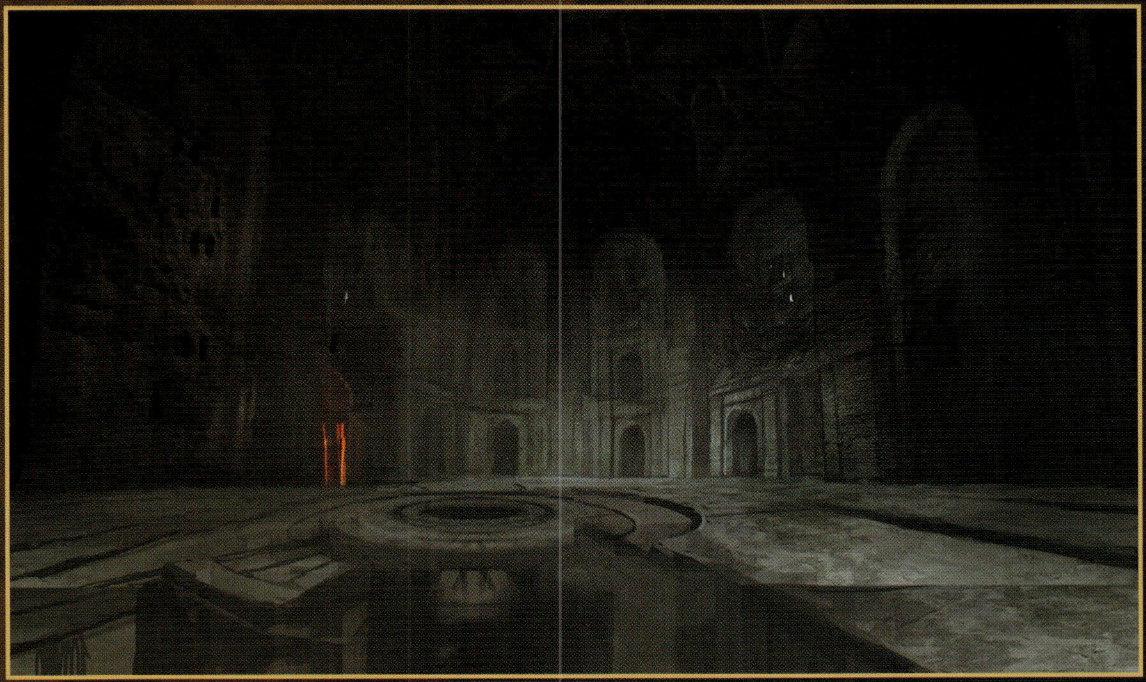

LIFT ROOM CONCEPT

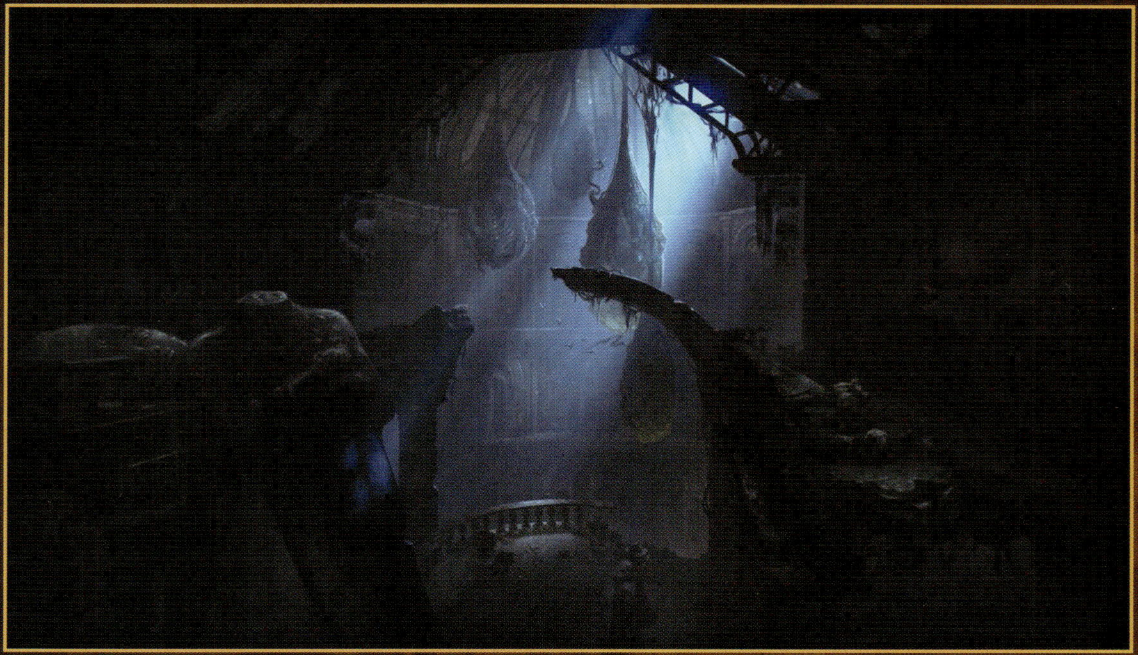

CATHEDRAL CEILING CONCEPT

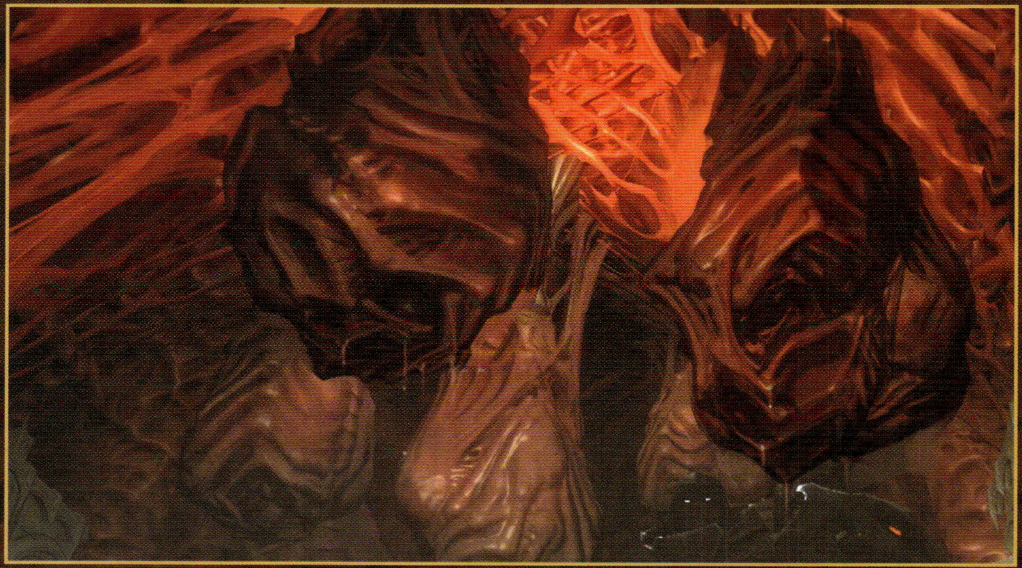

BATGROWTH CONCEPT

Eden

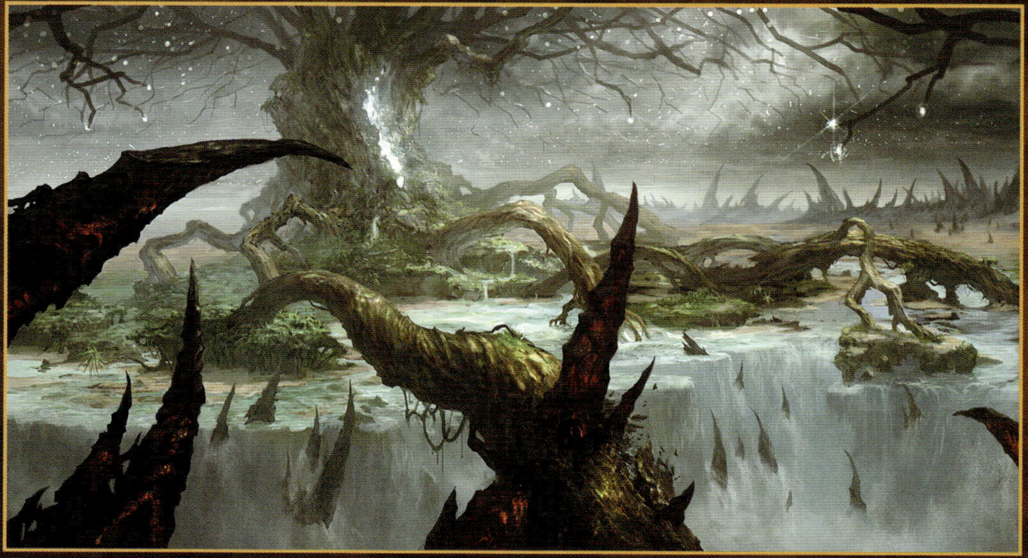

EDEN CONCEPT

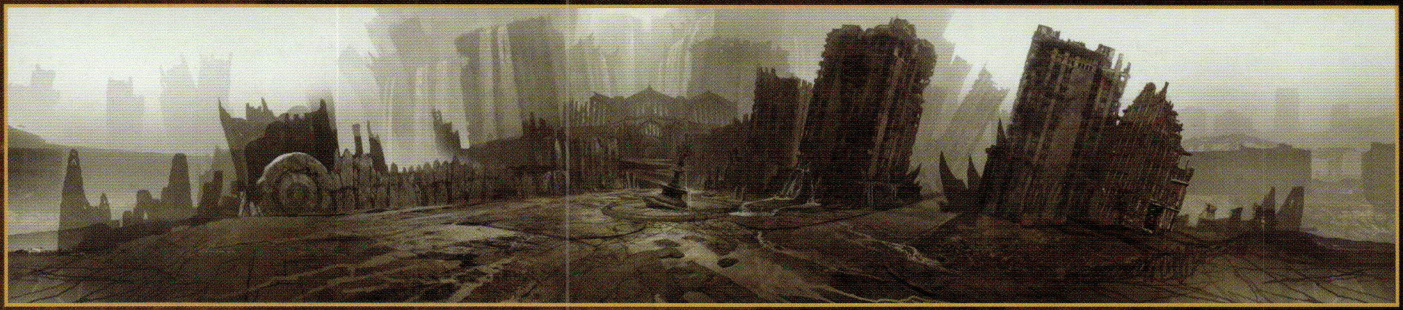

SUBWAY STATION

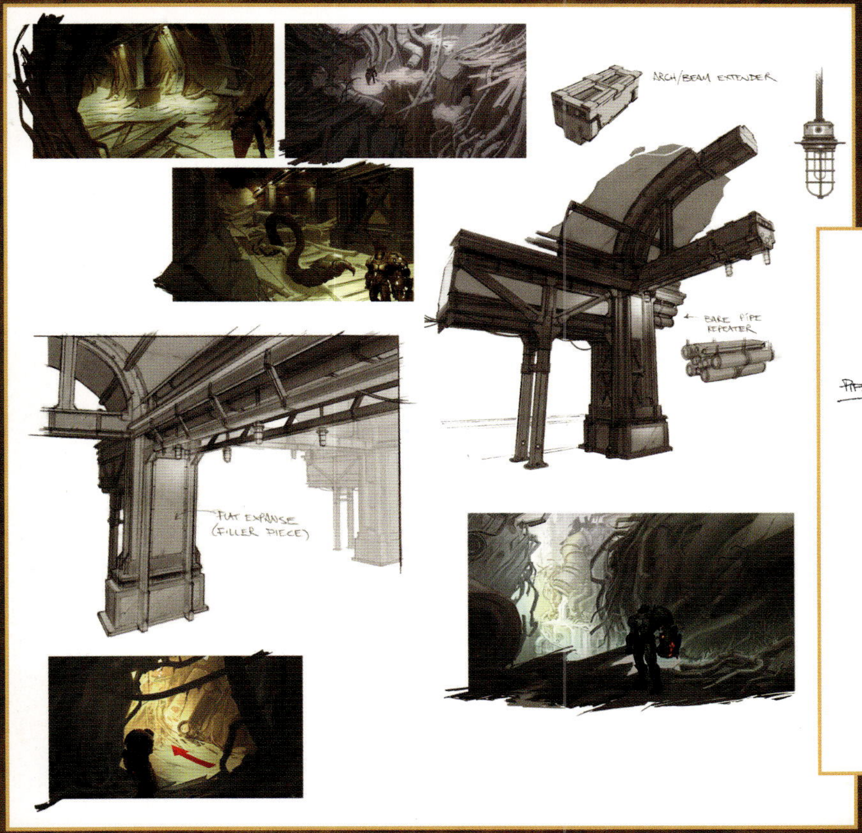

SUBWAY DESIGNS

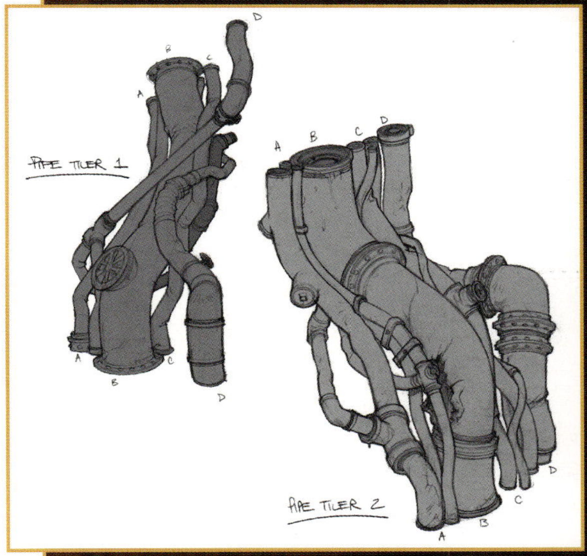

PIPE DESIGNS

The Hollow

A century ago, before the last breath of humanity was drawn, the subway teemed with activity. Countless souls passed through the dark tunnels, unaware that their world was nearing its end.

The savage tremors of the Apocalypse twisted the subway's tracks into knots, and the seas reclaimed the passageways. Now the subway stands as a watery grave for the city's last travelers. Drawn by the musk of death, the lowly vermin of Hell scrabble through the corridors. I call this place The Hollow, for reasons of my own.

INTERIOR CONCEPTS

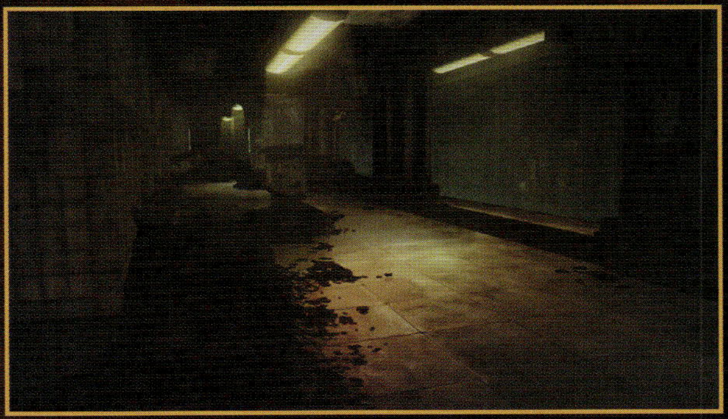

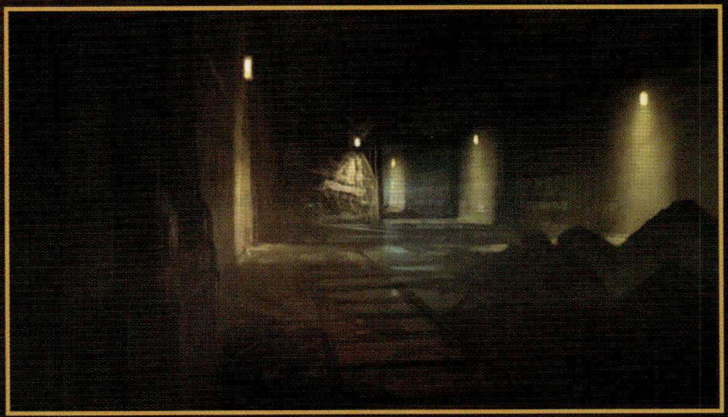

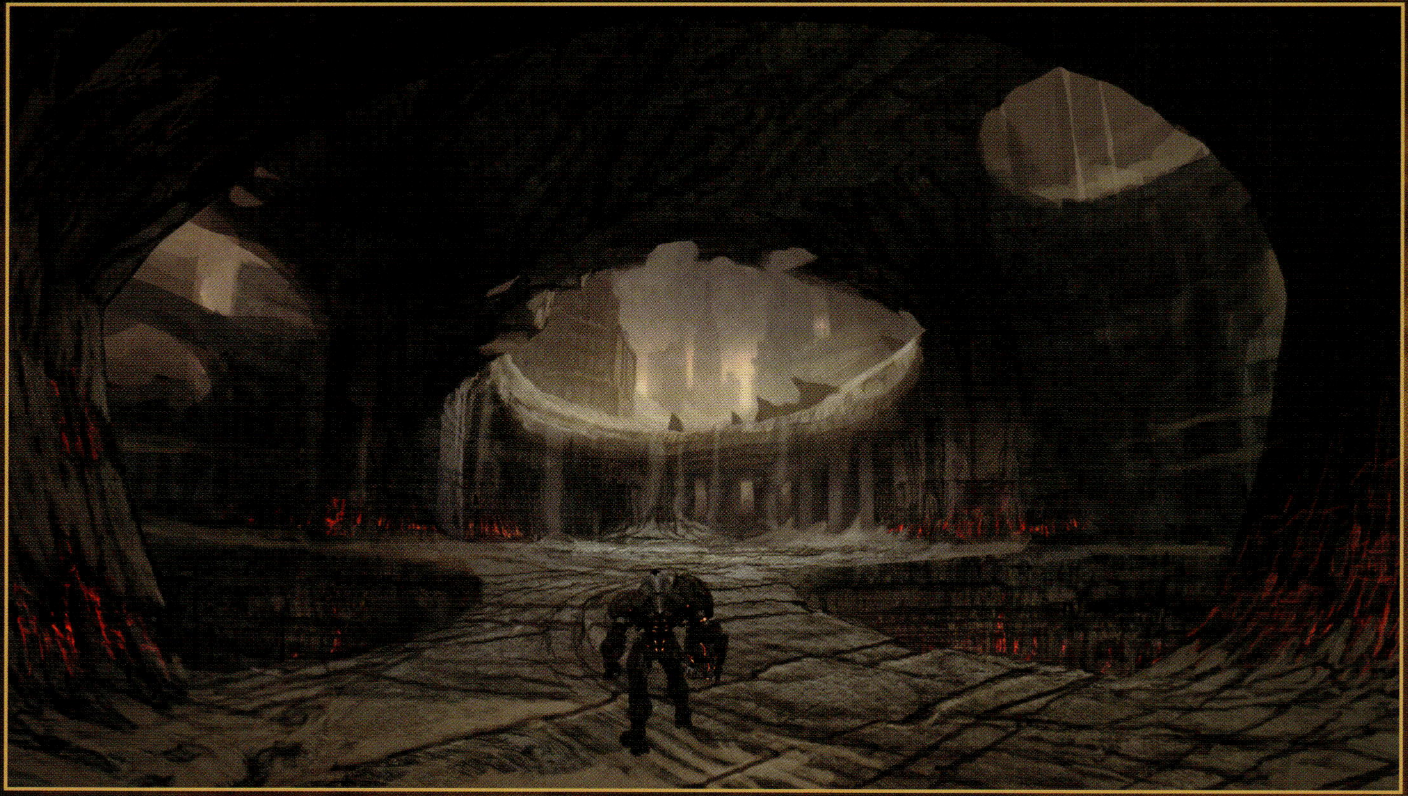

TUNNEL CONCEPT

Ashlands

On the outskirts of the city there is a desolate wasteland where the remains of charred buildings and scorched bones are blown into dunes. These are the Ashlands, where the air is thick with death and the ground littered with decay. I have heard the demons speak of titanic beasts that lurk below the surface of this wasteland. They also speak of a vast arena that rises above the Ashland's cinders, where some manner of twisted blood-sport is enjoyed by the servants of Darkness.

When I look upon the Ashlands I see only a curtain of soot, swirling and black, like ink spilled in churning water. I do not need demons to tell me that only evil lurks in those sinister dunes.

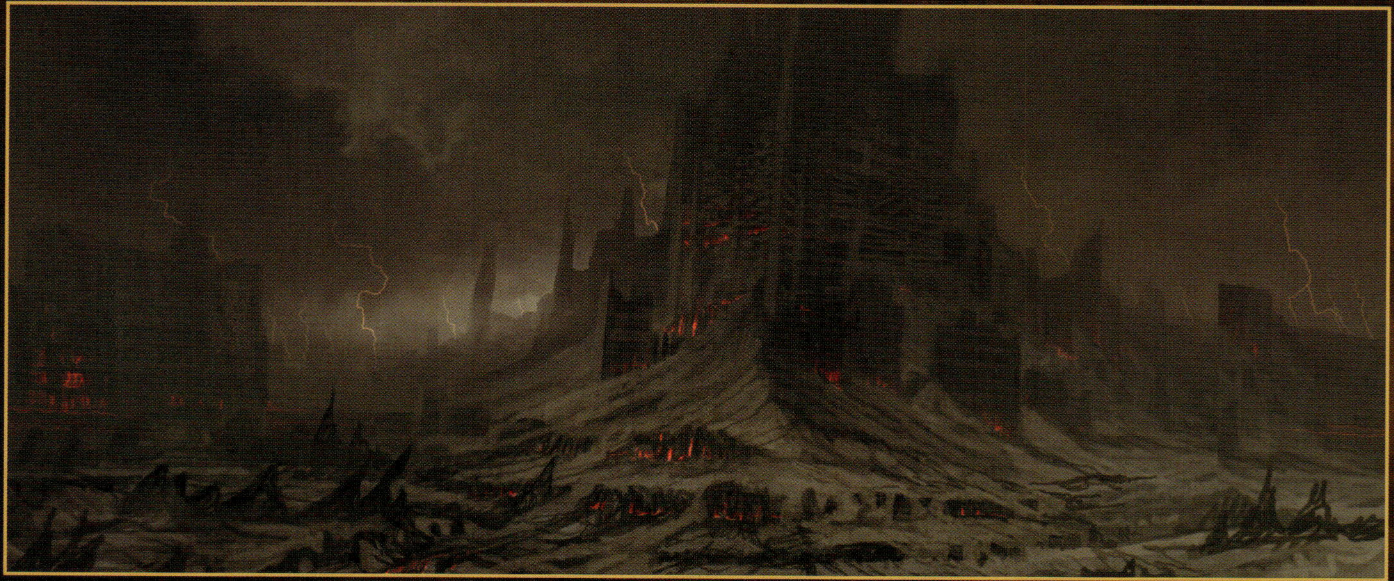

ASHLANDS CONCEPT

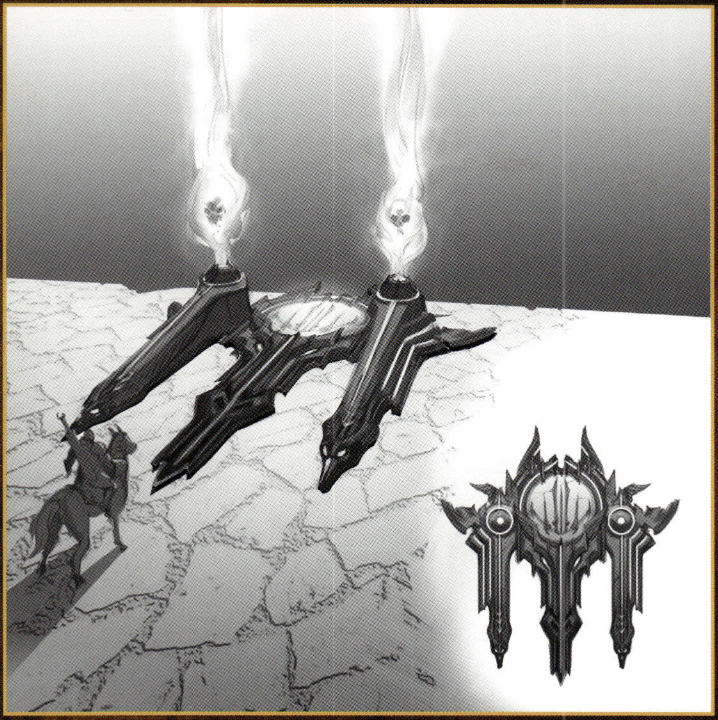

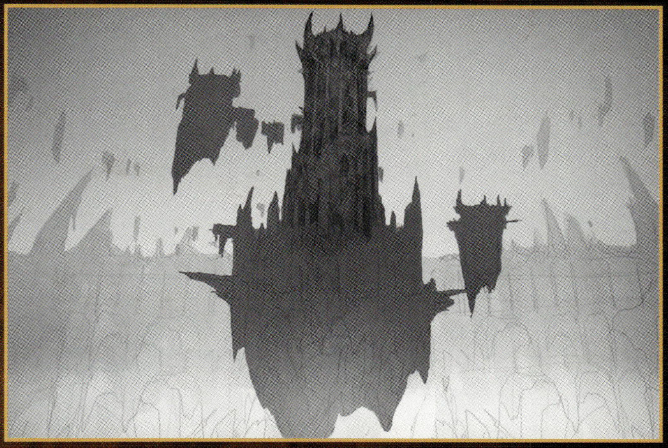

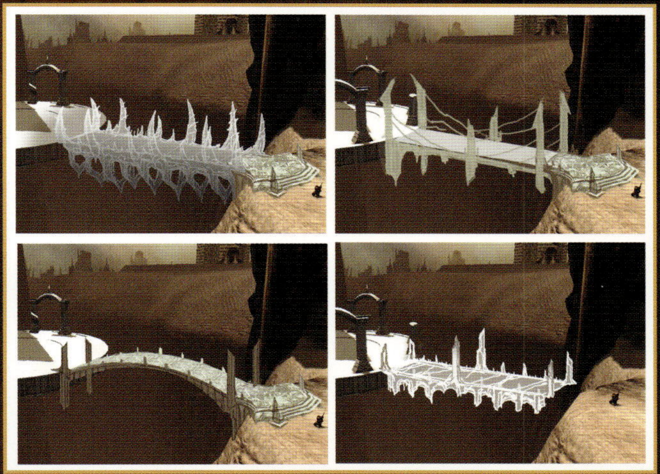

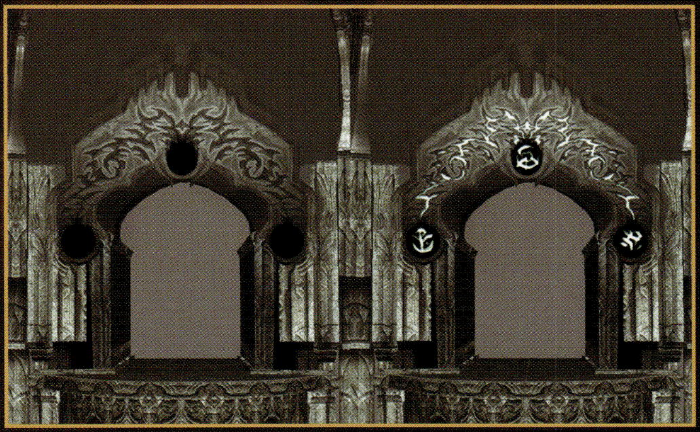

SOULBRIDGE DESIGNS

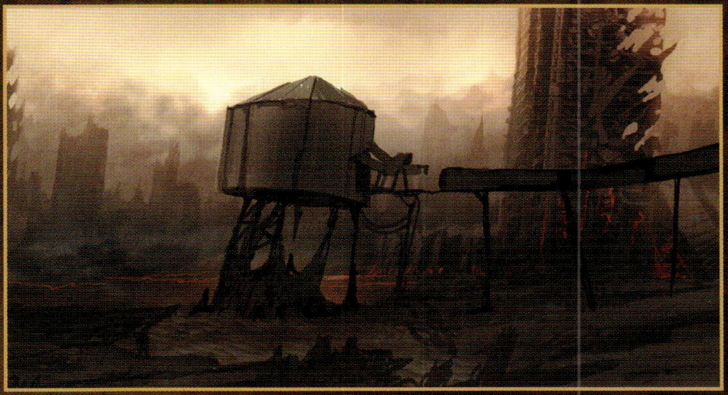

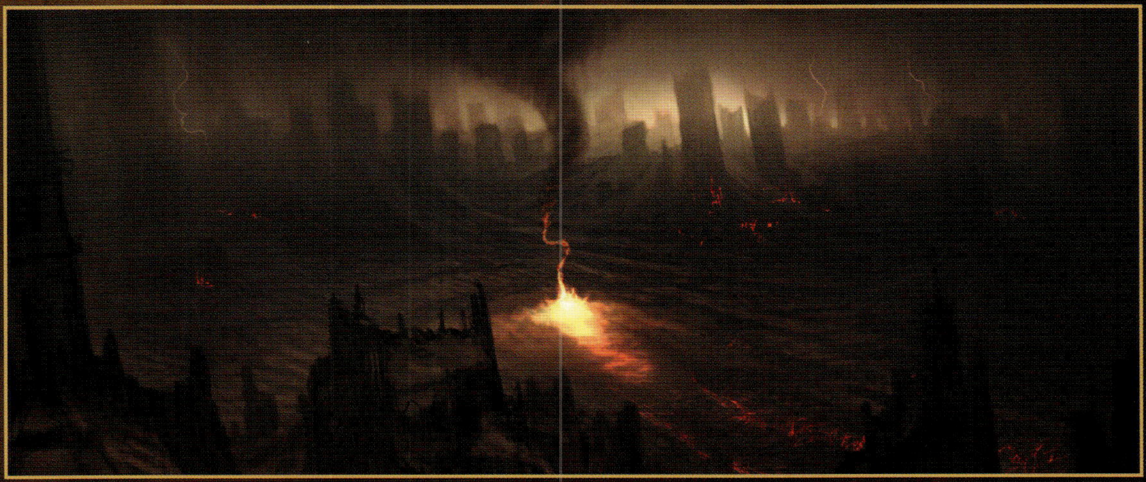

ASHLANDS CONCEPTS

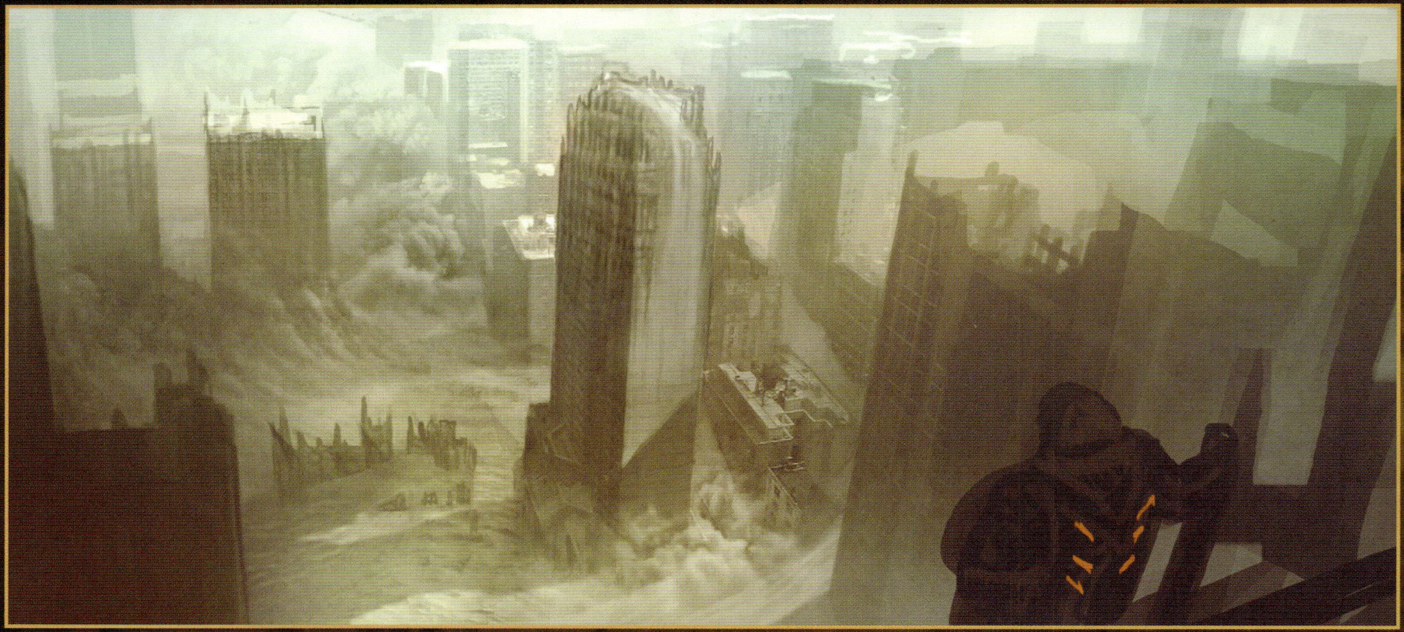

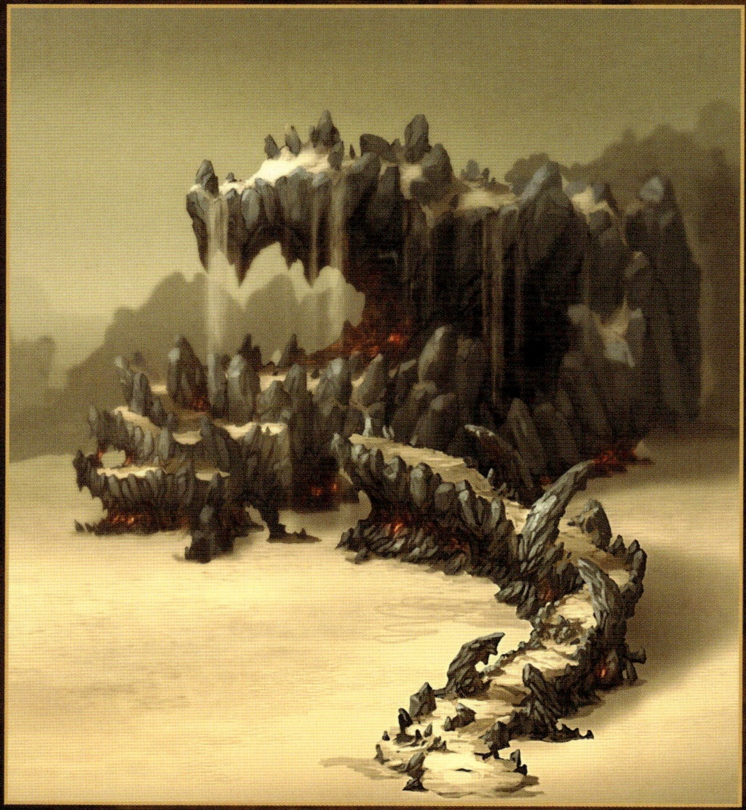

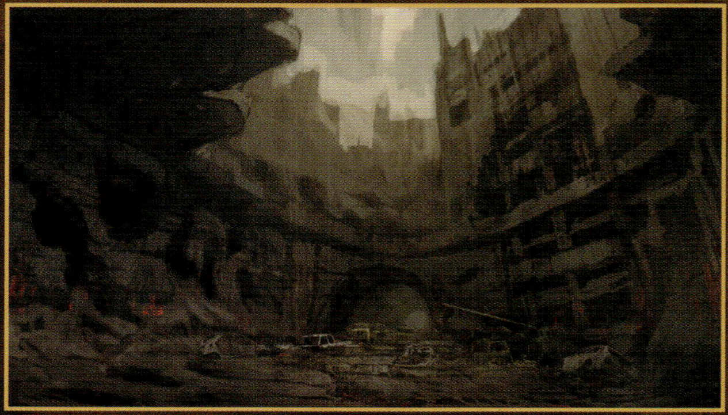

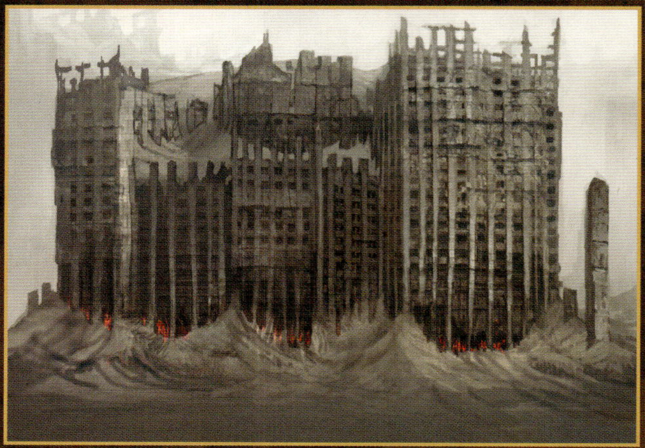

ASHLANDS CONCEPTS

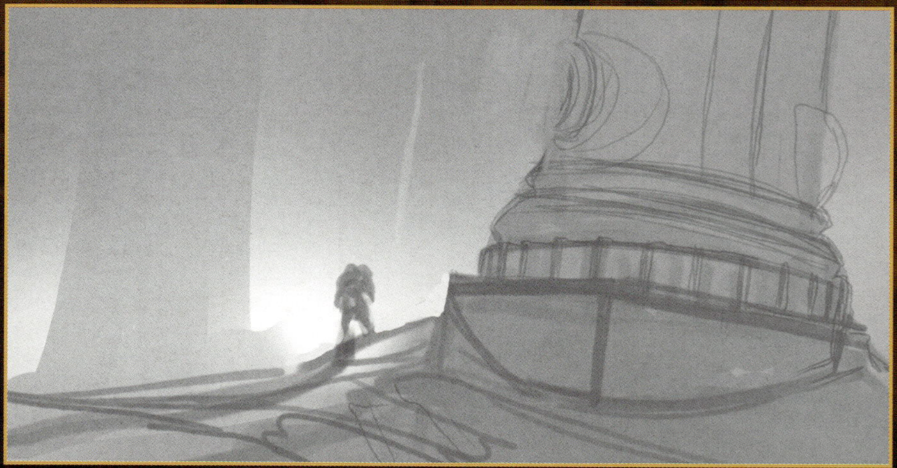

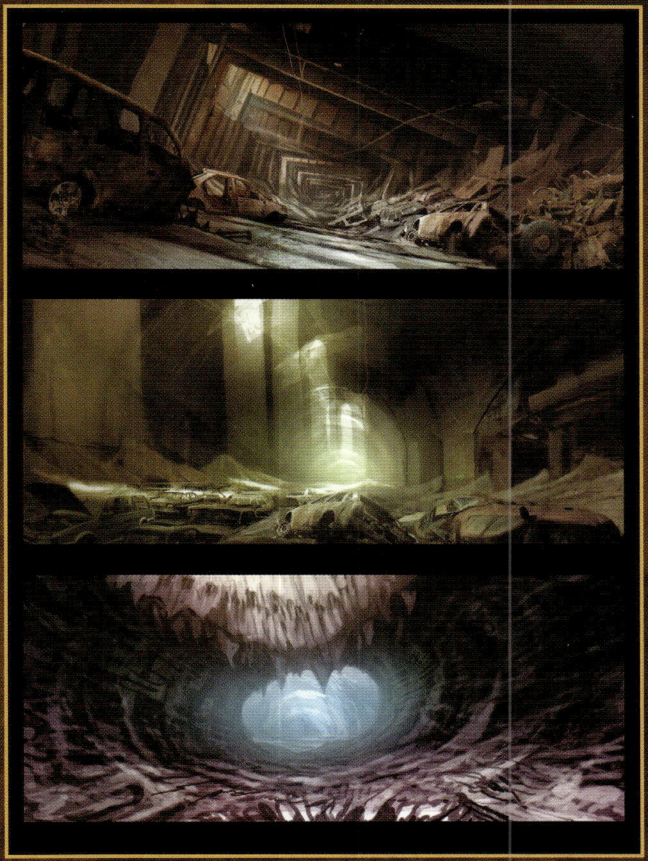

ASHLANDS CONCEPTS

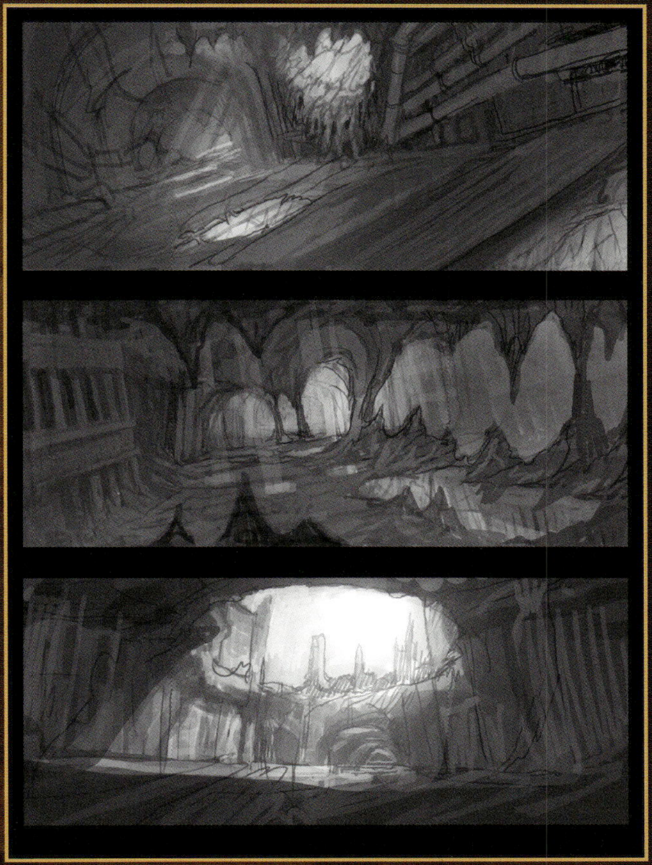

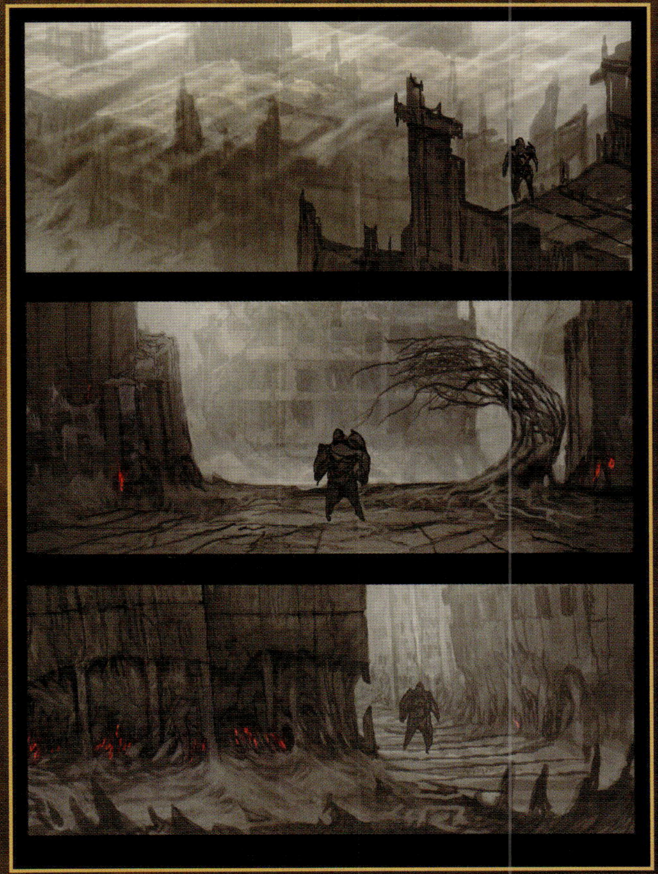

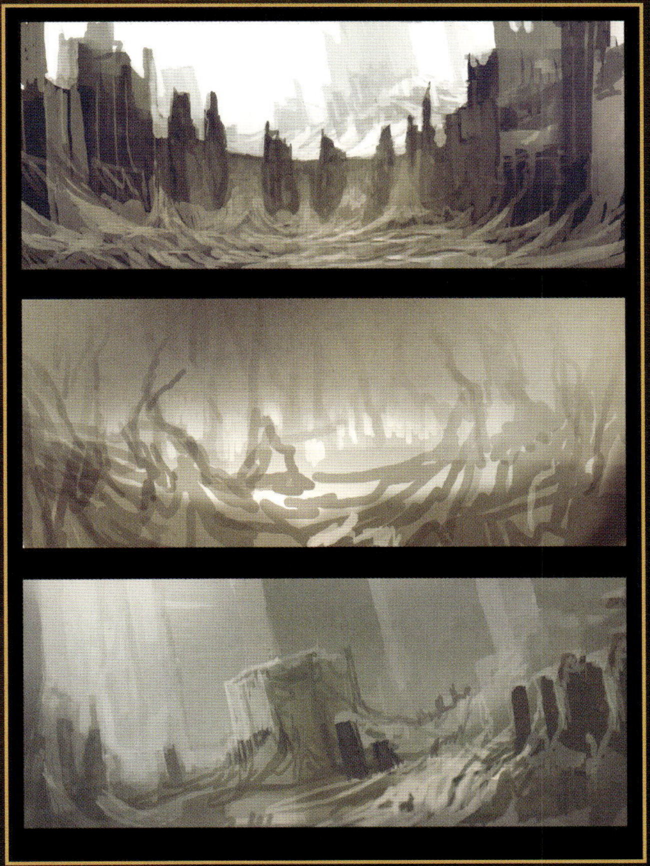

ASHLANDS CONCEPTS

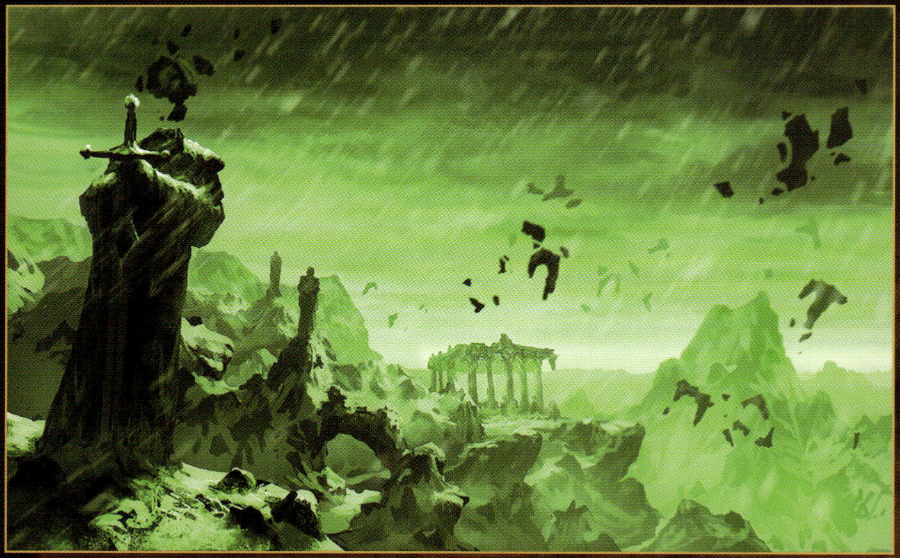

ASHLANDS CONCEPTS

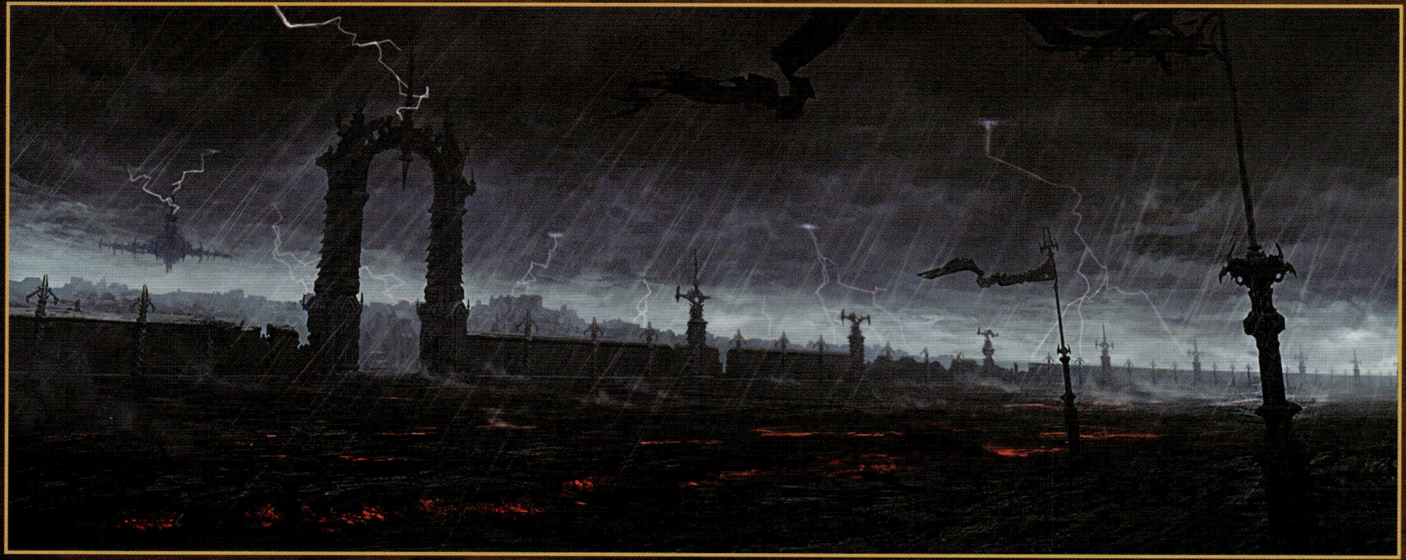

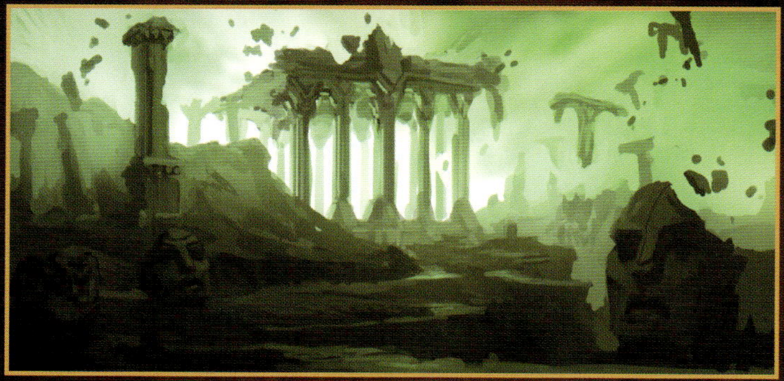

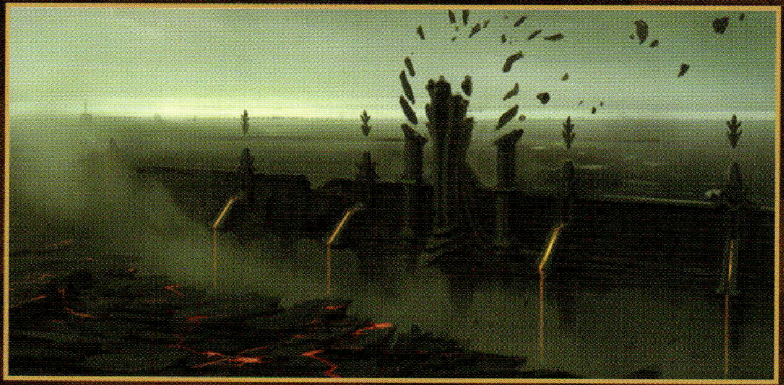

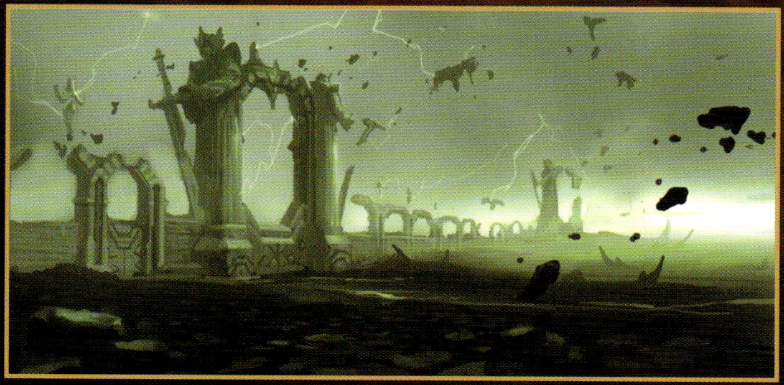

ASHLANDS CONCEPTS

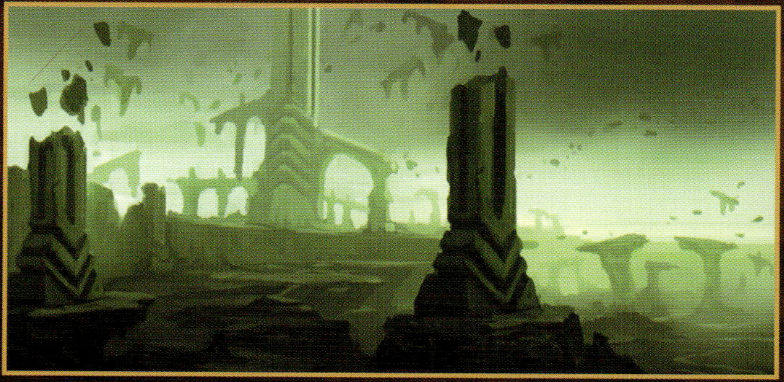

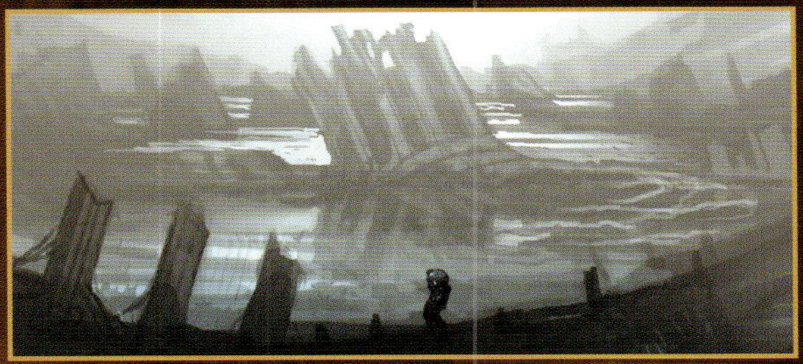

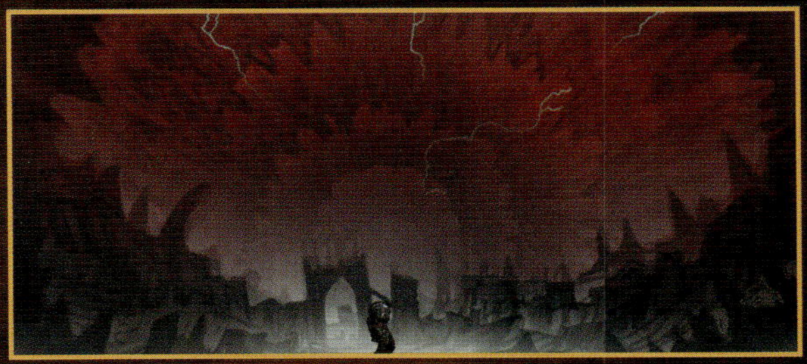

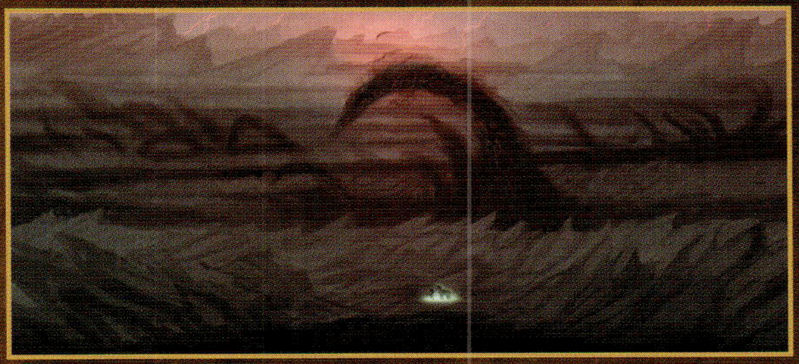

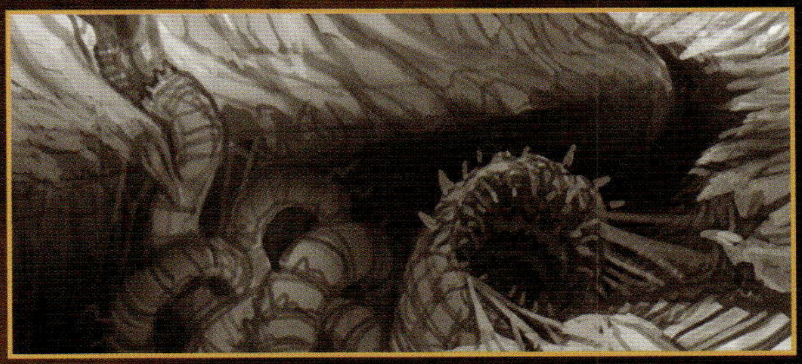

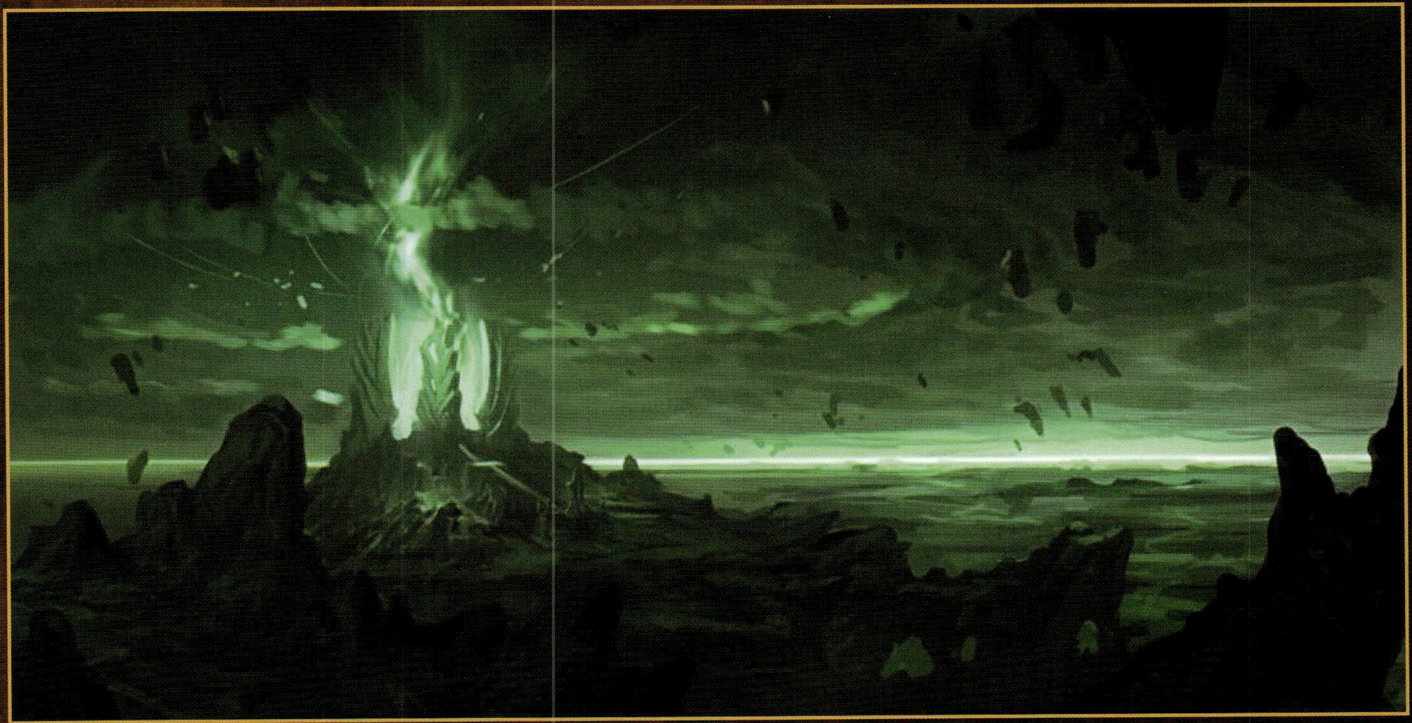

ASHLANDS CONCEPTS

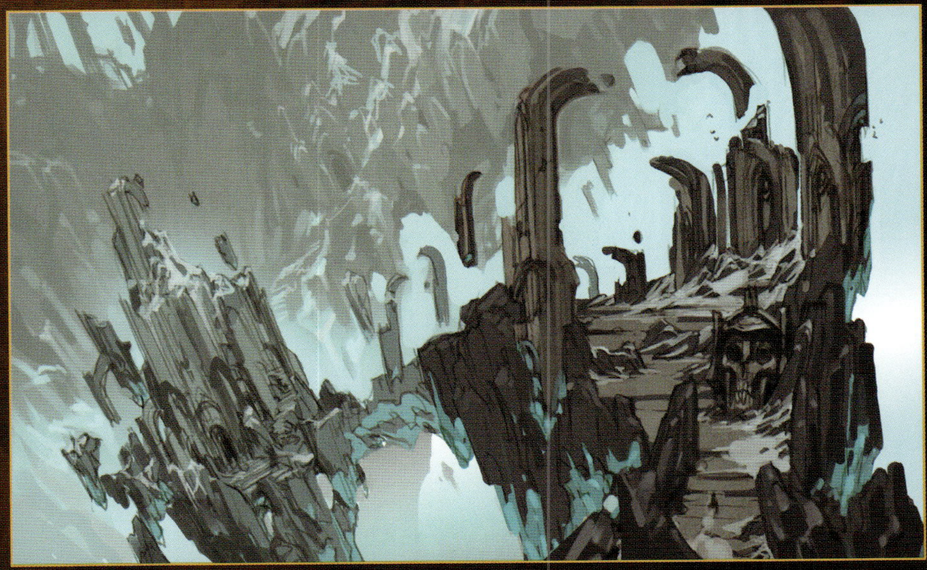

ASHLANDS CONCEPTS

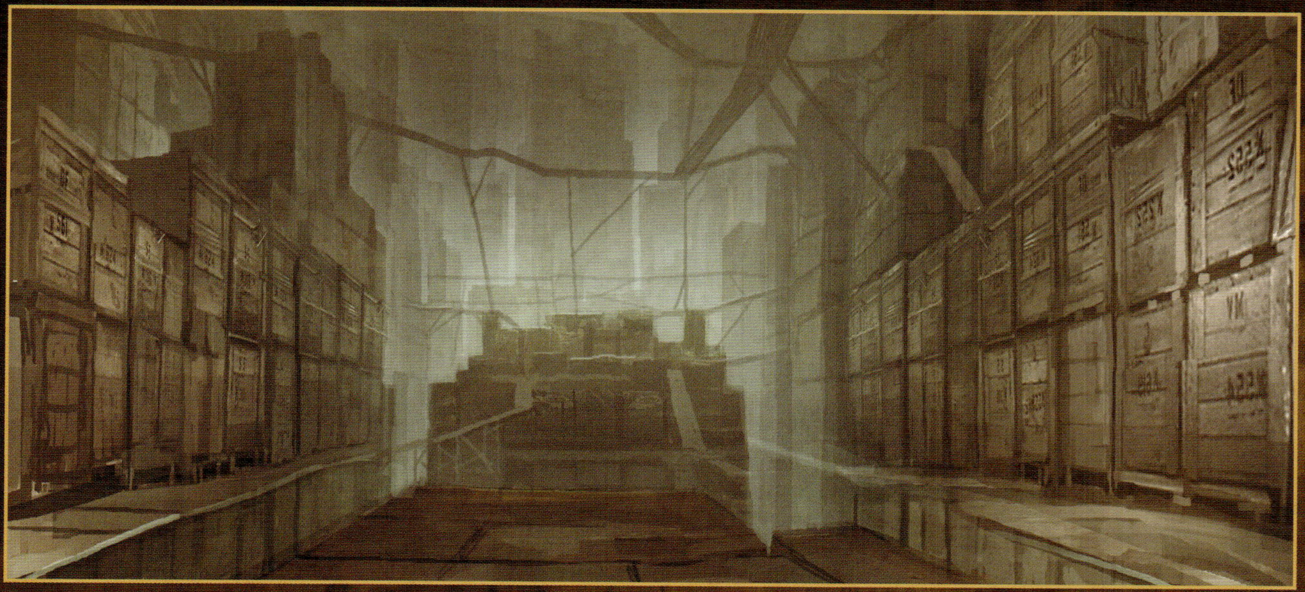

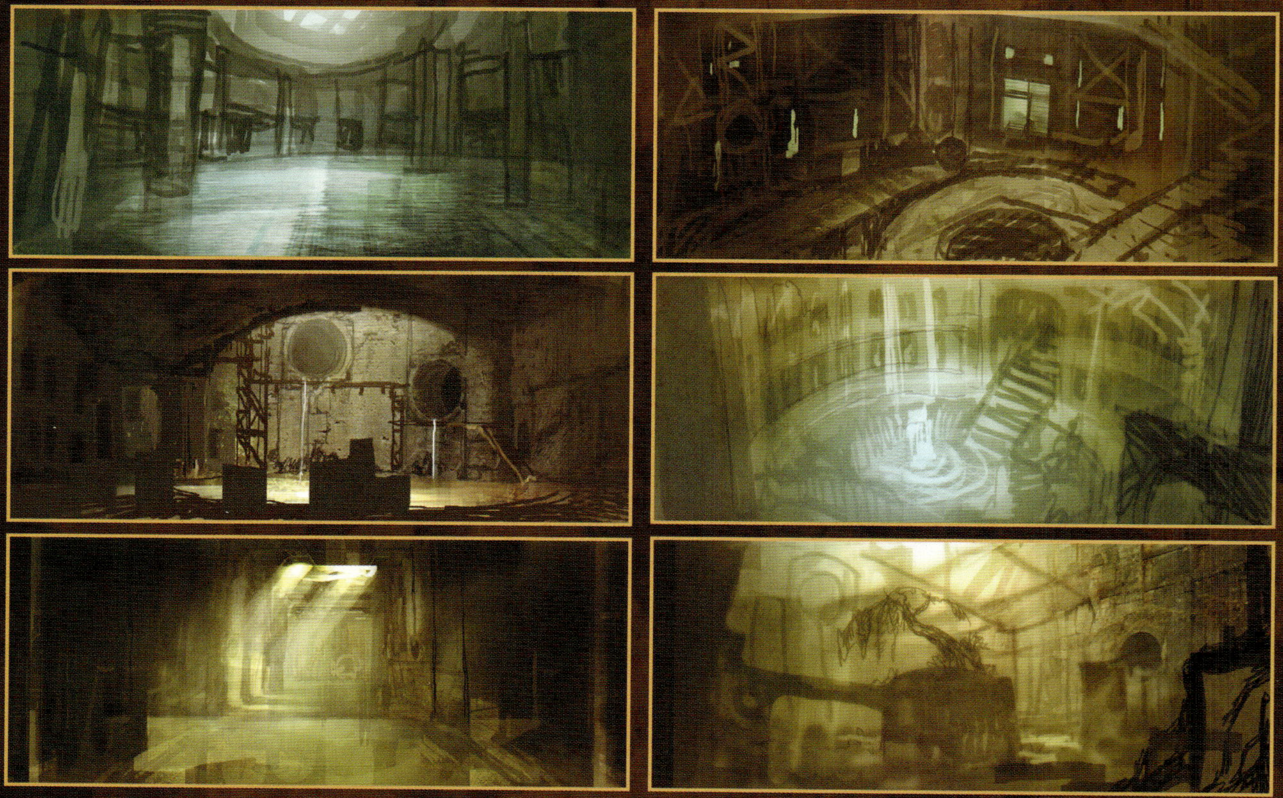

COLLECTOR INTERIOR CONCEPTS

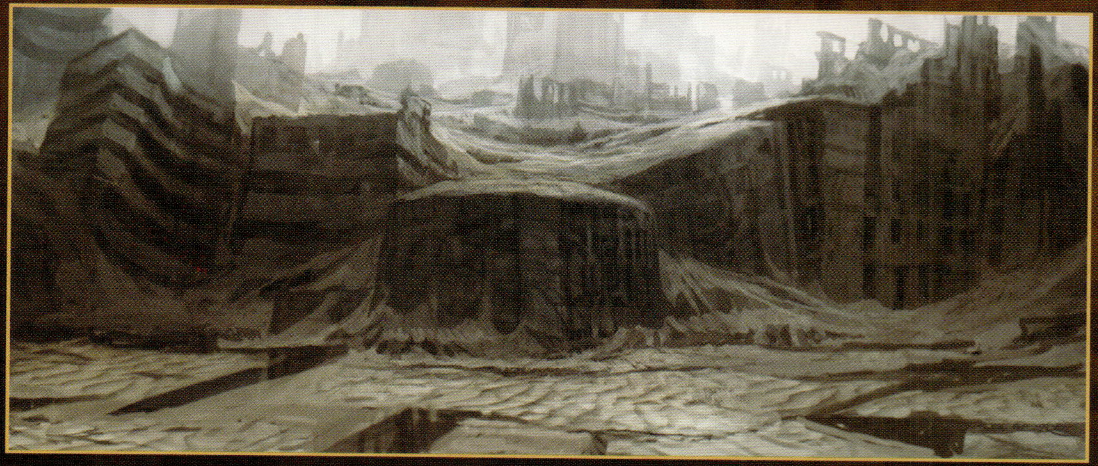

ASHLANDS CONCEPT

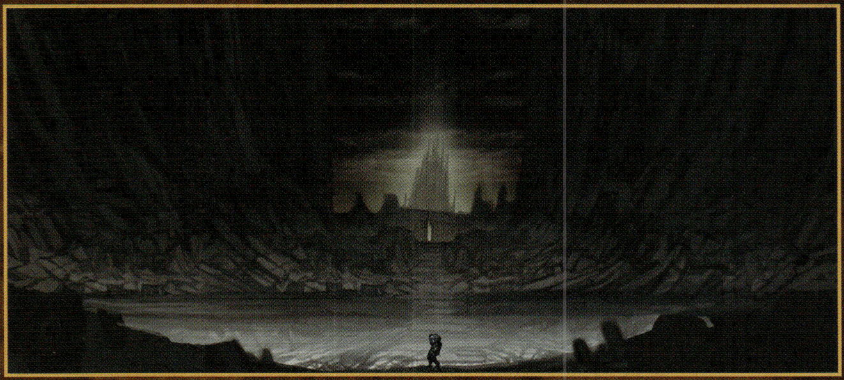

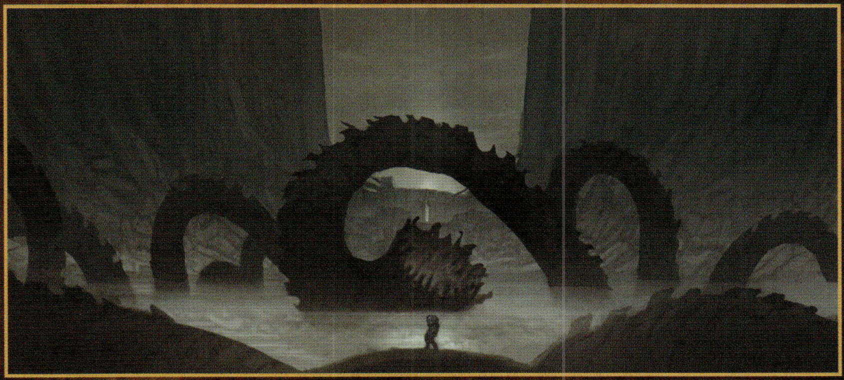

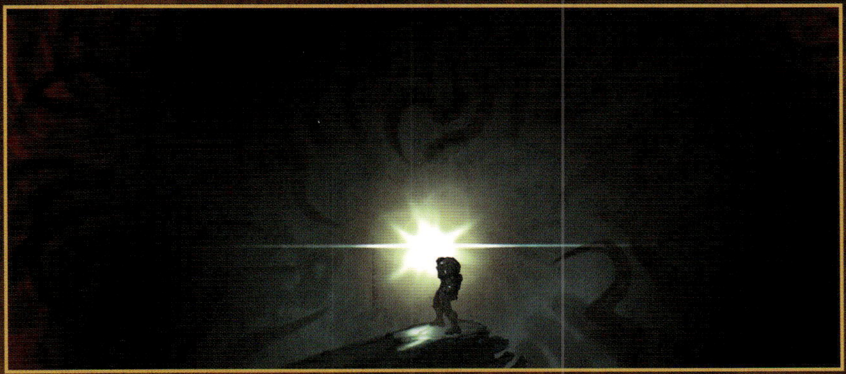

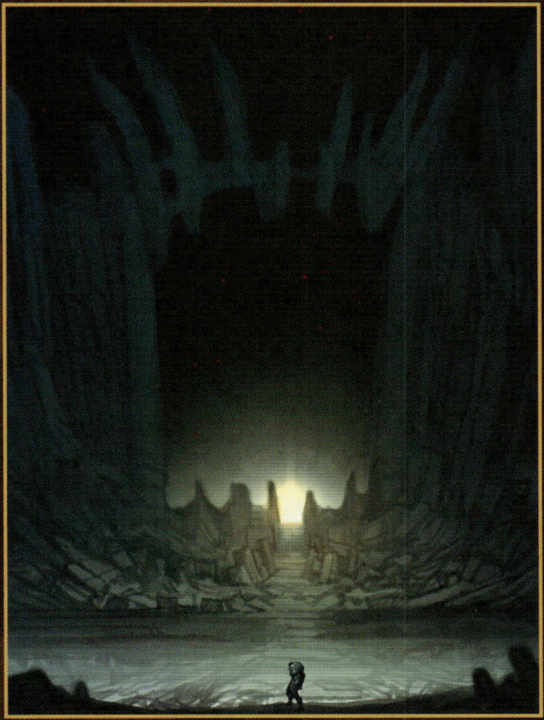

ASHLANDS CONCEPTS

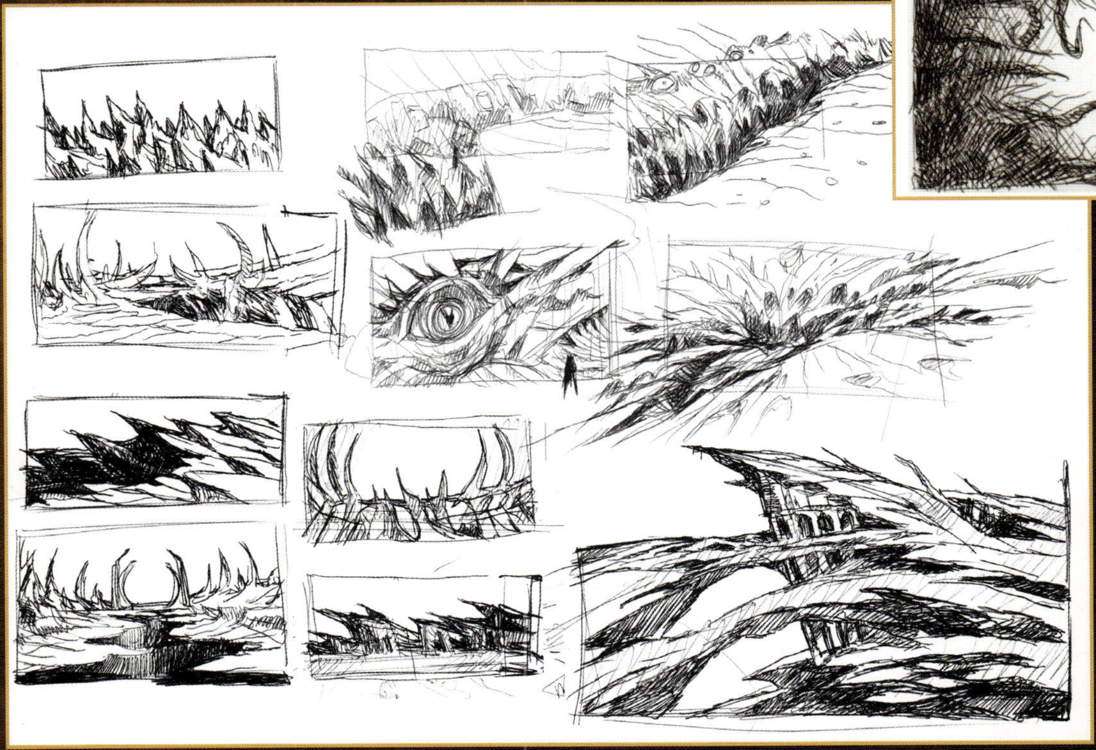

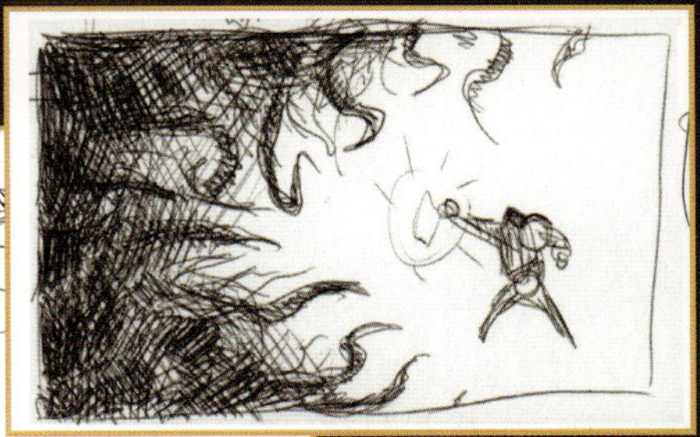

ASHLANDS FORMS

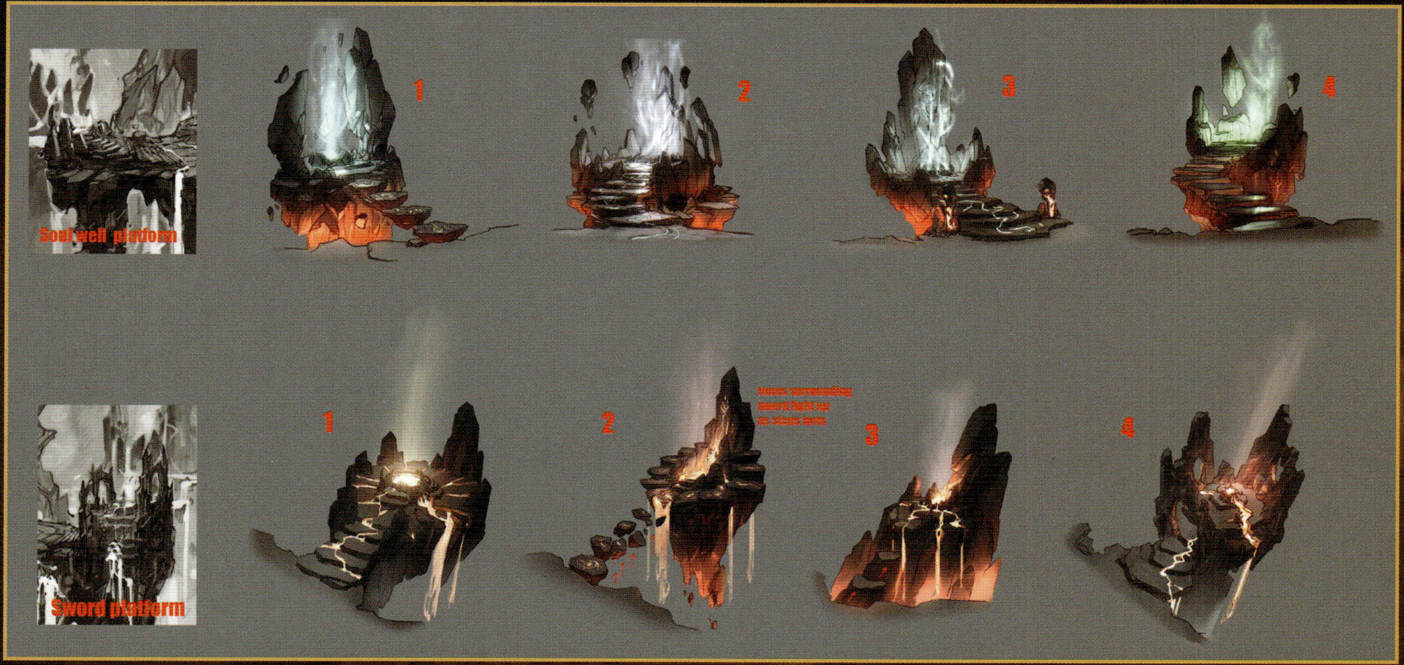

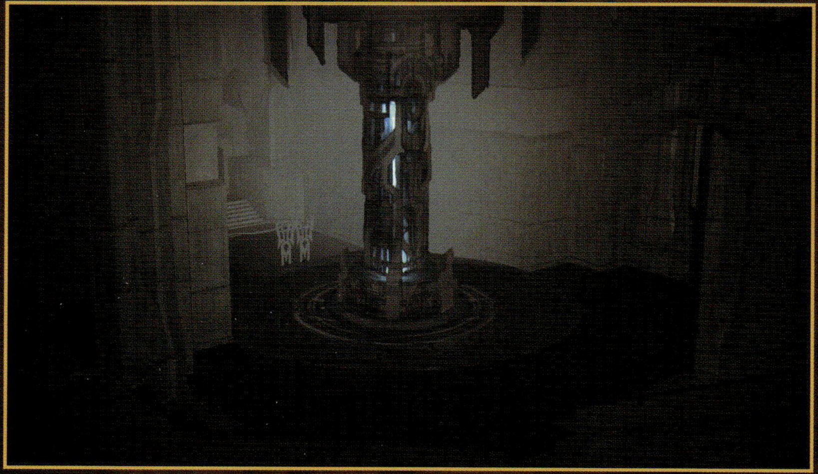

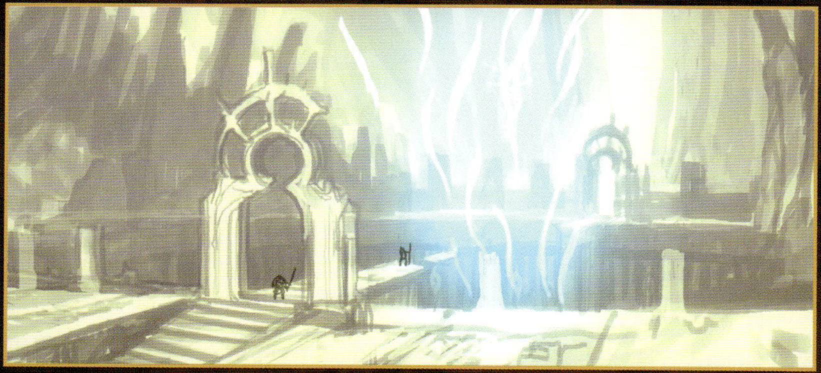

WELL OF SOULS CONCEPTS

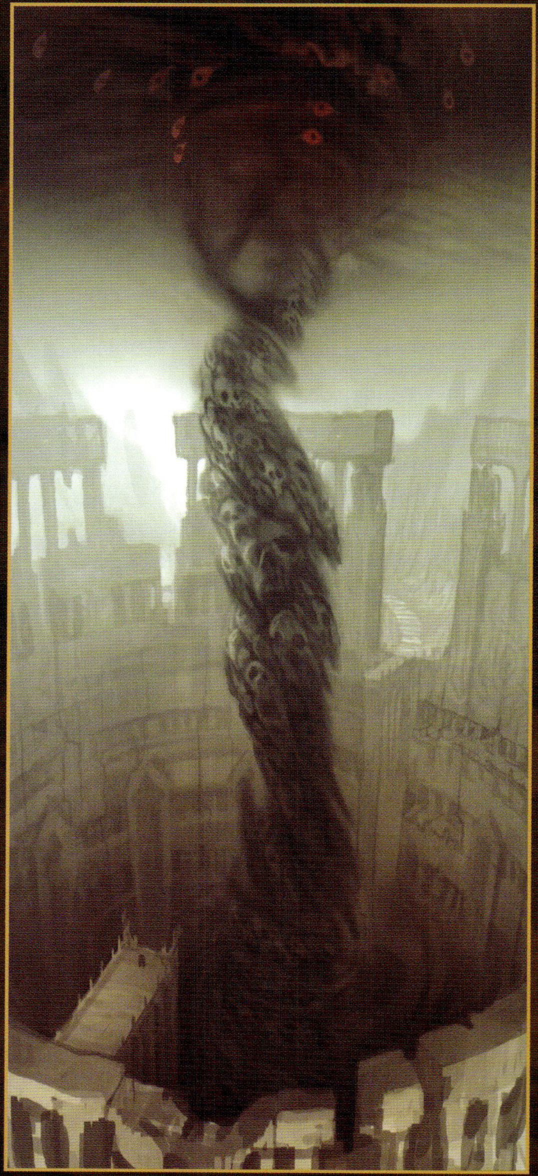

Well of Souls

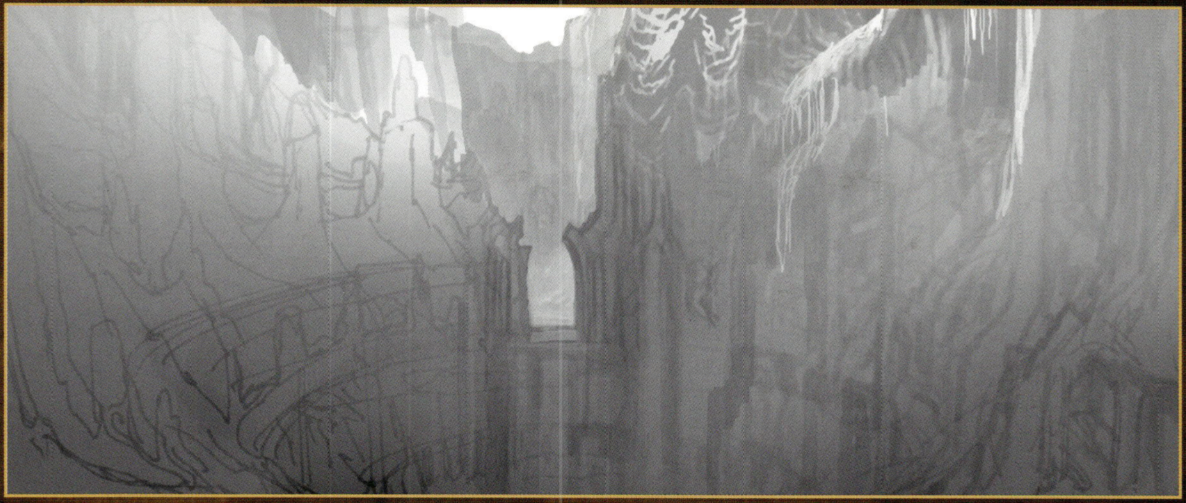

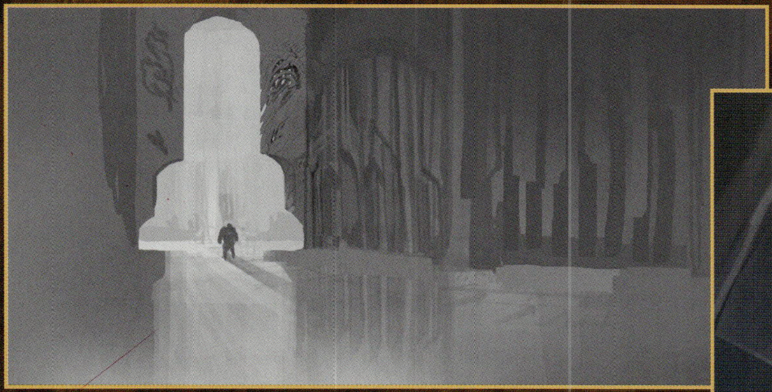

WELL OF SOULS CONCEPTS

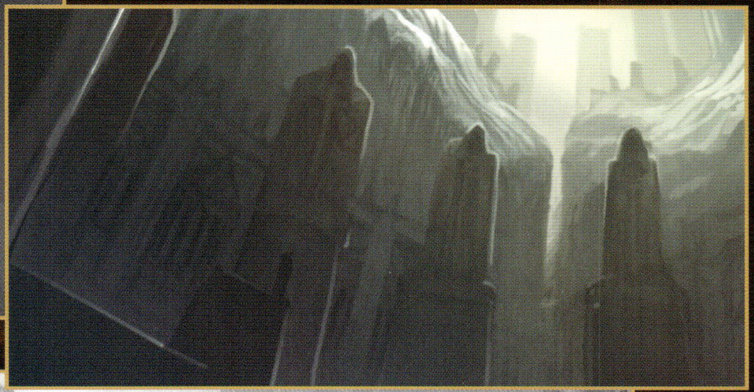

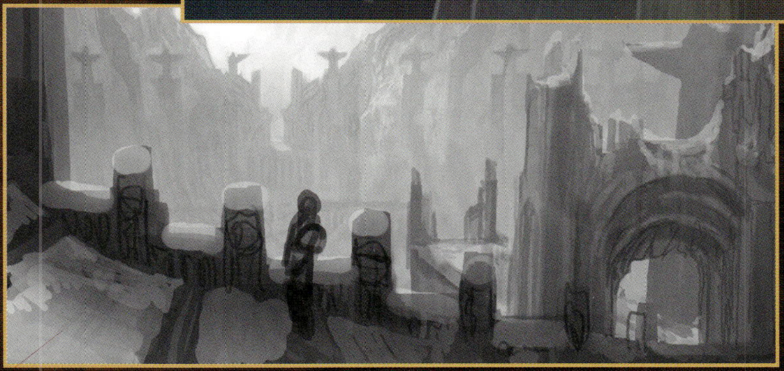

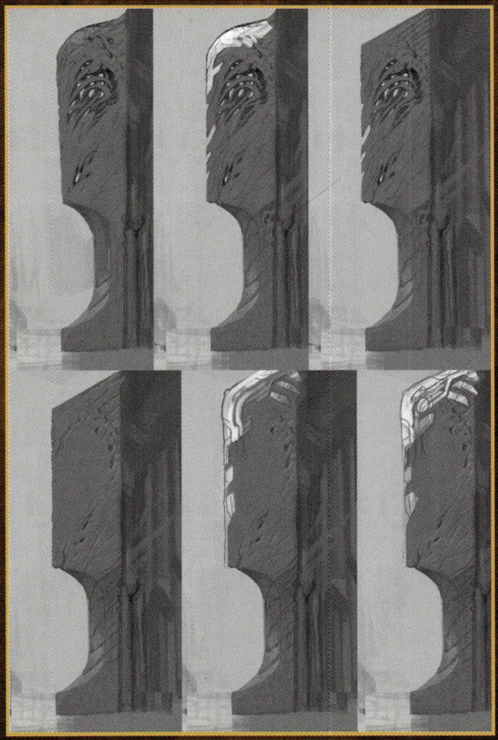

COLUMN CONCEPTS

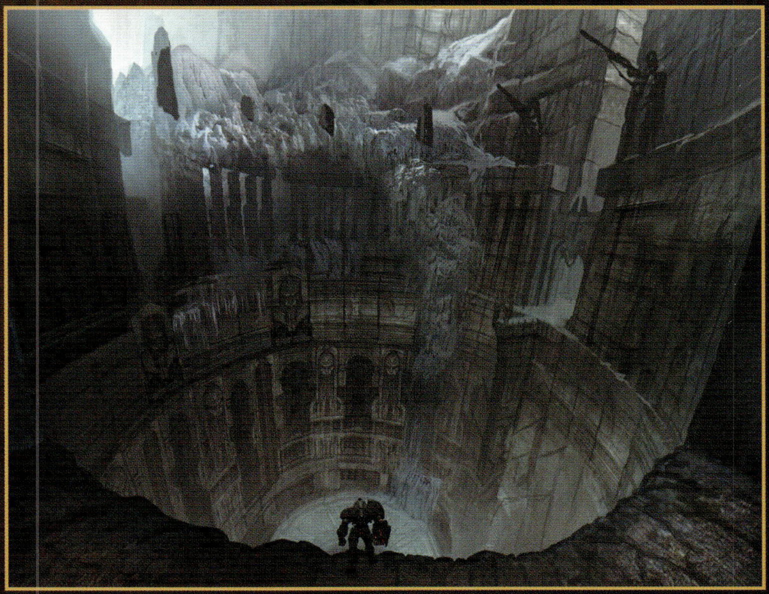

The Black Throne

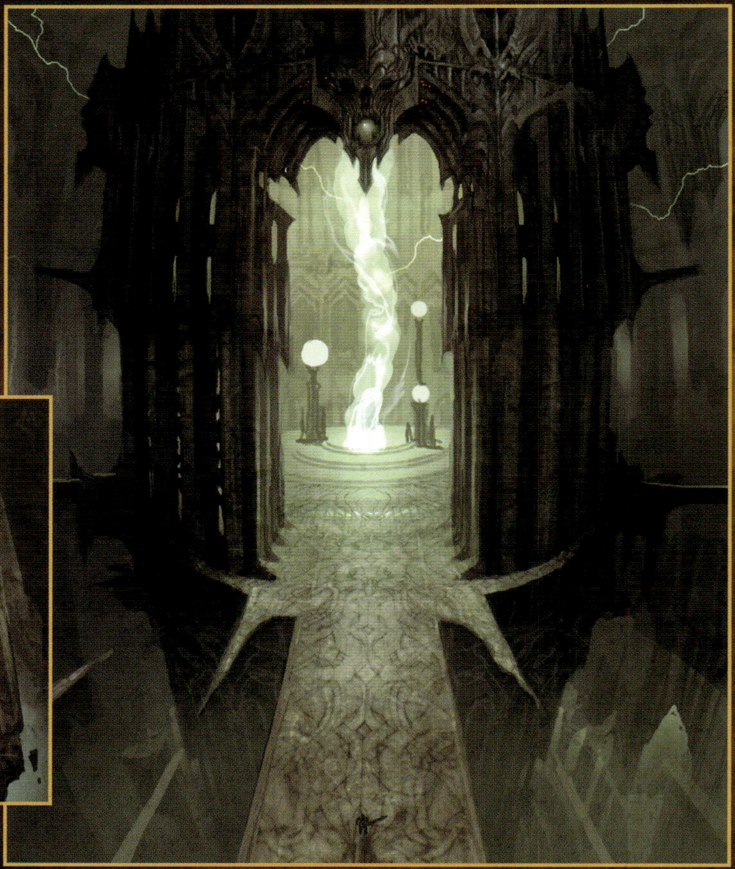

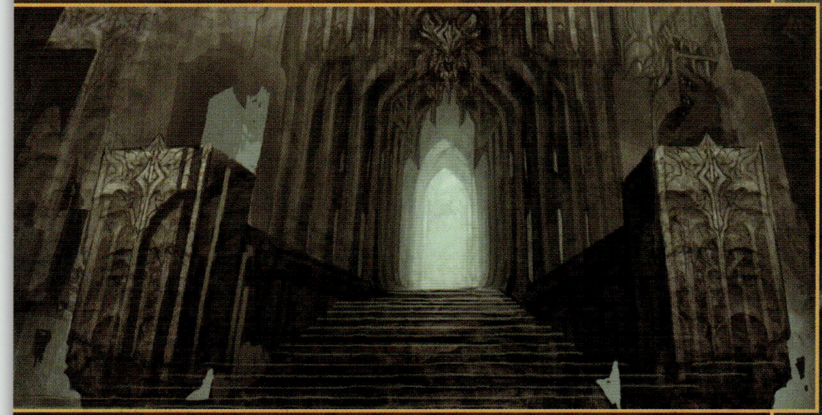

ENTRANCE CONCEPT

SHAFT CONCEPT

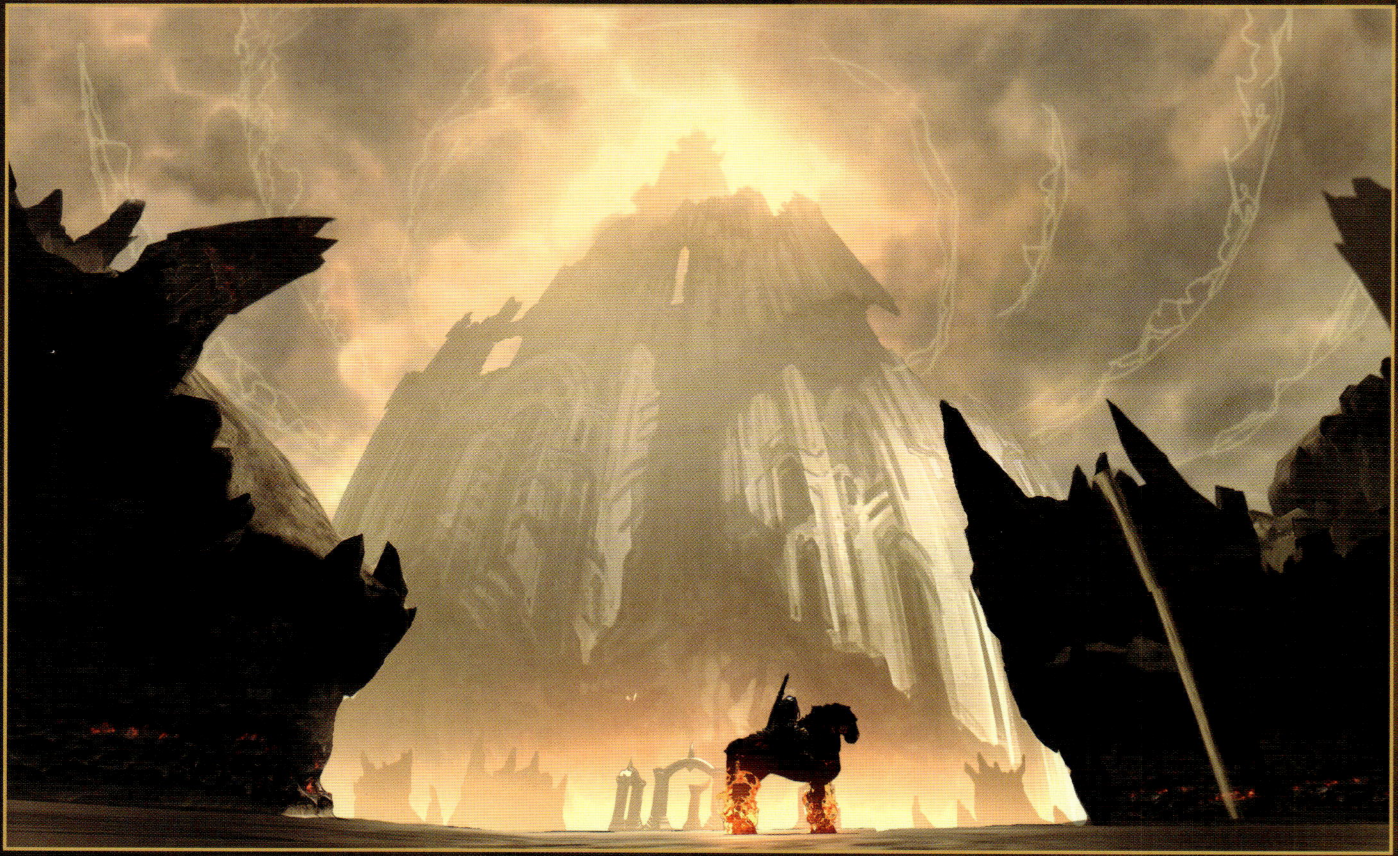

TOWER CONCEPT

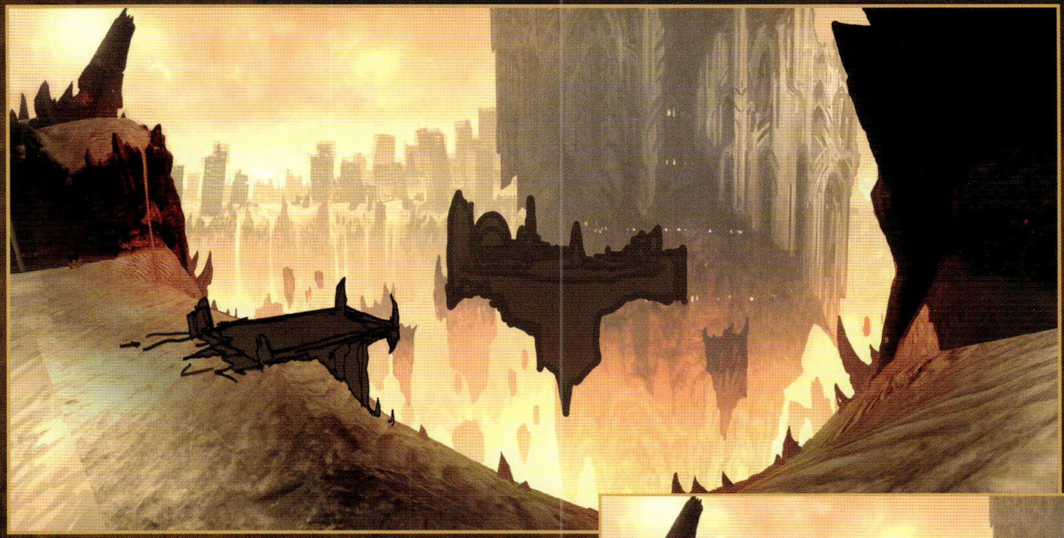

PIT CONCEPTS

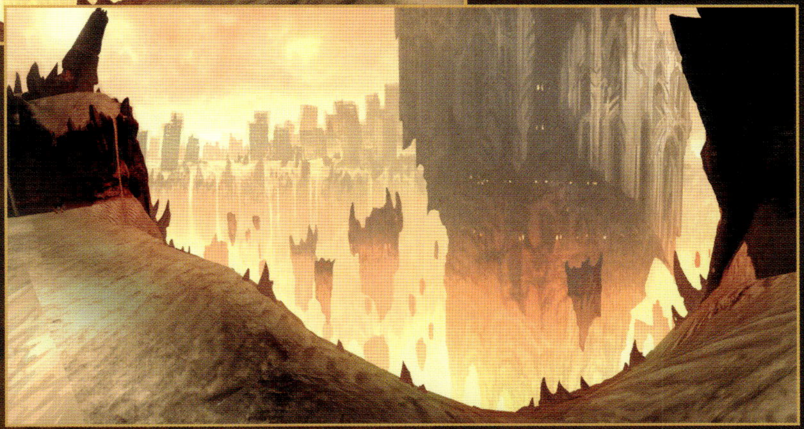

Rooted above a gaping wound cut deep into the earth, The Black Throne stands as both a stronghold of Hell's power and a symbol of the Dark One's victory. It rises high above the broken city, obsidian-colored brick stretching into unholy flame, a never-ending inferno reflecting but a fraction of the Destroyer's might.

Those who do not bow before the monolith are broken. I know this all too well.

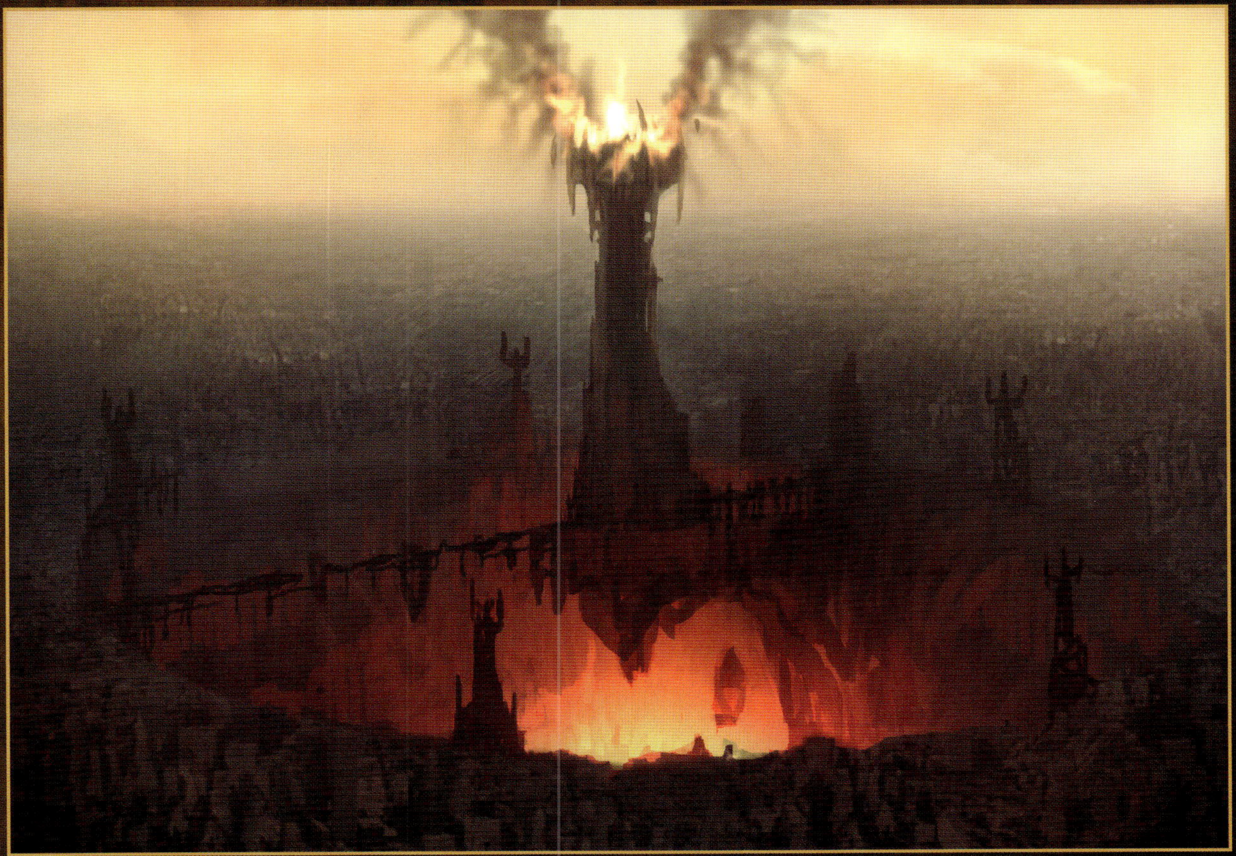

TOWER CONCEPT

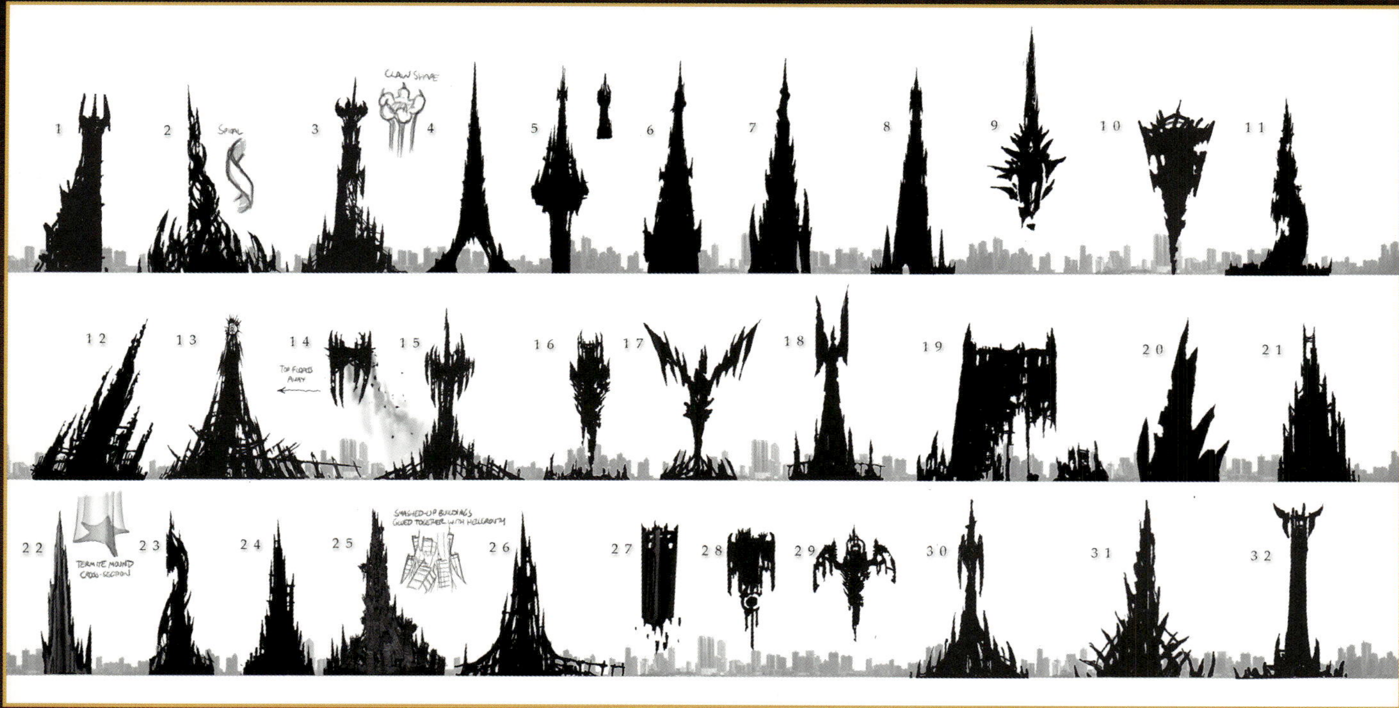

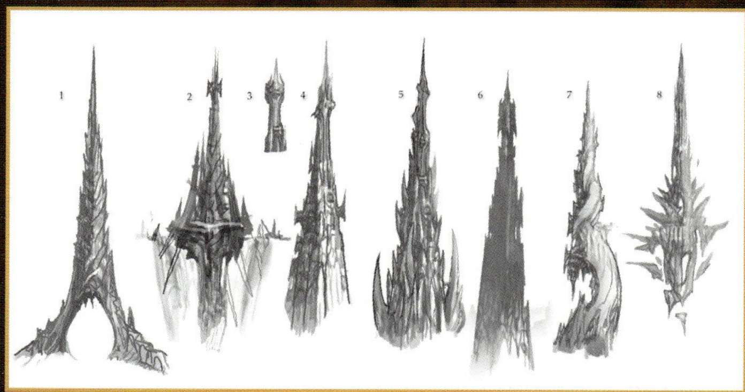

DEVELOPMENT SKETCHES

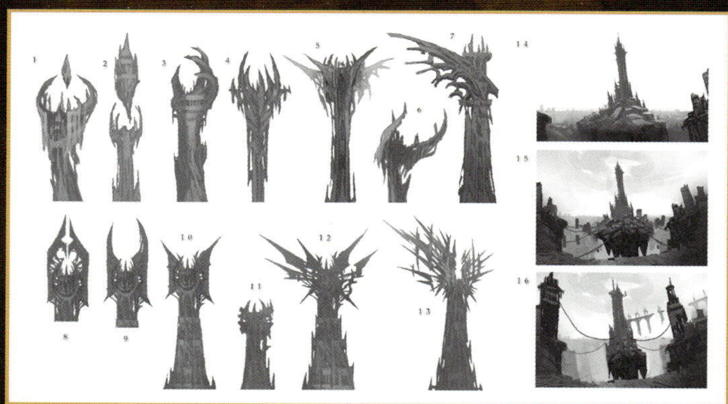

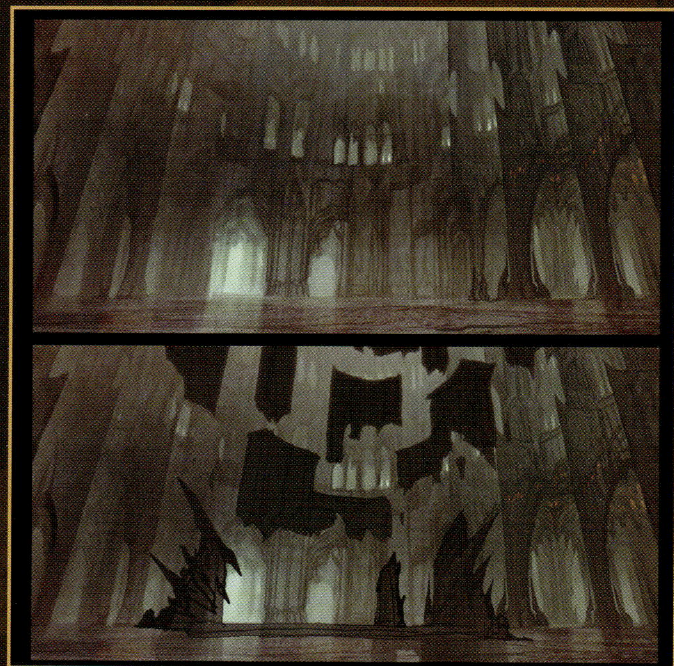

TOWER INTERIORS

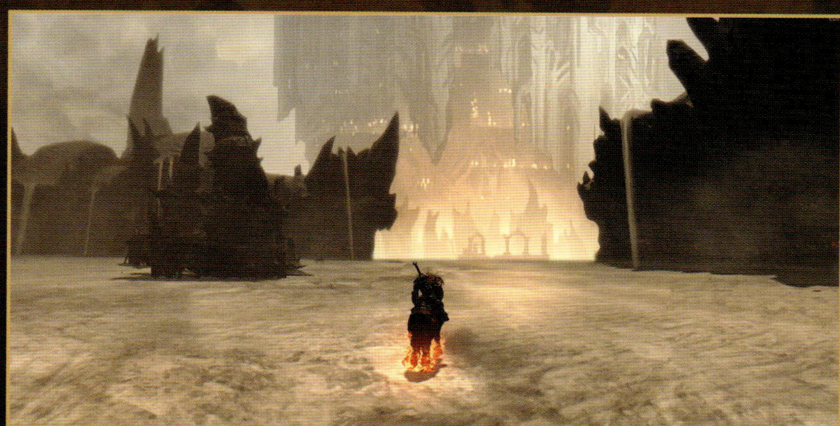

TOWER CONCEPT

PLATFORM SKETCHES

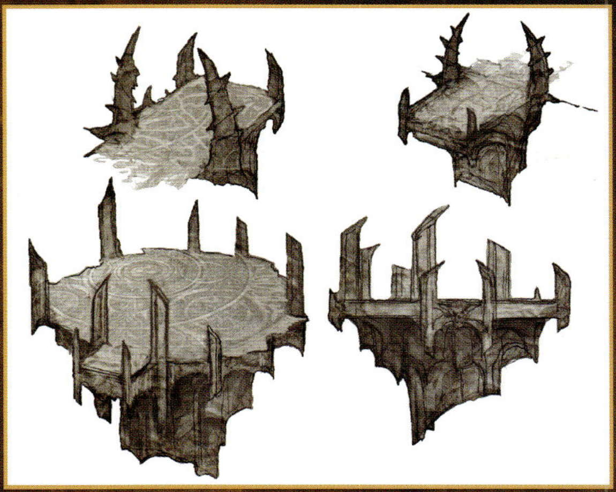

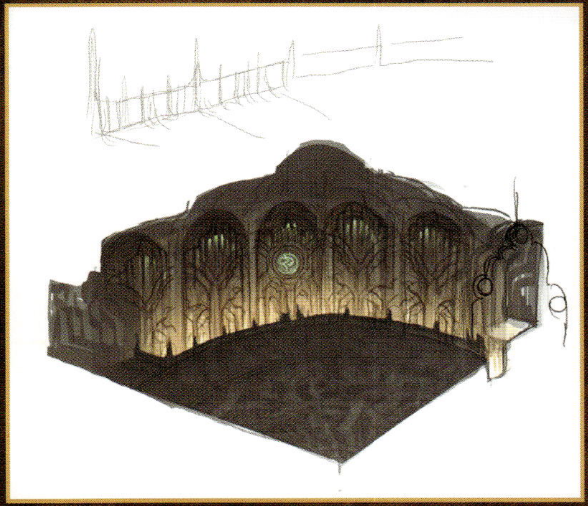

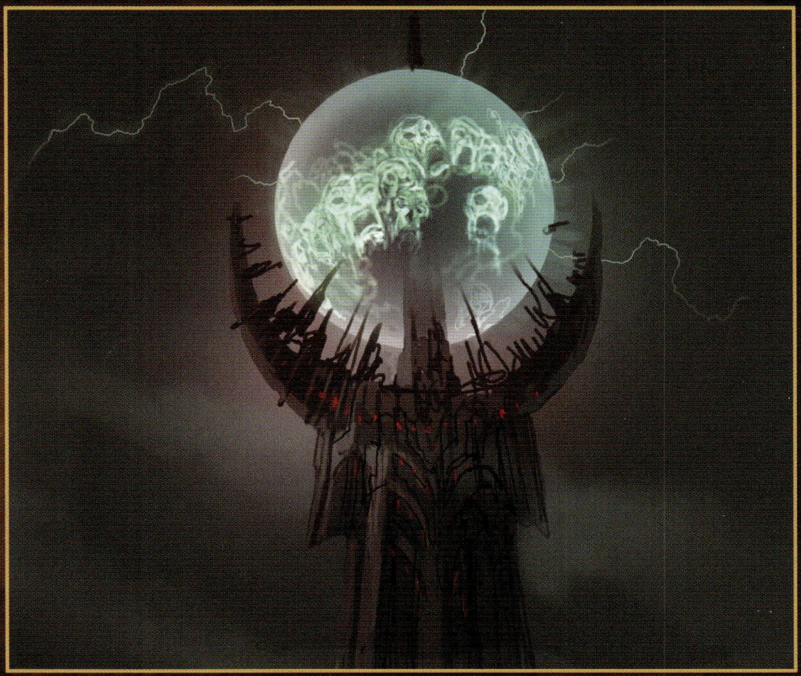

TOWER CONCEPTS

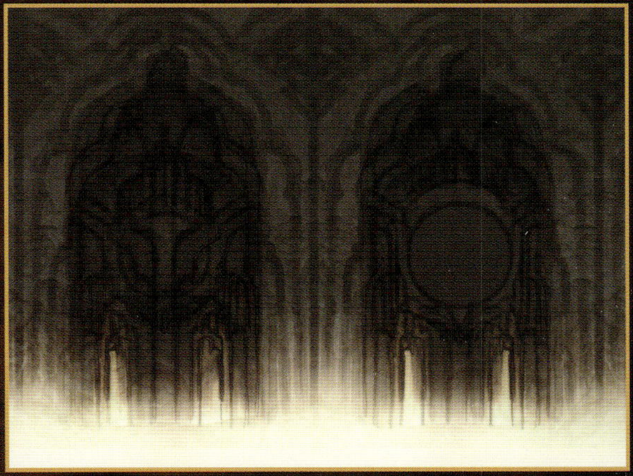

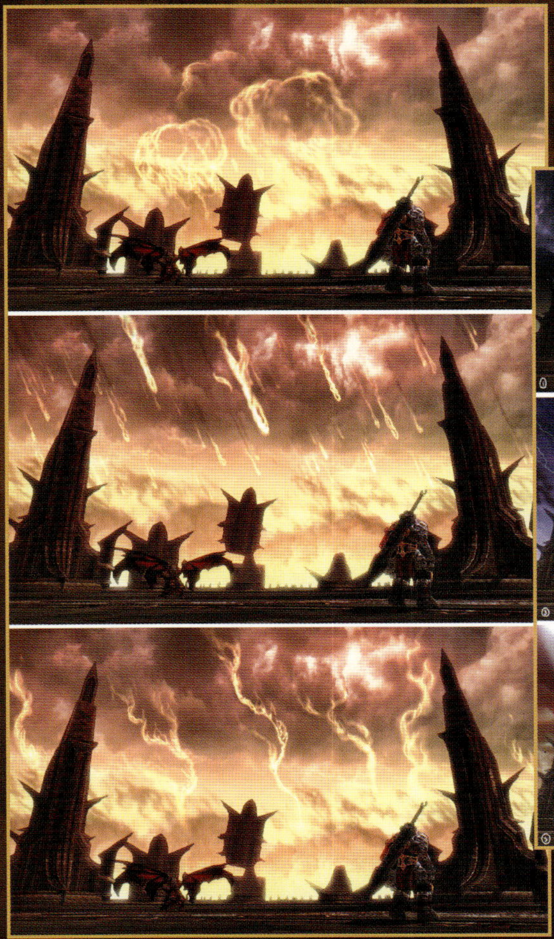

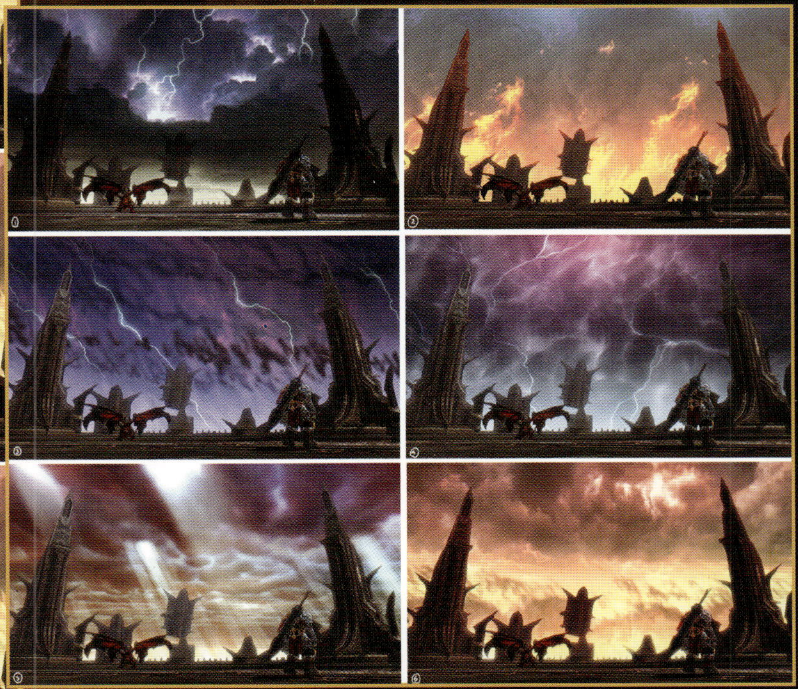

BOSS FIGHT CONCEPTS

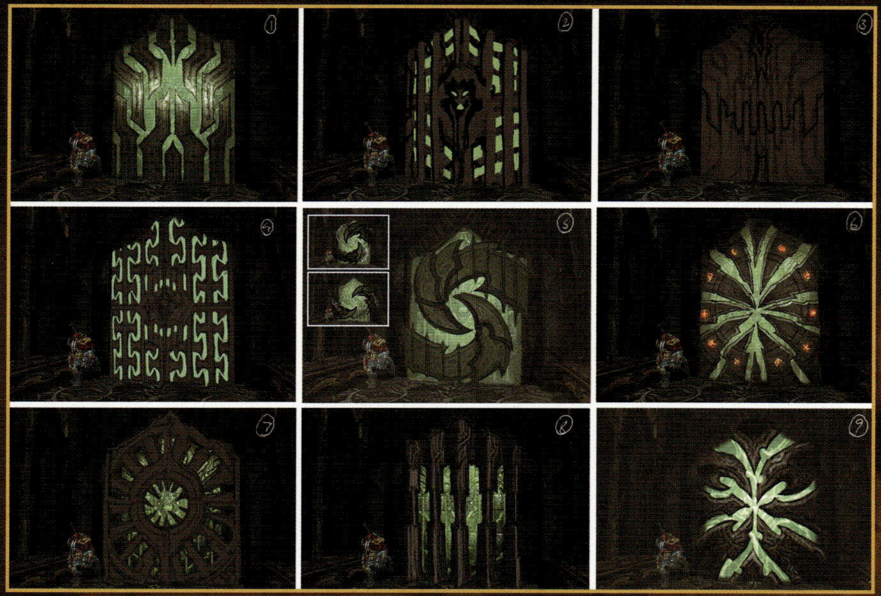

DOOR DESIGNS

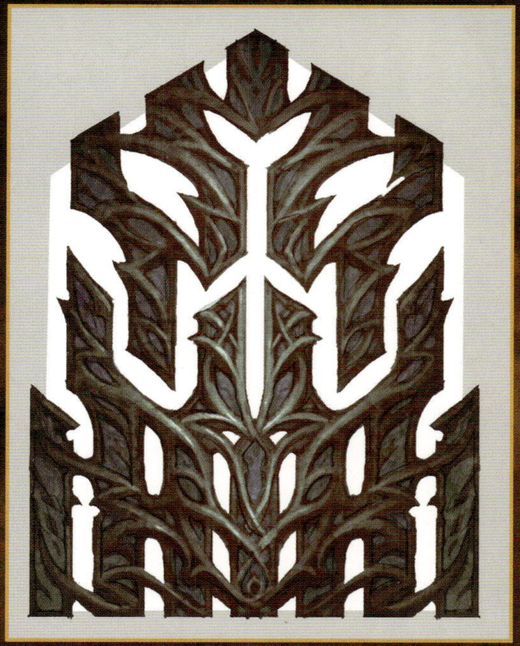

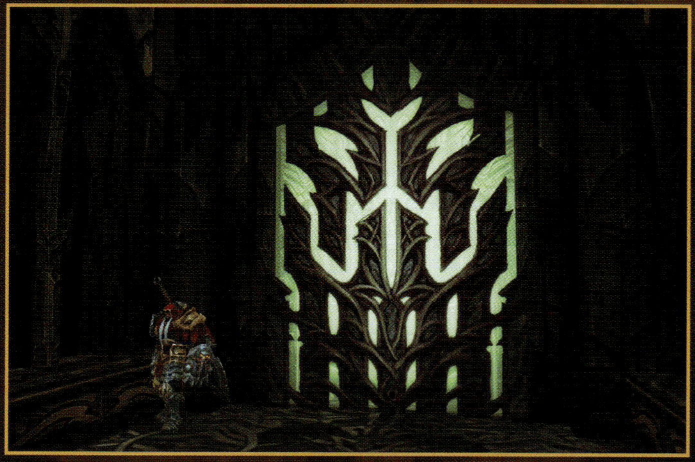

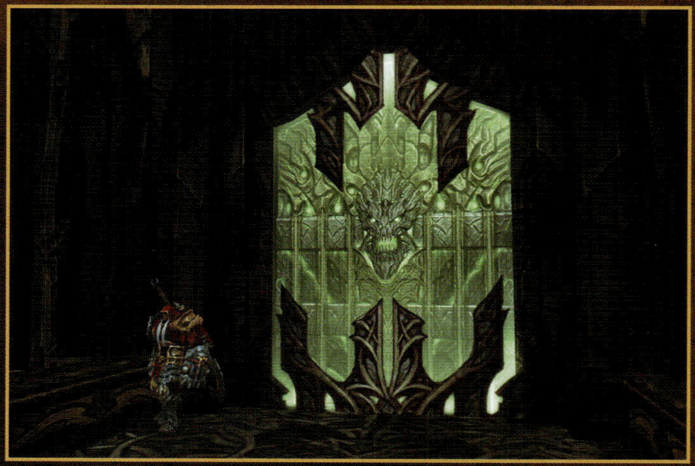

DOOR DESIGNS

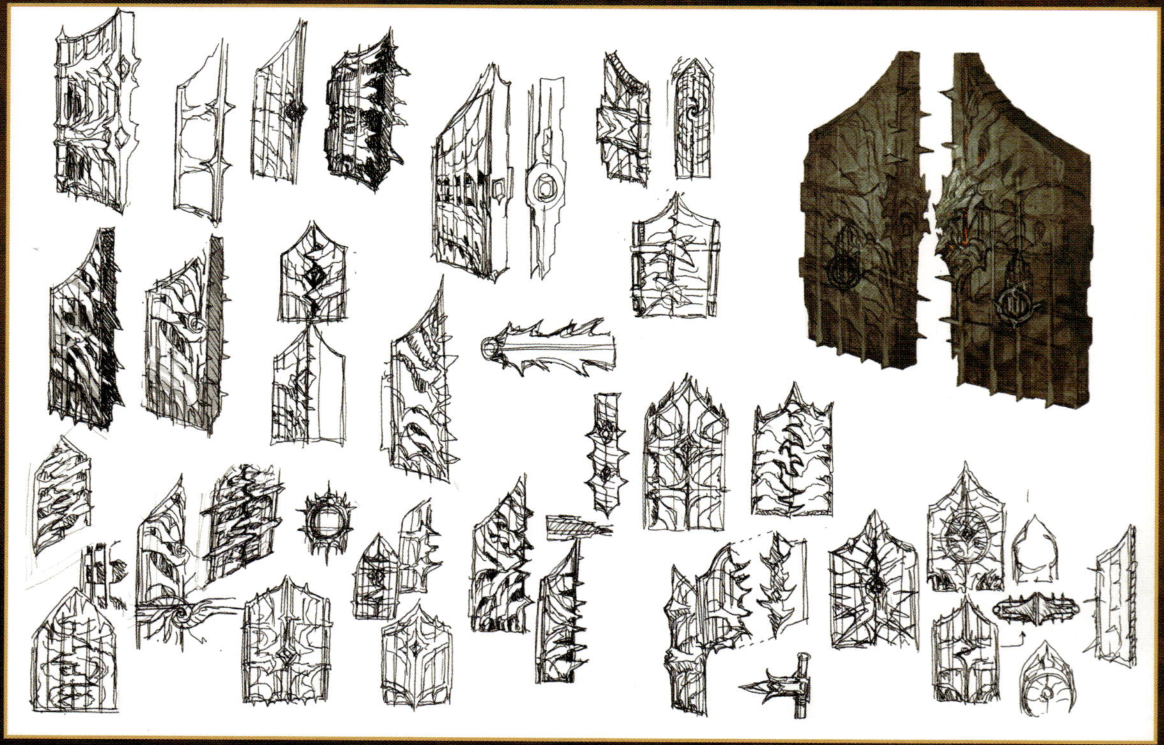

DOOR DEVELOPMENT SKETCHES

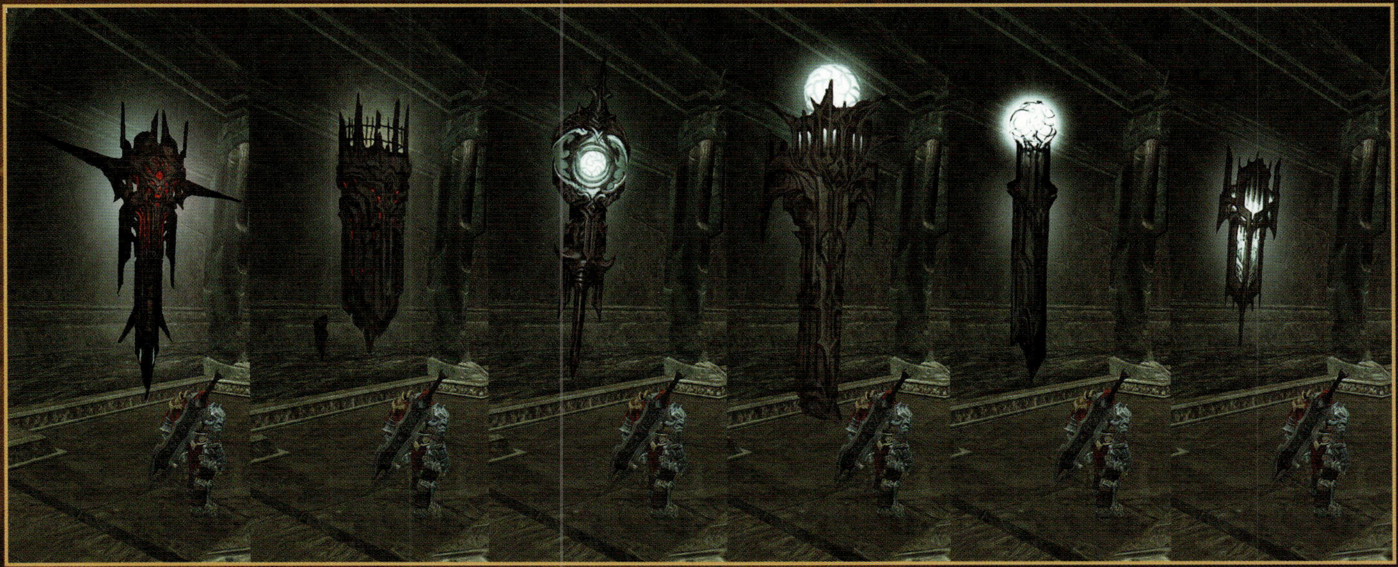

LIGHT DESIGNS

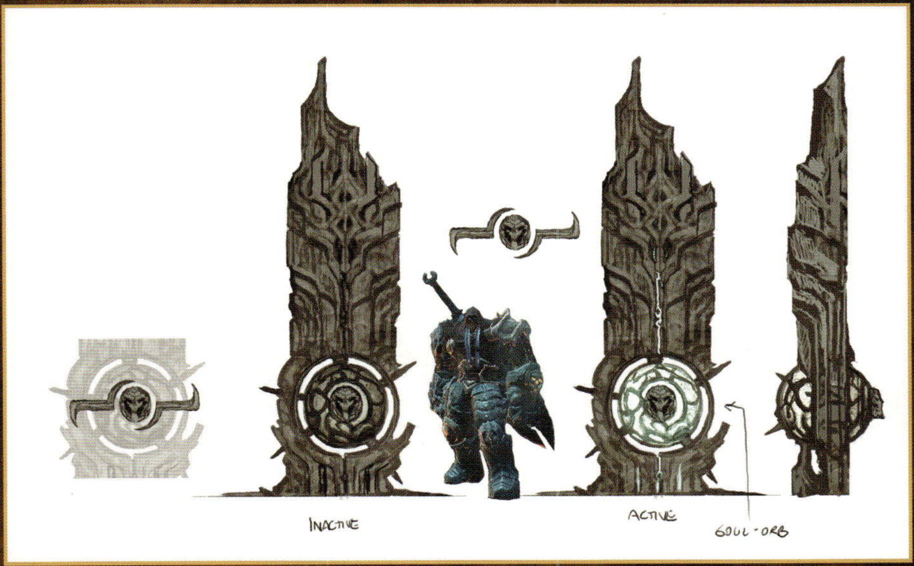

SWITCH DESIGNS

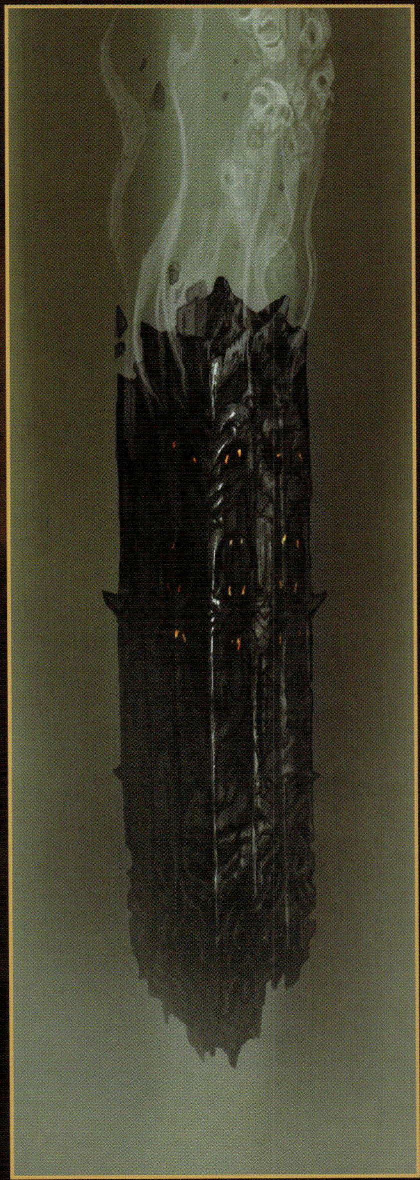

FLOATING PILLAR

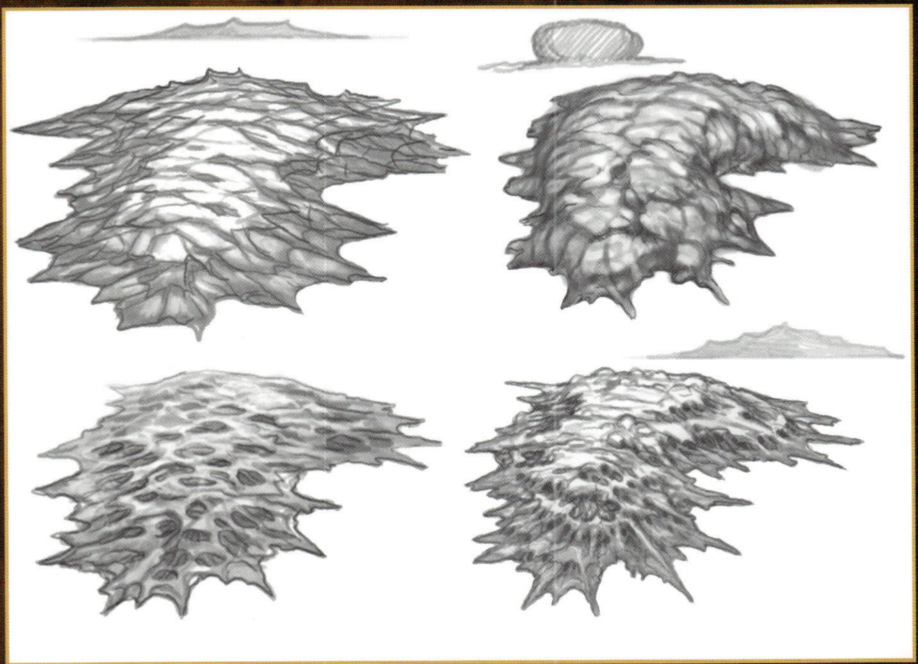

GOO CONCEPTS

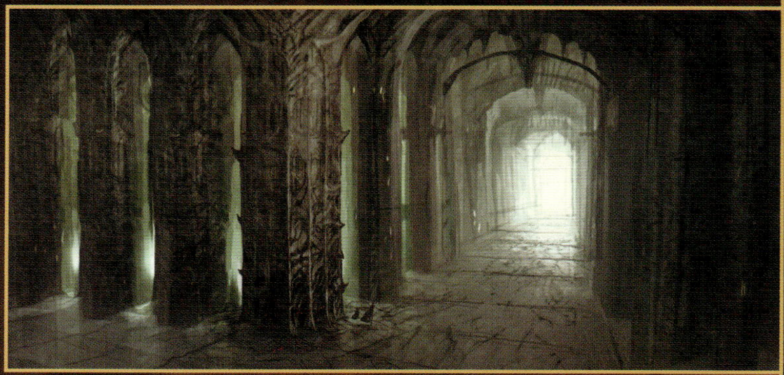

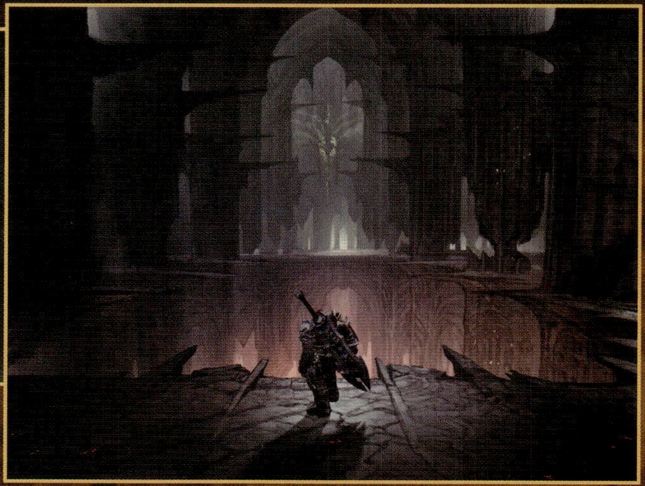

INTERIOR CONCEPTS

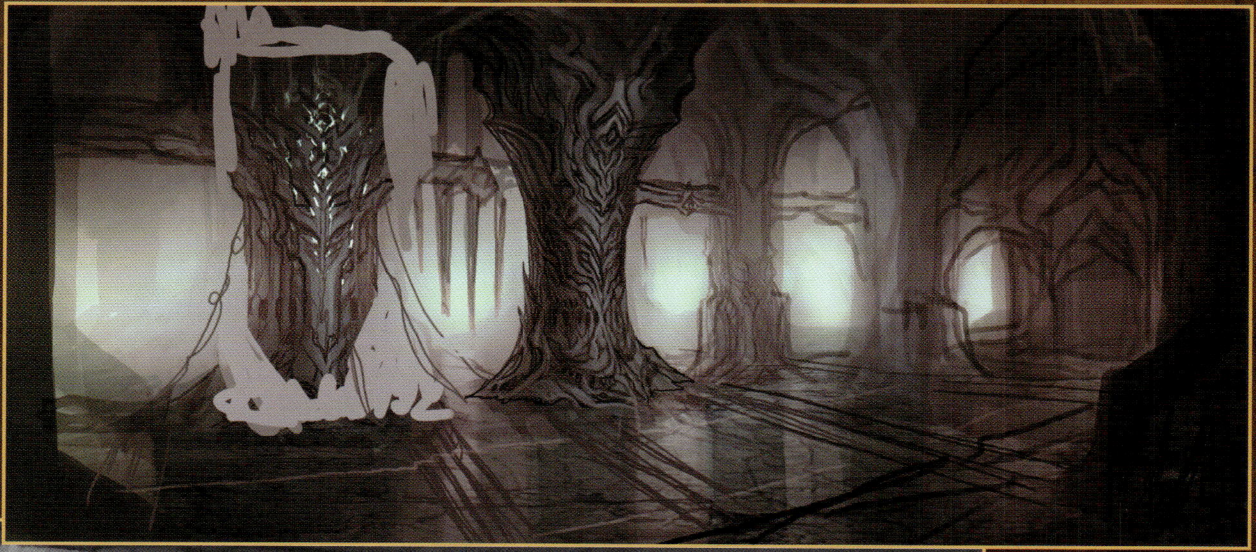

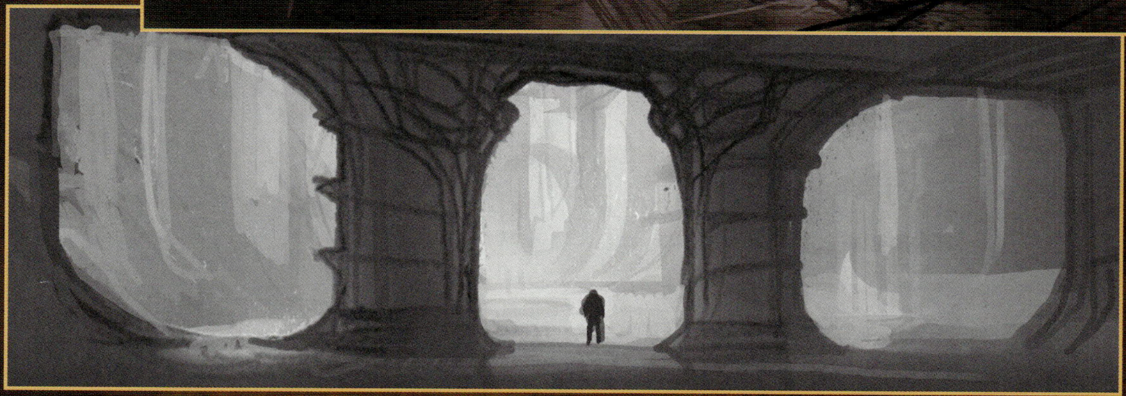

INTERIOR CONCEPTS

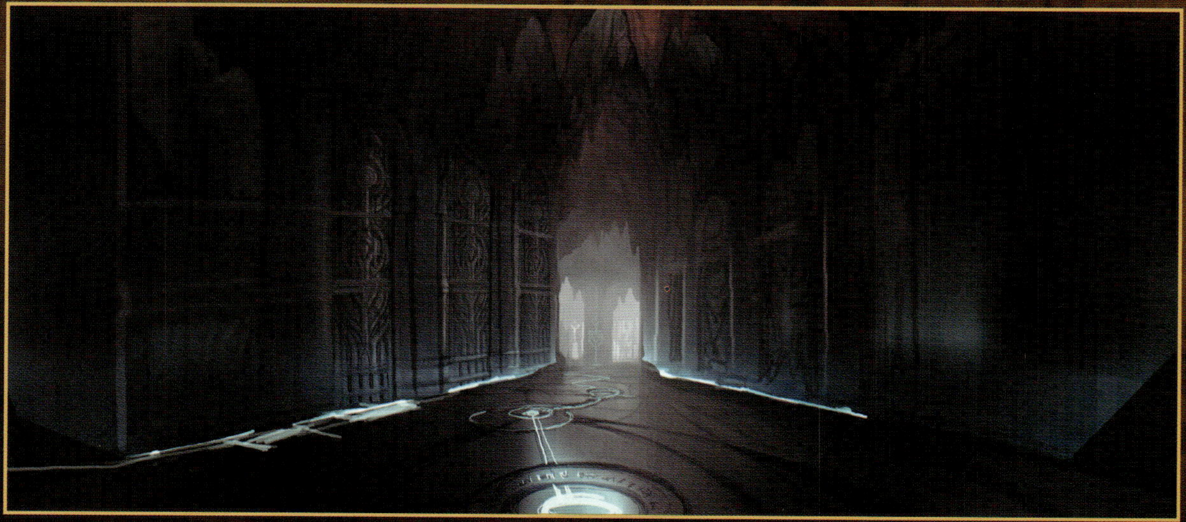

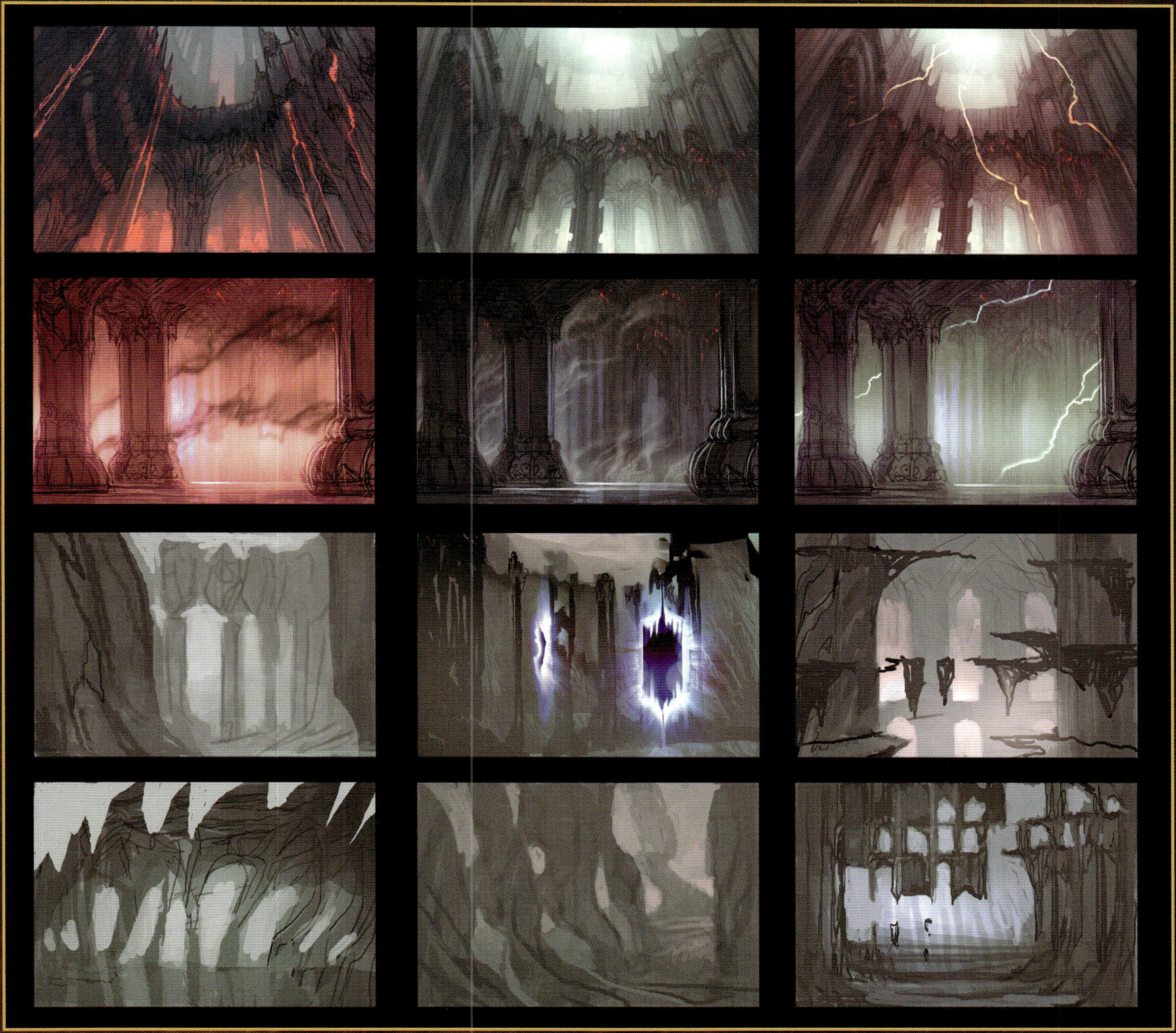

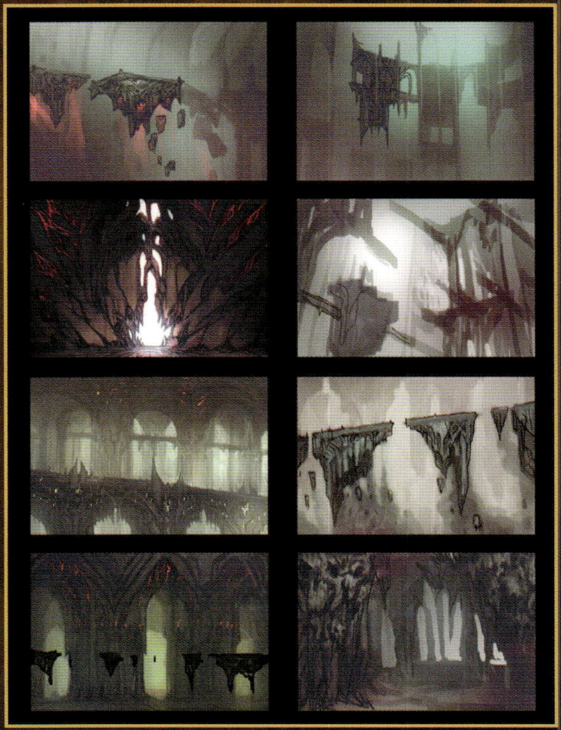

DARK TOWER CONCEPTS

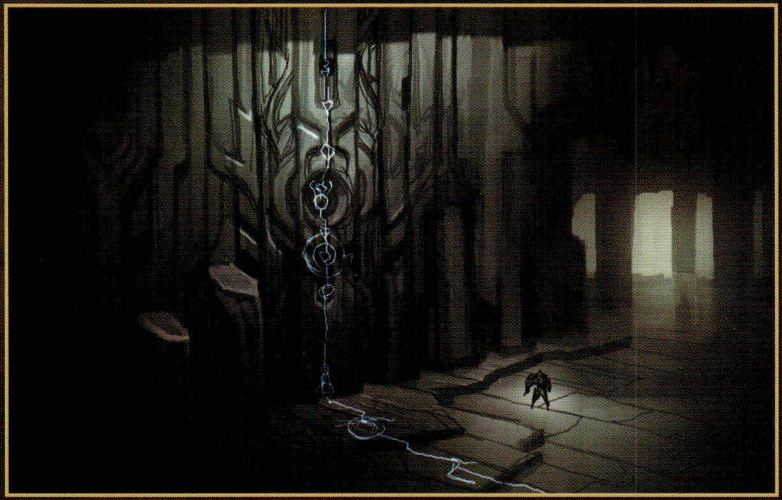

INTERIOR CONCEPT

Angelic Fortress

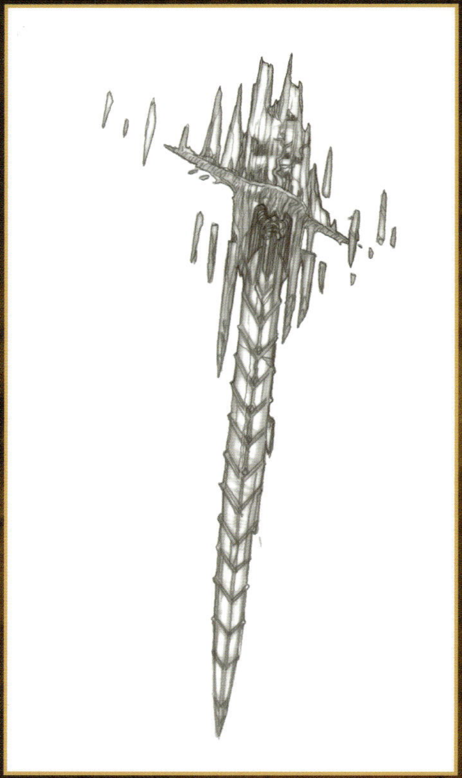

FORTRESS CONCEPT

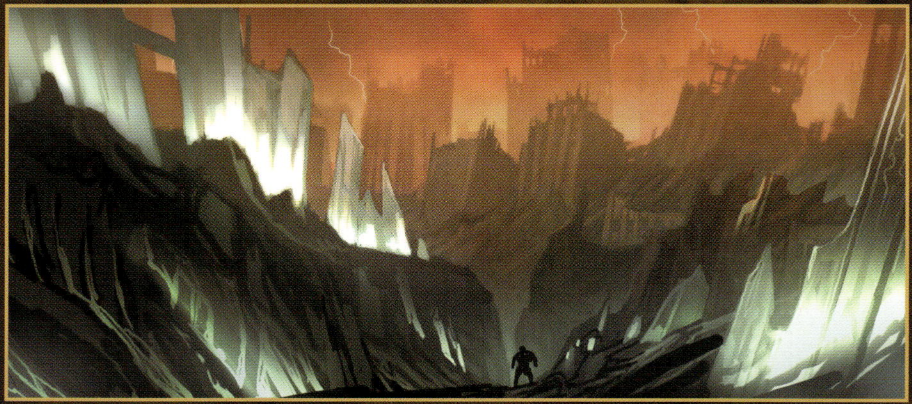

COLUMN DESIGNS

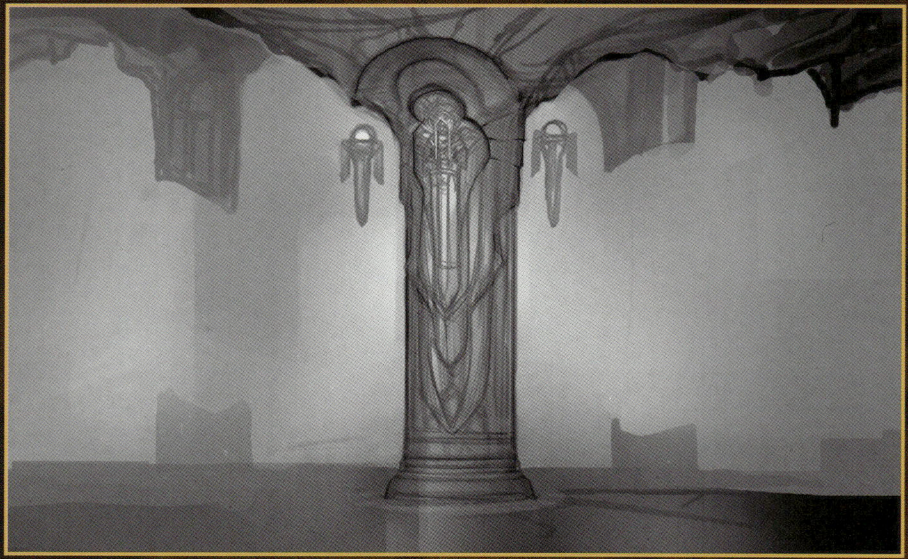

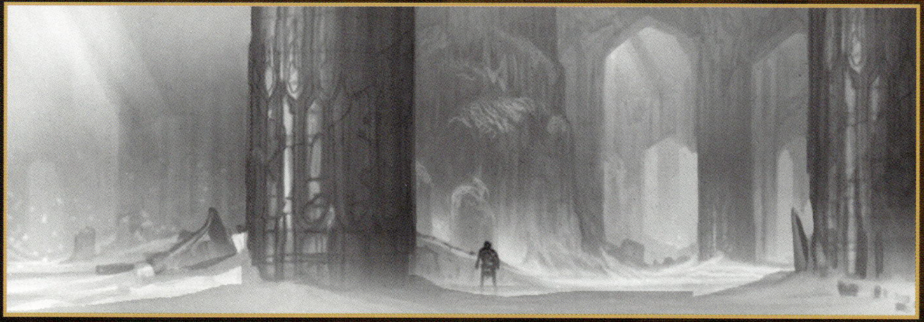

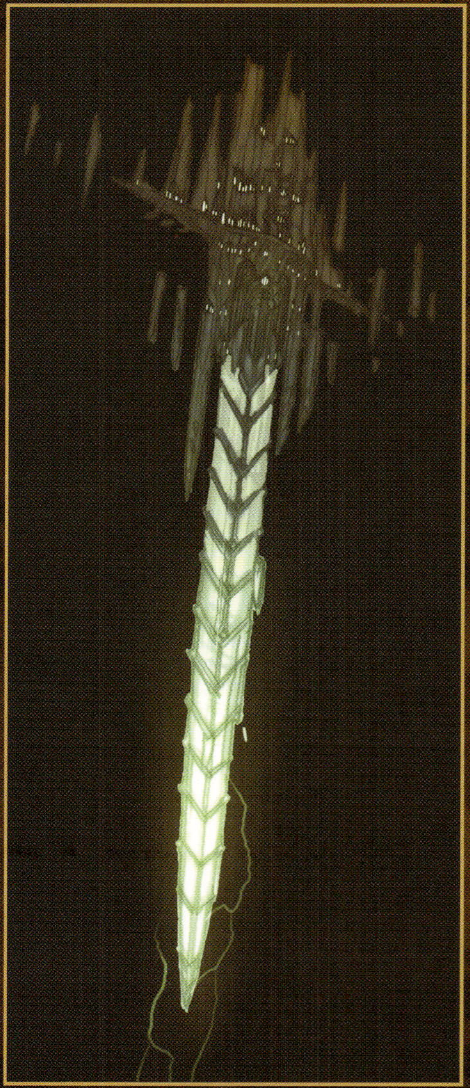

FLOATING FORTRESS CONCEPT

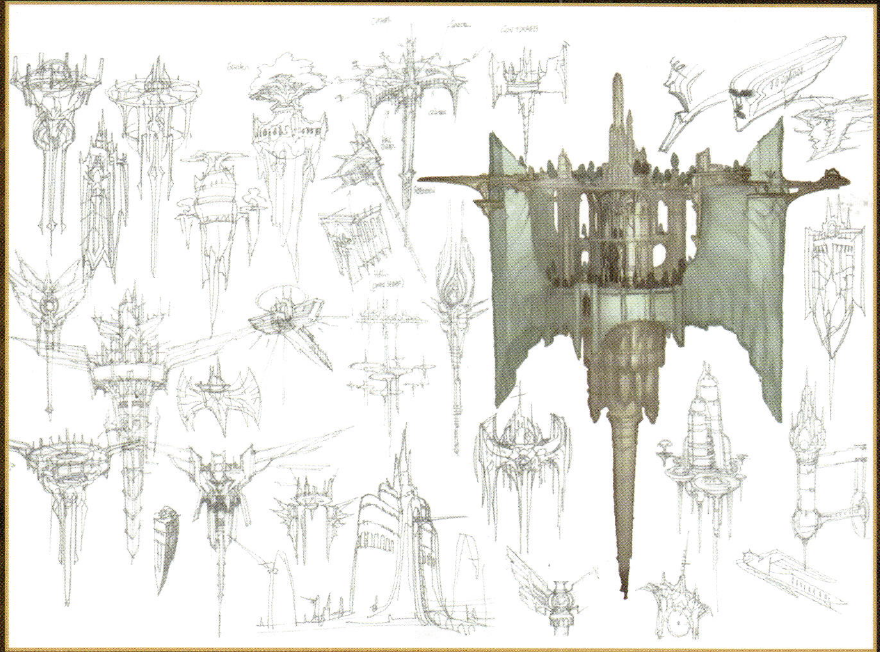

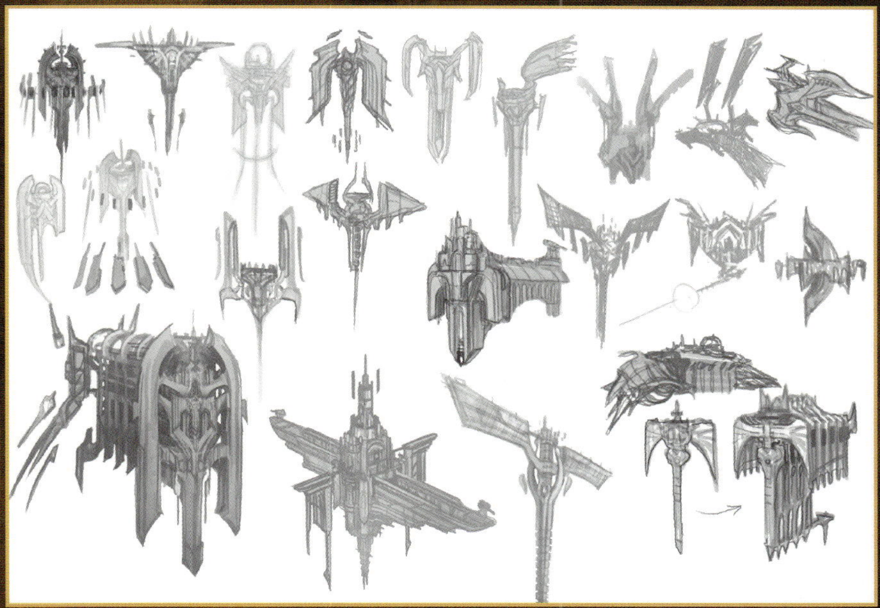

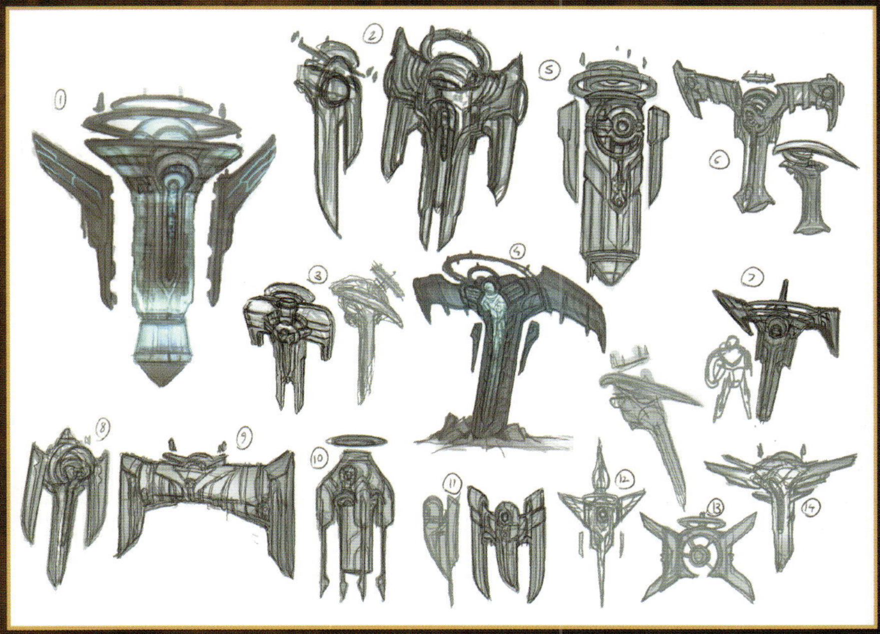

DEVELOPMENT SKETCHES

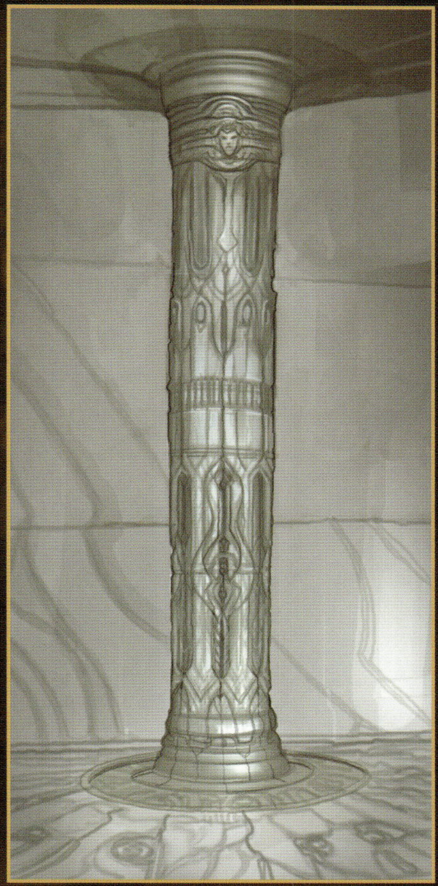

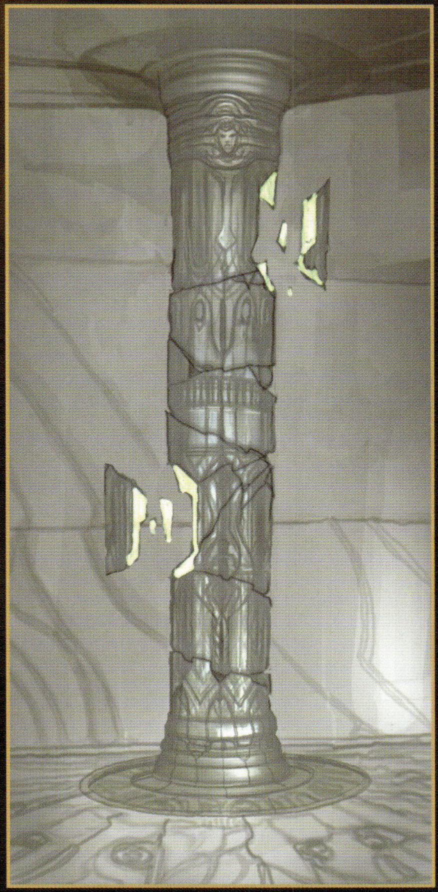

COLUMN DESIGNS

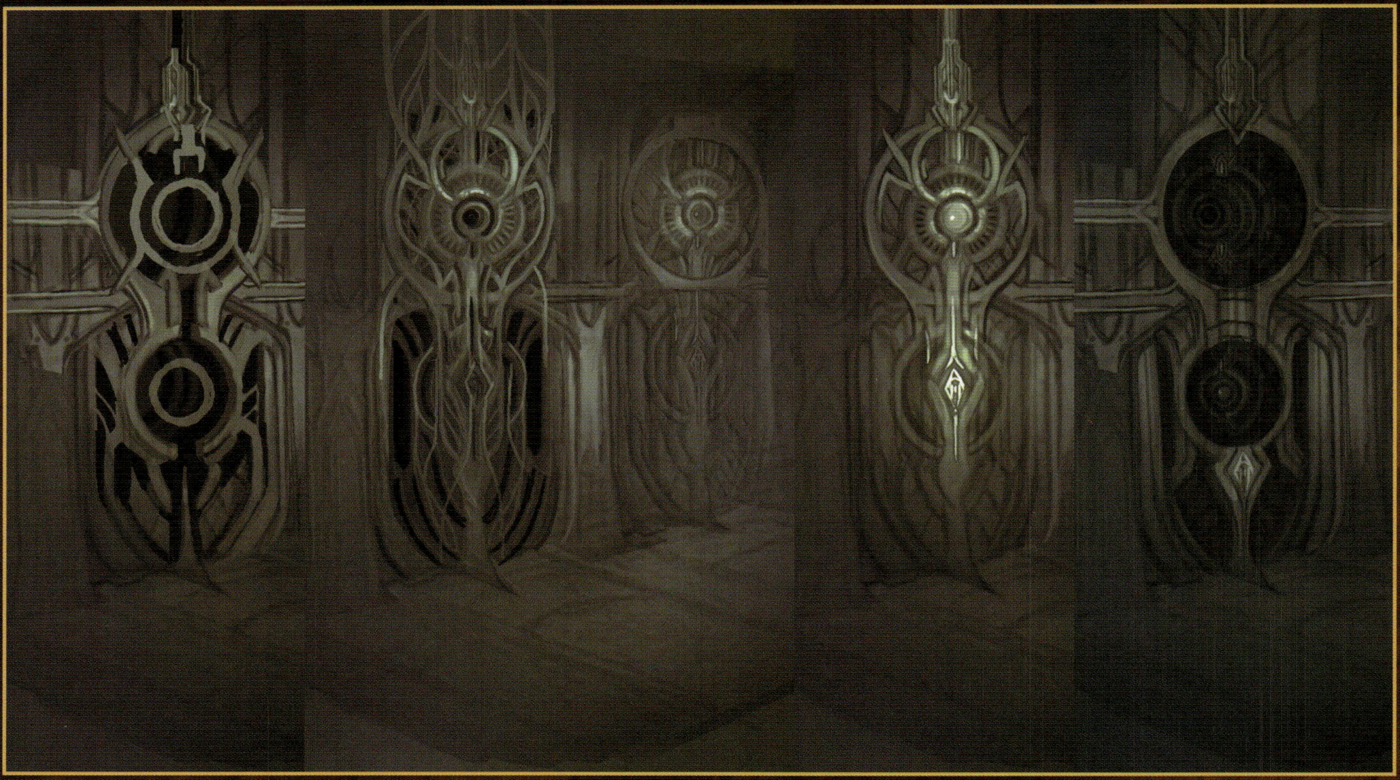

WALL DESIGNS

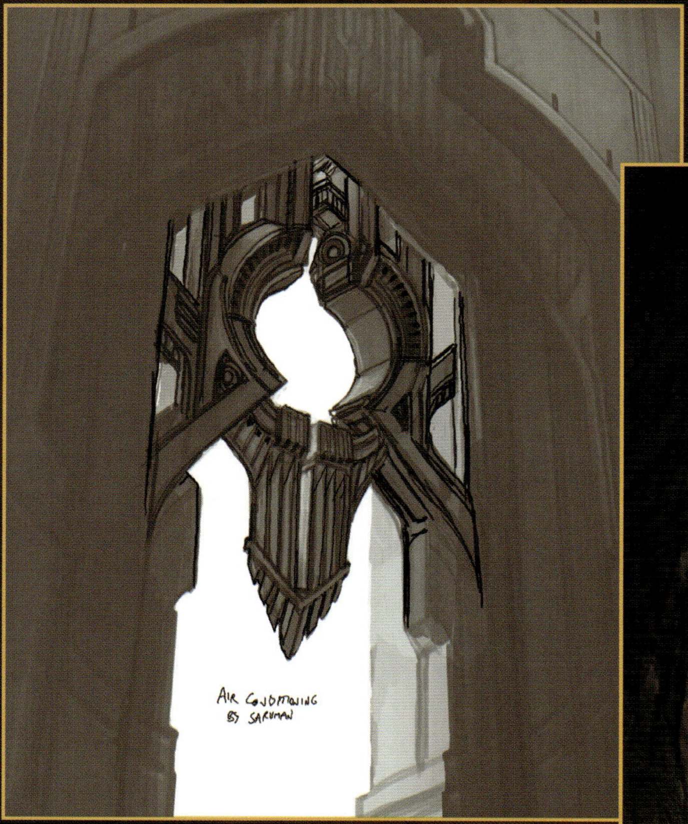

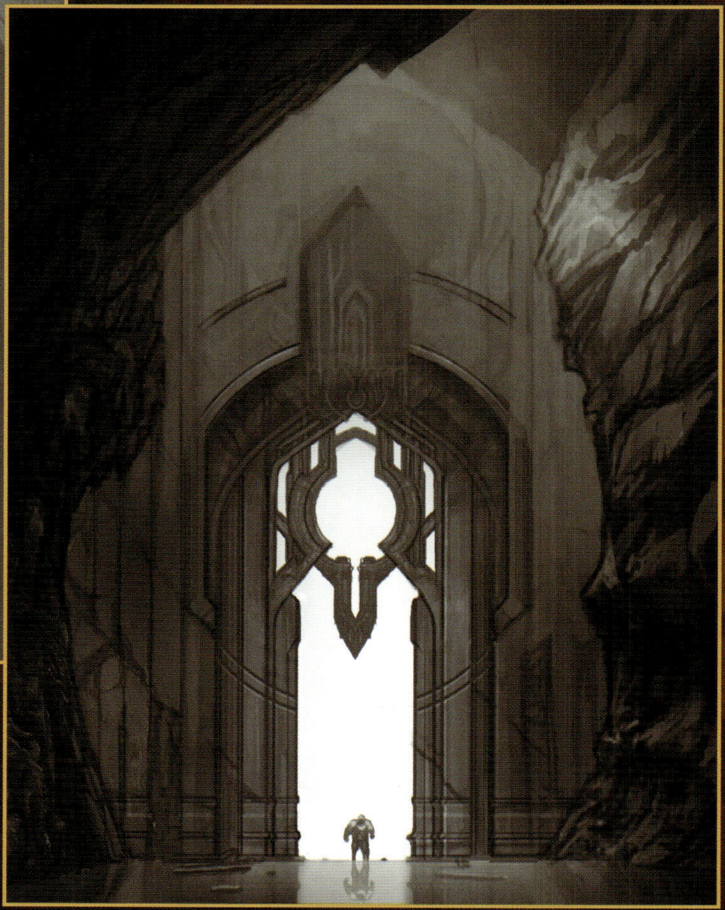

ARCHWAYS

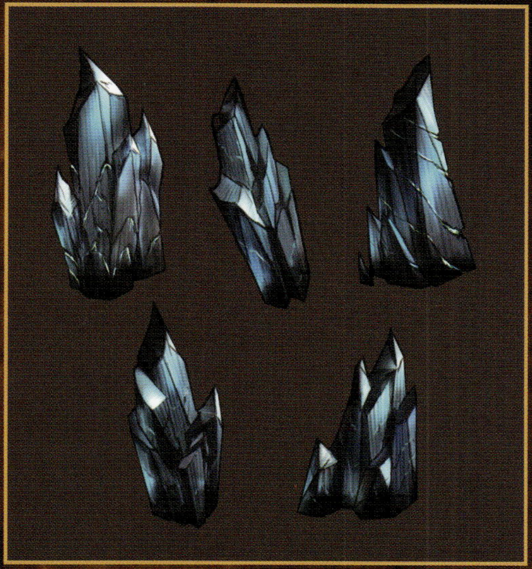

CRYSTAL DESIGNS

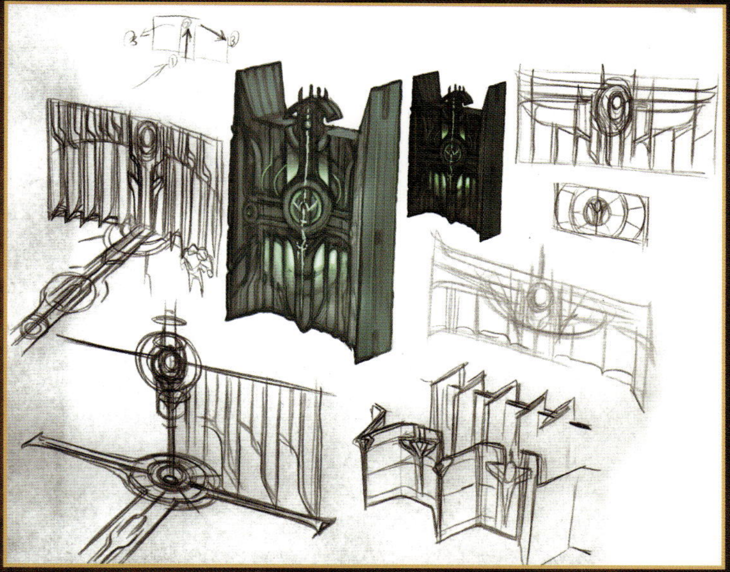

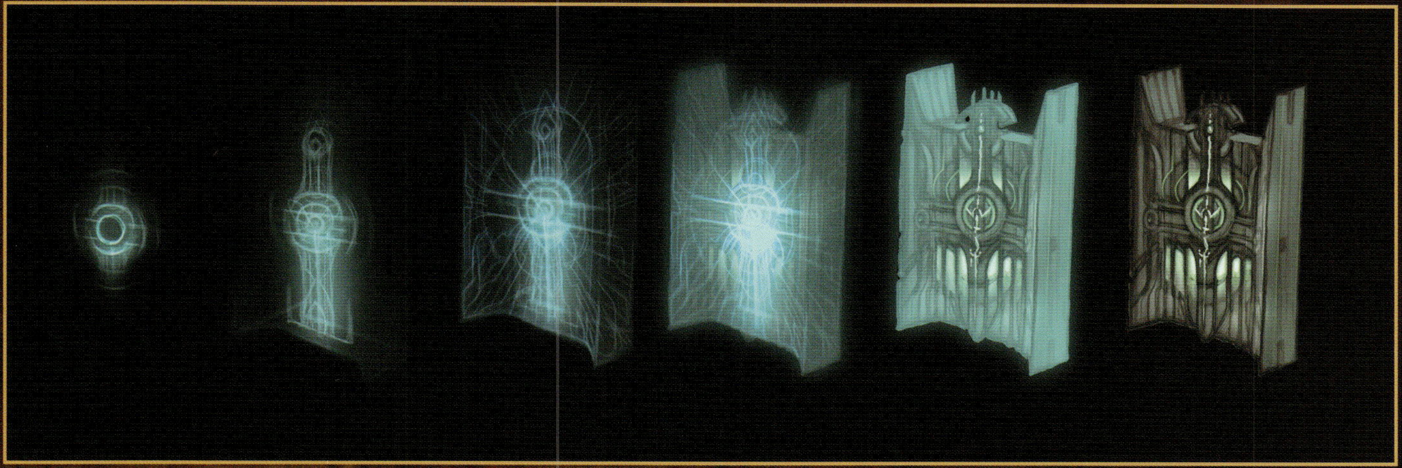

ANGEL GATE DEVELOPMENT SKETCHES

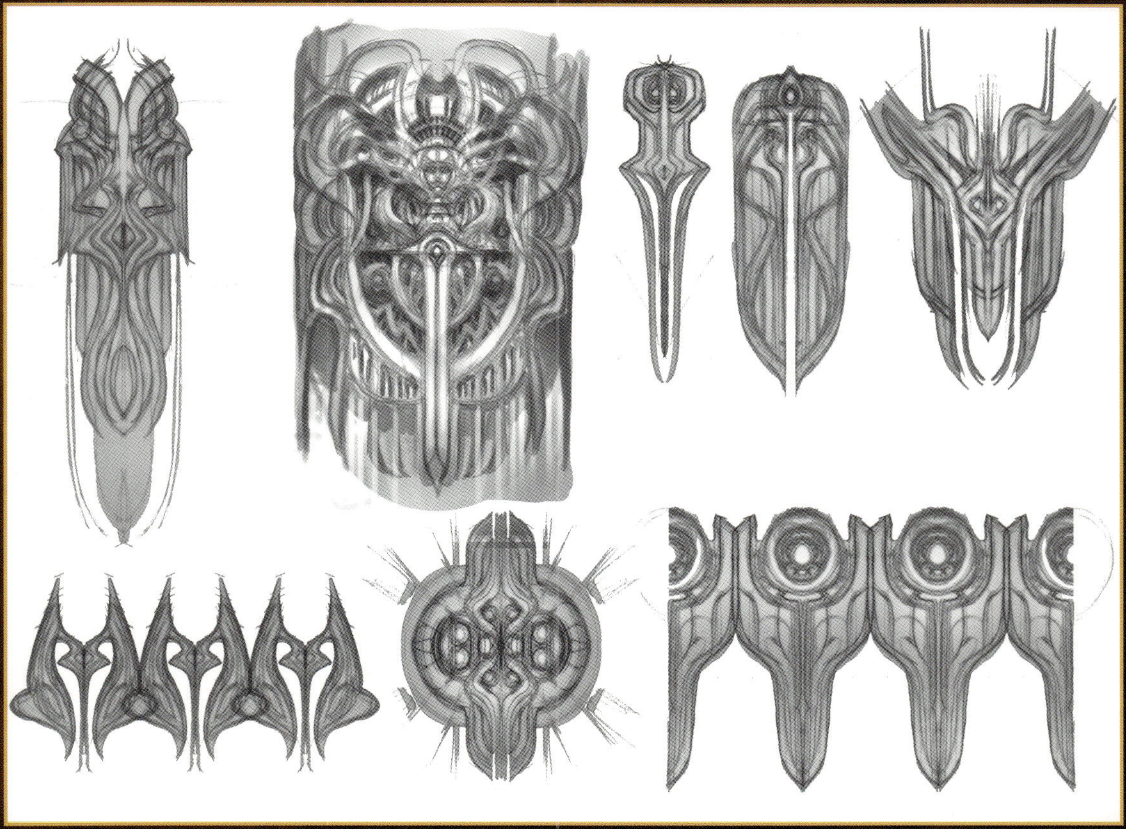

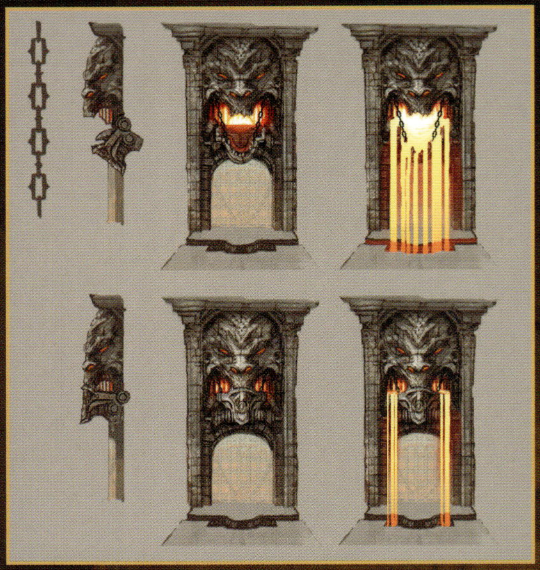

GATE DESIGNS

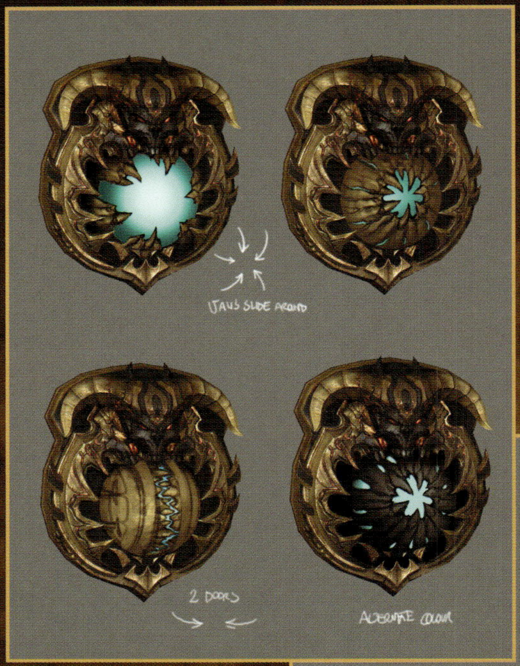

EMITTER DESIGNS

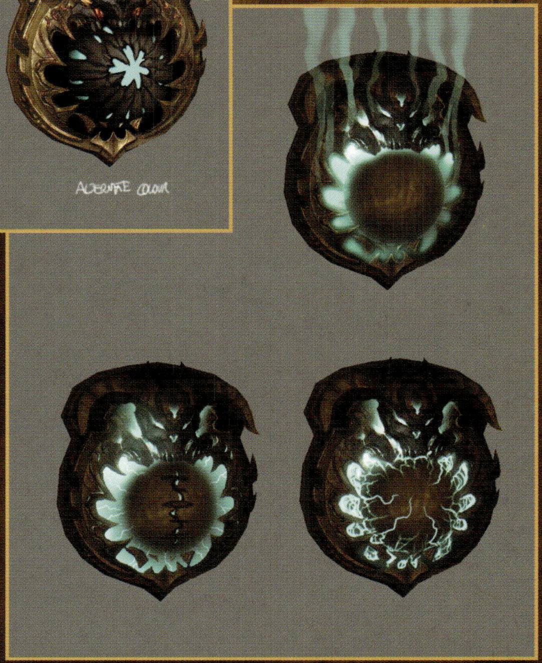

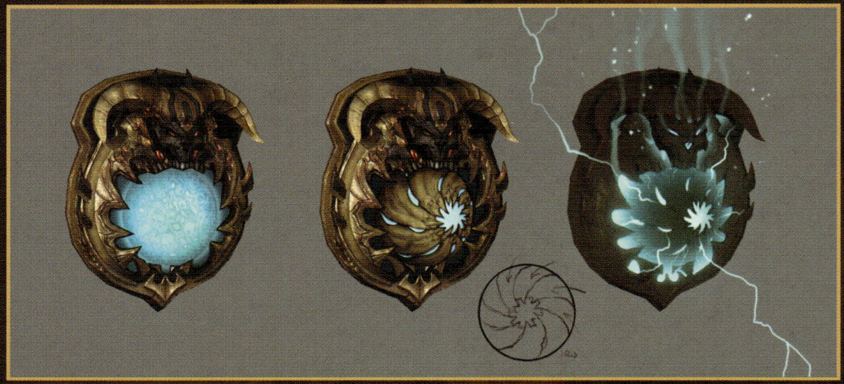

EMITTER DESIGNS

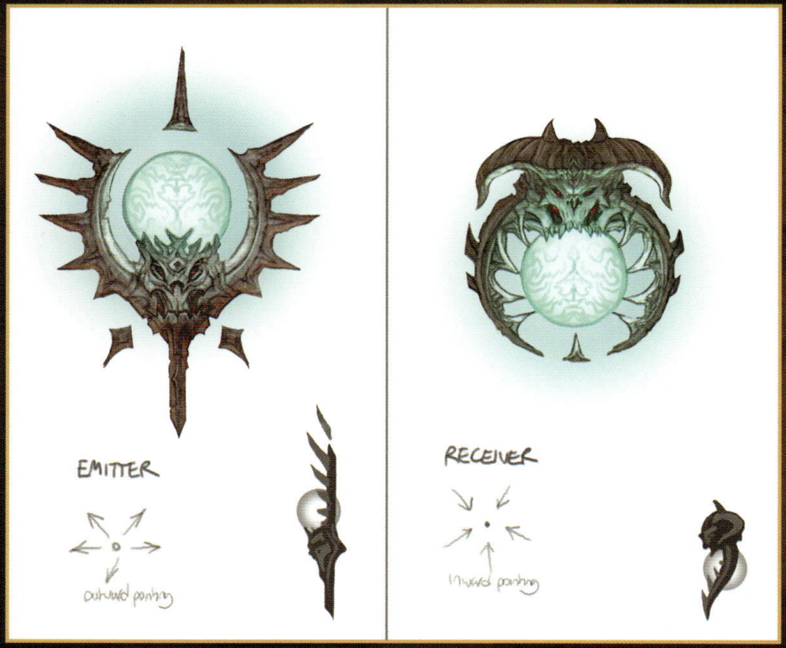

EMITTER & RECEIVER DESIGNS

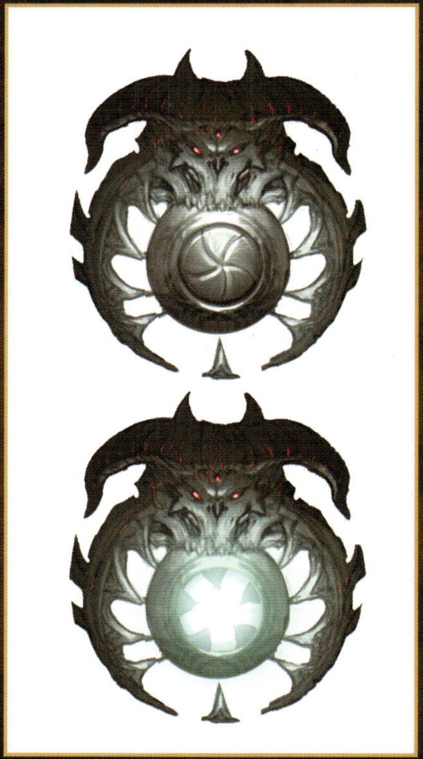

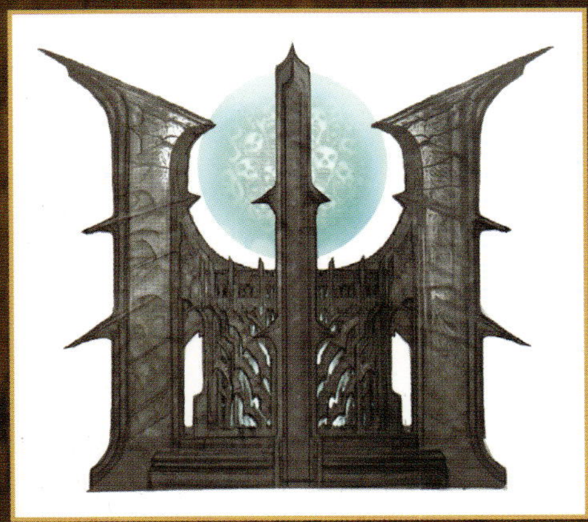

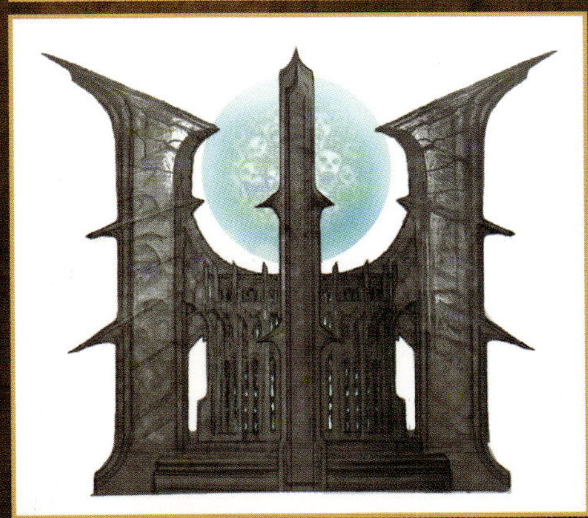

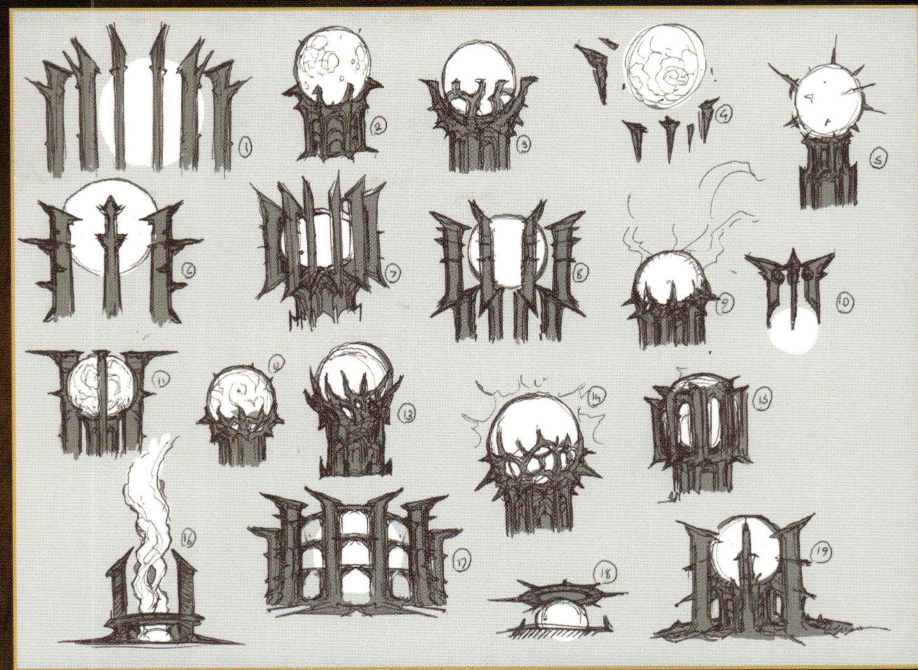

SOUL SOURCE DESIGNS

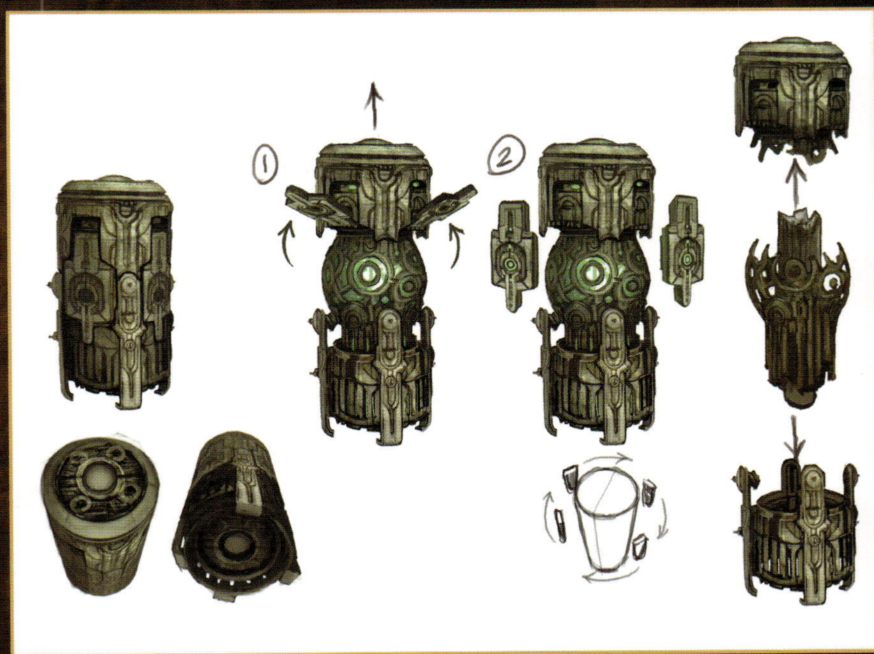

URN DESIGN

CHAIN LINK DESIGNS

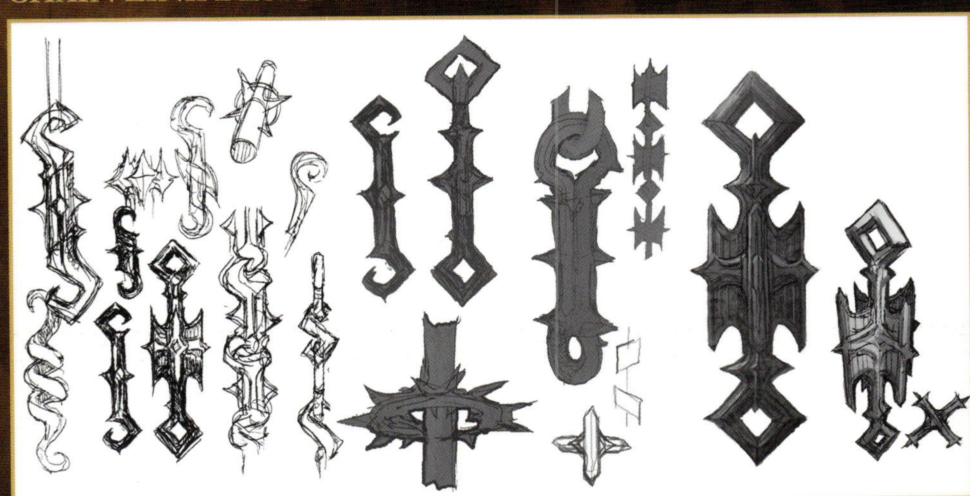

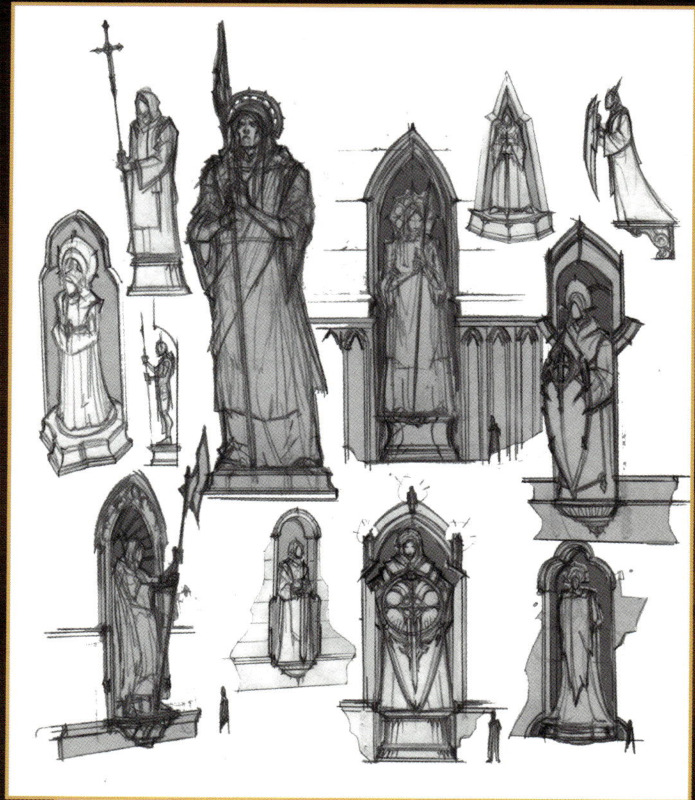

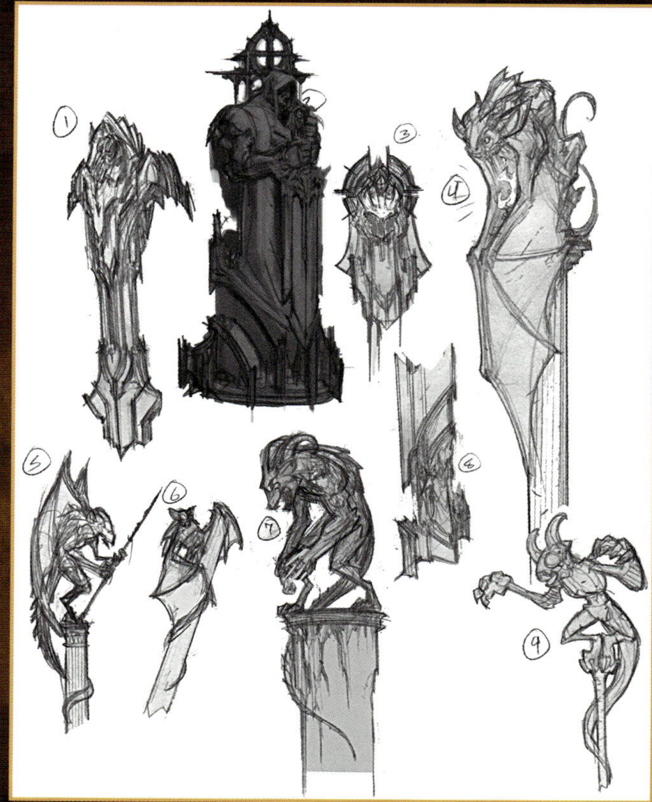

STATUE CONCEPTS

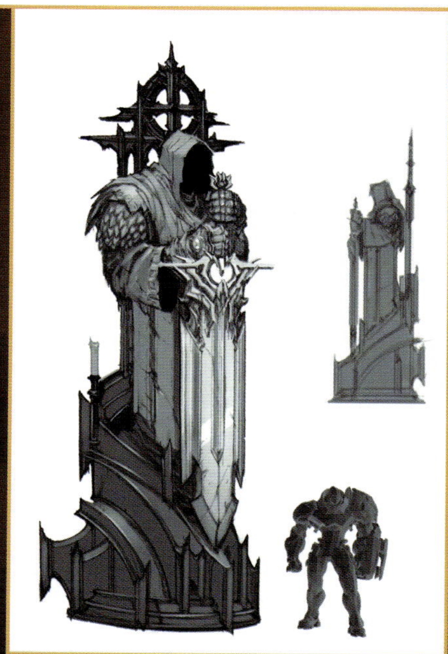

STATUE DESIGNS

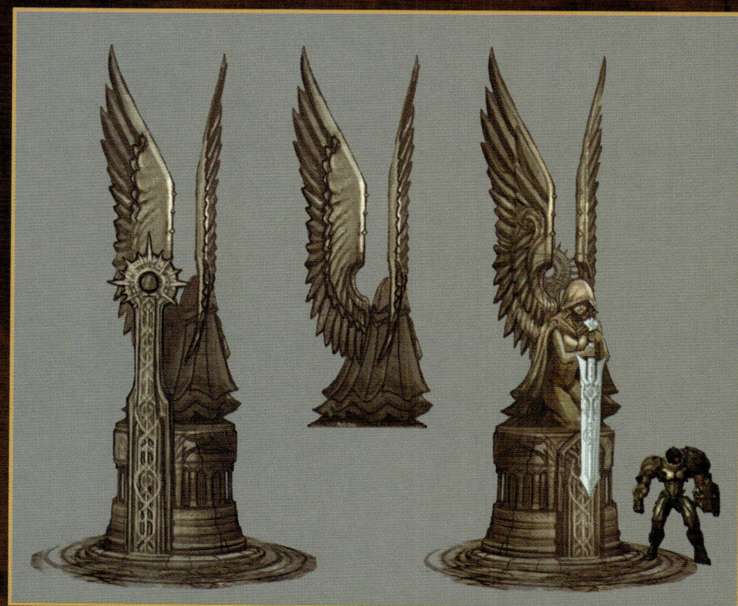

COLUMN DESIGNS

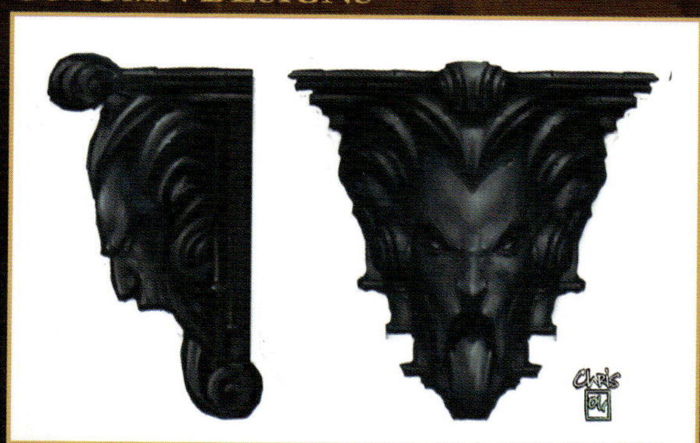

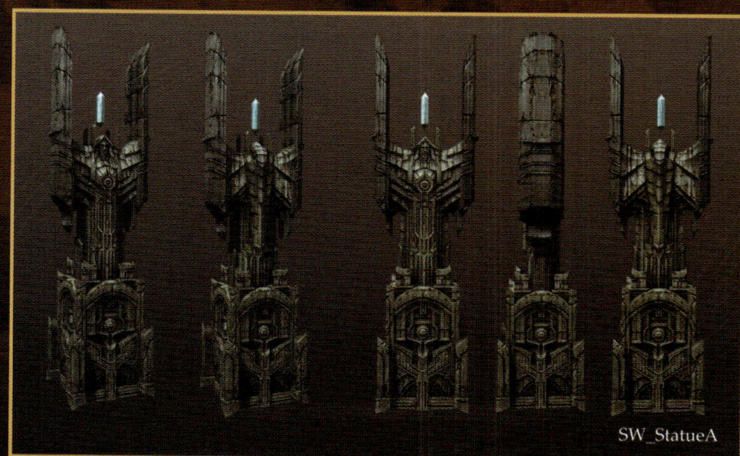

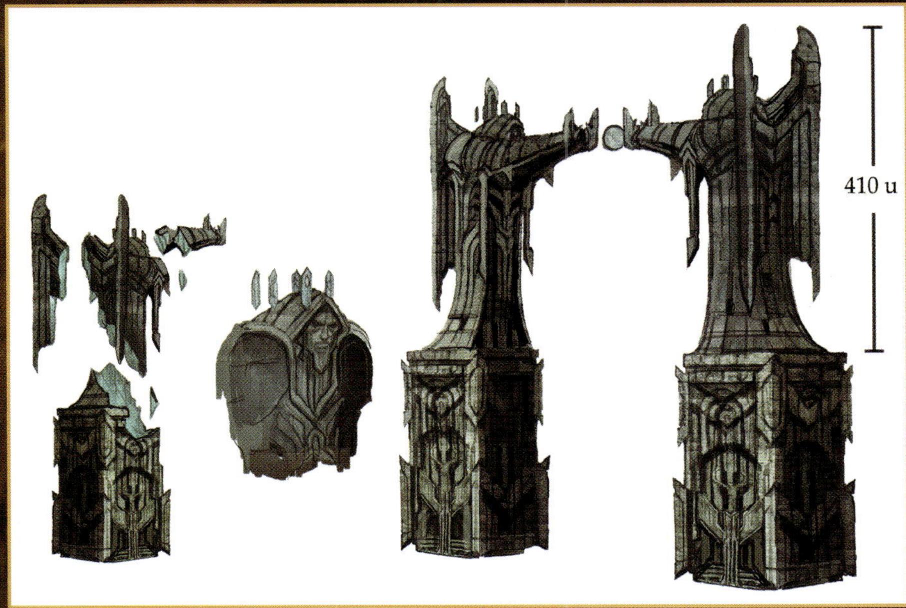

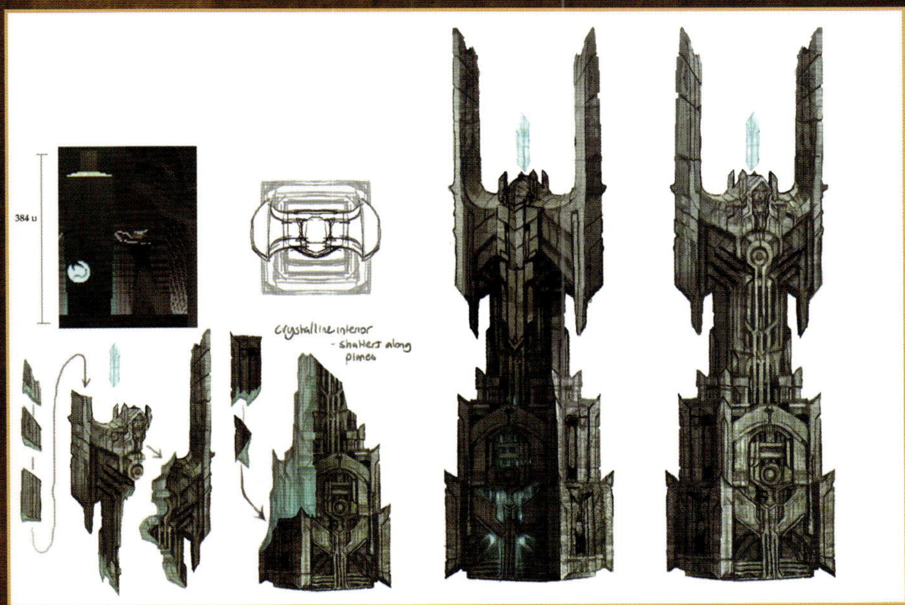

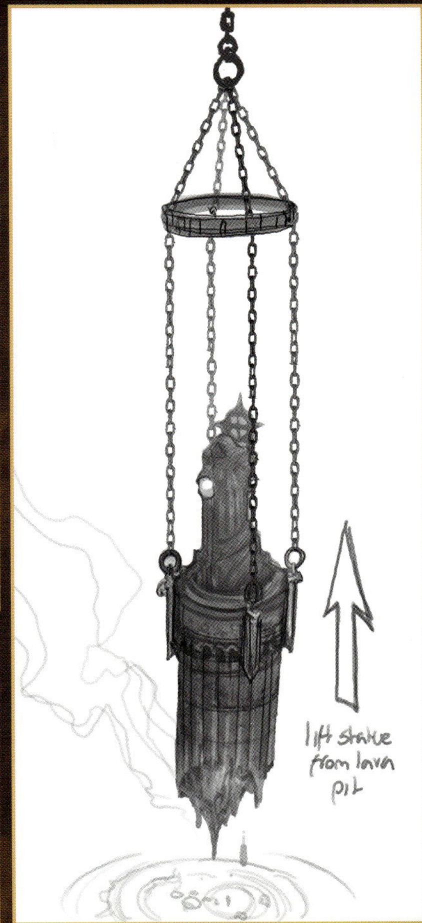

STATUE DESIGNS

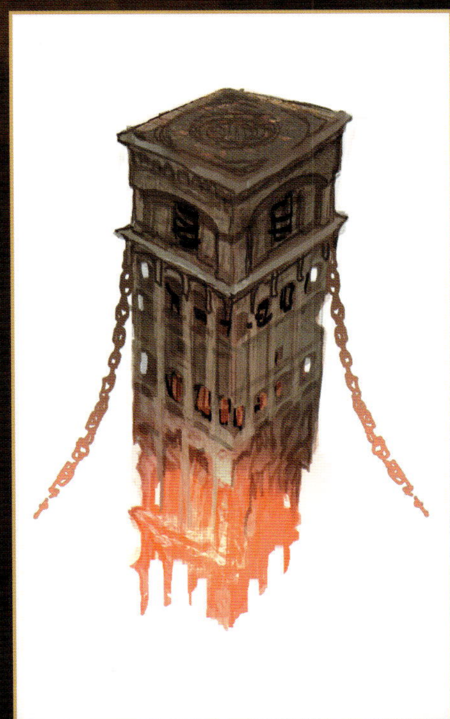

COLUMN DESIGN

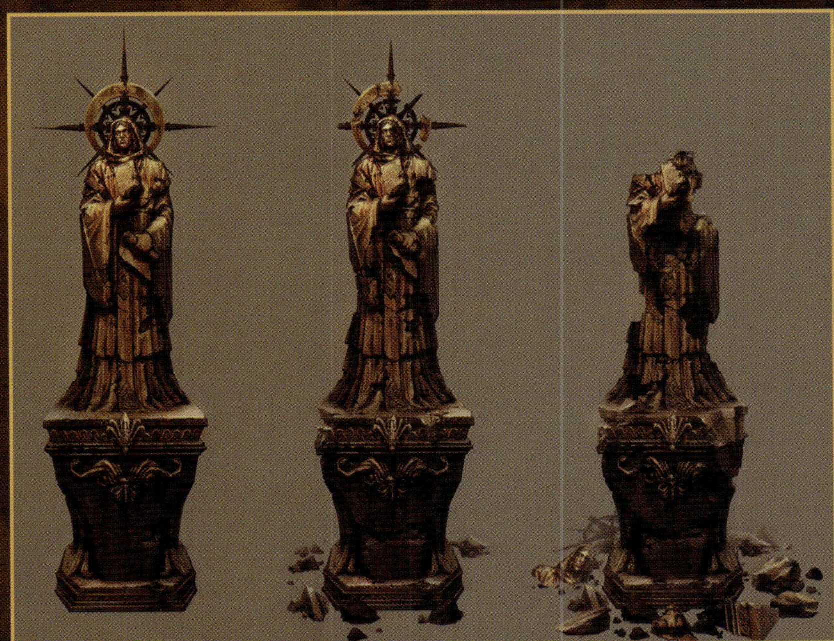

STATUE DESIGN

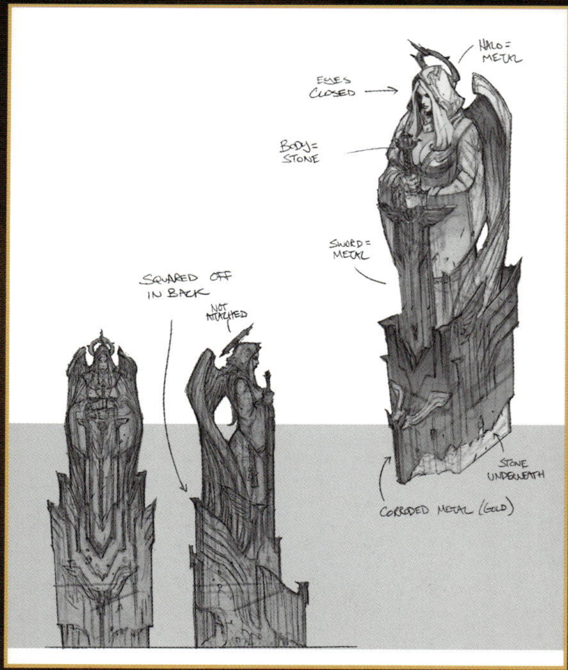

STATUE DESIGN

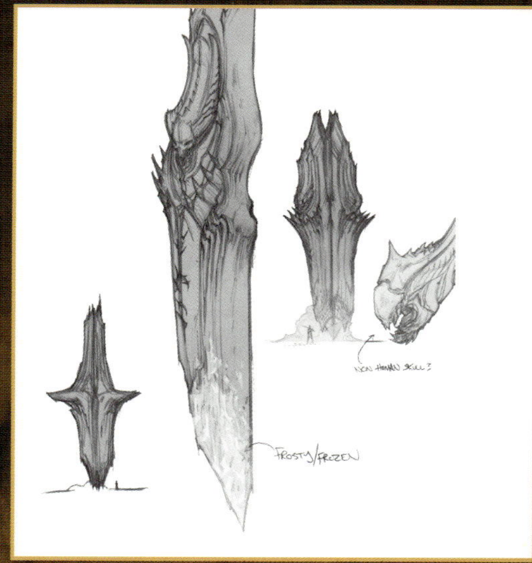

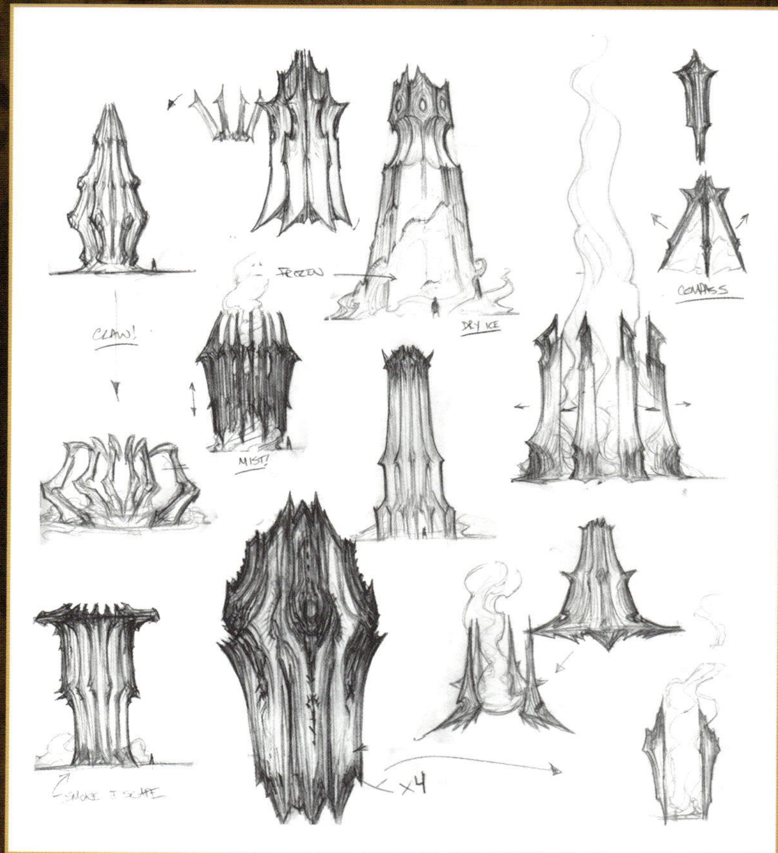

SHADOWGATE DESIGNS

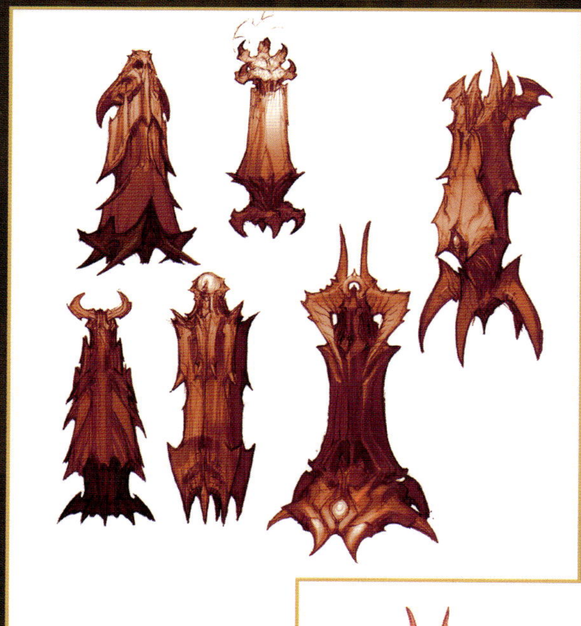

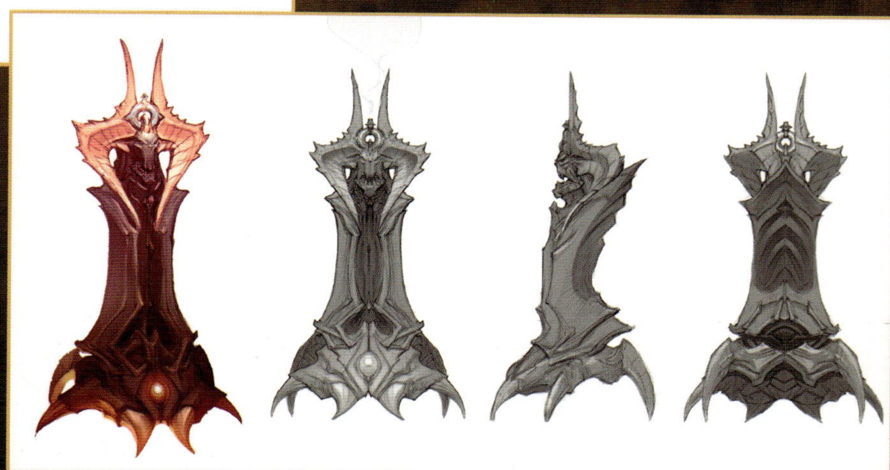

DEMON SHRINE DESIGNS

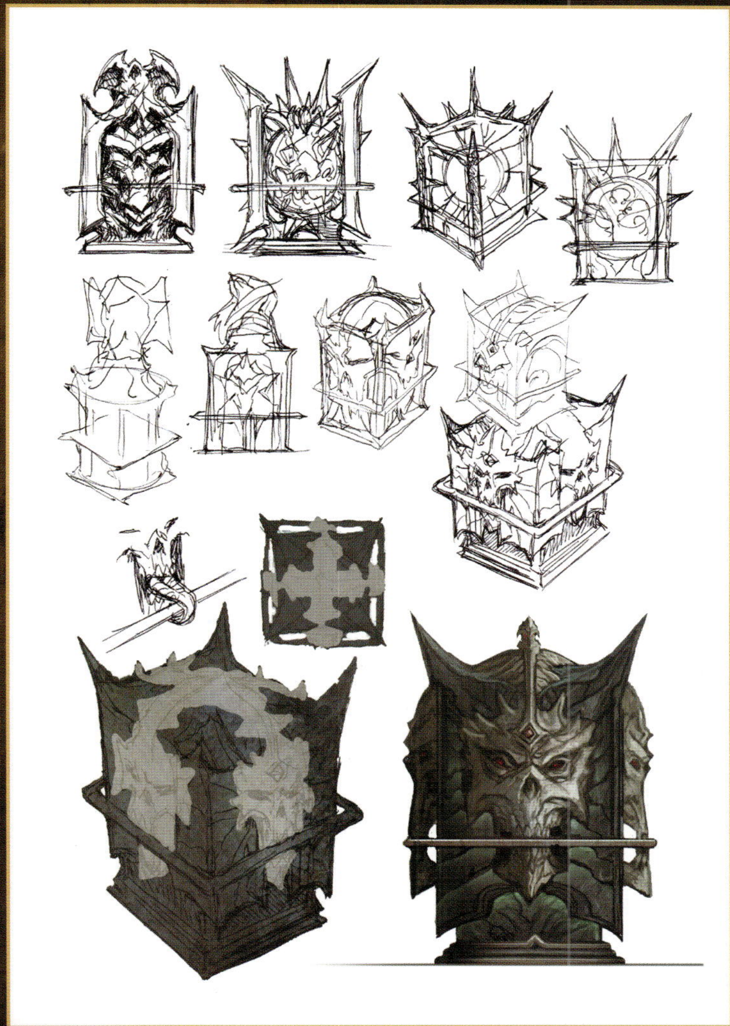

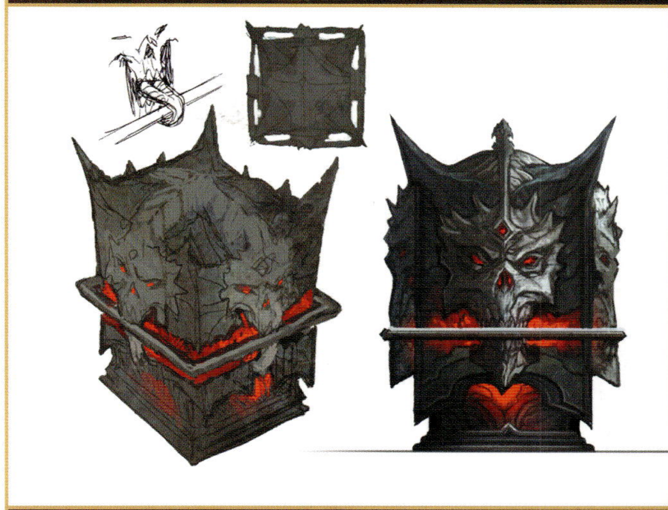

PUSHBLOCK CONCEPTS

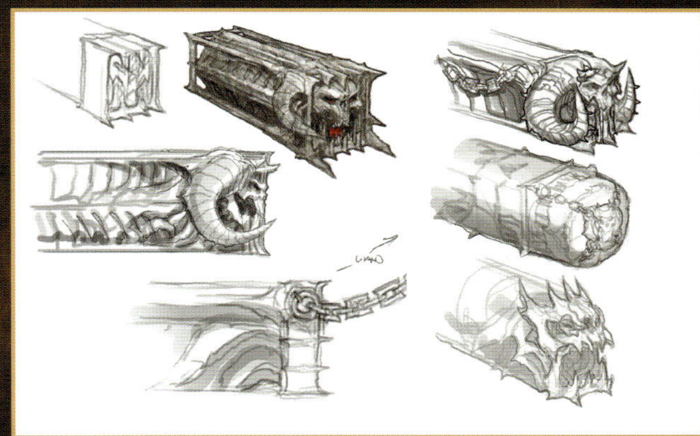

HAMMER COLUMN CONCEPTS

BREAKABLE OBJECT DESIGNS

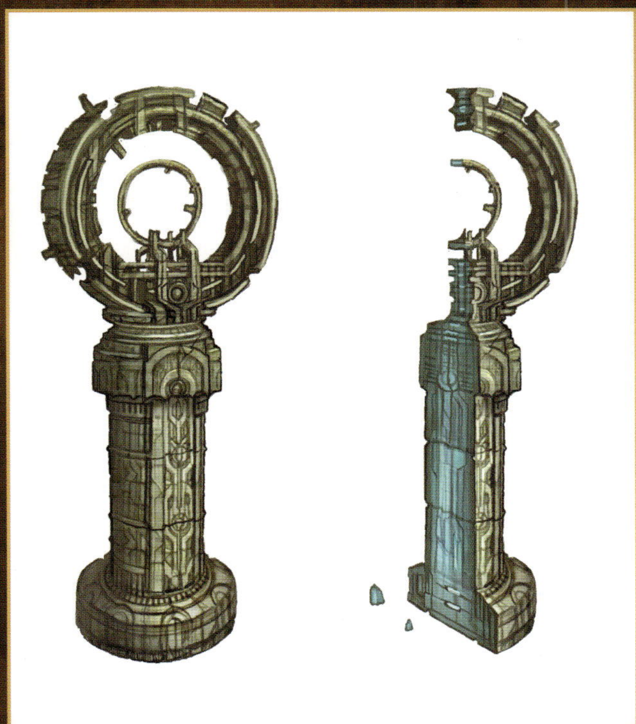

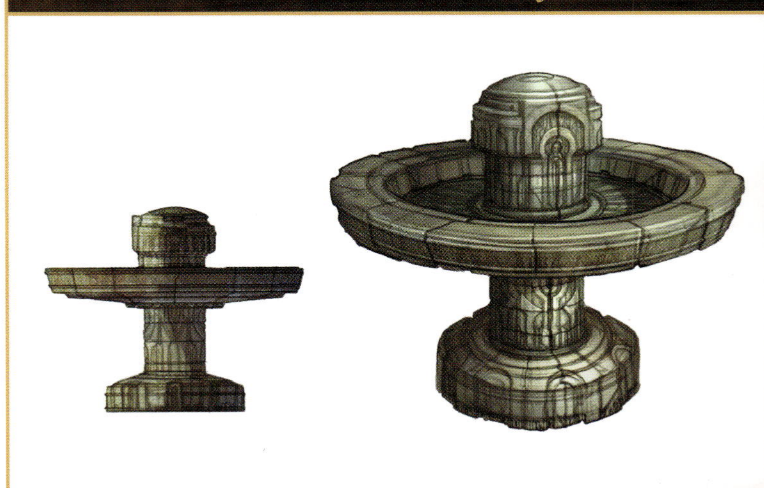

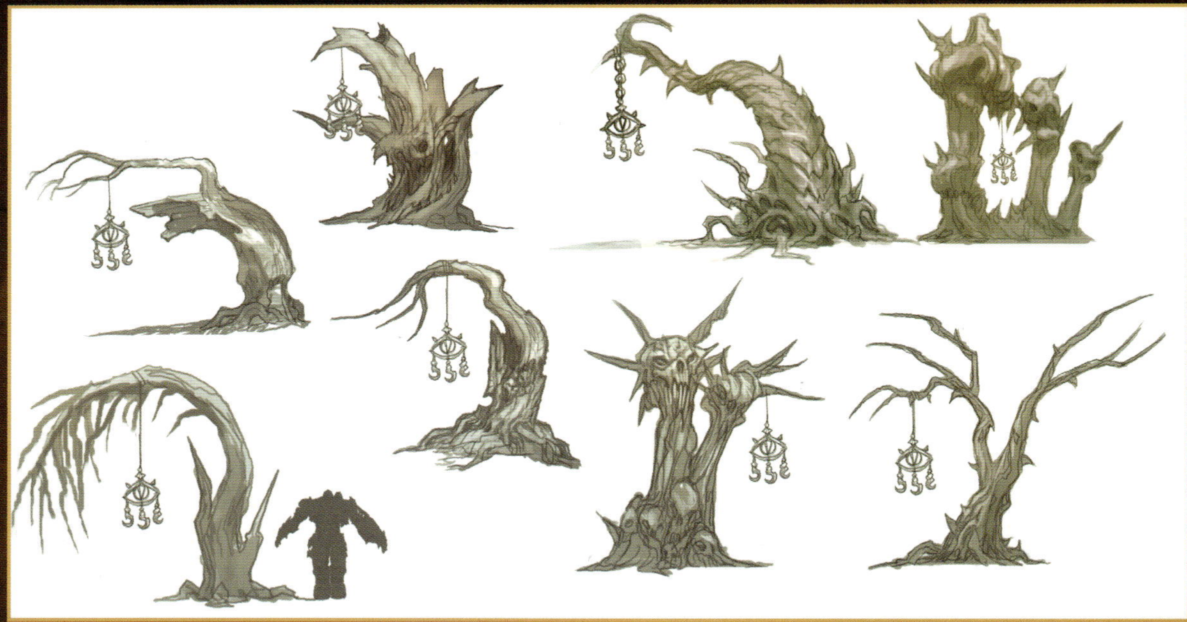

VULGRIM SUMMONIG RUNE CONCEPTS

VULGRIM LOCATION CONCEPTS

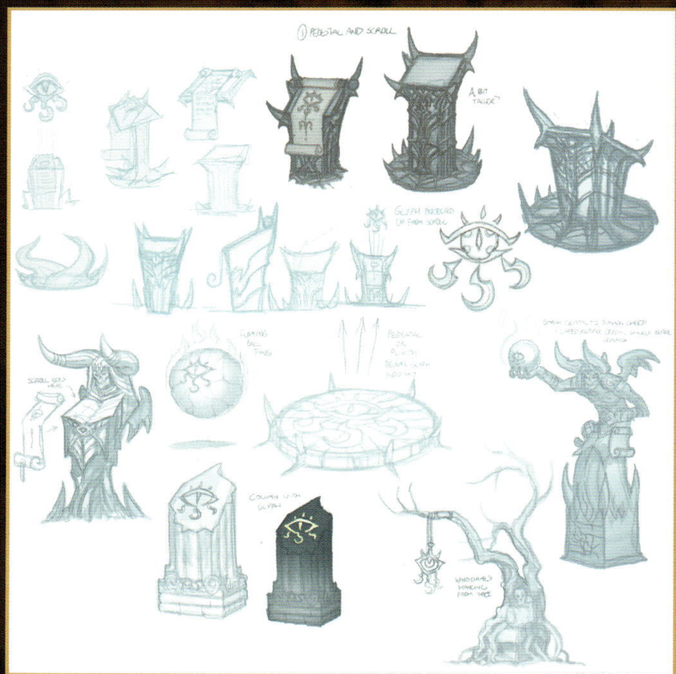

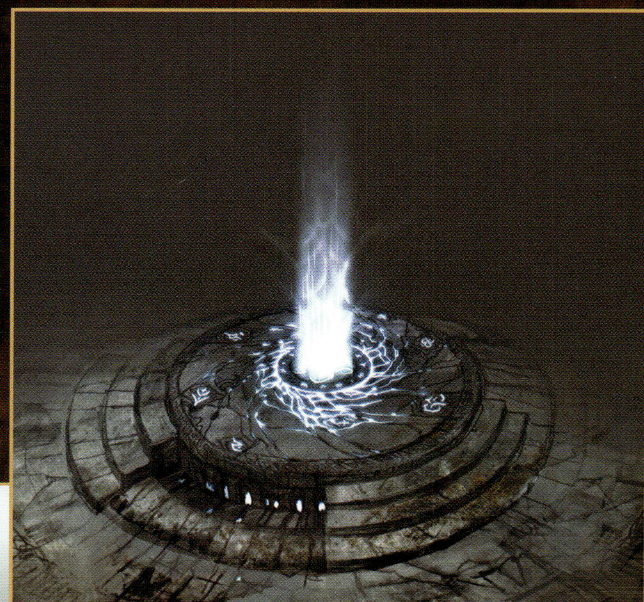

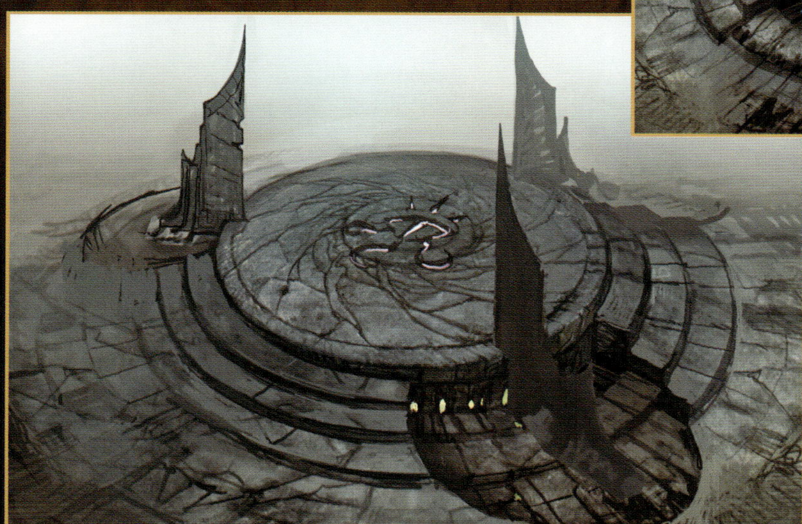

VULGRIM LOCATION DESIGNS

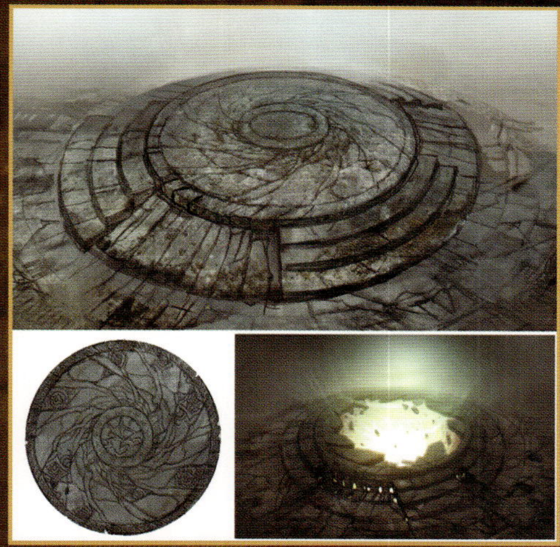

VULGRIM LOCATION DESIGNS

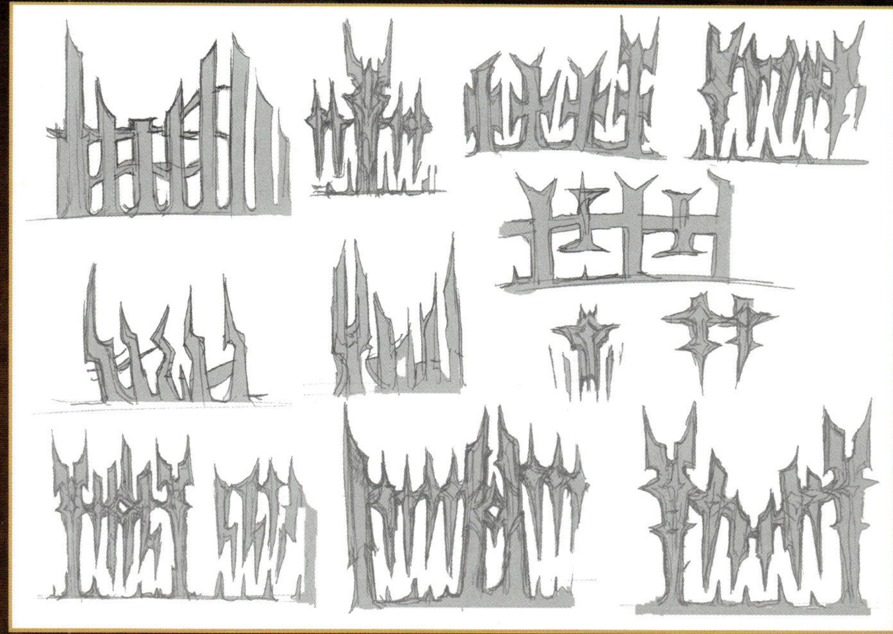

FENCE CONCEPTS

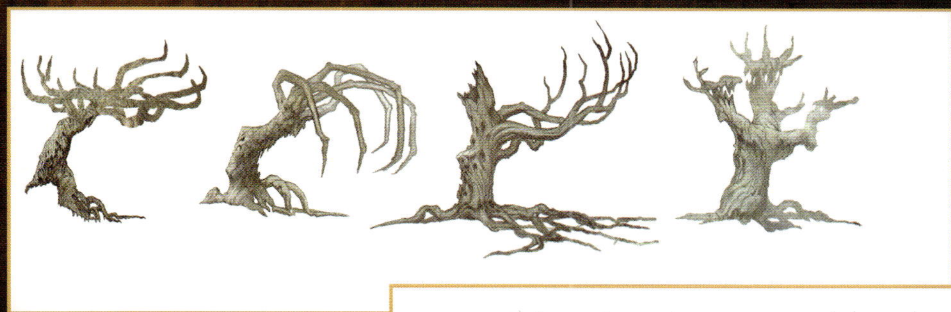

TREE CONCEPTS

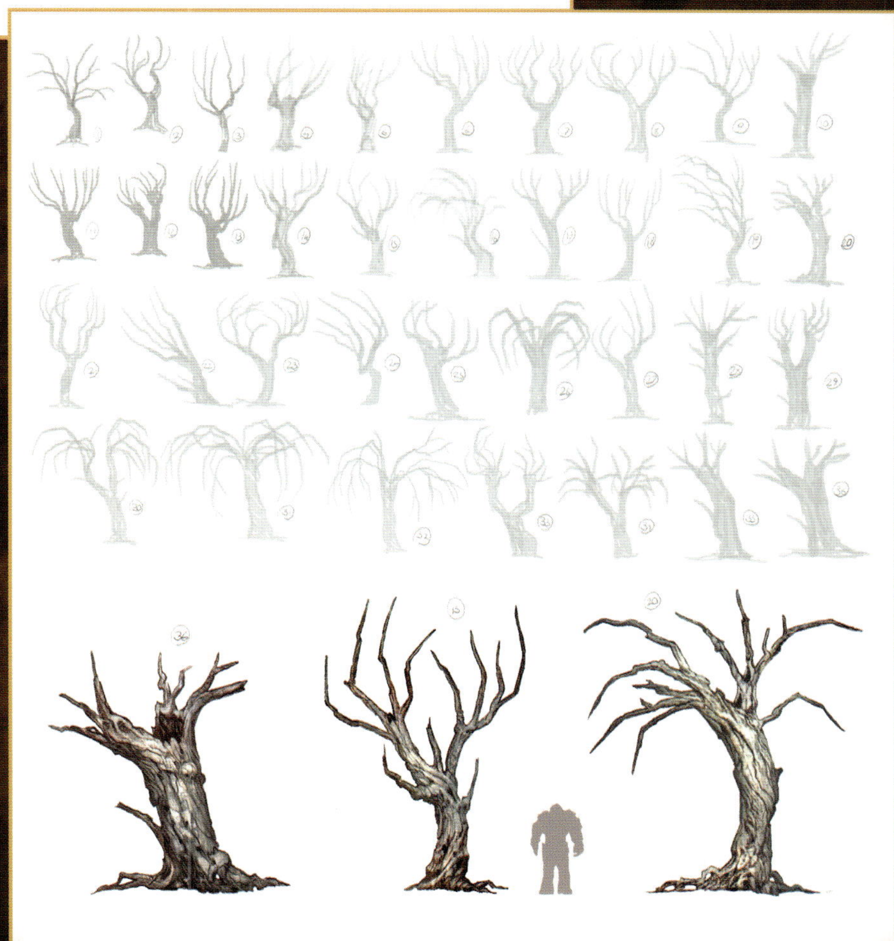

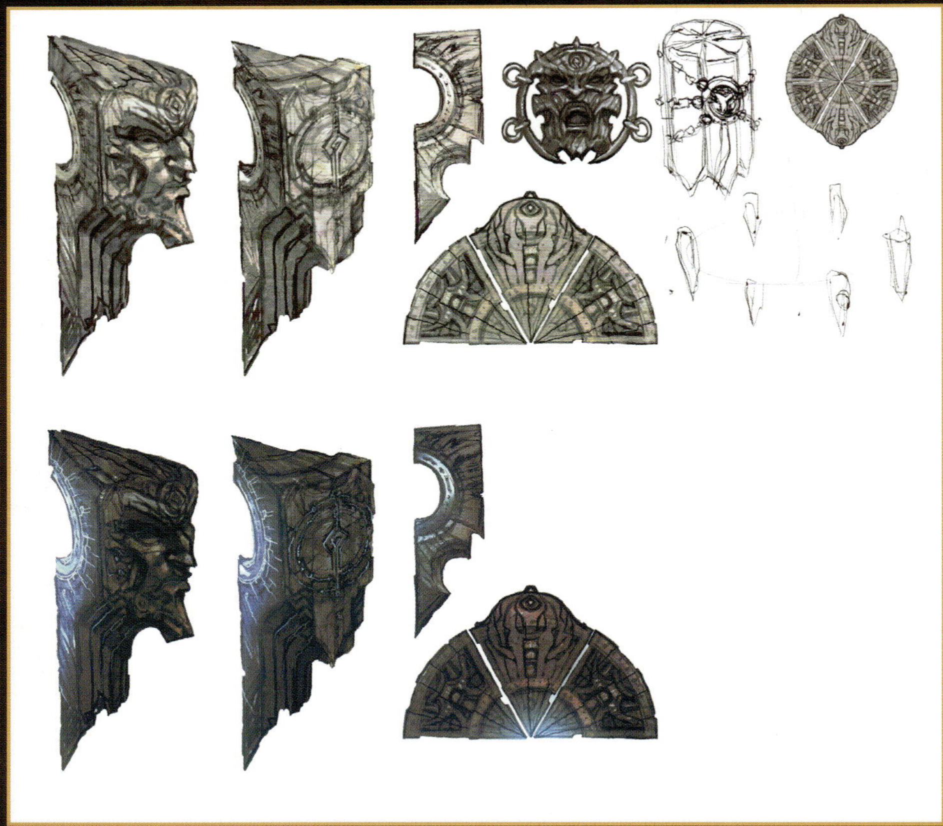

ALTAR DESIGNS

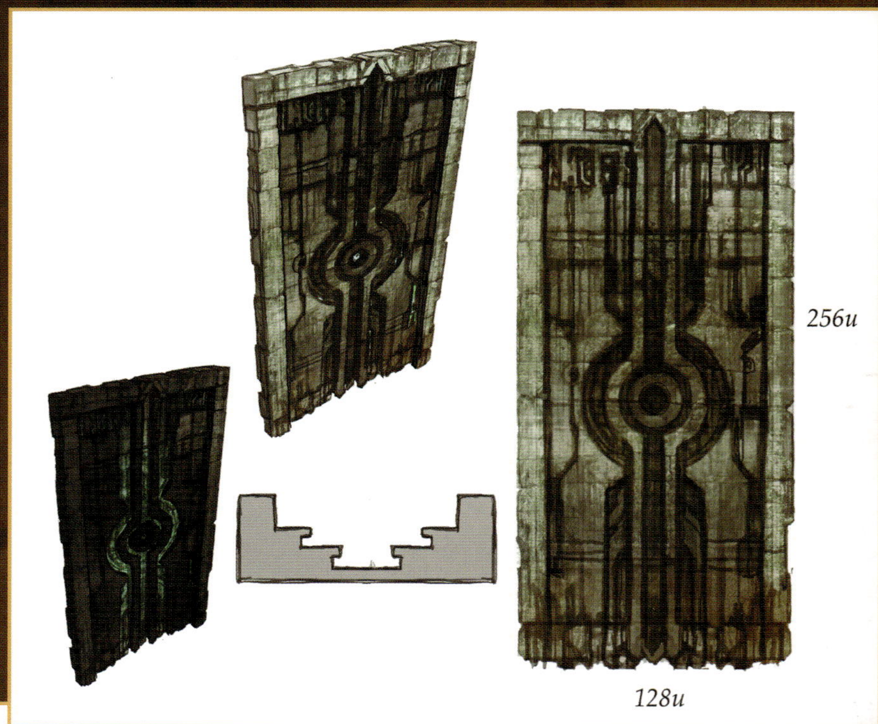

DOOR DESIGNS

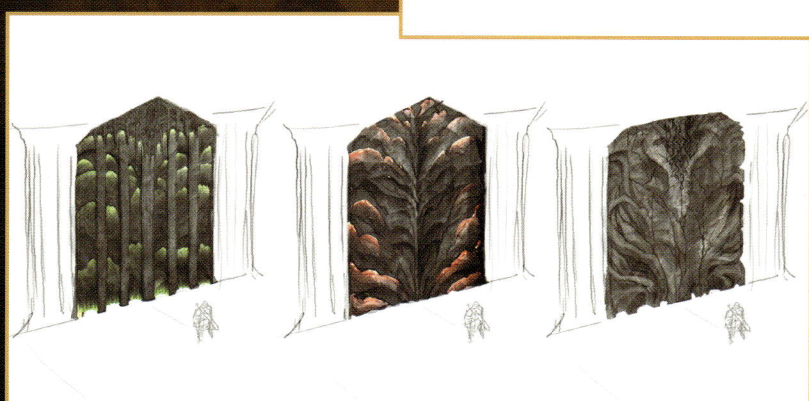

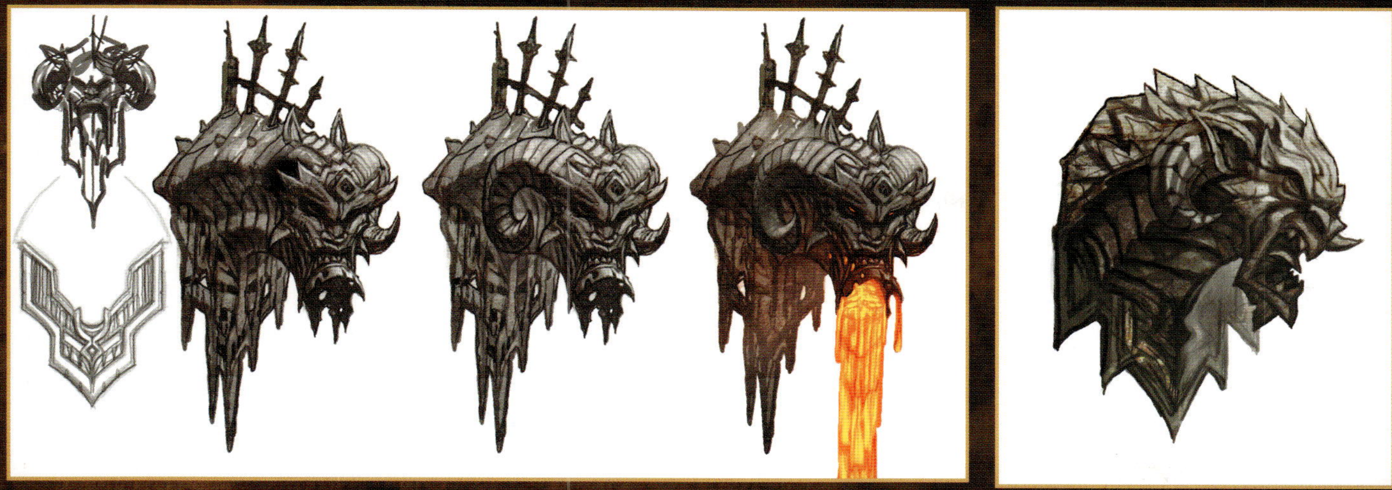

PILLAR HEAD DESIGNS

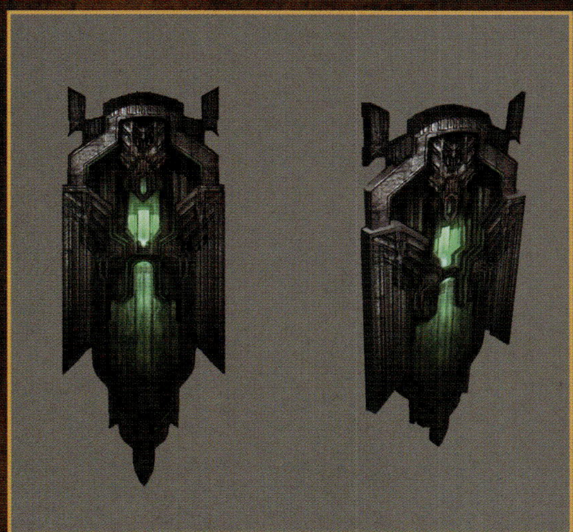

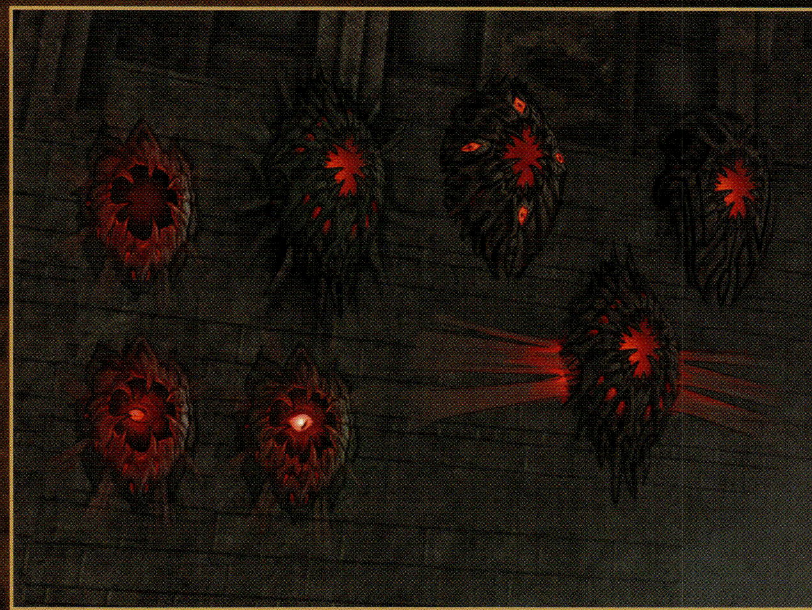

ATTACH POINT CONCEPTS

CROSSBLADE SWITCH DESIGNS

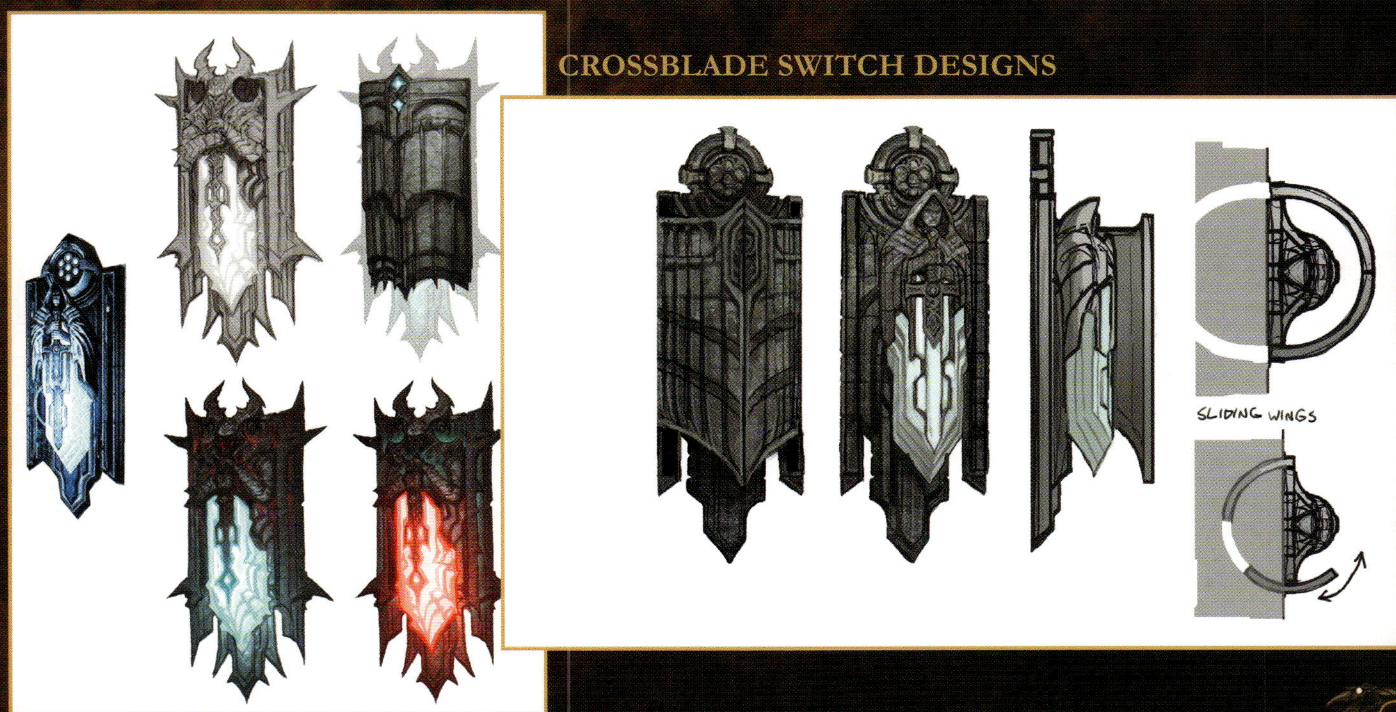

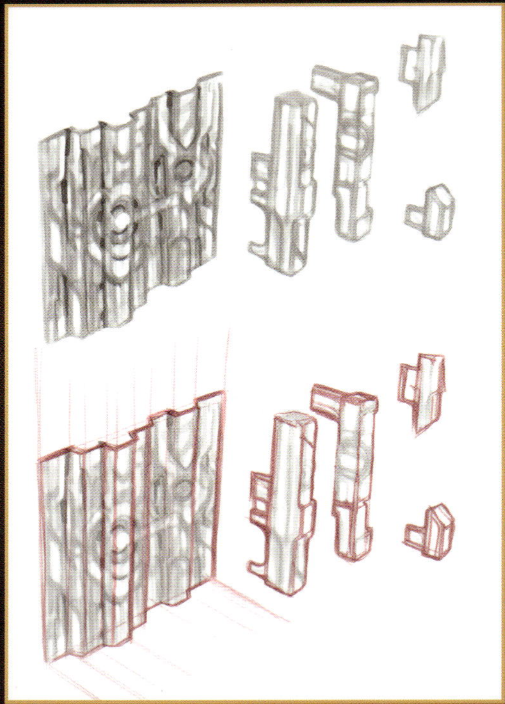

WALL DESIGNS

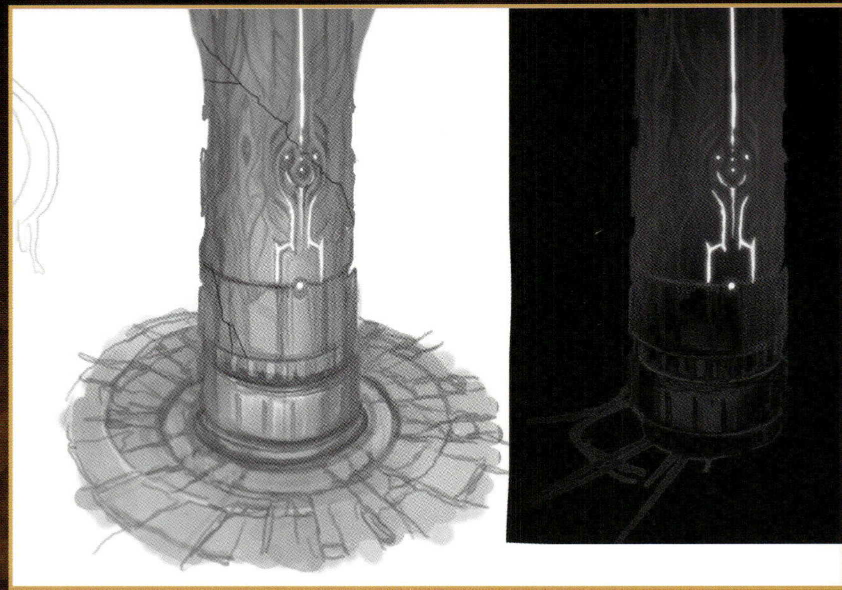

COLUMN DESIGNS

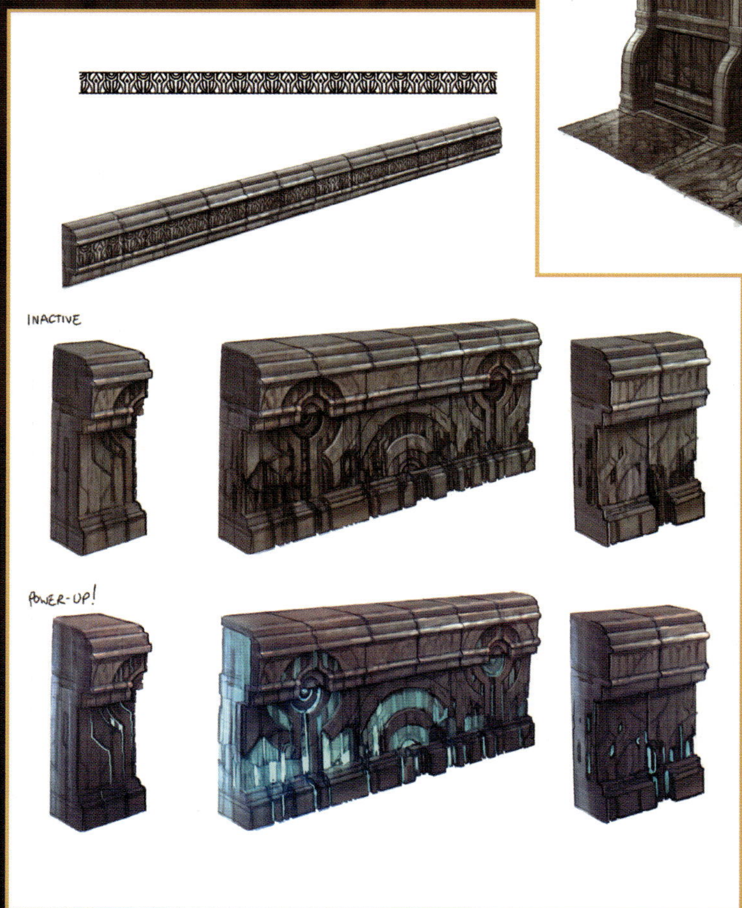

WALL DESIGNS

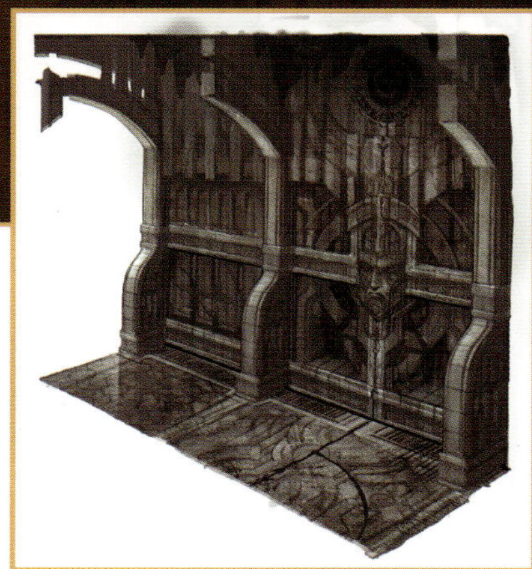

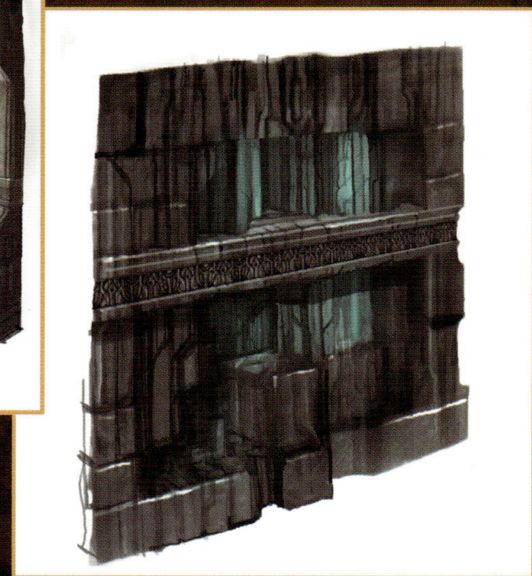

COLUMN DESIGN

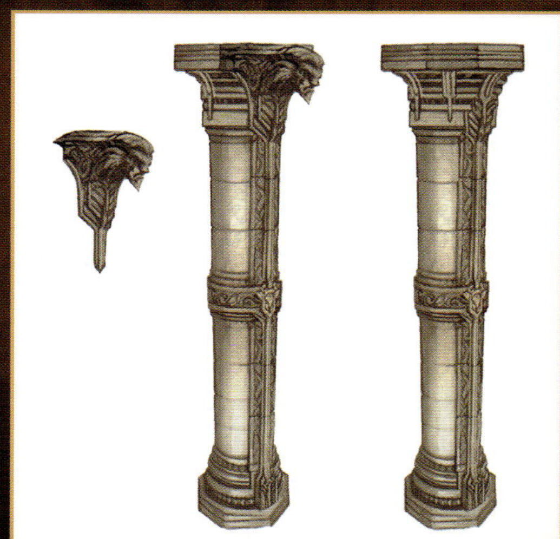

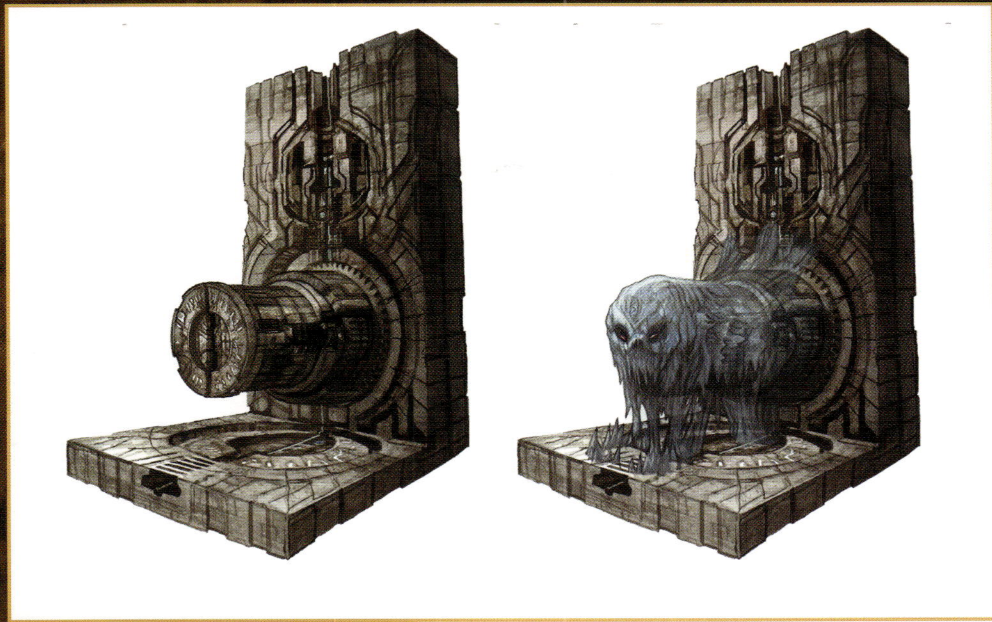

POWER CONDUIT DESIGNS

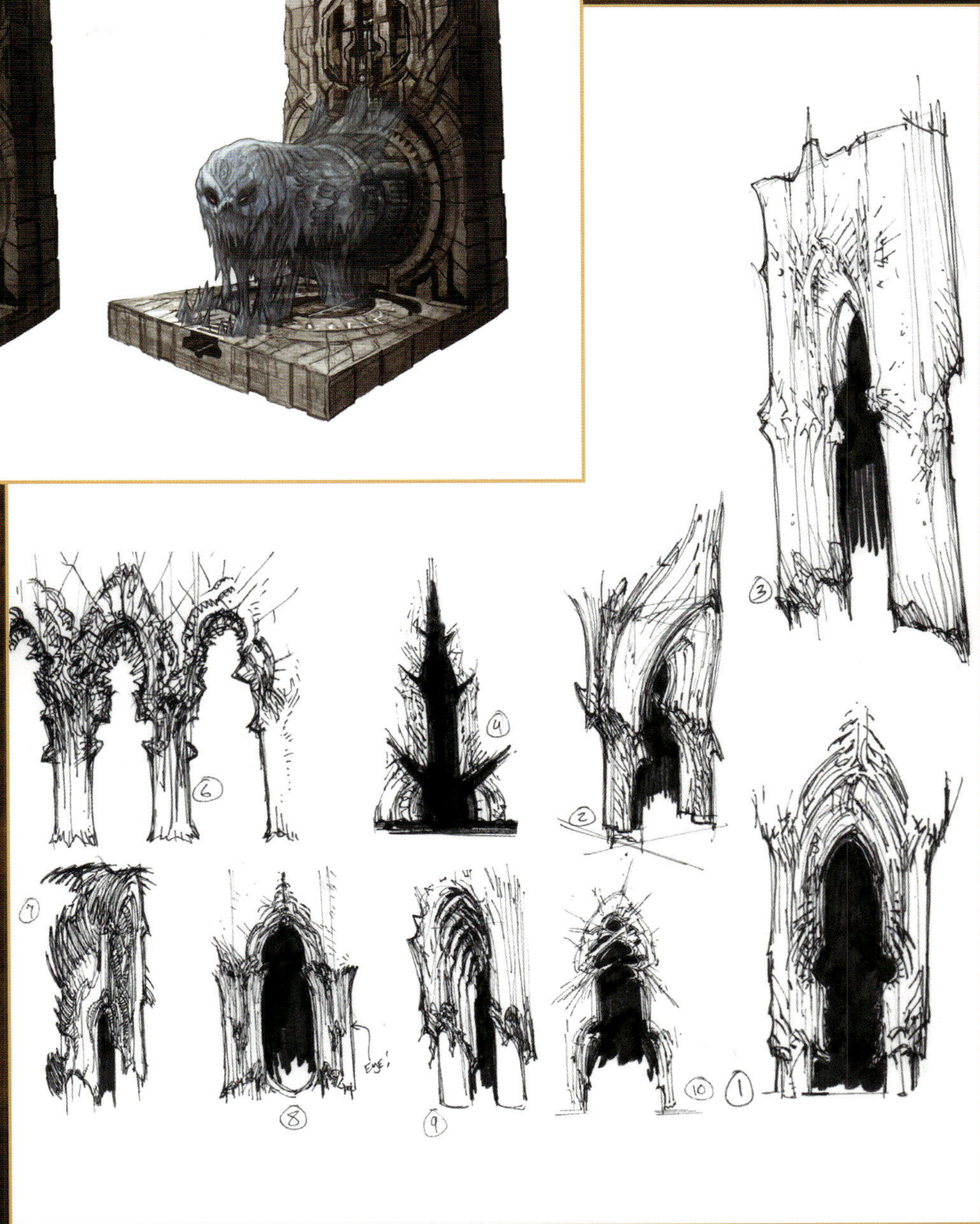

ARCH CONCEPTS

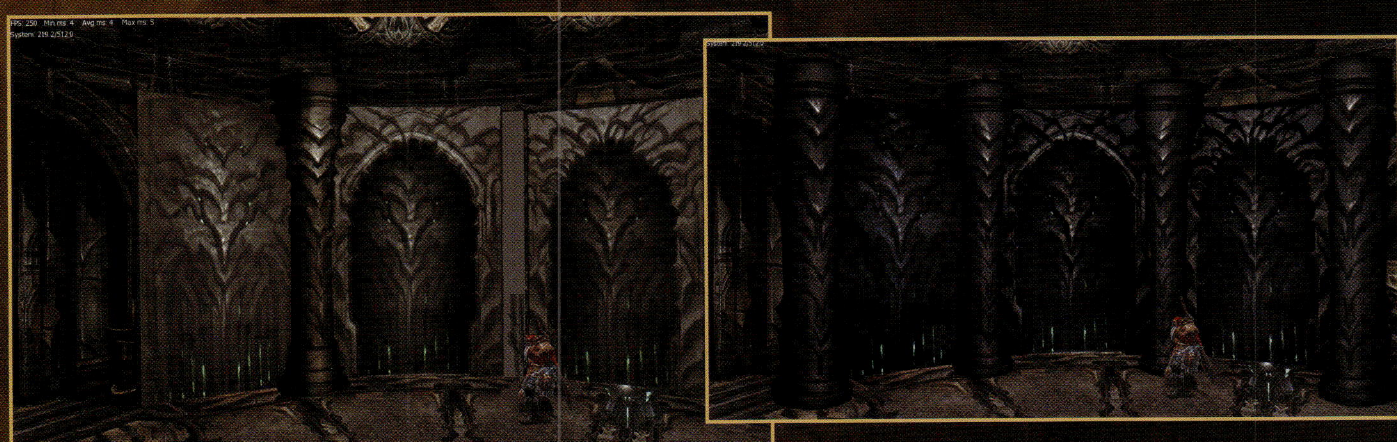

WALL DESIGNS

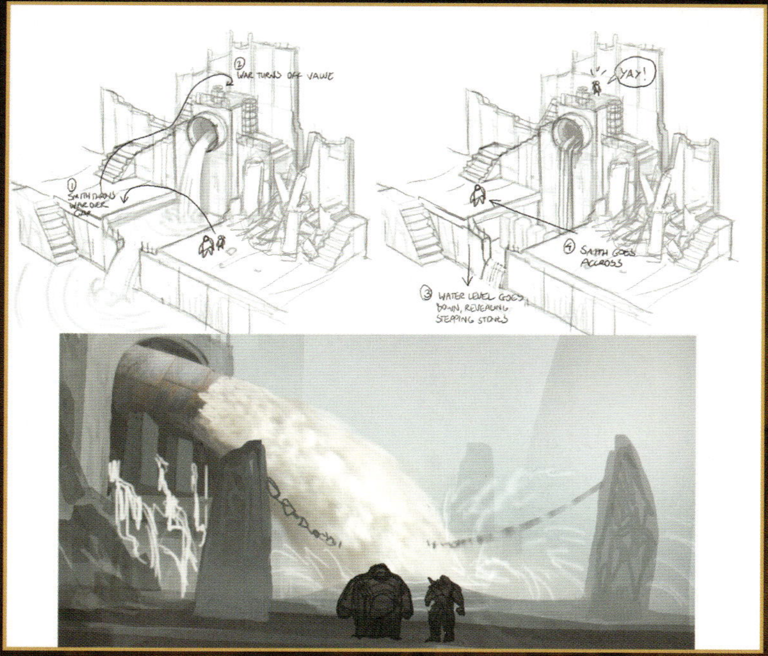

STEPPING STONES CONCEPT

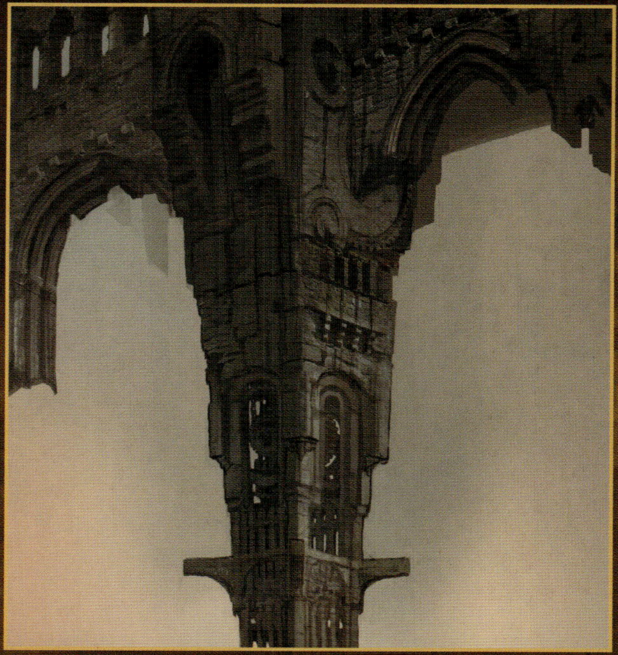

COLUMN DESIGN

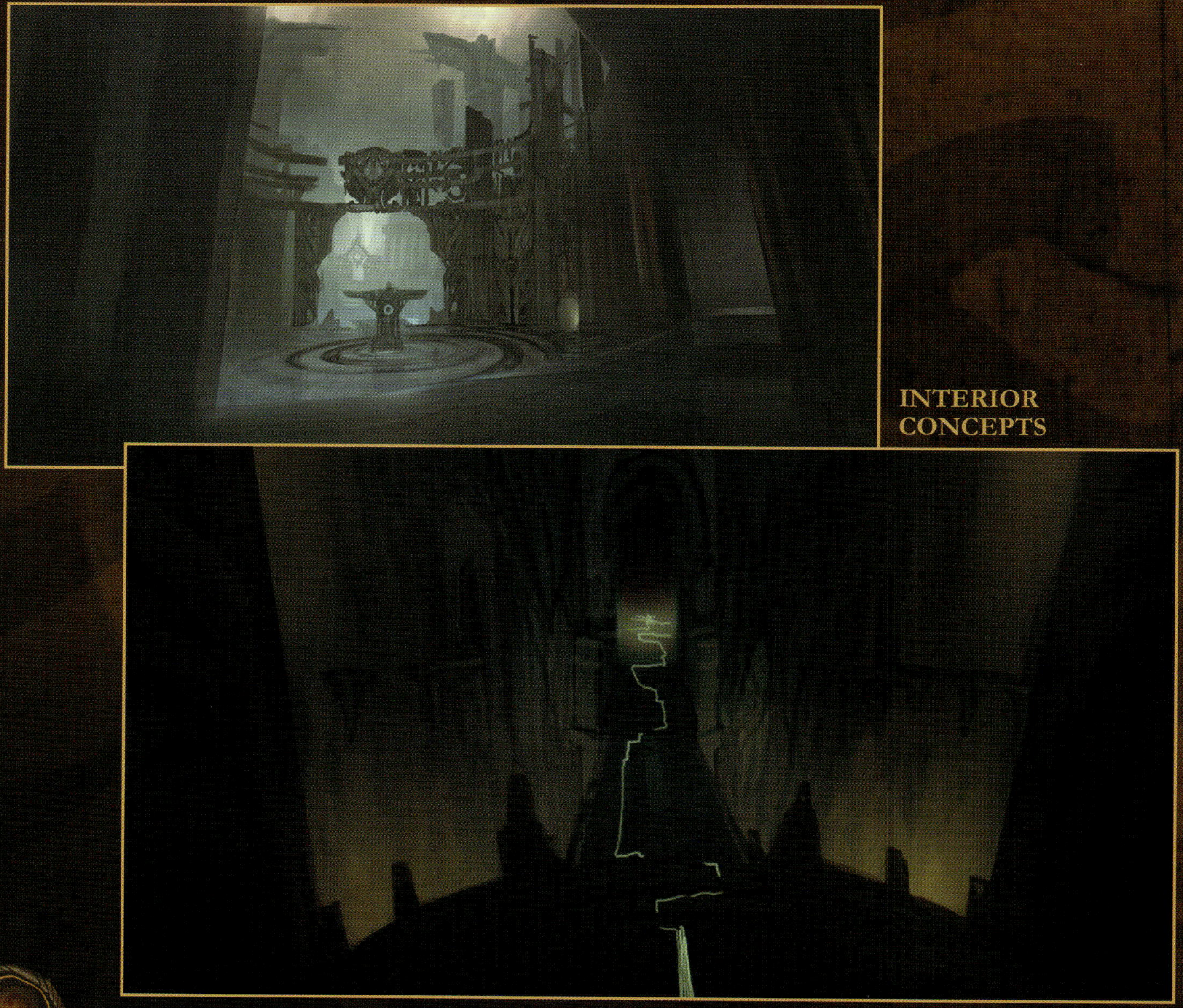

INTERIOR CONCEPTS

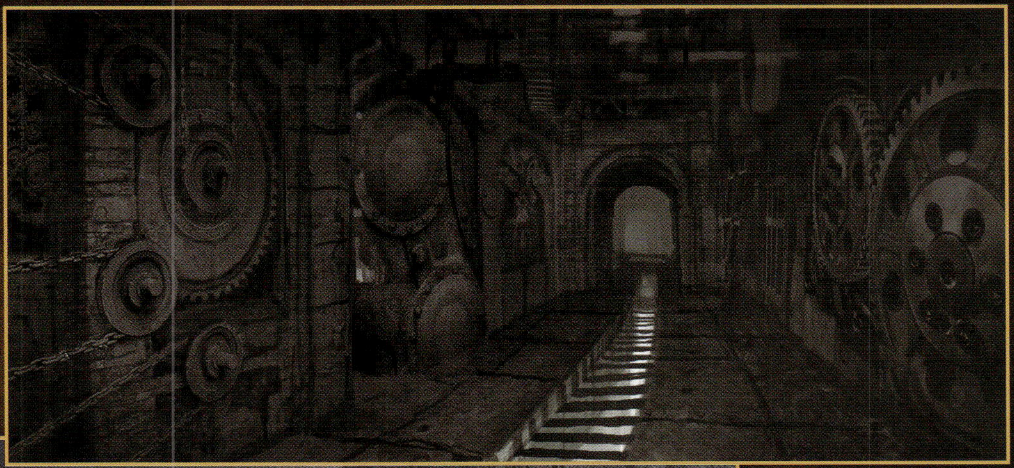

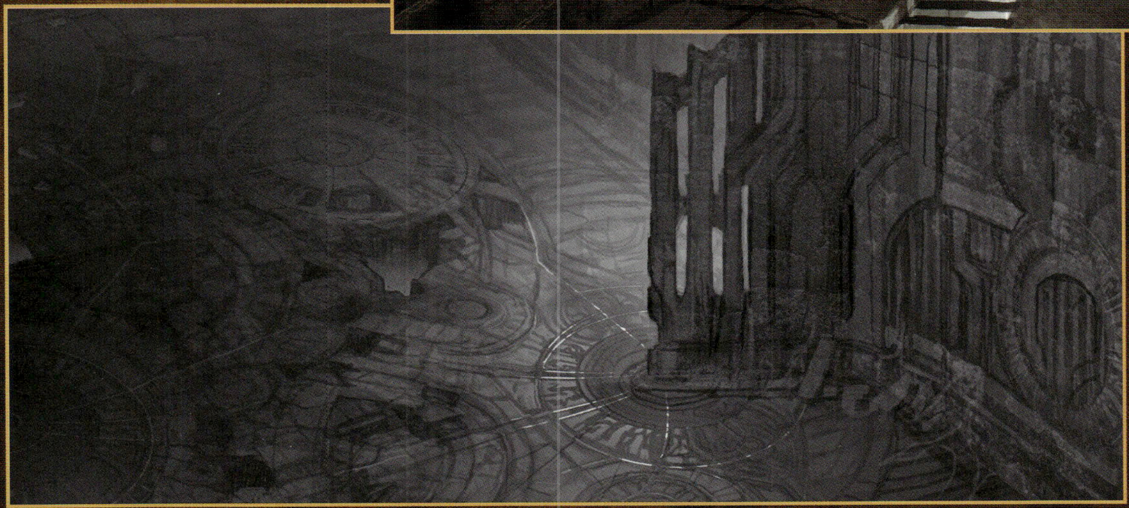

INTERIOR CONCEPTS

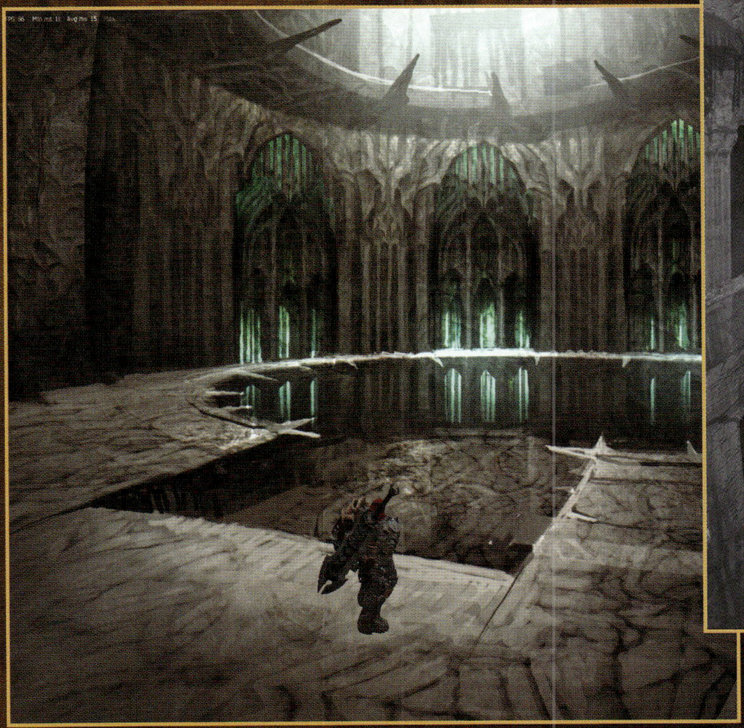

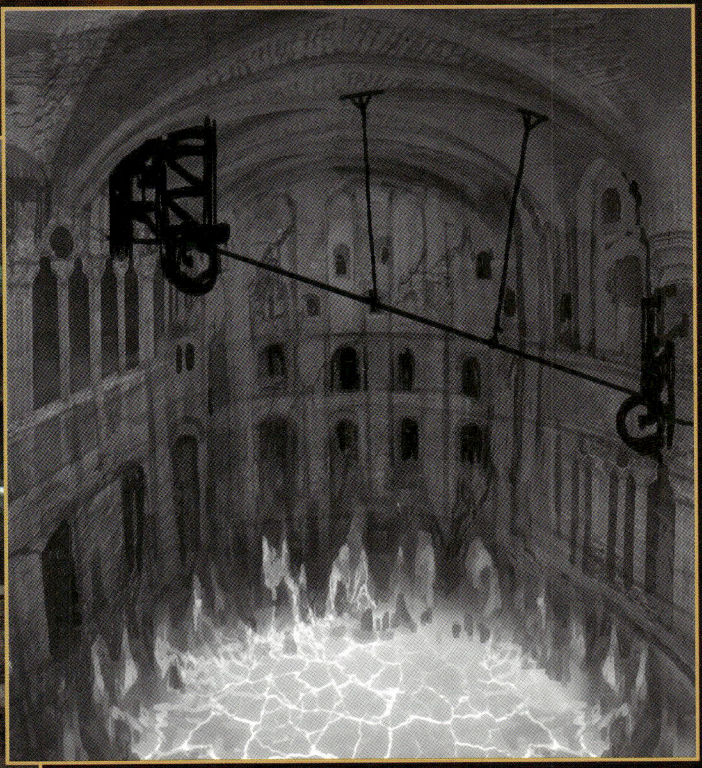

INTERIOR CONCEPTS

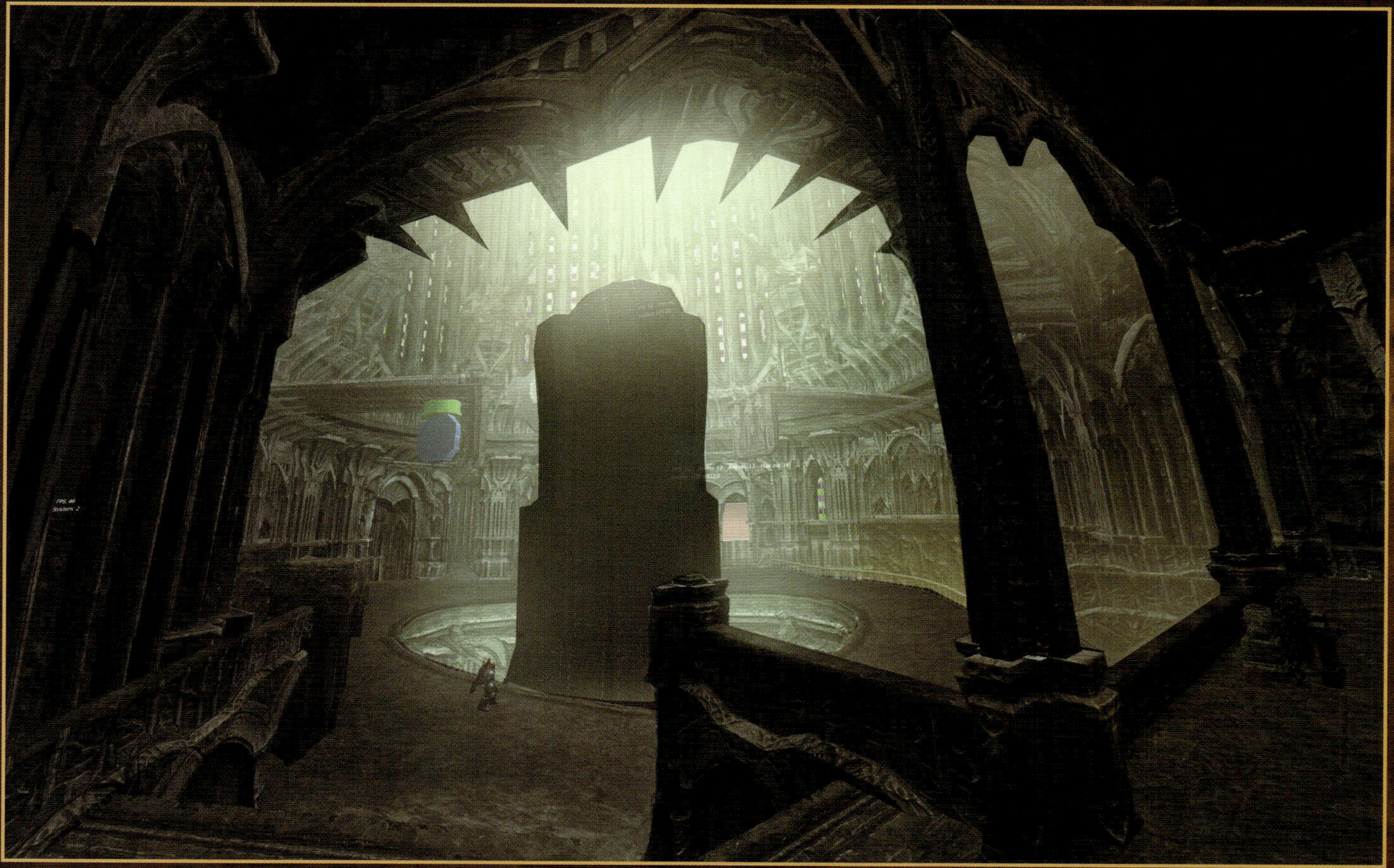

INTERIOR CONCEPT

TEMPEST CLOAK CONCEPTS

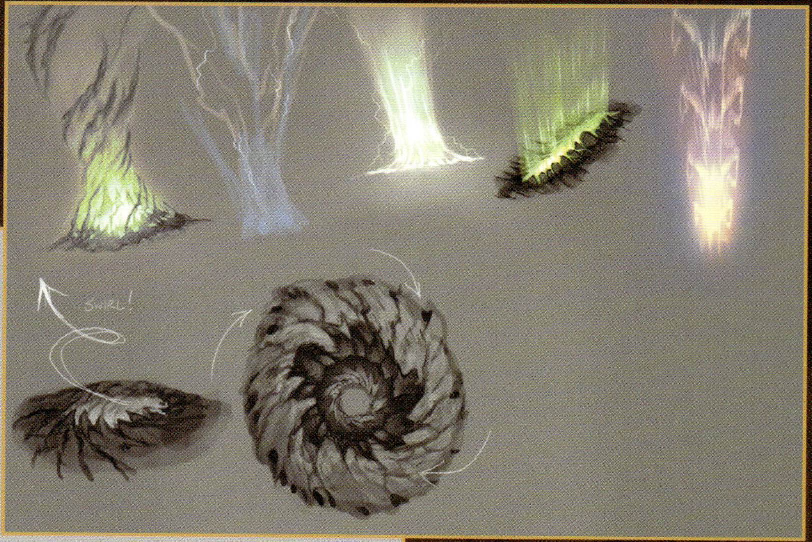

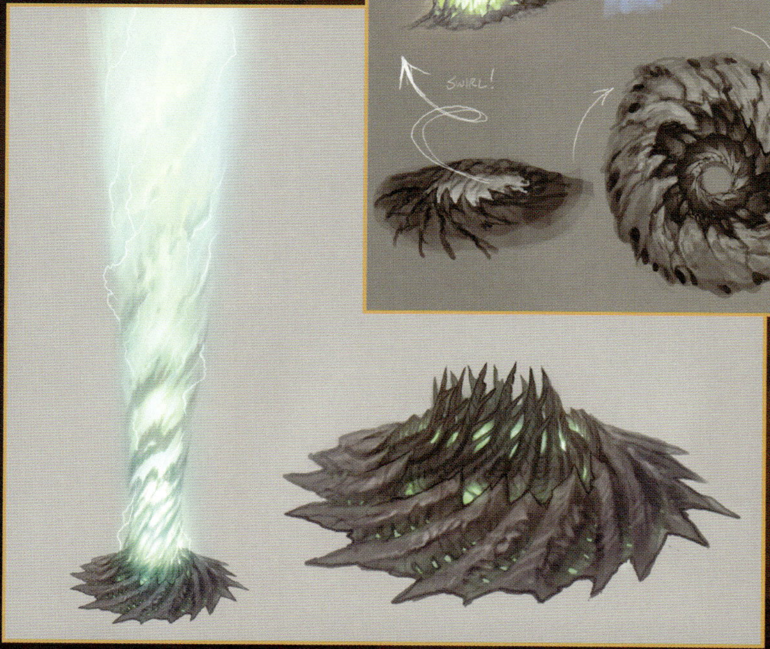

INTERIOR CONCEPT

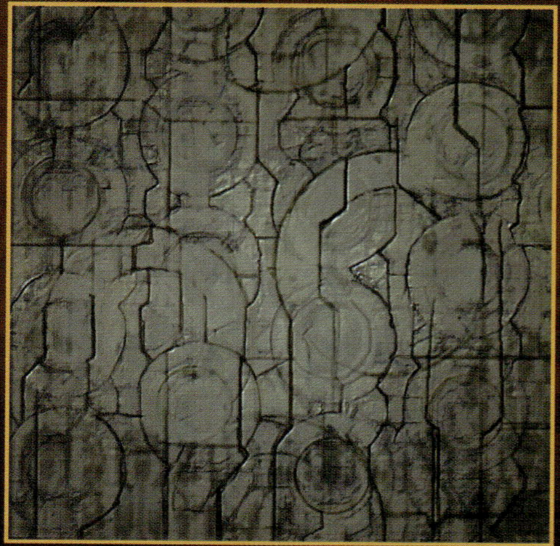

CEILING TEXTURE

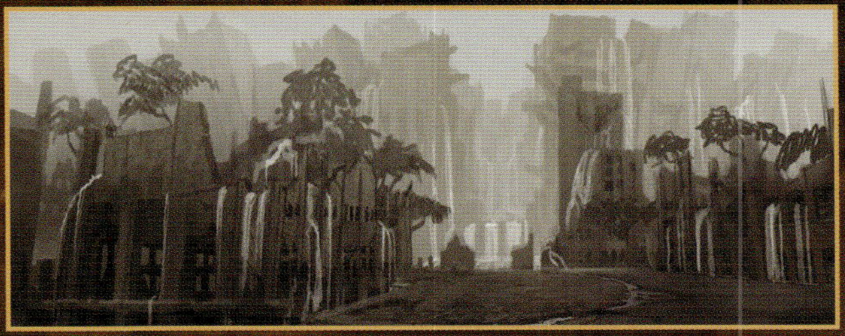
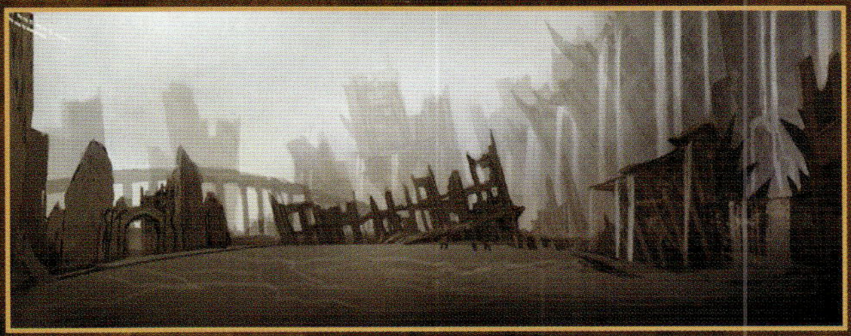
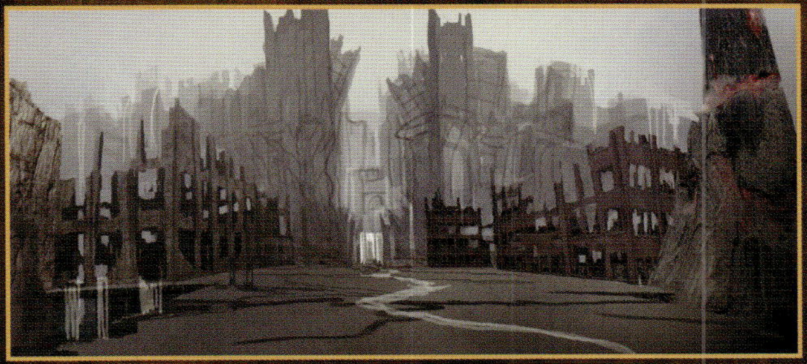
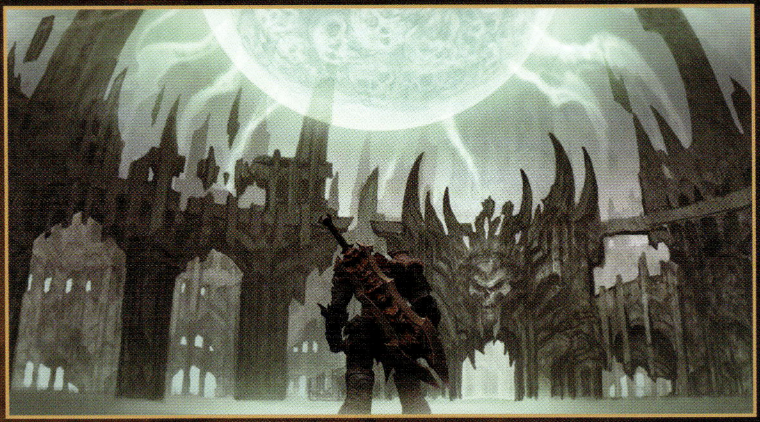
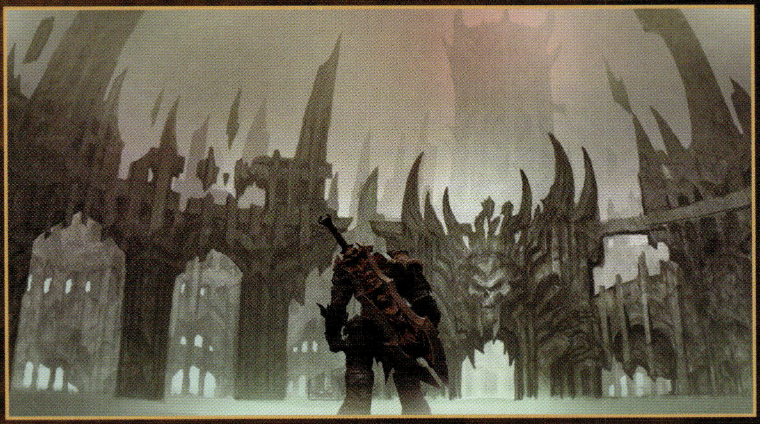

EXTERIOR CONCEPTS

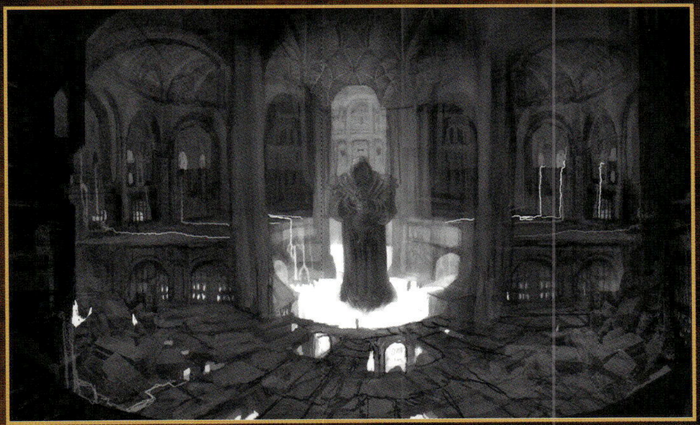
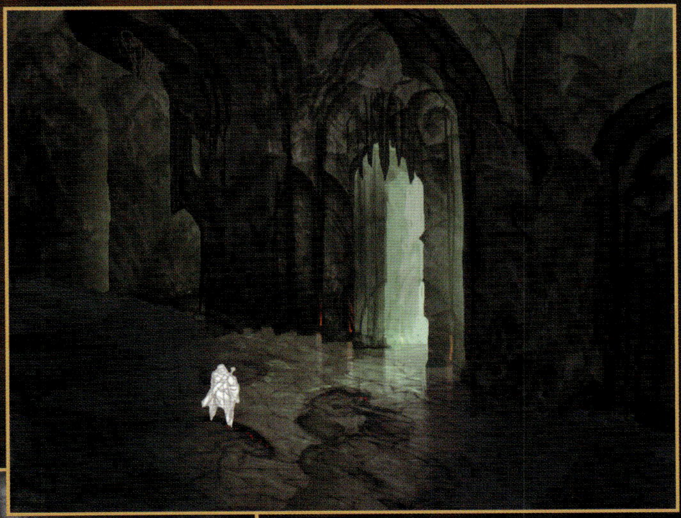
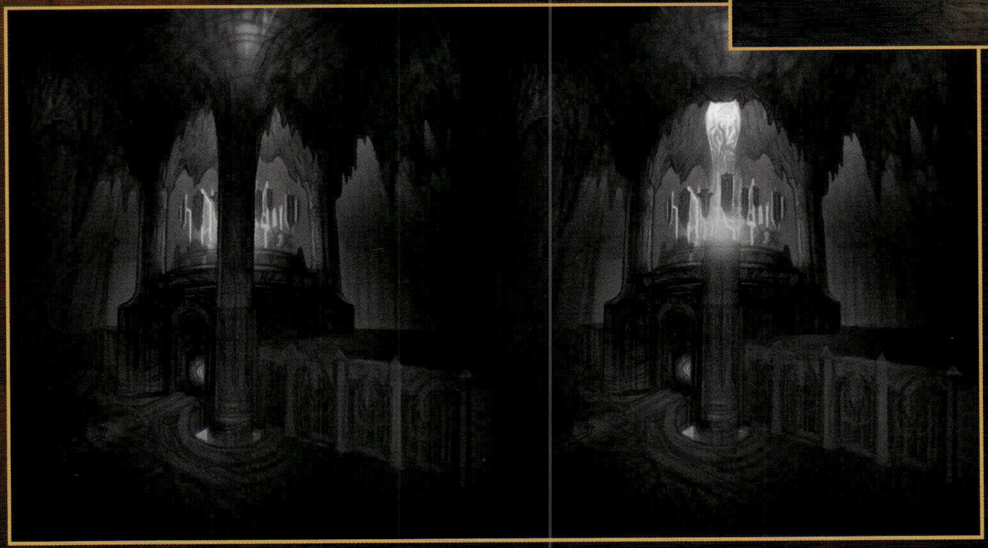

INTERIOR CONCEPTS

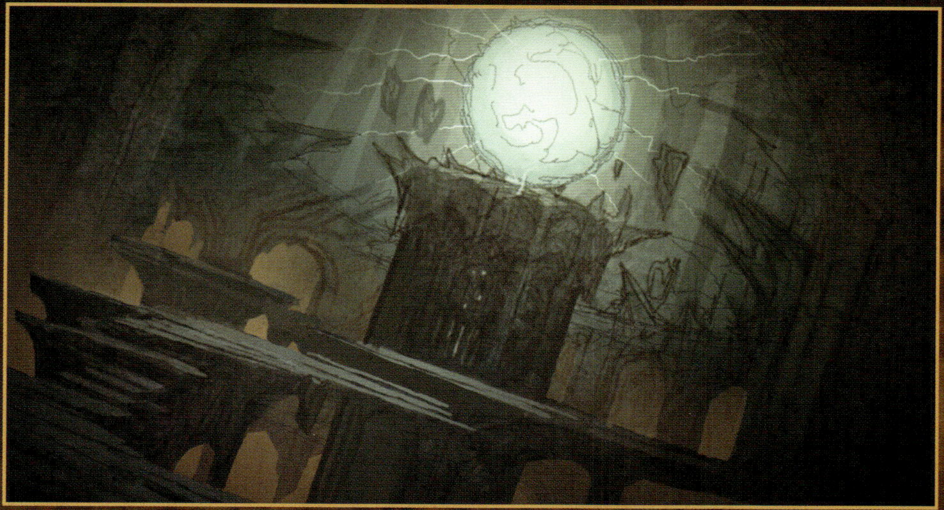

SOUL SOURCE CONCEPT

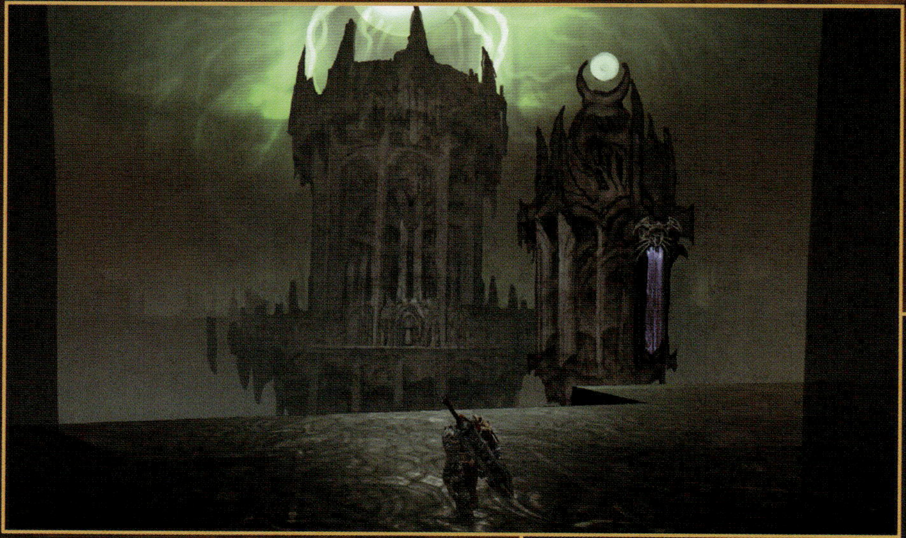

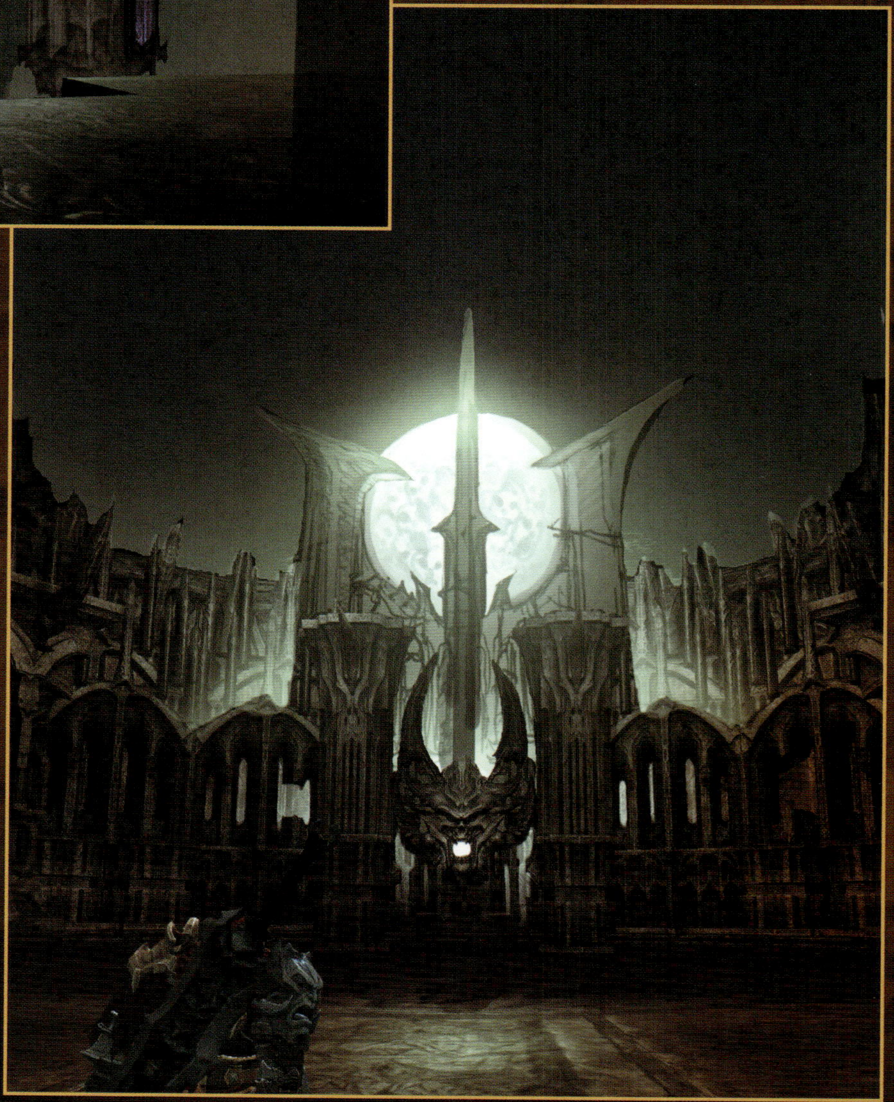

SOUL SOURCE CONCEPTS

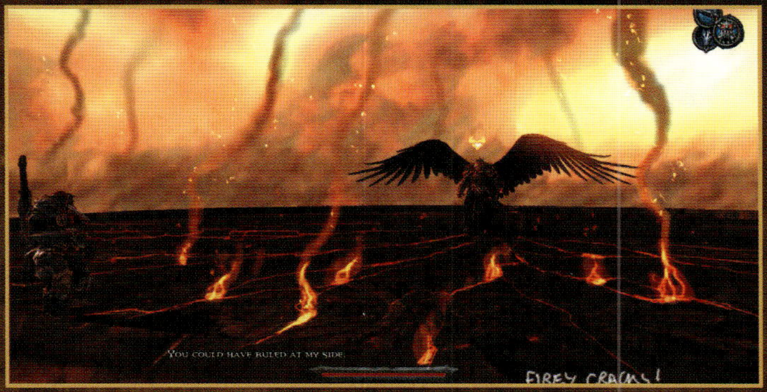

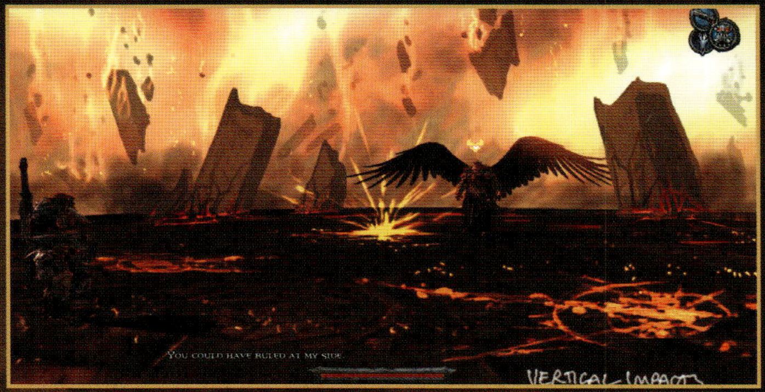

FINAL BATTLE CONCEPTS

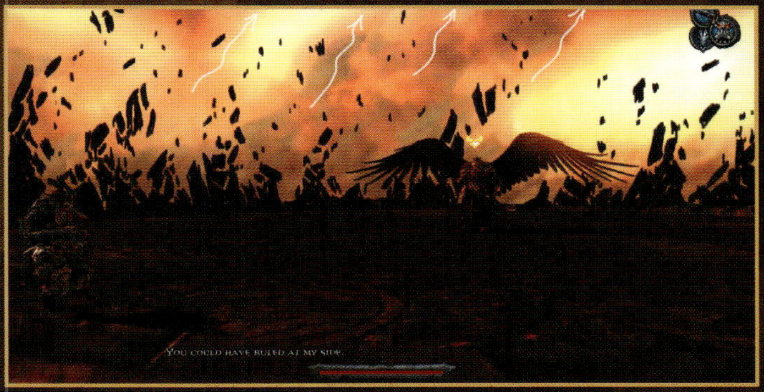

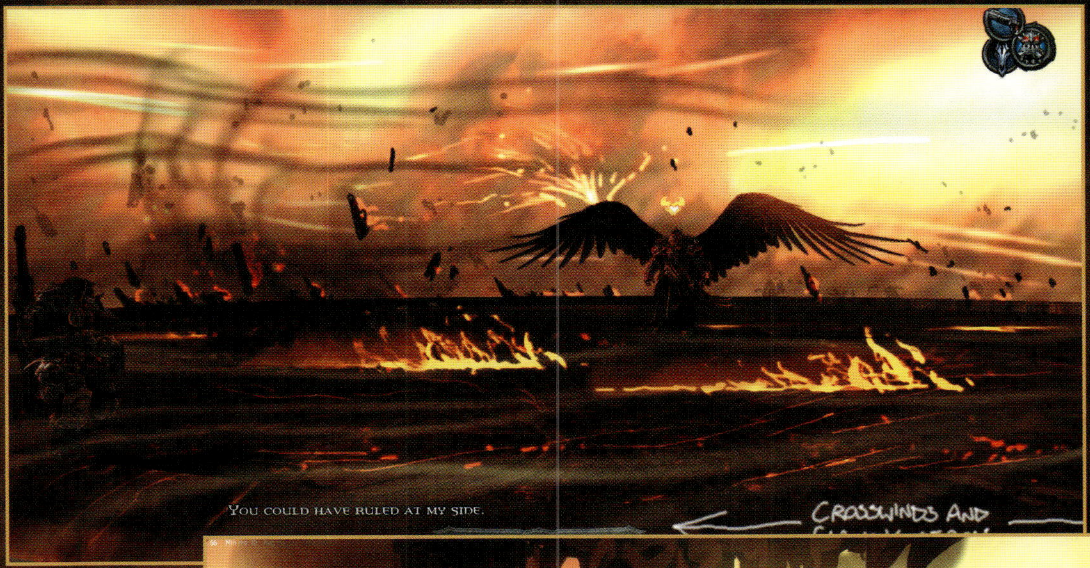

FINAL BATTLE CONCEPTS

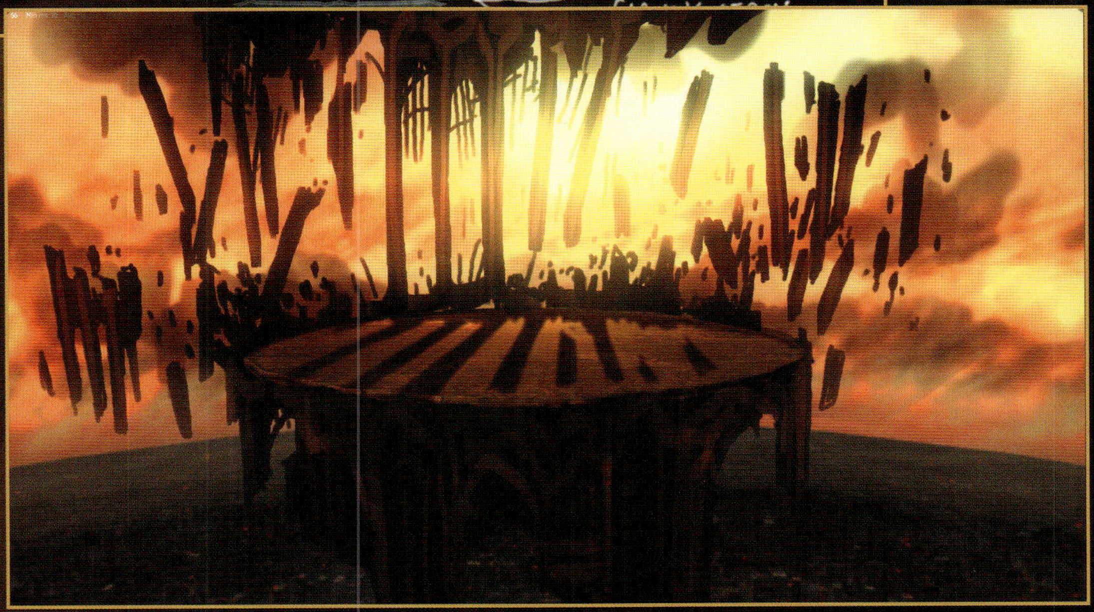

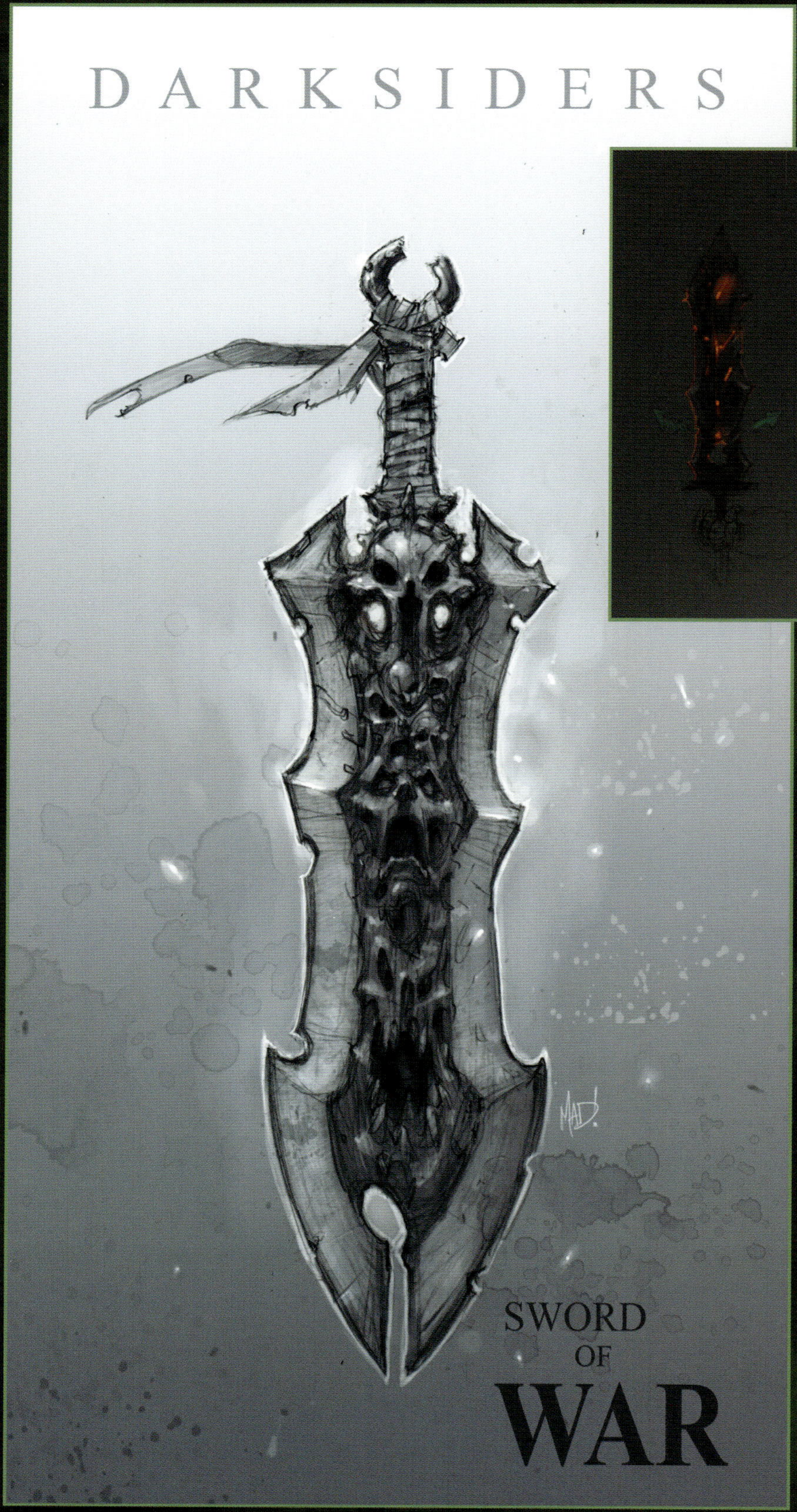

PENCIL ART

SWORD CONCEPT

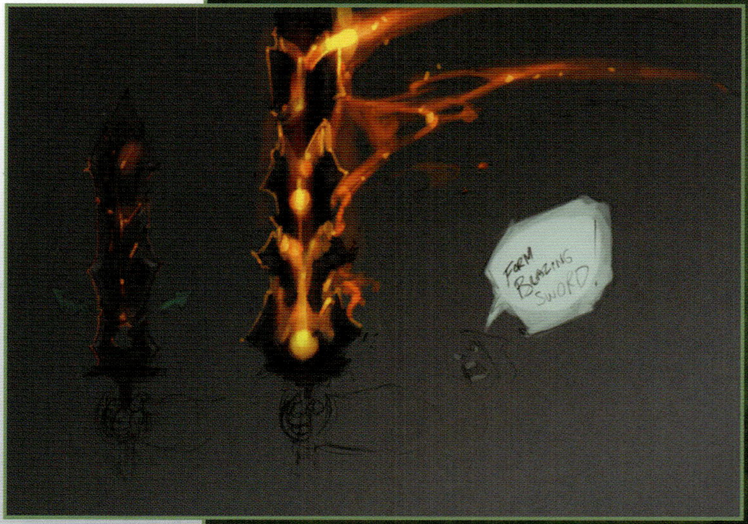

Chaoseater

Chaoseater is a sword unlike any other. This unforgiving weapon has slaughtered countless enemies, their fate foretold by the death-masks artfully etched along its massive blade. And many a battle has been decided by Chaoseater's viciously honed edge, which can slice through the thickest demon bone as if it were candle wax.

As with most ancient arcane weapons, Chaoseater's true power can only be unleashed by a master equal to its blood-stained legend. Such a master is the Horseman War. Even after centuries of torment, I tremble to think that War's grim face and upraised sword could be the last things I ever see…

SWORD CONCEPTS

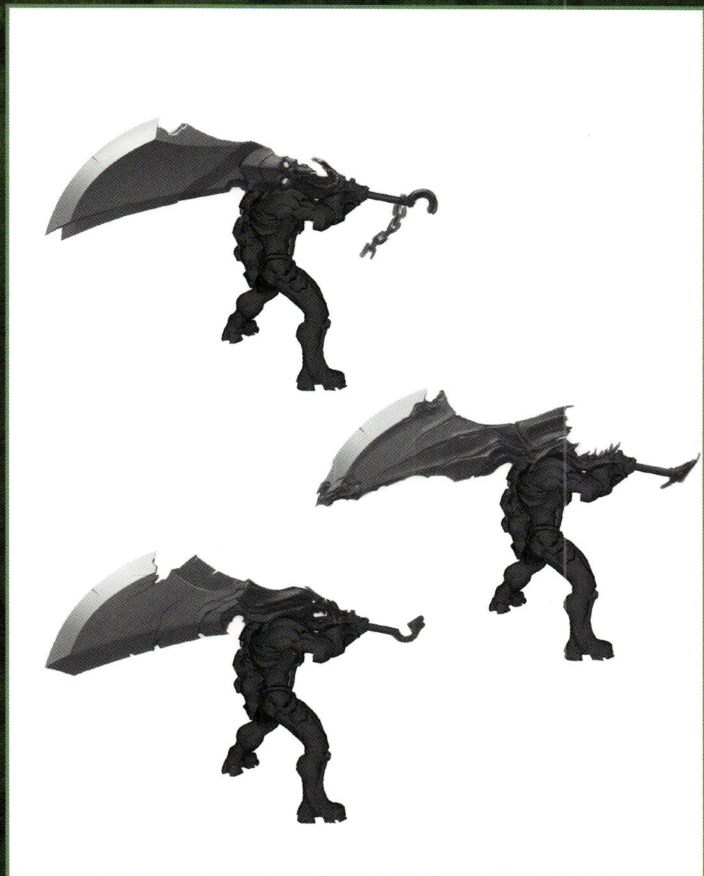

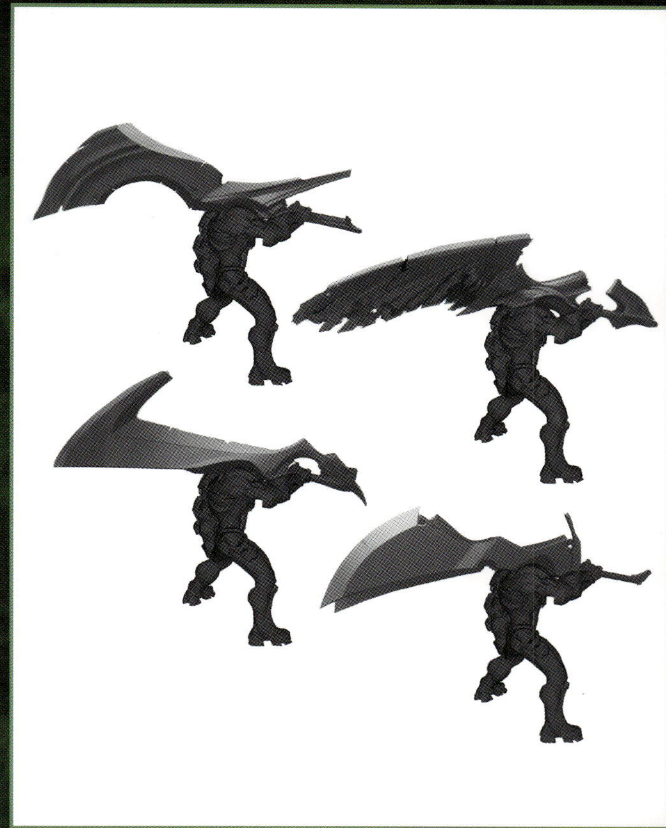

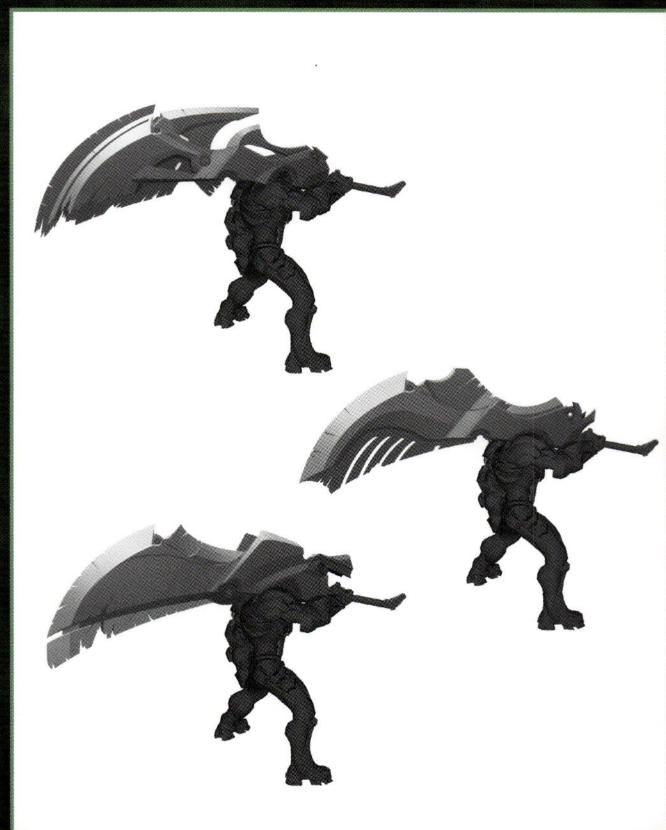

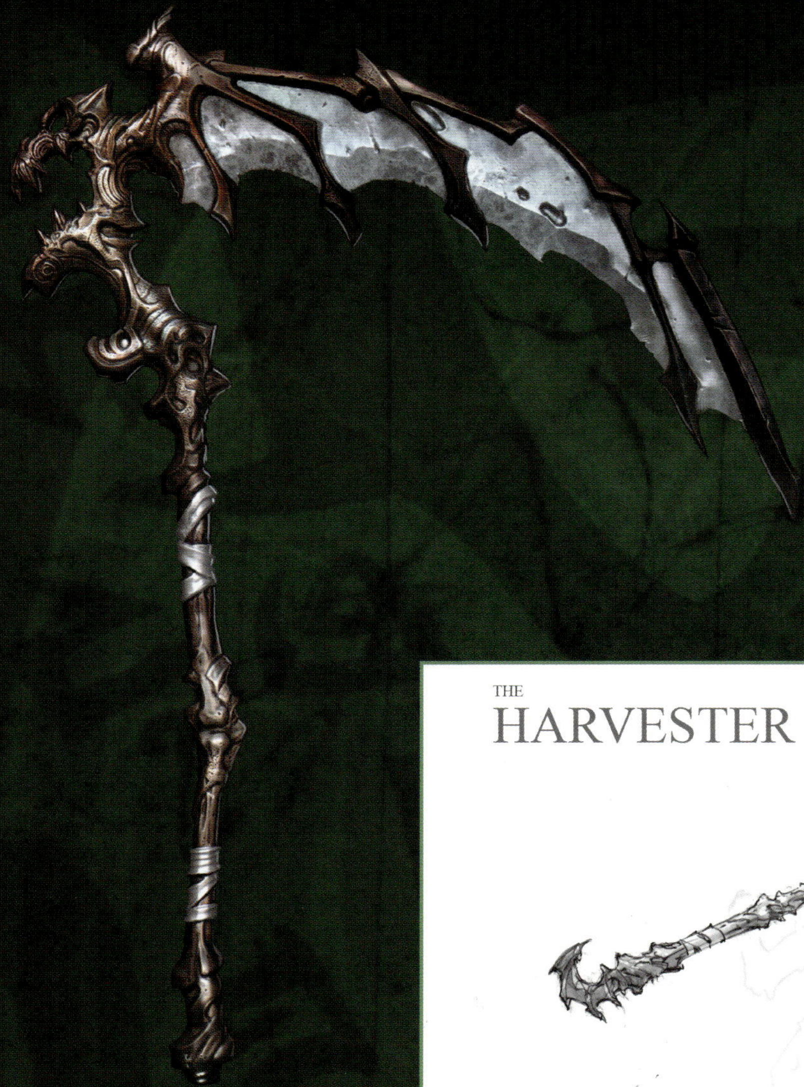

The Harvester

Death's Scythe, the Harvester, boasts a blade that resembles a barbed wing—a fitting shape, for few weapons cut through the air with more graceful—and life-ending—precision. This fabled weapon was made many ages ago, to fill the bony hands of the Horseman Death.

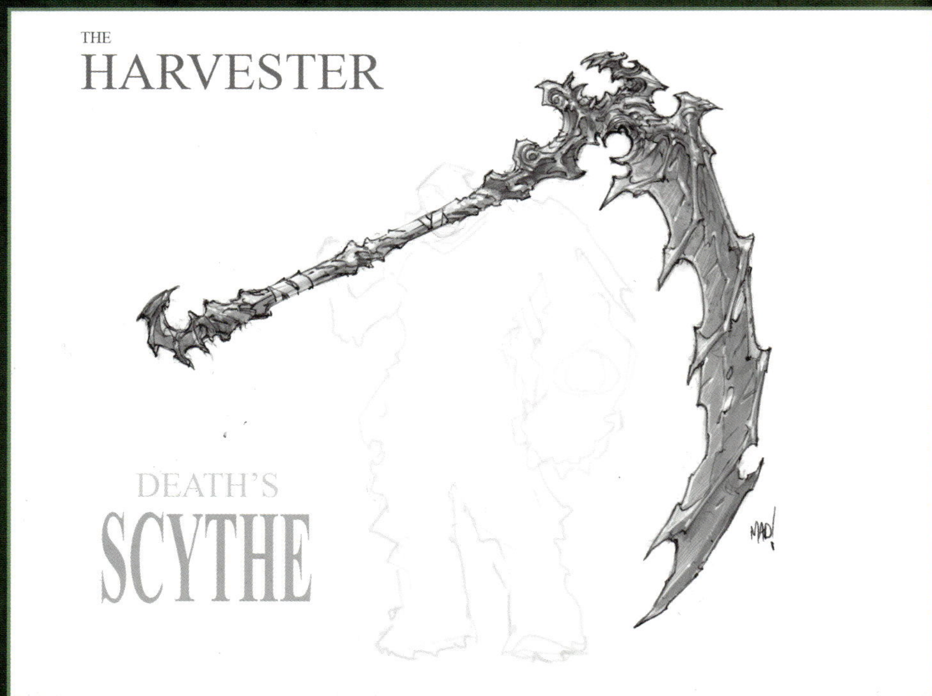

PENCIL ART

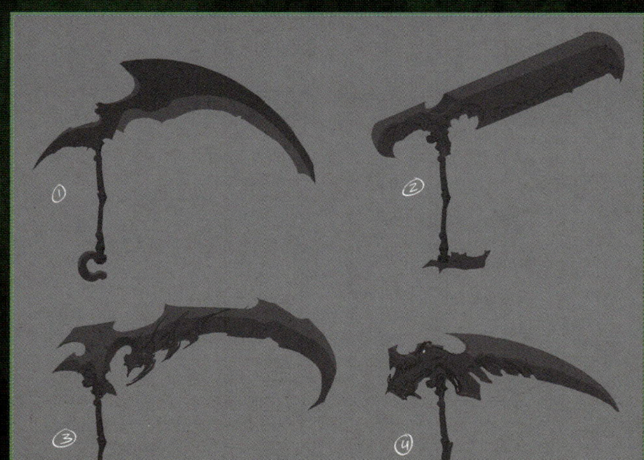

SCYTHE CONCEPTS

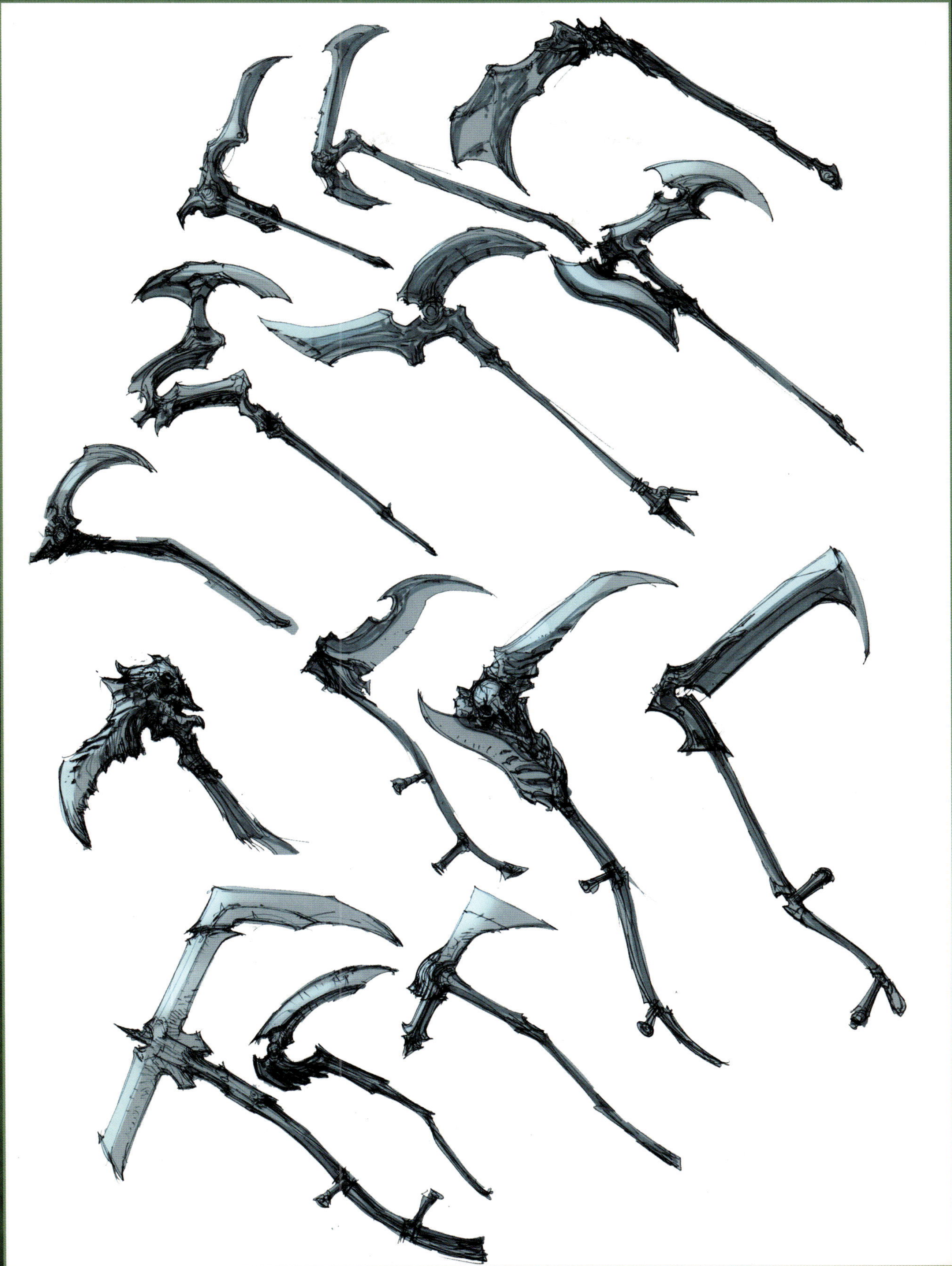

SCYTHE CONCEPTS

Crossblade

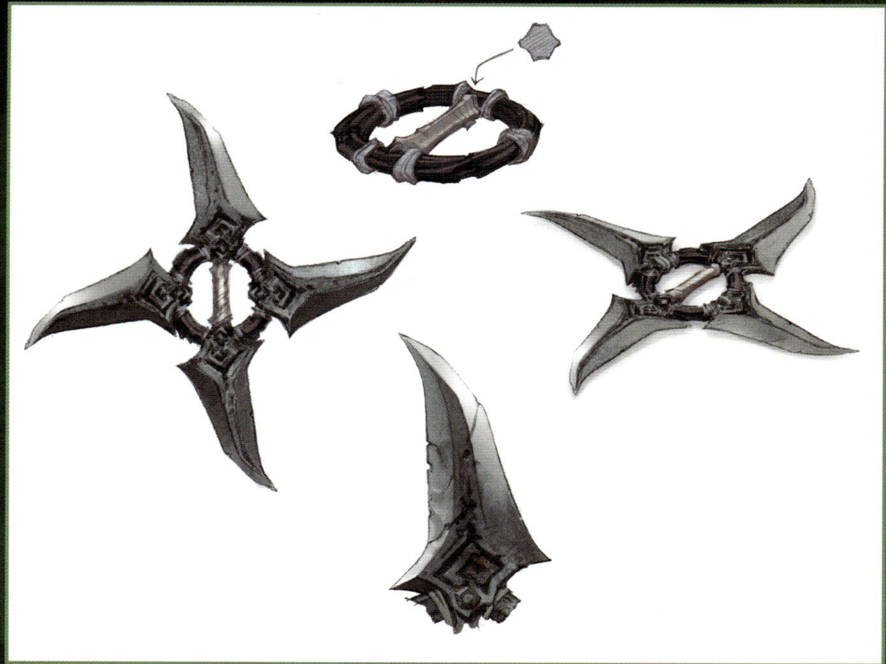

CROSSBLADE DESIGNS

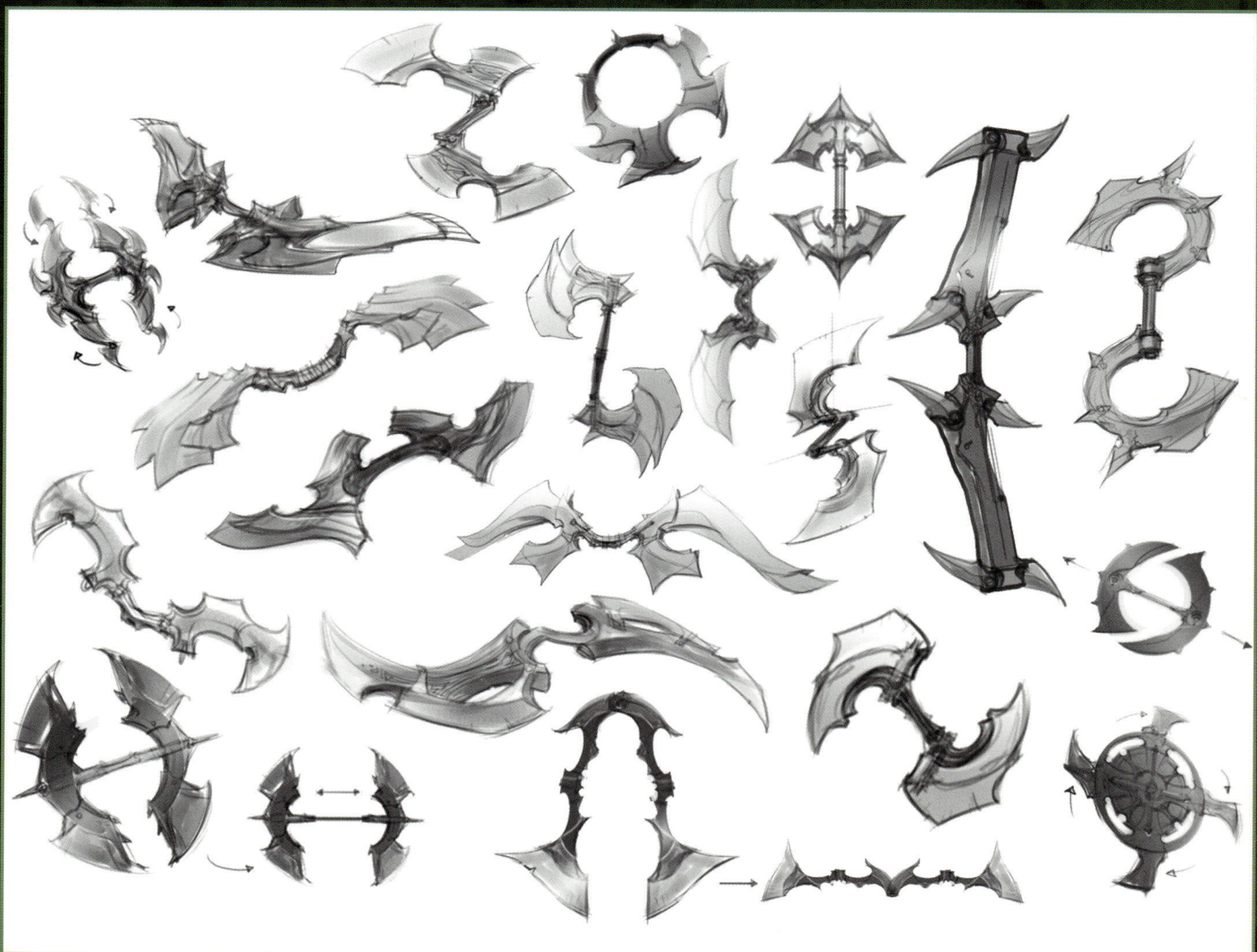

DEVELOPMENT SKETCHES

DEVELOPMENT SKETCHES

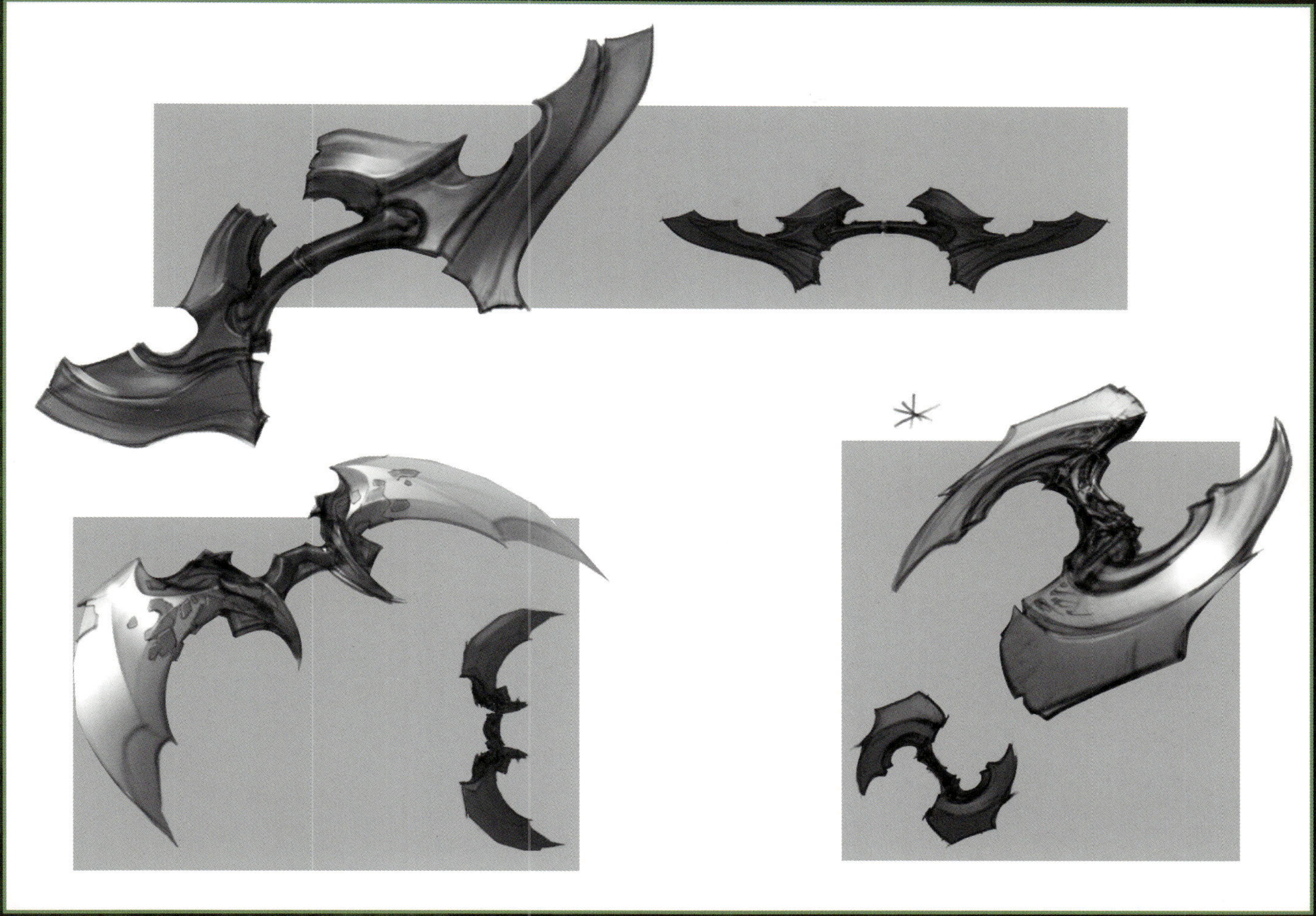

There are many profane weapons scattered about the ash of Man's kingdom. Few can match the speed and lethality of the Crossblade. It is a cluster of four blades that can be thrown with brutal force. After arcing deep into flesh, the Crossblade returns to its wielder's hand, ready to be thrown again.

And if that were not enough, the weapon carries an additional, malevolent secret. The Crossblade can absorb the properties of certain elements it passes through—such as fire and plague—and translate them into further mutilation. Even the mightiest of the Dark One's legions would dread a warrior who brandished a weapon of such devastating power.

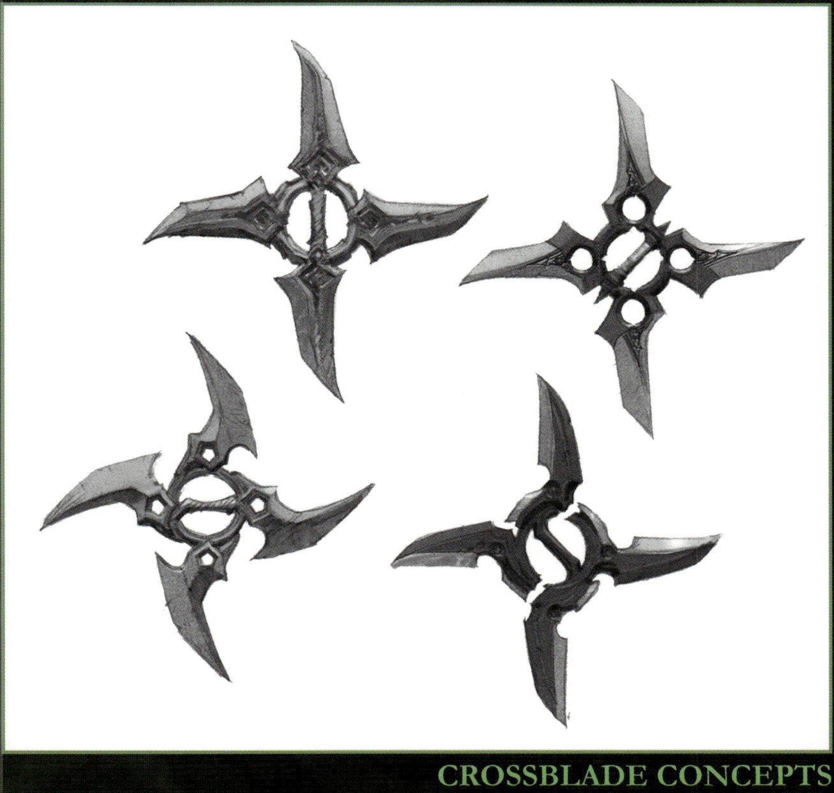

CROSSBLADE CONCEPTS

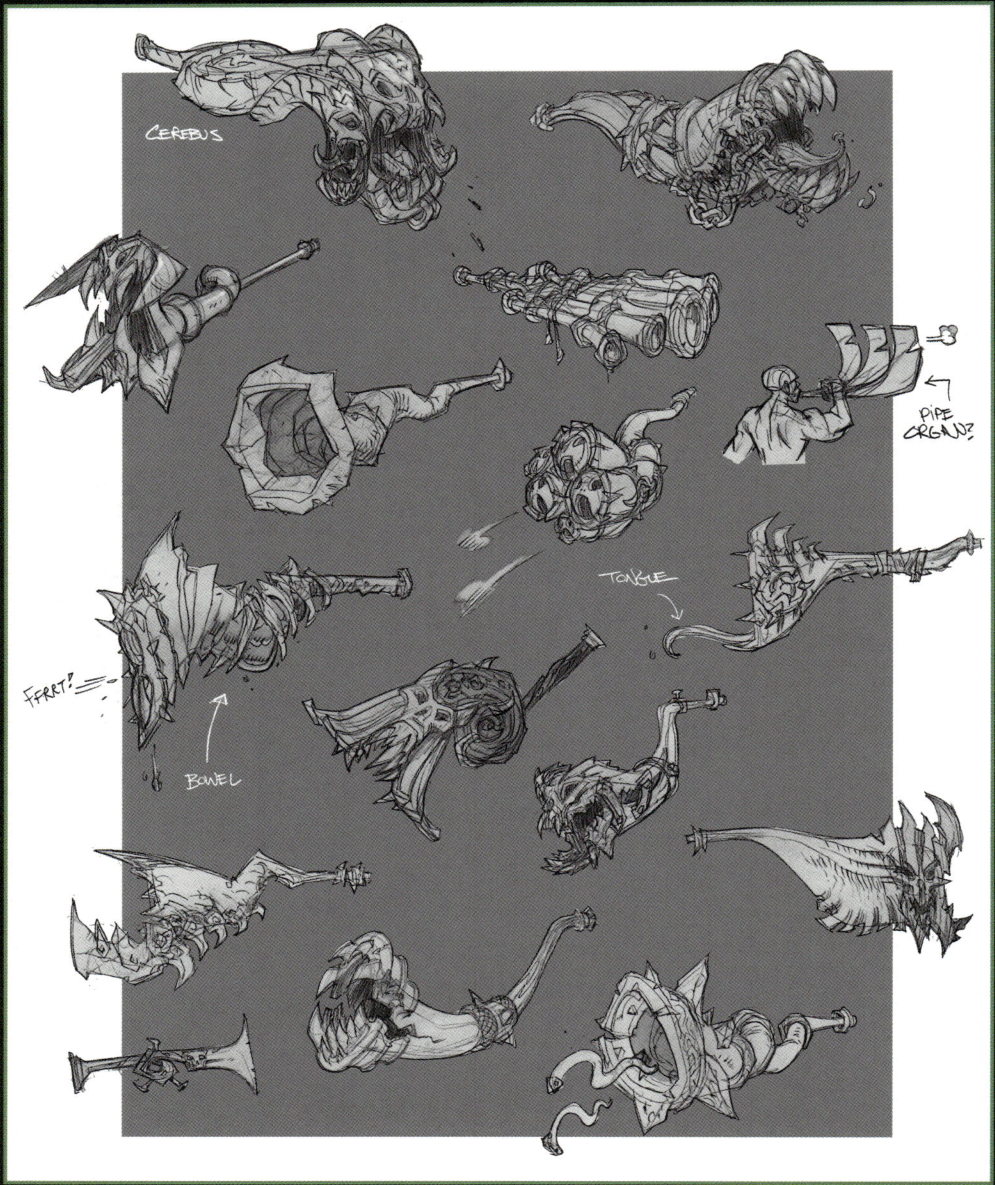

DEVELOPMENT SKETCHES

Even when silent, the Earthcaller appears to be screaming. Its mouth has been carved to resemble two demon faces twisted with rage. The horn is a powerful artifact, able to channel fury into raw sonic power.

Far more than a weapon, the Earthcaller is able to awaken the Tormented Gates. I believed this artifact lost. Now I pray that it does not fall into the wrong hands.

Earthcaller

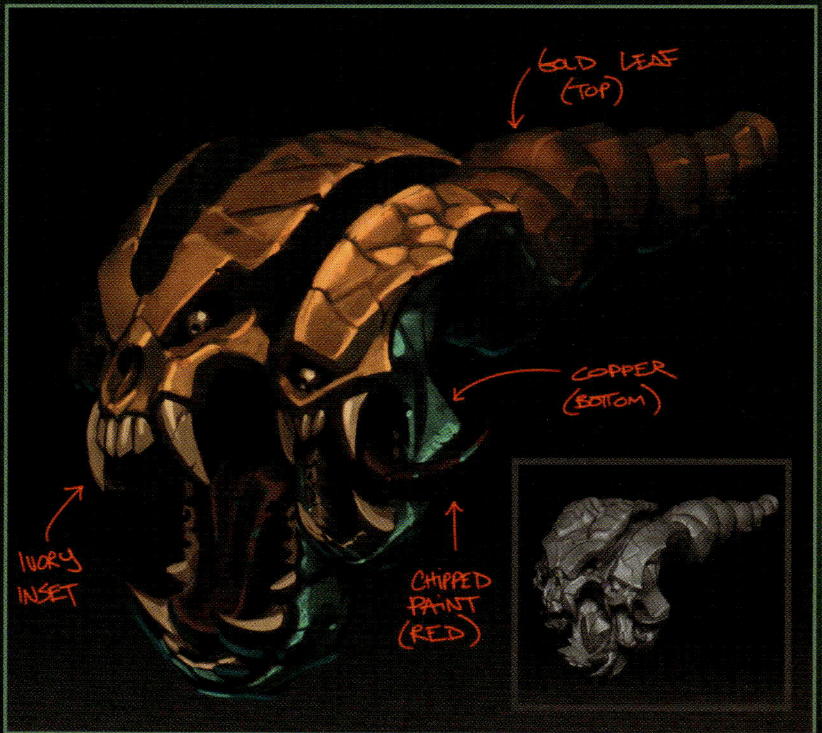

HORN DESIGN

Mask of Shadows

There is a realm hidden behind our own, where shadows swirl to conceal relics of unimaginable power, sequestered from the physical world. The Mask of Shadows allows one to peer into this domain, and to acquire the artifacts—and power—shrouded within.

But beware. The Destroyer's kingdom may extend even to this unknown dimension. And wherever demons are found, even darker things lurk, just out of sight.

CG TURNAROUNDS

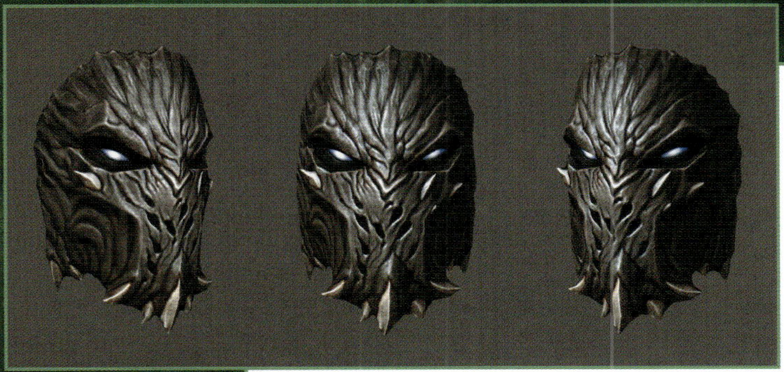

MASK CONCEPTS

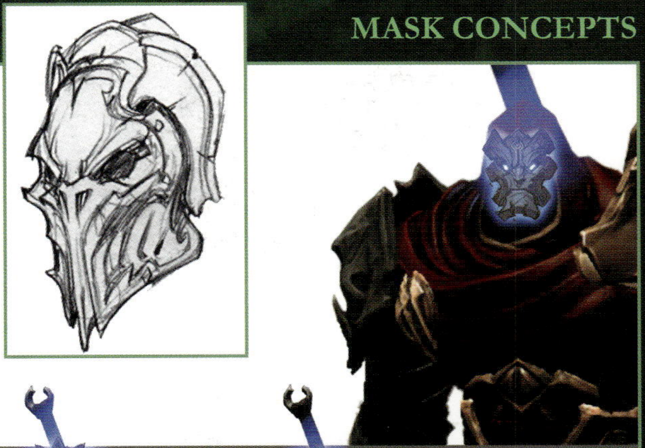

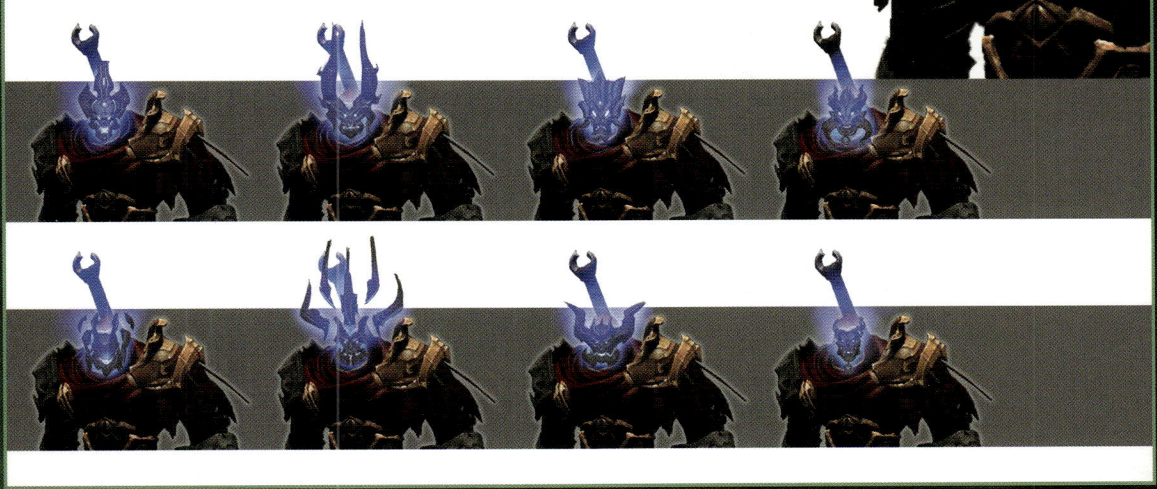

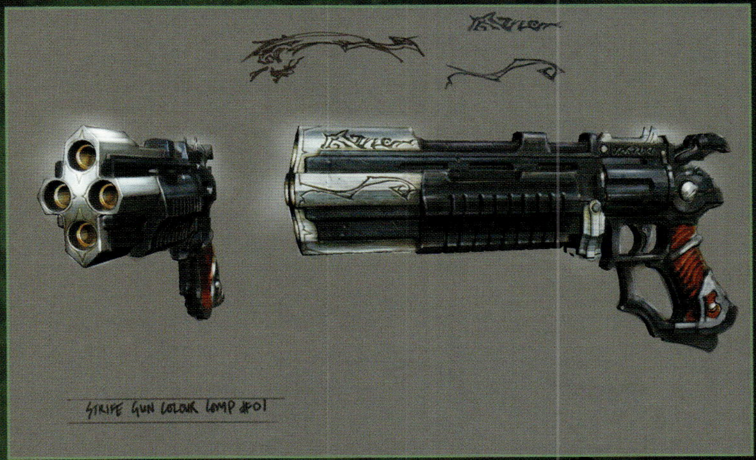

GUN DESIGN

Mercy

On the battlefields of the ruined Earth, the pistol known as Mercy would seem modest. With four barrels ornamented by simple depictions of smoke and flame, it is easily dwarfed by weapons wielded by angels and demons alike. Yet it is far deadlier than any firearm I have seen.

Mercy generates its own supply of lethal bullets. The rate of fire is defined only by how quickly its master can pull the trigger. In skilled hands, the gun's endless fusillade of bullets can cut down an entire enemy regiment. Although this weapon has yet to surface on Earth , I feel it, somewhere, close at hand.

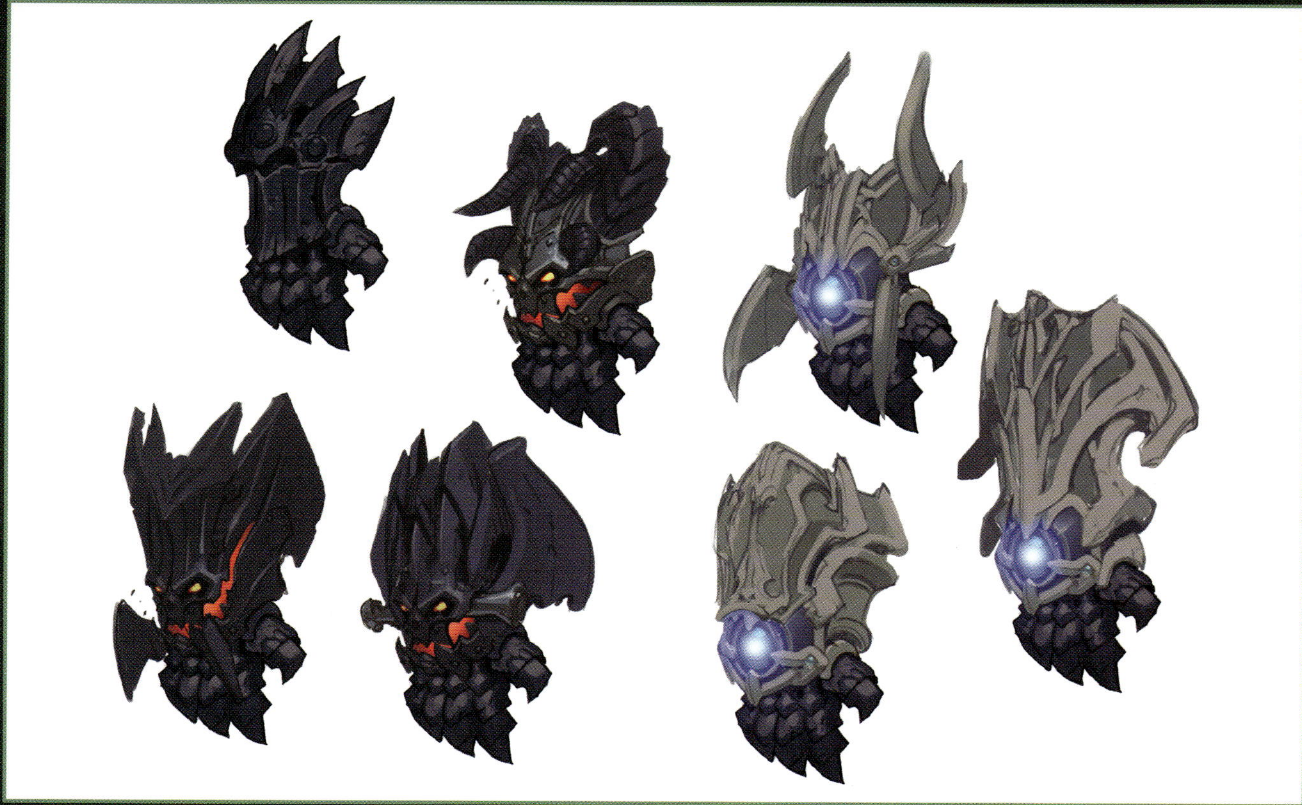

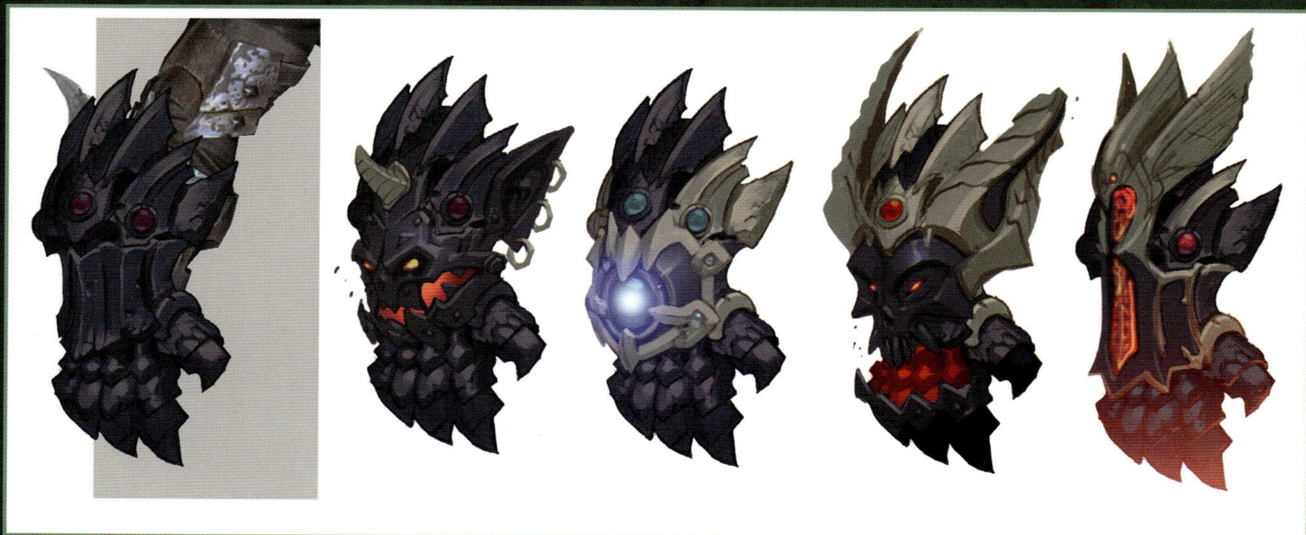

GAUNTLET CONCEPTS

Tremor Gauntlet

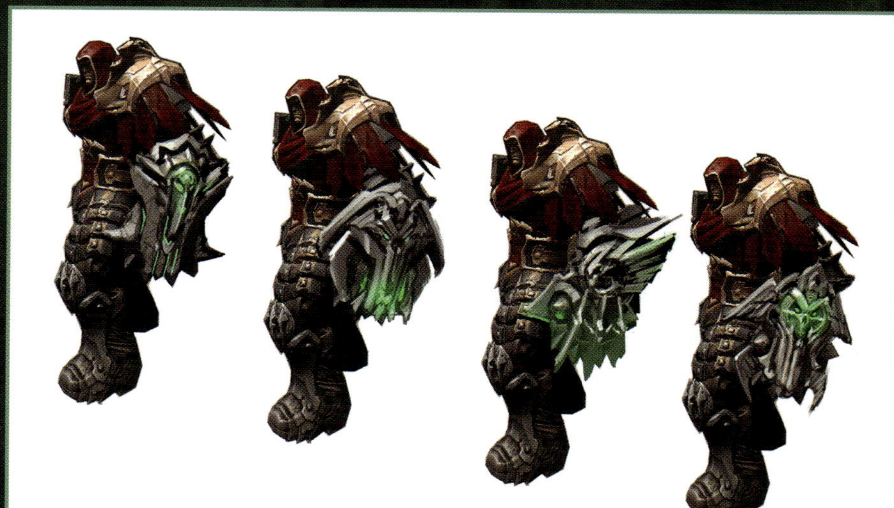

Among the relics lost beneath the earth, the Tremor Gauntlet is uniquely frightening. It is an ancient glove lined with spikes, a glaring demon face etched onto its surface. The demon's eyes glow red with a single purpose—to amplify power. To possess the Tremor Gauntlet is to become the weapon.

For the Tremor Gauntlet's master, each finger has the fortitude to break enemies in half. Imagine armor imploding at the force of a blow, and massive barriers crumbling to dust. It is the stuff of demons' dreams. For the rest of us, let us hope it remains only in our nightmares.

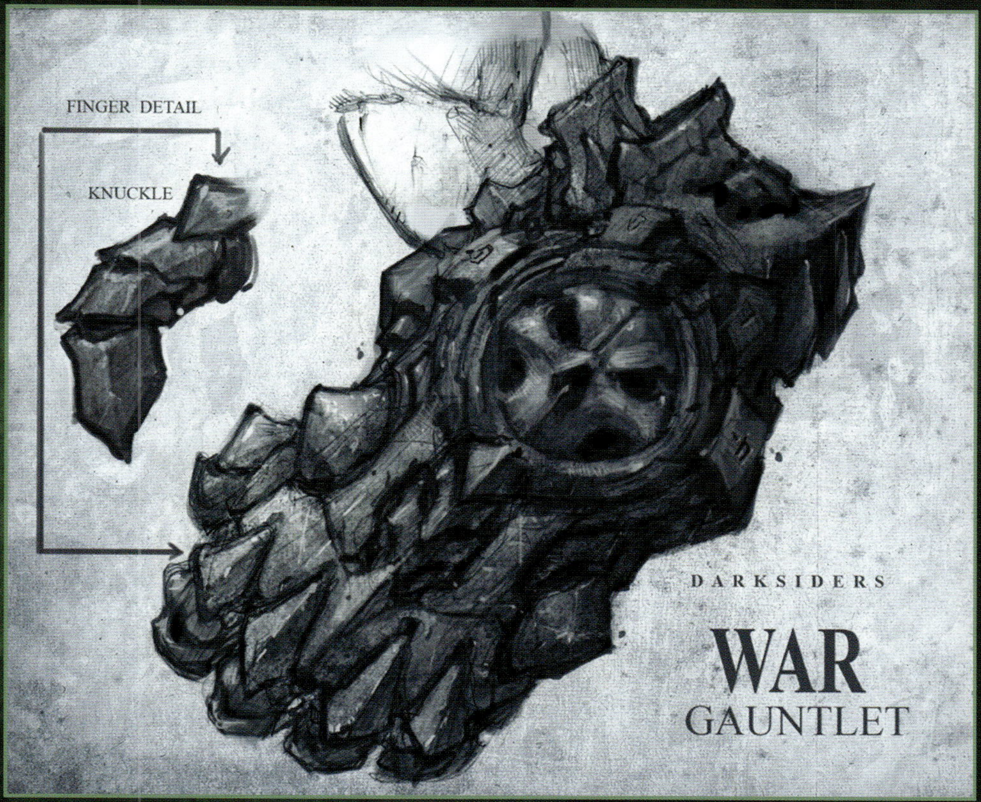

GAUNLET DESIGN

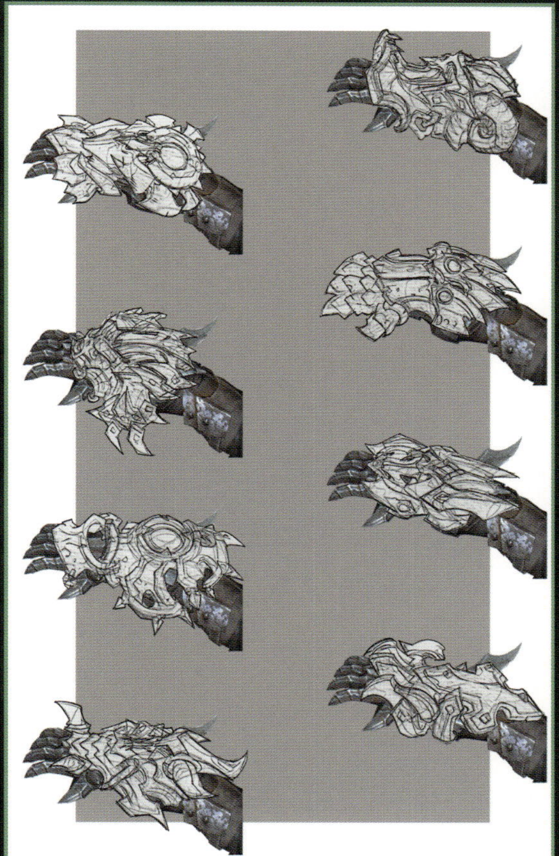

DEVELOPMENT SKETCHES

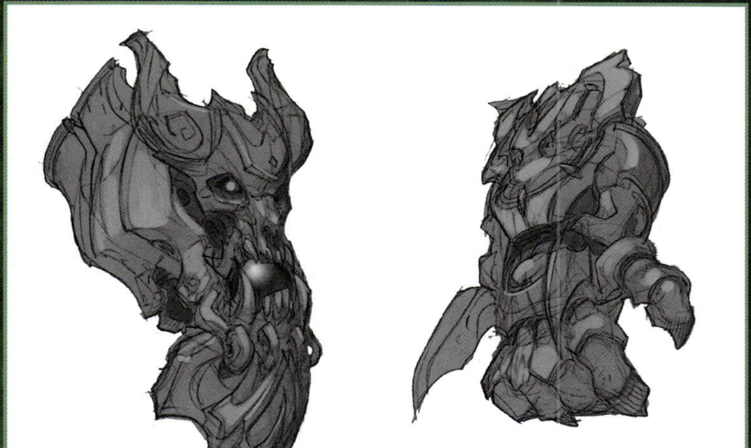

DEVELOPMENT SKETCHES

Abyssal Chain

Death is not always a cacophony of death cries and armor-beating. Sometimes it is a muffled tchink…a silent pause… and a sharp point through the heart.

The Abyssal Chain is a supernatural gauntlet forged to deliver such a fate. It fires a spearhead out of its engraved mouth with blinding speed, unspooling a chain behind it. This chain can be retracted to drag a dying foe to an even fouler fate. Or, it can pull the Hook and its master skyward to swing across the wastes.

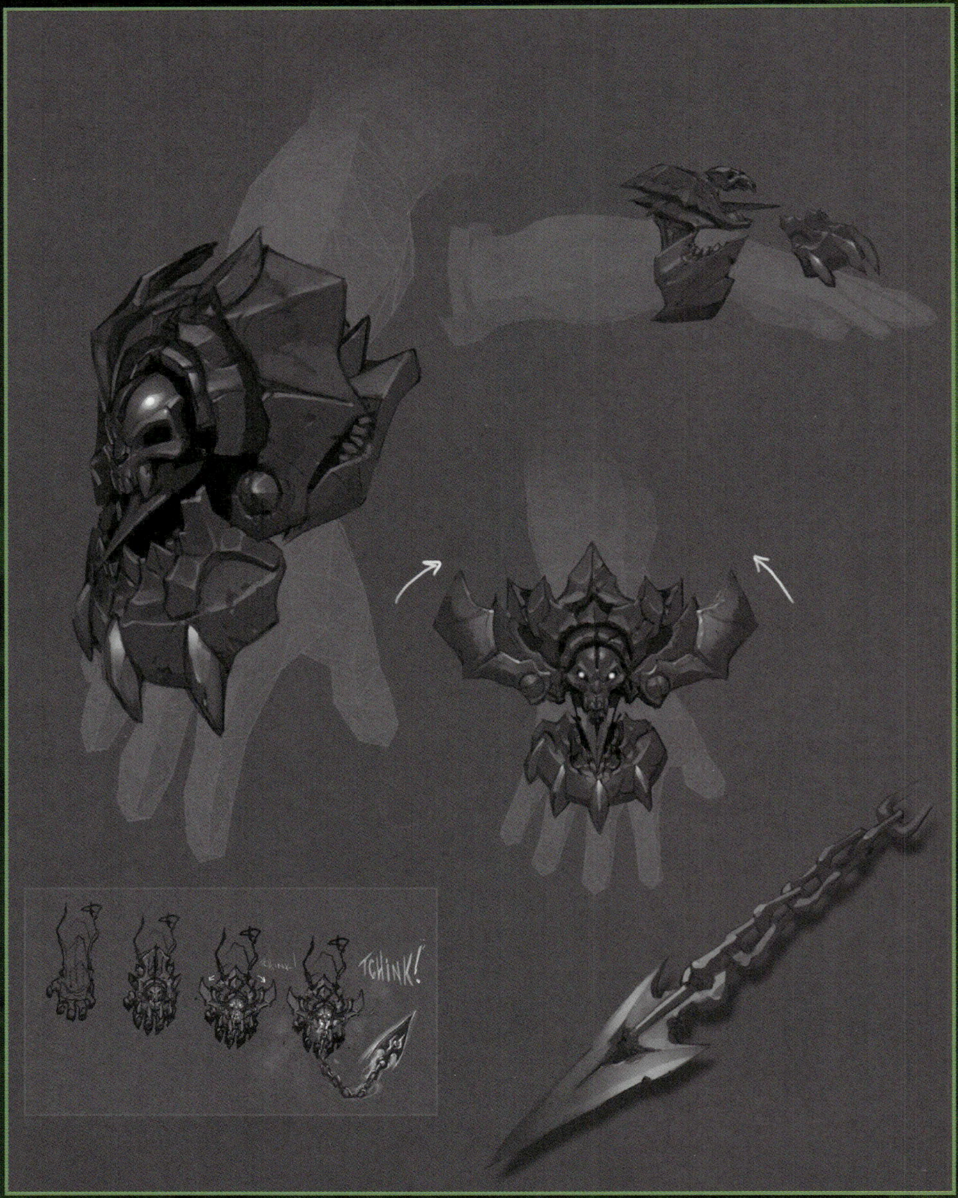

CHAIN DESIGN

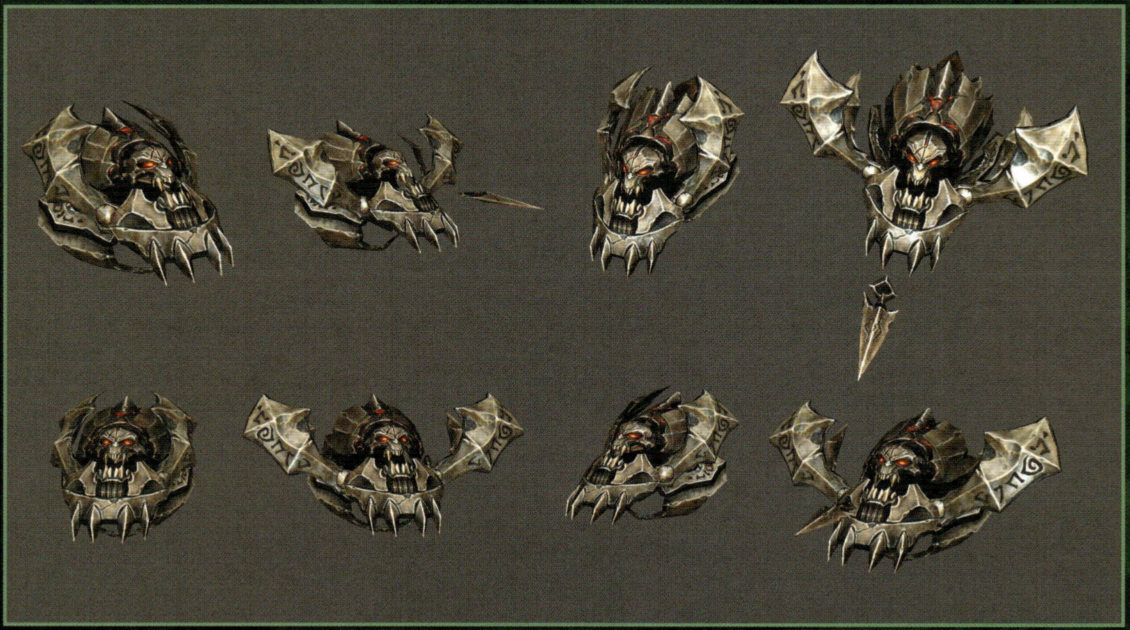

CG RENDERS

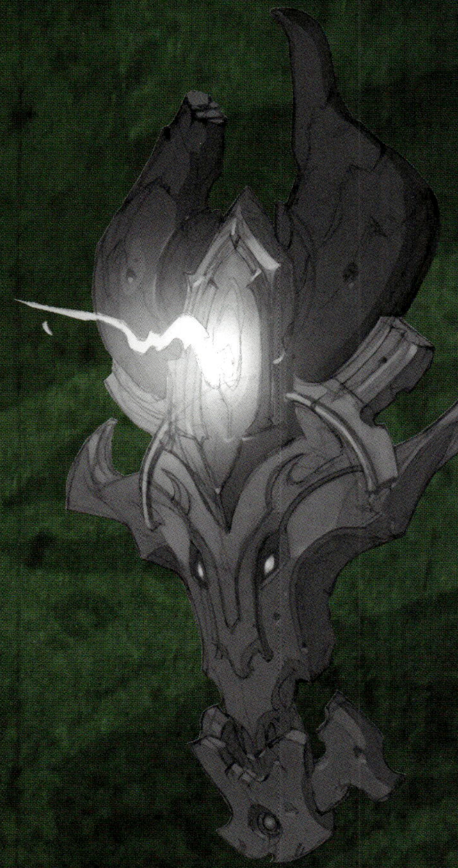

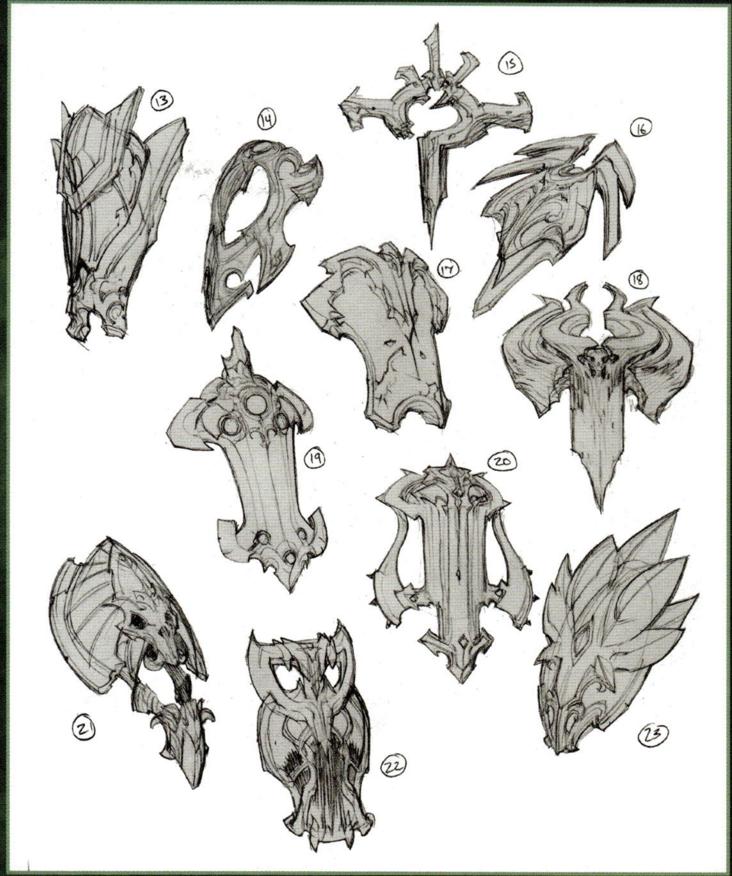

DEVELOPMENT SKETCHES

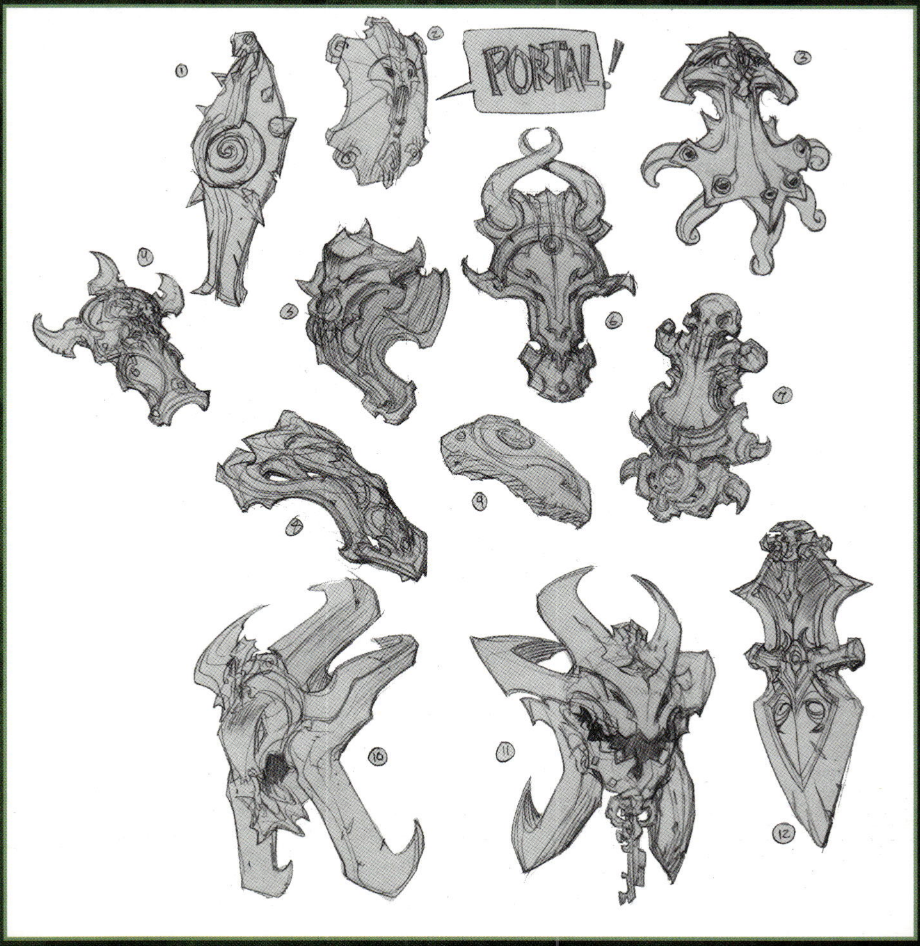

DEVELOPMENT SKETCHES

Voidwalker

The Voidwalker does what no mere weapon can: It opens a hole in reality itself.

This arcane artifact seethes with energy, which can be fired through the veil of the universe. When two such perforations are made, dimensional space curves back upon itself--and Voidwalker's holes are connected. To step into one hole is to exit the other to a new location. Thus, the Voidwalker's master can weave his way through the byzantine wastes, to access every bloody nook and corpse-filled cranny.

Armageddon Blade

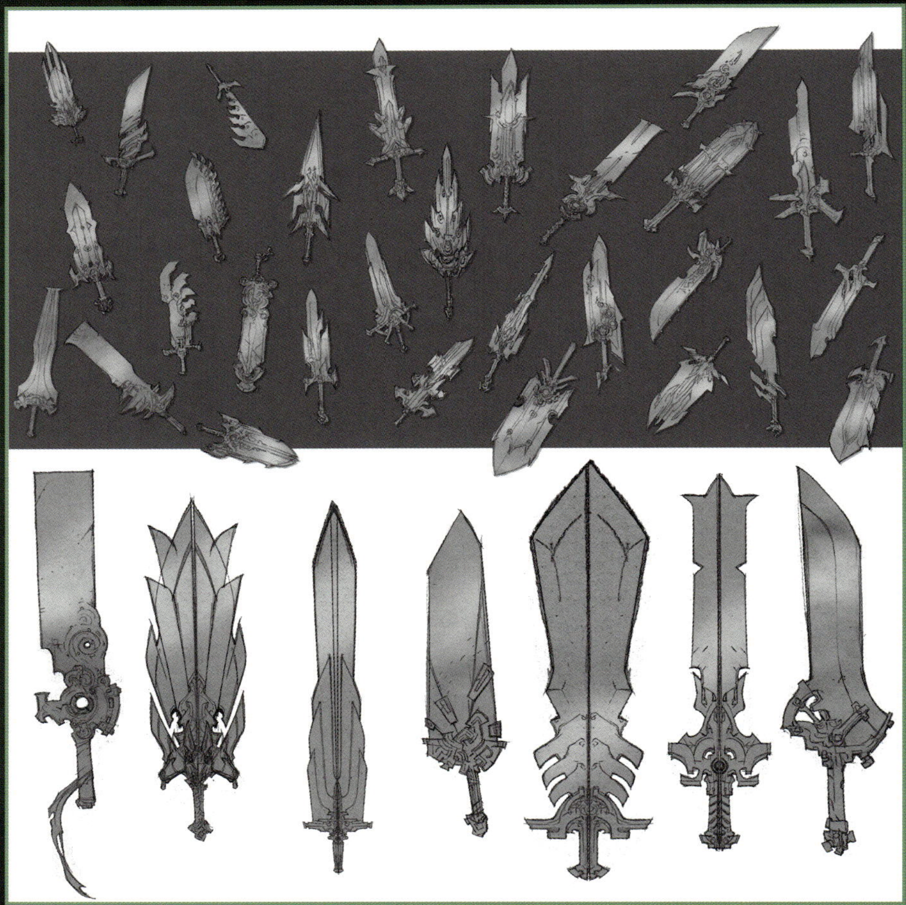

DEVELOPMENT SKETCHES

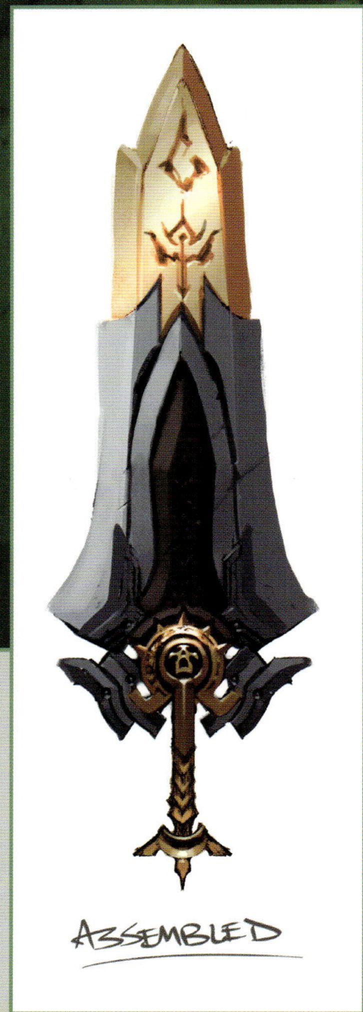

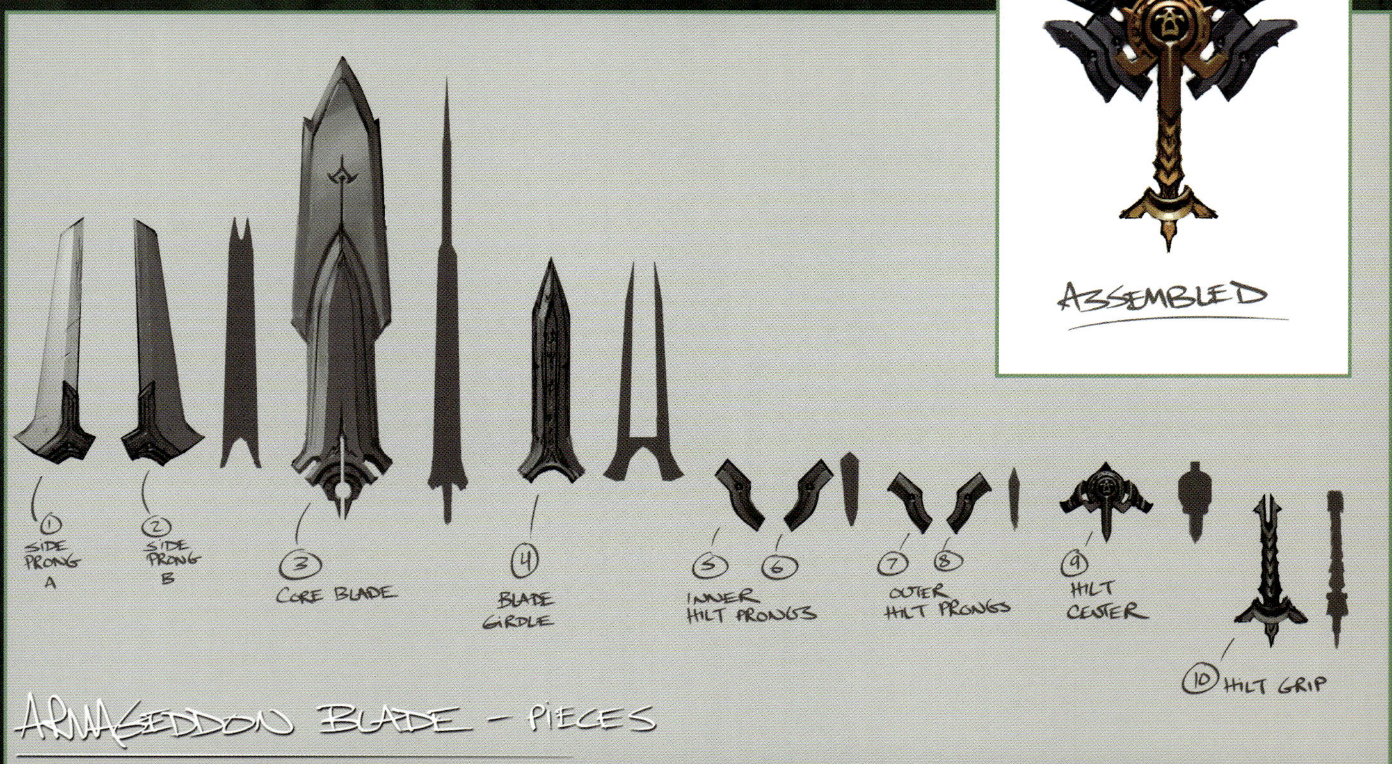

SWORD PIECES

Swords

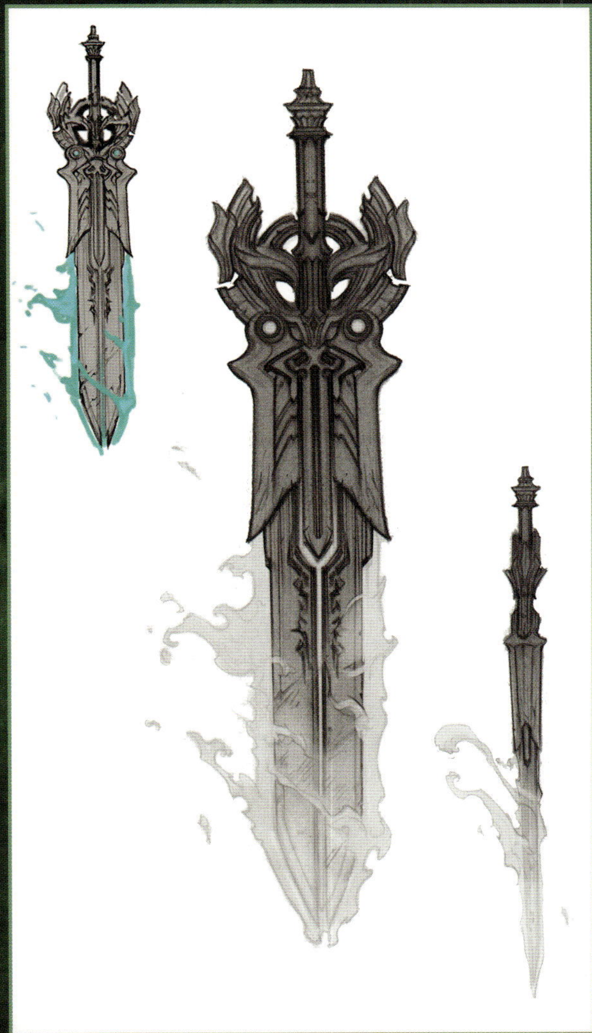

URIEL'S SWORD DESIGN

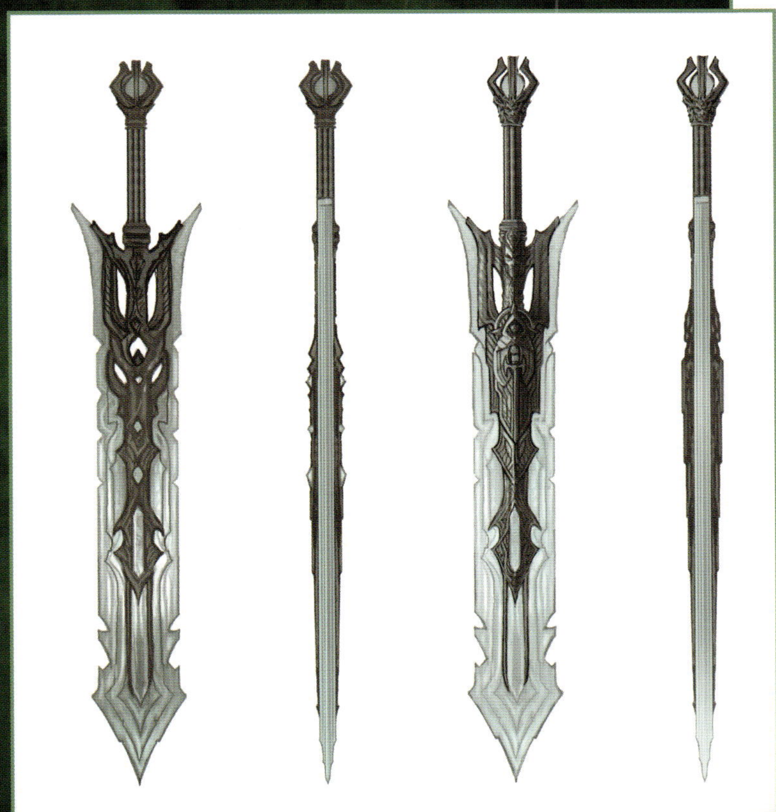

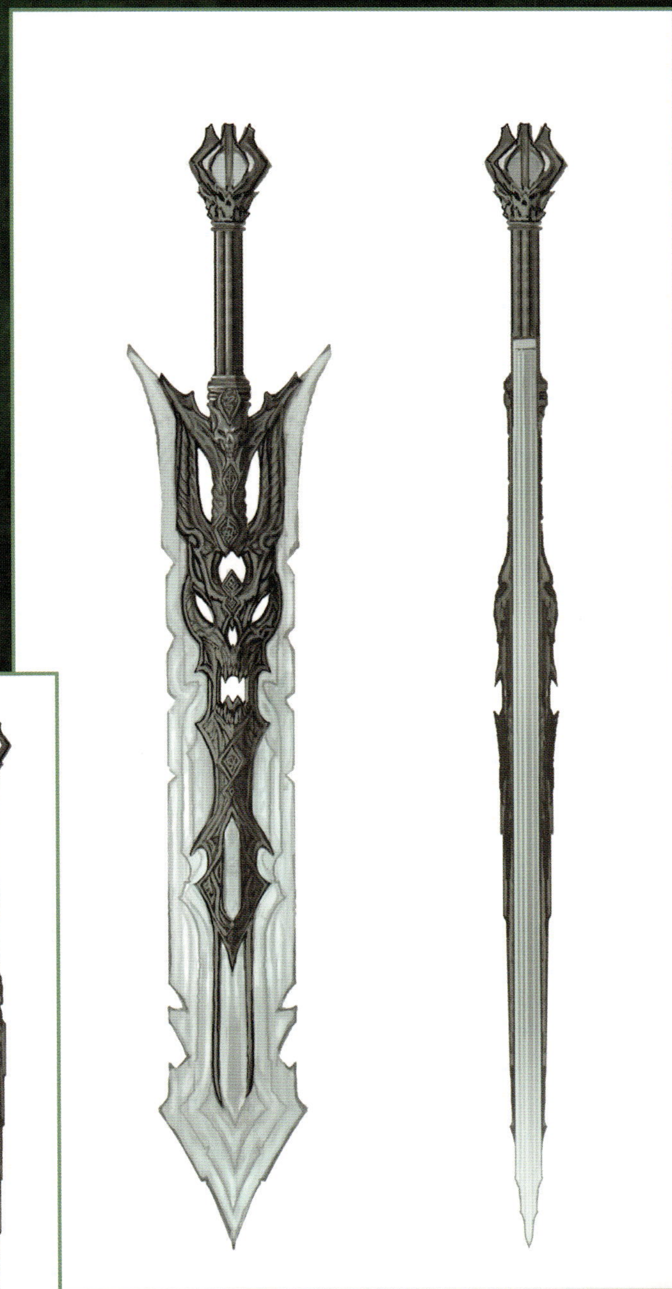

CHURCH SWORD DESIGN

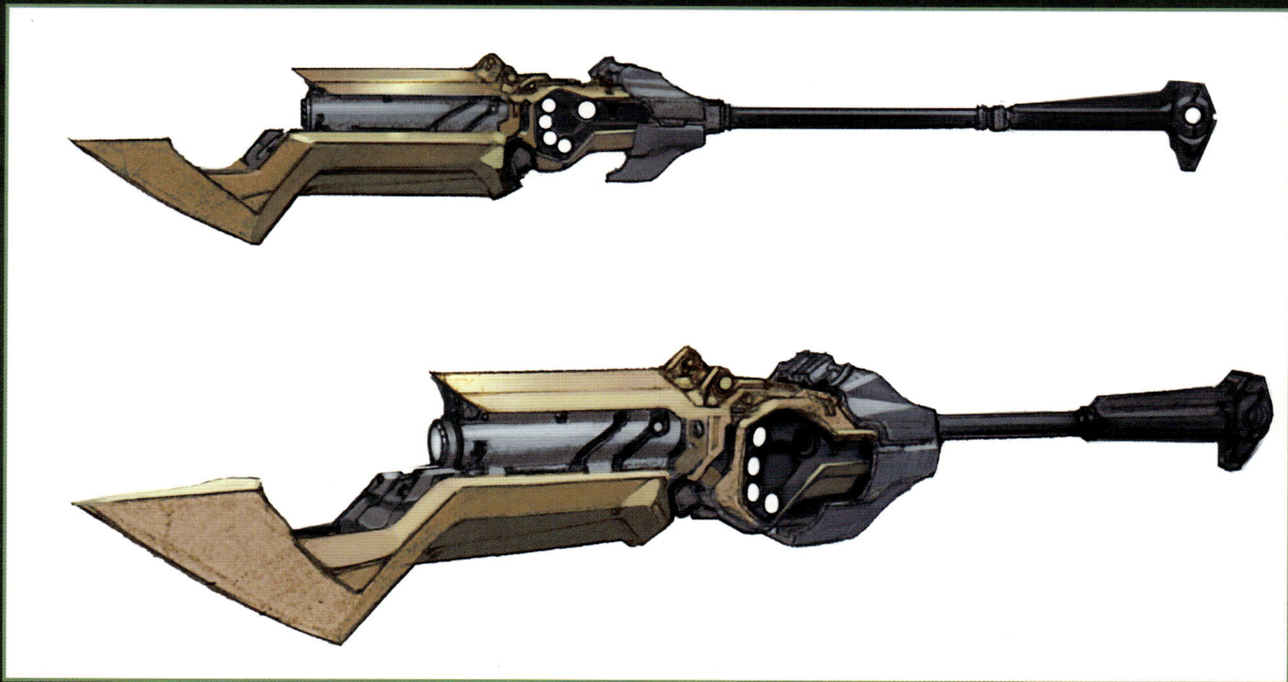

ANGEL SWORD DESIGN

Angel Weapons

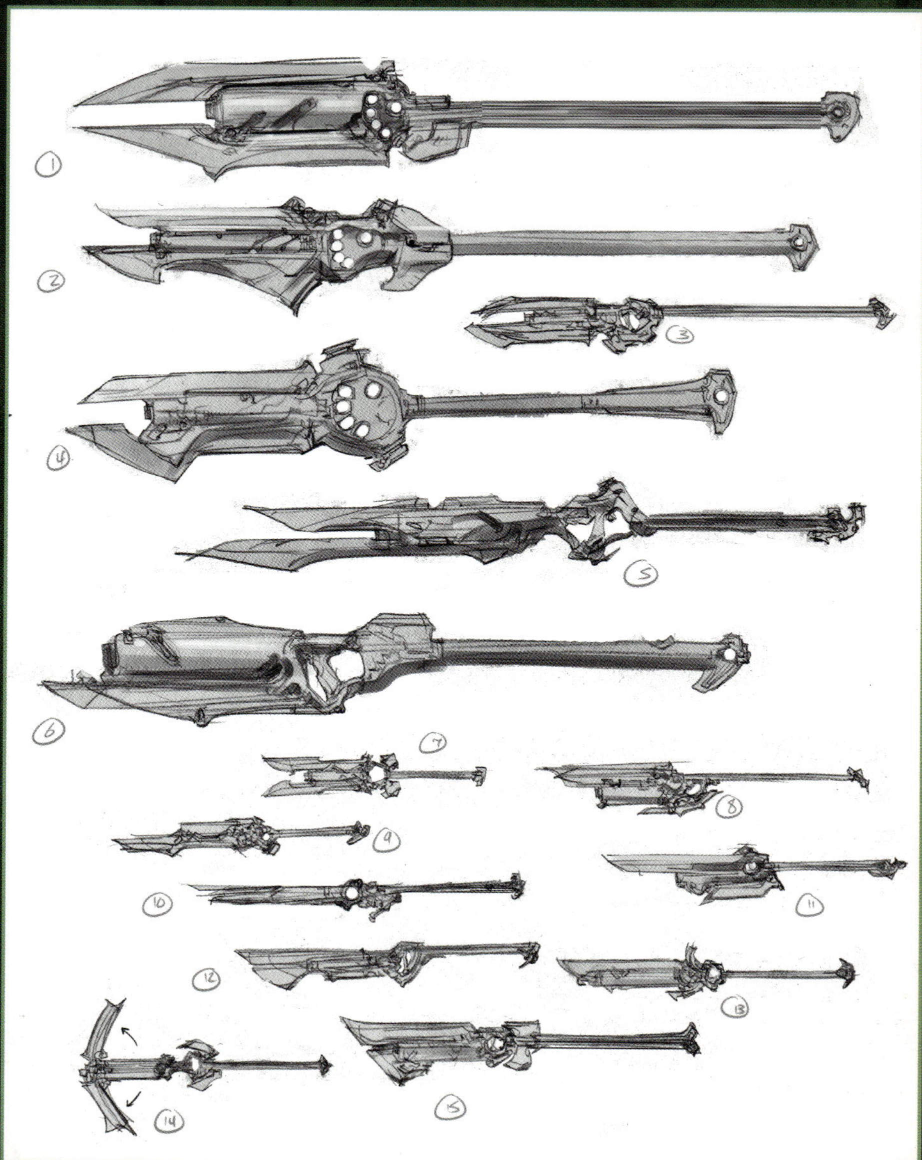

DEVELOPMENT SKETCHES

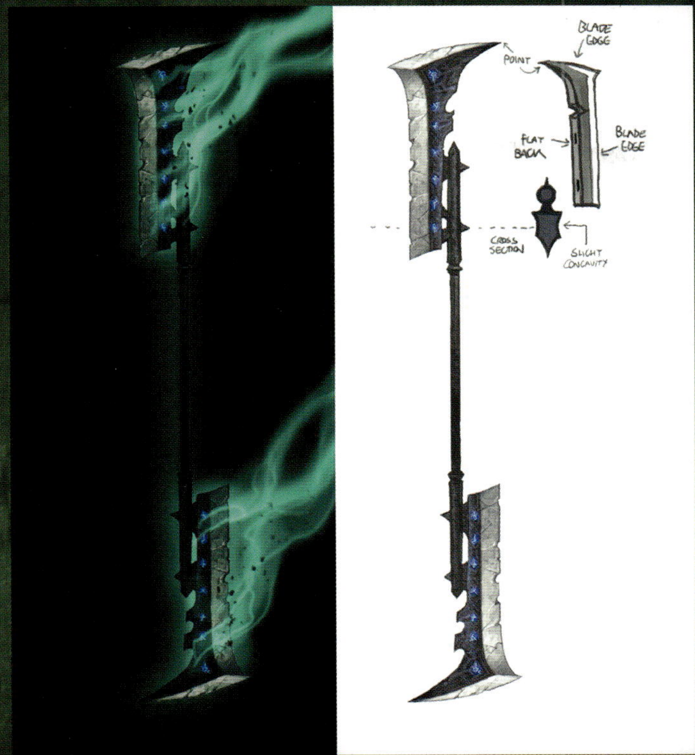

FALLEN ANGEL WEAPON DESIGN

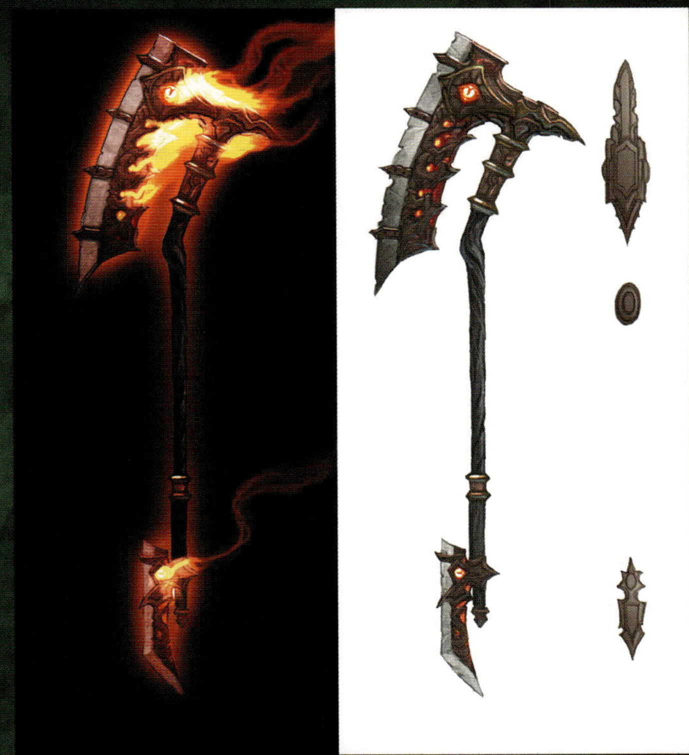

FORSAKEN AXE DESIGN

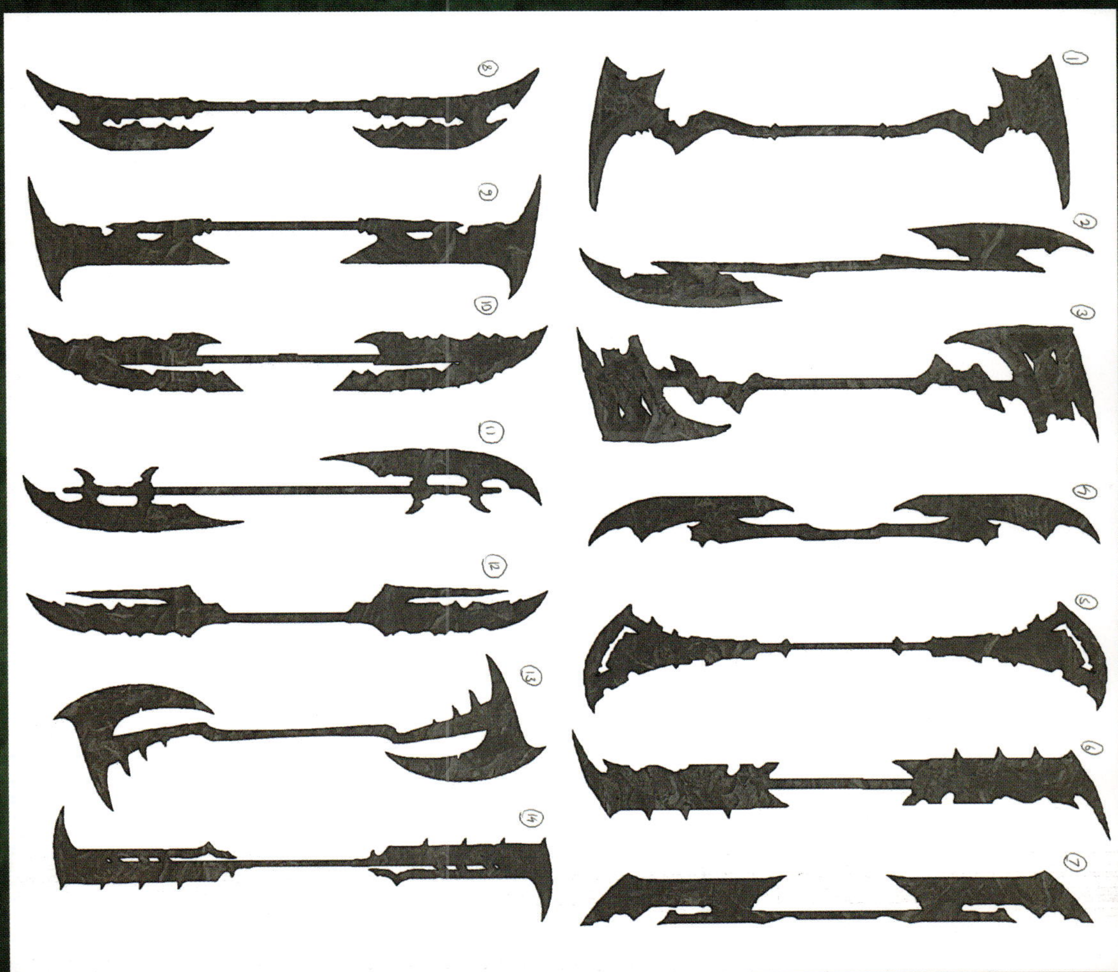

DEVELOPMENT SKETCHES

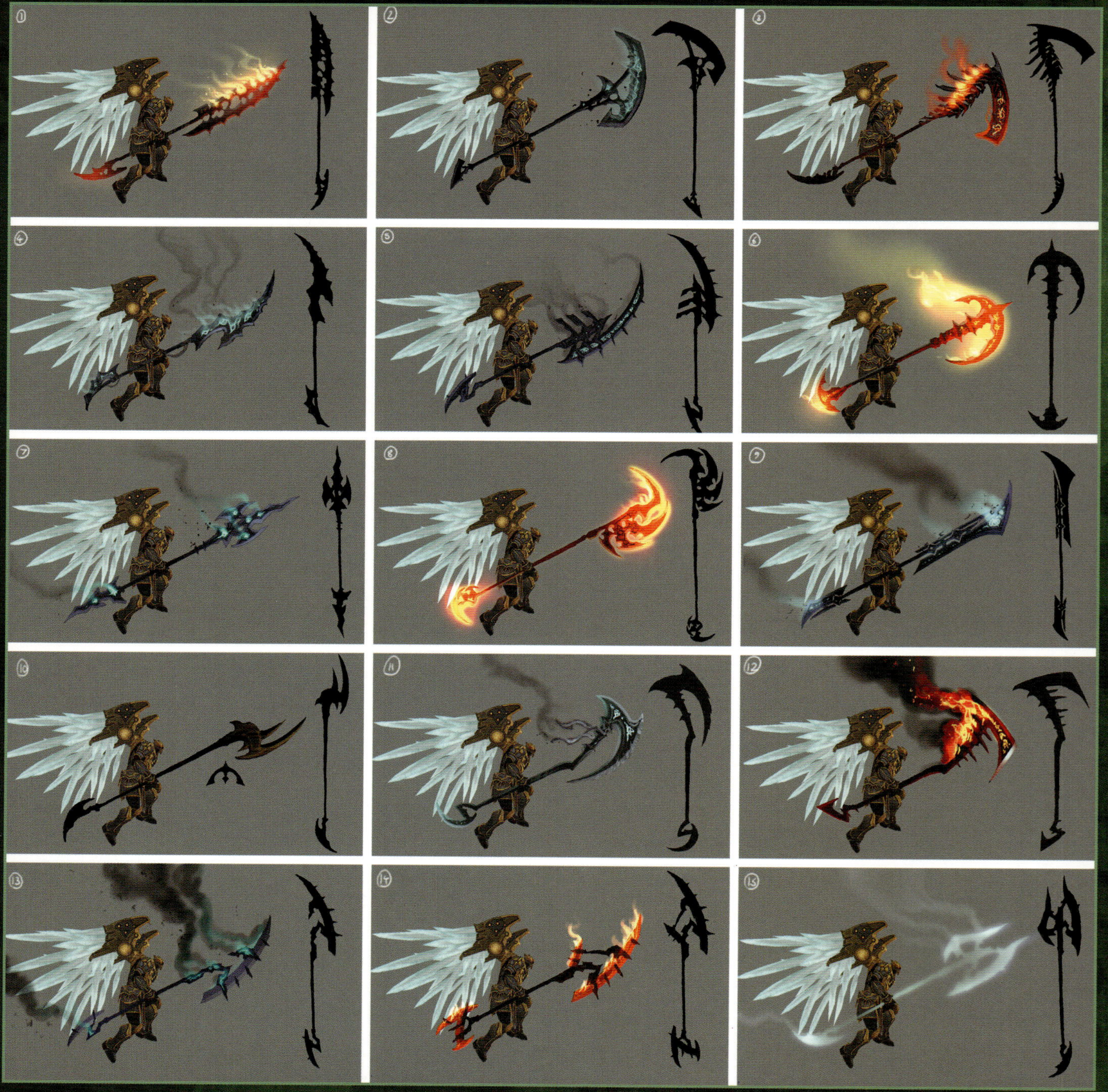

FORSAKEN WEAPON CONCEPTS

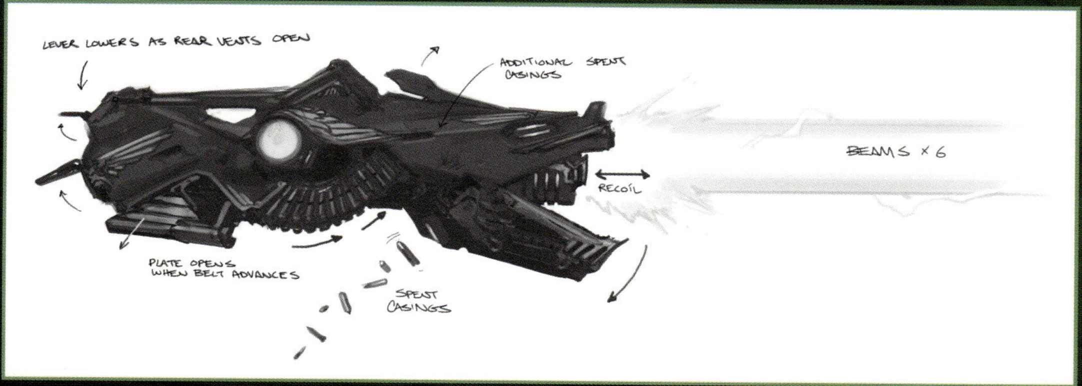

GUN DESIGN

Redemption

What angels lack in claws, teeth, and cruelty, they more than make up for with an arsenal of weaponry. Blazing with the radiance of the White City, Heaven's ordnance can burn away demons and their shadows.

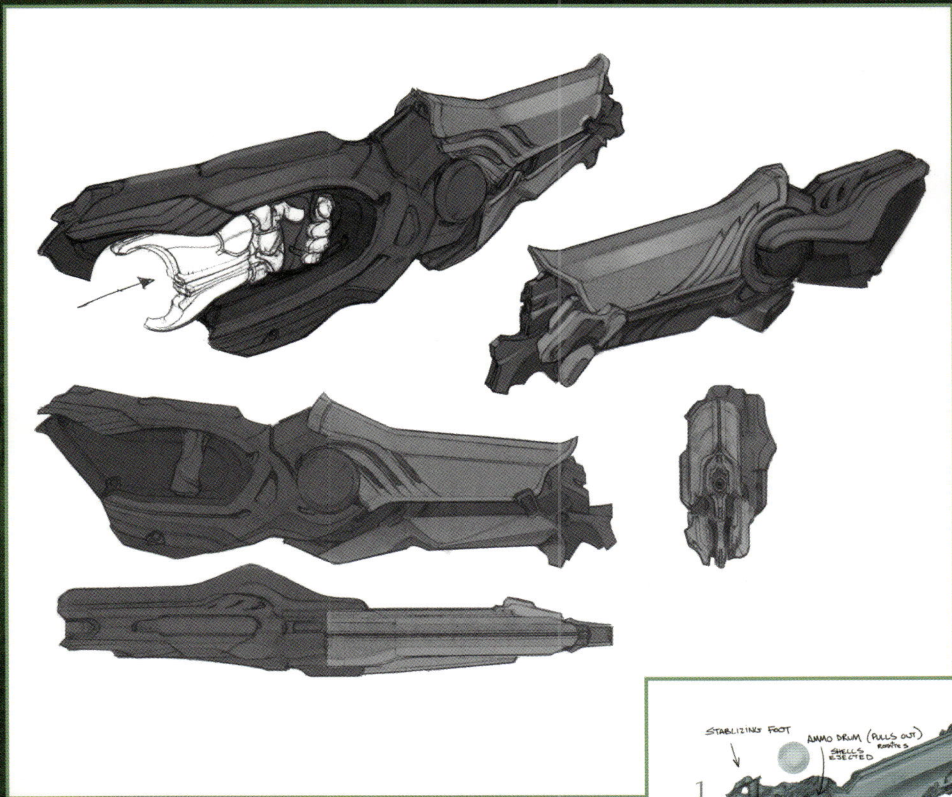

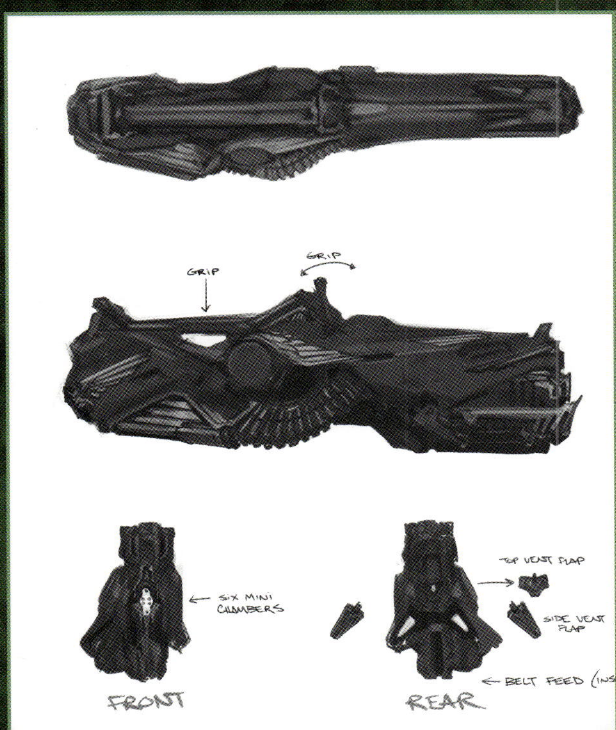

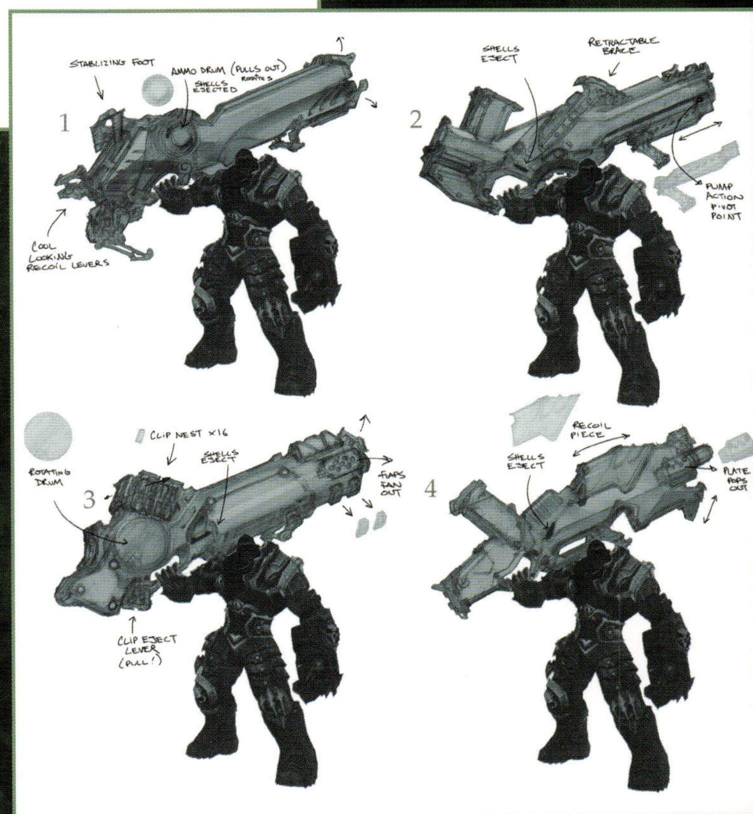

DEVELOPMENT SKETCHES

Redemption is among the greatest of these weapons. More cannon than gun, it fires powerful rounds that punch holes of purifying fire into the dark sky. The spreading flame of each shot is perhaps the truest light now cast upon this Earth.

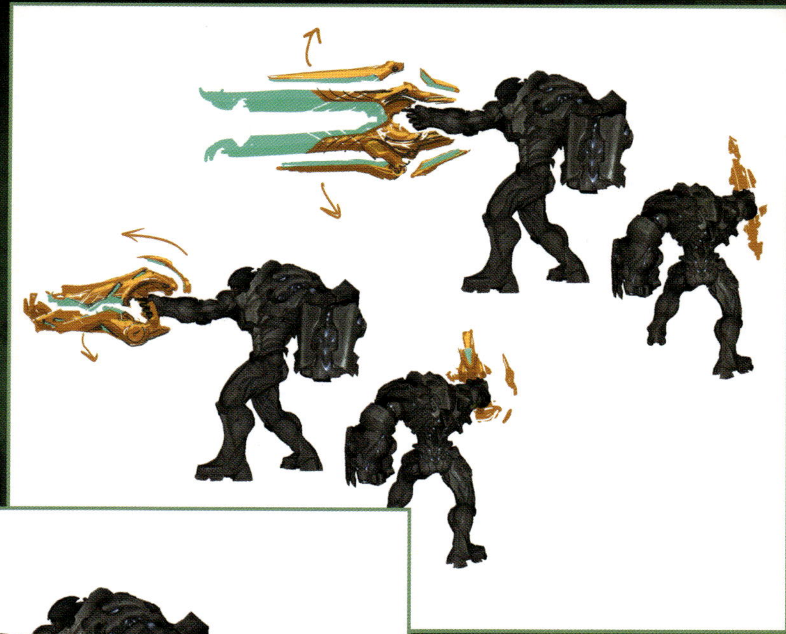

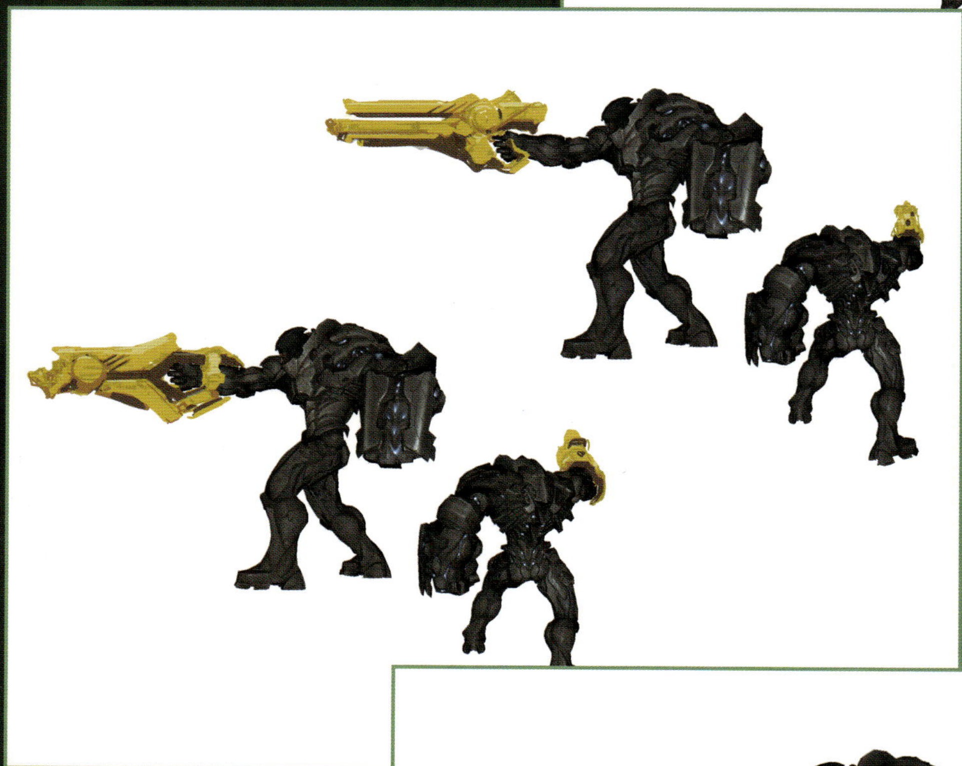

GUN CONCEPTS

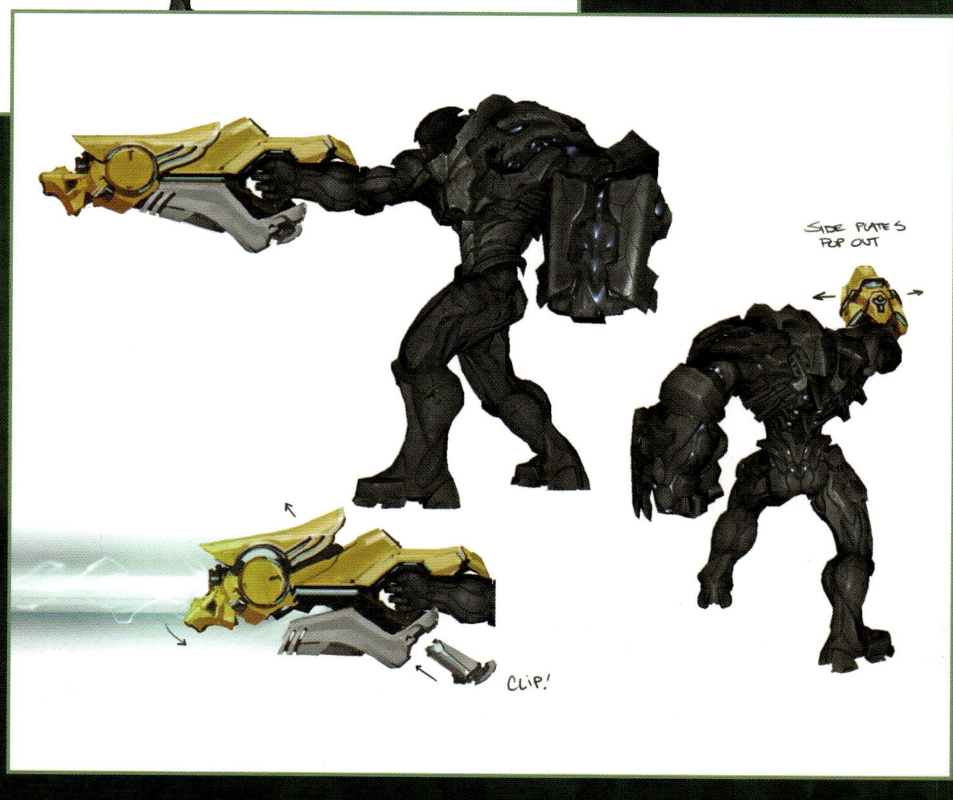

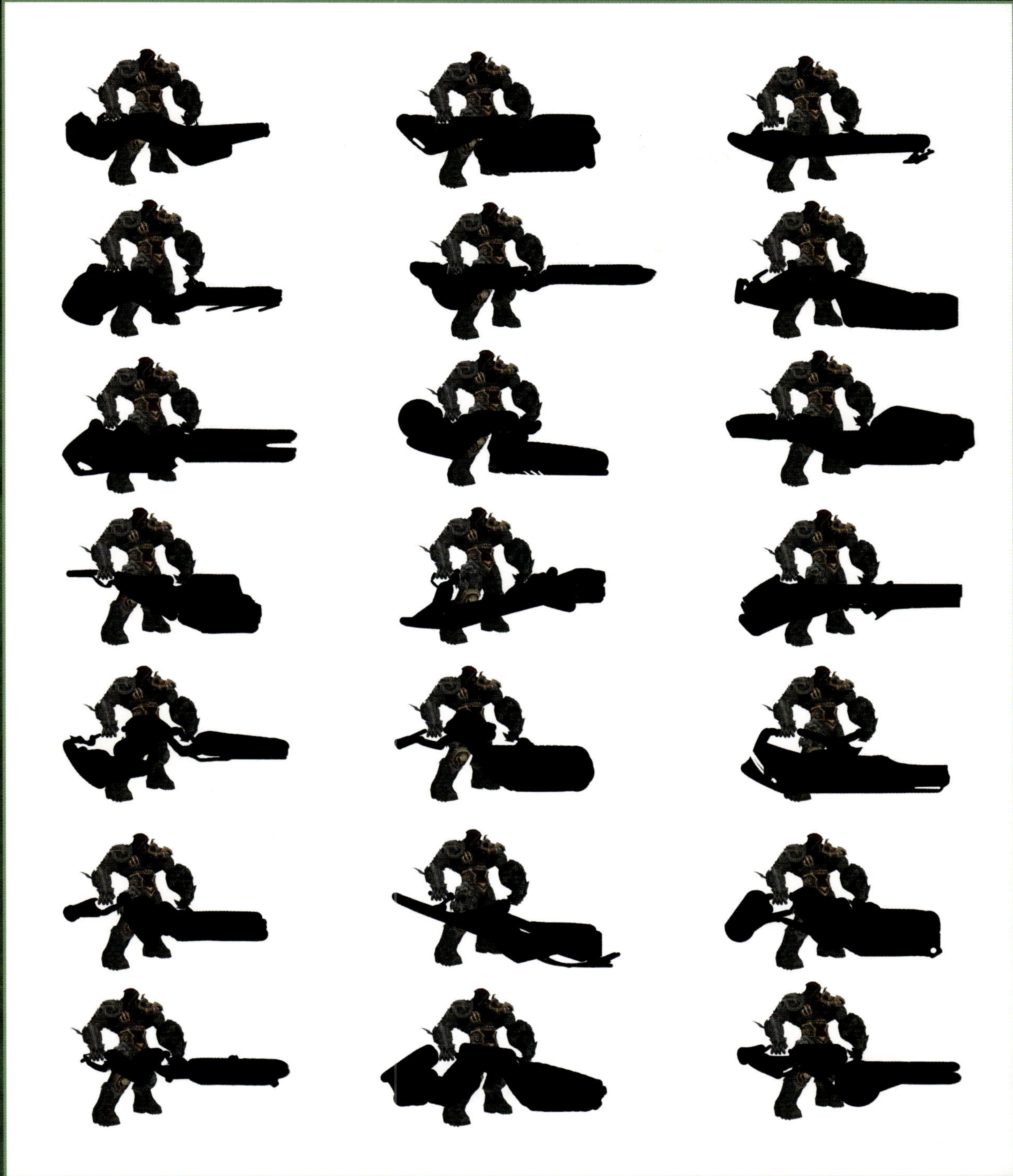

GUN CONCEPTS

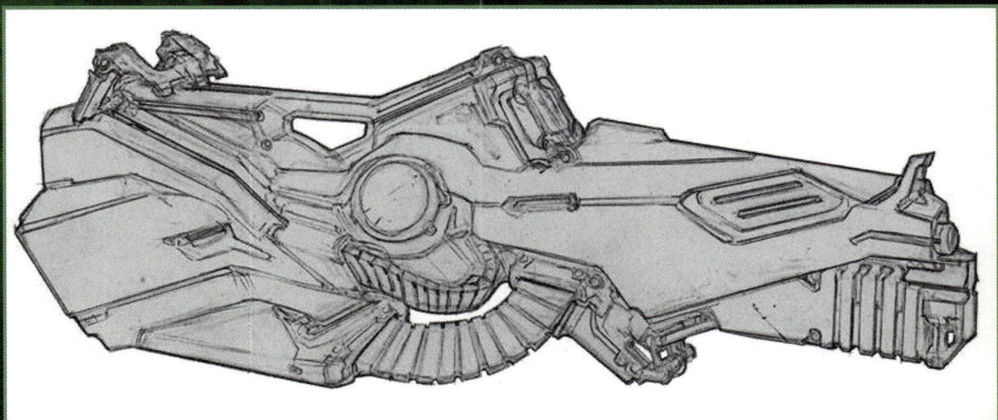

GUN DESIGN

Demon Weapons

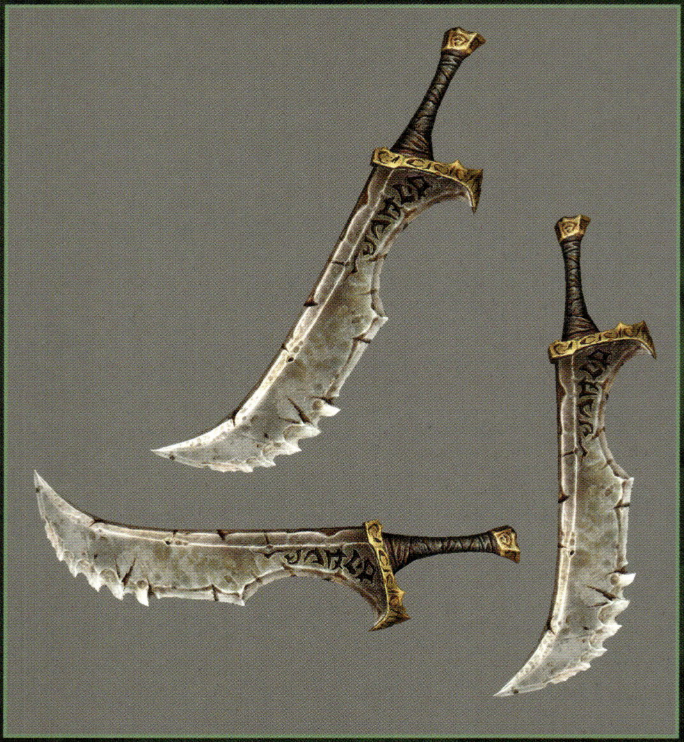

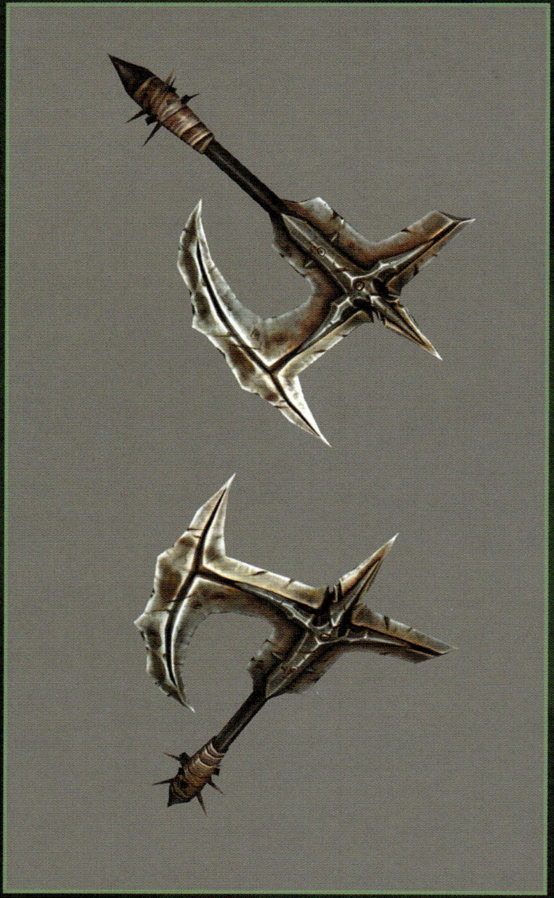

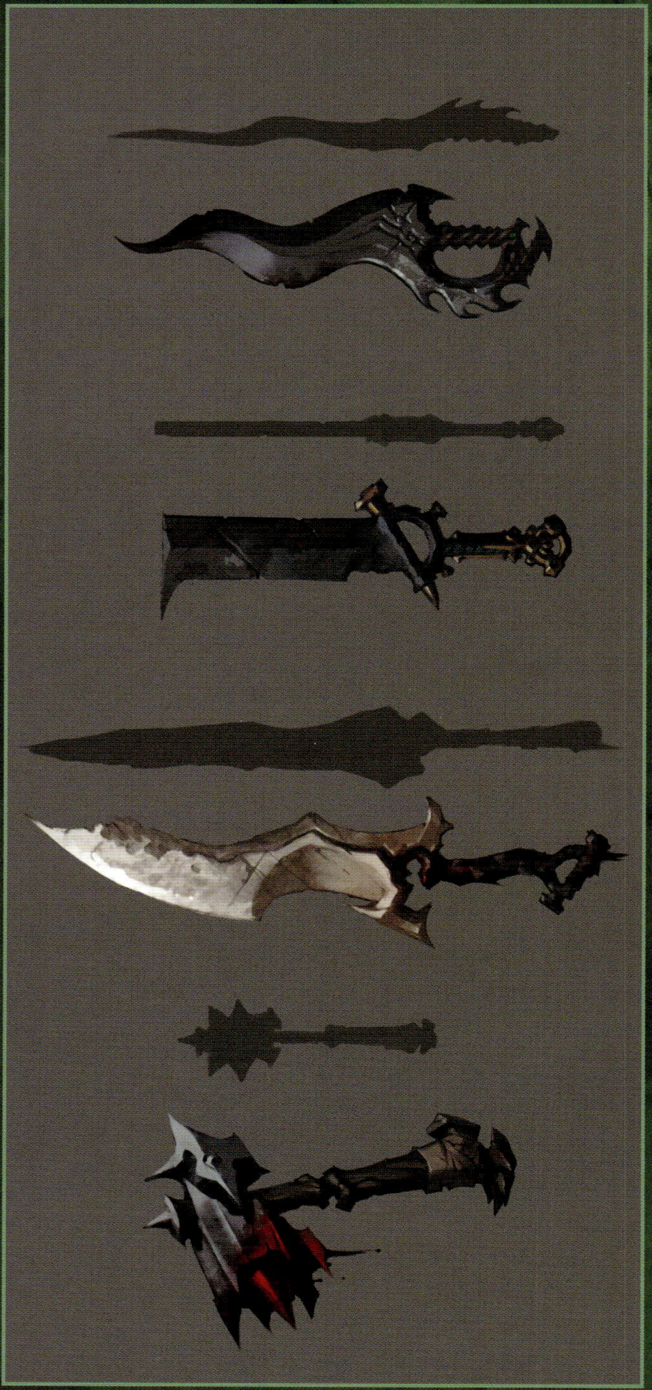

WEAPON DESIGNS

GUN DESIGN

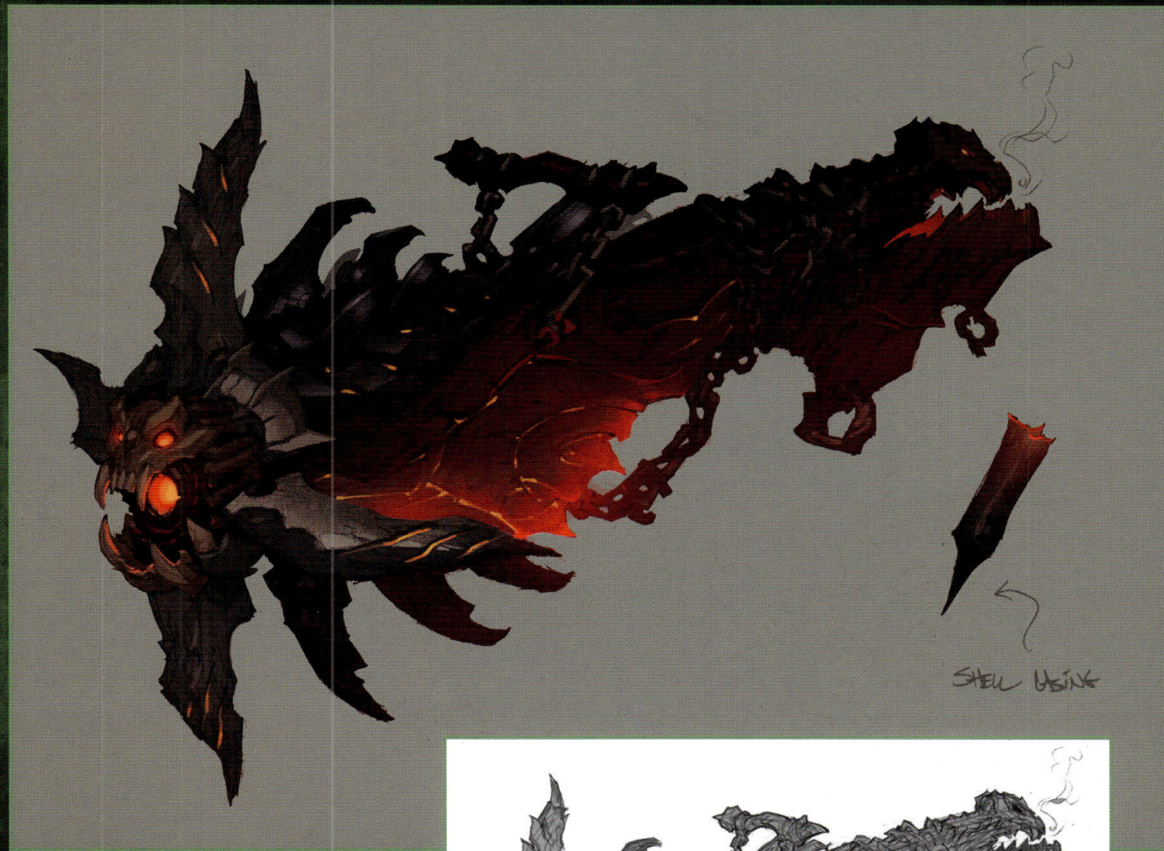

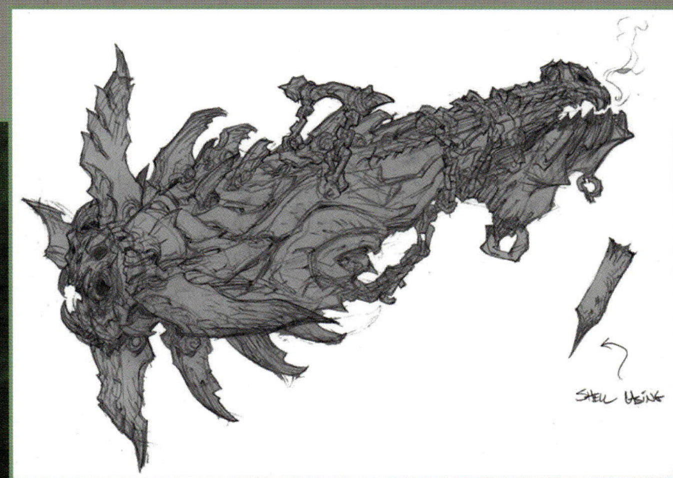

Fracture Cannon

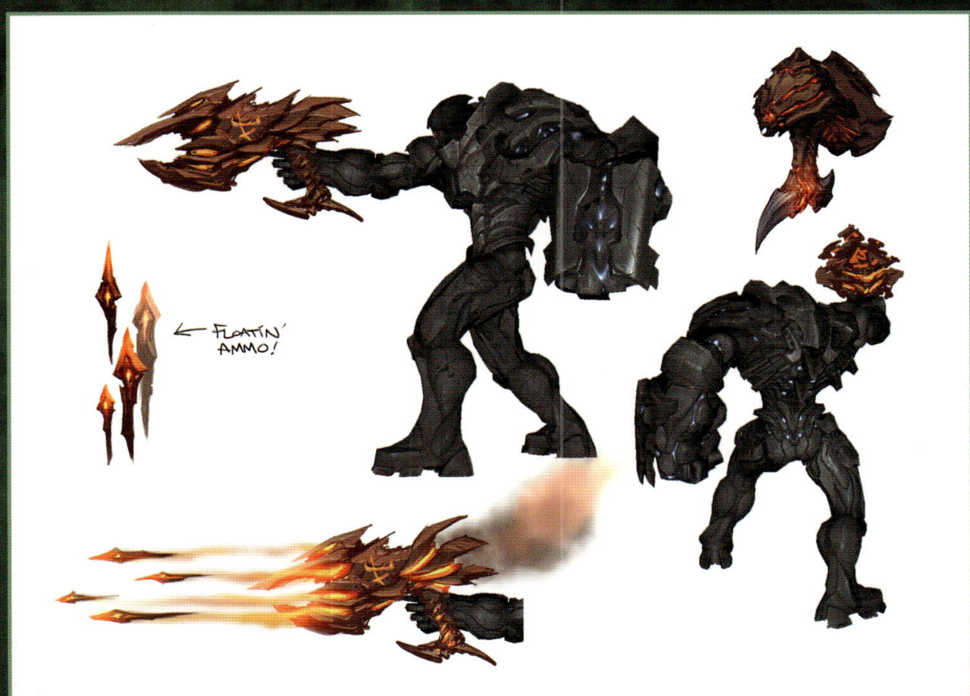

GUN CONCEPTS

It takes but one glance to understand the Fracture Cannon's terrible purpose. It is a ghoulish instrument of death, with a massive barrel, notched spikes, chains, and a fiendish skull. The cannon fires obsidian bolts that tear through flesh like wet paper—and explode into greedy flame. Even at range, the rolling thunder of each shot can shatter armor as well as bone. It is a small mercy that few are strong enough to wield this immense weapon.

Hordeseeker

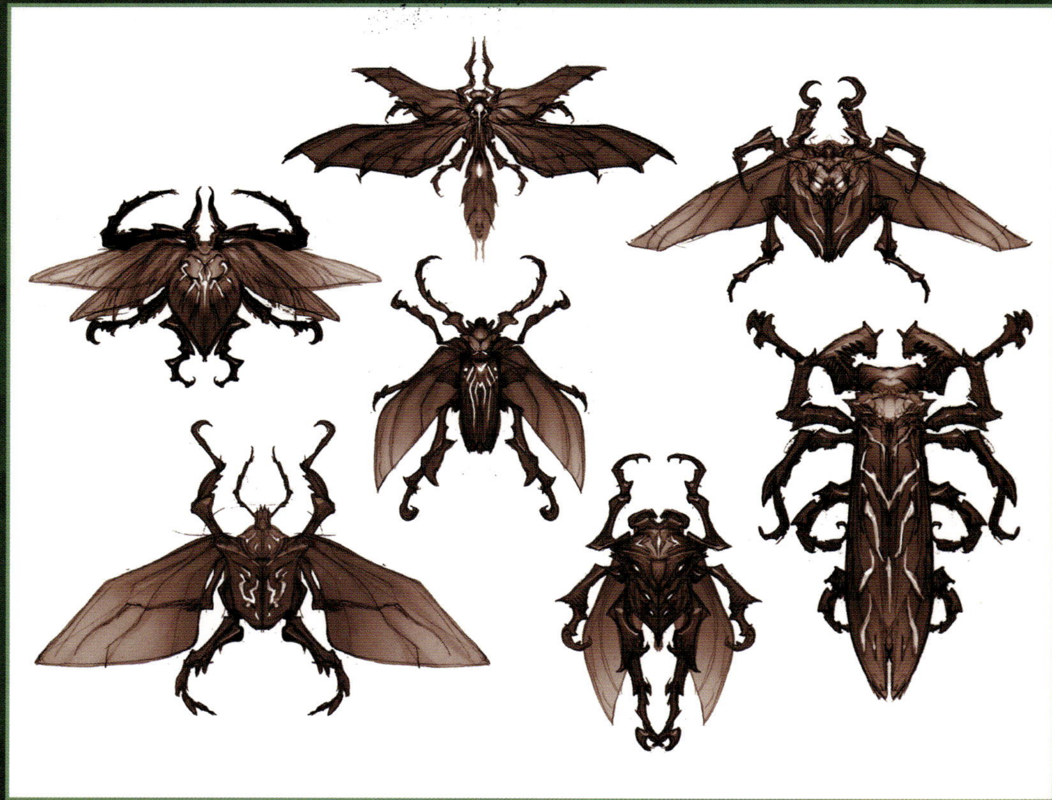

DEVELOPMENT SKETCHES

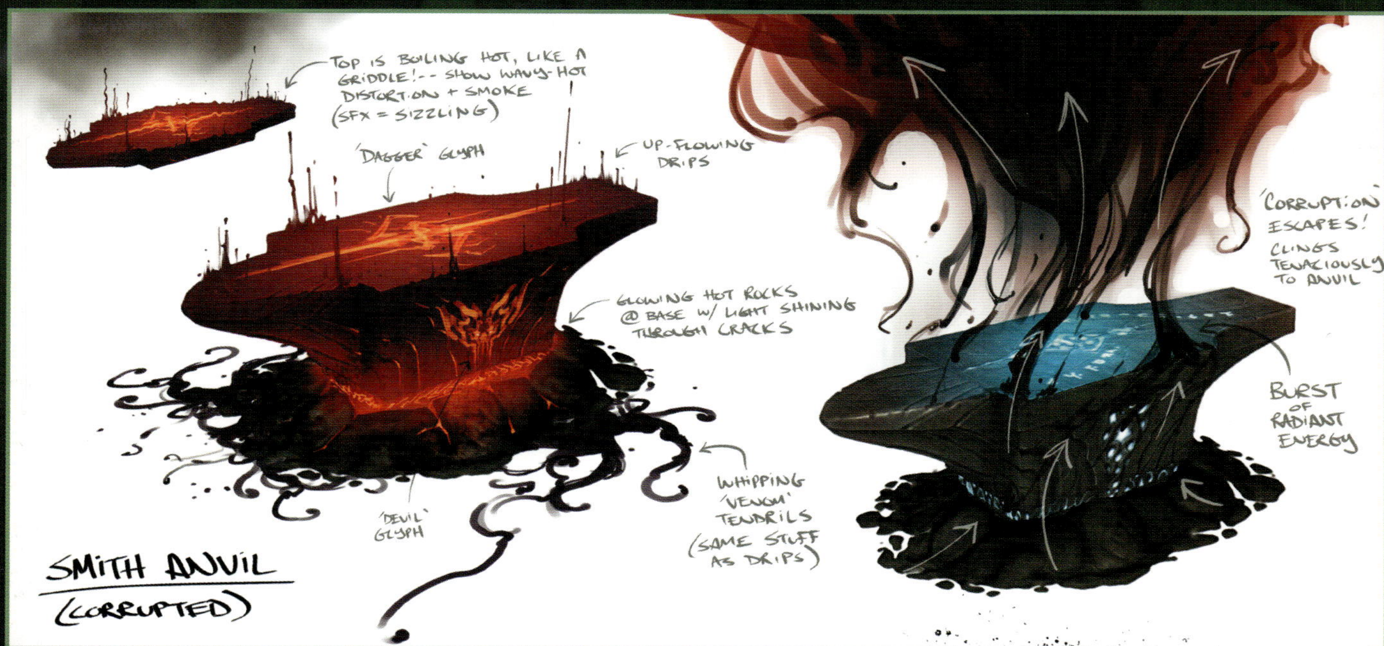

ANVIL DESIGN

Anvil

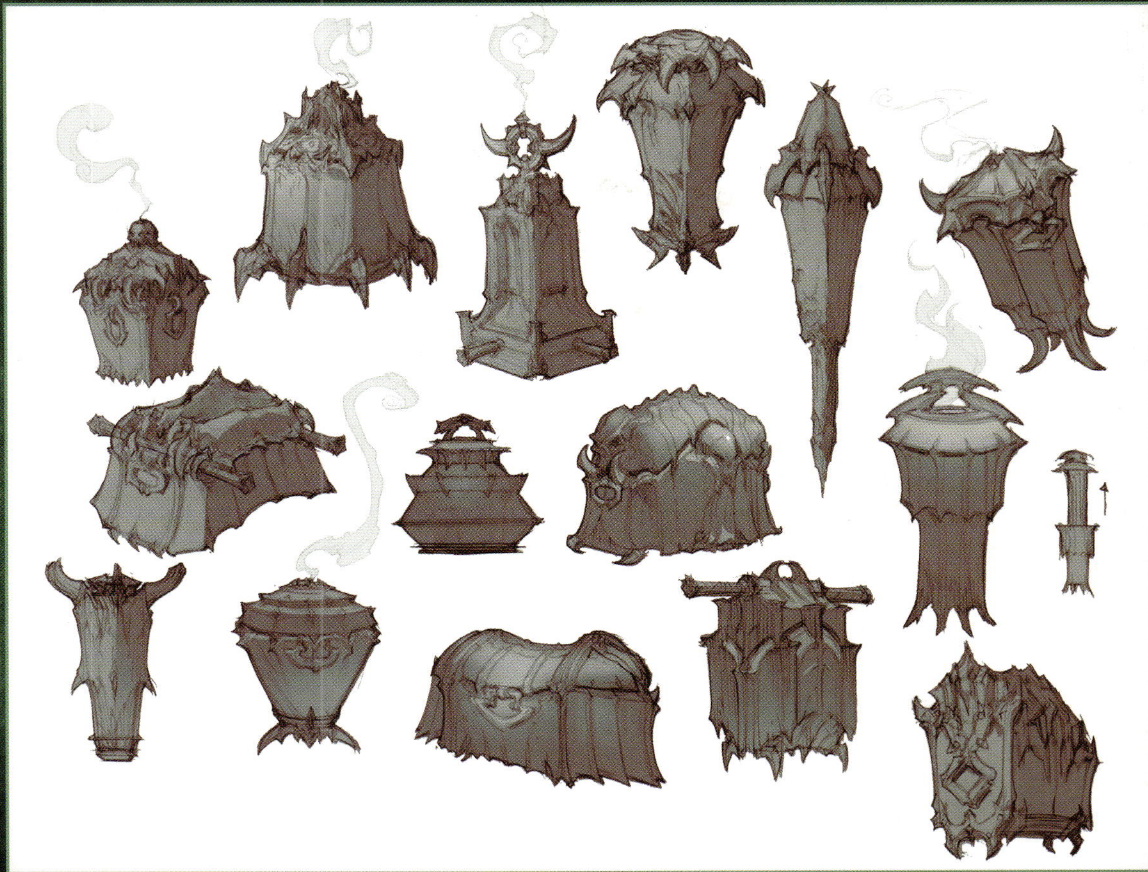

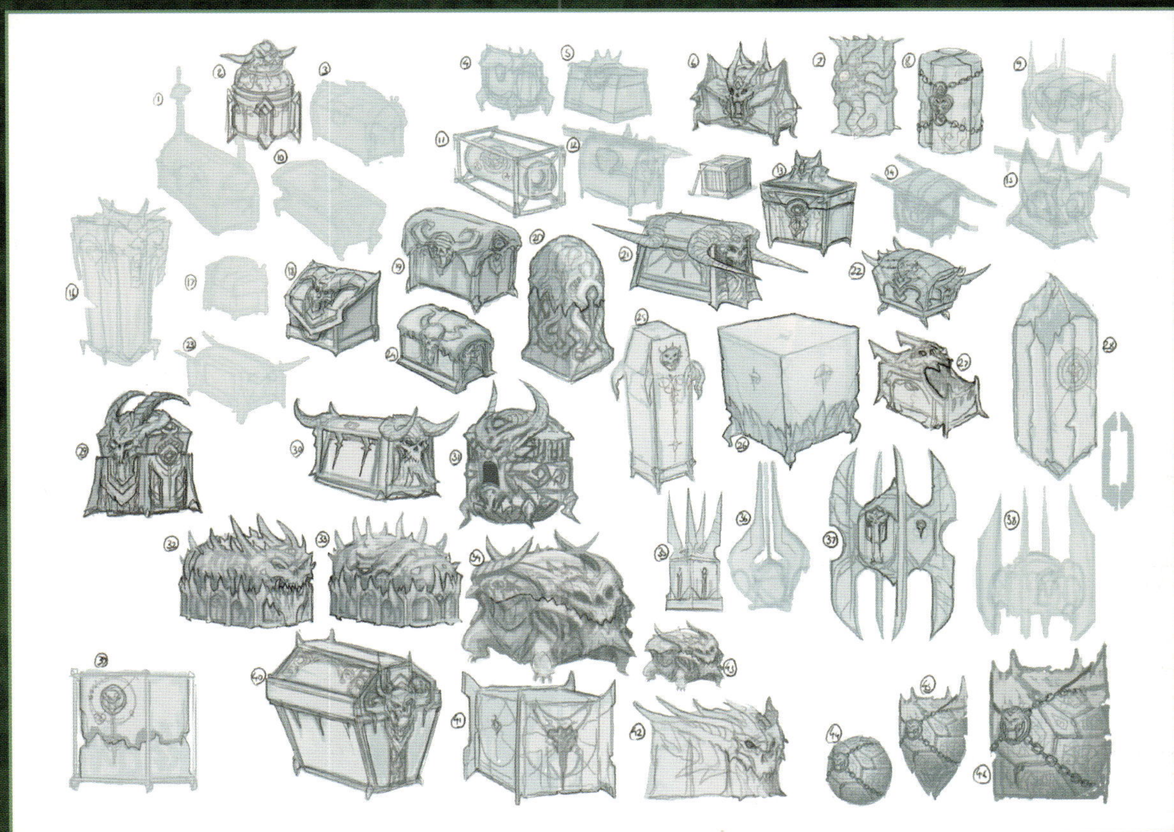

DEVELOPMENT SKETCHES

Caskets

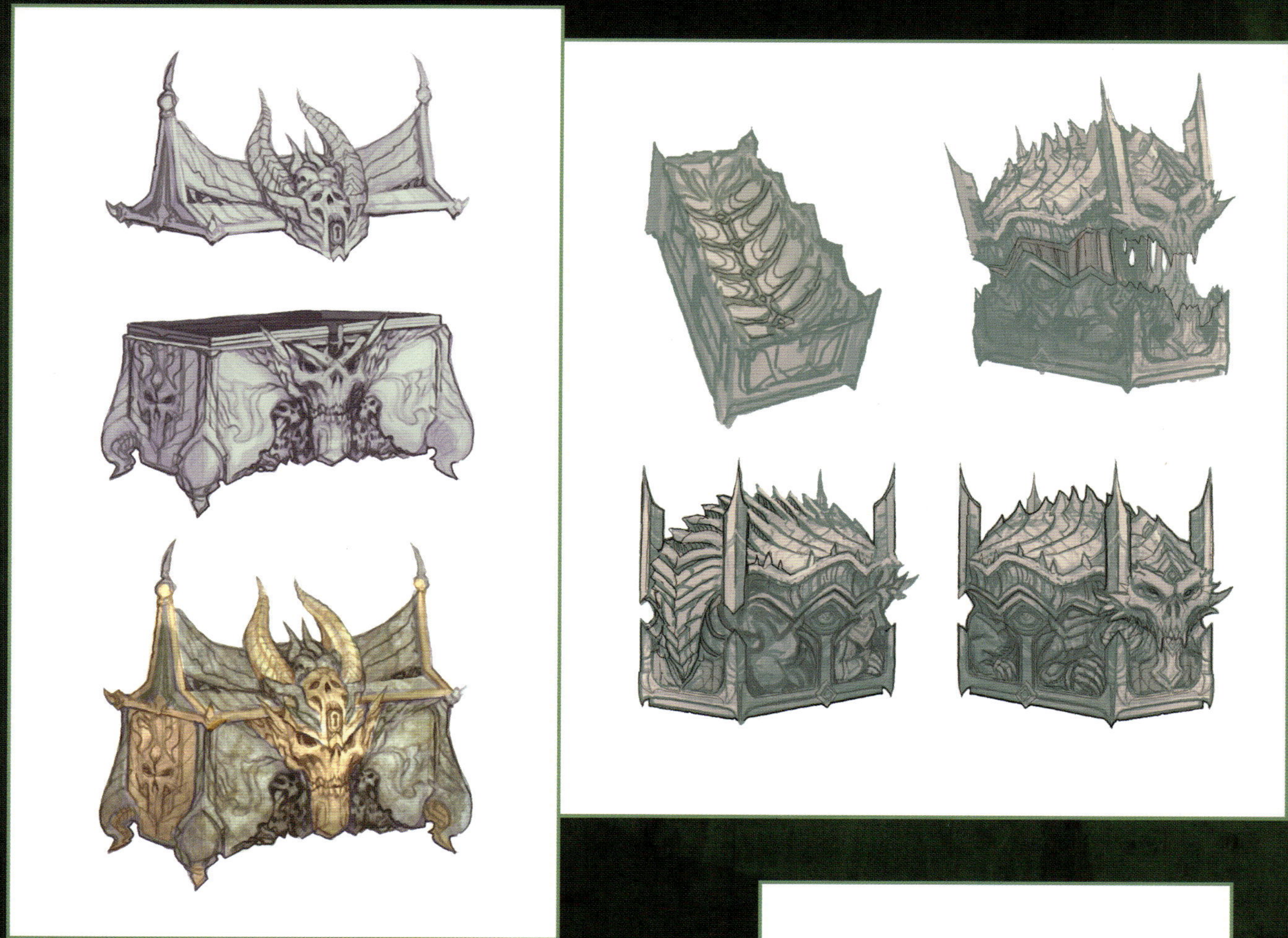

CASKET DESIGNS

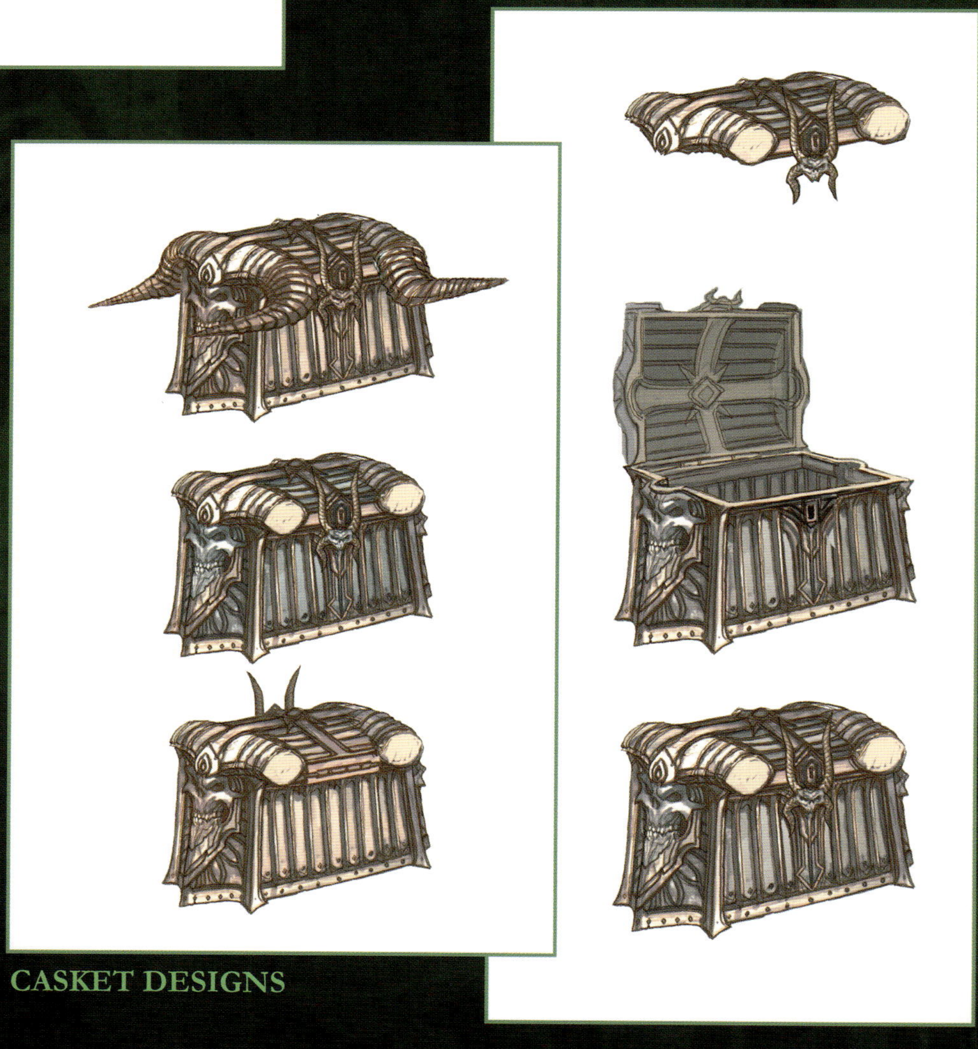

CASKET DESIGNS

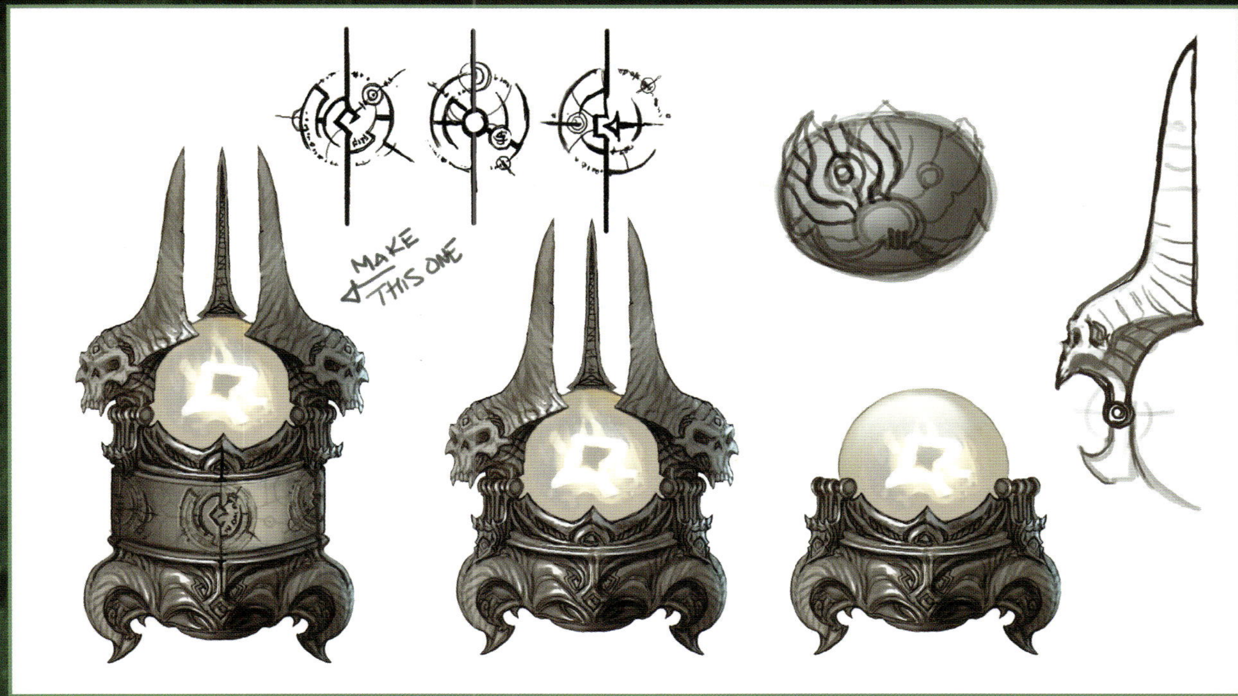

RARE CASKET DESIGNS

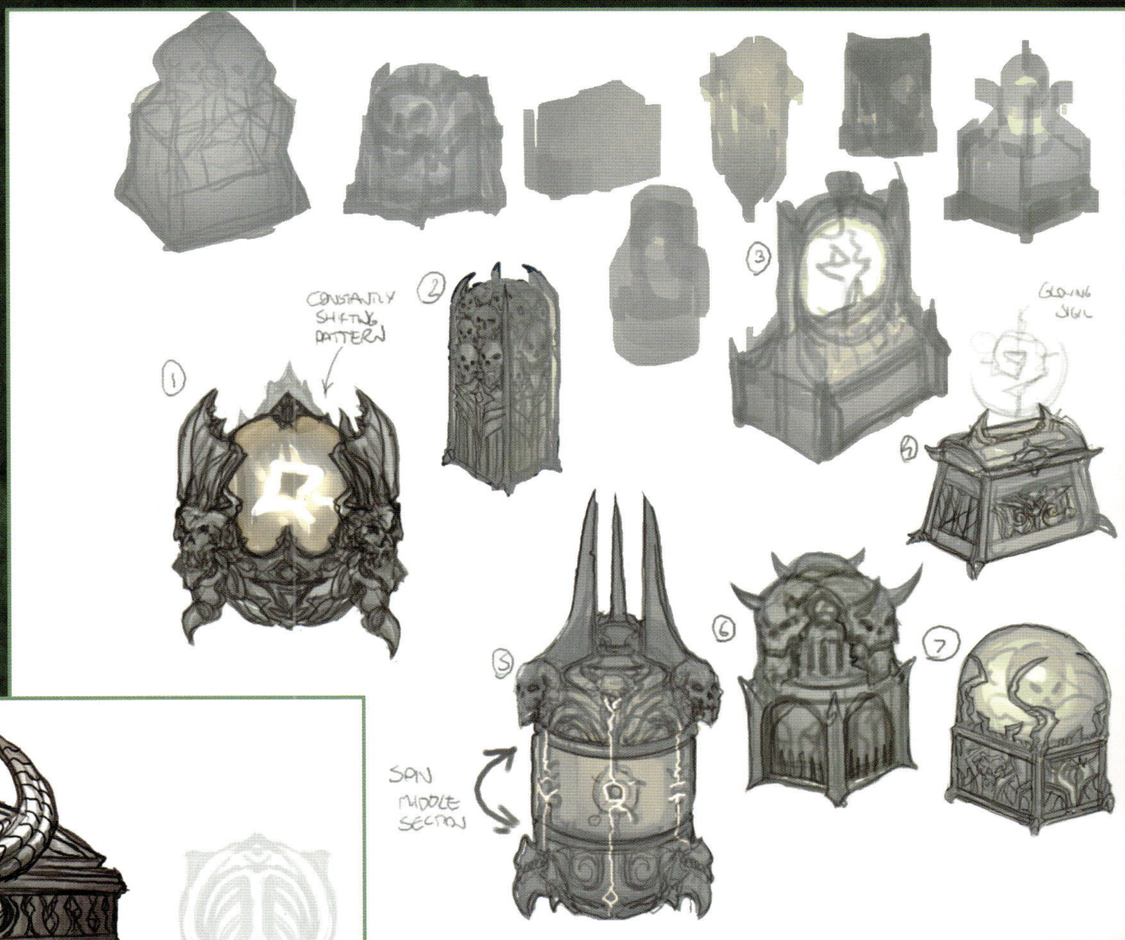

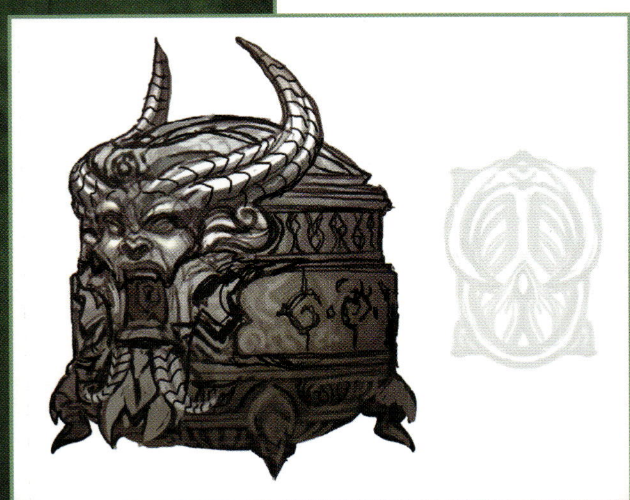

DEVELOPMENT SKETCHES

Artifacts

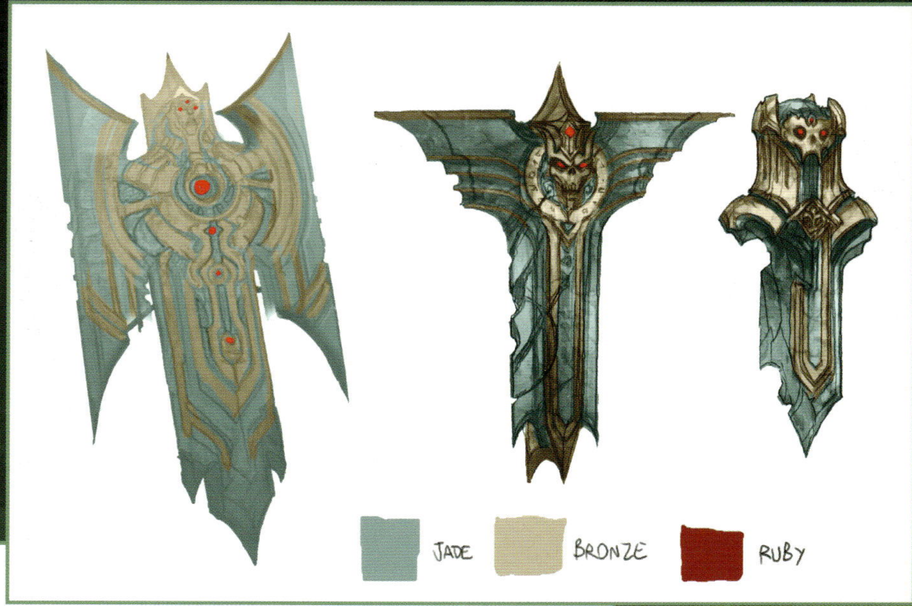

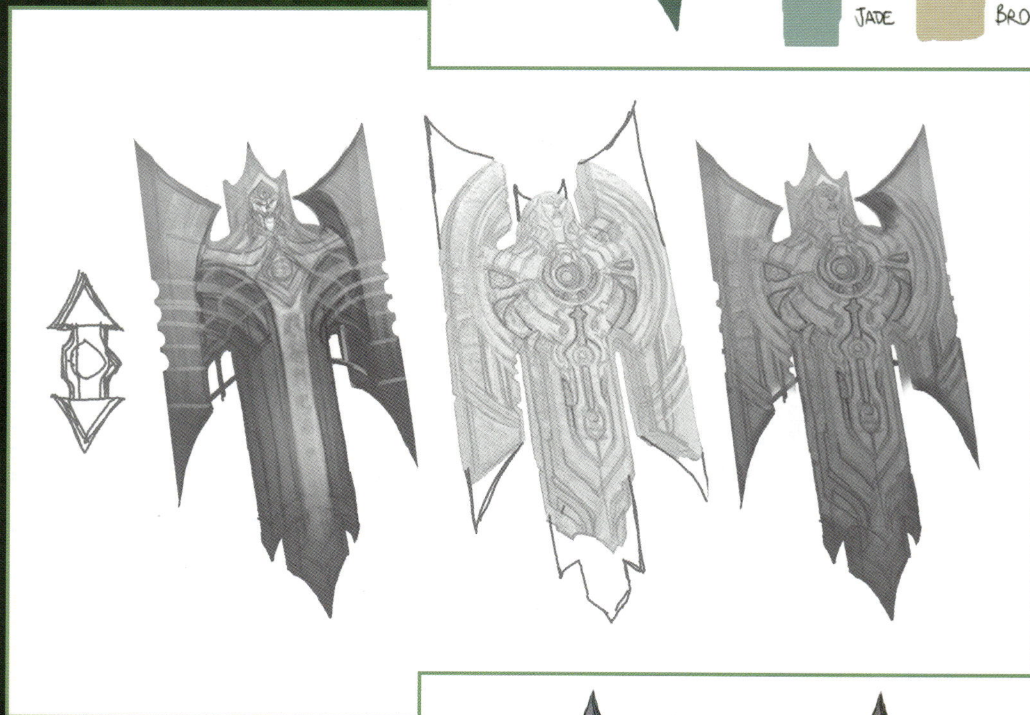

ARTIFACT DESIGNS

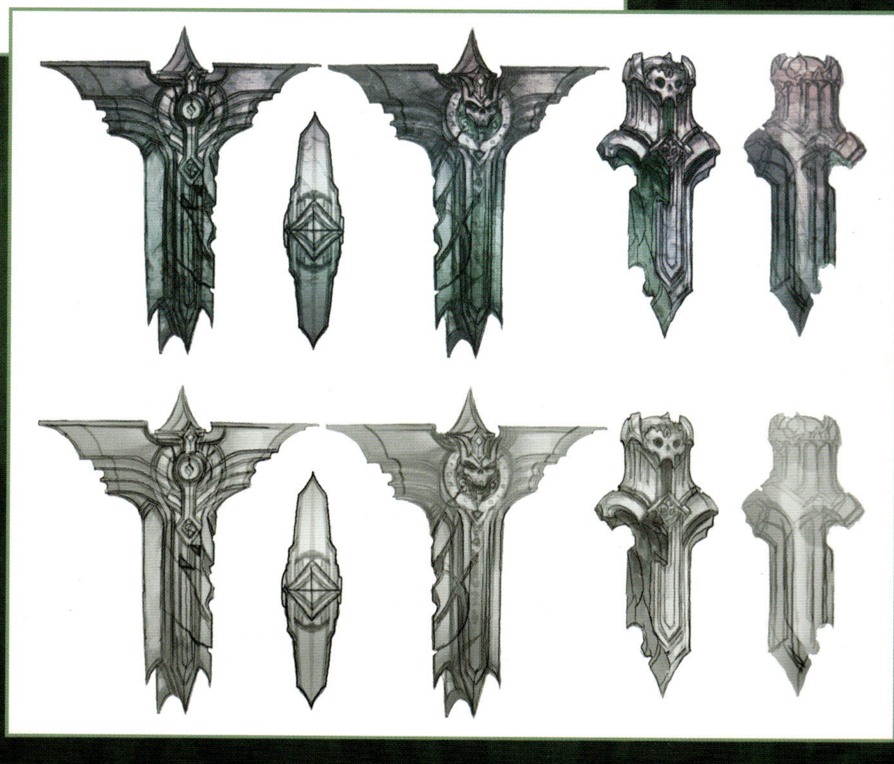

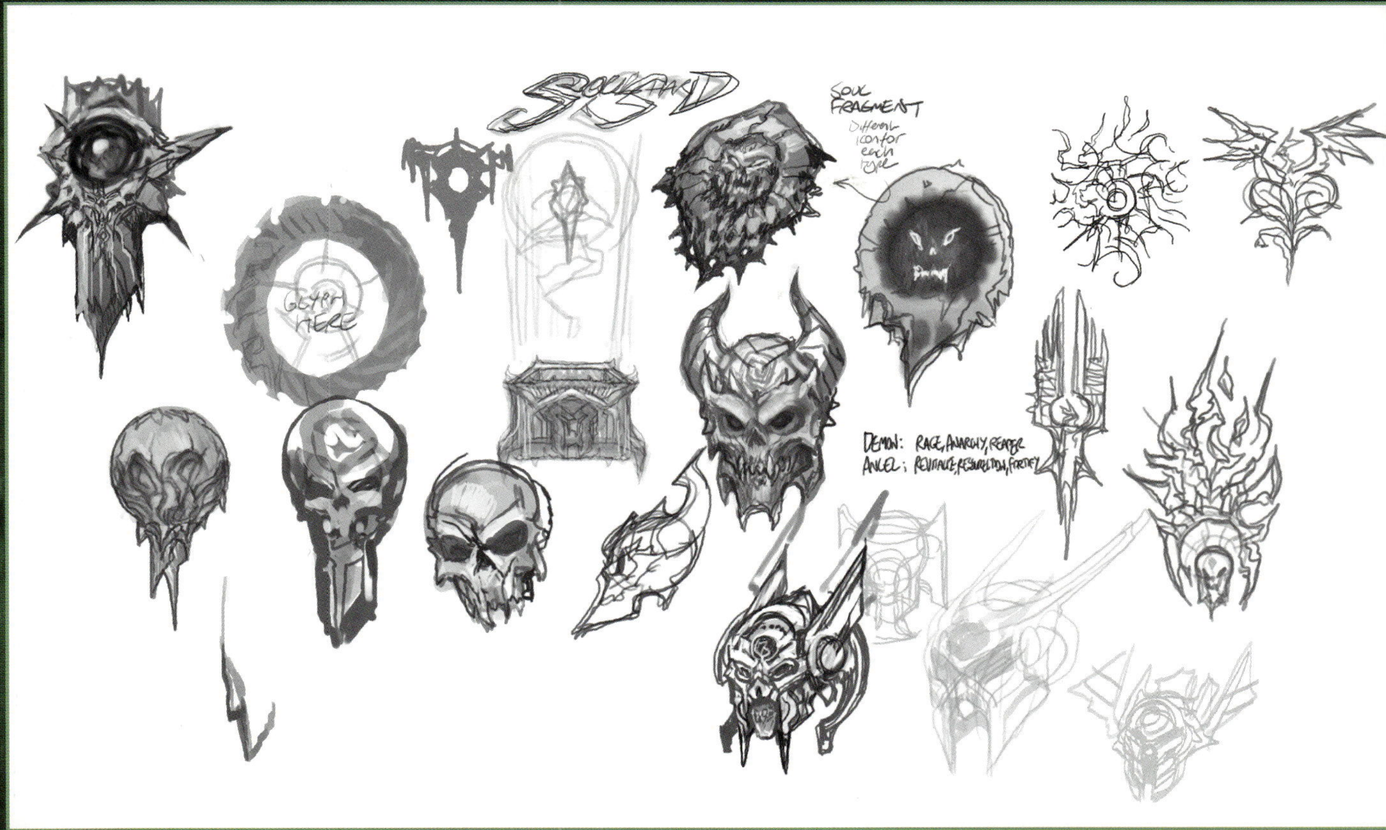

ITEM CONCEPTS

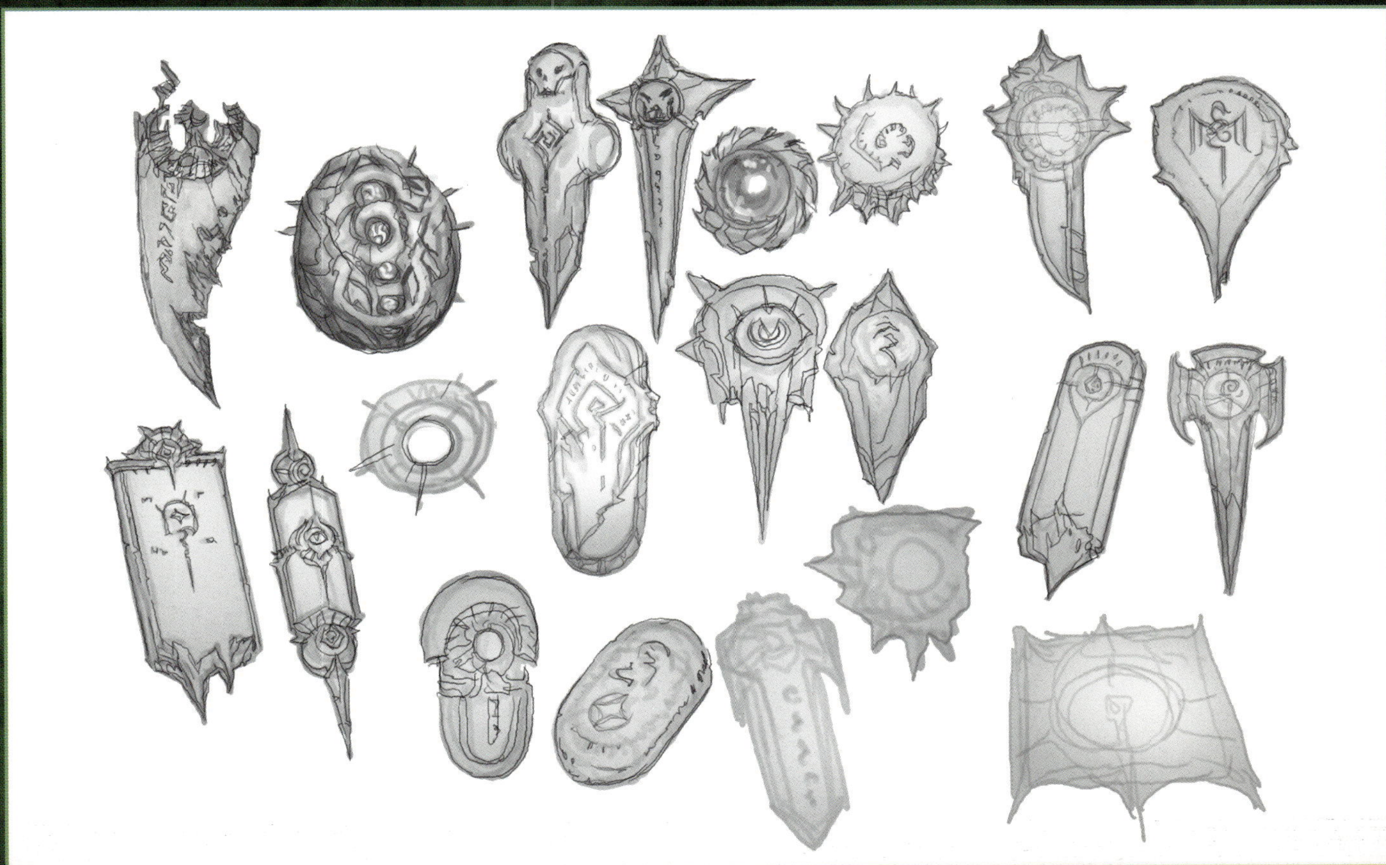

ITEM CONCEPTS

ITEM CONCEPTS

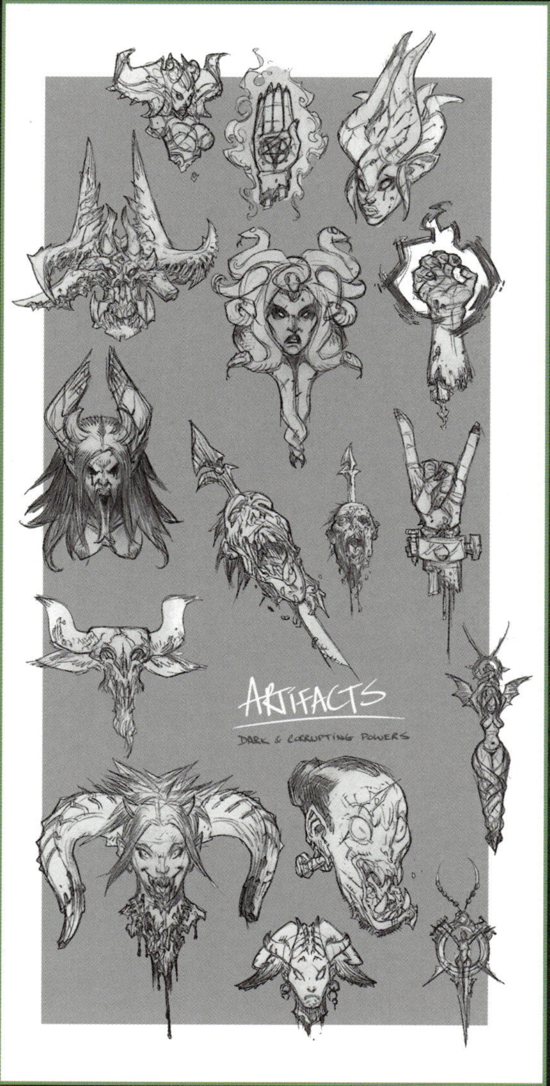

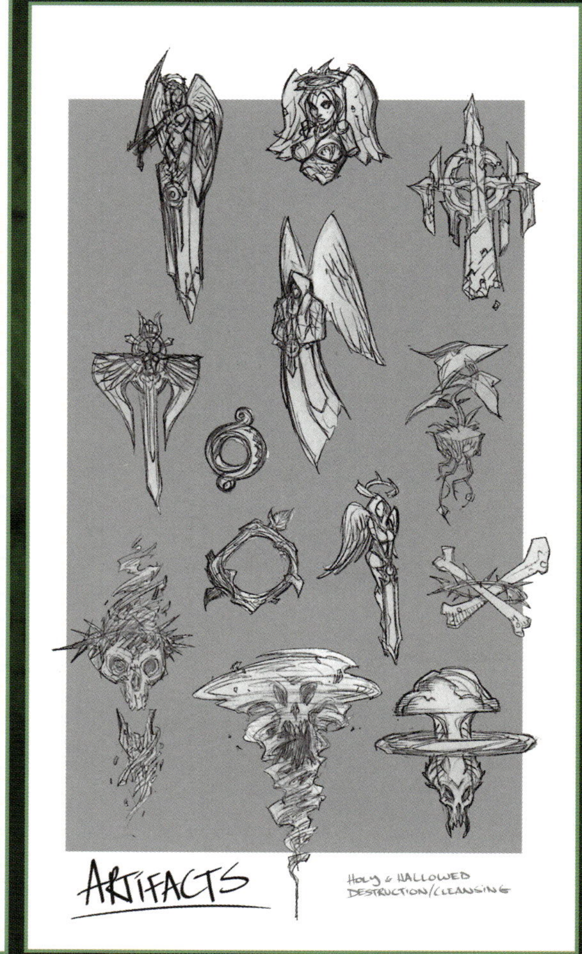

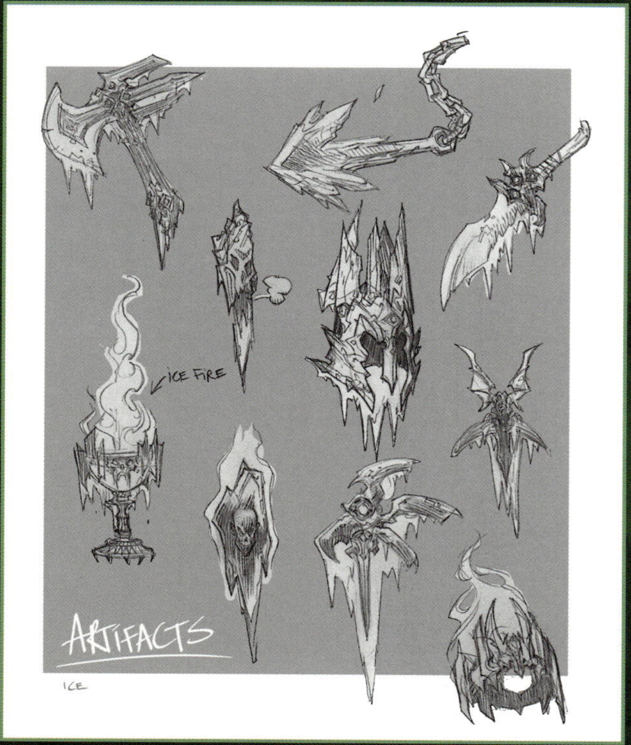

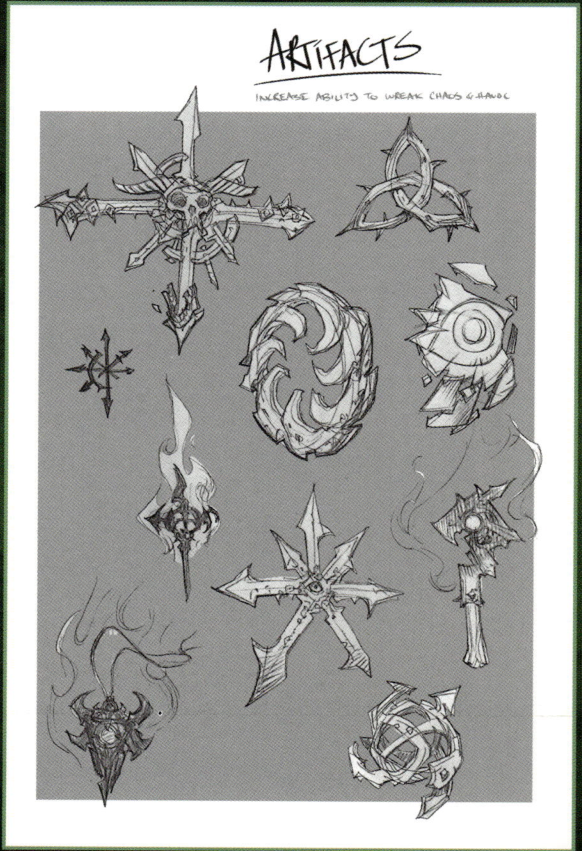

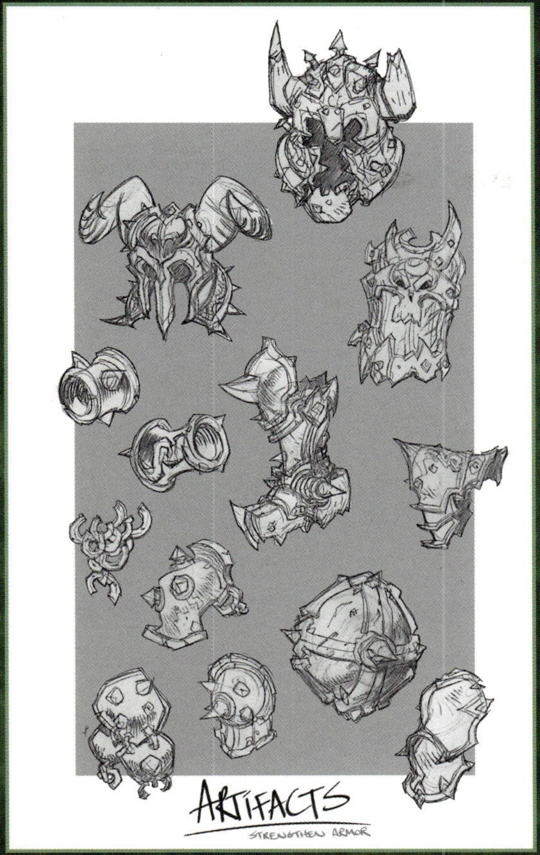

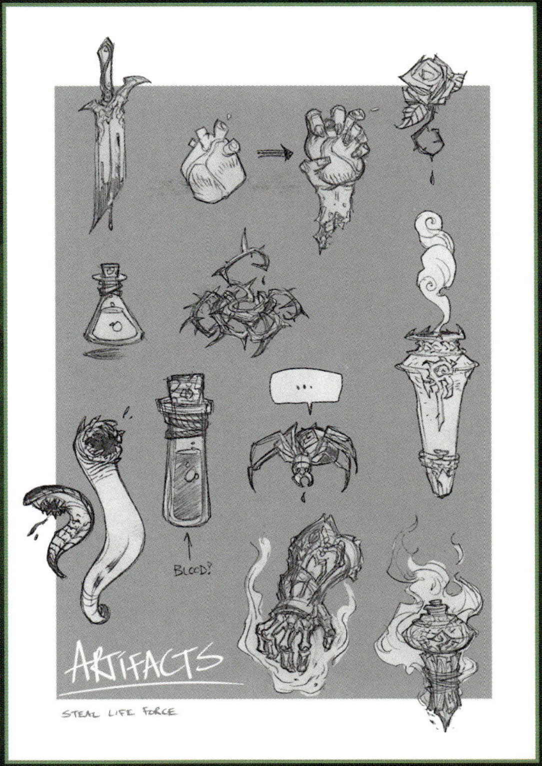

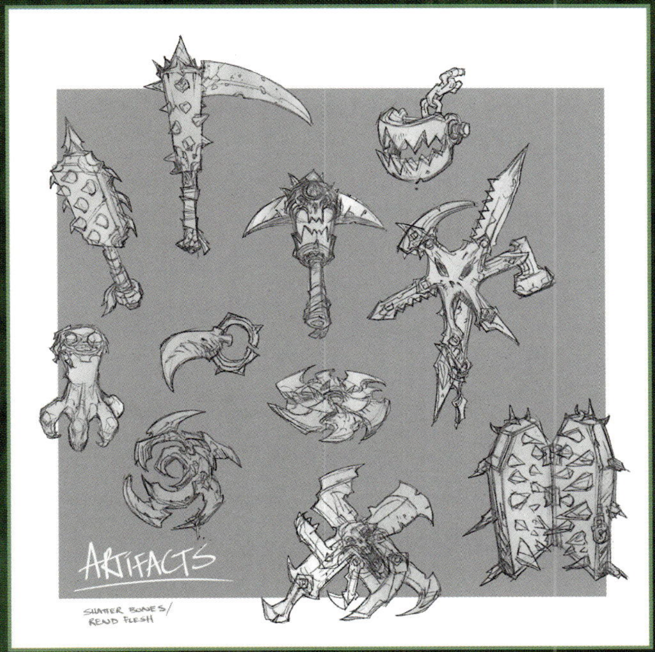

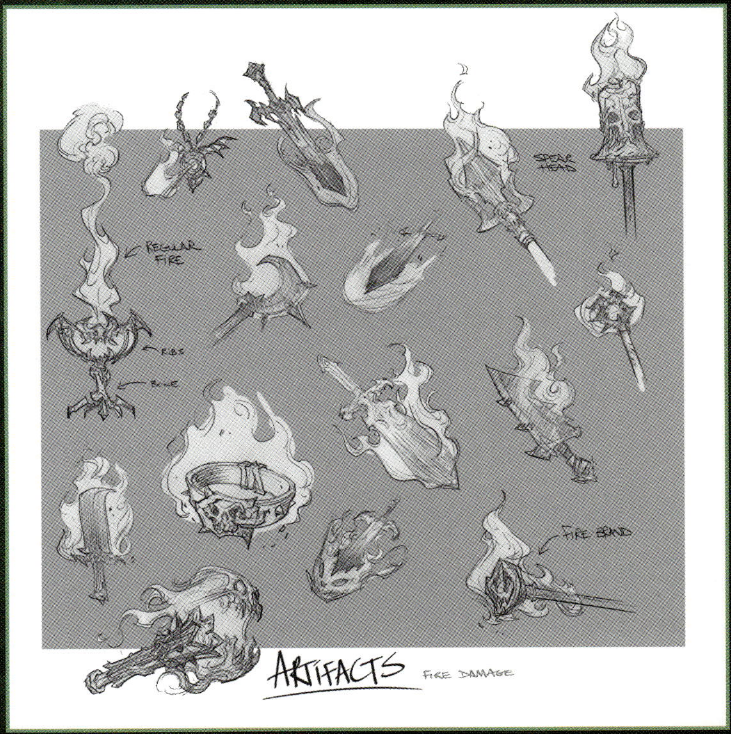

ITEM CONCEPTS

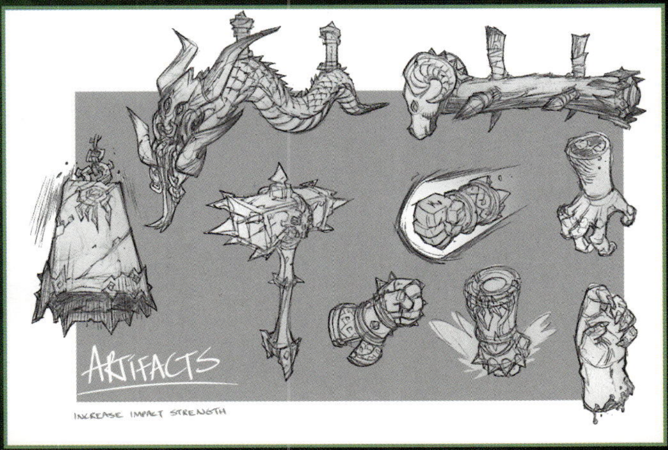

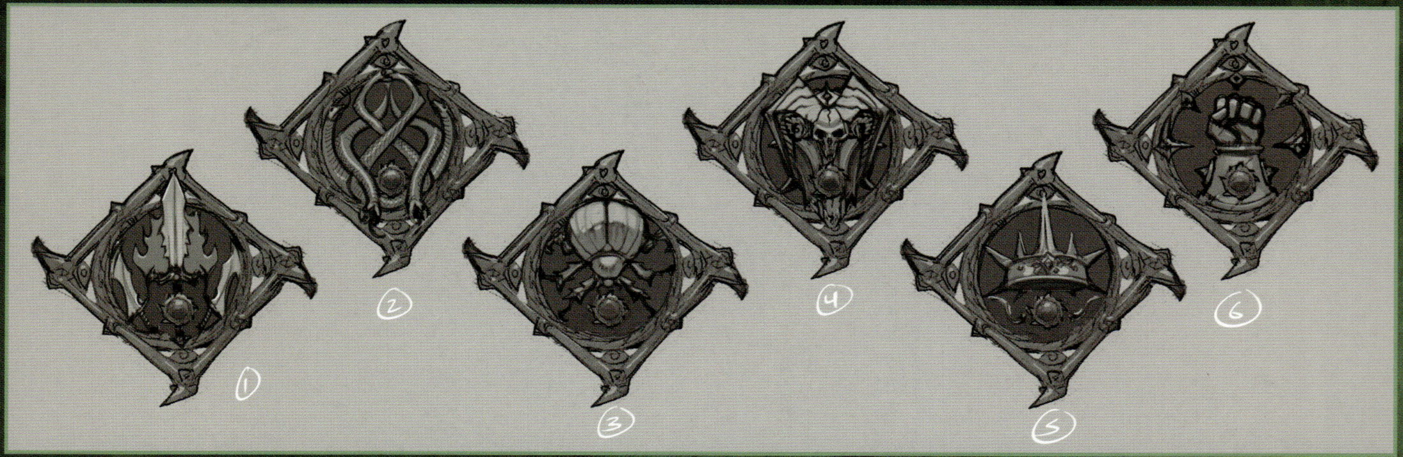

SEAL DESIGNS

The Seven Seals

SEVENTH SEAL DESIGNS

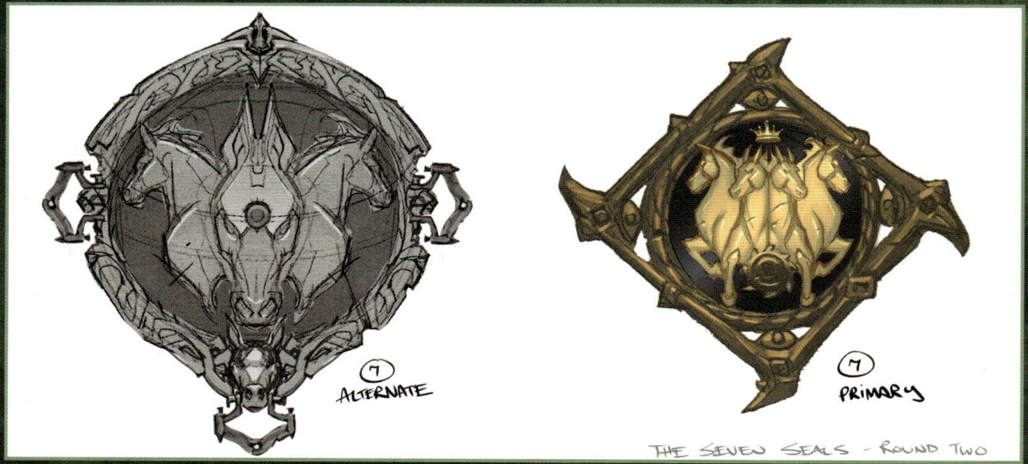

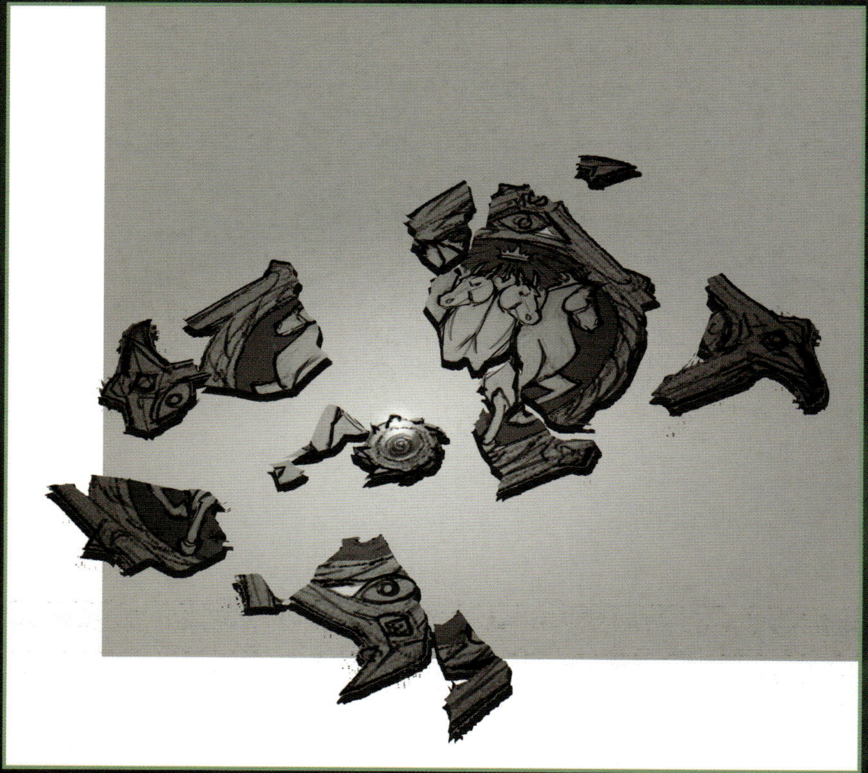

BROKEN SEAL CONCEPT

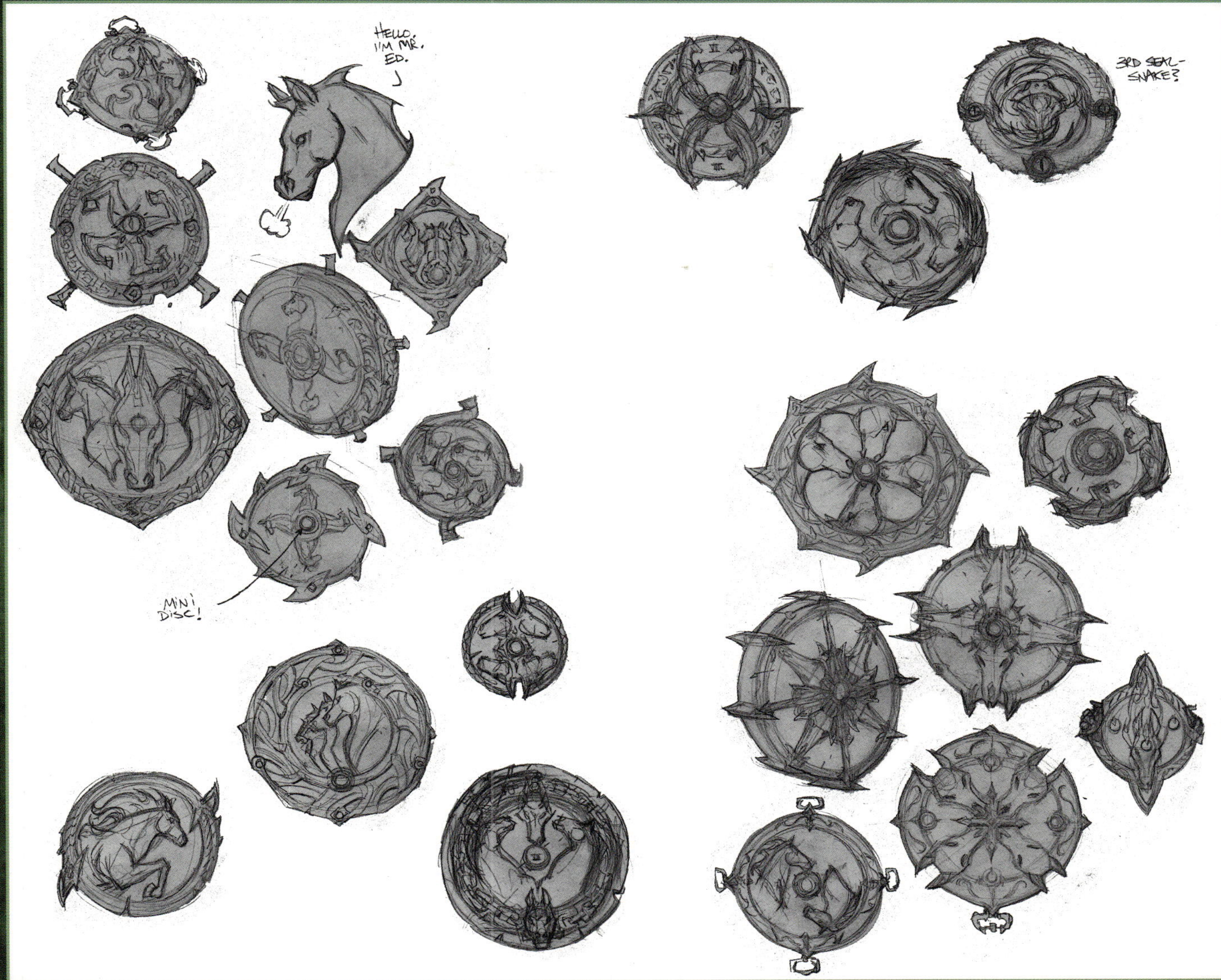

DEVELOPMENT SKETCHES

Heart of the Chosen

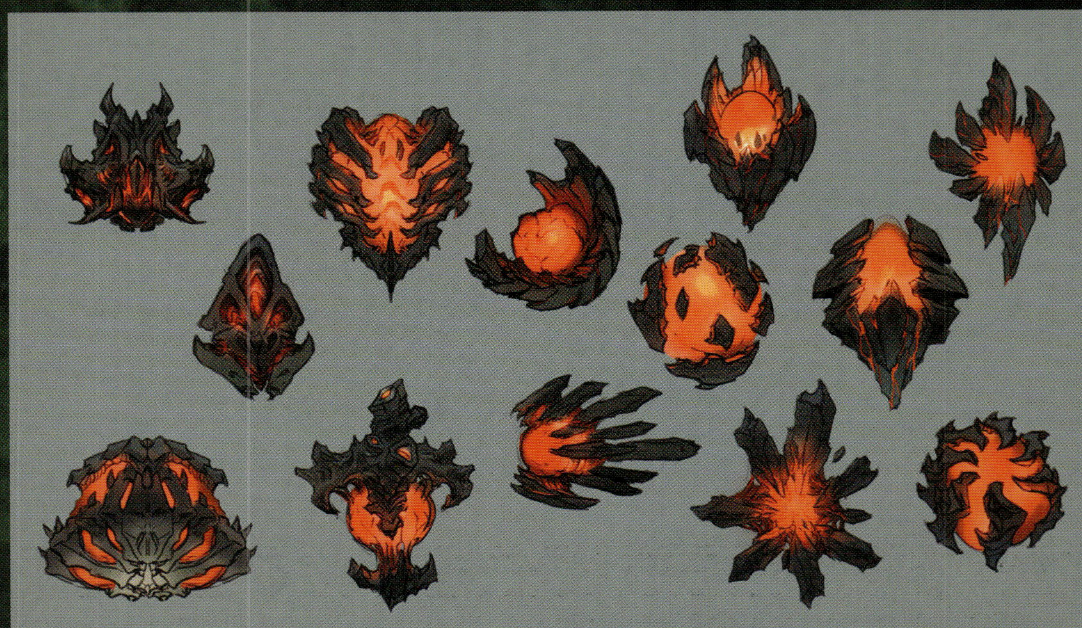

DEVELOPMENT SKETCHES

Iconography

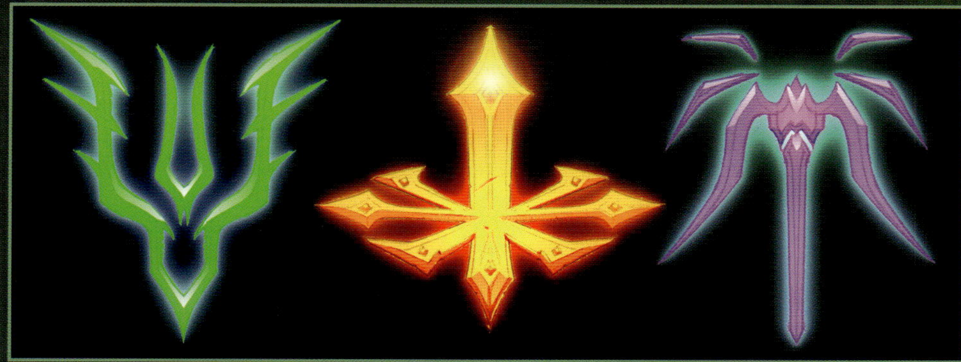

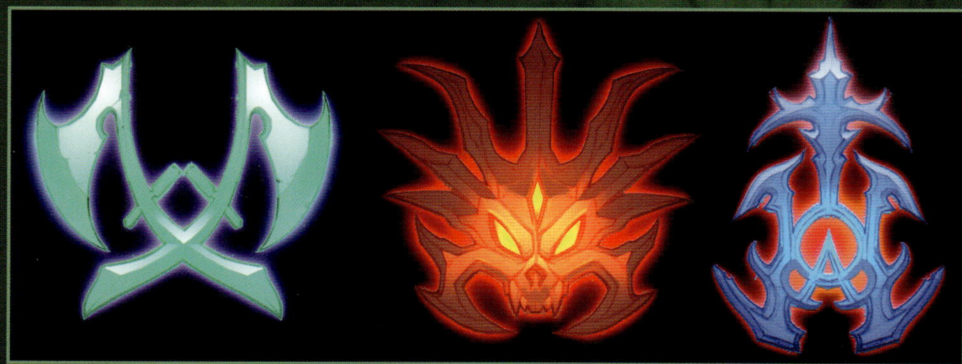

ICON DESIGNS

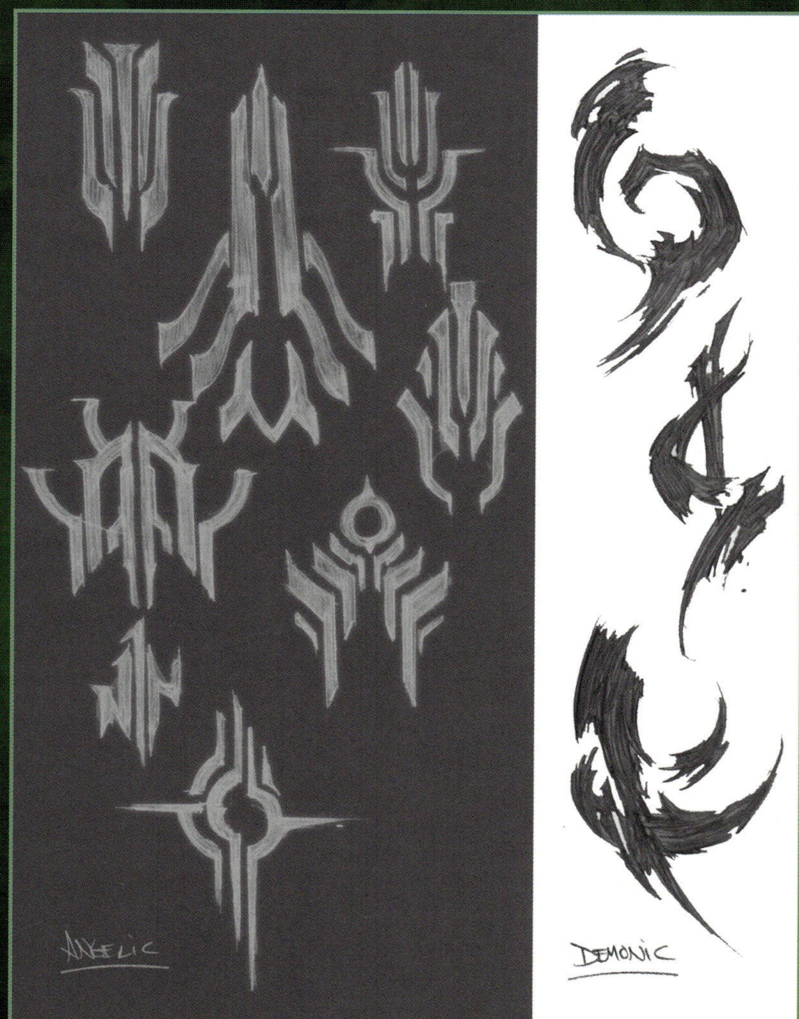

RUNE DESIGNS

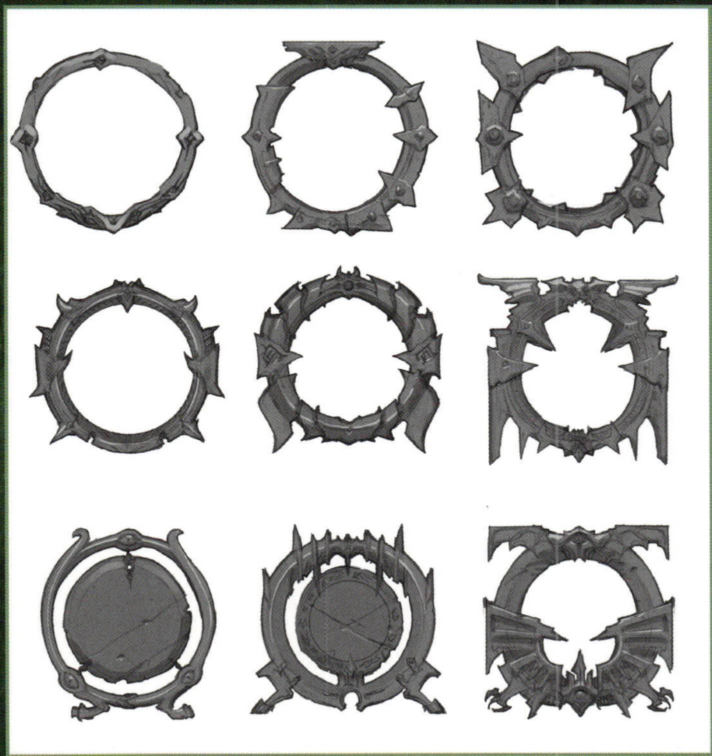

UPGRADE CONCEPTS

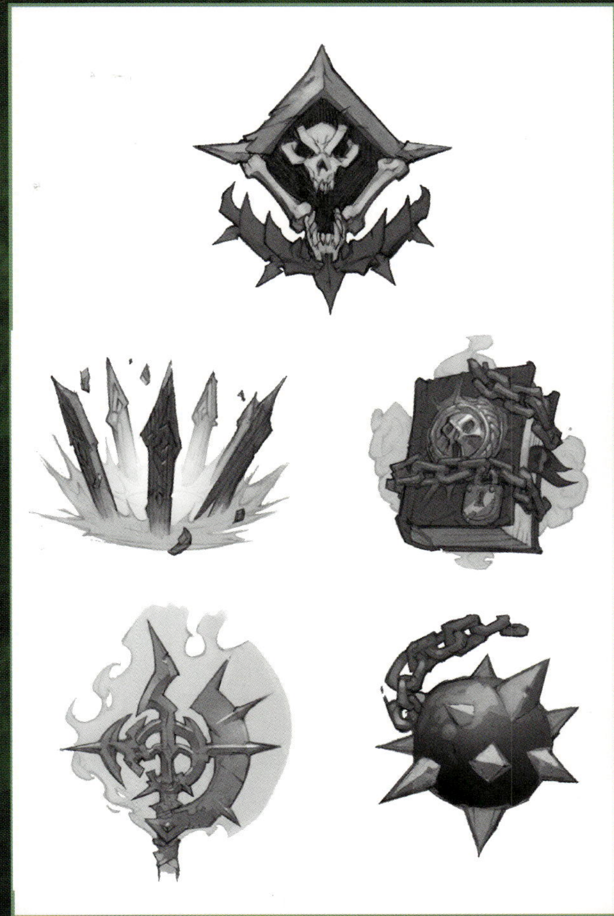

ICON DESIGNS

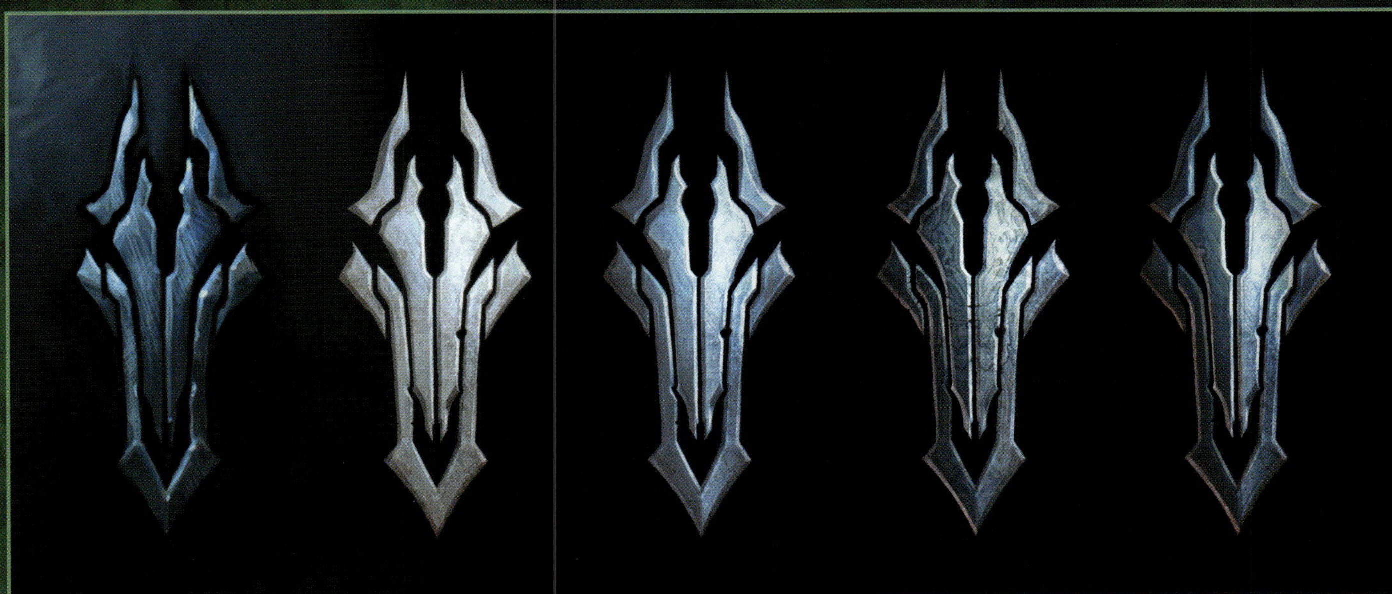

RUIN RUNE DESIGNS

Weapons

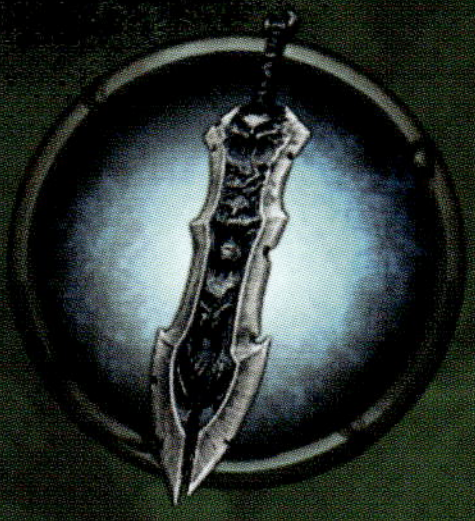
Chaoseater

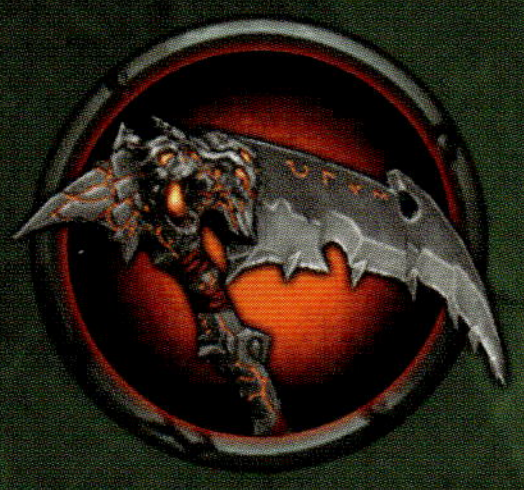
Scythe

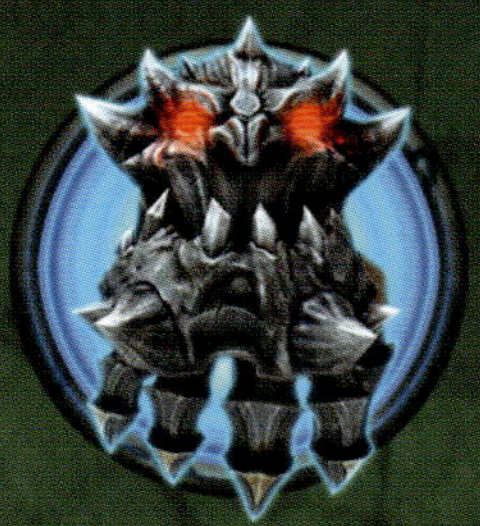
Tremor Gauntlet

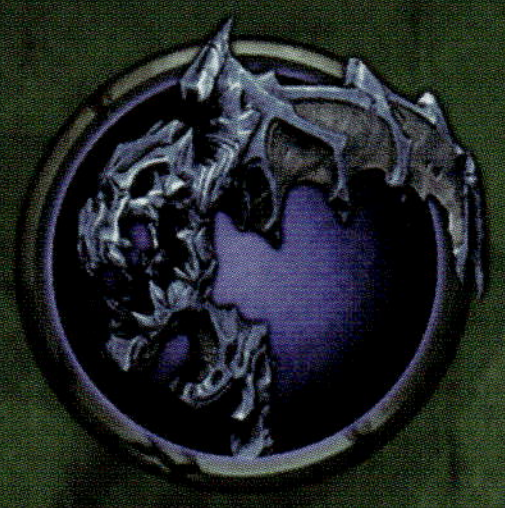
Harvester

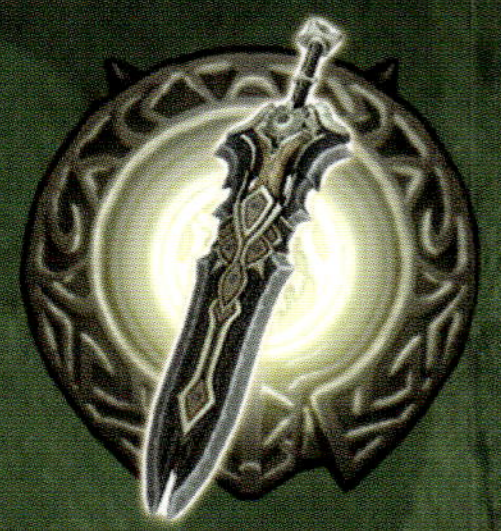
Armageddon Blade

Gear Items

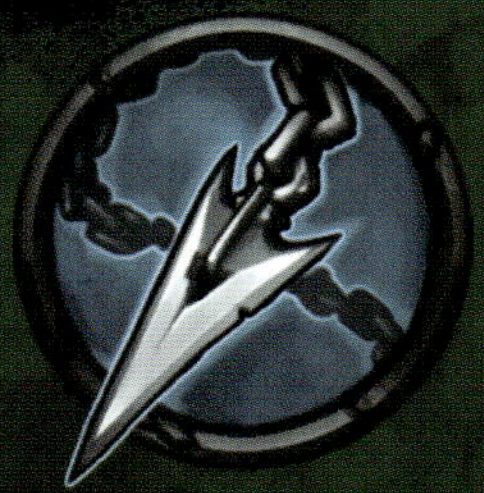
Abyssal Chain

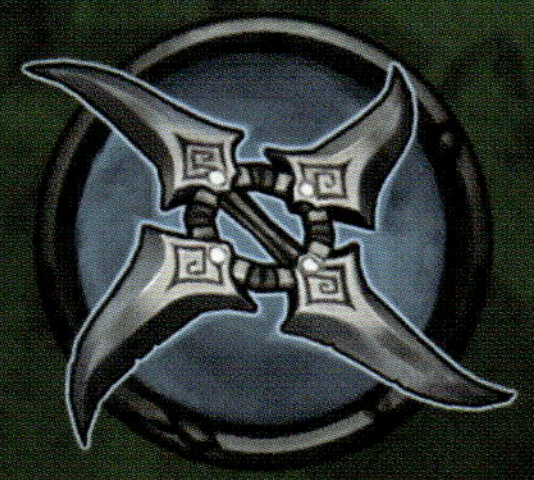
Crossblade

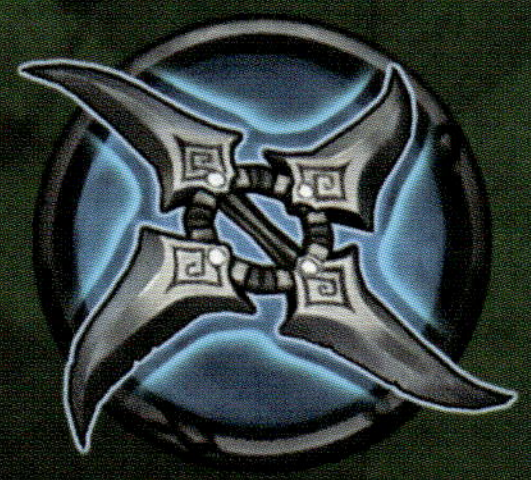
Crossblade (Ricochet Blade)

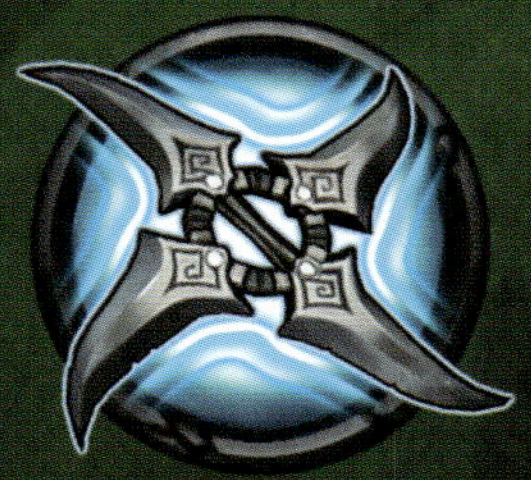
Crossblade (Ricochet Haze)

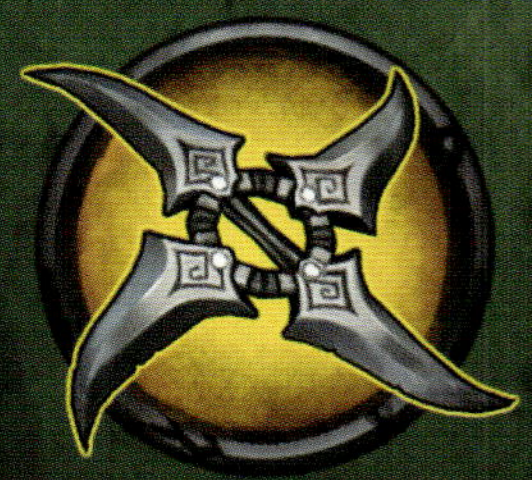
Crossblade (Shredder)

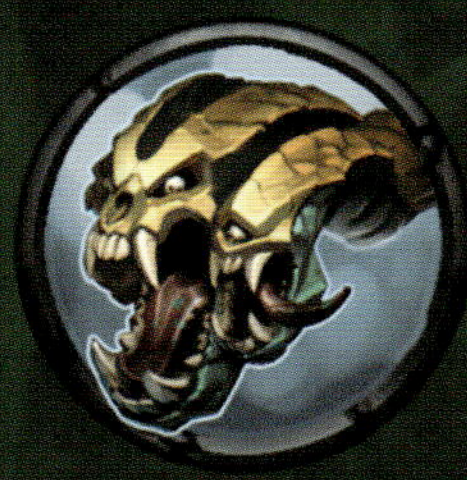
Earthcaller

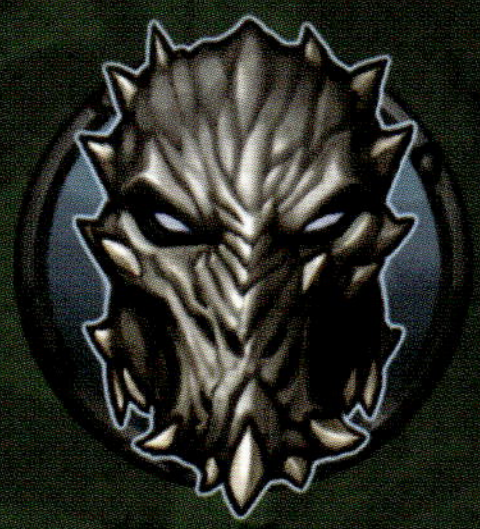
Mask of Shadows

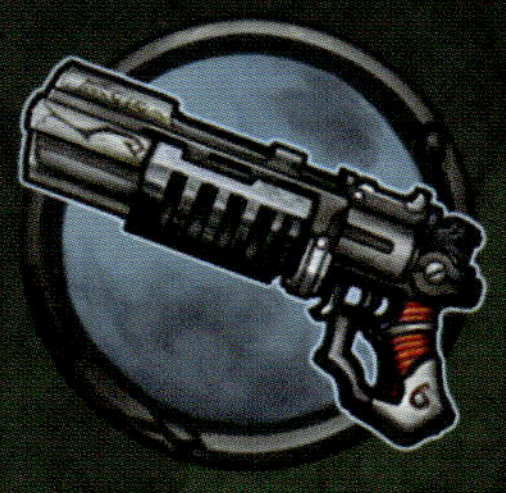
Mercy

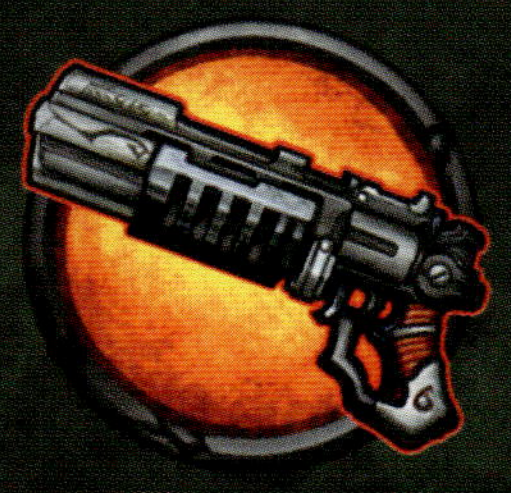
Mercy (Impact Rounds)

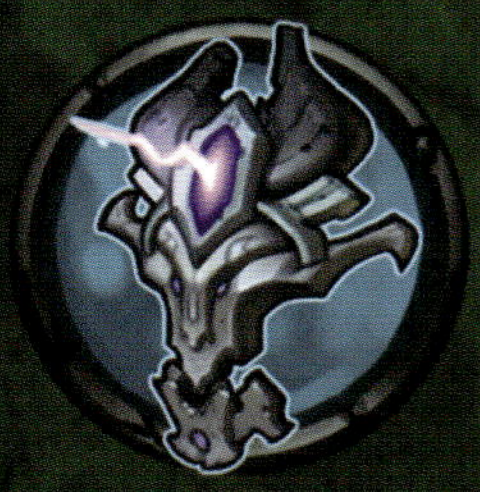
Voidwalker

Wrath Abilities

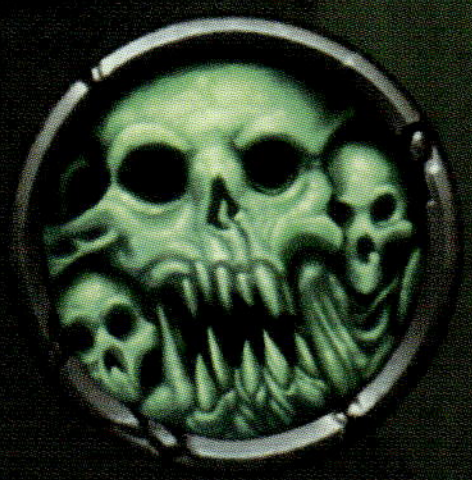
Affliction

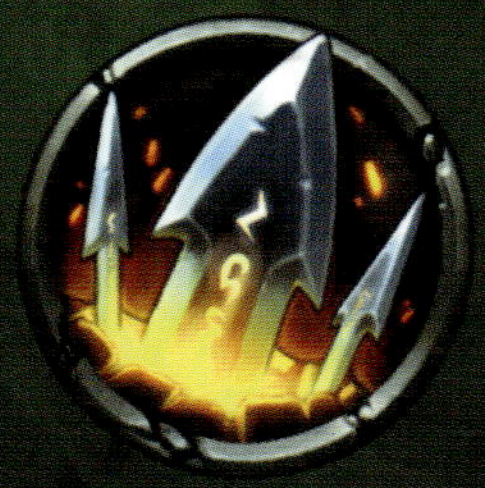
Blade Geyser

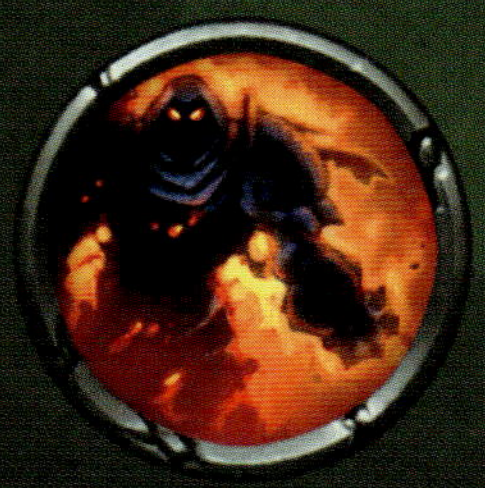
Immolation

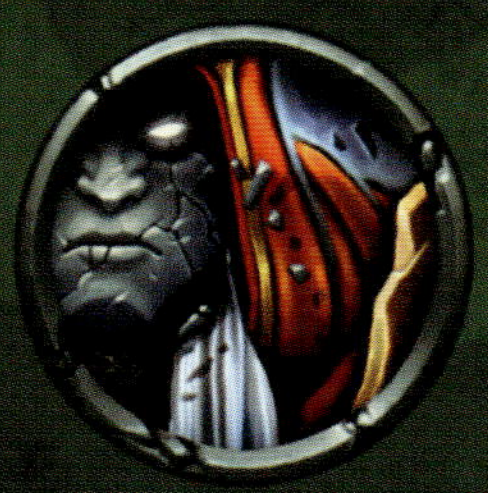
Stone Skin

Consumable Items

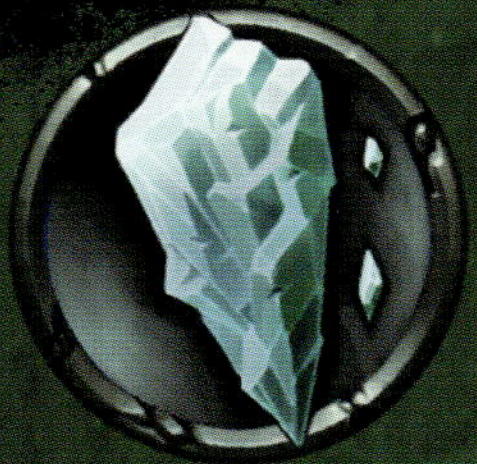
Empty Vessels

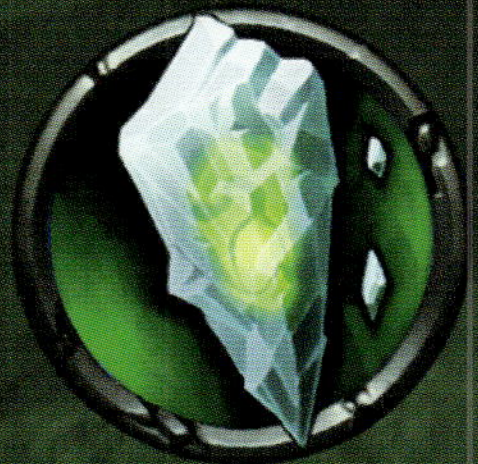
Life Essence

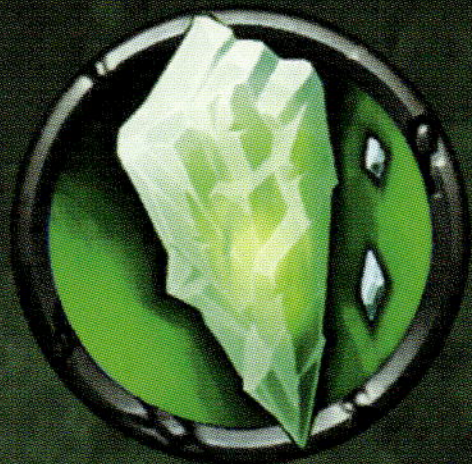
Greater Life Essence

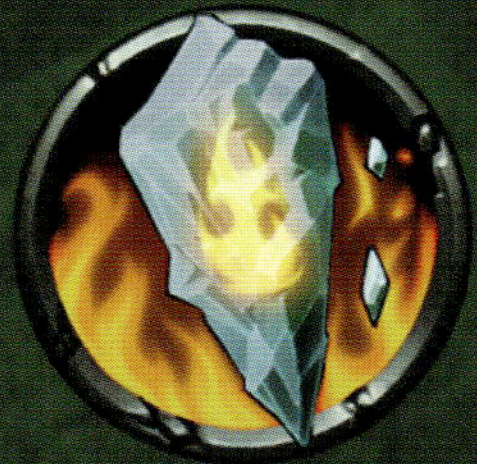
Rage

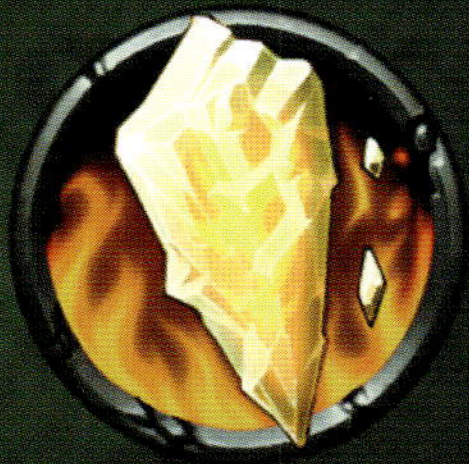
Greater Rage

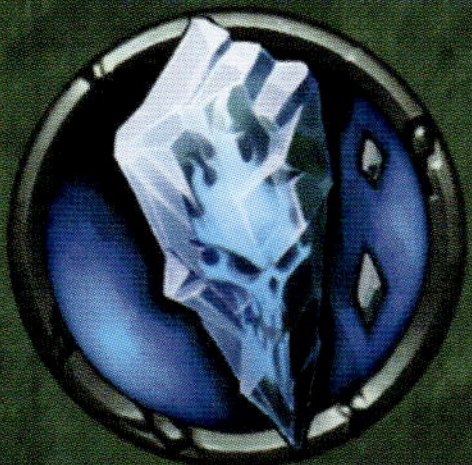
Undying

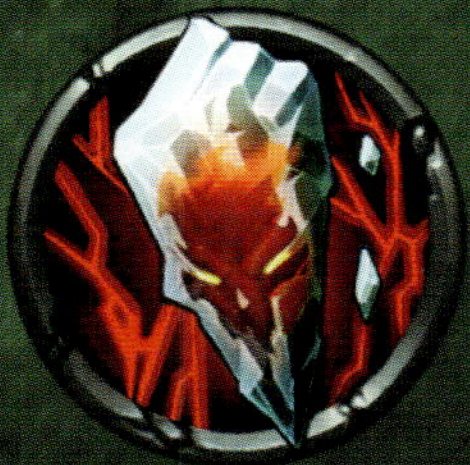
Possession

Weapon Enhancements

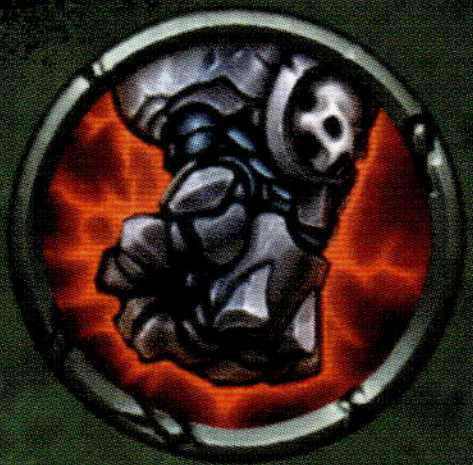
Bane

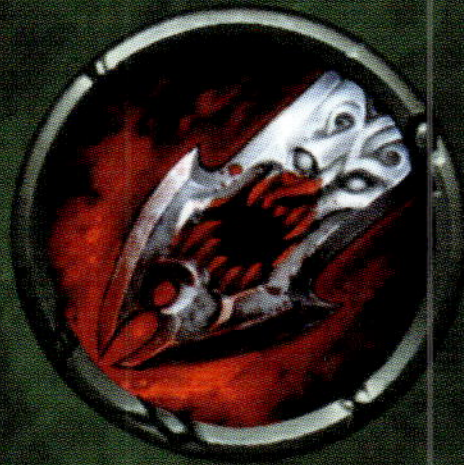
Bloodthirst

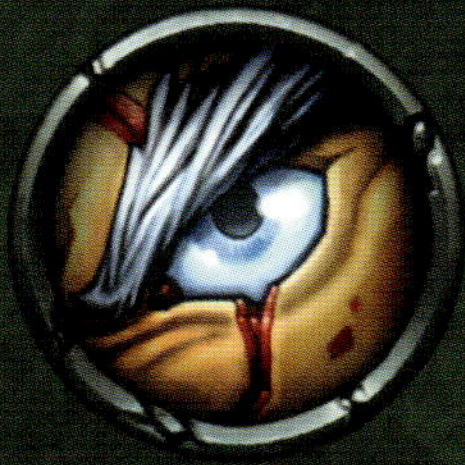
Carnage

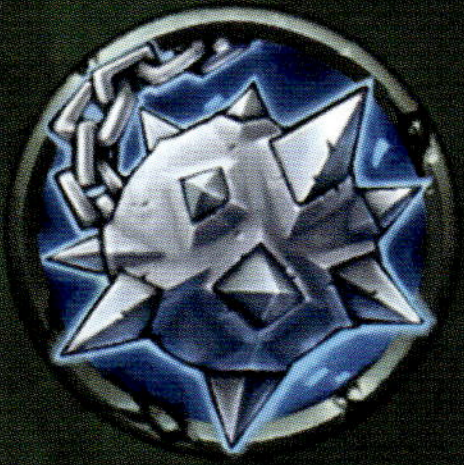
Combat Lore

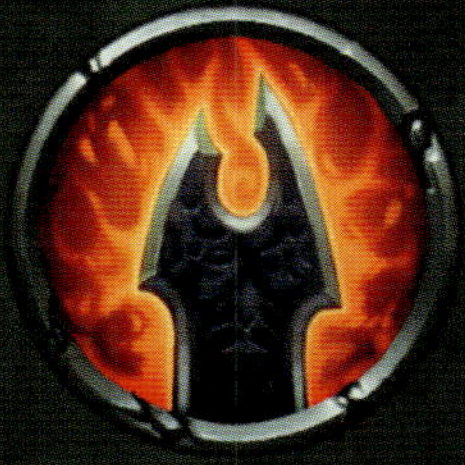
Hellfire

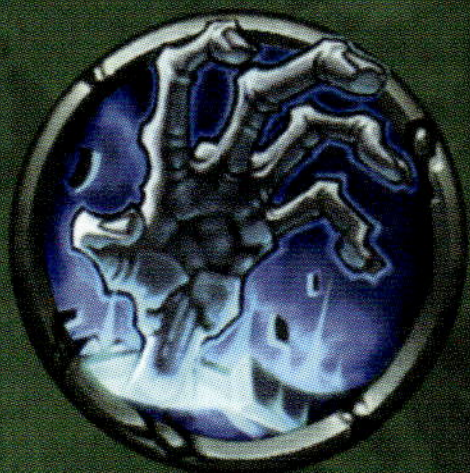
Ravager

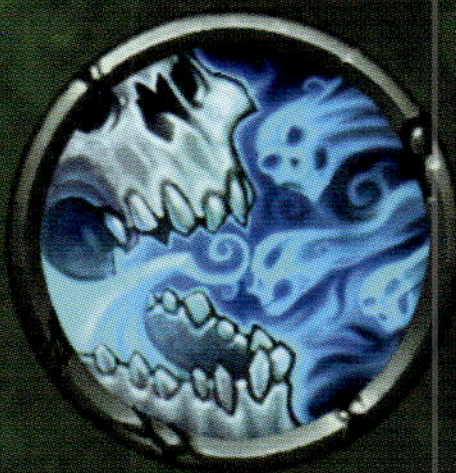
Reaper

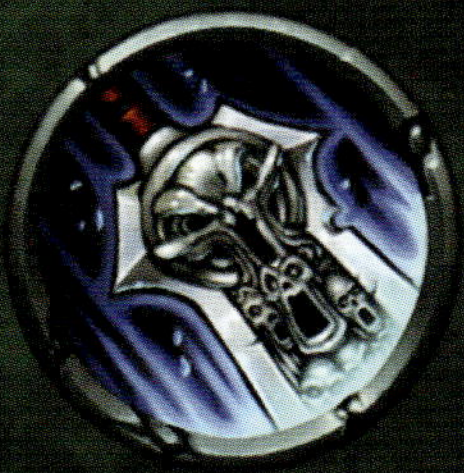
Weapon Master

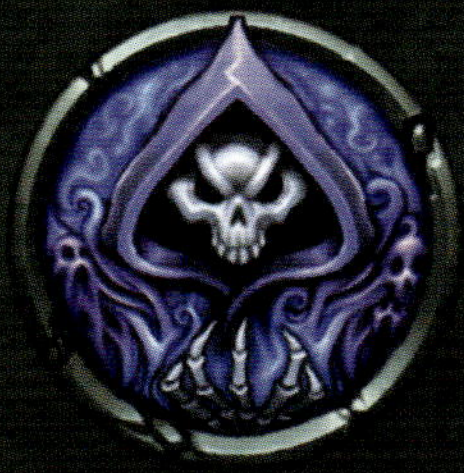
Death's Blessing

Fury's Embrace

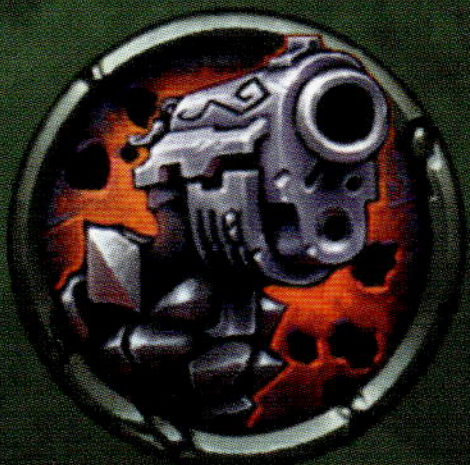
Strife's Offering

Miscellaneous Items

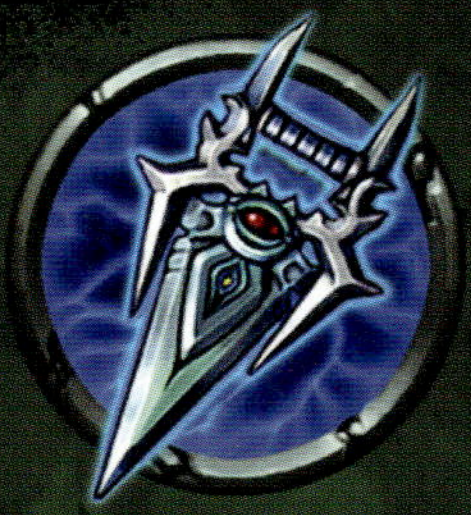

Beholder's Key

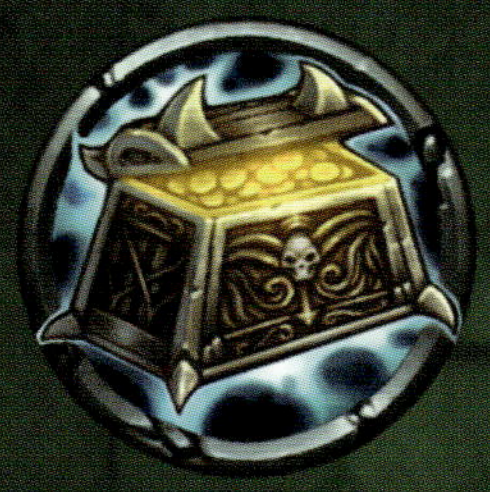

Hoardseeker

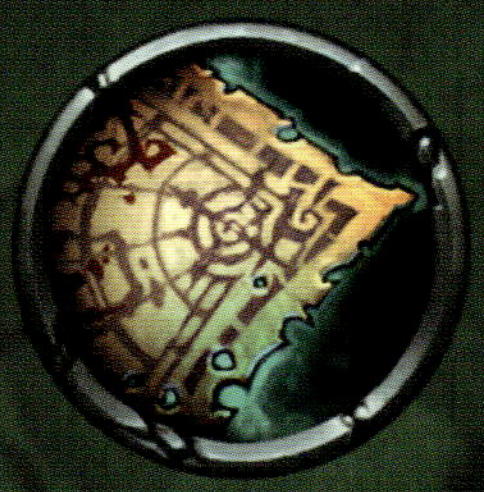

Map

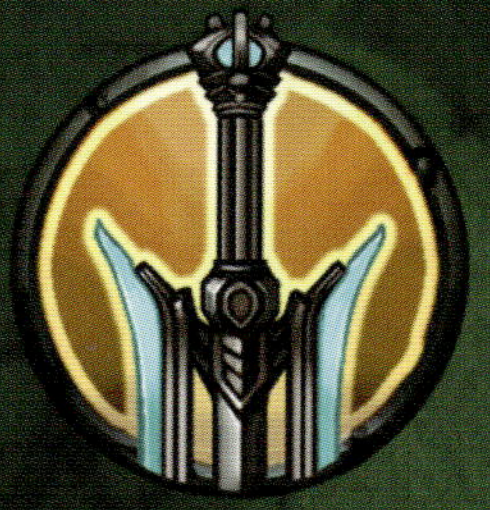

Crystal Sword

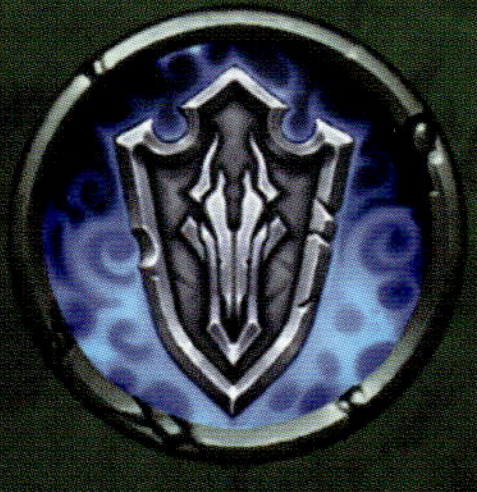

Abyssal Armor

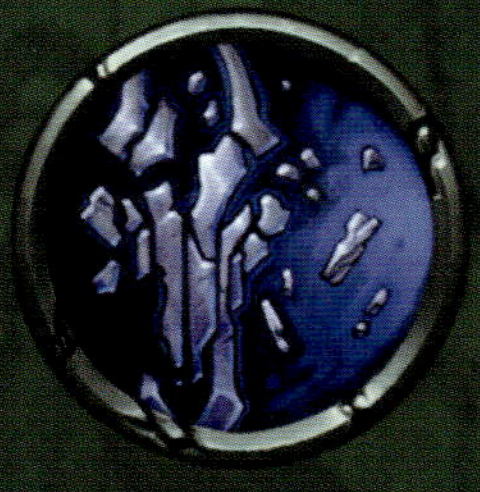

Abyssal Armor Piece

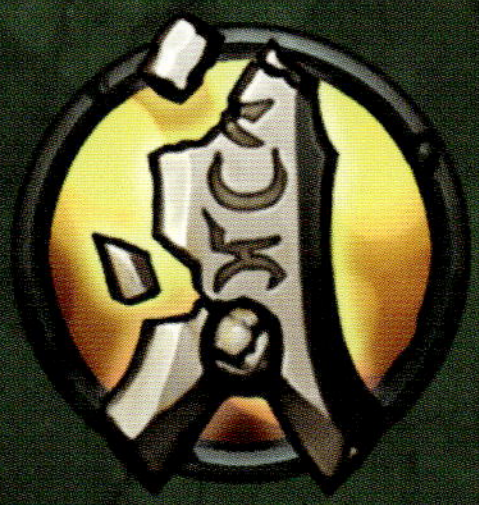

Armageddon Blade Shard

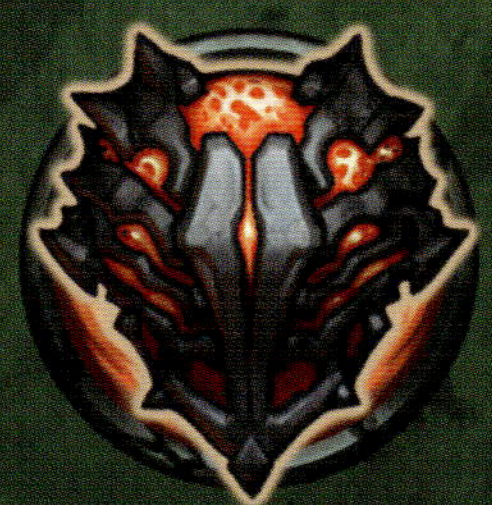

Heart of the Chosen

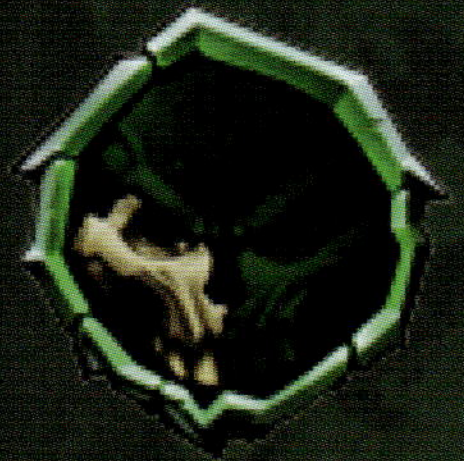

Lifestone Shard

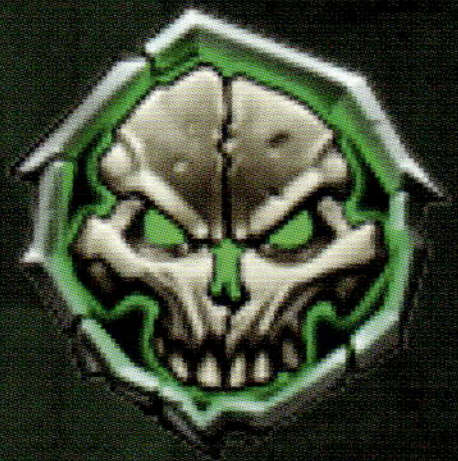

Lifestone

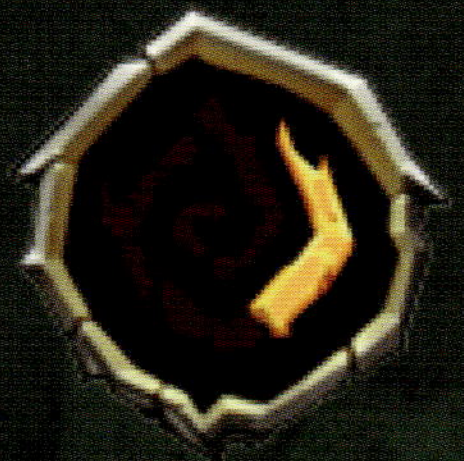

Wrath Shard

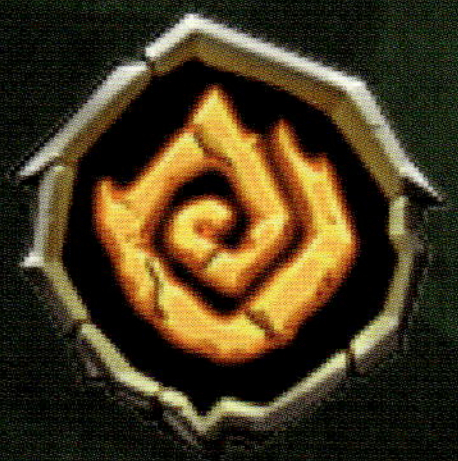

Wrath Core

Artifacts

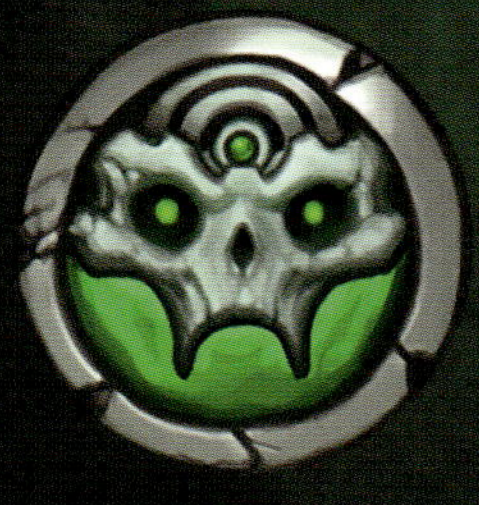

Soldier Artifact

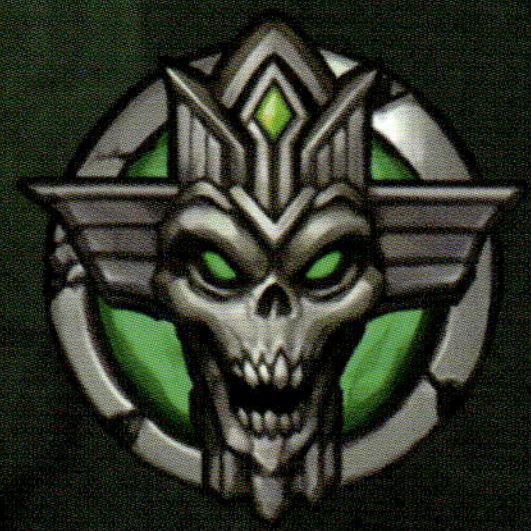

Champion Artifact

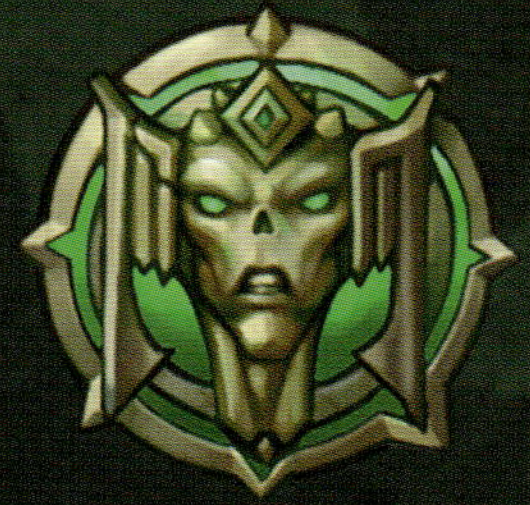

Overlord Artifact

Passive Abilities

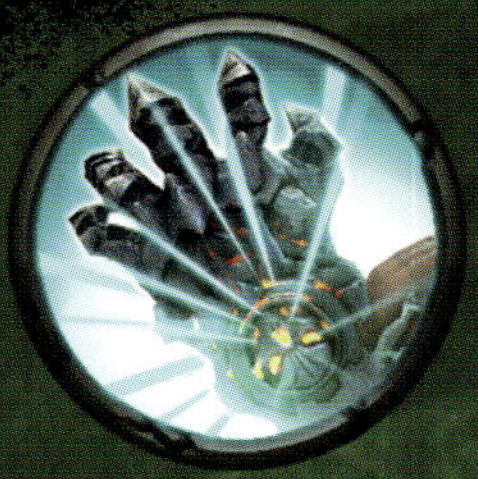

Block Counter

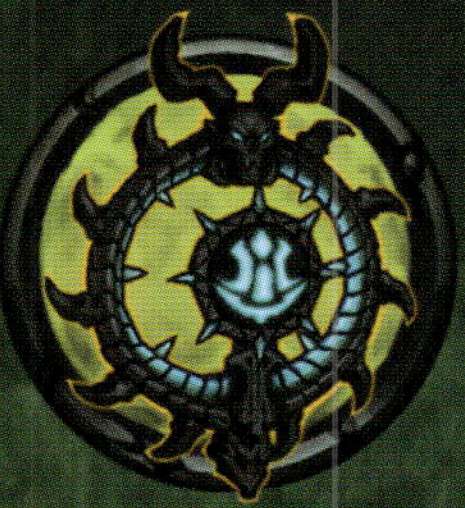

Chronomancer

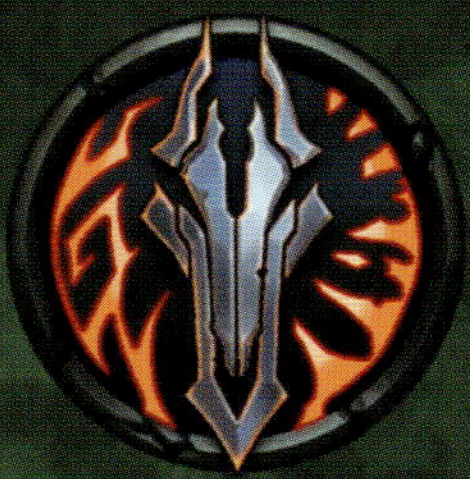

Ruin

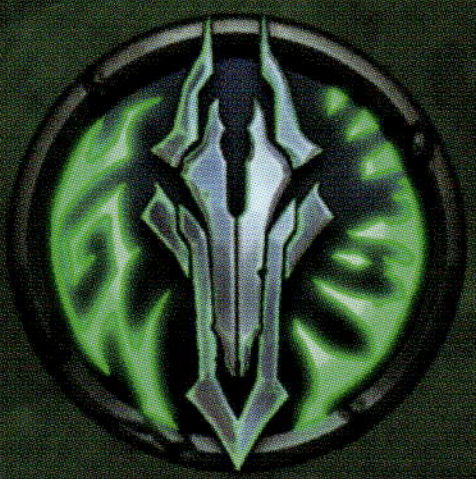

Ruin + Soul Bridge

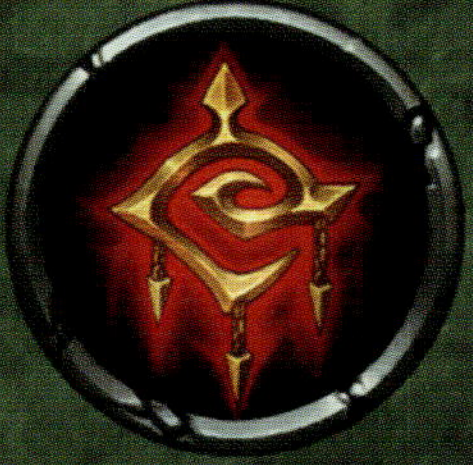

Serpent Holes

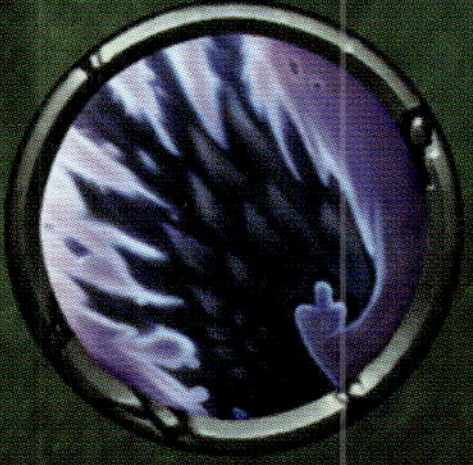

Shadowflight

Other Icons

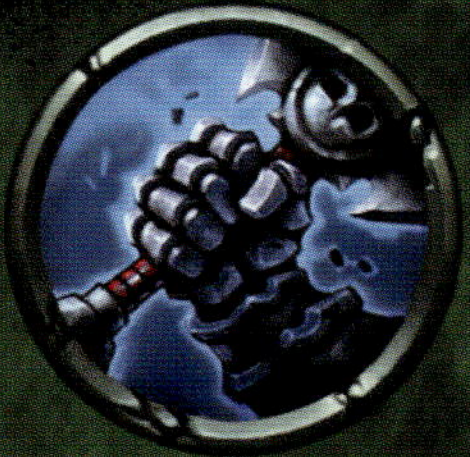

War

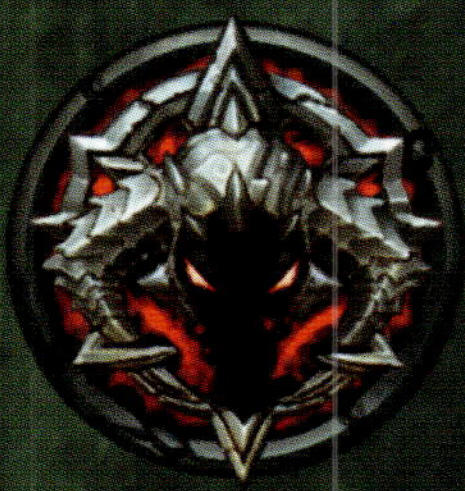

Chaos

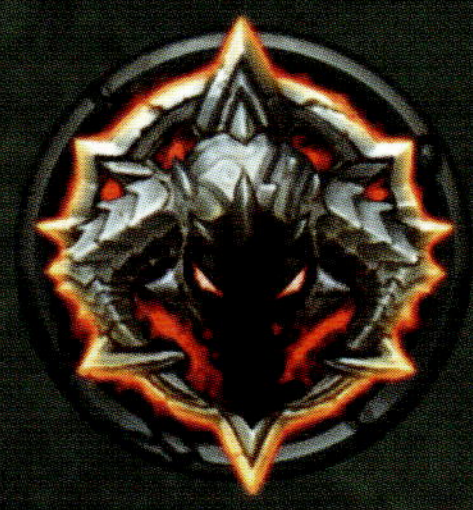

Chaos Rage

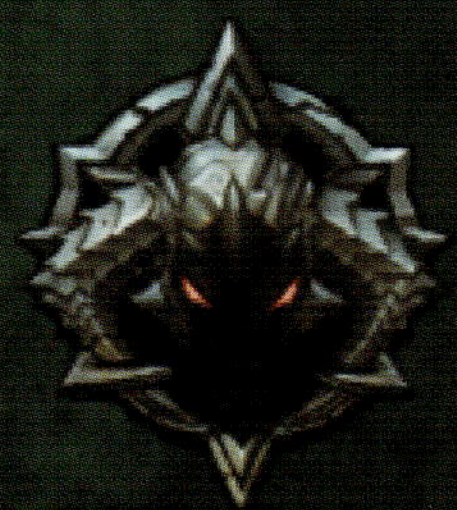

Chaos Indicator

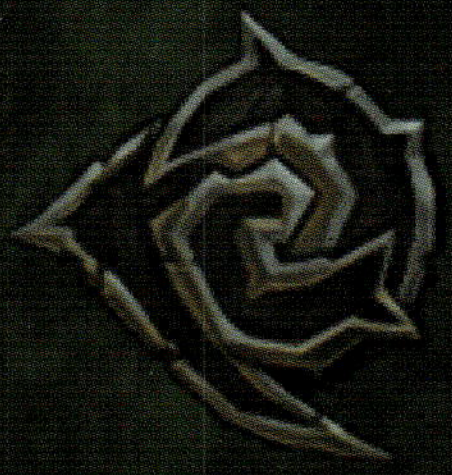

Chaos Meter

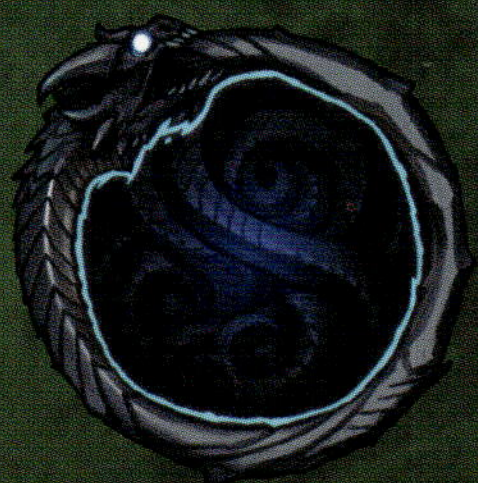

Upgrade Level 1

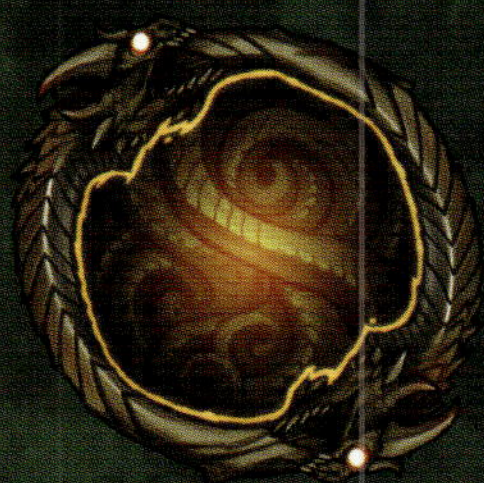

Upgrade Level 2

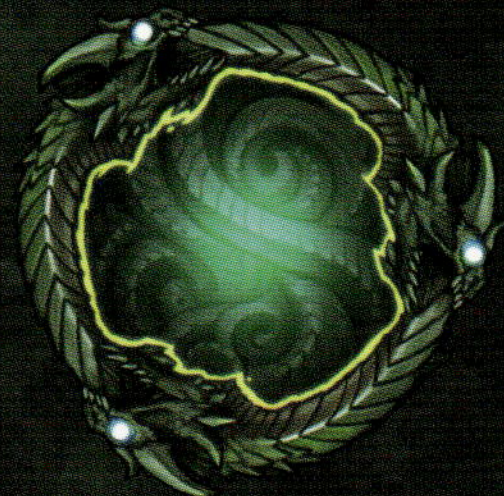

Upgrade Level 3

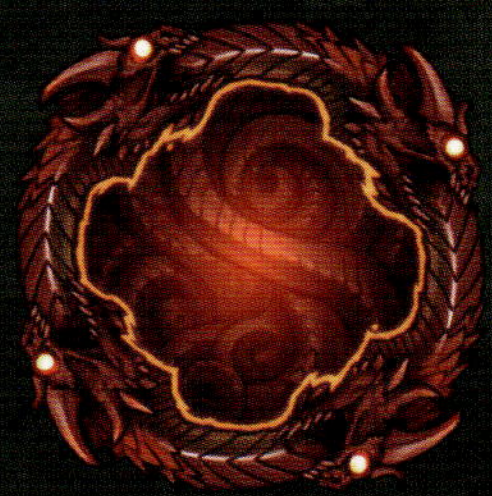

Upgrade Level 4

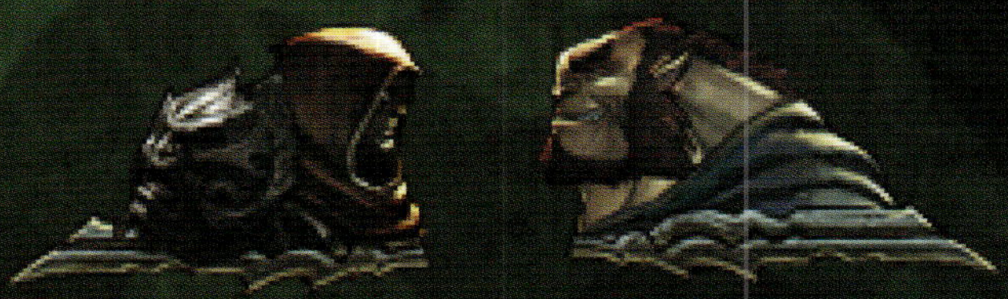

Tally Icons

Early Icon Designs

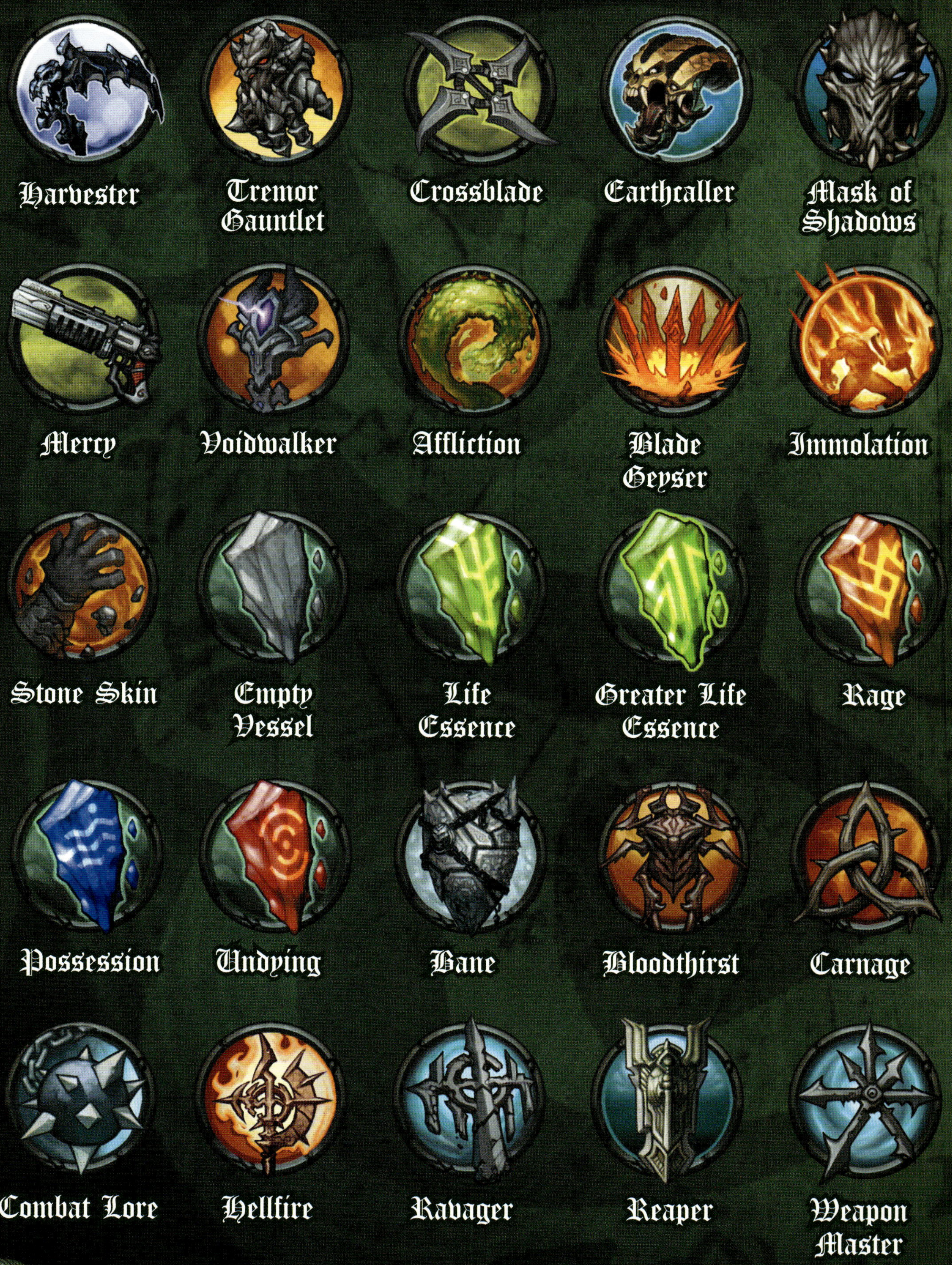

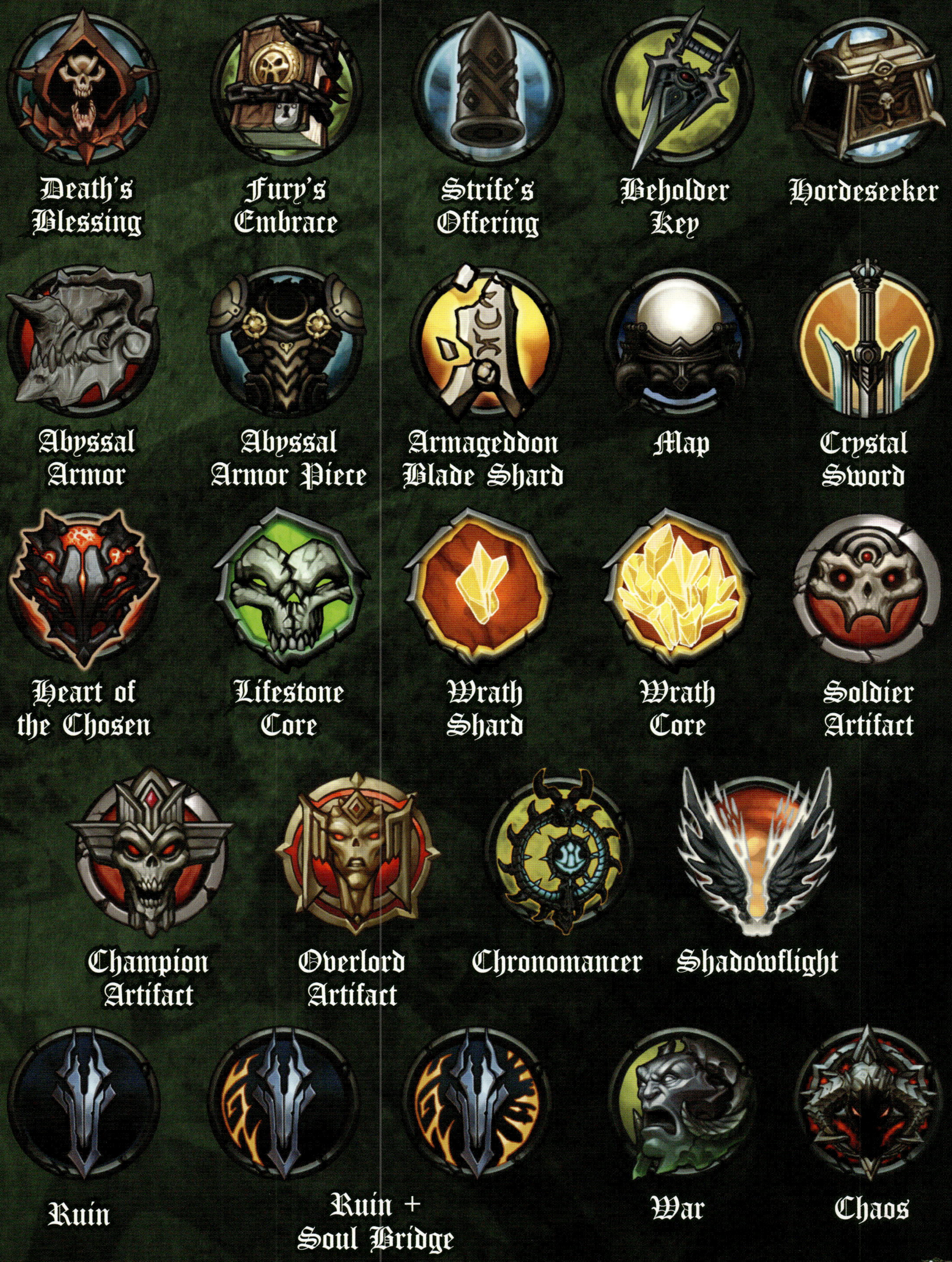
Death's Blessing
Fury's Embrace
Strife's Offering
Beholder Key
Hordeseeker
Abyssal Armor
Abyssal Armor Piece
Armageddon Blade Shard
Map
Crystal Sword
Heart of the Chosen
Lifestone Core
Wrath Shard
Wrath Core
Soldier Artifact
Champion Artifact
Overlord Artifact
Chronomancer
Shadowflight
Ruin
Ruin + Soul Bridge
War
Chaos

Logos

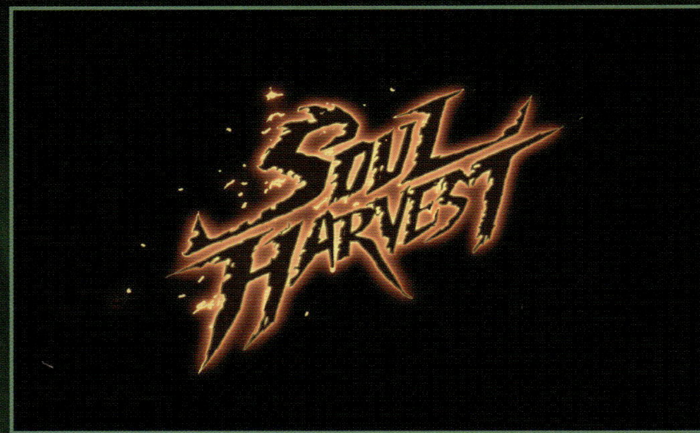

EARLY GAME TITLE

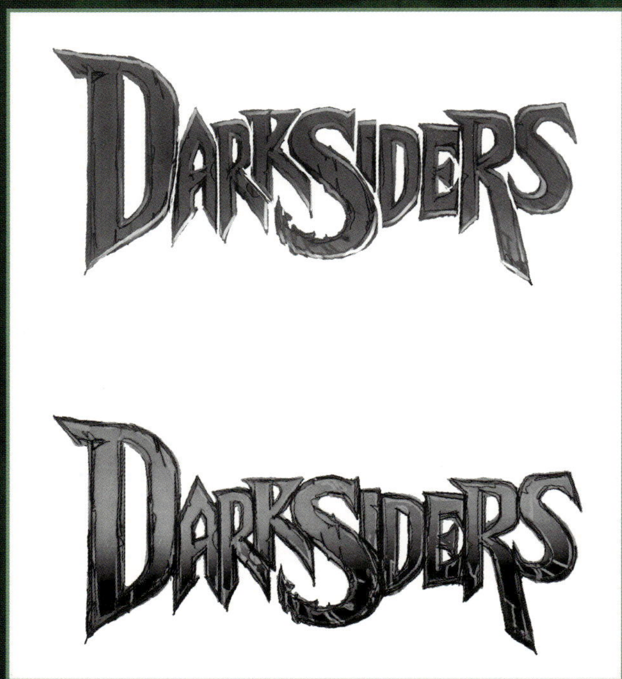

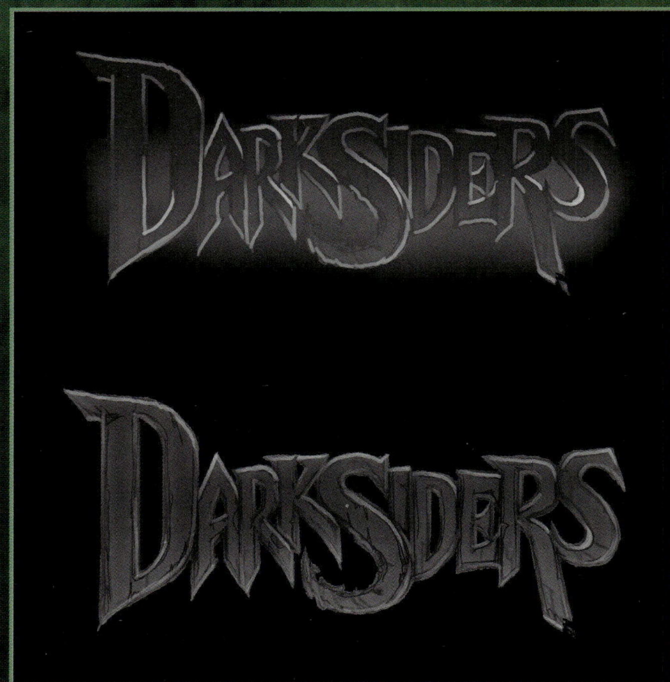

LOGO DESIGNS

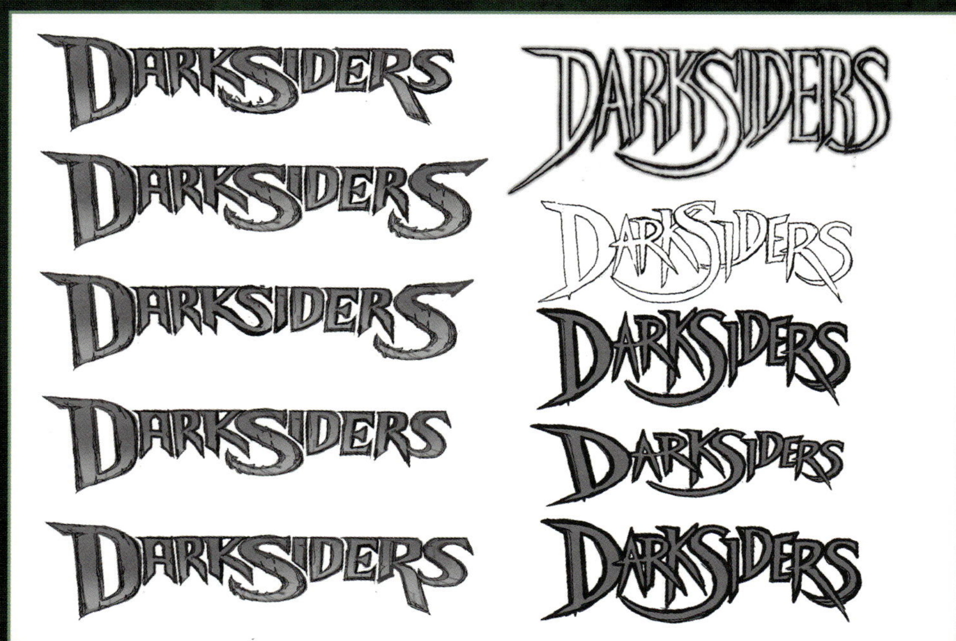

LOGO DESIGNS

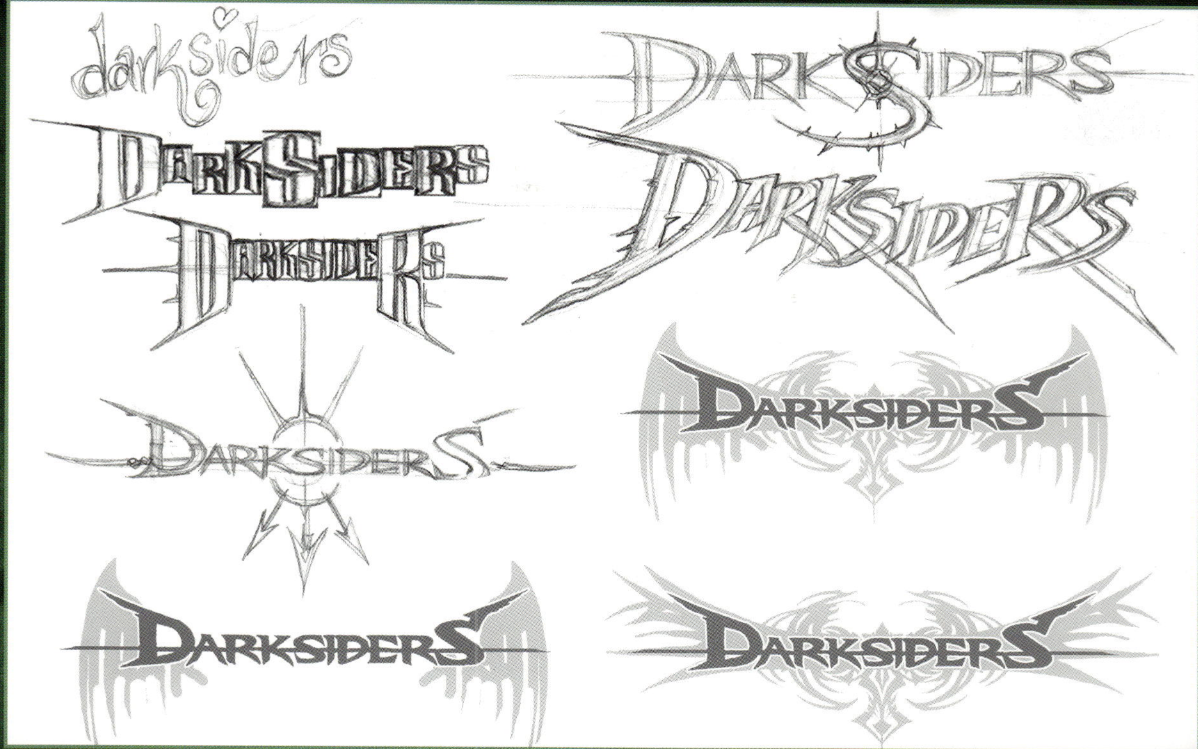

LOGO DESIGNS

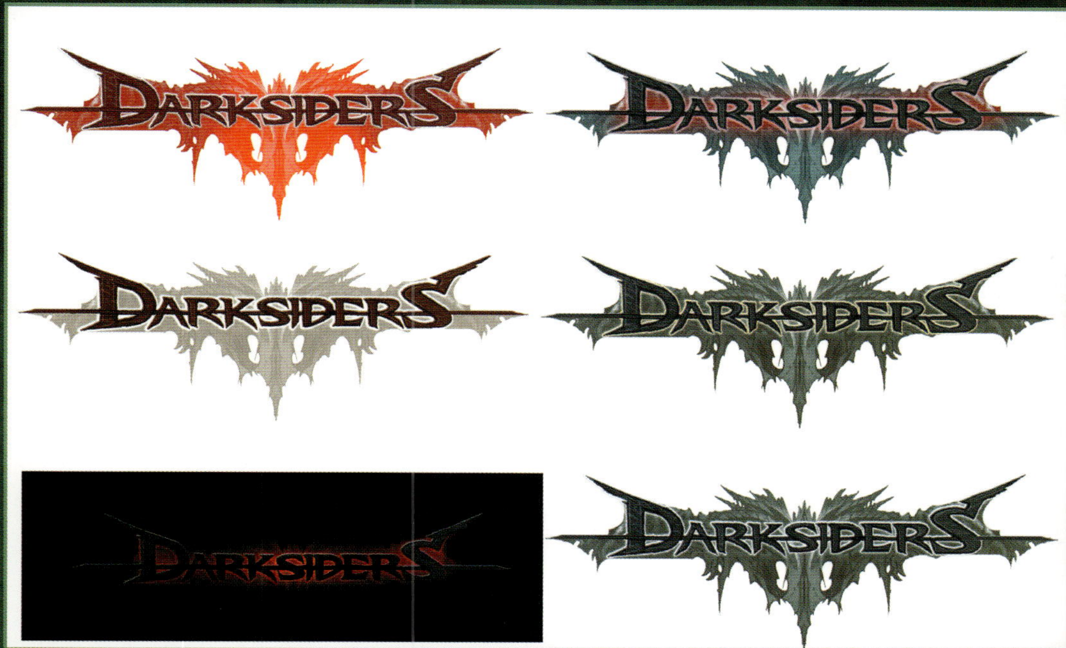

LOGO DESIGNS

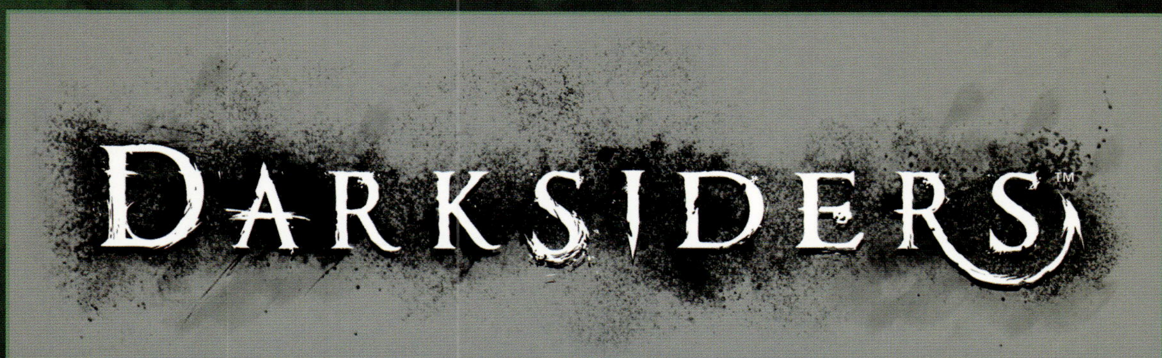

FINAL LOGO

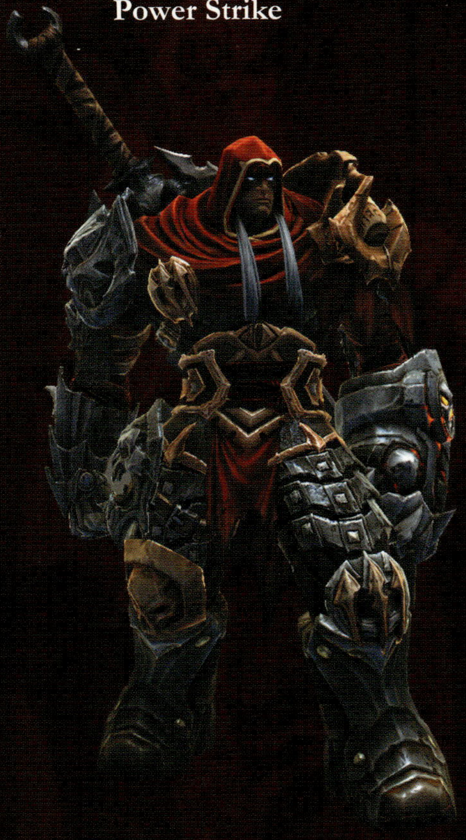

War

The legendary horseman of the Apocalypse

SIGNATURE ATTACK:
Power Strike

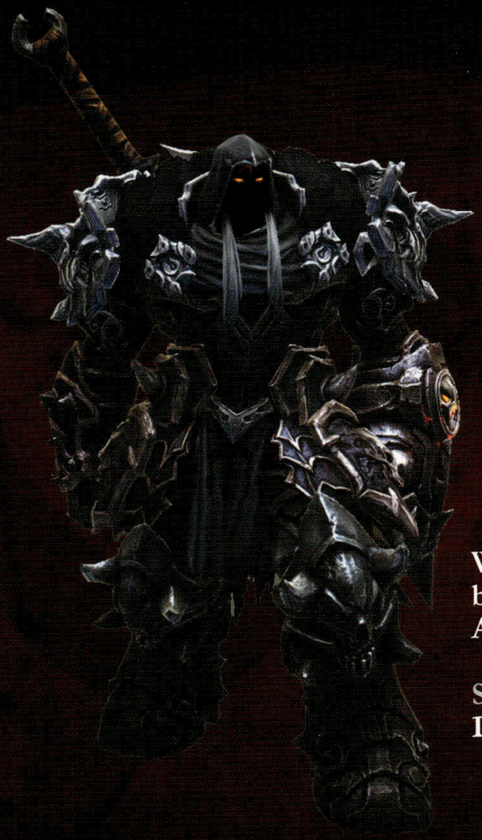

Abyssal Armor

War equipped with the bloodforged Abyssal Armor set.

SIGNATURE ATTACK:
Demon Edge

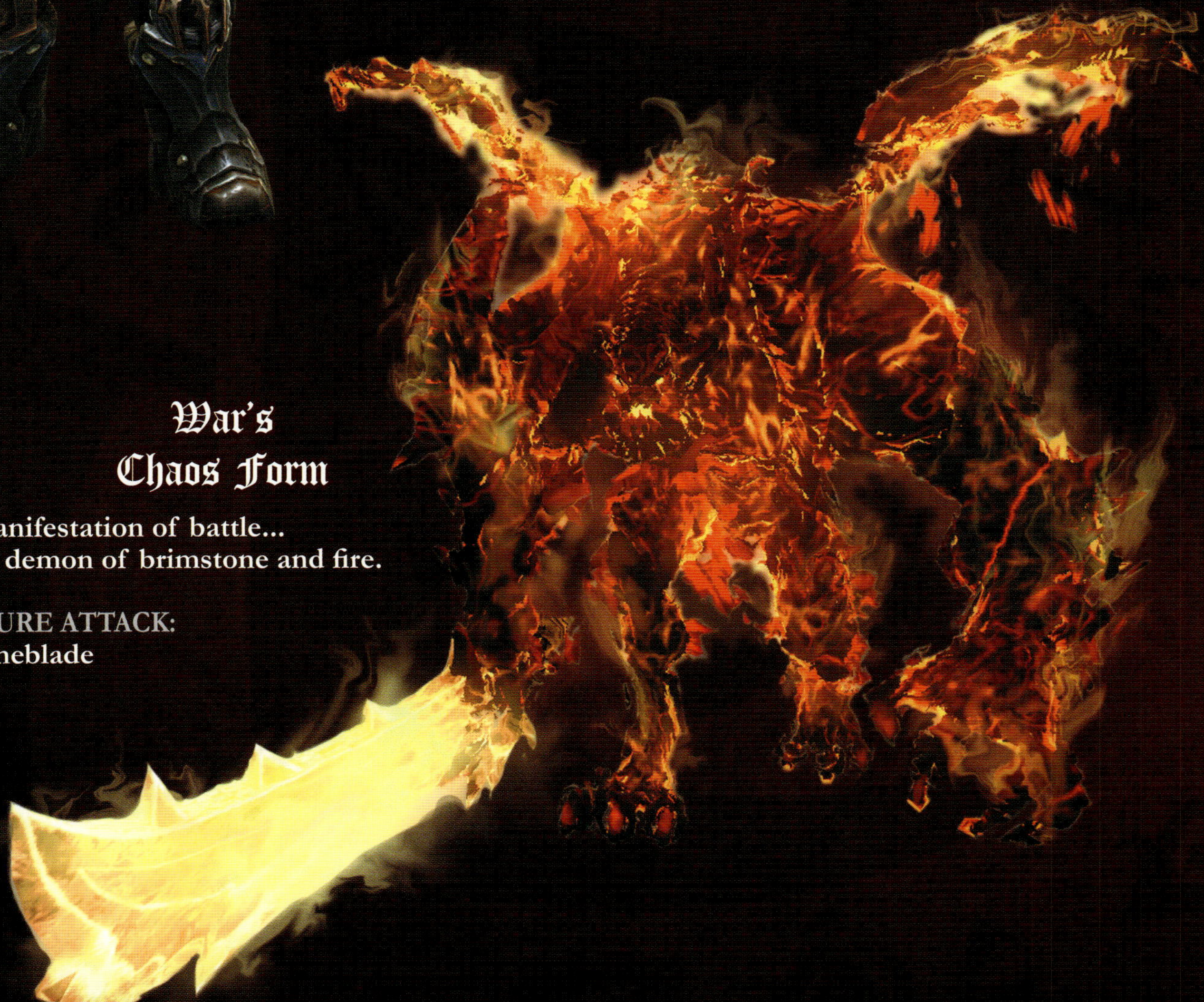

War's Chaos Form

War's manifestation of battle...
a 13 foot demon of brimstone and fire.

SIGNATURE ATTACK:
Brimstoneblade

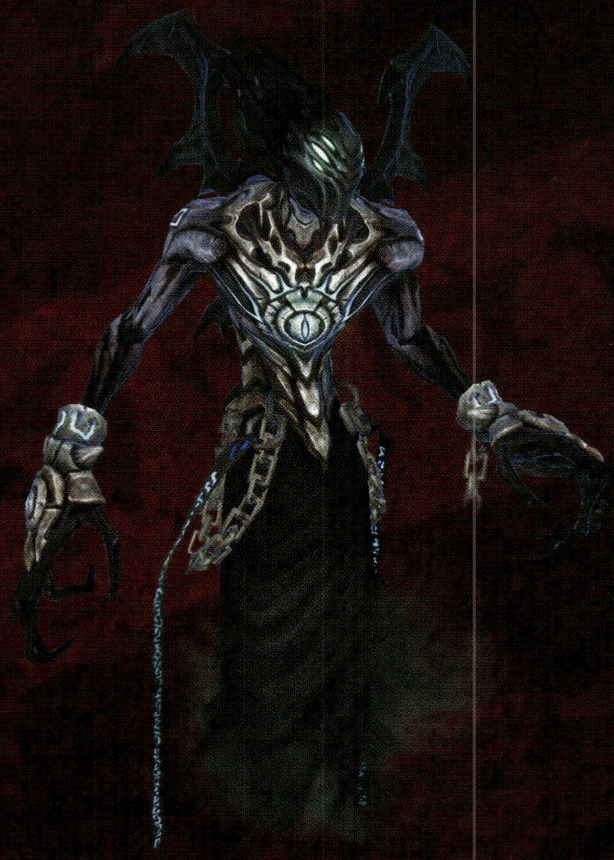

Watcher

A twisted, spiteful demon used to manipulate their shackled victims.

SIGNATURE ATTACK:
Onyx Flame

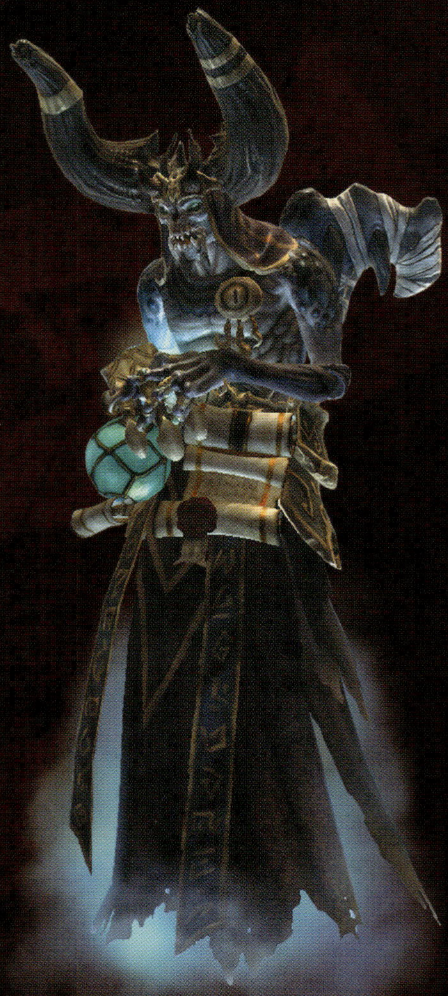

Vulgrim

Smarmy and devious trader of souls, he cares not who the buyer is.

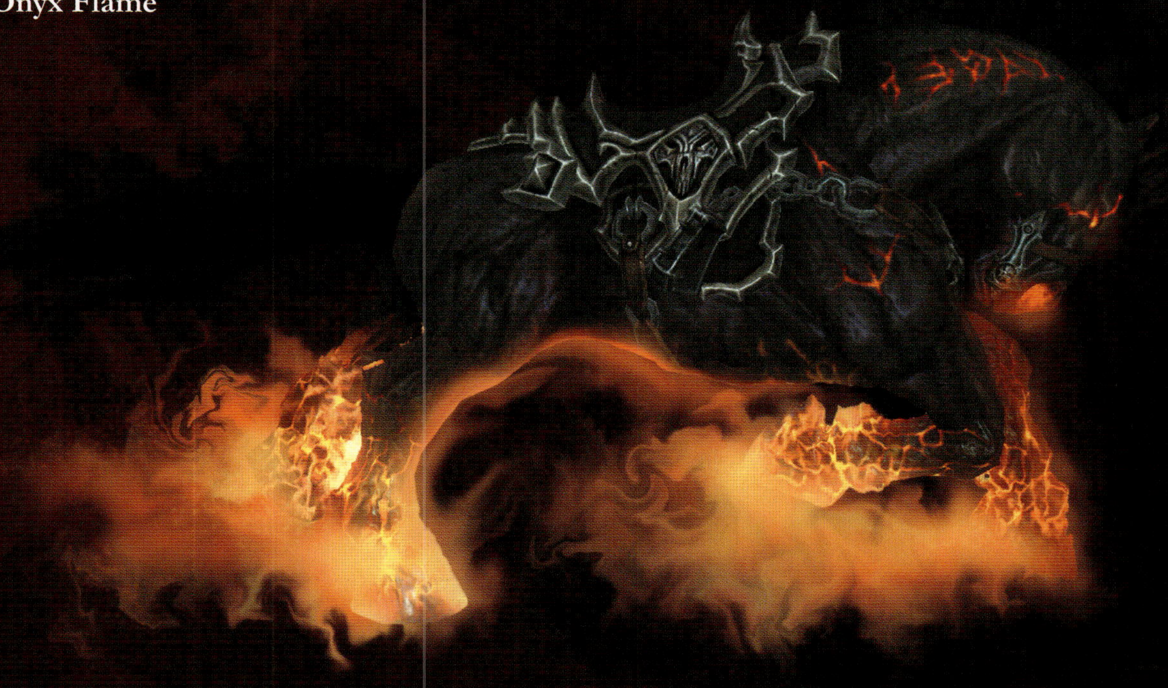

Ruin

War's terrifying and powerful steed.

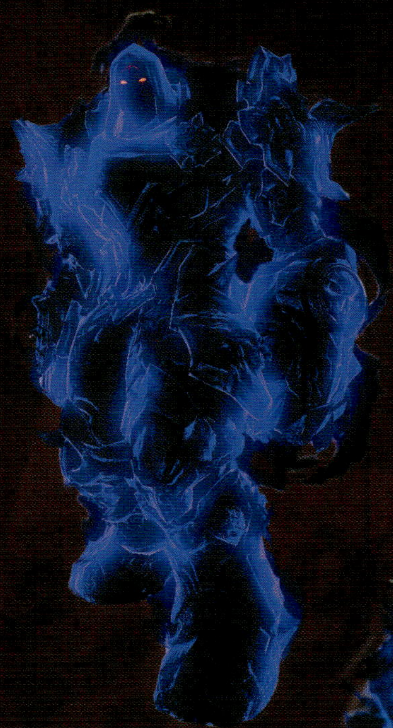

Shadow War

War's dark alter ego.

SIGNATURE ATTACK:
Shadow Havoc Form

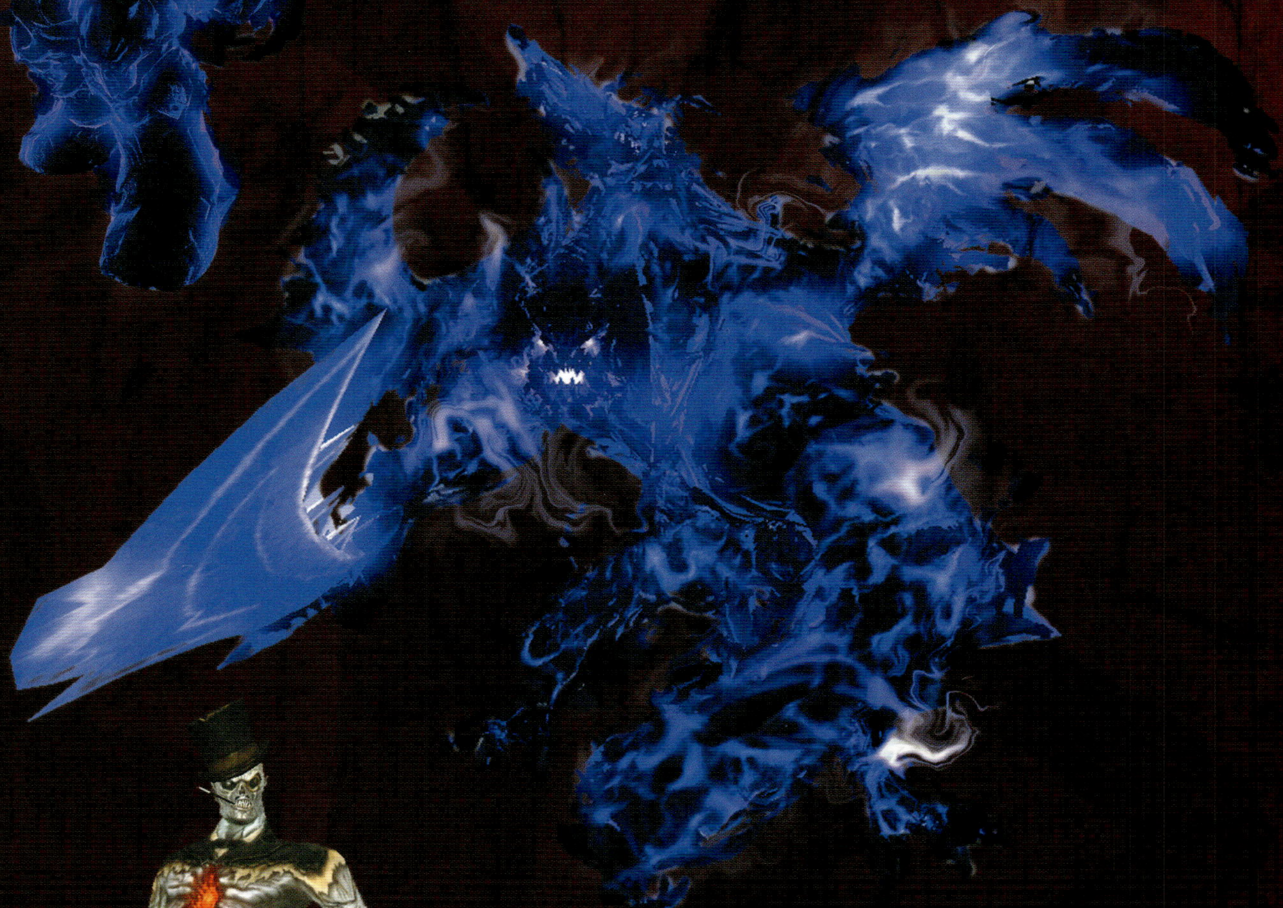

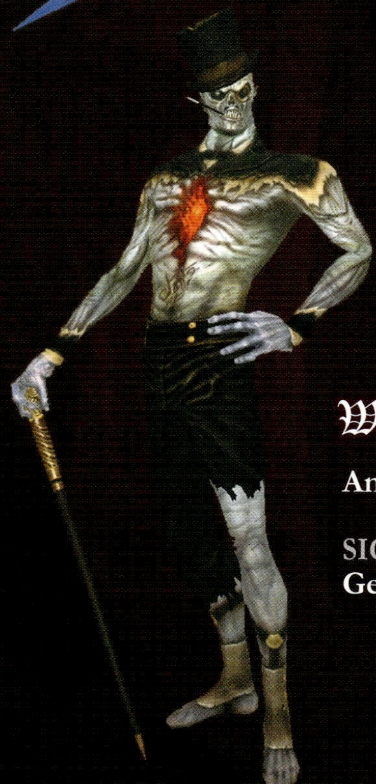

Wicked K

An undead with class.

SIGNATURE ATTACK:
Gentleman's Ruckus

Shadow War's Havoc Form

The shadow incarnation of War's Chaos Form.

SIGNATURE ATTACK:
Shadowsabre

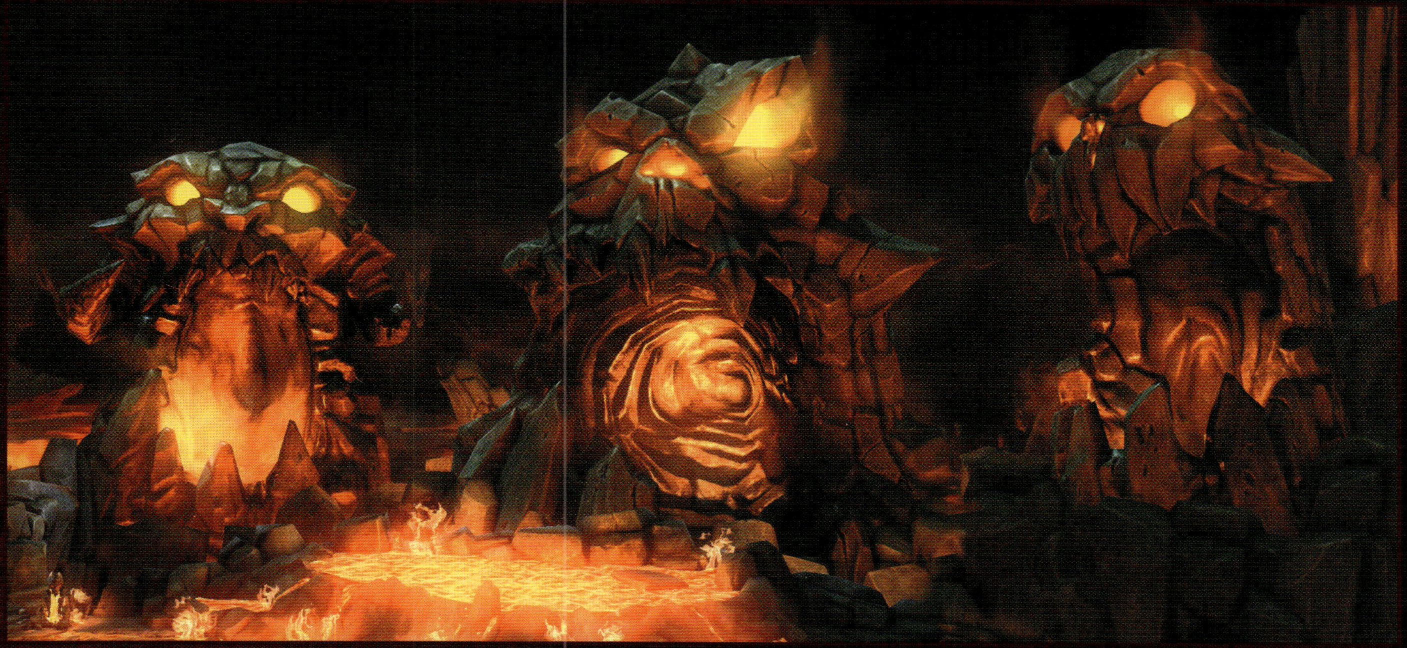

Charred Council 3 ageless entities who rule the balance between Heaven, Hell and the third kingdom; Earth.

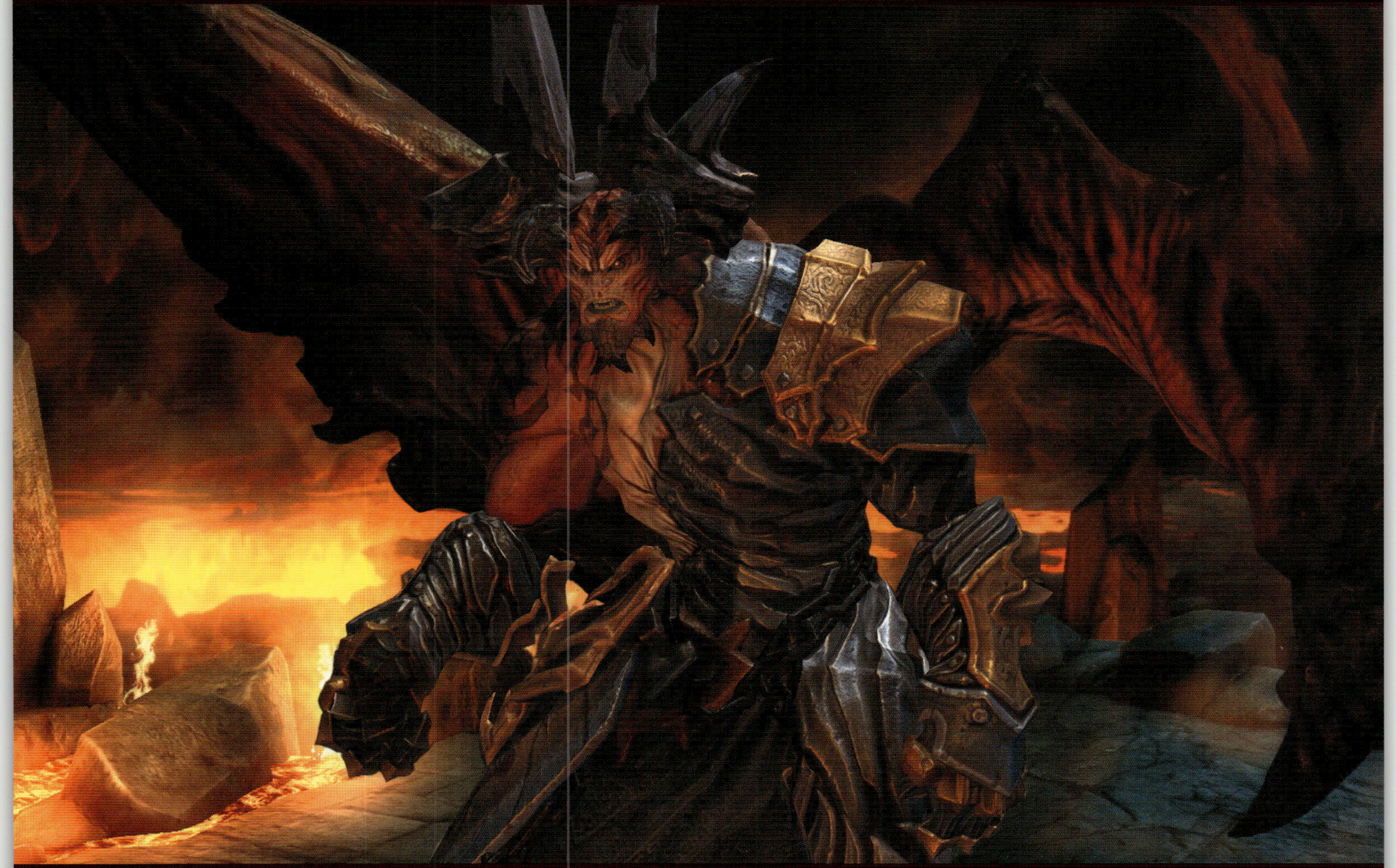

Samael An imprisoned demon who helps War regain is lost powers

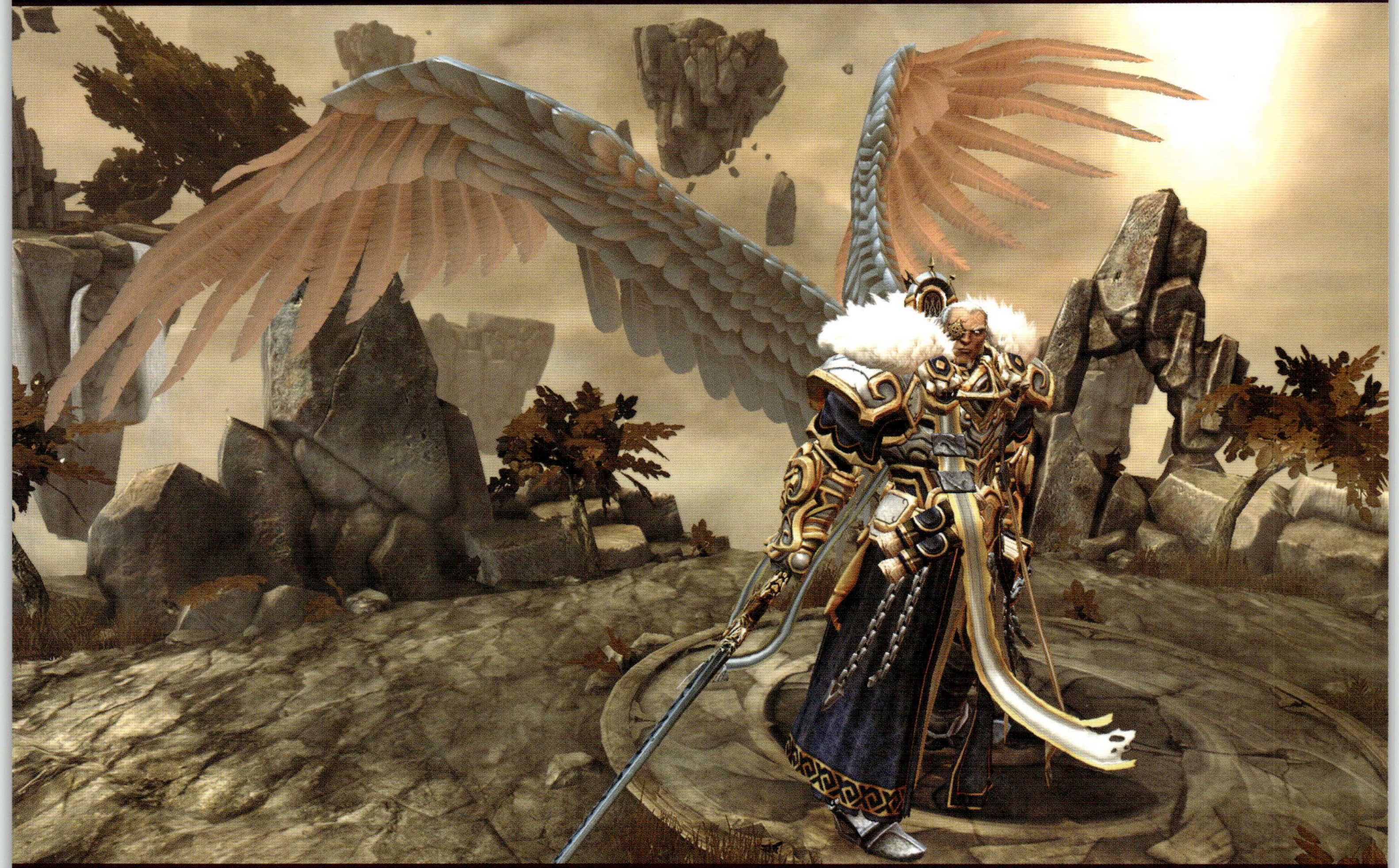

Abaddon Commander of Heaven's army. SIGNATURE ATTACK: Heavenly Glory

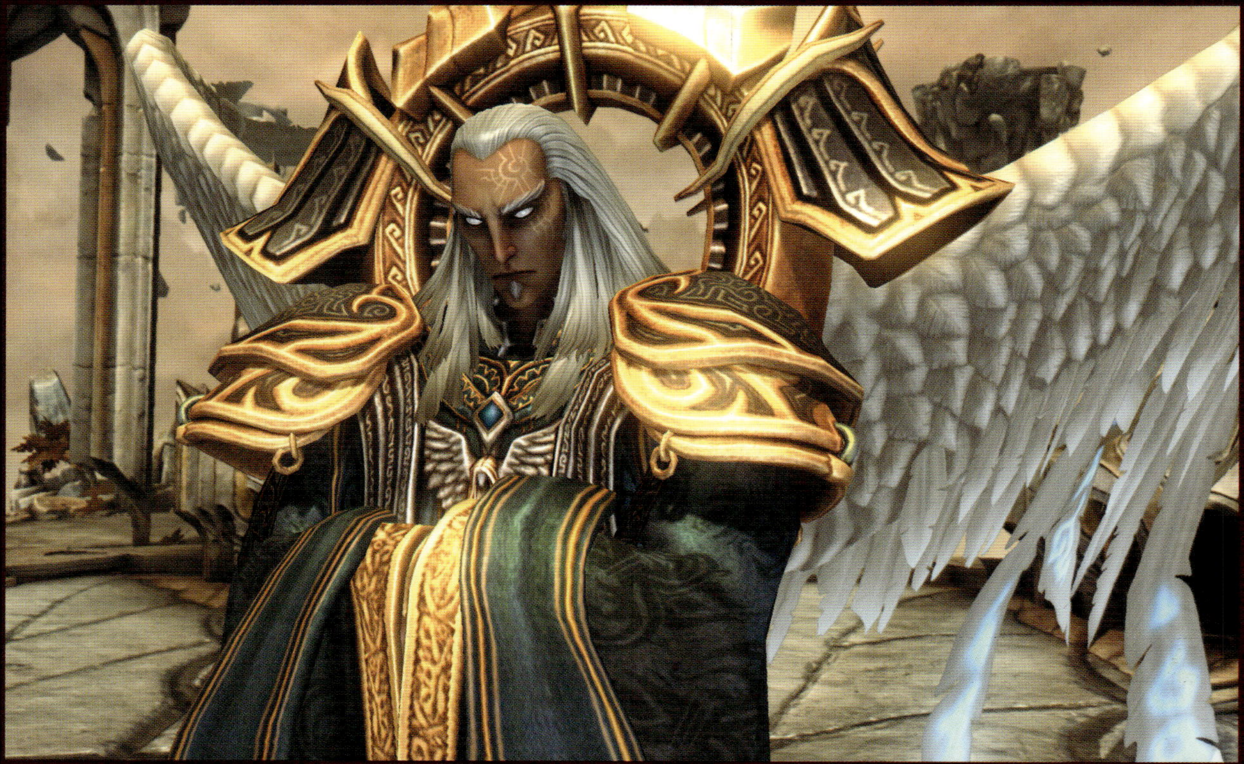

Azreal The archangel of death, imprisoned in the Black Throne.

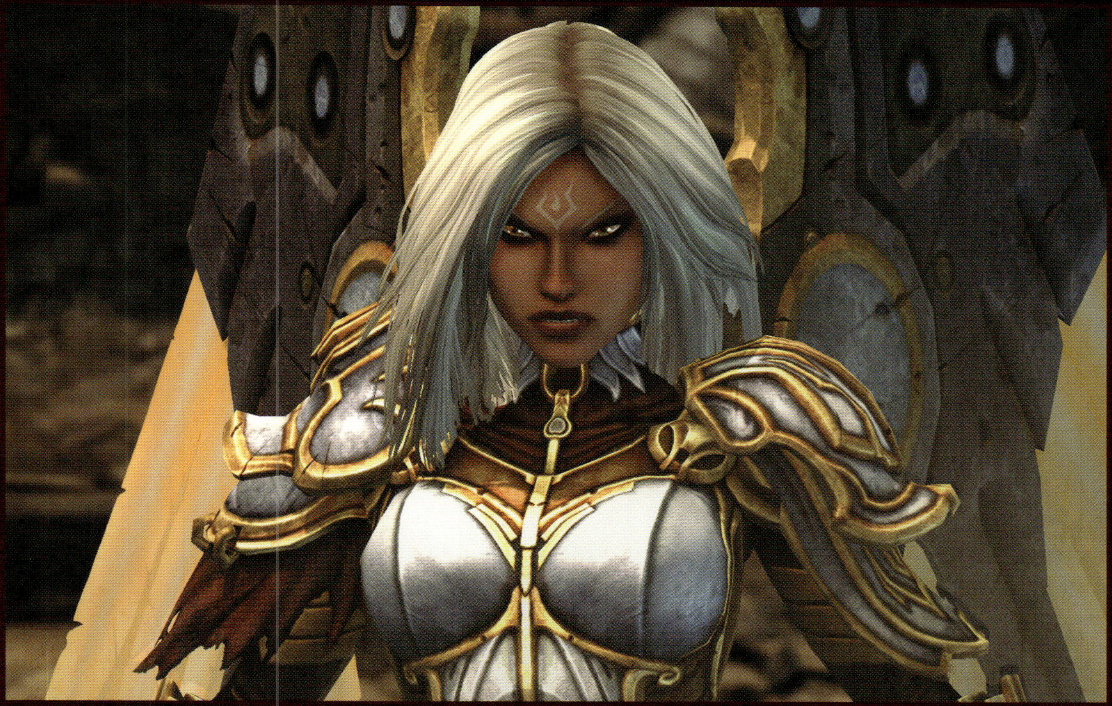

Uriel

One of Heaven's champions and second in command to Abaddon.

SIGNATURE ATTACK: Bladestorm

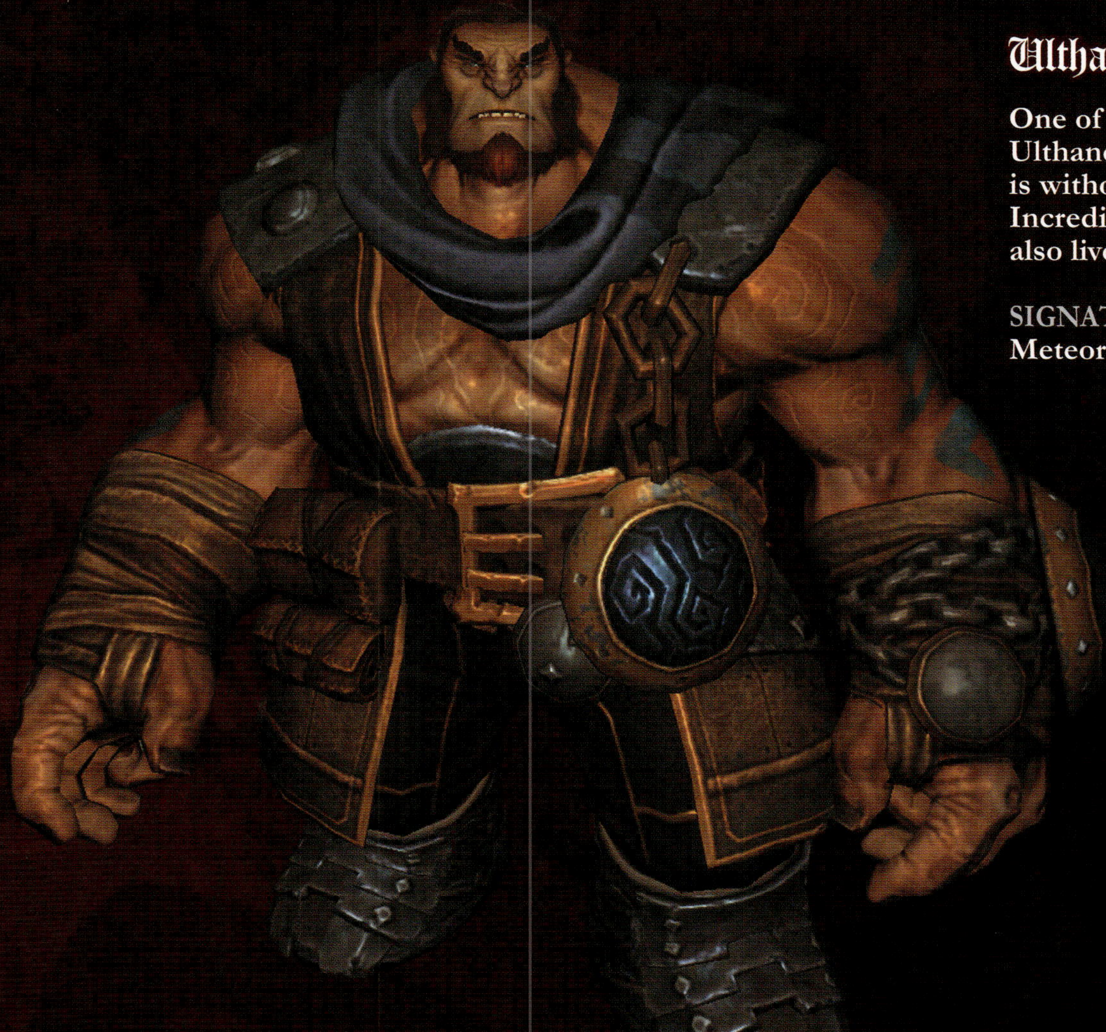

Ulthane

One of the old ones, Ulthane's forging ability is without approach. Incredibly powerful but also lives like a hermit.

SIGNATURE ATTACK: Meteor Hammer Throw

Angels

Light Angel

Righteous soldiers of Heaven.

SIGNATURE ATTACK:
Light Cannon

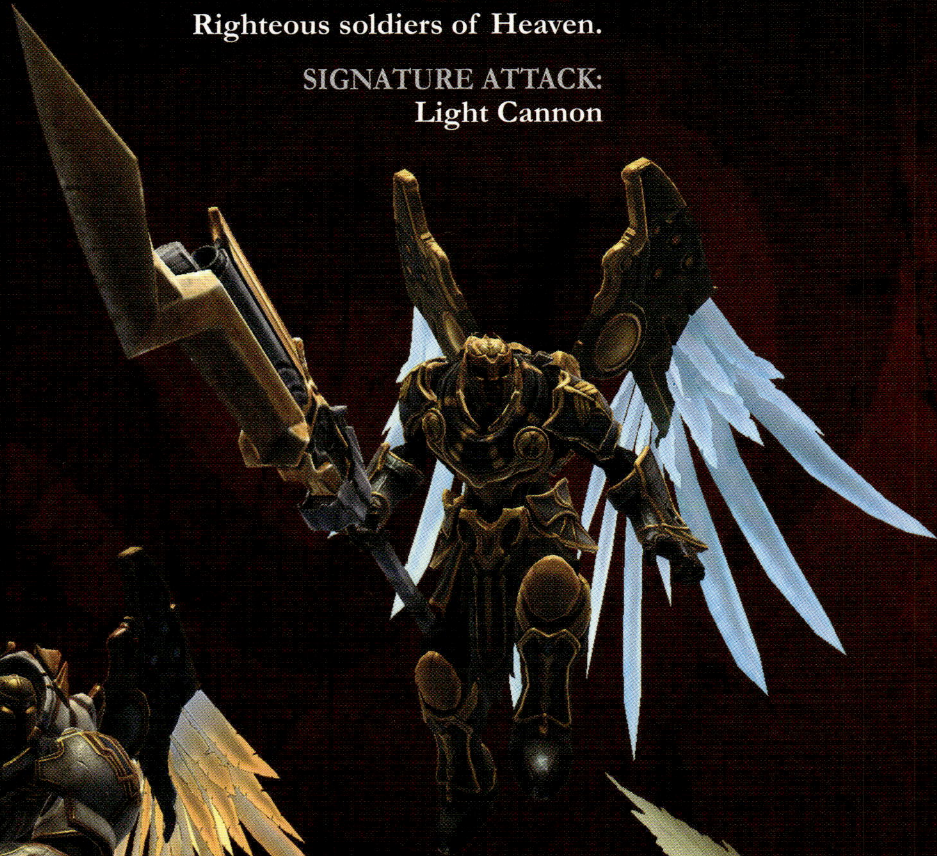

Stormbolter

Heaven's flying squadron.

SIGNATURE ATTACK:
Skybolt

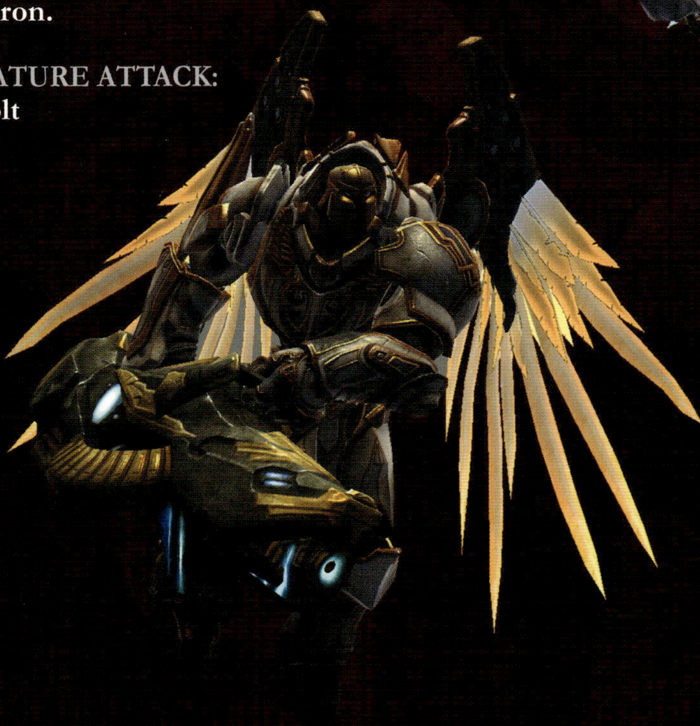

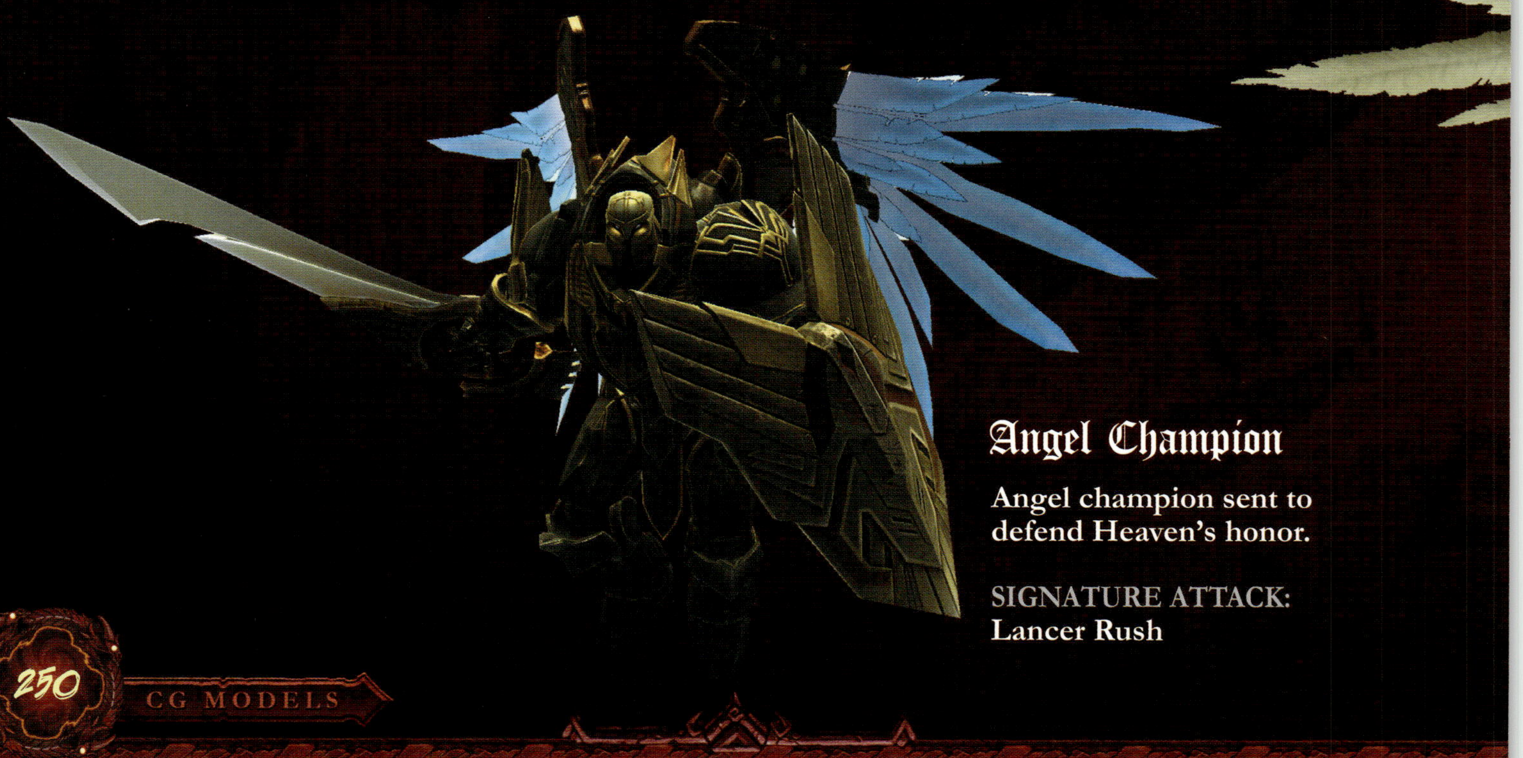

Angel Champion

Angel champion sent to defend Heaven's honor.

SIGNATURE ATTACK:
Lancer Rush

Forsaken

Elite angels corrupted by evil power.

SIGNATURE ATTACK:
Sonic Moon

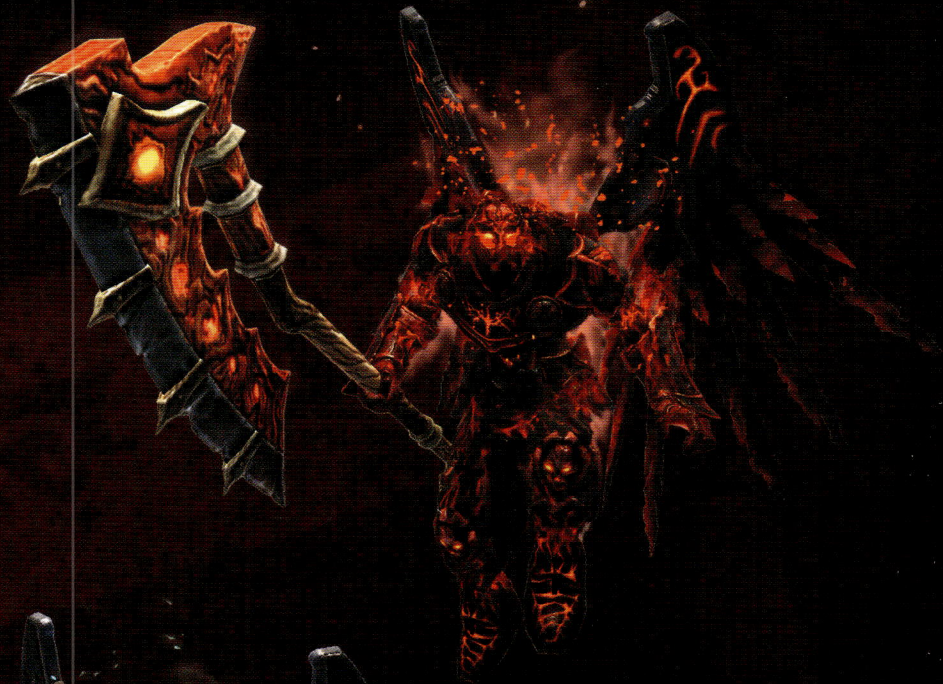

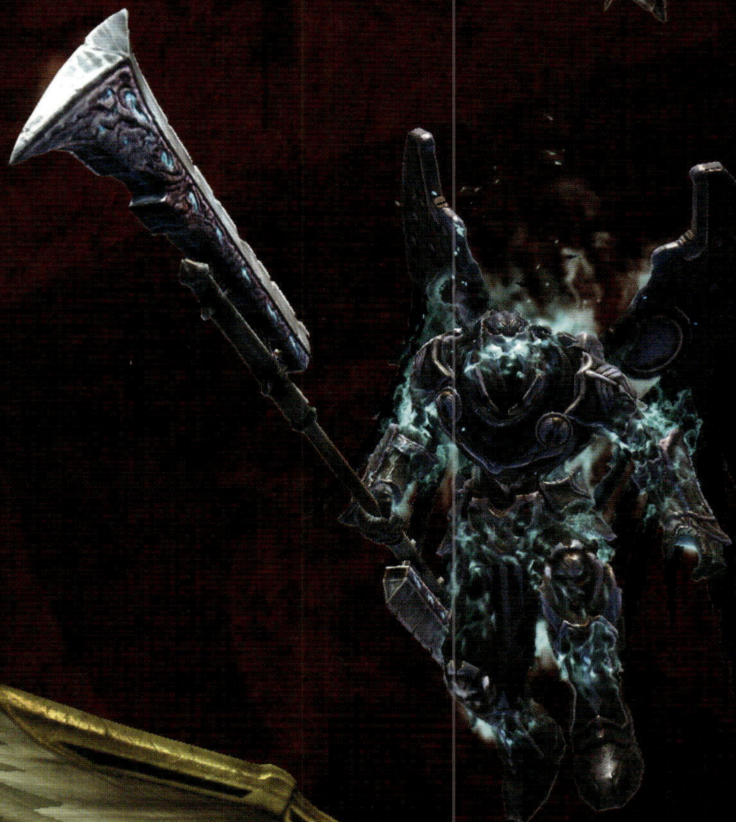

Fallen Angel

Outcast abandoned by heaven left to wander the earth.

SIGNATURE ATTACK:
Soul Grinder

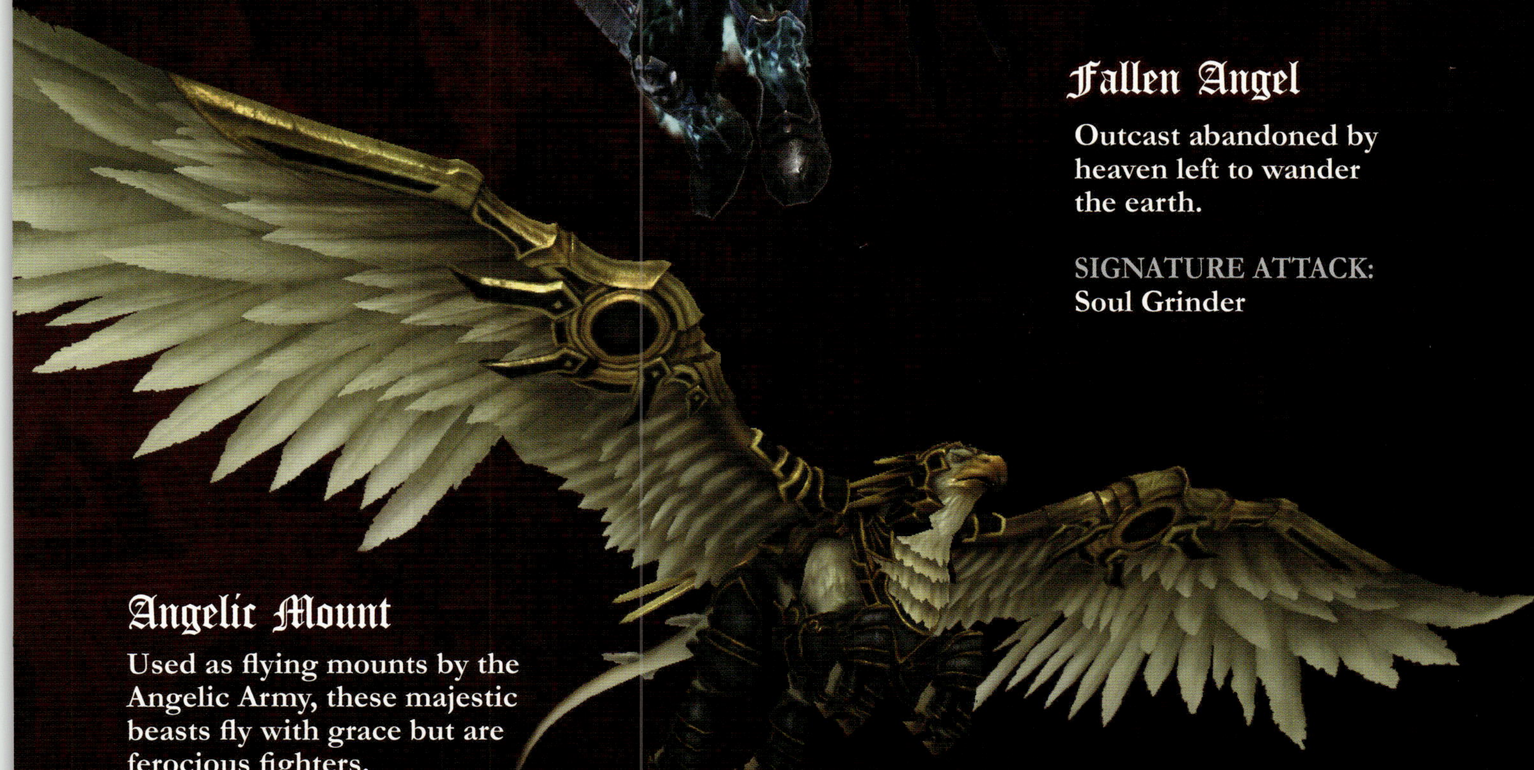

Angelic Mount

Used as flying mounts by the Angelic Army, these majestic beasts fly with grace but are ferocious fighters.

SIGNATURE ATTACK:
Chasing Shot

The Wicked

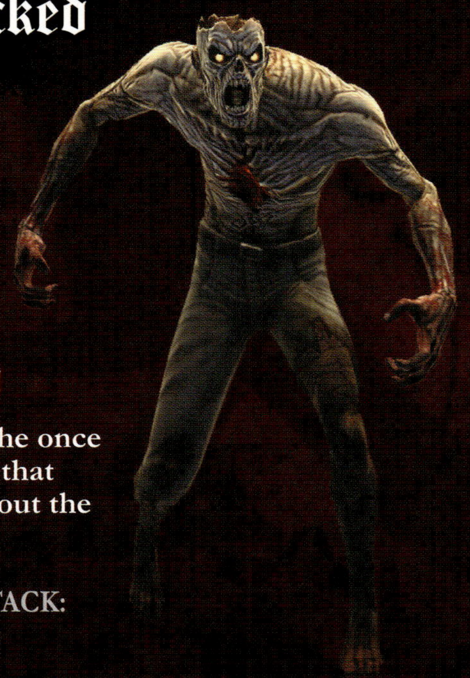

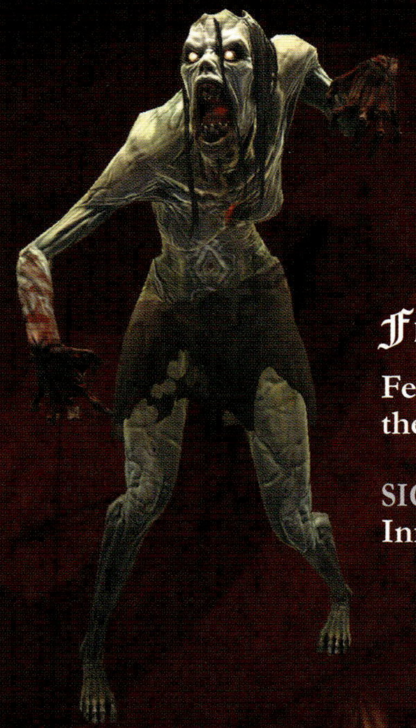

Female Wicked

Female version of the Wicked.

SIGNATURE ATTACK: Infection Strike

Male Wicked

Male version of the once human creatures that shamble throughout the world.

SIGNATURE ATTACK: Desperate Lunge

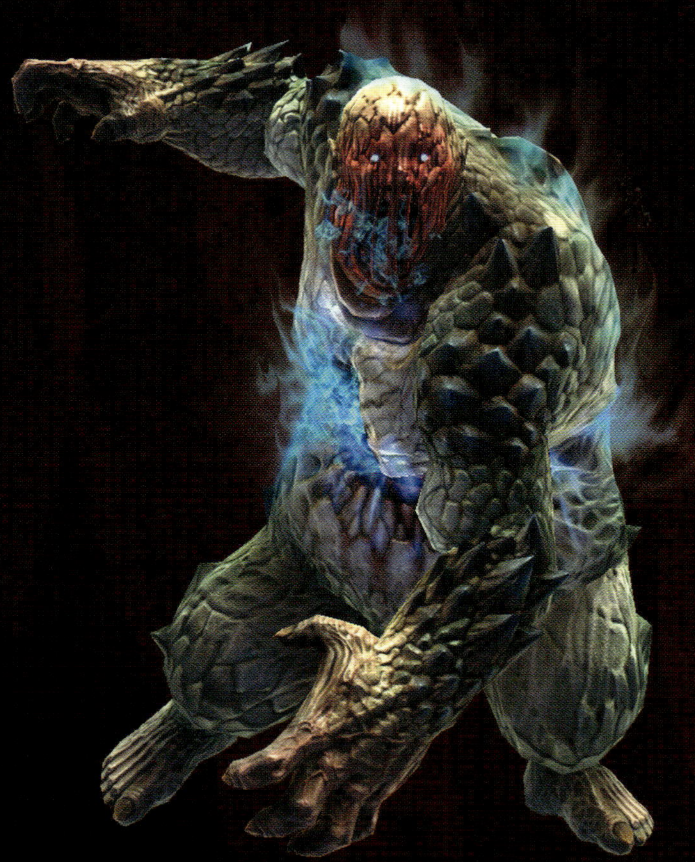

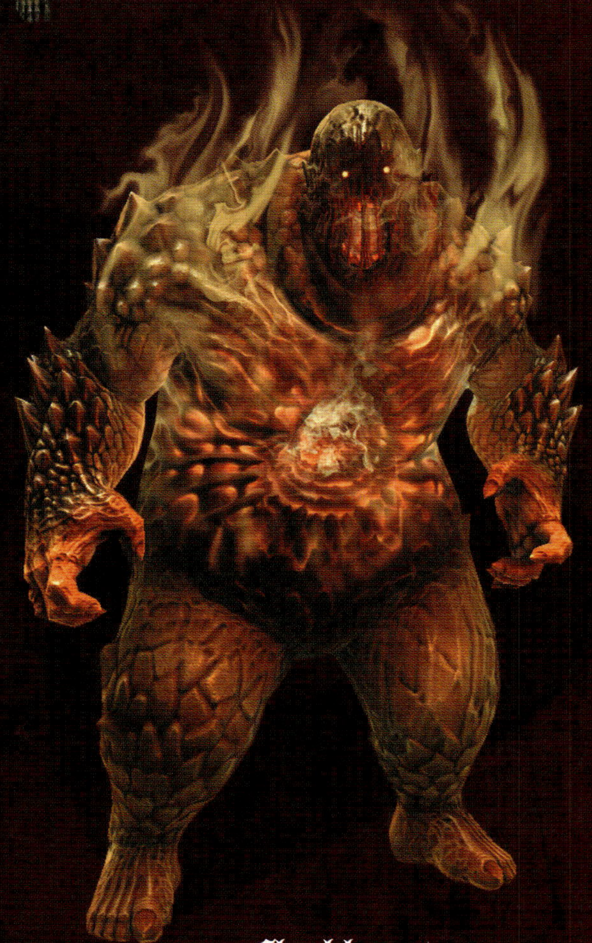

Fleshburster

Fiery Golem bent on destruction.

SIGNATURE ATTACK: Kamikazian

Ravenous

Soul eating demon with an insatiable appetite.

SIGNATURE ATTACK: Soul Gorge

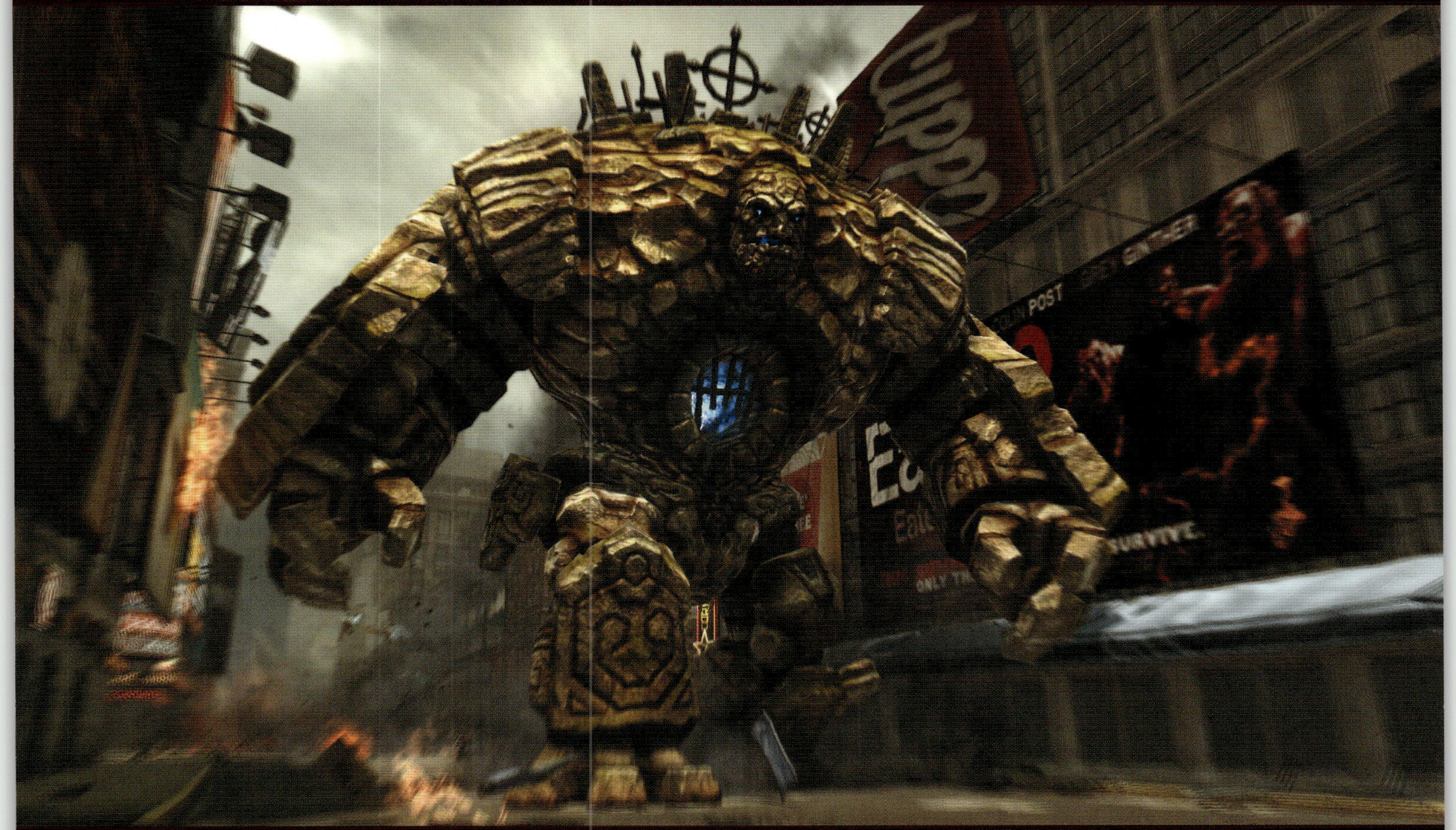

Tormented Gate

Ancient, non-aggressive entities made from living rock. Unkillable, but forced to do the destroyer's bidding.

SIGNATURE ATTACK: Atomic Stomp

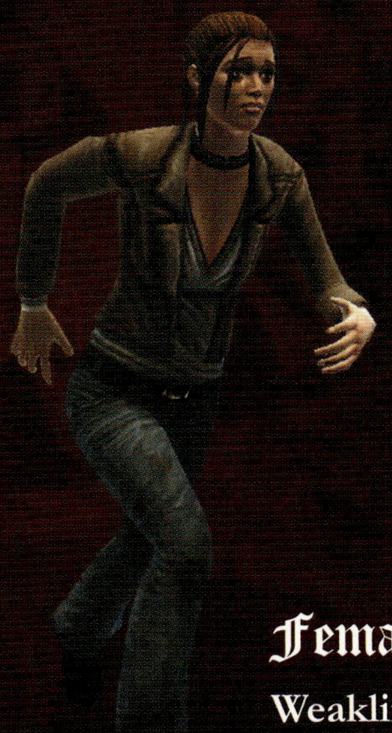

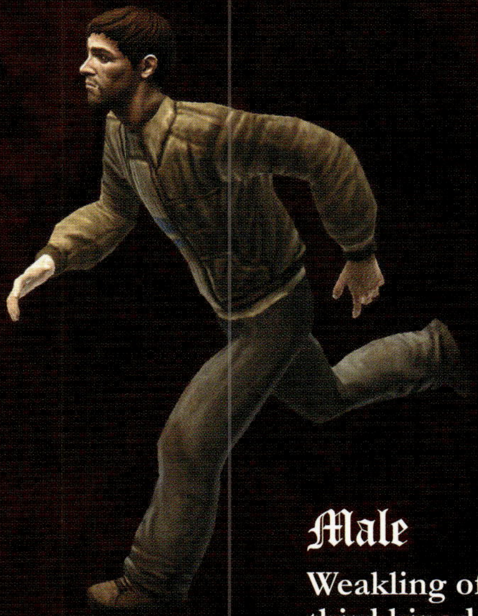

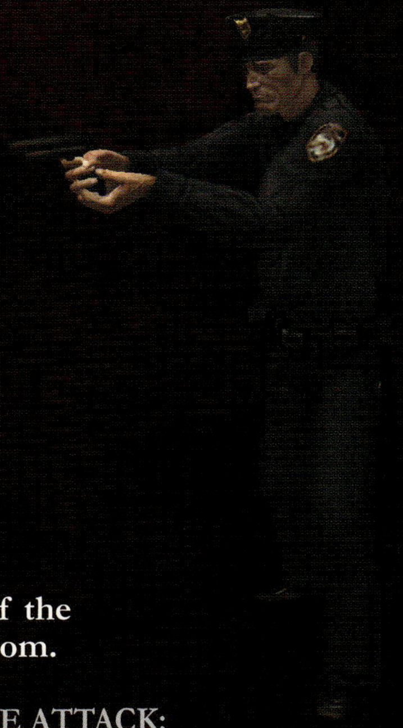

Cop

Brave, but futile protector of the third kingdom.

SIGNATURE ATTACK: Pistol Whip

Male

Weakling of the third kingdom.

SIGNATURE ATTACK: Sprint

Female

Weakling of the third kingdom.

SIGNATURE ATTACK: Hope

Humans

Phantom Guards

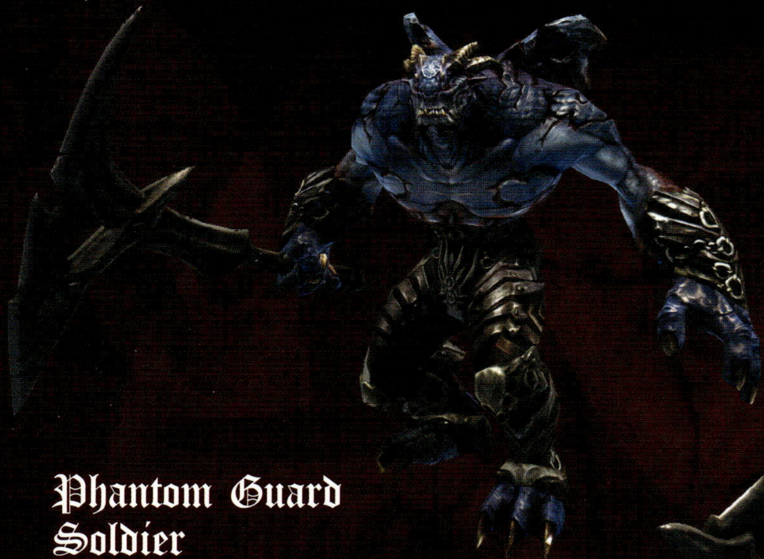

Phantom Guard Soldier

Minion grunts from the demon realm.

SIGNATURE ATTACK:
The Cleaver

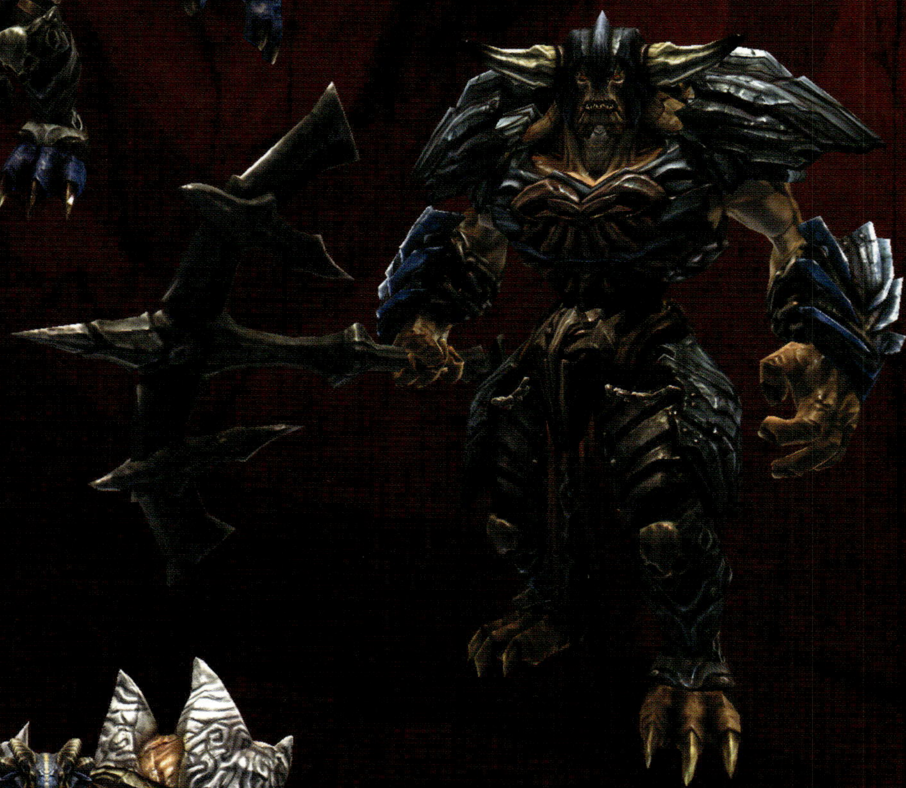

Phantom Captain

Commander of the demonic legions.

SIGNATURE ATTACK:
Gutbuster Uppercut

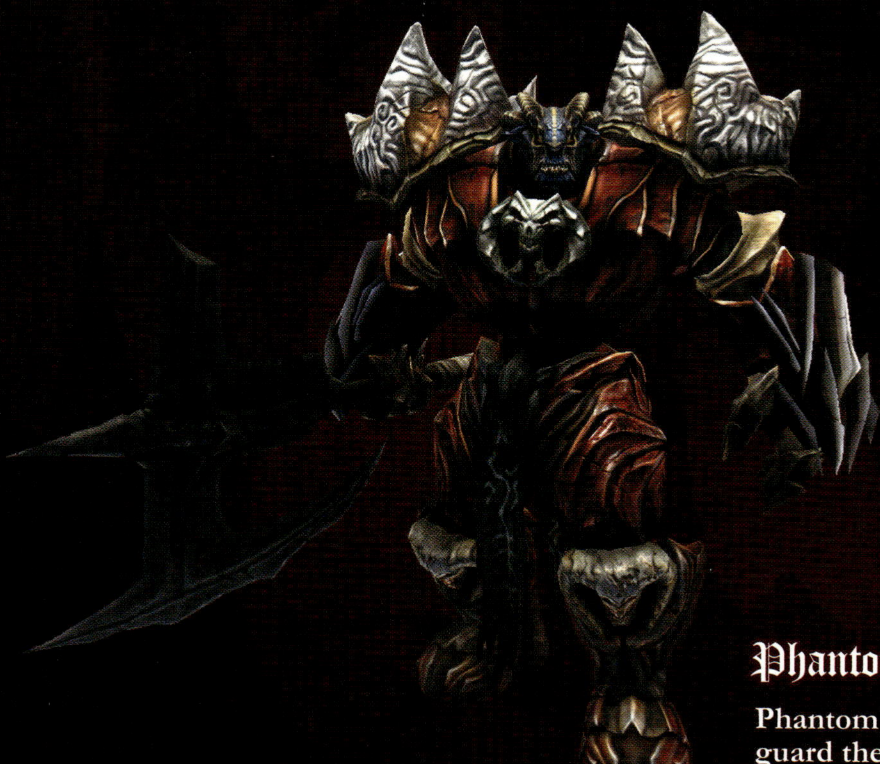

Phantom General

Phantom general assigned to guard the prison of Samael.

SIGNATURE ATTACK:
Storm Geyser

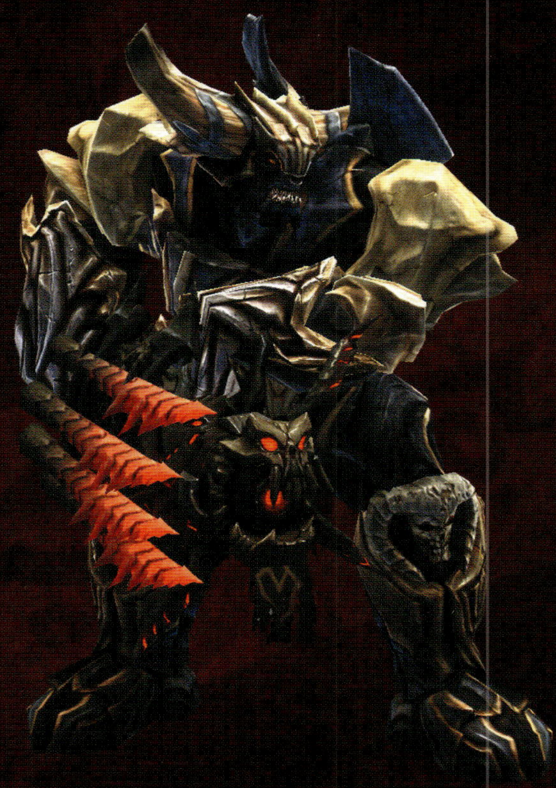

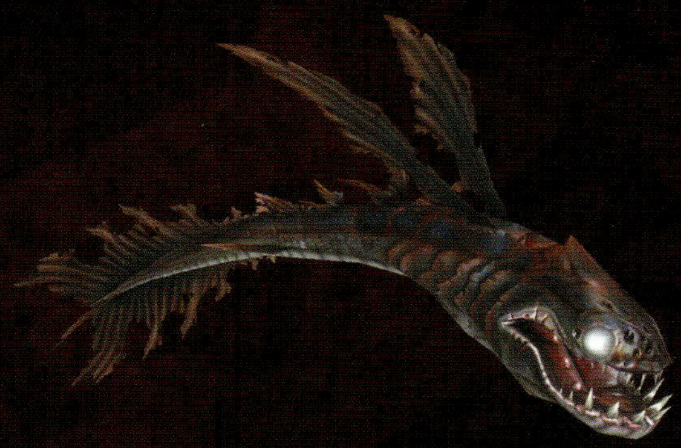

Deep Lurker

Electric demon fish that infest waters of Earth.

SIGNATURE ATTACK:
Aquashock

Devastator

A power, tank-like brute who carries the formidable fracture cannon weapon into battle. Slow, but dangerous at a distance.

SIGNATURE ATTACK:
Fracture Bolt

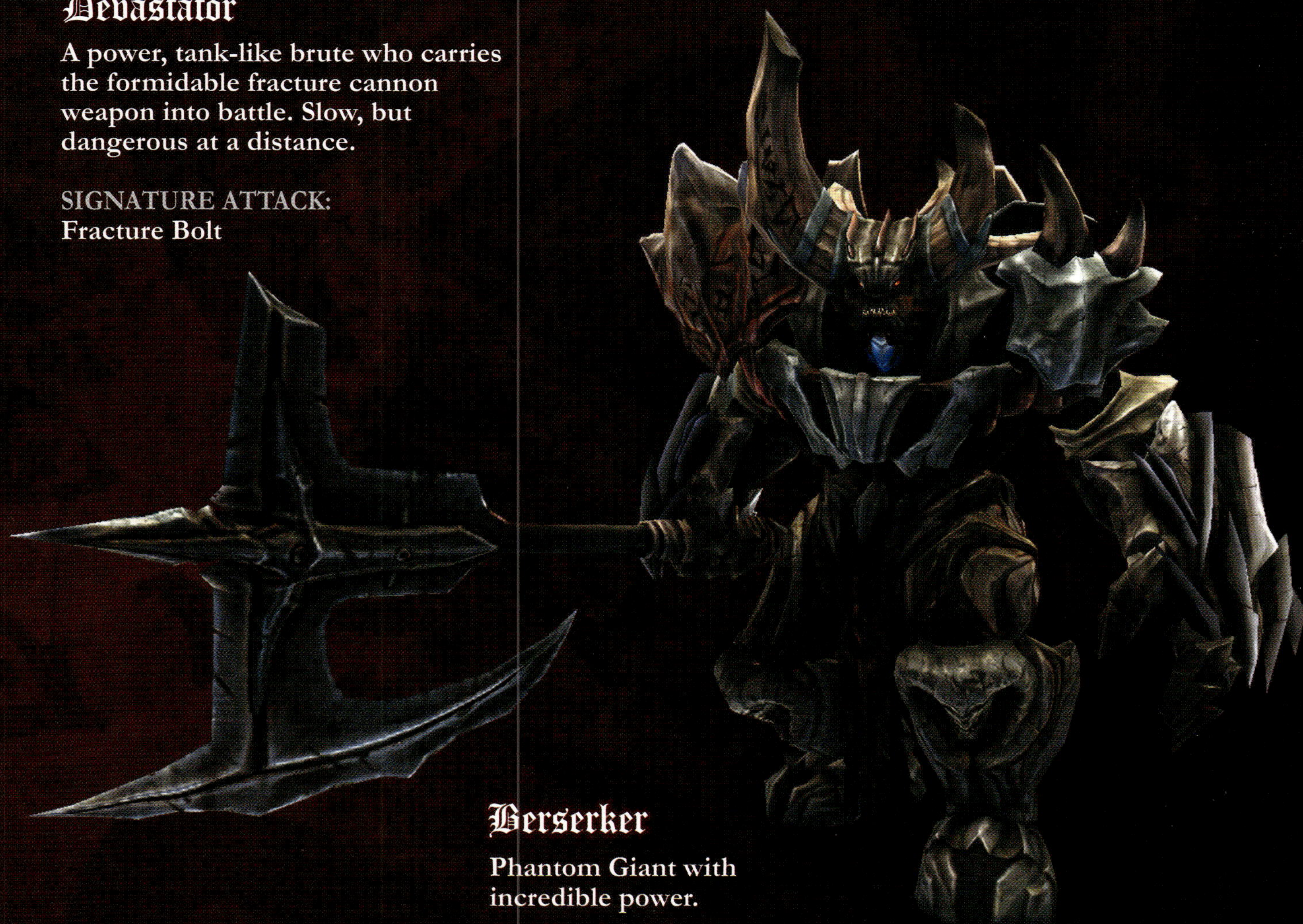

Berserker

Phantom Giant with incredible power.

SIGNATURE ATTACK:
Rampage Blade

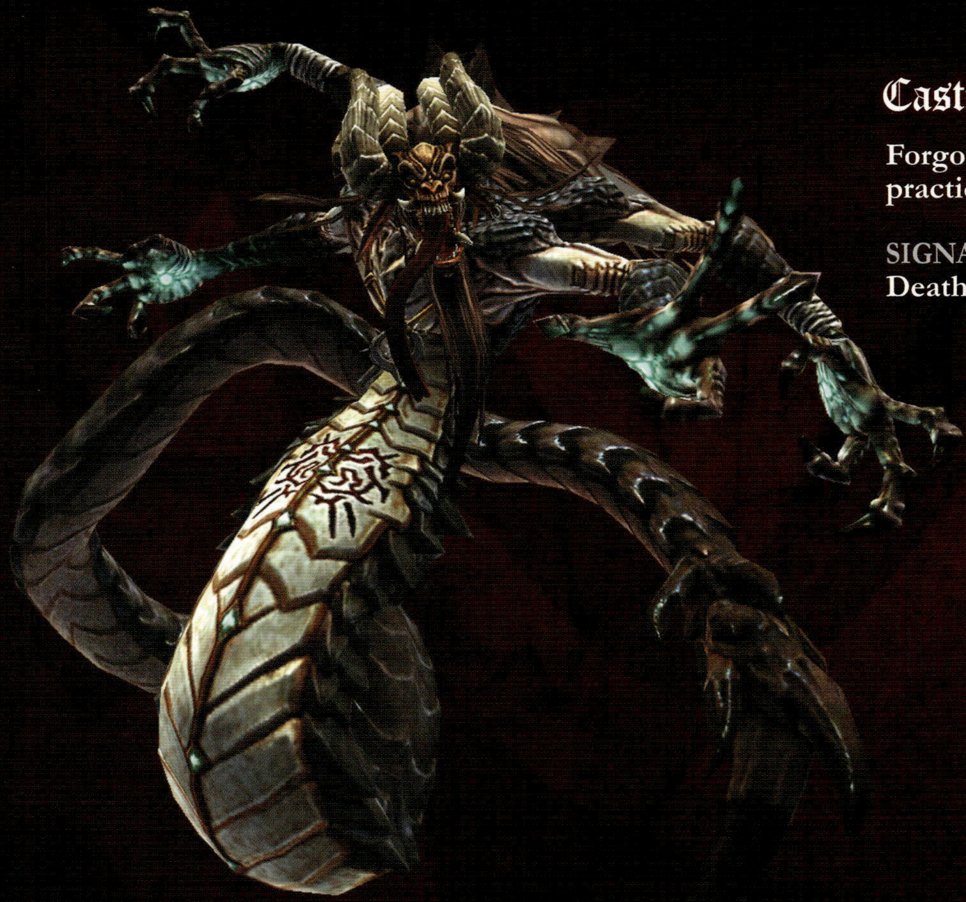

Caster

Forgotten shaman that practices the forbidden arts.

SIGNATURE ATTACK:
Death From Below

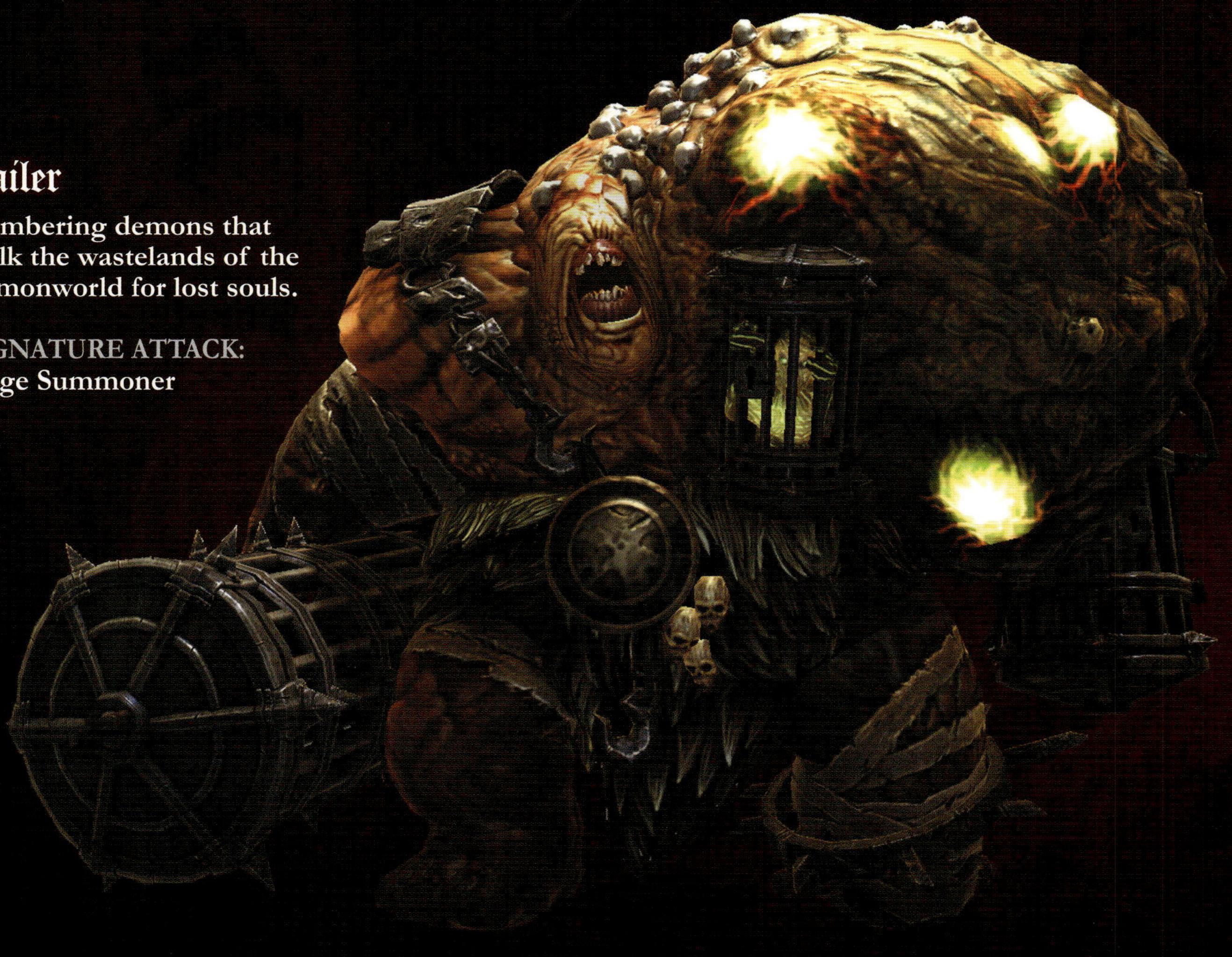

Jailer

Lumbering demons that walk the wastelands of the demonworld for lost souls.

SIGNATURE ATTACK:
Cage Summoner

Minions

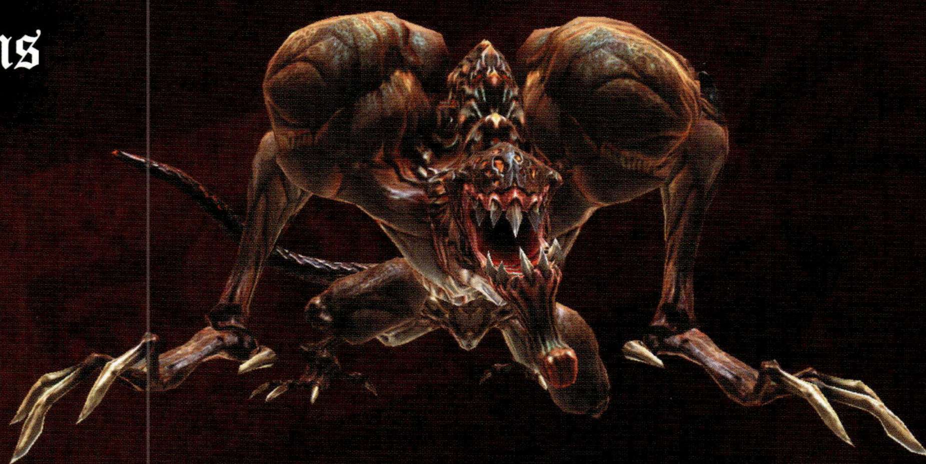

Minion

Grotesque scavengers of bloodied battle fields.

SIGNATURE ATTACK:
Lurching Claw

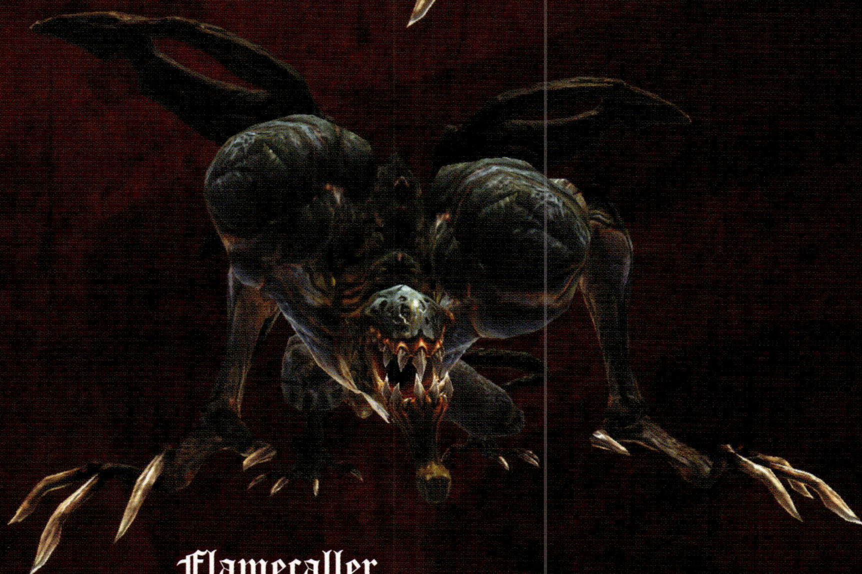

Flamecaller

Demonic Archers that lurk in the shadows.

SIGNATURE ATTACK:
Molten Core

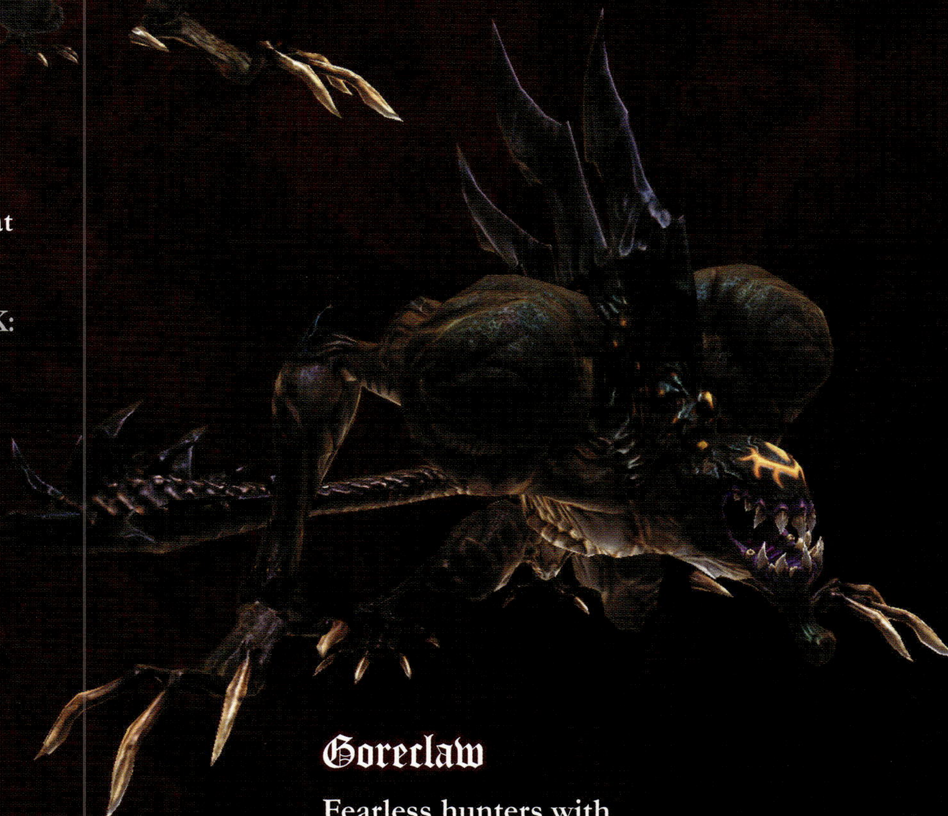

Goreclaw

Fearless hunters with unfathomable hunger.

SIGNATURE ATTACK:
Barrelblades

Undead

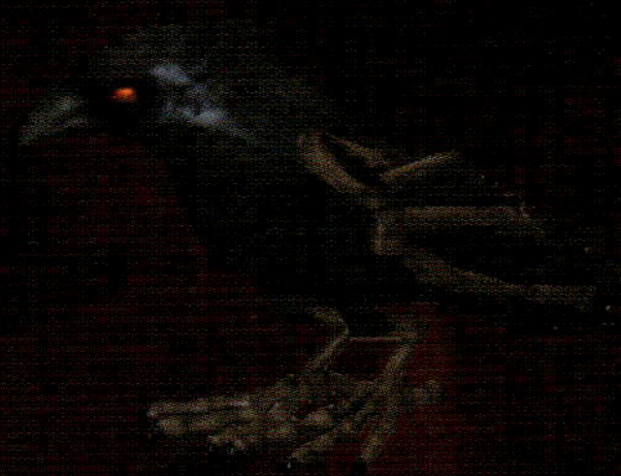

Crow

A possessed version of the third kingdom's vermin bird.

Undead Soldier

Undead knights summoned to serve the demonic army.

SIGNATURE ATTACK:
Thrasher

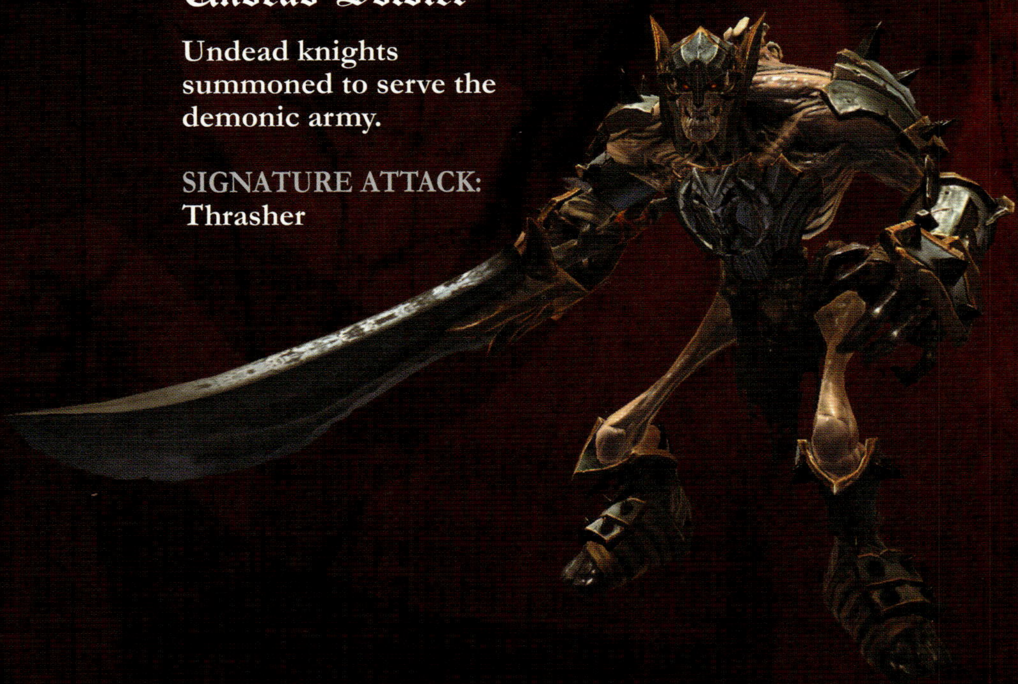

Conscript

Undead brute with armor made from demonic crystal.

SIGNATURE ATTACK:
Shatterblade

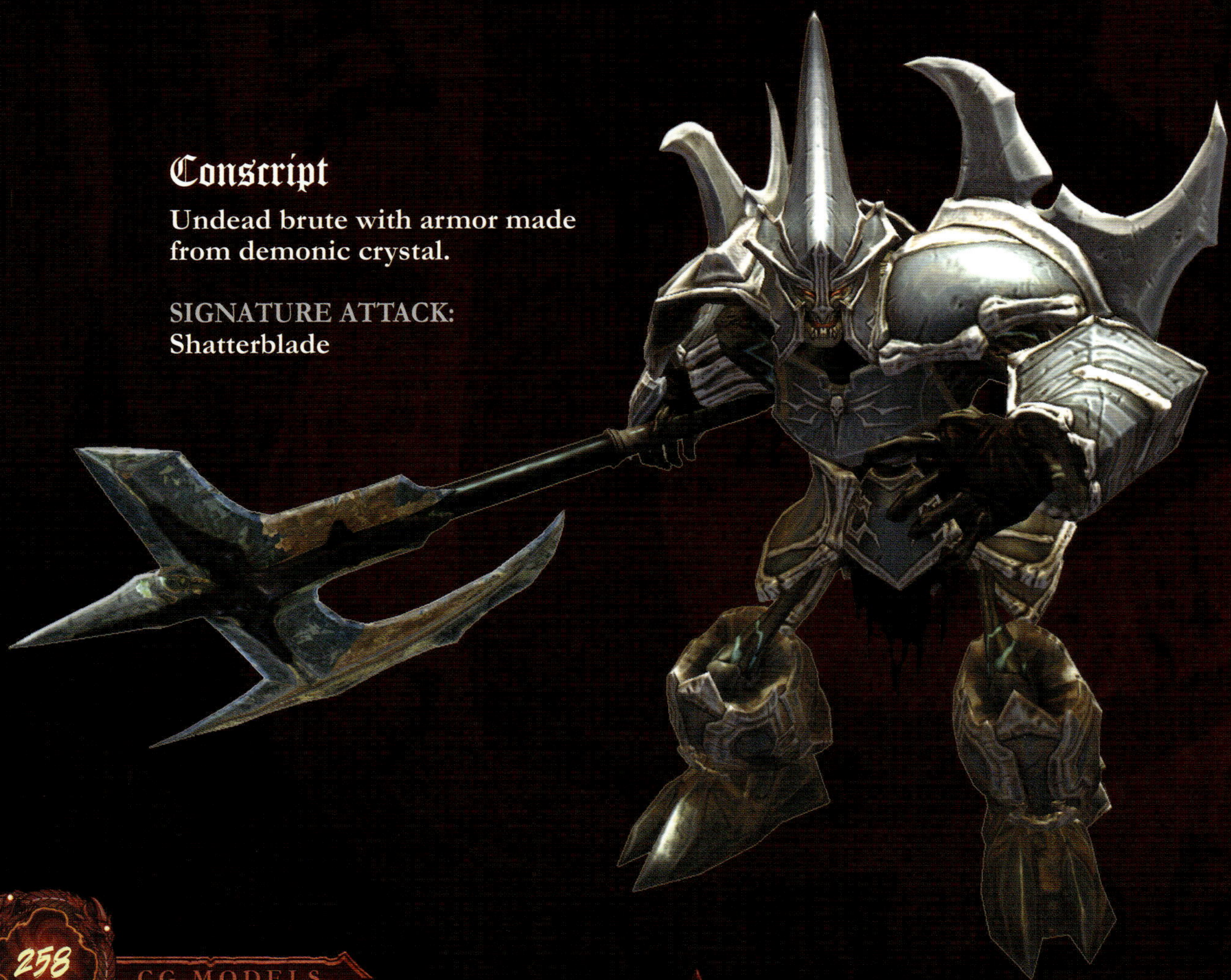

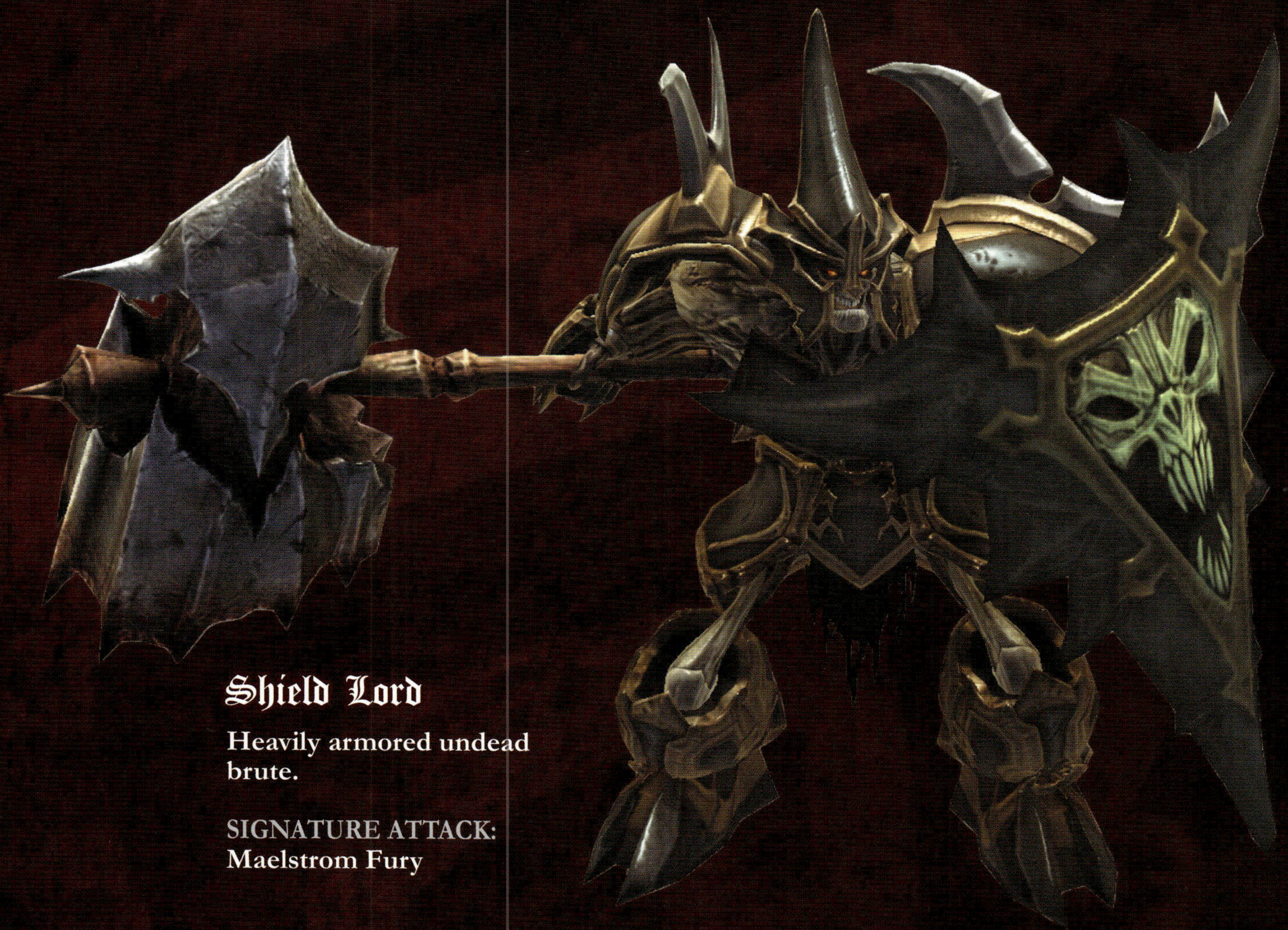

Shield Lord

Heavily armored undead brute.

SIGNATURE ATTACK:
Maelstrom Fury

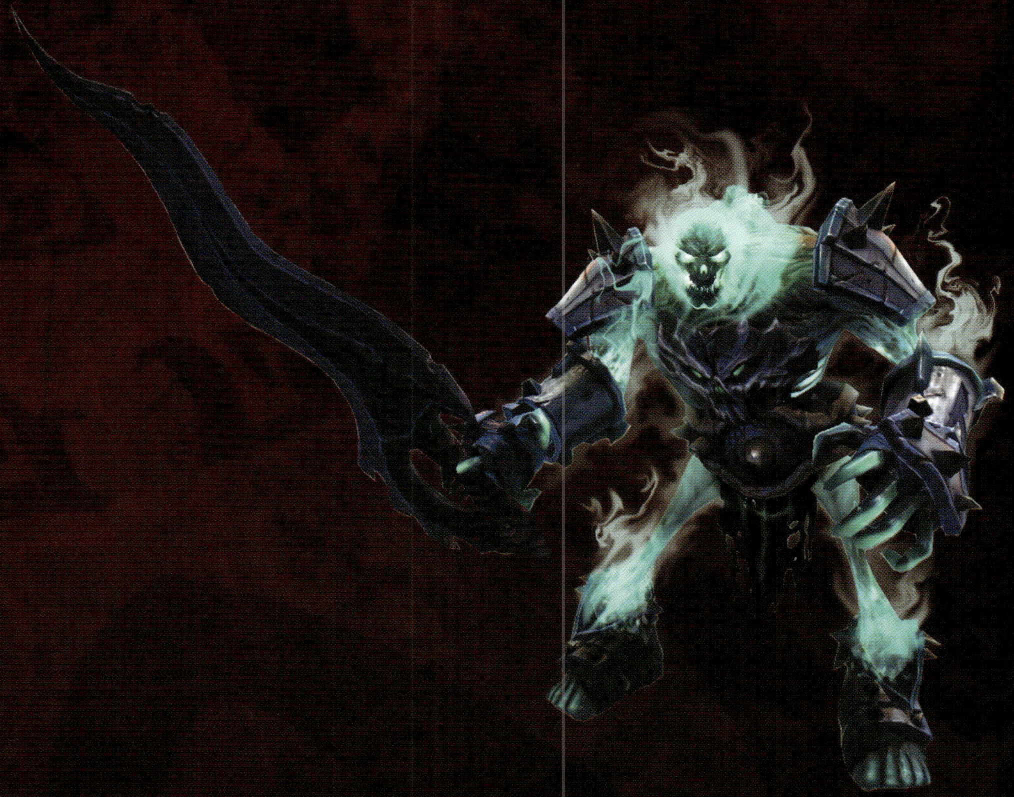

Undead Lord

Elite undead knights from the depths of Hell.

SIGNATURE ATTACK:
Bone Crusher

Broodlings

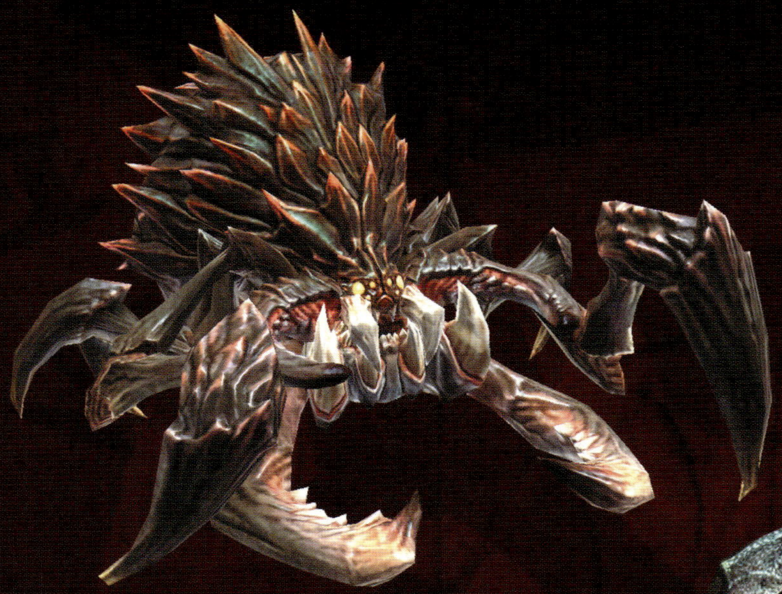

Broodling

Vicious baby spiders spawned from Silitha's egg sacks.

SIGNATURE ATTACK: Face Shredder

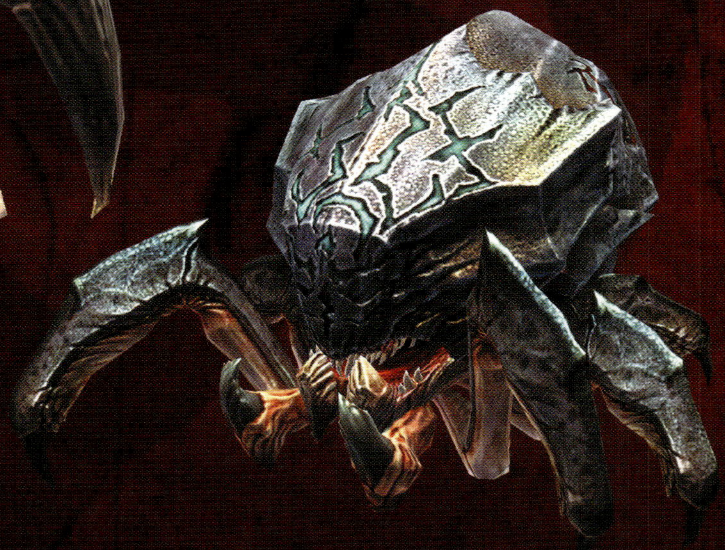

Loom Warden

One of the protectors of Silitha, these heavily armored beasts cannot be harmed while their shells remain.

SIGNATURE ATTACK: Feeding Frenzy

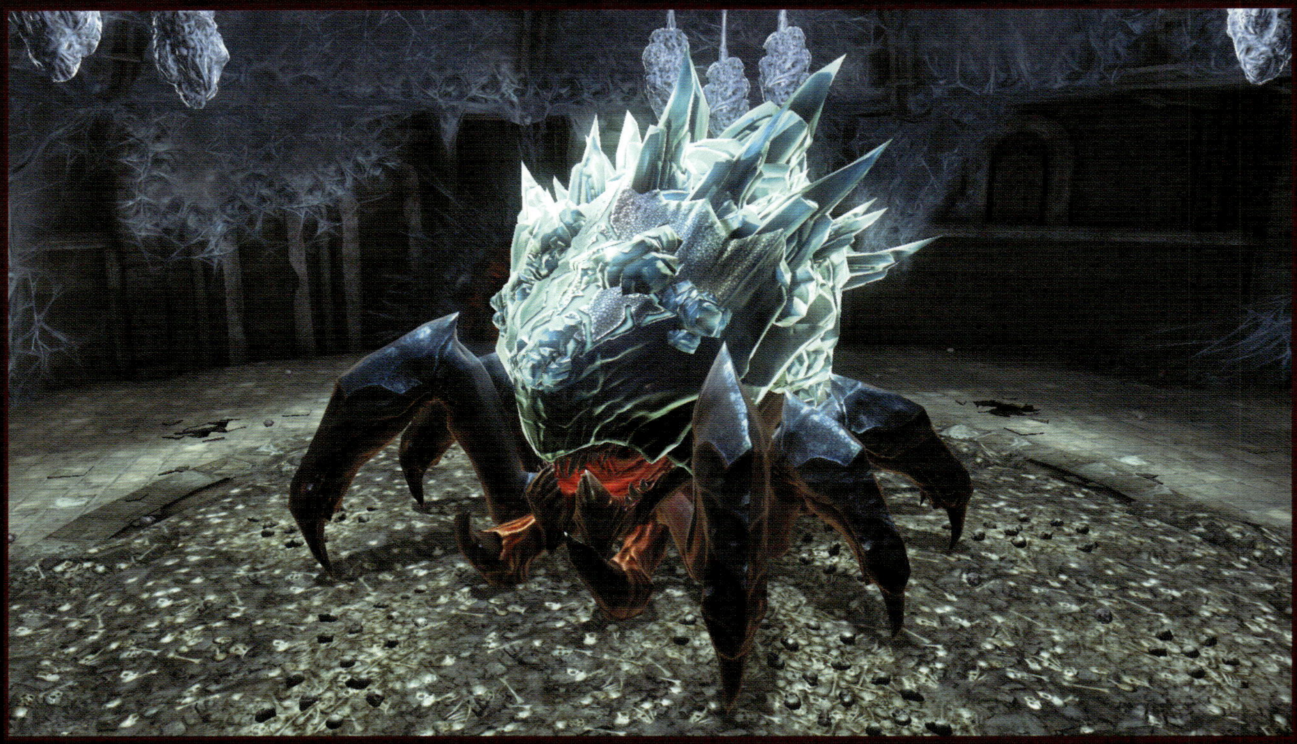

Broodmother Crystal shelled guardian of Silitha. SIGNATURE ATTACK: Seismic Slam

Wraiths

Wraith Scout

Demon princess of the underworld.

SIGNATURE ATTACK:
Blade Flurry

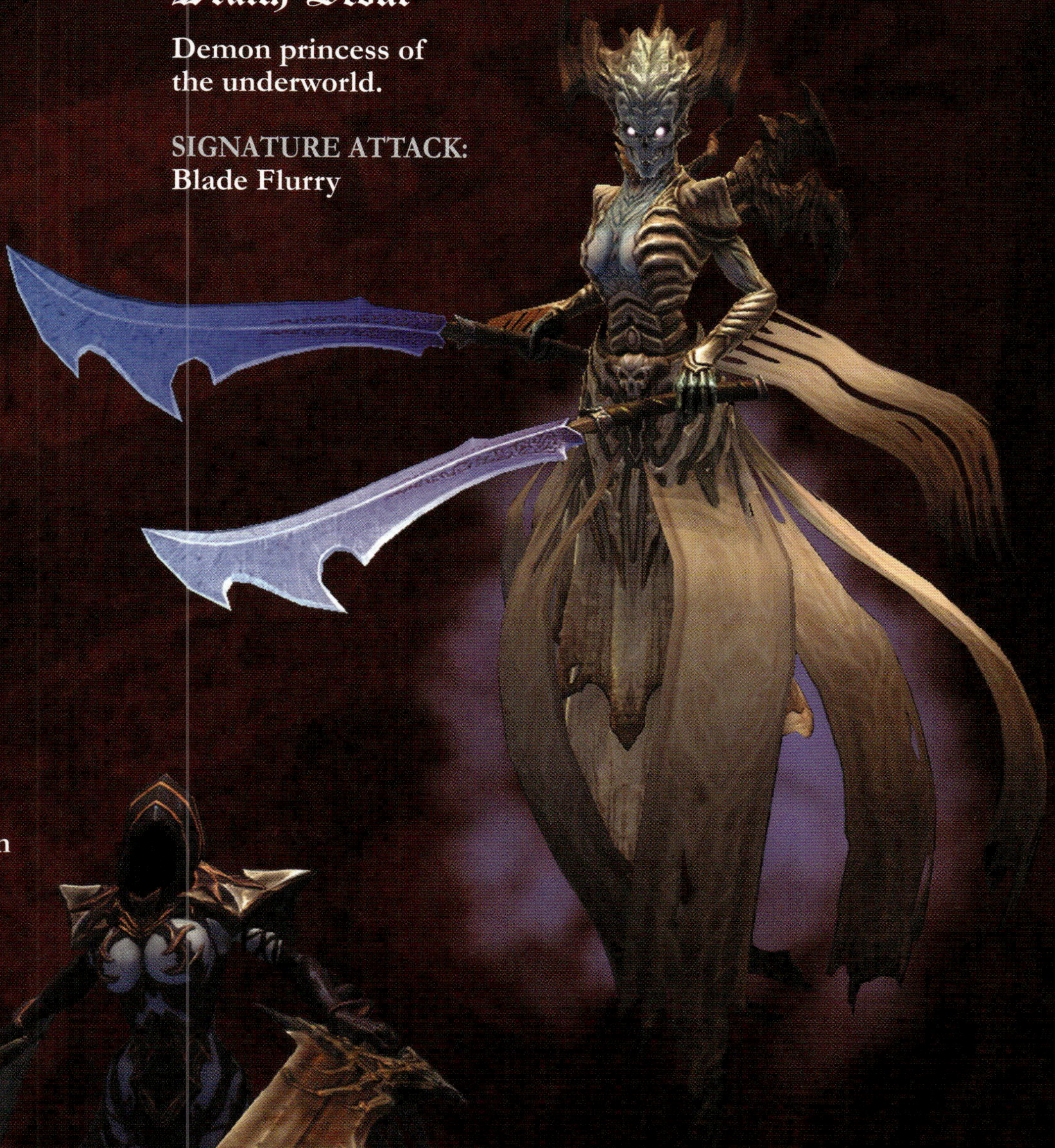

Wraith Soldier

Vengeful spirt with twin blades of torture.

SIGNATURE ATTACK:
Dancing Blade

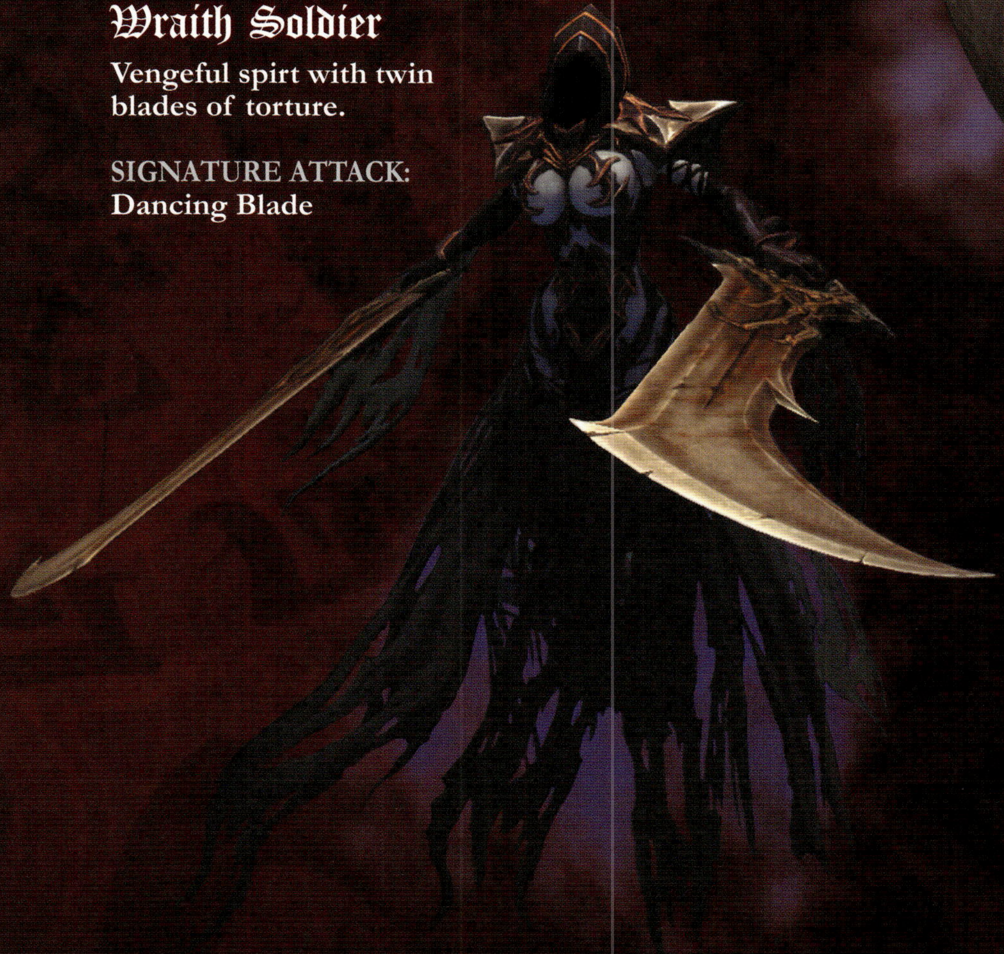

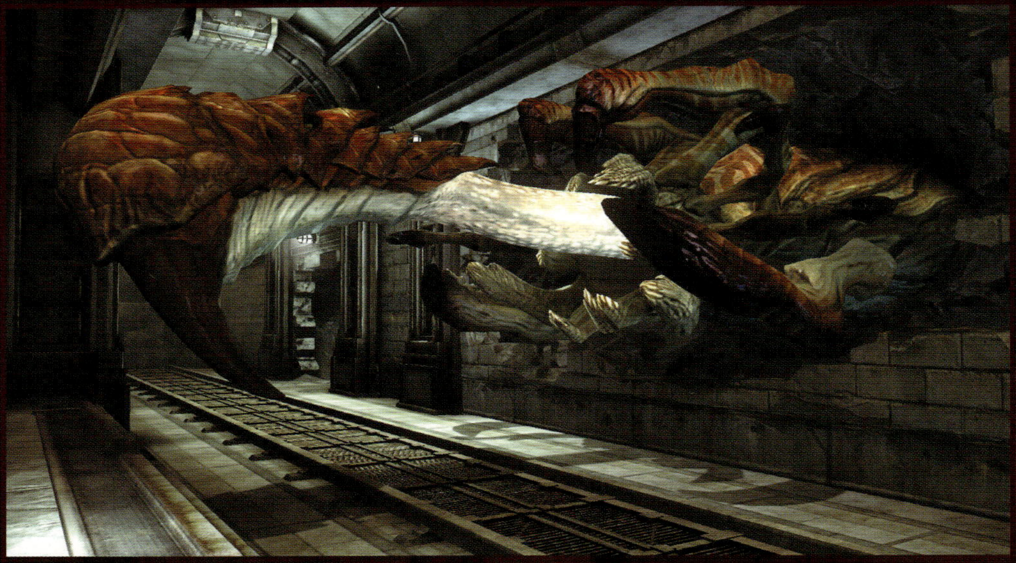

Torture Coil

Massive, underground beast with unparallel strength. It lies in the deepest reaches of The Hollows and breaks through the wall to destroy anything it senses moving.

SIGNATURE ATTACK: The Constrictor

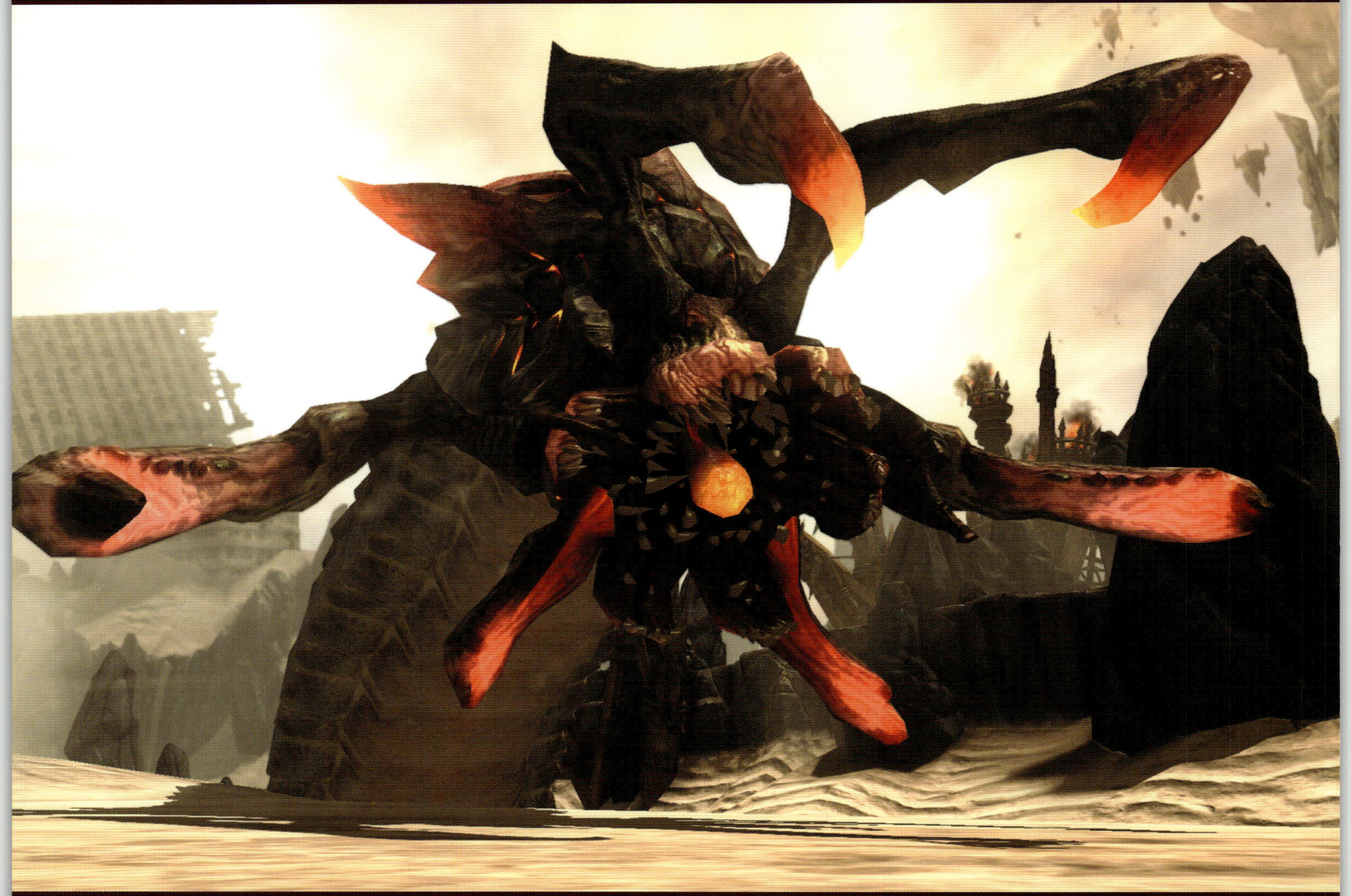

Ash Titan

Giant sand worms that scour beneath the Ashlands.

SIGNATURE ATTACK: The Earth Swallow

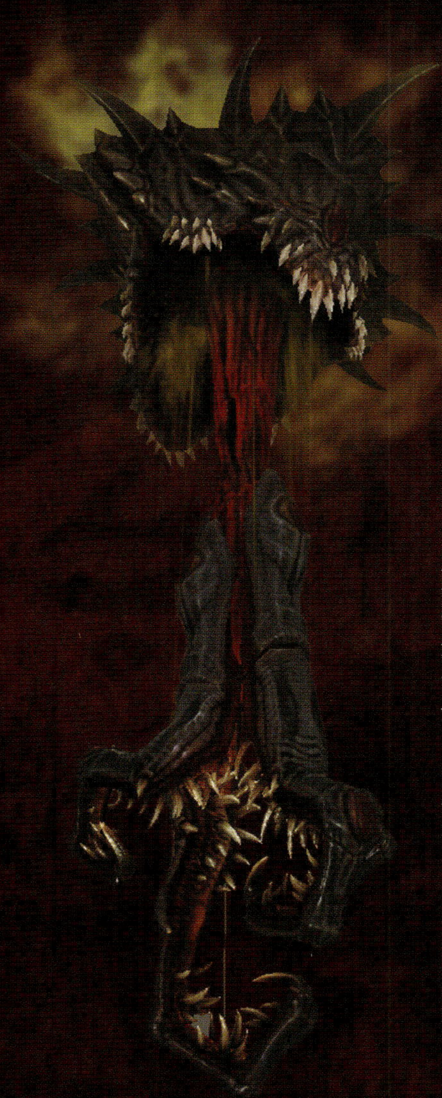

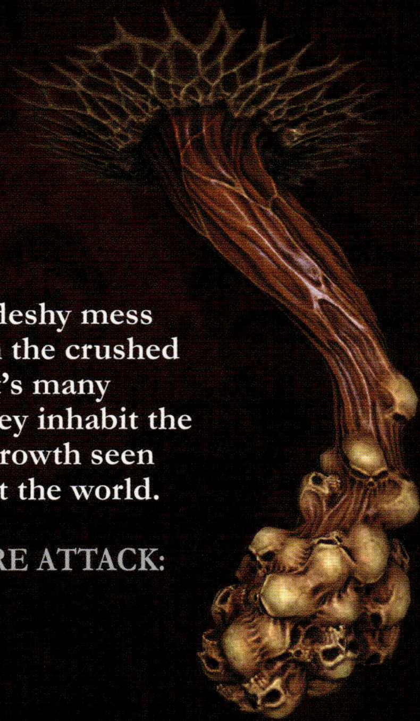

Lasher

A twisted fleshy mess made from the crushed bones of it's many victims, they inhabit the demonic growth seen throughout the world.

SIGNATURE ATTACK:
Fleshlash

Goremaw

Feeding talons who cannot be killed, only injured. Lie in wait for their unknowing pray to walk beneath them.

SIGNATURE ATTACK:
The Gore Grinder

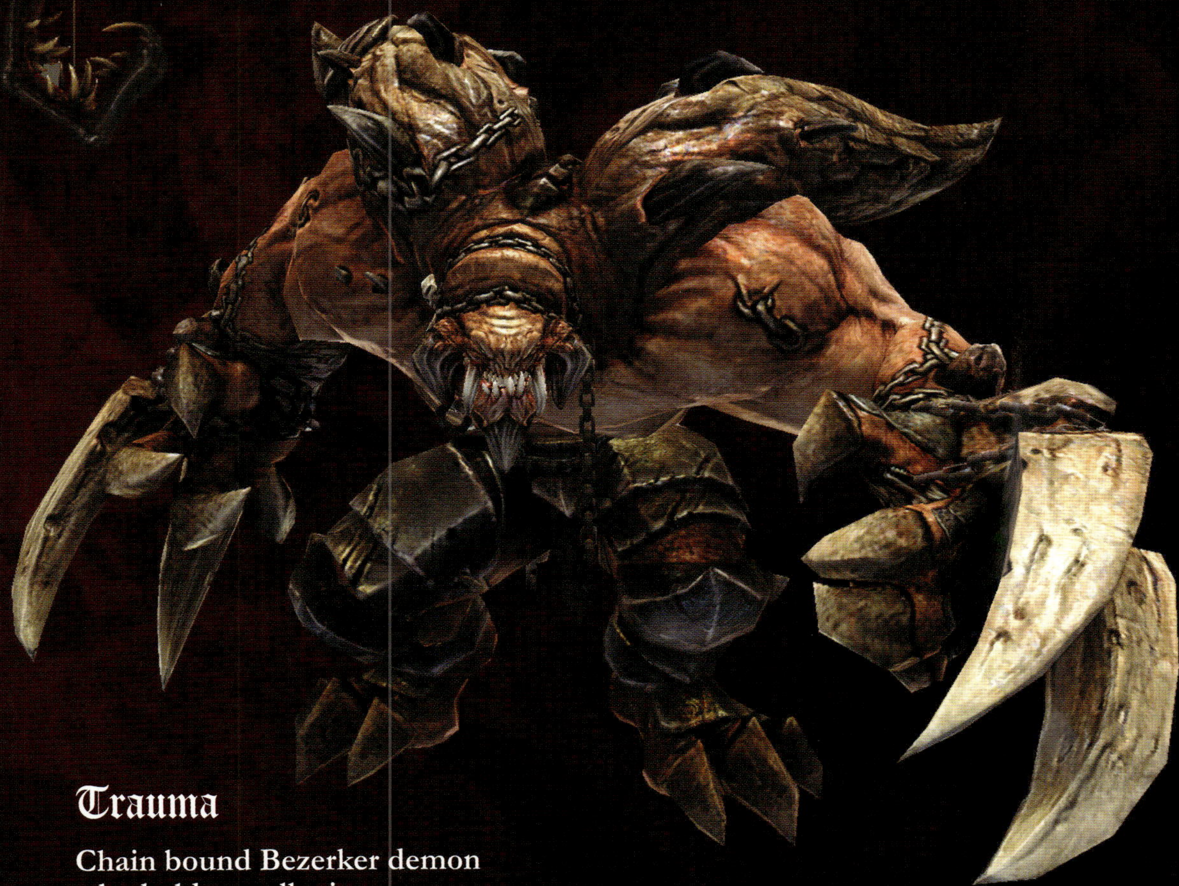

Trauma

Chain bound Bezerker demon who holds no allegiances

SIGNATURE ATTACK: Lunging Claw

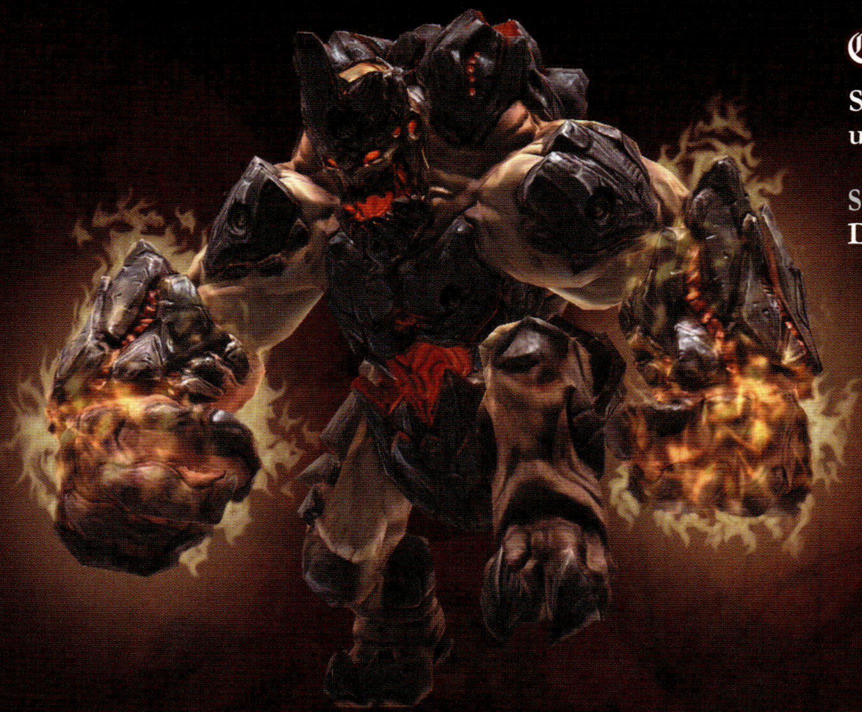

Earthcracker

Strongarm of the underworld forces.

SIGNATURE ATTACK:
Dozer Charge

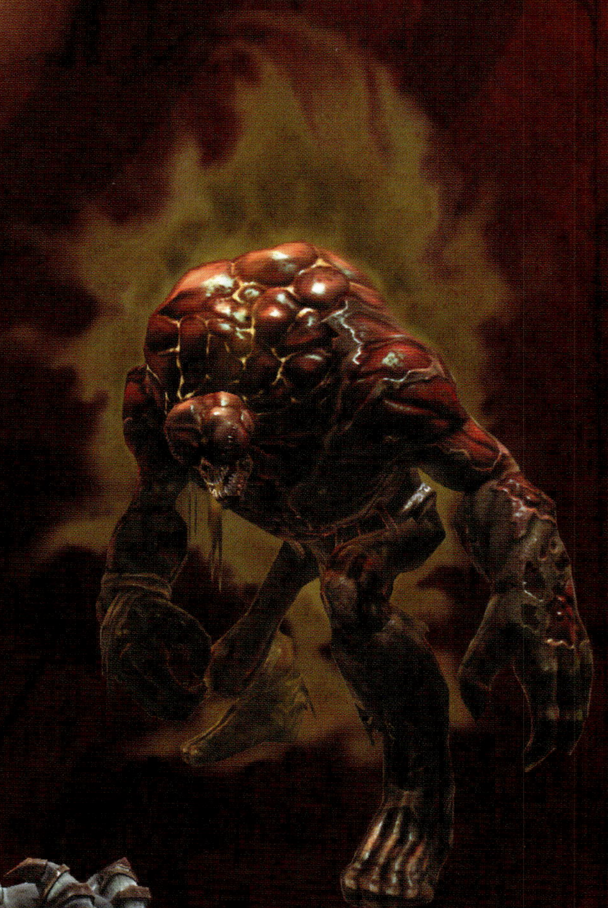

Rot Mauler

Disease ridden outcast of the underworld.

SIGNATURE ATTACK:
Plague Breathe

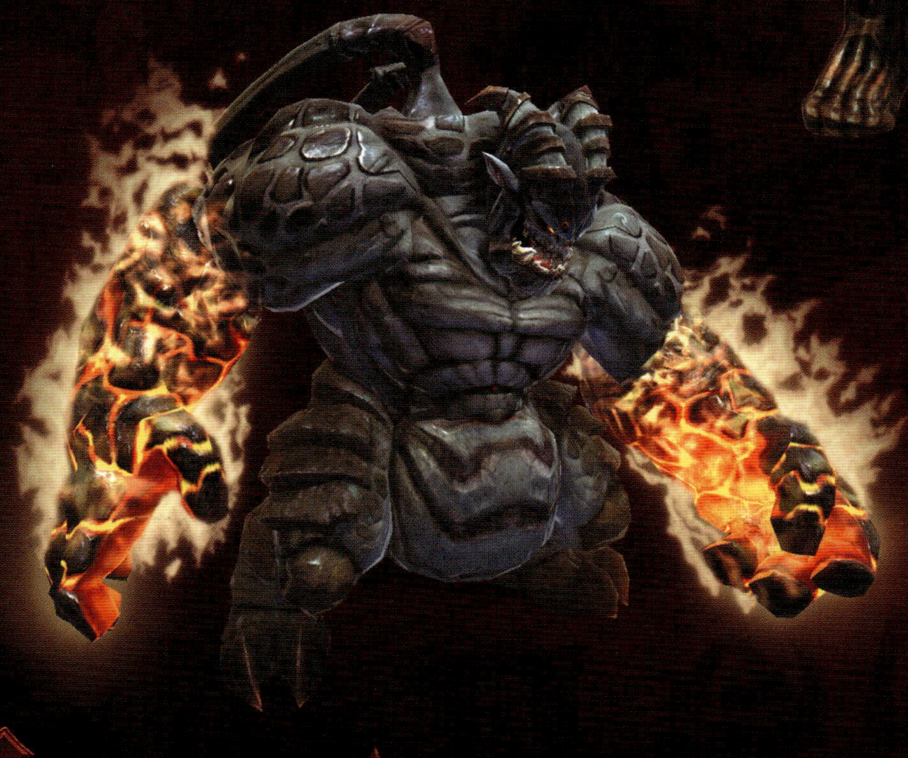

Gholen

Fire demon lord with molten hands.

SIGNATURE ATTACK:
Flamesummon

Guardian

Ancient construct that protects the Black Throne.

SIGNATURE ATTACK:
Bull Dozer Spin

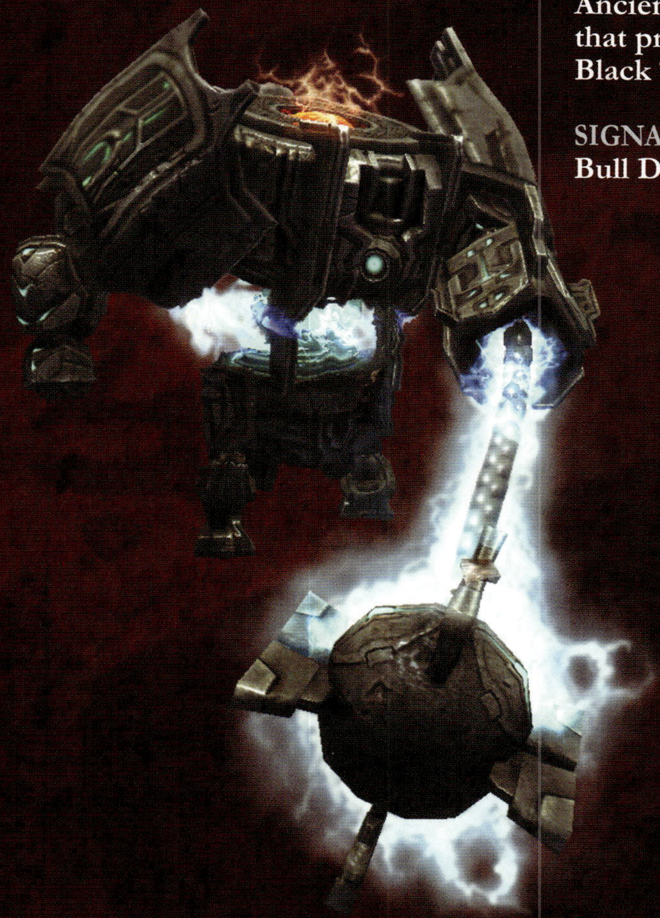

Grappleclaw

Savage beasts with relentless ferocity.

SIGNATURE ATTACK:
Frenzy

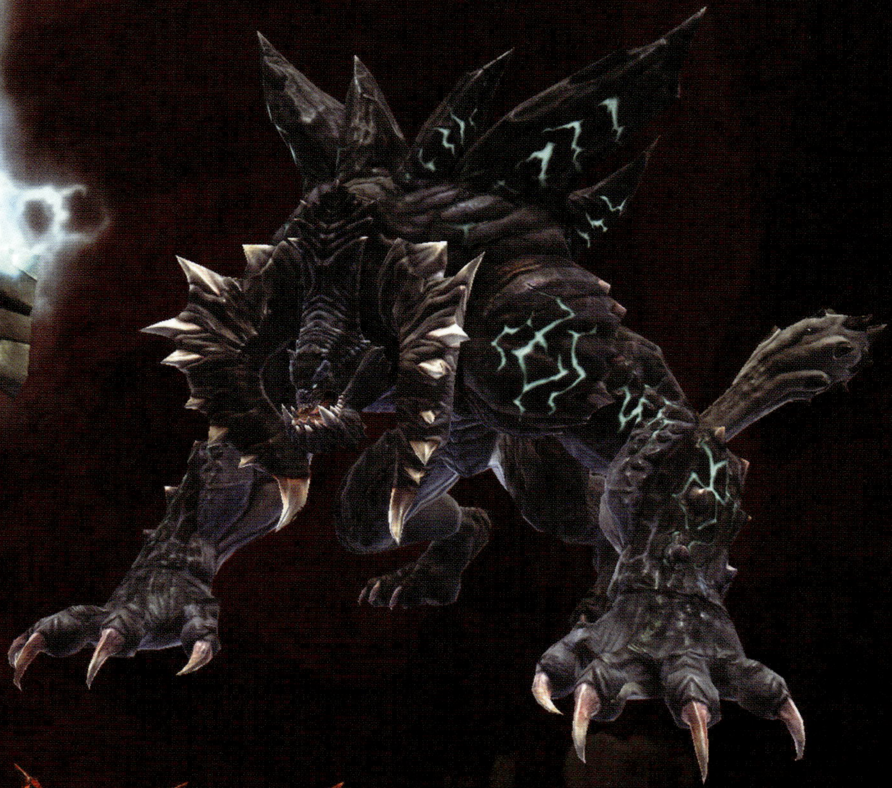

Grappleclaw
(Rare version)

Savage hunters that scour the land.

SIGNATURE ATTACK:
Flamewind Leap

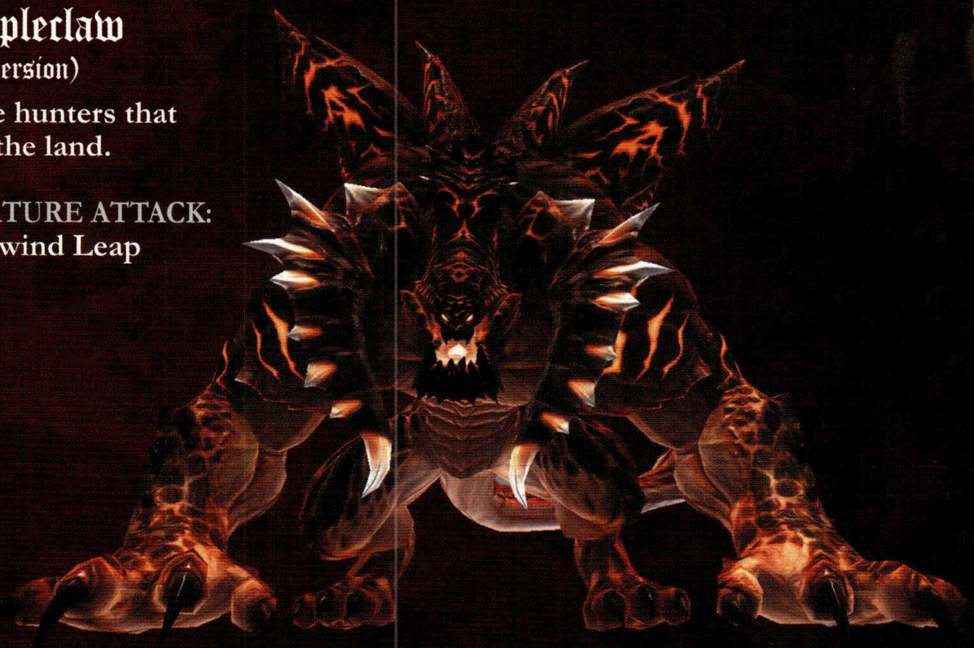

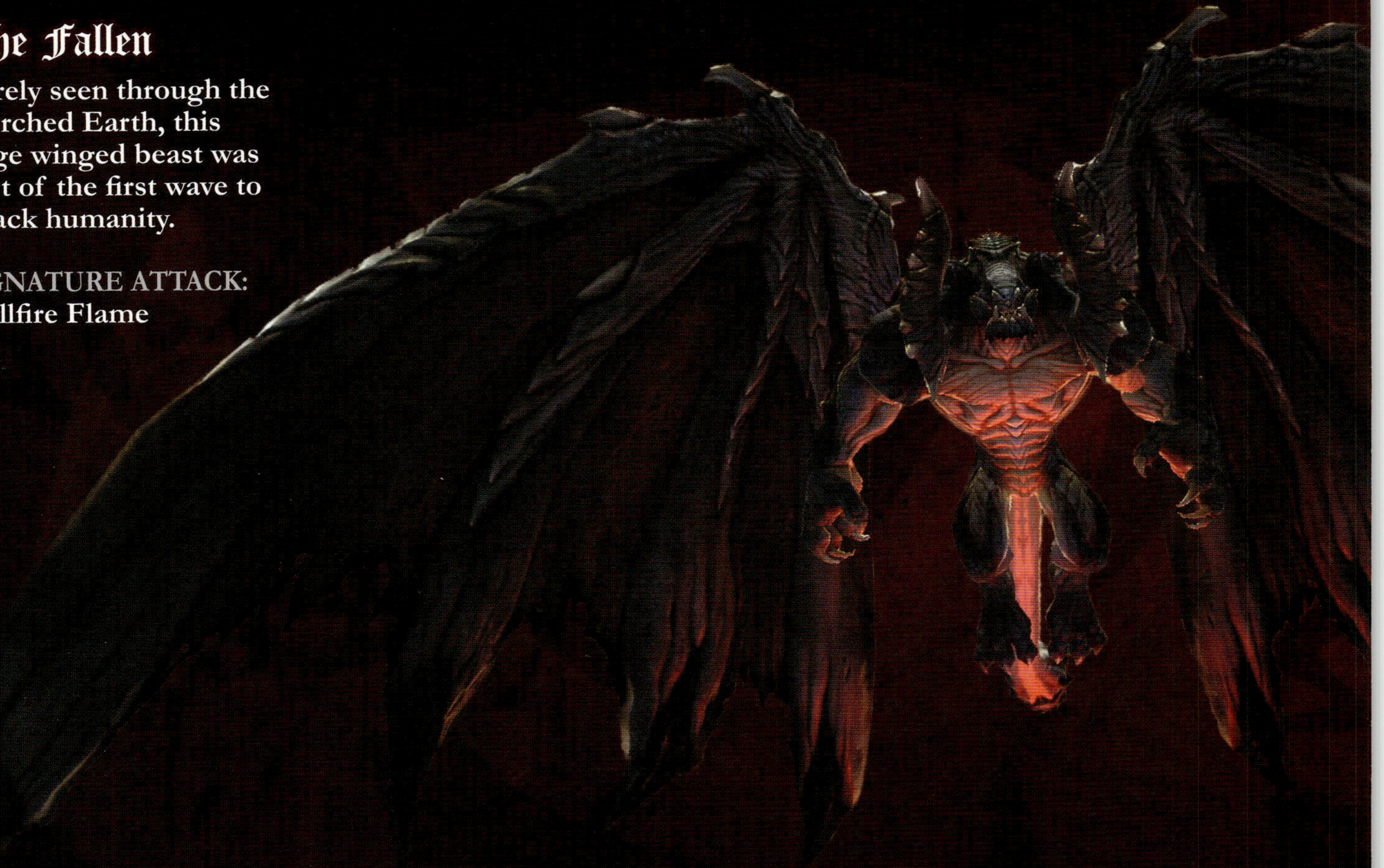

The Fallen

Rarely seen through the scorched Earth, this huge winged beast was part of the first wave to attack humanity.

SIGNATURE ATTACK:
Hellfire Flame

Locust

Small, robust winged creatures that move in hoards.

SIGNATURE ATTACK:
Pincer Stab

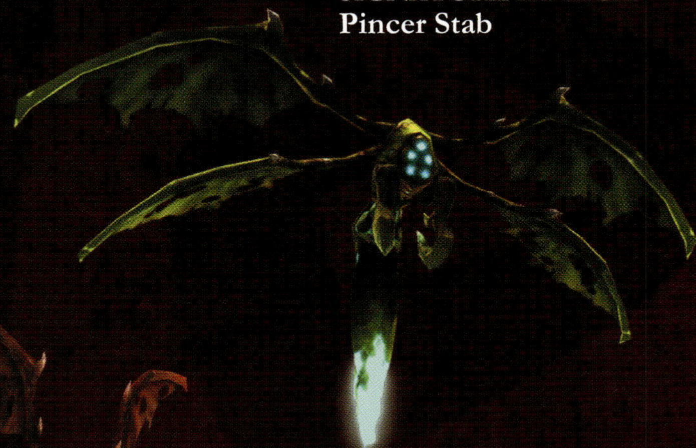

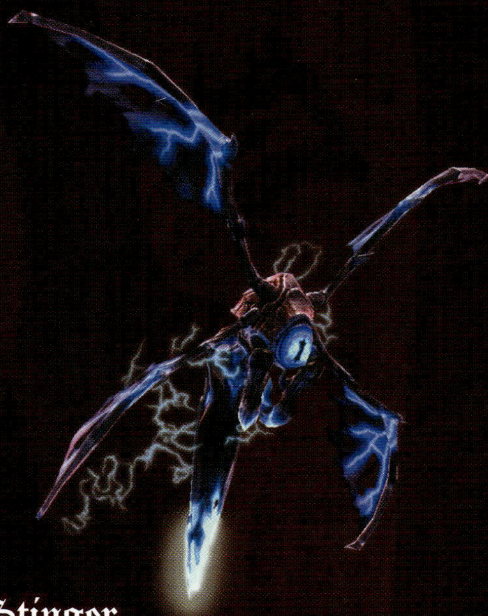

Stinger

Locust hybrid that can emit bursts of electrical energy.

SIGNATURE ATTACK:
Plasmasphere

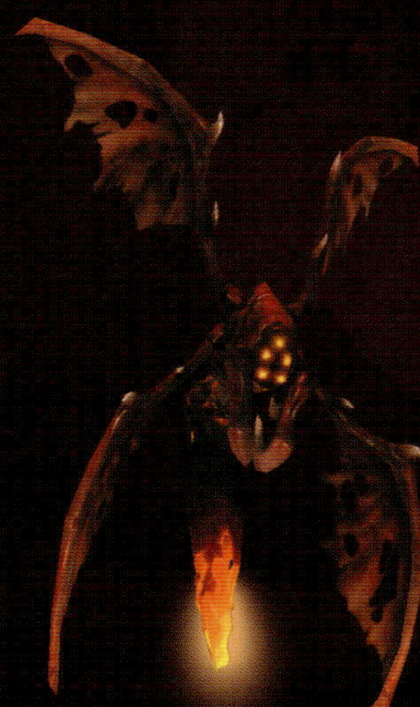

Redtip

A hybrid of the locust which shoots molten projectiles.

SIGNATURE ATTACK: Fire Bolt

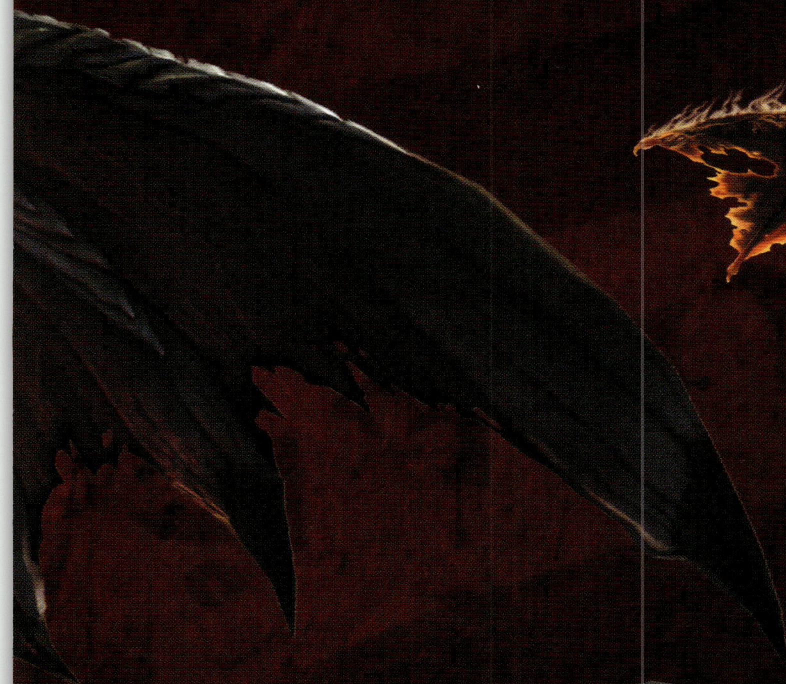

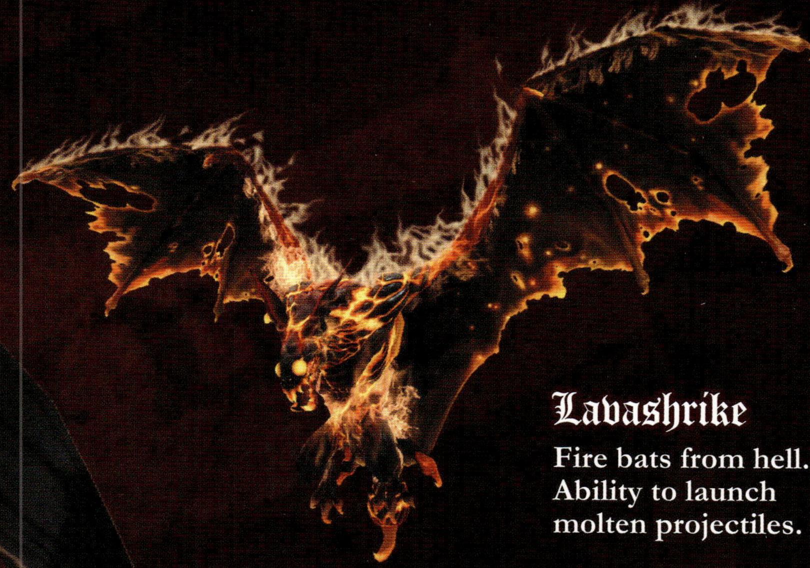

Lavashrike

Fire bats from hell.
Ability to launch
molten projectiles.

SIGNATURE ATTACK:
Molten Breathe

Duskwings

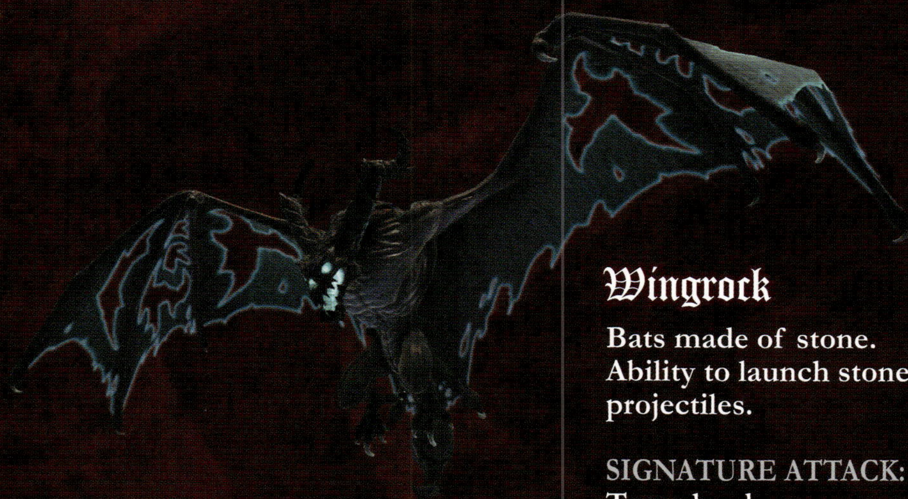

Wingrock

Bats made of stone.
Ability to launch stone
projectiles.

SIGNATURE ATTACK:
Terrashard

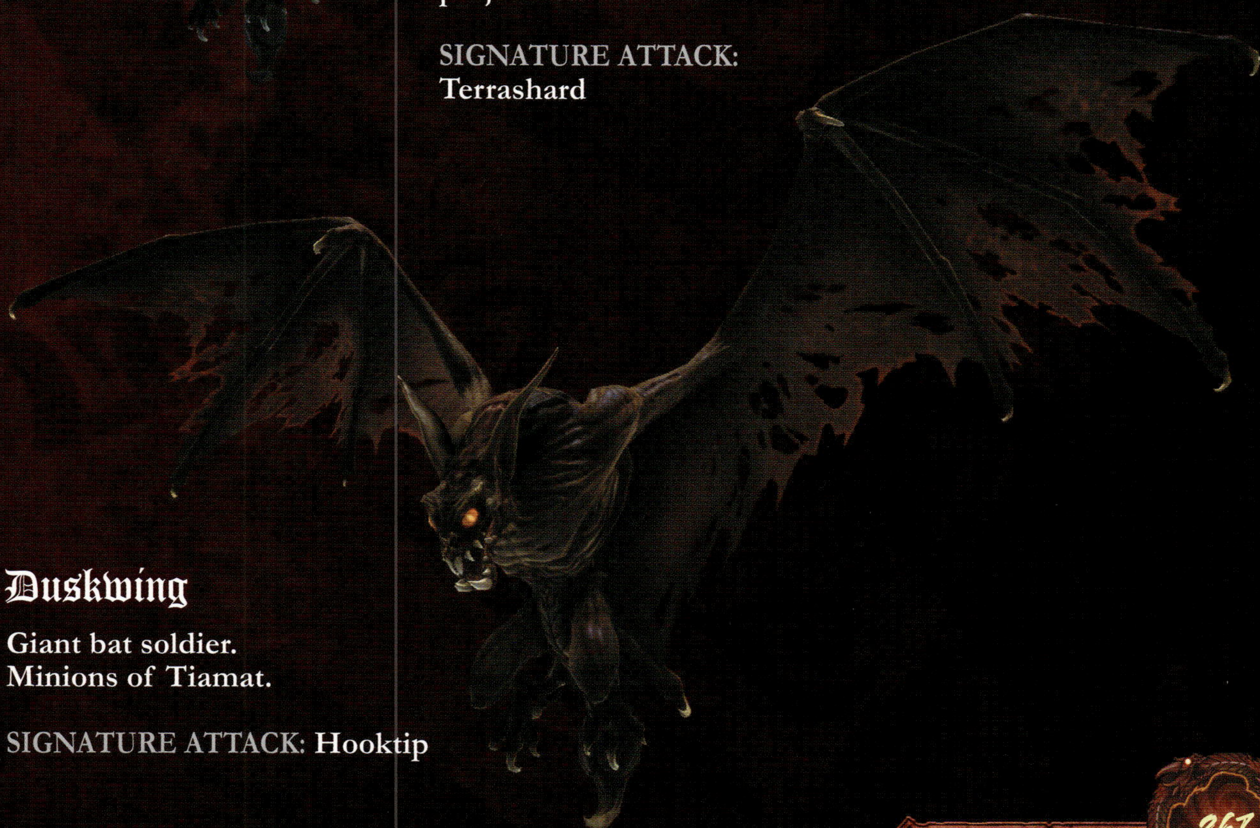

Duskwing

Giant bat soldier.
Minions of Tiamat.

SIGNATURE ATTACK: Hooktip

Abyssal Riders

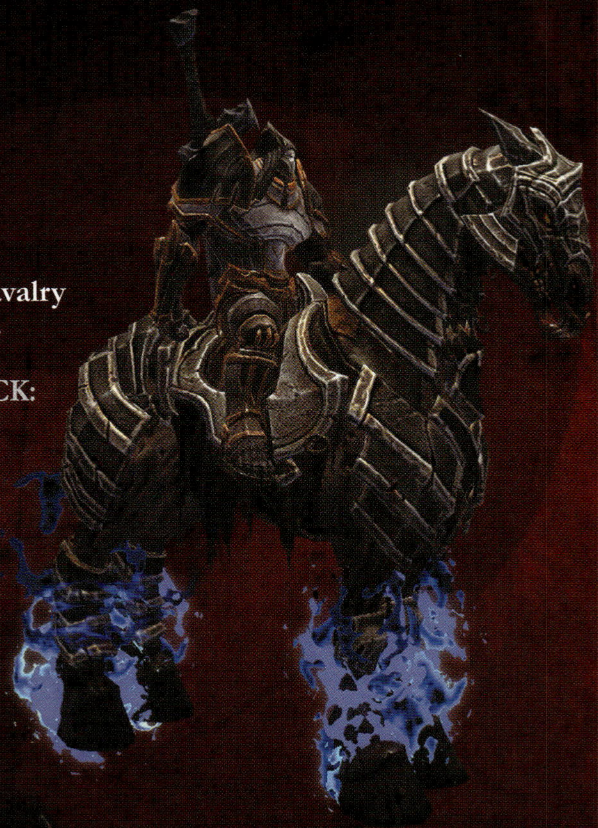

Abyssal Champion

Heavily armored cavalry of the demon army.

SIGNATURE ATTACK:
Napalm Flash

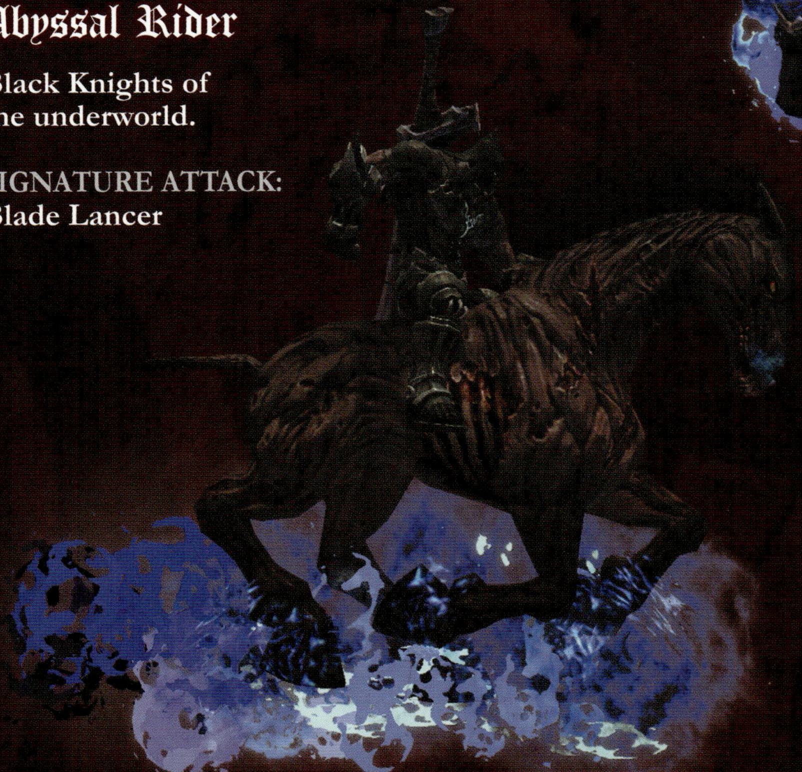

Abyssal Rider

Black Knights of the underworld.

SIGNATURE ATTACK:
Blade Lancer

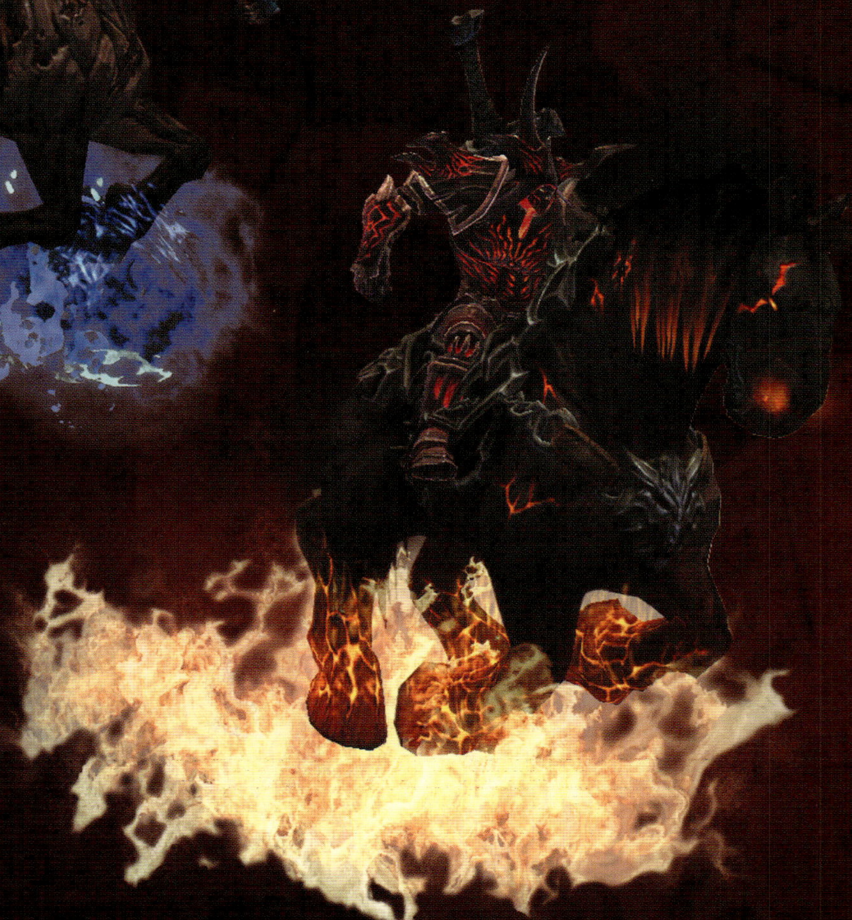

Abyssal Gladiator

Dark rider that has enslaved Ruin.

SIGNATURE ATTACK:
Napalm Fist

Tiamat

Ancient queen of the bats.

SIGNATURE ATTACK: Flying Sweep

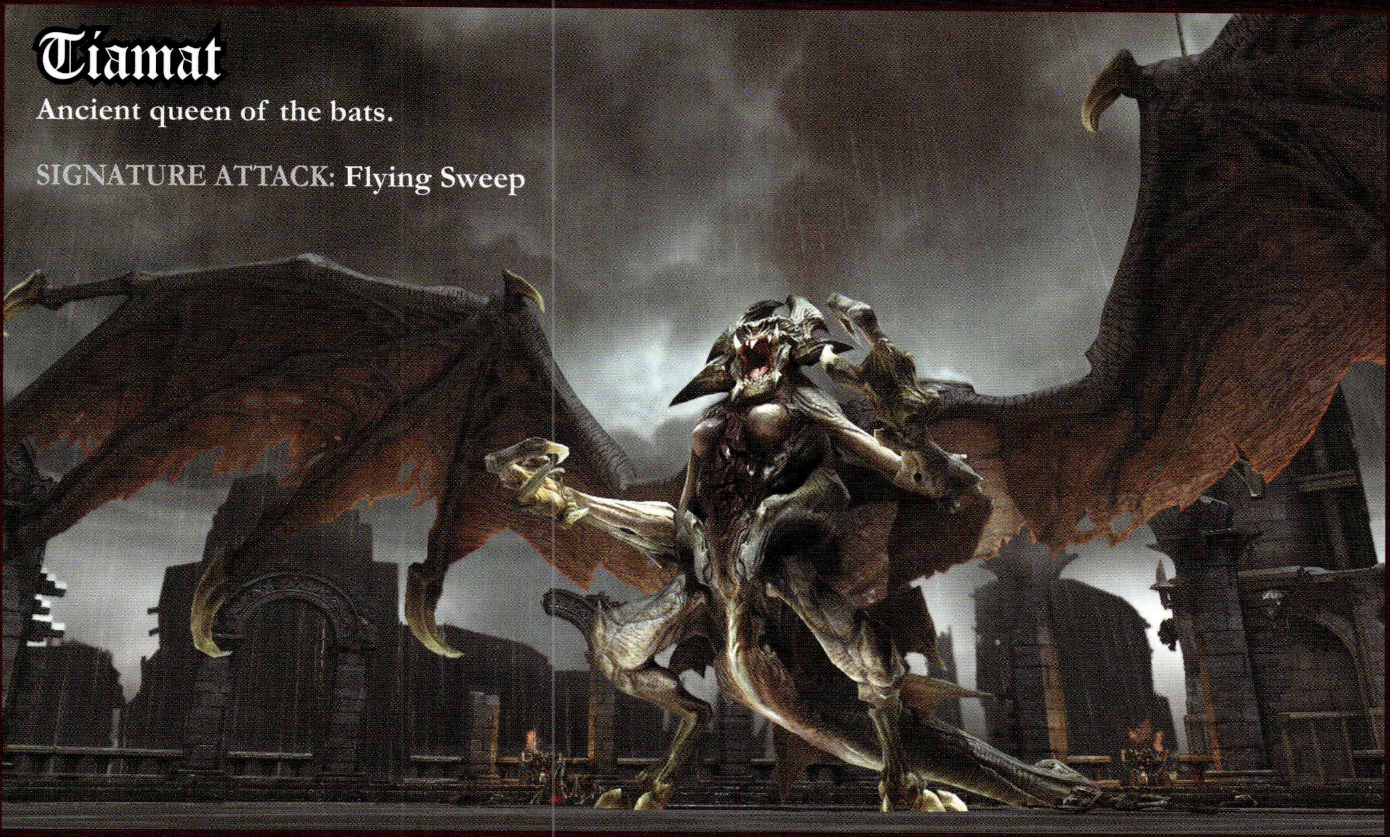

Griever

One of the 4 chosen who lurks within the dark depths of the hollows

SIGNATURE ATTACK: Groundshaker

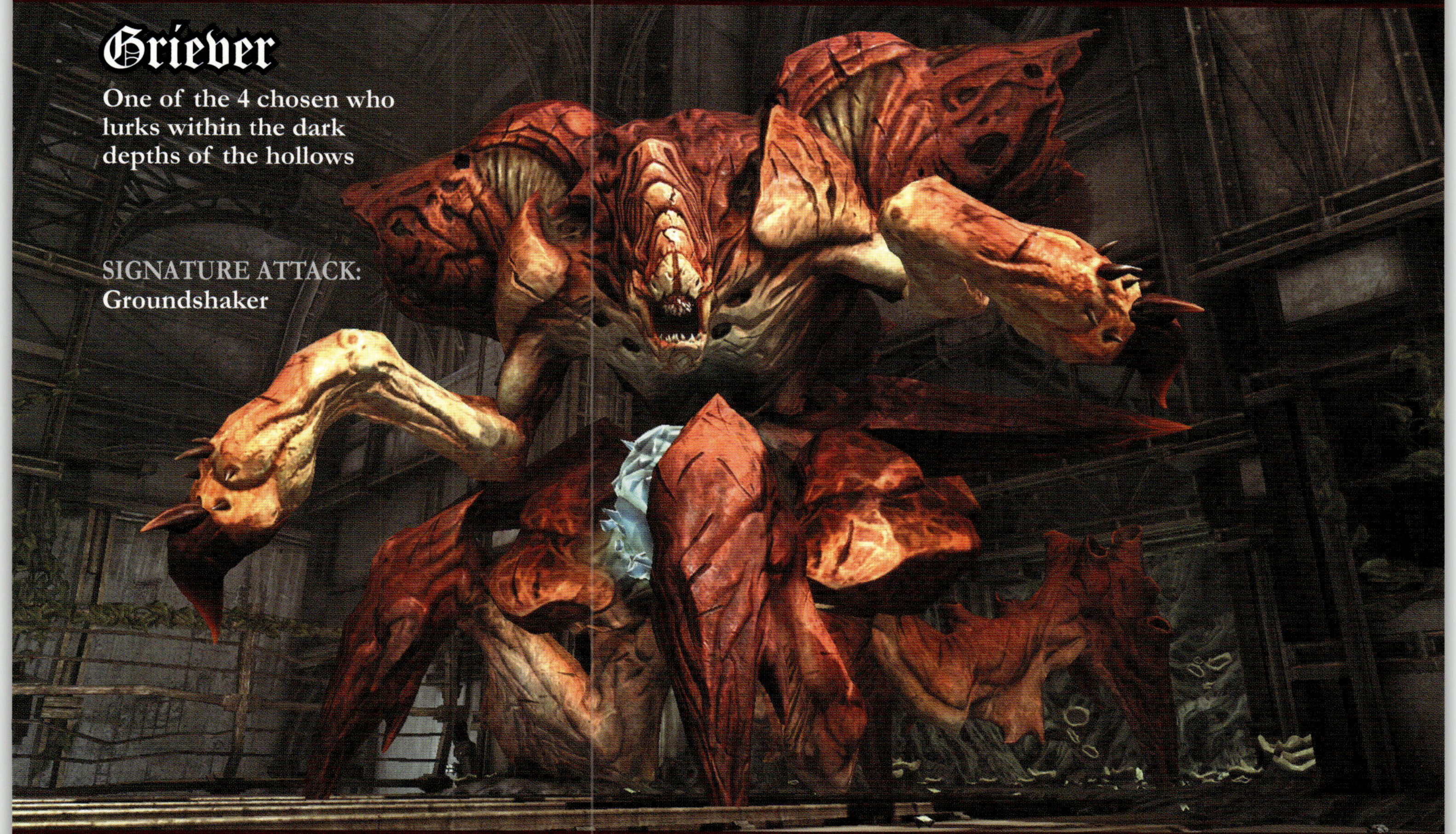

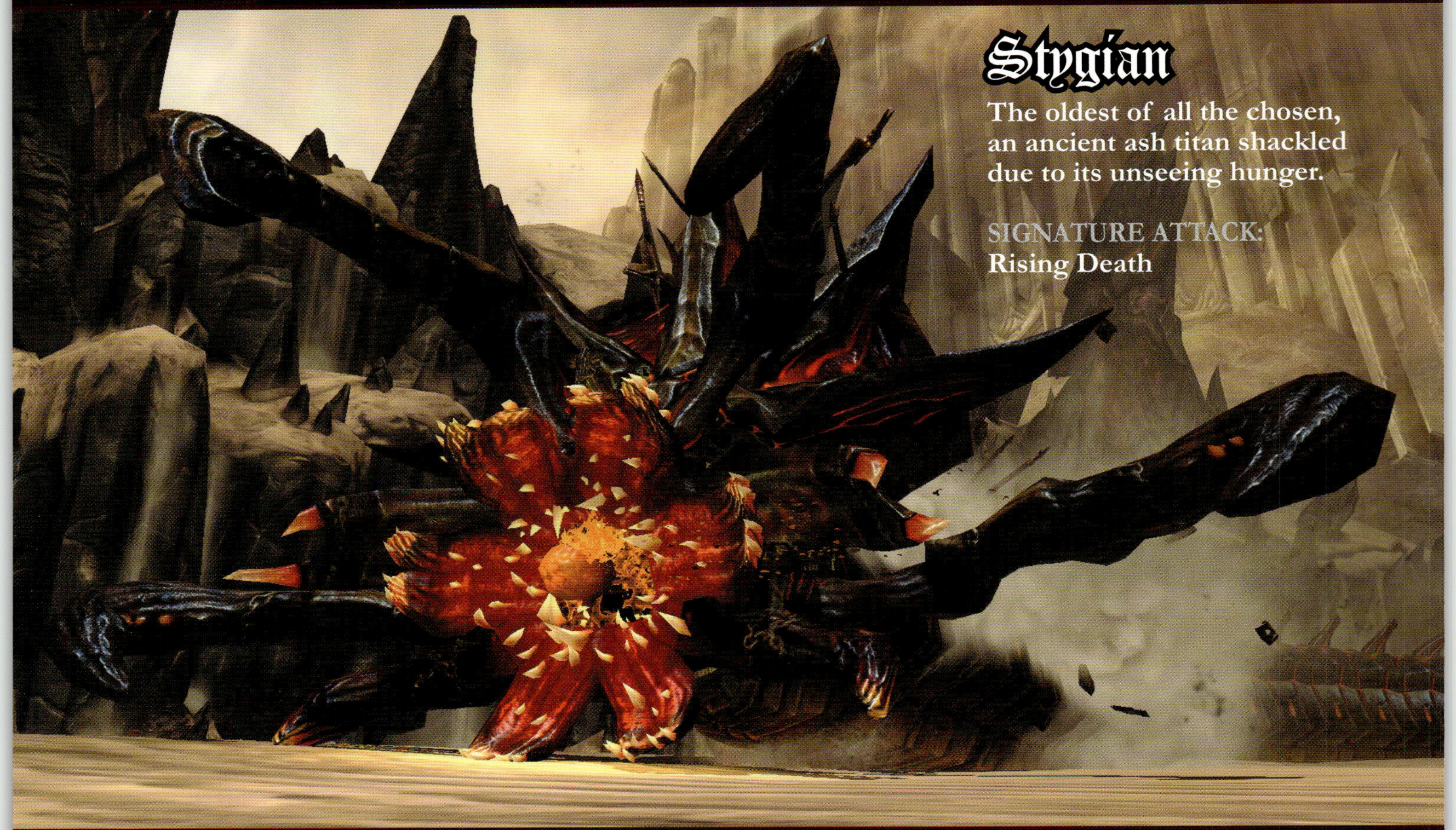

Stygian

The oldest of all the chosen, an ancient ash titan shackled due to its unseeing hunger.

SIGNATURE ATTACK:
Rising Death

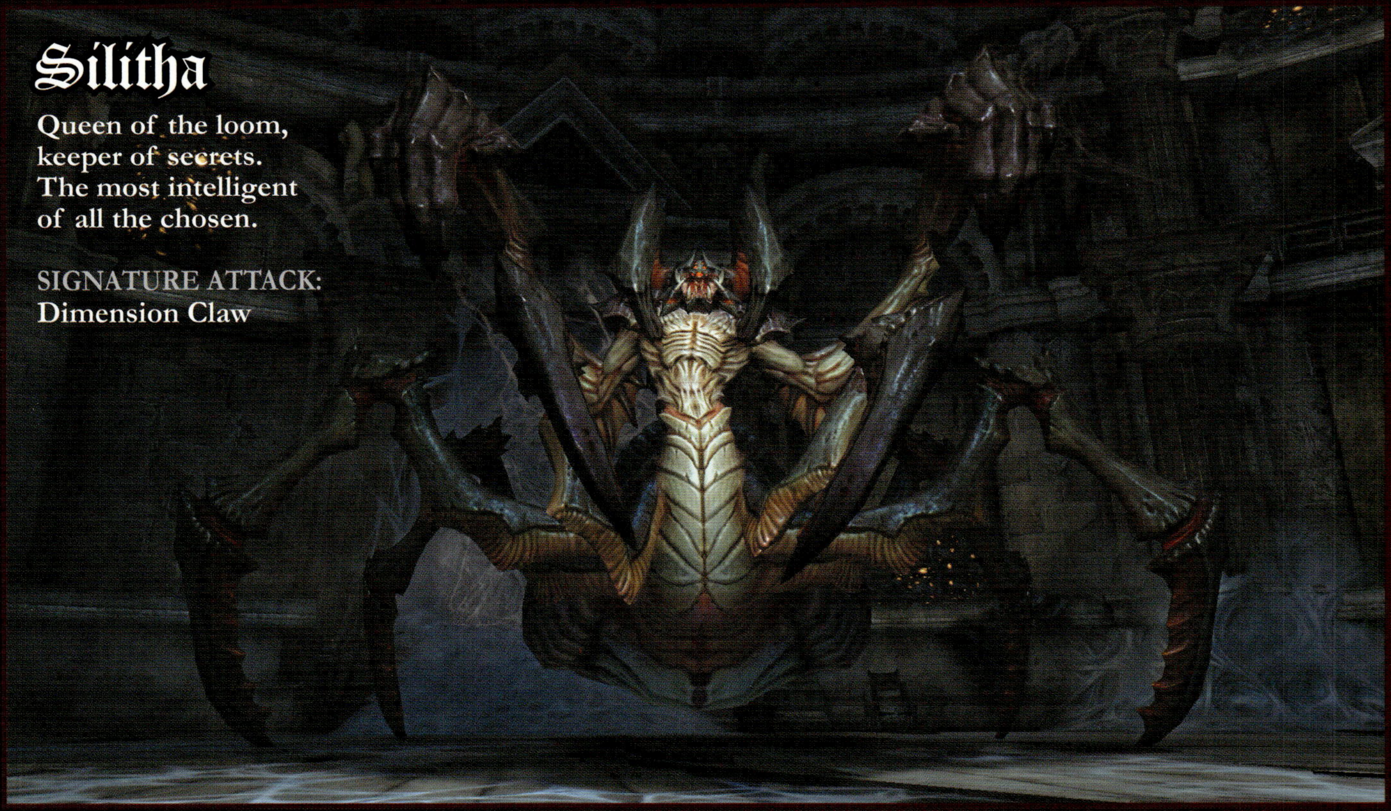

Silitha

Queen of the loom, keeper of secrets. The most intelligent of all the chosen.

SIGNATURE ATTACK:
Dimension Claw

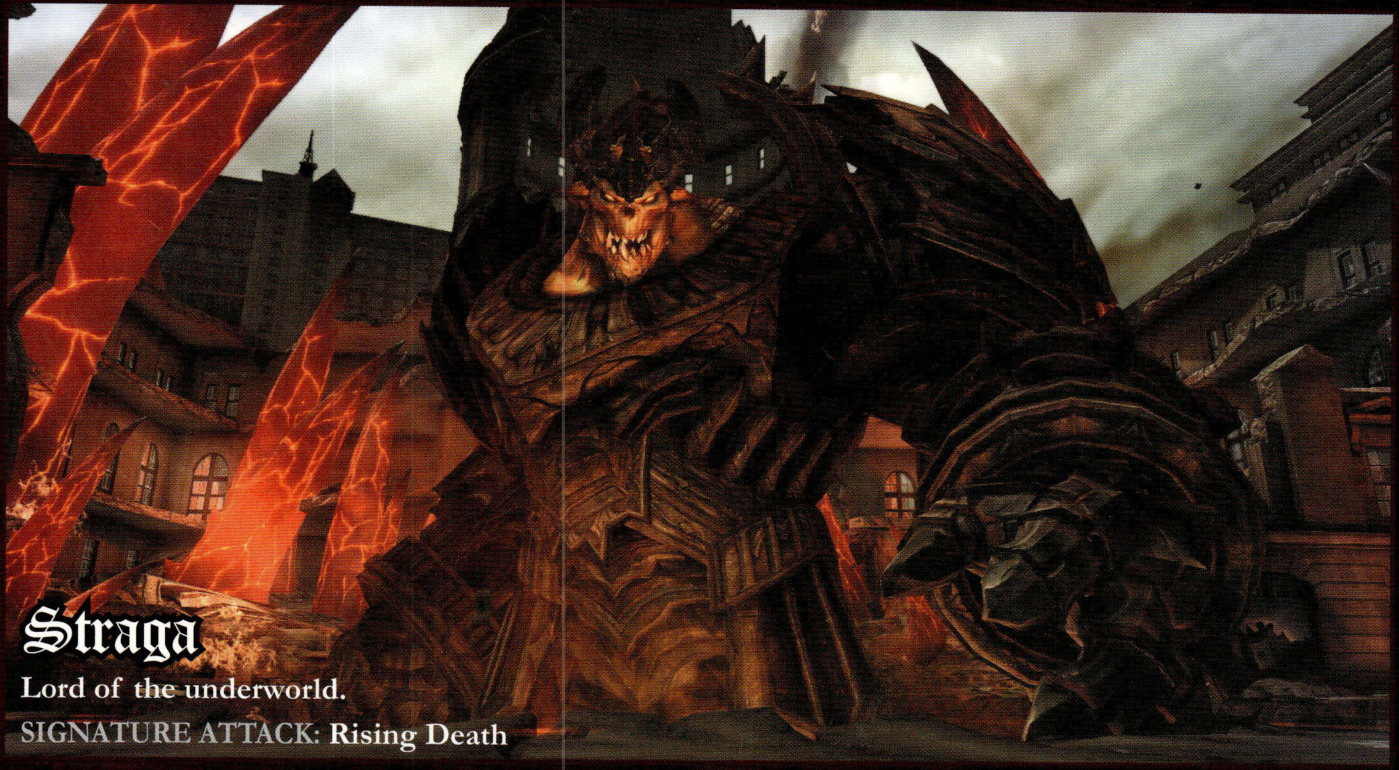

Straga

Lord of the underworld.

SIGNATURE ATTACK: Rising Death

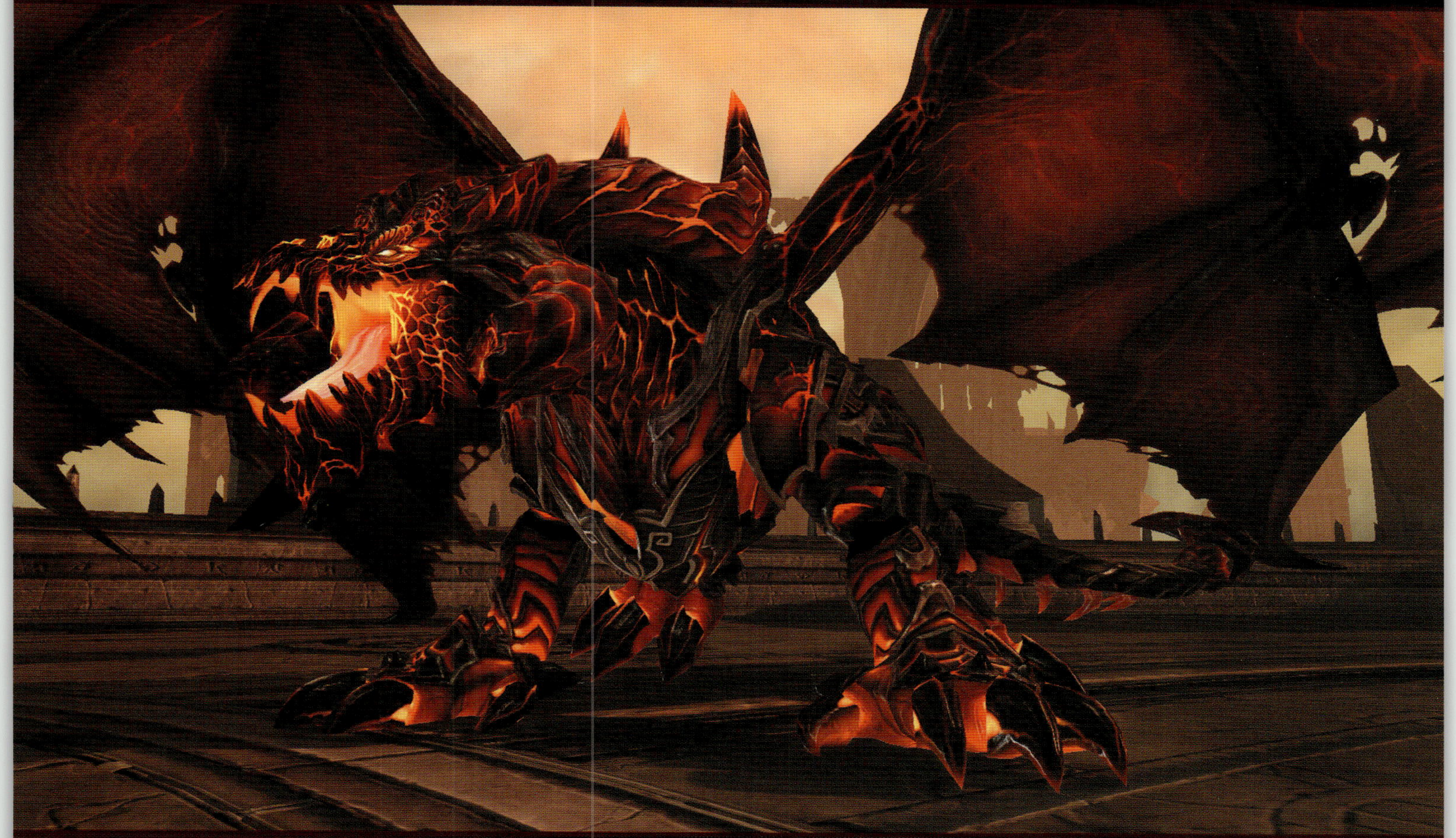

The Destroyer

Ruler of Hell.

SIGNATURE ATTACK:
Blazing Crusher

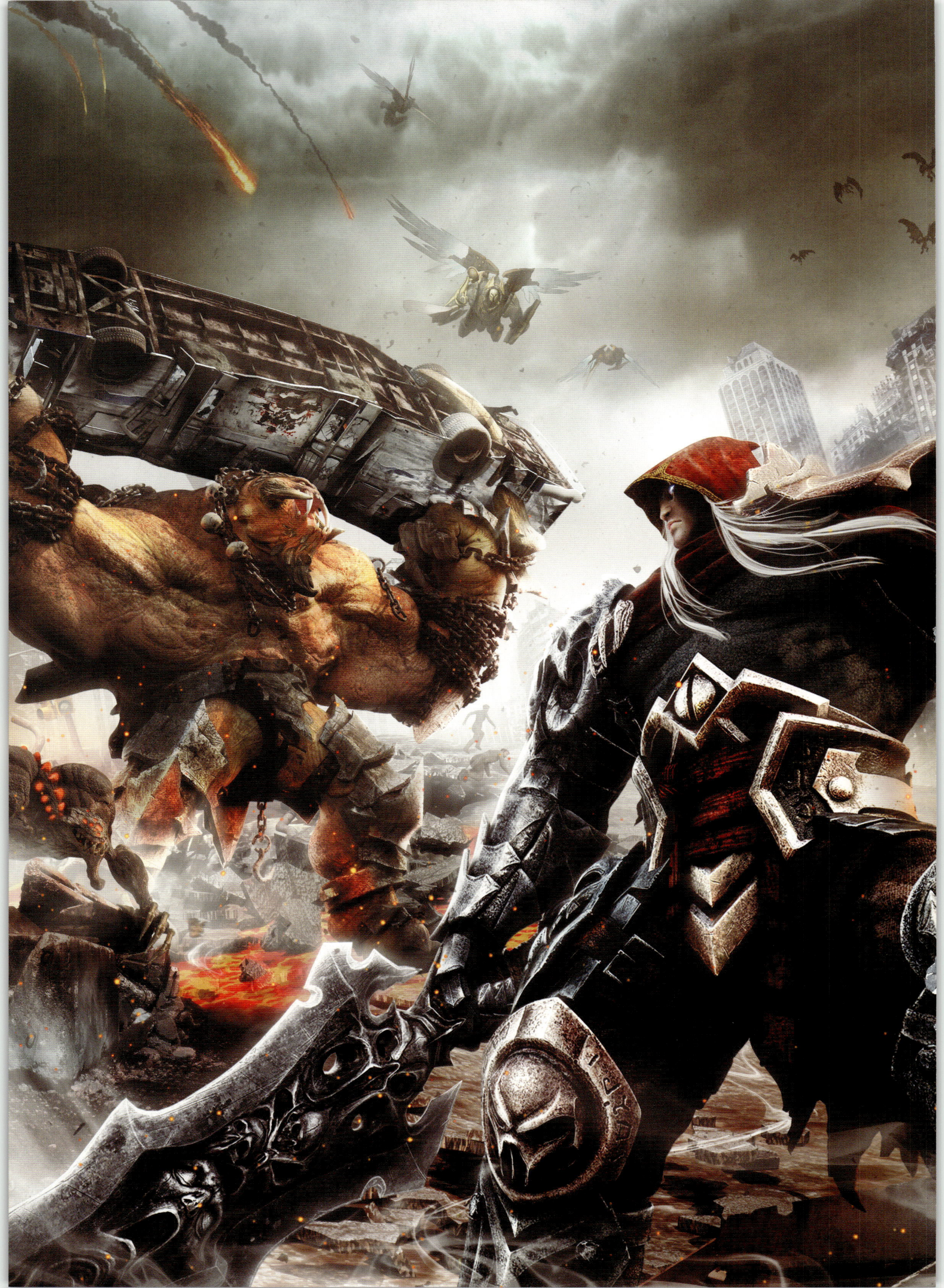

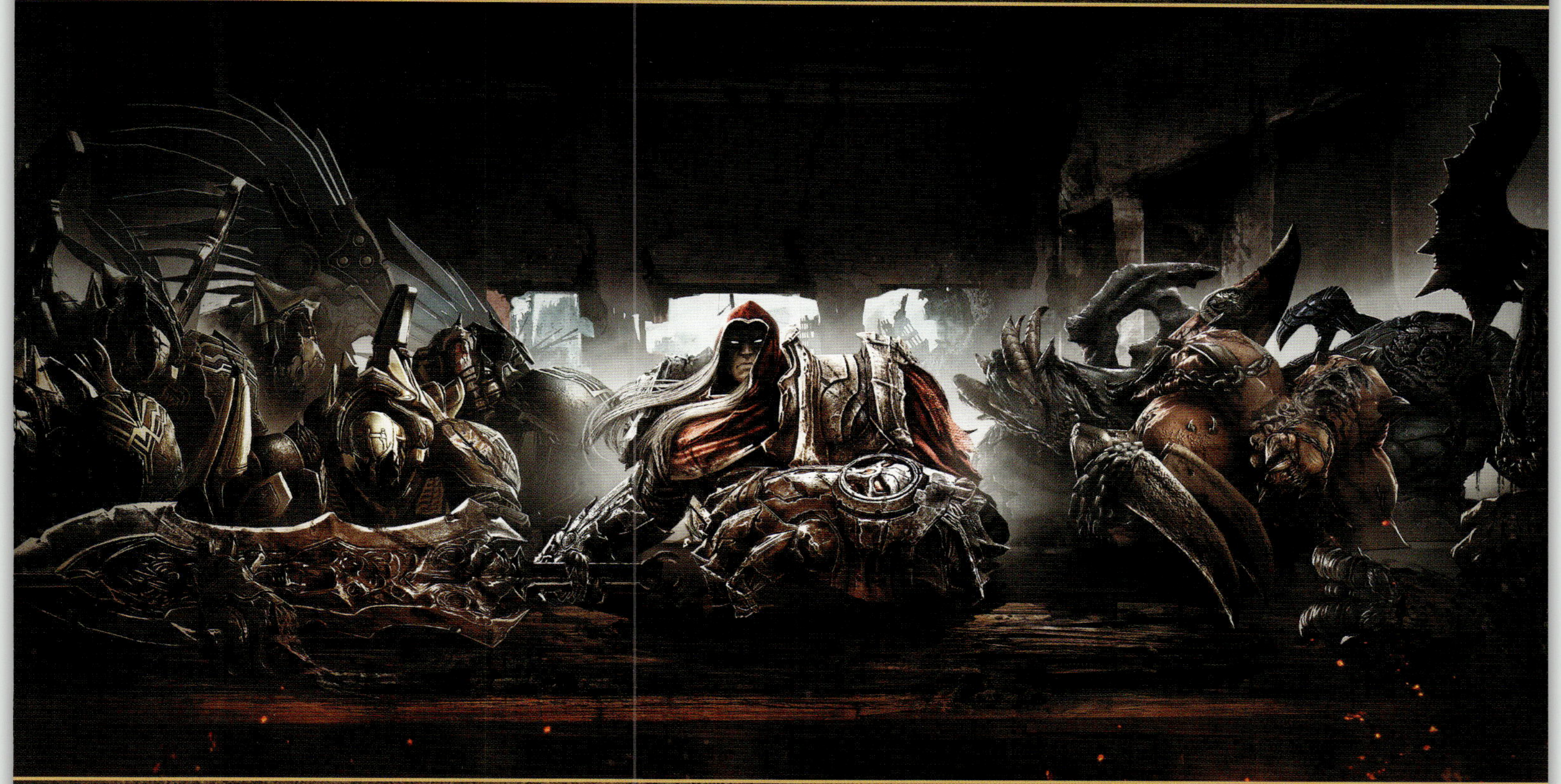

"THE LAST SUPPER"

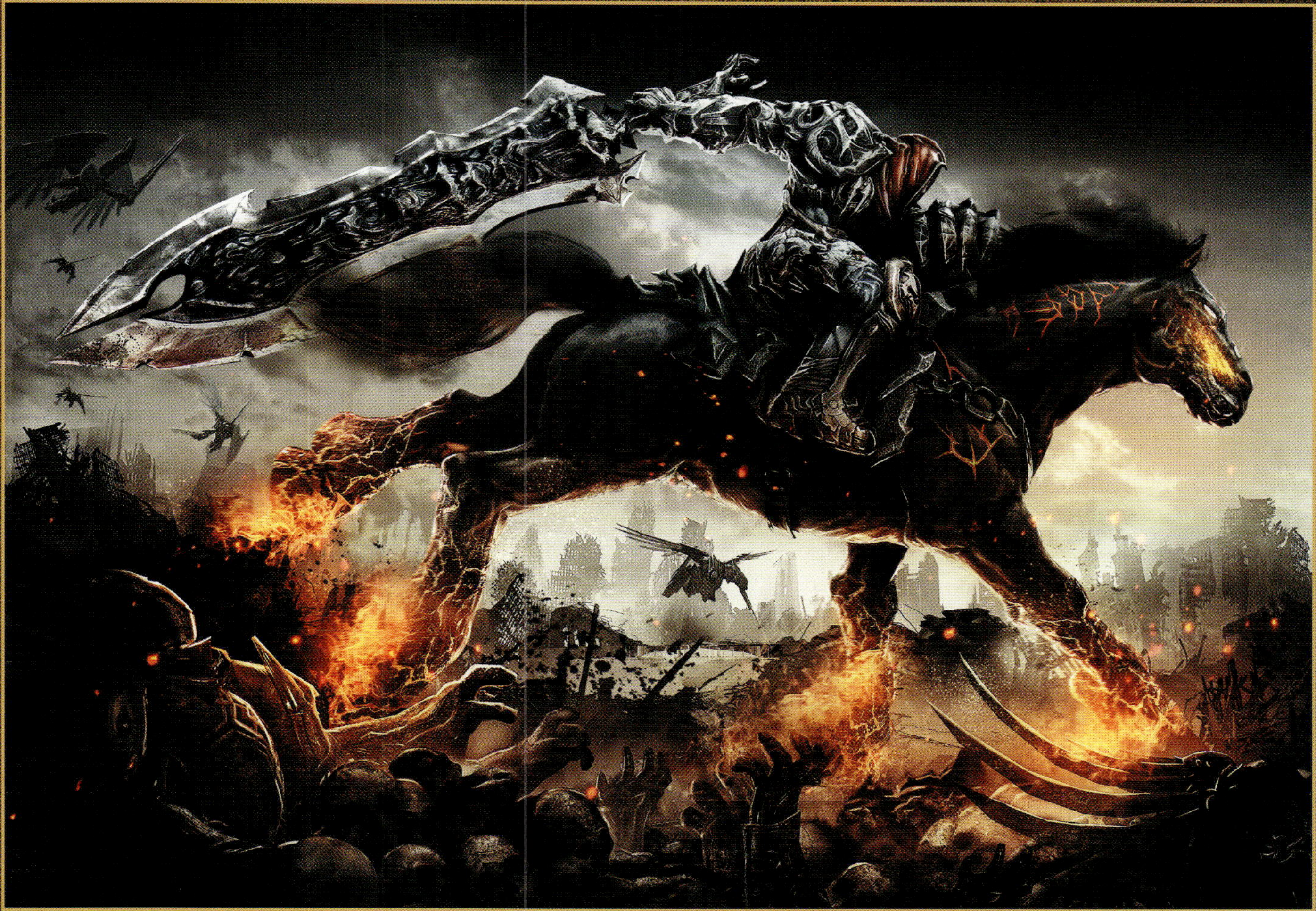

"WAR AND RUIN"

<<"IN THE BEGINNING"

“CHARGING ATTACK” >>

“WAR AND RUIN”

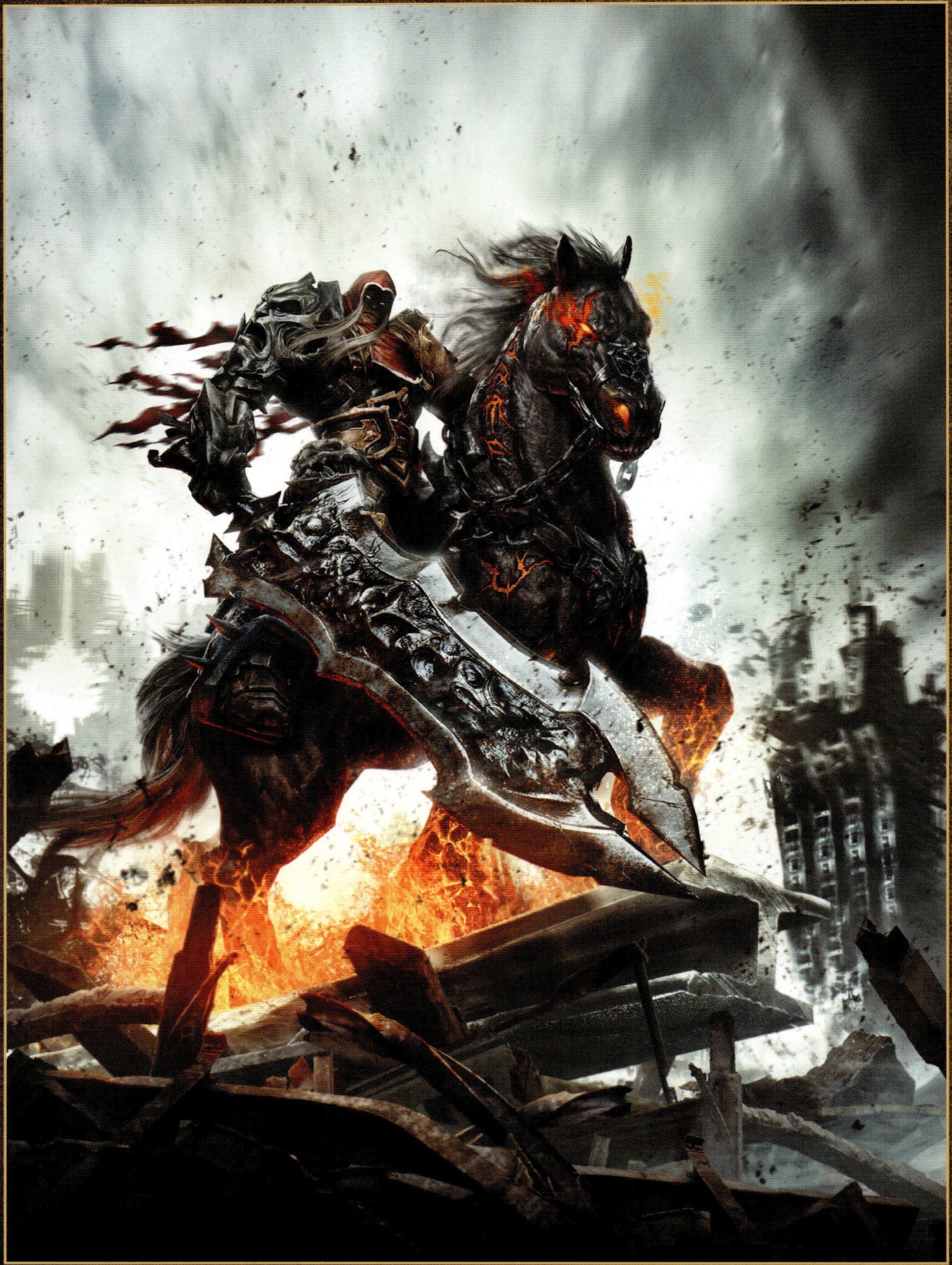

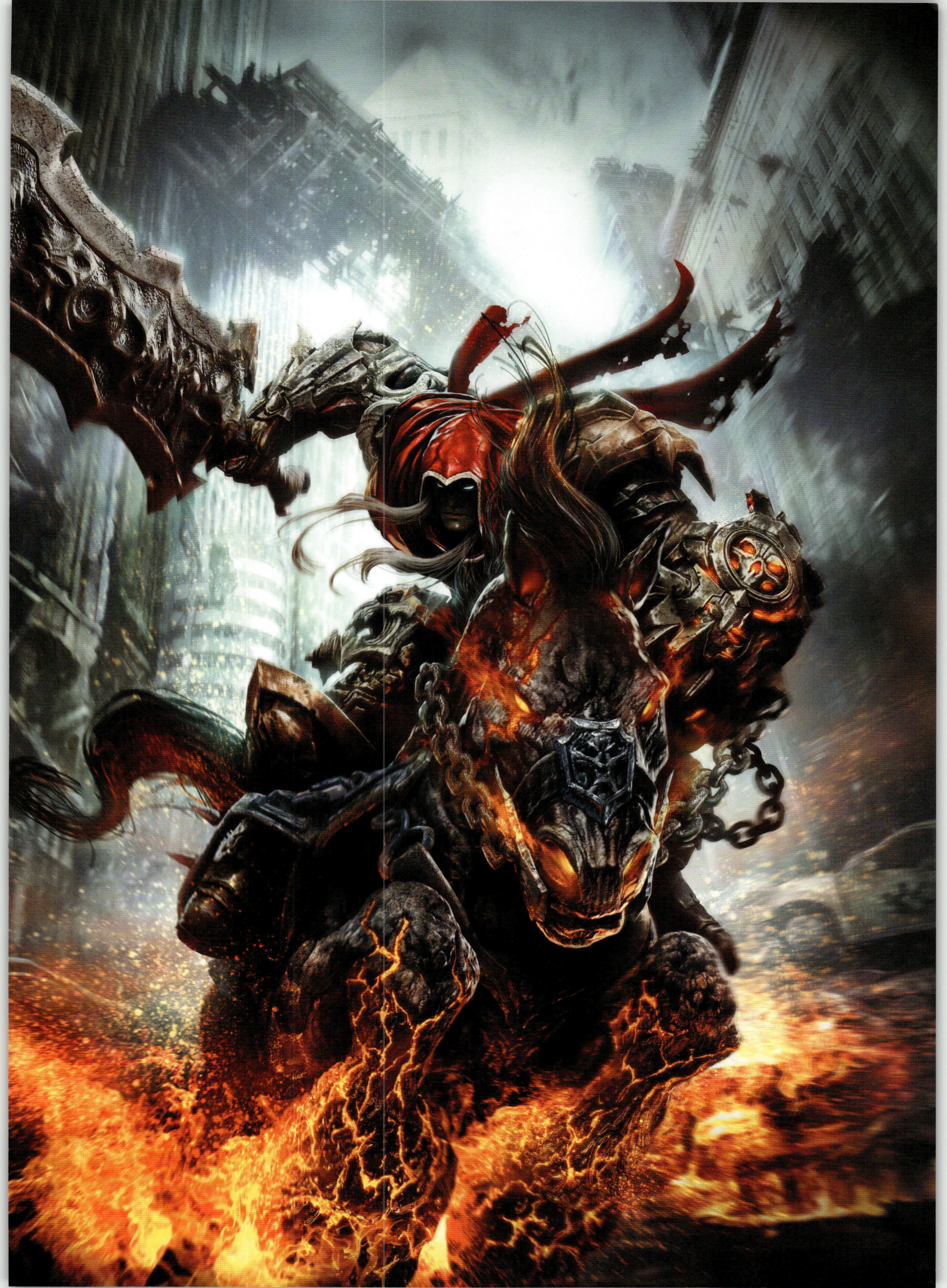

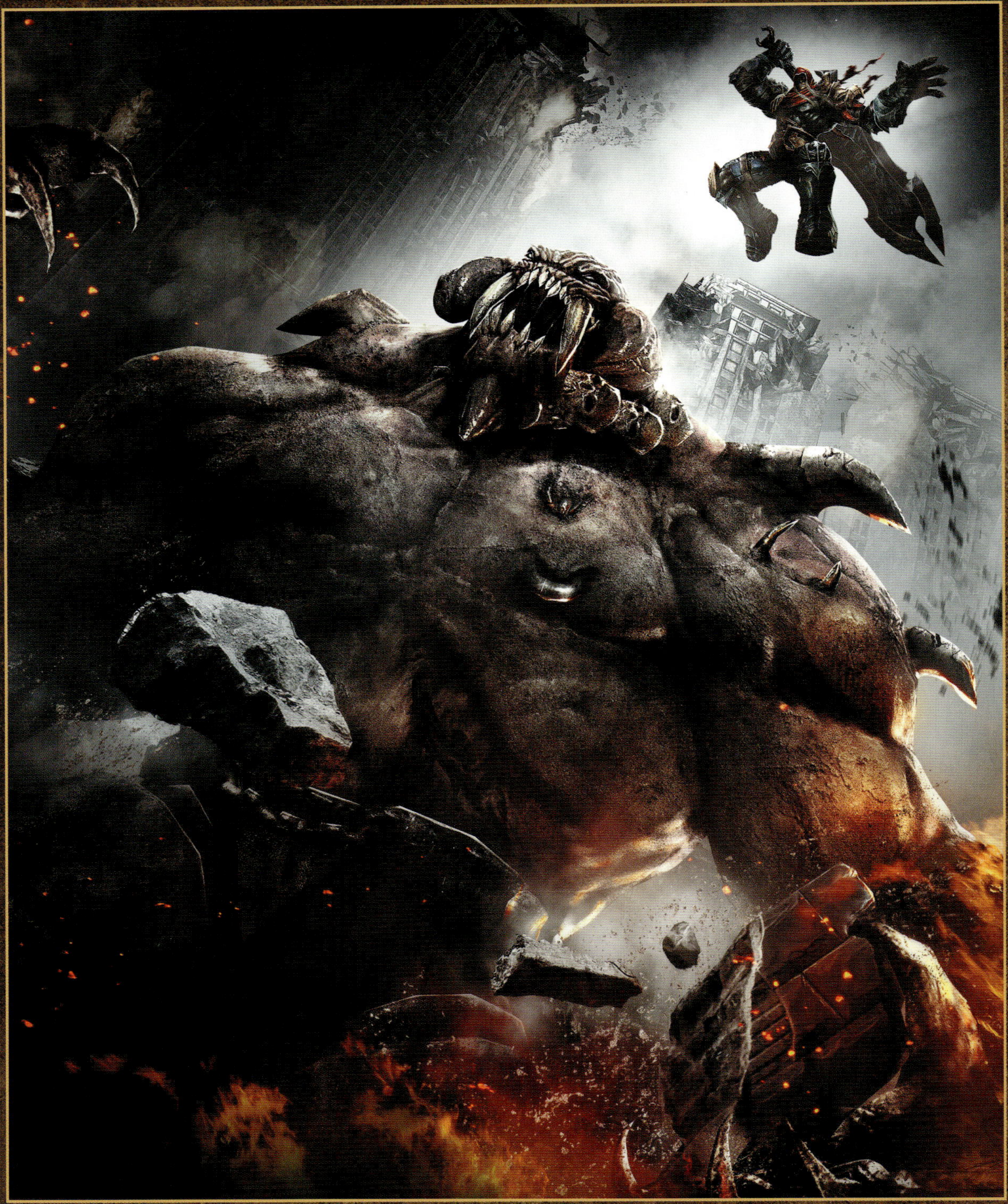

"GIANT KILLER"

"RUNNING THROUGH" (previous spread)

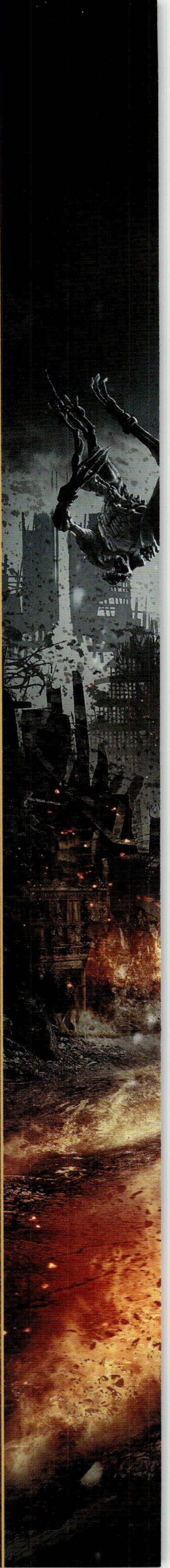

"BATTLE IN THE STREETS" >>

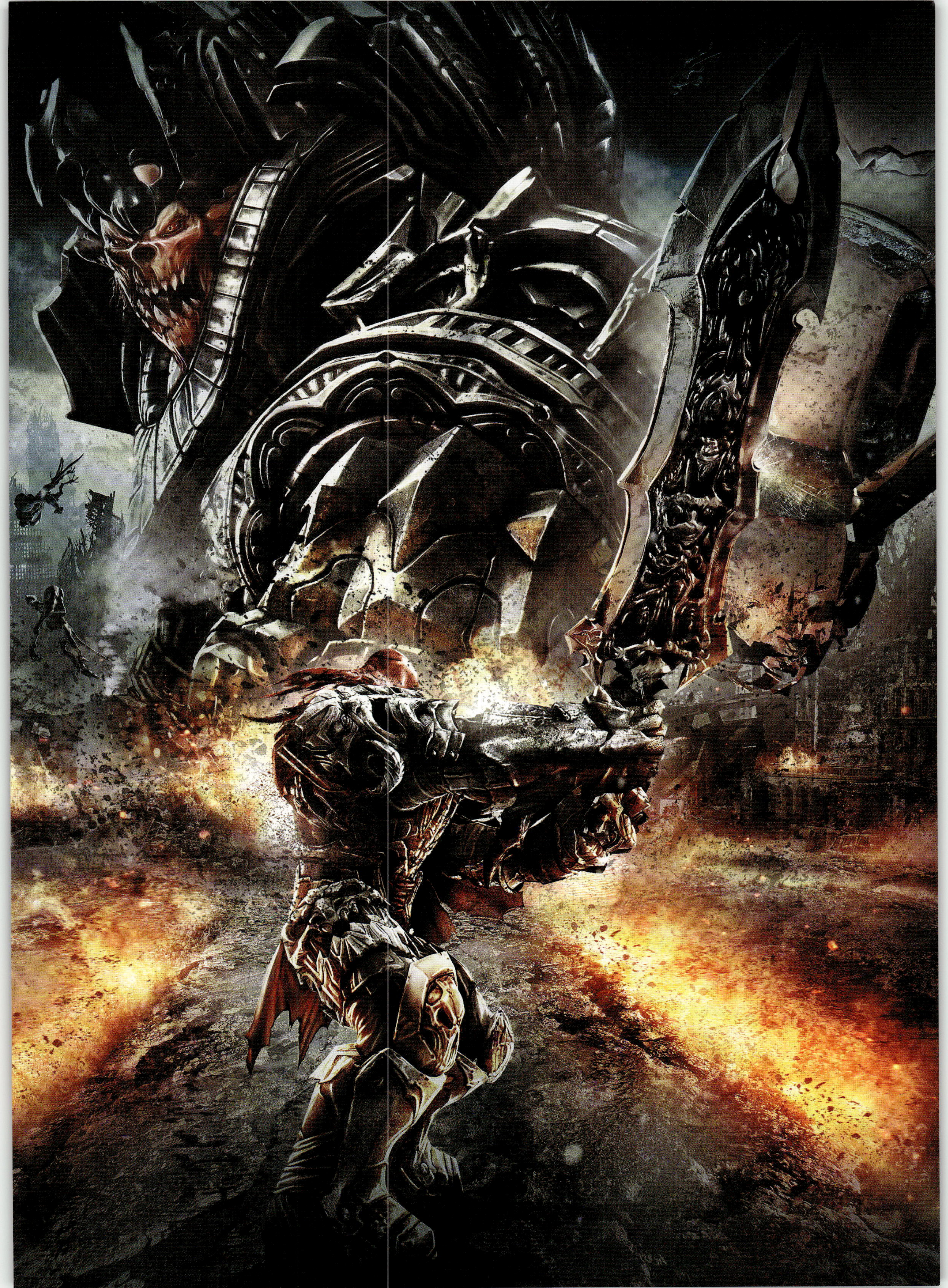

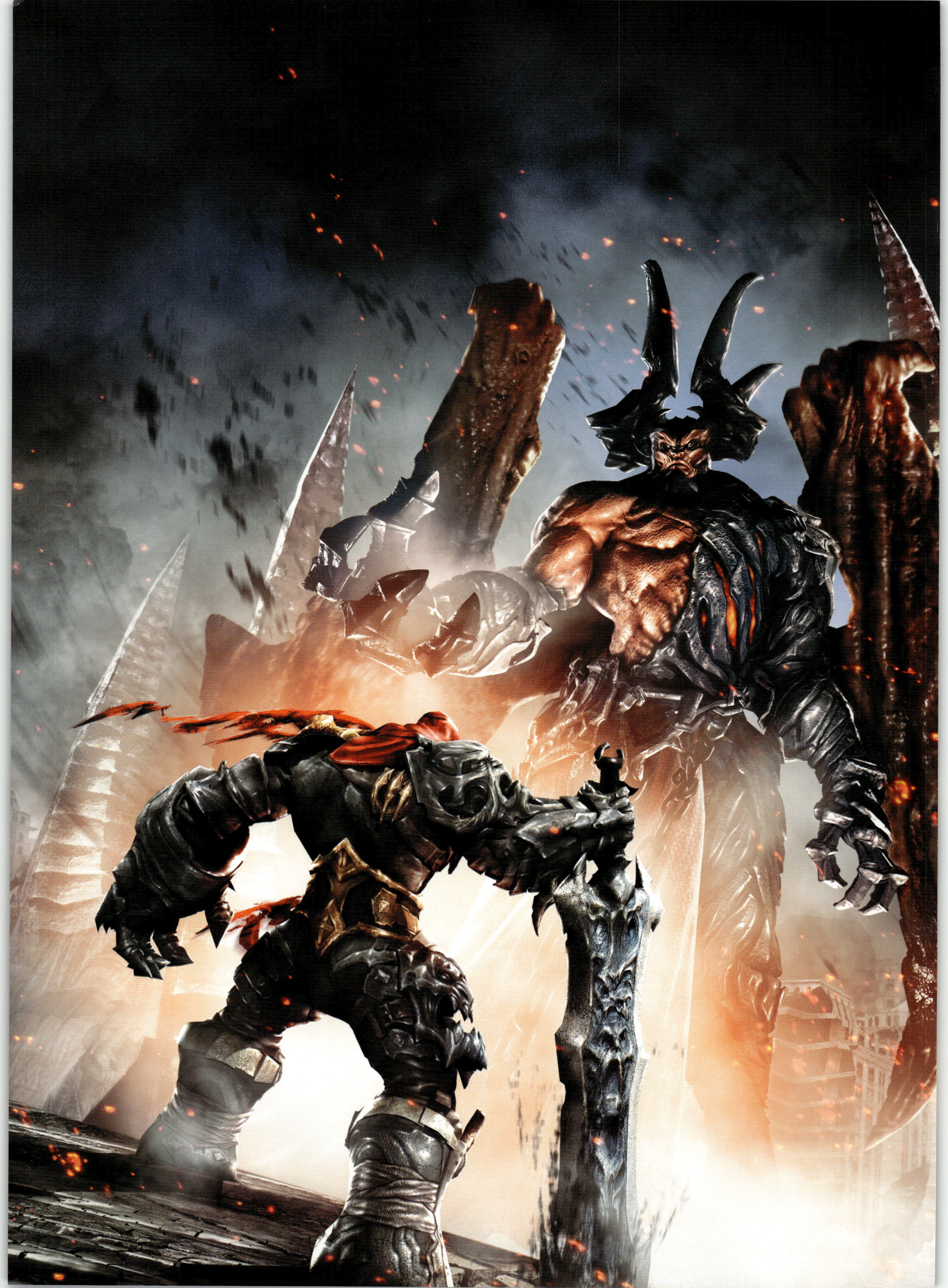

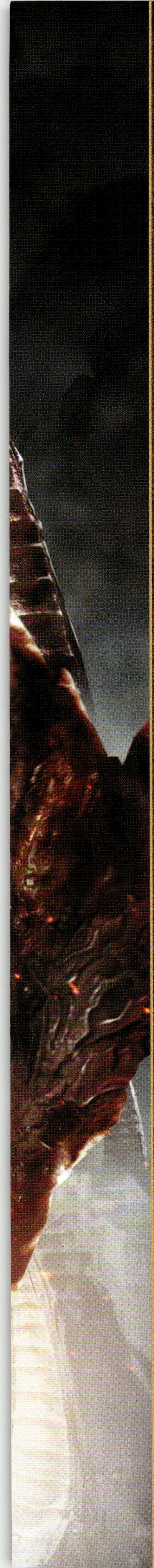
<< “MEETING SAMAEL”

“BRINGING DOWN THE QUEEN”

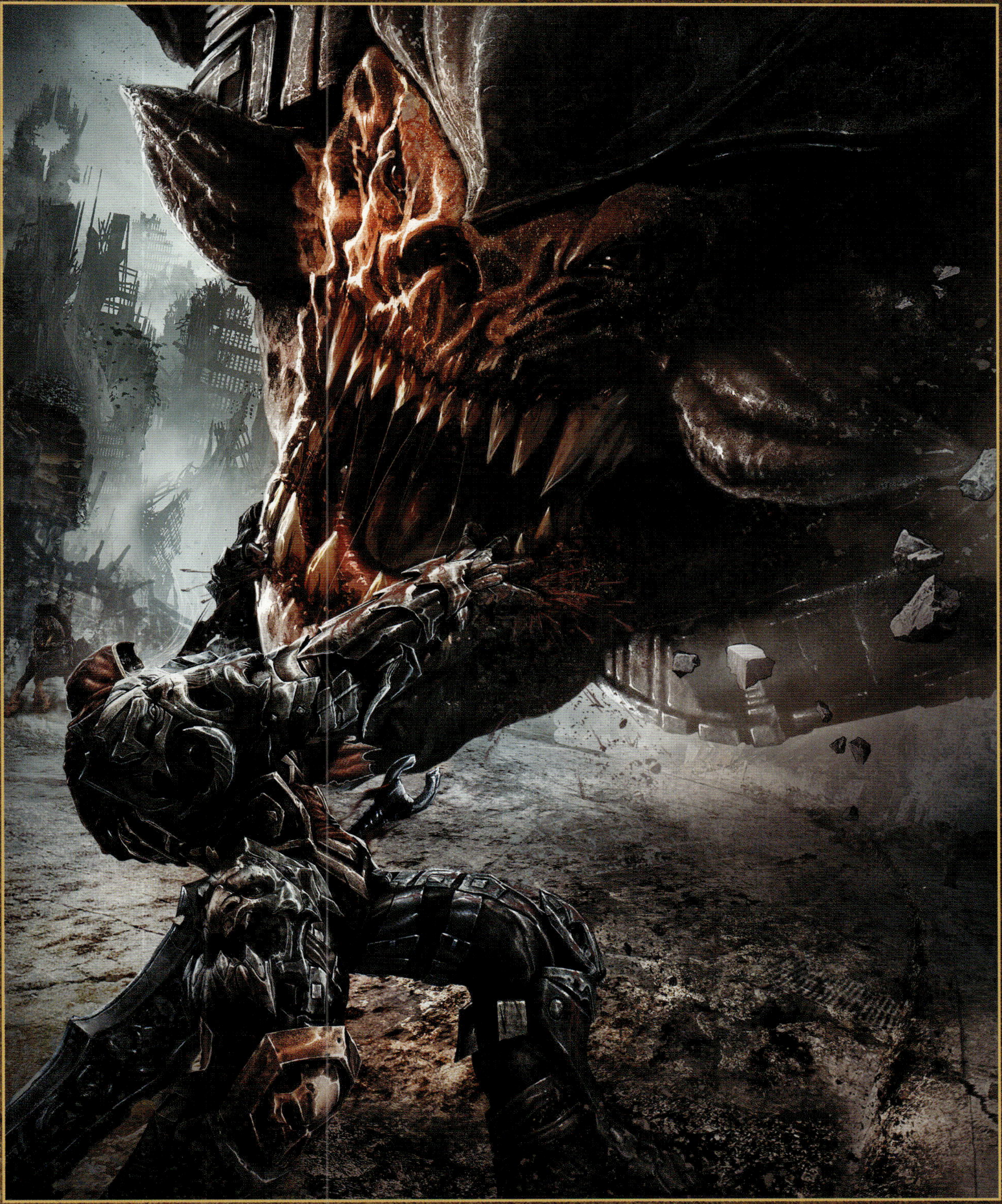

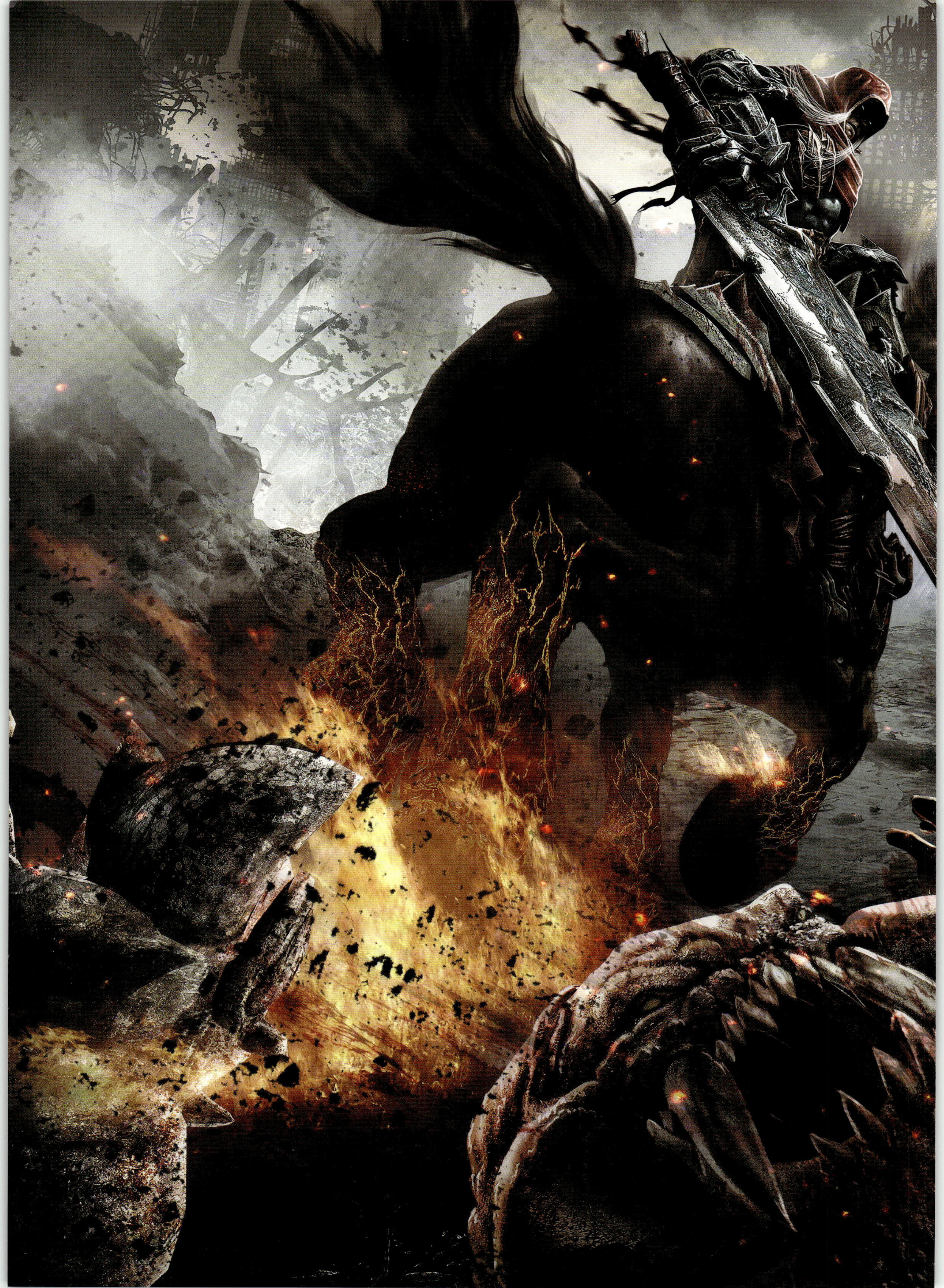

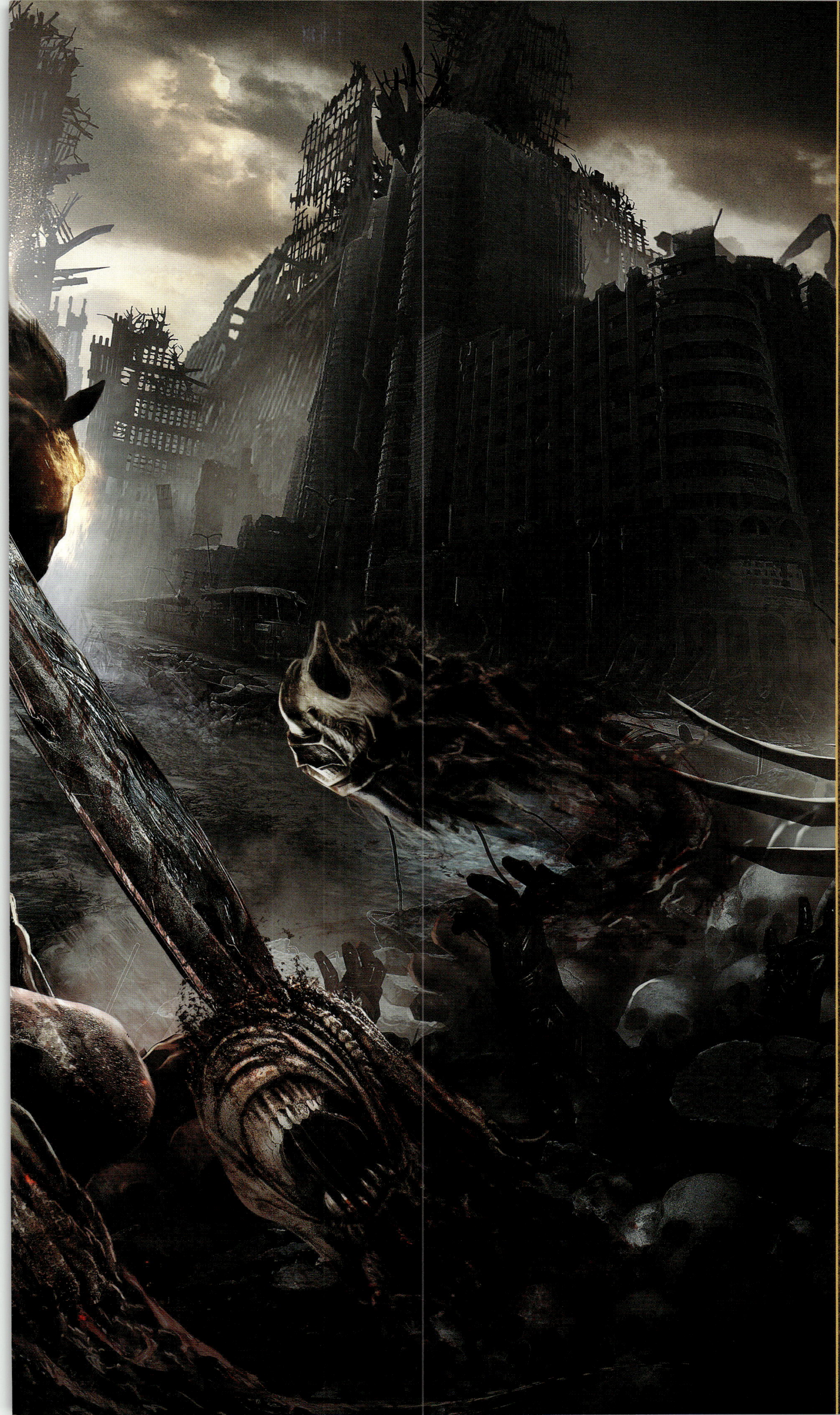

<<
"HEADS WILL ROLL"

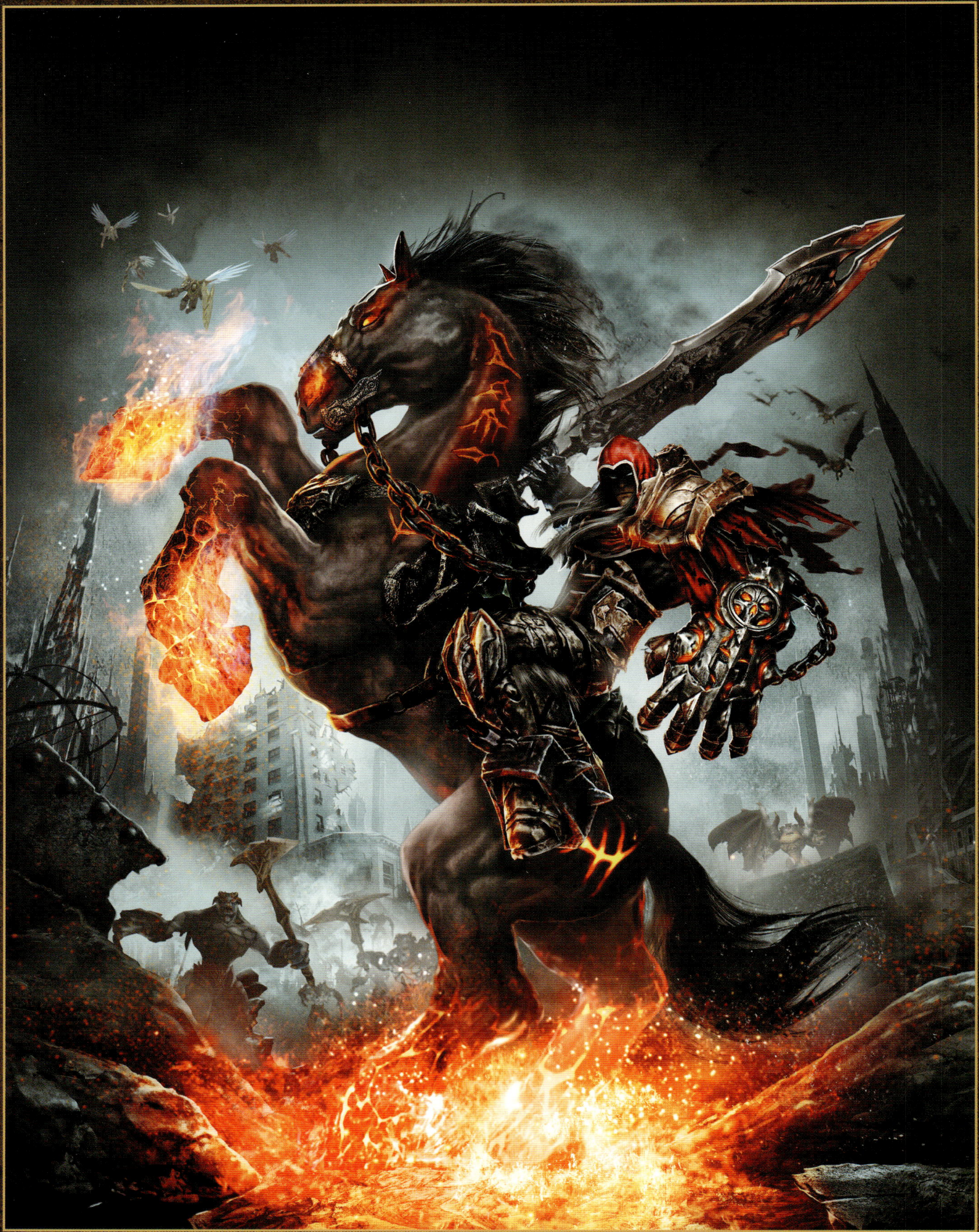

EARLY BOX ART

FINAL BOX ART >>

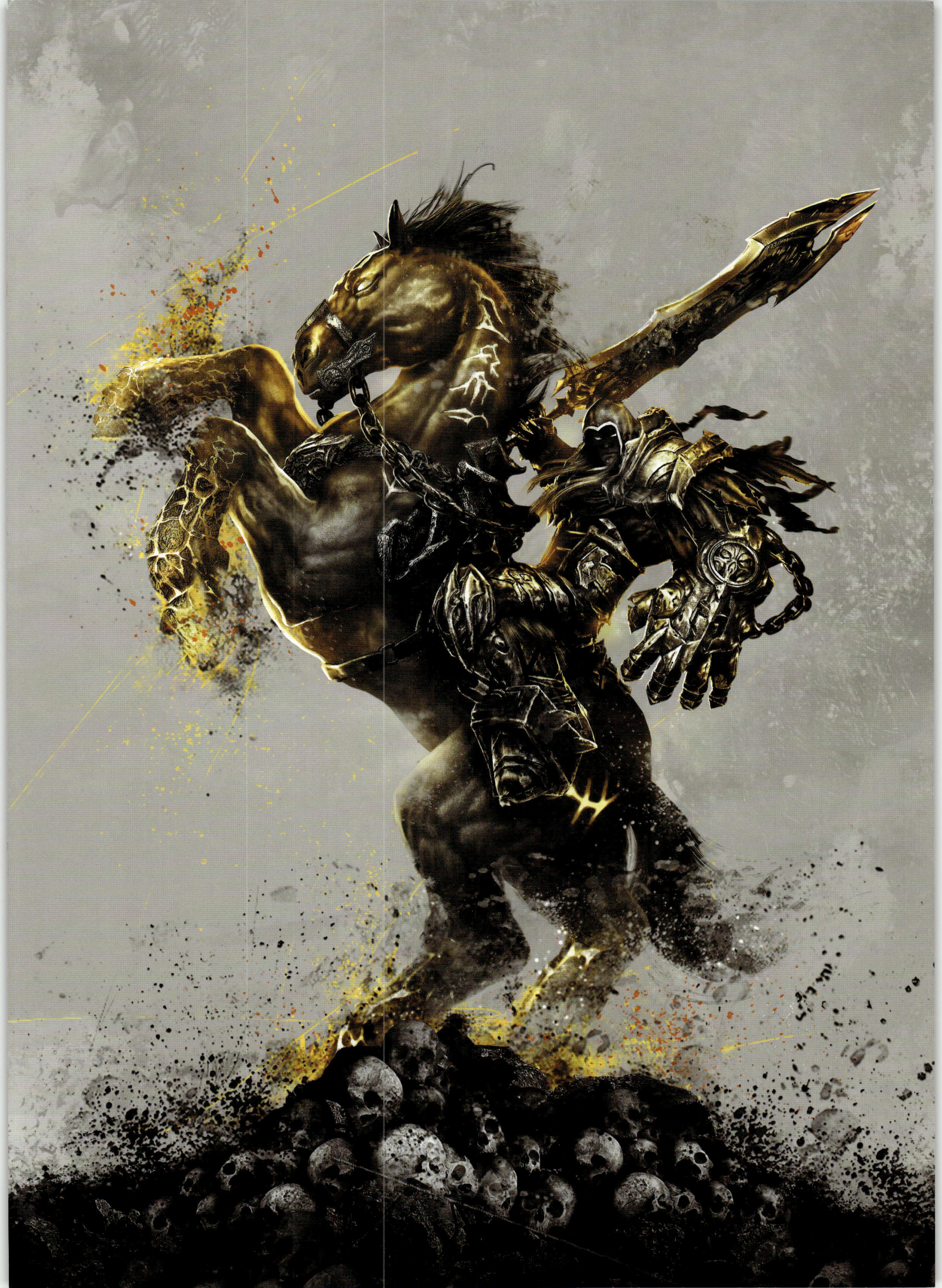

Game Credits

General Manager
David Adams

Creative Director
Joe Madureira

The Leads
Timothy Bell—Producer
Colin Bonstead—Lead Programmer
Haydn Dalton—Lead Designer
Marvin Donald—Lead Animator
Timothy Donley—Production Manager
Sam Gage—Lead VFX Artist
Gray Ginther—Lead Character Artist
John Pearl—Lead Environment Artist
Tarlochan Randhawa—Art Director
Jeremy Robins—Lead SFX Artist
Ryan Stefanelli—Lead Level Designer

Animators
Carl Coss, Chad Hranchak, Steve Madureira, Bradley Marques, Chris Mead, Jeremy Pantoja, Leisel Spence

Character Artists
Brian King, Pio Ravago III, LeRoy Strauss

Concept Artists
Phu Giang, Joe Madureira, Paul Richards, Nicholas Southam

Environment Artists
Gary Bergeron, Nga Yan Chan, Andrew Clark, Josh Coons, John Flath, William Fuller, Christopher Peacock, Leah Pearl, Mike Rodriguez, Ryan Verne, Cliff Young, Gabe Zumberge

Environment Art Interns
Jonathan Armstrong, Marc Edwards, John Lapio, Melissa Smith, Sarah Tempas

UI Artist
Colin Post

VFX Artist
Ryan Rosanky

Combat Design
David Adams, Brandon Boldenow, Jacob Crow, Howard Tang, John Tran

Level Design
Clint Bogue, John Hughes, Michael Lin, Robert Reininger III

Production
Jacqueline Marroquin, Anjanette Stach, Bri Thatcher

Programming
David Adams, Tony Bennett, Keith Blackstone, Gary Bland,
Josh Coyne, Scott Hofmann, Kevin King, Paul Masters, Andy Modrovich, Richard Osborne, Aaron Pendley, Ryan Ripstra

Sound Effects
Andrew Brock, Pedro Seminario

Additional Animation
Edward Lee Bowman II, Bret Church, Jeremy Fones, Eric Johnson, Jason Krueger, Jae Yoon Oh, Chuck Suong

Additional Art
Daniel Beaulieu, Shawn Brack, Brian "BoBo" Jones, Eric Miller, John Mueller, Derek Robinette, Leif Robles, Adam Schuman, James "Bobby" Simpson, Thomas Spampinato, Eric Spitler, Michael Tarwater, Billy Wardlaw

Additional Design
Bo Bell, Travis Koleski, Michael Maza, Tom Potter, Scott Rogers

Additional Production
Kay Gilmore, Grant McDaniel

Additional Cutscene SFX
Matt Bauer, Clark Crawford, Vincent Pontarelli

Additional Localization
M. Angelo Barken, Gary Gibson, Tamir Nadav

Additional SFX
Kenneth Bassham

Additional VFX
Ben Erickson Travis Koleski, John Edwards, FXVille

QA Testers
Capen Apple, Ryan Collins, Chris Doerr, Sean Lander,
Jonathan Lo, Justin McMorris, Rene Ogando, Sam Pearson, Jonathan Tackett, Randy Taintor, Joel Usher, Scott Winslow, Victor Wren

IT Manager
Jason Petty

IT Support Specialist
Brian Ray

HR Generalist
Traci Reston

Senior Recruiter
Michael Nichols

Office Administrator
Nash Cook

Design Consultant
Eric Williams – Short Short Super, LLC

VOICE TALENT

Featuring
Troy Baker (as Abaddon, Straga, Tortured Gate)
Moon Bloodgood (as Uriel)
Mark Hamill (as The Watcher)
Phil LaMarr (as Vulgrim)
Lani Minella (as Silitha and Tiamat)
Liam O'Brien (as War)
Vernon Wells (as Samael)

Also With
JB Blanc, Joel McCrary, Jamieson Price, Isaac Singleton, Jessica Straua, Keith Szarabajka, Fred Tasciore, Victor Wexler

VO Director
Keith Arem, Joe Madureira

PCB PRODUCTIONS

Voice Direction and Engineering
Keith Arem

VO Production Coordinator
Valerie Michelle Arem

MUSIC

Musical Score by
Cris Velasco, Mike Reagan, Scott Morton

STORY

Story
Joe Madureira

Script
Joe Kelly, Joe Madureira

ATTITUDE STUDIOS

Vice President, Attitude Games
Francois Lourdin

Technical Production Director
Jean Chrysostome Lepercque

Director, Storyboard Artist
Tarik Hamdine

Framing
Alexandre Labe

Editing
David Gibault

Lead Animation
Marco Pacifici

Animation
Arnaud Coia, Jérôme Ernoult, Julien Hassenforder, Nicolas Juncos, Patrick Le Bayon, Vincent Le Ster, Thibault Pluvinage, Ludovic Roz, David Vandenbroecke

Tech Support
Mikael Auffret, Raphael Bot-gartner

US Sales Agent
Nick Jacob

DIGIC PICTURES

Producer
Alex Sandor Rabb

Director (Intro Movie)
Istvan Zorkoczy

Director (War Movie)
Ivan Sarosacz

CG Supervisor
Robert Kovacs

Art Director
Peter Fendrik

Coordinator
Gyorgy Horvath

Lead Modeler
Tamas Varga

Modelers
Boglarka Piroth, Tamas Tothfalussy, Daniel Ulrich

Painters
Akos Haszon, Lajos Nagy, Karoly Porkolab, Kornel Ravadits

Lead Character TD
Andras Tarsoly

Lead Animator
Gabor Horvath

Animators
Zoltan Hollosy, Csilla Jelen, Daniel Keresztes,
Gabor Kiss, Zsolt Merey Kadar
Lead Technical Director
Szabolcs Horvatth
Technical Directors
Attila Chovanecz, Peter B. Kovacs, Kalman Ruszkai, Imre Tuske

Compositing
Balazs Horvath

Development
Gabor Medinacz, Gabor Tanay

Systems Administrator
Gabor Kali

Motion Capture
Stepan Kment (Bohemia Interactive)

FXVille
Team Lead, Art Director
Joe Olson
Senior Technical Artist
John Scrapper
Senior Artist, Producer
Jonathan Peters
Principal Artist
Garrett Smith
Junior Artist
Reed Shingledecker

MASS MEDIA
President & CEO
David Todd
Programmers
Lee Chidgey, Ken Jordan, Alex Rowell,
Roman Scharnberg, Stan Vasilyev

SILICON KNIGHTS
Core
Patrick Ingoldsby
Lead Environment Artist
Vasilios Papagianis, Alex Golebiowski, Evan
Yovanovich,
Chian Chia, Graham Yaxley, Mark Tomé,
Jason Zorn, Dino Litonjua
Secondary
Tony Tsang, Francisco Alvarez, Irwin Gamalinda,
Neal Giddings, Ben Cheung, Kyle Kotevich, Qiong Pan,
Chris Marleau, Rhodanim Belo, Edwin Yee, John Chan,
Ken Liao, Pamela Pagayonan
Coordinating
Sean Llewellyn, Producer
Carman Dix, Art Director

SKYWALKER SYMPHONY CHORUS
Music Contractor
Janet Ketchum
Conductor
Ian Robertson
Chorus Manager
Deborah Benedict
Boy Soprano
Zachary Weisberg

TECHNICOLOR
Vice President
Chan Park
VP, Sales and Marketing
Cindy Airey
Animation Director
Robert Castaneda
Senior Producer
David Yang
Producer
Ivan Glaze
Producer
Prithi Amarnath
Associate Producer
Max Neutra
Lead Animators
Gavin Dell, Somu Achary, Selvan Venkatesan

Lead Facial Animators
Ido Gondelman, Arun Nagendra Kamath
Previz Artists
Jeff Benoit, Patrick Rodriguez, Mark Villagracia
Animators
Ramachandran B, Robert Bardy, Vishnu Chakravarthy,
Alina Chau, Anish Kulangara George, Matthew Johnson,
Michael Raphael Joseph, Swaraj Kanthikar,
Guruprasad Kochukrishnan, John Kubasco,
Praveen PS Kumar, Sarah Lappena, Paul Lee,
Mark Levine, Praveen Madhyastha, Pillai Manoj,
Amit Jalaja Mohan, Srikanth Muralidhar, John Nguyen,
Mahesh Pachangam, Ravi Panwar, Siddarth Rathore,
Ashwarth Sadhu, Jeff Schanz, Raviteja Varma
Senior Engineer
David Vodhanel
Engineers
Edward Harmon, Gary Mosman
Junior Engineer
Matthew Bozarth
Lead Technical Artist
Dan Goldman
Technical Artist
Nicholas Joseph

WINKING ENTERTAINMENT LTD
Project Managers
Eddy Yau, Jimmy Chang, Jin Liu
Artists
Kang Lin, Asasin He, Fisher Zin, Ken Gao, Y.Z. Guo, Yu Lou,
Terry Han, F.L. Feng, Bloodorc Zhang, Idnomore Mu,
Vagar Zhang, Randy Wang, Seaman Liu, Snake Xiao,
Windflow Qu, Peter Peng, Nick Qin

EPIC GAMES CHINA

THQ
President & CEO
Brian J. Farrell
EVP, Core Game Brands
Danny Bilson
SVP, Finance and Administration,
Worldwide Studios
Steve DeCosta
VP, Product Development,
Worldwide Studios
Jeff Brown
VP, Creative Management
Tim Campbell
Director, Project Management
Kathleen Nicholls
Director, Creative Management
Lenny Brown
Director, Creative Management
Laddie Ervin
Director, Business Development
Andrew Walker
Senior Global PD Operations Manager
Ian Sedensky
Project Manager
Rob Shepherd
Associate Creative Manager
Daniel McGuffey
Associate Creative Manager
Eric Weiss
Music Director, Worldwide Studios
Victor Rodriguez
Senior Video Animation
Dave Colacioppo
Associate Video Editor
Tyler Endicott
Video Production Coordinator
Roberto "Tito" Blasini
Director of Localization
Philippe Juton
European Localization Director
Susanne Dieck
European Localization Engineer
Bernd Kurtz
European Localization Technician
Andreas Herbertz
Localization Project Manager
Dan Kukucka
Localization Project Manager
Miles Davies
Localization Project Manager
Catherine Duperron
Localization Executive Producer
Andrew Johnson
Localization Project Manager
Reshide Ameti
Associate Localization Manager
Masae Yamakura
Localization Project Manager
Yuki Kokubo
Operations Coordinator
Rachel Lee
VP, PD Finance
Laura Lloyd
Manager, PD Finance
Steffanie Bullis
Senior Financial Analyst
Elena Gramont
Manager, PD Finance
Barbara Spring
Executive Assistant
Jessica Peters
Administrative Assistant
Melissa Saito

THQ XDG (External Development Group)
Director of PD, XDG and Asia Online
Kevin Chu
Director of Engineering
Daniel Sass
Project Manager
Sandy Zhen-Yeh
Project Manager
Dilber Mann
Associate Project Manager
Mike Kelleher

THQ QUALITY ASSURANCE
VP, Product Development
Richard Browne

Senior QA Manager
Michael Motoda

QA Supervisors
Jeff Braun, Anne Farmer

Senior QA Lead
Sal Urena

QA Leads
Robert Faria, Jared Beauchamp

Senior Testers
Eric Dalehite, Nolan Ellis

Testers
Lars Bakke, Colin Bannon, Adam Benson, Edward Buckley, Chris Flores, Jay Chaney, Matt Fenwick, Andres Hernandez, Patrick Jarrett, Ricardo Jimenez, Tyler Johnston, Elisha Miller, Hector Reyna, Luis Salas, John Schulenburg, Zack Watson, Erika Wehrly, Jesse West

Compliance QA Supervisor
Michael Booker, Jennifer Henschel

Compliance QA Project Leads
Matthew J. Cooper, Eugene Park

Compliance QA Specialists
Mellissa Moore, Justin Schwartz, Andrew Dodson, David Lejeune, Troy Hieda, Roberto Candelario, Don Smith, Dustin Wiemer, Edwin DeNicholas, Jeff Kersten, Josh Geary, Mark Sagun, Patrick Thomson, Robert Razo

Submission Coordinators
Brian Skidmore, Darryl Matthews, Malik Aziz, Scott Ritchie

Senior Supervisor, Mastering
Anthony Dunnet

Mastering Lab Technicians
Glen Peters, Heidi Salguero, Ryan Fell, Ian Clark, Robert LeBeau

QA Operations Manager
Richard Jones

QA Operations Technicians
Luis Arevalo, Ryan Cashman, Justin Drolet, Michael Zlotnicki

QA Facilities Coordinator
Christopher Ramirez

QA Tools Programmer
Jonathan Gill

Database Administrator
T. Ryan Arnold

QA Data Analyst
Steve Nelson

QA HR Administrator
Omar Flores

HR Manager
Lori Ceballos

QA Administrative Assistant
Jennifer Osborn

Customer Service Supervisor
Colin Thompson

Customer Service Representatives
Jodie Geiselman, Peter Svenkerud, Christopher Brown

Senior Manager, Usability
Karl Steiner

THQ PUBLISHING

EVP, Global Publishing
Ian Curran

VP, Global Brand Management
Kevin Kraff

Global Brand Manager
Clint Chapman

Associate Brand Manager
Waleed Kamel

Director, Marketing Communications
Rob Cassel

Senior Public Relations Manager
Craig Mitchell

Senior Creative Services Manager
Brian Balistreri

Senior Creative Services Manager
Kirk Somdal

Global Traffic Specialist
Erica Wagner

Director, Trade Marketing
Julie Gibbs

Senior Channel Marketing Manager
Jeff Pugh

Senior Channel Marketing Manager
Laura Campos

VP, Sales—Americas
Terri Schiek

Director, Marketing Development
Adrienne Lauer

Director of Video Services
Robert Benjamin

Director of Fiction Development
Paul DeMeo

Senior Video Editor
Fernando Velloso

Writer
David Slagle

THQ INTERNATIONAL

VP, European & UK Marketing
Richard Williams

Head of Marketing, UK & Europe
Jon Rooke

Head of PR, UK & Europe
Sam Forrest

Head of Digital, UK & Europe
Huy Beynon

Product Marketing Manager
Mark Cook

UK & EUROPE

PR Manager, UK & Europe
Simon Watts

Digital Manager, UK & Europe
Mike Richardson

Marketing Manager, France
Benoit Bohet

Product Marketing Manager, France
Jerome Blazy

Marketing Director, Germany
Paul Ashcroft

Head of Product Management, Germany
Claus Schmidt

Marketing Director, Spain
Pablo Camacho

Product Marketing Manager, Spain
Javier Manu

Marketing Director, Italy
Paolo Pastorelli

Territory Manager, BENLUX
Jeroen Pompen

Senior Product Marketing Manager, BENLUX
Joey Smits

Managing Director, Export
Annie Sullivan

Sales & Marketing Manager, Export
Luke Keighran

Executive Assistant, Export
Eleanor Ridley

VP, Marketing, Asia Pacific
Travis Plane

Director of Export, Asia Pacific
Paul Donovan

Director of Market Development, Asia Pacific
Tim Page

Marketing Manager, Asia Pacific
Chris Wright

Associate Export Manager, Asia Pacific
Lyndall Dakic

Associate Product Manager, Asia Pacific
Luke Faulkner

Marketing Manager, Korea
Young Kwon

Associate Product & Licensing Manager, Japan
Medhi Camion

Instruction Manual
Greg Off

THQ BUSINESS & LEGAL AFFAIRS

EVP, Business & Legal Affairs
Ed Kaufman

VP, Business & Legal Affairs
Brandy Carrillo

Director, Business & Legal Affairs
Debbie Fingerman

Legal Counsel, Business & Legal Affairs
Adam Landenberger

Associate Legal Counsel
Garrett Lilley

Sr. Legal Specialist
Kate Dianaty

Legal Specialist
Kathleen Lilly

Contracts Analyst
Marla Park

Legal Assistant
Janet D'Andrea

SPECIAL THANKS

Andy Ashcraft, Max Carlson, Ken Cheung, Tom Cramer, Michael Herring, Steve Hoelle, Neal Kettler, Chris Lichtner, Darren Mason, Brian Mazza, Jack Sorensen, Jeff Stanislawski, Damian Stones, Roy Tessler, Rodney Walden, Malcom Wheeler, Abel Zhang

And to the families of the Vigil Games team for their incredible patience and support throughout the Darksiders development process.

Development Babies
Jadon Isaac Bennett, Addison Christine Bogue, Clint Bonstead, Travis Conrad Dalton, Benjamin Fones, Sarah Elise Madureira, Kaylen Osborne, Fox Petty, Aria Bella Robins, Robert Joseph Reininger IV, Caden Michael Stefanelli, David Young

Darksiders created by
Vigil Games

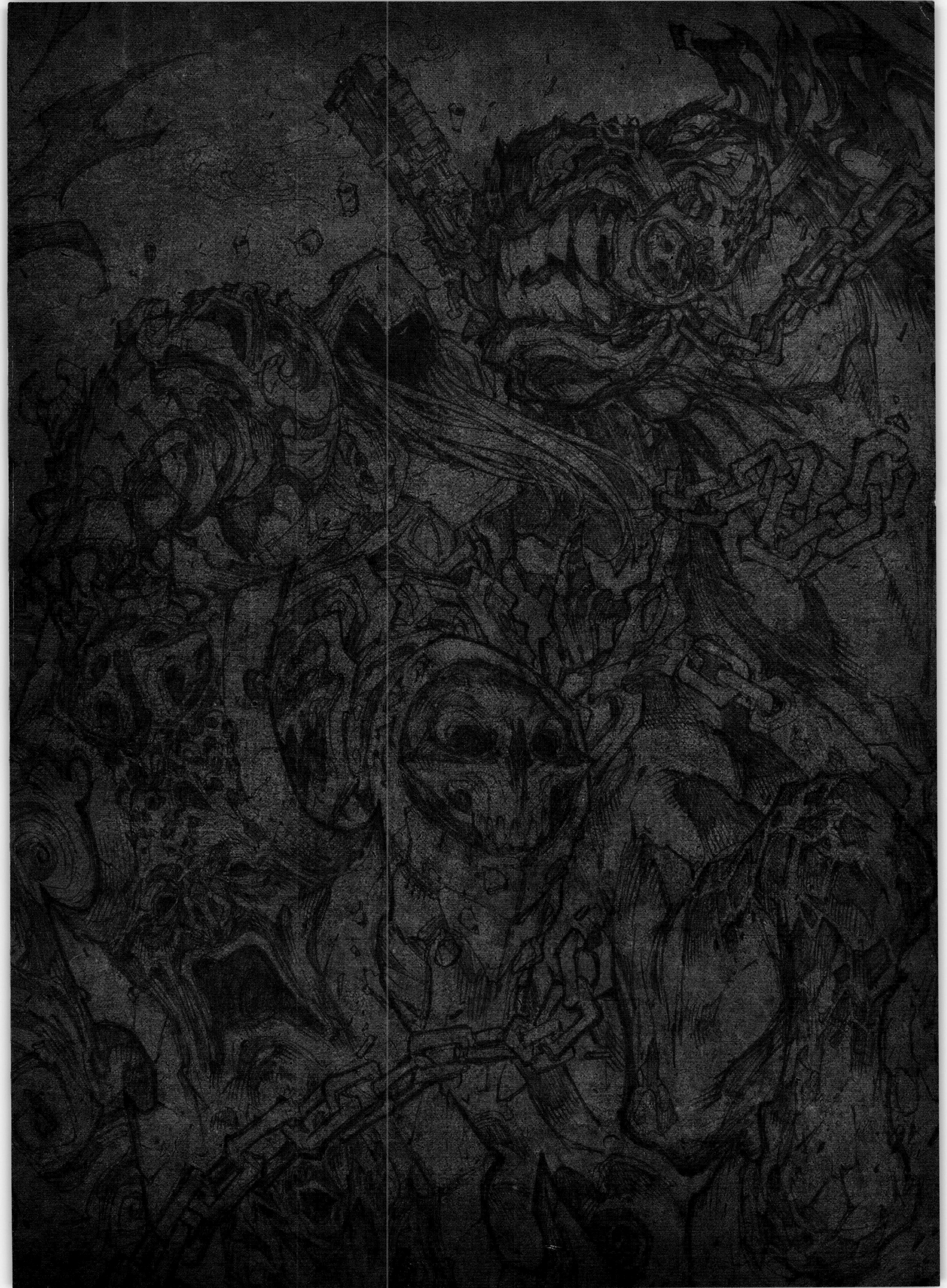

The Art of DARKSIDERS™

Cover Art by **JOE MADUREIRA** with **PIO RAVAGO III**
Book Layout and Design: **MATT MOYLAN**

UDON STAFF:
Chief of Operations: **ERIK KO**
Managing Editor: **MATT MOYLAN**
Project Manager: **JIM ZUBKAVICH**
Marketing Manager: **STACY KING**

THQ LICENSING:
GERMAINE GIOIA, JOSH AUSTIN, ARELI FERNANDEZ of THQ Inc.

SPECIAL THANKS:
JOE MADUREIRA, DAVID ADAMS, and the entire team at Vigil Games

Published by UDON Entertainment Corp.
P.O. Box 5002 RPO Major Mackenzie, Richmond Hill, Ontario, L4S 0B7 CANADA.

www.UDONentertainment.com

Printed by Suncolor Printing Co. Ltd.
E-mail: suncolor@netvigator.com

Second Printing: May 2011

ISBN-13: 978-1-926778-10-5
ISBN-10: 1-926778-10-3

Printed in Hong Kong

www.thq.com